lonely planet

Scotland

**Neil Wilson
Graeme Cornwallis
Tom Smallman**

LONELY PLANET PUBLICATIONS
Melbourne • Oakland • London • Paris

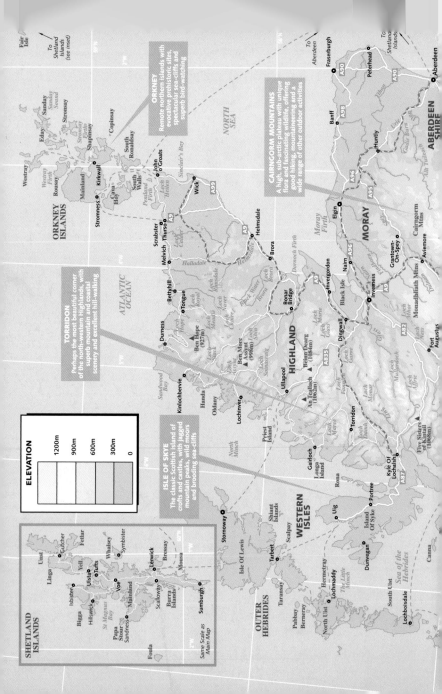

ATLANTIC
OCEAN

INNER
HEBRIDES

Berneray

Barra

Eigg
Muck
Coll
Tiree

Staffa
Iona
Erraid

Island
Of Mull

Tobermory

Colonsay

Oronsay

Islay

Port
Askaig

Jura

Gigha

Mull of
Kintyre

Campbeltown

NORTHERN
IRELAND

Derry

Ballycastle

Larne

Belfast

Stranraer

Cairnryan

Newton
Stewart

Kirkcudbright

DUMFRIES &
GALLOWAY

Dumfries

Moffat

BORDERS

Hawick

Jedburgh

Kelso

Coldstream

Berwick
Upon
Tweed

Holy
Island

Newcastle

ENGLAND

Carlisle

Galashiels

Peebles

LOTHIAN

Haddington

Dunbar

Lammermuir Hills

Edinburgh

Pentland Hills

FIFE

Dunfermline

Kirkcaldy

Cupar

St
Andrews

Dundee

Forfar

ANGUS

Arbroath

Montrose

Stonehaven

Braemar

Grampian Mtns

Pitlochry

Aberfeldy

Blairgowrie

Dunkeld

PERTHSHIRE

Perth

Crieff

Kinross

STIRLING

Stirling

Falkirk

Glasgow

Motherwell

Lanark

AYRSHIRE

Kilmarnock

Troon

Ayr

Girvan

Dumbarton

Greenock

Dunoon

Bute

Brodick

Arran

Ardrossan

Lochgilphead

ARGYLL

Oban

Lochaline

Fort
William

Glencoe

Ben Nevis
▲(1343m)

Tarbet

Loch Lomond

Loch Fyne

Scotland
2nd edition – January 2002
First published – March 1999

Published by
Lonely Planet Publications Pty Ltd ABN 36 005 607 983
90 Maribyrnong St, Footscray, Victoria 3011, Australia

Lonely Planet Offices
Australia Locked Bag 1, Footscray, Victoria 3011
USA 150 Linden St, Oakland, CA 94607
UK 10a Spring Place, London NW5 3BH
France 1 rue du Dahomey, 75011 Paris

Photographs
Many of the images in this guide are available for licensing from
Lonely Planet Images.
email: lpi@lonelyplanet.com.au

Front cover photograph
The Callanish Standing Stones on Lewis Island (Grant Dixon)

ISBN 1 86450 157 X

text & maps © Lonely Planet Publications Pty Ltd 2002
photos © photographers as indicated 2002

Printed by The Bookmaker International Ltd
Printed in China

Contents – Text

THE HIGHLANDS

THE HEBRIDES

ORKNEY & SHETLAND ISLANDS 460

LANGUAGE 496

GLOSSARY 500

INDEX 504

MAP LEGEND 512

METRIC CONVERSION inside back cover

Contents – Maps

MAP INDEX

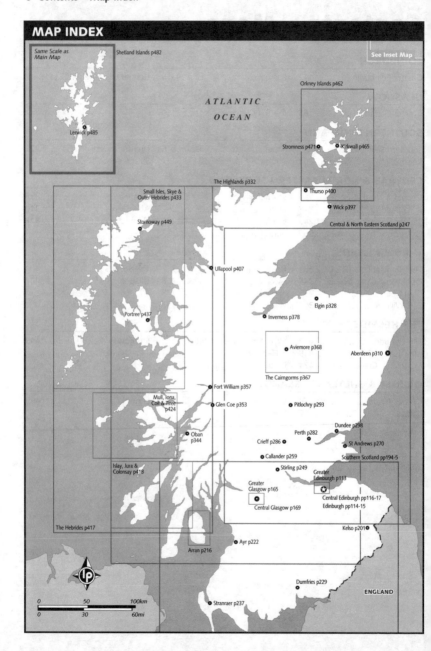

Same Scale as Main Map

See Inset Map

Shetland Islands p482

Lerwick p485

ATLANTIC OCEAN

Orkney Islands p462

Stromness p471 ● ● Kirkwall p465

The Highlands p332

● Thurso p400

● Wick p397

Central & North Eastern Scotland p247

Small Isles, Skye & Outer Hebrides p433

Stornoway p449 ●

● Ullapool p407

● Elgin p328

Portree p437 ●

● Inverness p378

● Aviemore p368

Aberdeen p310 ●

The Cairngorms p367

● Fort William p357

Mull, Iona, Coll & Tree p424

● Glen Coe p353

● Pitlochry p293

● Oban p344

● Perth p282

Dundee p298 ●

Crieff p286 ●

St Andrews p270 ●

Islay, Jura & Colonsay p418

● Callander p259

Southern Scotland pp194-5

● Stirling p249

Greater Edinburgh p113

Greater Glasgow p165 ●

Central Edinburgh pp116-17

Central Glasgow p169

Edinburgh pp114-15

The Hebrides p417

Kelso p201 ●

Arran p216

● Ayr p222

Dumfries p229 ●

ENGLAND

● Stranraer p237

0   50   100km
0   30   60mi

The Authors

Neil Wilson

After working as a petroleum geologist in Australia and the North Sea and doing geological research at Oxford University, Neil gave up the rock business for the more precarious life of a freelance writer and photographer. Since 1988 he has travelled in five continents and written around 30 travel and walking guidebooks for various publishers. He has worked on Lonely Planet's *Georgia, Armenia & Azerbaijan*, *Malta*, *Czech & Slovak Republics*, *Prague*, *Slovenia* and *Edinburgh* guides. Although he was born in Glasgow, in the west of Scotland, Neil defected to the east at the age of 18 and has lived in Edinburgh ever since.

Graeme Cornwallis

Born and raised in Edinburgh, Graeme later wandered around Scotland before coming to rest in Glasgow. While studying astronomy at Glasgow University, he developed a passion for peaks, particularly the Munros. He eventually bagged all 284 summits over 914m (3000 ft) in Scotland at least once and completion of the second round is currently in sight. Graeme has travelled extensively throughout Scotland and has a good background knowledge of the country and its fascinating history. He has also travelled extensively in Scandinavia and widely in Asia, North & South America and the Pacific. Mountaineering successes include trips to the Bolivian Andes, arctic Greenland and Norway. When he's not hiking, climbing or travelling, Graeme teaches mathematics and physics at home in Glasgow.

FROM THE AUTHORS

Neil Wilson Many thanks to Laura Smith at VisitScotland, to John Yellowlees at ScotRail, and to the helpful and enthusiastic staff at TICs throughout the country. Thanks also to Carol Downie, and to Michael and Charlie, for help and advice on Edinburgh restaurants and nightlife. Finally, thanks to co-author Graeme and to Emma Sangster and Rachel Beattie at Lonely Planet.

Graeme Cornwallis Firstly, I'd like to thank the Lonely Planet authors who worked on previous editions of the *Britain* guide, and the first and current editions of this book, particularly Tom Smallman and Neil Wilson.

Many thanks to Susan Brush for her companionship and moral support, and Grant and Margaret Cornwallis for general assistance. I'm indebted to John Heath of Aultbea, Wester Ross, who shared his in-depth knowledge of the North-Western Highlands and his hospitality.

Thanks also to the following who helped in various important ways: Laura Smith (VisitScotland), Paul Duffy (Scottish Citylink), Moira Dyer (Greater Glasgow & Clyde Valley Tourist Board), Chirsty MacKinnon (Portree TIC) and Iain Cornwallis (Dunblane).

I am indebted to the staff, who were happy to assist, at many TICs around the country; particularly impressive was Lochboisdale TIC (South Uist).

Stuart Graham (SNH) and family, Iain Cusick (Lamlash, Arran), Myrtle Potter (Dunning, Perthshire), Sandy MacLennan (Glen Nevis), Heather Martin and Steve Wells (Inverness), and Alistair Young and Dawn Rose (Ord, Skye), were most hospitable while I toured around the country. Gordon Innes, Jenny Rouse, Julian Morris and Al Kerr (all in Glasgow) assisted with their up-to-date knowledge of city restaurants. And thanks to Mary at Balloch Country Park for sending some vital information in the post. Finally, thanks to Clay Lucas for his enlivening update of the Glasgow entertainment section.

THANKS FROM THE PUBLISHER

Many thanks to the travellers who used the last edition and contacted us with helpful hints, advice and interesting anecdotes:

Rato Allenspach, Mauro Barbero, Mathias Berenger, Holly & Rob Borham, Dr Thomas Braeuniger, Mike Breslin, Julie Carroll, Steve Charlton, Diane Collins, Pete Connors, Cathleen Conway, W B Cooper, Lynda Cotton, Joanne Cumine, Pam Currie, Ella Delderfield, Barbara Dijke, Renee & John Elliott, Svend Erik Steenfeldt, Christopher Farmer, Carol Forsyth, Bjorn Fuchtenkord, Sheryl Fullner, Ingvar Grans, David Gyger, Thera Hamel, Dorsey & Hal Holappa, Nevil Hopley, Joanne Horvath, Matt Hoskins, Andreas Huber, Andrew Inglis, Susan Irwin, Jodie Ivers, Agnes Jackson, Kerry Jamieson, N Johnson, Mattias Karlsson, Jenny Kohn, Thomas Lehmann, Heather & Denis Liuzzi, Sarah Luchansky, Liz Macleod, Jayne Marshall, Charlotte Martensson, Patricia Mastrobuono, Phillip Mattle, Barbero Mauro, M McColl, Martin Miller, D W Moore, Heather Moore, Lisa Munroe, Roberta Murray, Gabe Murtagh, Shaun Paisley, Antoine Pécard, Marco Perezzani, Sonya Polis, Stephanie Potts, Alison Rae, Andy & Philippa Rands, Viola Retzlaff, Sally T Ringe, Fernando Rocco, Jenny Ross, Adam Rudes, Ron Schweikert, George Scott, Ruth Spellman, Richard Spencer, Mr & Mrs Stanley, Dave Stewart, Tracy Stewart, Jamie Strachan, Vanessa Stubbs, Marina Taylor Hehn, Christine Teelken, Gordon & Deborah Trousdale, Michele Tulino, Andrew Veech, Mary Beth Walker, Pat Waugh, M Webb, Elena Wiens, Scott Williamson, D Yudhope.

This Book

This is the 2nd edition of Lonely Planet's *Scotland*. Tom Smallman and Graeme Cornwallis wrote the 1st edition. Neil Wilson was the coordinating author of this edition and updated the Introduction, Facts About Scotland, Activities, Getting There & Away, Getting Around and Edinburgh chapters. Graeme Cornwallis updated the Facts for the Visitor and Glasgow chapters, less the Glasgow entertainment section which was updated by Clay Lucas. The remaining regional chapters were updated by both Neil and Graeme.

From the Publisher

This edition of *Scotland* was produced in Lonely Planet's London office and coordinated by Emma Sangster (editing) and Rachel Beattie (mapping and design).

Emma was assisted with the editing and proofing by a team comprising Charlotte Beech, Heather Dickson, Susan Grimshaw, Claire Hornshaw, Arabella Shepherd, Clare Tomlinson and Sam Trafford. Sam also produced the index.

Rachel was assisted with the mapping by Fiona Christie, Liam Molloy, Ed Pickard and Jolyon Philcox. Jimi Ellis drew the climate charts, Annika Roojun designed the cover and Lachlan Ross drew the back-cover map. Lonely Planet Images provided the photographs and illustrations were drawn by Asa Andersson, Jane Smith and Patrick Watson.

Many thanks to Emma Koch for the language chapter, and to Lou Byrnes, Paul Clifton, Tom Hall, Sally Schafer, Rachel Suddart, Sam Trafford, David Andrew and Miranda Wills for their expert advice. Thanks also to Amanda Canning, Tim Fitzgerald, Paul Piaia, Tim Ryder and Sara Yorke for all their help, especially during the last weeks.

Foreword

ABOUT LONELY PLANET GUIDEBOOKS

The story begins with a classic travel adventure: Tony and Maureen Wheeler's 1972 journey across Europe and Asia to Australia. Useful information about the overland trail did not exist at that time, so Tony and Maureen published the first Lonely Planet guidebook to meet a growing need.

From a kitchen table, then from a tiny office in Melbourne (Australia), Lonely Planet has become the largest independent travel publisher in the world, an international company with offices in Melbourne, Oakland (USA), London (UK) and Paris (France).

Today Lonely Planet guidebooks cover the globe. There is an ever-growing list of books and there's information in a variety of forms and media. Some things haven't changed. The main aim is still to help make it possible for adventurous travellers to get out there – to explore and better understand the world.

At Lonely Planet we believe travellers can make a positive contribution to the countries they visit – if they respect their host communities and spend their money wisely. Since 1986 a percentage of the income from each book has been donated to aid projects and human rights campaigns.

Updates Lonely Planet thoroughly updates each guidebook as often as possible. This usually means there are around two years between editions, although for more unusual or more stable destinations the gap can be longer. Check the imprint page (following the colour map at the beginning of the book) for publication dates.

Between editions up-to-date information is available in two free newsletters – the paper *Planet Talk* and email *Comet* (to subscribe, contact any Lonely Planet office) – and on our Web site at www.lonelyplanet.com. The *Upgrades* section of the Web site covers a number of important and volatile destinations and is regularly updated by Lonely Planet authors. *Scoop* covers news and current affairs relevant to travellers. And, lastly, the *Thorn Tree* bulletin board and *Postcards* section of the site carry unverified, but fascinating, reports from travellers.

Correspondence The process of creating new editions begins with the letters, postcards and emails received from travellers. This correspondence often includes suggestions, criticisms and comments about the current editions. Interesting excerpts are immediately passed on via newsletters and the Web site, and everything goes to our authors to be verified when they're researching on the road. We're keen to get more feedback from organisations or individuals who represent communities visited by travellers.

Lonely Planet gathers information for everyone who's curious about the planet – and especially for those who explore it first-hand. Through guidebooks, phrasebooks, activity guides, maps, literature, newsletters, image library, TV series and Web site we act as an information exchange for a worldwide community of travellers.

Research Authors aim to gather sufficient practical information to enable travellers to make informed choices and to make the mechanics of a journey run smoothly. They also research historical and cultural background to help enrich the travel experience and allow travellers to understand and respond appropriately to cultural and environmental issues.

Authors don't stay in every hotel because that would mean spending a couple of months in each medium-sized city and, no, they don't eat at every restaurant because that would mean stretching belts beyond capacity. They do visit hotels and restaurants to check standards and prices, but feedback based on readers' direct experiences can be very helpful.

Many of our authors work undercover, others aren't so secretive. None of them accept freebies in exchange for positive write-ups. And none of our guidebooks contain any advertising.

Production Authors submit their manuscripts and maps to offices in Australia, USA, UK or France. Editors and cartographers – all experienced travellers themselves – then begin the process of assembling the pieces. When the book finally hits the shops, some things are already out of date, we start getting feedback from readers and the process begins again...

WARNING & REQUEST

Things change – prices go up, schedules change, good places go bad and bad places go bankrupt – nothing stays the same. So, if you find things better or worse, recently opened or long since closed, please tell us and help make the next edition even more accurate and useful. We genuinely value all the feedback we receive. A well-travelled team reads and acknowledges every letter, postcard and email and ensures that every morsel of information finds its way to the appropriate authors, editors and cartographers for verification.

Everyone who writes to us will find their name in the next edition of the appropriate guidebook. They will also receive the latest issue of *Planet Talk*, our quarterly printed newsletter, or *Comet*, our monthly email newsletter. Subscriptions to both newsletters are free. The very best contributions will be rewarded with a free guidebook.

Excerpts from your correspondence may appear in new editions of Lonely Planet guidebooks, the Lonely Planet Web site, *Planet Talk* or *Comet*, so please let us know if you *don't* want your letter published or your name acknowledged.

Send all correspondence to the Lonely Planet office closest to you:

Australia: Locked Bag 1, Footscray, Victoria 3011
USA: 150 Linden St, Oakland, CA 94607
UK: 10a Spring Place, London NW5 3BH
France: 1 rue du Dahomey, 75011 Paris

Or email us at: talk2us@lonelyplanet.com.au

For news, views and updates see our Web site: www.lonelyplanet.com

HOW TO USE A LONELY PLANET GUIDEBOOK

The best way to use a Lonely Planet guidebook is any way you choose. At Lonely Planet we believe the most memorable travel experiences are often those that are unexpected, and the finest discoveries are those you make yourself. Guidebooks are not intended to be used as if they provide a detailed set of infallible instructions!

Contents All Lonely Planet guidebooks follow roughly the same format. The Facts about the Destination chapters or sections give background information ranging from history to weather. Facts for the Visitor gives practical information on issues like visas and health. Getting There & Away gives a brief starting point for researching travel to and from the destination. Getting Around gives an overview of the transport options when you arrive.

The peculiar demands of each destination determine how subsequent chapters are broken up, but some things remain constant. We always start with background, then proceed to sights, places to stay, places to eat, entertainment, getting there and away, and getting around information – in that order.

Heading Hierarchy Lonely Planet headings are used in a strict hierarchical structure that can be visualised as a set of Russian dolls. Each heading (and its following text) is encompassed by any preceding heading that is higher on the hierarchical ladder.

Entry Points We do not assume guidebooks will be read from beginning to end, but that people will dip into them. The traditional entry points are the list of contents and the index. In addition, however, some books have a complete list of maps and an index map illustrating map coverage.

There may also be a colour map that shows highlights. These highlights are dealt with in greater detail in the Facts for the Visitor chapter, along with planning questions and suggested itineraries. Each chapter covering a geographical region usually begins with a locator map and another list of highlights. Once you find something of interest in a list of highlights, turn to the index.

Maps Maps play a crucial role in Lonely Planet guidebooks and include a huge amount of information. A legend is printed on the back page. We seek to have complete consistency between maps and text, and to have every important place in the text captured on a map. Map key numbers usually start in the top left corner.

Although inclusion in a guidebook usually implies a recommendation we cannot list every good place. Exclusion does not necessarily imply criticism. In fact there are a number of reasons why we might exclude a place – sometimes it is simply inappropriate to encourage an influx of travellers.

Introduction

Scotland has a brand image that advertising agencies would kill for. There can be few people around the world who cannot conjure up some image of Scotland in their mind's eye, be it bagpipes, *Brigadoon* or *Braveheart*.

The reality, of course, is somewhat different. Although you'll find an abundance of Tartan-clad piper dolls, Loch Ness monster tea towels and Rabbie Burns snow-globes, they are thankfully confined to a few souvenir shops. The true Scotland is a modern European country whose many attractions include a fascinating history, sophisticated cities, wild mountain scenery and sparkling, island-studded seas.

Although an integral part of Great Britain since 1707, Scotland has maintained a separate and distinct identity throughout the last 300 years. The return of a devolved Scottish parliament to Edinburgh in 1999 marked a growing confidence and sense of pride in the nation's achievements. For a small, windswept country on the north-western fringes of Europe, Scotland has made a contribution to western civilization out of all proportion to its size. The long list of influential Scottish scientists, philosophers, writers, explorers and inventors would fill a separate book, and it was Scots who gave the world steamships, television, the telephone and countless other world-changing inventions. Oh, and golf, too.

The well-beaten tourist trail takes in Edinburgh, Pitlochry, Loch Ness and the Isle of Skye, and in high season these places can be jammed to bursting. But there are plenty of alternatives where you can escape the crowds, from the peaceful Border valleys to the whisky-scented islands of Islay and Jura, and from the Pictish stones of Angus to the desolate peaks of Sutherland and the remote northern isles of Orkney.

If you want to escape the crowds it's also worth considering an out-of-season visit. October brings a riot of autumn colour to the deciduous woodlands of Loch Lomond and the Trossachs, while a fresh layer of crisp snow lends grandeur to the mountains of Glencoe and Glen Shiel. And what could be cosier than curling up in front of a log fire in a Scottish country-house hotel while the frost sparkles on the pine trees outside?

The Scottish weather can be a little unpredictable, to say the least, but thank goodness for that – if Scotland had a Mediterranean climate the country would be overdeveloped, overcrowded and overrun with tourists. Take along waterproofs and a sense of adventure, and when the sun deigns to shine you will realise why Scots around the world are so attached to their homeland.

Facts about Scotland

HISTORY
First Immigrants
Scotland's earliest inhabitants were hunter-gatherers who began to push northwards from England, Ireland and northern Europe as the glaciers retreated in the wake of the last Ice Age around 10,000 BC. Over the next few thousand years these colonisers came in waves to different parts of the country. There are indications of Baltic cultures in eastern Scotland and Irish cultures on the western islands. Mesolithic flints from northern France have been found at many sites.

Recent archaeological investigations at Cramond, on the north-western edge of Edinburgh, have uncovered evidence of habitation there that has been dated to 8500 BC – the earliest known traces of human activity in Scotland.

Prehistoric Civilisations
The Neolithic era, beginning in the 4th millennium BC, brought a new way of life, with agriculture, stock breeding and trading. These changes caused an increase in population and more complex patterns of social organisation evolved to control them. With organised groups of workers, more ambitious construction projects became possible.

Neolithic people usually built wooden houses. It's only in treeless regions where they were forced to use stone that their architecture has survived. These northern islands contain rare examples of Neolithic domestic architecture; there's an entire village at Skara Brae in Orkney dating from around 3100 BC.

Between the late Neolithic and the early Bronze Age the Beaker People reached the British Isles from mainland Europe. They were so named after the shape of their earthenware drinking vessels which were customarily buried with their dead. They also introduced bronze for knives, daggers, arrowheads, and articles of gold and copper. Many of Scotland's standing stones and stone circles can be attributed to the Beaker People. Some sources claim that they were the original Celts.

Celtic settlers from Europe reached Scotland around 500 BC, heralding the arrival of the Iron Age. In the Highlands, which escaped Roman influence, it lasted well into the Christian era.

Roman Attempts at Colonisation
The Roman invasion of Britain began in 55 BC, when Julius Caesar's legions first crossed the English Channel. However, the Roman onslaught ground to a halt in the north, not far beyond the present-day Scottish border. Between AD 78 and 84, the Roman governor Agricola (whose son-in-law, Tacitus, gave the name Caledonia to the northern part of Scotland after the Caledones, the first tribe he came across) marched northwards and spent several years trying to subdue the wild tribes the Romans called the Picts (from the Latin *pictus*, meaning painted). Little is known about the Picts, who inhabited northern and eastern Scotland and probably reached Scotland via Orkney. The only material evidence of their culture is their unique symbol stones. These boulders, engraved with the mysterious symbols of an otherwise unknown people, can be found in many parts of eastern Scotland.

In the far north, Orkney was a centre of maritime power and posed a threat not only to the Romans but also to the other northern tribes. For defence against raiding parties, *brochs* (fortified stone towers) were constructed. Broch architecture was perfected in Orkney in the 1st century BC, and there are over 500 examples concentrated in Orkney, Shetland, the Western Isles and the north of Scotland. The best preserved, at Mousa in Shetland, dates from around 50 BC.

By the 2nd century, Emperor Hadrian had decided to cut his losses in the north and built the wall (AD 122–8) that bears his name, stretching across northern England between Carlisle and Newcastle. Two decades later Hadrian's successor, Antoninus Pius, invaded Scotland again and built a turf rampart, the Antonine Wall, between the Firth of Forth and the River Clyde. Roman legions were stationed there for about 40 years, before they once again withdrew. Apart from one more brief incursion by Septimus Severus early in the 3rd century AD, the Romans abandoned further attempts to subdue Scotland.

Feuding Celtic Tribes & Christianity
When the Romans finally left Britain in the 4th century, there were at least two indigenous peoples in the northern region of the British isles: the Picts in the north and east, and the Celtic Britons in the south.

In the 6th century another Celtic tribe, the Scots (from Scotti, the name given to them by the Romans), invaded Scotland from northern Ireland and established a kingdom in Argyll called Dalriada. These Irish Celts introduced the Gaelic language into western and northern Scotland. In the 7th century Angles, a tribe from north-eastern England, invaded south-eastern Scotland, capturing Dun Eiden (Edinburgh) in 638.

The 8th-century English monk and historian Bede attributes Christianity's arrival in Scotland to St Ninian, who established a centre in Whithorn (in Dumfries & Galloway) in 397. It's more than likely, however, that some of the Romanised Britons in southern Scotland adopted Christianity after the religion was given state recognition in 313. The Irish missionary St Columba founded a second important early-Christian centre on the tiny island of Iona, off Mull, in 563. By the late 8th century, most of the tribes in Scotland had converted to Christianity.

From the 780s onwards, Norsemen in longboats from Scandinavia began to pillage the Scottish coast and islands, eventually taking control of Orkney, Shetland, the Western Isles and parts of northern and western Scotland. Between 795 and 806, Norse raiders sacked the religious settlement at Iona three times, causing the monks to flee to Ireland with St Columba's bones. The Norsemen continued to control the entire western seaboard until Alexander III broke their power at the Battle of Largs in 1263.

Kenneth MacAlpin & the Makings of a Kingdom
The Picts and Scots were drawn together by the threat of invasion by the Norsemen, and by their common Christianity. In 843 Kenneth MacAlpin, the king of Dalriada (and son of a Pictish princess), took advantage of the Picts' custom of matrilineal succession to take over the Pictish throne, thus uniting Scotland north of the Firth of Forth into a single kingdom. He made Scone (near Perth) his capital, and brought to it the sacred Stone of Destiny used in the coronation of Scottish kings; he also brought relics of St Columba to the monastery at Dunkeld, symbolising the importance of the Celtic Church. Thereafter the Scots gained cultural and political ascendancy.

Nearly 200 years later, Kenneth MacAlpin's great-great-great-grandson, Malcolm II (reigned 1005–18), defeated the Northumbrian Angles led by King Canute at the Battle of Carham (1018) near Roxburgh on the River Tweed. This victory brought Edinburgh and Lothian under Scottish control and extended Scottish territory as far south as the Tweed.

Canmore Dynasty
Malcolm II's grandson was Malcolm III Canmore (reigned 1058–93). Malcolm III's father Duncan was murdered by Macbeth (as described in Shakespeare's eponymous play), and Macbeth himself was killed by Malcolm at Lumphanan in 1057. With his Saxon queen, Margaret, Malcolm Canmore founded a solid dynasty of able Scottish rulers. They introduced new Anglo-Norman systems of government and religious foundations.

Malcolm's son David I (reigned 1124–53) increased his power by adopting the Norman feudal system, granting land to noble Norman families in return for military service. By 1212 Walter of Coventry remarked that the Scottish court was 'French in race and manner of life, in speech and in culture'.

But the Highland clans, inaccessible in their glens, remained a law unto themselves for another 600 years. A cultural and linguistic divide grew up between the Gaelic-speaking Highlanders and the Lowlanders who spoke the Scots tongue – a language related to English, with French, Norse and Gaelic influences.

In the Lowlands, small commercial centres such as Berwick, Roxburgh, Stirling, Edinburgh and Forfar prospered through trade with England, Scandinavia and the Low Countries. These towns later became independent, self-governing burghs, trading wool and cattle for Flemish cloth or wine from Burgundy. Most of the population, however, eked out a subsistence from land and sea.

Wars of Independence

Two centuries of the Canmore dynasty came to an end in 1286 when Alexander III fell to his death over a sea-cliff at Kinghorn in Fife. He was succeeded to the throne by his four-year-old granddaughter, Margaret (the Maid of Norway), who was engaged to the son of King Edward I of England.

Margaret died in 1290 during the sea voyage to Scotland from her home in Norway, and there followed a dispute over the succession to the throne. There were no less than 13 'tanists', or claimants, but in the end it came down to a choice of two: Robert de Brus, lord of Annandale, and John Balliol, lord of Galloway. Edward I of England, as the greatest feudal lord in Britain, was asked to arbitrate – he chose Balliol, whom he thought he could manipulate more easily. Instead of withdrawing, as the Scots nobles expected, Edward sought to tighten his feudal grip on Scotland, treating the Scots king as his vassal rather than his equal. The humiliated Balliol finally turned against Edward, and allied Scotland with the French in 1295, thus beginning the enduring 'Auld Alliance'.

The English king's response was bloody. In 1296 he marched on Scotland with an army of 30,000 men, razed the ports of Berwick and Dunbar and butchered the citizens, and captured the castles of Berwick, Edinburgh, Roxburgh and Stirling. Balliol was incarcerated in the Tower of London, oaths of allegiance were demanded from Scottish nobles, and in a final blow to Scottish pride Edward I removed the Stone of Destiny, the coronation stone of the kings of Scotland, from Scone and took it back to London.

Bands of rebels led by local warlords attacked and harried the English occupiers. One such band, led by William Wallace, defeated the English army at the Battle of Stirling Bridge in 1297, but Wallace was captured and executed in London in 1305. The Scots nobles, inspired by Wallace's example, looked around for a new leader and turned to Robert the Bruce, grandson of the lord of Annandale who had been rejected by Edward in 1292. Bruce murdered his rival, John Comyn, in February 1306 and had himself crowned king of Scotland at Scone the following month.

Bruce mounted a campaign to drive the English out of Scotland but suffered repeated defeats. According to legend, while Bruce was on the run he was inspired by a spider's persistence in spinning its web to renew his own efforts. He went on to win a famous victory over the English, led by Edward II, at the Battle of Bannockburn in 1314. Continued

The stuff of legend, and Hollywood films: William Wallace

The Declaration of Arbroath

During the Wars of Independence, a group of Scottish nobles sent a letter to Pope John XXII requesting support for the cause of Scottish independence. Bearing the seals of eight earls and 31 barons, and written in Latin by the abbot of Arbroath in 1320, it is the earliest document that seeks to place limits on the power of a king.

Having railed against the tyranny of Edward I of England and having sung the praises of Robert the Bruce, the declaration famously concludes:

> Yet even the same Robert, should he turn aside from the task and yield Scotland or us to the English king or people, him we should cast out as the enemy of us all, and choose another king to defend our freedom; for so long as a hundred of us remain alive, we will yield in no least way to English dominion. For we fight, not for glory nor for riches nor for honour, but only and alone for freedom, which no good man surrenders but with his life.

raids on northern England forced Edward II to sue for peace, and, in 1328, the Treaty of Northampton gave Scotland its independence, with Robert I, the Bruce, as its king.

The Stewart Dynasty

Bannockburn and the Treaty of Northampton had no lasting effect. After the death of Robert I in 1329, the country was ravaged by civil disputes and continuing wars with England. Edinburgh was occupied several times by English armies, and in 1385 the Kirk of St Giles was burned to the ground.

Robert was succeeded by his five-year old son, David II (reigned 1329–71), who returned from exile in France in 1341 and made Edinburgh his main residence. When David II died without a son in 1371, the crown passed to his nephew, Robert II (reigned 1371–90), the child of his sister Marjory and her husband Walter the Steward. Thus was born the Stewart dynasty, which would rule Scotland and Britain for the next 300 years.

The early Stewart kings were ruthless in their attempts to break the power of the magnates. These were not peaceful years. Time and again the king met with an untimely death and clans such as the Douglases and the Donalds (lords of the Isles after the Norsemen were driven from the Hebrides in 1266) grew to wield almost regal power.

James IV & the Renaissance

James IV (reigned 1488–1513) married the daughter of Henry VII of England, the first of the Tudor monarchs, thereby linking the two royal families through 'the Marriage of the Thistle and the Rose'. This didn't prevent the French from persuading James to go to war with his in-laws, and he was killed at the Battle of Flodden in 1513, along with 10,000 of his subjects.

Renaissance ideas flourished during James IV's reign. Scottish poetry thrived, created by 'makars' (makers of verses) such as William Dunbar, the court poet of James IV, and Gavin Douglas. The intellectual climate provided fertile ground for the rise of Protestantism, a reaction against the perceived wealth and corruption of the medieval Roman Catholic Church, that would eventually lead to the Reformation.

Much graceful Scottish architecture dates from this period, and examples of the Renaissance style can be seen in alterations made to the palaces at Holyrood, Stirling, Linlithgow and Falkland. The building of collegiate churches and universities brought opportunities for education at home along French lines. St Andrews University was founded in 1410, Glasgow in 1451 and Aberdeen in 1495.

Mary Queen of Scots & the Reformation

In 1542, King James V lay on his deathbed in Falkland Palace in Fife – broken-hearted, it is said, after his defeat by the English at Solway Moss. His French wife, Mary of Guise, had borne him two sons, but both had died in infancy. On 8 December a messenger brought word that his wife had given birth to a baby girl at the Palace of Linlithgow. Fearing the end of the Stewart dynasty, and recalling its origin through Robert the Bruce's daughter, James sighed, 'It cam' wi' a lass, and it will gang wi' a lass.' He died a few days later, leaving his week-old daughter, Mary, to inherit the throne as queen of Scots.

Mary (reigned 1542–67) was sent to France, and Scotland was ruled by regents, who rejected overtures from Henry VIII of England urging them to wed the infant queen to his son. Henry was furious, and sent his armies to take vengeance on the Scots. Parts of Edinburgh were razed, Holyrood Abbey was sacked, and the great Border abbeys of Melrose, Dryburgh and Jedburgh were burned down. The Rough Wooing, as it was called, failed to persuade the Scots of the error of their ways. In 1558, Mary was married to the French dauphin and became queen of France as well as Scotland.

While Mary was in France, being raised as a Roman Catholic, the Reformation tore through Scotland. The wealthy Catholic Church was riddled with corruption, and the preachings of John Knox, a pupil of the Swiss reformer Calvin, found sympathetic ears. In 1560 the Scottish parliament created a Protestant Church that was independent of Rome and the monarchy. The Latin Mass was abolished and the pope's authority denied.

Following the death of her sickly husband, the 18-year-old Mary returned to Scotland, arriving at Leith on 19 August 1561. A week later she was formally welcomed to her capital city, dining in Edinburgh Castle before proceeding down the Royal Mile to the Palace of Holyroodhouse, where she held a famous audience with John Knox. The great reformer harangued the young queen and tried her Catholic faith; she later agreed to protect the Protestant Church in Scotland while continuing to hear Mass in private.

She married Henry Stewart, Lord Darnley, in the Chapel Royal at Holyrood and gave birth to a son (later James VI) in Edinburgh Castle in 1565. Any domestic bliss was short-lived and, in a scarcely believable train of events, Darnley was involved in the murder of Mary's Italian secretary Rizzio (rumoured to be her lover). Darnley himself was then murdered at his Edinburgh home,

probably by Mary's new lover and second-husband-to-be, the earl of Bothwell.

Mary's enemies – led by her bastard half-brother Lord James Stewart, the earl of Moray – finally confronted her at Carberry Hill, just east of Edinburgh, and Mary was forced to abdicate in 1567. Her son, the infant James VI (reigned 1567–1625), was crowned at Stirling, and a series of regents ruled in his place. When Queen Elizabeth I of England died childless in 1603, James VI of Scotland inherited the English throne in the so-called Union of the Crowns, thus becoming James I of Great Britain (usually written as James VI/I). James moved his court to London and, for the most part, the Stewarts ignored Scotland from then on. Indeed, when Charles I (reigned 1625–49) succeeded James in 1625, he couldn't be bothered to come north to Edinburgh to be formally crowned as king of Scotland until 1633.

Covenanters & Civil War

The 17th century was a time of civil war in Scotland and England. The arrogant attempts by Charles I to impose episcopacy (the rule of bishops) and an English liturgy on the Scottish Church set off public riots in Edinburgh. The Presbyterian Scottish Church believed in a personal bond with God that had no need of mediation through priests, popes and kings, and, on 28 February 1638, hundreds of people gathered in Greyfriars Kirkyard to sign a National Covenant affirming their rights and beliefs. Scotland was divided between the Covenanters and those who supported the king.

In the 1640s civil war raged in England too, where the struggle was between the Royalists and the Parliamentarians, led by Oliver Cromwell. Although the Scots opposed Charles I's religious beliefs and autocratic rule, they were appalled when Oliver Cromwell's Parliamentarians executed the king in 1649. They offered his son the Scottish Crown as long as he signed the Covenant, which he did. Charles II (reigned 1649–85) was crowned at Scone on 1 January 1651, but was soon forced into exile by Cromwell, who invaded Scotland and captured Edinburgh.

Following Charles II's restoration in 1660, he reneged on the Covenant; episcopacy was reinstated and hard-line Presbyterian ministers were deprived of their churches. Many clergymen rejected the bishops' authority and started holding outdoor services, or conventicles. Charles' brother and successor, James VII/II (1685–9) was a Catholic who made worshipping as a Covenanter a capital offence.

With the arrival in England of the Protestant William of Orange in 1688, the Catholic Stuart monarchy was doomed (the French spelling 'Stuart' was introduced to Scotland by Mary Queen of Scots, who was brought up in France). Scottish royalists held on to Edinburgh Castle in the name of King James during the Long Siege of 1689. Their leader, the duke of Gordon, held a famous conference with John Graham of Claverhouse (known as 'Bonnie Dundee') at the west postern of the castle. Dundee then rode off to raise a Jacobite army and began five more months of civil war that ended with his death at the Battle of Killiecrankie.

Union with England in 1707

The civil wars left the country and its economy ruined. During the 1690s, famine killed up to a third of the population in some areas. Anti-English feeling ran high, exacerbated by the failure of an investment venture in Panama (the so-called Darien Scheme, set up by the Bank of England to boost the economy), which resulted in widespread bankruptcy in Scotland.

The failure of the Darien Scheme made it clear to the wealthy Scottish merchants and stockholders that the only way they could gain access to the lucrative markets of developing colonies was through union with England. The English parliament favoured union through fear of Jacobite sympathies in Scotland being exploited by their enemies the French, and threatened to end the Scots' right to English citizenship and ban the duty-free export of Scottish goods to England. They also offered a financial incentive to investors who had lost money in the Darien Scheme. Despite popular opposition, the Act of Union – which brought England and Scotland under one parliament, one sovereign and one flag, but preserved the independence of the Scottish Church and legal system – took effect on 1 May 1707.

On receiving the Act in Edinburgh, the chancellor of Scotland, Lord Seafield – leader of the parliament that the Act abolished – is said to have murmured, 'Now there's an end to an auld sang.' Robert Burns later castigated the wealthy politicians who engineered the Union in characteristically stronger language: 'We're bought and sold for English gold – such a parcel of rogues in a nation!'

The Jacobites

The Jacobite rebellions of the 18th century sought to displace the Hanoverian monarchy (chosen by the English parliament in 1701 to succeed the house of Orange) and restore a Catholic Stuart king to the British throne. The name Jacobite comes from Jacob, the Latin form of the name James – the Jacobites were originally supporters of the exiled James VII/II. Jacobitism was mainly a Highland movement; it drew little support from the staunchly Presbyterian Lowlands.

James Edward Stuart, known as the Old Pretender, was the son of James VII/II. With French support he arrived in the Firth of Forth with a fleet of ships in 1708, causing panic in Edinburgh, but was seen off by English men-of-war. Another attempt in 1715 fizzled out after the inconclusive Battle of Sheriffmuir.

In 1745 the Old Pretender's son, Charles Edward Stuart (better known as Bonnie Prince Charlie), landed in Scotland to claim the crown for his father. Supported by an army of Highlanders, he marched southwards and captured Edinburgh (except for the castle) in September 1745, holding court at Holyrood before defeating the Hanoverian forces of Sir John Cope at Prestonpans, 9 miles east of Edinburgh. He got as far south as Derby in England, but success was short-lived; a Hanoverian army led by the duke of Cumberland harried him all the way back to the Highlands, where Jacobite dreams were finally extinguished at the Battle of Culloden in 1746.

After 'the '45' (as it became known), the government sought to suppress the Highland clans, banning Highland dress and the playing of the pipes. Many Jacobites were transported or executed, or died in prison; others forfeited their lands, or willingly emigrated to the developing colonies in North America. General Wade and his successor General Roy drove new military roads through the glens, and garrisons were established at Fort William, Fort Augustus and Fort George (near Inverness).

The Scottish Enlightenment

Following the removal of the Scottish parliament in 1707, Edinburgh declined in political importance, but its cultural and intellectual life flourished. During the period known as the Scottish Enlightenment (roughly 1740–1830) Edinburgh became known as 'a hotbed of genius'. The philosophers David Hume and Adam Smith and the sociologist Adam Ferguson emerged as influential thinkers, nourished on generations of theological debate. Medic William Cullen produced the first modern pharmacopoeia, chemist Joseph Black advanced the science of thermodynamics, and geologist James Hutton challenged long-held beliefs about the age of the Earth.

After centuries of bloodshed and religious fanaticism, people applied themselves with the same energy and piety to the making of money and the enjoyment of leisure. There was a revival of interest in Scottish history and vernacular literature, reflected in Robert Fergusson's satires and Alexander MacDonald's Gaelic poetry. The poetry of Robert Burns, a true man of the people, achieved lasting popularity. Sir Walter Scott, the prolific novelist and ardent patriot, unearthed the Scottish crown jewels and had them put on public display in Edinburgh Castle.

The Highland Clearances

With the banning of private armies following the Jacobite rebellions of the early 18th century, the relationship of Highland chief to clansman became an economic, not a military, one. Lands that had been confiscated after the '45 were returned to their owners in the 1780s, but by then the chiefs had tasted the aristocratic good life of the Lowlands, and were tempted by the easy profits to be made from sheep farming.

Their clansmen – no longer of any use as soldiers and uneconomic as tenants – were evicted from their homes and farms to make way for flocks of sheep. A few stayed to work the sheep farms; many more were forced to seek work in the cities, or to eke a living from smallholdings (crofts) on poor coastal land. And many thousands emigrated – some willingly, some under duress – to the developing colonies of North America, Australia and New Zealand. All over the Highlands and islands today, only a ruckle of stones among the bracken remains where once there were whole villages. The Mull of Oa, on the Island of Islay, for example, once supported a population of 4000 – today there are barely 40 people there.

The Industrial Revolution

In the second half of the 18th century, the development of the steam engine (by James Watt, a Scot) ushered in the Industrial Revolution. The Carron Ironworks near Falkirk, established in 1759, became the largest ironworks and gun factory in Britain, and the growth of the textile industry saw the construction of huge weaving mills in Lanarkshire, Dundee, Angus and Aberdeenshire; Dunfermline was famous for its fine linen. The world's first steamboat, the *Charlotte Dundas*, sailed on the newly opened Forth and Clyde Canal in 1802, and the world's first sea-going steamship, the *Comet*, was launched on the Clyde in 1812.

Glasgow, deprived of its lucrative tobacco trade with America following the American War of Independence (1776–83), developed into an industrial powerhouse, the 'second city' of the British Empire (after London). Cotton mills, iron and steelworks, chemical works, shipbuilding yards and heavy-engineering works proliferated along the River Clyde in the 19th century, powered by the coal mines of Lanarkshire, Ayrshire, Fife and Midlothian.

The Edinburgh & Glasgow Railway opened in 1842, and over the following decades new railway lines snaked their way to almost every corner of the country (many of these local lines were closed in the 1950s and '60s). By the start of the 20th century, Scotland was a world leader in the production of textiles, iron, steel and coal, and above all in shipbuilding and marine engineering. 'Clyde-built' was synonymous with engineering excellence, and Scottish-built ships plied the oceans the world over. Many of the world's most famous ocean liners, including the *Queen Mary*, the *Queen Elizabeth* and the *QE2*, were built on the Clyde.

Tourism & Politics

In the second half of the 19th century, encouraged by the writings of Sir Walter Scott,

Radicals and Reds

Scotland – and especially Glasgow – has a long history of radical politics. These were founded on the emergence of a well-educated, literate and articulate working class in the late 18th century, and the long-held Scottish belief in self-improvement.

The Paisley handloom weavers of the 1780s and 1790s formed literary and political debating societies, and supported the French Revolution and Tom Paine's *Declaration of the Rights of Man*. In 1787, the weavers of Calton in Glasgow stormed through the streets in protest against low wages; six of them were killed by troops.

In 1812, weavers all over Scotland silenced their looms in a nine-week strike; the strike leaders were eventually arrested and imprisoned for the crime of 'taking part in a combination to raise wages'. Resentment at government oppression in the wake of the Napoleonic Wars came to a head in the so-called 'Radical War' or 'Scottish Insurrection' of 1820, when troops confronted radical protesters in the streets of Glasgow; three of the leading agitators were executed.

James Keir Hardie (1856–1915), the bastard son of a poor housemaid, was born in the Lanarkshire mining village of Holytown. He first went down the mines at the age of ten, but was an avid reader and self-improver. By the age of 22 he had become an active campaigner for better wages and working conditions, and was blacklisted by the mine owners. He founded the Scottish Labour Party in 1888, and its successor the Independent Labour Party in 1893, specifically to represent the interests of the working classes in parliament. He would barely recognise his party's present incarnation, New Labour, which took power in Westminster in 1997.

By the early years of the 20th century, Scotland had a fully fledged alternative political culture. The Independent Labour Party was joined by Marxist organisations such as the Social Democratic Federation and the Socialist Labour Party, who advocated class war and direct action. The Glasgow schoolteacher and socialist revolutionary John Maclean (1879–1923) delivered lectures on Marxist theory to audiences of thousands. Maclean was appointed 'Bolshevik consul in Scotland' by Lenin following the Russian Revolution of 1917, and was an outspoken critic of Britain's involvement in WWI; he was arrested for sedition on half-a-dozen occasions.

The most notorious event in the history of Scottish radicalism was the Bloody Friday Riot of 1919. Fearing mass unemployment after WWI, the Clyde Workers Committee called a strike in support of a shorter working week. Strikers demonstrating in Glasgow's George Square began a riot after they were repeatedly charged by police. Fearing a Bolshevik-style revolution, the government sent in tanks, a howitzer and machine-gunners; fortunately, no-one was hurt.

In the General Election of 1922, Scotland returned no less than 29 Labour MPs, one Communist and a left-wing Prohibitionist, most of them from Glasgow and the west of Scotland – the region's socialist sympathies earned it the nickname of 'Red Clydeside'. Backed by the influx of 'Clydeside Reds' at Westminster, Lossiemouth-born James Ramsay Macdonald (1866-1937) was elected leader of the Labour Party and became Britain's first Labour prime minister in 1924.

the patronage of Queen Victoria and Prince Albert, and the spread of the railways, Scotland became a popular tourist destination. Victoria and Albert spent their summer holidays at Balmoral in Aberdeenshire (a tradition maintained by the royal family to this day), and it became fashionable for wealthy southerners to visit the Highlands to enjoy the salmon-fishing, grouse-shooting and deer-stalking. Strathpeffer, near Inverness, became a fashionable spa town, known as 'Harrogate of the North'.

Elsewhere, the new urban society saw a growing bourgeoisie take precedence in politics over the still-powerful landed aristocracy, and political life became more closely integrated with England's. There was much constitutional and parliamentary reform throughout the Victorian era. Legislation to improve the education system was connected with reform and dissension in the Church. Desire for betterment might send a farmer's child, barefoot and with a sack of oatmeal on his back, to university.

In the great industrial cities, conditions among the working classes were hard. In the notorious Gorbals district of Glasgow, where typhoid epidemics were rife, people lived in overcrowded tenements on barely subsistence wages. Despite prosperity from the thriving shipyards, coal mines, steelworks and textile mills, Glasgow and Clydeside harboured many unemployed, unskilled immigrants from Ireland and the Highlands.

The 20th Century

Industry continued to thrive through WWI, with Clydeside a major shipbuilding and munitions centre. The postwar slump didn't make itself felt in Scotland until the 1920s, but the Great Depression of the 1930s hit so hard that heavy industry never recovered. In 1900 Scotland had built 750,000 tons of shipping; in 1933, the figure had fallen to a mere 60,000 tons, and a quarter of the country's work force was unemployed.

Although German bombers blitzed Clydebank in 1941, killing 1200 people, Scotland largely escaped the trauma and devastation wrought on the industrial cities of England by WWII. Indeed, the war brought a measure of renewed prosperity to Scotland as the shipyards and engineering works geared up to supply the war effort. But the postwar period saw the collapse of shipbuilding and heavy industry, on which Scotland had become overreliant.

The discovery of oil and gas in the North Sea in the 1970s brought new prosperity to Aberdeen and the surrounding area, and to the Shetland Islands. However, most of the oil revenue was siphoned off to England. This, along with takeovers of Scots companies by English ones (which then closed the Scots operation, asset-stripped and transferred jobs to England), fuelled increasing nationalist sentiment in Scotland. The Scottish Nationalist Party (SNP) developed into a third force in Scottish politics, taking 30% of the popular vote in the 1974 General Election.

From the 1970s on, light engineering and high-tech electronics companies began to replace the defunct coal mines and steelworks of the Central Lowlands, but many are foreign owned. The fishing industry, profitable until Britain joined the European Union (EU), is in decline, crippled by fishing quotas imposed from Brussels and by over-fishing. Depopulation of the rural areas continues, although grant schemes subsidise new business initiatives away from agriculture and fishing.

Self-Rule

In 1967 the SNP won a landmark election victory when it took the Hamilton seat from Labour, and support for independence grew when oil – and the revenues it generated – began to flow from the Scottish sector of the North Sea in the 1970s. Both Labour and Conservative governments had toyed with offering Scotland devolution, or some degree of self-government, and in 1979 a referendum was held on whether to set up a directly elected Scottish Assembly. Fifty-two per cent of those who voted said 'yes' to devolution but the Labour prime minister, James Callaghan, decided that everyone who didn't vote should be counted as a 'no'. By this devious reasoning, only 33% of the electorate had voted 'yes', so the Scottish Assembly was rejected.

From 1979 to 1997, Scotland was ruled by a Conservative government in London for which the majority of Scots hadn't voted. Separatist feelings, always present, grew stronger. Following the landslide victory of the Labour Party in May 1997, another referendum was held on the creation of a Scottish parliament. This time the result was overwhelmingly and unambiguously in favour.

Elections to the new parliament took place on 6 May 1999, and the Scottish parliament convened for the first time on 12 May in the Assembly Rooms of the Church of Scotland at the eastern end of the Royal Mile in Edinburgh; Donald Dewar (1937–2000), formerly the Secretary of State for Scotland, was nominated as first minister (the Scottish parliament's equivalent of prime minister). The parliament was officially opened by Queen Elizabeth II on 1 July 1999. A new parliament building is being constructed at Holyrood in Edinburgh, and is expected to open in spring 2003.

GEOGRAPHY & GEOLOGY

Scotland covers 30,414 square miles, about half the size of England. It can be divided into three areas: the Southern Uplands, Central Lowlands, and the Highlands and islands.

South of Edinburgh and Glasgow lie the Southern Uplands, with fertile coastal plains and ranges of hills bordering England. The Central Lowlands comprise a broad slice from Edinburgh and Dundee in the east to Glasgow and Ayr in the west, and contain the industrial belt and most of the population.

The Highland Boundary Fault, a geological division, runs north-east from Helensburgh (west of Glasgow) to Stonehaven (south of Aberdeen) on the east coast. North of it lie the Highlands and islands, a mountainous area that makes up roughly two-thirds of the country. Mountains over 914m in height – there are almost 300 of them in Scotland – are known as Munros, after Sir Hugh Munro, the man who first compiled and published a list of them. Some rise directly from the steep-sided fjords, or sea lochs, of the

west coast. Ben Nevis, near Fort William, is Britain's highest mountain at 1344m.

The main Highlands watershed is near the west coast, giving long river valleys running east, many containing freshwater lochs and some arable land. The Great Glen is a fault line running north-east from Fort William to Inverness, containing a chain of freshwater lochs (including Loch Ness) connected by the Caledonian Canal.

Of Scotland's 790 islands, 130 are inhabited. The Western Isles comprise the Inner Hebrides and the Outer Hebrides. To the north are two other island groups, Orkney and Shetland, the northernmost outposts of the British Isles.

Edinburgh is the capital and financial centre, Glasgow the biggest city, and Aberdeen and Dundee the two largest regional centres. Inverness is the 'capital' of the Highlands.

CLIMATE

'Variable' is a vague but appropriate way to describe the many moods of Scotland's cool temperate climate. The weather changes quickly – a rainy morning can often be followed by a sunny afternoon. There are also wide variations over small distances; while one glen broods under cloud, the next may be basking in sunshine. As some locals are wont to say, 'If you don't like the weather, just wait for five minutes.' May, June and September are generally the driest months but you can expect rain at any time. Storms are rare from April to August.

Considering how far north the country lies (Edinburgh is on the same latitude as Labrador in Canada), you might expect a colder climate, but the winds from the Atlantic are warmed by the Gulf Stream. The east coast tends to be drier than the west – rainfall averages around 650mm – and is often warmer in summer and colder in winter. Temperatures rarely drop below 0°C on the coast, although winds off the North Sea can rattle your teeth. The west coast is milder and wetter, with over 1500mm of rain and average summer highs of 19°C. The western Highlands around Fort William are the wettest place in Britain, with annual rainfall as high as 3000mm.

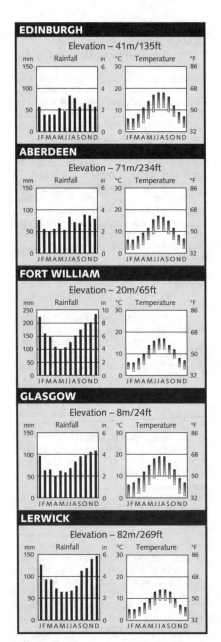

EDINBURGH
Elevation – 41m/135ft

ABERDEEN
Elevation – 71m/234ft

FORT WILLIAM
Elevation – 20m/65ft

GLASGOW
Elevation – 8m/24ft

LERWICK
Elevation – 82m/269ft

ECOLOGY & ENVIRONMENT

Although Scotland's wild, open countryside looks natural, it isn't. It's almost entirely 'artificial' in that most of the original forest (ie 99%) has been cleared, and the hillsides are kept bare by the managed grazing of sheep and deer. Artificial or not, the scenery is nonetheless still very beautiful.

In many areas of Scotland you'll notice thick conifer plantations. The Thatcher government encouraged landowners to plant these fast-growing trees, despite serious ecological drawbacks. As well as destroying wildlife habitat, conifers increase soil acidity and may have a detrimental effect on weather patterns. In the far north, fragile bog habitats have been destroyed by forestry planting.

Since the 1980s, many sea lochs and sheltered inlets on the west coast have been disfigured by salmon cages – salmon farming is worth £300 million a year to the Scottish economy. The industry has been blamed for spreading disease and parasites in wild fish populations, and for causing pollution and toxic algal blooms. While around 70 million farmed salmon were produced in Scotland in 1999, only 55,000 wild salmon were caught by rod and net, the lowest figure since records began.

So-called 'superquarries' are another controversial development of recent decades. Plans for a vast, £70 million quarry on the island of Harris in the Outer Hebrides were finally blocked by the Scottish Executive in 2000, after a 10-year legal battle. A superquarry already scars the north-western shore of Loch Linnhe at Glensanda, opposite the island of Lismore.

The seas around Scotland have suffered from pollution. Until relatively recently, most Scottish cities discharged untreated waste straight into the sea – in Dundee, more than 30 Victorian-era outfall pipes discharged raw sewage directly into the Firth of Tay until the construction of a new waste treatment plant in 2001. In the Firth of Forth, where the clean-up process has been going on for some time, the water quality has improved to the point where the beaches are among the cleanest in the country, and salmon are once again entering the river.

In Caithness, the Dounreay nuclear-waste-reprocessing plant has had a poor safety record over several decades. Following a series of accidents and disclosures about errors and cover-ups – around 170kg of weapons-grade uranium remains unaccounted for – the British government decided to close it down in 1998. However, reprocessing will continue until about 2006 when the waste runs out; after that it'll take until 2095 to dismantle the plant safely, clean up the site and encase the remains in concrete.

The remote islands of St Kilda, 60 miles west of the Outer Hebrides, set in a pristine ocean wilderness that supports 21 species of whale and dolphin, became Scotland's first World Heritage Site in 1986. Greenpeace claims the site is threatened by oil exploration and applied to put it on a Unesco list of sites in danger; the application was turned down in 1999.

Shetland appears to have pretty much recovered from the sinking of the oil tanker *Braer* in 1993; the coastline was spared serious damage because storms dispersed the spilled oil. Marine biologists are monitoring what long-term effects the pollution has had on marine life. Oil tankers still ply the waters around Shetland and the Outer Hebrides, so the threat of a similar accident remains real.

The organisations listed below are concerned with the environment.

Friends of the Earth Scotland (FoE Scotland; ☎ 0131-554 9977, W www.foe-scotland.org.uk) 72 Newhaven Rd, Edinburgh EH6 5QG. This voluntary organisation campaigns on environmental issues and publishes an annual beach guide *Sand, Sea and Sewage* rating the cleanliness of Scotland's beaches.

John Muir Trust (JMT; ☎ 0131-554 0114, W www.jmt.org) 12 Wellington Place, Leith, Edinburgh EH6 7EQ. This charity believes that the only way to protect and preserve public access to the wild areas of Scotland is to own them. It has purchased several properties, including Ben Nevis, and manages them in partnership with local communities.

National Trust for Scotland (NTS; ☎ 0131-243 9300, W www.nts.org.uk) Wemyss House, 28 Charlotte Square, Edinburgh EH2 4ET. This voluntary conservation body cares for around 74,870 hectares of countryside (as well as owning historic buildings) and has reciprocal membership agreements with the National Trust for England, Wales and Northern Ireland.

Royal Society for the Protection of Birds (RSPB; ☎ 0131-311 6500, W www.rspb.org) Dunedin House, 25 Ravelston Terrace, Edinburgh EH4 3TP. The RSPB manages a number of nature reserves around Scotland that open to the public.

Scottish Environment Protection Agency (SEPA; ☎ 01786-457700, W www.sepa.org.uk) Erskine Court, Castle Business Park, Stirling FK9 4TR. The SEPA is a public body responsible for environmental protection. It has an emergency hotline (☎ 0800 807060) for reporting pollution incidents.

Scottish Natural Heritage (SNH; ☎ 0131-447 4784, W www.snh.org.uk) 12 Hope Terrace, Edinburgh EH9 2AS. This government agency is responsible for the conservation of Scotland's wildlife, habitats and landscapes. It designates and manages National Nature Reserves (NNRs) and Sites of Special Scientific Interest (SSSIs), and will be responsible for the development of national parks in Scotland.

Scottish Wildlife Trust (SWT, ☎ 0131-312 7765, W www.swt.org.uk) Cramond House, 16 Cramond Glebe Rd, Edinburgh EH4 6NS. This voluntary agency owns or manages over 120 nature reserves.

The Woodland Trust Scotland (☎ 01764-662554, W www.woodland-trust.org.uk) Glenruthven Mill, Abbey Rd, Auchterarder, Perthshire PH3 1DP. This is the Scottish arm of a UK charity dedicated to the conservation of native woodlands.

FLORA & FAUNA
Flora

Although much of Scotland was originally covered by the Caledonian forest – a mix of Scots pine, oak, silver birch, willow, alder and rowan – deforestation has reduced this once-mighty forest to a few small pockets of indigenous trees; barely 1% remains.

Almost three-quarters of the country is uncultivated bog, rock and heather. In mountainous areas, such as the Cairngorms, alpine plants thrive, while in the far north there are lichens and mosses found nowhere else in Britain. Acidic peat covers almost 810,000 hectares, most notably in the Flow

Country of Caithness and Sutherland, now a conservation area.

Although the thistle is commonly associated with Scotland, the national flower is the Scottish bluebell (known in England as the harebell), which carpets the floor of native woodlands in spring. Yellow flag, wild thyme and yarrow abound in the summer. Heather, whose tiny pink and purple flowers emerge in August, covers much of the hills and moors. Other conspicuous flowering plants include vivid pink rhododendrons and bright yellow gorse (or whin), which both flower in May.

Fauna

Red deer are found in Scotland in large numbers, but the reindeer (apart from the herd of introduced domestic reindeer living in a semiwild state in the Cairngorms), beaver and auroch (wild ox) are all long extinct; the last wolf was shot in Sutherland in 1700. There has been talk of reintroducing the beaver and, more controversially, the wolf. A few Scottish wildcats remain in parts of the Highlands but they're rarely seen.

Sheep graze the grass-covered hills, and much of the Lowlands is given over to agriculture. Hairy Highland cattle are well adapted to survive the cold. Take care in approaching these diminutive bovids – they look cuddly but have foul tempers.

Foxes and red squirrels are found throughout the country, with pine martens in the forests. Otters are rare, though less so than in England, and their numbers are increasing. American mink, escaped from fur farms, are multiplying fast. Scotland contains almost the entire British population of blue mountain hares.

Native reptiles include the common adder (venomous) and the common lizard.

Scotland has an immense variety of bird species. Large numbers of grouse graze the heather on the moors, and gamekeepers burn vast areas to encourage the new shoots that attract this popular game bird. In heavily forested areas you may be lucky enough to see a capercaillie, a black, turkey-like bird, the largest member of the grouse family.

Birds of prey, such as the golden eagle, osprey, peregrine falcon and hen harrier, are protected. Millions of greylag geese winter on the Lowland stubble fields.

Since Scotland has 80% of Britain's coastline, it's not surprising to find millions of seabirds including gannets, kittiwakes, puffins, shags, fulmars and guillemots. Whale-watching trips follow more substantial photographic prey and both common and grey seals can be found around the coast. The fabled wild Scottish salmon, sea trout and brown trout are found in many rivers and lochs.

Endangered Species

Scotland is home to many animals and birds that are rare elsewhere in the UK, but they too are constantly threatened by the changing environment. The habitat of the once common corncrake, for example, was almost completely destroyed by modern farming methods. Farmers now receive a subsidy for mowing in a corncrake-friendly fashion and there are good prospects for its survival. Other threats don't even have an economic justification; the osprey nest at Boat of Garten has to be watched continuously to prevent egg collectors stealing the eggs.

Wildlife species that were slaughtered to the point of extermination in the 19th century – golden eagles, buzzards, pine martens, polecats and wildcats among them – are protected by law and are only now recovering. However, many of these species are a natural enemy of game birds and in order to preserve the latter for sporting shooters, some unscrupulous estate owners and gamekeepers poison birds of prey.

To combat these threats, Scottish Natural Heritage has established a Species Action Programme to restore populations of endangered species. Both the red kite and the white-tailed sea eagle, both absent from Scotland since the 19th century, have been successfully reintroduced.

Conservation Areas

Scotland's first ever national park, Loch Lomond and the Trossachs National Park, is due to open in April 2002. There are also plans to create a second national park in the Cairngorms.

National Scenic Areas (NSAs) are regions of exceptional natural beauty, especially in the Highlands, and are considered of national significance. National Nature Reserves (NNRs), also of national importance, protect habitats and species. The largest of these is in the Cairngorm Mountains. Sites of Special Scientific Interest (SSSIs) are significant for their geology, flora, fauna or habitats or combinations thereof. All NNRs are also SSSIs and are managed by the SNH. (Keeping up with the acronyms?)

Local Nature Reserves (LNRs) cover sites of local conservation interest for public use, while Regional Parks are large areas of countryside set aside for public recreation. Country Parks are smaller and usually close to towns.

GOVERNMENT & POLITICS

The Scottish parliament is a single-chamber system with 129 members (known as MSPs), elected through a system of proportional representation, and led by a first minister, currently Henry McLeish. It sits for four-year terms (the next elections are in 2003) and is responsible for education, health, housing, transport, economic development and other domestic affairs. It also has the power (as yet unused) to increase or decrease the rate of income tax in Scotland by up to 3%. The Scottish Executive – composed of the first minister, Scottish ministers, junior ministers and Scottish law officers – is the Scottish government, which proposes new laws and deals with the areas of responsibility outlined above, while the body of MSPs constitutes the Scottish legislature, which debates, amends and votes on new legislation.

The UK government in Westminster still controls areas such as defence, foreign affairs and social security. Scotland is represented in Westminster by 72 Scottish members of parliament (MPs) in the House of Commons, out of a total of 659. The Scotland Office, headed by the secretary of state for Scotland, is the Westminster department charged with ensuring Scotland's interests are represented in the UK government.

In contrast to Westminster, where the main political contest is between the Labour and Conservative parties with the Liberal Democrats coming a poor third, Scotland has four main parties – the Labour Party, the SNP, the Scottish Conservative and Unionist Party (also known as the Tory Party, or just the Tories), and the Liberal Democrats (Lib Dems) – and the main struggle for power is between Labour and the SNP.

The Conservative Party was largely opposed to devolution (the transfer of government powers from Westminster to Scotland), a policy proposed by the Labour Party in the hope of appeasing demands for independence. The long-term goal of the Scottish Nationalists is complete independence for Scotland.

In the 1997 UK elections, Scotland returned no Conservative MPs at all and in the 2001 UK elections the Tories managed to claw back just one seat in Scotland, with a majority of only 48 votes. In the 1999 Scottish parliament elections, Labour won 56 seats, the SNP 35, Conservatives 18, and the Lib Dems 17; the Scottish Socialist Party and the Green Party took one seat each.

ECONOMY

Scotland's economy is in a process of transition, as the old heavy industries are replaced by service sector and high-tech engineering and electronics industries – the concentration of computer factories in Fife has been dubbed 'Silicon Glen', in a pale imitation of California's Silicon Valley. Most of the country's coal mines and all of its steelworks have closed, and the shipbuilding industry hangs by a thread. The service sector now accounts for around two-thirds of the Scottish economy, manufacturing 22%, construction 6%, agriculture, fishing and forestry 3%, and mining a mere 2%.

As the new industries – mostly funded by foreign companies – have taken off, unemployment has fallen steadily from highs of 15% in the mid-1980s to less than 6% in 2000. Financial and business services have provided more new jobs in Scotland than electronics and North Sea oil combined, and Edinburgh is now second only to London as a financial centre. Tourism is one of the most important contributors to the Scottish economy, injecting more than £2 billion annually and employing one in 15 of the workforce. Oil and gas production in the North Sea is still rising, and is likely to continue for several decades to come. The biggest single employer in Scotland, however, is government – one in four Scots works in the public sector.

Scotland's manufacturing output is accounted for mainly by electronics, textiles, clothing (especially woollen knitwear), and food and drink – Scotch whisky is one of the country's most lucrative exports. Some traditional cottage industries, such as the weaving of Harris tweed, survive and thrive on a small scale.

In the Highlands some sheep and cattle farming continues, boosted by salmon and shellfish farming on the west coast, but tourism is the main income-provider. The fertile Lowland plains produce barley, oats, wheat, potatoes, turnips, cattle and sheep.

POPULATION & PEOPLE

Scotland's population at the 1991 census was 5.1 million – that's just 9% of the UK total, in a country that occupies one-third of the UK's land area. The population has been fairly stable since the 1950s, with a slight decrease since the 1974 high-point of 5.24 million, largely through migration in search of better job opportunities elsewhere. Over 65% of the population is concentrated in the Central Lowlands.

Glasgow is the largest city with 609,370 people, followed by Edinburgh which has 453,430, Aberdeen with 211,250 and Dundee with 142,700 (June 2000 estimates). In recent decades there has been a drift of population away from the former industrial areas of Glasgow and Lanarkshire, and into the booming east-coast cities of Edinburgh, Aberdeen and Inverness – Inverness is the UK's fastest-growing city, with a population increase from 41,800 in 1991 to 68,700 in 2001.

The Highland region is Britain's most sparsely populated area, with an average of 20 people per square mile – 30 times fewer than the UK average. A major problem since WWII has been the depopulation of the rural Highlands and, especially, the Western Isles, as younger people leave to find jobs and don't return. The population of the Western Isles fell by 5% in the short period between 1990 and 1998.

Ethnically, the Scots are a mixture of Anglo-Saxon, Celtic and Scandinavian stock. Immigration has added to the country's ethnic mix. Following the 19th-century famines in Ireland, many Irish people settled here, especially in Glasgow and the west. There are also many smaller ethnic communities including Italians, Poles, Indians, Pakistanis and Chinese.

EDUCATION

Scots have always put a high value on education. After the Protestant Reformation of the 16th century, the Scottish Church set out to spread literacy to every corner of the country. By the second half of the 18th century there was a school in almost every parish, joining the grammar schools in the burghs and the universities in Glasgow, Edinburgh, St Andrews and Aberdeen (at this time England still had only two universities, Oxford and Cambridge). In the late 18th century, almost everyone in the Central Lowlands could read and write – a remarkable achievement paralleled in few other parts of the world at that time.

From its beginnings, the Scottish education system was meritocratic – it provided the opportunity for anyone, regardless of their social background, to progress to the highest levels if they had the ability. Thus arose the Scots myth of the 'lad o' pairts' – the young man (they were all men in those days) of varied talents who could make a success of life as long as he had the intelligence and determination.

As a result of this rosy-hued history, it has often been claimed that Scotland's education system is one of the best in the world, but for the last century and a half that claim has probably been an exaggeration – it is no better and no worse than those in many other European countries.

The modern education system in Scotland is separate from that in England and Wales. Primary education from the ages of five to 12, and secondary education from 12 to 16 are compulsory; pre-school nursery education is optional. Scottish Certificate of Education (SCE) Standard Grade examinations are held at the end of the fourth year of secondary school.

Students can stay on at secondary school for a fifth and sixth year if they choose, to sit SCE Higher Grade exams, which are required for entrance to further education, training or university. Honours degree courses at Scottish universities last for four years.

State schools are supplemented by a number of independent, fee-paying schools, and there are more than a dozen universities, the most prestigious being the ancient establishments of Aberdeen, St Andrews, Edinburgh and Glasgow.

SCIENCE & PHILOSOPHY

The Scots have made a contribution to modern civilisation that is out of all proportion to the size of their country. Although Scotland accounts for only 10% of the British population, it has produced more than 20% of Britain's leading scientists, philosophers, engineers and inventors. Scots pioneered the modern disciplines of economics, sociology, geology, electromagnetic theory, anaesthesiology and antibiotics, and pioneered the steam engine, the pneumatic tyre, the telephone and the television.

Famous Scots-born scientists include John Napier (1550–1617), the inventor of logarithms; James Hutton (1726–97), the founder of modern geology; James Clerk Maxwell (1831–79), who developed the theory of electromagnetism and is widely recognised as the 'father of electronics'; and William Thomson, Lord Kelvin (1824–1907). Among his many achievements – which include becoming a student at Glasgow University at age 10, and a professor by age 22 – Lord Kelvin formulated

the second law of thermodynamics and supervised the laying of the first transatlantic telegraph cable. Scotland's greatest philosophers and thinkers include David Hume (1711–76), author of *A Treatise on Human Nature*, and Adam Smith (1723–90), who wrote *The Wealth of Nations*.

Edinburgh University, founded in 1853, is one of the world's leading academic institutions; its alumni include Charles Darwin (1809–82), who formulated the theory of evolution through natural selection, and James Burnett, Lord Monboddo (1714–99), who famously published a pre-Darwinian treatise, *Of the Origin and Progress of Language*, which proposed that humans were descended from orang-utans.

Edinburgh's medical schools have produced the likes of William Hunter (1718–83), the pioneering surgeon and anatomist; Sir James Young Simpson (1811–70), who discovered the anaesthetic properties of chloroform; Joseph Lister (1827–1912), a leader in the field of antisepsis; and Dr Elsie Inglis (1864–1917), a pioneering woman doctor and founder of the Scottish suffragette movement.

For more information, see also the later boxed text about 'Scottish Inventions & Discoveries'.

ARTS

Between them, Edinburgh and Glasgow dominate the arts scene in Scotland. Both have an energetic cultural calendar, partly reflected by their respective festivals, which showcase an extraordinary range of artists and performers. Historically, however, although the Scots have had a disproportionate impact on science, technology, medicine and philosophy, they are, with the notable exception of literature, under-represented in the world of the arts.

The arts never seem to have caught the Scottish popular imagination – or at least not in a form recognised by modern culture vultures. Perhaps the need for creative expression took different, less elitist paths – in the *ceilidh* (see the boxed text 'Tartanalia'), in folk music and dance, and in oral poetry and folk stories.

Scottish Inventions & Discoveries

It would be difficult to imagine life without many of the long list of things that the Scots either discovered or invented.

Given the weather in Scotland, perhaps it's not surprising that it was a Scot – the chemist Charles Macintosh (1766–1843) – who invented the waterproof material for the raincoat that still bears his name.

James Watt (1736–1819) didn't invent the steam engine (that was done by an Englishman, Thomas Newcomen) but it was Watt's modifications and improvements – notably the separate condenser – that led to its widespread usefulness in industry.

ASA ANDERSSON

A two-wheeled Scottish invention

The chemical engineer James Young (1811–83), known as 'Paraffin' Young, developed the process of refining crude oil and established the world's first oil industry, based on extracting oil from the oil shales of West Lothian.

Not only did John Logie Baird (1888–1946) from Helensburgh invent television, but it was his own company that produced (with the BBC) the world's first TV broadcast, the first broadcast with sound and the first outside broadcast. He also developed the concept of colour TV and took out a patent on fibre optics.

Alexander Graham Bell (1847–1922) was born in Edinburgh and emigrated to Canada and the USA, where he made a series of inventions, the most famous being the telephone in 1876.

In 1996, a team of Scottish embryologists working at the Roslin Institute near Edinburgh scored a first when they successfully cloned a sheep, Dolly, from the breast cell of an adult sheep. They added to this success when Dolly was mated naturally with a Welsh ram; in April 1998 she gave birth to a healthy lamb, Bonnie.

Literature

Scotland has a long and distinguished literary history, from the days of the medieval makars ('makers' of verses, ie poets), William Dunbar and Gavin Douglas, to the modern 'brat pack' of Iain Banks, Irvine Welsh, Ian Rankin and Christopher Brookmyre.

William Dunbar (1460–1513) was court poet to King James IV. His most famous works include *The Thrissil and the Rois* (The Thistle and the Rose), a celebration of James IV's marriage to the English princess Margaret Tudor, and the haunting *Lament for the Makaris*.

Gavin Douglas (1476–1522) was the son of the earl of Angus, and served as Provost of St Giles in Edinburgh between 1502 and 1514. His poetic style ranged from colloquial to courtly and his major works include the *Tretis of the Tua Mariit Wemen and the Wedo* (Treatise of the Two Married Women and the Widow) and a masterful translation of Virgil's *Aeneid*.

Robert Burns (1759–96) is Scotland's best-loved and most famous poet. His works have been translated into dozens of languages and are known and admired the world over. For a brief biography, see the boxed text under Alloway in the Southern Scotland chapter.

From the sublime to the ridiculous – if Burns was famous for the excellence of his poetry, William Topaz McGonagall (c.1825–1902) was renowned for the excruciating awfulness of his. Born in Edinburgh, he grew up in Orkney and Dundee, and lived most of his life in the latter. His *Poetic Gems* – including the appalling *Railway Bridge of the Silvery Tay* – are so bad they have become internationally famous.

Scottish Inventions & Discoveries

The list of famous Scots goes on and on: James Gregory (1638–75), inventor of the reflecting telescope; John McAdam (1756–1836), who developed road-building and surfacing techniques; Thomas Telford (1757–1834), one of the greatest civil engineers of his time; Robert William Thomson (1822–73), who patented the pneumatic tyre in 1845; John Boyd Dunlop (1840–1921), who reinvented the pneumatic tyre in 1888; Sir Alexander Fleming (1881–1955), co-discoverer of penicillin; and Sir Robert Watson-Watt (1892–1973), a direct descendant of James Watt, who developed the radar system that helped Britain to victory in WWII.
Other Scottish inventions and discoveries include:

• anaesthetics	• antiseptics	• breech-loading rifles
• bicycles	• carbon dioxide	• colour photography
• decimal fraction point	• electric light	• fire alarms
• gas-masks	• grand pianos	• golf
• insulin	• iron ploughs	• iron and steel ships
• kaleidoscope	• lawnmowers	• logarithms
• marmalade	• morphine	• penicillin
• postage stamp (adhesive)	• refrigeration	• shrapnel
• speedometers	• steam-powered ships	• telescopes
• ultrasound	• vacuum flasks	• water softeners

Scotland has also produced a significant number of Nobel Prize winners. Sir William Ramsay (1852–1916), whose work helped in the development of the nuclear industry, received the chemistry prize in 1904. Physiologist John Macleod (1876-1935), whose work led to the discovery of insulin, received the prize for medicine in 1923. Sir Alexander Fleming (1881-1955), co-discoverer of penicillin, also received it for medicine (in 1945). Other prize winners include: Charles Wilson, John Orr, Alexander Robertus Todd and Sir James Black.

James Boswell (1740–95), an Edinburgh advocate, is best known for his *Life of Johnson*, a biography of Dr Samuel Johnson, the English lexicographer who compiled the first dictionary of the English language. His *Journal of a Tour to the Hebrides* is a lively and engaging account of his expedition with Johnson to the western isles of Scotland.

Sir Walter Scott (1771–1832) is Scotland's greatest and most prolific novelist. The son of an Edinburgh lawyer, Scott was born in Guthrie St (off Chambers St; the house no longer exists) and lived at various New Town addresses before moving to his country house at Abbotsford (see Around Melrose in the Southern Scotland chapter). In 1787 the young Scott met Robert Burns in the house of an Edinburgh University professor. Scott's early works were rhyming ballads, such as *The Lady of the Lake*, and

his first historical novels – Scott effectively invented the genre – were published anonymously. He almost single-handedly revived interest in Scottish history and legend in the early 19th century, and was largely responsible for organising King George IV's visit to Scotland in 1822. Plagued by debt in later life, he wrote obsessively – to the detriment of his health – in order to make money, but will always be best remembered for classic tales such as *The Antiquary, The Heart of Midlothian, Ivanhoe, Redgauntlet* and *Castle Dangerous.*

Along with Scott, Robert Louis Stevenson (1850–94) ranks as Scotland's best-known novelist. Born at 8 Howard Place in Edinburgh, into a family of famous lighthouse engineers, Stevenson studied law at Edinburgh University but was always intent on pursuing the life of a writer. An inveterate traveller, but dogged by ill-health, he finally settled in Samoa in 1889, where he was revered by the natives as 'Tusitala' – the teller of tales. Stevenson is known and loved around the world for those tales – *Kidnapped*, *Catriona*, *Treasure Island*, *The Master of Ballantrae* and *The Strange Case of Dr Jekyll and Mr Hyde*.

Sir Arthur Conan Doyle (1859–1930), the creator of Sherlock Holmes, was born in Edinburgh and studied medicine at Edinburgh University. He based the character of Holmes on one of his lecturers, the surgeon Dr Joseph Bell, who had employed his forensic skills and powers of deduction on several murder cases in Edinburgh.

Scotland's finest modern poet was Hugh MacDiarmid (born Christopher Murray Grieve; 1892–1978). Originally from Dumfriesshire, he moved to Edinburgh in 1908 where he trained as a teacher and later a journalist, but spent most of his life in Montrose, Shetland, Glasgow and Biggar. His masterpiece is *A Drunk Man Looks at the Thistle*, a 2685-line Joycean monologue.

Born in Edinburgh and educated at the university, Norman MacCaig (1910–96) is widely regarded as the greatest Scottish poet of his generation. A primary school teacher for almost 40 years, MacCaig wrote poetry that is witty, adventurous, moving, evocative and filled with sharp observation; poems such as *November Night, Edinburgh* vividly capture the atmosphere of his home city.

The poet and storyteller George Mackay Brown (1917–96) was born in Stromness in the Orkney Islands, and lived there almost all his life. Although his poems and novels are rooted in Orkney, his work, like that of Burns, transcends local and national boundaries. His novel *Greenvoe* is a warm, witty and poetic evocation of everyday life in an Orkney community.

Lewis Grassic Gibbon (born James Leslie Mitchell; 1901–35) is another Scots writer whose novels vividly capture a sense of place – in this case the rural north-east of Kincardineshire and Aberdeenshire. His most famous work is the trilogy of novels called *A Scot's Quair*.

Dame Muriel Spark (b. 1918) was born in Edinburgh and educated at James Gillespie's High School for Girls, an experience that provided material for perhaps her best-known novel, *The Prime of Miss Jean Brodie*, a shrewd portrait of 1930s' Edinburgh. A prolific writer, Dame Muriel's latest novel *Aiding and Abetting*, based on the mysterious disappearance of Lord Lucan in 1974, was published in 2000.

The most widely known Scots writers today include the award-winning James Kelman (b. 1946) and Irvine Welsh (b. 1961). The grim realities of contemporary Glasgow are vividly conjured up in Kelman's short story collection, *Not Not While the Giro*; his controversial novel *How Late It Was, How Late* won the 1994 Booker Prize.

The novels of Irvine Welsh, who grew up in Edinburgh's working-class district of Muirhouse, describe a very different world from that inhabited by Miss Jean Brodie – the modern city's underworld of drugs, drink, despair and violence. Most well known for his debut novel *Trainspotting*, Welsh's best work is probably *Marabou Stork Nightmares*, in which a soccer hooligan – paralysed and in a coma – reviews his violent and brutal life.

Other leading contemporary writers include the artist and author Alasdair Gray (b. 1934), whose acclaimed novel *Lanark* is set in a run-down city based on modern Glasgow; and poet and playwright Liz Lochhead (b. 1946), whose work explores human relationships, especially as seen from a woman's point of view.

Architecture

There are interesting buildings all over Scotland, but Edinburgh has a particularly rich heritage of 18th- and early 19th-century architecture, and Glasgow is noted for its superb Victorian buildings.

Prehistoric The northern islands of Scotland have some of the best surviving examples of prehistoric buildings in Europe. The best known are the stone villages of Skara Brae (from 3100 BC) in Orkney and Jarlshof (from 1500 BC) in Shetland, and the characteristic stone towers *(brochs)* that can be seen in the north and west, including

MARK DAFFEY

Romantic Eilean Donan Castle, Loch Duich, Dornie

GRAEME CORNWALLIS

In ruins: Lochranza Castle, Isle of Arran

NEIL WILSON

The king of Scotland's castles? A view of Edinburgh Castle from Princes St

Not the road to nowhere but the West Highland Way to Fort William

Heather and Scots pine cones

A pair of guillemots on Fair Isle

A hairy Highland encounter

A disused fishing boat and lobster traps lie abandoned on Lewis.

Glenelg (south of Kyle of Lochalsh), Dun Carloway (Lewis) and Mousa (Shetland); these are thought to date from the Iron Age (2nd century BC to 1st century AD).

Early Christian (4th to 11th centuries)
Little has survived from this era, apart from a few religious buildings and the beautiful Celtic crosses at Kildalton (8th century) and Iona (10th century). Scotland has only three examples of the traditional round towers commonly associated with Celtic churches in Ireland – at Egilshay (Orkney), Abernethy (Fife) and Brechin (Angus) – which probably date from the 10th century.

Romanesque (12th century) The Romanesque style – with its characteristic round arches and chevron decoration – was introduced to Scotland along with the monasteries that were founded during the reign of David I (1124–53). Good examples survive in the abbeys of Dunfermline and Jedburgh, St Magnus Cathedral in Kirkwall and the parish churches at Leuchars and Dalmeny.

Gothic (12th to 16th centuries) The more elaborate Gothic style, distinguished by its tall, pointed arches, ornate window tracery and ribbed vaulting, was brought to Scotland and adapted by the monastic orders. Examples of Early Gothic architecture can be seen in the ruins of the great Border abbeys of Jedburgh and Dryburgh, at Holyrood Abbey in Edinburgh, and in Glasgow Cathedral. The more decorative Middle and Late Gothic styles appear in Melrose Abbey, the cathedrals of Dunkeld and Elgin, and the parish churches of Haddington (St Mary's) and Stirling (Holy Rude).

Post-Reformation (16th and 17th centuries) After the Reformation many abbeys and cathedrals were deliberately damaged or destroyed, as the new religion frowned on ceremony and ornament.

During this period the old style of castle, with its central keep and curtain wall (eg Caerlaverock and Dirleton castles), was superseded by the tower house, a characteristic feature of the Scottish countryside (good examples include Castle Campbell, Loch Leven Castle and Neidpath Castle). The Renaissance style was introduced in the royal palaces of Linlithgow and Falkland, and in the remarkable Italianate courtyard at Crichton Castle.

Georgian (18th & early 19th centuries)
The leading Scottish architects of the 18th century were William Adam (1684–1748) and his son Robert Adam (1728–92), whose revival of classical Greek and Roman forms influenced architects throughout Europe. Among the many neoclassical buildings they designed are the Old College of the University of Edinburgh, Edinburgh's Charlotte Square (possibly the finest example of Georgian architecture anywhere), Hopetoun House near South Queensferry, Mellerstain House in Berwickshire, and Culzean Castle in Ayrshire.

The New Town of Edinburgh, and other planned towns such as Inveraray (Argyll) and Blair Atholl (Perthshire), are characterised by their elegant Georgian architecture.

Victorian (mid- to late 19th century)
Alexander 'Greek' Thomson (1817–75) changed the face of 19th-century Glasgow with his neoclassical designs; masterpieces such as the Egyptian Halls and Caledonia Road Church in Glasgow combine Egyptian and Hindu motifs with Greek and Roman forms.

In Edinburgh, William Henry Playfair (1790–1857) continued the neoclassical tradition of Robert Adam in the Greek temples of the National Monument on Calton Hill, the Royal Scottish Academy and the National Gallery of Scotland, before moving on to the neo-Gothic style in Edinburgh University's New College on The Mound.

The 19th-century boom in country-house building was led by architects William Burn (1789–1870) and David Bryce (1803–76). The resurgence of interest in Scottish history and identity, led by writers such as Sir Walter Scott, saw architects turn to the towers, pointed turrets and crow-stepped gables of the 16th century for inspiration. The so-called Scottish baronial style produced many fanciful houses such as Balmoral, Scone Palace and Abbotsford, and the fashion was also followed by many civic buildings, including Edinburgh's Royal Infirmary.

The 20th Century Scotland's most famous 20th-century architect and designer is Charles Rennie Mackintosh, one of the most influential exponents of the Art Nouveau style. The most acclaimed example of his work is Glasgow School of Art, which still looks modern a century after it was built. The Art Deco style of the 1930s made little impact in Scotland, with only a few examples, such as St Andrews House in Edinburgh and the beautifully restored Luma Tower in Glasgow.

During the 1960s Scotland's larger towns and cities suffered badly under the onslaught of the motor car and the unsympathetic impact of large-scale, concrete building developments. However, modern architecture discovered a new confidence in the 1980s and 1990s, exemplified by the impressive gallery housing the Burrell Collection in Glasgow, and the new Scottish parliament building currently under construction in Edinburgh.

Painting

Scotland has produced few internationally known figures in the visual arts, although the National Gallery in Edinburgh and the galleries in Glasgow, Aberdeen, Perth and Dundee have important Scottish collections.

Scottish painting only really emerged in the mid-17th century with portraits by George Jameson (c. 1589–1644) and John Wright (1617–1700). Scottish portraiture reached its peak during the Scottish Enlightenment in the second half of the 18th century with the figures of Allan Ramsay (1713–84) and Henry Raeburn (1756–1823).

At the same time, Alexander Nasmyth (1758–1840) emerged as an important landscape painter whose work had an immense influence on the 19th century. One of the greatest artists of the 19th century was Sir David Wilkie (1785–1841), whose paintings depicted simple, rural Scottish life.

The Trustees' Academy in Edinburgh, particularly under the direction of Robert Scott Lauder (1803–69), was very influential and taught many of the great 19th-century painters, most notably William McTaggart (1835–1910). Exhibitions at the Royal Scottish Academy (RSA) in Edinburgh also helped to promote Scottish painters.

Since the end of the 19th century, Glasgow has dominated the Scottish scene, partly thanks to the Glasgow School of Art, which has produced several outstanding artists. These included Charles Rennie Mackintosh (1868–1928), whose Art Nouveau style upset more traditionalist painters, and Mary Armour (b.1902) who was a student there in the 1920s.

In the 1890s, the Glasgow Boys, who included Sir James Guthrie (1859–1930) and EA Walton (1860–1922) in their ranks, were stylistically influenced by the French impressionists. They were succeeded by the Scottish Colourists whose striking paintings drew upon French post-impressionism and Fauvism. In the same period the Glasgow Girls, exponents of decorative arts and design, drew upon Art Nouveau and Celtic influences. Among their members were Jessie Newbery (1864–1948), Anne Macbeth and the MacDonald sisters, Margaret and Frances.

The Edinburgh School of the 1930s were modernist painters who depicted the Scottish landscape. Chief among them were William Gillies (1898–1978), Sir William MacTaggart (1903–81; grandson of his earlier namesake) and Anne Redpath (1895–1965). Following WWII, artists such as Alan Davie (b.1920) and Sir Eduardo Paolozzi (b.1924) gained international reputations in abstract expressionism and pop art, but their work isn't particularly 'Scottish'. Today's new wave of painters include the 'New Glasgow Boys' (eg Peter Howson and Ken Currie) whose work is characterised by a concern for social issues.

Music

Classical Sir John Clerk of Penicuik (1676–1755), a leading Scottish patron of the arts, was a notable composer, violinist and harpsichordist, who studied in Europe under the master Arcangelo Corelli. He paved the way for a flowering of Scottish music during the Enlightenment, when Edinburgh composers William McGibbon (c.1690-1756) and James Oswald (1710–69) adapted traditional Scots tunes to the classical Italian style. Thomas Erskine (1732–81), sixth earl of Kelly (known as 'Fiddler Tam'), was one of the most important British composers of the 18th century, and the first Scottish musician to produce a symphony.

Sir Alexander Campbell MacKenzie (1847–1935), the son of a noted Edinburgh violinist and himself a professional violinist by the age of 11, was one of the finest British musicians and composers of his time; his best works include his *Piano Quartet* and the choral oratorio *Rose of Sharon*.

Scotland did not have a full-time symphony orchestra until the 1930s, and institutions such as Scottish Opera and Scottish Ballet were not founded until the 1960s.

Folk Scotland has always had a strong folk tradition and in the 1960s and '70s Robin Hall and Jimmy MacGregor, the Corries and the hugely talented Ewan McColl worked the pubs and clubs up and down the country. The Boys of the Lough, headed by Shetland fiddler Aly Bain, were one of the first professional bands to promote the traditional Celtic music of Scotland and Ireland; they have been followed by the Battlefield Band, Runrig (who write songs in Gaelic), Alba, Capercaillie and others.

Rock & Pop Scottish artists who have been successful in rock and pop music include Gerry Rafferty, who wrote *Baker St*, Fish (lead singer of Marillion) and Midge Ure, who helped organise the Band Aid famine relief in the 1980s. Iain Anderson, front man for Jethro Tull, was born in Edinburgh. Nazareth, Barbara Dickson, Big Country and The Rezillos all hailed from Fife. Sheena Easton came from Bellshill and now lives in Beverley Hills. Aberdeen's greatest musical export is Annie Lennox. The Jesus & Mary Chain came from East Kilbride. Twin brothers Craig and Charlie Reid from Fife have enjoyed huge success, both at home and abroad, as The Proclaimers.

Glasgow has produced an amazing range of musical talent, including such performers as the BMX Bandits, Aztec Camera, Hue & Cry, Simple Minds, Wet Wet Wet, Primal Scream, Texas, Belle and Sebastian, Travis – and, of course, Lulu, who had her first hit as a teenager in 1964 and is still going strong.

Edinburgh's contribution to the contemporary music scene includes: the rock band Idlewild; reggae-soul-pop singer Finlay Quaye; Shirley Manson, lead singer of Garbage; and the red-hot jazz saxophonist Tommy Smith.

Cinema

Scotland has never really had its own film industry, but in the last few years the government-funded agency Scottish Screen (☎ 0141-302 1730) has been created to nurture native talent and promote and develop all aspects of film and TV in Scotland.

Perthshire-born John Grierson (1898–1972) is acknowledged around the world as the father of the documentary film. His legacy includes the classic *Drifters* (about the Scottish herring fishery) and *Seaward the Great Ships*, about Clyde shipbuilding. Film-maker Bill Douglas (1934–91), the director of an award-winning trilogy of films documenting his childhood and early adult life, was born in the former mining village of Newcraighall just south of Edinburgh.

Glasgow-born writer-director Bill Forsyth (b. 1946) is best known for *Local Hero* (1983), a gentle comedy about an oil magnate seduced by the beauty of the Highlands, and *Gregory's Girl* (1980), about an awkward, teenage schoolboy's romantic exploits. The directing credits of Gillies MacKinnon (b. 1948), another Glasgow native, include *Small Faces* (1996), *Regeneration* (1997) and *Hideous Kinky* (1998).

Michael Caton-Jones (b. 1958), director of *Memphis Belle* (1990) and *Rob Roy* (1995), was born in West Lothian and is a graduate of Edinburgh University.

In the 1990s, the rise of the director-producer-writer team of Danny Boyle (English), Andrew Macdonald and John Hodge (both Scottish) – who wrote the scripts for *Shallow Grave* (1994), *Trainspotting* (1996) and *A Life Less Ordinary* (1997) – marked the beginnings of what might be described as a home-grown Scottish film industry. Other cinematic talents to emerge in this decade include actor and director

Peter Mullan *(My Name is Joe*; 1998) and director Lynne Ramsay *(Ratcatcher*; 1999).

Scotland's most famous actor is, of course, Sir Sean Connery (b. 1930), the original and best James Bond, and star of dozens of other hit films including *Highlander* (1986), *The Name of the Rose* (1986), *Indiana Jones and the Last Crusade* (1989) and *The Hunt for Red October* (1990). Connery started life as 'Big Tam' Connery, sometime milkman and brickie, born in a tenement in Fountainbridge, Edinburgh. He strongly supports the development of Scottish film-making, and his new production

Tartanalia

Bagpipes The bagpipe is one of the oldest musical instruments still in use today. Although no piece of film footage on Scotland is complete without the drone of the pipes, their origin probably lies outside the country.

The Highland bagpipe comprises a leather bag kept inflated by the blowpipe and held under the arm; the piper forces air through the pipes by squeezing the bag. Three of the pipes, appropriately known as the drones, play all the time without being touched by the piper. The fourth pipe, the chanter, is the one on which the melody is played.

Queen Victoria did much to repopularise the bagpipes with her patronage of all things Scottish. When staying at Balmoral she liked to be wakened by a piper playing outside her window.

Ceilidh The Gaelic word *ceilidh* (pronounced kay-lee) means 'visit' – a ceilidh was originally a social gathering in the house after the day's work was over. A local bard (poet) presided over the telling of folk stories and legends, and there was also music and song. These days, a ceilidh means an evening of entertainment including music, song and dance.

ASA ANDERSSON

A Scotsman in the full regalia

Highland Games Highland games are held in Scotland throughout the summer, and not just in the Highlands – the Edinburgh International Highland Games take place in late July and early August. Assorted sporting events with piping and dancing competitions attract locals and tourists alike.

company, Fountainbridge Films, is working on a biopic of Mary Queen of Scots.

Other Scottish actors who have achieved international recognition include Robert Carlyle, who starred in *Trainspotting* (1996), *The Full Monty* (1997) – the UK's most commercially successful film – and *The World Is Not Enough* (1999); Ewan MacGregor, who appeared in *Trainspotting* and *Star Wars: The Phantom Menace* (1999); and John Hannah, whose films include *Four Weddings & a Funeral* (1994) and *Sliding Doors* (1998). Other famous names include Deborah Kerr, Ian Bannen, Gordon Jackson, Alistair Sim, James Robertson Justice and Dame Flora Robson.

It's less widely known that Scotland produced some of the stars of silent film, including Eric Campbell (the big, bearded villain in Charlie Chaplin's films) and Jimmy Finlayson (the cross-eyed character in Laurel and Hardy films); though born in England, Stan Laurel himself grew up and made his acting debut in Glasgow.

SOCIETY & CONDUCT

Outside Scotland, Scots are often stereotyped as being a tight-fisted bunch, but

Tartanalia

Some events are peculiarly Scottish, particularly those that involve bouts of strength-testing. The apparatus used can be pretty primitive – tossing the caber involves heaving a tree trunk into the air. Other popular events are throwing the hammer and putting the stone.

Tartan The oldest surviving piece of tartan – a patterned woollen material now made into everything from kilts to key-fobs – dates back to the Roman period. Today, tartan is popular the world over, and beyond – astronaut Al Bean took his MacBean tartan to the moon and back. Particular *setts* (tartan patterns) didn't come to be associated with particular clans until the 17th century, although today every clan, and indeed every Scottish football team, has one or more distinctive tartans.

The Kilt The original Scottish Highland dress was not the kilt but the *plaid* – a long length of tartan cloth wrapped around the body and over the shoulder. The wearing of Highland dress was banned after the Jacobite rebellions but revived under royal patronage in the following century. George IV and his English courtiers donned kilts for their visit to Scotland in 1822. Sir Walter Scott, novelist, poet and dedicated patriot, did much to rekindle interest in Scottish ways. By then, however, many of the old setts had been forgotten – some tartans are actually Victorian creations. The modern kilt only appeared in the 18th century and was reputedly invented by Thomas Rawlinson, an Englishman!

The Scottish Flag Scottish football and rugby supporters can never seem to make up their minds which flag to wave – the Saltire or the Lion Rampant. The Saltire, or St Andrew's Cross – a diagonal white cross on a blue ground – is one of the oldest national flags in the world, dating from at least the 12th century. Originally a religious emblem – St Andrew was crucified on a diagonal cross – it became a national emblem in the 14th century. According to legend, white clouds in the form of a saltire appeared in a blue sky during the battle of Nechtansmere between Scots and Saxons, urging the Scots to victory. It was incorporated in the Union Flag of the United Kingdom following the Act of Union in 1707.

The Lion Rampant – a red lion on a golden-yellow ground – is the Royal Banner of Scotland. It is thought to derive from the arms of King William I the Lion (reigned 1143–1214), and strictly speaking should be used only by a Scottish monarch. It is incorporated in the British Royal Standard, quartered with the three lions of England and the harp of Ireland.

nothing could be further from the truth – most are in fact extremely generous. Scots may appear reserved, but they are passionate in their beliefs, be they about politics, religion or football. They generally treat visitors courteously, and the class distinctions that so bedevil England are less prevalent. The influence of religion is declining fast, but in the Western Isles it still affects everyday life, and sectarian tension between Protestants and Catholics occasionally erupts into violence on the football terraces. The Scots take their drinking seriously, spending an average 9% of their weekly income on booze and cigarettes, the highest consumption in Britain.

Dos & Don'ts

Though using the term British is fine, the Scots understandably don't like being called English. If subjects such as religion or Scottish nationalism come up in a pub conversation, as a visitor it's probably best to practise your listening skills, at least until you're sure of the situation.

RELIGION

It's probably true that religion has played a more influential part in Scotland's history than in other parts of mainland Britain. This remains true today: while barely 2% of people in England and Wales regularly attend church services, the figure for Scotland is 10%.

Two-thirds of Scots belong to the Presbyterian Church (or Kirk) of Scotland. There are two Presbyterian minorities: the Free Church of Scotland (known as the Wee Frees) and the United Free Presbyterians, found mainly in the Highlands and islands. The Episcopal (Anglican) Church of Scotland, once widespread North of the Tay, now has only about 35,000 members.

There are about 800,000 Roman Catholics, mainly in the Glasgow area, many of them descended from 19th-century Irish immigrants. Some islands, such as Barra, and areas of Aberdeenshire and Lochaber, were converted to Roman Catholicism as a result of secret missionary activity after the Reformation. Although not

remotely on a par with the situation in Northern Ireland, sectarian tensions between Protestants and Catholics can still be felt in Glasgow, especially at Rangers and Celtic football matches.

In Edinburgh and Glasgow there are also small communities of Moslems, Hindus and Jews.

LANGUAGE

Scotland's official language is standard English, with a smattering of loan-words from Scots, French and Gaelic. Certain regional Scottish accents – notably in Glasgow and Aberdeenshire – are notoriously difficult for visitors to understand.

Scots

From around the 8th to the 19th centuries the common language of Lowland Scotland was the 'Scots tung'.

Lowland Scots (sometimes called Lallans), like modern English, evolved from Old English and has Dutch, French, Gaelic, German and Scandinavian influences. As distinct from English as Norwegian is from Danish, it was the official language of the state in Scotland until the Act of Union in 1707, and was the language used by Robert Burns in his poetry. English rose to predominance as the language of government and of 'polite society' following the Union. The spread of education and literacy in the 19th century eventually led to the Scots language being perceived as backward and unsophisticated – school children were often beaten for using Scots instead of English.

The Scots tongue persisted, however, and today it is undergoing a revival – Scots language dictionaries have been published, there are university degree courses in Scots language and literature, and Scots is studied as part of the school curriculum.

Gaelic

Scottish Gaelic belongs to the Celtic language family, along with Irish Gaelic, Welsh, Manx, Cornish and Breton; it is the oldest continuously used language in Scotland. The 1991 census recorded 65,000

Gaelic speakers in Scotland, mostly in the western Highlands and the Hebrides.

The Gaelic tongue was brought to Scotland by Irish tribespeople (known to the Romans as the Scotti) who colonised Argyll in the 5th century AD. Gaelic was the language of the Celtic church and in the following centuries it spread along with Christianity to most of Scotland, except for Orkney and Shetland (where a Scandinavian dialect, called 'Norn', was spoken) and parts of the south-east – Scottish place names beginning with 'Kil', from Kilmarnock in Ayrshire to Kildonan in Sutherland, are derived from *cill,* the Gaelic word for 'church'. This predominance lasted until the 12th century when the Anglo-Saxon precursor of Lowland Scots spread throughout the Lowlands. Gaelic then went into a long period of decline, retreating to the north-west Highlands and the Hebrides. It was only in the 1970s that it began to make a comeback; in Gaelic-speaking areas today there are bilingual schools and colleges, and bilingual road signs.

See the Language section at the back of the book for more information on Scottish Gaelic and for useful words and phrases.

Facts for the Visitor

HIGHLIGHTS

Planning a trip can be difficult for the first-time visitor. Scotland may be small but its long, turbulent history has left it with a rich heritage of medieval castles and cathedrals, historic cities, towns and villages, stately homes and elegant gardens. Added to this are the Lowland hills, the beautiful coastal regions, and the spectacular Highlands and islands.

Historic Cities, Towns & Villages

Edinburgh
One of the world's great cities, with a dramatic site and extraordinary architectural heritage.

Kirkcudbright
This attractive town supports an artist's colony (Dumfries & Galloway).

Kirkwall
The original part of the city is a fine example of an ancient Norse town (Orkney).

Melrose
Charming market town, with a ruined abbey and good walks (the Borders).

New Lanark
Proposed as a UNESCO World Heritage Site and famous for the social experiments of Robert Owen (Lanarkshire).

St Andrews
Old university and golfing town, with ruined castle and harbour, overlooking a sweeping stretch of sand (Fife).

Stirling
An ancient fortress city that played a pivotal role in Scotland's history, with a castle more interesting than Edinburgh's.

Cathedrals & Churches (Kirks)

Dunkeld Cathedral
One of the most beautifully sited cathedrals in Scotland (Perthshire & Kinross).

Glasgow Cathedral
This Gothic cathedral was the only mainland cathedral to survive the Reformation intact.

Greyfriars Kirk
In one of Edinburgh's most evocative locations and where Greyfriars Bobby sat in vigil over his master's grave (Edinburgh).

St Magnus Cathedral
This red sandstone cathedral was built by the same masons who built Durham Cathedral in England (Kirkwall, Orkney).

St Giles' Cathedral
A Norman-style cathedral from where John Knox launched the Scottish Reformation (Edinburgh).

Museums & Galleries

Burrell Collection
A fascinating moderate-sized collection developed by a wealthy shipowner, housed in a superb museum sited in parkland (Glasgow).

Kelvingrove Art Gallery and Museum
Has an excellent collection of European and Scottish art (Glasgow).

Museum of Scotland
Five floors tracing the history of Scotland from geological beginnings to the 1990s, with many imaginative and stimulating exhibits; the interior design is an attraction in itself (Edinburgh).

National Gallery of Modern Art
Concentrates on 20th century art with works by Picasso, Magritte, Matisse etc (Edinburgh).

National Gallery of Scotland
Houses a large collection of European art from 15th-century Renaissance to 19th-century post-impressionism, and a special section on Scottish art (Edinburgh).

Historic Houses

Hopetoun House
One of Scotland's finest stately homes, overlooking the Firth of Forth (Edinburgh).

John Knox's House
One of the most interesting buildings on the Royal Mile (Edinburgh).

Mellerstain House
Considered Robert Adam's finest mansion (the Borders).

Provost Skene's House
A pre-Reformation gem (Aberdeen).

Tenement House
Small apartment giving a vivid insight into late-19th-/early-20th-century middle-class life (Glasgow).

Traquair House
Extraordinary building dating from the 10th century, seemingly untouched by time (the Borders).

Castles

Blair
One of the most popular tourist attractions in Scotland (Perthshire & Kinross).

Caerlaverock
An unusual triangular castle with a moat (Dumfries & Galloway).

Edinburgh
Former royal residence atop an extinct volcano, overlooking the city centre.

Glamis
Where Shakespeare set *Macbeth* (Dundee & Angus).

Hermitage
Brutal but romantic castle surrounded by bleakly beautiful countryside (the Borders).

Stirling
Favoured royal residence of the Stewarts.

Thirlestane
A fairy-tale castle that's still inhabited (the Borders).

Coast

The scenery from Oban to John o'Groats is one of the world's greatest natural spectacles, with arches, caves, stacks and hidden coves in many places along the coast. Some of the most spectacular cliffs in Britain are to be found in Hoy (Orkney), Clo Mor (Cape Wrath) and around Duncansby Head (John o'Groats).

Islands

Barra
Tiny but beautiful, it encapsulates the Outer Hebridean experience (Outer Hebrides).

Colonsay
Fine sandy beaches, good walks and a mild climate with only half as much rain as on the mainland (Argyll).

Harris
A mountainous and spectacular island, with beautiful beaches and isolated crofts (Outer Hebrides).

Iona
Very touristy during the day, but spend the night here to experience the magic of this holy island (Argyll).

Mull
Rough mountains, magnificent coastline, quaint villages and medieval castles (Argyll).

Orkney
Beautiful beaches, wildflowers and the fascinating Stone Age ruins (Orkney).

St Kilda
A World Heritage Site with prolific bird life (Outer Hebrides).

Skye
The wonders of Skye include sandy beaches, spectacular peaks, castles, and wildlife, from otters and deer to golden eagles, seals and whales.

Staffa
Boat trips from Mull to see Fingal's Cave and the incredible rock formations that inspired Mendelssohn's *Hebridean Overture* (Argyll).

Prehistoric Remains

Callanish Standing Stones
A cross-shaped avenue and circle on a dramatic site (Lewis).

Mousa Broch
The best preserved broch (defensive tower) in Britain (Shetland).

Ring of Brodgar
Well-preserved stone circle, part of an extensive ceremonial site that includes standing stones and a chambered tomb (Orkney).

Skara Brae
The extraordinarily well-preserved remains of a village inhabited 5000 years ago – including dressers, fireplaces, beds and boxes all made from stone (Orkney).

Train Journeys

The West Highland Line
Scotland's most famous railway line, with particularly dramatic sections crossing Rannoch Moor and from Fort William to Mallaig.

Inverness-Kyle Line
An excellent trip through wild moors and glens, leading to the bridge to Skye.

SUGGESTED ITINERARIES

Depending on the time at your disposal, you might want to try some of the following:

Three days
Visit Edinburgh and St Andrews.

One week
Visit Edinburgh, St Andrews, Glasgow, Oban, Glencoe and Fort William.

Two weeks
Visit Edinburgh, St Andrews, Glasgow, Loch Lomond, Oban, Glencoe, Fort William and the Isle of Skye.

One month
As for two weeks, but include the Outer Hebrides, Ullapool, the north coast, Orkney, Inverness, the Cairngorms and Aberdeen.

Two months
As for one month but stay longer in each place or include walking a long-distance path such as the West Highland Way, visits to the Borders, Dumfries and Galloway, or some of the more remote islands such as Shetland or Islay.

PLANNING
When to Go
Whenever you visit Scotland, you're likely to see both sun and rain. The best time to visit is May to September. April and October are also acceptable weather risks, though some attractions are closed in October. In summer, daylight hours are long; the midsummer sun sets around 11pm in the Shetland Islands and even in Edinburgh there are seemingly endless evenings.

Edinburgh becomes impossibly crowded during the festival in August. Book well ahead if you plan to visit then; alternatively, stay in Glasgow (or elsewhere) and travel into Edinburgh.

In winter the weather's cold, windy and often wet – and daylight hours are short. Though travel in the Highlands can be difficult, roads are rarely closed and Scotland's ski resorts are popular. Although many facilities close for the winter season, there's always one tourist information centre (TIC) open for an area (though several within that area may close) and more B&Bs and hotels are staying open year-round. Travel in the islands can be a problem then because high winds easily disrupt ferries. Edinburgh and Glasgow are still worth visiting in winter.

What Kind of Trip?
Your particular interests will have a large bearing on the kind of trip it'll be, as will the amount of time and money at your disposal. Many visitors to Scotland restrict themselves to Edinburgh, but the rest of the country is too beautiful to overlook. You'll get more out of your visit if you take time to explore some of the less-touristy towns, and the wonderful, more remote parts of Scotland are best appreciated on a longer stay.

It's easy enough to get to the main centres by bus or train, but some attractions have no public transport, so walking or cycling may be your only way to see them. If you're driving, the country's A-roads offer plenty to see and can be travelled at the national speed limit of 60/70mph. However, getting around remote parts of the country is time-consuming because of twisty, single-track roads;

give yourself time to do them justice, especially if you want to take in some of the islands too.

With limited time, your best bet might be to take a coach tour, or one of the hop-on, hop-off bus tours operated by Haggis Backpackers or Macbackpackers (see the Getting Around chapter).

Maps
If you're driving north from England you'll probably already have a road atlas to Britain showing Scotland in adequate detail for touring. There's a range of excellent road atlases and not much to distinguish between them in terms of accuracy or price, though the graphics differ – pick the one you find easiest to read. If you plan to go off the beaten track, you'll need one that shows at least 3 miles to the inch (1cm to 1.9km).

Alternatively, TICs have free maps at a scale of at least one inch to 10 miles (1cm to 6.4km) which are adequate for most purposes. For general touring the clear *Collins Touring Map of Scotland* (£3.99) shows most tourist attractions.

What to Bring
Since anything you think of can be bought in Scottish cities, pack light and pick up what you need as you go along. Clothing in particular is good value.

A travelpack – a combination of a backpack and shoulder bag – is the most popular item for carrying gear, especially if you plan to do any walking. A travelpack's straps zip away inside the pack when not needed, making it easy to handle in airports and on crowded public transport. Most travelpacks have sophisticated shoulder-strap adjustment systems and can be used comfortably, even for long hikes.

A tent is unlikely to be very useful; the weather hardly encourages camping, and long-distance walks are well served by hostels, camping barns and B&Bs. A sleeping bag is useful in some hostels and when visiting friends; get one that doubles as a quilt. Sheets are included in overnight fees at most hostels. A padlock is handy for locking your bag to a train or a bus luggage rack and may also be needed to secure your hostel locker. A Swiss Army knife (or any pocketknife that includes a bottle opener and strong corkscrew) is useful for all sorts of things.

For city sightseeing, a small daypack is harder for snatch thieves to grab than a shoulder bag. Other possibilities include a compass, a torch (flashlight), an alarm clock, an adapter plug for electrical appliances, sunglasses and good sun lotion.

Use plastic carrier bags to keep things organised, and dry, inside your backpack. Airlines lose bags from time to time, but there's a much better chance of getting them back if they're tagged with your name and address *inside* as well as on the outside.

Don't forget some form of waterproof jacket with a hood – umbrellas aren't recommended and usually get destroyed by the wind. If you're going to be walking, treat your boots with a waterproofing agent as many trails cross boggy ground.

RESPONSIBLE TOURISM

Except in Scotland's remote and mountainous reaches, congestion on the roads and in the cities and towns can be a major problem – even outside the peak tourist season. Visitors will do residents, themselves and the environment a favour if, wherever possible, they forgo driving in favour of using public transport, cycling or walking.

If the natural environment is to support the growing number of visitors, especially the remote and fragile areas, then human activity will need to be sensitive to that environment. The country code involves some important principles – minimising your impact, leaving no trace of your passing (not damaging wildlife, plants or trees), leaving no litter (take out what you take in) and sticking to the walking trails.

TOURIST OFFICES
Local Tourist Offices
The Scottish Tourist Board/Visit Scotland (STB; ☎ 0131-332 2433, fax 315 4545, ⓔ info@stb.gov.uk, Ⓦ www.visitscotland .com) has its headquarters at 23 Ravelston Terrace, Edinburgh EH4 3TP. They deal with postal and telephone enquiries only. The STB has a branch at 19 Cockspur St, London SW1 5BL, off Trafalgar Square, but for telephone enquiries, call the Edinburgh office.

Most towns have TICs that open 9am or 10am to 5pm Monday to Friday, and at weekends in summer. In small places, particularly in the Highlands, TICs only open from Easter to September. Note that tourist offices only promote their members, who pay high fees for membership, and may not provide the best available service.

Tourist Offices Abroad
Overseas, the British Tourist Authority (BTA, Ⓦ www.bta.org.uk) represents the STB and stocks masses of information, much of it free. For information in foreign languages, check out Ⓦ www.visitbritain.com.

Contact the BTA before leaving home because some discounts are available only to people who have booked before arriving in Britain. Travellers with special needs (disability, diet etc) should also contact the nearest BTA office. Addresses are listed on its Web site. Some overseas offices are:

Australia
(☎ 02-9377 4400, fax 9377 4499,
ⓔ visitbritainaus@bta.org.uk)
Level 16, The Gateway, 1 Macquarie Place,
Circular Quay, Sydney, NSW 2000
Canada
(☎ 888 VISIT UK, fax 905-405 1835,
ⓔ travelinfo@bta.org.uk)
5915 Airport Rd, Suite 120, Mississauga,
Ontario L4V 1T1
France
(☎ 01 44 51 56 20, fax 01 44 51 56 21)
Maison de la Grande Bretagne, 19 Rue des
Mathurins, F-75009 Paris (entrance in Rues
Tronchet and Auber)
Germany
(☎ 01801-468642, fax 069-97 112444,
ⓔ gb-info@bta.org.uk)
Westendstrasse 16–22, D-60325 Frankfurt
Ireland
(☎ 01-670 8000, fax 670 8244)
18–19 College Green, Dublin 2
Netherlands
(☎ 020-689 0002, fax 689 0003,
ⓔ BritInfo.NL@bta.org.uk)
Aurora Gebouw (5e), Stadhouderskade 2, NL-1054 ES Amsterdam

New Zealand
(☎ 09-303 1446, fax 377 6965,
e bta.nz@bta.org.uk)
17th Floor, NZI House, 151 Queen St, Auckland 1

USA
(☎ 1 800 GO 2 BRITAIN,
e travelinfo@bta.org.uk)
Chicago: 625 N Michigan Ave, Suite 1001, Chicago IL 60611 (persona l callers only)
New York: 551 Fifth Ave, Suite 701, New York, NY 10176-0799

VISAS & DOCUMENTS
Passport

Your most important travel document is a passport, which should remain valid until well after your trip. If it's about to expire, renew it before you go. This may not be easy to do abroad, and some countries insist your passport remains valid for up to six months after your arrival.

Applying for or renewing a passport can be an involved process taking from a few days to several months, so don't leave it till the last minute. Bureaucracy usually grinds faster if you do everything in person rather than relying on the mail or agents. You'll need to supply some or all of the following: passport photos, birth certificate, population register extract, signed statements and payment.

Australian citizens can apply at post offices, or the passport office in their state capital; Canadians can apply at regional passport offices; New Zealanders can apply at any district office of the Department of Internal Affairs; and US citizens must apply in person (but may usually renew by mail) at a US Passport Agency office or some courthouses and post offices.

Citizens of EU countries just need a national identity card (which usually involves less paperwork and processing time) for travel to Britain, but carrying a passport is still advisable.

Visas

A visa is a stamp in your passport permitting you to enter a country for a specified period of time. Depending on your nationality, the procedure ranges from a mere formality to an endurance test. Sometimes you can get a visa at borders or airports, but it's far better to have the paperwork completed before your arrival.

There are various visa types, including tourist, transit, business and work visas. Transit visas are usually cheaper than tourist or business visas, but they only allow a very short stay and can be difficult to extend.

Visa requirements can change, and you should always check with embassies or a reputable travel agent before travelling. If you're travelling widely, carry plenty of spare passport photos (you'll need up to four every time you apply for a visa).

For more information, see the Foreign Office Web site at W visa.fco.gov.uk or the Lonely Planet Web site at W www.lonely planet.com.au.

British Visas Visa regulations are always subject to change so it's essential to check the situation with your local British embassy, high commission or consulate before leaving home.

Currently, if you're a citizen of Australia, Canada, New Zealand, South Africa or the USA, you're given 'leave to enter' Britain at your place of arrival. Tourists from these countries are permitted to stay for up to six months, but are prohibited from working. The Working Holidaymaker scheme, for Commonwealth citizens aged 17 to 27 inclusive, allows visits of up to two years but arrangements must be made in advance through a British embassy.

EU citizens can live and work in Britain free of immigration control and don't need a visa to enter the country.

British immigration authorities have always been tough and are getting even tougher; dress neatly and carry proof that you have sufficient funds with which to support yourself. A credit card and/or an onward ticket will help. People have been refused entry because they happened to be carrying papers (such as references) that suggested they intended to work.

No visas are required for Scotland if you arrive from England or Northern Ireland. If you arrive from the Republic of Ireland or any other country, normal British customs and immigration regulations apply.

Visa Extensions To extend your stay in the UK contact the Home Office, Immigration and Nationality Directorate (☎ 0870 606 7766), Block C, Whitgift Centre, Croydon, London CR9 1AT *before* your existing permit expires. You'll need to send your passport with your application.

Onward Tickets
Although you don't need an onward ticket to be granted 'leave to enter' on arrival (see Visas earlier), this could help if there's any doubt over whether you have sufficient funds to support yourself and purchase an onward ticket in Britain.

Travel Insurance
This not only covers you for medical expenses, theft or loss, but also for cancellation of, or delays in, any of your travel arrangements. There's a variety of policies and your travel agent can provide recommendations. The international student travel policies handled by STA Travel and other reputable student travel organisations are usually good value.

Make sure the policy includes health care and medication in the countries you may visit to/from Scotland. Go for as much as you can afford, especially if you're also visiting the Channel Islands, the USA, Switzerland, Germany or Scandinavia, where medical costs are high.

Always read the small print carefully:

- Some policies specifically exclude 'dangerous activities' such as scuba diving, motorcycling, skiing, mountaineering and even trekking.
- You may prefer a policy that pays doctors or hospitals directly rather than forcing you to pay on the spot and claim the money back later. If you have to claim later, make sure you keep all documentation. Some policies ask you to call back (reverse charges) to a centre in your home country where an immediate assessment of your problem is made.
- Not all policies cover ambulances, helicopter rescue or emergency flights home.
- Most policies exclude cover for pre-existing illnesses.

Driving Licence & Permits
Citizens of the EU, Iceland, Norway and Liechtenstein can use their home driving licence until its expiry date. For non-EU citizens, home driving licences are legal for 12 months from the last date of entry to Britain; you can then apply for a British licence at post offices.

Camping Card International
Your home automobile association also issues a Camping Card International, basically a camping-ground ID. It's also issued by local camping federations, and sometimes at camp sites. It incorporates third party insurance for damage you may cause, and many camping grounds offer a small discount if you have one.

Hostel Card
If you're travelling on a budget, membership of the Scottish Youth Hostel Association/Hostelling International (SYHA/HI) is a must (those aged over 18 £6, those aged under 18 £2.50, life membership £60). There are over 70 SYHA hostels in Scotland and members are eligible for a wide list of discounts.

Student & Youth Cards
The most useful card is the plastic ID-style International Student Identity Card (ISIC), which displays your photograph. This can perform wonders, including producing discounts on many forms of transport. Even if you have your own transport, the card soon pays for itself through reduced or free admission to attractions and cheap meals in some student restaurants.

There's a worldwide industry in fake student cards, and many places now stipulate a maximum age for student discounts or, more simply, substitute a 'youth discount' for a 'student discount'. If you're aged under 26 but not a student, you can apply for the Euro<26 card, which goes by various names in different countries, or an International Youth Travel Card (IYTC) issued by the ISTC. These cards are available through student unions, hostelling organisations or youth-oriented travel agencies. They don't automatically entitle you to discounts, but you won't find out until you flash the card.

Seniors Cards

Discount cards for over 60s are available for rail and bus travel. See the Getting Around chapter for details.

Vaccination Certificates

You may need these if you're travelling onwards through parts of Asia, Africa and South America, where yellow fever is prevalent.

Other Documents

Nationals of EU countries should carry Form E111, which allows free emergency medical treatment in Britain. Enquire from your national health service or travel agent well in advance. Australian Medicare doesn't cover any medical treatment in Scotland.

If you're visiting Britain on the Working Holidaymaker scheme bring any course certificates or letters of reference that might help you find a job.

Copies

It's wise to keep photocopies of all your important documents (passport, air tickets, insurance policy, travellers cheques serial numbers) in a separate place in case of theft; stash £50 alongside, just in case.

It's also a good idea to store details of your vital travel documents in Lonely Planet's free online Travel Vault in case you lose your photocopies (or can't be bothered with them). Your password-protected Travel Vault is accessible online from anywhere in the world – create it at **W** www.ekno.lonely planet.com.

EMBASSIES & CONSULATES
Your Own Embassy

It's important to realise what your own embassy – the embassy of the country of which you are a citizen – can and can't do to help you if you get into trouble. Generally speaking, it won't be much help in emergencies if the trouble you're in is remotely your own fault. Remember that you are bound by the laws of the country you are in. Your embassy will not be sympathetic if

you end up in jail after committing a crime locally, even if such actions are legal in your own country.

In genuine emergencies you might get some assistance, but only if other channels have been exhausted. For example, if you need to get home urgently, a free ticket home is exceedingly unlikely – the embassy would expect you to have insurance. If you have all your money and documents stolen, it might assist with getting a new passport, but a loan for onward travel is out of the question.

Some embassies used to keep letters for travellers or have a small reading room with home newspapers, but these days the mail holding service has usually been stopped and even newspapers tend to be out of date.

UK Embassies & High Commissions Abroad

Some UK embassies abroad include:

Australia
  High Commission: (☎ 02-6270 6666)
  Commonwealth Ave, Yarralumla, Canberra, ACT 2600
Canada
  High Commission: (☎ 613-237 1530)
  80 Elgin St, Ottawa, Ontario K1P 5K7
France
  Embassy: (☎ 01 44 51 31 00)
  35 rue du Faubourg St Honoré, 75383 Paris
Germany
  Embassy: (☎ 030-20457 0)
  Wilhelmstrasse 70, 10117 Berlin
Japan
  Embassy: (☎ 03-5211 1100)
  1 Ichiban-cho, Chiyoda-ku, Tokyo 102-8381
New Zealand
  High Commission: (☎ 04-472 6049)
  44 Hill St, Wellington 1
South Africa
  High Commission: (☎ 21-461 7220)
  91 Parliament St, Cape Town 8001
USA
  Embassy: (☎ 202-588 6500)
  3100 Massachusetts Ave NW, Washington DC 20008

Consulates in Scotland

Most foreign diplomatic missions are in London, but some countries also have consulates in or near Edinburgh:

Australia (☎ 624 3333) 69 George St, EH2 2JG (NB For passport applications and document witnessing only – for emergencies contact the Australian High Commission in London, ☎ 020-7887 5335)

Belgium (☎ 01968-679970) 2 West St, Penicuik, Midlothian

Canada (☎ 220 4333) Standard Life House, 30 Lothian Rd, EH1 2DH

Denmark (☎ 337 6352) 215 Balgreen Rd, EH11 2RZ

France (☎ 225 7954) 11 Randolph Crescent, EH3 7TT

Germany (☎ 337 2323) 16 Eglinton Crescent, EH12 5DG

Ireland (☎ 226 7711) 16 Randolph Crescent, EH3 7TT

Italy (☎ 226 3631) 32 Melville St, EH3 7HA

Japan (☎ 225 4777) 2 Melville Crescent, EH3 7HW

Netherlands (☎ 220 3226) Thistle Court, 1–2 Thistle St, EH2 2HT

Spain (☎ 220 1843) 63 North Castle St, EH2 3LJ

Sweden (☎ 220 6050) 22 Hanover St, EH2 2EP

Switzerland (☎ 226 5660) 66 Hanover St, EH2 1HH

USA (☎ 556 8315) 3 Regent Terrace, EH7 5BW

CUSTOMS

Travellers arriving in the UK from other EU countries don't have to pay tax or duty on goods for personal use. The maximum amounts of tobacco and alcohol that each person can bring into the country duty-free are 800 cigarettes, 400 cigarillos, 200 cigars, 1kg of smoking tobacco, 10L of spirits, 20L of fortified wine (eg port or sherry), 90L of wine and 110L of beer. People under the age of 17 are not allowed to import any alcohol or tobacco.

Travellers from outside the EU can bring in, duty-free, a maximum of 200 cigarettes *or* 100 cigarillos *or* 50 cigars *or* 250g of tobacco; 2L of still table wine; 1L of spirits *or* 2L of fortified wine, sparkling wine or liqueurs; 60mL of perfume; 250mL of toilet water; and £145 worth of all other goods, including gifts and souvenirs. Anything over this limit must be declared to customs officers on arrival.

Restricted goods, which you cannot bring into the UK without a special licence, include firearms, CB radios, animals and birds (including pets), certain plants, and most meats, meat products, eggs, milk and cream. For more details of restrictions, see the HM Customs and Excise Web site at **W** www.hmce.gov.uk. Quarantine regulations are posted on this Web site.

MONEY
Currency

The British currency is the pound sterling (£), with 100 pence (p) to a pound. One and 2p coins are copper; 5p, 10p, 20p and 50p coins are silver; the £1 coin is gold-coloured; and the £2 coin is gold- and silver-coloured. The word pence is usually abbreviated and pronounced 'pee'.

Notes (bills) come in £5, £10, £20, £50 and £100 denominations and vary in colour and size. Some places might not accept £50 and £100 notes. Several Scottish banks (the Clydesdale Bank, Royal Bank of Scotland and Bank of Scotland) issue their own bank notes, including a £1 note. You shouldn't have trouble changing them in shops etc immediately south of the Scotland-England border, but elsewhere it may be difficult. Although all UK banks will accept them, foreign banks will not.

Exchange Rates

The following currencies convert at these approximate rates:

country	unit		sterling
Australia	A$1	=	£0.36
Canada	C$1	=	£0.46
euro	€1	=	£0.61
Japan	¥100	=	£0.57
New Zealand	NZ$1	=	£0.29
USA	US$1	=	£0.70

For up-to-date exchange rates, check the Internet at **W** www.oanda.com.

Exchanging Money

Be careful using bureaux de change; they may offer good exchange rates but frequently levy outrageous commissions and fees. Make sure that you establish the rate, the percentage commission and any fees in advance. Extra commission for exchanging euros has been reported, so it may be better to carry cash in US dollars rather than euros.

The bureaux de change at international airports are exceptions to the rule. They charge less than most high-street banks and cash sterling travellers cheques for free. They also guarantee that you can buy up to £500 worth of most major currencies.

Personal cheques are still widely used in Britain, but they must be validated and guaranteed by a plastic cheque card. Increasingly, retail outlets are linked to the Switch/Delta debit-card networks; money is deducted direct from your current account. Look for a current account that pays interest (or at least doesn't charge for ordinary transactions while you're in credit), gives you a cheque book and guarantee card, and offers access to Automatic Teller Machines (ATMs) and the Switch/Delta network.

Cash Nothing beats cash for convenience... or risk. It's still a good idea, though, to travel with some local currency in cash, if only to tide you over until you get to an exchange facility. There's no problem if you arrive at Edinburgh, Glasgow, Glasgow Prestwick or Aberdeen airports; all have good-value exchange counters open for incoming flights.

If you're travelling in several countries, some extra cash in US dollars is a good idea; it can be easier to change a small amount of cash (just before leaving a country, for example) than a travellers cheque.

Banks rarely accept foreign coins, although some airport foreign exchanges will. Before you leave one country for the next, try to use up your change.

Travellers Cheques Travellers cheques offer some protection from theft. American Express (Amex) or Thomas Cook cheques are widely accepted and have efficient replacement policies. Keep a record of the cheque numbers and the cheques you've cashed somewhere separate from the cheques themselves.

Although cheques are available in various currencies, there's little point using US$

cheques in Scotland (unless you're travelling from the USA), since you'll lose on the exchange rate when you buy the cheques and again each time you cash one. Bring pounds sterling to avoid changing currencies twice. In Scotland, travellers cheques are usually only accepted by banks.

Take most cheques in large denominations, say £100; commission is usually charged per cheque. It's only towards the end of a stay that you may want to change a small cheque to make sure you don't get left with too much local currency.

Credit Cards, Debit Cards & ATMs If you're not familiar with the options, ask your bank to explain the workings and relative merits of credit, credit/debit, debit and charge cards.

Plastic cards are ideal for major purchases and can allow you to withdraw cash from selected banks and automatic teller machines (ATMs – called cashpoints in Scotland). ATMs are usually linked to international money systems such as Cirrus, Maestro or Plus, so you can insert your card, punch in a personal identification number (PIN) and get instant cash. But ATMs aren't fail-safe, especially if the card was issued outside Europe, so it's safer to go to a human teller – it can be a headache if an ATM swallows your card.

Credit cards usually aren't hooked up to ATM networks unless you specifically request a PIN number from your bank. You should also ask which ATMs abroad will accept your particular card. Cash cards, which you use at home to withdraw money from your bank account or savings account, are becoming more widely linked internationally – ask your home bank for advice.

Charge cards such as Amex and Diners Club don't have credit limits but may not be accepted in small establishments or off the beaten track. Some Amex cards allow you to cash up to £1000 worth of personal cheques at Amex offices in any seven-day period.

Credit and credit/debit cards like Visa and MasterCard are more widely accepted. If you have too low a credit limit to cover major expenses like car hire or airline tickets, you can pay money into your account so it's in credit when you leave home.

Visa, MasterCard, Amex and Diners Club cards are widely recognised, although some places make a charge for accepting them (generally for small transactions). B&Bs usually require cash.

You can use Visa, MasterCard, Amex, Cirrus, Plus and Maestro in ATMs belonging to the Royal Bank of Scotland, Clydesdale Bank, Bank of Scotland and TSB. These banks also accept cards from English banks, including HSBC, Lloyds TSB and Barclays. Cash withdrawals from some ATMs have been subject to charges of £1, but this may be phased out in the near future so check with your bank or take out larger amounts.

Combine plastic and travellers cheques so you have something to fall back on if an ATM swallows your card or the local banks don't accept your card.

International Transfers You can instruct your home bank to send you a draft. Specify the city, the bank and the branch to which you want your money directed, or ask your home bank to tell you where there's a suitable one. The whole procedure will be easier if you've authorised someone back home to access your account.

Money sent by telegraphic transfer (usually at a cost of £7) should reach you within a week; by mail, allow at least two weeks. When it arrives, it will most likely be converted into local currency – you can take it as it is or buy travellers cheques.

You can also transfer money by either Moneygram or Thomas Cook. American travellers can also use Western Union (☎ 0800 833833).

Security

Keep your money in a money-belt or something similar, out of easy reach of snatch thieves. You might want to stitch an inside pocket into your skirt or trousers to keep an emergency stash; keep about £50 apart from the rest of your cash in case of a crisis. Take care in crowded places and never leave wallets sticking out of trouser pockets or day-packs.

Costs

Scotland can be expensive, but backpacker accommodation is widely available, so budget travellers will be able to keep their costs down. Edinburgh is more expensive than most other mainland towns, but prices also rise quite steeply in remote parts of the Highlands and islands where supplies depend on ferries. Petrol can cost up to 20p a litre more on remote islands than in the central Lowlands.

Some typical high-season (July and August) costs are listed below:

Hostel bed	£10 to £16 per person
Bed & breakfast	£20 per person
Mid-range hotel	£45 per person
Quality restaurant	£15 a head
Gourmet restaurant	£25 a head
Loaf of bread	40p to 80p
Pint of beer	£2
Bottle of wine	£4 (in supermarket)
Bottle of quality wine	£15 (in restaurant)
1L petrol	78p
Car hire	from £20 a day
Local phone call	20p
Newspaper	30p

While in Edinburgh you'll need to budget £18 to £25 a day for bare survival. A one-day bus travel card is £2.20, and drinks and the most basic sustenance cost at least £6, with any sightseeing or nightlife costs (around £10 to £15) on top.

Costs obviously rise if you stay in a central B&B or hotel and eat restaurant meals – a bar or cheap restaurant meal will be around £9. Add a couple of pints of beer and entry fees to tourist attractions or a nightclub and you could easily spend £50 per day – without being extravagant.

Once you start moving around the country, particularly if you have a transport pass or are walking or hitching, the costs drop. Fresh food costs roughly the same as in Australia and the USA. However, without including long-distance transport, and assuming you stay in hostels and an occasional cheap B&B, you'll still need around £25 per day.

If you hire a car or use a transport pass, stay in B&Bs, eat one sit-down meal a day and don't stint on entry fees, you'll need £45 to £55 per day, but add £3 for snacks and drinks, £4 for miscellaneous items and at least £5 for admission costs. If you're travelling by car you'll probably average a further £10 to £15 per day on petrol and parking (not including hire charges).

Unless otherwise indicated, admission costs are given as adult/child throughout this book.

Tipping & Bargaining

In general, if you eat in a Scottish restaurant you should leave a tip of at least 10% unless the service was unsatisfactory. Waiting staff are often paid derisory wages on the assumption that the money will be supplemented by tips. If the bill already includes a service charge of 10 to 15%, you needn't add a further tip.

Taxi drivers expect to be tipped (about 10%). It's less usual to tip minicab drivers.

Bargaining is virtually unheard of, even at markets, although it's fine to ask if there are discounts for students, young people or youth-hostel members. Some 'negotiation' is also OK if you're buying an expensive item such as a car or motorcycle.

Taxes & Refunds

Value-added tax (VAT) is a 17.5% sales tax that is levied on all goods and services except fresh food and books. Restaurant prices must by law include VAT.

Non-EU citizens can sometimes claim a refund of VAT paid on goods – a considerable saving. EU residents may also be eligible but must have spent *less* than 365 days out of the two years prior to making the purchase living in Britain, and must leave the EU for at least one year within three months of making the purchase. Non-EU nationals are only required to leave the EU within three months of making the purchase.

Not all shops participate in the VAT refund scheme, and different shops have different minimum-purchase conditions (normally around £40).

On request, participating shops give you a special form/invoice; they'll need to see your passport. This form must be presented with the goods and receipts to customs when you depart (VAT-free goods can't be posted or shipped home). After customs has certified the form, it should be returned to the shop for a refund less an administration fee.

Several companies offer a centralised refunding service to shops. Participating shops carry a sign in their windows. You can avoid bank charges for cashing a sterling cheque by using a credit card for purchases and asking to have your VAT refund credited to your card account. Cash refunds are sometimes available at major airports.

POST & COMMUNICATIONS
Post

Most post offices open 9am to 5.30pm Monday to Friday and 9am to 12.30pm Saturday.

Mail sent within the UK can go either 1st or 2nd class. First-class mail is faster (normally next-day delivery) and more expensive (27p up to 60g, 41p up to 100g) than 2nd-class mail (19/33p). Air-mail postcards/letters (40g to 60g) to European countries cost 36/65p, to South Africa, the USA and Canada 45p/£1.35 and Australia and New Zealand 45p/£1.49. An air-mail letter generally takes five days to get to the USA or Canada and around a week to Australia or New Zealand.

If you don't have a permanent address, mail can be sent to poste restante in the town or city where you're staying. Amex offices also hold card-holders' mail for free.

Telephone

Although British Telecom (BT) is still the largest telephone operator, with the most public phone booths, there are also several competing companies.

You'll normally see two types of phone booth: one takes money (and doesn't give change), while the other uses prepaid phone cards and credit cards. Some phones accept both coins and cards.

All phones come with reasonably clear instructions in several languages. If you're likely to make several calls (especially international) and don't want to find yourself with coins but no card, buy a BT phonecard.

Ranging in value from £2 to £20, they're widely available from various retailers, including post offices and newsagents.

Some codes worth knowing are:

☎ 0345	local call rate
☎ 0800	toll-free call
☎ 0845	local call rate
☎ 0870	national call rate
☎ 0891	premium rate
☎ 0990	national call rate

Local & National Calls Local calls are charged by time; national calls are charged by time and distance. Daytime rates are from 8am to 6pm, Monday to Friday; cheap rate is from 6pm to 8am, Monday to Friday, and the cheap weekend rate is from midnight Friday to midnight Sunday. The latter two rates offer substantial savings.

For directory enquiries call ☎ 192 (11p per minute from public telephones but 40p per call for up to two searches from a private phone). To get the operator call ☎ 100.

The *Yellow Pages* business directory (with maps) is online at W www.yell.co.uk.

International Calls Dial ☎ 155 for the international operator. To get an international line (for international direct dialling) dial 00, then the country code, area code (drop the first zero if there is one) and number. Direct dialling is cheaper, but some budget travellers prefer the operator-connected reverse-charge (collect) calls.

You can also use the Home Country Direct service (see the boxed text across) to make a reverse-charge or credit-card call via an operator in your home country.

For most countries (including Europe, USA and Canada) it's cheaper to phone overseas between 8pm and 8am Monday to Friday and at weekends; for Australia and New Zealand, however, it's cheapest from 2.30pm to 7.30pm and midnight to 7am every day (savings are considerable).

There's a wide range of local and international phonecards. Lonely Planet's eKno global communication service provides low-cost international calls – for local calls you're usually better off with a local

phonecard. eKno also offers free messaging services, email, travel information and an online travel vault, where you can securely store all your important documents. You can join online at W www.ekno.lonelyplanet.com, where you will find the local-access numbers for the 24-hour customer-service centre. Once you have joined, always check the eKno Web site for the latest access numbers for each country and updates on new features.

Mobile Phones The UK uses the GSM 900 network, which covers the rest of Europe, Australia and New Zealand, but isn't compatible with the North American GSM 1900 or the totally different system in Japan (though some North Americans have GSM 1900/900 phones that work in Scotland). If you have a GSM phone, check with your

Country-Direct Numbers

Many countries have arrangements for direct-dial connections from the UK to a domestic operator for reverse-charge (collect), account and credit-card calls.

Dial ☎ 0800 89 then:

Australia/Optus	☎ 0061
Australia/Telstra	☎ 0611
Canada	☎ 0016
France	☎ 0033
Germany	☎ 0049
Ireland	☎ 0353
Japan/Dial Japan	☎ 0443
Japan/Japan Direct	☎ 0081
Japan/Japan Straight	☎ 0080
Japan/Auto Home Dial	☎ 0860
Netherlands	☎ 0031
New Zealand/NZ Direct	☎ 0064
New Zealand/Call NZ	☎ 0640
South Africa	☎ 0027
USA/AT&T	☎ 0011
USA/Hawaii Direct	☎ 0808
USA/MCI	☎ 0222
USA/Sprint	☎ 0877
USA/Worldcom	☎ 0456

service provider about using it in the UK, and beware of calls being routed internationally (very expensive for a 'local' call). You can also rent a mobile phone – ask TICs for details – or buy a 'pay-as-you-go' phone for as little as £20. In this case you can't use your existing number however.

Fax, Email & Internet Access

Most hotels have fax machines that guests can use and larger ones have business centres with fax, printing, email and Internet services. Most backpacker hostels offer Internet access to their customers; alternatively, use one of the cybercafes found in Edinburgh, Glasgow and some other places such as Stirling, Callander and small places in the Highlands and islands including Port Ellen (Islay), Galmisdale (Eigg), Sligachan (Skye), Staffin (Skye) and Lochmaddy (North Uist). However, as there's little competition, some cybercafes charge very high rates. Internet terminals can also be found in some pubs.

DIGITAL RESOURCES
Web Sites

There are plenty of sites of interest to cyber-travellers. Web sites are given throughout this book where appropriate.

The best place to start is the Lonely Planet Web site (**W** www.lonelyplanet.com.au), which offers a speedy link to numerous sites of interest. For official tourist information, visit the Scottish Tourist Board at **W** www .visitscotland.com. There's also 'The Internet Guide to Scotland' at **W** www.scotland-inverness.co.uk, with frequently updated info for tourists. The National Museums of Scotland are on the Internet at **W** www.nms.ac.uk.

For news, weather, sport, entertainment, travel, outdoor activities, places to eat, pubs and visitor attractions, check out **W** www.scotlandonline.com. Similar, but less extensive, sites include **W** www.onl inescotland.com and **W** www.scotland.com.

For over 15,000 links to Web sites on Scottish or related topics, see **W** www.scotsmart .com. Another list of links is at **W** www.tiac .net/users/namarie/scotland.html. A good commercial genealogy service is **W** www .scottish-roots.co.uk. Australasians of Scottish descent may want to check out **W** www.scots heritage.com.au, the Web site for the magazine *Scots*.

CitySync

CitySync Edinburgh is Lonely Planet's digital city guide for Palm OS handheld devices. For more details, see **W** www.citysync.com.

BOOKS
Lonely Planet

Check out Lonely Planet's *Edinburgh* city guide and *Walking in Scotland*. For travel elsewhere in Britain, LP publishes *Britain*, *Wales*, *London* and *Cycling Britain*.

Guidebooks

The highly recommended *Touring Guide to Scotland* (2001), published by the Scottish Tourist Board, details over 1500 tourist attractions and is well worth £4.99.

People of a literary bent might like to look at the *Oxford Literary Guide to Great Britain and Ireland*, which details the writers who have immortalised the towns and villages.

There are numerous local guidebooks, the most useful being mentioned in the regional chapters. See the Activities chapter for details of cycling and walking guidebooks and books on tracing your ancestors.

For guides on accommodation and food see those sections later in the chapter.

Travel

One of the greatest Scottish travelogues is *Journal of a Tour to the Hebrides* with *Samuel Johnson*, by James Boswell. The famous lexicographer and his Scottish biographer visited Skye, Coll and Mull in 1773, and met Flora MacDonald (who had helped Bonnie Prince Charlie escape after the battle of Culloden).

More recently, *Native Stranger*, by Alistair Scott (1995), recounts the efforts of a Scot who knew 'more about the Sandinistas' but got to grips with the realities of modern Scotland by travelling the length and breadth of the land.

In Bill Bryson's highly entertaining and perceptive modern travelogue covering Britain, *Notes from a Small Island* (1997), the author visits Scotland. *The Kingdom by the Sea*, by Paul Theroux (1995), and Jonathan Raban's *Coasting* (1987), both written in 1982, are now a little dated, but nonetheless readable. Older but also still readable is John Hillaby's *Journey Through Britain*, which describes a two-month walk from Land's End to John o'Groats in 1968, great for measuring the changes which have taken place since then.

For a look behind the tourism gloss, Nick Danziger's *Danziger's Britain* (1997) should be required reading. The picture it paints of modern Britain is thoroughly depressing, and includes descriptions of life for the marginalised in the Highlands and Glasgow. This guy has seen the world and if this is how he says it is, then it's hard to argue with him.

History & Politics

Scotland – A Concise History, by Magnus Linklater and Fitzroy Maclean, is a recommended introduction and is noted for its superb illustrations, but for detailed popular history you can't beat Professor TC Smout's excellent *A History of the Scottish People 1560-1830* and *A Century of the Scottish People 1830-1950*. Andrew Marr's *The Battle for Scotland*, an interesting political history of Scotland from the 19th century to 1992, and Tom Steel's *Scotland's Story*, readable and well illustrated but stopping in the early 1980s, are both out of print.

If you were wondering what happened to the Stewart dynasty, *The Forgotten Monarchy of Scotland* gives a fairly outrageous history of the royal line-up to the present day. It's written by the self-styled Prince Michael of Albany, who claims descent from Bonnie Prince Charlie.

To flesh out some of the great figures of Scottish history there are many well-written biographies, including Antonia Fraser's *Mary Queen of Scots* and Fitzroy Maclean's *Bonnie Prince Charlie*. Nigel Tranter's well-researched and highly recommended historical novels cover the Dark Ages, medieval and Renaissance times; *The Wallace* is a magnificent account of the activities of Scotland's greatest hero.

In Bed with an Elephant, by Sir Ludovic Kennedy (1996; out of print), himself a Scot, is an entertaining, sometimes personal account of Scottish culture, Scotland's turbulent history and the country's relationship with its powerful southern neighbour, England (the elephant referred to in the title).

For an illuminating, entertaining and honest account of 19th-century life, take a look at *Hundred Years in the Highlands*, by Osgood Mackenzie.

General

Gavin Maxwell wrote several books about his life among otters and other wildlife in the Highlands; *Ring of Bright Water* is probably the best known. The naturalist Mike Tomkies wrote an evocative series of books, including *A Last Wild Place*, about his experiences while living in a remote West Highland cottage in the 1980s, but it's now out of print.

The Silver Darlings, Neil Gunn's story of the north-east's great fishing communities in the days before EU quotas, is worth seeking out but it's also out of print.

With some beautiful photographs, *Wild Scotland*, by James McCarthy, is an informative guide to Scotland's natural heritage and conservation.

For information on all things Scottish consult the *Collins Encyclopaedia of Scotland*, edited by Julia & John Keay (1998; out of print).

FILMS

Scotland has been the setting for many popular and classic films. Earlier ones include Alfred Hitchcock's *The 39 Steps* (1935), the classic comedy *Whisky Galore!* (1949), *Tunes of Glory* (1960), *The Prime of Miss Jean Brodie* (1969), *Kidnapped* (1972) and the cult horror film *The Wicker Man* (1973).

Highlander (1986), starring Sean Connery and Christopher Lambert, was set in 16th-century Scotland and filmed around Fort William and in Glen Coe and Glen Uig.

Rob Roy, the 1995 rendition of the outlaw's tale, featured some dodgy Scottish accents from Liam Neeson and Jessica Lange. However, Billy Connolly's accent was real enough when he played John Brown, Queen Victoria's Scottish servant, in *Mrs Brown* (1997).

When *Braveheart*, Mel Gibson's Hollywood treatment of the William Wallace story, won an Oscar in 1996, the Scottish Tourist Board (STB) cheered, anticipating a glut of tourists lured by the glorious background scenery. What the STB didn't mention, however, was that while part of *Braveheart* was filmed around Fort William, most of it was shot in Ireland (which had been wooing Hollywood film makers with tax breaks).

The same year saw the release of *Loch Ness*, a romantic comedy focusing on the monster myth, and *Trainspotting*, the film version of Irvine Welsh's controversial novel.

NEWSPAPERS & MAGAZINES

The Scots have published newspapers since the mid-17th century. Scotland's home-grown dailies include the *Scotsman* and the popular Labour tabloid, the *Daily Record*. *The Herald*, founded in 1783, is the oldest daily newspaper in the English-speaking world. The *Sunday Post*, noted for its conservative and rose-tinted nostalgia, is the country's best-selling Sunday paper, with a circulation of 1.6 million.

If you visit the Highlands and islands take a look at the weekly broadsheet the *Oban Times*, which gives a wonderfully parochial view of local goings on. There's also the excellent *West Highland Free Press*, available every Thursday.

Most papers sold in England and Wales are available in Scotland. Some of them are supposedly designed specifically for Scottish readership, but differences from English editions are usually marginal.

The monthly *Scots Magazine*, with articles on all aspects of Scottish life, has been in circulation since 1739. *Scottish Memories* is a romanticised monthly magazine that highlights people and moments from Scottish history.

You can also buy many foreign papers and magazines, especially in central Edinburgh.

These include the *International Herald Tribune*, *Time* and *Newsweek*.

RADIO & TV

Most radio and all TV stations are linked to the UK-wide networks.

Radio

The BBC (W www.bbc.co.uk) caters for most tastes though much of the material comes from England. Its main music station, Radio 1 (FM 97.6–99.8MHz) aims at a teenage and twentysomething audience; Radio 2 (FM 88–90.2MHz) provides music aimed at older listeners; Radio 3 (FM 90.2–92MHz) is for classical music and opera; Radio 4 (FM 92.4–94.6MHz; LW 198kHz) offers a mix of news, current affairs, drama and comedy; Radio Five Live (AM 693 and 909kHz) intersperses sport with current affairs.

BBC Radio Scotland (AM 810kHz, FM 92.4–94.7MHz) provides a mix of music, drama, news and sport from a Scottish point of view. It also oversees regional stations in Aberdeen, the Highlands, Orkney and Shetland, and a Gaelic language channel, Radio nan Gaidheal.

There are numerous independent radio stations throughout Scotland; wherever you go there'll be a local commercial station offering local news alongside the music. However, picking up radio stations in the Highlands can be a nightmare.

UK-wide commercial stations can be picked up in major urban areas. These include Classic FM (classical music), Virgin Radio (pop) and Talk Radio ('shock jock' chat and phone-ins).

Radio frequencies and programmes are published in the daily press.

TV

Britain still turns out some of the best quality TV programmes in the world. BBC1 and BBC2 are publicly funded by an annual TV licence and don't carry advertising. ITV1 and Channels 4 and 5 are commercial stations and do.

There are two Scottish-based commercial TV broadcasters. Scottish Television (STV) covers southern Scotland and some of the western Highlands, and Grampian TV transmits to the Highlands from Perth to the Western Isles and Shetland. Both include Gaelic-language programmes. Border TV covers Dumfries & Galloway and the Borders, as well as north-west England.

These channels are up against competition from Rupert Murdoch's satellite TV company Sky and assorted cable channels. Cable churns out mostly missable rubbish but BSkyB is gradually monopolising sports coverage with pay-per-view screenings of the most popular events.

VIDEO SYSTEMS

With many tourist attractions selling videos as souvenirs it's worth bearing in mind that Britain, like much of Europe, uses the Phase Alternative Line (PAL) system which isn't compatible with NTSC or SECAM unless converted (at great expense).

PHOTOGRAPHY & VIDEO
Film & Equipment

Both print and slide film are widely available; if there's no specialist photographic shop around, Boots, the chemist chain, is the likeliest stockist. The cost for a 36- exposure print films is from £4.49, excluding processing; a 36- exposure slide films cost from £4.49 excluding processing, to £6.99 including processing. A three-pack of 90-minute Digital 8/Hi8 video cassettes costs around £15; a 30-minute DV-Mini cassette costs around £13.

A cheaper, fast and efficient mail-order service by telephone is offered by Mathers (☎ 01204-522186).

Most towns have several shops where you can get print films processed in as little as one hour.

Technical Tips

With dull, overcast conditions common throughout the whole of Scotland, high-speed film (ISO 200 or ISO 400) is useful. In summer, the best times of day for photography are usually early in the morning and late in the afternoon when the glare of the sun has passed.

Restrictions

Many tourist attractions either charge for taking photos or prohibit photography altogether. Use of a flash is frequently forbidden to protect delicate pictures and fabrics. Video cameras are often disallowed because of the inconvenience they can cause to other visitors.

TIME

Scotland follows Greenwich Mean Time (GMT) in winter and British Summer Time (BST) in summer. BST is GMT plus one hour – the clocks go forward at 2am on the last Sunday in March, and back again at 2am on the last Sunday in October.

When it's noon in Edinburgh in summer, it's 4am in Los Angeles, 7am in New York, 1pm in Paris (and the rest of Europe), 1pm in Johannesburg, 8pm in Tokyo, 9pm in Sydney and 11pm in Auckland.

Most public transport timetables use the 24-hour clock.

ELECTRICITY

In Scotland, as in the rest of Britain, electricity is supplied at 240V, 50Hz AC. Plugs have three square pins and adapters are necessary for non-British appliances; these are widely available in electrical stores in towns and cities. North American appliances, which run on 110V, will also need a transformer if they don't have one built in.

WEIGHTS & MEASURES

Despite dogged resistance from a minority of the population, Britain has officially moved to the metric system. However, exceptions to the weights and measures legislation include road distances (still quoted in miles, not kilometres) and pubs, where draught beer is still sold by the pint (568mL), although spirits are sold in measures of 25mL or 35mL. Petrol (gasoline) is sold by the litre but milk can still be bought in pints. This book uses miles to indicate distance (with kilometres given in brackets), but the heights of mountains are given in metres, as is often the local custom.

For conversion tables, see the inside back cover.

LAUNDRY

Most high streets have a laundrette, usually a disheartening place to spend much time. The average cost for a single wash and dry will be about £3. Bring soap powder with you; it can be expensive if bought in a laundrette. A service wash, where someone does it for you, costs about £2 more. Hostels and camp sites usually have self-service laundry facilities.

TOILETS

Although many city-centre facilities can be grim (graffitied or rendered vandal-proof in solid stainless steel), those at main train stations, bus terminals, large supermarkets and motorway service stations are generally good, usually with facilities for the disabled and children.

Some disabled toilets can only be opened with a special key which can be obtained from some tourist offices, or by sending a cheque or postal order for £2.50 to RADAR (see Disabled Travellers later), together with a brief description of your disability.

HEALTH

Travel health largely depends on predeparture preparations, day-to-day health care while travelling and how you handle any medical problem or emergency that may develop. In reality, few travellers experience anything worse than an upset stomach.

Predeparture Planning

Make sure that you have adequate health insurance; see Travel Insurance earlier for details. You don't need an International Certificate of Vaccination to enter Scotland, but you may need one to return home. However, a Yellow Fever Vaccination Certificate is required if entering from an infected area (see the Visas & Documents section earlier).

Make sure you're healthy before you start travelling. If you're going on a long trip make sure your teeth are OK. If you wear glasses be sure to take a spare pair and your prescription.

If you require a particular medication take an adequate supply, as it may not be available locally. Take part of the packaging showing the generic name, rather than the brand, which will make getting replacements easier. It's a good idea to have a legible prescription or letter from your doctor to show that you legally use the medication to avoid any problems.

Basic Rules

Care in what you eat and drink is the most important health rule; stomach upsets are the most likely travel health problem (between 30% and 50% of travellers in a two-week stay experience this), but the majority of these upsets are relatively minor. Unfortunately, food poisoning can sometimes be a problem so it's important not to become complacent.

Water Tap water is always safe unless there's a sign to the contrary (eg on trains). Don't drink straight from a stream – you can never be certain there are no people or cattle upstream.

Medical Problems & Treatment

Sunburn Even in Scotland, including when there's cloud cover, it's possible to get sunburned surprisingly quickly – especially if you're on water, snow or ice. Use 15+ sunscreen, wear a hat and cover up with a long-sleeved shirt and trousers.

Heat Exhaustion Dehydration or salt deficiency can cause heat exhaustion. In hot conditions and if you're exerting yourself (eg walking) make sure you get sufficient nonalcoholic liquids. Salt deficiency is characterised by fatigue, lethargy, headaches, giddiness and muscle cramps. Vomiting or diarrhoea can rapidly deplete your liquid and salt levels.

Fungal Infections To prevent fungal infections, wear loose, comfortable clothes, wash frequently and dry carefully. Be sure to always wear flip-flops (thongs) in shared bathrooms.

If you get an infection, consult a chemist. Try to expose the infected area to air or sunlight as much as possible and wash all towels and underwear in hot water as well as changing them often.

Hypothermia Hypothermia can occur when the body loses heat faster than it can produce it, resulting in the body's core temperature falling. It's surprisingly easy to progress from very cold to dangerously cold through a combination of wind, wet clothing, fatigue and hunger, even if the air temperature is above freezing.

Walkers in Scotland should always be prepared for difficult conditions. It's best to dress in layers, and a hat is important since a lot of heat is lost through the head. A strong, waterproof outer layer is essential. Carry basic supplies, including food that contains simple sugars to generate heat quickly.

Symptoms of hypothermia include exhaustion, numb skin (particularly toes and fingers), shivering, slurred speech, irrational or violent behaviour, lethargy, stumbling, dizzy spells, muscle cramps and sudden bursts of energy.

To treat mild hypothermia, get the person out of the wind and rain, remove wet clothing and replace it with dry, warm clothing. Give them hot liquids – not alcohol – and some high-calorie, easily digestible food. Do not rub victims; instead, allow them to slowly warm themselves. This should be enough to treat the early stages of hypothermia and prevent the onset of critical serious hypothermia.

Diarrhoea A change of water, food or climate can cause the runs; diarrhoea caused by contaminated food or water is more serious. Dehydration is the main danger with any diarrhoea, particularly in children or the elderly, and it can occur quite quickly. Fluid replacement (at least equal to the volume being lost) is the most important thing to remember. Weak black tea with a little sugar, soda water, or soft drinks allowed to go flat and diluted 50% with clean water are all good. With severe diarrhoea a rehydrating solution is preferable to replace minerals and salts lost. Keep drinking small amounts often and stick to a bland diet as you recover.

Motion Sickness Eating lightly before and during a trip will reduce the chances of motion sickness. If you're prone to motion sickness, try to find a place that minimises disturbance – near the wing on aircraft, close to midships on boats, near the centre on buses. Fresh air usually helps; reading and cigarette smoke don't. Commercial motion-sickness preparations, which can cause drowsiness, have to be taken before the trip commences; when you're feeling sick it's too late. Ginger (available in capsule form) and peppermint (including mint-flavoured sweets) are effective natural preventatives.

Insect Bites & Stings Bee and wasp stings are usually painful rather than dangerous. However, in people who are allergic to them severe breathing difficulties may occur and require urgent medical care. Calamine lotion or Stingose spray will give relief, and ice packs will reduce the pain and swelling.

Midges – small blood-sucking flies – and clegs (horseflies) are a major problem in the Highlands and islands during summer. Bring mosquito repellent, some antihistamine tablets and a head net. Always check all over your body if you've been walking through a potentially tick-infested area as ticks can cause skin infections and other more serious diseases. To remove a tick, press down around the tick's head with tweezers, grab the head and gently pull upwards.

HIV & AIDS Infection with the human immunodeficiency virus (HIV) may lead to acquired immune deficiency syndrome (AIDS), which is fatal. Any exposure to blood, blood products or body fluids may put the individual at risk. The disease is often transmitted through sexual contact or dirty needles – vaccinations, acupuncture, tattooing and body piercing can be potentially as dangerous as intravenous drug use. HIV/AIDS can also be spread through infected blood transfusions, but in Scotland these are screened and are safe.

Sexually Transmitted Diseases (STDs) Gonorrhoea, herpes and syphilis are among these diseases; sores, blisters or rashes around the genitals, discharge or pain when urinating are common symptoms. In some

STDs, such as chlamydia, symptoms may be less marked or not observed at all, especially in women. Syphilis symptoms eventually disappear completely, but the disease continues and can cause severe problems in later years. While abstinence from sexual contact is the only 100% effective prevention, using condoms is also effective. Each individual STD requires treatment with specific antibiotics, but there's no cure yet for herpes or AIDS.

Women's Health

Gynaecological Problems Use of antibiotics, synthetic underwear, sweating and contraceptive pills can lead to fungal vaginal infections. Characterised by a rash, itch and discharge, these can be treated with a vinegar or lemon-juice douche, or with live yoghurt. Nystatin, miconazole or clotrimazole pessaries or vaginal cream are the usual treatment.

STDs are a major cause of vaginal problems. Their symptoms include a smelly discharge, painful intercourse and sometimes a burning sensation when urinating. Medical attention should be sought and male sexual partners must also be treated.

Medical Emergency

Dial ☎ 999 or ☎ 112 (both free) for an ambulance. Not all hospitals have an accident and emergency department; look for red signs with an 'H', followed by 'A&E'.

Pharmacies should have a notice in the window advising where you'll find the nearest late-night or Sunday branch.

WOMEN TRAVELLERS

Women are unlikely to have any problems in Scotland, although common-sense caution should be observed, especially in towns and cities. Solo hitching anywhere in Scotland isn't wise. Women can enter most pubs alone, but there are still a few places where this may attract undesirable attention.

Many parts of central Edinburgh and Glasgow are best avoided late at night; women have been attacked in The Meadows (Edinburgh) and near the cathedral in Glasgow. Be aware of red-light districts in both

cities – Coburg St (Leith, Edinburgh) and Anderston/Blythswood Square (Glasgow).

Condoms are usually available in women's toilets in bars, chemists and service stations. The contraceptive pill is available only on prescription, however, the 'morning-after' pill (effective for up to 72 hours after unprotected sexual intercourse) is now available over-the-counter at chemists. Family planning associations are listed in phone books.

The Rape and Abuse Line can be contacted toll-free every evening at ☎ 0808 800 0123 (calls are answered by women).

Organisations

For general advice on health issues, contraception and pregnancy, visit a Well Woman clinic – ask at local libraries or doctors' surgeries for the details. In Edinburgh, contact Well Woman Services (☎ 0131-343 1282), 18 Dean Terrace, Stockbridge.

GAY & LESBIAN TRAVELLERS

Although many Scots are fairly tolerant of homosexuality, hostility may be encountered and overt displays of affection aren't wise if conducted away from acknowledged 'gay' venues or districts. The age of homosexual consent is now 16.

Edinburgh and Glasgow have small but flourishing gay scenes. The Web site at Ⓦ www.gayscotland.com and the monthly magazine *Scotsgay* (Ⓦ www.scotsgay.com) keep gays, lesbians and bisexuals informed about gay-scene issues.

The main information source is the LGBT Centre (☎ 0131-557 2625), 58a Broughton St, Edinburgh; otherwise, contact the Gay & Lesbian Switchboard (☎ 0131-556 4049, ⓔ mail@lgls.org) or the Lesbian Line (☎ 0131-557 0751). Pride Scotland can be found at Ⓦ www.pridescotland.org.

DISABLED TRAVELLERS

For many disabled travellers, Scotland is a strange mix of user-friendliness and unfriendliness. Few new buildings are inaccessible to wheelchair users, so large, new hotels and modern tourist attractions are usually fine. However, most B&Bs and guesthouses are in hard-to-adapt older buildings. This means that travellers with mobility problems may pay more for accommodation than their more able-bodied fellows.

It's a similar story with public transport. Newer buses sometimes have steps that lower for easier access, as do trains, but it's always wise to check before setting out. Tourist attractions sometimes reserve parking spaces near the entrance for disabled drivers.

Many ticket offices, banks etc are fitted with hearing loops to assist the hearing-impaired; look for the symbol of a large ear. A few tourist attractions, such as Glasgow Cathedral, have Braille guides or scented gardens for the visually impaired.

Information & Organisations

Get in touch with your national support organisation (preferably the travel officer, if there is one) before leaving home. These often have complete libraries devoted to travel, and can put you in touch with travel agents who specialise in tours for people with special needs.

The STB produces a guide, *Accessible Scotland*, for disabled travellers, and many TICs have leaflets with accessibility details for their area. For more information, including specialist tour operators, contact Disability Scotland (☎ 0131-229 8632, W www.disabilityscotland.org.uk), Princes House, 5 Shandwick Place, Edinburgh EH2 4RG.

The Royal Association for Disability and Rehabilitation (RADAR) publishes a guide (£8 including postage) on travelling in the UK which gives a good overview of facilities. Contact RADAR (☎ 020-7250 3222, W www.radar.org.uk), Information Dept, 12 City Forum, 250 City Rd, London EC1V 8AF. The Holiday Care Service (☎ 01293-774535, W www.holidaycare.org .uk), 2nd Floor, Imperial Bldgs, Victoria Rd, Horley, Surrey RH6 7PZ, also publishes a guide (£7.50) to accessible accommodation and travel in Britain and can offer general advice.

Rail companies offer a Disabled Persons' Railcard (see Rail in the Getting Around chapter for more details).

SENIOR TRAVELLERS

Seniors are entitled to discounts on things such as public transport and admission fees to tourist attractions, provided they show proof of age. Sometimes a special pass is needed. The minimum qualifying age is generally 60 to 65 for men, 55 to 65 for women.

In your home country, a lower age may entitle you to special travel packages and discounts (on car hire, for instance) through organisations and travel agents that cater for senior travellers. Start hunting at your local senior-citizens advice bureau.

In Scotland, rail companies offer a Senior Citizens Railcard for people of 60 and over (see Rail in the Getting Around chapter).

TRAVEL WITH CHILDREN

Successful travel with young children requires effort but can certainly be done. Try not to overdo things and consider using self-catering accommodation as a base. Children under a certain age can often stay free with their parents in hotels, but be prepared for hotels and B&Bs that won't accept children. Modern, purpose-built hotels usually provide cots.

Include children in the planning process; if they've helped to work out where you'll be going, they'll be more interested when they get there. Include a range of activities – balance a visit to Edinburgh Castle with one to the Museum of Childhood.

The *List* magazine has a section on children's activities and events in and around Glasgow and Edinburgh; also check the local newspapers.

See Lonely Planet's *Travel with Children*, by Maureen Wheeler, for more information.

USEFUL ORGANISATIONS

Membership of Historic Scotland and the National Trust for Scotland is worth considering, especially if you're going to be in Scotland for a while. Both are non-profit organisations dedicated to the preservation of the environment, and both care for hundreds of spectacular sites, which are open free of charge to members. See below for further details.

Historic Scotland

Historic Scotland (HS; ☎ 0131-668 8800, W www.historic-scotland.net), Longmore House, Salisbury Place, Edinburgh EH9 1SH, manages more than 330 historic sites, including top attractions such as Edinburgh and Stirling castles. A year's membership costs £28/21 for an adult/senior, giving free entry to HS sites, and half-price entry to English Heritage properties in England and Cadw properties in Wales. It also offers short-term 'Explorer' membership – three/seven/14 days for £12/17/22.

There are standard HS opening times, and unless indicated otherwise, standard opening times apply. Properties open 9.30am to 6.30pm daily April to September; they close two hours earlier (opening at 2pm on Sunday) October to March; and some places are open longer hours in October and November. Last admission is 30 minutes before closing time.

National Trust for Scotland

The National Trust for Scotland (NTS; ☎ 0131-243 9555, W www.nts.org.uk), 28 Charlotte Square, Edinburgh EH2 4ET, is separate from the National Trust (NT; England, Wales and Northern Ireland), although there are reciprocal membership agreements. The NTS cares for 100 properties and 73,340 hectares of countryside.

A year's membership of the NTS costing £28 (£12 for those aged under 26, £19 for seniors) offers free access to all NTS and NT properties.

DANGERS & ANNOYANCES
Crime

Scotland has the usual big-city crimes (often alcohol related), so normal caution is advised. Pickpockets and bag snatchers operate in crowded public places, although this isn't a big problem. To make it harder for them, place your wallet in a front pocket when in urban areas.

Carry valuables next to your skin or in a sturdy pouch on your belt. Don't leave valuables lying around in your room, even in hotels. Never leave valuables in a car, and remove all luggage overnight. Report thefts

to the police and ask for a statement, or your travel insurance won't pay out; thefts from cars may be excluded.

Midges & Clegs

The most painful problems facing visitors to the Highlands and islands are midges and clegs. The midge is a tiny blood-sucking fly only 2mm long, which is related to the mosquito. Midges are at their worst during the twilight hours, and on still, overcast days. They proliferate from late May to mid-September, but especially mid-June to mid-August – which unfortunately coincides with the main tourist season. Cover yourself up, particularly in the evening, wear light-coloured clothing (midges are attracted to dark colours) and, most importantly, use a reliable insect repellent containing DEET or DMP.

The cleg, or horse fly, is about 13mm (half an inch) in length and slate grey in colour. A master of stealth, it loves to land unnoticed on neck or ankle, and can give a painful bite. It can even bite through hair or light clothing. Unlike midges, they are most active on warm, sunny days, and are most common in July and August.

Beggars

The cities have their share of beggars. If you don't want to give money directly, but would like to help the homeless and long-term unemployed, you could buy a copy of the magazine *The Big Issue* (£1) from homeless street vendors, who benefit directly from sales. Also, consider giving to Shelter Scotland (☎ 0131-413 7070), a charity that helps the homeless and gratefully accepts donations.

Military Jets

One of the most annoying and frightening aspects of touring the Highlands is the sudden appearance and sound of military jets. It's something you never get used to.

Racial Discrimination

In general, tolerance prevails and visitors are unlikely to have problems associated with their skin colour. However, Scots are no less racist than other Britons, and taunts and – rarely – attacks do occur (the murder of an asylum seeker was in the news at the time of writing). Although few visitors will be aware of anti-English sentiment, it does exist, mainly in remote areas and on some islands.

EMERGENCIES
Dial ☎ 999 or ☎ 112 (both free) for police, ambulance, fire brigade, mountain rescue or coastguard.

LEGAL MATTERS
The 1707 Act of Union prexserved the Scottish legal system as separate from the law in England and Wales. Although there has been considerable convergence since then, Scots Law remains distinct.

Police have the power to detain anyone suspected of having committed an offence punishable by imprisonment (including drugs offences) for up to six hours. They can search you, take photographs and fingerprints, and question you. You are legally required to provide your correct name and address – not doing so, or giving false details, is an offence – but you are not obliged to answer any other questions. After six hours, the police must either formally charge you or let you go. If you are detained and/or arrested, you have the right to inform a solicitor and one other person, though you have no right to actually see the solicitor or to make a telephone call. If you don't know a solicitor, the police will inform the duty solicitor for you.

If you need legal assistance contact the Scottish Legal Aid Board (☎ 0131-226 7061, fax 220 4878), 44 Drumsheugh Gardens, Edinburgh.

Drugs
Possession of a small amount of cannabis is an offence punishable by a fine, but possession of a larger amount of cannabis – which will be construed as having intent to supply – or any amount of harder drugs is much more serious, with a sentence of up to 14 years in prison. Police have the right to search anyone they suspect of possessing drugs.

Driving Offences
You're allowed to have a maximum blood-alcohol level of 35mg/100mL when driving, but the safest approach is not to drink at all.

Traffic offences (illegal parking, speeding etc) usually incur a fine for which you're usually allowed 30 days to pay.

See also Road Rules under Car & Motorcycle in the Getting Around chapter.

BUSINESS HOURS
Offices generally open 9am to 5pm Monday to Friday. Shops may open longer hours, and most open 9am to 5pm Saturday. An increasing number of shops also open Sunday, typically from 10am to 4pm. Even in small towns, supermarkets stay open until 8pm daily and a few city supermarkets are open 24 hours. In country towns, some shops have an early-closing day – usually Tuesday, Wednesday or Thursday afternoon.

Post offices open 9am to 5.30pm Monday to Friday and 9am to 12.30pm Saturday. Bank hours vary, but are generally 9.30am to 4pm Monday to Friday. Some banks open Saturday, generally from 9.30am to 12.30pm.

Church Regulations
In the Highlands and islands the Free Church of Scotland and the Free Presbyterian Church observe the Sabbath strictly, and in some areas all shops and petrol stations are closed on Sundays, and there are no Sunday ferry services.

PUBLIC HOLIDAYS & SPECIAL EVENTS
Public Holidays
Although bank holidays are general public holidays in the rest of the UK, in Scotland they only apply to banks and some other commercial offices.

Bank holidays occur at the start of January, the first weekend in March, the first and last weekend in May, the first weekend in August and Christmas Day and Boxing Day.

Christmas Day, New Year's Day and 2 January are also general public holidays. Scottish towns normally have their own

Scotland's Festivals

Following its inception in 1947 as a counterpoint to the austerity and problems of reconstruction after WWII, the **Edinburgh International Festival** has grown into the world's largest, most important arts festival. It attracts top performers in 'serious' music, dance and drama who play to capacity audiences.

The **Fringe Festival** began unofficially at the same time and grew in tandem to become the largest such event in the world. It showcases wannabe stars, and over 500 amateur and professional groups present every possible kind of avant-garde performance in venues all around the city.

A separate event but a major attraction in its own right, the **Edinburgh Military Tattoo** is held in the same period and takes place on the Esplanade of Edinburgh Castle. The show is an extravaganza of daredevil displays, regimental posturing and swirling bagpipes and ends with a single piper playing a lament on the battlements. For bookings, contact the Tattoo Office (☎ 0131-225 1188, fax 225 8627, Ⓦ www.edintattoo.co.uk), 32 Market St, Edinburgh EH1 1QB.

To make sure that every B&B and hotel room for over 40 miles is full, several other festivals take place at roughly the same time. The 10-day **Edinburgh International Jazz & Blues Festival** (Ⓦ www.jazzmusic.co.uk) attracts top musicians from around the world who perform at various venues in late July/early August. The two-week **Edinburgh International Film Festival** (Ⓦ www.edfilmfest.org.uk), dating from 1947, is Scotland's chief film festival. Authors and many literary enthusiasts gather in Charlotte Square during the **Edinburgh Book Festival** (Ⓦ www.edbookfest.co.uk). These latter two festivals are during the second half of the month.

The festival period is a great time to be in Edinburgh. The city is at its best, and the Fringe isn't at all elitist. In most cases the performers and front-of-house people are friendly and relaxed – they're grateful to have an audience – so there's no need to feel intimidated. Just be prepared to take the bad with the good...

The International Festival runs from mid-August to early September. If you're more interested in this festival the last week is a good time to go, because the Fringe and Tattoo finish at the end of August, reducing the number of visitors. If you want to attend the International Festival, it's best to book ahead; the programme is published in late March and is available from the Edinburgh Festival Office (☎ 0131-473 2000, fax 473 2002, Ⓔ eif@eif.co.uk, Ⓦ www.eif.co.uk), The Hub, Castlehill, Royal Mile, Edinburgh EH1 2NE. Prices are generally reasonable, and some unsold tickets are sold half-price on the day of performance (from 1pm) from venues or The Hub.

The Fringe is less formal, and many performances have empty seats left at the last moment. It's still worth booking for well-known names, or if the production has received good reviews. Programmes are available, from June, from the Fringe Office (☎ 0131-226 5257, fax 220 4205, Ⓦ www.edfringe.com), 180 High St, Edinburgh EH1 1QS.

Hogmanay, the Scottish celebration of the New Year, is another major fixture in Edinburgh's festival calendar with concerts, the biggest street party in Europe and a massive bonfire on Calton Hill. For details contact The Hub (see earlier) or see the Web site at Ⓦ www.edinburghshogmanay.org.

For all these festivals, booking accommodation months ahead is strongly advised.

Glasgow also has a series of major festivals, the largest of which is the **West End Festival** with open-air concerts and other events during two weeks in mid-June. Contact The White House (☎ 0141-341 0844, fax 341 0855, Ⓦ www.glasgowwestend.co.uk), Dowanhill Park, Havelock St, Glasgow G11 5JE.

Highland games occur all over Scotland, but the biggest and most famous is the **Braemar Gathering** in Aberdeenshire in the north-east. Thousands, including the royal family, descend on Braemar on the first Saturday in September to watch Scotland's finest take part in these traditional sports in Memorial Park. There's also music and dancing and a hill race. For information contact WA Meston (☎ /fax 01339-755377, Ⓦ www.braemargathering.org), Coilacriech, Ballater, Aberdeenshire AB35 5UH.

spring and autumn holiday; dates vary from year to year and from town to town.

Special Events

Countless diverse events are held around the country all year. Even small villages have weekly markets, and many still enact traditional customs and ceremonies, some dating back hundreds of years.

The STB publishes a comprehensive list, *Events in Scotland*, twice a year. Historic Scotland (see Useful Organisations earlier in this chapter) also publishes an annual list of events at its sites.

The Traditional Music & Song Association (☎ 0131-667 5587, fax 662 9153, e e.cowie@ tmsa.demon.co.uk) publishes an excellent annual listing of music, dance and cultural festivals around Scotland; it's also on the Web at w www.tmsa.demon.co.uk.

See the boxed text opposite for details of the main festivals.

January
Hogmanay Celebrations to greet the New Year, including a huge street party in Edinburgh
The Ba' Two teams chase each other and a ball until one team reaches its goal, New Year's Day, Kirkwall, Orkney
Up Helly Aa Re-enactment of a Viking fire festival, last Tuesday in January, Shetland
Burns Night Suppers all over the country celebrating Robbie Burns, 25 January

April
Rugby Sevens Seven-a-side rugby tournament, the Borders

May
Spirit of Speyside Whisky Festival (w www .spiritofspeyside.com) Four days of distillery tours, whisky-tasting, food, art and outdoor activities
Scottish FA Cup Final Deciding match in Scotland's premier football knock-out tournament, Hampden Park, Glasgow
Orkney Folk Festival (w www.orkney.com) Concerts, ceilidhs, workshops, Orkney

June to August
Riding of the Marches Horse riding, with parades, brass bands etc, commemorating conflict with England, various towns in the Borders

June
West End Festival Two huge weeks of music and the arts, Glasgow
Royal Highland Show (w www.rhass.org.uk) Scotland's national agricultural show, Edinburgh

July
International Jazz Festival (w www.jazzfest .co.uk) Jazz from around the world, Glasgow

July & August
Edinburgh International Jazz & Blues Festival Ten days of excellent music in the capital

August
Edinburgh Military Tattoo Pageantry and military displays, running for three weeks
Edinburgh International and Fringe Festivals Premier international arts festivals, running for three weeks mid-August to early September
Edinburgh International Film Festival Two weeks of movies during the latter half of August
Edinburgh Book Festival A two-week celebration of literature, also in the latter half of August
World Pipe Band Championships Gathering of over 100 pipe bands, Glasgow

September
Braemar Gathering Kilts, cabers and bagpipes, attended by the queen, Braemar; other games held all over Scotland, June to September

October
Royal National Mod (w www.the-mod.co.uk) A largely competitive Gaelic music festival, in various locations

LANGUAGE COURSES

With the remarkable revival of Scottish Gaelic since the 1980s, a number of courses on the language and culture are available, including:

An Ceathramh (☎ 01408-641474, e Ancea thramh@tesco.net) Muie East, Rogart, Sutherland IV28 3UB. A centre for adult tuition in Gaelic offering intensive courses throughout summer.
Cothrom na Fèinne (☎ 01599-566240) Balmacara Mains, Kyle IV40 8DN. Residential courses take place during the first week of the month, May to October. Individually tailored weekends are available November to April.
Sabhal Mór Ostaig (☎ 01471-888000, w www .smo.uhi.ac.uk) Sleat, Isle of Skye IV44 8RQ. Offers courses in Gaelic language, song, piping and the fiddle.

WORK

Low-paid seasonal work is available in the tourist industry, usually in restaurants and pubs. Hostel noticeboards sometimes advertise casual work and hostels themselves sometimes employ travellers to staff the reception, clean up etc. Without skills, it's difficult to find a job that pays well enough to save money. Whatever your skills, it's worth registering with a number of temporary agencies.

EU citizens don't need a work permit. The Working Holidaymaker scheme, for Commonwealth citizens aged 17 to 27 inclusive, allows visits of up to two years, but arrangements must be made in advance through a British embassy. Commonwealth citizens with a UK-born parent may be eligible for a Certificate of Entitlement to the Right of Abode, which entitles them to live and work in the UK. Contact your nearest British Embassy for details.

Commonwealth citizens with a UK-born grandparent, or a grandparent born before 31 March 1922 in what's now the Republic of Ireland, could qualify for a UK Ancestry-Employment Certificate, allowing them to work full time for up to four years in the UK.

Students from the USA who are at least 18 years old and studying full time at a college or university can get a Blue Card permit allowing them to work for six months in the UK. It costs US$250 and is available through the British Universities North America Club (BUNAC; ☎ 203 264 0901, e wib@bunac usa), PO Box 430, Southbury CT 06488. BUNAC also runs programmes for Australians, Canadians and New Zealanders. For more details, check out w www.bunac.org.uk.

ACCOMMODATION

This will almost certainly be your single-greatest expense. Even camping can be expensive at some official sites. For budget travel, the two main options are hostels and cheap B&Bs. Mid-range B&Bs are often in beautiful old buildings and many rooms have private bathrooms. Guesthouses and small hotels are more likely to have private bathrooms. If money's no object, there are some superb hotels, the most interesting in converted castles and mansions.

TICs have an accommodation booking service (£3, local and national). A 10% refundable deposit is also required for most bookings. The service is worth using in July and August, but isn't necessary otherwise, unless you plan to arrive in a town after business hours when the local TIC is closed. If you arrive late, it may still be worth going to the TIC, since some leave a list in the window showing which B&Bs had rooms free when they closed.

Regional tourist boards publish reliable (if not comprehensive) accommodation lists which include STB-approved and -graded accommodation. STB gradings reflect the level and quality of facilities. Places paying to be members of the tourist board have a plaque at the front, but note that some of the best B&Bs don't participate at all. In practice, seeing the place, even from the outside, will give a clue as to what to expect. Always ask to look at your room before checking in.

Single rooms are in short supply and many accommodation suppliers are reluctant to let a double room (even when it's quiet) to one person without charging a supplement.

Camping

Free wild camping is usually acceptable in unenclosed land, well away from houses and roads; try to seek permission. The draconian Land Reform Act may make wild camping illegal (see the boxed text 'Access & the Law' in the Activites chapter).

Commercial camping grounds are geared to caravans and vary widely in quality. A tent site costs from £4 to £12. If you plan to use a tent regularly, invest in *Scotland: Caravan & Camping* (£3.99), available from most TICs.

Bothies, Camping Barns & Bunkhouses

Bothies are simple shelters, often in remote places. They are not locked, there's no charge, and you can't book. Take your own cooking equipment, sleeping bag and mat. Users should stay one night only, and leave it as they find it.

A camping barn (*bod* in Shetland) – usually a converted farm building – is where walkers

PAUL BIGLAND

GLENN BEANLAND

NEIL WILSON

GLENN BEANLAND

MARTIN MOOS

Different styles: a Victorian turret, Peebles; the ruined western end of St Andrews Cathedral; the town of Inverness; the remarkably complete Jedburgh Abbey; and a close look at Melrose Abbey

GRAEME CORNWALLIS

Lagavulin, one of three Scotch whisky distilleries near Port Ellen on the Isle of Islay

ANDREW MARSHALL & LEANNE WALKER

A swan-necked copper pot still, used for distillation

ANDREW MARSHALL & LEANNE WALKER

Steeped barley is spread on the floor to germinate.

MARTIN MOOS

The end result: bottles and bottles of whisky!

can stay for around £5 per night. Take your own cooking equipment, sleeping bag and mat. Bunkhouses, a grade or two up from camping barns, have stoves for heating and cooking and may supply utensils. They may have mattresses, but you'll still need a sleeping bag. Most charge from £8.

Hostels

If you're travelling on a budget, the numerous hostels offer cheap accommodation and are great centres for meeting fellow travellers. Hostels have facilities for self-catering and some provide cheap meals. From May to September and on public holidays, hostels can be booked-out, sometimes by large anti-social groups. Book as far in advance as possible.

Scottish Youth Hostel Association (SYHA) The SYHA (☎ 01786-891400, fax 891333, ₩ www.shya.org.uk), 7 Glebe Crescent, Stirling FK8 2JA, has a network of good and reasonably priced hostels. It produces a handbook (£1.50) giving details on over 70 hostels, including transport links. In big cities, costs are £12/10.50 to £14/12.50 for seniors/juniors (including continental breakfast), while the rest start at £6.50/5. Throughout this book, higher hostel prices for adults are given first, followed by the reduced price for under-18s. Prices vary by season and are higher in summer; the SYHA Web site has full details.

SYHA hostels aren't always in town centres – fine if you're walking the countryside or have your own transport, a pain if not. At simple hostels, you're usually locked out between 10.30am and 5pm, and the front door is locked at 11pm. You can access city hostels all day (to 2am), but reception isn't always open during these times.

For bookings, contact the central reservation service on ☎ 0870 155 3255 or e reservations@syha.org.uk.

Independent & Student Hostels There are a large number of independent hostels, most with prices around £10. The *Independent Hostel Guide*, available from some TICs, lists over 90 hostels in Scotland, and is either free or available for a nominal

cost (20p). Alternatively, send an A5-sized stamped, addressed envelope to Pete Thomas, Croft Bunkhouse & Bothies, 7 Portnalong, Isle of Skye IV47 8SL.

University Accommodation

Many Scottish universities offer their student accommodation to visitors during the holidays. Most rooms are comfortable, functional single bedrooms, some with shared bathroom, but there are also twin and family units, self-contained flats and shared houses. Full-board, half-board, B&B and self-catering options are available. Rooms are usually available late June to late September. B&B costs around £18 to £25 per person.

Local TICs have details.

B&Bs, Guesthouses & Hotels

B&Bs provide the cheapest private accommodation. At the bottom end (£12 to £18 per person) you get a bedroom in a private house, a shared bathroom and an enormous cooked breakfast (juice, cereal, bacon, eggs, sausage, baked beans and toast). Small B&Bs may only have one room to let. More upmarket B&Bs have private bathrooms and TVs in each room.

Guesthouses, often large converted houses with half a dozen rooms, are an extension of the B&B concept. They range from £15 to £30 per person per night, depending on the quality of the food and accommodation. Pubs may also offer cheap B&B and can be good fun since they often place you at the hub of the community. However, they can be noisy and aren't always ideal for lone women travellers.

At the other end of the scale there are some wonderfully luxurious places, including country-house hotels in superb settings, and castles complete with crenellated battlements, grand staircases and the obligatory rows of stags' heads. For these you can pay from around £60 to well over £100 per person. The *Which? Hotel Guide* (£15.99) covering Britain lists many of the finest hotels. Recommendations are generally trustworthy because hotel owners don't have to pay to appear in the guide.

Short-Term Rental

There's plenty of self-catering accommodation, and staying in a house in the city or cottage in the country gives you an opportunity to get a feel for a region and its community. The minimum stay is usually one week in the summer peak season, three days or less at other times.

Outside weekends and July/August, it's not essential to book a long way ahead. Details are in the accommodation guides available from TICs. Alternatively, buy a copy of the STB's *Scotland: Self-Catering* (£5.99). Expect a week's rent for a two-bedroom cottage to cost from £150 in winter, £175 April to June, and £250 July to September. Places in the city range from £175 to over £700 per week.

FOOD

Scotland's chefs have an enviable range of fresh meat, seafood and vegetables at their disposal. The country has gone a long way to shake off its once dismal culinary reputation. Most restaurants are reasonably good and there are some that are internationally renowned.

The quality of cooking at hotel restaurants and B&Bs that provide evening meals is variable. In small villages the alternatives are usually bleak, although village bakeries have a good range of pies, cakes and snacks. In towns there are Indian and Chinese alternatives, as well as fast-food chains. Most pubs offer food, with either a cheap bar menu or a more formal restaurant, or both. Many supermarkets and department stores have reasonable (and reasonably priced) cafes.

Lunch is served from noon to 2.30pm, dinner from 6pm or 7pm to 8pm or 9pm. Scotland is notorious for places that will not serve you if you arrive five seconds after 'kitchen closing time'.

Some of the best places to eat are members of the Taste of Scotland scheme, but they have to pay substantial fees for inclusion. The annual *Taste of Scotland Guide* (£8.99) is worth buying to track down these restaurants and hotels.

For vegetarians, if you like pizza, pasta and curry you should be able to get a reasonable meal pretty well anywhere. Most restaurants have at least a token vegetarian dish, although vegans will find the going tough. *Vegetarian Britain*, by Alex Bourke and Alan Todd, lists over 500 places to stay and eat in Britain.

Scottish Breakfast

Surprisingly few Scots eat porridge and even fewer eat it in the traditional way as a savoury dish not a sweet one; that is with salt to taste, then eaten with milk, but no sugar. You'll rarely be offered porridge in a B&B. Generally, a glass of fruit juice accompanies a bowl of cereal or muesli, followed by a cooked breakfast which may include: bacon, sausage, black pudding (a type of sausage made from dried blood), grilled tomato, grilled mushrooms, fried bread or tattie (potato) scones (if you're lucky), and an egg or two.

More upmarket hotels may offer porridge followed by kippers (smoked herrings). As well as toast, there may be oatcakes (oatmeal biscuits) to spread your marmalade on. In the Aberdeen area there may also be butteries – delicious butter-rich bread rolls.

Snacks

As well as ordinary scones (similar to American biscuits), Scottish bakeries usually offer cheese, tattie and girdle scones.

Bannocks are a cross between scones and pancakes. Savoury pies include the *bridie* (a pie filled with meat, potatoes, onions and sometimes other vegetables) and the Scotch pie (minced meat in a plain round pastry casing – best eaten hot). A *toastie* is a toasted sandwich.

Dundee cake, a rich fruit cake topped with almonds, is highly recommended. Black bun is another type of fruit cake, eaten over Hogmanay (New Year's Eve).

Soups

Scotch broth, made with mutton stock, barley, lentils and peas, is highly nutritious and very tasty, while cock-a-leekie is a hearty soup made with chicken and leeks. Warming vegetable soups include leek and potato soup, and lentil soup (traditionally made using ham stock – vegetarians beware!).

Seafood soups include the delicious *cullen skink*, made with smoked haddock, potato, onion and milk, and *partan bree* (crab soup).

Meat & Game

Steak eaters will enjoy a thick fillet of world-famous Aberdeen Angus beef, while beef from Highland cattle is much sought after. Venison, from the red deer, is leaner and appears on many menus. Both may be served with a wine-based or creamy whisky sauce. Mince (minced beef cooked with onion) and tatties (potatoes) is traditional Scottish home cooking and is very filling.

Gamebirds such as pheasant and the more expensive grouse, traditionally roasted and served with game chips and fried breadcrumbs, are also available. They're definitely worth trying, but watch your teeth on the shot, which isn't always removed before cooking.

Then there's haggis, Scotland's much-maligned national dish...

Fish & Seafood

Scottish salmon is famous worldwide, but there's a big difference between farmed salmon and the leaner, more expensive, wild fish. Smoked salmon is traditionally dressed with a squeeze of lemon juice and eaten with fresh brown bread and butter. Trout, the salmon's smaller cousin – whether wild, rod-caught brown trout or farmed rainbow trout – is delicious fried in oatmeal.

As an alternative to kippers (smoked herrings) you may be offered Arbroath smokies (lightly smoked fresh haddock), traditionally eaten cold. Herring fillets fried in oatmeal are good, if you don't mind picking out a few bones. Mackerel pate and smoked or peppered mackerel (both served cold) are also popular.

Juicy langoustines (also called Dublin Bay prawns), crabs, lobsters, oysters, mussels and scallops are also widely available in Scotland.

Cheese

The Scottish cheese industry is growing. Cheddar is its main output but there are speciality cheese-makers whose products are definitely worth sampling. Many are based on the islands, particularly Arran, Bute, Gigha, Islay, Mull and Orkney. Brodick Blue is a blue cheese made from ewes' milk on Arran. There are several varieties of cream cheese (Caboc, St Finan, Howgate) which are usually rolled in oatmeal. There are also some small-scale producers of Highland smoked cheese.

Scottish oatcakes make the perfect accompaniment to cheese.

Haggis – Scotland's National Dish

Scotland's national dish is frequently ridiculed by foreigners because of its ingredients, which don't inspire confidence. However, once you get over any delicate sensibilities towards tucking in to chopped lungs, heart and liver mixed with oatmeal and (traditionally) boiled in a sheep's stomach, with the accompanying glass of whisky it can taste surprisingly good.

Haggis should be served with tatties and neeps (mashed potatoes and turnips), with a generous dollop of butter and a good sprinkling of black pepper.

Although it's eaten year-round, haggis is central to the celebrations of 25 January, in honour of Scotland's national poet, Robert Burns. Scots worldwide unite on Burns Night to revel in their Scottishness. A piper announces the arrival of the haggis and Burns' poem *Address to a Haggis* is recited to this 'Great chieftan o' the puddin-race'. The bulging stomach is then lanced with a *dirk* (dagger) to reveal the steaming offal within.

Vegetarians (and quite a few carnivores, no doubt) will be relieved to know that veggie haggis is available in some restaurants in Scotland.

Puddings

Traditional Scottish puddings are irresistibly creamy, calorie-enriched concoctions. *Cranachan* is whipped cream flavoured with whisky, and mixed with toasted oatmeal and raspberries. *Atholl brose* is a mixture of cream, whisky and honey flavoured with oatmeal. *Clootie dumpling* is delicious, a rich steamed pudding filled with currants and raisins.

DRINKS
Nonalcoholic Drinks

In terms of consumption, coffee has recently overtaken tea as Scotland's most popular beverage. In the last five or six years the cities have been swamped by a gurgling tide of espresso machines as cafes and coffee shops have opened on almost every street corner, dispensing cappuccinos and lattes to a caffeine-craving public. Fortunately, a few old-style tearooms survive where you can still get a decent pot of or-ange pekoe with which to wash down your shortbread.

Despite having some of the purest tap water in the world, Scotland has been quick to jump aboard the bottled water bandwagon, with several brands of Scottish mineral water (notably Highland Spring) available in shops, bars and restaurants.

Alternatively there's Irn-Bru (see the boxed text 'The Other National Drink').

Alcoholic Drinks

The legal minimum age for buying alcoholic drinks in Scotland is 18.

Wine, beer and spirits for home consumption are sold in supermarkets and neighbourhood off-licences (liquor stores) rather than bars. Opening hours are generally 10am to 10pm Monday to Saturday and 12.30pm to 8pm Sunday.

Most restaurants are licensed to sell alcoholic drinks. Those that are not are often advertised as BYO (Bring Your Own) – buy a bottle of wine at an off-licence and take it with you to the restaurant, which usually charges £1 to £3 'corkage'.

See also Pubs under Entertainment later in this chapter.

Whisky Scotch whisky (always spelt without an 'e' – whiskey *with* an 'e' is Irish or American) is Scotland's best-known product and biggest export. The spirit has been distilled in Scotland at least since the 15th century. See the earlier boxed text 'How to Be An Instant Malt Whisky Buff'.

As well as whiskies, there are also several whisky-based liqueurs such as Drambuie. If you must mix your whisky with anything other than water try a whisky-mac (whisky with ginger wine). After a long walk in the rain there's nothing better to warm you up.

At a bar, older Scots may order a 'half' or 'nip' of whisky as a chaser to a pint or half-pint of beer (a 'hauf and a hauf'). Only tourists ask for 'Scotch' – what else would you be served in Scotland? The standard measure in pubs is either 25mL or 35mL.

Beer There's a wonderfully wide range of beers, from light (almost like lager) to extremely strong and treacly. What New Worlders call beer is actually lager; to the distress of local connoisseurs, lagers constitute a huge chunk of the market. Fortunately, thanks to the Campaign for Real Ale (CAMRA) organisation, the once-threatened traditional beers are thriving.

The best ales are hand-pumped from the cask, not carbonated and drawn under pressure. They're usually served at cellar temperature, which may come as a shock to lager drinkers, and have subtle flavours that a cold, chemical lager can't match. Most popular is what the Scots call 'heavy', a dark beer similar to English bitter. Most Scottish brews are graded in shillings so you can tell their strength, the usual range being 60 to 80 shillings (written 80/-). The greater the number of shillings, the stronger the beer.

The market is dominated by the big brewers – Youngers, McEwans, Scottish & Newcastle and Tennent's. Look out for beer from local breweries, some of it very strong – the aptly named Skullsplitter from Orkney is a good example, which is 8.5% alcohol by volume. Caledonian 80/-, Maclays 80/- and Belhaven 80/- are others worth trying.

How to Be a Malt Whisky Buff

'Love makes the world go round? Not at all! Whisky makes it go round twice as fast.'
From *Whisky Galore*, by Compton Mackenzie (1883–1972)

Whisky-tasting today is almost as popular as wine-tasting was in the yuppie heyday of the late 1980s. Being able to tell your Ardbeg from your Edradour is de rigeur among the whisky-nosing set, so here are some pointers to help you impress your friends.

What's the difference between malt and grain whiskies? Malts are distilled from malted barley – that is, barley that has been soaked in water, then allowed to germinate for around 10 days until the starch has turned into sugar – while grain whiskies are distilled from other cereals, usually wheat, corn or unmalted barley.

So what is a single malt? A single malt is a whisky that has been distilled from malted barley and is the product of a single distillery. A pure (vatted) malt is a mixture of single malts from several distilleries, and a blended whisky is a mixture of various grain whiskies (about 60%) and malt whiskies (about 40%) from many different distilleries.

Why are single malts more desirable than blends? A single malt, like a fine wine, somehow captures the essence of the place where it was made and matured – a combination of the water, the barley, the peat smoke, the oak barrels in which it was aged, and (in the case of certain coastal distilleries) the sea air and salt spray. Each distillation varies from the one before, like different vintages from the same vineyard.

How should a single malt be drunk? Either neat, or preferably with a little water added. To appreciate the aroma and flavour to the utmost, a measure of malt whisky should be cut (diluted) with one-third to two-thirds as much spring water (still, bottled spring water will do). Ice, tap water and (God forbid) mixers are for philistines. Would you add lemonade or ice to a glass of Chablis?

Give me some tasting tips! Go into a bar and order a Lagavulin (Islay) and a Glenfiddich (Speyside). Cut each one with half as much again of still, bottled spring water. Taking each one in turn, hold the glass up to the light to check the colour; stick your nose in the glass and take two or three short, sharp sniffs. For the Lagavulin you should be thinking: amber colour, peat-smoke, iodine, seaweed. For the Glenfiddich: pale, white-wine colour, malt, pear drops, acetone, citrus. Then taste them. Then try some others. Either you'll be hooked, or you'll never touch whisky again.

Where's the cheapest place to buy Scotch whisky? A French supermarket, unfortunately. In the UK, where a bottle of single malt typically costs £20 to £30, taxes account for around 72% of the price, making Scotland one of the most expensive places in Europe to enjoy its own national drink.

If you're serious about spirits, the Scotch Malt Whisky Society (☎ 0131-554 3451, Ⓦ www .smws.com), The Vaults, 87 Giles St, Edinburgh EH6 6BZ, runs an intensive one-day Whisky School that covers the basics of whisky-tasting and evaluation. The cost is £210, including lunch, canapes and drinks. Membership of the society costs from £75 per year and includes use of members' rooms in Edinburgh and London.

Long before hops arrived in Scotland, beer was flavoured with heather. Reintroduced, heather ale is surprisingly good and available in some pubs.

The Other National Drink

What do Scotland and Peru have in common?

Answer: they are the only countries in the world where a locally manufactured soft drink outsells Coca Cola. In Peru it's Inca Cola, but in Scotland it's Barr's Irn-Bru, which commands 25% of the Scottish fizzy drinks market (Coke has 24%). A Barr's advertising campaign in the 1980s promoted Irn-Bru as 'Scotland's other national drink'.

Barr's have been making soft drinks in Scotland since 1880, but it was in 1901 that they launched a new beverage called 'Iron-Brew' (labelling regulations forced a change of spelling to 'Irn-Bru' in 1946). As with Coke, the recipe (32 ingredients, including caffeine and ammonium ferric citrate – the source of the iron in the name) remains a closely guarded secret known by only two people. Scots swear by its efficacy as a cure for hangovers, which may account for its massive sales. You can even get Irn-Bru along with your Big Mac in Scottish branches of McDonalds.

In recent years Barr's have begun to build their brand overseas, exporting the quirky, humorous and award-winning advertising campaign that positions Irn-Bru drinkers as mischievous and rascally. Irn-Bru is hugely popular in Russia, where it is the third favourite soft drink after Coke and Pepsi (maybe it's that hangover thing again), and in the Middle East, but it has yet to challenge Coke and Pepsi in the USA. Big Red, beware...

Tasting notes

Colour is a rusty, radioactive orange. Nosing reveals a bouquet of bubble gum, barley sugar and something vaguely citrussy , maybe tangerine? Carbonation is medium, and mouth-feel...well, you can almost feel the enamel dissolving on your teeth.

Stout is a dark, rich, foamy drink; Orkney Dark Island is a Scottish brand.

Beers are usually served in pints (from £1.20 to £2.20), but you can also ask for a 'half' (a half pint). Potency can vary from 3.2% to 8.5%.

Wine For centuries people made wine from wild flowers, fruit and tree sap. This cottage industry is continued at Moniack Castle, near Beauly in the Highlands, and at Cairn o' Mohr winery in the Carse o' Gowrie.

Good international wines are widely available and reasonably priced (except in pubs and restaurants). In supermarkets, an ordinary but drinkable bottle can be found for around £4.

ENTERTAINMENT

Scotland has its own national ballet, opera and orchestra as well as many fine theatres and repertory companies. Cinemas around the country show commercial films, and the big cities have independent cinemas showing art-house, foreign and cult movies. Glasgow and Edinburgh have lively club scenes, but nightclubs are by no means confined to the major cities. Many pubs offer entertainment ranging from live traditional Scottish folk music to pop, rock and jazz music, disco and quiz nights.

In Glasgow and Edinburgh, look out for the *List*, a twice-monthly listings magazine (£1.95).

Pubs

The local pub is the place to go for a drink and often live music; you'll get a warm reception at most country pubs. Given how much Scotland is epitomised by its pubs, it's odd how unenthusiastic the big breweries seem to be in hanging on to them. Traditional pubs are being reinvented as brasseries and Irish or Australian theme bars. Just ask at your hostel, B&B or hotel for better recommendations.

Some pubs in the more depressed areas of big towns have a reputation for late-night brawls and should be avoided by the non-pugnacious visitor.

Pubs generally open from 11am to between 11pm and 1am Monday to Saturday and from 12.30pm Sunday. Some have a late licence at weekends. The bell for last orders rings about 15 minutes before closing time. Watch out for the early evening 'Happy Hour', with lower prices for drinks. Infuriatingly, many pubs in the Highlands and islands close between 2.30pm and 5pm – and they may be completely closed in winter. There's nothing worse, especially if you've been travelling for some time.

Ceilidhs

Some tourist centres in the Highlands stage a *ceilidh* (pronounced **kay**-lee), or Highland show, featuring Scottish song and dance, most nights during the summer. Some local restaurants also combine a show with dinner.

If you fancy trying an eightsome reel, informal local *ceilidhs* with dancing that you can join in usually take place on Friday or Saturday. Ask at the local TIC for details. It's not as difficult as it looks and there's often a 'caller' to lead everyone through their paces.

ASA ANDERSSON

An evening of song, music and dance: the *ceilidh*

SPECTATOR SPORTS

Most Scots men are sports mad and watch matches with fierce, competitive dedication, identifying closely with teams and individuals that compete both locally and internationally. The most popular games are football (soccer), rugby union, shinty, lawn bowls, curling and golf, the last two of which the Scots claim to have invented.

Football

Also known as soccer to distinguish it from rugby football, this is Scotland's largest spectator sport. The Scottish Football League is the main national competition and has a number of divisions. The best clubs form the Scottish Premier League. In the 1990s it was dominated by Glasgow Rangers who, in 1997, equalled the record of nine successive championships set by its main rival, Glasgow Celtic, in the 1960s and 70s. Celtic was the first British team to win the European Cup (1967) and, so far, the only Scottish club to have done so. Celtic were Premier League champions in 2001.

The Scottish Football Association (SFA) Cup is a knock-out competition. The final is held mid-May, traditionally at Hampden Park in Glasgow which, after major renovations, again hosts this important annual sporting event. The national team has resumed playing home internationals at Hampden.

The domestic football season lasts from August to May and most matches are played at 3pm on Saturday, 1pm or 6pm on Sunday, or 7.30pm on Tuesday or Wednesday.

When the Scots play abroad, the game unites the country; at home it highlights differences and trouble can occur, especially when Catholic Celtic plays Protestant Rangers in Glasgow.

Rugby Union

Rugby union football is administered by the Scottish Rugby Union based at Murrayfield in Edinburgh, where international games are played. Each year, starting in January, Scotland takes part in the Six Nations Rugby Union Championship. The most important fixture is the clash against England for the Calcutta Cup.

At club level, the season runs from September to May, and among the better union teams are those from the Borders such as Hawick, Kelso and Melrose. At the end of the season, teams play a Rugby Sevens (seven-a-side) variation of the 15-player competition.

Golf
Although games that involve hitting a ball with a stick have been played in Europe since Roman times, it was the Scottish version that caught on. Apparently dating from the 15th century, golf was popularised by the Scottish monarchy. St Andrews in Scotland is the home of golf, since the Royal and Ancient club (the recognised authority on the rules) and the famous Old Course are both there.

Shinty
Shinty (*camanachd* in Gaelic) is an amateur ball-and-stick sport similar to Ireland's hurling. It's fast, very physical and played most of the year. It's administered by the Camanachd Association and the Camanachd Cup is the most prized trophy. The final, a great Gaelic get-together, draws a large crowd and is televised on STV.

Curling
Scotland is the home of curling, which involves propelling circular polished granite stones over ice as close to the centre of a target as possible. A team is made up of four players and one reserve. Almost all games are played indoors and the Royal Caledonian Curling Club, in Edinburgh, is the governing body.

SHOPPING
Making things to sell to tourists is big business in Scotland, and almost every visitor attraction seems to have been redesigned to funnel you through the gift shop. Among the tourist kitsch are some good-value, high-quality goods, but check labelling thoroughly as many 'Scottish' products are made in other countries.

Tartan, Tweed & Other Fabrics
Scottish textiles, particularly tartans, are popular and tartan travelling rugs or scarves are often worth buying. There are said to be over 2000 designs, some officially recognised as clan tartans. Many shops have a list and can tell you if your family belongs to a clan, but these days if you can pay for the cloth you can wear the tartan. There are some universal tartans, such as the Flower of Scotland, that aren't connected with a clan.

The traditional highland dress is the 4m- to 5m-long plaid, which was banned for many years after the 1745 Jacobite rebellion. The kilt is a 19th-century romanticisation, but it still has a remarkable degree of popularity. For about £350 to £400, you can have a kilt made in your clan tartan, but this shouldn't be worn without a *sporran* (purse), which can cost from £40 for a plain version or up to £1000 for an ornate silver-dress sporran. Full kilts are traditionally worn only by men, while women wear kilted or tartan skirts.

There are mill shops in many parts of Scotland, but the best-known textile manufacturing areas are the Borders and in the central Lowlands, particularly around Stirling and Perth. Scotland is also renowned for a rough woollen cloth known as tweed – Harris tweed is world famous. There are various places on this Hebridean island where you can watch your cloth being woven.

Sheepskin rugs and jackets are also popular.

Knitwear
Scottish knitwear can be great value and is sold throughout Scotland. Shetland is most closely associated with high-quality wool and at knitwear factory shops you can buy genuine Shetland sweaters for as little as £20. The most sought-after sweaters bear the intricate Fair Isle pattern – the genuine article from this remote island costs at least £40.

Jewellery & Glassware
Silver brooches set with cairngorms (yellow or wine-coloured gems traditionally found in the mountains of the same name), or amethyst, are popular. Jewellery decorated with Celtic designs featuring mythical creatures and intricate patterns is particularly attractive, although some pieces are actually made in Cornwall. Glassware, particularly Edinburgh crystal and Caithness glass, is another good souvenir.

Food & Drink

Sweet, butter-rich Scottish shortbread makes a good gift. The biggest manufacturer, Walkers, is famous for baking such prodigious quantities of the stuff that the Speyside town of Aberlour smells of nothing else. Dark, fruity Dundee cake lasts well and is available in a tin, but heavy to take home by air. Heather honey can give you a reminder of Scotland when your visit is over.

If you haven't far to go, smoked salmon or any other smoked product (venison, mussels, etc) is worth buying, but some countries don't allow you to import meat and fish.

If you're leaving the EU, you're better off buying duty-free souvenir bottles of whisky at the airport rather than in High St shops, unless it's a rare brand. If you go on a distillery tour, you may be given around £3 discount to buy a bottle there. Miniature bottles make good presents.

Activities

Scotland is a great place for outdoor recreation and although it isn't cheap to travel in, many activities open up some of the most beautiful corners of the country and are often within reach of the tightest budget. In fact, those travelling on a shoestring may find themselves hiking or cycling out of necessity. Fortunately, a walk or ride through the countryside will almost certainly be a highlight of a Scottish holiday. For those who have the money, other activities such as golf or fishing are available as part of holiday packages that include bed, board and transport.

Most activities are well organised and have clubs and associations that can give visitors invaluable information and, sometimes, substantial discounts. Many of these organisations have national or international affiliations, so check with local clubs before leaving home. The Scottish Tourist Board (STB) and British Tourist Authority (BTA) have brochures on most activities, which can provide a starting point for further research.

BIRD-WATCHING
Scotland is a bird-watcher's paradise. There are over 80 ornithologically important nature reserves managed by Scottish Natural Heritage (SNH), the Royal Society for the Protection of Birds (RSPB) and the Scottish Wildlife Trust (SWT). See Ecology & Environment in the Facts about Scotland chapter for addresses. Further information can be obtained from the Scottish Ornithologists Club (☎ 0131-556 6042, W www.the-soc.org.uk), 21 Regent Terrace, Edinburgh EH7 5BT.

In the Highlands and islands there are spectacular birds of prey such as the osprey, peregrine falcon, golden eagle and the reintroduced red kite and white-tailed sea eagle. A good location to view ospreys is the Boat of Garten Nature Reserve near Aviemore. Seabirds can be seen all around the coast, with huge concentrations at Duncansby Head near John o'Groats and at the Clo Mor Cliffs on Cape Wrath. Bass Rock, offshore from North Berwick, near Edinburgh, supports a huge breeding colony of gannets.

The islands are home to thousands of seabirds as well as a stopover to migrating birds. In the Hebrides, Islay is a wintering ground for greylag and barnacle geese and North Uist has huge populations of migrant waders.

Orkney has colonies of nesting seabirds at Mull Head and Gultak, and Deer Sound attracts wildfowl. Other Orkney Islands – Stronsay, Westray and North Ronaldsay – also attract breeding seabirds and migratory birds.

The Shetland Islands are also famous for their varied birdlife. On Sumburgh Head, Shetland, there are puffins, kittiwakes, fulmars, guillemots, razorbills and shags. Fair Isle, Whalsay and Out Skerries are in the path of thousands of migrating birds and Foula has around 500,000 seabirds including great skuas.

CANAL BOATING
The small canal network in central Scotland was created during the Industrial Revolution as a means of transporting freight – mostly coal. But they were soon made obsolete by the spread of the railways and finally killed off by modern roads. By WWII, the canals were in terminal decline, and in the following decades many sections were filled in. Today, however, the canals are being revived as part of the tourist industry.

The Forth and Clyde Canal runs 35 miles (56km) between Grangemouth in the east and Bowling near Dumbarton in the west. The 31-mile (50km) Union Canal links central Edinburgh with Falkirk. At one time these two canals were connected at Falkirk and, as part of the Millennium Project to restore the canals, that link will be restored by means of the spectacular Falkirk Wheel (due in December 2001).

The Falkirk Wheel

The Union Canal, linking central Edinburgh to the Forth and Clyde Canal at Falkirk, was completed in 1822, allowing cheap coal from the mines of western-central Scotland to be carried by barge to the Scottish capital. It was also used to carry slate and stone for the building of Edinburgh's expanding New Town. However, the expansion of the railways in the mid-19th century rendered the canals obsolete and they fell into disuse. In the 20th century, several sections were filled in, notably the flight of 11 locks that linked the Union to the Forth and Clyde Canal at Falkirk.

The £78-million Millennium Link Project, initiated in 1997, set out to restore the Forth and Clyde and Union canals to full working order, in the hope that their use for pleasure boating would provide a boost to the economy of central Scotland. The Forth and Clyde Canal was officially reopened in May 2001, and the Union Canal is scheduled to open by spring 2002.

The centrepiece of the project is the Falkirk Wheel, a unique engineering structure that was designed to replace the flight of locks that once linked the two canals at Falkirk. It is the world's first rotating boat lift, raising vessels (plus almost 300 tonnes of water) 35m in one steel caisson, while descending boats are carried down in the second caisson on the opposite side of the wheel. From summer 2002, visitors will be able to take trips on the Falkirk Wheel on special excursion boats.

For further information, check out the Web site at W www.millenniumlink.org.uk.

The 60-mile (96km) Caledonian Canal, which slices through the Great Glen from Fort William to Inverness, and the 9-mile (14.5km) Crinan Canal in Argyll were built as short-cuts for sea-going vessels, allowing them to avoid the long and arduous passages around Cape Wrath and the Mull of Kintyre. Their continued use by fishing boats and yachts means that they did not slip into disuse like the Lowland canals, and are still in active use.

Information

Scotland's canals are owned and operated by the British Waterways Board (☎ 0141-332 6936, W www.scottishcanals.co.uk), Canal House, 1 Applecross St, Glasgow G4 9SP, which publishes free *Skippers' Guides* to all the canals (available online), and *The Waterways Code for Boaters*, a free booklet packed with useful information and advice. It also publishes a list of hire-boat and canal-holiday companies.

Boat Hire

At the time of research there were very few boats available for hire on the Lowland canals, but this is expected to change in the future. **Lowland Narrowboats** (☎ *0131-660 2587*, W *www.lowlandnarrowboats.com*), 121 Waverley Crescent, Bonnyrigg, Midlothian EH19 3BW, has a six-berth narrowboat for hire on the Union Canal, costing from £340 to £800 per week depending on the season.

The Caledonian Canal, with its mixture of canal reaches, open lochs and stunning scenery, is fully geared to boating holidays. The main operator here is **Caley Cruisers** (☎ *01463-236328*, W *www.caleycruisers .com*), Canal Rd, Inverness IV3 6NF, which has a fleet of 50 motor cruisers ranging from two to eight berths available for hire from March to October.

At the height of the summer season (July and August), a 32-foot, two- to three-berth cruiser costs around £615 per week, and a 39-foot boat sleeping six to eight people costs £1825 per week. Early and late in the season these rates fall to around £330 and £1115 respectively.

Travelling the Waterways

No particular expertise or training is needed, nor is a licence required to operate a canal-cruising boat. You're normally given a quick once-over of the boat and an explanation of how things work, a brief foray out onto the loch or canal and then you're on your way. Proceed with caution at first, although you'll soon find yourself working the locks like a veteran.

CANOEING

Scotland, with its islands, sea lochs and indented coastline, is ideal for sea-kayaking, while its inland lochs and Highland rivers are great for both Canadian and white-water canoeing.

For information contact the Scottish Canoe Association (☎ 0131-317 7314, 🆆 www.scot-canoe.org), Caledonia House, South Gyle, Edinburgh EH12 9DQ. It publishes coastal navigation sheets as well as organising tours including introductory ones for beginners.

CYCLING

Travelling by bicycle is an excellent way to explore Scotland. Bikes aren't allowed on motorways but you can cycle on all other roads unless the road is marked 'private'. A-roads tend to be busy and are best avoided. B-roads are usually quieter and many are pleasant for cycling. The best roads are the unclassified roads or country lanes linking small villages; they're not numbered – you simply follow the signposts. There are also forest trails and dedicated cycle routes along canal towpaths and disused railway tracks. Cycle routes have been suggested throughout this book.

You can bring your own bike or hire one when you arrive.

Information

The STB publishes a useful free booklet, *Cycle Scotland*, with some suggested routes, lists of cycle-holiday companies and other helpful information. Many regional TICs have information on local cycling routes and places to hire bikes. They also stock cycling guides and books.

The Cyclists' Touring Club (CTC; ☎ 01483-417217, fax 426994, 🄴 cycling@ctc.org.uk, 🆆 www.ctc.org.uk), Cotterell House, 69 Meadrow, Godalming, Surrey GU7 3HS, is a membership organisation offering comprehensive information about cycling in Britain. It provides suggested routes, lists of local cycling contacts and clubs,

recommended accommodation, organised cycling holidays, a cycle-hire directory, and a mail-order service for maps and books.

For up-to-date detailed information on Scotland's cycle-route network contact Sustrans (☎ 0117-929 0888, 🆆 www.sustrans.org.uk), 53 Cochrane St, Glasgow G1 1HL. Sustrans is a charity that promotes sustainable transport, and its flagship project is the National Cycle Network – around 5000 miles (8050km) of traffic-free cycling routes all over Britain. In Scotland, the backbone of the network is the route from Carlisle (in north-western England) to Inverness, via Ayr, Glasgow, Pitlochry and Aviemore.

There are plenty of operators hiring out bikes from around £7 to £15 per day or £50 per week, plus a deposit refundable when the bike is returned.

Transporting Your Bicycle

To Scotland Ferries transport bicycles for a small fee and airlines usually accept them as part of your 20kg luggage allowance. When buying your ticket, check with the ferry company or airline about any regulations or restrictions that apply on the transportation of bicycles.

Bicycles can be transported by bus provided there's enough room in the luggage compartment and that they're folded or dismantled and boxed.

Generally, bikes can be taken free on local rail services on a first-come, first-served basis. On most long-distance routes it's necessary to make a reservation (usually around £3.50) for your bike. Some trains carry only one or two bikes so make your reservation (and get your ticket) at least 24 hours before travelling. Check bike-carriage details with the rail company for the whole of your planned journey as far in advance as possible.

In Scotland Bikes (but not tandems or trailers) are carried for free on all ScotRail trains, provided space is available. Reservations are required on the more popular routes, including Glasgow/Edinburgh to Inverness and Aberdeen, Glasgow to Stranraer, the West

Highland Line and the Inverness to Kyle of Lochalsh line, and can be made at main stations or through ScotRail telesales on ☎ 0845 755 0033.

Most CalMac ferries charge a one-way fare of £1 or £2 for a bike and many passenger-only ferries carry bikes for free.

Where to Cycle
Cyclists in search of the wild and remote will enjoy north-western Scotland. Its majestic Highlands and mystical islands offer quiet pedalling through breathtaking mountainscapes. There are fewer roads in this part of Scotland and generally less traffic. Roads are well graded but sometimes very remote, so carry plenty of food and plan ahead. Of the isles, Skye has a bridge to the mainland and suffers the worst of seasonal traffic; good ferries between the islands offer easy escape routes.

For the less intrepid cyclist, the beautiful forests, lochs, glens and hills in the central and southern areas of Scotland are more easily accessible and have a more intimate charm. Cyclists can seek out the smaller roads and tracks to avoid the traffic.

Hebridean Islands The scenic Hebridean Islands off the western coast, linked by a comprehensive ferry system, provide superb cycling opportunities. Allow two to three weeks to give yourself time to enjoy the scenery. Interesting circular routes are possible on most islands. The route outlined here comprises some 280 miles (450km) of cycling, and any tour will need to be planned around the times of ferry crossings; some are summer only.

From Ardrossan, near Ayr, take the ferry to the Isle of Arran, and cycle northwards to Lochranza for another ferry to Claonaig on the Kintyre peninsula. You can then head farther northwards through Lochgilphead to Oban to catch the ferry to Craignure on the Isle of Mull.

Mull is worth exploring before taking the ferry from Tobermory to Kilchoan. Cycle eastwards along the Ardnamurchan peninsula to Salen, then northwards to Mallaig. Ferries leave from here to Armadale on the Isle of Skye. You can then cycle northwards to Uig, or follow numerous other routes around the island.

From Uig, take a ferry to Tarbert (Isle of Harris) in the Outer Hebrides. These outer isles are wild and remote places with many quiet roads to explore. Cycle south to Benbecula and onto South Uist where you can catch the ferry back to Oban and its train station.

Glasgow to Gourock There's a 14-mile (22.5km) cycling route that starts in Glasgow and runs westwards via Paisley, Kilmacolm and Greenock to Gourock on the peninsula jutting into the Firth of Clyde. It's partly on minor roads, partly on a disused railway line.

Loch Leven A lovely 20-mile (32km) circuit runs around Loch Leven in the West Highlands (near Glen Coe), taking in Kinlochleven, Glen Coe, North Ballachulish and Ballachulish; the views are stunning.

The Machars Peninsula You can cycle around The Machars peninsula in Galloway between Newton Stewart and Glenluce via Whithorn. The 50-mile (80km) route is off the beaten track and goes through rich green pastures and attractive villages with the coast visible most of the way. It's easy cycling but it can be windy and you should be prepared for rain.

Tweed Cycle Way This is 62 miles (100km) along minor roads through the beautiful Tweed Valley from Biggar in the Borders, to Berwick-upon-Tweed in Northumberland.

DIVING
It may lack coral reefs and warm, limpid waters but Scotland offers some of the most spectacular and challenging scuba diving in Europe, if not the world. Beneath the waves of the western coast lies a surprisingly colourful undersea world of soft corals and jewel anemones, and a varied marine wildlife that includes conger eels, lobsters, cuttlefish, sea urchins, starfish and seals.

The sea bed around St Abbs in the Scottish Borders is Scotland's first voluntary marine nature reserve.

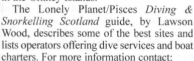
JANE SMITH

In addition to its natural attractions, there are also hundreds of fascinating shipwrecks, the most famous of which are the seven WWI German warships that lie on the bed of Scapa Flow in the Orkney Islands.

The Lonely Planet/Pisces *Diving & Snorkelling Scotland* guide, by Lawson Wood, describes some of the best sites and lists operators offering dive services and boat charters. For more information contact:

Scottish Sub Aqua Club (☎ 0141-425 1021, W www.scotsac.com) The Cockburn Centre, 40 Bogmoor Place, Glasgow G51 4TQ
British Sub Aqua Club (☎ 0151-350 6200, W www.bsac.com) Telford's Quay, South Pier Rd, Ellesmere Port, Cheshire CH65 4FL

GOLF
Scotland is the home of golf. The game has been played here for centuries and there are more courses per capita in Scotland than in any other country.

Courses are tested for their level of difficulty, and most are playable year-round. Some private clubs only admit members, friends of members, or golfers who have a handicap certificate or a letter of introduction from their club, but the vast majority are open to visitors.

Most clubs give members priority in booking tee-off times; it's always advisable to book in advance. It should be easier to book a tee-off time on a public course but weekends, on all courses, are usually busy. Also, check whether there's a dress code and whether the course has golf clubs for hire (not all do) if you don't have your own.

St Andrews is the headquarters of the game's governing body, the Royal and Ancient Golf Club, and the location of the world's most famous golf course, the Old Course. Muirfield is home to the world's oldest golf club, the Honourable Company of Edinburgh Golfers. Carnoustie, east of Dundee, has one of the longest courses and toughest finishes; golf has been played here since at least 1650. The course at Loch Lomond is home to the World Invitational Championship. Other major courses are Troon and Turnberry in Ayrshire, Gleneagles in Perthshire and Musselburgh in East Lothian.

Information
The BTA has a useful *Golfing Holidays* booklet that focuses on golfing trips and major golf tournaments in Britain. *Golf in Scotland* is a free brochure listing 400 courses and clubs with details of where to stay.

The Scottish Tourist Board/visitscotland (☎ 0131-332 2433, W www.visitscotland .com), 23 Ravelston Terrace, Edinburgh EH4 3EU, publishes a free brochure, the *Guide to Golf in Scotland*, and has an online course directory and booking facility on its Web site.

Costs
A round of golf on a public course costs about £10. Private courses are more expensive with green fees ranging from £12 to £20 – and up to more than £60 on championship courses. Many clubs offer a daily or weekly ticket. Some regions offer a Golf Pass, costing between £50 and £75 for five days (Monday to Friday) depending on the area, which allows play on a range of courses.

Golf clubs cost about £7 per round to hire.

FISHING
Fishing – coarse, sea and game – is enormously popular in Scotland, whose waters are filled with salmon, trout (sea, brown and rainbow), pike, arctic char and many other species. Its streams, rivers, lochs and firths have probably the greatest variety of marine habitats and some of the cleanest waters in Europe.

There's no close season for coarse fishing or sea angling, but for wild brown trout the close season is early October to mid-March.

The close season for salmon and sea trout varies between districts; it's generally from early November to early February.

You don't need a licence to fish in Scotland but much of the land and the fishing rights to most waters are privately owned, so you must obtain a permit from the owners or their agents. These are often readily available at the local fishing tackle shop or hotel. Permits usually cost from around £15 per day but some salmon rivers – notably the Tweed, the Tay and the Spey – can be much more expensive.

The STB/visitscotland's booklet *Fish Scotland* is a good introduction and is stocked by TICs. For more in-depth information you should try *Scotland for Game, Sea and Coarse Fishing*, available from Pastime Publications (☎ 0131-556 1105), 6 York Place, Edinburgh EH1 3EP.

Other organisations that can help include:

Scottish Federation of Sea Anglers (☎ 01292-264735) Brian Burn, Flat 2, 16 Bellevue Rd, Ayr KA7 2SA

Scottish National Anglers Association (☎ 0131-339 8808) David Wilkie, Administration Office, Caledonia House, South Gyle, Edinburgh EH12 9DQ

HORSE RIDING & PONY TREKKING

Seeing the country from the saddle is highly recommended, even if you're not an experienced rider. There are riding schools catering to all levels of proficiency.

Pony trekking is a popular holiday activity. A half-day's trekking should cost around £15, and riding hats are included. Many pony trekkers are novice riders so most rides are at walking speed with the occasional trot. If you're an experienced rider there are numerous riding schools with horses for hire – TICs have details.

The STB/visitscotland publishes a *Riding & Trekking Scotland* brochure, which lists riding centres around Scotland. For more information contact:

Trekking & Riding Society of Scotland (☎ 01821-650210, W www.ridinginscotland .com) Steadingfield, Wolfhill, Perthshire PH2 6DA

British Horse Society (☎ 08701-202244, W www.bhs.org.uk) British Equestrian Centre, Stoneleigh Park, Kenilworth, Warwickshire CV8 2LR. The society publishes *Where to Ride and Train* (£5.95), which lists places throughout the UK, and can send lists specific to a particular area.

ROCK CLIMBING

Scotland has a long history of rock climbing and mountaineering, with many of the classic routes on Ben Nevis and Glen Coe having been pioneered in the late 19th century.

The country's main rock-climbing areas include Ben Nevis, with routes up to 400m in length, Glen Coe, the Cairngorms, the Cuillins of Skye, Arrochar and the Isle of Arran, but there are hundreds of smaller crags all over the country. Some of the more remote crags in the Highlands and Outer Hebrides have only been explored in the last decade. One unusual feature of Scotland's rock-climbing scene is the sea stacks around the coast, most famously the 140m-high Old Man of Hoy.

Rock Climbing in Scotland, by Kevin Howett, and the Scottish Mountaineering Club's regional *Rock & Ice Climbs* guides are excellent references, and you can pick up useful information in most climbing equipment shops.

For more detailed information you can contact the Mountaineering Council of Scotland (☎ 01738-638227, W www.mountaineering-scotland.org.uk), The Old Granary, West Mill St, Perth PH1 5QP.

You can also check out the Scottish Mountaineering Club's Web site at W www .smc.org.uk.

SAILING

The western coast of Scotland, with its myriad islands, superb scenery and challenging winds and tides, is widely acknowledged as one of the finest cruising grounds in the world.

Experienced skippers with suitable qualifications can charter a yacht from one of dozens of agencies; prices for bareboat charter start at around £600 per week for a four-berth yacht. Beginners can take a Royal Yachting Association training course (from £325 for five days). Courses in dinghy sailing, powerboating, windsurfing and canoeing are also available at many centres around the coast.

For details of yacht charter agencies, sailing schools and courses, ask for the STB/visitscotland's *Sail Scotland* brochure or check out the Web site at W www.sailscotland.co.uk.

SKIING & SNOWBOARDING

There are five ski centres in Scotland but the slopes are far smaller and the weather considerably less reliable than anything you'll find in the Alps or Pyrenees. On a sunny day, however, with good snow, it can be very pleasant.

Scotland offers both downhill and cross-country skiing as well as snowboarding. The high season is from January to April but it's sometimes possible to ski from as early as November to as late as May. However, high winds and poor weather can sometimes make the Scottish winter-sports scene something of an endurance test.

Package holidays are available but it's easy to make your own arrangements, with all kinds of accommodation on offer in and around the ski centres. You can easily turn up at the slopes, hire some kit, buy a day pass and off you go. It can be extremely busy at weekends, especially if there's a good weather forecast, but you can sometimes have a slope to yourself mid-week.

Information

Contact STB/visitscotland (☎ 0131-332 2433) for its detailed *Scottish Snow* brochure and accommodation list. General information can be obtained from Snowsport Scotland (☎ 0131-445 4151, W www.snsc.demon.co.uk), Hillend, Biggar Rd, Edinburgh EH10 7EF.

Each ski centre has its own Web site and contact number for snow reports and general information. There's an answerphone service for calls outside business hours.

Cairngorm
☎ 01479-861261
W www.cairngormmountain.com
Glencoe
☎ 01855-851226
W www.ski-glencoe.co.uk

Glenshee
☎ 013397-41320
W www.ski-glenshee.co.uk
The Lecht
☎ 019756-51440
W www.lecht.co.uk
Nevis Range
☎ 01397-705825
W www.nevis-range.co.uk

The Ski Hotline weather-report service can be useful. Phone ☎ 09001-654 followed by 654 for all centres, 660 for Nevis Range, 658 for Glencoe, 656 for Glenshee, 657 for The Lecht, and 655 for Cairngorm. For cross-country the number is ☎ 0891-654659. These number cost 60p per minute. Alternatively you can check the Web site at W www.ski-scotland.com, which is updated daily during the ski season.

Resorts

The biggest ski centres are Glenshee and Cairngorm. **Glenshee** (920m), on the A93 road between Perth and Braemar, offers the largest network of lifts and widest range of runs in Scotland. It also has snow machines for periods when the real thing doesn't appear.

Cairngorm (1097m) has almost 30 runs spread over an extensive area. The town of Aviemore, with its pubs, restaurants and shops, is nearby and there's a ski bus service from here and from the surrounding villages to the slopes. Cairngorm is probably the most popular resort for snowboarders.

Glencoe (1108m) is the oldest of the resorts, with only five tows and two chairlifts. It's easily accessible from Glasgow, and has some spectacular scenery.

Nevis Range (1221m) near Fort William offers the highest ski runs, the grandest setting, and some of the best off-piste potential in Scotland. A gondola takes you to the foot of the main skiing area, which has eight tows and three chairlifts.

The Lecht (793m) is the smallest and most remote centre, on the A939 road between Ballater and Grantown-on-Spey. However, the short runs are good for beginners and families.

Access to the centres is probably easiest by car – there are plenty of car parks. Slopes are graded in the usual way, from green (easy) through blue and red to black (very difficult); and each centre has a ski patrol. You should ensure that your travel insurance covers you for winter sports.

All the ski resorts have funparks for snowboarders.

Costs

It's easy to hire ski equipment and clothing when you arrive but you should book lessons, if you want them, in advance. The prices vary but on average expect to pay £13 to £15 per day for hire of skis, boots and poles or snowboard and boots; and £8 to £12 per day for ski clothing.

Lift passes cost £15 to £20 per day, or £64 to £80 for a five-day pass (Monday to Friday only, passport photo required). In a group, ski lessons cost around £12 per person for two hours; private lessons cost £20 to £25 per hour. A one-day beginner's package, including lift pass, equipment hire and four hours' instruction, costs around £30 to £45, depending on the resort. Charges are lower for under 18s (under 16s at The Lecht). Cairngorm is generally the most expensive of the lot, Lecht the cheapest.

SURFING

Most overseas visitors don't think of Scotland as a place for a beach holiday – for good reasons, notably the climate and water temperature. You definitely have to be hardy, or equipped with a wetsuit, to do anything more than take a quick dip. On the other side of the equation, there is some truly magnificent coastline, some beautiful sandy beaches and some of the best surfing breaks in Europe.

Summer water temperatures are roughly around 13°C; winter temperatures are 5° to 6°C colder. So getting in the water, at least in summer, is feasible if you have a wetsuit. A 3mm fullsuit (steamer) plus boots is sufficient in summer, while winter requires a 5mm suit, plus boots, hood and gloves.

Sadly, many beaches suffer from pollution, often thanks to local towns draining their storm water and sewage offshore. It's worth checking with a local before taking the plunge.

For most visiting surfers, the most unusual aspect of surfing here is the impact of the tides. The tidal range is large, which means there is often a completely different set of breaks at low and high tides. As is usually the case, the waves tend to be biggest and best on an incoming tide. The waves in spring, autumn and winter tend to be bigger and more consistent than in summer; conditions in summer are pretty unreliable.

The entire Scottish coast has surf but it's the north and west, particularly around Thurso and in the Outer Hebrides, that has outstanding world-class possibilities. Lewis has the best and most consistent surf in Britain, with around 120 recorded breaks and waves up to 5m. Thurso has a couple of famous breaks, one in front of the harbour wall with lefts and rights, known as Reef, and one at Beach. Thurso East (Castle Reef) is the big one – a huge right that sometimes works up to 5m. The eastern coast of Scotland is easily accessible but the swells are unreliable and short-lived.

For more information contact Hebridean Surf (☎/fax 01851-705862, ⓔ hebsurf@ madasafish.com, ⓦ www.hebrideansurf .co.uk), 28 Francis St, Stornoway, Lewis HS1 2ND.

WALKING

Every weekend many people invade the countryside for short and long walks, often ending up somewhere that sells tea or beer. There are footpaths around many villages and towns and plans for more in the pipeline. Keen walkers should consider a week based in one interesting spot (perhaps in a self-catering cottage, hostel or camp site) with a view to exploring the surrounding countryside.

The best time is usually May to September for mountains, although walking the West Highland Way or Southern Upland Way is normally fine between April and October. (Winter walking in the higher areas of Scotland is 'technical' – requiring, at the very least, an ice-axe, crampons and mountaineering experience.)

July and August is holiday time in Britain, so everywhere is likely to be busier than normal – although only a few parts of Scotland ever get *really* crowded. Midges can also be a problem at this time. The most pleasant time is May to mid-June – before the midges emerge. September (and sometimes October) is also good, although days are colder and shorter.

Highland hikers should be properly equipped and cautious as the weather can become vicious at any time of year. After rain, peaty soil can become boggy; always wear stout shoes and carry a change of clothing.

Some of the walks described here are quite serious mountain/wilderness undertakings and shouldn't be embarked upon lightly.

Access

Scotland has a formal system of registered rights of way and there is a tradition of relatively free access to open country, especially on mountains and moorlands (see the boxed text 'Access & the Law' later in the section). There is much cooperation between organisations such as the Scottish Landowners' Federation, the Mountaineering Council of Scotland and the Ramblers' Association to promote responsible access to the countryside.

Providing you don't cause damage and that you leave the land if (in the unlikely event) you're asked to do so by the owner, you shouldn't have any trouble. You should, however, avoid areas where you might disrupt or disturb wildlife, deer stalking and grouse shooting (mainly from 12 August to the third week in October) and lambing (generally mid-April to the end of May).

Rights of way exist but local authorities aren't required to list and map them so they're not shown on Ordnance Survey (OS) maps. However, in its guide, *Scottish Hill Tracks*, the Scottish Rights of Way & Access Society (SRWS) publicises those routes which have, or deserve to have, legal status and defends those under threat. Access is free at all times to areas owned by the

National Trust for Scotland (NTS) and to most owned by the Forestry Commission.

Information

Every TIC has details (free or for a nominal charge) of suggested walks that take in local points of interest. Other useful sources of information are:

Mountaineering Council of Scotland
(☎ 01738-638227, ⓦ www.mountaineering-scotland.org.uk) The Old Granary, West Mill St, Perth PH1 5QP
Ramblers' Association Scotland (☎ 01577-861222, ⓦ www.ramblers.org.uk/scotland) Kingfisher House, Auld Mart Business Park, Milnathort, Kinross KY13 9DA
Scottish Rights of Way & Access Society
(☎ 0131-558 1222, ⓦ www.scotways.co.uk) 24 Annandale St, Edinburgh EH7 4AN

Guidebooks Scores of books are available that describe walks ranging from half-hour strolls to week-long expeditions.

Lonely Planet's *Walking in Scotland* is a comprehensive resource, covering short walks and long-distances paths. Its *Walking in Britain* covers Scottish walks too.

For general advice, the STB produces a *Walking Scotland* brochure, describing numerous routes in various parts of the country, plus safety tips and other information.

Great Walks Scotland, by Hamish Brown et al, describes a good range of routes of varying difficulty all over the country. Or try *100 Best Routes on Scottish Mountains*, by Ralph Storer.

The Scottish Mountaineering Club publishes a series of guides including *The Munros Hillwalkers Guide*. It also publishes several *District Guides* listing mainly high-level walks for those with experience.

The High Mountains Companion is a condensed text of Irvine Butterfield's *The High Mountains of Britain & Ireland*. Both books cover the British Isles but concentrate on the mountains of Scotland.

Highly recommended if you like mountains but can't stomach the intensity of Munro bagging is *The First Fifty*, by Muriel Gray. She likes to debunk the mystique and fastidiousness that can sometimes envelop other writers and books concerning walking in Scotland.

And just in case you thought all walks in Scotland were up the biggest mountains, there's *Exploring Scottish Hill Tracks*, by Ralph Storer, with a marvellous range of circular routes and longer expeditions for walkers and mountain bikers, many following traditional cattle-drovers' routes through the glens.

The Ordnance Survey (OS) Pathfinder series of walking guides – including *Fort*

Munros & Munro Bagging

The Scottish Highlands cover the most extensive tract of hill country in the British Isles. In addition to their appeal to scenery seekers, they present many challenges for hillwalkers and mountaineers.

Unpredictable weather conditions at any time of year and often remote summits, together with few opportunities for shelter, mean that those who venture into the hills should be properly equipped and aware of their own capabilities. The Scottish mountains are relatively modest in height with the highest, Ben Nevis, reaching only 1343m above sea level, but conditions in winter can be arctic, and snow can fall on the high summits even in summer.

At the end of the 19th century, Sir Hugh Munro compiled a list of all the summits in Scotland over 900m, with nearly 300 gaining the status of 'Munros'. After various revisions to the list there are now 284 Munros in the eponymous tables. 'Munro bagging' – ticking off the list as you 'bag' each summit – is now a popular leisure activity. For some, it's an obsession.

Sir Hugh himself narrowly failed to complete the full round and the first person to succeed in this monumental task was the Reverend AE Robertson in 1930, a Gaelic-speaking minister of the Church of Scotland. Since then, his feat has been matched by around 3000 others and the number continues to increase.

Munro bagging has created a boom in books devoted to walking and climbing in the Scottish mountains so there's no shortage of advice on the subject.

To the uninitiated, it may seem strange that Munro baggers see a day (or longer) plodding around in mist, cloud and driving rain to the point of exhaustion as time well spent. However, for those who can add one or more ticks to their list, the vagaries of the weather are part of the enjoyment – at least in retrospect.

Munro bagging is, of course, more than merely ticking names on a list. It takes you to some of the wildest, most beautiful parts of Scotland and, for many, provides years of healthy enjoyment and spiritual reward.

Visitors to Scotland may wish to experience something of the magic of the Scottish mountains but, with limited time, choices must be made. All parts of the Highlands and islands have their own devotees and there are many Munros within easy reach of Scotland's major cities.

Some areas are outstanding for their own particular reasons. These include the Torridon Hills in Wester Ross, ancient mountains rising steeply from sea level; Ben Nevis and Glencoe, offering an infinite variety of walks and climbs as well as the highest peak and biggest cliffs in Britain; and the Cairngorms, a sub-arctic wilderness of stony plateau far from public roads. The traverse of the Cuillin Hills on the Isle of Skye provides the finest mountaineering challenge of all, taking in seven Munros with serious rock climbing punctuating the route. Completion of the traverse in a day is a considerable achievement, but is really only possible in good settled weather.

The weather is the key. When the sun shines, it's easy to understand the lure of the Scottish mountains but wind, rain and even snow are likely at any time of year. Skill and judgement are then at a premium in deciding whether to carry on, to turn back or even not to set out at all. On such occasions, it's worth reminding yourself that the hills will be there for another day.

Hugh Gore

William & Glen Coe, Inverness, Loch Ness & the North-East Highlands and *Skye & the North-West Highlands* – each cover about 30 walking routes of varying length and difficulty, with OS map excerpts, colour photos and background information.

Maps The Ordnance Survey (OS) caters to walkers with a wide variety of maps at different scales. Its Landranger series at 1:50,000 – 1¼ inches to 1 mile or 2cm to 1km – is good, but if you want more detail it also publishes Pathfinder/Tourist maps at 1:25,000 (2½ inches to 1 mile or 4cm to 1km). TICs usually stock a selection.

Alternatively, look out for the excellent walkers' maps published by Harveys; they're at scales of 1:40,000 and 1:25,000.

Munro baggers should look out for the Bartholomew map of the Munros (£3.99).

Organised Walks

There are plenty of operators offering guided walks; the STB has a comprehensive list. Scot Trek (☎ 0141-334 9232, W www .scot-trek.co.uk), 9 Lawrence St, Glasgow G11 5HH, organises walking holidays from June to November that include the Cairngorms and the West Highland Way.

Multiday Walks

Southern Upland Way Coast to coast the Southern Upland Way is 212 miles (340km) from Portpatrick in the west to Cockburnspath in the east. It's suitable for walkers of different abilities and passes through varied countryside that contains a wealth of local history, literature and wildlife.

The route includes some long, extremely demanding stretches, so walkers tackling the entire length must be both experienced and fit. Parts of the route are sparsely populated, with shelter and transport virtually nonexistent. Proper equipment is essential;

JANE SMITH

in summer you can expect to experience everything from snow to a heat wave. Although the entire route is waymarked, walkers must be able to navigate with a map and compass when visibility is bad.

Walkers are advised to walk south-west to north-east (with the prevailing wind at your back) and allow anything between 12 and 20 days. The route takes in cliff-top paths, old Roman roads, hill ridges and drovers' trails. It passes over high hilltops and wide moors, through valleys, forests, farms and villages.

Short, less demanding sections of the walk can be undertaken as one- or two-day walks, for example Portpatrick to New Luce (23 miles; 37km) and Yair Bridge to Melrose (7½ miles; 12km).

An excellent official guide to the walk is published by the government Stationery Office and comes complete with two 1:50,000 OS route maps. Aurum Press also publishes the *Southern Upland Way*, by Anthony Burton.

Accommodation is quite difficult to find in parts and many walkers use tents. Book accommodation in advance, especially in the busy summer months. Local TICs can help, and supply a free accommodation leaflet.

For more details visit online at W www .southern-upland-way.com.

West Highland Way This classic hike stretches for 95 miles (152km) through the Scottish Highlands, from Milngavie (pronounced mull-**guy**), 7 miles (11km) northwest of the centre of Glasgow to Fort William.

The route passes through a tremendous range of landscape that includes some of Scotland's most spectacular scenery. It begins in the Lowlands, but the greater part of the trail is among the mountains, lochs and fast-flowing rivers of the Highlands. After following the eastern shore of Loch Lomond, and passing Crianlarich and Tyndrum, the route crosses wild Rannoch Moor and reaches Fort William via Glen Nevis, in the shadow of Britain's highest peak, Ben Nevis.

The path is easy to follow and it uses the old drove roads, along which cattle were herded in the past, an old military road (built by troops to help subdue the Highlands in the 18th century) and disused railway lines. Best walked from south to north, the walk can be done in about six or seven days.

You need to be properly equipped with good boots, maps, a compass, and food and drink for the northern part of the walk. Midge repellent is also essential.

The Harveys map, *West Highland Way*, is the most accurate and contains useful additional tourist information. *The West Highland Way*, by Robert Aitken (The Stationery Office), comes with a 1:50,000 OS route map and is the most comprehensive guide. *West Highland Way* (Aurum Press), by Anthony Burton, also contains OS maps.

Accommodation shouldn't be too difficult to find, though it's quite limited between Bridge of Orchy and Kinlochleven. In summer, book B&Bs in advance. There are some youth hostels on or near the path, as well as bunkhouses. It's also possible to camp in some parts. A free accommodation list is available from TICs.

For more information check out the Web site at W www.west-highland-way.co.uk.

The Speyside Way This is a Lowland route running alongside the River Spey, one of Scotland's famous salmon-fishing rivers. It starts at Buckie and follows the coast to Spey Bay, east of Elgin, then runs inland along the river to Aviemore in the Cairngorms (with branches to Tomintoul and Dufftown). At only 66 miles (105km), it can be done in three or four days. With more time it could possibly be combined with some high-level walking in the Cairngorms.

This route has also been called the 'Whisky Trail' as it passes near a number of distilleries, including Glenlivet and Glenfiddich, some of which are open to the public. If you stop at them all, the walk may take longer than the usual three or four days!

Although there's no specific guidebook, the Automobile Association's (AA's) *Exploring Britain's Long Distance Paths* and the *National Trail Companion* cover most things; there's also the *Speyside Way* leaflet produced by Moray Council Ranger Service (☎ 01340-881266).

Check out the route at W www.speyside way.org.

The Great Glen Way This 73-mile (117km) route along the Great Glen from Inverness to Fort William – where walkers could connect with the West Highland Way – is scheduled to open officially in spring 2002. It is described in detail in *The Great Glen Way*, by Jacquetta Megarry.

In the meantime, there are plenty of good waymarked day walks, described in the *Great Glen Forest Walks* leaflet available from local TICs. You can look for the fabled Loch Ness Monster as you go!

For more details on this walk visit the Web site at W www.greatglenway.com.

Fife Coastal Path This trail starts at North Queensferry, just across the Forth Bridge from Edinburgh, and follows the northern shore of the Firth of Forth for 46 miles (73km); allow two to three days. It is still being developed, and will eventually connect with the Tay Bridge and Dundee, a total distance of 78 miles (125km).

The route is mostly on flat or undulating country, with a few steep sections. It isn't fully waymarked and you're unlikely to meet other walkers, so keep a close eye on the map. Highlights, apart from the stunning scenery and quiet fishing villages, include the attractive town of St Andrews.

There's no specific guidebook but ask for details from Kirkcaldy TIC (☎ 01592-267775) or at the Edinburgh TIC. The AA book *Exploring Britain's Long Distance Paths* describes the route, and the *National Trail Companion* covers accommodation.

St Cuthbert's Way This 62-mile (100km) walk from Melrose in the Borders to Lindisfarne (Holy Island) in Northumberland, England, links sites associated with the life of St Cuthbert. From Melrose it crosses the Eildon Hills to join the Tweed Valley before reaching the border near the twin towns of Kirk and Town Yetholm.

Crossing the border into England, it traverses the northern Cheviot Hills to Fenwick and on to the causeway linking the mainland with Lindisfarne. Before crossing the causeway check the times of the tides at the TIC in Wooler. The walk can be done in about six or seven days.

The official trail guide is Harvey Walker's *St Cuthbert's Way*. Leaflets on the route, accommodation and facilities are available free from TICs.

The Pilgrims Way In Galloway, the Pilgrims Way follows a 25-mile (40km) trail through The Machars peninsula from Glenluce Abbey in the north-west to the Isle of Whithorn in the south-east. The trail links sites associated with St Ninian, who introduced Christianity to Scotland, and along the route you'll see standing stones and burial mounds from the Bronze Age, Iron-Age forts, early-Christian chapels and medieval castles, as well as great scenery.

The walk can be done in two to three days and is described in *A Way to Whithorn: A Guide to the Whithorn Pilgrims Way*, by Andrew Patterson.

The Clyde Walkway When this route is complete it will run about 40 miles (65km) from Glasgow to the Falls of Clyde at New Lanark, closely following the River Clyde. The sections between Glasgow and Bothwell Castle and from Crossford to New Lanark are complete; the former connects with two shorter trails in Glasgow, the Kelvin Walkway and Allander Walkway, which in turn offer an attractive route to Milngavie at the start of the West Highland Way. Contact the TIC in Glasgow for details.

Short Walks

As well as those mentioned here, descriptions of other walks are given throughout this guide.

Isle of Arran This island is often called 'Scotland in miniature' and there's enough there to keep any walker happy for a week or two. When the sun shines, Arran masquerades as an island in the Mediterranean but it can get cold, wet and windy, so come well prepared. Get a copy of the leaflet *Walks on Arran* from the TIC in Brodick.

The island's highest mountain, Goat Fell (874m), is one of the most visited points on the island and there are several routes to the summit. The most popular are from Brodick Castle to the south, and from Corrie on the eastern side of the mountain. A quieter, more pleasing approach goes from The Saddle, the pass between Glen Rosa and Glen Sannox, on the western side. Allow seven to eight hours. There are numerous possibilities for linking up with paths to other peaks including Cir Mhor, Ciogh na h'Oighe, Castheal Abhail and Beinn Tarsuinn.

In the north-west of Arran are the Pirnmill Hills. Although not quite as high as Goat Fell, and less rugged in appearance, they are far less frequently visited. Finally, there are some lovely coastal walks, worthwhile at any time but particularly when the hills are shrouded in cloud. Possibly the best of these is the walk from Lochranza to Sannox, called the Cock of Arran Coast Walk. Even in miserable weather, this 8-mile (13km) route is interesting. It takes about four to five hours.

Glen Coe The lofty peaks and ridges that flank Glen Coe should be left to the mountaineer, but there's a good rough walk circumnavigating Buachaille Etive Beag. The appeal of this route is the remote, rugged landscape. The 9-mile (14.5km) walk itself is quite a challenge and you might be glad of trekking poles for balance when negotiating stream crossings. Allow at least five hours.

Ben Nevis There's something irresistible about an attempt on Ben Nevis (1343m), the highest peak in the country. Despite its popularity, the walk, which begins virtually at sea level, shouldn't be undertaken lightly. You should be well equipped with good boots and waterproofs, have adequate food and drink, carry a map and compass (and know how to use them!) and be aware that it can be cold and dangerous. Snow can fall on the summit even in midsummer and cloud envelops the peak two days out of three.

The route is about 4½ miles (7km) each way, but the ascent (and descent) and inevitable stops along the way mean that up

Access & the Law

Access to the countryside has been a thorny issue in Scotland for many years. In Victorian times, belligerent landowners attempted to prevent walkers from using well-established trails and moves to counter this led to successful litigation for the walkers and the formation of what later became the Scottish Rights of Way Society.

In 1865, the Trespass Scotland Act was passed, creating (among other things) the criminal offence of camping or lighting fires on private land without the owner's permission. Trespassing was also covered by earlier civil law, which allowed (in extreme cases) interdicts to be made, damages awarded and/or removal of the trespasser by minimum force.

Nowadays, legal action against trespassers is rare and this has led to the incorrect assumption that there is no law of trespass in Scotland. Most sensible people observe local restrictions when lambing or deer stalking is taking place, so conflict with farmers and landowners is avoided.

The Criminal Justice and Public Order Act (1994) didn't clarify matters and pressure from both landowners and walkers groups started to mount. In the mid-1990s, the Access Forum was set up to discuss the difficulties and arrange compromises. However, in February 2001, when the Scottish Executive published both the Draft Access Code and the Draft Land Reform Bill, it was revealed that legislators had bowed under pressure from unknown landowners. Some draconian restrictions on movement were included in the draft, which would make Scotland a laughing stock if they became law. Thousands of objections to the draft bill showed the depth of anger many people felt at things like 'closure of the countryside due to weather conditions' (section 4.8.1) and 'exclusion orders' (section 4.16). What happens next remains to be seen.

If you want to find out more about the Scottish Rights of Way & Access Society (Scotways; ☎/fax 0131-558 1222, ℮ info@scotways.com), check out their Web site at ⓦ www.scotways.com, or write to them at 24 Annandale St, Edinburgh EH7 4AN. Membership costs £10.

---

to eight hours should be allowed for the round trip. Ionad Nibheis Visitor Centre or the SYHA hostel are good starting points. If you don't want to go to the summit there's the Ben Nevis Low-Level Circuit from Halfway Lochan.

Cairngorms This extensive mountain range is popular with climbers and hillwalkers year round. These are the wildest uplands anywhere in Britain, with arctic tundra, superb high corries and awesome rock formations. The wildlife is pretty good too.

Cairn Gorm (1245m) is the most accessible summit but the high plateau is not the place for a casual stroll. You're only about 650 miles (1040km) from the Arctic Circle here, and at altitudes of 1000m or more in winter you're certainly in an arctic environment. Weather conditions are notoriously bad and navigation on the featureless summit plateaus can be difficult. Unless you're

an experienced mountaineer the routes should only be attempted in summer. Even then, walkers should be prepared for poor conditions.

The Cairn Gorm High Circuit is one of the most popular routes in the Cairngorms because of its easy access from Aviemore. From the ski-area car park (at 625m altitude) it takes about 1½ hours to climb up to the summit of Cairn Gorm at the start of the circuit, which runs around the rim of Coire an t-Sneachda and Cairn Lochan, then down the ridge that runs alongside Lurcher's Gully and back to the car park. The total distance is around 7 miles (11km).

Don't be put off if you're not a peak bagger. On the northern side of the range near Aviemore, Rothiemurchus Estate and Glenmore Forest Park there are many walking opportunities suitable for all walkers.

You can obtain detailed information from the TIC in Aviemore.

Getting There & Away

Whichever way you're travelling, make sure you take out travel insurance. (See the Facts for the Visitor chapter.)

Bus travel between Scotland and other parts of the UK and Europe is usually the cheapest option, but it can be bone-crunching and exhausting and the savings are not huge, especially compared with the budget air fares you should be able to find.

From the rest of the world you will probably have to fly into London or another European hub and catch a connecting flight to a Scottish airport. The cost of the connecting flight adds little to the overall cost of the trip when bought in conjunction with the main ticket. However, there are times when to save the most money you may have to transfer from one London airport to another, or you may have to shift to the bus or train. When making an assessment, don't forget the hidden expenses – getting to and from airports, departure taxes, and food and drink consumed en route – and weigh up the inconvenience against the potential savings.

AIR
Airports & Airlines

The main international airports are Glasgow (☎ 0141-887 1111, W www.baa.co.uk); Glasgow Prestwick International (☎ 01292 511211, W www.glasgow.pwk.com); Edinburgh (☎ 0131-333 1000, W www.baa.co.uk); and Aberdeen (☎ 01224-722331, W www.baa.co.uk). Other airports include Dundee (☎ 01382-643242); Inverness (☎ 01463-232471, W www.hial.co.uk); and Sumburgh (☎ 01950-60654, W www.hial.co.uk). There are frequent direct flights to Scotland from other parts of the UK and Ireland, Europe and North America, and a limited number of services from Africa, the Middle East and Asia.

The main airlines serving Scotland are British Airways (BA; ☎ 0845 773 3377, W www.britishairways.co.uk); British Midland (☎ 0870 607 0555, W www.flybmi.com) and KLM UK (☎ 0870 507 4074,

W www.klmuk.com). A list of other airlines follows:

Aer Lingus ☎ 0845 973 7747,
  W www.aerlingus.com
Air Canada ☎ 0870 524 7226,
  W www.aircanada.ca
Air France ☎ 0845 084 5111,
  W www.airfrance.com
Air Transat ☎ 1 866 847 112
American Airlines ☎ 0345 789789,
  W www.aa.com
Atlantic Airways ☎ 0845 6072 7727
  W www.atlantic.fo
Braathens ☎ 0191-214 0991,
  W www.braathens.no
British European ☎ 0870 567 6676,
  W www.british-european.com
Canada 3000 ☎ 416-679 3000 in Ontario,
  ☎ 1 888 3000 669 in all other provinces
Continental Airlines ☎ 0800 776464,
  W www.continental.com
Lufthansa ☎ 0845 773 7747,
  W www.lufthansa.com

Scandinavian Airlines (SAS) ☎ 0845 6072 7727,
W www.scandinavian.net
ScotAirways ☎ 0870 606 0707
W www.scotairways.co.uk

There are also several discount, 'no-frills' airlines whose flights do not appear on the computerised reservations systems used by travel agents and Web sites such as W www.travelocity.com and W www.expedia .com. To check their fares you have to call their reservations numbers or check their Web sites (which often offer extra discounts for tickets bought on the Internet). Flying mid-week and booking several months in advance, fares from London to Edinburgh or Glasgow can be as low as £45 return.

easyJet (☎ 0870 600 0000, W www.easyjet.com)
  A feisty carrier with bright orange aircraft, easy-Jet has direct flights into Edinburgh and Glasgow from London Luton, Amsterdam and Belfast. It also has flights from London Luton to Aberdeen and Inverness.
Go (☎ 0845 605 4321, W www.go-fly.com) Originally a spin-off of BA but now independent, Go flies into Edinburgh and Glasgow from London Stansted, Bristol, Dublin and Belfast.
Ryanair (☎ 0870 156 9569, W www.ryanair .com) An Ireland-based airline, Ryanair flies direct to Glasgow Prestwick from London Stansted, Dublin, Brussels Charleroi, Paris Beauvais and Frankfurt Hahn, and from Dublin to Edinburgh.

Buying Tickets

World aviation has never been so competitive, making air travel better value than ever. But you have to research the options carefully to make sure you get the best deal. The Internet is an increasingly useful resource for checking air fares.

Full-time students and those aged under 26 (under 30 in some countries) have access to better deals than other travellers. You have to show a document proving your date of birth or a valid International Student Identity Card (ISIC) when buying your ticket and boarding the plane.

Generally, there is nothing to be gained by buying a ticket direct from the airline.

Discounted tickets are released to selected travel agents and specialist discount agencies, and these are usually the cheapest deals going.

One exception to this rule is the expanding number of no-frills carriers mentioned earlier, which mostly only sell direct to travellers. Unlike the 'full-service' airlines, no-frills carriers often make one-way tickets available at around half the return fare, meaning that it is easy to put together an open-jaw ticket when you fly to one place but leave from another.

The other exception is booking on the Internet. Many airlines, full-service and no-frills, offer some excellent fares to Web surfers. They may sell seats by auction or simply cut prices to reflect the reduced cost of electronic selling.

Many travel agencies around the world have Web sites, which can make the Internet a quick and easy way to compare prices. There are also an increasing number of online agents such as W www.travelocity .co.uk and W www.deckchair.com which operate only on the Internet. Online ticket sales work well if you are doing a simple one-way or return trip on specified dates. However, online superfast fare generators are no substitute for a travel agent who knows all about special deals, has strategies for avoiding layovers and can offer advice on everything from which airline has the best vegetarian food to the best travel insurance to bundle with your ticket.

You may find the cheapest flights are advertised by obscure agencies. Most such firms are honest and solvent but there are some rogue fly-by-night outfits around. Paying by credit card generally offers protection, as most card issuers provide refunds if you can prove you didn't get what you paid for. Similar protection can be obtained by buying a ticket from a bonded agent, such as one covered by the Air Travel Organiser's Licence (ATOL) scheme in the UK. Agents who only accept cash should hand over the tickets straight away and not tell you to 'come back tomorrow'.

After you've made a booking or paid your deposit, call the airline and confirm that the booking was made. It's generally

Air Travel Glossary

Alliances Many of the world's leading airlines are now intimately involved with each other, sharing everything from reservations systems and check-in to aircraft and frequent-flyer schemes. Opponents say that alliances restrict competition. Whatever the arguments, there is no doubt that big alliances are the way of the future.

Courier Fares Businesses often need to send urgent documents or freight securely and quickly. Courier companies hire people to accompany the package through customs and, in return, offer a discount ticket which is sometimes a bargain. However, you may have to surrender all your baggage allowance and take only carry-on luggage.

Fares Airlines traditionally offer 1st class (coded F), business class (coded J) and economy class (coded Y) tickets. These days there are so many promotional and discounted fares available that few passengers pay full fare.

Lost Tickets If you lose your airline ticket, an airline will usually treat it like a travellers cheque and, after inquiries, issue you with another one. Legally, however, an airline is entitled to treat it like cash and if you lose it then it's gone forever. Take very good care of your tickets.

Onward Tickets An entry requirement for many countries is that you have a ticket out of the country. If you're unsure of your next move, the easiest solution is to buy the cheapest onward ticket to a neighbouring country or a ticket from a reliable airline which can later be refunded if you do not use it.

Open-Jaw Tickets These are return tickets where you fly out to one place but return from another. If available, this can save you backtracking to your arrival point.

Overbooking Since every flight has some passengers who fail to show up, airlines often book more passengers than they have seats. Usually excess passengers make up for the no-shows, but occasionally somebody gets 'bumped' onto the next available flight. Guess who it is most likely to be? The passengers who check in late. If you do get 'bumped', you are normally offered some form of compensation.

Reconfirmation Some airlines require you to reconfirm your flight at least 72 hours prior to departure. Check your travel documents to see if this is the case.

Restrictions Discounted tickets often have various restrictions on them – such as needing to be paid for in advance and incurring a penalty to be altered or cancelled. Others are restrictions on the minimum and maximum period you must be away.

Round-the-World Tickets RTW tickets give you a limited period (usually a year) in which to circumnavigate the globe. You can go anywhere the carrying airlines go, as long as you don't backtrack. The number of stopovers or total number of separate flights is decided before you set off and they usually cost a bit more than a basic return flight.

Ticketless Travel Airlines are gradually waking up to the realisation that paper tickets are unnecessary encumbrances. On simple one-way or return trips, reservations details can be held on computer and the passenger merely shows ID to claim their seat.

Transferred Tickets Airline tickets cannot be transferred from one person to another. Travellers sometimes try to sell the return half of their ticket, but officials can ask you to prove that you are the person named on the ticket. On an international flight, tickets are compared with passports.

not advisable to send money (even cheques) through the post unless the agent is very well established – some travellers have reported being ripped off by fly-by-night mail-order ticket agents.

Many travellers change their routes halfway through their trips, so think carefully before you buy a ticket that is not easily refunded.

Travellers with Specific Needs

If they're warned early enough, airlines can often make special arrangements for travellers, such as wheelchair assistance at airports or vegetarian meals on the flight. Children aged under two travel for 10% of the standard fare (or free on some airlines) as long as they don't occupy a seat. They don't get a baggage allowance. 'Skycots', baby food and nappies should be provided by the airline if requested in advance. Children aged between two and 12 can usually occupy a seat for half to two-thirds of the full fare, and do get a baggage allowance.

The disability-friendly Web site, **W** www .everybody.co.uk, has an airline directory that provides information on the facilities offered by various airlines.

Departure Tax

All UK domestic flights and those from Scotland to destinations within the EU carry a £10 departure tax. For flights to other destinations abroad the tax is £20. This is usually included in the price of your ticket.

England & Wales

There are more than a hundred flights a day between London and Edinburgh and Glasgow, and several daily from other UK airports. BA has flights to Glasgow and Edinburgh from London, Bristol, Birmingham, Cardiff, Manchester, Plymouth and Southampton, and to Aberdeen and Inverness from London.

British Midland flies from London Heathrow to Aberdeen, Edinburgh and Glasgow; to Edinburgh from East Midlands Airport, Leeds/Bradford and Manchester, and to Glasgow from East Midlands Airport, Guernsey, Jersey, Leeds/Bradford and Manchester.

KLM UK and Go fly to Edinburgh from London Stansted, and easyJet flies from London's Luton airport to Edinburgh, Glasgow, Inverness and Aberdeen. British European (under the name Jersey European) flies from London City and Birmingham to Edinburgh; from Birmingham, Exeter, Guernsey and Jersey to Glasgow; and from London City to Aberdeen. ScotAirways flies from London City to Edinburgh, Glasgow and Dundee.

Prices vary enormously. A standard economy return ticket from London to Edinburgh or Glasgow costs around £265 from British Midland, while Jersey European, easyJet and Go offer return flights, travelling mid-week or on a Saturday and booking a month or two in advance, from as little as £45.

For students or travellers aged under 26, popular travel agencies in the UK include STA Travel (☎ 020-7361 6262, **W** www.sta travel.co.uk), which has an office at 86 Old Brompton Rd, London SW7; and usit Campus (☎ 0870 240 1010, **W** www.usit campus.co.uk), which has an office at 52 Grosvenor Gardens, London SW1. Both of these agencies have branches throughout the UK, and sell tickets to all travellers but cater especially to young people and students.

Ireland

Aer Lingus has daily flights from Dublin to Edinburgh and Glasgow. BA flies direct from Dublin to Edinburgh, from Belfast and Londonderry to Glasgow, and from Belfast to Aberdeen and Edinburgh, the lowest return fares start at around £70. Go and easy-Jet have direct flights from Belfast to Edinburgh; return fares cost from £35. Ryanair flies from Dublin to Glasgow Prestwick and Edinburgh, and has special offer flights from as little as IR£10 return, flying mid-week in low season. British European flies from Cork and Shannon airports to Glasgow and Edinburgh; all flights travel via Birmingham.

The Irish youth and student travel agency usitNOW (☎ 01-602 1600, **W** www.usit now.ie), 19 Aston Quay, O'Connell Bridge,

Dublin 2, has offices in most major cities in Ireland.

Continental Europe

The major airlines operate several direct flights a day into Edinburgh from Amsterdam, Brussels, Frankfurt and Paris, plus one or two daily from Copenhagen, Düsseldorf and Munich. In addition, it's possible to reach Edinburgh via London Stansted from various European cities using Go and easyJet, including Athens, Barcelona, Copenhagen, Geneva, Madrid, Munich, Naples, Nice, Prague, Reykjavik, Rome, Venice and Zurich. There are daily flights to Glasgow from Amsterdam (KLM UK and easyJet) and Malta (Air Malta; ☎ 020-7292 4949, W www.airmalta.com).

The best fare from continental Europe is with easyJet, which offers direct flights from Amsterdam to Edinburgh from around €55 return. Flying from Munich to Edinburgh via London Stansted with Go costs from around €190.

Travelling via London, there is not much variation in air-fare prices for departures from the main European cities. All the major airlines usually offer some sort of deal, and travel agencies generally have a number of deals on offer, so shop around.

Expect to pay the equivalent of about £120 to £200 on major airlines for discounted return tickets to Edinburgh or Glasgow. Across Europe many travel agencies have ties with STA Travel, where cheap tickets can be purchased. Outlets in major cities include: STA Travel in Berlin (☎ 030 311 0950, W www.statravel.de), Goethesttrasse 73, 10625 Berlin; Voyage Wasteels in Paris (☎ 0 803 88 70 04 – this number can only be dialled from within France – fax 01 43 25 46 25, W www.wasteels.fr), 11 rue Dupuytren, 756006 Paris; and Passaggi in Rome (☎ 06-474 0923, fax 482 7436), Stazione Termini FS, Galleria di Tesla, Rome.

In Belgium, Connections (☎ 02-550 01 00, W www.connections.be), 19–21 rue du Midi, 1000 Brussels, and Nouvelles Frontières (☎ 02-547 44 44, W www.nouvelles-frontieres.be), 2 blvd Maurice Lemmonier, 1000 Brussels, are recommended agencies.

NBBS Reizen (☎ 020-620 5071, W www.nbbs.nl), 66 Rokin, Amsterdam, is the official student travel agency in the Netherlands. Another recommended agency in Amsterdam is Malibu Travel (☎ 020-626 3230, W www.etn.nl/malibu), Prinsengracht 230.

Scandinavia

Icelandair (☎ 020-7874 1000, W www.icelandair.com) has daily flights between Reykjavik and Glasgow, while British Midland flies from Edinburgh to Copenhagen. Aberdeen has flight connections with the Faroe Islands (Atlantic Airways), Stavanger (British Midland, SAS and Braathens) in Norway, and Esbjerg (British Midland) in Denmark. A return flight from Stavanger to Aberdeen costs from around Nkr1700; from Reykjavik to Glasgow costs from Ikr30,000.

The USA

There are no direct flights from the USA to Edinburgh, but there are a couple that land at Glasgow – Continental Airlines from New York, and American Airlines from Chicago. Flight time from New York to Glasgow is around 7½ hours, and return fares start from around US$650.

Due to a system – currently being challenged – in which the landing fees for airlines are considerably higher at Scottish airports than at Heathrow, the majority of transatlantic flights to the UK still arrive at London. This also means that flights from US cities to Scotland via London are cheaper – from around US$560 – but the flight time is two to three hours longer.

Rather than fly via London, it's worth considering flying via Iceland. Icelandair has direct flights from New York, Boston, Baltimore/Washington, Minneapolis and Orlando (from October to March) to Reykjavik, where you can connect with a flight to Glasgow. Fares start at around US$530.

Discount travel agents in the USA are known as consolidators (although you won't see a sign on the door saying 'Consolidator'). San Francisco is the ticket consolidator capital of America, although some good deals can be found in Los Angeles,

New York and other big cities. Consolidators can be found through the *Yellow Pages* or the major daily newspapers. *The New York Times*, the *Los Angeles Times*, the *Chicago Tribune* and *The Examiner* (San Francisco) all produce weekly travel sections in which you will find a number of travel agency ads. Ticket Planet is a leading ticket consolidator in the USA and is recommended. Visit its Web site at [W] www .ticketplanet.com.

Council Travel, America's largest student travel organisation, has around 60 offices in the USA; its head office (☎ 800-226 8624) is at 205 E 42 St, New York, NY 10017. Call it for the office nearest you or visit its Web site at [W] www.ciee.org. STA Travel (☎ 800-777 0112) has offices in Boston, Chicago, Miami, New York, Philadelphia, San Francisco and other major cities. Call the toll-free 800 number for office locations, or visit its Web site at [W] www.sta travel.com.

Canada
The charter operator Air Transat has one direct flight a week from Toronto to Edinburgh, while between them Air Canada, Air Transat (☎ 1 866 847 112, [W] www.air transat.com) and Canada 3000 (☎ 416-679 3000 in Ontario, ☎ 1 888 3000 669 in all other provinces) have two to four flights a day to Glasgow. There are also two flights a week from Calgary and one a week from Vancouver to Glasgow. Return fares from Toronto start at around C$550.

Canadian discount air-ticket sellers are also known as consolidators and their air fares tend to be about 10% higher than those sold in the USA. The *Globe & Mail*, *Toronto Star*, *Montreal Gazette* and *Vancouver Sun* carry travel agents ads and are a good place to look for cheap fares.

Travel CUTS (☎ 800-667-2887) is Canada's national student travel agency and has offices in all major cities. Its Web address is [W] www.travelcuts.com.

Australia
For flights between the UK and Australia, there are a lot of competing airlines and a wide variety of air fares. Round-the-World (RTW) tickets are often real bargains (from around A$3000) and since Australia is pretty much on the other side of the world from Europe, it can sometimes work out cheaper to keep going right round the world on a RTW ticket than do a U-turn on a return ticket.

Expect to pay from A$1800 in the low season to A$3000 in the high season for a return ticket to London. Adding a connecting flight from London to Edinburgh should only add around A$100 to the cost of the ticket.

Cheap flights from Australia to Europe generally go via South-East Asian capitals, involving stopovers at Kuala Lumpur, Bangkok or Singapore. If a long stopover between connections is necessary, transit accommodation is sometimes included in the price of the ticket. If it's not, it may be worth considering a more expensive ticket that does include it.

Quite a few travel offices specialise in discount air tickets. Some travel agents, particularly smaller ones, advertise cheap air fares in the travel sections of weekend newspapers, such as *The Age* in Melbourne and *The Sydney Morning Herald*.

Two well-known agents for cheap fares are STA Travel and Flight Centre. STA Travel (☎ 03-9349 2411) has its main office at 224 Faraday St, Carlton, VIC 3053, and offices in all major cities and on many university campuses. Call ☎ 131 776 Australiawide for the location of your nearest branch or visit its Web site at [W] www.sta travel.com.au. Flight Centre (☎ 131 600 Australiawide, [W] www.flightcentre.com .au) has a central office at 82 Elizabeth St, Sydney, and there are dozens of offices throughout Australia.

New Zealand
Round-the-World (RTW) fares for travel to or from New Zealand are usually the best value (prices from around NZ$4300), often cheaper than a return ticket. Depending on which airline you choose, you may fly across Asia, with possible stopovers in India, Bangkok or Singapore, or across the

USA, with possible stopovers in Honolulu, Australia or one of the Pacific Islands.

Prices are similar to those from Australia (from around NZ$2600 Auckland to London) but the trip is even longer – two 12-hour flights minimum.

Travel agents advertise fares in the travel section of *The New Zealand Herald*. Flight Centre (☎ 09-309 6171, W www.flight centre.com.au) has a large central office in Auckland at National Bank Towers (on the corner of Queen and Darby Sts) and many branches throughout the country. STA Travel (☎ 09-309 0458, W www.sta.travel .com.au) has its main office at 10 High St, Auckland, and has other offices in Auckland as well as in Hamilton, Palmerston North, Wellington, Christchurch and Dunedin.

Asia

There are no direct flights from Asia to Scottish airports. Travelling via London, a return flight from Hong Kong to Edinburgh will cost from around HK$7500, and from Tokyo around ¥140,000.

Although most Asian countries are now offering fairly competitive air-fare deals, Bangkok, Singapore and Hong Kong are still the best places to shop around for discount tickets. Hong Kong's travel market can be unpredictable but some excellent bargains are available if you are lucky.

Hong Kong has a number of excellent, reliable travel agencies and some not-so-reliable ones. A good way to check on a travel agent is to look it up in the phone book: fly-by-night operators don't usually stay around long enough to get listed. Many travellers use the Hong Kong Student Travel Bureau (☎ 2730 3269), 8th floor, Star House, Tsimshatsui. You could also try Phoenix Services (☎ 2722 7378), 7th floor, Milton Mansion, 96 Nathan Rd, Tsimshatsui.

Africa

There are no direct flights from Africa to Scotland. Travelling via London, return fares from Johannesburg to Edinburgh start at around R4300.

Nairobi and Johannesburg are probably the best places in east and southern Africa to buy tickets. Some major airlines have offices in Nairobi, which is a good place to determine the standard fare before you make the rounds of the travel agencies. Getting several quotes is a good idea as prices are always changing. Flight Centres (☎ 02-210024) in Lakhamshi House, Biashara St, has been in business for many years.

In Johannesburg the South African Student's Travel Services (☎ 011-716 3045) has an office at the University of the Witwatersrand. STA Travel (☎ 011- 447 5551) has an office in Johannesburg on Tyrwhitt Ave in Rosebank.

BUS

Long-distance buses (coaches) are usually the cheapest method of getting to Scotland from other parts of the UK. The main operators are National Express (☎ 0870 580 8080, W www.gobycoach.com), and its subsidiary Scottish Citylink (☎ 0870 550 5050, W www.citylink.co.uk), with numerous regular services from London and other departure points in England, Wales and Northern Ireland (see the Edinburgh and Glasgow chapters).

Fares on the main routes are competitive, with many smaller operators undercutting Scottish Citylink/National Express. The cheapest London to Glasgow/Edinburgh coach is the daily overnight service operated by Silver Choice Travel (☎ 0141-333 1400, W www.silverchoicetravel.co.uk). It charges £24 for an Apex return, which must be bought at least seven days in advance, and is not valid for travel on Friday or Sunday; its standard return fare is £30, and the journey time is nine hours. The return fare with Scottish Citylink is £36 but its services are more frequent. For information on bus passes and discount cards see the Getting Around chapter.

Scottish Citylink runs a daily bus service from Edinburgh to various destinations in Ireland, including Belfast (£42 return, 7½ hours) and Dublin (£52 return, 10½ hours) via Glasgow and the high-speed ferry link between Stranraer and Belfast.

Backpackers Buses

From July to September, Edinburgh-based Haggis Backpackers (☎ 0131-557 9393, W www.haggisadventures.com) offers a hop-on hop-off bus service between London and Edinburgh, visiting places of interest en route. Buses depart three times a week from 258 Vauxhall Bridge Rd (near Victoria); the minimum round trip takes seven days but you can take up to three months if you like. The round-trip fare is £129; a two-day one-way trip from London to Edinburgh costs £39.

Going Forth (☎ 0131-478 6500, W www.goingforth.com) also offers a two-day, one-way guided trip from London to Edinburgh for £40; buses depart once a week on Saturday, June to September.

Celtic Connection (☎ 0131-225 3330, W www.celticconnection.freeserve.co.uk) runs a shuttle minibus service on Monday and Friday from Dublin and Belfast to Glasgow and Edinburgh for £29 one way, including the ferry crossing. Seats are sold on a standby basis and can't be booked until three days before the date of travel.

The budget bus company Slowcoach (☎ 020-7373 7737, W www.straytravel.com) operates between youth hostels in England and ventures into Scotland as far as Loch Lomond, Stirling and Edinburgh. You can get on and off the bus where you like (there's no compulsion to stay at a hostel), and your pass remains valid for two months. Buses leave London three times a week throughout the year; the price (£109) includes some activities and visits en route. The London to Edinburgh trip takes a minimum of four days, including visits to Bath, Stonehenge, Wales, the Lake District, Loch Lomond and Stirling.

TRAIN

Travelling to Scotland by train is usually faster and more comfortable, but more expensive, than taking the bus. Taking into account check-ins and the travel time between city centre and airport, the train offers a competitive alternative to air travel on the London to Edinburgh route. You can get timetable and fares information for all UK trains from the National Rail Enquiry Service (☎ 0845 748 4950).

Rest of the UK

GNER operates a fast and frequent rail service between London Kings Cross and Edinburgh (four hours), passing through Peterborough, York and Newcastle, with around 20 departures a day between 7am and 7pm. A standard return costs around £85 but special offers sometimes have fares as low as £39. The Virgin Trains service between London Euston and Glasgow, calling at Birmingham, Crewe and Preston, is somewhat slower at 5½ hours.

The Caledonian Sleeper service, connecting Edinburgh, Glasgow, Stirling, Perth, Dundee, Aberdeen, Fort William and Inverness with London Euston is operated by Scotrail and runs nightly (after 11pm) from Sunday to Friday. A standard return (sharing a two-bunk compartment) from London to Edinburgh or Glasgow costs £119, and a first-class return (single-bunk compartment) costs £165; the seven-day advance purchase Apex fare is £89. You also have the option of travelling on the sleeper in a first-class coach with a reclining seat, rather than a bunk; this costs £35/65 for an Apex/standard return. The journey lasts about 7½ hours.

Services to Edinburgh from other parts of England and Wales usually require changing trains at some point. Typical discount return fares and journey times include: Bristol (£105, seven hours), Cardiff (£105, 7½ hours), Leeds (£54, three hours) and Manchester (£46.60, four hours).

ScotRail offers various 'Rail and Sail' deals between Edinburgh and Glasgow and Belfast via the ferry crossings at Stranraer and Troon. Off-peak returns cost from £45, and the journey time is about five hours.

Continental Europe

You can travel from Paris or Brussels to Scotland by train using the Eurostar (☎ 0870 518 6186 in the UK, ☎ 0 836 35 35 39 in France, W www.eurostar.com) service as far as London Waterloo station, but then you'll have to take the tube from Waterloo to Kings Cross or Euston stations to connect with the Edinburgh or Glasgow train. The total journey time from Paris is about eight hours, and the standard return fare from Paris to London is around €500; even with discount fares to London of around €120, flying is usually faster and cheaper.

Buying Tickets

If the Byzantine Empire had designed a railway system, it could not have come up with anything more impenetrably complex than the labyrinthine structure created by the privatisation of British Rail in the mid-1990s. Rail services are provided by 25 different train operating companies (TOCs), while the rails themselves, along with the stations and signalling systems, are owned and operated by a completely separate company called Railtrack (though the situation was in flux at the time of writing).

There's a bewildering range of ticket types with various restrictions attached, depending on when you book and when you're travelling. You can check timetables and fares with the National Rail Enquiry Service (☎ 0845 748 4950), who will then give you the phone number of one of the TOCs where you can make a credit-card booking.

ScotRail operates most train services within Scotland, as well as the Caledonian Sleeper service to London; you can book tickets by credit card on ☎ 0845 755 0033, or book online at ⓦ www.scotrail.co.uk. GNER (☎ 0845 722 5225, ⓦ www.gner.co.uk) operates the main, east-coast London Kings Cross to Edinburgh route, and Virgin Trains (☎ 0845 722 2333, ⓦ www.virgintrains .co.uk) runs services from London Euston, Wales and north, central, south and southwest England to Glasgow and Edinburgh.

For most journeys it's easy enough to buy a ticket at the station just before departure but as the London–Edinburgh route is very popular it's safer to make a seat reservation.

Rail Passes

Unfortunately, Eurail passes are not recognised in Britain. There are local equivalents but they in turn aren't recognised in the rest of Europe. See the Getting Around chapter for details of passes valid for train travel in Scotland.

The BritRail pass, which includes travel in Scotland, must be bought outside Britain. There are many variations available, but the most useful for a visit to Britain that takes in Scotland is probably the BritRail Flexipass. It provides unlimited train travel on a certain number of days within a specified 60-day period. Prices are for adult 1st class/over-60s 1st class/standard class:

4 days	US$350/300/235
8 days	US$510/435/340
15 days	US$770/655/515

Youth passes are valid for those aged between 15 and 25 (standard class only) and cost US$185/240/360 for 4/8/15 days.

CAR & MOTORCYCLE

See the Getting Around chapter for details of road rules, driving conditions and information on renting and buying vehicles.

The fastest driving route to Scotland from London (400 miles) is via the M1 and M6 to Carlisle, and then the M74 as far as Abington, where you fork right on the A702 for the final leg to Edinburgh, or keep straight on for Glasgow. From Leeds (200 miles) and Newcastle (107 miles), the M1/A1 along the east coast and the A68 via Jedburgh are the main routes to the Scottish capital.

Drivers of vehicles registered in other EU countries will find bringing a car or motorcycle into the UK fairly straightforward. The vehicle must have registration papers and a nationality plate, and the driver must have insurance. Although the International Insurance Certificate (Green Card) is no longer compulsory, it still provides excellent proof that you are covered. Driving to Scotland from mainland Europe via the Channel Tunnel or ferry ports, head for London and follow the busy M25 orbital road to the M1 motorway, then follow the route as described from London.

Arriving in or leaving Edinburgh or Glasgow by car during the morning and evening rush hours (7.30am to 9.30am and 4.30pm to 6.30pm Monday to Friday) is an experience you can live without. Try to time your journey to avoid these periods.

HITCHING

Hitching is never entirely safe in any country in the world, and we don't recommend it. Travellers who decide to hitch should understand that they are taking a small but potentially serious risk. People who do choose to hitch will be safer if they travel in pairs and let someone know where they are planning to go. See also Hitching in the Getting Around chapter.

BOAT
Northern Ireland

From Northern Ireland, the main car ferry links to Scotland are the Belfast–Stranraer, Larne–Cairnryan and Belfast–Troon crossings, operated by Stena Line (☎ 028 90 747 747 from Northern Ireland, W www.stena line.com), P&O Irish Sea (☎ 0870 242 4777, W www.poirishsea.com) and SeaCat (☎ 0870 552 3523, W www.steam-packet .com) respectively. There are standard and high-speed ferries on the Stranraer and Cairnryan routes, high-speed only on the Troon crossing.

Fares vary widely depending on the season, and there are special deals worth looking out for. A one-way Apex fare on the slow ferry from Belfast to Stranraer costs around £125 for a car and two people. One-way Apex fares on the high-speed catamaran between Belfast and Troon start at £96 for a car and two passengers. One-way fares for foot passengers start at around £17.

The Larne–Cairnryan high-speed catamaran is the fastest crossing – one hour compared with 2½ hours for the Troon–Belfast route or the Larne–Cairnryan slow ferry. The drive from Cairnryan or Stranraer to Glasgow or Edinburgh is 85 or 132 miles respectively. From Troon to Glasgow is just 35 miles.

The car ferry service between Ballycastle (Northern Ireland) and Campbeltown (Argyll), which was launched in 1997, ceased operation in 2000. At the time of research there was a possibility that it may start up again in 2002. Check the Web site

at W www.cambeltownferry.com for the latest details.

Continental Europe

At the time of writing there were firm plans to open a direct ferry link between Scotland and mainland Europe. Starting in spring 2002, Superfast Ferries will run a roll-on roll-off car ferry between Rosyth, 12 miles north-west of Edinburgh, and a port in Zeebrugge in Belgium. One crossing a day is planned, and the journey time is expected to be around 16 hours. Superfast's sales agent in the UK is Viamare Travel (☎ 020-7431 4560, fax 7431 5456, W www.superfast scotland.com), Graphic House, 2 Sumatra Rd, London NW6 1PU.

Scandinavia

From late May to early September the Smyril Line (their UK agent is P&O Scottish Ferries, ☎ 01244-572615, W www .smyril-line.com) operates its weekly 'North Atlantic Link' car ferry between Shetland (Lerwick), the Faroe Islands (Torshavn), Iceland (Seydisfjordur), Norway (Bergen) and Denmark (Hantsholm). It leaves from Lerwick on Mondays for Bergen, and on Wednesdays for Torshavn and Seydisfjordur.

The one-way fare from Bergen to Lerwick in low/high season is Dkr1030/1460 per person for a couchette, and Dkr820/1170 for a car up to 5m. From the Faroes to Shetland the equivalent fares are Dkr480/680 and Dkr390/570; and from Iceland Dkr1060/1500 and Dkr730/1060. A special through-fare (one-way) from Aberdeen to Bergen via Lerwick on P&O Scottish Ferries and Smyril Line costs from £95/115 per person for a couchette plus £112/130 for a car up to 5m.

The Aberdeen–Lerwick crossing takes 14 hours; Lerwick to Bergen takes 13½ hours, Lerwick to Torshavn is 13 hours, and Torshavn to Seydisfjordur is 15 hours.

ORGANISED TOURS

There are hundreds of companies around the world offering package tours of Scotland. Ask a travel agent, or contact the Scottish

Tourist Board/visitscotland or the British Tourist Authority (see Tourist Offices in the Facts for the Visitor chapter).

Ancestral Journeys (☎ 01383-720522, ⓔ ances tralconnections@compuserve.com) 105 St Margaret St, Dunfermline KY12 7PH. This company will research your Scottish ancestry and organise a personalised tour, with a professional genealogist and historian, that combines sightseeing with visiting the places where your ancestors lived. Prices start US$1850 per person for a week, including 10 hours of genealogical research.

Footprints (☎ 01683-221592, ⓔ enquiries@ footprints-scotland.co.uk) Moffat, Dumfriesshire DG10 9BN. Footprints runs small, personalised tours starting in Edinburgh or Glasgow, exploring Scotland's prehistoric past with an archaeological expert. Highlights include visits to Pictish symbol stones, Iron-Age forts and stone circles. Three-day tours cost from £360 per person.

Saltire Tours (☎ 0131-442 2324, ⓔ chris@ saltiretours.co.uk) 3 Baberton Mains Cottage, Edinburgh EH14 5AB. This is a small company providing a wide range of imaginative tours from art and architecture to castles and whisky to Sir Walter Scott. Tours can be tailored to fit any budget.

Taste of Scotland (☎ 01592-260101, fax 261333, ⓔ admin@robertthebruce.com) 9 Nicol St, Kirkcaldy KY1 1N. Taste of Scotland offers bespoke luxury tours, staying in top hotels, eating at the best restaurants and travelling in a Rolls-Royce with a qualified guide and driver.

From the USA

There are a number of recommended organised tours operating from the USA, including:

About Travel (☎ 605-362 1741, ⓔ cheryl@ aboutravel.com) 3548 S Gateway Blvd #302, Sioux Falls SD 57106. This company offers eight-day trips to the Edinburgh Festival, including tickets to two major shows, various Fringe performances and the Military Tattoo. Prices for a 15-day tour start at US$3195.

Celebrity Tours Inc (☎ 914-244 1300 or ☎ 1-800-663 5578, ⓔ info@celebritytours.net) 2 Ascot Circle, Mount Kisco NY 10459. Celebrity Tours can organise tours that combine a visit to Edinburgh with playing golf at the Old Course in St Andrews and other famous courses in Scotland. An eight-day golf tour of Scotland costs from US$3075.

From New Zealand

Organised tours to Scotland from New Zealand include:

Scottish Heritage Travel (☎03-318 8066, fax 318 8464, ⓔ travel@scottish-heritage.co.nz) Kinnairdy, Coal Track Rd, R.D. 1, Christchurch 8021. These people run a wide range of special interest tours, including whisky distillery tours and visits to clan gatherings. A two-night package to Edinburgh for the Military Tattoo costs from £155 per person.

Getting Around

Public transport in Scotland is generally good, but it can be expensive compared to other European countries. During the 1980s and 1990s UK government policy was openly hostile to public transport. Car ownership was favoured and local rail and bus services suffered – the chaotic privatisation of British Rail was but one illustration of this attitude.

Buses are usually the cheapest way to get around. Unfortunately, they're also the slowest, and on main routes you're often confined to major roads which screen you from the small towns and landscapes that make travelling in Scotland worthwhile. With discount passes and tickets bought in advance, trains can be competitive in price; they're also quicker and often take you through beautiful countryside.

Traveline (☎ 0870 608 2608) provides timetable information for all public transport services in Scotland and throughout Great Britain. Unfortunately, Traveline does not provide any information on fares, nor can it book tickets for you – it will give you the telephone number of the relevant operator, so you can call to check fares and make bookings.

It's worth considering car rental for at least part of your trip. However, even if you're not driving, with plenty of time and a mix of buses, trains, ferries, the odd taxi, walking and occasionally hiring a bike, you can get almost anywhere.

AIR

Most domestic air services in Scotland are geared to business needs, or are lifelines for remote island communities. You might feel it's worth flying to Barra in the Outer Hebrides just to experience landing on a beach – one of the few airports in the world where flight schedules are dictated by tide times! Otherwise, flying is a pricey way to cover relatively short distances, and only worth considering if you're short of time and want to visit the outer reaches of Scotland, in particular the Outer Hebrides, Orkney and Shetland.

The main domestic operators in Scotland are British Regional Airlines and Loganair/British Airways Express, who both fly under the franchise of British Airways (☎ 0845 773 3377, W www.british-regional .com; W www.loganair.com), with flights from Glasgow to Barra, Benbecula, Campbeltown, Inverness, Islay, Kirkwall, Sumburgh, Stornoway and Tiree; from Edinburgh to Kirkwall, Sumburgh, Stornoway and Wick; and from Aberdeen and Inverness to Kirkwall and Sumburgh. Loganair/British Airways Express operates inter-island flights in Orkney and Shetland.

British Midland (☎ 0870 607 0555, W www.flybmi.com) flies from Edinburgh to Aberdeen, and Highland Airways (☎ 01851-701282, W www.highlandairways.co.uk) runs a service between Inverness and Stornoway (daily except Sunday).

Most airlines offer a range of tickets including full fare (flexible but very expensive), Apex (which must be booked at least 14 days in advance) and special offers on some services. There are also youth fares (for under 25s) but Apex and special-offer fares are usually cheaper.

An Apex fare from Glasgow/Inverness to Kirkwall in the Orkney Islands on British Airways costs from £140/100 respectively. A flight from Edinburgh to Sumburgh in the Shetland Islands costs from £140; flights between Orkney and Shetland cost from £60 return. A single/return from Inverness to Stornoway with Highland Airways is £55/110 (payment by credit card only).

Air Passes

If you're flying into the UK on British Airways you may be eligible for a UK Airpass, which is sold in conjunction with international return flights – it can't be purchased in the UK. This allows you to buy tickets on certain BA domestic flights for an additional

£59 each. However, these tickets must be booked at least seven days before your arrival in the UK.

BA/British Regional Airlines has a Highland Rover air pass that allows travel on direct flights within Scotland and between Scotland and Northern Ireland, and is valid from a minimum of seven days up to three months. It can be bought from BA offices and agents anywhere.

Domestic Departure Tax

There's a £10 airport departure tax added to the price of domestic flight tickets – check that this is included in the price you're quoted.

BUS

Scotland's national bus network has one major player, Scottish Citylink (☎ 0870 550 5050, W www.citylink.co.uk), which is supplemented by numerous smaller regional operators. Long-distance express buses are usually referred to as coaches.

Some regions operate telephone inquiry travel lines which try to explain the fast-changing situation with timetables; where possible, these numbers have been given in the regional chapters. Before planning a journey off the main routes it's advisable to phone for the latest information – Traveline (☎ 0870 608 2608) provides bus timetable (but not fares) information for the whole of Scotland.

Bus Passes & Discounts

Scottish Citylink offers a range of discount cards, which give up to 30% off standard adult fares on its coach services. Cards are available for full-time students, people aged between 16 and 25, and people aged 50 or over, and cost £6 for one year. You will need a passport photo and proof of ID – an ISIC card is accepted as proof of student status and a passport is OK for proof of age. These cards also offer a discount on National Express services within Scotland.

Scottish Citylink Explorer Pass This pass can be bought in the UK by both UK and overseas citizens. It provides unlimited,

free travel on all Citylink services within Scotland for three consecutive days of travel (£33), any five days travel out of 10 consecutive days (£55), or any eight days travel out of 16 (£85). It also gives discounts on various regional bus services and on CalMac and P&O Scottish ferries. It is not valid on National Express coaches.

Citylink also offers discounts to holders of the Euro<26 card, and the Young Scot card (☎ 0870 513 4936, W www.youngscot .org), which provides discounts all over Scotland and Europe.

Backpackers Buses

Haggis Backpackers (☎ 0131-557 9393, W www.haggisadventures.com), 60 High St, Edinburgh, runs a bus service on a circuit between hostels in Edinburgh, Pitlochry, Inverness, Loch Ness, Carbisdale Castle, Ullapool, Isle of Skye, Fort William, Glencoe, Oban and Stirling (although there's no obligation to stay in the hostels). You can start your tour at any point, and hop on and off the bus wherever and whenever you like, booking up to 24 hours in advance. There's no fixed time for completing the circuit, but you can only cover each section of the route once. Buses depart Edinburgh on Monday, Wednesday, Friday and Saturday year-round, and tickets cost £69/55 in summer/winter.

Macbackpackers (☎ 0131-558 9900, W www.macbackpackers.com), 105 High St, Edinburgh, runs a similar jump-on, jump-off service, with daily departures year-round and a fare of £55.

Postbus

Many small places can only be reached by Royal Mail postbuses – minibuses, or sometimes just four-seater cars, driven by postal workers delivering and collecting the mail. They follow circuitous routes through some of the most beautiful areas of Scotland, and are particularly useful for walkers – there are no official stops, and you can hail a postbus anywhere on its route. Fares are typically £2 to £5 for a one-way journey. For more information contact Royal Mail Customer Service (☎ 0845 774 0740, or ☎ 01752-387112 from outside the UK), or check the online routes and timetable information at **W** www.postbus.royalmail.com.

TRAIN

Scotland's rail network stretches to all of the country's major cities and towns, but the railway map has a lot of large, blank areas in the Highlands and the Southern Uplands – you'll need to switch to the bus or hire a car to explore these. The West Highland line from Glasgow to Fort William and Mallaig, and the Inverness to Kyle of Lochalsh line are two of the most scenic train journeys in the world.

For information on train timetables and fares in Scotland, call the National Rail Enquiry Line on ☎ 0845 748 49 50.

Bicycles are carried free on all ScotRail trains, but space is generally quite limited. Reservations are compulsory on certain rail routes, including the Glasgow to Oban/Fort William/Mallaig line and the Inverness to Kyle of Lochalsh line; they are recommended on many others. You can make reservations for you bicycle from eight weeks to two hours in advance at main train stations, or when buying tickets by phone.

Rail Itinerary

The following itinerary is for four days.

Journey Times

from	to	time
Edinburgh	Glasgow	50 minutes
Glasgow	Fort William	3¾ hours
Fort William	Mallaig	1½ hours
Mallaig	Armadale (Skye)	30 minutes by ferry
Armadale	Kyle of Lochalsh	by bus (22 miles)
Kyle of Lochalsh	Inverness	2½ hours
Inverness	Perth	2½ hours
Perth	Edinburgh	1½ hours

Route

This itinerary includes the West Highland Line, the most scenic rail journey in the country, and the Kyle Line across the Highlands from Kyle of Lochalsh to Inverness. The ScotRail Travelpass (see under Train Passes in the Train section of this chapter) covers the whole of this route except for the bus from Armadale to Kyle of Lochalsh.

It takes less than one hour from Edinburgh to Glasgow's Queen St station, where trains depart on the West Highland Line to Fort William and Mallaig. The route passes Loch Lomond on the way to Crianlarich, then crosses the wilderness of Rannoch Moor – it is possible to devise interesting walks linking the stations on the moor. The stretch of line along Glen Spean enjoys views of Ben Nevis, Britain's highest peak. From Fort William, the train crosses the Great Glen and offers superb views of Loch Shiel at Glenfinnan station before reaching the spectacular coastal section along Loch nan Uamh to Arisaig, Britain's most westerly train station. The final stretch north to Mallaig has superb views over the sea to the islands of Skye, Rhum and Eigg.

From Mallaig, a ferry takes you across to Armadale in Skye, where you can catch a bus to Kyle of Lochalsh (check bus times in advance with the Portree Tourist Office on ☎ 01478-612137), the terminus of the Kyle Line from Inverness. From Inverness there are frequent departures south to Perth, where it's worth stopping to see nearby Scone Palace before continuing to Edinburgh.

Train Passes

ScotRail offers a range of good-value passes for train travel in Scotland. You can buy them at BritRail outlets in the USA, Canada and Europe, at the British Travel Centre in Regent St, London, at train stations throughout Britain, at certain UK travel agents (eg, usitCampus and Thomas Cook) and from ScotRail Telesales (☎ 0845 755 0033).

The Freedom of Scotland Travelpass gives free, unlimited travel on all ScotRail and Strathclyde Passenger Transport trains, all Caledonian Macbrayne ferry services, and on certain Scottish Citylink coach services (on routes not covered by rail). It is available for four days' travel out of eight (£79/69 in high/low season) or eight days' travel out of 15 (£99/89). High season is from mid-May to mid-September. Holders of Railcards (see Railcards later in this section) get a 33% discount on these prices – if you're eligible, a Railcard will more than pay for itself when you buy a Travelpass.

The Highland Rover pass gives free train travel in the Highlands from Glasgow to Oban, Fort William and Mallaig, and from Inverness to Kyle of Lochalsh, Aviemore, Aberdeen and Thurso; it also gives free travel on the Oban/Fort William to Inverness bus, and a discount on ferries to Mull and Skye. It is only available for four days travel out of eight (£49/39).

The Central Scotland Rover covers train travel between Glasgow, Edinburgh, North Berwick, Stirling and Fife. It costs £29 for three days' travel out of seven.

Railcards

A range of discount Railcards, which give 33% off standard adult fares, is available for travel on all train services in the UK. There are cards for full-time students (studying in the UK), people aged between 16 and 25, families (up to four adults and four children), and people aged 60 or over, costing £18 (£20 for the Family Railcard) for one year. You will need a passport photo and proof of ID – an ISIC card is accepted as proof of student status and a passport is OK for proof of age. You can pick up a Railcard application form from main train stations, or get one from ScotRail telesales.

People with disabilities (UK citizens only) can apply for a Disabled Persons Railcard (£14) – application forms can be obtained from the Disabled Persons Railcard Office, PO Box 1YT, Newcastle-upon-Tyne NE99 1YT. Applications can take up to three weeks to process.

You can recoup the cost of a Railcard with just one return trip from London to Edinburgh or Glasgow, or one Freedom of Scotland Travelpass. Railcard discounts apply to Cheap Day Return tickets (see Tickets later in this section) but not to Apex tickets.

Tickets

ScotRail (☎ 0845 755 0033 for ticket sales and reservations, ⓦ www.scotrail.co.uk) operates most train services in Scotland. Reservations are recommended for intercity trips, especially on Fridays and public holidays; for shorter journeys, just buy a ticket at the station before you go. On certain routes – including the Glasgow–Edinburgh express – and in places where there's no ticket office at the station, you can buy tickets on the train.

There are two classes of train travel: first and standard. First class costs 30% to 50% more than standard and, but on very crowded trains, isn't really worth the extra money.

Children under five years old travel free; those aged between five and 15 pay half-price for most tickets. However, when travelling with children it is almost always worth buying a Family Railcard. At the weekend on certain intercity routes you can upgrade a standard class ticket to first class for only £3 per single journey – just ask the conductor on the train.

There is a bewildering variety of ticket types on offer.

Single – valid for a single (ie one-way) journey at any time on the particular day specified; expensive

Day Return – valid for a return journey at any time on the particular day specified; relatively expensive

Cheap Day Return – valid for a return journey on the day specified on the ticket, but there are time restrictions (you're not usually allowed to travel on a train that leaves before 9.15am); relatively cheap

Open Return – for outward travel on a stated day and return on any day within a month

Apex – one of the cheapest return fares; standard class only; reservations compulsory and you must travel on the booked services; you must book at least 48 hours in advance, but seats are limited so book as soon as possible (up to eight weeks in advance)

SuperSaver – the cheapest ticket where advance purchase isn't necessary; can't be used on Friday after 2.30pm, Saturday in July and August or on bank holidays, or on days after these before 2.30pm. The return journey must be within one calendar month.

Saver – higher priced than the SuperSaver, but can be used any day and there are fewer time restrictions

SuperAdvance – similarly priced to the SuperSaver but with fewer time/day restrictions; however, tickets must be bought before 2pm on the day before travel and both the outward and return journey times must be specified; limited availability so book early

CAR & MOTORCYCLE

Travelling by private car or motorcycle allows you to get to remote places, and to travel quickly, independently and flexibly. Unfortunately, the independence you enjoy tends to isolate you and cars are nearly always inconvenient in city centres. Scotland's roads are generally good and far less busy than in England, so driving is more enjoyable.

Motorways (designated 'M') are toll-free dual carriageways and deliver you quickly but bypass the most interesting countryside; they are limited mainly to central Scotland. Main roads (designated 'A') are dual or single carriageways and are sometimes clogged with slow-moving trucks or caravans; the A9 from Perth to Inverness is notoriously busy.

Life on the road is more relaxed and interesting on the secondary roads (designated 'B') and minor roads (undesignated). These wind through the countryside from village to village. You can't travel fast, but you won't want to. In some areas roads are only single track with passing places indicated by a pole. It's illegal to park in these places. Remember that passing places are not only for allowing oncoming traffic to pass, but also for overtaking – check your rear-view mirror frequently, and pull over to allow faster vehicles to pass if necessary.

Road Distances (in miles)

	Aberdeen	Dundee	Edinburgh	Fort William	Glasgow	Inverness	Kyle of Lochalsh	Mallaig	Oban	Scrabster	Stranraer	Ullapool
Aberdeen	---											
Dundee	70	---										
Edinburgh	129	62	---									
Fort William	165	121	146	---								
Glasgow	145	84	42	104	---							
Inverness	105	131	155	66	166	---						
Kyle of Lochalsh	188	177	206	76	181	82	---					
Mallaig	189	161	180	44	150	106	34	---				
Oban	180	118	123	45	94	110	120	85	---			
Scrabster	218	250	279	185	286	119	214	238	230	---		
Stranraer	233	171	120	184	80	250	265	232	178	374	---	
Ullapool	150	189	215	90	225	60	88	166	161	125	158	---

In the Highlands and islands the main hazards are suicidal sheep wandering onto the road (be particularly wary of lambs in spring)...and the distracting beauty of the landscape!

At around 80p per litre (equivalent to US$4.30 for a US gallon), petrol is expensive by American or Australian standards, and diesel is only a few pence cheaper. Distances, however, aren't great. Petrol prices also tend to rise as you get farther from main population centres. In remote areas petrol stations are few and far between and sometimes closed on Sunday.

Road Rules

Anyone using the roads a lot should get hold of the *Highway Code* (£1.49), which is available in bookshops and some TICs.

A foreign driving licence is valid in Britain for up to 12 months from the time of your last entry into the country. If you're bringing a car from Europe make sure you're adequately insured.

Briefly, vehicles drive on the left-hand side of the road; front-seat belts are compulsory and if belts are fitted in the back seat then they must be worn; the speed limit is 30mph (48kph) in built-up areas, 60mph (96kph) on single carriageways and 70mph (112kph) on dual carriageways; you give way to your right at roundabouts (traffic already on the roundabout has the right of way); and motorcyclists must wear helmets.

See Legal Matters in the Facts for the Visitor chapter for information on drink-driving rules.

Rental

Car rental is relatively expensive and often you'll be better off making arrangements in your home country for a fly/drive deal. The big international rental companies charge from around £120 a week for a small car (Ford Fiesta, Peugeot 106); rates offered by local companies, such as Arnold Clark (☎ 0131-228 4747) in Edinburgh, start at around £18 a day or £90 a week.

The reservations numbers for the main international companies include Avis (☎ 0870 606 0100), Budget (☎ 0845 606

6669), Europcar (☎ 0870 607 5000), Hertz (☎ 0870 844 8844) and Thrifty Car Rental (☎ 0870 066 0514). TICs have lists of local car-hire companies.

To rent a car, drivers must usually be between 23 and 65 years of age – outside these limits special conditions or insurance requirements may apply.

If you are planning on visiting the Outer Hebrides, Orkney or Shetland, it will often prove cheaper to hire a car on the islands, rather than pay to take a rental car across on the ferry.

Purchase

It is possible to buy a reasonable car or camper van in the UK for around £1000 to £2000. Vehicles require a Ministry of Transport (MOT) safety certificate (the certificate itself is usually referred to simply as an MOT) issued by licensed garages and valid for one year; full third-party insurance – shop around but expect to pay at least £300; registration – a standard form signed by the buyer and seller, with a section to be sent to the Ministry of Transport; and a tax disc (£160 for one year, £88 for six months; £105/57.75 for vehicles with engines less than 1200cc), available from main post offices on presentation of a valid MOT certificate, insurance and registration documents. Note that cars that are 25 or more years old are tax exempt.

You're strongly recommended to buy a vehicle with valid MOT and tax. MOT and tax remain with the car through a change of ownership; third-party insurance goes with the driver rather than the car, so you'll still have to arrange this (and beware of letting others drive the car). For further information about registering, licensing, insuring and testing your vehicle, contact a post office or Vehicle Registration Office for leaflet V100.

Car Parking

Many towns in Scotland, big and small, could easily be overrun by cars. As a result, there are often blanket bans on, or at least active discrimination against, bringing cars into town centres. It's a good idea to go along with it even if, sometimes, you will have to walk further.

The parking will be easier and you'll enjoy the places more if it's not cluttered up with cars, yours and others. This particularly applies in small villages – park in the car parks, not on the street.

In bigger cities there are often short-stay and long-stay car parks. Prices are often the same for stays of up to two or three hours, but for lengthier stays the short-stay car parks rapidly become much more expensive. The long-stay car parks may be slightly less convenient but they're much cheaper.

A double yellow line means no parking at any time; a single line means no parking for at least an eight-hour period somewhere between 7am and 7pm; and a broken line means there are some restrictions – nearby signs spell these out. In some cities there are also red lines, which mean no stopping, let alone parking.

Motorcycle Touring

Scotland is ideal for motorcycle touring, with lots of winding roads of good quality and stunning scenery to stimulate the senses. Just make sure your wet-weather

---

Driving Itinerary

If you're only visiting Scotland for a short holiday, you can pack in a lot more if you have your own set of wheels and plan your route carefully. The following itinerary is for seven days.

Road Distances

from	to	distance
Edinburgh	St Andrews	58 miles; 93km
St Andrews	Aberdeen	83 miles; 134km
Aberdeen	Inverness	106 miles; 171km
Inverness	Fort William	65 miles; 105km
Fort William	Glasgow	102 miles; 164km
Glasgow	Stirling	26 miles; 42km
Stirling	Edinburgh	35 miles; 56km

Route

Take the A90 and M90 out of Edinburgh and over the Forth Road Bridge, then turn east onto the A91 north of Kinross, following signs to St Andrews. If you have time, stop off at Falkland Palace on the way. It's worth spending the night in St Andrews, famed around the world as the home of golf.

From St Andrews, head north on the A919 and A92 following signs for Tay Bridge and Dundee. Stop to visit Scott of Antarctica's ship *Discovery* at the north end of the bridge. Continue on the A929 and the smaller A928 to Glamis Castle, one of the most famous of Scotland's many castles. From Glamis take the A94 north-east to the affluent 'Granite City' of Aberdeen.

You can take one of several routes from Aberdeen to Inverness. The direct route is along the A96 via Huntly and Elgin. Alternatively, if you have an extra day to spare, consider taking the route through the Grampian Mountains via Ballater, Tomintoul and Grantown-on-Spey on the A93, A939, A95 and A9 – about 150 miles. Balmoral Castle, the queen's Scottish residence (which can be visited when the royal family is not at home), is a short distance off this route.

From Inverness, head south-west along Loch Ness on the A82, stopping at the Loch Ness Monster Exhibition and Urquhart Castle. Continue to Fort William, leaving yourself time for an evening walk in Glen Nevis. To climb Ben Nevis, Britain's highest peak, you will need to allow a whole day. Continue south on the A82 from Fort William to Glasgow, stopping at Glen Coe and Loch Lomond. Spend the following day in this lively city before taking the M80 to Stirling, a drive of less than an hour. Look around Stirling's magnificent castle the next day before returning to Edinburgh.

gear is up to scratch. Crash helmets are compulsory.

The Auto-Cycle Union (☎ 01788-566400, fax 573585, e admin@acu.org.uk, W www.acu.org.uk), ACU House, Wood St, Rugby, Warwickshire CV21 2YX, publishes a useful booklet about motorcycle touring in Britain.

Motoring Organisations

It's well worth becoming a member of a British motoring organisation. The two largest in the UK, both offering 24-hour breakdown assistance, are the Automobile Association (AA; ☎ 0800 917 0992 to join, W www.theaa.com) and the Royal Automobile Club (RAC; ☎ 0800 550550 to join, W www.rac.co.uk). One year's membership starts at £38 for the AA and £34 for the RAC. Both these companies can also extend their cover to include Europe. If you're a member of a motoring organisation back home, you should check to see if it has a reciprocal arrangement with an organisation in Britain. This could entitle you to touring maps and information, help with breakdowns, and technical and legal advice, all usually free of charge.

WALKING & CYCLING

Walking and cycling are popular and rewarding ways to explore Scotland. For information see the Activities chapter.

HITCHING

Hitching is never entirely safe in any country and we don't recommend it. Travellers who decide to hitch are taking a small but potentially serious risk. However, many people choose to hitch, and the advice that follows should help to make their journeys as fast and safe as possible.

Hitching is reasonably easy in Scotland, except around the big cities and built-up areas, where you'll need to use public transport. Although the north-west is more difficult because there's less traffic, waits of over two hours are unusual (except on Sunday in 'Sabbath' areas). On some Scottish islands, where public transport is infrequent, hitching is so much a part of getting

around that local drivers may stop and offer you lifts without you even asking.

It's against the law to hitch on motorways or the immediate slip roads; make a sign and use approach roads, nearby roundabouts or the service stations.

BOAT

The main ferry services in Scotland are to the Western Isles and to Orkney and Shetland. The main car-ferry operators are CalMac and P&O, but there are many other car and passenger-only ferries serving smaller islands and short sea crossings. Taking a car on a ferry to the farther-flung islands can be expensive; you can save some money by hiring one once you arrive on the island.

Caledonian MacBrayne (CalMac; ☎ 0870 565 0000, W www.calmac.co.uk) is the most important ferry operator on the west coast, with services from Oban to the islands of Barra, South Uist, Coll, Tiree, Lismore, Mull and Colonsay, from Ullapool to the Outer Hebrides, and from Mallaig to Skye and on to the Outer Hebrides. CalMac's Island Rover ticket gives unlimited travel on its ferry services, and costs £43/63 per person for eight/15 days, plus £210/315 for a car, or £105/158 for a motorbike. Bicycles travel for free.

P&O Scottish Ferries (☎ 01224-572615, fax 574411, W www.posf.co.uk) has ferries from Aberdeen and Scrabster (near Thurso) to Orkney, from Orkney to Shetland and from Aberdeen to Shetland. Pentland Ferries (☎ 01856-831226, W www.pentland ferries.com) has a shorter (one hour) crossing from the Scottish mainland to St Margaret's Hope in Orkney.

See the relevant chapters for full details of ferry services and fares.

LOCAL TRANSPORT

There are comprehensive local bus networks in Edinburgh, Glasgow, Aberdeen and some other larger towns. Glasgow also has an extensive suburban rail network as well as an underground line. Taxis are reasonably priced and over a short distance may be competitive with a local bus, if there are three or four people to share the cost.

ORGANISED TOURS

Since travel is so easy to organise in Scotland, there's little need to consider a tour. Still, if your time is limited and you prefer to travel in a group, there are some interesting possibilities.

Road

There are plenty of coach tours available from the big cities, particularly Edinburgh and Glasgow. From Edinburgh, Scotline (☎ 0131-557 0162, fax 556 2029, **W** www .scotlinetours.com), 87 High St, offers a range of day trips by coach to St Andrews, Loch Lomond and the Trossachs, Loch Ness and Glencoe. Adult/child fares range from £14/7 to £25/12 including lunch but not admission fees.

Rabbie's Trail Burners (☎ 0131-226 3133, fax 225 7028, **W** www.rabbies.com), 207 High St, Edinburgh, offers one- to five-day tours of the Highlands in 16-seat minicoaches. The three-day tour takes in Glencoe, Lochaber, Kintail, Skye and Loch Ness, and costs £95 in the high season. Accommodation is extra – you can choose from hostels (£9 to £12 per night) or B&Bs (£16 to £22) up to five-star hotels (over £70), and book rooms when you buy your ticket.

Scotsell (☎ 0141-772 5928), 2D Churchill Way, Bishopbriggs, Glasgow G64 2RH, can organise self-drive car-touring holidays to the islands. A seven-night tour of the Outer Hebrides, using your own vehicle, costs from £433 per person, including hotel accommodation and ferry tickets. Car rental is available at extra cost.

Mountain Innovations (☎/fax 01479-831331, **W** www.scotmountain.co.uk), Fraoch Lodge, Deshar Rd, Boat of Garten PH24 3BN, organises good-value activity holidays in the Highlands, including walking, mountain biking, kayaking, skiing and horseriding. Packages include car hire, accommodation, food and guides. A five-day tour that takes in the Cairngorms, Speyside, Loch Ness, Torridon, Glen Nevis and Glen Coe costs from £135 per person.

Backpackers Tours

Several companies – including Haggis Backpackers and Macbackpackers (see the Bus section earlier in this chapter) and Going Forth (☎ 0131- 478 6500, **W** www .goingforth.com), 9 South St Andrew St – run three- to seven-day guided tours of the Highlands and islands all year round, taking in the main attractions of Glencoe, Eilan Donan Castle, Skye and Loch Ness. Prices range from £55 to £230, including hostel accommodation and various visits and activities. Macbackpackers' five-day Skye Trekker tour (£165, Easter to September only) includes two days' trekking through the Cuillin mountains of Skye, and a night camping out in the wild. Haggis and Going Forth have tours starting from London as well as from Edinburgh.

Celtic Connection (☎ 0131-225 3330, **W** www.celticconnection.freeserve.co.uk) offers three- to seven-day tours that take in both Scotland and Ireland, starting in Dublin and Belfast.

Rail

The Royal Scotsman (☎ 0131-555 1021, **W** www.royalscotsman.com) is a luxury train, complete with opulent, wood-panelled sleeping cabins (16 twin and four single) and dining cars, hauled by a diesel locomotive, that makes three- and five-day tours of the Highlands from April to October. Rates, including on-train accommodation, gourmet meals and fine wines, start at £1390 per person.

ScotRail Short Breaks (☎ 0870 161 0161) offers two-night trips to the Highlands, costing from £89 per person including accommodation, and a week-long tour of the Highlands and islands for £455, including rail, coach and ferry travel and accommodation.

From June to September, the Jacobite Steam Train (☎ 01463-239026, **W** www .westcoastrailway.co.uk) runs along the scenic West Highland Line between Fort William and Mallaig – one of the great railway journeys of the world. A standard-class day return ticket costs £22/12.50 for adults/children.

Cruises

There are many companies offering cruises and yacht charters around Scotland's beautiful west coast – acknowledged as one of the most spectacular cruise areas in the world.

Top of the range is Hebridean Island Cruises (☎ 01756-704704, fax 704794, W www.hebridean.co.uk), which offers four- to 14-night luxury cruises aboard the *Hebridean Princess*, departing from Oban. A four-night 'Taste of the Hebrides' tour costs from £885 per person.

Douglas Lindsay (☎ 01631-770246, fax 770246, W www.corryvreckan.co.uk) runs cruises aboard the beautiful 20m (65ft) yacht *Corryvreckan*, based at Oban. The yacht has five double guest-cabins, and rates include delicious gourmet meals. You don't need any experience of sailing, but you can take part in the sailing and steering if you want to. Prices are from £495 to £525 per person per week, all inclusive.

Caledonian Discovery Ltd (☎ 01397-772167, fax 772765, e fingal@sol.co.uk, W www.lochaber.co.uk/fingal) has a 37m (120ft) barge, *Fingal of Caledonia*, which sails between Inverness and Corpach (near Fort William) on the Caledonian Canal from mid-April to mid-October. Rates are £465 per person per week in the high season (June to August), including all meals and activities such as canoeing, windsurfing, swimming and cycling.

Edinburgh & the Lothians

☎ 0131 • pop 453,430

Edinburgh enjoys an incomparable location, set amid volcanic hills on the southern edge of the Firth of Forth. Its superb architecture ranges from extraordinary 16th-century tenements to monumental Georgian and Victorian masterpieces, all dominated by a castle on a precipitous crag in the city's heart. Sixteen thousand buildings are listed as architecturally or historically important, and the city itself is a World Heritage Site.

Geology and architecture combine to create a remarkable symphony in stone in Edinburgh. Old Town, with its crowded tenements, stands in contrast to the orderly grid of New Town, with its disciplined Georgian terraces. There are vistas from nearly every street – sudden views of the Firth of Forth, the castle, the Pentland Hills, Calton Hill with its memorials, and rugged Arthur's Seat.

All the great dramas of Scottish history have played at least one act in Edinburgh, the royal capital since the 11th century. Even after the union of 1707 with England, it remained the centre of government administration (now the Scottish Executive), the separate Scottish legal system and the Presbyterian Church of Scotland. With the opening of the devolved Scottish parliament in 1999, Edinburgh once again wields real political power.

In some ways, however, it's the least Scottish of Scotland's cities – partly because of the impact of tourism, partly because of its sophisticated, cosmopolitan population. Edinburgh has a reputation for being civilised and reserved, especially in comparison with extrovert, gregarious Glasgow. Nevertheless, the vibrant pub scene, large student population and annual arts festivals make the Scottish capital a lively and sociable city.

On the down side, life can be grim for many inhabitants of the bleak council housing estates surrounding the city and there are problems with drugs and prostitution.

HIGHLIGHTS

- Patrolling the battlements at Edinburgh Castle and sticking your fingers in your ears when the One O'Clock Gun goes off
- Exploring Scotland's history in the brilliant Museum of Scotland
- Taking a hike up Calton Hill just before sunset for a stunning view over the city and the Firth of Forth
- Stepping aboard the former Royal Yacht *Britannia* at Leith and nosing around HM the Queen's private quarters
- Visiting the picture-postcard village of Cramond
- Taking a cruise on the Firth of Forth to Inchcolm island, with its ruined abbey and colonies of seals and seabirds
- Pondering the secrets of the Knights Templar at the beautiful and mysterious Rosslyn Chapel

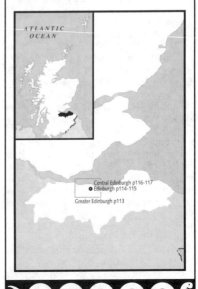

ATLANTIC OCEAN

Central Edinburgh p116-117
Edinburgh p114-115
Greater Edinburgh p113

HISTORY

Castle Rock, a volcanic crag with three vertical sides, dominates the city centre. This natural defensive position attracted the first settlers; the earliest signs of habitation date back to around 900 BC.

The Angles, from the kingdom of Northumbria in north-eastern England, captured the rock in 638. It was called Dun Eiden (meaning 'Fort on the Hill Slope') by the Scots and it is thought that the Angles took the existing Gaelic name 'Eiden' and tacked it onto their own Old English word for fort, 'burh', to create the name Edinburgh.

Edinburgh began to grow in the 11th century when markets developed on the ridge east of the fort, and from 1124 David I held court at the castle and founded the abbey at Holyrood.

The city's first effective town wall was constructed around 1450 and enclosed Old Town as far east as Netherbow and the area around Grassmarket. This overcrowded area – by then the most populous town in Scotland – became a medieval Manhattan, forcing its densely packed inhabitants to build upwards instead of outwards, and creating tenements that in places soared to 12 storeys high.

A golden era that saw the foundation of the Royal College of Surgeons and the introduction of printing ended with the death of James IV at the Battle of Flodden in 1513. England's Henry VIII attempted to force a marriage between Mary (James V's daughter) and his son but the Scots sent the infant Mary to France to marry the dauphin instead. The city was sacked by the English, and the Scots turned to the French for support.

The capital played an important role in the Reformation, led by the Calvinist firebrand John Knox. Mary, Queen of Scots, held court in the Palace of Holyroodhouse for six brief years, but when her son James VI succeeded to the English throne in 1603, he moved his court to London. The Act of Union in 1707 further reduced Edinburgh's importance, but cultural and intellectual life continued to flourish.

In the second half of the 18th century a planned new town was created across the valley to the north of Old Town. During the period known as the Scottish Enlightenment (roughly 1740–1830), Edinburgh became known as 'a hotbed of genius', inhabited by leading scientists and philosophers such as David Hume and Adam Smith.

The population exploded in the 19th century – Edinburgh quadrupled in size to 400,000, not much less than it is today – and Old Town's tenements were taken over by refugees from the Irish famines. A new ring of crescents and circuses was built to the north of New Town, and grey Victorian terraces spread south of Old Town. In the 20th century the slum dwellers were moved into new housing estates that now foster severe social problems.

Edinburgh entered a new era following the 1997 referendum vote in favour of a devolved Scottish parliament, which first convened in July 1999. The parliament is temporarily housed in the Church of Scotland Assembly Rooms, near the castle, while a controversial new parliament building – a futuristic design that has gone way over budget – is under construction at Holyrood at the foot of the Royal Mile.

ORIENTATION

The most important landmark is Arthur's Seat, the 251m rocky peak south-east of the city centre. Old and New Towns are separated by Princes Street Gardens, with the castle dominating both of them.

The Royal Mile (Lawnmarket, High St and Canongate) is Old Town's main street and runs from the castle to the Palace of Holyroodhouse. The city's main shopping street, Princes St, runs along the northern side of Princes Street Gardens. At its eastern end, Calton Hill is crowned by several monuments.

The Edinburgh and Scotland Information Centre (ESIC) lies between Waverley train station and Princes St, above Princes Mall shopping centre. The bus station in New Town is trickier to find; it's off the north-eastern corner of St Andrew Square, north of the eastern end of Princes St.

Bear in mind that long streets may be known by different names along their length. For example, the southern end of Leith Walk is variously called Union Place and Antigua St on one side, Elm Row and Greenside Place on the other.

Maps

Lonely Planet's fold-out *Edinburgh City Map* is perfect for sightseeing. It is plastic-coated, virtually indestructible and indicates all the major landmarks, museums and shops. There's also a street index.

The ESIC (see Tourist Offices below) issues a handy free pocket map of the city centre. For coverage of the whole city, the most detailed maps are Nicolson's *Edinburgh Citymap* (£3.50) and the Ordnance Survey's (OS) *Edinburgh Street Atlas* (£5.99). You can buy these at the ESIC and at many bookshops and newsagents.

The OS's 1:50,000 Landranger map *Edinburgh, Penicuik & North Berwick* (Sheet No 66; £5.25) covers the city and the surrounding region to the south and east at a scale of 1¼ inches to 1 mile (2cm to 1km); it is useful for walking in the Pentland Hills and exploring East Lothian. *Edinburgh Seven Hills* (£3.95), by Harvey Maps, is a walker's map with useful enlargements of Arthur's Seat and the other hills that lie within the city.

INFORMATION
Tourist Offices

The Edinburgh and Scotland Information Centre (ESIC; ☎ 473 3800, fax 473 3881, e esic@eltb.org), above Princes Mall at 3 Princes St, opens 9am to 8pm Monday to Saturday and 10am to 8pm Sunday in July and August; 9am to 7pm Monday to Saturday and 10am to 7pm Sunday in May, June and September; and 9am to 5pm Monday to Wednesday, 9am to 6pm Thursday to Saturday and 10am to 5pm Sunday the rest of the year. The centre has an accommodation booking service, a currency exchange, a gift and book shop, and counters selling tickets for Edinburgh city tours and Scottish Citylink bus services. There are also tourist information desks at Edinburgh airport and at the Old Craighall Junction service area on the main A1 road, about 5 miles (8km) east of the city centre.

Consulates & High Commissions

Scotland's capital houses several consulates and high commissions; see the Facts for the Visitor chapter.

Money

The ESIC bureau de change opens the same hours as the ESIC. It charges no commission for changing foreign cash or travellers cheques into pounds but you'll get a better rate at a bank or American Express (AmEx). There's also a bureau de change in the main post office.

AmEx (☎ 718 2501), 139 Princes St, opens 9am to 5.30pm Monday to Friday and 9am to 4pm Saturday. It charges no commission on cash and AmEx travellers cheques, and generally offers a good rate of exchange (slightly better on cash than on cheques).

Thomas Cook (☎ 226 5500), 52 Hanover St, opens 9am to 5.30pm Monday to Saturday and charges 2% commission, with a minimum charge of £3, on both cash and travellers cheques. Rates of exchange are the same for both cash and cheques.

Most banks also change money. The Royal Bank of Scotland (☎ 556 8555) and the Bank of Scotland (☎ 442 7777) both have branches on St Andrew Square.

Post

Edinburgh's main post office (☎ 0845 722 3344) is inconveniently hidden away inside the sprawling St James Centre, off Leith St at the eastern end of Princes St. It opens 9am to 5.30pm Monday, 8.30am to 5.30pm Tuesday to Friday, and 8.30am to 6pm Saturday. Items addressed to poste restante can be picked up here. There are more convenient city centre branches at 40 Frederick St in New Town, and in St Mary's St off the Royal Mile.

Email & Internet Access

There are many cybercafes spread around the city. Convenient ones include:

easyEverything (☎ 220 3580, w www.easy -everything.com) 58 Rose St. Open 24 hours. This is a huge place with 450 PCs and a dynamic pricing system – the quieter the place is, the cheaper it gets. Average cost is £1 for around 35 minutes, minimum charge £2.

e-corner (☎ 558 7858, W www.e-corner.co.uk) Platform 1, Waverley Station. Open 7.30am to 9pm Monday to Friday, 8am to 9pm Saturday and Sunday. Access costs £1 for 20 minutes and £2 an hour.

Frugal Cafe (☎ 228 7567, W www.frugalcafe .com) 1a Brougham Place. Open 8.30am to 10pm daily. This is the best-value Internet cafe in town – access costs 1p per minute at all times.

International Telecom Centre (☎ 558 7114, W www.btinternet.com/~itc1) 52 High St, Royal Mile. Open 9am to 11pm daily. Access costs 1p per minute before 7pm, £1 for 30 minutes after 7pm. A fax service and cheap international phone calls are also offered.

Web 13 (☎ 229 8883, W www.web13.co.uk) 13 Bread St. Open 9am to 10pm daily. Access costs £1 per 20 minutes.

Travel Agencies

Two agencies that specialise in budget and student travel are usit Campus (☎ 668 3303), 53 Forrest Rd, and STA Travel (☎ 226 7747), 27 Forrest Rd; both issue ISIC cards.

Bookshops

James Thin (☎ 556 6743) is at 53–9 South Bridge and is the city's principal home-grown bookstore. In New Town, there are big branches of the nationwide Waterstone's chain at Nos 13 and 128 Princes St and 83 George St, and another James Thin branch at 59 George St. The Stationery Office Bookshop (☎ 606 5566) at 71 Lothian Rd has a good selection of books on Scottish history and travel (including LP guides), and probably the widest range of OS maps in town.

Libraries

The Central Library (☎ 242 4800) on George IV Bridge has a room devoted to Edinburgh (one floor down) and another to all things Scottish (in the basement). It opens 10am to 8pm Monday to Thursday, to 5pm Friday, and 9am to 1pm Saturday.

The National Library of Scotland (☎ 226 4531, W www.nls.uk), opposite the Central Library, houses a reference-only, general reading room. It opens 9.30am to 8.30pm weekdays (from 10am Wednesday) and 9.30am to 1pm Saturday. There's a branch

south of the city in Newington, at 33 Salisbury Place on the corner of Causewayside which contains the Scottish Science Library (open 9.30am to 5pm Monday, Tuesday Thursday and Friday, and 10am to 8.30pm Wednesday) and the Map Library (open 9.30am to 5pm Monday, Tuesday, Thursday and Friday, 10am to 5pm Wednesday, and 9.30am to 1pm Saturday).

Universities

Edinburgh has three universities. The oldest biggest and most prestigious is the University of Edinburgh, with over 15,000 undergraduates. Its information centre (☎ 650 1000, W www.ed.ac.uk) at 7–11 Nicolson St, next to the Edinburgh Festival Theatre opens 9.15am to 5pm weekdays.

Heriot-Watt University (☎ 449 5111, W www.hw.ac.uk) has its main campus south-west of the city at Riccarton, near Currie. Napier University (☎ 444 2266 W www.napier.ac.uk) has its main campuses at 10 Colinton Rd in Merchiston and at 219 Colinton Rd in Craiglockhart.

Laundry

Most of Edinburgh's backpacker hostels will wash and dry a load of laundry for you for around £3; some have self-service coin-operated washing machines where you can do the laundry yourself.

There are self-service, coin-operated laundries all over the city – expect to pay around £3 for a wash and dry. Check the *Yellow Pages* under Launderettes to find the nearest. The best of the bunch is the Sundial Launderette (☎ 556 2743), at 7–9 East London St in New Town. It has an excellent cafe next door called The Lost Sock Diner. The launderette opens 8am to 7pm Monday to Friday, 8am to 4pm Saturday, and 10am to 2pm Sunday.

North-east of the city centre, there's the Bendix Launderette & Dry Cleaners (☎ 554 2180) at 342 Leith Walk. Canonmills Dry Cleaners & Launderette (☎ 556 3199), at 7 Huntly St, is convenient for people staying in Eyre Place. South of the centre in Marchmont is another Sundial Launderette (☎ 229 2137) at 17 Roseneath St.

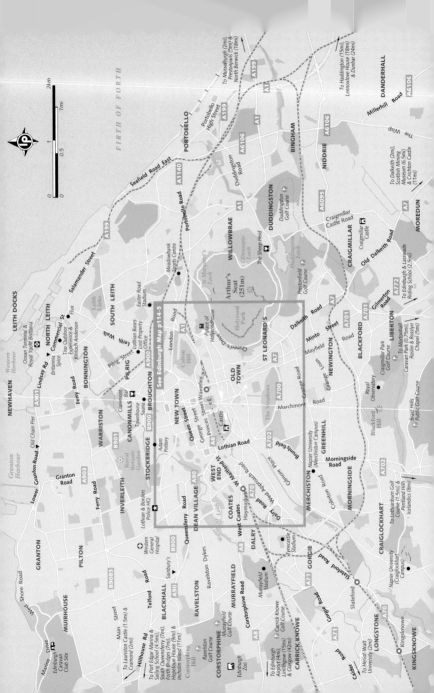

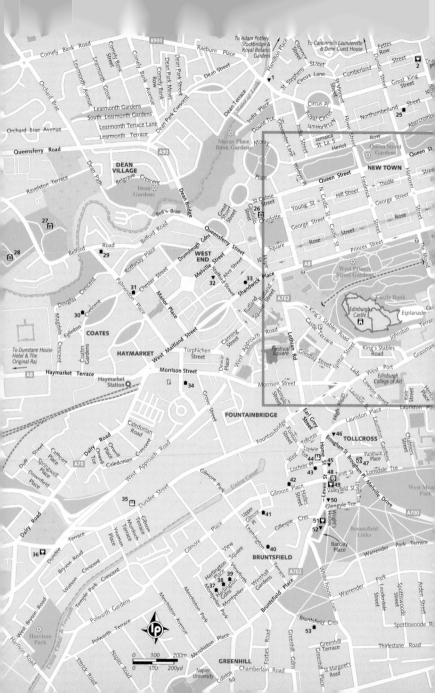

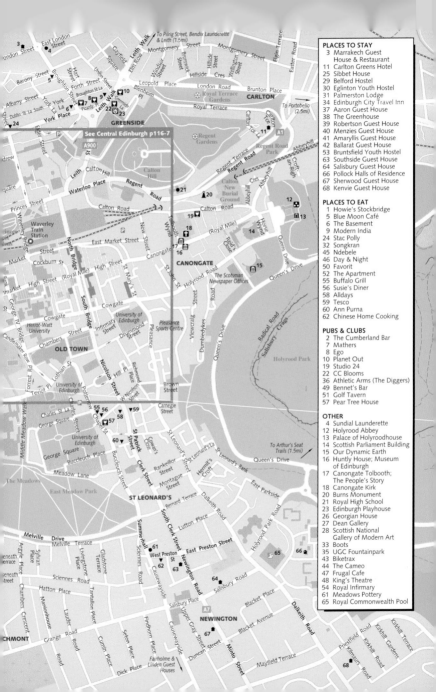

CENTRAL EDINBURGH

JONATHAN SMITH

Taking in Leith, Edinburgh's seaport, from the summit of Calton Hill

The Scott Monument: Edinburgh's memorial to novelist Sir Walter Scott, who died in 1832

JONATHAN SMITH

A glimpse of the stylish city's superb architecture

A view down the length of Princes St

A monumental sight at sunrise, Calton Hill

A distinctive flag along the Royal Mile

Left Luggage

There's a left-luggage office at Waverley train station, beside platform 1/19. The charge per item is £3.50 for up to three hours, £4 for three to 12 hours, £4.50 for 12 to 24 hours, and £4.50 per subsequent 24-hour period. It opens 7am to 11pm daily.

While the new bus station at St Andrew Square is under construction, there are temporary luggage lockers at the south-western corner of St Andrew Square.

Medical Services

The main general hospital for Edinburgh is the Royal Infirmary of Edinburgh (☎ 536 4000) at 1 Lauriston Place. It has a 24-hour accident and emergency department.

Chemists can advise you on minor ailments. At least one local chemist opens round the clock and details of this will be displayed in the windows of other chemists. Alternatively, look in the local newspaper or in the *Yellow Pages*. Boots (☎ 225 6757), 48 Shandwick Place (the extension of Princes St in the West End), opens 8am to 9pm Monday to Saturday, and 10am to 5pm Sunday.

Medications are readily available either over the counter or on prescription, so there's no need to stock up. All prescription drugs cost a flat rate of £6.10.

Emergencies

In an emergency, dial ☎ 999 or ☎ 112 (no money needed at public phones) and ask for police, ambulance, fire brigade or coastguard.

The Edinburgh Dental Institute (☎ 536 4900), also part of the Royal Infirmary complex, has an emergency dental clinic, open 9am to 3pm Monday to Friday.

The Edinburgh Rape Crisis Centre (☎ 556 9437) can offer support after an attack.

Dangers & Annoyances

Edinburgh is safer than most cities of a similar size, but it has its share of crime (often drug-related), so the normal big-city precautions apply.

Lothian Rd, Dalry Rd, Rose St and the western end of Princes St, at the junction with Shandwick Place and Queensferry and Hope Sts, can get a bit rowdy on Friday and Saturday nights after people have been drinking. Calton Hill offers good views during the day but is probably best avoided at night. Women on their own should avoid walking across the Meadows after dark.

If you lose anything or leave something behind in a pub or restaurant, check first with the establishment concerned, then with the lost property department (☎ 311 3141) at the police headquarters on Fettes Ave, north of the centre near the Western General Hospital. It opens 8am to 5pm Monday to Friday. Anything lost in the street or left behind in a city taxi should also end up here.

The lost property office (☎ 554 4494) of the Lothian Buses bus company, at 1–4 Shrub Place on Leith Walk, opens 10am to 1.30pm Monday to Friday.

EDINBURGH CASTLE

The brooding, black crags of Castle Rock, shouldering above the western end of Princes St, are the very reason for Edinburgh's existence. This rocky hill – the glacier-worn stump of an ancient volcano – was the most easily defended hilltop on the invasion route between England and central Scotland, a route followed by countless armies from the Roman legions of the 1st and 2nd centuries AD through to the Jacobite troops of Bonnie Prince Charlie in 1745.

The castle has played a pivotal role in Scottish history, both as a royal residence – King Malcolm Canmore (reigned 1057–93) and Queen Margaret made their home here in the 11th century – and as a military stronghold. When the army of Bonnie Prince Charlie passed through Edinburgh in 1745, they made only a cursory attempt to take the castle; that was the last time the castle saw military action and from then until the 1920s it served as the British army's main base in Scotland.

Edinburgh Castle (☎ 225 9846, *Castle Hill; adult/concession/child £7.50/5.50/2 including audioguide; open 9.30am-6pm daily Apr-Sept, 9.30am-5pm daily Oct-Mar, closed 25-26 Dec, last ticket sold 45 mins before closing)*, managed by Historic Scotland (HS; see Useful Organisations in the Facts for the Visitor chapter), is now Scotland's most

EDINBURGH

popular pay-to-enter tourist attraction. The **Esplanade**, a parade ground dating from 1820, is now a car park with superb views south over the city towards the Pentland Hills.

The **Entrance Gateway** dates from between 1886 and 1888, and is flanked by statues of Robert the Bruce and William Wallace. Inside, a cobbled lane leads up beneath the 16th-century **Portcullis Gate** and past the cannon of the Argyle and Mills Mount batteries. The battlements here have great views over New Town to the Firth of Forth.

At the far end of Mills Mount Battery is the famous **One O'Clock Gun**, a gleaming WWII 25-pounder that fires an ear-splitting time signal at exactly 1pm every day (except Sundays, Christmas Day and Good Friday).

At the western end of the castle, a road leads down to the **National War Museum of Scotland** (☎ 225 7534, Edinburgh Castle; admission included in Edinburgh Castle ticket; open 9.45am-5.30pm daily Apr-Nov,

9.45am-4.30pm daily Dec-Mar). This museum brings Scotland's military history vividly to life. The exhibits have been personalised by telling the stories of the original owners of the objects on display, making it easier to empathise with the experiences of war than any dry display of dusty weaponry ever could.

South of Mills Mount, the road curls up leftwards through **Foog's Gate** to the highest part of Castle Rock, crowned by the tiny **St Margaret's Chapel**, the oldest surviving building in Edinburgh. It's a simple Romanesque structure that was probably built by David I or Alexander I in memory of their mother Queen Margaret sometime around 1130 (she was canonised in 1250). Beside the chapel lies **Mons Meg**, a giant 15th-century siege gun built at Mons in what is now Belgium in 1449.

The main group of buildings on the summit of Castle Rock are arranged around Crown Square, dominated by the hushed shrine of the **Scottish National War Memorial**. Opposite is

The Stone of Destiny

On St Andrew's Day 1996, with much pomp and ceremony, a block of sandstone – 26½ inches by 16½ inches by 11 inches in size, with rusted iron hoops at either end – was installed in Edinburgh Castle. For the previous 700 years it had lain in London, beneath the Coronation Chair in Westminster Abbey. Almost every English, and later British, monarch from Edward II in 1307 to Elizabeth II in 1953 had parked their backside firmly over this stone during their coronation ceremony.

The legendary Stone of Destiny – said to have originated in the Holy Land, and on which Scottish kings placed their feet during their coronation (not their bums; the English got that bit wrong) – was stolen from Scone Abbey near Perth by King Edward I of England in 1296. It was taken to London and there it remained for seven centuries – except for a brief removal to Gloucester during WWII air raids, and a three-month sojourn in Scotland after it was stolen by Scottish students at Christmas in 1950 – an enduring symbol of Scotland's subjugation by England.

The Stone of Destiny returned to the political limelight in 1996, when the then Scottish Secretary and Conservative Party MP, Michael Forsyth, arranged for the return of the sandstone block to Scotland. A blatant attempt to boost the flagging popularity of the Conservative Party in Scotland prior to a general election, Forsyth's publicity stunt failed miserably. The Scots said thanks very much for the stone and then, in May 1997, voted every Conservative MP in Scotland into oblivion.

Many people, however, believe that Edward I was fobbed off with a shoddy imitation in 1296 and that the true Stone of Destiny remains safely hidden somewhere in Scotland. This is not impossible – some descriptions of the original state that it was made of black marble and decorated with elaborate carvings. Interested parties should read Stone of Destiny (1997) by Pat Gerber, which details the history of Scotland's most famous lump of rock.

the **Great Hall**, built for James IV (reigned 1488–1513) as a ceremonial hall and used as a meeting place for the Scottish parliament until 1639. Its most remarkable feature is the original, 16th-century hammer-beam roof.

On the eastern end of the square is the **Royal Palace**, built during the 15th and 16th centuries, where a series of historical tableaux leads to a strongroom housing the **Honours of Scotland** (the Scottish crown jewels), which are the oldest surviving crown jewels in Europe. Locked away in a chest following the Act of Union in 1707, the crown (made in 1540 from the gold of Robert the Bruce's 14th-century coronet), sword and sceptre lay forgotten until they were unearthed at the instigation of the novelist Sir Walter Scott in 1818. Also on display here is the **Stone of Destiny** (see the boxed text opposite).

Among the neighbouring **Royal Apartments** is the bedchamber where Mary, Queen of Scots, gave birth to her son James VI, who was to unite the crowns of Scotland and England in 1603.

The **Castle Vaults** beneath the Great Hall (entrance at western end) were used variously as storerooms, bakeries and prisons – French prisoners carved the graffiti on the walls in the 18th century.

THE ROYAL MILE

Edinburgh's Old Town stretches along a ridge to the east of the castle, a jagged, jumbled pile of masonry riddled with closes, wynds, vaults and tunnels, and cleft along its spine by the cobbled ravine of the Royal Mile. The mile-long street earned its regal appellation in the 16th century because it was used by the king to travel between the castle and the Palace of Holyroodhouse. There are four sections – Castlehill, Lawnmarket, High St and Canongate – whose names reflect their historical origins.

Until the founding of New Town in the 18th century, old Edinburgh was remarkable for its incredible concentration of humanity. Constrained between the boggy ground of the Nor' Loch to the north and the city walls to the south and east, the only way for the town to expand was upwards. The five- and six-storey tenements that were raised along the Royal Mile in the 16th and 17th centuries were the skyscrapers of their day, remarked upon with wonder by visitors. All classes of society, from beggars to magistrates, lived cheek by jowl in these urban ants' nests, the wealthy occupying the middle floors – high enough to be above the noise and stink of the streets, but not so high that climbing the stairs would be too tiring – while the poor squeezed into attics, basements, cellars and vaults amid the rats, rubbish and raw sewage.

The Old Town tenements still support a thriving city-centre community, but today the street level is crammed with tourists and tacky souvenir shops. Most people stick to the main High St but it's worth taking a little time to duck up the countless closes (narrow alleys) that lead off into quiet courtyards with unexpected views of sea and hills.

Castlehill

A short distance downhill from the Castle Esplanade, a former school houses the **Scotch Whisky Heritage Centre** (☎ 220 0441, 354 Castlehill; adult/child £6.50/3.25 includes tour & tasting; open 9.30am-5.30pm daily). The centre explains the making of whisky from barley to bottle, in a series of exhibits that combine sight, sound and smell.

The quaint building across the street is the **Outlook Tower and Camera Obscura** (☎ 226 3709, Castlehill; adult/child/family £4.25/2.10/12; open 9.30am-6pm Mon-Fri & 10am-6pm Sat & Sun Apr-Oct, 10am-5pm daily Nov-Mar). The 'camera' itself is a curious device (originally dating from the 1850s, although revised in 1945), which uses lenses and mirrors to throw a live image of the city onto a large horizontal screen. The accompanying commentary is entertaining, and the whole exercise has a quirky charm. The Outlook Tower offers great views over the city.

With Edinburgh's tallest spire (71.7m), the **Highland Tolbooth Kirk** is a prominent feature of Old Town's skyline. The interior has been refurbished and it now houses

The Hub (☎ 473 2000, Ⓦ www.eif.co.uk/ thehub, Castlehill; admission free; ticket centre open 10am-5pm Mon-Sat), the ticket office and information centre for the Edinburgh Festival. There's also a good cafe here.

Opposite the kirk are the Assembly Rooms of the Church of Scotland, which are the temporary home of the debating chamber of the new **Scottish parliament** (the visitors' entrance is in Milne's Court, beside the Ensign Ewart pub). See the entry for the Scottish Parliament Visitor Centre under High St later in this section.

Lawnmarket

A corruption of 'Landmarket' (selling goods from the land outside the city), Lawnmarket takes its name from the large cloth market that flourished here until the 18th century; this was the poshest part of Old Town, where many of its most distinguished citizens made their homes.

One of these was the merchant Thomas Gledstanes, who in 1617 purchased the tenement later known as **Gladstone's Land** (☎ 226 5856, 477 Lawnmarket; adult/child £3.50/2.50; open 10am-5pm Mon-Sat & 2pm-5pm Sun Apr-Oct) and now cared for by the National Trust for Scotland (NTS; see Useful Organisations in the Facts for the Visitor chapter). It contains fine painted ceilings, walls and beams, and some splendid furniture from the 17th and 18th centuries. The volunteer guides provide a wealth of stories and detailed history.

Tucked down a close just east of Gladstone's Land you'll find the **Writers' Museum** (☎ 529 4901, Lady Stair's Close, Lawnmarket; admission free; open 10am-5pm Mon-Sat, plus 2pm-5pm Sun during Edinburgh Festival). Located in Lady Stair's House (built in 1622), it contains manuscripts and memorabilia belonging to Robert Burns, Sir Walter Scott and Robert Louis Stevenson.

High St

High St, which stretches from George IV Bridge down to the Netherbow at St Mary's St, is the heart and soul of Old Town, home to the city's main church, the Law Courts,

the city council and – until 1707 – the Scottish parliament.

On the corner of the Royal Mile and George IV Bridge is the **Scottish Parliament Visitor Centre** (☎ 348 5000, Ⓦ www .scottish.parliament.uk, George IV Bridge; admission free; open 10am-5pm Mon-Fri, open earlier when parliament is sitting). The centre explains the workings of the new parliament, which was officially opened on 1 July 1999 – the first Scottish parliament for almost 300 years. You can visit the debating chamber when parliament is not sitting (usually from 10am to noon and 2pm to 4pm Monday and Friday), or you can phone ahead (☎ 348 5411, no more than a week in advance) to arrange free tickets for the public gallery while parliament is sitting.

Dominating High St is the great grey bulk of **St Giles Cathedral** (☎ 225 9442, High St; admission free but donations welcome; open 9am-7pm Mon-Fri & 9am-5pm Sat & 1pm-5pm Sun Easter-Sept, 9am-5pm Mon-Sat & 1pm-5pm Sun Oct-Easter). Properly called the High Kirk of Edinburgh (it was only a true cathedral – the seat of a bishop – from 1633 to 1638 and from 1661 to 1689), St Giles was named after the patron saint of cripples and beggars. There has been a church on this site since the 9th century. A Norman-style church was built in 1126 but was destroyed by English invaders in 1385; the only substantial remains are the central piers that support the tower. The present church dates largely from the 15th century – the beautiful crown spire was completed in 1495 – but much of it was restored in the 19th century.

St Giles was at the heart of the Scottish Reformation. John Knox served as minister here from 1559 to 1572, preaching his uncompromising Calvinist message, and when Charles I attempted to re-establish episcopacy in Scotland in 1637 by imposing a new liturgy, he only hardened the Scots' attitude against him. As the service from Charles I's *Book of Common Prayer* was read out for the first time in St Giles, a local woman called Jenny Geddes hurled her stool at the dean and called out, 'De'il colic the wame o' thee – wouldst thou say Mass at ma lug?'

The devil buckle your belly – would you say Mass in my ear?) – and ignited a riot whose aftermath led to the signing of the National Covenant at Greyfriars the following year. A plaque marks the spot where Jenny launched her protest, and a copy of the National Covenant is displayed on the wall.

One of the most interesting corners of the kirk is the **Thistle Chapel**, built between 1909 and 1911 for the Knights of the Most Ancient & Most Noble Order of the Thistle. The elaborately carved Gothic-style stalls have canopies topped with the helms and arms of the 16 knights.

Around St Giles is the cobbled expanse of **Parliament Square**, flanked to the south by **Parliament House**, the meeting place of the Scottish parliament from 1639 to 1707 (the neoclassical facade was added in the early 19th century). After the Act of Union the building became the centre of the Scottish legal system, housing the Court of Session and the High Court, a function which it still serves today. The most interesting feature is the 17th-century **Parliament Hall**, where the parliament actually met. Now used by lawyers and their clients as a meeting place, it boasts its original oak hammer-beam roof and magnificent 19th-century stained-glass windows.

By the side of the street, outside the western door of St Giles, a cobblestone **Heart of Midlothian** is set in the paving. Passers-by traditionally spit on it for luck (don't stand downwind!). This was the site of the Tolbooth, originally built to collect tolls, but subsequently a meeting place for parliament, the town council and the General Assembly of the Reformed Kirk, before becoming law courts and, finally, a notorious prison and place of execution.

At the other end of St Giles is the **Mercat Cross**, a 19th-century copy of the 1365 original, where merchants and traders met to transact business and Royal Proclamations were read.

Across the street from the Cross is the **City Chambers**, originally built by John Adam (brother of Robert) in 1761 to serve as the Royal Exchange – a covered meeting place for city merchants – to replace the Mercat Cross. However, the merchants continued to prefer their old stamping grounds in the street, and the building became the offices of the city council in 1811. Part of it was built over the sealed-off remains of Mary King's Close (see the later boxed text 'Underground Edinburgh').

At the south-western corner of the intersection with South Bridge is the **Tron Kirk** (1637); it owes its name to a *tron* or public weighbridge that once stood on the site.

Halfway down the next block is 'the noisiest museum in the world' – the **Museum of Childhood** (☎ 529 4142, 42 High St; admission free; open 10am-5pm Mon-Sat year-round, plus 2pm-5pm Sun July & Aug). Often overrun with screaming kids, it covers serious issues related to childhood – health, education, upbringing and so on – but also has an enormous collection of toys, dolls, games and books.

The Royal Mile narrows at the foot of High St beside the jutting facade of **John Knox House** (☎ 556 9579, 43-45 High St; adult/child £2.25/75p; open 10am-5pm Mon-Sat year-round, plus noon-5pm Sunday July & Aug). It is the oldest surviving tenement in Edinburgh, dating from around 1490; John Knox is thought to have lived here from 1561 to 1572. The labyrinthine interior has some beautiful painted timber ceilings and an interesting display on Knox's life and work.

High St ends at the intersection with St Mary's and Jeffrey Sts, where Old Town's eastern gate, the **Netherbow Port** (part of the Flodden Wall) once stood. Though it no longer exists, its former outline is marked by brass strips set in the road.

Canongate

Canongate – the stretch of the Royal Mile from Netherbow to Holyrood – takes its name from the Augustinian canons (monks) of Holyrood Abbey. From the 16th century it was home to aristocrats attracted to the Palace of Holyroodhouse. Originally governed by the monks, Canongate was an independent burgh separate from Edinburgh until 1856.

Underground Edinburgh

As Edinburgh expanded in the late 18th and early 19th centuries, many old tenements were demolished and new bridges were built to link Old Town to the newly built areas to its north and south. South Bridge (built between 1785 and 1788) and George IV Bridge (built between 1829 and 1834) lead southwards from the Royal Mile over the deep valley of Cowgate, but so many buildings have been built closely around them that you can hardly tell they are bridges – George IV Bridge has a total of nine arches but only two are visible; South Bridge has no less than 18 hidden arches.

These subterranean vaults were originally used as storerooms, workshops and drinking dens. But as early-19th-century Edinburgh's population was swelled by an influx of penniless Highlanders cleared from their lands, and Irish refugees from the potato famine, the dark, dripping chambers were given over to slum accommodation and abandoned to poverty, filth and crime.

The vaults were eventually cleared in the late 19th century, then lay forgotten until 1994 when the South Bridge vaults were opened to guided tours (see Organised Tours later in this chapter). Certain chambers are said to be haunted and one particular vault was investigated by paranormal researchers in 2001.

Nevertheless, the most ghoulish aspect of Edinburgh's hidden history dates from much earlier – from the plague that struck the city in 1645. Legend has it that the disease-ridden inhabitants of Mary King's Close (a lane on the northern side of the Royal Mile on the site of the City Chambers – you can still see its blocked-off northern end from Cockburn St) were walled up in their houses and left to perish. When the lifeless bodies were eventually cleared from the houses, they were so stiff that workmen had to hack off limbs to get them through the small doorways and narrow, twisting stairs.

From that day on, the close was said to be haunted by the spirits of the plague victims. The few people who were prepared to live there reported seeing apparitions of severed heads and limbs, and the largely abandoned close fell into ruin. When the Royal Exchange (now the City Chambers) was constructed between 1753 and 1761, it was built over the lower levels of Mary King's Close, which were left intact and sealed off beneath the building.

Interest in the close revived in the 20th century when Edinburgh's city council began to allow occasional guided tours to enter. Then in the 1990s, Mercat Tours (see Organised Tours later in this chapter) was given permission to take tour groups into the close. Since then, visitors have reported many supernatural experiences – the most famous ghost is 'Sarah', a little girl whose sad tale has prompted people to leave gifts of dolls in a corner of one of the rooms.

One of the surviving symbols of Canongate's former independence is the **Canongate Tolbooth** (☎ 529 4057, 163 Canongate; admission free; open 10am-5pm Mon-Sat year-round, plus 2pm-5pm Sun during the Edinburgh festival). Built in 1591, it served successively as a collection point for tolls (taxes), a council house, a courtroom and a jail. With its picturesque turrets and projecting clock, it's an interesting example of 16th-century architecture. It now houses a fascinating museum called **The People's Story**, recording the life, work and pastimes of ordinary Edinburgh folk from the 18th century to the present day.

Across the street from the Tolbooth is **Huntly House**. Built in 1570, it now houses the **Museum of Edinburgh** (☎ 529 4143, 142 Canongate; admission free; open 10am-5pm Mon-Sat year-round, plus 2pm-5pm Sun during the Edinburgh festival). It covers the history of the city from prehistory to the present. Exhibits of national importance include an original copy of the National Covenant of 1638, but the big crowd-pleaser is the dog collar and feeding bowl that once belonged to Greyfriars Bobby, the city's most famous canine citizen.

Downhill on the left is the attractive curved gable of the **Canongate Kirk**, built in 1688. The kirkyard contains the graves of several famous people, including the economist Adam Smith (1723–90), author of *The Wealth of Nations*, Mrs Agnes MacLehose (the 'Clarinda' of Robert Burns' love poems), and the 18th-century poet Robert Fergusson (1750–74). Fergusson was much admired by Robert Burns, who paid for the gravestone and penned the epitaph – take a look at the inscription on the back.

HOLYROOD

The district at the foot of the Royal Mile is undergoing a major upheaval during the construction of the new Scottish parliament buildings (due for completion in late 2003).

Palace of Holyroodhouse & Holyrood Abbey

The **Palace of Holyroodhouse** (☎ 556 1096, *Canongate; adult/child/family £6.50/3.30/ 16.30; open 9.30am-6pm daily Apr-Oct, 9.30am-4.30pm daily Nov-Mar)* is the queen's official residence in Scotland. It is closed to the public when the royal family is visiting and during state functions (usually in mid-May, and mid-June to around early July; telephone first to check).

The palace developed from a guesthouse attached to Holyrood Abbey, which was extended by King James IV in 1501. The oldest surviving section of the building, the north-western tower, was built in 1529 as a royal apartment for James V and his wife, Mary of Guise. Mary, Queen of Scots, spent six eventful years living here, during which time she debated with John Knox and witnessed the murder of her secretary Rizzio.

The guided tour leads you through a series of impressive royal apartments, ending in the **Great Gallery**. The 89 portraits of Scottish kings were commissioned by Charles II and supposedly record his unbroken lineage from Scota, the Egyptian pharaoh's daughter who discovered the infant Moses in a reed basket on the banks of the Nile.

But the highlight of the tour is **Mary Queen of Scots' Bed Chamber** in the 16th-century tower house. This bedroom was home to the unfortunate Mary from 1561 to 1567. It was here too that her jealous husband restrained the pregnant queen while his henchmen murdered her secretary – and favourite – David Rizzio. A plaque in the neighbouring room marks the spot where he bled to death. The exit from the palace leads into the ruins of Holyrood Abbey.

King David I founded **Holyrood Abbey** here in the shadow of Salisbury Crags in 1128. It was probably named after a fragment of the True Cross (*rood* is an old Scots word for cross) said to have been brought to Scotland by his mother St Margaret. Most of the surviving ruins date from the 12th and 13th centuries, although a doorway in the far south-eastern corner has survived from the original Norman church.

Scottish Parliament Building

The new Scottish parliament building is being built on the site of a former brewery and is due to open by early 2003. The temporary **Parliament Building Visitor Centre** (☎ *no phone, Holyrood Rd; admission free; open 10am-4pm daily)* records the development of the project from the initial architectural design competition to the current state of construction. The competition to design the new parliament was won in July 1998 by the Catalan architect Enric Miralles, who envisaged a group of lenticular buildings with curved roofs inspired by upturned boats seen on a beach in northern Scotland.

Our Dynamic Earth

The modernistic white marquee pitched beneath Salisbury Crags marks Edinburgh's newest tourist attraction, Our Dynamic Earth (☎ *550 7800, Holyrood Rd; adult/ child/family £7.95/4.50/20; open 10am-6pm daily Apr-Oct, 10am-5pm Wed-Sun Nov-Mar)*. It's billed as an interactive, multimedia 'journey of discovery' through Earth's history from the Big Bang to the present day. Hugely popular with kids of all ages, it's a slick extravaganza of whizz-bang special effects cleverly designed to fire up young minds with curiosity about all things geological and environmental. Its true purpose, of course, is to disgorge you into a gift shop where you can buy model dinosaurs and souvenir T-shirts.

EDINBURGH

Holyrood Park & Arthur's Seat

In Holyrood Park, Edinburgh is blessed in having a little bit of wilderness in the heart of the city. The former hunting ground of Scottish monarchs, the park covers 263 hectares of varied landscape, including crags, moorland and loch. The highest point is the 251m summit of **Arthur's Seat**, the deeply eroded remnant of a long-extinct volcano. The park can be circumnavigated by car or bike along Queen's Drive (closed to motorised traffic on Sunday), and you can hike from Holyrood to the summit in 45 minutes.

NORTH OF THE ROYAL MILE

Cockburn St, lined with trendy fashion, jewellery and music shops, leads down from the Royal Mile to Waverley Bridge; a right turn into Market St leads to the **Fruitmarket Gallery** (☎ 225 2383, **W** www.fruitmarket.co.uk, 45 Market St; admission free; open 11am-6pm Mon-Sat, noon-5pm Sun). One of Edinburgh's most innovative and popular galleries, the Fruitmarket showcases contemporary Scottish and international artists; it also has an excellent arts bookshop and cafe.

Across the street is the **City Art Centre** (☎ 529 3993, 2 Market St; admission free except for occasional exhibitions; open 10am-5pm Mon-Sat year-round, plus noon-5pm Sun Jul & Aug). The largest of Edinburgh's smaller galleries, it comprises six floors of exhibitions, with a variety of themes, including an extensive collection of Scottish art.

SOUTH OF THE ROYAL MILE
Grassmarket

The site of a market from the 15th century until the start of the 20th, Grassmarket has always been a focal point of Old Town. As well as being a cattle market, this was the main place of execution in the city, and over 100 martyred Covenanters are commemorated by a monument at the eastern end, where the gallows used to stand. The notorious murderers Burke and Hare operated from a now-vanished close off the western end. In 1827 they enticed at least 18 victims

to their boarding house, suffocated them and sold the bodies to Edinburgh's medical schools.

Nowadays, the broad, open square, edged by tall tenements and dominated by the looming castle, has many lively pubs and restaurants, including the White Hart Inn which was once patronised by Robert Burns. **Cowgate** – the long, dark ravine leading eastwards from Grassmarket – was once the road along which cattle were driven from the pastures around Arthur's Seat to the safety of the city walls. Today, it is the heart of Edinburgh's nightlife, with around two dozen clubs and bars within five minutes' walk of each other (see Entertainment later in this chapter).

Greyfriars

Candlemaker Row leads up from the eastern end of Grassmarket towards one of Edinburgh's most famous churches. **Greyfriars Kirk** was built on the site of a Franciscan friary and opened for worship on Christmas Day 1620. In 1638, the National Covenant was signed, rejecting Charles I's attempts to impose episcopacy and a new English prayer book, and affirming the independence of the Scottish Church. Many who signed were later executed in Grassmarket and, in 1679, 1200 Covenanters were held prisoner in terrible conditions in an enclosure in the kirkyard. There's a small exhibition inside.

Hemmed in by high walls and overlooked by the brooding presence of the castle, **Greyfriars Kirkyard** is one of Edinburgh's most evocative spots, a peaceful green oasis dotted with elaborate monuments. Many famous Edinburgh names are buried here, including the poet Allan Ramsay (1686–1758), architect William Adam (1689–1748) and William Smellie (1740–95), the editor of the first edition of the *Encyclopedia Brittanica*.

However, the memorial that draws the biggest crowds is the tiny statue of **Greyfriars Bobby**, in front of the pub beside the kirkyard gate. Bobby was a Skye terrier who maintained a vigil over the grave of his master, an Edinburgh police officer, from 1858 to 1872. The story was immortalised (and romanticised) in a novel by Eleanor Atkinson in 1912, and in 1963 was made into a movie by – who else? – Walt Disney. Bobby's grave – marked by a small, pink granite stone – is just inside the entrance to the kirkyard. You can see his original collar and bowl in the Museum of Edinburgh (see the Canongate section earlier in this chapter).

Chambers St

The broad and elegant Chambers St stretches eastwards from Greyfriars Bobby, dominated by the long facade of the **Royal Museum and Museum of Scotland** (☎ 247 4219, Ⓦ www.nms.ac.uk, Chambers Street; admission free except for special exhibitions; open 10am-5pm Mon & Wed-Sat, 10am-8pm Tues, noon-5pm Sun, closed 25 Dec). The golden stone and striking modern architecture of the Museum of Scotland – opened in 1998 – is one of the city's most distinctive new landmarks. The five floors of the museum trace the history of Scotland from geological beginnings to the 1990s, with many imaginative and stimulating exhibits – audioguides are available in several languages. Highlights include the Monymusk Reliquary, a tiny silver casket dating from AD 750, which is said to have been carried into battle with Robert the Bruce at Bannockburn in 1314, and a set of charming, 12th-century chess pieces made from walrus ivory. Don't forget to take the lift to the Roof Terrace for a fantastic view of the castle.

The modern Museum of Scotland connects with the original, Victorian **Royal Museum**, dating from 1861, whose stolid, grey exterior gives way to a bright and airy, glass-roofed entrance hall. The museum houses an eclectic collection covering natural history, archaeology, scientific and industrial technology, and the decorative arts of ancient Egypt, Islam, China, Japan, Korea and the west. One of the prize exhibits is the *Wylam Dilly* (1813), the world's oldest steam locomotive. Volunteers give free, 45-minute guided tours of the Royal Museum (at 3pm daily except Tuesday and Thursday) and the Museum of Scotland (at 2pm daily and also at 6pm Tuesday).

At the eastern end of Chambers St, beyond College Wynd, is Edinburgh University's **Old College** (also called Old Quad; it now houses the Law Faculty), a neoclassical masterpiece designed by Robert Adam in 1789 but not completed till 1834. Inside the Old College, at the College Wynd end, is the **Talbot Rice Art Gallery** (☎ 650 2210, Ⓦ www.trg.ed.ac.uk, Old College, South Bridge; admission free; open 10am-5pm Tues-Sat, daily during Edinburgh Festival), which houses a small, permanent collection of old masters, plus regular exhibitions of new work.

NEW TOWN

New Town lies north of Old Town, on a ridge running parallel to the Royal Mile and separated from it by the valley of Princes Street Gardens. Its regular grid of elegant, Georgian terraces is a complete contrast to the chaotic tangle of tenements and wynds that characterise Old Town.

Between the end of the 14th century and the start of the 18th, the population of Edinburgh – still confined within the walls of Old Town – increased from 2000 to 50,000. The tottering tenements were unsafe and occasionally collapsed, fire was an ever-present danger, and the overcrowding and squalor became unbearable.

So when the Act of Union in 1707 brought the prospect of long-term stability, the upper classes were keen to find healthier, more spacious living quarters, and in 1766, the lord provost of Edinburgh announced an architectural competition to design an extension to the city. It was won by an unknown 23-year-old, James Craig, a self-taught architect whose simple and elegant plan envisaged the main axis being George St, with grand squares at either end, and with building restricted to one side only of Princes and Queen Sts so that the houses enjoyed views over the Firth of Forth to the north and to the castle and Old Town to the south.

During the 18th and 19th centuries, New Town continued to sprout squares, circuses, parks and terraces, with some of its finest neoclassical architecture designed by Robert Adam. Today, Edinburgh's New Town remains the world's most complete and unspoilt example of Georgian architecture and town planning. Along with Old Town, it was declared a UNESCO World Heritage Site in 1995.

Princes St

Princes St is one of the world's most spectacular shopping streets. Built up on one side only – the northern side – it catches the sun in summer and allows expansive views across **Princes Street Gardens** to the castle and the crowded skyline of Old Town.

The western end of Princes St is dominated by the red-sandstone edifice of the Caledonian Hotel, and the tower of **St John's Church**, worth visiting for its fine Gothic Revival interior. It overlooks **St Cuthbert's Parish Church**, built in the 1890s on a site of great antiquity – there has been a church here since at least the 12th century, and perhaps since the 7th century. There is a circular **watch tower** in the graveyard – a reminder of the Burke and Hare days when graves had to be guarded against robbers.

At the eastern end is the prominent clock tower – traditionally three minutes fast so that you don't miss your train – of the Balmoral Hotel, and the beautiful **Register House** (1788), designed by Robert Adam, with a statue of the duke of Wellington on horseback in front. It houses the National Archives of Scotland.

Princes Street Gardens lie in a valley that was once occupied by the Nor' Loch (North Loch), a boggy depression that was drained in the early 19th century. They are split in the middle by **The Mound** – around two million cart-loads of earth were dumped here during the construction of New Town, to provide a road link across the valley to Old Town. It was completed in 1830.

The eastern half of the gardens is dominated by the massive Gothic spire of the **Scott Monument** (☎ 529 4068, East Princes Street Gardens; admission £2.50; open 9am-8 pm Mon-Sat & 10am-6pm Sun June-Sept; 9am-6pm Mon-Sat & 10am-6pm Sun Mar-May & Oct; 9am-4pm Mon-Sat & 10am-4pm Sun Nov-Feb), built by public subscription in memory of the novelist Sir Walter Scott after his death in 1832. You

can climb the 287 steps to the top for a superb view of the city.

Royal Scottish Academy

The distinguished Greek Doric temple at the corner of The Mound and Princes St, its northern pediment crowned by a seated figure of Queen Victoria, is the home of the Royal Scottish Academy (RSA; ☎ 558 7097, The Mound; admission free, £2-5 for special exhibitions; open 10am-5pm Mon-Sat, 2pm-5pm Sun). Designed by William Playfair and built between 1823 and 1836, it was originally called the Royal Institution; the RSA took over the building in 1910. The galleries display a collection of paintings, sculptures and architectural drawings by academy members dating from 1831, and it also hosts temporary exhibitions throughout the year.

National Gallery of Scotland

Immediately south of the RSA is the National Gallery of Scotland (☎ 624 6200, The Mound; admission to permanent collection free, £2-5 for special exhibitions; open 10am-5pm Mon-Sat & 2pm-5pm Sun, or noon-6pm Mon-Sat & 11am-6pm Sun during Edinburgh Festival). Also designed by William Playfair, this imposing classical building with its Ionic porticoes dates from the 1850s. It houses an important collection of European art from the Renaissance to postimpressionism. There are paintings by Verrocchio (Leonardo da Vinci's teacher), Tintoretto, Titian, Holbein, Rubens, Van Dyck, Vermeer, El Greco, Poussin, Rembrandt, Gainsborough, Turner, Constable, Monet, Pissaro, Gauguin and Cezanne.

The USA is also represented by the works of Frederick Church, John Singer Sargent and Benjamin West. The section dedicated to Scottish art includes portraits by Allan Ramsay and Sir Henry Raeburn, rural scenes by Sir David Wilkie and impressionistic landscapes by William MacTaggart. Annually, in January, the gallery exhibits its collection of Turner watercolours, bequested by Henry Vaughan in 1900.

Antonio Canova's statue of the Three Graces (in Room 10) is owned jointly with

London's Victoria & Albert Museum. In Greek mythology the Three Graces – Aglaia (Brightness), Euphrosyne (Joyfulness) and Thalia (Bloom) – were the daughters of Zeus and Euryonome, and embodied beauty, grace and youth.

At the time of research, the RSA and National Gallery were undergoing major refurbishment that will see the two buildings linked by an underground mall, and their gallery space increased by 1395 square metres, giving them twice the temporary exhibition space of the Prado in Madrid, and three times that of the Royal Academy in London. The work is due for completion in summer 2002.

George St & Charlotte Square

Until recently, George St – the major axis of New Town – was the centre of Edinburgh's financial industry, and Scotland's equivalent of Wall St. Now many of the big financial firms have moved to premises in the new office district west of Lothian Rd, and George St's banks and offices are being turned into shops, pubs and restaurants.

At the western end of George St is Charlotte Square, the architectural jewel of New Town, designed by Robert Adam shortly before his death in 1791. The northern side of the square is Adam's masterpiece and one of the finest examples of Georgian architecture anywhere. **Bute House**, in the centre at No 6, is the official residence of Scotland's first minister.

Next door is the **Georgian House** *(NTS; ☎ 226 2160, 7 Charlotte Square; adult/child £5/4; open 10am-5pm Mon-Sat & 2pm-5pm Sun Mar-Oct, 11am-4pm Mon-Sat & 2pm-4pm Sun Nov-24 Dec)*, which has been beautifully restored and refurnished to show how Edinburgh's wealthy elite lived at the end of the 18th century. The walls are decorated with paintings by Allan Ramsay, Sir Henry Raeburn and Sir Joshua Reynolds. A 35-minute video brings it all to life rather well.

The headquarters of the **National Trust for Scotland** *(NTS; ☎ 243 9300,* W *www .nts.org.uk, 28 Charlotte Square; admission free; open 10am-5pm Mon-Sat, noon-5pm Sun)* is on the southern side of the square.

As well as a shop, cafe, restaurant and information desk, the building contains a restored 1820s drawing room with Regency furniture and a collection of 20th-century Scottish paintings.

St Andrew Square

St Andrew Square is not as architecturally distinguished as its sister at the opposite end of George St. Dominating the square is the fluted column of the **Melville Monument**, commemorating Henry Dundas, 1st Viscount Melville (1742–1811), who was the most powerful Scottish politician of his time, often referred to when alive as the 'Uncrowned King of Scotland'. The impressive Palladian mansion of **Dundas House**, built between 1772 and 1774, on the eastern side of the square, was built for Sir Laurence Dundas. It has been the head office of the Royal Bank of Scotland since 1825 and has a spectacular iron dome (you can go into the banking hall for a look).

A short distance along George St is the **Church of St Andrew & St George**, built in 1784, with an unusual oval nave. It was the scene of the Disruption of 1843, when 451 dissenting ministers left the Church of Scotland to form the Free Church.

Just north of the square at the junction with Queen St is the Venetian Gothic palace of the **Scottish National Portrait Gallery** *(☎ 624 6200, 1 Queen St; admission free; open 10am-5pm Mon-Sat & noon-5pm Sun, hours extended during Edinburgh Festival)*. Its galleries illustrate Scottish history through portraits and sculptures of famous Scottish personalities, from Robert Burns and Bonnie Prince Charlie to Sean Connery and Billy Connolly.

CALTON HILL

Calton Hill (100m), rising dramatically above the eastern end of Princes St, is Edinburgh's acropolis, its summit scattered with grandiose memorials, mostly dating from the first half of the 19th century. It is also one of the best viewpoints in Edinburgh, with a panorama that takes in the castle, Holyrood, Arthur's Seat, the Firth of Forth, New Town and the full length of Princes St.

On the southern side of the hill, on Regent Rd, is the modernist facade of **St Andrew's House**, built between 1936 and 1939, which housed the civil servants of the Westminster government's Scottish Office until they were moved to the new Scottish Executive building in Leith in 1996.

Just beyond St Andrew's House and on the opposite side of the road is the imposing **Royal High School** building, dating from 1829 and modelled on the Temple of Theseus in Athens. Former pupils include Robert Adam, Alexander Graham Bell and Sir Walter Scott. It now stands empty. To its east, on the other side of Regent Rd, is the **Burns Monument** (1830), a Greek-style memorial to Robert Burns.

You can reach the summit of Calton Hill via the road beside the Royal High School or by the stairs at the eastern end of Waterloo Place. The largest structure on the summit is the **National Monument**, an over-ambitious attempt to replicate the Parthenon and intended to honour Scotland's dead in the Napoleonic Wars. Construction – paid for by public subscription – began in 1822, but funds ran dry when only 12 columns were complete.

Looking a bit like an upturned telescope – the similarity is intentional – and offering better views, the **Nelson Monument** *(☎ 556 2716, Calton Hill; admission £2.50; open 1pm-6pm Mon & 10am-6pm Tues-Sat Apr-Sept, 10am-3pm Mon-Sat Oct-Mar)* was built to commemorate Admiral Lord Nelson's victory at Trafalgar in 1805.

The design of the **City Observatory**, built in 1818, was based on the ancient Greek Temple of the Winds in Athens. Its original function was to provide a precise, astronomical time-keeping service for marine navigators, but smoke from Waverley train station forced the astronomers to move to Blackford Hill in the south of Edinburgh in 1895.

CRAMOND

With its moored yachts, stately swans and whitewashed houses spilling down a hillside at the mouth of the River Almond, Cramond is the most picturesque corner of Edinburgh. It is also rich in history – it has

long been known that the Romans built a fort here in the 2nd century AD (the village's name comes from Caer Amon, 'the fort on the River Almond'), but recent archaeological excavations have revealed evidence of a Bronze-Age settlement as long ago as 8500 BC, the oldest known site in the whole of Scotland.

Cramond, which was originally a mill village, has a historic 17th-century church and a 15th-century tower house as well as some rather unimpressive Roman remains, but most people just come to enjoy the walks along the river to the ruined mills and to take the little rowing-boat ferry across the river to the Dalmeny Estate. A little downstream from the ferry landing is **The Maltings** *(☎ 312 6034, Cramond Village; admission free; open 2pm-5pm Sat & Sun June-Sept, daily during Edinburgh Festival)*, which hosts a small exhibition on Cramond's history.

Take bus No 40 or 41 from The Mound, Hanover St (northbound) or Charlotte Square to Cramond Glebe Rd, then walk 400m northwards.

The Cramond Ferry operates on demand from 9am to 1pm and 2pm to 7pm Saturday to Thursday, April to September; and from 10am to 1pm and 2pm to 4pm Saturday to Thursday, October to March, except for Christmas Day and New Year's Day. The fare is 50/10p for adults/children. Prams are carried, but bikes and dogs are not allowed.

DEAN VILLAGE

If you follow Queensferry St northwards from the western end of Princes St, you come to **Dean Bridge**, designed by Thomas Telford and built between 1829 and 1832. Down in the valley just west of the bridge is Dean Village (*dene* is a Scots word for valley). It was founded as a milling community by the canons of Holyrood Abbey in the 12th century and by 1700 there were 11 water mills here operated by the Incorporation of Baxters (the bakers' trade guild). One of the old mill buildings has been converted into flats, and the village is now an attractive residential area.

Scottish National Gallery of Modern Art & Dean Gallery

Set in an impressive neoclassical building surrounded by a sculpture park some 500m west of Dean Village is the **Scottish National Gallery of Modern Art** (☎ 624 6200, 75 Belford Rd; admission free except for special exhibitions; open 10am-5pm Mon-Sat, noon-5pm Sun). The collection concentrates on 20th-century art, with various European movements represented by the likes of Matisse, Picasso, Kirchner, Magritte, Miró, Mondrian and Giacometti. American and English artists are also represented, but most space is given to Scottish painters – from the Scottish colourists of the early 20th century to contemporary artists such as Peter Howson and Ken Currie. There's an excellent cafe downstairs, and the surrounding park features sculptures by Henry Moore, Sir Eduardo Paolozzi and Barbara Hepworth among others.

Directly across Belford Rd from the National Gallery of Modern Art, another neoclassical mansion houses its adjunct, the **Dean Gallery** (☎ 624 6200, 73 Belford Rd; admission free except for special exhibitions; open 10am-5pm Mon-Sat, noon-5pm Sun). The dean holds the Gallery of Modern Art's collection of Dada and surrealist art, including works by Dali, Giacometti and Picasso, and a large collection of sculpture and graphic art created by the Edinburgh-born sculptor Sir Eduardo Paolozzi.

LEITH

Leith – 2 miles (3km) north-east of the city centre – has been Edinburgh's seaport since the 14th century and remained an independent burgh with its own town council until it was incorporated by the city in the 1920s. Like many of Britain's dockland areas, it fell into decay in the decades following WWII but has been undergoing a revival since the late 1980s. Old warehouses have been turned into luxury flats and a lush crop of trendy bars and restaurants has sprouted along the waterfront. The area was given an additional boost in the late 1990s when the Scottish Office (a government department, now renamed the Scottish Executive) moved to a new building on Leith docks. The city council has now formulated a major redevelopment plan for the entire Edinburgh waterfront from Leith to Granton, the first phase of which is Ocean Terminal (due to have opened by the time you read this), a shopping and leisure complex that includes the former Royal Yacht *Britannia* and a berth for visiting cruise liners. Parts of Leith are still a bit rough – Salamander St, for example, is a notorious red-light district – but it's a distinctive corner of the city and well worth exploring.

Royal Yacht Britannia

One of Edinburgh's biggest tourist attractions is the former Royal Yacht *Britannia* (☎ 555 5566, W www.royalyachtbritannia.co.uk, Ocean Drive, Leith; adult/child/family £7.75/3.75/20; open 10am-3.30pm Mon-Fri Oct-Mar; 9.30am-4pm Mon-Fri Apr-May; 9.30am-4.30pm Mon-Fri June-Sept; 9.30am-4.30pm Sat & Sun year-round; closed 1 Jan & 25 Dec). She was the British royal family's floating home during their foreign travels from her launch in 1953 until her decommissioning in 1997, and is now moored permanently in front of Ocean Terminal.

The tour, which you take at your own pace with an audioguide (also available in French, German, Italian and Spanish), gives an intriguing insight into the Queen's private tastes – *Britannia* was one of the few places where the royal family could enjoy true privacy. The entire ship is a monument to 1950s decor and technology, and the accommodation reveals Her Majesty's preference for simple, unfussy surroundings – the Queen's own bed is surprisingly tiny and plain. In fact, the initial interior design was rejected by the Queen for being too flashy.

There was nothing simple or unfussy about the running of the ship, though. When the Queen travelled, along with her went 45 members of the royal household, five tons of luggage and a Rolls-Royce that was carefully squeezed into a specially built garage on the deck. The ship's company consisted of an admiral, 20 officers and 220 yachtsmen. The decks (of Burmese teak) were scrubbed daily, but all work near the royal accommodation was carried out in complete silence and had to be finished by 8am. A thermometer was kept in the Queen's bathroom to make sure that the water was the correct temperature, and when in harbour one yachtsman was charged with ensuring that the angle of the gangway never exceeded 12 degrees. And note the mahogany windbreak that was added to the balcony deck in front of the bridge – it was put there to stop wayward breezes from blowing up skirts and inadvertently revealing the royal undies.

Shuttle buses run from Waverley Bridge to *Britannia* every 20 minutes during opening times.

GREATER EDINBURGH
Craigmillar Castle
Two-and-a-half miles (4km) south-east of the city centre lies Craigmillar Castle *(HS; ☎ 661 4445, Craigmillar Castle Rd; adult/child £2/75p; open 9.30am-6.30pm daily Apr-Sept; 9.30am-4.30pm Mon-Wed & Sat, 9.30am-1pm Thur & 2pm-4.30pm Sun Oct-Mar).* Dating from the 15th century, the tower house rises above two sets of machicolated walls that enclose an area of 0.6 hectares. Mary, Queen of Scots, took refuge here after the murder of Rizzio; it was here too that plans to murder her husband Darnley were laid. Look for the prison cell complete with built-in sanitation, something some 'modern' British prisons only finally managed in 1996. Take bus No 33 from Princes St to Old Dalkeith Rd and walk 500m up Craigmillar Castle Rd.

Edinburgh Zoo
Opened in 1913, and located 2½ miles (4km) west of the city centre, Edinburgh Zoo *(☎ 334 9171, W www.edinburghzoo .org.uk, 134 Corstorphine Rd; adult/child £7/4; open 9am-6pm daily Apr-Sept; 9am-5pm daily Oct & Mar; 9am-4.30pm daily Nov-Feb)* is one of the world's leading conservation zoos. Edinburgh's captive breeding programme has saved many endangered species, including Siberian tigers, pygmy hippos and red pandas. The main attractions are the penguins (kept in the world's biggest penguin pool), the sea lion and red panda

feeding times, the animal handling sessions, and the new Lifelinks 'hands on' zoology centre.

To get to the zoo take bus No 12, 16, 26, 31, 86 or 100 (the Airlink airport bus) westbound from Princes St.

Lauriston Castle
Lauriston Castle *(☎ 336 2060, Cramond Rd South; adult/child £4.50/3; open 11am-1pm & 2pm-5pm Sat-Thur Apr-Oct, 2pm-4pm Sat & Sun Nov-Mar)*, 3 miles (5km) north-west of the city centre, started life in the 16th century as a tower house, built by Archibald Napier (whose son, John, invented logarithms). The castle was extended and 'modernised' in 19th-century baronial style and now contains a collection of fine art and furniture. It's set in peaceful grounds with great views northwards across the Firth of Forth to Fife. Take bus No 40 from Hanover St to Cramond Rd South.

Royal Botanic Garden
Just north of Stockbridge is the lovely Royal Botanic Garden *(☎ 552 7171, W www .rbge.org.uk, 20a Inverleith Row; admission free; open 9.30am-4pm daily Nov-Jan; 9.30am-5pm daily Feb & Oct; 9.30am-6pm daily Mar & Sept; 9.30am-7pm daily Apr-Aug).* Twenty-eight beautifully landscaped hectares include splendid Victorian palm houses, colourful swathes of rhododendron and azalea, and a world-famous rock garden. The Terrace Cafe offers good views towards the city centre. Take bus No 8, 17, 23, 27 or 37 to East Gate.

ACTIVITIES
Edinburgh is lucky to have several good **walking** areas within the city boundary, including Arthur's Seat, Calton Hill, Blackford Hill, Hermitage of Braid, Corstorphine Hill, and the coast and river at Cramond. The Pentland Hills, which rise to over 500m, stretch south-westwards from the city for 15 miles (25km), offering excellent high- and low-level walking.

You can follow the Water of Leith Walkway from the city centre to Balerno (8 miles; 13km), and continue across the Pentlands to Silverburn (6½ miles; 10.5km) or Carlops (8 miles; 13km), and return to Edinburgh by bus. Another good option is to walk along the towpath of the Union Canal, which begins in Fountainbridge and runs all the way to Falkirk (31 miles; 50km). You can return to Edinburgh by bus at Ratho (8½ miles; 13.5km) and Broxburn (12 miles; 19km), and by bus or train from Linlithgow (21 miles; 34km).

Edinburgh and its surroundings offer many excellent opportunities for **cycling**. The main off-road routes from the city centre out to the countryside follow the Union Canal towpath and the Water of Leith Walkway from Tollcross south-westwards to Balerno (7½ miles; 12km) on the edge of the Pentland Hills, and the Innocent Railway Cycle Path from the southern side of Arthur's Seat eastwards to Musselburgh (5 miles; 8km) and on to Ormiston and Pencaitland. There are several routes through the Pentland Hills that are suitable for mountain bikes – for details ask at any bike shop or contact the Pentland Hills Ranger Service (☎ 445 3383).

Top-quality bikes can be hired from the friendly and helpful **Edinburgh Cycle Hire & Scottish Cycle Safaris** (☎/fax 556 5560, W www.cyclescotland.co.uk, 29 Blackfriars St; £10-15 per day, £50-70 per week; open 10am-6pm Mon-Sat). The price includes helmet, lock and repair kit; there are occasionally older bikes available for £5 per day. You can hire tents and touring equipment too. They also organise cycle tours in Edinburgh and all over Scotland – check their Web site for details.

There are no less than 19 **golf courses** in Edinburgh. Two of the best city courses are the challenging **Braid Hills Public Golf Course** (☎ 452 9408, Braid Hills Approach; green fees £10/12.50 weekdays/weekends) and the scenic **Lothianburn Golf Course** (☎ 445 5067, 106a Biggar Rd, Fairmilehead; green fees £16.50/22.50 weekdays/weekends).

There are many scenic bridle paths suitable for **horse riding** in the countryside around Edinburgh, and a number of riding schools offer two- and three-hours treks as well as tuition. Try **Pentland Hills Icelandics**

(☎ 01968-661095, W www.phicelandics.co.uk, Windy Gowl Farm, Carlops, Midlothian) or the **Edinburgh & Lasswade Riding Centre** (☎ 663 7676, Kevock Rd, Lasswade).

The Firth of Forth provides sheltered waters for all kinds of **sailing**. **Port Edgar Marina & Sailing School** (☎ 331 3330, W www.portedgar.co.uk, Shore Rd, South Queensferry; boat rental sessions 10am-noon & 2pm-4pm year-round, plus 7pm-9pm Mon-Fri, Apr-Oct) rents out Topper/420/Wayfarer sailing dinghies at £9.80/18.20/25.40 for a two-hour session. It also offers a wide range of sailing, canoeing and power-boating tuition courses.

The Firth of Forth is a bit on the chilly – and polluted – side for enjoyable **swimming**, but there are several indoor alternatives. The city's main facility is the **Royal Commonwealth Pool** (☎ 667 7211, 21 Dalkeith Rd; adult/child £2.70/1.40; open 9am-9pm Mon, Tues, Thur & Fri, 10am-9pm Wed, 10am-4pm Sat & Sun), which has a 50m pool, diving pool, children's pool, flumes and fitness centre.

ORGANISED TOURS
Walking Tours
There are lots of organised walks around Edinburgh, many of them related to ghosts, murders and witches. For starting times, phone or check the Web sites listed below.

Black Hart Storytellers (☎ 221 1249, W www.blackhart.uk.com) Tours cost £5; not suitable for children. Many people who take the 'City of the Dead' tour of Greyfriars Kirkyard have reported encounters with the 'McKenzie Poltergeist'.

Cadies & Witchery Tours (☎ 225 6745, W www.witcherytours.com) Adult/child £7/4. The becloaked and pasty-faced Adam Lyal leads a 'Murder & Mystery' tour of Old Town's darker corners. These tours are famous for their 'jumper-ooters' – costumed actors who 'jump oot' when you least expect it. Ooooh, scary.

McEwan's 80/- Literary Pub Tour (☎ 226 6665, W www.scot-lit-tour.co.uk) Adult/students & over-65s £7/5. An enlightening two-hour trawl through Edinburgh's literary history – and its associated howffs – in the entertaining company of Messrs Clart and McBrain. One of the best of Edinburgh's walking tours.

Mercat Tours (☎ 557 6464, W www.mercat-tours.co.uk) Adult/child £5/3. Mercat offers a wide range of tours, including history walks in Old Town and Leith, 'Ghosts & Ghouls', and visits to haunted Mary King's Close, hidden underground vaults and darkened graveyards.

Bus Tours
Open-topped buses leave from Waverley Bridge outside the main train station and offer hop-on/hop-off tours of the main sights, taking in New Town, Grassmarket and the Royal Mile. They're a good way of getting your bearings – although with a bus map and a Day Saver bus ticket (£2.20) you could do much the same thing but without the commentary. *Guide Friday* (☎ 556 2244) charges £8.50/2.50 for adults/children, and *Lothian Buses'* (☎ 555 6363) bright red Edinburgh Tour buses cost £7.50/2.50; tours depart every 10 minutes from Waverley Bridge. *Mac Tours* (☎ 220 0770) have a similar offering, but in a vintage bus, with departures every 20 minutes (£7.50/2.50).

SPECIAL EVENTS
Edinburgh hosts an amazing series of festivals throughout the year, notably the Edinburgh International Festival, the Fringe Festival and the Military Tattoo, which are all held about the same time. See the boxed text 'Special Events' in the Facts for the Visitor chapter.

PLACES TO STAY
A boom in hotel building has seen Edinburgh's tourist capacity swell markedly in recent years, but you can guarantee that the city will still be filled to the gills during the Festival and Fringe period (August) and over Hogmanay/New Year. If you want a room during these periods, book as far in advance as possible. In general, it's best to book ahead at Easter and between mid-May and mid-September.

If you arrive in Edinburgh without a room, there are several agencies that can help. The ESIC booking service (☎ 473 3800) will try to find a room to suit and will charge you a £4 fee if successful. If you

have the time, get hold of its free accommodation brochure, the *Edinburgh Holiday Guide*, and ring round yourself.

For £5, three branches of Thomas Cook will make hotel reservations: the Edinburgh airport office (☎ 333 5119); the office (☎ 557 0905) in Waverley Steps near the ESIC; and the office (☎ 557 0034) on Platform 1 of Waverley train station.

In the following sections, the price breakdown is based on the cost per person for bed and breakfast (B&B), sharing a double room

Camping
Edinburgh has two well-equipped camp sites reasonably close to the city centre.

Edinburgh Caravan Club Site (☎ 312 6874, Marine Drive) Bus: No 8A from North Bridge or Broughton St. Pitch £2-3, plus £3.75-4.75 per person. Open year round This site is 3 miles (5km) north-west of the city centre, overlooking the Firth of Forth.

Mortonhall Caravan Park (☎ 664 1533 fax 664 5387, W www.meadowhead.co.uk mortonhall, 38 Mortonhall Gate, Frogston Rd East) Bus: No 11 from Princes St (westbound). Pitch (including 1 car & 2 people £9-13.25. Open Mar-Oct. Located in attractive parkland 5 miles (8km) south-east of the centre, Mortonhall has an on-site shop, bar and restaurant.

SYHA Hostels
The Scottish Youth Hostels Association (SYHA; ☎ 01786-891400, fax 01786 891333, reservations ☎ 0870 155 3255 W www.syha.org.uk), 7 Glebe Crescent Stirling FK8 2JA, runs around 80 hostels throughout Scotland, including four in Edinburgh.

You need to be a member of SYHA or Hostelling International (HI) – if not, you can join on the spot at any SYHA hostel (£6/2.50 for adults/under-18s). Under-fives are not allowed; breakfast is included.

Bruntsfield Youth Hostel (☎ 447 2994, Bruntsfield Crescent) Bus: No 11 or 16 from Princes St. Adults £9.75-11, under-18s £8.50-9.75. Situated in an attractive location overlooking a park, the hostel was renovated in June 2000. New facilities includ-

email access and computer games. It's about 2½ miles (4 km) from Waverley train station – catch a bus from the garden side of Princes St and get off at Forbes Rd.

Eglinton Youth Hostel (☎ *337 1120, 18 Eglinton Crescent)* Adults £12-14, under-18s £10.50-12.50. This hostel is a mile (1.6km) west of Waverley train station. It's a pleasant place but can get a bit crowded and noisy, and the kitchen and bathroom facilities have trouble coping with a full house.

The ***Central Youth Hostel*** (☎ *556 5566, 11/2 Robertson's Close, Cowgate)* and the ***Pleasance Youth Hostel*** (☎ *668 3423, New Arthur Place)* both open in July and August only.

Independent Hostels

There's a growing number of independent backpackers' hostels, many of them right in the centre of town. Most have 24-hour access and no curfew.

Near Waverley Station The following places are within five minutes' walk of Edinburgh's main train station.

City Centre Tourist Hostel (☎ *556 8070, fax 220 5141,* W *www.edinburghhostels.com, 3rd floor, 5 West Register St)* Beds £12-20. The City Centre is a small (around 40 beds), clean and bright hostel, with pine-wood bunks and comfy mattresses in four-, six-, eight- and 10-bed dorms. There's a small kitchen and TV lounge, and a laundry (£3 per load).

St Christopher's Inn (☎ *020-7407 1856, fax 020-7403 7715,* W *www.st-christophers.co.uk, 9-13 Market St)* Dorm beds from £12. The 108-bed St Christopher's is just across the street from the Market St entrance to Waverley station. The price includes a continental breakfast.

Edinburgh Backpackers Hostel (☎ *220 1717, fax 539 8695, Cockburn St)* Dorm beds from £11.50, doubles £37.50. Just up the hill from St Christopher's, Edinburgh Backpackers is clean, bright and friendly.

Old Town These hostels are right in the heart of things, and close to pubs and clubs.

Brodies Backpackers Hostel (☎/*fax 556 5770,* W *www.brodieshostels.co.uk, 12 High St, Royal Mile)* Dorm beds £13.90/15.90 weekdays/weekends July-Sept, £9.90/11.90 Dec-Apr, £11.90/13.90 the rest of the year. Brodies is a small (50 beds), friendly place with four dorms (three mixed and one women-only). It has hotel-quality mattresses and duvets, a kitchen and a cosy lounge area with a fireplace. There is no TV, which makes for good socialising. They'll wash, dry and fold your laundry for £3.50 per load.

The following three places are all run by Scotland's Top Hostels (W www.scotlands-top-hostels.com). All charge between £10.50 and £12.50 for dorm beds, depending on season.

High Street Hostel (☎ *557 3984, fax 556 2981,* e *high-street@scotlands-top-hostels.com, 8 Blackfriars St)* This long-established and well-equipped hostel, housed in a 17th-century building, has a reputation as a party place, so if you're not in a party mood you might find it a bit noisy.

Royal Mile Backpackers (☎ *557 6120, fax 556 3999,* e *royal-mile@scotlands-top-hostels.com, 105 High St)* The small and cosy RMB isn't far from the High Street Hostel and shares its facilities.

Castle Rock Hostel (☎ *225 9666, fax 226 5078,* e *castlerock@scotlands-top-hostels.com, 15 Johnston Terrace)* With its bright, spacious, single-sex dorms, superb views and friendly staff, the 200-bed Castle Rock has prompted plenty of positive feedback from travellers. It has a great location only a minute's walk from the castle, Internet access for £1 an hour, laundry for £2.50 per load, and big-screen video nights.

West End The following are about 20 minutes' walk west of Waverley station – if you're arriving by train from Glasgow or the north, get off at Haymarket station, which is much closer.

Belford Hostel (☎ *225 6209, fax 539 8695,* e *info@hoppo.com, 6/8 Douglas Gardens)* Dorm beds £11.50-14. Housed in a converted church, the Belford is under the same management as Edinburgh Backpackers. Although some people have complained of noise – there are only thin partitions between rooms, and no ceilings – it's well run and cheerful, with good facilities.

Palmerston Lodge (☎/fax 220 5141, ⓦ *www.rooms-in-edinburgh.co.uk, 25 Palmerston Place)* Dorm beds £10-15, private rooms £25-50. Situated in a listed building on the corner of Chester St, this quiet hostel-cum-B&B has no bunks, only single beds, and there are showers and toilets on every floor. The rates include a continental breakfast – there are no kitchen facilities for guests.

University Accommodation

Edinburgh has a large student population and during vacations, universities and colleges offer accommodation in student halls of residence. Most are a fair way from the centre and cost as much as lower-end, more central B&Bs.

Pollock Halls of Residence (☎ 0800 028 7118, fax 667 7271, ⓦ *www.edinburghfirst .com, 18 Holyrood Park Rd)* Singles from £23.90, includes breakfast. This is a modern complex belonging to the University of Edinburgh, with 1200 rooms (500 en suite). It's busy and often noisy, but close to the city centre and with Arthur's Seat as a backdrop.

Napier University (☎ 455 4331, fax 455 4411, ⓦ *www.napier.ac.uk, 219 Colinton Rd)* Flats £300-460 per week. Napier lets out self-catering flats for four to five people year-round. Some have disabled access and all have free car parking.

B&Bs & Guesthouses

The main concentrations of B&Bs and guesthouses are in Tollcross, Bruntsfield, Newington and Pilrig.

New Town The following places are on the northern edge of New Town, only 10 minutes' walk from Princes St.

Marrakech Guest House (☎ 556 4444, fax 557 3615, ⓔ *marr@rapidial.co.uk, 30 London St)* B&B £20-30. The friendly, family-run Marrakech is handy for New Town and for Broughton St nightlife. There's an excellent Moroccan restaurant in the basement (see Places to Eat later in this chapter).

Dene Guest House (☎ 556 2700, fax 557 9876, ⓔ *deneguesthouse@yahoo.com, 7 Eyre Place)* B&B from £19.50. The Dene is a friendly and informal guesthouse, set in a charming Georgian town house.

Tollcross Half a mile south from the western end of Princes St, along Lothian Rd, lies Tollcross.

Amaryllis Guest House (☎/fax 229 3293, ⓔ *ghamaryllis@aol.com, 21 Upper Gilmore Place)* Singles £25-35, doubles £36-60. The gay-friendly Amaryllis has five rooms, all with TV and some with en-suite facilities. There's private parking out front, and Princes St is only 10 to 15 minutes' walk away.

Ballarat Guest House (☎ 229 7024, fax 622 1265, 14 Gilmore Place) B&B from £28. Named after a former gold-mining town in Australia, the Ballarat is a small (five rooms) and friendly family guesthouse with a no-smoking policy.

Bruntsfield Another half a mile south from Tollcross is Bruntsfield.

Aaron Guest House (☎ 229 6459, fax 228 5807, ⓦ *www.aaron-guesthouse.com, 10 Hartington Gardens)* Singles £35-50, doubles £55-85. Located at the end of the street, this comfortable and friendly place is handy for drivers since it has a private car park. It's nonsmoking and caters for vegetarians.

The Greenhouse (☎ 622 7634, ⓔ *green house_edin@hotmail.com, 14 Hartington Gardens)* B&B £25-40. The Greenhouse is a nonsmoking, wholly vegetarian and vegan guesthouse, which uses organic and GM-free foods as much as possible. Even the soap and shampoo are free of animal products.

Menzies Guest House (☎/fax 229 4629, ⓔ *hazim@cableinet.co.uk, 33 Leamington Terrace)* Singles £20-40, doubles £28-60. This is a clean, friendly and well-run place with seven rooms spread over three floors.

Robertson Guest House (☎ 229 2652, fax 220 0130, ⓦ *www.robertson-guesthouse .com, 5 Hartington Gardens)* B&B £23-50. Tucked away in a quiet back street, the Robertson offers a good range of food in the mornings, including yoghurt, fresh fruit and a cooked vegetarian breakfast.

Newington There are lots of guesthouses on and around Minto St and Mayfield Gardens (the continuation of North Bridge and Nicolson St) in Newington. This is the main traffic artery from the south and carries traffic from the A7 and A68 (both routes are signposted). The best places are in the side streets on either side of the main road.

Fairholme Guest House (☎ 667 8645, fax 668 2435, Ⓦ www.fairholme.co.uk, 13 Moston Terrace) Doubles £25-40. A pleasant, quiet Victorian villa with four rooms and free parking, the gay-friendly Fairholme has been recommended by several readers.

Kenvie Guest House (☎ 668 1964, fax 668 1926, Ⓦ www.kenvie.co.uk, 16 Kilmaurs Rd) B&B £20-32. Situated in a quiet side street but close to a main bus route, the Kenvie is bright and welcoming, with TV and coffee in all rooms.

Linden House (☎ 667 9050, Ⓔ linden housegh@aol.com, 13 Mayfield Rd) Singles/doubles £20-35. Readers have recommended the Linden for its well-appointed rooms (with en-suite facilities, TV and coffee-making kit) and friendly, helpful owners.

Salisbury Guest House (☎/fax 667 1264, Ⓔ brenda.wright@btinternet.com, 45 Salisbury Rd) B&B £23-35. This semi-detached Georgian villa has 12 rooms, large gardens, private parking, and is quiet, comfortable and nonsmoking. It closes over Christmas and the New Year.

Sherwood Guest House (☎ 667 1200, fax 667 2344, Ⓔ sherwood@fastfacts.net, 42 Minto St) Singles £40-60, doubles £50-70. One of the better B&B guesthouses on Minto St, the Sherwood is a refurbished Georgian villa with limited off-road parking. It is wholly nonsmoking and has a TV in every room.

Southside Guest House (☎ 668 4422, fax 667 7771, Ⓦ www.southsideguesthouse.co.uk, 8 Newington Rd) Singles £40-50, doubles £70-100. Forget traditional guesthouses – the Southside is deeply trendy and has seven, stylish rooms that just ooze interior design. There's a good cafe too.

Pilrig North-east of New Town and west of Leith Walk, Pilrig St has lots of guesthouses, all within about a mile (1.6km) of the centre. To get here, take bus No 11 from Princes St.

Ardmor House (☎/fax 554 4944, Ⓔ robin@ardmorhouse.freeserve.co.uk, 74 Pilrig St) Singles/doubles from £35/50. The gay-friendly Ardmor is a stylish renovated Victorian house with five bedrooms, all with en-suite facilities.

Balmoral Guest House (☎ 554 1857, fax 553 5712, Ⓔ mpimbert@aol.com, 32 Pilrig St) B&B £20-30. Travellers have written to recommend this comfortable B&B located in an elegant Georgian terrace.

The seven-bedroom *Barrosa Guest House* (☎ 554 3700, 21 Pilrig St), the lovely Victorian *Balquhidder Guest House* (☎ 554 3377, 94 Pilrig St) and the larger *Balfour House* (☎ 554 2106, 92 Pilrig St) have similar room rates to the Balmoral.

Hotels

Old Town Apart from backpacker hostels, there are few inexpensive places to stay in Old Town.

Apex International Hotel (☎ 300 3456, fax 220 5345, Ⓦ www.apexhotels.co.uk, 31-35 Grassmarket) Doubles/twins £120-160. Centrally located and with good business facilities, the modern, 175-room Apex has a rooftop restaurant and off-street parking.

Crowne Plaza (☎ 0800 027 1022, Ⓦ www.crowneplazaed.co.uk, 80 High St) Singles/doubles from £155/180. This luxury hotel was built in the 1990s but blends well with the Royal Mile's 17th-century architecture. The interior is, nonetheless, as modern as you would expect. Check the Web site for cheaper deals on rooms.

Edinburgh (City Centre) Premier Lodge (☎ 0870 700 1370, fax 0870 700 1371, Ⓦ www.premierlodge.com, 94 Grassmarket) Rooms from £49.95. The Premier Lodge is a budget chain hotel with a great Old Town location. Rooms are small but comfy and can sleep up to two adults and two children. Breakfast is not included in the price.

Ibis Hotel (☎ 240 7000, fax 240 7007, Ⓦ www.ibishotel.com, 6 Hunter Square) Rooms £60. The Ibis is a spruce, modern, chain hotel, just off the Royal Mile, and offers a flat room rate that includes a self-service breakfast buffet.

Point Hotel (☎ 221 5555, fax 221 9929, W www.point-hotel.co.uk, 34 Bread St) Singles/doubles from £95. Housed in the beautiful former showrooms of the St Cuthbert Co-operative Association (built 1937), the Point is famous for its striking contemporary interior design.

The Scotsman Hotel (☎ 556 5565, fax 652 3652, W www.thescotsmanhotelgroup .co.uk, 20 North Bridge) Singles/doubles from £150. The former offices of *The Scotsman* – opened in 1904 and hailed as 'the most magnificent newspaper building in the world' – are now home to Edinburgh's newest luxury hotel. The rooms on the northern side enjoy superb views over New Town and Calton Hill.

Tailor's Hall Hotel (☎ 622 6801, fax 622 6818, W www.festival-inns.co.uk, 139 Cowgate) Singles/doubles/triples £85/105/130. The Tailor's Hall, with bright, modern rooms decorated in blue, pink and natural pine, is located bang in the middle of Edinburgh's clubland, and has three big bars of its own downstairs. Good for partying, but not a place for the quiet life.

Travelodge (☎ 557 6281, fax 557 3681, 33 St Mary's St) Rooms £49.95. Yet another centrally located budget hotel, convenient for the Royal Mile and the pubs and clubs of Cowgate, the Travelodge's twin rooms accommodate up to two adults and two kids.

New Town This area is home to the city's most prestigious hotels.

Balmoral Hotel (☎ 556 2414, fax 557 3747, e reservations@thebalmoralhotel .com, 1 Princes St) Singles/doubles from £130/150. The Balmoral offers some of the best accommodation in Edinburgh, including suites with 18th-century decor and superb views of the city. All 188 rooms have two phone lines, a modem point and satellite TV.

Caledonian Hilton Hotel (☎ 459 9988, fax 225 6632, W www.caledonianhotel.co .uk, 4 Princes St) B&B from £125-195. An Edinburgh institution, the century-old 'Cally' is a vast, red-sandstone palace of Edwardian pomp and splendour. It has a spa, swimming pool and gym, and full business and conference facilities.

Carlton Greens Hotel (☎ 556 6570, fax 557 6680, e carltongreens@british-trust-hotels.com, 2 Carlton Terrace) Singles £35-60, doubles £70-90. Set at the leafy, eastern end of Calton Hill, the flower-bedecked Carlton Greens is a quiet, relaxing place with views of Arthur's seat.

Hanover Hotel (☎ 226 7576, fax 226 3260, 40 Rose St) Singles/doubles from £90/130. The 96-room Hanover is a modern, welcoming hotel right in the middle of Edinburgh's shopping district.

Parliament House Hotel (☎ 478 4000, fax 478 4001, e phadams@aol.com, 15 Calton Hill) Singles/doubles from £90/130. Tucked away on a quiet corner of Calton Hill, the cosily traditional Parliament House is only five minutes' walk from Princes St.

rick's (☎ 622 7800, fax 622 7801, W www.ricksedinburgh.co.uk, 55a Frederick St) Rooms £105.75. Describing itself as 'not a hotel', just a restaurant with rooms (10 of them), rick's was voted one of the world's coolest places to stay by *Condé Nast Traveller* magazine. All walnut and designer fabrics – nice...

West End & Haymarket Hotels in this district are convenient for Princes St and Haymarket train station.

Dunstane House Hotel (☎/fax 337 6169, W www.dunstane-hotel-edinburgh.com, 4 West Coates) Singles £35-55, doubles £67-98. Readers have recommended the friendly Dunstane House Hotel, a large villa dating from 1850 with many original features, including beautiful rooms with four-poster beds. Parking is available.

Edinburgh City Travel Inn (☎ 228 9819, fax 228 9836, W www.travelinn.co.uk, 1 Morrison Link) Rooms £49.95. Part of the Travel Inn budget chain, this place is sleek, modern and comfortable, and is only three minutes' walk from Haymarket train station. Rooms take up to two adults and two children, but breakfast is not included.

The Original Raj (☎ 346 1333, fax 337 6688, e originalrajhotel@aol.com, 6 Wes.

Coates) Rooms £35-55 per person. Enjoy some oriental splendour at the Raj – Edinburgh's only Indian-themed hotel. It has 17 colourfully decorated rooms and must be the only hotel in the city where you can get samosas for breakfast.

Leith Several new hotels have been built in Leith in recent years.

Express by Holiday Inn (☎ 555 4422, fax 555 4646, e info@hiex-edinburgh.com, Britannia Way, Ocean Drive) Rooms £59.95. The Express is a big, modern, comfortable hotel with ample free parking, close to Ocean Terminal and the Scottish Executive. Rooms accommodate up to two adults and two children (aged up to 18).

Malmaison Hotel (☎ 468 5000, fax 468 5002, e edinburgh@malmaison.com, 1 Tower Place, Leith) Singles/doubles from £130. This stylish, award-winning hotel, located in a 19th-century Seaman's Mission in Leith, has an attractive waterfront location and an excellent French brasserie.

Travel Inn (☎ 555 1570, fax 554 5994, w www.travelinn.co.uk, 51/53 Newhaven Place) Rooms £40.95. This branch of the Travel Inn budget hotel chain overlooks Newhaven Harbour, about 20 minutes by bus from the city centre. There is lots of parking.

PLACES TO EAT

In the last few years there has been a huge boom in the number of restaurants and cafes in Edinburgh, and there is a wide range of cuisines to choose from. In addition, most pubs serve food, offering either bar meals or a more formal restaurant, or both, but be aware that pubs without a restaurant licence are not allowed to serve those aged under 16. Lunch is generally served from 12.30pm to 2.30pm, dinner from 7pm to 10pm.

The price gradings in this section are based on the average cost of a two-course dinner for one, excluding drinks – budget means less than £10, mid-range means £10 to £20, and top end means over £20. Note that many mid-range and top-end places offer good-value set lunches that would be graded as budget or mid-range respectively. Some of these are listed in the later boxed text 'Lunch for Less'.

Places to Eat – Budget

Old Town & Around There's a good range of inexpensive restaurants in and around Old Town.

Bar Italia (☎ 228 6379, 100 Lothian Rd) Pizzas & pastas £6-7.75. Open noon-midnight Mon-Thur, noon-1am Fri & Sat, 5pm-midnight Sun. A classic Italian restaurant of the old school, Bar Italia comes complete with red-and-white-check tablecloths, candles in Chianti bottles and smartly dressed, wise-cracking waiters who occasionally burst into song. Good-value Italian nosh and a lively atmosphere make it a popular venue for birthdays and office parties.

Café Odile (☎ 225 1333, 23 Cockburn St) Mains £4.95-5.45, set lunch £6.50-7.90. Open 10am-5pm Tues-Sat. This attractive white room, tucked away upstairs at the back of the Stills Gallery, provides a cool escape from the bustle of the Royal Mile. The menu of French home cooking includes mouth-watering soups and savoury tarts, and a chocoholic's paradise of desserts. The set lunch is available from noon to 2.30pm.

Favorit (☎ 220 6880, 19-20 Teviot Place) Sandwiches £3.65-3.95, salads £4.65-4.95. Open 8am-3am daily. A stylish cafe-bar with a slightly retro feel, Favorit caters for everyone: workers grabbing breakfast on the way to the office, coffee-slurping students skiving off afternoon lectures, and late-night clubbers with an attack of the munchies. They also do the best bacon butties in town. There's a second branch *(30 Leven St)* in Tollcross.

Khushi's (☎ 556 8996, 16 Drummond St) Mains £3-5. Open noon-3pm & 5pm-9pm Mon-Thur, noon-3pm & 5pm-9.30pm Fri & Sat. Established in 1947, Khushi's is an authentic Punjabi canteen and something of an Edinburgh institution. Its speciality is basic Indian dishes cooked in the traditional way, served with no frills at very low prices. It's not licensed, but you can bring your own booze (no corkage) or get a jug of beer from the pub next door.

Petit Paris (☎ 226 2442, 38-40 Grassmarket) Mains £4.75-8.95. Open noon-3pm & 5.30pm-11pm year-round except Sun Oct-Easter. Like the name says, this is a little piece of Paris, complete with check tablecloths, friendly waiters and good value grub – the *moules et frites* (mussels and chips) are excellent. There's a lunch and pre-theatre deal of the plat du jour and a coffee for £5, and from Sunday to Thursday you can bring your own wine (£2 corkage per bottle).

New Town & Around This area is a bit short on cheap eats.

Blue Moon Café (☎ 557 0911, 1 Barony St) Starters £1.95-4.95, mains £4-5.95. Open 11am-10pm Mon-Fri, 9.30am-10pm Sat & Sun. The Blue Moon is the focus of Broughton Street's gay social life, always busy, always friendly, and serving up delicious nachos, salads, sandwiches and baked potatoes. It's famous for its brilliant, homemade hamburgers, which come plain or topped with cheese or chilli sauce, and delicious daily specials such as smoked haddock mornay.

Marrakech (☎ 556 4444, 30 London St) Dinner £11. Open 6pm-10pm Mon-Sat. A friendly and homely little Moroccan restaurant, in the basement of the hotel of the same name (see Places to Stay earlier in this chapter), the Marrakech dishes up delicious *tajines* (a slow-cooked casserole of lamb with almonds and dried fruit, usually prunes or apricots) accompanied by homebaked, caraway-scented bread. Round off the meal with a pot of mint tea.

Tampopo (☎ 220 5254, 25a Thistle St) Mains £6.20-7.50. Open noon-2.30pm & 6pm-9pm Tues-Fri, noon-3pm & 6pm-9pm Sat. This tiny, no-frills, one-man-operated Japanese restaurant serves filling noodle dishes for £6.20 to £6.80, and a sushi platter with green tea for £7.50.

Places to Eat – Mid-Range
Old Town & Around There's an amazing variety of restaurants and cafes in Old Town.

The Apartment (☎ 228 6456, 7-13 Barclay Place) Mains £5.25-8.95. Open 5.45pm-11pm Mon-Fri, noon-3pm & 5.45pm-11pm Sat & Sun. Cool, classy and almost always full, the Apartment is just too popular for its own good. Fantastic bistro food and a buzzy, busy atmosphere make it hard to get a table. Book in advance – by at least three weeks, preferably – and don't be surprised if you still have to wait. But it's worth being patient for treats such as marinated lamb meatballs with merguez and basil-wrapped goat's cheese, roasted monkfish marinated in yoghurt with sweet red chilli, new potato and spring onion, or deliciously sweet grilled scallops with a smoked salmon and hazelnut butter.

blue bar cafe (☎ 221 1222, 10 Cambridge St) Mains £11-13.50. Open noon-3pm & 6pm-11pm Mon-Sat. Set above the foyer of the Traverse Theatre, this bright white place is a lighter and less formal version of the Atrium (see Places to Eat – Top End later). The food is simple but perfectly cooked and presented – try rump of lamb with pureed peas and bubble and squeak – and the atmosphere loud and chatty, with all those luvvies from the theatre downstairs.

Buffalo Grill (☎ 667 7427, 12-14 Chapel St) Mains £6.95-12.95. Open noon-2pm & 6pm-10.15pm Mon-Fri, 6pm-10.15pm Sat, 5pm-10pm Sun. The BG is cramped, noisy, fun and always busy, so book ahead. An American-style menu offers burgers, steaks and side orders of fries and onion rings, along with fish and chicken dishes, prawn tempura and the vegetarian Andybut burger. But steaks are the main event – from eight to 16 ounces – cooked perfectly to order. You can have your steak plain or marinated (lemon pepper or teriyaki) and served as it is or with a choice of extras from jalapeno chillies to oysters. You can buy booze in the restaurant, or bring your own wine – £1 corkage per bottle.

Café Hub (☎ 473 2067, Castlehill, Royal Mile) 2-course/3-course lunch £8/10. Open 9.30am-10pm Tues-Sat, 9.30am-6pm Sun & Mon. A Gothic hall beneath the Tolbooth Kirk – now home to the Edinburgh Festival offices – has been transformed with some zingy yellow paint, cobalt blue furniture and lots of imagination into this bright and breezy bistro. Drop in for some cake and cappuccino, or try something more filling – sweetcorn and smoked sausage chowder (£2.85) or a hummus and roast veg sandwich (£3.65) – or linger over the good-value set lunch.

Pancho Villa's (☎ 557 4416, 240 Canongate, Royal Mile) Mains £5.95-8.95. Open noon-2.30pm & 6pm-10pm Mon-Thur, noon-10.30pm Fri & Sat, 6pm-10.30pm Sun. With a Mexican manager and lots of Latin-American staff, it's not surprising that Pancho's is one of the most authentic-feeling Mexican places in town. It's also the city's best-value Mexican, with a set lunch for just £5. The dinner menu includes delicious steak fajitas and great vegetarian spinach enchiladas. It's often busy, so book ahead.

The Point Hotel (☎ 221 5555, 34 Bread St) 2-course lunch £7.90, 3-course dinner £12.90. Open noon-2pm & 6pm-10pm Mon-Wed, noon-2pm & 6pm-10pm Thur & Fri, 6pm-11pm Sat. The Point's now legendary lunch and dinner menus offer exceptional value – delicious Scottish/international cuisine served in an elegant room with crisp, white linen and attentive service. They must make their profit on the drinks, though the house wine costs only £10.95 per bottle. Reservations are strongly recommended.

Songkran (☎ 225 7889, 24a Stafford St) Mains £5.25-8.95. Open noon-2.30pm & 5.30pm-11pm Mon-Sat, 5.30pm-11pm Sun. You'd better book a table and be prepared for a squeeze to get in to this tiny New Town basement. The reason for the crush is some of the best Thai food in Edinburgh – try the tender *yang* (marinated and barbecued beef, chicken or prawn), the crisp and tart orange chicken, or the chilli-loaded warm beef salad. This place serves up the real thing.

Suruchi (☎ 556 6583, 14a Nicolson St) Mains £6.95-12.95. Open noon-2pm & 5.30pm-11.30pm, closed Sun lunch. A laid-back Indian eatery with warm buff walls, hand-made turquoise tiles, lazy ceiling fans and chilled-out jazz guitar, the Suruchi offers a range of exotic dishes as well as the traditional tandoori standards. Try *shakuti* from Goa (lamb or chicken with coconut,

poppy seeds, nutmeg and chilli), or vegetarian *kumbhi narial* (mushrooms, coconut and coriander). An amusing touch is provided by the menu descriptions – they're translated into broad Scots ('a beezer o' a curry this… gey nippie oan the tongue').

The Tower (☎ 225 3003, Museum of Scotland, Chambers St) Starters £4.95-9.95, mains £8.95-18.95, 2-course theatre supper menu £12. Open noon-11pm daily. Chic and sleek, with a keek at the castle oot the windae. Set atop the new museum building, the trendy Tower offers grand views and a menu of quality Scottish food, simply prepared – try half a dozen Loch Fyne oysters followed by an Aberdeen Angus steak.

New Town & Around There's a good selection of restaurants in this area.

Café Marlayne (☎ 226 2230, 76 Thistle St) Starters £1.50-5.90, mains £8.60-11.90. Open noon-2pm & 6pm-10pm Tues-Sat. All weathered-wood and warm yellow walls, little Café Marlayne is a cosy nook offering French farmhouse cooking – *escargots* with garlic and parsley, oysters with lemon and tabasco, *boudin noir* (black pudding) with sautéed apples, peppered duck breast with balsamic vinegar – at very reasonable prices.

Howie's Stockbridge (☎ 225 5553, 4-6 Glanville Place) Lunch £7.50, dinner £14.95. Open noon-2.30pm & 6pm-10pm daily. This branch of Howie's – all chrome, blond wood and feng shui – is a trendier incarnation of their no-nonsense Dalry and Bruntsfield restaurants, designed to pander to the fashionable New Town crowd. But the 'Scottish fusion' food is as good, and as good value, as ever. And who can resist a place with quaffable house wine at £6.10 per bottle?

Modern India (☎ 556 4547, 20 Union Place, Leith Walk) Starters £2.95-6.95, mains £7.95-14.95. Open 11am-2pm & 5pm-midnight Mon-Thur, 5pm-1am Fri & Sat, 4pm-midnight Sun. Stylish and… well, modern, this restaurant marks a radical departure from the standard Scottish curry house. 'Modern Indian' cuisine includes things such as roast monkfish tails with an achari

Lunch for Less

Many restaurants in Edinburgh offer good-value lunches.

The Basement (☎ 557 0097, 10a-12a Broughton St) Food served noon-10.30pm daily. The Basement is a groovy bar with a separate restaurant area. It offers a two-course lunch for only £5.95, available from noon to 3pm Monday to Friday. The grub is sort of international – *bruschetta*, nachos, spaghetti, chicken in orange and ginger sauce – but goes Thai on Wednesday and Mexican at the weekend.

Britannia Spice (☎ 555 2255, 150 Commercial St, Britannia Way) Lunch served noon-2.15pm daily. No, not Geri Halliwell's latest incarnation, but an award-winning curry house with ocean-liner decor, serving a wide range of dishes from northern India, Bangladesh, Nepal, Thailand and Sri Lanka. The waist-widening, all-you-can-eat buffet lunch costs £7.95.

ASA ANDERSSON

Chinese Home Cooking (☎ 668 4946, 34 West Preston St) Lunch served noon-2pm Mon-Fri. You'll be hard pushed to find better value than the good, down-to-earth Chinese food served in this basic, no-nonsense restaurant, where the three-course set lunch costs only £4.50.

La P'tite Folie (☎ 225 7983, 61 Frederick St) Lunch served noon-3pm Mon-Sat. This is a delightful little French place whose menu includes the classics – French onion soup, *moules marinières, Coquilles St Jacques* – and a range of plats du jour. The two-/three-course lunch is a bargain at £5.90/6.90.

The Old Chain Pier (☎ 552 1233, 1 Trinity Crescent) Food served noon-8pm daily. The Old Chain Pier is a lovely little pub overlooking – nay, overhanging – the Firth of Forth on the waterfront near Granton Harbour. The excellent bar menu includes soup of the day for £1.60, a creamy and filling mussel and smoked haddock stew for only £3.95, and a succulent steak and onion baguette with chips for £4.95. The menu of real ales is no less enticing than the food.

Pierre Victoire (☎ 225 1721, 10 Victoria St) Lunch served noon-3pm. The place that launched a thousand cheap-eats, and still one of the best-value restaurants in town, Pierre's three-course set lunch (£4.95) includes a basket of French bread, but potatoes, vegetables and drinks are all extra. A glass of house wine is £2.30, so ask for a jug of water if you're counting the pennies.

marinade, and chicken tikka salsa – a superb Indian-Mexican fusion. Well worth a visit.

Mussel Inn (☎ 225 5979, 61-65 Rose St) Lunch £8.50, dinner £14. Open noon-10pm Mon-Sat, 1.30pm-10pm Sun. Owned by shellfish farmers on the west coast, the Mussel Inn provides a direct outlet for fresh Scottish seafood. The busy restaurant is all bright beech wood, and tables spill out onto the pavement in summer. A kilogram pot of mussels with a choice of sauces – try leek, bacon, white wine and cream – costs £8.95, while a smaller platter of queen scallops costs £5.45.

Nargile (☎ 225 5755, 73 Hanover St) Lunch £7.50, dinner £13.50. Open noon-3pm & 5.30pm-10.30pm Mon-Thur, noon-3pm & 5.30pm-11pm Fri & Sat. Throw away any preconceptions about kebab shops – this Turkish restaurant is a class act. Enjoy a spread of delicious *mezeler* (think Turkish tapas) followed by meltingly sweet, marinaded lamb chargrilled to crispy perfection. Finish off with *baklava* (nut-filled pastry soaked in honey) and a Turkish coffee. If it wasn't for the prices, you could almost be in Turkey.

Rhodes & Co (☎ 220 9190, 3 Rose St) Dinner £16.50. Open noon-3pm & 6pm-10pm Mon-Sat, noon-3pm Sun. Housed in the former Jenners tearooms, Rhodes & Co – set up by the famous TV chef Gary Rhodes, though he doesn't actually cook here – offers solid, top-quality British cuisine with an inventive touch. Traditional roast pork with apple sauce becomes soft knuckle of ham with caramelised apple and cider *jus*, and the fish in the fish and chips is actually monkfish tail, delicately fried in the lightest and crispest of batters.

Stac Polly (☎ 556 2231, 29-33 Dublin St) Lunch £10-13, dinner £20-23. Open noon-2.30pm & 6pm-11pm Mon-Fri, 6pm-11pm Sat & Sun. Named after a mountain in north-western Scotland, Stac Polly's kitchen adds sophisticated twists to fresh Highland produce. Meals such as garden pea and fresh mint soup with garlic cream and parmesan crouton, followed by pan-fried saddle of venison with orange, tarragon and green peppercorn sauce, keep the punters coming back for more. The restaurant's famous baked filo pastry parcels of haggis, served with plum sauce, are so popular they've almost become a national dish. What would Burns think?

Leith Several restaurants have cropped up in north-eastern Edinburgh.

Fishers (☎ 554 5666, 1 The Shore, Leith) Mains £11.50-16.95. Open noon-10.30pm daily. This cosy little bar-turned-restaurant,

tucked beneath a 17th-century signal tower, is one of the city's best seafood places. Fishers' fishcakes (£4.50) are almost an Edinburgh institution, and the rest of the hand-written menu (you might need a calligrapher to decipher it) rarely disappoints. Booking is recommended – if you can't get a table here, try their new branch, *Fishers in the City* (☎ 225 5109, 58 Thistle St).

Daniel's Bistro (☎ 553 5933, 88 Commercial St, Leith) Pasta dishes £5.85-6.25, mains £7.95-10.95, set lunch/dinner from £4.95/11.45. Open 10am-10pm daily. The eponymous Daniel comes from Alsace, and his all-French kitchen staff combine top Scottish and French produce with Gallic know-how to create a wide range of delicious dishes. The fish soup is excellent, and main courses range from seafood crepes to Alpine *raclette* (grilled cheese with baked potatoes). It opens all day, so you can nip in for a snack and a coffee in the afternoon.

The Raj (☎ 553 3980, 91 Henderson St, The Shore, Leith) Mains £6-10. Open noon-2.30pm & 5.30pm-11pm Sun-Thur, noon-2.30pm & 5.30pm-midnight Fri & Sat. Run by celebrity chef Tommy Miah (author of *True Taste of Asia*), the Raj is an atmospheric curry house overlooking the Water of Leith and serving Indian (including Goan) and Bangladeshi cuisine. Specialities include the tongue-tingling green Bengal chicken (marinated with lime juice, mint and chilli) and spicy Goan lamb garam fry. If you want to eat at home or in your hotel room, try their Curry-in-a-Hurry delivery service (freephone ☎ 0800 073 1983) between 5.30pm and 11pm daily.

Places to Eat – Top End
Old Town & Around East of the castle, there's a couple of recommended quality restaurants.

The Atrium (☎ 228 8882, 10 Cambridge St) Set 3-course dinner £38.50. Open noon-2pm & 6.30pm-10pm Mon-Fri, 6.30pm-10pm Sat. Elegantly dressed in wood and white linen, the Atrium is one of Edinburgh's most fashionable restaurants, counting Mick Jagger and Jack Nicholson among its past guests. The cuisine is modern Scottish with a

Mediterranean twist, with the emphasis on the finest of fresh, seasonal produce – fillet of sea bream with mussels and white-bean stew, or pan-fried Gressingham duck with *bok choi*, caramelised pork and a lentil and coriander sauce.

Igg's (☎ 557 8184, 15 Jeffrey St) Starters £5.75, mains £15.75. Open noon-2.30pm & 6pm-10.30pm Mon-Sat. A sumptuous dining room with crisp, white linen and rich, yellow walls make Igg's a good choice for a special night out. The menu is mostly Spanish, with tapas-style starters and interesting main courses such as pan-fried fillet of barracuda on a spicy plum risotto with spinach and red pepper coulis. Lunches are much cheaper, with main courses for around £7.

New Town & Around North of Old Town there are a couple of other top-end eateries.

Caffè D.O.C. (☎ 220 6846, 49a Thistle Street) Mains £12-16. Open 10.30am-3pm & 7pm-10pm Tues-Sat. As the name suggests – D.O.C. stands for *denominazione d'origine controllata*, the Italian equivalent of the French *appellation d'origine contrôlée* – this simple and elegant little restaurant, ideal for a quiet dinner for two, offers a wide range of excellent Italian wines. Wash down sea-bass baked with herbs (£14.80) with a bottle of Vernaccia di San Gimignano (£14).

Café Royal Oyster Bar (☎ 556 4124, 17a West Register St) Mains £14.75-24.70. Open noon-2pm & 7pm-10pm daily. Pass through the revolving doors on the corner of West Register St and you're transported back to Victorian times – a palace of glinting mahogany, polished brass, marble floors, stained glass, Doulton tiles, gilded cornices and table linen so thick that it creaks when you fold it. The Oyster Bar is a place for a very special occasion. The menu is mostly classic seafood, from oysters on ice, to *Coquilles St Jacques Parisienne* or lobster thermidor, augmented by a handful of beef and game dishes.

Leith This area is home to several trendy eateries.

(fitz) Henry (☎ 555 6625, 19 Shore Place, Leith) Starters £4-8, mains £13-16. Open noon-2.30pm & 6.30pm-10.30pm Mon-Fri, 6.30pm-10.30pm Sat. A deeply trendy brasserie tucked away in a warehouse in deepest Leith, (fitz) Henry exudes an atmosphere of wicked decadence. The menu is full-on French, allowing you to choose a politically incorrect, but thoroughly delicious, dinner of foie gras followed by roasted veal. Other delights on the menu include roasted calf's liver, rabbit *en cocotte à la Provençal*, and rare grilled tuna with puy lentil salad and mustard vinaigrette.

Martin Wishart (☎ 553 3557, 54 The Shore, Leith) Starters £6.50-9, mains £13.50-18. Open noon-2pm & 7pm-10pm Tues-Fri, 7pm-10pm Sat. In 2001 this restaurant became the only one in Edinburgh to win a Michelin star. The eponymous chef has worked with Albert Roux, Marco Pierre White and Nick Nairn, and brings a modern-French approach to the best Scottish produce – lobster and truffle ravioli with buttered Savoy cabbage and shellfish cream, fillet of Scottish beef with artichoke and French beans and a red wine and shallot jus. Book as far ahead as possible.

Places to Eat – Vegetarian

Many restaurants, of all descriptions, offer vegetarian options on the menu, some good, some bad, some indifferent. The places listed here are all 100% veggie and all fall into the 'good' category.

Ann Purna (☎ 662 1807, 45 St Patrick's Square) Mains £4.75-7.95. Open noon-2pm & 5.30pm-11pm Mon-Fri, 5.30pm-11pm Sat & Sun. This little gem of an Indian restaurant serves exclusively vegetarian dishes from southern India. If you're new to this kind of food, opt for a *thali* – a self-contained platter that contains about half a dozen different dishes, including a dessert.

Bann UK (☎ 226 1112, 5 Hunter Square) Starters £3.90, mains £9.80. Open 11am-1am Sun-Thur, 11am-3am Fri & Sat. If you want to convince a carnivorous friend that cuisine à la veg can be every bit as tasty and inventive as a meat-muncher's menu, take them to Bann, a darkly stylish restaurant with chunky furniture and burgundy and pale cream walls. Dishes such as Thai potato fritters with coconut and coriander relish, and veggie-haggis and leek sausages with red onion gravy, are guaranteed to win converts. They also do an all-day veggie breakfast for £6.50.

Henderson's (☎ 225 2131, 94 Hanover St) Mains £3.75-4.50, 3-course dinner with coffee £13.50. Open 8am-10.45pm Mon-Sat plus Sun during the Edinburgh Festival. Established in 1963, Henderson's is the grandmother of Edinburgh's vegetarian restaurants. The food is mostly organic and guaranteed GM-free, and special dietary requirements can be catered for. The place still has something of a '70s feel to it (but in a good way), and the daily salads and hot dishes are as popular as ever. Favourite dishes include veggie haggis with neeps and tatties, and the ratatouille of roasted vegetables.

Susie's Diner (☎ 667 8729, 51-53 West Nicolson St) Mains £3-6. Open 9am-8pm Mon, 9am-9pm Tues-Sat. Susie's is a down-to-earth, self-service, vegetarian restaurant with scrubbed wood tables, rickety chairs and a friendly atmosphere. The menu changes daily but includes things such as tofu, aubergine and pepper casserole, stuffed roast tomatoes, and Susie's famous falafel plates – reputedly 'the best falafel in the Western world'.

Cafes

Cafe culture has swept through Edinburgh in the last decade, and it is as easy to get your daily caffeine fix as it is in New York or Paris. Most cafes offer some kind of food, from cakes and sandwiches to full-on meals.

Elephant House (☎ 220 5355, 21 George IV Bridge) Open 8am-11pm daily. Here you'll find counters at the front, tables and views of the castle at the back, and little effigies and images of elephants everywhere. Excellent cappuccino (£1.70) and tasty, home-made food – pizzas, quiches, pies, sandwiches and cakes – at reasonable prices make the Elephant House deservedly popular with local students, shoppers and office workers. Light meals, such as spinach and ricotta pie with salad, cost £3.75.

The Lower Aisle (☎ 225 5147, St Giles Cathedral, High St, Royal Mile) Open 8.30am-4.30pm Mon-Fri, 9am-2pm Sun. Hidden in a vault beneath St Giles Cathedral (entrance on the side opposite the Royal Mile), the Lower Aisle is a good place to escape the crowds, except at lunchtime when it's packed with lawyers and secretaries from the nearby courts.

Made In Italy (☎ 622 7328, 42 Grassmarket) Open 8am-11pm Mon-Thur, 8am-1.30am Fri & Sat, 10am-11pm Sun. Look out for this traditional-style cafe, where you can sit inside at the counters or outside at the pavement tables, and enjoy real Italian coffee (large cappuccino £1.75) and real Italian ice cream. If you're hungry, they do good pizzas and panini sandwiches too.

Ndebele (☎ 221 1141, 57 Home St) Open 10am-10pm daily. This South African cafe is hidden deep in darkest Tollcross, but is worth seeking out for the changing menu of unusual African dishes (including at least one veggie option) – try a boerewors sandwich (sausage made with pork, beef and coriander).

Self-Catering

There are grocery stores and food shops all over the city, many of them open 9am to 10pm daily. Many petrol stations also have shops that sell groceries. *Day & Night* (☎ 221 9059, 141 Lauriston Place), *Alldays* (☎ 667 7481, 91-93 Nicolson St) and *Spar* (☎ 346 4493, 37a-39 Dalry Rd) all open 24 hours.

There are several large supermarkets spread throughout the city too. The most central ones are *Safeway* (☎ 556 1190, St James Centre) and *Tesco* (☎ 456 2400, 94 Nicolson St). *Sainsbury's* (☎ 332 0704, 185 Craigleith Road) has an ATM and stays open until 10pm on Friday and Saturday. The food hall in *Marks & Spencer* (☎ 225 2301, 54 Princes St) sells high-quality ready-cooked meals.

ENTERTAINMENT

Edinburgh has a number of fine theatres and concert halls, and there are independent art-house cinemas as well as mainstream movie theatres. Many pubs offer entertainment ranging from live Scottish folk music to pop, rock and jazz as well as karaoke and

Trad vs Trendy

At one end of Edinburgh's broad spectrum of hostelries lies the traditional 19th-century bar, which has preserved much of its original Victorian decoration and generally serves cask-conditioned real ales and a staggering range of malt whiskies. At the other end is the modern 'style bar', with a cool clientele and styling so sharp you could cut yourself on it. The bar staff here are more likely to be serving schnapps, shooters and absinthe cocktails. Here are some suggestions from each end of the range.

ASA ANDERSSON

Top 5 Traditional Bars

The Athletic Arms (The Diggers) (☎ 337 3822, 1-3 Angle Park Terrace) Named after the cemetery across the street – the grave-diggers used to nip in and slake their thirst after a hard day's interring – the Diggers dates from the 1890s. Its heyday as a real-ale drinker's mecca has passed but it's still staunchly traditional – the decor has barely changed in 100 years – and it's packed to the gills with football and rugby fans on match days.

The Abbotsford (☎ 225 5276, 3 Rose St) One of the few pubs in Rose St that has retained its Edwardian splendour, the Abbotsford has long been a hang-out for writers, actors, journalists and media people, and has many loyal regulars. Dating from 1902, and named after Sir Walter Scott's country house, the pub's centrepiece is a splendid, mahogany island bar.

Bennet's Bar (☎ 229 5143, 8 Leven St) Situated beside the King's Theatre, Bennet's has managed to retain almost all of its beautiful Victorian fittings, from the leaded, stained-glass windows and ornate mirrors to the wooden gantry and the brass water taps on the bar (for your whisky – there are over 100 malts to choose from).

quiz nights, while the new generation of style bars purvey house, dance and hip-hop to the pre-clubbing crowd.

The most comprehensive source of what's-on info is *The List* (£1.95; ⓦ www .list.co.uk), an excellent, fortnightly listings and reviews magazine covering both Edinburgh and Glasgow. It's available from most newsagents.

Bars

Edinburgh has over 700 bars which are as varied as the population... everything from Victorian palaces to rough-and-ready drinking dens, and from bearded, real-ale howffs to trendy cocktail bars.

Royal Mile & Around The pubs on the Royal Mile are – not surprisingly – aimed mainly at the tourist market, but there are some good places hidden up the closes and along the side streets.

The Jolly Judge (☎ 225 2669, 7A James Court) A snug little howff tucked away down a close, the Judge exudes a cosy 17th-century character (low, painted ceilings), and has the added attraction of a cheering fire in cold weather.

Trad vs Trendy

Café Royal Circle Bar (☎ 556 1884, 17 West Register St) Perhaps *the* classic Edinburgh bar, the Café Royal's main claims to fame are its magnificent oval bar and the series of Doulton tile portraits of famous Victorian inventors. Check out the bottles on the gantry – staff line them up to look like there's a mirror there, and many a drink-befuddled customer has been seen squinting and wondering why he can't see his reflection.

The Sheep Heid (☎ 656 6951, 43-45 The Causeway, Duddingston) Possibly the oldest inn in Edinburgh – with a licence dating back to 1360 – the Sheep Heid feels more like a country pub than an Edinburgh bar. Set in the semi-rural shadow of Arthur's Seat, it's famous for its 19th-century skittles alley and the lovely little beer garden.

Top 5 Trendy Bars

Baracoa (☎ 225 5846, 7 Victoria St) This is the place to come for Latin sounds, Cuban cocktails and Havana cigars. There's a two-for-one happy hour from 5pm to 7pm, and salsa classes (£3.50) from 7pm on Tuesday and Thursday.

Iguana (☎ 220 4288, 41 Lothian St) Iguana opened in 1996, making it positively prehistoric for a style bar, but a combination of timeless decor, cool sounds and good value have kept it popular. The crowd consists mostly of students, nurses and medics during the day, and clubbers in the evening.

Oxygen (☎ 557 9997, 3 Infirmary St) Czech beer and Morgans Spiced aren't the only things that come in bottles here. This place is so breathtakingly cool that they serve bottled oxygen to keep you from passing out.

Pivo Caffé (☎ 557 2925, 2-6 Calton Rd) Aiming to add a little taste of Bohemia to Edinburgh's bar scene, Pivo (the Czech word for beer) serves goulash and dumplings, bottled and draught Czech beers, and two-pint cocktails – try a 'long absinthe' (absinthe with lemonade and lime).

Tonic (☎ 225 6431, 34a North Castle St) As cool and classy as a perfectly mixed martini, Tonic prides itself on the authenticity of its cocktails, of which there are many – the menu goes on forever. Check out the Phillipe Starck bar stools – do you sit on them, or use them as ashtrays?

The Malt Shovel (☎ 225 6843, 11-15 Cockburn St) A traditional-looking pub – all dark wood and subdued tartanry – offering a good range of real ales and over 100 malt whiskies, the Malt Shovel is famed for its regular Tuesday night jazz from Swing 2001 (or possibly 2002 by the time you read this).

Royal Mile Tavern (☎ 557 9681, 127 High St) An elegant, traditional bar lined with polished wood, mirrors and brass, the Royal Mile serves real ale, good wines and fine food – *moules marinières* and crusty bread is a lunchtime speciality.

The World's End (☎ 556 3628, 4 High St) So named because this part of High St once lay next to Old Town's limit – part of the 16th-century Flodden Wall can still be seen in the basement – the World's End is an old local pub, with plenty of regulars as well as tourists. They do good bar food, including excellent fish and chips.

Grassmarket & Around The pubs of Grassmarket have outdoor tables on sunny summer afternoons, but in the evenings are favoured by boozed-up lads on the pull, so steer clear if that's not your thing.

Cowgate – Grassmarket's extension to the east – is Edinburgh's clubland.

The Three-Quarter (☎ 622 1622, 4 Grassmarket) Sited in a converted church, the Three-Quarter is a vast and lively sports bar and cafe where the faithful can worship at the altar of the large-screen satellite TVs. Altogether now, *In nomine* rugby, *et* footie, *et* spirituous liquors...

The Last Drop (☎ 225 4851, 74 Grassmarket) The name commemorates the gallows that used to stand nearby, but the Last Drop is now a swinging party pub, popular with students and backpackers.

Bow Bar (☎ 226 7667, 80 West Bow) A busy, traditional pub serving a range of excellent real ales and a vast selection of malt whiskies, it's often standing room only at the Bow Bar on Friday and Saturday evenings.

The Three Sisters (☎ 622 6800, 39 Cowgate) This huge pub is actually three bars – one American, one Irish and one Gothic – with a big cobbled courtyard for outdoor drinking in summer. It's a bit of a mad party place but you can come back the morning after and soothe your hangover with a big, fried breakfast – and a free Bloody Mary if you order before 11am.

Bannerman's Bar (☎ 556 3254, 212 Cowgate) A long-established favourite, Bannerman's straggles through a warren of old vaults, and pulls in crowds of students, locals and backpackers. The beer is good but their weekend breakfasts are best avoided.

Pear Tree House (☎ 667 7533, 38 West Nicolson St) The Pear Tree is another student favourite, with comfy sofas and board games inside, plus the biggest beer garden in the city centre. There's live music in the garden on Sunday afternoons in summer.

Rose St & Around Rose St was once a famous pub crawl, where generations of students, sailors and rugby fans would try to visit every pub on the street (around 17 of them) and down a pint of beer in each one.

The Kenilworth (☎ 226 4385, 152-154 Rose St) A gorgeous, Edwardian drinking palace, complete with original fittings –

from the tile floors, mahogany circle bar and gantry, to the ornate mirrors and gas lamps – the Kenilworth was Edinburgh's original gay bar back in the 1970s. Today, it attracts a mixed crowd of all ages, and serves a good range of real ales and malt whiskies.

Robertsons 37 Bar (☎ 225 6185, 37 Rose St) No 37 is to malt whisky connoisseurs what the Diggers once was to real-ale fans. Its long gantry sports a choice of more than 100 single malts and the bar provides a quiet and elegant environment in which to sample them.

Guildford Arms (☎ 556 4312, 1 West Register St) Located next door to the Café Royal (see the earlier boxed text 'Trad vs Trendy'), the Guildford is another classic Victorian pub full of polished mahogany, brass and ornate cornices.

New Town & Broughton St This is an area that's packed full of busy pubs and bars.

The Cumberland Bar (☎ 558 3134, 1-3 Cumberland St) Under the same management as the Bow Bar in Victoria St, the Cumberland pays the same attention to serving well-looked-after, cask-conditioned ales. Though relatively new, the bar has an authentic, traditional wood-brass-and-mirrors look, and there's a nice little beer garden outside.

Kay's Bar (☎ 225 1858, 39 Jamaica St) Housed in a former wine-merchant's office, tiny Kay's Bar is a cosy haven with a coal fire and a fine range of real ales. Good food is served in the back room at lunchtime, but you'll have to book a table – Kay's is a popular spot.

Mathers (☎ 556 6754, 25 Broughton St) Mathers is the forty-something generation's equivalent of the twenty-something's **The Basement** across the street – a friendly, relaxed pub with Edwardian decor serving real ales and good pub grub (see the earlier boxed text 'Lunch for Less').

The Standing Order (☎ 225 4460, 62-66 George St) One of several converted banks on George St, the Standing Order is a cavernous beer hall with a fantastic vaulted ceiling, and some cosy rooms off to the right –

look for the one with the original 27-tonne safe. Despite its size, it can be standing-room only at weekends.

Bruntsfield *Golf Tavern (☎ 229 5040, 30 Wright's Houses)* Overlooking the pitch-and-putt course on Bruntsfield Links and housed in a 19th-century building, though there have been licenced premises on this spot since the 15th century, this is an attractive place with luxurious leather sofas, and pulls in a young, studenty crowd at weekends.

Leith & Granton *Port o'Leith (☎ 554 3568, 58 Constitution St)* This is a good, old-fashioned, friendly local boozer. The Port is swathed with flags and cap bands left behind by visiting sailors – the harbour is just down the road. Pop in for a pint and you'll probably stay till closing time.

The Starbank Inn (☎ 552 4141, 64 Laverockbank Rd) Along with the Old Chain Pier (see the earlier boxed text 'Lunch for Less'), the Starbank is an oasis of fine ales and good, home-made food on Edinburgh's windswept waterfront. In summer there's a sunny conservatory, and in winter a blazing fire to toast your toes in front of.

Clubs
Edinburgh's club scene has got some fine DJ talent and is well worth exploring. Most of the venues are concentrated in and around the twin sumps of Cowgate and Calton Rd – so it's downhill all the way...

La Belle Angele (☎ 225 7536, 11 Hastie's Close, Cowgate) Home to Manga, Edinburgh's unmissable drum 'n' bass club, and jazz-funk session Big Beat (held on Friday monthly), the Belle also has a great house and garage night in Ultragroove (held on Saturday monthly).

The Bongo Club (☎ 558 7604, 14 New St) Famous for the hip-hop clubs El Segundo and Headspin, at the time of writing the word was that the Bongo may have to move out of its New St premises. Check the location in *The List*.

Ego (☎ 478 7434, 14 Picardy Place) A glitzy two-floor venue in a former casino, Ego dishes up everything from the wild

electronic jazz of Keep It Unreal to the glammy cheese-fest of Disco Inferno.

Gaia (☎ 229 9438, 28 Kings Stables Rd) Gaia pulls in a pissed-up, studenty, dance-till-you-puke crowd, gamely thrashing away to a soundtrack of pop, funk, disco and house while trying not to barf up the gallon of cheap promo drinks they just downed. Grand fun.

Club Mercado (☎ 226 4224, 36-39 Market St) At Club Mercado's house night Eye Candy (held on Saturday fortnightly), the dress code is 'dress glam, or scram', while the Time Tunnel (held every Friday) carries jaded office workers back to the '60s, '70s and '80s.

Studio 24 (☎ 558 3758, 24 Calton Rd) The programme at Studio 24 covers all bases, from house to goth to nu metal. The big night for serious clubbers, though, is the hard-house club Oxygen (held on Saturday fortnightly).

The Venue (☎ 557 3073, 17-23 Calton Rd) Spread over three floors, and hosting live gigs as well as clubs, the Venue is one of Edinburgh's top nightspots. Try Cerotonin (held on Friday monthly) for techno and trance, Scratch (held on Saturday monthly) for hip-hop, or Rhombus (held on Saturday monthly) for jazz, funk, reggae and soul.

Gay & Lesbian
Edinburgh has a small – but perfectly formed – gay and lesbian scene, centred on the area around Broughton St (known affectionately as 'The Pink Triangle') at the eastern end of New Town.

Blue Moon Cafe (☎ 556 2788, 1 Barony St) Open 11am-11.30pm Mon-Fri, 9am-12.30am Sat & Sun. Set in the heart of the Pink Triangle, the Blue Moon is a friendly caff offering good food and good company.

CC Blooms (☎ 556 9331, 23 Greenside Place, Leith Walk) Open 6pm-3am Mon-Sat, 8pm-3am Sun. The raddled old queen of the Edinburgh gay scene, CC's offers two floors of deafening dance and disco. It's a bit overpriced and overcrowded but worth a visit – if you can get past the bouncers and the crowds of drunks looking for a late drink.

Planet Out (☎ 524 0061, 6 Baxter's Place, Leith Walk) Open 4pm-1am Mon-Fri, 2pm-1am Sat & Sun. Planet Out pulls in a younger crowd than CC's, and has a better party atmosphere at weekends – it's a bit quieter during the week, when you can chill out on the sofas and chat.

Claremont Bar (☎ 556 5662, 133-135 East Claremont St) Open 11am-1am Mon-Sat, 12.30pm-1am Sun. Scotland's only sci-fi theme pub (no, you have to see it), the Claremont is a friendly, gay-owned bar and restaurant. The first and third Saturdays of the month are men-only nights, when leather, rubber, skinheads and bears are the order of the evening. If that's not your bag, Monday nights see the weekly meeting of the Edinburgh Doctor Who Appreciation Society (honest!).

The Townhouse Sauna & Gym (☎ 556 6116, W www.townhouse-sauna.co.uk, 53 East Claremont St) Admission £6-9. Open noon-11pm Sun-Thur, noon-midnight Fri & Sat. Gay-owned and operated, the Townhouse is Scotland's biggest gay sauna, spread over four floors of a Georgian town house. Facilities include two sauna cabins, steam room, Jacuzzi, gym, video lounge and bar.

Rock, Jazz & Folk Music

Check out *The List* and the *The Gig Guide* (a free leaflet available in bars and music venues) to see who's playing where.

Henry's Jazz Bar (☎ 538 7385, 8a Morrison St) Edinburgh's hottest jazz joint, Henry's has something going on every night, from traditional and contemporary jazz to soul, funk, hip-hop and drum 'n' bass.

Henderson's vegetarian restaurant (see Places to Eat earlier) has live music, mainly jazz and classical guitar, at 7.30pm most evenings.

The Liquid Room (☎ 225 2564, 9c Victoria St) Tickets £9-15. One of the city's top live-music venues, boasting a superb sound system, the Liquid Room stages all kinds of music from local bands to the Average White Band. Check the programme at W www.liquidroom.com.

Timberbush (☎ 476 8080, 28 Bernard St, Leith) Admission free. A cool cafe-bar that serves good food, Timberbush also stages live rock and cover bands from 9pm on Friday night, live bands or DJs Wednesday, Thursday and Saturday, and jazz on Sundays.

Whistle Binkie's (☎ 557 5114, 4-6 South Bridge) Open 7pm-3am daily. This crowded cellar bar, just off the Royal Mile, has live music every night, from rock, blues and folk. Open mic night, from 10pm on Monday, showcases new talent – check W www .whistlebinkies.com for what's on.

The capital is a great place to hear traditional Scottish (and Irish) folk music, with a mix of regular spots and impromptu sessions.

Pleasance Cabaret Bar (☎ 650 2349, 60 The Pleasance) Admission £6. The Pleasance is home to the Edinburgh Folk Club, which runs a programme of visiting bands and singers at 8pm on Wednesday.

The Royal Oak (☎ 557 2976, 1 Infirmary St) Admission free Mon-Sat, £3 Sun. The popular 'Wee Folk Club' in the downstairs lounge, with a tiny bar and room for only 30 punters, is ticket only, so get there early (9pm start) if you want to be sure of a place. Saturday night is an open-session night – bring your own instruments (or a good singing voice).

Sandy Bell's (☎ 225 2751, 25 Forrest Rd) Admission free. This unassuming bar has been a stalwart of the traditional music scene since the Corrs were in nappies. There's music almost every evening at 9pm, and also from 2.30pm on Sunday afternoon.

Cinema

Film buffs will find plenty to keep them happy in Edinburgh's art-house cinemas, while popcorn munchers can choose from a range of multiplexes.

The Cameo (box office ☎ 228 4141, information ☎ 228 2800, 38 Home St) Admission £2.50-5.20. The three-screen, independently owned Cameo is a good, old-fashioned cinema showing an imaginative mix of mainstream and art-house movies. There's a good programme of midnight movies, late-night double bills and Sunday matinees, and the seats in Screen 1 are big enough to get lost in.

The Filmhouse (☎ 228 2688, 88 Lothian Rd) Admission £2.20-5.20. The Filmhouse is the main venue for the annual International Film Festival and screens a full programme of art-house, classic, foreign, and second-run films, with lots of themes, retrospectives and 70mm screenings. It has wheelchair access to all screens.

UGC Fountainpark (information & credit-card booking ☎ 0870 902 0417, Fountainpark Complex, Dundee St) Admission £3.50-5.50. The UGC is a massive 12-screen multiplex complete with cafe-bar, movie-poster shop and scarily overpriced popcorn.

Classical Music, Opera & Ballet
The following are the main venues for classical music.

Edinburgh Festival Theatre (☎ 529 6000, 13-29 Nicolson St) Tickets £6-46. The modern Festival Theatre is the city's main venue for opera, dance and ballet, but also stages musicals, concerts, drama and children's shows.

St Giles Cathedral (☎ 225 9442, High St, Royal Mile) Tickets free-£6. The big kirk on the Royal Mile hosts a regular and varied programme of classical music, including popular lunch-time and evening concerts and organ recitals. The cathedral choir sings at the 10am and 11.30am Sunday services.

Usher Hall (☎ 228 1155, Lothian Rd) Tickets £5.50-19. Box office open 10am-5pm Mon-Sat, until 8.15pm on day of performance. The architecturally impressive Usher Hall hosts concerts by the RSNO and performances of popular music.

Theatre, Musicals & Comedy
Royal Lyceum Theatre (☎ 248 4848, 30b Grindlay St) Tickets £7-17.50. Box office open 10am-8pm Mon-Sat (until 6pm on nonperformance days). A grand Victorian theatre located beside the Usher Hall, the Lyceum stages drama, concerts, musicals and ballet.

Traverse Theatre (☎ 228 1404, 10 Cambridge St) Tickets £4-10. Box office open 10am-6pm Mon, 10am-8pm Tues-Sat, 4pm-8pm Sun. The Traverse is the main focus for new Scottish writing and stages an adventurous programme of contemporary drama and dance. The cafe-bar here is a hip place to hang out.

King's Theatre (☎ 220 4349, 2 Leven St, Bruntsfield) Tickets £7-16.50. The King's is a traditional theatre with a programme of musicals, drama, comedy and its famous annual Christmas pantomime.

Edinburgh Playhouse (☎ 557 2692, bookings ☎ 0870 606 3424, 18-22 Greenside Place) This restored theatre at the top of Leith Walk stages broadway musicals, dance shows, opera and popular-music concerts.

The Stand Comedy Club (☎ 558 7272, 5 York Place) Tickets £1-7. The Stand, founded in 1995, is Edinburgh's main comedy venue. It's a cabaret bar with performances every night and a free Sunday lunch-time show.

Scottish Evenings
Several places offer an evening of traditional Scottish music and dancing.

Carlton Hotel (☎ 472 3000, North Bridge) The Carlton offers a *Hail Caledonia* Scottish evening for £39.50 per person, which includes a five-course dinner, entertainment and a nip of whisky. The action kicks off at 7pm daily from May to September, and ends around 10.30pm, depending on how much the audience gets into the swing of things.

SPECTATOR SPORTS
Edinburgh has two rival football teams playing in the Scottish Premier League. Heart of Midlothian (aka Hearts) and Hibernian (aka Hibs). The domestic football season lasts from August to May, and most matches are played at 3pm on Saturday or 7.30pm on Tuesday or Wednesday.

Tynecastle Stadium (☎ 200 7200, W www.heartsfc.co.uk, Gorgie Rd) Hearts – winners of the Scottish Cup in 1998 – have their home ground south-west of the centre in Gorgie.

Easter Road Stadium (☎ 661 2159, W www.hibs.co.uk, 12 Albion Place) Hibernian's home ground is north-east of the centre. Hibs – who have not won the Scottish

Cup since 1902 – came close in 2001, making it to the final only to lose 3-0 to Glasgow Celtic.

Each year, from January to March, Scotland's national rugby team takes part in the Six Nations Rugby Union Championship. The most important fixture is the clash against England for the Calcutta Cup. At club level, the season runs from September to May.

Murrayfield Stadium (☎ 346 5000, W *www.sru.org.uk, 112 Roseburn St)* About 1½ miles (2.5km) west of the centre, this is the venue for international rugby matches.

Most other spectator sports, including athletics and cycling, are hosted at *Meadowbank Sports Centre* (☎ 661 5351, 139 London Rd)*, Scotland's main sports arena, east of the centre.

Horse-racing enthusiasts should head 6 miles (10km) east to *Musselburgh Racecourse* (☎ 665 2859, W *www.musselburgh -racecourse.co.uk, Linkfield Rd, Musselburgh)*, Scotland's oldest racecourse (founded 1816), where meetings are held throughout the year.

SHOPPING

Princes St is Edinburgh's principal shopping street, lined with all the big high-street stores, with many smaller shops along pedestrianised Rose St. There are also two big shopping centres – Princes Mall, at the eastern end of Princes St, and the nearby St James Centre at the top of Leith St.

A new shopping complex, with a flagship *Harvey Nichols* store, is due to open on the eastern side of St Andrew Square in autumn 2002, and the new *Ocean Terminal* in Leith is the biggest shopping centre in Edinburgh.

For more off-beat shopping – including fashion, music, crafts, gifts and jewellery – head for the cobbled lanes of Cockburn, Victoria and St Mary's Sts, all near the Royal Mile in Old Town, or the urban 'villages' of Stockbridge and Morningside.

Cashmere & Wool Woollen textiles and knitwear are one of Scotland's classic exports. Scottish cashmere – a fine, soft wool from young goats and lambs – provides the most luxurious and expensive knitwear and has been seen gracing the torsos of pop-star Robbie Williams and England footballer David Beckham.

Designs On Cashmere (☎ 556 6394, 28 High St, Royal Mile)* and *The Cashmere Store* (☎ 225 5178, 2 St Giles St, Royal Mile)* are good places to start, with a wide range of traditional and modern knitwear, while the colourful designs at *Joyce Forsyth Designer Knitwear* (☎ 220 4112, 42 Candlemaker Row)* will drag your ideas about woollens firmly into the 21st century.

Edinburgh Woollen Mill (☎ 226 3840, 139 Princes St)* is an old stalwart of the tourist trade, with a good selection of traditional jerseys, cardigans, scarves, shawls and rugs.

Crafts & Souvenirs During the Festival period, there's a good *Crafts Fair* in the churchyard at St John's Church, on the corner of Princes St and Lothian Rd, with a wide range of jewellery, ceramics and leather goods.

The Meadows Pottery (☎ 662 4064, 11a Summerhall Place)* sells colourful stoneware, all hand-thrown on the premises. *The Adam Pottery* (☎ 557 3978, 76 Henderson Row)*, also produces its own ceramics, mostly decorative, or in a wider range of styles.

Flux (☎ 554 4075, 55 Bernard St, Leith)* is an outlet for contemporary Scottish arts and crafts, including stained glass, metalware, jewellery and ceramics.

The Edinburgh History Shop (☎ 477 3522, 24 St Mary's St)* has a range of unusual and high-quality gifts, from old maps and history books to traditional horn spoons and casts of the stone carvings in Rosslyn Chapel.

Department Stores Founded in 1838 *Jenners* (☎ 225 2442, 48 Princes St)* is the *grande dame* of Scottish department stores. It stocks a wide range of quality goods, both classic and contemporary. *John Lewis* (☎ 556 9121, St James Centre)* is the place to go for good-value clothes and household goods.

Aitken & Niven (☎ 225 1461, 77-79 George St)*, founded in 1905, is another independent Scottish store, with a good range of quality tartans and tweeds, and a wide selection of rugby shirts and accessories.

The city-centre branch of *Marks & Spencer (☎ 225 2301, 54 Princes St)* has an excellent food hall.

Outdoor Equipment There's a couple of good places specialising in outdoor gear.

Tiso (☎ 225 9486, 123-125 Rose St) has four floors of equipment, including camping, hiking, climbing, canoeing, skiing and snowboarding gear. At their macho branch, *Tiso Outdoor Experience (☎ 554 0804, 41 Commercial St)* in Leith, you can try before you buy with their Goretex test shower, boot-bashing footpath, rock-climbing wall, ice-climbing wall and stove-testing area.

Tartan & Highland Dress There are dozens of shops along the Royal Mile and Princes St where you can buy kilts and tartan goods. One of the best is *Kinloch Anderson (☎ 555 1390, 4 Dock St, Leith)*, founded in 1868 and still family-run; they are a supplier of kilts and Highland dress to the royal family.

Geoffrey (Tailor) Inc (☎ 557 0256, 57-59 High St, Royal Mile) can fit you out in traditional Highland dress, or run up a kilt in your own clan tartan. Their offshoot, 21st Century Kilts, offers modern fashion kilts in a variety of fabrics.

GETTING THERE & AWAY
Air
Edinburgh airport (☎ 333 1000), 8 miles (13km) west of the city, has numerous services to other parts of the UK, Ireland and Europe. British Airways (BA; ☎ 0845 773 3377), British Midland (☎ 0870 607 0555) and KLM uk (☎ 0870 507 4074) are the main operators.

Bus
At the time of writing, buses and coaches arrive and depart from various temporary bus stops on St Andrew Square and Waterloo Place; a new bus station on the eastern side of the square is due to open in late 2002. The Scottish Citylink ticket office is in the ESIC, on top of Princes Mall at the eastern end of Princes St.

Standard return fares and journey times to Edinburgh include:

destination	return fare	best time (hrs)
Aberdeen	£25	3¼
Dundee	£13	1¾
Fort William	£28	4
Inverness	£24	4
Glasgow	£5	1¼
Stirling	£10.50	1¼

Train
The main terminus in Edinburgh is Waverley train station, located in the heart of the city. Trains arriving at, and departing from, the west also stop at Haymarket station, which is more convenient for the West End. The Edinburgh Rail Travel Centre in Waverley station opens 8am to 11pm Monday to Saturday and 9am to 8pm Sunday. For fare and timetable enquires, phone the National Rail Enquiry Service (☎ 0845 748 4950) or check the timetable on the Railtrack Web site at W www.railtrack.co.uk.

ScotRail operates a regular shuttle service (departures every 15 minutes) between Edinburgh and Glasgow (£7.50 cheap day return, 50 minutes), and frequent daily services to all Scottish cities, including Aberdeen (£44.90 standard return, 2½ hours), Dundee (£17.40, 1½ hours) and Inverness (£37.10, 3¼ hours).

Great North Eastern Railway (always referred to as GNER) operates a fast and frequent rail service between London (four hours) and Edinburgh, with around 20 departures daily between 7am and 7pm. A standard return costs around £85, but special offers sometimes offer fares as low as £39.

Car & Motorcycle
Arriving in or leaving Edinburgh by car during the morning and evening rush hours (7.30am to 9.30am and 4.30pm to 6.30pm Monday to Friday) is an experience you can live without. Try to time your journey to avoid these periods.

GETTING AROUND
To/From the Airport

The Lothian Buses Airlink service runs from Waverley Bridge, just outside the train station, to Haymarket and the airport (£3.30/5 one way/return; 30 minutes). Buses run between 4.50am and 12.20am, with departures every 10 minutes from 7am to 9.30pm. The Airsaver ticket (£4.20/2.50 for adults/children) can be purchased on the bus and gives a one-way trip on the Airlink bus plus unlimited travel for one day on all Lothian Bus services in the city.

An airport taxi to the city centre costs around £13 and takes about 20 minutes. Both buses and taxis depart from just outside the arrivals hall at stand Nos 17 and 18.

Bus

Bus timetables, route maps and fare guides are posted at all main bus stops, and you can pick up the free *Edinburgh Travelmap*, showing all the city's bus routes, from the Traveline office (☎ 225 3858, 0800 232323), 2 Cockburn St, which has information on all of Edinburgh's public transport. It opens 8.30am to 5pm Monday to Friday.

Adult fares range from 50p to £1; children aged under five travel free and those aged five to 15 pay a flat fare of 50p. On Lothian Buses you must pay the driver the exact fare, but First Edinburgh buses will give change. Lothian Bus drivers also sell a Daysaver ticket (adult/child £2.20/1.50) that gives unlimited travel on Lothian buses for a day. Night-service buses, which run hourly between midnight and 5am, charge a flat fare of £1.60.

Information on timetables and fares is also available online at W www.lothianbuses.co.uk and W www.firstedinburgh.co.uk.

Car & Motorcycle

Though useful for day trips beyond the city, a car in central Edinburgh is more of a liability than a convenience. There is restricted access on Princes St, George St and Charlotte Square, many streets are one-way and finding a parking place in the city centre is like striking gold. Queen's Drive around Holyrood Park is closed to motorised traffic on Sunday.

Parking There's no parking on main roads into the city from 7.30am to 6.30pm Monday to Saturday. On-street parking in the city centre is controlled by parking meters and self-service ticket machines from 8.30am to 6.30pm Monday to Friday and 8.30am to 1.30pm Saturday, and costs £1 per hour, with a two-hour maximum. If you break the rules, you'll get a parking ticket – the fine is £40, reduced to £20 if you pay up within 14 days. Cars parked illegally will be towed away. There are large, long-stay car parks at the St James Centre, Greenside Place, New St, Castle Terrace and Morrison St. Motorcycles can be parked for free at designated areas in the city centre.

Car Rental All the big, international car rental agencies have offices in Edinburgh (see Car in the Getting Around chapter).

There are many smaller, local agencies that offer better rates. One of the best is Arnold Clark (☎ 228 4747) at 1–13 Lochrin Place in Tollcross, which charges from £18 per day/£90 per week for a Fiat Seicento, including VAT and insurance. The daily rate includes 250 miles (400km) per day; excess is charged at 4p per mile. For periods of four days and more, mileage is unlimited.

Taxi

Edinburgh's taxis can be hailed in the street, ordered by phone, or picked up at one of the many central ranks. Taxis are fairly expensive – the minimum charge is £1.20 for the first 340 yards (311m), then 20p for every subsequent 240 yards (220m) – a 2-mile (3km) trip will cost around £4. The main local companies are Capital Taxis (☎ 228 2555), Central Radio Taxis (☎ 229 2468), City Cabs (☎ 228 1211) and Radiocabs (☎ 225 9000).

Bicycle

Although there are plenty of steep hills to negotiate, Edinburgh is an ideal place for cycling – nothing is more than half an hour away and outside the centre the traffic is fairly tolerable. See also Activities earlier in this chapter.

Biketrax (☎ 228 6633), at 11 Lochrin Place, rents out a wide range of cycles and equipment, including kids' bikes, tandems, recumbents, pannier bags, child seats – even unicycles! A mountain bike costs £15 for one day (24 hours), £10 for extra days, and £60 for one week, £40 for extra weeks. You'll need a £100 cash or credit-card deposit and some form of ID. It opens 9.30am-6pm Mon-Fri, 9.30am-5.30pm Sat, noon-5pm Sun.

Edinburgh Cycle Hire & Scottish Cycle Safaris (☎/fax 556 5560), at 29 Blackfriars St, is a friendly and helpful agency that rents top-quality bikes for £10 to £15 per day, £50 to £70 per week, including helmet, lock and repair kit; there are occasionally older bikes available for £5 per day. You can hire tents and touring equipment too. They also organise cycle tours in Edinburgh and all over Scotland.

The Lothians

Edinburgh is small enough that, when you need a break from the city, the beautiful surrounding countryside isn't far away and is easily accessible by public transport. The old counties around Edinburgh are called Midlothian, West Lothian and East Lothian, and are often referred to simply as 'the Lothians'.

MIDLOTHIAN
South Queensferry

South Queensferry lies on the southern bank of the Firth of Forth, 8 miles (13km) west of Edinburgh city centre. Located at the narrowest part of the firth, ferries plied across the water to Fife from the earliest times, ceasing only in 1964 when the graceful Forth Road Bridge – now the fifth longest in Europe – was opened.

Predating the Forth Road Bridge by 74 years, the magnificent **Forth Bridge** – only outsiders ever call it the Forth Rail Bridge – is one of the finest engineering achievements of the 19th century. Completed in 1890 after seven years' work, its three huge cantilevers span 1447m and took 59,000 tonnes of steel, 8 million rivets and the lives of 58 men.

In the pretty, terraced High St in South Queensferry is the small **Queensferry**

Museum (☎ 331 5545, 53 High St, South Queensferry; admission free; open 10am-1pm & 2.15pm-5pm Mon & Thur-Sat, noon-5pm Sun). It contains some interesting background information on the bridges, and a model of the 'Burry Man', part of the summer gala festivities. On the first Friday of August, some hapless local male spends nine hours roaming the streets covered from head to toe in burrs and clutching two floral staves in memory of a medieval tradition.

Places to Eat & Drink There are several good pubs along High St. The **Hawes Inn** (☎ 331 1990, Newhalls Rd, South Queensferry), famously mentioned in Robert Louis Stevenson's novel Kidnapped, serves food from noon to 10pm daily; it's opposite the Inchcolm ferry, right beside the railway bridge.

Getting There & Away To get to South Queensferry, take First bus No 88 (25 minutes) westbound from Princes St (eastern end) or Charlotte Square; there's a bus every 20 minutes. It's a 10-minute walk east from the bus stop to the Hawes Inn and the Inchcolm ferry.

There are also frequent trains (15 minutes) from Edinburgh Waverley and Haymarket stations to Dalmeny station. From the station exit, the Hawes Inn is only a five-minute walk along a footpath (across the road, behind the bus stop) that leads north beside the railway and under the bridge.

Inchcolm
The island of Inchcolm lies east of the Forth bridges, less than a mile off the coast of Fife. Only 800m long, it is home to the ruins of **Inchcolm Abbey** (HS; ☎ 01383-823332, Inchcolm, Fife; adult/child £2.80/1; open 9.30am-6.30pm daily Apr-Sept). Inchcolm is one of Scotland's best-preserved medieval abbeys, founded by Augustinian priors in 1123.

The ferry boat Maid of the Forth (☎ 331 4857) sails from Hawes Pier in South Queensferry to Inchcolm. There are daily sailings from mid-July to early September, and at weekends only from April to June and October. The return fare is £9.75/4 for adults/children, including admission to Inchcolm Abbey. It's a half-hour sail to Inchcolm and you're allowed 1½ hours ashore. As well as the abbey, the trip gives you the chance to see the island's grey seals, puffins and other seabirds.

Hopetoun House

Two miles (3km) west of South Queensferry lies one of Scotland's finest stately homes, Hopetoun House *(☎ 331 2451; adult/child £5.30/2.70; open 10am-5.30pm daily Apr-Sept, 10am-5.30pm Sat & Sun Oct)*. It has a superb location in lovely grounds beside the Firth of Forth. There are two parts, the older built to Sir William Bruce's plans between 1699 and 1702 and dominated by a splendid stairwell, the newer designed between 1720 and 1750 by three members of the Adam family, William and sons Robert and John. The rooms have splendid furnishings and staff are on hand to make sure you don't miss details such as the revolving oyster stand for two people to share.

Hopetoun House can be approached along the coast road from South Queensferry, or, from Edinburgh, turn off the A90 onto the A904 just before the Forth Bridge and follow the signs.

Scottish Mining Museum

About 9 miles (14.5km) south-east of Edinburgh city centre is the impressive Scottish Mining Museum *(☎ 663 7519, Lady Victoria Colliery, Newtongrange; adult/child £4/2.20; open 10am-5pm daily)*. Exhibits explain the story of coal and the history of coal mining in Scotland, including the harsh life of a 19th-century mining family, before you visit the pithead, a noisy re-creation of a working coalface, and the massive winding engine. Former coal miners act as guides.

First Edinburgh bus Nos 80, 80A, 86 and 89 run from Princes St, Edinburgh, to Newtongrange.

Rosslyn Chapel

On the eastern edge of the village of Roslin, 7 miles (11km) south of Edinburgh city centre, is one of Scotland's most beautiful and enigmatic churches – **Rosslyn Chapel** *(Collegiate Church of St Matthew; ☎ 440 2159, W www.rosslyn-chapel.com, Roslin, Midlothian; admission £4; open 10am-5pm daily Mar-Oct, 10am-4.30pm daily Nov-Mar)*. Built in the mid-15th century for William St Clair, third earl of Orkney, the chapel does not conform to the architectural fashion of its time. The ornately carved interior is a monument to the mason's art and is rich in symbolic imagery. As well as flowers, vines, angels and biblical figures, the carved stones include many examples of the pagan 'Green Man'; other figures are associated with Freemasonry and the Knights Templar. Intriguingly, there are also carvings of plants from the Americas which predate Columbus' voyage of discovery. The symbolism of these images has led some researchers to conclude that Rosslyn is some kind of secret Templar repository, and it has been claimed that hidden vaults beneath the chapel could conceal anything from the Holy Grail or the head of John the Baptist to the body of Christ himself. The chapel is owned by the Episcopal Church of Scotland and services are still held here on Sunday mornings.

Wilson's bus No 315 runs hourly on weekdays, every two hours on Saturdays and twice a day on Sundays, from St Andrew Square in Edinburgh.

Crichton Castle

Crichton Castle *(HS; ☎ 01875-320017 Pathhead, Midlothian; adult/child £2/75p; open 9.30am-6.30pm daily Apr-Sept)* is 10 miles (16km) south-east of Edinburgh. Partly ruined, it enjoys a delightful location overlooking a valley and has a beautiful Italianate courtyard with faceted stonework. Take bus No 29 or 30 from Waterloo Place in Edinburgh to Pathhead village, then walk 2 miles (3km) south on the B6367 road.

Pentland Hills

Rising on the southern edge of Edinburgh, these hills stretch 16 miles (25.5km) south-west to near Carnwath in Lanarkshire. The hills rise to 579m at their highest point and offer excellent, not-too-strenuous walking with great views. There are several access points along the A702 road on the southern side of the hills. MacEwan's bus No 100 runs four times daily along the A702 from Edinburgh to Biggar.

EAST LOTHIAN

Beyond the former coalfields of Dalkeith and Musselburgh, the fertile farmland of East Lothian stretches eastwards along the coast to the seaside resort of North Berwick and the fishing harbour of Dunbar. In the middle lies the attractive county town of Haddington.

Haddington & Around
☎ 01620 • pop 8000

Haddington, straddling the River Tyne 18 miles (29km) east of Edinburgh, dates back to the 12th century when it was made a royal burgh by David I. Most of the modern town, however, was built in the 17th to 19th centuries during the period of prosperity that resulted from the Agricultural Revolution. It's still a prosperous market town and the administrative centre for East Lothian.

The prettiest part of Haddington is the tree-lined Court St, with its wide pavement and grand 18th- and 19th-century buildings. Haddington gets congested with traffic, especially on Market and High Sts where, during the day at least, cars jostle for the limited parking spaces.

Things to See & Do From the eastern end of High St, Church St leads to St Mary's Collegiate Church (☎ 823109, Sidegate; admission free; open 11am-4pm Mon-Sat, 9.30am-4.40pm Sun). Built in 1462, it is the largest parish church in Scotland. Buried in the churchyard is Jane Welsh (1801–66), wife of Thomas Carlyle. The Jane Welsh Carlyle Museum (☎ 823738, 2 Lodge St; adult/child £1/75p; open 2pm-5pm Wed-Sat Apr-Sept) is the house in which she lived until her marriage.

A mile south of Haddington is Lennoxlove House (☎ 823720, Lennoxlove Estate; adult/child £4/2; guided tours 2pm-4.30pm Wed, Thur & Sun Easter-Oct). The oldest part of the house dates from around 1345, with extensions added over the following

centuries. It contains some fine furniture and paintings, and memorabilia relating to Mary, Queen of Scots. Chief among these are her death mask and a silver casket given to her by Francis II of France, her first husband. The house has been the seat of the duke of Hamilton since 1947.

Places to Stay & Eat
The town has a camping ground nearby and several guesthouses.

Monk's Muir (☎ 860340, fax 861770; off the main A1 road 2½ miles/4km east of town) Tent pitches £8.40-9.90. This secluded and attractive camp site, close to the town, opens year-round.

Hamilton's (☎ 822465, fax 825613, 28 Market St) Singles/twins £18/20. Mrs Hamilton offers B&B in a central Victorian terrace.

The Waterside Bistro & Restaurant (☎ 825764, 115 Waterside) With a lovely location overlooking the river, The Waterside is a great place to have lunch on a summer's day, watching the swans and ducks go by. The bistro does good-quality light meals, while the upstairs restaurant is more formal.

Getting There & Away First Edinburgh bus No 106 runs between Edinburgh and Haddington every 20 minutes. The nearest train station is at Drem, 3 miles (5km) to the north.

North Berwick & Around
☎ 01620 • pop 4860

North Berwick, 24 miles (38km) east of Edinburgh, is an attractive Victorian seaside resort with long sandy beaches, three golf courses and a small harbour. The TIC (☎ 892197), on Quality St, opens 9am to 6pm Monday to Saturday.

Things to See & Do North Berwick's big new attraction is the Scottish Seabird Centre (☎ 890202, W www.seabird.org, The Harbour; adult/child/family £4.50/3.20/12.50; open 10am-6pm daily Apr-Sept, 10am-4pm daily Oct-Mar). The centre uses remote-control video cameras on the Bass Rock and other islands to relay live images of nesting gannets and other seabirds, and screens films and multimedia shows. There are also high-powered telescopes on the viewing deck that you can use to scan the coast and islands.

Beside the harbour are the remains of the **Auld Kirk**, the 12th-century Church of St Andrews, the first parish church of North Berwick. Off High St, a short steep path climbs up **North Berwick Law** (184m), a conical hill that dominates the town. When the weather's fine there are great views.

Several small islands lie offshore. **Bass Rock**, 3 miles (5km) east, was once used as a prison for Covenanters but is now home to thousands of gannets and other seabirds. Puffins nest in burrows on nearby **Craig Rock** and **Fidra Island**.

Fred Marr (☎ *892838)* runs trips out daily in summer (at weekends the rest of the year). Trips around Bass Rock and Fidra Island cost £5/3 and take about one hour 10 minutes. Fred will also drop you off on Bass Rock for two to three hours, then return and pick you up (£12).

Dirleton Castle Two miles (3km) west of North Berwick, Dirleton Castle *(HS; ☎ 850330, Dirleton, East Lothian; adult/ child £2/1; open 9.30am-6.30pm daily Apr-Sept, 9.30am-4.30pm Mon-Sat & 2.30pm-4.30pm Sun Oct-Mar)* is surrounded by beautiful gardens, and has massive round towers, a drawbridge and a horrific pit dungeon.

Tantallon Castle Built around 1350, spectacular Tantallon Castle *(HS; ☎ 892727; adult/child £2.80/1; open 9.30am-6.30pm daily Apr-Sept, 9.30am-4.30pm Sat-Wed, 9.30am-1pm Thur Oct-Mar)*, 3 miles east of North Berwick, was a fortress residence of the Douglas Earls of Angus (the 'Red Douglases'). On one side it's an almost sheer drop to the sea below, and fulmars nest in the cliffs.

Places to Stay North Berwick has lots of places to stay, though they can fill up quickly at weekends when golfers are in town.

Gilsland Caravan & Camping Park (☎ *892205, Grange Rd)* Tents from £3.50 per person. Open mid Mar-Oct. This sheltered site is close to the town and the beach.

Palmerston (☎ *892884, fax 895561, 28[St Andrew St)* B&B from £22 per person. This is a central B&B with spacious ensuite rooms and private parking.

Craigview (☎ *892257, 5 Beach Rd)* B&B from £22.50 per person. Popular Craigview overlooks the harbour and Bass Rock, and offers vegetarian breakfasts.

Getting There & Away First Edinburgh bus No 124 runs between Edinburgh and North Berwick every 20 minutes during the day, and hourly in the evenings (£4, one hour). There are frequent trains to Edinburgh (£7, 33 minutes).

Dunbar
☎ 01368 • pop 5800

Dunbar is a small fishing port and holiday resort on the east coast, 30 miles (48km, from Edinburgh. It was the site of two important battles, both resulting in Scottish losses. Edward I invaded in 1296 and General Monck defeated a larger Scots army in 1650, facilitating Cromwell's entry into Edinburgh. John Muir (1838–1914), pioneer conservationist and 'father' of the US national park system, was born here.

The TIC (☎ 863353), 143 High St, opens 9am to 5pm weekdays October to March and daily April to September (extended hours in July and August).

Things to See & Do Dunbar was an important Scottish fortress town in the Middle Ages, but little remains of **Dunbar Castle** except for some tottering ruins, inhabited by seabirds, overlooking the harbour. From the castle, a 2-mile (3km) cliff-top trail follows the coastline west to the sands of Belhaven Bay and **John Muir Country Park** *(☎ 863886)*.

John Muir House (☎ *862595, 128 High St; admission free; open 11am-1pm Mon-Sat & 2pm-5pm daily June-Sept)* is Muir's childhood home and has a small exhibition and audio-visual display on his life. The **Dunbar Town House Museum** (☎ *863734 High St; admission free; open 12.30pm-4.30pm daily Apr-Oct)* gives an introduction to local history and archaeology.

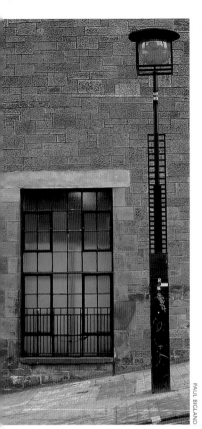

PAUL BIGLAND

MARTIN MOOS

MARTIN MOOS

MARTIN MOOS

ity sights: Mackintosh Building, Glasgow School of Art; Greyfriar's Bobby, Edinburgh's famous dog; busking bagpiper along Edinburgh's Royal Mile; and a taste of Edinburgh's nightlife

Kelvingrove Art Gallery & Museum is Glasgow's grand Victorian cathedral of culture.

Cycling alongside Loch Lomond, Britain's largest freshwater lake

Dunbar Leisure Pool *(☎ 865456, Castle Park; adult/child £3.50/2; open 10am-9pm Tues & Wed, 10am-5pm Thur-Sun)*, on the hilltop above the harbour, is an attractive modern swimming pool with flumes and a children's pool.

Places to Stay Dunbar has something to please everyone, including those listed here.

Belhaven Bay Caravan Park *(☎ 865956, fax 865022, Belhaven Bay)* Tents from £3.50 per person. Located next to John Muir Country Park, the Belhaven opens mid-March to October.

Springfield Guest House *(☎ 862502, Belhaven Rd)* B&B £18-30 per person. West of the centre, this family-run guest-house is in an elegant Victorian villa.

Getting There & Away Dunbar is well served by buses from Edinburgh, including bus Nos 251, 253 and 256. GNER trains run from Edinburgh Waverley train station (£11.50, 40 minutes) every half-hour or so.

WEST LOTHIAN
Linlithgow
☎ 01506 • pop 9500

This ancient royal burgh, 15 miles (24km) west of Edinburgh, is one of Scotland's oldest towns, though much of it 'only' dates from the 15th to 17th centuries. Its centre retains a certain charm, except for the appallingly ugly modern buildings just west of the Cross (marketplace).

The TIC (☎ 844600), in the Burgh Halls at the Cross, opens 10am to 5pm daily April to October.

Things to See & Do The town's main attraction is the magnificent ruin of **Linlithgow Palace** *(HS; ☎ 842896, Church Peel; adult/child £2.80/1; open 9.30am-6.30pm daily Apr-Sept, 9.30am-4.30pm Mon-Sat & 2pm-4.30pm Sun Oct-Mar)*. Begun by James I in 1425, the building of the palace continued for over a century. It was a favourite royal residence – James V was born here in 1512, and his daughter Mary (later Queen of Scots) in 1542. Cromwell billeted his troops here in the 1650s and Bonnie Prince Charlie

briefly visited in 1745 – legend has it that a cooking fire left by retreating Jacobite soldiers caused the blaze that gutted the palace in 1746.

Beside the palace is the Gothic **St Michael's Church** *(☎ 842188, Church Peel; admission free; open 10am-4.30pm daily May-Sept and Easter weekend)*. Built between the 1420s and 1530s, it is topped by a controversial aluminium spire that was added in 1964. The church is said to be haunted by a ghost that foretold King James IV of his impending defeat at Flodden in 1513.

The **Linlithgow Story** *(☎ 670677, Annet House, 143 High St; adult/child £1/60p, admission free Sun; open 10am-4pm Mon & Wed-Sat, 1pm-4pm Sun Easter-Oct)* is a small museum which tells the story of the Stewart monarchy and the history of the town.

Just 150m south of the town centre lies the Union Canal and the **Linlithgow Canal Centre** *(☎ 671215, W www.lucs.org.uk, Manse Road Canal Basin; admission free; open 2pm-5pm Sat & Sun Easter-Sept)*. A little museum records the history of the canal, and there are three-hour **canal boat trips** west to the Avon Aqueduct (adult/child £6/3; departures at 2pm Saturday and Sunday Easter to June and September to October, and 2pm daily July and August). Shorter, 20-minute cruises leave every half-hour (adult/child £2.50/1.50; departures between 2pm and 4.30pm Saturday and Sunday Easter to June and September to October, and 2pm to 4.30pm daily July and August).

Places to Eat Linlithgow offers a few good eateries.

The Four Marys *(☎ 842171, 65-76 High St)* Mains £4.95-6.95. An attractive traditional pub that serves real ales and good pub grub – try the haggis, neeps and tatties for £4.95.

Marynka *(☎ 840123, 57 High St)* 2-course dinner £16.50. Open Mon-Sat. This is a pleasant little gourmet restaurant, a few doors down from The Four Marys and a little more formal.

Champany Inn (☎ 834532) Mains £5.95-12.95. This is an excellent lunch spot famous for its steaks and lobsters. The 'Chop and Ale House' is a less expensive alternative to the main dining room. The inn is located 2 miles (3km) north-east of town, on the A804 road towards Queensferry.

Getting There & Away Buses (Nos 38, 38A, 38B and 138 from St Andrew Square and trains between Edinburgh and Falkirk stop at Linlithgow, which is 15 miles (24km) from the Scottish capital. Buses stop at the Cross, and the train station is 250m east of the town centre.

Glasgow

☎ 0141 • pop 612,000

Although Glasgow lacks the instantly inspiring beauty of Edinburgh, it's one of Britain's largest, liveliest and most interesting cities, with a legacy of appealing Victorian architecture and several distinguished suburbs of terraced squares and crescents. 'Glasgow – The Friendly City' say the billboards, and it's true, thanks mainly to the warmth, vibrancy and energy of its inhabitants.

In the early 1970s, the name Glasgow came to be synonymous with unemployment, economic depression and urban violence. It was known for the bloody confrontations that occurred between rival supporters of Protestant Rangers and Catholic Celtic football teams, and as the home of the Glasgow Kiss (a particularly unfriendly head butt). Over the following years, however, the city reinvented itself, rediscovering its rich cultural roots and proclaiming a new pride through a well-orchestrated publicity campaign. By 1990, it had been elected European City of Culture and, in 1999, served as the UK's City of Architecture and Design. Currently, Glasgow is the third most popular destination in Britain for foreign tourists, after London and Edinburgh.

Although influenced by thousands of Irish immigrants, Glasgow is the most Scottish of cities, with a unique blend of friendliness, urban chaos, black humour and energy. In the late 20th century the city saw an incredible outburst of musical talent and produced such groups as Simple Minds, Tears for Fears, Deacon Blue, Aztec Camera, Wet Wet Wet and Texas, as well as comedians such as Billy Connolly and Stanley Baxter.

It also boasts excellent art galleries and museums (including the famous Burrell Collection) – most of them free – as well as numerous good-value restaurants, nearly 800 pubs and bars and a lively arts scene.

HISTORY

Glasgow grew up around the cathedral founded by St Mungo in the 6th century and,

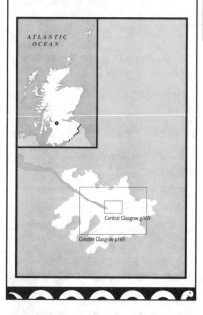

HIGHLIGHTS

- Gazing upon the beautifully displayed treasures of the Burrell Collection
- Marvelling at the architecture of Charles Rennie Mackintosh
- Journeying through a time warp at The Tenement House
- Viewing the outstanding exhibits at Kelvingrove Art Gallery & Museum
- Visiting the Scottish mainland's only cathedral to have survived the turbulent Reformation
- Jumping headlong into the nightlife of the pubs and clubs

ATLANTIC OCEAN

Central Glasgow p169

Greater Glasgow p165

in 1451, the city became the site of the University of Glasgow, the second university to be founded in Scotland. Unfortunately, with the exception of the cathedral, virtually

GLASGOW

nothing of the medieval city remains. It was swept away by the energetic people of a new age – the age of capitalism, the Industrial Revolution and the British Empire.

In the 18th century, much of the tobacco trade between Europe and the USA was routed through Glasgow and provided a great source of wealth. Other New World imports included rum and sugar. Even after the tobacco trade declined in the 19th century, the city continued to prosper as a centre of textile manufacturing, shipbuilding and the coal and steel industries.

The new industries created a huge demand for labour, and peasants poured in from Ireland and the Highlands to crowd the city's tenements. In the mid-18th century, the population had reached 17,500. By the end of that century, it had risen to 100,000. After 20 years, that figure had doubled and, by 1860, it was home to 400,000 people. The outward appearance of prosperity, however, was tempered by the dire working conditions in the factories, particularly for women and children. In the second half of the 19th century, the city experienced four major cholera outbreaks and life expectancy was a mere 30 years.

While the workers suffered, the textile barons and shipping magnates prospered, and Glasgow could justifiably call itself the second city of the empire. Grand Victorian public buildings were constructed, and some of the wealthier citizens spent their fortunes amassing the large art collections that now form the basis of the city's superb galleries.

In the first half of the 20th century, Glasgow was the centre of Britain's munitions industry, supplying arms and ships for the two world wars. After those boom years, however, the port and heavy industries began to decline and, by the early 1970s, the city looked doomed. Glasgow has always been proud of its predominantly working-class nature but, unlike middle-class Edinburgh with its varied service industries, it had few alternatives when recession hit and unemployment spiralled.

Certainly, there's increasing confidence in the city but, behind all the optimism, the

general standard of living remains relatively low and life is tough for those affected by the comparatively high unemployment, inadequate housing and generally poor diet. In the city centre, visitors will notice dilapidated buildings sprouting trees and other flora. The city has been slated as the heart-attack capital of the world and, although there have been campaigns to raise awareness of the problem, deep-fried chocolate bars can still be seen on chip-shop menus.

ORIENTATION

Glasgow's tourist sights are spread over a wide area. The city centre is built on a grid system on the northern side of the River Clyde. The two train stations (Central and Queen St), the Buchanan Bus Station and the TIC are all on or within a couple of blocks

GREATER GLASGOW

PLACES TO STAY

1	One Devonshire Gardens
2	The Town House
3	Kirklee Hotel
4	Terrace House Hotel
12	Bunkum Backpackers; Chez Nous Guest House; Iona Guest House
14	Amadeus Guest House
15	Alison Guest House; Craig Park Guest House
16	Seton Guest House
19	Holly House
20	Glasgow Guest House
23	Reidholme Guest House
24	Boswell Hotel
25	Dunkeld Hotel

PLACES TO EAT

5	Café Antipasti
6	Puppet Theatre; Stravaigin II
7	Di Maggios
9	University Café
10	Ashoka; Ubiquitous Chip; Grosvenor Café; Mitchell's; Brel's; Cul de Sac; STA Travel

OTHER

8	West End Cycles
11	Curlers
13	Queen's Cross Church
17	People's Palace
18	Glasgow Science Centre
21	Pollok House
22	Burrell Collection
26	Scottish Football Museum

GREATER GLASGOW

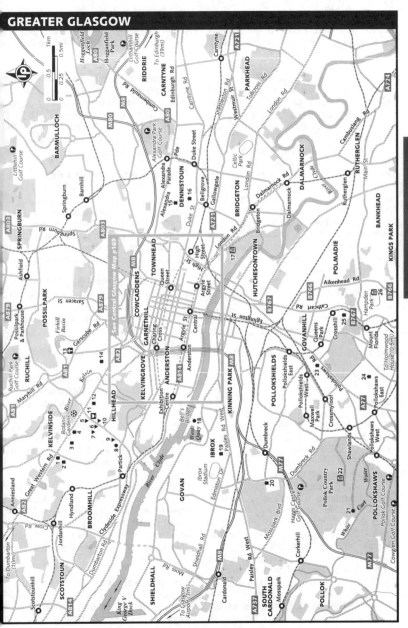

GLASGOW

of George Square, the main city square. Running alongside a ridge in the northern part of the city, Sauchiehall (soch-ie-**hall**) St has numerous high-street shops and a pedestrian shopping centre at its eastern end, as well as pubs and restaurants farther west. Argyle St, running parallel to the river, and pedestrianised Buchanan St, at right angles to Argyle St, are also important shopping streets. Merchant City is the city's main commercial district, east of George Square.

The university and the Glasgow Youth Hostel (Scottish Youth Hostel Association, SYHA) hostel are near Kelvingrove Park, north-west of the city centre in an area known as the West End. Pollok Country Park and the Burrell Collection are in the South Side, south-west of the centre.

Motorways bore through the suburbs and the M8 sweeps round the northern and western edges of the centre, passing the airport 10 miles (16km) west.

INFORMATION

The List, available from newsagents (£1.95), is Glasgow's and Edinburgh's invaluable fortnightly guide to films, theatre, cabaret, music, clubs – the works. The 136-page *Eating & Drinking Guide*, published by the *List* every April, covers Glasgow and Edinburgh and costs £4.95.

Tourist Offices

At 11 George Square, the main TIC (☎ 204 4400, fax 221 3524, e info@seeglasgow .com, w www.seeglasgow.com) has a bureau de change and charges £2/3 for local/national accommodation bookings. It opens 9am to 6pm Monday to Saturday, with extended opening hours until 7pm in June and September, and 8pm in July and August. It's also open on Sunday between Easter to September, from 10am to 6pm. There's another branch (☎ 848 4440) at Glasgow International Airport.

Travel information is also available from the St Enoch Square Travel Centre, St Enoch Square. It opens 8.30am to 5.30pm, Monday to Saturday. You can also try Buchanan Bus Station, Killermont St, which opens 6.30am (7am on Sunday) to

10.30pm daily. All telephone enquiries should be made to Traveline Scotland (☎ 0870 608 2608, 8am to 8pm daily).

Money

The Clydesdale Bank, 7 St Enoch Square has four 24-hour ATMs and is open Monday to Saturday (10am to 3pm on Saturday).

American Express (AmEx; ☎ 222 1401) 115 Hope St, opens commercial hours Monday to Friday, and until 2pm on Saturday (closing noon on Saturday from October to June).

Post & Communications

At the main post office, 47 St Vincent St you can collect poste restante, buy and sell currency, cash travellers cheques and arrange Moneygram money transfers. Opening hours are 8.30am to 5.45pm on weekdays, and 9am to 5.30pm on Saturday. Post offices in some supermarkets are also open on Sunday.

EasyEverything (☎ 222 2364) at 57 St Vincent St offers Internet access at variable rates – the quieter the place is, the cheaper it gets. Average cost is £1 for about 35 minutes.

Bookshops

Waterstone's (☎ 332 9105) at 153 Sauchiehall St has a coffee shop and five floors of just about anything you might want to read It opens 8.30am to 9pm Monday to Friday 9am to 8pm Saturday and 10.30am to 7pm Sunday.

Borders (☎ 222 7700) at 98 Buchanan St also has a cafe and sells international newspapers and magazines. It opens from 8am to 11pm daily (9pm on Sunday).

Left Luggage

Facilities are available at Buchanan Bus Station (☎ 333 3708), Killermont St, from 6.30am to 10.30pm daily. It costs £2 for the first hour, or £3 per day. Lockers at Central Station cost £3/4/5 (small/medium/large) for 24 hours.

Medical Services

To see a doctor, visit the out-patients department at any general hospital. Glasgow Royal Infirmary (☎ 211 4000), 84 Castle St is by the cathedral. The Southern General Hospital (☎ 201 1100), Govan Rd, is the main South Side hospital.

Dental emergencies are handled at the Glasgow Dental Hospital (☎ 211 9600), 378 Sauchiehall St.

Emergency
As anywhere in Scotland, the free emergency numbers are ☎ 999 or ☎ 112.

Dangers & Annoyances
Keep clear of Orange marches, which are exhibitions of solidarity with the Protestant Northern Irish cause; violence can result when Catholics try to 'break the ranks'. These events aren't for tourists.

GEORGE SQUARE & THE MERCHANT CITY
The TIC on George Square is a good starting point for exploring the city. The square is surrounded by imposing Victorian architecture, including the old post office, the Bank of Scotland and the City Chambers. There are statues of Robert Burns, James Watt, Lord Clyde and, atop a 24m-high Doric column, Sir Walter Scott.

The grand **City Chambers** *(☎ 287 4018, George Square; admission free; entry for 45-minute guided tours only, 10.30am-2.30pm Mon-Fri)*, the seat of local government, were built in the 1880s at the high point of the city's wealth. Their interior is even more extravagant than their exterior, and the chambers were used for filming *The House of Mirth*, starring Gillian Anderson.

A Walk Through the Merchant City
An interesting hour-long walk will take you from George Square to Glasgow Cathedral through the Merchant City, a planned 18th-century civic development. The Tobacco Lords were the entrepreneurs who opened up European trade with the Americas, importing tobacco, rum and sugar in the 18th century and their profits went to build these warehouses, offices and gracious homes. The more recent redevelopment trend has turned the warehouses into apartments for Glaswegian yuppies, and stylish shopping centres such as the Italian Centre have sprung up to serve their retail needs.

Once you've seen the City Chambers, cross George Square and walk one block south down Queen St to the **Gallery of Modern Art** (see that section later). This four-floor colonnaded building, built in 1827, was once the Royal Exchange, where business transactions were negotiated.

The gallery faces Ingram St, which you should cross and then follow east for four blocks to **Hutchesons' Hall** *(☎ 552 8391, 158 Ingram St; admission free; open 10am-5pm Mon-Sat)*. Built in 1805 to a design by David Hamilton, this elegant building is now maintained by the National Trust for Scotland (NTS).

Retrace your steps one block and continue south down Glassford St past **Trades Hall** *(☎ 552 2418, 85 Glassford St; admission free; open 9am-5pm Mon-Fri & 9am-noon Sat, but closed during functions)*, designed by Robert Adam in 1791 to house the trades guild. This is the only surviving building in Glasgow by this famous Scottish architect; the exterior is best viewed from Garth St, one block west on Ingram St. Turn right into Wilson St and first left along Virginia St, lined with the old warehouses of the Tobacco Lords; many of these have now been converted into flats. The **Tobacco Exchange** became the Sugar Exchange in 1820 but it's now in poor condition.

Back on Wilson St, the bulky **Sheriff Court House** fills a whole block. It was originally built as Glasgow's town hall; the former cells now house the extraordinarily trendy Corinthian nightclub (see Entertainment later in this chapter). Continue east past **Ingram Square**, another warehouse development, to the **City Halls**, now used for concerts. The city's markets were once held here. Turn right from Albion St into Blackfriars St. Emerging onto the High St, turn left and follow High St up to the cathedral.

GLASGOW CATHEDRAL & PRECINCTS
The oldest part of the city is concentrated around Glasgow Cathedral, to the east of

the modern centre. The area was given a facelift in the 1990s, with the opening of St Mungo's Museum of Religious Life and Art (see that section later). The money for the restoration of the cathedral was sensibly spent on updating the heating system rather than on giving the blackened exterior a high-pressure hose-down. Nearby, Provand's Lordship (see that section later), the city's oldest house, completes a trio of interesting sights. The crumbling tombs of the city's rich and famous crowd the necropolis, behind the cathedral.

It takes about 15 to 20 minutes to walk from George Square but numerous buses pass nearby, including Nos 16, 36, 37, 39, 41 and 42.

Glasgow Cathedral

The cathedral (☎ 552 6891, Cathedral Square; admission free; open 9.30am-6pm Mon-Sat & 2pm-5pm Sun Apr-Sept, 9.30am-4pm Mon-Sat & 2pm-4pm Oct-Mar), managed by Historic Scotland (HS; see Useful Organisations in the Facts for the Visitor chapter), a shining example of pre-Reformation

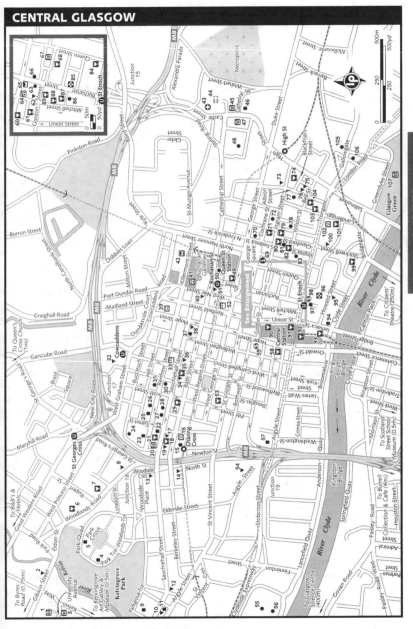

CENTRAL GLASGOW

GLASGOW

Gothic architecture, is the only mainland Scottish cathedral to have survived the Reformation. Most of the current building dates from the 15th century, and only the western towers were destroyed in the turmoil.

This has been hallowed ground for over 1500 years. The site was blessed for Christian burial in 397 by St Ninian. In the following century, St Kentigern, also known as St Mungo, accompanied the body of a holy man from Stirlingshire to be buried here. He stayed to found a monastic community, and built a simple church. The first building was consecrated in 1136, in the presence of King David I, but it burned down in 1197 and was rebuilt as the lower church.

The entry is through a side door into the **nave**, which is hung with some regimental colours. The wooden roof above has been restored many times since its original construction but some of the timber dates from the 14th century. Much of the cathedral's stained glass is modern and to your left, you'll see Francis Spear's 1958 work *The Creation*, which fills the west window.

The cathedral is divided by the late 15th-century stone choir screen, decorated with seven pairs of figures to represent the Seven Deadly Sins. Beyond is the **choir**. The four stained-glass panels of the east window, depicting the apostles and also by Francis Spear, are particularly effective. At the north-eastern corner is the entrance to the 15th-century **upper chapter house**, where Glasgow University was founded. It's now used as a sacristy.

The most interesting part of the cathedral, **the lower church**, is reached by a stairway. Its forest of pillars creates a powerful atmosphere around St Mungo's tomb, the focus of a famous medieval pilgrimage that was believed to be as meritorious as a visit to Rome. Edward I paid three visits to the shrine in 1301.

Sunday services are at 11am and 6.30pm.

St Mungo's Museum of Religious Life & Art

This award-winning museum (☎ 553 2557, 2 Castle St; admission free; open 10am-5pm Mon-Thur & Sat, 11am-5pm Fri & Sun),

near the cathedral, was opened in 1993. From its inception, it has been a highly controversial project as it's understandably challenging to select works of art outlining all the world's main religions – but the result is well worth it and the museum is small enough not to be overwhelming.

The building may look like a bit of restored antiquity, but in fact it was built to house the museum – a £6.5 million reconstruction of the bishop's palace that once stood here. A 12-minute video will provide an overall view before you delve into the exhibits. There are three galleries, representing religion as art, religious life and, on the top floor, religion in Scotland. In the main gallery Dali's *Christ of St John of the Cross* hangs beside statues of the Buddha and Hindu deities. Outside, you'll find Britain's only Zen garden. See Places to Eat for details of the restaurant.

The recommended ***restaurant*** downstairs provides both vegetarian and meat dishes. Soup and a roll cost £1.75 and main dishes are £2.95.

Provand's Lordship

Across the road from St Mungo's Museum is the oldest house in Glasgow – Provand's Lordship (☎ 552 8819, 3 Castle St; admission free; open 10am-5pm Mon-Thur & Sat, 11am-5pm Fri & Sun). Built in 1471 as a manse for the chaplain of St Nicholas Hospital, it's said to have been visited by Mary Queen of Scots, James III and James IV. It's now a museum with various period displays connected with the house, but the furniture comes from elsewhere. The displays are as diverse as a 16th-century room of one of the chaplains who lived here, and a 20th-century sweet shop. There's also a medieval-theme garden in the grounds.

GALLERY OF MODERN ART

The Gallery of Modern Art (☎ 229 1996, Queen St; admission free; open 10am-5pm Mon-Thur & Sat, 11am-5pm Fri & Sun) features contemporary paintings, ceramics, furniture and sculpture, including items from Scottish artists such as Peter Howson, Ken Currie, John Bellany, Eduardo Paolozzi,

Bruce McLean, David Hockney and Jasper Johns. There are also permanent exhibits from abroad and the occasional temporary exhibition.

The Rooftop Café (☎ 221 7484) opens from 10am to 4.30pm daily for soup and snacks.

BURRELL COLLECTION

Glasgow's top attraction is the Burrell Collection *(☎ 287 2550, Pollok Country Park; admission free, parking £1.50; open 10am-5pm Mon-Thur & Sat, 11am-5pm Fri & Sun)*. It was amassed by wealthy industrialist Sir William Burrell before it was donated to the city. It's now housed in a prize-winning museum in the Pollok Country Park, 3 miles (5km) south of the city centre. This idiosyncratic collection includes everything from Chinese porcelain and medieval furniture to paintings by Renoir and Cézanne. It's not so big as to be overwhelming, and the stamp of the collector lends an intriguing coherence.

The building was the result of a design competition in 1971. If the contest had not been run during a postal strike, necessitating an extension of the closing deadline, Barry Gasson's winning entry would not have been completed. From the outside, the building seems somewhat of a hybrid but the truly spectacular interior provides a fitting setting for an exquisite collection of tapestries, oriental porcelain, paintings and European stained glass. Floor-to-ceiling windows admit a flood of natural light, and the trees and landscape outside only enhance the effect created by the exhibits.

Carpeted floors maintain the silence to contemplate the beautifully displayed treasures. Carved-stone Romanesque doorways are incorporated into the structure so one actually walks through them. Some galleries are reconstructions of rooms from Hutton Castle, the Burrell residence. Even the public seating is of superb design and production quality.

The light and airy cafe on the lower ground floor includes the same floor-to-ceiling windows, hung with heraldic glass medallions. Lunches are available in the adjacent *restaurant* (main courses £5.50 to £7.95). Weather permitting, you may prefer to save a good chunk of change (even a cup of coffee costs £1.10) and bring a picnic lunch.

There are occasional guided tours. Numerous buses pass the park gates (including Nos 45, 47, 48 and 57 from the centre), and there's a twice-hourly bus service between the gallery and the gates (a pleasant 10-minute walk). Alternatively, catch a train to Pollokshaws West from Central Station (four per hour; you want the second station on the line taking trains destined for East Kilbride or Kilmarnock).

Pollok House

Also in Pollok Country Park, and a 10-minute walk from the Burrell Collection, is Pollok House *(NTS; ☎ 616 6410, 2060 Pollokshaws Rd; adult/child £4/3 Apr-Oct, admission free Nov-Mar; open 10am-5pm daily Apr-Oct, otherwise 11am-4pm daily)*. It contains a fine collection of Spanish paintings, including works by El Greco and Goya. The house is Georgian (1750) and there's a tearoom in the old kitchen, which has an unusual circular centre light and a full range of kitchen implements.

MACKINTOSH BUILDINGS

There are a number of superb Art Nouveau buildings designed by the Scottish architect and designer Charles Rennie Mackintosh (CRM). Tours of most of these buildings run at weekends, once monthly, May to October, for £239/394 singles/doubles (including two nights' hotel accommodation, breakfasts, lunches, dinners, transport and guide). Contact the CRM Society (see the boxed text 'Charles Rennie Mackintosh' later) for details.

Glasgow School of Art

Widely recognised as Mackintosh's greatest building, the Glasgow School of Art *(☎ 353 4526, 167 Renfrew St; adult/child £5/3; open for guided tours only, 11am & 2pm weekdays, 10.30am, 11.30am & 1pm Sat)* still houses the educational institution. It's hard not to be impressed by the thoroughness of the design; the architect's pencil seems to have shaped everything inside and outside the building. The interior design is strikingly austere, with simple colour combinations (often just black and cream) and those uncomfortable-looking high-backed chairs for which he is famous. The library, designed as an addition in 1907, is a masterpiece. Parts of the school may be closed to visitors if they're in use and tour times may vary.

Willow Tea Rooms

More Mockintosh than Mackintosh, the Willow Tea Rooms (☎ 332 0521, 217 Sauchiehall St; admission free; open 9.15am-4.15pm Mon-Sat, noon-4.15pm Sun) is a reconstruction of the tearoom Mackintosh designed and furnished in 1904 for restaurateur Kate Cranston.

The restaurant closed in 1926 and the premises were then occupied by a series of retail businesses. Reconstruction took two years and the Willow opened as a tearoom again in 1980. Sauchiehall means 'lane of willows', hence the choice of a stylised willow motif. See Places to Eat for details of the tearoom.

Queen's Cross Church

Now the headquarters of the CRM Society, Queen's Cross Church (☎ 946 6600, 870 Garscube Rd; admission free; open 10am-5pm Mon-Fri, 2pm-5pm Sun) is the only one of Mackintosh's church designs to be built, with excellent stained glass and relief carvings. It's the wonderful simplicity of the design that is particularly inspiring. There's also an information centre, a small display and a gift shop.

Other Mackintoshiana

In the former Glasgow Herald building, **The Lighthouse** (☎ 225 8414, 11 Mitchell Lane;

Charles Rennie Mackintosh

The distinctive style of CRM

JANE SMITH

The quirky, linear and geometric designs of this famous Scottish architect and designer have had almost as much influence on the city as have Gaudi's on Barcelona. Many of the buildings Mackintosh designed in Glasgow are now open to the public, and you'll see his tall, thin, Art Nouveau typeface repeatedly reproduced.

Born in 1868, Mackintosh studied at the Glasgow School of Art. In 1896, when he was aged only 27, his design won a competition for the School of Art's new building. The first section was opened in 1899 and is considered to be the earliest example of Art Nouveau in Britain, as well as Mackintosh's supreme architectural achievement. This building demonstrates his skill in combining function and style.

Mackintosh applied himself to every facet of design, from whole facades to the smallest window fastener. As a furniture designer and decorative artist, he designed the interiors for Kate Cranston's chain of Glasgow tearooms between 1896 and 1911. The Willow Tea Rooms has been fully restored and is again open as a tearoom.

Although Mackintosh's genius was quickly recognised on the Continent (he contributed to a number of exhibitions in France, Germany and Austria), he did not receive the same encouragement in Scotland. His architectural career here lasted only until 1914 when he moved to England to concentrate on furniture design. He died in 1928, but it's only in the last 30 years that Mackintosh's genius has been widely recognised. If you want to know more about the man and his work, contact the Charles Rennie Mackintosh Society (☎ 946 6600, fax 945 2321, [e] info@crmsociety.com, [w] www.crmsociety.com), Queen's Cross Church, 870 Garscube Rd, Glasgow G20 7EL.

adult/child £2.50/free; open 10.30am-5pm Mon & Wed-Sat, 11am-5pm Tues, noon-5pm Sun) has an interesting high-tech Mackintosh Interpretation Centre, temporary exhibitions of avant-garde furniture, and great rooftop views from the former water tower.

The principal rooms from CRM's home have been reconstructed as the **Mackintosh House** *(☎ 330 5431, Hillhead St; admission free; open 9.30am-12.30pm & 1.30pm-5pm Mon-Sat)*, with original furnishings, at the Hunterian Museum & Art Gallery (see that section later).

At the Art Gallery and Museum in Kelvingrove Park (see that section later), there's an interesting display of Mackintosh paintings, furniture and decorative art.

Scotland Street School Museum *(☎ 287 0500, 225 Scotland St; admission free; open 10am-5pm Mon-Thur, 11am-5pm Fri & Sun)* is an impressive Mackintosh building which is dominated by two glass towers. It's now a museum of education, which may sound dull but it's fascinating. There are reconstructions of classrooms from Victorian times, and the 1940s, '50s and '60s.

Although designed in 1901 as an entry to a competition run by a German magazine, the **House for an Art Lover** *(☎ 353 4770, Bellahouston Park, 10 Dumbreck Rd; adult/child £3.50/2.50; open 10am-4pm Sun-Thur, 10am-3pm Sat)* was not completed until 1996. It has permanent Mackintosh displays and a cafe. Bus Nos 3, 9, 54, 55 and 56 all run from the city centre.

Twenty-three miles (37km) north-west of Glasgow at Helensburgh is the **Hill House** *(NTS; ☎ 01436-673900, Upper Colquhoun St; adult/child £6/4.50; open 1.30pm-5pm daily Apr-Oct)*, Mackintosh's domestic masterpiece, now in the hands of the National Trust for Scotland. See Helensburgh in The Highlands chapter.

THE TENEMENT HOUSE

For an extraordinary time-capsule experience, visit the small apartment in the Tenement House *(NTS; ☎ 333 0183, 145 Buccleuch St; adult/child £3.50/2.50; open 2pm-5pm daily Mar-Oct)*. It gives an insight into middle-class city life in the late-19th/early-20th century, with box-beds, the original kitchen range and all the fixtures and fittings of the family who lived here for over 50 years.

It's an interesting place, but surely the Toward family wouldn't have kept it quite so squeaky clean and orderly as the NTS manages now. Despite the additional exhibition area in the ground-floor flat, it can get crowded.

GLASGOW SCIENCE CENTRE

The superb ultra-modern Glasgow Science Centre *(☎ 420 5000, 50 Pacific Quay; adult/child £6.50/4.50; open 10am-6pm daily)* opened in summer 2001 and is Scotland's flagship millennium project at a cost of £75 million. It brings science and technology alive through hundreds of interactive exhibits on four floors; look out for the illusions, and the cloud chamber, showing tracks of natural radiation. Friendly and well-trained staff members assist with queries. There's also a rotating observation tower over 400ft high (adult/child £5.50/4; open 10am to 9pm Thursday to Saturday), a planetarium and an egg-shaped titanium-covered IMAX cinema (adult/child £5.50/4; open 10am to 9pm Thursday to Saturday). Combined and family tickets are available. Take an Arriva (☎ 0870 241 3197) bus No 24 from Renfield St or a First Glasgow bus No 30 from Union St to the Scottish Exhibition and Conference Centre (SECC), then cross Bell's Bridge.

WEST END

In the West End you'll find Glasgow University, several museums and galleries, lots of restaurants and the extensive Kelvingrove Park. The area swarms with students during term time, but it's quieter during the holidays.

Hunterian Museum & Art Gallery

When the Hunterian was opened in 1807 it was Scotland's first public museum. Now part of the university and housed in two separate buildings on either side of University Ave, it contains the collection of

GLASGOW

William Hunter (1718–83), famous physician, medical teacher and one-time student of the university.

The Hunterian Museum (☎ 330 4221, University Ave; admission free; open 9.30am-5pm Mon-Sat), in the main university building, comprises a disparate collection of artefacts including a notable coin collection, fossils and minerals, dinosaur eggs, Romano-British stone slabs and carvings, various other archaeological displays and some of Captain Cook's curios from his voyages to the South Seas.

Behind an imposing pair of cast-aluminium doors by Edinburgh-born Paolozzi is the painting collection of the Hunterian Art Gallery (☎ 330 5431, 82 Hillhead St; admission free; open 9.30am-5pm Mon-Sat), opened in its new home in 1980. The Scottish Colourists – Samuel Peploe, JD Fergusson, Francis Cadell – are well represented. There are also McTaggart's impressionistic Scottish landscapes, and a gem by Thomas Millie Dow. There's a special collection of James McNeill Whistler's limpid prints, drawings and paintings, but there are also some of his personal possessions. It's interesting to compare some of his own furniture and household goods to the contents of the **Mackintosh House**, the final section in the gallery. Look out for three impressive paintings by Chardin.

Set up as a reconstruction of architect Charles Rennie Mackintosh's Glasgow home (which had to be demolished), the style of the Mackintosh House is quite startling even today. You ascend from the gallery's sombre ground floor into the cool, white, austere drawing room. There's something other-worldly about the very mannered style of the beaten silver panels, the long-backed chairs, and the surface decorations echoing Celtic manuscript illuminations. The Northampton guest bedroom is impossibly elegant and dazzling, in blue and white stripes. The Mackintosh House is closed from 12.30pm to 1.30pm.

There's a coffee bar by the museum's entrance and the student refectory is next to the art gallery. Bus Nos 44, 44A and 44D pass this way from the city centre (Hope St).

Kelvingrove Art Gallery & Museum

Opened in 1902, this grand Victorian cathedral of culture (☎ 287 2699, Kelvingrove Park; admission free; open 10am-5pm, 11am-5pm Fri & Sun) should not be missed, particularly for its excellent collection of Scottish and European art. However, the museum may close for around 18 months from November 2002 due to a proposed £25-million redevelopment project.

The impressive central hall is dominated at one end by organ pipes; recitals take place about three times per month. An authentic museum smell emanates from the natural history of Scotland section, popular with school tours. Also downstairs there are some old-fashioned presentations of otherwise interesting artefacts, including archaeological finds of prehistoric and Roman Scotland, European arms and armour, and musical instruments.

The art gallery upstairs houses the city's collection of 19th- and 20th-century works. Scottish painters of luminous landscapes and still lifes are comprehensively represented – Arthur Melville, McTaggart, Cadell, Joseph Crawhall and Joan Eardley. The Scottish Colourists and 'The Glasgow Boys' are well represented. Other paintings include Rembrandt's wonderful Man in Armour, and works by Botticelli, Monet, Van Gogh and Picasso. There are also displays of silver.

The art gallery and museum are grandly set back from the road in Kelvingrove Park, just west of the Kelvin Way, and it has an inexpensive cafe. Any bus heading for Dumbarton Rd, such as Nos 6, 9, 62 and 64, passes this way; Kelvin Hall is the nearest underground station.

Museum of Transport

Across Argyle St from the Hunterian Museum & Art Gallery and is the surprisingly interesting and very comprehensive Museum of Transport (☎ 287 2720, 1 Bunhouse Rd; admission free; open 10am-5pm Mon-Thur & Sat, 11am-5pm Fri & Sun). Exhibits include an excellent reproduction of a 1938 Glasgow street scene, a display of cars made in Scotland, plus assorted railway locos, trams, bikes (including the world's first pedal-powered bicycle from 1847) and model ships. One of the models is the unique circular ship, the *Livadia*. There's a display about the Clyde shipyards.

OTHER THINGS TO SEE

On Glasgow Green, the city's oldest park, **The People's Palace** *(☎ 554 0223, Glasgow Green; admission free; open 10am-5pm Mon-Thur & Sat, 11am-5pm Fri & Sun)* was built in the late 19th century as a cultural centre for Glasgow's East End. It's now a splendid museum of social history, telling the story of the city from 1750 to the present. The refurbished Winter Gardens are also worth seeing.

The **Royal Highland Fusiliers Museum** *(☎ 332 0961, 518 Sauchiehall St; admission free; open 9am-4.30pm Mon-Thurs, 9am-4pm Fri, weekends by appointment only)* charts the history of this and previous regiments from 1678 to the present. Exhibits include uniforms, medals, pictures and other militaria. Wrought ironwork within the museum was designed by Mackintosh.

Fossil Grove *(☎ 950 1448, Victoria Park, Dumbarton Rd; admission free; open noon-5pm daily Apr-Sept)* has sections of 350-million-year-old fossilised trees, lying as they were found. Information boards provide explanations for this Site of Special Scientific Interest. To get here, take bus No 44 or 44D from the city centre to Victoria Park Drive North or bus No 9 or 62 to Dumbarton Rd.

Holmwood House *(NTS; ☎ 637 2129, 61-63 Netherlee Rd, Cathcart; adult/child £3.50/2.50; open 1.30pm-5.30pm daily Apr-Oct)* is an interesting building designed by Alexander 'Greek' Thomson and built between 1857 and 1858. Despite ongoing renovations, it's well worth a visit. Look out for sun symbols downstairs and stars upstairs in this attractive house with its adaptation of classical Greek architecture. To get to Cathcart train station, take a 'Cathcart Circle' train via Queen's Park or a train to Neilston (four hourly from Central Station). Otherwise, take bus No 44, 44A, 44D or 66 from the city centre. Then you should follow Rhannan Rd for about half a mile (1km) to Holmwood House.

The **Scottish Football Museum** *(☎ 616 6100, Hampden Park; adult/child £5/2.50; open 10am-5pm Mon-Sat, 11am-5pm Sun)* features temporary and permanent exhibits describing the history of the game in Scotland and the influence of Scots on the world game. You can view a press box and changing rooms. There's also a library and archive (opening 2002) and a cafe. A 45-minute tour of Hampden Park (see the boxed text 'Hampden Park – Scotland's Field of Dreams' later in this chapter) costs £2.50/1.25, when available. Hampden Park is off Aikenhead Rd, Mount Florida, in South Side. To get there, you can take a train to Mount Florida station (trains bound for Neilston or Newton, four per hour) or take bus No 5, 31, 37, 74 or 75 from Stockwell St.

The Barras, Glasgow's flea market on Gallowgate, shouldn't be missed. There are almost a thousand stalls and people come here just for a wander as much as for shopping, which gives the place a holiday air. It takes place only on Saturday and Sunday. The Barras is notorious for designer frauds, so be cautious. Watch your wallet too.

WALKING & CYCLING

There are numerous green spaces within the city. **Pollok Country Park** surrounds the Burrell Collection and has numerous woodland trails. Nearer the centre of the city, the Kelvin Walkway follows the River Kelvin through Kelvingrove Park, the Botanic Gardens and on to Dawsholm Park.

There are several long-distance pedestrian/cycle routes that originate in Glasgow and follow off-road routes for most of the way. The TIC has a range of maps and leaflets detailing these routes, most of which start from Bell's Bridge (by the SECC). For the latest information on the expanding National Cycle Network, contact Sustrans on ☎ 0131-623 7600, or check out the Web at Ⓦ www.sustrans.org.uk.

The Glasgow–Loch Lomond Route traverses residential and industrial areas, following a disused railway to Clydebank, the Forth and Clyde canal towpath to Bowling, then a disused railway to Dumbarton,

GLASGOW

reaching Loch Lomond via the towpath by the River Leven. This route continues all the way to Inverness, from Balloch via Aberfoyle, Loch Vennachar, Callander and Strathyre to link with the Glen Ogle Trail, Killin, Pitlochry and Aviemore.

The Glasgow–Greenock/Gourock Route runs via Paisley, this first section partly on roads. From Johnstone to Greenock the route follows a disused railway line; the final section to Gourock has now been built. Sculpture from the Sustrans public arts project brightens parts of the way.

The Glasgow–Irvine, Ardrossan and West Kilbride Cycle Way runs via Paisley, then off-road as far as Glengarnock. From here to Kilwinning it follows minor roads, then the route is partly off-road. Ferries to the Isle of Arran, popular with cyclists, leave from Ardrossan. An extension via Ayr, Maybole and Glentrool leads to the Solway coast and Carlisle.

The Glasgow to Edinburgh Route has now opened. It partly follows the Clyde walkway and a disused railway line. Also, in the future, cycle routes should be completed to Callander via the Bridge of Allan and to Carlisle via the Clyde Valley and Annandale.

The long-distance footpath known as the West Highland Way begins in Milngavie, 8 miles (13km) north of Glasgow, and runs for 95 miles (153km) to Fort William (see Walking in the Activities chapter).

ORGANISED TOURS

Mercat Tours (☎ 772 0022) runs 1½-hour guided walking tours, leaving from the TIC daily at 7pm from March to November, 2pm daily in July and August and also at 9pm from April to October, for £5/4. The latter, known as the Ghosts & Ghouls Walking Tour, includes a night visit to the cathedral and graveyard, which requires some nerve.

Walkabout Glasgow Tours (☎ 204 4400) provide an entertaining 31-minute audio commentary for a 1½- to 3½-hour walking route through the city. Headphones cost £5 per day from the TIC.

For a 90-minute combined land and river tour, contact *glasgowDucks (☎ 0870 013 6140; adult/child £11.50/9.50)*. Departures

from the Glasgow Science Centre are at 10am, noon, 3pm and 5pm Thursday to Sunday.

The *Waverley (☎ 221 8152)*, the world's last ocean-going paddle steamer, cruises the Firth of Clyde from the Waverley Terminal daily in April, July and August. It serves several towns and the islands of Bute, Great Cumbrae and Arran. Tickets cost between £6 and £30 depending on where you're going.

SPECIAL EVENTS

Not to be outdone by Edinburgh, Glasgow has developed several festivals of its own, starting each January with the two-week Celtic Connections music festival (☎ 353 8000).

The Bearsden & Milngavie Highland Games (☎ 942 5177) are held in early June. The West End Festival of music and the arts (☎ 341 0844) runs for two weeks in June and it's currently Glasgow's biggest festival. The excellent International Jazz Festival (☎ 552 3552) is held in early July.

Glasgay (☎ 334 7126, W www.glasgay.co .uk) is a gay performing arts festival, held around October/November.

Other festivals include the classical RSNO Proms (☎ 353 8000) in June and the World Pipe Band Championships (☎ 221 5414) in mid-August, with around 200 pipe bands.

PLACES TO STAY

Finding somewhere decent in July and August can be difficult – for a B&B, get into town reasonably early and use the TIC's booking service. Unfortunately, many of Glasgow's B&Bs are expensive by Scottish standards (you may have to pay up to £35 for a single), but several new hostels have opened in recent years. At weekends, many of the expensive business hotels slash their prices by up to 50%, making them great value for tourists.

Places to Stay – Budget

Craigendmuir Park (☎ 779 2973/4159, fax 779 4057, Campsie View, Stepps) From £7.50 per tent. Open year-round. The nearest camp site to town, this is a 15-minute walk from Stepps station. It takes caravans and tents.

Hostels & Colleges There are plenty of hostels and colleges to take advantage of in Glasgow. Most are to be found in the West End.

Glasgow Youth Hostel (☎ 332 3004, fax 332 5007, 7-8 Park Terrace) Beds adult/child £10/8.50. Once a hotel, the SYHA hostel has mostly four-bed dorms, many with en-suite facilities, as well as four doubles. In summer, it's advisable to make a booking. Reception opens at 2pm, but the door's locked at 2am. From Central Station take bus No 44 and ask for the first stop on Woodlands Rd.

Glasgow Backpackers Hostel (☎ 332 9099, fax 220 1869, 17 Park Terrace, e glasgow@scotlands-top-hostels.com) Beds from £10; twin rooms from £11.50 per person. Open July-Sept. Near the youth hostel, this independent hostel is in an impressive Georgian terrace and provides free tea and coffee.

Bunkum Backpackers (☎/fax 581 4481, 26 Hillhead St, e jjkinnell@aol.com) Dorm beds £9, twin rooms for £12 per person. This hostel is close to Glasgow University and the Byres Rd action spots.

Euro Hostel (☎ 222 2828, fax 222 2829, 318 Clyde St, e info@euro-hostels.com) B&B £13.75-25 per person. The 380-bed Euro Hostel, in a former student hall of residence, has 24-hour reception, en-suite rooms and provides a buffet breakfast. There's a microwave facility, but no kitchen. Internet access costs around £1.50 to £3 per hour.

University of Glasgow (☎ 330 5385, fax 334 5465, e vacation@gla.ac.uk) B&B £17.75-31 per person; self-catering per night £14-35, per week £84-210. Open mid-Mar to mid-Apr & July-Sept. The University of Glasgow has a range of B&B accommodation around the city (confirm locations when booking).

The University of Strathclyde (☎ 553 4148, fax 553 4149, e rescat@mis.strath.ac.uk) opens the following halls of residence to tourists from mid-June to mid-September:

Campus Village (☎ 552 0626, fax 553 4194, Rottenrow East) Bed-only rate from £13.50, en-suite B&B singles/doubles £24/40. Opposite Glasgow Cathedral, the Campus Village office opens 24 hours, but phone ahead to make arrangements. There's a coin-operated laundry next to the office.

Jordanhill Campus (☎ 950 3508, fax 950 3320, 76 Southbrae Drive). Singles from £16. If you don't mind staying farther out of town, the university's cheapest B&B accommodation is at Jordanhill Campus. Bus No 44 from Central Station goes to the college gates.

Baird Hall (☎ 332 6415, 460 Sauchiehall St) B&B from £16.50. The university's impressive Art Deco Baird Hall is in a great location and offers some B&B accommodation year-round.

Places to Stay – Mid-Range & Top End

City Centre There are several similarly priced places along Renfrew St.

McLay's Guest House (☎ 332 4796, fax 353 0422, 268 Renfrew St) Singles/doubles £21/38, with bathroom £27/46. With 62 rooms, this labyrinthine place is brilliantly located behind Sauchiehall St.

The Old School House (☎ 332 7600, fax 332 8684, 194 Renfrew St) B&B singles/doubles from £29/46, with bathroom £35/54. The rooms in this listed building have been pleasantly restored and all but one are en suite.

Victorian House (☎ 332 0129, fax 353 3155, 212 Renfrew St) Singles/doubles £23/38, with bathroom £32/54. This is a large guesthouse just down the road from the School of Art.

Willow Hotel (☎ 332 2332, fax 353 0961, 228 Renfrew St) offers B&B in en-suite rooms for £24/44 to £32/50.

Babbity Bowster (☎ 552 5055, fax 552 7774, 16-18 Blackfriars St) Singles/doubles £50/70. This place is a very lively pub/restaurant (see Entertainment later in this chapter) with six bedrooms, each with a bathroom. It's a great place to stay but forget it if you like to turn in early with a nice cup of cocoa.

Premier Lodge (☎ 221 1000, fax 248 1000, 10 Elmbank Gardens) Singles/doubles £52/58 including breakfast. This hotel is located in the tower above Charing Cross train station.

Glasgow Marriott (☎ 226 5577, fax 221 7676, 500 Argyle St) B&B £67.50-148.50 Sun-Thur, £39-59 Fri-Sat. This is a very comfortable city-centre hotel.

East End There's a batch of reasonable-value B&Bs located to the east of the Necropolis.

The rooms in the following three guest houses have shared bathrooms. *Alison Guest House* (☎/fax 556 1431, 26 Circus Drive) has singles for £16-20 and doubles for £30-32; *Craigpark Guest House* (☎ 554 4160, 33 Circus Drive) offers B&B for £16-18; *Seton Guest House* (☎ 556 7654, fax 402 3655, 6 Seton Terrace) has singles/doubles from £17/34.

Cathedral House Hotel (☎ 552 3519, fax 552 2444, 28 Cathedral Square) Singles/doubles from £49/69. One of the best places to stay in Glasgow is the small Cathedral House Hotel, housed in a Victorian baronial-style building complete with turrets, with eight well-appointed rooms, all en suite. It's very close to the cathedral and easily accessible from the M8. There's also a restaurant with contemporary Scottish cuisine (two courses around £11).

West End Many of the places to stay in this area are situated on or around Great Western Rd. There are several B&Bs on Hillhead St (just south of Great Western Rd and near Byres Rd).

Chez Nous Guest House (☎ 334 2977, 33 Hillhead St). Singles £16-30, doubles £40-60. There are 31 rooms here, fifteen of which have attached bathroom.

Iona Guest House (☎ 334 2346, fax 334 7561, 39 Hillhead St) B&B from £23/36. The Iona is much smaller than Chez Nous, but with very pleasant rooms.

Amadeus Guest House (☎ 339 8257, fax 339 8859, 411 North Woodside Rd) B&B £18-30. This place is just north of Great Western Rd and the M8. Some rooms have en-suite shower.

Kirklee Hotel (☎ 334 5555, fax 339 3828, 11 Kensington Gate) Singles/doubles from £48/64. The highly recommended Kirklee Hotel is more upmarket than most

in the area and you'll probably be treated as well as the plants in the window boxes – which are very well treated indeed. All rooms have a bathroom.

Terrace House Hotel (☎ 337 3377, fax 400 3378, 14 Belhaven Terrace) Singles £39-62, doubles £58-78. You'll find the Terrace House Hotel just off Great Western Rd, a little nearer the city centre. There are nine rooms, all with attached bathrooms.

Town House (☎ 357 0862, fax 339 9605, 4 Hughenden Terrace) Singles/doubles from £58/68. This place is similar to Kirklee Hotel and Terrace House Hotel, with 10 en-suite rooms. It's very well run and an excellent choice.

Alamo Guest House (☎ 339 2395, 46 Gray St) Singles/doubles from £20/34. This place has 10 rooms and is good value.

Smith's Hotel (☎ 339 7674, fax 334 1892, 963 Sauchiehall St) Singles £20-35, doubles £36-50. Established in 1928, this is a pleasant family-run hotel.

One Devonshire Gardens (☎ 339 2001, fax 337 1663, 1 Devonshire Gardens) Singles/doubles from £159.50/184.50. Reputedly the best hotel in Glasgow and with the atmosphere of a luxurious country house, the five-star One Devonshire Gardens is sumptuously decorated and occupies three classical terrace houses. There are 27 rooms, all en suite and very well appointed. As one might expect, there's also an excellent restaurant here, with main courses from around £17 to £21.

South Side In quiet suburbs near Pollokshaws Rd, Pollok Country Park and the Burrell Collection, there are several places to stay.

Reidholme Guest House (☎ 423 1855, 36 Regent Park Square) B&B £20-22. There are six rooms here, but only one has an en-suite bathroom.

Dunkeld Hotel (☎ 424 0160, fax 423 4437, 10 Queen's Drive) Singles £30-45 doubles £44-60. In this recommended hotel, all rooms have a private bathroom and set dinners cost £11.

Boswell Hotel (☎ 632 9812, fax 636 4472, 27 Mansionhouse Rd) Singles/doubles

£42.50/60 weekdays, £35/50 weekends. On the other side of Pollokshaws Rd, just south of Queen's Park and off Langside Ave, the Boswell Hotel is also known as a watering hole, with its three bars and occasional live music. All rooms have attached bath/showers.

North of Pollok Country Park, in the Bellahouston area between the M8 and M77, and in Ibrox, north of the M8, there are a couple of small B&Bs. *Glasgow Guest House (☎/fax 427 0129, 56 Dumbreck Rd)* has en-suite singles/doubles from £25/40. B&B at the comfortable and nicely decorated *Holly House (☎ 427 5609, fax 427 5608, 54 Ibrox Terrace)* costs £30/19 with/without private bathroom.

PLACES TO EAT

Thirty years ago, when the pubs in Scotland closed at 10pm, Glaswegians went to restaurants to take advantage of extended licensing hours, and not for the food. Things are very different now and Glasgow not only has an excellent range of places to eat but many are also very moderately priced.

The West End probably has the greatest range of restaurants, everything from Glasgow's most famous place to eat, the upmarket Ubiquitous Chip, to cheap cafes where they really do serve chips with everything. In the city centre, however, and along Sauchiehall St, there are no shortage of places to eat either.

If you're on a budget, have your main meal at lunchtime – the set lunches offered by many restaurants and pubs are usually very good value at £3 to £6.

Many Glasgow restaurants post excellent offers on the Internet (changing daily) at W www.5pm.co.uk.

West End

The main restaurant/pub area in the West End is just west of Glasgow University, around Byres Rd. The nearest underground station is Hillhead.

Café Antipasti (☎ 337 2737, 337 Byres Rd) Lunch £3.45-4.25, evening dishes £5.40-8.55. This is a pleasant and busy place, with good food too.

University Café (☎ 339 5217, 87 Byres Rd) Meals under £4.20. This university institution is very cheap; there's fish and chips and salad, excellent pizza and superb home-made ice-cream.

Just off Byres Rd, on the east side, Ashton Lane is packed with places to eat, including some of Glasgow's best restaurants.

Grosvenor Café (☎ 339 1848, 35 Ashton Lane) Evening specials around £10. The Grosvenor Café is cheaper during the day, when you can get soup, filled rolls and hot meals. Try the pizza with fried egg for £1.50. It's cosy and popular with families.

Ashoka (☎ 357 5904, 19 Ashton Lane) 2-course pre-theatre menu £7.95. This is a fairly good Indian restaurant.

Ubiquitous Chip (☎ 334 5007, 12 Ashton Lane) 3-course dinner with coffee £33.95. This restaurant has earned a solid reputation for its excellent Scottish cuisine, fresh seafood and game, and for the length of its wine list. Set among potted plants of arboreal proportions this is an excellent place for a night out. There's a cheaper restaurant here, *Upstairs at the Chip*, where two courses at lunchtime will cost less than £10.

Mitchells (☎ 339 2220, 35 Ashton Lane) Main courses £11.95-14.25. Open Mon-Sat. This is an informal bistro with some excellent Scottish dishes.

On the west side of Byres Rd, directly across from Ashton Lane, is Ruthven Lane where, among the wacky shops, there are a number of interesting places to eat.

Stravaigin II (☎ 334 7165, 8 Ruthven Lane) Main courses mostly £8-10. The home-made Scottish food here includes vegetarian options.

Puppet Theatre (☎ 339 8444, 11 Ruthven Lane) Lunch mains £5-10.50, dinner mains £7.95-22.50. The Puppet Theatre is a classy and expensive place featuring Scottish cuisine.

Di Maggio's (☎ 334 8560, 61 Ruthven Lane) Pizza & pasta £3.95-6.95. Down the lane from Puppet Theatre is Di Maggio's, good for pizzas and pasta (with vegetarian options).

Those staying in the vicinity of Kelvingrove Park will find a scattering of good

GLASGOW

restaurants on or around Gibson St and Great Western Rd.

Stravaigin (☎ 334 2665, 28 Gibson St) 3-course menu £25.95. The highly recommended and award-winning Stravaigin serves meals cooked to order. There's also a cheaper menu upstairs; the fish supper with Caledonian 80/- batter (£6.25), Thai red curry with chicken (£6.65) and oven-baked west-coast mackerel (£6.95) are particularly good.

Bay Tree Café (☎ 334 5898, 403 Great Western Rd) Main courses under £4.50. Open 9am-9pm daily. The vegetarian Bay Tree Café is excellent value. The salads are generous and there's a good range of hot drinks. The cafe is famous for its all-day Sunday brunch, served from 9am to 8pm, including vegetarian burger, tattie scone, mushrooms, beans and tomato (£4.50). Falafel with pitta bread and dip costs £4.25. If you're in a hurry, the cafe also serves takeaways.

There are several other places scattered around the West End, just west of the M8.

Insomnia Café (☎ 564 1530, 38 Woodlands Rd) Main courses £4-6.50. Scotland's first 24-hour cafe, has never closed since it first opened in October 1995. Breakfast is a la carte or £5.50 fixed-price; there's also a wide range of meals, herbal teas and coffees.

Thai Fountain (☎ 332 1599, 2 Woodside Crescent) 2-course lunch £7.80, most main courses £9-13. Thai Fountain is an excellent place and is renowned for its food. There are vegetarian choices and all main courses are half-price from 5.30pm to 7pm on weekdays and 5.30pm to 6.30pm on Saturday.

The Buttery (☎ 221 8188, 652 Argyle St) 3-course dinner £34.95. Open Mon-Sat. This elegant place, with a Scottish menu, is one of the best restaurants in the city.

The Belfry (☎ 221 0630, 652 Argyle St) 2-course lunch or dinner £11. Open noon-2.30pm & 6pm-10pm Mon-Sat. Downstairs from The Buttery is this cheaper bistro. Reservations are advised.

Mitchell's (☎ 204 4312, 157 North St) Lunch main courses £6.50-7.95, 3-course pre-theatre meals £11.95. Near the Mitchell Library is Mitchell's, an excellent bistro with a Scottish and international menu.

Mother India (☎ 221 1663, 28 Westminster Terrace) Main courses £5.75-9.50, 2-course lunch & pre-theatre menus both £8.50. Open Wed-Fri for lunch and daily for dinner. By Sauchiehall St, Mother India has wide-ranging vegetarian choices and is highly recommended.

Snaffle Bit (☎ 339 7163, 975 Sauchiehall St) Snacks & meals £1.30-3.95. This is a popular place for a bar meal, such as homemade soup (£1.30) or steak pie (£3.95).

City Centre

There are lots of restaurants to choose from in Glasgow's city centre.

Chinatown Restaurant (☎ 353 0037, 42 New City Rd) Most main courses £9-15. You'll see many people from the Glaswegian Chinese community eating in this highly recommended and authentic restaurant. Vegetarian dishes are great value at £6.80 to £7.80.

Ciao Italia (☎ 332 4565, 441 Sauchiehall St) Express lunch & drink £4.95. Dinner & drink around £10. This is an efficient Italian restaurant.

Loon Fung (☎ 332 1240, 417 Sauchiehall St) Set dinners from £18, 3-course lunch £7.90. This is one of the best Chinese restaurants in town.

Centre for Contemporary Arts (☎ 332 7521, 346 Sauchiehall St) Snacks around £2-6. The pleasant cafe at the Centre for Contemporary Arts reopened in October 2001 after major refurbishment and offers sandwiches and light meals.

Bradford's (☎ 332 5071, 245 Sauchiehall St) Breakfast from £3.85, light meals £3.50-5.85. The main branch of Glasgow's well-known bakery chain Bradford's has a good tearoom upstairs.

Willow Tea Rooms (☎ 332 0521, 217 Sauchiehall St) Light meals around £4-6. Open 9am-5pm Mon-Sat and 11am-5pm Sun (last orders 4.15pm daily). Located above a jewellery shop, the Willow Tea Rooms was designed by Charles Rennie Mackintosh in 1903. At lunch- and tea-time the queues can extend into the gift shop and jeweller's downstairs. Avoid them by arriving when it opens and splash out on a superior breakfast of smoked salmon, scrambled eggs and toast

(£5.35). There's another branch (☎ 204 5242) at 97 Buchanan St.

Delifrance (☎ 353 2700, 119 Sauchiehall St) This branch of the patisserie chain serves good filled baguettes, but they're rather pricey (from £3.65); takeaways are cheaper.

Blue Lagoon (☎ 332 7071, 109 West Nile St) At Blue Lagoon, takeaway fish and chips or chicken and chips is only £2.60.

Jade House (☎ 332 1932, 7 Bath St) 3-course lunches £5.95, 3-course dinners £9.50. Open Mon-Sat. This is a very pleasant Chinese restaurant with an extensive a la carte menu. Vegetarian and takeaway meals are available.

At Princes Square, the stylish shopping centre on Buchanan St, the basement is given over to pricey restaurants ranging from American to Italian.

Yes (☎ 221 8044, 22 West Nile St) 2-course/3-course dinner £24.95/29.50. This stylish restaurant, bar and brasserie has a great reputation. It has an express-lunch menu (all dishes served in under 15 minutes), with main courses for £8.95. In the evening, you can enjoy a three-course meal in the brasserie for £12.95 while listening to live piano music (6pm to 7.30pm Monday to Saturday).

The Granary (☎ 226 3770, 82 Howard St) Main courses £3.55-4.25. Near the St Enoch Centre, the Granary is a pleasant and inexpensive place. It's mainly vegetarian but also has a few nonveg choices.

Aulds on the Terrace (☎ 221 6988, St Enoch Centre) Snacks 49p-£3.58. This coffee shop is popular with shoppers and does a wide range of snacks (sandwiches, toasties, baked potatoes, salads).

GLASGOW

The Glesca Patois

Glasgow enjoys a rich local dialect and a knowledge of the vernacular might make your visit there a wee bit more interesting.

For many, the pub is a focal point of social life. Order a 'half and a half', and you'll get a whisky and a half pint of beer. Seasoned drinkers may refer to their whisky as a 'wee goldie', or a 'nippy sweetie'. A pint of heavy will get you dark draught beer. A 'heavy bevvy' on the other hand will get you a major hangover with a 'loupin' heid' (headache), 'dry boke' (nausea) and/or feeling 'awfy no weel' (very under the weather) the next day.

There may be some football supporters in the pub. The 'Bhoys' (Celtic football club) wear green colours and are traditionally supported by the 'Tims' (Catholics). The 'Gers' (Rangers football club) wear blue and are the 'Huns' (Protestant) team.

Football can be a touchy subject in Glasgow. Tell anyone who asks that you're a 'Jags' (Partick Thistle) supporter and you're on neutral ground. Billy Connolly, the comedian, who grew up in Partick, claims that he always thought the full team name was 'Partick Thistle Nil'. Enough said.

When males spot a 'wee stoater' (good-looking young woman) in the bar, they might be inclined to try their 'patter' (witty chat) on her. Impress her, and they might get a 'lumber' (pick-up). Inane conversation about the weather, 'the nights are fair drawin' in' (the days are getting shorter), or 'it's stoatin' doon ootside' (it's raining very heavily), will not impress, and almost certainly result in a 'KB' (knock-back, rejection). Should her boyfriend, 'the Big Yin', arrive unexpectedly, and offer to 'mollocate', 'wanner' or 'stiffen' the would-be lothario, or alternatively to give him his 'heid in your hauns' (head in your hands), then violence is probably imminent.

At that point it's best to 'shoot the crow' (go) before a 'stooshie' (brawl) develops, and, in future, to give that particular pub the 'body swerve' (a wide berth).

However, Glaswegians are very friendly to travellers. You may be addressed as 'Jimmy' or 'Hen', depending on your sex. If you refer to their city as 'Glesca', and never 'Glasgie', they may even mistake you for a local.

John McKenna

Tivoli (☎ *552 1690, 39 Stockwell St*) is a cafe with takeaways including filled rolls from 75p and fish and chips for £3.75. Try its excellent ice-cream – banana splits are £3.25.

Café Gandolfi (☎ *552 6813, 64 Albion St*) Main courses £4.80-11.60. In the Merchant City, near the City Halls, this cafe was once part of the old cheese market. It's now an excellent, friendly bistro and up-market coffee shop – very much the place to be seen. Arbroath smokies (smoked haddock) baked with tomatoes and cream cost £4.50.

Artà (☎ *552 2101, 13 Walls St*) 2-course pre-theatre Wed-Sun £9.95. This is an extraordinary hacienda-style place that has to be seen to be believed. Tapas cost £2.50 to £7.50, pizza and paella are £8.50 to £12, and vegetarian options are available. See Modern Bars under Entertainment for details of what else Artà has to offer.

Loop (☎ *572 1472, 64 Ingram St*) Light meals £5.95, main courses £6.95-15.50. Loop is a bright and modern bistro-style place with an excellent Scottish and international menu.

ENTERTAINMENT

A decade ago, Glasgow offered you the choice of posh boozer or squalid boozer. These days there are as many different styles of bar as there are punters to guzzle in them.

Space only allows us to list a few of the best bars and clubs here; a month of solid drinking wouldn't get you through the rest. For more information, splash out £1.95 on *The List* magazine.

Pubs

Traditional Pubs Old-style pubs with old-world character are easily found in Glasgow.

Waxy O'Connors (☎ *354 5154, 46 West George St*) If you've been trying to avoid those acid flashbacks, steer clear of Waxy O'Connors: this labyrinthine maze of six bars on three levels is an Escher drawing brought to life. Sadly, it's also an Irish-themed bar, but even that doesn't ruin the surreal fun.

The Drum & Monkey (☎ *221 6636, 93-95 Vincent St*) Jazz fans can get their fix on Sunday afternoons at the Drum & Monkey; the rest of the week, jazz records accompany the dark wood and marble columns of this beautiful drinking emporium.

The Horse Shoe (☎ *229 5711, 17 Drury St*) This charming pub has one of Europe's longest bars; more important are the real ales served over it. It also offers the best value three-course lunch in town (£2.80).

Scotia (☎ *552 8681, 112 Stockwell St*) Drinks have been poured down throats at Scotia, Glasgow's oldest pub, since 1792. And while the last good airing feels like it happened back in the mid-1850s, Scotia's cheery charm outweighs the grungy atmosphere. There's live folk music on Wednesday and blues on Sunday.

Blackfriars (☎ *552 5924, 36 Bell St*) Merchant City's most relaxed and atmospheric pub, Blackfriars' friendly staff and chilled-out house make it special. There is free jazz at weekends.

Babbity Bowster (☎ *552 5055, 16-18 Blackfriars St*) Babbity Bowster has live music most nights, and is perfect for a quiet daytime drink.

Uisge Beatha (☎ *564 1596, 232-246 Woodlands Rd*) If you enjoy a drink among dead things, you'll love Uisge Beatha (Gaelic for whisky, literal translation: 'water of life') in the West End. Stuffed animals line those walls not filled by disturbing paintings of meadows or depressed lords, and with 100 whiskies and four quirky rooms to choose from, this unique pub is one of Glasgow's best.

Halt Bar (☎ *564 1527, 160 Woodlands Rd*) Glasgow University students pile into the Halt Bar for the cheap drinks, rough-and-ready vibe and live music.

Modern Bars If sleek, slick and chic is more your style, Glasgow has dozens of modern bars to choose from.

Artà (☎ *552 2101, 13-19 Walls St*) Opulent Artà is decadence on a scale the Romans would've appreciated. This spectacularly cavernous place is a must-see for any style diva (see also Places to Eat earlier).

Corinthian (☎ *552 1101, 191 Ingram St*) A breathtaking domed ceiling makes Corinthian an awesome venue, though the lavish bill might also leave you awe-struck.

Originally a bank and later Glasgow's High Court, this majestic building also houses two plush clubs – Life and Q – downstairs in old court cells. There is a strict dress code for these clubs.

Strata (☎ 221 1888, 45 Queen St) The glamorous young things strutting their booty about Strata try a bit too hard, but it's forgivable because this bar's design really is superb.

Bar 10 (☎ 221 8353, 10 Mitchell Lane) Designed by the Hacienda's Ben Kelly, Bar 10 is as laid back as you could ask in a hip city bar; friendly, tuned-in staff complete the happy picture.

Underworld (☎ 221 5020, 95 Union St) Underworld's nightly flood of worker ants is slightly terrifying, but at other times this bar below Central Station is the perfect subterranean watering hole.

Crystal Palace (☎ 221 2624, 36 Jamaica St) The craven hoards that stampede Crystal Palace each night have one thing in mind – cheap booze. And with bottles of wine at £5 and space for 1000 drinkers, this two-level barn serves them admirably.

Brunswick Cellars (☎ 572 0016, 239 Sauchiehall St) Be careful wandering downstairs into Brunswick Cellars: it's dark. The payoff is the cosy vibe of candlelit punters. Or maybe we just imagined that – it was quite hard to see.

Nice 'n' Sleazy (333 0900, 421 Sauchiehall St) Close to the Glasgow School of Art, students come here to discuss primers, Duchamp and Nietzche over Glasgow's cheapest drinks. There are often young bands in the downstairs bar (Mogwai, and Belle and Sebastian started here).

Gay & Lesbian

Glasgow's vibrant gay scene is huge, and many straight clubs and bars have gay and lesbian nights. Check out the *List*, the free *Scots Gay* magazine, and the Web site at W www.gay-glasgow.co.uk .

Polo Lounge (☎ 553 1221, 84 Wilson St) Staff claim 'the city's best talent' is found here; a quick glance at the many glamour pusses – male and female – proves their claim. The downstairs club is packed at weekends; other nights just the main bars open.

Moda (☎ 553 1221, Cnr Virginia & Wilson Sts) Blonde wood and fake tan are the chief attributes of Moda, a place where beautiful folk strike a pose over daytime drinks, or recuperate before returning to the Polo Lounge next door or going downmarket at Delmonica's.

Delmonica's (☎ 552 4803, 68 Virginia St) Metres from the Polo Lounge, Delmonica's is a world away, with its predatorial feeling of people on the pull. It's packed on weekday evenings.

Revolver (☎ 553 2456, 5a John St) Hip little Revolver, downstairs on cosmopolitan John St, sports a relaxed crowd and, crucially, a free jukebox.

Candle Bar (☎ 552 8717, 20 Candleriggs) The Candle Bar's gaudy interior draws a brash young set, though regular karaoke nights bring all sorts out of the woodwork.

Bennet's (☎ 552 5761, W www.bennets.co.uk, 80 Glassford St) Glasgow's longest-running gay club, Bennet's opens Wednesday to Sunday with a mix of '70s and '80s disco and pop.

Clubs

There once was a time when Glasgow's club dress code was black shoes; these dark ages have thankfully passed and anywhere worth spending your money couldn't care less about footwear.

Glaswegians hit the clubs after the pubs close, so many offer discounted entry and cheaper drinks before 11pm. Clubs charge for entry; you might avoid this by asking for passes at bars – many are linked to nights or share DJs. Entry varies from £3 to £5, though large venues might try to make you part with £6 or more. There's usually a £1 to £2 student discount. Most close around 3am.

MAS (☎ 221 7080, 29 Royal Exchange Square) Run by the same folk as the achingly cool *Republic Biere Halle (9 Gordon St)*, MAS is less style-obsessed and puts together Glasgow's best hard house instead.

The Tunnel (☎ 204 1000, 84 Mitchell St) This is the venue to hear big-name DJs such as Paul Oakenfold and Judge Jules; resident mixers pump out trance and hard house at other times.

GLASGOW

The 13th Note (☎ 243 2177, 260 Clyde St) This club plays everything from jazz to hip hop to Latin disco.

Archaos (☎ 204 3189, 25 Queen St) Archaos' Gatecrusher feel and mix of house and garage pulls a young crowd on weekdays and a hipper, older crowd at the weekend.

Privilege (☎ 204 5233, 69 Hope St) Privilege's main drawcard is its 'Shagtag' Thursdays. The numerical flirting game works thus: everyone's given a numbered board and text. Spot someone you fancy, scribble their number on your board and hold tight until they spot it and chemistry runs its unpredictable course.

The Arches (☎ 221 4001, Midland St, Off Jamaica St) The Arches holds 2000 people and, as the name cunningly suggests, is designed around hundreds of arches slammed together. The music is house or funk.

The Cathouse (☎ 248 6606, 15 Union St) Cake on the foundation and rejoin your Goth brethren at the three-level Cathouse, Glasgow's top indie and alternative venue.

The Shack (☎ 332 7522, 193 Pitt St) Renowned as Glasgow's top student pick-up joint, The Shack plays current chart-topping horrors and the odd indie classic.

The Garage (☎ 332 1120, 490 Sauchiehall St) Students who consider themselves a cut above The Shack pile into The Garage for cheap beer and low-brow house.

King Tut's Wah Wah Hut (☎ 221 5279, 272a St Vincent St) Oasis made Britpop history by debuting here, though it's probably just the cheap drinks keeping the Hut popular these days.

Concerts, Theatre & Film

Theatre Royal (☎ 332 9000, 282 Hope St, W www.theatreroyalglasgow.com) This is the home of Scottish Opera, and the Scottish Ballet often performs here.

Glasgow Royal Concert Hall (☎ 287 5511, 2 Sauchiehall St, W www.grch.com) The Royal Scottish National Orchestra as well as pop and rock bands play at this modern concert hall.

King's Theatre (☎ 287 5511, 294 Bath St) Tickets £5-28.50. The King's Theatre hosts mainly musicals; on rare occasions,

there are variety shows, pantomimes and comedies.

SECC (☎ 0870 040 4000; W www.secc .co.uk) Rock and pop bands on the international circuit usually play in the Armadillo (Clyde Auditorium) at the SECC – the Scottish Exhibition and Conference Centre – a bizarre looking place by the River Clyde, which holds up to 3000 people.

Barrowland Ballroom (☎ 552 4601, 244 Gallowgate) Some bands choose this place, a vast dance hall in the East End that's far funkier than the SECC.

Citizens' Theatre (☎ 429 0022, 119 Gorbals St, W www.citz.co.uk) Tickets cost adults £6-12, concessions £3-6. This is one of the top theatres in Scotland and it's well worth trying to catch a performance here.

Tron Theatre (☎ 552 4267, 63 Trongate W www.tron.co.uk) Tron Theatre stages contemporary Scottish and international performances. There's also a good cafe here.

Centre for Contemporary Arts (☎ 332 0522, 350 Sauchiehall St, W www.cca -glasgow.com) After a £10-million facelift this interesting centre and pleasant cafe reopened for business in October 2001.

Glasgow Film Theatre (☎ 332 8128, 12 Rose St, W www.scot-art.org/gft) Tickets cost adults £3.75-£4.75, concessions £2-3.50. The two-screen Glasgow Film Theatre, off Sauchiehall St, screens art-house cinema and classics.

Odeon Renfield Street (☎ 332 3413, 56 Renfield St) The nine-screen Odeon Renfield Street shows mainstream films for £4.50 (concessions £3.50).

SPECTATOR SPORTS

Celtic Football Club (☎ 551 8653, W www .celticfc.co.uk), Celtic Park, Parkhead (in the East End), has a 60,832-seat stadium with a restaurant. Celtic are a strong force in Scottish football and were the Scottish League champions in 2001. Adult tickets cost between £15 and £25; child tickets cost £11.

Rangers Football Club (☎ 0870 600 1993 W www.rangers.co.uk), Ibrox Stadium, 150 Edmiston Dr (in the South Side), is no stranger to controversial players. The restaurant, however, has a good reputation; snacks

Hampden Park – Scotland's Field of Dreams

Scotland's National Football Stadium is most unusual since it's home to an amateur club, Queen's Park, founded in 1867 as Scotland's first football club.

Always shy of professionalism, Queen's Park didn't join the Scottish League until 1900. In 1903, it moved to its newly built Hampden Stadium, which has since been modified and upgraded several times. Initially, the stadium could hold 40,000 standing and 4000 seated spectators. Its main use has been for international matches, particularly against England, and Scottish Cup Finals, passionate sporting contests that have spawned legendary characters. The 1937 Scotland-England game drew an incredible 149,547 spectators, the highest ever official football match attendance in Britain.

With the completion of the latest refurbishment, the stadium includes the Scottish Football Museum and Hampden now draws a regular stream of visitors.

are also available in the stadium during matches. Tours of the stadium and trophy room run every 45 minutes from 10.30am to 3.45pm on Sundays (£6.50/4.50). Rangers' stadium holds 50,500 people; tickets cost between £10 and £22.

SHOPPING

Shops that sell outdoor equipment include *Tiso's* (☎ 248 4877, 129 Buchanan St) and *Adventure 1* (☎ 353 3788, 38 Dundas St).

GETTING THERE & AWAY

Glasgow is 405 miles (652km) from London, 97 miles (156km) from Carlisle, 42 miles (68km) from Edinburgh and 166 miles (267km) from Inverness.

Air

Glasgow International Airport (☎ 887 1111, W www.baa.co.uk/glasgow), 10 miles (16km)

west of the city, handles domestic traffic and international flights. Ryanair (☎ 0870 156 9569) flies from Glasgow Prestwick airport, 30 miles (48km) south-west of Glasgow, to London Stansted airport (1¼ hours, five to eight flights per week), from £11 one way. Discounted fares for rail travel to Glasgow Central or for coaches and trains to central London from Stansted are usually available for Ryanair ticket holders; enquire when booking.

Bus

All long-distance buses arrive and depart from Buchanan Bus Station.

Buses from London are very competitive. Silver Choice (☎ 01355-230403, W www .silverchoicetravel.co.uk) is currently the best deal with tickets from £20/24 single/ return. Departures are daily at 10pm from both Victoria Coach Station in London and

Buchanan Bus Station in Glasgow, and the run takes around nine hours. The service is very popular so you'll need to book well in advance.

National Express (☎ 0870 580 8080, W www.gobycoach.com) leaves from the same stations and has four or five daily services from £26/28. The best option is to catch the 8am bus from London, so that you arrive in good time to organise accommodation. There's one direct overnight bus from Heathrow airport. From May to October it departs at 11.05pm; call National Express for departure times the rest of the year.

National Express also has numerous links with other English cities. Services include: three daily buses from Birmingham (£33.50/36, 5¾ hours); one from Cambridge (£39.50/41.50, 9¾ hours); numerous from Carlisle (£13/14, two hours); two from Newcastle (£21/22, four hours); and one from York (£23.50/25.50, 7½ hours).

National Express/Scottish Citylink (☎ 0870 550 5050, W www.citylink.co.uk) have buses to most major towns in Scotland. There are numerous services to Edinburgh (single/return £3/5, 1¼ hours, every 20 or 30 minutes during the day). Eighteen to 20 buses per day run to Stirling (£3.60/5, 40 minutes), 15 or 16 to Inverness (£14/19.50, from 3½ hours), two to five to Oban (£11.20/15, three hours), 18 or 19 to Aberdeen (£15/21, 3¼ to four hours), four to Fort William (£11.80/16, three hours) and three to Portree on Skye (£20/27, 6¼ to seven hours). There's a twice-daily summer service (late-May to September) to Stranraer, connecting with the ferry to Belfast in Northern Ireland (£29/39, six hours).

Stagecoach Express (☎ 333 1100, W www .stagecoach-westscotland.co.uk) runs hourly buses to Edinburgh (£3/4, 1¼ hours). Stagecoach Express (☎ 01592-416060) also runs buses to St Andrews (£6.45, 2½ hours, hourly) and Dundee (£6.45, 2½ hours, twice hourly) via Glenrothes.

Walkers should check out First Edinburgh (☎ 01324-613777), which runs buses every hour or two to Milngavie (£1.15, 30 minutes), the start of the West Highland Way.

Train

As a general rule, Central Station serves southern Scotland, England and Wales, and Queen St serves the north and east. There are buses every 10 minutes between them (50p, free with a through train ticket). There are up to eight direct trains a day from London's Euston station; they're not cheap, but they're much quicker (five to six hours) and more comfortable than the bus. There are also up to eight direct services from London King's Cross. Fares change name and price rapidly but there are usually a few seats with return fares in the £30 to £40 range. At the time of writing, the best fare was Virgin Value (☎ 0845 722 2333, W www.virgin.com/trains) at £29 return, but seats must be booked at least 14 days in advance.

ScotRail (W www.scotrail.co.uk) has the West Highland line heading north to Oban and Fort William (see those sections in The Highlands chapter) and other direct links to Dundee (£19.70 single), Aberdeen (£28 single) and Inverness (£30.60 single). There are numerous trains to Edinburgh (£7.30 single, 50 minutes). Train travellers are advised to purchase a Freedom of Scotland travelpass or a Highland Rover pass (see Train Passes in the Getting Around chapter).

For all rail enquiries call ☎ 0845 748 4950.

Car

There are numerous car-rental companies; the big names have offices at Glasgow International Airport. Melvilles Motor (☎ 0870 160 9999, W www.melvilles.co .uk) charges from £22/100 per day/week for a Clio, Micra, Punto or Corsa. Arnold Clark (☎ 848 0202, W www.arnoldclark.co.uk), at the airport, has Fiat Seicentos for only £18/90 per day/week.

GETTING AROUND

The Roundabout Glasgow ticket (£3.50/1.75) covers all underground and train transport in the city for a day. First Glasgow (☎ 423 6600, W www.firstglasgow.com) has a FirstDay CityWide ticket that allows hop-on/off travel on all its buses; it can be bought from drivers for £2/1.80 before/after 9.30am and is valid until midnight. ▶

you're going farther afield, such as Balloch, Helensburgh, Dumbarton or Hamilton, get the £2.50/2.20 Network Wide ticket.

From the Airport
There are buses every 10 or 15 minutes from the Glasgow International Airport to Buchanan Bus Station (single £3.30). Buses continue to Edinburgh (£6 from the airport). A taxi would cost about £14.

Bus
City bus services are frequent. You can buy tickets when you board buses, but on most you must have the exact change. Routes vary and currently there isn't a route map available; contact an information office for the latest details (see under Tourist Offices earlier). For short trips in the city, fares cost 55p. From 2001, seven First Glasgow routes (Nos 9, 12, 40, 41, 56/57, 62 and 66) started running an hourly service all night, but this may not continue.

From March to October, City Sightseeing (☎ 204 0444) runs tourist buses every 30 minutes (9.30am to 4.30pm or 5pm) along the main sightseeing routes, starting at George Square. You get on and off as you wish and a day ticket costs £7/3 (buy from the driver or the TIC). Guide Friday (☎ 248 7644) is similar with a slightly longer route.

Train
There's an extensive suburban network of trains in and around Glasgow; tickets should be bought before travel if the station is staffed, or from the conductor if it isn't.

There's also an underground line that serves 15 stations in the centre, west and south of the city (90p). It runs Monday to Saturday from around 6.30am to around 11.30pm, and on Sunday from 11am to 5.45pm. The Discovery Ticket (£2.50) gives unlimited travel on the system for a day.

Taxi
There's no shortage of taxis. If you order from Glasgow Wide Taxis (☎ 429 7070) by phone, you can pay by credit card (£1 surcharge). There's also the option of Croft Radio Cars on ☎ 633 2222.

Bicycle
West End Cycles (☎ 357 1344 or freephone ☎ 0800 072 8015), 16 Chancellor St, is at the southern end of Byres Rd and rents mountain bikes (with locks) for £12 per day or £50 per week. Two forms of ID and a £50 deposit are required.

Around Glasgow

Glasgow is surrounded by a grim hinterland of postindustrial communities. Industrial archaeologies could have a field day here and some might see a perverse beauty in the endless suburbs of grey council house architecture. But it's here, possibly, that the Glasgow area's gritty black sense of humour is engendered.

RENFREWSHIRE
Paisley
☎ 0141 • pop 77,000
This is the town that gave its name to the well-known fabric design of swirling stylised teardrops or pinecones called the Paisley Pattern. Now effectively a suburb west of Glasgow, Paisley grew up around its abbey. By the 19th century the town was a major producer of printed cotton and woollen cloth.

The famous design was, in fact, copied from shawls brought back from India. At one time, Paisley was the largest producer of cotton thread in the world; the Coats family of threadmakers have enjoyed a long association with the town.

Information The helpful TIC (☎ 889 0711), 9a Gilmour St, is open 9.30am to 5.30pm (noon to 5pm on Sunday) mid-April to September, and 9am to 5pm Monday to Saturday the rest of the year. Ask for leaflets on local nature walks.

Fernie Guided Tours of Paisley (☎ 561 8078) runs two-hour walking tours starting at the abbey from 10.45am and 1.30pm Monday to Saturday, for £5/3 adult/child.

Walking Tour Start your walking tour at Gilmour St train station and follow Gilmour St towards The Cross (keep the taxi stance on your right). Turn left into Gauze St, cross the river, and you'll see **Paisley Abbey** (☎ 889 7654, Abbey Close; admission free; open 10am-3.30pm Mon-Sat) on your right. The abbey was founded in 1163 by Walter Fitzallan, the first high steward of Scotland and ancestor of the Stuart dynasty. It was badly damaged by fire during the Wars of Independence in 1306, but rebuilt soon after. Most of the nave is 14th or 15th century. The building was a ruin from the 16th century until the 19th-century restoration, completed in 1928. There are two royal tombs in the abbey, excellent stained-glass windows, and the 10th-century Celtic **Barochan Cross**. On the other side of Abbey Close, you'll see the grand **Town Hall**. From the abbey, turn right along Abbey Close, then left into the High St.

At the western end of the High St, there's the **University of Paisley** and the **Museum and Art Gallery** (☎ 889 3151, High St; admission free; open 10am-5pm Tues-Sat, 2pm-5pm Sun), with a large display of Paisley shawls and an interesting outline of the history of the Paisley Pattern. It also has collections of local and natural history, ceramics and 19th-century Scottish art.

From the museum, continue along the High St into Wellmeadow St, with the **Thomas Coats Memorial Church** on your right.

Turn right into West Brae and Oakshaw St West for the **Coats Observatory** (☎ 889 2013, 49 Oakshaw St West; admission free; open 10am-5pm Tues-Sat, 2pm-5pm Sun). There are interesting displays about astronomy, earthquake recording, weather and climate, all continuously monitored here since 1882. Telescope viewing is from 7.30pm to 9.30pm, Thursday, October to March.

Retrace your steps to the High St, past the museum, and turn right down Storrie St, taking the second left into George St, then left again into George Place. Here, you'll find the **Sma' Shot Cottages** (☎ 889 1708, 11-17 George Place; admission free; open 1pm-5pm Wed & Sat Apr-Sept), including an 18th-century weaver's cottage and a 19th-century artisan's house, both with period furniture and other items of historic interest. There's also a row of mill workers'

houses from the 1840s and a tea room with home baking.

From the cottages, turn left up Shuttle St, then right along New St, to the **Paisley Arts Centre** (☎ 887 1010, New St; free admission to bar & bistro, shows £3.50-6; opening hours vary), in a converted church dating from 1738. It has a theatre, bar and bistro. Continue past the arts centre, turn left into Causeyside St, and you'll return to Gilmour St.

Places to Stay & Eat There's not much point in staying overnight in Paisley, being so close to Glasgow. However, there are several good guest houses.

Myfarrclan (☎ 884 8285, fax 581 1566, 146 Corsebar Rd) B&B en-suite singles/doubles from £45/60. This is a luxurious but rather twee choice.

Gleniffer House (☎ 848 5544, fax 01505-325822, Glenpatrick Rd, Elderslie) B&B en-suite rooms from £20-35. This 200-year-old building is about two miles (3km) west of Paisley town centre.

There are lots of inexpensive places to eat in central Paisley.

Sportsters (☎ 848 7108, 7 Gilmour St) Baked potatoes £3.95. This is a pub with loud live music and televised football.

O'Neill's (☎ 847 5401, 27 New St) Sandwiches from £2.95, main courses £4.25-5.95. O'Neill's Irish theme pub gets a bit wild late at night.

Modern India (☎ 887 6877, 8 New St) Buffets 7pm-10pm Sun-Thur £9.95. The Modern is a reasonable-value Indian restaurant.

Finally, *Caprice* (☎ 889 9432, 11 Gilmour St) offers either takeaway or a three-course lunch for £4.95 (Mondays to Saturdays).

Getting There & Away Trains leave Glasgow's Central Station up to eight times each hour for Paisley's Gilmour St station (£2 single, £2.50 off-peak day return). There are frequent buses from Central Rd

Kilbarchan
☎ 01505 • pop 4000

Kilbarchan is just off the A737 Glasgow to Irvine road and about 5 miles (8km) west of Paisley.

The interesting **Weaver's Cottage** *(NTS; ☎ 705588, The Cross; adult/child £2/1.30; open 1.30pm-5.30pm daily Apr-Sept, Sat-Sun Oct)*, dating from 1723, has a rare cruck roof, which supported the original thatch. Initially two cottages, the weavers living here produced Paisley shawls, muslin and tartan for buyers from Paisley. There's a video presentation, 18th- and 19th-century furnishings and demonstrations of hand-loom weaving (Friday to Sunday). The loom is nearly 200 years old.

Bobbins (☎ 705509, 25 Steeple St) Snacks around £2-4. For a pleasant snack, visit Bobbins, not far from the weaver's cottage.

The best way to get to Kilbarchan is by Arriva (☎ 0870 241 3197) bus No 36, which runs frequently from Union St in Glasgow (single/return £1.80/2.95).

WEST DUNBARTONSHIRE
Dumbarton
☎ 01389 • pop 22,634

This town was the ancient capital of the Britons of Strathclyde, but time has passed it by. Dumbarton stands at the gateway to Loch Lomond and the Highlands, where the River Clyde becomes the Firth of Clyde, 14 miles (22km) west of Glasgow. It was important both as a strategic and trading centre around 1500 years ago.

The year-round TIC (☎ 742306) is by the A82 at Milton, 2 miles (3km) east of town; ask for the free *Historic Dumbarton & Clydebank* leaflet.

On top of spectacular **Dumbarton Rock**, here's **Dumbarton Castle** *(HS; ☎ 732167, Castle Rd; adult/child £2/75p; open standard HS hours, closed Thur afternoons & Fri & Sun mornings in winter)*, now mostly a barracks. The **Scottish Maritime Museum** *(☎ 763444, Castle St; adult/child £1.50/75p; open 10am-4pm Mon-Sat)* has a working experimental ship-model tank and a tearoom.

Places to eat include fish and chip shops, Chinese and Indian restaurants, and (on Castle St) coffee shops and a bistro.

Trains to Dumbarton Central run four times an hour from Glasgow Queen St (£2.75 single, £3.30 off-peak return, 30 minutes) towards Helensburgh or Balloch.

INVERCLYDE
The ghosts of once-great shipyards still line the banks of the Clyde west of Glasgow.

The only place of any interest at all along the coast west of here is Greenock, although there are a couple of items of interest in the otherwise unprepossessing town of **Port Glasgow**. You could stop to see the replica of the *Comet*, Greenock Rd, Europe's first commercial steamship, launched here in 1812. There's also **Newark Castle** *(HS; ☎ 01475-741858, adult/child £2/75p; open standard HS hours Apr-Sept)*, a fine 16th-century house.

Greenock
☎ 01475 • pop 50,013

James Watt, who perfected the steam engine, was born in Greenock in 1736. The Greenock Cut, a 5-mile-long (8km) circuit from Overton, is a good walk through the hills above the town – it follows an old aqueduct (approximately 2½ hours).

Cruises around the firth are run by *Clyde Marine (☎ 721281)*, mid-June to August; departures from Greenock Victoria Harbour (a five-minute walk from Greenock Central station) sail to Rothesay, Millport, Lochranza on Arran, Tighnabruaich, Tarbert on Loch Fyne and the heads of Loch Long and Loch Goil.

There's a good walk up to Lyle Hill, above Gourock Bay, where there's the Free French memorial, commemorating sailors who lost their lives in the Battle of the Atlantic during WWII, and a great view over the Firth of Clyde.

Information & Orientation The Inverclyde Information Office (☎ 712555), 7 Clyde Square, near the High St and behind the Town Hall, stocks tourist information and is open year-round.

Most things of interest in Greenock are near the High St, where the A78 to Largs branches off the end of the A8 Glasgow road. The central train station is close to the A8, near the waterfront at Customhouse Quay. The 24-hour Tesco supermarket is on Dalrymple St and the post office is on Nicolson St.

GLASGOW

Shipbuilding on the Clyde

One of the earliest permanent Lower Clyde shipyards was established in 1711 by John Scott at Greenock. Initial construction was for small-scale local trade but, by the end of the 18th century, large ocean-going vessels were being built. As the market expanded, shipyards also opened at Dumbarton and Port Glasgow.

The *Comet*, Europe's first steamship, was launched at Port Glasgow in 1812 and, soon afterwards, other local yards became involved in the lucrative steamship-building trade. By the 1830s and '40s, the Clyde had secured its position as world-leader in shipbuilding with the development of iron-hulled ships, which were 25% cheaper to run than wooden-hulled ones. Steel hulls came into use by the 1880s, allowing construction of larger ships with the latest and best engines.

In 1899, John Brown & Co, a Sheffield steelmaker, took over a Clydebank yard and by 1907 had become part of the world's largest shipbuilding conglomerate, producing ocean-going liners. Output from the Clyde shipyards steadily increased up to WWI. Yarrow & Co set up a warship-building yard farther upriver at Scotstoun. With the advent of WWI, there was huge demand for new shipping from both the Royal Navy and Merchant Navy.

During and after the war, many small companies disappeared and shipbuilding giants such as Lithgows Ltd took their place. The depression years of the 1920s and '30s saw many yards mothballed or closed. The *Queen Mary* sat unfinished at John Brown's yard for over two years, but was finally launched in 1934. Another boom followed during WWII – the Mulberry harbour used in the Normandy landings was built on the Clyde.

After the war, the market was in good shape, but yard owners were reluctant to invest in a new plant. When they did eventually invest, it was for the wrong type of shipping (passenger liners were going out of fashion), and many yards went into liquidation in the 1960s. In 1972, Upper Clyde Shipbuilders was liquidated, causing complete chaos, a sit-in and a bad headache for Ted Heath's government.

Lithgow's, Scott's and Yarrow's managed to survive by manufacturing oil tankers, submarines, cargo ships and naval vessels. Scott-Lithgow, formed from an amalgamation in 1967, attempted to diversify into oil-rig manufacture in the early 1980s, but the company ran into serious difficulties and had to be rescued by Trafalgar House. The rescue failed and the yard was closed, creating further unemployment and misery.

In 1985, Yarrow Shipbuilders Ltd was sold to GEC, but the old name lingers on. Now the great shipyards of the Clyde are mostly derelict and empty and there were further job losses in 2001. The remains of a once mighty industry includes Yarrow Shipbuilders in Glasgow, BAE Systems Marine in Scotstoun and Govan, Ferguson Shipbuilders in Port Glasgow, as well as several specialised marine subcontractors.

Museums Displays in the **McLean Museum and Art Gallery** (☎ 715624, 15 Kelly St; admission free; open 10am-5pm Mon-Sat) chart the history of steam power and Clyde shipping.

The **HM Customs & Excise Museum** (☎ 881451, Custom House Quay; admission free; open 10am-4pm Mon-Fri) traces the interesting history of the Customs and Excise service. Robert Burns and Adam Smith were former employees. The Custom House was completed in 1819 and is well worth a visit.

Places to Stay & Eat Greenock has a choice of both basic and more luxurious accommodation.

James Watt College (☎ 731360, fax 730877, Ardmore Hall, Custom House Way, B&B £20-25. Fairly central and down on the waterfront, this hall of residence has 168 single rooms, many en suite.

Tontine Hotel (☎/fax 723316, 6 Ardgowan Square) Singles £50-82, doubles £50-102. This grand hotel, with well-appointed rooms, each with private bath, is just off the A8 near the Clyde Port Container Terminal.

In central Greenock, there are lots of restaurants, cafes and pubs on West Blackhall St, including *Paccino's Diner & Takeaway*; which serves baked potatoes from £2.25 and main courses from £3.50 to £6.95.

Morgan's (☎ 724511, 49 West Blackhall St) Main courses £4.95-6.50. Morgan's is a pleasant place serving Scottish and international dishes.

Cathay Royale (☎ 720832, 134 West Blackhall St) 2-course lunch from £4.50. Cathay Royale serves Asian food.

There's also an *Italian restaurant* on West Blackhall St.

Getting There & Away Greenock is 27 miles (43km) west of Glasgow. There are three trains an hour from Glasgow Central (£3.80), and hourly buses. The Glasgow to Greenock pedestrian/cycle route follows an old railway track for 10 miles (16km) – see Walking & Cycling under Glasgow earlier for details.

Gourock
☎ 01475 ● pop 11,692
Gourock is a seaside resort 3 miles (5km) west of Greenock. Although the small central area is fairly run-down, the suburbs are pleasant, the town's location is wonderful and it's an important transport hub.

Places to Stay & Eat Kempock St, near the train station and ferry terminal, has banks, grocery stores and various cheap takeaway outlets.

Three in One (☎ 639918, 17 Kempock St) Pizzas from £2.40. This is a fairly basic takeaway outlet.

Taj Mahal (☎ 633268, 89 Kempock St) Buffets £9.95. Taj Mahal offers Monday and Tuesday evening eat-as-much-as-you-like buffets with a choice of seven starters,

seven main courses and five desserts plus tea and coffee.

Cathay Princess (☎ 632541, 25 Kempock Place) 4-course meals £19. Cathay Princess is more upmarket. Takeaways are available.

For accommodation, you'd be best to head for Glasgow or Dunoon, though there are options in Gourock. *Spinnaker Hotel* (☎ 633107, 121 Albert Rd) does B&B for £25 to £40 and also serves bar meals (£4.50 to £8.40). Six of its eight rooms are en suite.

Getting There & Away CalMac ferries (☎ 650100) leave hourly every day for Dunoon (£2.75, cars £6.85, 20 minutes) on Argyll's Cowal peninsula. CalMac also runs a passenger-only service to Kilcreggan (£1.60, 12 minutes, three to 12 daily) and Helensburgh (£1.60, 30 minutes, three or four daily). Western Ferries (☎ 01369-704452) has a half-hourly service to Dunoon (£2.80, cars £8.20, 20 minutes) from McInroy's Point, 2 miles (3km) from the train station; Citylink buses run to here.

Gourock train station is next to the CalMac terminal; there are three trains an hour to Glasgow Central (£4.10).

Scottish Citylink (☎ 0870 550 5050) runs hourly buses to Glasgow (£4.50) from McInroy's Point via the Shore St Health Centre by the train station.

Wemyss Bay
☎ 01475 ● pop 1715
Eight miles (13km) south of Gourock is Wemyss Bay (pronounced weemz), where you can jump off a train and onto a ferry for Rothesay on the Isle of Bute (see the Argyll & Bute section in The Highlands chapter).

Wemyss Bay Hotel (☎ 520285, 23 Greenock Rd) is one of the few places to eat. The only other place near the pier is a *fish and chip shop* opposite the Victorian train station. The station's appealing structure, opened in 1865, is one of the finest of its age.

Trains to Glasgow run hourly (£4.30). CalMac ferries (☎ 520521) to Rothesay connect with most trains and cost £3.25 per passenger and £13.15 for a car.

GLASGOW

Southern Scotland

Southern Scotland is a large, beautiful region, although in many ways it's something of a 'no man's land'. Historically, it was the buffer between the rambunctious and imperialist English and the unruly Scots.

Although today's inhabitants are proudly and indisputably Scottish, they are unique – like but unlike the Scots farther to the north, like but unlike the northern English to the south. This duality is perhaps not incompatible with the fact that this region was home to the two men – Robert Burns and Sir Walter Scott – who, in the late 18th and early 19th centuries, did most to reinvent and popularise Scottishness.

The Romans attempted to draw a clean line across the map with Hadrian's Wall, leaving the Celtic Picts to their own devices. The great Anglo-Saxon kingdoms of Bernicia and Northumbria, however, dominated the east and the south-west and succeeded in driving many Celts farther north. Another wave of Anglo-Saxons arrived from northern England after 1066, bringing with them a language that evolved into Lowlands Scots – like but unlike English, as Robert Burns so vividly illustrated.

The Norman invasion of England led to war with the Scots, although in times of peace, especially in the south, the aristocracy intermarried, leading to complicated land holdings on both sides of the border. The wars of Scottish independence fought at the end of the 13th century, and the beginning of the 14th, took a terrible toll on southern Scotland. And although the Scots succeeded in consolidating their independence, and great monastic estates were established, the south was still periodically trampled on by opposing armies.

Worse still, large parts of today's Borders and Dumfries & Galloway regions were neglected – neither the English nor the Scottish had any real interest in bringing stability to their enemy's border. There were periods of relative calm when great monasteries were constructed (and reconstructed),

HIGHLIGHTS

- Cycling through the scenic Tweed Valley
- Visiting the old buildings and *wynds* of attractive Jedburgh
- Viewing beautiful Dryburgh Abbey
- Experiencing the captivating atmosphere of Traquair House
- Surveying the lochs and pine-covered mountains of Galloway Forest Park
- Hiking through the varied scenery along the Southern Upland Way

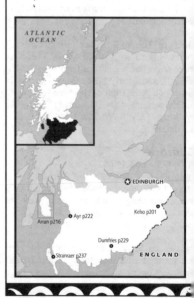

but the Debatable Lands, as they were known, were virtually ungoverned and ungovernable from the late 13th to the mid 17th centuries. The great families, with their complex blood feuds, fought and robbed the English, the Scots and each other. It's been argued that this continuous

Coldingham Bay with the small fishing village of St Abbs in the distance

A larger-than-life postbox on the small Isle of Arran

Underneath the arches of Dryburgh Abbey

The ruined Romanesque remains of Kelso Abbey

St Cuthbert's Way in winter, near to the ruins of the Premonstratensian abbey at Dryburgh

Standing stones on Machrie Moor, Isle of Arran

Streetlife in the market town of Melrose

tate of guerrilla warfare had an indelible ffect on the region and its people.

Following the 1707 union, peace allowed new surge of development. The Borders, artly thanks to the abbeys, had traditionally een an important wool growing and pro- essing region, and during the 19th century he knitting and weaving industries that sur- ive today were created.

The countryside varies: gentle open fields n the east, beautiful hilly countryside flank- ng the River Tweed and the high Glenken and Jalloway hills in the west. The region is cer- ainly not undiscovered by tourists – it's too bvious a stopover for those heading to/from Jlasgow and Edinburgh. However, it's easy o escape the crowds, particularly in the south- vest. Away from the main roads there's little raffic, which makes for good cycling.

Ayrshire was the birthplace of Scotland's ational poet, Robert Burns, though it's he least spectacular part of the region. The sle of Arran, in the Firth of Clyde, is noted or its magnificent scenery. In Dumfries & Jalloway, the coast and the mountains ap- roach the grandeur of the north. The Bor- ers have beautiful countryside, particularly round the River Tweed, and pleasant towns uilt around monastic ruins.

WALKING

he region's most famous walk is the 12-mile (341km) **Southern Upland Way**, Iritain's first official coast-to-coast foot- ath. Another long-distance walk is the 100- iile (161km) **St Cuthbert's Way**, inspired y the travels of St Cuthbert, which crosses ome superb scenery between Melrose and indisfarne (in England). In Galloway, the **ilgrims Way** follows a 25-mile (40km) ail from Glenluce Abbey to the Isle of Vhithor, and the 15-mile (24km) **Berwick- hire Coastal Path** leads from Berwick-on- weed (just across the border in England) to t Abbs. The Scottish Borders Tourist Board roduces a useful free booklet called *Walk- ig in the Scottish Borders*.

CYCLING

Vith the exception of the main north–south -roads and the A75 to Stranraer, traffic is

sparse, which, along with the beauty of the countryside, makes this ideal cycling country. Bear in mind that the prevailing winds are from the south-west. A free booklet called *Cycling in the Scottish Borders* is produced by the Scottish Borders Tourist Board.

The **Tweed Cycle Way** is a waymarked route running 62 miles along the beauti- ful Tweed Valley following minor roads from: Biggar to Peebles (13 miles; 21km); to Melrose (16 miles; 26km); to Coldstream (19 miles; 30.5km); and to Berwick-upon- Tweed (14 miles; 22.5km). Jedburgh Tourist Information Centre (TIC) has information.

Another interesting route is outlined in the *Scottish Border Cycle Way*, although this isn't waymarked. This route runs 210 miles (338km) from Portpatrick to Berwick-upon-Tweed – via Three Lochs, Talnotry, Castle Douglas, Dumfries, Ruth- well, Gretna Green, Newcastleton, Hawick, Jedburgh and Coldstream. Contact Jed- burgh TIC for information. Another route is detailed in the guide *Four Abbeys Cycle Route*, a 55-mile (88.5km) circular tour taking in Melrose, Dryburgh, Kelso and Jedburgh. The guide is available from the Scottish Bor- ders Tourist Board and local TICs.

A decent map will reveal numerous other possibilities. The Tweed Valley is hard to ig- nore, but the Galloway Hills (north of New- ton Stewart) and coastal routes to Whithorn (south of Newton Stewart) are also excellent.

Borders Region

There's a tendency to think that the real Scotland starts north of Perth, but the cas- tles, forests and glens of the Borders have a romance and beauty of their own. The re- gion survived centuries of war and plunder and was romantically portrayed by Robert Burns and Sir Walter Scott.

Although parts, especially to the west, are wild and empty, the fertile valley of the River Tweed has been a wealthy region for 1000 years.

The population was largely concentrated in a small number of *burghs* (towns), which also supported large and wealthy monastic

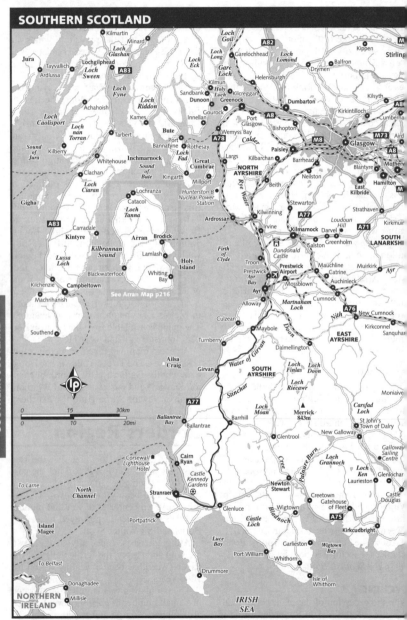

SOUTHERN SCOTLAND

See Arran Map p216

SOUTHERN SCOTLAND

communities. These provided an irresistible magnet during the border wars, and they were destroyed and rebuilt numerous times.

The monasteries met their final fiery end in the mid-16th century, burned by the English yet again, but this time English fire combined with the Scottish Reformation and they were never again rebuilt. The towns thrived once peace arrived, and the traditional weavers provided the foundation for a major textile industry, which still survives.

If you pause here on your way north, you'll find the lovely Tweed Valley, with its rolling hills, castles, ruined abbeys and sheltered towns. This is excellent cycling and walking country.

The Borders Region lies between the Cheviot Hills, along the English border, and the Pentland, Moorfoot and Lammermuir Hills, which form the border with Lothian and overlook the Firth of Forth. The most interesting country surrounds the River Tweed and its tributaries.

There's a good network of local buses coordinated by the Scottish Borders Council, which also publishes bus guides available from TICs.

COLDSTREAM
☎ 01890 • pop 1750

Sitting on the banks of the River Tweed, which forms the border with England, Coldstream is a small, relatively uninspiring town with a winding, undulating main street. It's best known for giving its name to the Coldstream Guards.

The TIC (☎ 882607), in the Town Hall on High St, opens 10am to 4pm Monday to Saturday and 2pm to 4pm Sunday, April to September (until 5pm, except Sundays, in July and August); and 1pm to 4pm, Monday to Saturday only, in October.

Things to See
The history of the Coldstream Guards, and the town itself, is covered in the **Coldstream Museum** (☎ 882630, 12 Market Square; admission free; open 10am-4pm Mon-Sat & 2pm-4pm Sun Apr-Sept, 1pm-4pm Mon-Sat Oct), just off High St.

Near the five-arched bridge across the river is an 18th-century cottage, formerly the **Toll House**, where eloping couples were once united in 'irregular marriages'.

On the western edge of Coldstream is the 1214-hectare **Hirsel Country Park**, seat of the earls of Home. Hirsel House isn't open to the public, but you can visit the grounds during daylight hours.

Four miles (6.5km) south-east of Coldstream, across the border near Branxton, is **Flodden Field**. There, in 1513, a Scots incursion under James IV was cut short when his army was routed by the English.

Places to Stay & Eat
Coldstream Caravan & Camping Site (☎ 882333, 100m south-west of Market Square) Tent pitches for 1/2 persons £4/6. This beautiful grassy site is beside Leet Water, a small tributary of the River Tweed.

Attadale (☎ 883047, 1 Leet St) B&B £17 per person. Attadale offers three rooms in a traditional terraced house.

Coldstream Guards

The Coldstream Guards were formed in 1650, in Berwick-upon-Tweed, for duty in Scotland as part of Oliver Cromwell's 'New Model Army', and were originally known as Colonel Monck's Regiment of Foot. The regiment took its present name from the town where it was stationed in 1659; its full title is the Coldstream Regiment of Foot Guards.

The regiment played a significant part in the restoration of the monarchy in 1660. It saw service at Waterloo against Napoleon, at Sebastopol during the Crimean War, in the Boer War, at the Somme and Ypres in WWI and at Dunkirk and Tobruk in WWII.

It remains the oldest regiment in continuous existence in the British army and is the only one directly descended from the New Model Army. The regiment's emblem is the Star of the Order of the Garter, its regimental motto is *nulli secundus* (second to none) and its colonel-in-chief is the British monarch.

Garth House (☎ 882477, 7 Market St) Rooms from £17.50-18.50 per person. This is an 18th-century place.

Crown Hotel (☎ 882558, Market Square) Rooms with/without bathroom £26/17.50 per person. The Georgian Crown Hotel, near the museum, is a family-run hotel with good-value bar meals.

Castle Hotel (☎/fax 882380, 11 High St) Rooms £25 per person. Castle Hotel also does good bar meals and has a restaurant; lunchtime mains cost around £4.95. All rooms are en suite.

Getting There & Away

The town is on the busy A697 road which links Newcastle upon Tyne in Northumberland with Edinburgh.

There are up to seven buses daily Monday to Saturday between Kelso and Berwick-upon-Tweed via Coldstream.

DUNS & AROUND

☎ 01361 • pop 2308

Duns is a quiet market town in the centre of Berwickshire. The original settlement stood on the slopes of nearby Duns Law, from which it gets its name.

Limited tourist information is available from Nairn's Newsagents on Market Square, open 5.30am to 5pm Monday to Saturday and 6am to 4pm Sunday.

Things to See

The **Jim Clark Room** (☎ 883960, 44 Newtown St; adult/child £1/free; open 10.30am-1pm & 2pm-4.30pm Mon-Sat & 2pm-4.30pm Sun Apr-Sept; 1pm-4pm Mon-Sat Oct) is a museum dedicated to the life of Jim Clark (1936–68), who lived (and is buried) at nearby Chirnside. A farmer by trade, he was twice world motor-racing champion in the 1960s before being killed in a crash while practising.

You can get to **Duns Law** (218m), in Duns Castle Estate, by following Castle St up from the square. There are good views of the Merse and Lammermuir Hills from the summit, where the **Covenanter's Stone** marks the spot where the Covenanting armies camped in 1639; a copy of the Covenant was later signed at Duns Castle.

The castle isn't open to the public, but you can visit the 77-hectare **nature reserve**, managed by the Scottish Wildlife Trust. There are nature trails and many species of bird, animal and plant life. The lake, with the unfortunate name of 'Hen Poo', is a wildfowl haunt.

Manderston House (☎ 883450, 2 miles/ 3km east of Duns on the A6105; adult/child £6/3; open 2pm-5pm Thur & Sun mid-May to Sept), in 23 hectares of beautiful gardens, is a classic Edwardian stately home. Among its features are impressive state rooms and a silver staircase.

Places to Stay & Eat

There are B&Bs in the streets radiating from Market Square.

Claymore (☎ 883880, 8 Murray St) Rooms from £18. Claymore has two rooms with shared facilities and offers evening meals.

White Swan Hotel (☎ 883338, 31-32 Market Square) B&B £20-22.50 per person. This basic but friendly hotel on the northern side of the main square has a lively bar.

Barniken House Hotel (☎ 882466, 18 Murray St) Singles/doubles £25/45. Barniken House is a grand Georgian villa with private parking and a children's play area.

The pubs are the best places for meals. One of the few serving evening meals is the **Black Bull Hotel** *(Black Bull St)*; its food is standard but filling and mains cost around £5. You can get bar lunches at the *Whip & Saddle (Market Square)* from noon to 2pm; it also serves good real ale.

Getting There & Away
Buses running between Kelso and Berwick-upon-Tweed stop at Duns (up to seven daily Monday to Saturday).

LAMMERMUIR HILLS
North of Duns, the low-lying Lammermuir Hills, with their extensive grouse moors, rolling farmland and wooded valleys, run east–west along the border with East Lothian. The hills are popular with walkers and there are numerous trails, including a section of the Southern Upland Way.

To the west, the way can be accessed at **Lauder**, where it passes through the grounds of **Thirlestane Castle** *(☎ 01578-722430, beside Leader Water; castle & grounds £5.20/3, grounds only £1.50; open 10.30am-5pm daily Apr-Oct, last admission 4.15pm)*, just outside town off the A68. Thirlestane is one of Scotland's most fascinating castles. The massive original keep was built in the 13th century but was refashioned and extended in the 16th century – with fairy-tale turrets and towers – but without compromising the scale and integrity of the building. Its chief architect was William Bruce, who also restored the Palace of Holyroodhouse in Edinburgh. The most impressive feature is the intricate plasterwork ceilings. It's still a family home and as a visitor you feel almost as if you're prying.

The hourly First Edinburgh bus No 95 from Edinburgh to Galashiels and Hawick passes through Lauder.

You can also get onto the Southern Upland Way from the tiny village of **Abbey St Bathan's** in the secluded, bucolic Whiteadder Valley, off the B6355. From here, the final 10-mile (16km) section of the trail heads north-east to Cockburnspath beside the coast.

THE COAST
The Borders coastline offers some attractiv scenery, rich flora and fauna, and a number o activities including cliff-top walks and scub diving. The main settlement, Eyemouth, is good base from which to explore the area.

Eyemouth
☎ 018907 • pop 3480
Eyemouth, at the mouth of the river fror which it gets its name, 5 miles (8km) nort of the Scotland–England border, is a bus fishing port and popular holiday destinatior

David I promoted herring fishing her back in the 12th century, and in the 18t century fishermen supplemented their in come through the lucrative smugglin trade. The community suffered its greates catastrophe in October 1881, when a storn destroyed the coastal fishing fleet killin 189 fishermen, 129 of whom were fron Eyemouth.

Information The TIC (☎ 50678) is in Eye mouth Museum on Manse Rd near the har bour. It opens 10am to 5pm Monday t Saturday and 12.30pm to 2.30pm Sunday April to June and September; 9.30am t 5.30pm Monday to Saturday and noon t 5pm Sunday in July and August; and 10am to 4pm Monday to Saturday only in Octobei

The Bank of Scotland and the Roya Bank of Scotland have ATMs, and there' a laundrette on Church St, open 9am t 12.30pm and 2pm to 4pm weekdays, morn ings only Saturday. Wednesday is early closing day.

Things to See & Do The Eyemouth Mu seum *(☎ 50678, Auld Kirk, Manse Rd adult/child £1.75/free; open same hours a TIC)* has displays on local history, particu larly relating to the town's fishing heritage The centrepiece is the large tapestry com memorating the 1881 fishing disaster.

If you're interested in **walking**, get a copy of the brochure *Walks in and Aroun Eyemouth*, available from the TIC, whicl describes a number of short walks. One o the most scenic is the 4-mile (6.5km) cliff top path south to Burnmouth.

pecial Events The town is packed at veekends in mid-June when the Eyemouth eafood Festival takes place. Activities inlude cooking demonstrations, *ceilidhs* and olk dancing. The week-long Herring Queen estival in late July is another calendar highight.

'laces to Stay & Eat There are a few opions to keep you happy here.

Hillcrest (☎ 50463, Coldingham Rd) Rooms £17 per person. The central Hillrest has two rooms with shared bathroom nd is handy for the harbour.

Churches Hotel (☎ 50401, fax 50747, ℮ info@churcheshotel.co.uk, Albert Rd) Singles £60-70, doubles £75-85. This stylish otel, run by well-known diver, author and underwater photographer Lawson Wood, has n excellent seafood restaurant.

The Old Bakehouse (☎ 50265, 4 Manse Rd) Mains £4.95-5.50. Open 9am-5pm daily, unch served noon-3pm. Opposite the TIC, his is one of the best places to eat in town. t serves snacks all day, plus good value set unches for £5.95.

The pubs along the quay have suitably nautical names – the *Contented Sole*, the *Whale Hotel* and the *Ship Hotel* – and serve reshly caught seafood. For good bread, oies, cakes and pastries, try *Lough's Home Bakery*, on High St.

Getting There & Away Bus No C4 runs nce a day from Monday to Friday to/from Kelso via Duns; bus Nos 34, 35, 36 and 235 go south to Berwick-upon-Tweed (15 minutes; twice hourly), which has the nearest rain station. Bus No 253 from Berwick to Edinburgh (1¾ hours; six Monday to Saturday, three Sunday) passes through Eyemouth.

South of Eyemouth

The small village of **Ayton**, 2 miles (3km) south-west of Eyemouth, is largely an 18thand 19th-century creation. It's known for the restored 1846 red sandstone **Ayton Castle** *(☎ 018907-81212; adult/child £3/free; open 2pm-5pm Sun early-May–mid-Sept)*. t's a family home and isn't overly geared o tourism.

Farther south, beyond the village of Foulden and about 3 miles (5km) west of the A1, is **Paxton House** *(☎ 01289-386291, along the B6461; adult/child £5/2.50; open 11.15am-5.30pm Apr-Oct, last tour 4.15pm, grounds open 10am-sunset Apr-Oct)*, beside the River Tweed and surrounded by over 32 hectares of parkland and gardens. It was built in 1758 by Patrick Home for his intended wife, the daughter of Prussia's Frederick the Great, though she stood him up. Designed by the Adam family – brothers John, James and Robert – it's acknowledged as one of the finest 18th-century Palladian houses in Britain. It contains a large collection of Thomas Chippendale and Regency furniture, and its picture gallery houses paintings from the national galleries of Scotland.

In the grounds, there are walking trails and a riverside museum on salmon fishing.

St Abb's Head & Coldingham Bay

About 3 miles (5km) north of Eyemouth, this picturesque area attracts anglers, scuba divers, bird-watchers and walkers.

The village of **Coldingham** is of little interest, but from there the B6438 road takes you downhill to the small fishing village of **St Abbs**, nestled below the cliffs.

The clear, clean waters around St Abbs form part of **St Abbs & Eyemouth Voluntary Marine Reserve** *(☎ 018907-71443, Rangers Cottage, Northfield, St Abbs)*, one of the best cold-water diving sites in Europe. The reserve is home to a wide variety of marine life, including grey seals and porpoises. **Scoutscroft Dive Centre** *(☎ 018907-71669, ℮ pete@divescoutscroft.freeserve.co.uk)*, St Abbs Rd, Coldingham, provides guided dives, equipment hire and courses; a halfday 'Discover Scuba' course costs £55.

Divers can charter boats from **D&J Charters** *(☎ 018907-71377)* or **St Abbs Boat Charter** *(☎ 018907-71681)*; the latter also does **bird-watching** trips.

North of the village and run by the National Trust for Scotland (NTS) is the 78-hectare **St Abb's Head National Nature Reserve** *(☎ 018907-71443, Rangers Cottage,*

Northfield, St Abbs), which has large colonies of guillemots, kittiwakes, herring gulls, fulmars, razorbills and some puffins. You get to the reserve by following the trail that begins beside the Northfield Farm car park and Head Start cafe, on the road just west of St Abbs.

Back in Coldingham, a signposted turnoff to the east leads ¾ mile (1.2km) down to quiet, away-from-it-all Coldingham Bay, which has a sandy beach and a cliff-top walking trail to Eyemouth (3 miles; 5km).

Coldingham Youth Hostel (☎ 018907-71298, *The Mount*) Dorm beds £6.10/4.95. Opens late-Mar–early-Nov. This hostel is on the cliff above the southern side of the bay.

Several places offer B&B, including *St Veda's House* (☎ 018907-71478, *Coldingham Bay*), just opposite the path down to the beach. B&B costs from £20 to £22 per person; it also does evening meals and has a bar.

Bus No 253 between Edinburgh and Berwick-upon-Tweed (six daily Monday to Saturday, three Sunday) stops in Coldingham and St Abbs, as does bus No 235 which runs at least hourly from Eyemouth.

Cockburnspath

The 16th-century Mercat Cross in Cockburnspath village square, about a mile inland from the coast, is the official eastern-end start of the Southern Upland Way.

KELSO

☎ 01573 • pop 6045

Kelso is a prosperous market town with a broad cobbled square, flanked by Georgian buildings, at the hub of narrow cobbled streets. There's an interesting mix of architecture, and the town has a lovely site at the junction of the Rivers Tweed and Teviot. It's busy during the day, but dies completely in the evening. It's a real town, however, not a tourist trap.

Information

The TIC (☎ 223464), at Town House, The Square, opens 11am to 4pm Monday to Saturday year-round plus 10am to 1pm Sunday April to October, and has extended hours June to September. Accommodation can be difficult to find during local festivals and when markets are held late June to mid September.

Kelso Abbey

Kelso Abbey *(admission free; open 9.30am 6pm Mon-Sat & 2pm-6pm Sun Apr-Dec* was built by the Tironensians, an order founded at Tiron in Picardy and brought t the Borders around 1113 by David I. Once one of the richest abbeys in southern Scotland, English raids in the 16th century reduced it to ruins. Today, there's little to see, though what remains is some of the finest surviving Romanesque architecture in Scotland.

Nearby, the octagonal **Kelso Old Parish Church** *(open 10am to 4pm weekdays)*, built in 1773, is intriguing.

Floors Castle

Floors Castle *(☎ 223333, about a mile west of Kelso; adult/child £5.50/3.25; open 10am-4.30pm daily Easter to Oct)* is an enormous mansion – Scotland's largest inhabited house – overlooking the Tweed. Built by William Adam in the 1720s, the original Georgian simplicity was 'improved' during the 1840s with the addition of rather ridiculous battlements and turrets. Floors makes no bones about being in the tourist business, and although the duke of Roxburghe's family is still in residence there's no sense that this is a real home; visitors are restricted to 10 rooms and a busy restaurant.

Follow Cobby Riverside Walk to reach the entrance to the castle grounds (see below).

Walking

The **Pennine Way**, which starts its long journey at Edale in the Peak District, ends at Kirk Yetholm Youth Hostel (see Around Kelso later in this chapter), about 6 mile (10km) south-east of Kelso on the B6352. Less ambitious walkers should leave The Square by Roxburgh St and take the signposted alley to **Cobby Riverside Walk**, a pleasant ramble along the river (past some expensive fishing spots) to Floors Castle (although you have to rejoin Roxburgh St to gain admission to the castle).

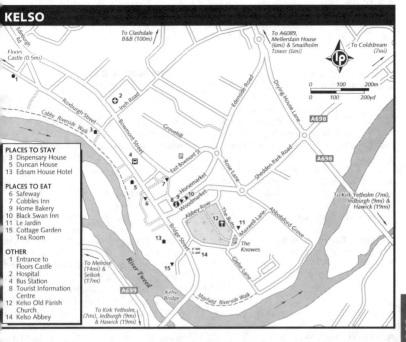

KELSO

To Clashdale B&B (100m)

Floors Castle (0.5mi)

To A6089, Mellerstain House (6mi) & Smailholm Tower (6mi)

To Coldstream (7mi)

Edinburgh Rd

Roxburgh Street

Cobby Riverside Walk

Inch Road

Bowmont Street

Grovehill

Edenside Road

Drying House Lane

Rose Lane

Shedden Park Road

A698

A698

East Bowmont St

Horsemarket

Woodmarket

Abbey Row

The Butts

Maxwell Lane

Abbotsford Grove

To Kirk Yetholm (7mi), Jedburgh (9mi) & Hawick (19mi)

Bridge Street

The Knowes

Glebe Lane

To Melrose (14mi) & Selkirk (17mi)

River Tweed

A699

Kelso Bridge

Mayfield Riverside Walk

To Kirk Yetholm (7mi), Jedburgh (9mi) & Hawick (19mi)

0 100 200m
0 100 200yd

PLACES TO STAY
3 Dispensary House
5 Duncan House
13 Ednam House Hotel

PLACES TO EAT
6 Safeway
7 Cobbles Inn
9 Home Bakery
10 Black Swan Inn
11 Le Jardin
15 Cottage Garden Tea Room

OTHER
1 Entrance to Floors Castle
2 Hospital
4 Bus Station
8 Tourist Information Centre
12 Kelso Old Parish Church
14 Kelso Abbey

Special Events

The Kelso Borders Show and the Marches Ride, both held in July, are two of the main events on Kelso's calendar.

Places to Stay

The nearest hostel is in Kirk Yetholm, about 6 miles (10km) to the south-east (see Around Kelso later in this chapter).

Clashdale (☎ 223405, 26 Inchmead Drive) B&B from £16 per person. Mr Watson has one single and one double room available, about five minutes' walk from the town centre. Room only, without breakfast, costs just £11 per person.

Dispensary House (☎ 228738, 106 Roxburgh St) B&B £25 per person. This B&B is set in a lovely Georgian townhouse overlooking the River Tweed.

Duncan House (☎ 225682, Chalkheugh Terrace) Rooms from £17 per person. This is another fine old house, near the town centre, with a view over the Rivers Tweed and

Teviot. There's a double, a twin and a family room, all with private bathrooms.

Ednam House Hotel (☎ 224168, fax 226319, Bridge St) Singles/doubles from £55/76. The comfortable, Georgian Ednam House is the top place in town, with fine gardens overlooking the river.

Places to Eat

Cottage Garden Tea Room (☎ 225889, 7 Abbey Court) Light meals £2-4. Open 10am-4.45pm Mon-Sat, 11am-4.45pm Sun. This place, tucked away in a quiet corner near the museum, has some outdoor seating. It serves tea, coffee, home-baked snacks and light lunches.

Le Jardin (☎ 228288, Knowes Around, 5a The Knowes) 2-course dinner £9-11. Open 6pm-10pm Thur-Sat, noon-2.30pm Sun. This cosy bistro, behind Kelso Abbey, offers a different menu each week, with dishes such as prawn and salmon casserole, and goat's cheese salad; there's always a vegetarian option.

Cobbles Inn (☎ 223548, 7 Bowmont St) Lunch mains £5.95-6.95. Food available noon-2pm and 6pm-9pm. This traditional pub, up an alley north of the main square, serves delicious bar meals, including an excellent cod fillet in beer batter.

Ednam House Hotel (☎ 224168, Bridge St) Bar lunches £6-6.50. Food available noon-2pm and 7pm-9pm Sun-Thur, 6pm-9.30pm Fri & Sat. Bar lunches are reasonably priced here; dinners aren't too bad either, with a main course and coffee costing £13.

The **Black Swan Inn** (Horsemarket), does bar meals from £5; the **Home Bakery**, just along the street, sells delicious pastries.

There's a **Safeway** supermarket on the corner of the main square.

Getting There & Away

The bus station is between Bowmont and Roxburgh Sts. See Coldstream earlier for details on the bus service to Berwick-upon-Tweed. First Borders (☎ 224121) bus No 20 links Kelso, Jedburgh and Hawick (seven daily Monday to Saturday, four Sunday).

AROUND KELSO

Bus No 65 between Melrose and Kelso stops in Smailholm village and passes about a mile from Mellerstain House.

Smailholm Tower

Perched on a rocky knoll above a small lake, the narrow stone Smailholm Tower (☎ 01573-460365, Sandyknowe Farm, Smailholm; adult/child £2/75p; open 9.30am-6.30pm daily Apr-Sept, 9.30am-4.30pm Sat & 2pm-4.30pm Sun Oct-Mar), managed by Historic Scotland (HS), provides one of the most evocative sights in the Borders and keeps the bloody uncertainties of its history alive. Although the displays inside are sparse, the panoramic view from the top is worth the climb.

The nearby farm, **Sandyknowe**, was owned by Sir Walter Scott's grandfather. As Scott himself recognised, his imagination was fired by the ballads and stories he heard as a child at Sandyknowe, and by the ruined tower a stone's throw away.

The tower is 6 miles (10km) west of Kelso, a mile south of Smailholm village on the B6397. You pass through the farmyard to get to the tower.

Mellerstain House

Mellerstain House (☎ 01573-410225, Gordon; adult/child £5/2; open 12.30pm-5pm Sun-Fri May-Sept plus Easter Weekend, last admission 4.30pm) is considered to be Scotland's finest mansion designed by Robert Adam and, in particular, is famous for its ornate interiors. Completed in 1778, it has a classically elegant style.

Town Yetholm & Kirk Yetholm

The twin villages of Town Yetholm and Kirk Yetholm, separated by Bowmont Water, are close to the English border, about 6 miles (10km) south-east of Kelso. Hill walking centres, they lie at the northern end of the **Pennine Way** and on **St Cuthbert's Way** between Melrose and Lindisfarne (Holy Island) in Northumberland.

Kirk Yetholm Youth Hostel (☎ 01573-420631, Kirk Yetholm, Kelso) Dorm beds £8.25/7. Open late-June–Sept. As the last stop on the Pennine Way, this place is often busy - book well in advance if you want a bed.

Bus No 81 runs up to six times a day Monday to Saturday to/from Kelso.

MELROSE
☎ 01896 • pop 2276

Melrose is the most charming of the Border towns, lying at the foot of the three heather-covered Eildon Hills. It's spick-and-span with a classic market square, some attractive parks and rugby ovals (Melrose is the birthplace of Rugby Sevens), and one of the great abbey ruins. However, urban sprawl from Galashiels is lapping at its western edges.

Information

The TIC (☎ 822555), Abbey House, Abbey St, opens 10am to 5pm Monday to Saturday and 10am to 1pm Sunday, April to June, September and October; and 9am to 6pm Monday to Saturday and 10am to 5pm Sunday, July and August.

The post office is around the corner from he TIC on Buccleuch St. You can check our email at Melrose Library at 18 Market quare; it opens 10am to 1pm and 2.30pm to pm Monday and Wednesday; and 2.30pm ɔ 5pm and 5.30pm to 7pm Friday.

Melrose Abbey

ounded by David I in 1136 for Cistercians rom Rievaulx in Yorkshire, this red sand-tone abbey *(HS; ☎ 822562; adult/child 3.30/1.20; open 9.30am-6.30pm daily Apr-ept, 9.30am-4.30pm Mon-Sat & 2pm-.30pm Sun Oct-Mar)* was repeatedly estroyed by the English in the 14th century. t was rebuilt by Robert the Bruce, whose eart is buried here. The ruins date from the 4th and 15th centuries and were repaired by ir Walter Scott in the 19th. They are pure iothic and are famous for their decorative tonework – see if you can glimpse the pig argoyle playing the bagpipes on the roof.

The sheltered **Priorwood Garden** *(NTS; ☎ 822493, next to the abbey; £1 donation equested; open 10am-5.30pm Mon-Sat & .30pm-5.30pm Sun Apr-Sept, 10am-4pm lon-Sat & 1.30pm-4pm Sun Oct-Dec)* fea-ures various plants used for dried-flower rrangements.

rimontium Exhibition

'his small but interesting exhibition ☎ 822651, The Ormiston, Market Square; dult/child £1.50/1; open 10.30am-4pm aily, closed 1pm-2pm Sat & Sun, Apr-Oct) ells the story of the Roman fort of Trimon-um (literally 'three hills') at nearby New-tead, and its associated archaeological igs. You can also join a 3½-hour guided 'rimontium Walk to the Roman sites round Melrose; walks start at 1.30pm 'uesday and Thursday and cost £2.50/2.

Walking

'here are many attractive walks in the **Eildon lills**, accessible via a footpath off Dingleton .d (the B6359) south of the town, or via the -ail along the River Tweed. The *Eildon Hills Valk* booklet is available from the TIC.

The **St Cuthbert's Way** long-distance path tarts in Melrose, while the coast-to-coast

Southern Upland Way passes through the town (see the Activities chapter). You can do a day's walk along St Cuthbert's Way as far as Harestanes (16 miles; 26km), on the A68 road near Jedburgh, and return to Melrose on the hourly Jedburgh–Galashiels bus.

Special Events

In mid-April, rugby followers fill the town to see the week-long Melrose Rugby Sevens competition.

Places to Stay

Camping & Hostels *Gibson Park Cara-van and Camp Site (☎ 822969, High St)* Sites £6.20. Open year round. It's best to book ahead if you want to pitch a tent here during July and August.

Melrose Youth Hostel (☎ 822521, Prior-wood) Dorm beds £11.25/10. Open Feb-Oct. This hostel is in a large, Georgian mansion on the edge of town, 100m south-east of the abbey. Breakfast is included in the price. From the market square, follow the sign-posts to the A68.

B&Bs & Hotels Melrose B&Bs and hotels aren't cheap by Scottish standards but they are of a high standard; this wouldn't be a bad place to treat yourself. There aren't many, so consider making a reservation.

Birch House (☎/fax 822391, High St) B&B £23-27 per person. Birch House is a large, friendly and open place which serves substantial breakfasts.

Braidwood (☎ 822488, Buccleuch St) B&B £20-23 per person. Mr Graham's town-house near the abbey offers high-standard facilities and a nice warm welcome. There's home baking too.

Burts Hotel (☎ 822285, fax 822870, e reservations@burtshotel.co.uk, Market Square) Singles/doubles £52/92. Set in an early-18th-century house that retains much of its period charm, Burts has been run by the same couple for 30 years and exudes warmth and friendliness.

Places to Eat

Marmion's Brasserie (☎ 822245, Buccleuch St) Mains £12.75-14.95. Open 9.30am-6pm

& 6.30pm-10pm daily. This atmospheric, oak-panelled nook serves snacks (£3-5) all day, but the lunch and dinner menus include gastronomic delights such as roast quail, braised lamb and sweetbreads.

The **Kings Arms Hotel**, on High St, and **Burts Hotel** and **Millar's Hotel**, on Market Square, all serve excellent bar meals. **Russell's Restaurant**, also on Market Square, is the place to go for coffees, teas and home-baked food.

Getting There & Away

Melrose has numerous bus links to Galashiels, Kelso and Jedburgh. First Borders bus No 62 runs hourly to Peebles (1¼ hours) and Edinburgh (2¼ hours), while bus No 65 goes hourly to Kelso.

AROUND MELROSE
Dryburgh Abbey

Dryburgh Abbey *(HS;* ☎ *01835-822381; adult/child £2.80/1; open 9.30am-6.30pm Mon-Sat & 2pm-6.30pm Sun Apr-Sept, closes 2 hrs earlier Oct-Mar)* is the most beautiful and most complete of the border abbeys, partly because the neighbouring town of Dryburgh no longer exists (another victim of the wars), and partly because it has a lovely site in a sheltered valley by the River Tweed. The abbey belonged to the Premonstratensians, a religious order founded in France, and was built from around 1150.

The pink-stoned ruins were chosen as the burial place for Sir Walter Scott, and later for Earl Haig, the Allied commander during WWI. There are some beautiful picnic spots.

The abbey is 5 miles (8km) south-east of Melrose on the B6404 which passes famous **Scott's View** overlooking the valley. You can hike there along the southern bank of the River Tweed, or take bus No 65 to the nearby village of Newtown St Boswells.

Abbotsford

The home of Sir Walter Scott is definitely not an architectural masterpiece – the best one can say is that it's disjointed – but it's in a beautiful setting and well worth visiting. It houses a fascinating collection of the great man's possessions.

Abbotsford *(☎ 01896-752043; adult/child £4/2; open 9.30am-5pm daily June-Sept 9.30am-5pm Mon-Sat & 2pm-5pm Sun Mar, May & Oct)* is about 3 miles (5km) west of Melrose on the B6360 road. Frequent buses run between Galashiels and Melrose; alight at the Tweedbank roundabout and walk west for a quarter of a mile. You can walk from Melrose to Abbotsford in an hour along the southern bank of the Tweed.

GALASHIELS
☎ 01896 • pop 13,766

Galashiels is a busy, unprepossessing mill town strung along the A6091, 3 miles (5km) west of Melrose. It's something of a transport hub and there's quite a bit of accommodation available, but there are few pressing reasons to stay.

The TIC (☎ 755551), 3 St John St, open 11am to 4pm Monday to Saturday in April, May and October; 10am to 5pm Monday to Saturday in June and September; and 10am to 6pm Monday to Saturday and 11am to 1pm Sunday in July and August.

The **Lochcarron Cashmere and Wool Centre** *(☎ 751100, Waverley Mill, Huddersfield St; admission £2.50/free; open 9am-5pm Mon-Sat year-round, plus noon-5pm Sun June-Sept)* offers tours of the woollen factory (at 10am, 11.30am, 1.30pm and 3pm, except Friday afternoon) and houses a museum on Galashiels' history.

There are frequent buses to/from Edinburgh, Melrose, Hawick, Kelso and Peebles.

SELKIRK
☎ 01750 • pop 5952

Selkirk is an unusual little town that climbs a steep ridge above the Ettrick Water, a tributary of the Tweed. Mills came to the area in the early 1800s, but it's now a quiet place (much quieter than Galashiels or the textile centre of Hawick). There's a statue of Sir Walter Scott at one end of High St and one of the explorer Mungo Park at the other.

The TIC (☎ 20054), tucked away along Halliwell's Close off Market Square, open 10am to 5pm Monday to Saturday and 2pm to 4pm Sunday, April to June, September and

October; and 9.30am to 5pm Monday to Saturday and 2pm to 5pm Sunday in July and August.

Things to See

The TIC is located in **Halliwell's House Museum** (☎ 20096, Halliwell's Close, Market Square; admission free; open same hours as TIC), which dates from 1712 and is the oldest building in Selkirk. The museum has an interesting display on local history and a programme of temporary exhibitions.

Also on Market Square is the 1804 **Sir Walter Scott's Court Room** (☎ 20096, Market Square; admission free; open 10am-4pm Mon-Sat & 2pm-4pm Sun Apr-Oct), where the great man served as sheriff of Selkirk County; it houses an exhibition on his life and writings.

You can see glass blowers in action at the **Selkirk Glass Visitor Centre** (☎ 20954, Dunsdalehaugh; admission free; open 9am-5pm Mon-Sat & 11am-5pm Sun), on the A7 north of the town centre.

Places to Stay & Eat

Victoria Park Camping & Caravan Site (☎ 20897, Victoria Park) Tent sites £7-8. Open Apr-Oct. This camp site enjoys an attractive setting beside Ettrick Water.

Sunnybrae House (☎ 21156, 75 Tower St) B&B £20. Sunnybrae is a short walk east from the northern end of Market Square and has large, comfy bedrooms and a private lounge.

County Hotel (☎ 21233, 3-5 High St) Singles/doubles £32.50/55. The family-run County has pleasant rooms (all en suite) and serves good-quality bar meals for around £5 to £6.

Court House Coffee Shop (☎ 22058, 28 Market Square) Sandwiches from £1. Open 9am-5pm Mon-Sat, 11am-4pm Sun. The Court House is well known for its high teas; it also does all-day breakfasts for £2.50.

At **Grieves Snack Attack** (Market Square), next to the Court House, you can get delicious pies, pastries and bannocks (flat, savoury cakes made from oatmeal or barley).

Getting There & Away

First Edinburgh bus No 95 runs hourly between Hawick, Selkirk, Galashiels and Edinburgh.

JEDBURGH

☎ 01835 • pop 4090

Jedburgh, on the northern slopes of the Cheviot Hills, is the most visited of the Borders towns and has a number of interesting sights, which it has capitalised on with great effect. It has a tendency to look like a film set, but it's an attractive town and many of the old buildings and *wynds* (alleys) have been intelligently restored.

Information

The large, efficient TIC (☎ 863435), Murray's Green, opens 10am to 5pm Monday to Saturday, October to May; 11am to 4pm Sunday in April and May; 9.30am to 6pm Monday to Saturday and 11am to 5pm Sunday in June and September; and 9am to 8pm weekdays, 9am to 7pm Saturday and 10am to 6pm Sunday in July and August.

The post office is on High St. You can check your email at the TIC (£1.50 for five minutes). Early closing day is Thursday.

Jedburgh Abbey

Jedburgh Abbey (HS; ☎ 863925, Abbey Bridge End; adult/child £3.30/1.20; open 9.30am-6.30pm daily Apr-Sept, 9.30am-4.30pm Mon-Sat & 2pm-4.30pm Sun Oct-Mar), founded in 1138 by David I as a priory for Augustinian canons, dominates the town. It was the site for a royal wedding and a coronation but it suffered the usual cycle of sacking and rebuilding. The red sandstone ruins are roofless, but substantial and impressive.

Mary Queen of Scots House

Mary reputedly stayed briefly at this house (☎ 863331, Queen St; adult/child £2.50/1.50; open 10.30am-3.30pm Mon-Sat & 1pm-4pm Sun Mar & Nov, 10am-4.30pm Mon-Sat & 11am-4.30pm Sun Apr-Oct) in 1566 after her famous ride to visit the injured earl of Bothwell, her future husband, at Hermitage Castle. The displays are interesting enough and evoke the sad saga of Mary's life, but they're sparse, and the text engraved on the glass panels is hard to read. Nevertheless, it's a beautiful 16th-century tower house and worth a visit.

Jedburgh Castle Jail & Museum

The former jail (☎ 863254, Castlegate; adult/child £1.25/free; open 10am-4.30pm Mon-Sat & 1pm-4pm Sun Easter-Oct), at the top of the hill south of the centre, is worth the walk. It was built in the 1820s on the site of the castle that had been destroyed by the Scots in 1409 to prevent the perfidious English using it.

The displays in the cell blocks give a good depiction of prison life, and the exhibition in the jailer's house does the same for Jedburgh's history.

Special Events

For two weeks in late June/early July the Jethart Callant Festival commemorates the perilous time when people rode out on horseback checking for English incursions.

Places to Stay

Elliot Park Camping & Caravanning Club Site (☎ 863393, Edinburgh Rd) Pitches £9.80-12.40. This secluded camp site is about a mile (1.6km) north of the town centre, on the banks of the Jed Water.

Reiver's Rest (☎ 864977, e relax@ reiversrest.co.uk, 91 Bongate) B&B £18 per person. Travellers have recommended this place, on the main A68 road about half a mile (0.8km) north of the town centre. It has covered parking for motorbikes and bicycles, and even has a sauna! Be sure to book ahead.

Glenfriars Hotel (☎/fax 862000, Friarsgate) Singles/doubles £35/64. The very comfortable Glenfriars Hotel, in a Georgian mansion a block west of High St, is quiet yet convenient for the town centre.

Hundalee House (☎/fax 863011) Singles £25-35, doubles £40-46. This beautiful manor house, set in 6 hectares of gardens, is another traveller's recommendation. It's a mile (1.6km) south of Jedburgh, on a minor road west of the A68.

Places to Eat

Castlegate Restaurant (☎ 862552, 1 Abbey Close) Mains £5.25-9.95, 3-course dinner £8.95. Open noon-2.30pm & 6pm-9pm daily. The Castlegate specialises in Scottish produce, including Angus steaks, venison and haggis. It's a good place for either a full meal or just a cup of tea.

Simply Scottish (☎ 864696, 6-8 High St, 3-course dinner £9.95. Open 10am-10pm Mon-Sat & 11am-9.30pm Sun Apr-Oct. This bistro-style place serves good-value snacks all day, plus an interesting table d'hôte menu in the evenings, including dishes such as venison casserole with red wine and mushrooms, and wild mushroom crepe with fresh herbs and cream.

The *Pheasant Lounge Bar* (High St) has a good range of bar meals from £5 to £7.

Getting There & Away

Jedburgh has good bus connections to Hawick, Galashiels and Kelso. Bus No 23 runs to/from Berwick-upon-Tweed via Kelso and Coldstream. Monro's bus No 29 runs five times daily from Edinburgh to Jedburgh in each direction.

HAWICK

☎ 01450 • pop 15,720

Straddling the River Teviot, Hawick (hoy-ick) is the largest town in the Borders and has long been a major production centre for knitwear and hosiery. Most people come to shop at the numerous factory outlets that dot the town. A list is available from the TIC.

The TIC (☎ 372547), 1 Tower Knowe, at the western end of High St, opens 10am to 5pm Monday to Saturday and noon to 5pm Sunday, April to October; till 5.30pm in June and September; and till 6pm in July and August.

In the same building is **Drumlanrig's Tower Visitor Centre** (☎ 373457, 1 Tower Knowe; adult/child £2.50/1.50; open same hours as TIC), which tells the story of cross-border warfare from the 16th century. Across the river, **Hawick Museum and Scott Art Gallery** (☎ 373457, Wilton Lodge Park; adult/child £1.25/free; open 10am-noon &

1pm-5pm Mon-Fri, 2pm-4pm Sat & Sun Apr-Sept, 1pm-4pm Mon-Fri & 2pm-4pm Sun Oct-Mar) has an interesting collection of mostly 19th-century manufacturing and domestic memorabilia.

Sarah's Coffee Shop, downstairs at Orrock Halls near the TIC, is a good place for tea and a scone.

First Borders bus No 115 runs to Melrose and Galashiels, while the hourly bus No 95 connects Hawick with Galashiels, Selkirk and Edinburgh.

HERMITAGE CASTLE

Hermitage Castle *(HS;* ☎ *013873-76222; adult/child £2/75p; open 9.30am-6.30pm daily Apr-Sept, 9.30am-4.30pm Mon-Sat & 2pm-4.30pm Sun Oct-Mar)* is a massive collection of stone, with a heavy cubist beauty; it sits isolated beside a rushing stream surrounded by bleak, empty moorland. Dating from the 13th century, but substantially rebuilt in the 15th, it embodies the brutal history of the Borders; the stones themselves almost speak of the past. It was Sir Walter Scott's favourite castle, probably best known as the home of the earl of Bothwell, and the spot to which Mary, Queen of Scots, rode in 1566 to see him after he had been wounded in a border raid.

It's also where, in 1338, Sir William Douglas imprisoned his enemy Sir Alexander Ramsay and deliberately starved him to death. Ramsay survived for 17 days by eating grain that trickled into his pit (which can still be seen) from the granary above. The castle is said to be haunted and it certainly has something of a spooky feel about it, especially when dark clouds gather.

The castle is about 12 miles (19km) south of Hawick on the B6357, and can be reached by bus No 128 to Langholm.

PEEBLES
☎ 01721 • pop 7080

Peebles is a prosperous little town set among rolling wooded hills on the banks of the River Tweed. Although it's not particularly notable, there's a broad, attractive High St and it makes a pleasant base from which to tour the Tweed Valley.

The TIC (☎ 720138), on High St, opens 9.30am to 5pm Monday to Saturday and 10am to 2pm Sunday in April, May and October; 9.30am to 5pm Monday to Saturday and 10am to 4pm Sunday, June and September; 9am to 8pm weekdays, 9am to 7pm Saturday and 10am to 6pm Sunday in July and August; and 9.30am to 12.30pm and 1.30pm to 4.30pm Monday to Saturday, the rest of the year.

Things to See
Tweeddale Museum & Gallery *(☎ 724820, High St; admission free; open 10am-noon & 2pm-5pm Mon-Fri, 10am-1pm & 2pm-4pm Sat Easter-Oct, Mon-Fri only Nov-Mar)* is in the Chambers Institute, which was given to the town by publisher William Chambers in 1859. It houses an interesting collection of displays including a copy of both the frieze taken from the Parthenon in Athens by Lord Elgin, and the 19th-century Alexander frieze.

Neidpath Castle *(☎ 720333; adult/child £3/1; open 11am-6pm daily July-Sept)* is a tower house perched on a bluff above the River Tweed. It's in a lovely spot with good views from the parapets, although there's little to see inside. The castle is a mile (1.6km) west of the centre on the A72 and can be reached by following a footpath along the river.

Places to Stay & Eat
Rosetta Caravan & Camping Park (☎ 720770, fax 720623, Rosetta Rd) Tent pitches £8. Open Apr-Oct. This camp site is about half a mile (0.8km) north of the centre, along High St.

Rowanbrae (☎ 721630, fax 723324, ℮ john@rowanbrae.freeserve.co.uk, Northgate) B&B £17.50-20. This nonsmoking B&B, in a lovely Victorian house, has three very comfortable rooms. The breakfasts are huge.

Green Tree Hotel (☎/fax 720582, ℮ green .tree.hotel@compuserve.com, 41 Eastgate) B&B £29.50 per person. Open for food noon-2pm, 5pm-8.30pm. The tidy Green Tree Hotel has eight rooms, all en suite, and serves good bar meals for around £6.

SOUTHERN SCOTLAND

Cross Keys Hotel *(☎ 724222, fax 724262, Northgate)* Singles £27-33, doubles £50-60. The Cross Keys is a renovated 17th-century coaching inn with five ensuite rooms around a cobbled courtyard. There's also a bar and restaurant, with live music at weekends.

Cringletie House Hotel *(☎ 730233, fax 730244,* **e** *enquiries@cringletie.com)* B&B £75-110. This elegant baronial mansion, 2 miles (3km) north of Peebles on the A703 road towards Edinburgh, is a comfortable country house hotel with an excellent ***restaurant*** *(lunch £7.95-19.50, 3-course dinner £32.50).*

Prince of India Restaurant *(☎ 724455, 86 High St)* Mains £5.20-7.80, 4-course set lunch £6.25. Open noon-2pm & 5pm-11.30pm daily. This curry house specialises in northern Indian food.

Sunflower Restaurant *(☎ 722420, 4 Bridgegate)* Lunch £7.50, dinner mains £9.95-14.95. Open 10am-5pm Sun-Wed, 10am-9pm Thur-Sat. The Sunflower's warm, yellow dining room serves good haddock and chips for lunch, and has a more interesting menu in the evenings, with dishes such as smoked haddock chowder, and venison with cranberry sauce and lentil mash.

For takeaway fish and chips, try ***Big Ed's Chippy*** *(Northgate)*, open 11am to 11.45pm daily; head for ***The Silver Spoon Tearoom*** *(Innerleithen Rd)*, open 9am to 4.30pm Monday to Saturday and 11am to 4pm Sunday, for tea and cakes.

Getting There & Around

Bus The bus stop is beside the post office on Eastgate. First Edinburgh bus No 62 runs hourly to Edinburgh (one hour), Galashiels (50 minutes) and Melrose (1¼ hours). Bus No C1 leaves once daily at 10.15am for Traquair (30 minutes), Selkirk (one hour 20 minutes) and Galashiels (2¼ hours), while the No 291 departs for Biggar (40 minutes) up to nine times daily.

Bicycle Scottish Border Trails (☎ 722934), 2 miles (3km) east of Peebles at Glentress, organises bicycle tours, both on and off road. It also hires out mountain bikes from £16 per

day and tourers from £10. Pre-booking is recommended.

AROUND PEEBLES
Traquair House

Traquair (tra-**kweer**) House *(☎ 01896-830323,* **w** *www.traquair.co.uk, Innerleithen; adult/child £5.30/2.80; open 10.30am-5.30pm daily June-Aug, 12.30pm-5.30pm daily Apr, May, Sept to 7 Oct)* is one of Britain's great country houses; there are many that are more aesthetically pleasing, but this one has a powerful, ethereal beauty – and an exploration here is like time travel.

Parts of the building are believed to have been constructed long before the first official record of its existence in 1107. The massive tower house was gradually expanded over the next 500 years, but has remained virtually unchanged since 1642.

Since the 15th century, the house has belonged to various branches of the Stuart family, and the family's unwavering Catholicism and loyalty to the Stuart cause is largely why development ceased when it did. The family's estate, wealth and influence was gradually whittled down after the Reformation, and there was neither the opportunity nor, one suspects, the will to make any changes.

One of the most fascinating rooms is the concealed room where priests secretly lived and gave Mass – up to 1829 when the Catholic Emancipation Act was finally passed. Other beautiful, time-worn rooms hold fascinating relics, including the cradle used by Mary for her son, James VI of Scotland (who also became James I of England), and many letters written by the Stuart pretenders to their supporters.

In addition to the house, there's a garden maze, an art gallery, a small brewery producing Bear Ale and an active craft community. The Scottish Beer Festival takes place here in late May and there's the Traquair Fair (admission £12/7) in early August.

Traquair is 1½ miles (2½ km) south of Innerleithen, about 6 miles (10km) south-east of Peebles. First Edinburgh bus No 62 runs hourly to Innerleithen and Peebles from Edinburgh. Bus No C1 goes once daily to Traquair from Peebles.

SOUTHERN SCOTLAND

South Lanarkshire

South and east of Glasgow are the large satellite towns of East Kilbride, Hamilton, Motherwell and Coatbridge. Farther upstream, the Clyde passes through a once-important coal-mining district, now significant for its fruit farms. Plums from the area around Crossford and strawberries from Kirkfieldbank are particularly tasty.

EAST KILBRIDE
☎ 01355 • pop 72,407
Known as polo-mint city because of its plethora of roundabouts, East Kilbride was the last place on earth anyone would want to visit – at least until the opening of the interesting **Museum of Scottish Country Life** *(☎ 224181, Wester Kittochside, Philipshill Rd; adult/child £3/free; open 10am-5pm daily)*. The fine exhibitions cover farming and rural lifestyles, with displays including household artefacts, clothing and toys. Workshops and activities range from wall-building to hay-making. There's also a cafe. To get here, take a frequent First Glasgow bus No 66 (£2/1.80 day ticket before/after 9.30am; 45 minutes) from Stockwell St in Glasgow to the Philipshill roundabout, then follow the signs.

BLANTYRE
☎ 01698 • pop 18,484
This town's most famous son is David Livingstone, the epitome of the Victorian missionary-explorer, who opened up central Africa to European religion. Born in 1813, in the one-roomed tenement that now forms part of the David Livingstone Centre, he worked by day in the local cotton mill from the age of 10, educated himself at night and took a medical degree in 1840 before setting off for Africa.

The interesting **David Livingstone Centre** *(☎ 823140, 165 Station Rd; adult/child £3/1; open 10am-5pm Mon-Sat, 12.30pm-5pm Sun)* tells the story of his life as a youngster in Blantyre through to his later days as a missionary and explorer, his battle against slave traders and his famous meeting with Stanley. It's by the River Clyde, just downhill

from Blantyre train station. There's an African theme cafe here serving reasonably priced soup and snacks.

It's a 20- to 30-minute walk along the riverside to **Bothwell Castle** *(HS; ☎ 816894; adult/child £2/75p; open 9.30am-6.30pm Apr-Sept, 9.30am-4.30pm Mon-Sat & 2pm-4.30pm Sun Oct-Mar, closed Thur afternoon & Fri Oct-Mar)*, regarded as the finest 13th-century castle in Scotland. Built of red sandstone, the substantial ruins, much fought over during the Wars of Independence, include a massive circular keep standing above the river. There's a good guidebook available for £1.75.

Trains run from Glasgow Central to Blantyre (£2.10 single, £2.60/3.50 peak/off-peak return, 20 minutes) twice hourly.

HAMILTON
☎ 01698 • pop 49,911
Less than 2 miles (3km) from the centre of Hamilton is **Chatelherault** *(☎ 426213, Carlisle Rd, Ferniegair; admission free; visitor centre open 10am-5pm Mon-Sat & noon-5pm Sun, closing 5.30pm Sun Apr-Oct, lodge closed Fri Oct-Mar)*, a country park with woodland trails and an excellent restored hunting lodge and kennels dating from 1732. **Cadzow Castle**, in the grounds, was completed in 1550.

Trains from Glasgow Central to Hamilton Central (two stops beyond Blantyre) run twice hourly (£2.50/2.90 single/off-peak return; 25 minutes), then catch a bus to the park (destinations Ferniegair or Larkhall; 15 minutes).

Hamilton Mausoleum *(☎ 328232, Hamilton Palace sports grounds; tours adult/child £1.10/70p; tours at 3pm Wed, Sat & Sun, 2pm Oct-Mar)* is the burial vault of the Hamilton family. It's a most unusual circular building, with a 15-second echo.

LANARK & NEW LANARK
☎ 01555 • pop 9500
Below the market town of Lanark, in an attractive gorge by the River Clyde, are the excellent restored **mill buildings and warehouses** *(W www.newlanark.org)* of New Lanark. This was once the largest cotton-spinning complex in Britain, but it

was better known for the pioneering social experiments of Robert Owen, who managed the mill from 1800. An enlightened capitalist, he provided his workers with housing, a cooperative store (which was the inspiration for the modern cooperative movement), a school with adult education classes and a social centre he called 'The New Institute for the Formation of Character'. New Lanark has been nominated as a UNESCO World Heritage Site.

In 1297, the Scots patriot William Wallace killed Hazelrigg, the sheriff of Lanark, here, precipitating the Wars of Independence.

Orientation & Information

The TIC (☎ 661661), Horsemarket, Ladyacre Rd, Lanark, is near the bus and train stations and opens year-round. The 20-minute walk down to New Lanark is worth it for the views, but there's a daily bus service from the train station (hourly). Returning to Lanark, currently the last bus leaves New Lanark at 4.42pm (6.57pm Sunday).

There are two banks with ATMs on High St and the post office is on the Edinburgh road (St Leonards St). The Lanark Health Centre can be contacted on ☎ 665522.

If you need a taxi, call Clydewide on ☎ 663221.

Things to See

In New Lanark, the **Visitor Centre** *(☎ 661345, New Lanark Mills; adult/child £4.75/3.25; open 11am-5pm daily)* includes admission to Robert Owen's house, Robert Owen's school (where a girl tells you the story of her life as a millworker in the 1820s), a restored millworker's house, the New Millennium Experience (an intriguing high-tech audio-visual ride), and a 1920s-style village store. There's also a gift shop with good-value woollens on sale.

Probably the best way to get the feel of this impressive place is to wander around the outside of the buildings and then walk up to the **Falls of Clyde** through the nature reserve. Visit the **Falls of Clyde Wildlife Centre** *(☎ 665262, New Lanark; admission free; open 11am-5pm daily)* by the river first; there's an exhibition about local bats,

badgers and peregrine falcons. Walk for a couple of miles (3km) to the power station then half a mile (800m) to the beautiful **Cora Linn** (waterfalls) and, beyond them, **Bonnington Linn**.

Craignethan Castle *(HS; ☎ 860364, Tillietudlem; adult/child 2/75p; open 9.30am-6.30pm daily Apr-Sept, reduced hours Oct-Nov)* is 5 miles (8km) north-west of Lanark. Remodelled as the last great medieval castle in Scotland in 1530, with a commanding position above the River Nethan, this extensive ruin includes a **caponier** (unique in the UK) and a virtually intact tower house with indoor latrines and spiral staircases. If you don't have your own transport, take an hourly Lanark–Hamilton bus to Crossford, then follow the footpath along the northern bank of the River Nethan (20 minutes).

Four miles (6km) south of Lanark, by the A73, there's the **Carmichael Heritage Centre** *(☎ 01899-308336, Westmains, Carmichael; adult/child £3.25/1.95; open 9.30am-5.30pm daily Apr-Oct)*, with an interesting wax-model collection of historical and modern figures. On site, there's a windmill for electrical requirements and a tearoom. Lanark to Biggar buses (☎ 01501-820598) pass this way, four to 16 times daily.

Places to Stay

If you want to stay in Lanark, the TIC has a free accommodation list for the area.

Mrs Buchanan's *(☎ 661002, 5 Hardacres)* B&B £16-20. This has pleasant accommodation on the northern edge of Lanark.

Mrs Berkley's *(☎ 665487, 159 Hyndford Rd)* Singles/doubles from £18/32. This is located 10 minutes from the station. Evening meals are available.

Newhouse Caravan & Camping Park *(☎/fax 870228, Newhouse Park Farm, Ravenstruther)* Tent pitches from £3. Open Mar-Oct. The park is located 3 miles (5km) east of Lanark, by the A70.

New Lanark Youth Hostel *(☎ 666710, fax 666719, Wee Row, Rosedale St)* Dorm beds from £8.50/7.25. Open Mar-Oct. This hostel, opened in 1994, is very pleasantly located near the river. Internet access is available for £1 per 10 minutes.

New Lanark Mill Hotel (☎ 667200, fax 667222, Mill One, New Lanark) Singles/doubles from £57.50/75. All rooms are en suite. The bar and restaurant do soup and snacks for under £4, but the restaurant also offers a three-course lunch/dinner for around £10.50/18.

Places to Eat

Crown Tavern (☎ 664639, 17 Hope St) Mains £5.75-14.50. You'll get a good bar meal in the traditional pub here.

Clydesdale Inn (☎ 678740, 15 Bloomgate) Bar meal mains £4-5. Meals, with vegetarian choices, are served all day.

East India Company (☎ 663827, 32 Wellgate) Mains £4.70-8.95, 3-course weekday lunch £4.50. Near St Nicholas' Church, this is a reasonable choice.

Treats (☎ 664466, 60 Bannatyne St) Jacket potatoes £1.75-3.80. Treats is a self-service cafe with good home baking.

Valerio's (☎ 665818, Bannatyne St) Fish and chips £3.69. Valerio's, near the bus station and the TIC, is a typical fish and chip shop.

In the New Lanark Visitor Centre there's the *Mill Pantry* for snacks and light meals (soup and bread £1.70); or you could try the New Lanark Mill Hotel bar and restaurant for something more substantial (see Places to Stay earlier).

Self-caterers can stock up at the large *Somerfield* supermarket, conveniently situated by the TIC.

Getting There & Away

Lanark is 25 miles (40km) south-east of Glasgow. Hourly trains run daily between Glasgow Central and Lanark (£4.10/4.90 single/day return; 55 minutes).

BIGGAR

☎ 01899 • pop 1994

Biggar is a pleasant town in a rural setting dominated by Tinto Hill (712m). The hill is a straightforward ascent by its northern ridge from Thankerton. The town is well worth a visit – it probably has more museums and attractions per inhabitant than anywhere else of its size!

Information

The seasonal TIC (☎ 221066), at 155 High St, opens 10am to 5pm Monday to Saturday and noon to 5pm Sunday from 9 April to 30 September. The post office and Royal Bank ATM are also on High St. The Health Centre (☎ 220383) is at South Croft Road.

Things to See

The Biggar Museums Trust (☎ 221050) looks after four major museums in the town (and two other places). **Moat Park Heritage Centre** *(☎ 221050, Kirkstyle; adult/child £2/1; open 10.30am-5pm Mon-Sat & 2pm-5pm Sun Easter-Oct)*, in a renovated church, covers the history of the area with geological and archaeological displays. There are also natural and folk history exhibits, including a 6.7-sq-metre patchwork. The **Greenhill Covenanter's House** *(☎ 221050, Burnbrae; adult/child £1/70p; open 2pm-5pm daily May-Sept)* is a reconstructed farmhouse, with 17th-century furnishings and artefacts relating to local Covenanters. **Gladstone Court** *(☎ 221050, North Back Rd; adult/child £2/1; open 10.30am-5pm Mon-Sat & 2pm-5pm Sun May-mid-Oct)* is an indoor street museum showing historic shops. The **Gasworks Museum** *(☎ 221050, Gasworks Lane; adult/child £1/50p; open 2pm-5pm daily June-Sept)* is the only coal-fired gasworks left in Scotland, originally opened in 1839.

Biggar Puppet Theatre *(☎ 220631, Broughton Rd; all seats £5, guided tours £2.50/2 adult/child; open 10am-4.30pm Tues-Sun Easter-Aug)* has miniature Victorian puppets and bizarre modern ones over 1m high that glow in the dark. There are several ultraviolet displays but you don't need your sunglasses.

Places to Stay & Eat

YMCA Camp Site (☎ 850228, Wiston) Camping £3 per person. Open year round. Campers can stay at this camp site at Wiston, 1½ miles (2.5km) south of Tinto Hill.

Elmwood (☎ 308740, 32 Sheriffflats Rd) B&B £17 per person. This B&B at Thankerton, 4 miles (6.5km) from Biggar, and near Tinto Hill, has two rooms with shared facilities.

Daleside (☎/fax 220097, 165 High St) B&B £18-25. This place offers three rooms with shared bathroom.

Elphinstone Hotel (☎ 220044, 145 High St) Singles/doubles from £29/48. The Elphinstone has three en-suite rooms. Bar meals are also available at this recommended inn.

Cornhill House (☎ 220001, fax 220112, Coulter) Singles/doubles £50/70. Cornhill House, located 2 miles (3km) south-west of Biggar, is a well-appointed place complete with turrets. Its excellent restaurant opens for lunch and dinner; main courses range from £5.25 to £17.

Coffee Spot (☎ 221902, 152 High St) Head to the Coffee Spot for filled baguettes and baked potatoes (from £1.35).

Oriental (☎ 221894, 3 Park Place) Mains from £6.95. This is a new place that doesn't come cheap.

Taj Mahal (☎ 220801, 101 High St) Mains from £3.95. This is the best place to eat in town.

There are a couple of *supermarkets* on High St.

Getting There & Away

Biggar is 33 miles (53km) south-east of Glasgow. Buses to Edinburgh (Stagecoach Western ☎ 01387-253496; MacEwan's ☎ 01387-256533) run three to nine times daily; tickets cost £3. There are four to 16 daily runs to Lanark (HAD Coaches ☎ 01501-820598) for £1.80. From Monday to Saturday, postbuses (☎ 01246-546329) run from Biggar to Tweedsmuir, Abington and Wanlockhead. There's also a weekday run to Lanark.

ABINGTON, CRAWFORD & CRAWFORDJOHN
☎ 01864

At **Abington**, 35 miles (56km) south of Glasgow by the M74, there's a 24-hour motorway service station with a TIC (☎ 502436), open from at least 10am to 5pm daily. Turn off the motorway here for **Wanlockhead** and **Crawfordjohn**. In Abington village, you'll find a general store, post office, tearoom and Royal Bank, but note that the nearest ATM is at the aforementioned Abington Services. Crawfordjohn has a **Heritage Venture** (☎ 504265; admission free; open 1pm-4pm weekends May-Sept, other times by arrangement), in a former church behind the school, with Covenanter's relics, wildlife and agricultural displays etc.

Crawford Arms Hotel (☎ 502267, 111 Carlisle Rd, Crawford) B&B without/with bathroom £19.50/23.50 per person. This hotel offers bar meals; mains cost around £5, starters and desserts about £2.

Holmlands Country House (☎ 502753, fax 502313, 22 Carlisle Rd, Abington) B&B £20-35 per person. This is the best place to stay in the area, in a pleasant secluded spot, sheltered from the motorway. Home baking and evening meals are available.

Colebrooke Arms (☎ 504239, 7 Main St, Crawfordjohn) Mains £4.25-12.95. The Colebrooke Arms serves a wide range of home-made bar meals.

Stagecoach Western (☎ 01387-253496) runs about six buses daily between Dumfries and Edinburgh, via Abington (Dumfries to Abington £2.90, Abington to Edinburgh £4.30). HAD Coaches (☎ 01501-820598) does a Monday to Saturday service from Lanark to Abington (£1.60) via Leadhills. There's a Monday to Saturday postbus service (☎ 01246-546329) from Abington and Crawfordjohn to Biggar and Wanlockhead.

DOUGLAS
☎ 01555 • pop 1616

The main road (A70) gives a rather negative impression of this interesting place. Douglas has close ties to Scottish history, begun during the Wars of Independence when the Good Sir James Douglas fought alongside Robert the Bruce.

With the almost total destruction of the grand Douglas family castle by fire in 1755 the village slipped into obscurity.

Turn off the A70 at the Douglas Arms Hotel and follow Main St to the **Douglas Heritage Museum** (☎ 851536, Bells Wynd; admission free; open 2pm-5pm weekends Easter-Sept, other times by arrangement), previously the dower house for Douglas Castle, later converted into a chapel. It contains Cameronian military memorabilia and a mock-up of an old shop.

St Bride's Chapel

Close to the heritage museum is the excellent St Bride's Chapel *(HS; Main St; admission free)*. The 14th-century choir stalls and nave were restored in 1880. They contain three Douglas family wall-tombs, including one for the Good Sir James, who was killed in Spain in 1330 while taking the Bruce's heart to the Holy Land. Look out for the lead-encased hearts of James and Archibald, 5th earl of Angus (also known as 'Bell-the-Cat', one of the most colourful figures in Scottish history), on the floor of the chapel. The superb 16th-century clock tower has the oldest working clock in Scotland (1565).

Mrs Cowan (☎ 851657), 2 Clyde Rd, behind the Crosskeys Inn, holds the key for the chapel.

Walking

There's an interesting walk up to the Hagshaw Wind Farm about a mile (1.6km) north-west of the village. Follow the minor road to Douglas West, then head up to the farm from the old schoolhouse. There are about 50 gigantic three-blade fans up there.

Places to Eat

JJ's Takeaway (☎ 851043, 56 Ayr Rd) Pizza from £2.40. Located behind the petrol station near the Douglas Arms Hotel, JJ's Takeaway does fish and chips, burgers and pizzas, both sit-in and takeaway. There's also a Chinese and an Indian restaurant in Douglas.

Getting There & Away

Douglas is about 7 miles (11km) north-west of Abington. Stokes (☎ 870344) runs hourly bus services to Lanark, while another service goes to Muirkirk, with connections for Cumnock and Ayr.

Ayrshire

The rolling hills and farmland of Ayrshire are best known for being the birthplace and home of poet Robert Burns.

These rich pastures were once also famous for the Ayrshire breed of dairy cattle, since largely replaced by Friesians (see the boxed text 'Ayrshire Cattle' later). Parts of the coast comprise attractive sandy beaches and low cliffs overlooking the mountainous Isle of Arran.

There are famous golf courses at Troon and Turnberry. It was at Prestwick Golf Club that the major golf tournament, the British Open Championship, was initiated in 1860.

NORTH AYRSHIRE
Largs
☎ 01475 • pop 10,000

Largs is a pleasant town facing the Isle of Great Cumbrae. There's a TIC (☎ 01292-678100) at the train station; it opens year-round. Main St, with banks, cafes and cheap eating places, is fairly short, running inland from the CalMac ferry terminal to just past the train and bus stations. The post office is just off Main St, on Aitken St. Largs hosts a **Viking festival** during the first week in September.

Things to See The main attraction in Largs is the award-winning **Vikingar!** *(☎ 689777, Greenock Rd; adult/child £3.80/2.90; open 10.30am-5.30pm Sun-Fri, 12.30pm-5.30pm Sat)*, a multimedia exhibition describing Viking influence in Scotland until its demise at the Battle of Largs in 1263. Tours with staff in Viking outfits run every half-hour. There's also a theatre, cinema, cafe, shop, swimming pool and leisure centre. To get here, follow the A78 coast road northwards from the TIC; you can't miss it, it's the only place with a longship outside.

Skelmorlie Aisle *(☎ 687081, Manse Court; admission free; open mid-May–early-Sept by arrangement)*, just off High St, is the remnant of Largs Old Kirk (1636) and is well worth a visit. It has an unusual painted barrel-vaulted ceiling depicting the seasons, and an elaborately carved stone tomb.

Hunterston B Nuclear Power Station *(☎ 0800 376 0676; admission free; open by arrangement for groups)*, 7 miles (11km) south of Largs, offers a 10-minute introductory video and a one-hour tour. Call the

SOUTHERN SCOTLAND

toll-free number for advice on times when individuals can see the power station or whether you can join a group tour.

Walking There's a good walk for a couple of miles (3km) into the hills east of Largs; start from Main St, turn left into Aitken St, then right up Gateside St and Flatt Rd, past the school. Follow the path high above the Gogo Water as far as Greeto Bridge and the waterfalls. You can climb up steeper slopes to the mast, at 300m, for great views of the Firth of Clyde and the town. Allow two to three hours.

Places to Stay & Eat There's a fine selection of places to stay and eat in Largs.

Biscayne House (☎ 672851, fax 676153, 110 Irvine Rd) Dorm beds £11, doubles £25. The hostel is over half a mile (1km) from the town centre.

St Leonard's (☎ 673318, 9 Irvine Rd) Rooms £18-25 per person. St Leonard's is a central B&B, but only one of its three rooms has a private bathroom.

Brisbane House Hotel (☎ 687200, fax 676295, 14 Greenock Rd) Singles £65-75, doubles £90-130. All rooms in this comfortable hotel are en suite. The great-value meals are recommended.

Toby's Bar (☎ 687183, 67 Gallowgate) Mains £3.95-6.95. This place does really good, cheap bar meals, with soup and bread at £1.95 and baked potatoes from £2.50.

Ayrshire Cattle

This hardy type of dairy cattle originated from cross-breeding in the 18th century and proved to be a great success, giving high milk yields even when feed was poor. Ayrshires are the only British-developed breed of dairy cattle.

By the early 19th century, Ayrshires were paramount in Britain. Large numbers of these variously coloured cattle were exported to Canada, the USA, Russia, Finland and Kenya. However, due to recent changes in the nature of dairy farming, the larger Friesian breed has overtaken the Ayrshire in popularity.

Nardini's Café (☎ 674555, Esplanade) 3-course lunch £6.25. The well-known Nardini's does great ice cream.

Baker's Oven (76 Main St) Breakfast £2.99. Breakfast here comprises a filled baguette and coffee.

There's a large *Safeway* supermarket beyond the southern end of Main St, just off Irvine Rd.

Getting There & Away Largs is 32 miles (51km) west of Glasgow by road. There are hourly trains to Largs from Glasgow Central (£4.90/6.10 single/off-peak return; one hour). Buses run to Ardrossan (£2.10), Ayr (£3.75), Glasgow, Greenock (£2.85) and Irvine (£2.50). Stagecoach Western and Arriva buses can be contacted on ☎ 01294-607007 and ☎ 0870 241 3197 respectively.

Isle of Great Cumbrae
☎ 01475 • pop 1200

Included here because it's reached from North Ayrshire, the island is administered as part of Argyll & Bute. There's actually nothing very great about it – it's only 4 miles (6km) long – but it's bigger than privately owned Little Cumbrae island, just to the south.

A frequent 15-minute CalMac ferry ride links Largs with Great Cumbrae (£3.15 to £3.60 return, £13.35 to £15.70 for a car). Buses (£2 return) meet the ferries for the 3½-mile (5.5km) journey to **Millport**, which has two sandy beaches. The town boasts Europe's smallest cathedral, **The Cathedral of the Isles** (☎ 530353, College St; admission free; open daylight hours daily), which was completed in 1851, and the interesting **Robertson Museum and Aquarium** (☎ 530581, adult/child £1.50/1; open 9.30am-12.15pm & 2pm-4.45pm weekdays year-round, plus Sat Jun-Sept, closing 4.15pm year-round), just east of town. A short way along the coast from the aquarium is the remarkable rock feature called **The Lion**.

The **Museum of the Cumbraes** (☎ 531191, Guildford St; admission free; open 11am-1pm & 2pm-4.30pm Tues, Thur & Fri Easter-Oct) is at the stables of **The Garrison**, previously the excise and militia headquarters. There's a seasonal TIC (☎ 01292-678100), 28 Stuart St (at the waterfront), and several bike-hire places, including Mapes (☎ 530444), at 3 Guildford St (£2.90 for two hours). Rural parts of the island are very pleasant; the narrow Inner Circle Rd is a good cycle route. Ask the TIC for maps of cycle routes.

On the main street around the bay, you'll find a post office, VG supermarket, bank (with ATM), two fish and chip shops and a couple of cafes.

Denmark Cottage (☎ 530958, fax 530988, 8 Ferry Rd) B&B £16-20 per person. This is a pleasant family home; rooms have shared bathroom.

College of the Holy Spirit (☎ 530353, fax 530204, College St) B&B £17.50-22.50 per person. This place is next to the cathedral and is an interesting and unusual choice for accommodation; evening meals are available.

Newton Bar & Hiccups Lounge (☎ 530920, 1 Glasgow St) Mains from £3.95. This place does cheap snacks, pizzas, burgers, traditional bar meals and takeaways.

Spice Island (☎ 530900, 15 Stuart St) 3-course lunch £5.95. Spice Island is a pleasant Indian restaurant.

Irvine
☎ 01294 • pop 35,000

In the early 1990s, Irvine Development Corporation flattened a large area and redeveloped it as **Irvine Harbourside**, an interesting place with brand-new 19th-century-style buildings, not far from the town centre and train station. The cobbled street **Linthouse Vennel** is lined with impressive and very expensive-looking buildings. The TIC (☎ 01292-678100), New St, is near the train station and opens year-round. Ask the TIC for information on the town's Burns Trail.

There are *Asda* and *Tesco* supermarkets in the Irvine Centre; banks with ATMs and the post office are on High St.

Things to See & Do The **Scottish Maritime Museum** *(☎ 278283, Gottries Rd, Harbourside; adult/child/family £2.50/ 1.75/5; open 10am-5pm daily)* has various ships you can clamber about on, and you can also see a restored shipyard-worker's flat. There are regular guided tours through-

out the day that visit sections not normally open to the public. *Puffers Coffee Shop* on site does snacks and daily specials.

The **Big Idea** *(☎ 0870 840 4030, Harbourside; adult/child/family £7.95/5.95/18-29; open 10am-5pm Mon-Fri, 10am-6pm Sat-Sun, last admission 4pm)* millennium exhibition claims to be the world's first inventor centre, with hundreds of interactive exhibits. Admission includes a free Inventor's Kit worth £4.95.

The **Magnum Leisure Centre** *(☎ 278381,* W *www.themagnum.co.uk, Harbourside; admission fees vary; open 9am-10pm Mon & Fri, 10am-10pm Tues-Thur, 9am-6pm Sat & Sun)* is Scotland's largest, and has swimming (with flumes), ice rinks, curling, football, squash, bowls, cinema, theatre, an inexpensive cafe and lots more. Swimming/ice skating charges start at £2/2.20.

Places to Stay & Eat The TIC keeps a list of accommodation options.

Harbour Guest House (☎ 276212, 1 Harbour St) Singles/doubles £18.50/30. For accommodation at Harbourside, try this seafront place in the heart of the impressive redeveloped area.

Laurelbank Guest House (☎ 277153, 3 Kilwinning Rd) B&B £16-20 per person. This friendly Victorian guesthouse is centrally located.

Ship Inn (☎ 279722, 120 Harbour St) Bar meals £4.85-6.95. The wonderful Ship Inn, near the Magnum Centre, is the oldest pub in Irvine, built in 1597. The bar meals here are very good indeed.

Marina Inn (☎ 274079, 110 Harbour St) Bar meals from around £5. This pub has live folk music every Tuesday.

Harbour Chippy (Gottries Rd) This is the place to go for good fish and chips (£3.05).

Getting There & Away Irvine is 26 miles (42km) from Glasgow. Trains run to Glasgow Central half-hourly (£4.40/5.30 single/ off-peak return, 35 minutes). In the other direction they go to Ayr. Buses depart from High St (Irvine Cross) for Ayr (£2.20, 30 minutes, twice hourly Monday to Saturday, every two hours Sunday), Glasgow (£2.55,

SOUTHERN SCOTLAND

1¼ hours, hourly Monday to Saturday, four Sunday), Greenock (£4.40, 1¼ hours, twice hourly Monday to Saturday, every two hours Sunday), Kilmarnock (90p, 26 minutes, every 10 or 15 minutes) and Largs (£2.50, 45 minutes, twice hourly Monday to Saturday, every two hours Sunday). Stagecoach Western buses can be contacted on ☎ 01294-607007.

Ardrossan

☎ 01294 • pop 11,000

The main reason for coming here is to catch a CalMac ferry to Arran. Trains leave Glasgow Central (£4.60, one hour) four or five times daily to connect with ferries.

Ardrossan is a very run-down area; there are several cheap, but mostly uninspiring, places to eat on the main street (Glasgow St) and in neighbouring Princes St. On Glasgow St, there's a post office, grocer and general store.

Edenmore Guest House (☎ 462306, fax 604016, 47 Parkhouse Rd) B&B £18-25 per person. If you need B&B in town, try Edenmore, just off the main A78. It also offers evening meals.

Sangeet Indian Restaurant (☎ 601191, 51 Glasgow Rd) 3-course meals £6.95, available 5pm-7pm Tues, Wed, Fri & Sat. Cheap takeaways are also available at this busy place.

Stacie's (54 Princes St) opens at 6am for breakfast.

ISLE OF ARRAN

☎ 01770 • pop 4800

Known as 'Scotland in miniature', parts of this island certainly are reminiscent of other areas of the country. There are challenging walks in the mountainous northern part of the island, often compared to the Highlands; the landscape in the south is gentler and similar to the rest of southern Scotland.

Since Arran is easily accessible from Glasgow and Ayrshire, being only an hour's ferry ride from Ardrossan, it's very popular. Despite its popularity, the 20-mile-long (32km-long) island seems to be big enough to absorb everyone. The bucket-and-spade brigade fill the southern resorts, cyclists take to the island's circular road, and hikers

tackle the hills, the highest being Goat Fell (874m). With seven courses, Arran is also popular with golfers.

Orientation & Information

The ferry from Ardrossan docks at Brodick, the island's main town. To the south, Lamlash is actually the capital, and, like nearby Whiting Bay, a popular seaside resort. From the village of Lochranza in the north there's a ferry link to Claonaig on the Kintyre peninsula.

Near Brodick pier, the helpful TIC (☎ 302140) opens 9am to 7.30pm daily June to September (10am to 5pm Sunday), with shorter hours at other times. Tourist information is also available on the ferry from Ardrossan at peak times. The hospital (☎ 600777) is in Lamlash. There's a laundry by the Collins Good Food Shop (next to the River Cloy).

The Pier Tearoom (☎ 830217), Lochranza, offers Internet access. For more information

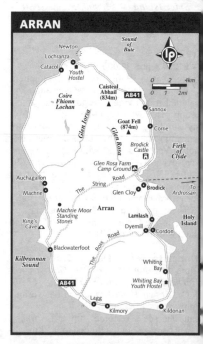

about Arran, check out the Web sites at W www.ayrshire-arran.com or W www .arrantourism.com.

Stagecoach Western (☎ *302000*) runs full-/half-day tours for £7.50/5 or £5/3. The full-day tours run from late May to September, departing Brodick pier at 11am daily. Half-day tours run in July and early August, departing Brodick pier at 1.45pm weekdays.

The week-long Arran Folk Festival (☎ 302623, W www.arranfolkfestival.org) takes place in early June. There are also local village festivals happening from June to September.

Arran is known for its local cheeses, and Arran mustard is also worth buying. Watch out for the woollens, though – real Aran (one 'r') sweaters come from the Irish island of Aran, not this one.

Things to See

The town of **Brodick** isn't particularly interesting, but it's in a pleasant location. There are several hotels, B&Bs, gift shops, a Coop supermarket and banks with ATMs. Taking the road 1½ miles (2.5km) north, you'll come to the small **Heritage Museum** (☎ *302636, Rosaburn; adult/child £2.25/1; open 10.30am-4.30pm daily April-Oct*) with a late-19th-century-style furnished cottage, an old blacksmith's workshop, local archaeology and geology exhibits, and a yearly special exhibition.

Brodick Castle and Park *(NTS; ☎ 302202; adult/child £6/4.50 to castle and park, £2.50/1.70 for park only; castle open 11am-4.30pm daily Apr-Oct, park open 9.30am-sunset year-round)* is 2½ miles (4km) north of Brodick. Parts of this ancient seat of the dukes of Hamilton date from the late 13th century. It's an interesting stately home, with a rather more lived-in feel than some NTS properties. It also has an excellent restaurant with home baking and meals for under £7. The Victorian kitchen and scullery, complete with displays of peculiar kitchen devices, are well worth a look. The grounds, now a country park with various trails among the rhododendrons, have an attractive walled garden dating from 1710.

As you go round Brodick Bay, look out for seals, often seen on the rocks around Merkland Point. Two types live in these waters, the Atlantic grey and the common seal. They're actually quite easy to tell apart – the common seal has a face like a dog; the Atlantic grey seal has a Roman nose.

The coast road continues to the small, pretty village of **Corrie**, where there's a shop and hotel, and one of the tracks up Goat Fell starts here. Corrie Village Shop (☎ 810209) sells wonderful **Marvin Elliot sculptures**. After **Sannox**, with a sandy beach and great views of the mountains, the road cuts inland.

Lochranza is a village in a small bay at the north of the island. From late March to late October, there's a direct ferry link to Claonaig on the Kintyre peninsula from here. There's also a shop and post office, youth hostel, camp site, several B&Bs and a couple of hotels.

On a promontory stand the ruins of the 13th-century **Lochranza Castle** *(admission free)*, said to be the inspiration for the castle in *The Black Island*, Hergé's Tintin adventure. The key is available from Lochranza Stores. Also in Lochranza is Scotland's newest distillery, **Isle of Arran Distillers** *(☎ 830264; tours £3.50/free adult/child; open 10am-4.30pm daily)*, which opened in 1995. The village has a boat race, fiddlers' rallies and other music events from June to August.

Two miles (3km) beyond Lochranza, the whitewashed cottages of **Catacol**, known as the Twelve Apostles, were built to house people cleared from land set aside for sheep and deer. Sunsets are wonderful here from April to August.

On the western side of the island, reached by the String Rd across the centre (or the coast road), are the **Machrie Moor standing stones**, upright sandstone slabs erected around 6000 years ago. It's an eerie place, and these are the most impressive of the six stone circles on the island. To get there, you'll need an Ordnance Survey (OS) map; walk along the 1½-mile (2.5km) track from the coast road, starting from the HS sign just north of Machrie village. There's another group at nearby **Auchagallon**, surrounding a Bronze Age burial cairn.

Blackwaterfoot is the largest village on the west coast; it has a shop/post office and two hotels. You can walk to **King's Cave** from here, via Drumadoon Farm – Arran is one of several islands that lay claim to a cave where Robert the Bruce had his famous arachnid encounter. This walk could be combined with a visit to the Machrie standing stones.

The landscape in the southern part of the island is much gentler; the road drops into little wooded valleys, and it's particularly lovely around **Lagg**. Walk from Lagg post office to **Torrylin Cairn** (10 minutes each way), a chambered tomb over 4000 years old, where at least eight bodies were found. By the roadside at **Kilmory**, you can visit the **Torrylin Creamery** (☎ 870240; admission free; open 10am-4pm Sun-Fri). There are displays about cheese-making. In the shop, you can buy a tasty one-pound Arran Dunlop cheese for £3.50. By the roadside at **East Bennan**, there's **Southbank Farm Park** (☎ 820221; adult/child £2.50/2; open 10am-5pm Tues, Thur & Sun Easter-Sept), with lots of beasts, including those wonderful hairy Highland cattle. **Kildonan** has pleasant sandy beaches, two hotels, a camp site and an ivy-clad ruined castle.

In **Whiting Bay**, you'll find small sandy beaches, a SYHA hostel, village shop, post office and craft shops. There are lots of hotels; most of them serve meals. Check out the pubs for live local music, from folk to pop and rock.

Just north of Whiting Bay is **Holy Island**, owned by the Samye Ling Tibetan Centre (Dumfriesshire) and used as a retreat, but day visits are allowed. The ferry runs from Lamlash (☎ 600998, £8, 15 minutes, four daily). No dogs, alcohol or fires are allowed on the island. There's a good walk to the top of the hill (314m), a two- to three-hour return trip.

Lamlash is a sailing centre, with hotels, restaurants, cafes, grocery stores and a post office. The bay was used as a safe anchorage by the Navy during WWI and WWII.

Walking & Cycling

The walk up and down **Goat Fell** takes five to six hours and, if the weather's good, there

are superb views from the 874m-high summit. It can, however, be very cold and windy up there, so go well prepared. There are paths from Brodick Castle and Corrie.

From the high point of the road between Sannox and Lochranza, you can head southwards (avoiding the forestry) and walk up a pleasant ridge to **Caisteal Abhail** (859m). The view is magnificent from the top. Don't be tempted to follow the eastern ridge to Ceun na Caillich (Witch's Step) – it involves moderate rock climbing and it's quite exposed.

However, you can go southwards to **Cir Mhór** (798m), scramble over its pointed summit, continue down its eastern ridge to a pass, then descend steeply into Glen Sannox. Only attempt this route in good weather; allow six hours. For both routes, carry OS map No 69 and a compass. Note that there's deer stalking on Caisteal Abhail from late August to late October; ask locally for advice.

Another good walk on a marked path goes up to **Coire Fhionn Lochan** from Mid Thundergay; it takes about an hour to reach the loch. You can continue up to the top of **Beinn Bhreac** (711m), taking another 1½ hours from the loch.

More moderate walks include the trail through **Glen Sannox**, which goes from the village of Sannox up the burn, a two-hour return trip. From Whiting Bay Youth Hostel there are easy one hour walks through the forest to the **Giant's Graves** and **Glenashdale Falls**, and back.

The 50-mile (80km) circuit on the coastal road is popular with cyclists and has few serious hills – more in the south than the north. Traffic isn't too bad, except in high season.

Places to Stay

Camping Without permission from the landowner camping isn't allowed, but there are several camp sites (open April to October). When choosing a site, note that midges can be a major pain in sheltered spots.

Glen Rosa Farm (☎ 302380, 2 miles, 3km from Brodick) Camp sites £2.50 per person. Glen Rosa Farm doesn't have showers and may, in fact, soon close! Phone to check.

Middleton Camping (☎ 600251, Cordon, Lamlash) £1.75 per tent, plus £3 per person

This is a fairly upmarket site in a quiet location.

Kildonan Hotel (☎ 820207, Kildonan) £4 per person, plus 50p per tent. Down by the sea, the camping at Kildonan Hotel includes the use of excellent facilities.

Lochranza Golf (☎ 830273, fax 830600, Lochranza) From £6 per tent. This site is located next to the par 70 Lochranza golf course.

Hostels There are three reasonably good hostels on Arran.

Lochranza Youth Hostel (☎/fax 830631, Lochranza) Beds from £8.50/5. Open Feb-Oct. Located in the north of the island, this is an excellent self-catering hostel.

Whiting Bay Youth Hostel (☎/fax 700339, Shore Rd, Whiting Bay) Beds from £8.25/7. Open Apr-Oct. Located in a rather austere-looking building, this hostel has good facilities.

Kildonan Hotel Bunkhouse (☎ 820207, Kildonan) Dorm beds £8. Right at the southern tip of Arran, this bunkhouse now has a kitchen. No bedding is provided so you'll need your own sleeping bag.

B&Bs & Hotels – Brodick It's best to get out of Brodick to some of the more attractive smaller villages, although there are numerous places to stay here, especially along Shore Rd, the main drag.

Glenfloral (☎/fax 302707, Shore Rd) B&B £17 per person with shared bathroom. Vegetarians are also catered for in this pleasant seafront guesthouse.

Tigh-na-Mara (☎ 302538, fax 302546, The Seafront) B&B £18-23.50 per person. Only two of the nine rooms are en suite, but there are great views.

Belvedere (☎ 302397, fax 302088, Alma Rd) B&B £20-25 per person. All rooms in this friendly guesthouse are en suite; a four-course dinner is available for £22, including wine, and vegetarians are catered for.

Pirate's Cove (☎ 302438, Corrie Shore) B&B £18-20 per person. Friendly Pirate's Cove, 3 miles (5km) north of Brodick, also serves traditional Scottish meals from £7.50.

Rosaburn Lodge (☎/fax 302383) B&B £20-30 per person. Half-a-mile (800m) from the centre of Brodick, by the River Rosa, this comfortable B&B has three en-suite rooms.

Kilmichael Country House Hotel (☎ 302219, fax 302068, Glen Cloy) Singles £75, doubles £120-150. The island's best hotel is also its oldest building – it has a glass window dating from 1650. It's a tastefully decorated hideaway, a mile (1.6km) outside Brodick, with eight rooms and an excellent restaurant (four-course dinners cost £29.50).

B&Bs & Hotels – Corrie There are a few places to stay in Corrie.

Corrie Hotel (☎ 810273, Corrie) Singles/doubles £21/42, en-suite rooms £26/52. This traditional stone building offers reasonable accommodation. Bar meals are available here for between £5.85 and £6.50. There's also a beer garden in July and August.

Blackrock Guest House (☎ 810282, Corrie) B&B £18-25 per person. Some rooms are en suite at this seafront guesthouse a half-mile (800m) north of the Corrie Hotel.

B&Bs & Hotels – Lochranza This is a scenically superb location in which to stay.

Castlekirk (☎ 830202, Lochranza) B&B £19 per person. Castlekirk is a converted church opposite the castle, with two rooms and an in-house art gallery.

Croftbank (☎ 830201, Lochranza) B&B £16-18 per person. Open Feb-Nov. This place can be found by the post office and offers acceptable B&B.

Lochranza Hotel (☎/fax 830223, Lochranza) En-suite singles/doubles from £30/50. The pleasant Lochranza Hotel has great views of the harbour and the rooms have been recently redecorated.

Apple Lodge (☎/fax 830229, Lochranza) Doubles £62-72. Apple Lodge is the finest place to stay in Lochranza, with three double rooms and excellent meals (three-course dinners cost £19). You'll be well looked after in very comfortable surroundings.

B&Bs & Hotels – Blackwaterfoot This is a good base for exploring the west coast.

Kinloch Hotel (☎ 860444, fax 860447, Blackwaterfoot) B&B £39.20-49 per person. This hotel has good leisure facilities (handy on a wet day), including a 15m swimming pool (£2.25 for nonresidents), sauna, solarium, squash court and multi-gym. Bar meals are available for between £6 and £14.50; dinner costs £17.50.

Morvern House (☎ 860254, Blackwaterfoot) Singles/doubles from £17/34. Morvern House is in the same building as the shop and post office, and offers standard B&B.

B&Bs & Hotels – Lagg This is one of the nicest places on Arran.

Lagg Inn (☎ 870255, fax 870250, Lagg) B&B £25-49 per person. Lagg Inn boasts a lovely location; some rooms are en suite and one has a four-poster bed. Food on offer includes seafood, game and Arran lamb; main courses cost from £5.55 to £10.95 and the two-/three-course dinner will set you back £15.95/18.95.

B&Bs & Hotels – Kildonan This is a very peaceful spot.

Breadalbane Hotel (☎/fax 820284, Kildonan) B&B £20-27.50 per person. Flats £100-250 per week. This friendly place has holiday flats with bedrooms, bathroom and kitchen, sleeping four to six people. Rates depend on the season; outside the high season the hotel may also let flats for less than a week.

B&Bs & Hotels – Whiting Bay This place has a wonderful coastal setting.

Burlington Hotel (☎ 700255, fax 700232, Shore Rd) B&B en-suite singles/doubles £30.50/51. You'll get great organic food in the fine restaurant here; two-/three-course dinners cost £15/17.95.

Rowallan (☎ 700729, fax 700377, School Rd) B&B singles/doubles from £23/40. This is a good B&B with dinner and Internet access available. The residents' lounge has an open fire.

Places to Eat

Creelers Seafood Restaurant (☎ 302810, Duchess Court) Mains £7-16. Open Tues-Sun. This award-winning restaurant is 1½

miles (2.5km) north of Brodick, by the Arran Aromatics shopping centre. It's a bistro-style place with an imaginative menu and some outside seating. There's also a shop selling seafood and smoked foods.

You can stock up on local cheeses from the cheese shop opposite, or have a snack in the pleasant *Home Farm Kitchen (☎ 302731 Duchess Court)*, with home baking and baked potatoes from £2.95, including salad

Stalkers Eating House (☎ 302579, Main St) Mains around £6. Back in Brodick, try this place on the waterfront. It does good value meals, including home-made steak pie (£6.15) and jacket potatoes (from £1.65), and there are solid Scottish puddings such as treacle sponge.

Brodick Bar (☎ 302169, Alma Rd) Main around £6. Located by the post office, this is a good choice for a bar meal. Soup and a roll costs £2.25.

Ormidale Hotel (☎ 302293, Glen Cloy) Mains £5.65-10.95. Situated in Glen Cloy this hotel has good bar food and occasional live music.

Lochranza Hotel (☎ 830223, Lochranza) Bar meals £6-12, 3-course set menu £15 Check out the daily specials on the white board, although cheaper snacks are on offer The three-course set restaurant meal i fairly good value.

Catacol Bay Hotel (☎ 830231, Catacol) Bar mains £5.50-8. Two miles (3km) from Lochranza, the bar here does excellent bar food. The restaurant does a Sunday afternoon buffet (noon-4pm) for £7.50 and you can eat as much as you like. In summer there are ceilidhs (Tuesday) and live music (once a week).

Breadalbane Hotel (☎ 820284, Kildonan) Mains £4-10.95. You'll get great home made bar food at this hotel.

Kildonan Hotel (☎ 820207, Kildonan) Bar meals around £5-11. The Kildonan Hotel does bar meals, but you can also have lobster salad, caught by the proprietor, for £10.50.

Coffee Pot (☎ 700382, Golf Course Rd Whiting Bay) Meals and snacks £1.90-5.50 The Coffee Pot has coffee pots from around the world and a good selection of home baking and meals.

Cameronia Hotel (☎ 700254, Shore Rd, Whiting Bay) Bar mains from £5.50. You'll find decent bar meals and real ales on offer at this hotel.

Glenisle Hotel (☎ 600559, Shore Rd, Lamlash) Lunch mains £5.25-6, 2-course dinners £14. The Glenisle Hotel dishes up good food that hasn't been cooked in a microwave!

Drift Inn (☎ 600656, Shore Rd, Lamlash) Most mains £5.45-6.60. You can enjoy your pub grub in the beer garden here.

Ferry Fry (The Pier), by the TIC, does pizzas from £2 and good takeaway fish and chips for £3.50.

Getting There & Away

CalMac (☎ 302166) runs a daily car ferry between Ardrossan and Brodick (£4.40, £25.50/31.50 off-peak/peak for a car, 55 minutes, four to six daily) and from late March to late October runs services between Claonaig and Lochranza (£4, £18.05/21.55 off-peak/peak for a car, 30 minutes, seven to nine daily). From late October to late March, the car ferry sails from Lochranza to Portavadie (Cowal) and Tarbert (Kintyre). Contact CalMac for details.

If you're going to visit several islands, it's worth planning your route in advance. CalMac has a wide range of tickets, including Island Hopscotch fares that work out cheaper than buying several single tickets.

Getting Around

The island's efficient bus services are operated by Stagecoach Western (☎ 302000) and Royal Mail (☎ 01246-546329). There are four to six buses daily from Brodick Pier to Lochranza (£1.65, 45 minutes). Buses for Blackwaterfoot run via Lochranza, the String Rd, or Whiting Bay (£1.65, 30 minutes or one hour 10 minutes respectively, five to 16 daily). Four to 13 buses daily run from Brodick to Lamlash and Whiting Bay (£1.60, 30 minutes). A Daycard costs £3. For a taxi, phone ☎ 302274 in Brodick or ☎ 600903 in Lamlash.

There are several places to rent bikes in Brodick, including Mini Golf Cycle Hire (☎ 302272), on Shore Rd, with bikes from only £4.50 per day. Blackwaterfoot Garage (☎ 860277) does bike hire for £7 per day. Whiting Bay Hires (mobile ☎ 07885 287779) has 18-speed mountain bikes for £9 per day.

EAST AYRSHIRE

There's not much to see in this county apart from depressed towns and farmland. However, near the eastern border with Lanarkshire, and by the A71 Irvine to Edinburgh road, there's **Loudoun Hill**, a trachyte volcanic remnant with extensive views. It's a great place for a picnic and you can watch the rock climbers too. The **Pulpit Rock** is a great climb, moderate in standard, but you'll need experience and equipment before attempting it. In 1297, William Wallace and his men ambushed a party of English troops in the narrow glen below the hill – the first successful skirmish for the Scots.

Kilmarnock, where Johnnie Walker whisky has been blended since 1820, has the excellent **Dean Castle** (☎ 01563-522702, W www .deancastle.com, Dean Rd; admission free, including guided tour; open noon-5pm daily, weekends only Nov-Mar), a 15-minute walk along Glasgow Rd from the bus and train stations. Ask the Kilmarnock to Glasgow bus driver to drop you at Dean Rd (Western Buses ☎ 01563-525192, half-hourly). Trains run to Kilmarnock from Glasgow Central (£3.90/4.10 single/off-peak return, hourly). The castle, restored in the first half of the 20th century, has a virtually windowless keep (from 1350) and an adjacent palace (from 1468) with a superb collection of medieval arms, armour, tapestries and musical instruments. The grounds, an 81-hectare park, are a good place for a picnic, or you can eat at the visitor centre's **tearoom**, where snacks and light meals cost under £4.

SOUTH AYRSHIRE
Ayr
☎ 01292 • pop 49,500

Ayr's long sandy beach has made it a popular family seaside resort since Victorian times. It's also known for its racecourse, the top course in Scotland, with more racing days than any other in Britain. The Scottish Grand National is held here in April. Ayr is the largest town on this coast and makes a convenient base for a tour of Burns territory.

Information The TIC (☎ 678100), 12 Sandgate, opens 9am to 6pm daily July and August, and 9am to 5pm Monday to Saturday the rest of the year.

There are banks with ATMs on High St and Sandgate. The post office is on Sandgate. Ayr Hospital (☎ 610555) is south of town, by the Dalmellington road.

Things to See Most things to see in Ayr are Burns-related. The bard was baptised in the

Auld Kirk (old church) off High St. Several of his poems are set here in Ayr; in *Tw. Brigs*, Ayr's old and new bridges argue wit. one another. The **Auld Brig** (Old Bridge was built in 1491 and spans the river ju. down from the church. In Burns' poem *Tai o'Shanter*, Tam spends a boozy evening i the pub that now bears his name, at 23 High St.

St John's Tower (☎ 612000, *Mont. gomerie Terrace; admission free, £2 key de posit; key available during office hou. from Parks & Environment, South Ayrshir Council, Burns Statue Square*) is the onl.

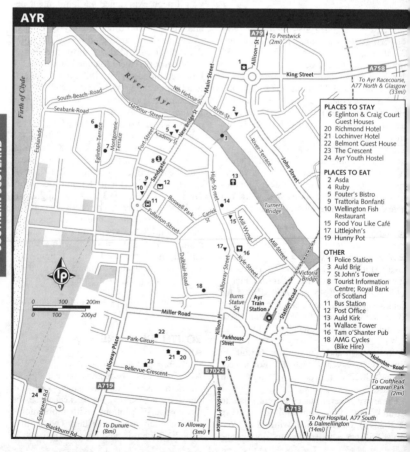

AYR

PLACES TO STAY
6 Eglinton & Craig Court Guest Houses
20 Richmond Hotel
21 Lochinver Hotel
22 Belmont Guest House
23 The Crescent
24 Ayr Youth Hostel

PLACES TO EAT
2 Asda
4 Ruby
5 Fouter's Bistro
9 Trattoria Bonfanti
10 Wellington Fish Restaurant
15 Food You Like Café
17 Littlejohn's
19 Hunny Pot

OTHER
1 Police Station
3 Auld Brig
7 St John's Tower
8 Tourist Information Centre; Royal Bank of Scotland
11 Bus Station
12 Post Office
13 Auld Kirk
14 Wallace Tower
16 Tam o'Shanter Pub
18 AMG Cycles (Bike Hire)

emnant of a church where a parliament was held in 1315, the year after the celebrated victory at Bannockburn. John Knox's son-in-law was the minister here, and Mary, Queen of Scots, stayed overnight in 1563.

The **Wallace Tower** (☎ *612000 office hours only, open by arrangement*) is a neo-Gothic structure, 34m high, and includes a statue of William Wallace.

Cycling With not too many steep hills, the area is well suited to cyclists. See the Glasgow chapter for the cycle way from that city. Ask at the TIC for its useful leaflet.

From Ayr, you could cycle to Alloway and spend a couple of hours seeing the Burns sights before continuing to Culzean via Maybole. You could either camp here, after seeing Culzean Castle, or cycle back along the coast road to Ayr, a round trip of about 22 miles (35km).

In Ayr, **AMG Cycles** (☎ *287580*), 55 Dalblair Rd, hires out bikes for £12.50 per day.

Places to Stay There are a number of good options in town.

Crofthead Caravan Park (☎ *263516, Holmston*) £6 per tent. Open Easter-Oct. This recently renovated camp site is 2 miles (3km) east of Ayr near the A70.

Ayr Youth Hostel (☎ *262322, fax 289061, 5 Craigweil Rd*) Adults/under-18s from £9.25/8. Open Apr-Oct. The hostel is housed in a magnificent turreted mansion by the beach and is less than a mile (1.6km) from the train and bus stations.

Eglinton Guest House (☎/*fax 264623, 23 Eglinton Terrace*) B&B £18-25 per person. A short walk west of the bus station, this comfortable, family-owned establishment offers dinner too.

Craig Court Guest House (☎/*fax 261028, 22 Eglinton Terrace*) B&B £17.50-22 per person. This friendly place is particularly nicely decorated and furnished, and the breakfast isn't bad either.

A five- to 10-minute walk from the station brings you to a quiet crescent of upmarket B&Bs and small hotels, including the following recommendations on Park Circus.

Belmont Guest House (☎ *265588, fax 290303, 15 Park Circus*) B&B with en-suite facilities £20-24. Located in a Victorian town house, there's a pleasant lounge and library for guests here.

Lochinver Guest House (☎/*fax 265086, 32 Park Circus*) B&B £18-27.50 per person. Some rooms have shared bathroom in this homely place.

Richmond Guest House (☎ *265153, fax 288816, 38 Park Circus*) Singles £27-30, doubles £44-50. This is a small, friendly and efficient place.

Park Circus continues into Bellevue Crescent and there's also a good choice here.

The Crescent (☎ *287329, fax 286779, 26 Bellevue Crescent*) Singles £30-32, doubles £48-52. All rooms are en suite in this excellent small hotel. It's a traditional but fully modernised and well-appointed Victorian townhouse.

Places to Eat The town has a good variety of eating establishments.

Fouters Bistro (☎ *261391, 2A Academy St*) Main dishes £4.95-14.95, 2-course set dinner Mon-Sat £9.95. The best place in town, in a former bank vault opposite the town hall, specialises in Ayrshire produce and local seafood.

Trattoria Bonfanti (☎ *266577, 64 Sandgate*) Pasta £4.95-6.50, pizza from £4.25. Trattoria Bonfanti does good range of pasta dishes and pizzas.

Ruby (☎ *267131, 22 New Bridge St*) 3-course lunch £5 Mon-Sat, £5.40 Sun. Ruby is a good Chinese restaurant specialising in seafood. It also does takeaways.

Littlejohn's (☎ *288666, 231 High St*) Mains £6.25-12.95. This chain restaurant, with wacky decor, offers lunch specials for £4.95.

Hunny Pot (☎ *263239, 37 Beresford Terrace*) Light meals £2.50-4.50. Open 9am-10pm Mon-Sat, 10.30am-9pm Sun. The pleasant Hunny Pot serves good coffees and light meals.

Food You Like Café (☎ *619998, 4 Mill St*) Mains £2.75-3.85. This place serves cheap and cheerful food, including breakfast for £1.15.

SOUTHERN SCOTLAND

Wellington Fish Restaurant (☎ *263859, 102 Sandgate).* Head here for the best fish and chips in Ayr (£3.50). It's located near the bus station,and you can sit in or take away.

There is a huge ***Tesco*** supermarket on Whitletts Rd, by Ayr Racecourse, and an ***Asda*** supermarket on Wallace St, near the river.

Getting There & Around Ayr is 33 miles (53km) from Glasgow. There are at least two trains an hour from Glasgow Central to Ayr (£5.20, 50 minutes), and some trains continue south to Stranraer (£10, 1½ hours from Ayr). The main bus operator in the area is Stagecoach Western (☎ 613500) – its hourly X77 service (Monday to Saturday) from Glasgow to Ayr costs £3.50 (one hour). It also runs buses from Ayr to Girvan (£3.30, one hour 10 minutes, twice hourly Monday to Saturday, hourly Sunday), Stranraer (£5.70, 1¾ hours, four to nine daily), Greenock (£5.65, 1¾ hours, twice hourly Monday to Saturday, every two hours Sunday), Irvine (£2.20, 30 minutes, twice hourly Monday to Saturday, every two hours Sunday), Kilmarnock (£3, 40 minutes, twice hourly Monday to Saturday, hourly Sunday), Largs (£3.75, 1¼ hours, twice hourly Monday to Saturday, every two hours Sunday), Muirkirk (change at Cumnock; £3.45, 1½ hours, hourly except Sunday) and Dumfries (£4.60, 2¼ hours, five to seven daily).

For a taxi, call Central Taxis on ☎ 267655.

Alloway
☎ 01292

Three miles (5km) south of Ayr, Alloway is where Robert Burns was born in 1759. Even if you're not a fan, it's still worth a visit since the Burns-related exhibitions also give a very good impression of life in Ayrshire in the late 18th century. All the sights are within easy walking distance of each other and come under the umbrella title **Burns National Heritage Park**.

The **Burns Cottage and Museum** *(☎ 441215, Alloway; adult/child £2.80/1.40; open 9am-6pm daily Apr-Oct, 10am-4pm Mon-Sat & noon-4pm Sun Nov-Mar)* stands by the main road from Ayr. A 10-minute video introduces you to Burns, his family

and the cottage. Born in the little box bed i this cramped thatched cottage, the poet spen the first seven years of his life here. There a good museum of Burnsiana by the cottag exhibiting everything from his writing con pendium to a piece of wood from his coffi Light meals are available in the tearoom.

From here, you can visit the ruins of **Al loway Auld Kirk**, the setting for part of *Ta o'Shanter*. Burns' father, William Burne (his son dropped the 'e' from his name) i buried in the kirkyard.

The nearby **Tam o'Shanter Experienc** *(☎ 443700, Murdoch's Lane; admissio free; open 9am-5.30pm daily Apr-Oct, 9am 5pm Nov-Mar)* has an audio-visual displa (£1.40/70p), a restaurant and a book/gif shop. The restaurant here does exceller home-made soup (£1.75, including a roll The **Burns Monument and Gardens** are ad jacent and open 9am to 5pm. The monu ment was built in 1823 and affords a viev of the 13th-century **Brig o'Doon**. There ar also statues of Burns' drinking cronies i the gardens.

Brig O'Doon House *(☎ 442466, fa 441999, Alloway)* Singles/doubles £75/10(Mains £6.95-14.95. This is a grand place decorated with stags' heads; the brasseri does two-course lunches for around £11.5 and three-course dinners for around £18.

Ivy House *(☎ 442336, fax 445572, Alloway)* B&B en-suite singles/double £110/190 including dinner. Ivy House, o the road to Ayr, is a small, luxurious hote with a fine restaurant.

Stagecoach Western (☎ 613500) bus N 57 runs hourly between Alloway and Ay from 8.45am to 5.50pm Monday to Satur day (£1.60 return). Otherwise, rent a bik and cycle here.

Troon
☎ 01292 • pop 15,425

Troon, a major sailing centre on the coast miles (11km) north of Ayr, has exceller sandy beaches and six golf courses. Th demanding championship course **Roya Troon** *(☎ 311555, e info@royaltroon.com Craigend Rd; open 9.30am-11am an 2.30pm-4pm Mon, Tues & Thur, May-Oct*

Robert Burns

Best remembered for penning the words of *Auld Lang Syne*, Robert Burns is Scotland's most famous poet, and a popular hero whose birthday (25 January) is celebrated as Burns Night by Scots around the world.

He was born in 1759 in Alloway. Although his mother was illiterate and his parents poor farmers, they sent him to the local school where he soon showed an aptitude for literature and a fondness for the folk song. He began to write his own songs and satires, some of which he distributed privately. When the problems of his arduous farming life were compounded by the threat of prosecution from the father of Jean Armour, with whom he'd had an affair, he decided to emigrate to Jamaica. He gave up his share of the family farm and published his poems to raise money for the journey.

The poems were so well reviewed in Edinburgh that Burns decided to remain in Scotland and devote himself to writing. He went to Edinburgh in 1787 to publish a second edition, but the financial rewards were not enough to live on and he had to take a job as a customs officer in Dumfriesshire. He contributed many

Robbie Burns: Scotland's famous son

songs to collections published by Johnson and Thomson in Edinburgh, and a third edition of his poems was published in 1793. Burns died of rheumatic fever in Dumfries in 1796, aged 37.

While some dispute the claim that Burns was a true literary genius, he was certainly an accomplished poet and songwriter, and has been compared to Chaucer for his verse tale *Tam o'Shanter*. Burns wrote in Lallans, the Scottish Lowland dialect of English that is not very accessible to the Sassenach (Englishman), or foreigner; perhaps this is part of his appeal. He was also very much a man of the people, satirising the upper classes and the church for their hypocrisy.

Many of the local landmarks mentioned in *Tam o'Shanter* can still be visited. Farmer Tam, riding home after a hard night's drinking in a pub in Ayr, sees witches dancing in Alloway churchyard. He calls out to the one pretty witch, but is pursued by them all and has to reach the other side of the River Doon to be safe. He just manages to cross the Brig o'Doon, but his mare loses her tail to the witches.

The Burns connection in southern Scotland is milked for all it's worth. Ask TICs if the leaflet leading you to every place that can claim some link with the bard has been republished. For more information about Burns, check the Web at W www.robertburns.org or, for tour itineraries, try W www.ayrshire-arran.com.

ffers two rounds of golf for £150, including lunch in the clubhouse (caddie hire is £30 extra).

Dundonald Castle *(HS; ☎ 01563-851489, Dundonald; adult/child £2/1; open 10am-6pm daily Apr-Sept)* is 4 miles (6km) northeast of Troon. It was the first home of the Stuart Kings, built by Robert II in 1371, and reckoned to be the third most important castle in Scotland, after Edinburgh and Stirling. HS spent over £1 million on renovations in the 1990s. There's a tearoom and an interesting visitor centre (50p) on site. Stagecoach Western (☎ 01563-525192) runs hourly buses (Monday to Saturday) between Troon and Kilmarnock, via Dundonald village.

Piersland House Hotel (☎ 314747, fax 315613, 15 Craigend Rd) B&B £59.50-84.50 per person. All bedrooms are en suite in this magnificent hotel, former home of the Johnny Walker whisky family. The fine restaurant has an adventurous Scottish menu; mains cost from £11.95.

There are twice hourly trains to Ayr (£1.90, 11 minutes) and Glasgow (£4.70, 45 minutes). Seacat (☎ 0870 552 3523, W www .steam-packet.com) sails two to three times daily to Belfast (£19 to £23 for passengers, £72 to £183 for a car and driver, 2½ hours).

Culzean Castle & Country Park

Well worth seeing, Culzean (*cull*-ane; NTS; ☎ 01655-884400; adult/child/family £8/6/20, park only adult/child £4/3; open 11am-5.30pm daily Apr-Oct & weekends only in Mar, Nov & Dec, park open 9.30am-sunset year round), 12 miles (19km) south of Ayr, is one of the most impressive of Scotland's great stately homes. Perched dramatically on the edge of the cliffs, this late-18th-century mansion was designed by Robert Adam to replace the tower house built here in the 16th century. Culzean Castle is the NTS's most visited property and it can get quite crowded at weekends from June to August. Tours (no extra charge) run at 11.30am and 3.30pm.

The original castle belonged to the Kennedy clan, who, after a feud in the 16th century, divided into the Kennedys of Culzean and Cassillis, and the Kennedys of Bargany. Because of the American connection (Eisenhower was an occasional visitor), most people wrongly assume that the Culzean Kennedys were closely related to JFK. Culzean Castle was given to the NTS in 1945.

Robert Adam, clearly the most influential architect of his time, was renowned for his meticulous attention to detail and the elegant classical embellishments with which he decorated his ceilings and fireplaces. The beautiful oval staircase here is regarded as one of his finest achievements.

On the 1st floor, the opulence of the circular saloon contrasts splendidly with the views of the wild sea below. The other rooms on this floor are also interesting, and Lor Cassillis' bedroom is said to be haunted by lady in green mourning a lost baby. Even th bathrooms are palatial, the dressing room be side the state bedroom being equipped wit a state-of-the-art Victorian shower that d rects jets of water from almost every angl The ground floor has an amazing armour (with around 1100 weapons) and an impres sive Georgian kitchen, with a vast array o copper pots.

Set in a 228-hectare park combining wood land, coast and gardens, there's much more t see than just the castle. An interesting exhi bition in the Gas House explains how ga was produced here for the castle. There's als a visitor centre, two ice houses, a swan pon a pagoda, a re-creation of a Victorian viner an orangery, a deer park and an aviar Wildlife in the area includes otters.

It's possible to stay in the castle fron April to October, but gracious living doesn come cheap. A night for two in the Eisen hower suite costs £375 (including afternoo tea) and the cheapest singles/doubles co £140/200.

Camping and Caravanning Clu (☎ 01655-760627, Culzean Country Park Members £3.65-4.80 per person, plus £4.3 for nonmembers. This camp site has goo facilities and is convenient for a visit to th castle.

Maybole is the nearest train station, bu since it's 4 miles (6km) away, it's best t come by bus from Ayr (£2.30, 30 minute six to nine daily). The bus passes the par gates but it's still a 20-minute walk throug the grounds to the castle.

Turnberry
☎ 01655 • pop 192

This peaceful coastal village is best know for its famous resort hotel and golf cours

Turnberry Hotel (☎ 331000, fax 33170 Turnberry) Singles £100-135, doubles £31 355. You'll have priority to play the worl famous golf course here if you stay at th luxurious Turnberry Hotel. If you can affor the overnight charges, plus green fees from £120 per day, the four-course dinner in th award-winning restaurant is a snip at £62.9

Kirkoswald

☎ 01655 • pop 500

In Kirkoswald village, you'll find the recently renovated **Souter Johnnie's Cottage** *(NTS; ☎ 760603, Main Rd; adult/child £2.50/1.70; open 11.30am-5pm daily Apr-Sept & weekends in Oct)*, with period furniture and a reconstruction of a shoemaker's workshop. The original real-life occupant, John Davidson, was immortalized by Burns as Souter Johnnie in *Tam o'Shanter*.

Two miles (3km) east of the village, by the A77, **Crossraguel Abbey** *(HS; ☎ 883113; adult/child £2/75p; open 9.30am-6.30pm daily Apr-Sept)* is a substantial ruin dating back to the 13th century.

Stagecoach Western (☎ 613500) runs Ayr to Girvan buses twice hourly Monday to Saturday (hourly Sunday) via Crossraguel and Kirkoswald (£2.30, 37 minutes).

Ailsa Craig & Girvan

Curiously shaped Ailsa Craig can be seen from much of South Ayrshire. Looking like a giant bread roll floating out to sea, it's now a bird sanctuary, and taking a cruise from Girvan on the MV *Glorious* (☎ 01465-713219)

Ailsa Craig

Ailsa Craig (340m) is an eroded granite and basalt volcanic remnant sitting in the Firth of Clyde, roughly halfway between Glasgow and Belfast, hence its endearing epithet 'Paddy's Milestone'. This small island is roughly circular and less than a mile in diameter. It's known to bird-watchers as the world's second largest gannet colony – around 10,000 pairs breed annually on the island's sheer cliffs.

The unusual blue-tinted granite from Ailsa Craig has been used by geologists to trace the movements of the great Ice Age ice sheet, and bits of the rock have been found as far afield as Wales. More recently, the rock has been quarried to make curling stones. Visitors can still see quarry workers' cottages and a narrow-gauge railway running from the jetty to the quarry.

is normally about as close as you'll get to the gannets that crowd this 340m-high rocky outcrop. It's possible to land if the sea is reasonably calm; a four-hour trip costs £10/7 per adult/child, while a six-hour trip costs £12 per person. A minimum of eight people is required, with at least one week's notice.

Girvan isn't terribly exciting, but it has all the usual tourist services, including a seasonal TIC (☎ 01292-678100) on Bridge St.

Mr Chips *(21 Bridge St)* does good fish suppers, and for a pleasant bar meal try the **Hamilton Arms Hotel** *(☎ 01465-712182, 12 Bridge St)* where mains cost around £6.

Trains run approximately hourly (with only three trains Sunday) from Girvan to Ayr (£3.30, 30 minutes) and Glasgow (£7, 1¾ hours). Girvan to Stranraer (£8.50, 50 minutes) trains run two to seven times daily. Buses run to Ayr (£3.30, one hour) twice hourly (hourly Sunday), to Stanraer (£3, 55 minutes) four to 10 times daily and to Newton Stewart (£3.55, one hour 10 minutes) two to five times daily.

Dumfries & Galloway

The tourist board bills this region as Scotland's surprising south-west, and it will surprise you if you expect beautiful scenery to be confined to the Highlands. The area has many of the features for which Scotland is famous – mountains (which reach 843m), rolling hills, lochs and a rugged coastline.

This is, however, one of the forgotten corners of Britain – and away from the main transport routes west to Stranraer and north to Glasgow – so traffic and people are sparse.

The Southern Uplands run through Dumfries & Galloway. Warmed by the Gulf Stream, this is the mildest corner of Scotland, a phenomenon that has allowed the development of some famous gardens. This is excellent cycling and walking country and is crossed by the coast-to-coast Southern Upland Way (see the Activities chapter).

Many notable historic and prehistoric attractions are linked by the Solway Coast

Heritage Trail from Annan in the east to the Mull of Galloway in the west (information available from TICs). Caerlaverock Castle, Threave Castle and Whithorn Cathedral and Priory are just three. Kirkcudbright is a beautiful town and makes a good base.

This stretch of coastline on the northern side of the wedge-shaped Solway Firth offers sheltered bays, mud-flats, salt marshes and some forested hills. Don't let its beauty beguile you too much; the Solway Firth is tidal, and when the tide's out you can walk out a long way, but when it turns it comes in very fast.

Stranraer, in the far west, is the ferry port to Belfast in Northern Ireland and is the shortest link from Scotland.

The economy of the region is struggling with the aftermath of the 2001 foot-and-mouth crisis, which resulted in the slaughter of most of the livestock in southern and eastern areas.

GETTING THERE & AROUND

Dumfries & Galloway council has a travel information line (☎ 0845 709 0510), from 9am to 5pm weekdays, with information on public transport.

Bus

National Express/Eurolines (☎ 0870 580 8080, W www.gobycoach.com) operates twice-daily coaches from London and Birmingham (via Manchester and Carlisle) to Stranraer. These coaches service the main towns and villages along the A75 (including Dumfries, Castle Douglas and Newton Stewart). Scottish Citylink (☎ 0870 550 5050, W www.citylink.co.uk) runs twice-daily buses from Stranraer to Glasgow/Edinburgh. Stagecoach Western (☎ 01387-253496) and MacEwan's (☎ 01387-256533) provide a variety of local bus services. Sometimes different bus companies have services along the same route but charge different prices, so ring the council travel information line to check.

The Day Discoverer (£5/2 adult/child) is a useful day ticket valid on most buses in the region and on Stagecoach Cumberland in Cumbria.

Train

Two lines from Carlisle to Glasgow cross the region via Dumfries and Moffat respectively. The line from Glasgow to Stranraer runs via Ayr. Call ☎ 0845 748 4950 for details.

DUMFRIES

☎ 01387 • pop 37,519

Dumfries is a large town on the River Nith with a strategic position that placed it smack in the path of a number of vengeful English armies. As a result, although it has existed since Roman times, the oldest standing building dates from the 17th century.

Dumfries has escaped modern mass tourism, although it was the home of Robert Burns from 1791 to his death in 1796 and there are several important Burns-related museums. The centre is of interest, with some pleasant 19th-century districts built in the area's characteristic red sandstone.

Orientation & Information

Most of the attractions and facilities are on the eastern side of the river. The bus station is situated by the main bridge; the train station is a 10-minute walk north-east. The TIC (☎ 253862), 64 Whitesands, opposite the car park by the river, opens 10am to 6pm Monday to Saturday mid-June to mid-September (noon to 5pm Sunday); otherwise, closing between 4pm and 5pm (closed Sunday November to mid-June). You can book National Express/Scottish Citylink buses here.

There's a bank with ATMs at 2 Bank St.

Burnsiana

Burns House (☎ 255297, Burns St; admission free; open 10am-5pm Mon-Sat & 2pm-5pm Sun Apr-Sept, 10am-1pm & 2pm-5pm Tues-Sat Oct-Mar) is a place of pilgrimage for Burns enthusiasts; it's here that the poet spent the last years of his life and there are some interesting relics, original letters and manuscripts.

The **Robert Burns Centre** (☎ 264808, Mill Rd; admission free, audio-visual presentation £1.50/75p; open 10am-8pm Mon-Sat & 2pm-5pm Sun Apr-Sept, 10am-1pm & 2pm-5pm Tues-Sat Oct-Mar) is an award-winning museum on the banks of the river in an old mill.

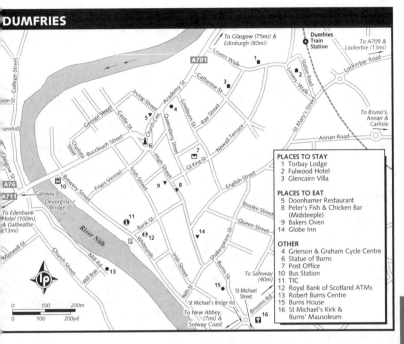

DUMFRIES

PLACES TO STAY
1 Torbay Lodge
2 Fulwood Hotel
3 Glencairn Villa

PLACES TO EAT
5 Doonhamer Restaurant
8 Peter's Fish & Chicken Bar (Midsteeple)
9 Bakers Oven
14 Globe Inn

OTHER
4 Grierson & Graham Cycle Centre
6 Statue of Burns
7 Post Office
10 Bus Station
11 TIC
12 Royal Bank of Scotland ATMs
13 Robert Burns Centre
15 Burns House
16 St Michael's Kirk & Burns' Mausoleum

...t tells the story of Burns and Dumfries in the
...790s. There's also a restaurant and gallery.
Burns' **mausoleum** is in the graveyard at
...t Michael's Kirk, and at the top of High St
...s a **statue** of the bard; take a close look at
...he sheepdog at his feet.

Places to Stay

...here are some good-value B&Bs near the
...rain station, in a quiet and pleasant suburb.

*Glencairn Villa (☎/fax 262467, 45 Rae
...t)* B&B singles/doubles from £16/36. Glen-
...airn Villa offers spacious and comfortable
...ccommodation.

*Fulwood Hotel (☎/fax 252262, 30
...overs Walk)* Singles £21-30, doubles £34-
...4. This Victorian villa, opposite the train
...tation, offers rooms with private bath, and
...egetarian breakfast on request.

*Torbay Lodge (☎/fax 253922, 31 Lovers
...Valk)* B&B £18-22 per person. This place
...as comfortable, elegant and well-appointed
...ooms.

*Edenbank Hotel (☎ 252759, fax 259473,
17 Lauriknowe)* Singles/doubles from
£33/60. The recently refurbished family-run
Edenbank Hotel, a short walk from the
town centre, has a range of rooms, including three singles with bathrooms. Evening
meals are available.

Places to Eat

*Doonhamer Restaurant (☎ 253832, 15
Church Crescent)* Pizza £4.50, pasta £4.40.
Doonhamer Restaurant serves snacks and
hot meals, from fish and chips to pizza and
pasta, including vegetarian dishes.

Hulabaloo (☎ 259679, Mill Rd) Mains
around £6. Open Tues-Sun (lunch only on
Sun). This restaurant, at the Robert Burns
Centre, has a small but adventurous menu.

Bruno's (☎ 255757, 3 Balmoral Rd)
Mains around £6. This Italian restaurant is
one of the best places to eat in town.

Globe Inn (☎ 252335, 56 High St) Bar
mains £3.80-5.20. This traditional pub, said

to be Burns' favourite watering hole, serves great home-cooked bar meals; steak pie is £4.50.

The recommended takeaway place is **Peter's Fish & Chicken Bar** *(Midsteeple, High St)*, with fish and chips for £2.95.

Baker's Oven, on pedestrianised High St, has a range of good-value baked goods, sandwiches and jacket potatoes. There's a huge **Safeway** supermarket on Brooms Rd.

Getting There & Away
Bus National Express/Eurolines bus Nos 920/921 run twice daily between London and Belfast, via Birmingham, Manchester, Carlisle, Dumfries, the towns along the A75 and Stranraer. There are also regular local buses to Kirkcudbright and towns along the A75 to Stranraer (£5, three hours). Scottish Citylink has two to four buses daily (X74) to/from Glasgow (£6.50, two hours). Stagecoach Western and MacEwans run two to seven buses daily to Edinburgh (£5.40 or £6.30, 2¾ hours), via Moffat and Biggar.

Train Dumfries is on a line that leaves the main west-coast line at Gretna and from Dumfries runs north-west along Nithsdale to join the Glasgow-Stranraer line at Kilmarnock. Monday to Saturday, there are trains every hour or two between Carlisle and Dumfries (£3.50/7 off-peak/peak, 35 minutes), and seven between Dumfries and Glasgow (£9.40, 1¾ hours); there's a reduced service Sunday.

Car & Motorcycle Edinburgh is 80 miles (128km) north-east of Dumfries on the A76 and A702. Glasgow is 75 miles (120km) north-west and can be reached either via Kilmarnock on the A76/77 or on the A701 and M74. Stranraer is 68 miles (109km) west on the A75, via Castle Douglas and Newton Stewart.

Getting Around
Grierson & Graham (☎ 259483), 10 Academy St, hires out bikes for £10 (24 hours) or £6 (9am to 5pm, weekdays). Or you could try Dixon's Taxis (☎ 720900).

CAERLAVEROCK CASTLE
The ruins of Caerlaverock Castle *(H. ☎ 01387-770244, by Glencaple; adul child £2.80/1; open 9.30am-6.30pm dai Apr-Sept, 9.30am-4.30pm Mon-Sat & 2pr 4.30pm Sun Oct-Mar)*, on a beautiful stretc of the Solway coast south-east of Dumfrie are among the loveliest in Britain. Su rounded by a moat, lawns and stands trees, the unusual pink-stoned triangul castle looks impregnable. In fact, it fell se eral times. The current castle dates from th late 13th century. Inside, there's an extrao dinary Scottish Renaissance facade to apar ments that were built in 1634.

Monday to Saturday, the castle can I reached from Dumfries by Stagecoac Western's bus No 371 (two to 11 daily). E car take the B725 south.

It's worth combining a visit to the cast with one to **Caerlaverock Wildlife and We lands Centre** *(☎ 01387-770200, by Gle caple; adult/child £4/2.50; open 10am-5p daily)*, a mile (1.6km) east. It protects 54 hectares of salt marsh and mud-flats, th habitat for numerous birds, including ba nacle geese.

SOUTH OF DUMFRIES
South of Dumfries, the Solway Coast Trail follows the A710 loop with side tri on minor roads to Rockcliffe and Kippfo before going inland to Dalbeattie then fo lowing the A711 to Kirkcudbright.

McEwan's (☎ 01387-256533) bus N 372 from Dumfries stops in New Abbe Kirkbean, Rockcliffe, Kippford and Da beattie; from there bus No 505 continues Kirkcudbright (but not on Sundays).

New Abbey & Around
☎ 01387
This small, picturesque village 7 mil (11km) south of Dumfries contains the r mains of the red sandstone, 13th-century Ci tercian **Sweetheart Abbey** *(HS; ☎ 85039 adult/child £1.50/50p; open 9.30am-6.30p daily Apr-Sept; 9.30am-4.30pm Mon-Wed Sat, 9.30am-1pm Thur & 2pm-4.30pm Fri Sun Oct-Mar)*. The abbey was founded b Devorgilla de Balliol in honour of her dea

usband (with whom she had founded Balliol College, Oxford). On his death, she had his heart embalmed and carried it with her until he died, 22 years later. She and the heart are buried in the presbytery – hence the name.

In wooded grounds just north of the village, **Shambellie House Museum of Costume** (☎ 850375; adult/child £2.50/free; open 11am-5pm daily Apr-Oct) displays a selection of Georgian to Edwardian clothes and furniture. There are also fine temporary exhibitions.

About 1½ miles (2.5km) south, there's a turn-off to Ardwall Farm. From the car park, a forested, sometimes muddy, track climbs 1¼ miles (2km) up **Criffel Hill** (569m); from the top there are fine views of the Dumfries countryside and across the Solway Firth to Cumbria.

In the village square, two recommended places to stay face each other.

Abbey Arms Hotel (☎ 850489, 1 The Square) B&B singles/doubles £22/44. You'll find en-suite doubles in this fine three-storey house. It also offers good bar meals from £3.50.

Criffel Inn (☎ 850244, fax 850305, 2 The Square) B&B £20-23.50 per person. Most rooms are en suite in this recommended inn; bar meals start at £5.50.

Kirkbean

About a mile (1.6km) south-east of this village, in the private estate of **Arbigland**, there's a cottage on a hillside overlooking the Solway Firth that was the birthplace of John Paul Jones (1747–92), a former pirate who became father of the US Navy. Now, the **John Paul Jones Cottage** (☎ 880613; adult/child £2/1; open 10am-5pm Tues-Sun Apr-Sept, daily July & Aug) is a museum, including a small exhibition, audiovisual display and video on his remarkable life.

Rockcliffe & Kippford

The A710 continues through undulating farmland, interspersed with the by-now-familiar yellow gorse, past wide **Sandyhills Bay** to Colvend. From there, a side road takes you to the sleepy villages of Rockcliffe and Kippford, beside the River Urr estuary.

Rockcliffe is on a beautiful, rocky cove from the northern end of which (near the toilet block) there's a short footpath to the **Mote of Mark** (NTS), a hill-top stronghold inhabited by Celts in the 5th to 7th centuries. The footpath is part of the 30-minute **Jubilee Path** (NTS) along the rugged coastline to Kippford, which was built to commemorate Queen Victoria's jubilee. Stagecoach Western runs five buses daily to Dumfries (£1.75, one hour).

Off the coast, **Rough Island** (NTS) is an 8-hectare bird sanctuary which, except during May and June when the birds are nesting, can be reached at low tide by foot over the sand flats. Kippford is a popular sailing centre.

Dalbeattie & Around
pop 4421

Most buildings in this small commercial centre are made from granite mined at the local quarry (which also provided the stone for the Bank of England in London). From Dalbeattie, you can either follow the scenic coast road to Kirkcudbright or head inland on the A745 to Castle Douglas. Off the B794, 2 miles (3km) north of town, the **Motte of Urr** (admission free; open at all times) is a 12th-century Norman motte-and-bailey castle, one of Scotland's largest.

About 4 miles (6km) south, off the Kirkcudbright road, is the 15th-century **Orchardton Tower** (☎ 0131-668 8800, Palnackie; admission free; open on request), the only circular tower house in Scotland; the keyholder lives in the nearby cottage.

CASTLE DOUGLAS & AROUND
☎ 01556 • pop 3855

Castle Douglas is an open, attractive little town that was laid out in the 18th century by Sir William Douglas, who had made a fortune in the Americas. Beside the town is the small but beautiful **Carlingwark Loch**. The TIC (☎ 502611), in a small park on King St, opens April to October (closed Sunday April to mid-June).

Sulwath Brewery

You can see traditional brewing processes at Sulwath Brewery (☎ 504525, 209 King St;

admission £3.50/free; open 10am-4pm Mon-Sat, closing 1pm Sat Nov-Mar). Admission includes a half-pint of Galloway real ale (tea or coffee is also available).

Threave Garden

Threave Garden *(NTS; ☎ 502575, Threave House; adult/child £4.50/3.50; visitor centre open 9.30am-5.30pm daily Apr-Oct & 10am-4pm Wed-Sun in Mar & Nov-23 Dec, garden open 9.30am-sunset year-round),* a mile (1.6km) west off the A75, houses the NTS horticultural school, and is noted for its spectacular spring daffodil display from mid-March to mid-May, though it's colourful from mid-May to October too.

Threave Castle

Two miles (3km) farther west, Threave Castle *(HS; ☎ 07711 223101; adult/child £2/75p, including ferry; open 9.30am-6.30pm daily Apr-Sept)* is an impressively grim tower on a small island in the middle of the lovely River Dee. Built in the late 14th century, it became a principal stronghold of the Black Douglases. It's now basically a shell, having been badly damaged by the Covenanters in the 1640s, but it's a romantic ruin nonetheless.

It's a 10-minute walk from the car park to the ferry landing where you ring a bell for the custodian to take you across to the island in a small boat.

Loch Ken

Loch Ken, stretching for 9 miles (14km) north-west of Castle Douglas beside the A713, is an important outdoor recreational area. The range of watersports includes windsurfing, sailing, canoeing, power-boating and fishing. Galloway Sailing Centre *(☎ 01644-420626),* on the eastern bank north of Parton village, provides equipment, training and accommodation. There are also walking trails and a rich variety of birdlife. The Royal Society for the Protection of Birds (RSPB) has a **nature reserve** *(☎ 01671-402861)* on the western bank, north of Glenlochar.

Places to Stay & Eat

Lochside Caravan & Camping Site (☎/fax 503806, Lochside Park) Sites for vans and tents from £7.95-9.55. This is an attractiv spot alongside Carlingwark Loch.

Galloway Sailing Centre (☎/fax 01644 420626, Loch Ken) Dorm beds £9.50. Si miles (10km) north of Castle Douglas, thi sailing centre offers year-round backpacke accommodation.

Woodlea (☎ 502247, 37 Ernespie Ra B&B £16-18 per person. Woodlea is a wel coming stone-built villa and a warm recep tion is guaranteed.

Douglas Arms Hotel (☎ 502231, fa 504000, King St) Singles/doubles fron £37.50/68.50. This place offers a range o comfortable en-suite rooms and good food bar meals cost from £3.75 to £13.95, and three-course dinner is available for £13.50

Getting There & Away

MacEwan's bus No 501 between Dumfrie (£1.95, 45 minutes) and Kirkcudbrigh (£1.25, 20 minutes) calls frequently Mon day to Saturday (five times Sunday). Bu No 520 runs one to three times daily alon the A713, connecting Castle Douglas wit New Galloway (£1.25, 30 minutes) and Ay (£4, 2¾ hours).

Getting Around

Ace Cycles (☎ 504542), 11 Church St, hire out touring and mountain bikes for £10 fo 24 hours.

KIRKCUDBRIGHT
☎ 01557 • pop 3588

Kirkcudbright's dignified streets of 17th and 18th-century merchants' houses, and it interesting harbour, make it an ideal base t explore the beautiful south coast. The lovel surrounding countryside has a distinctiv hummocky topography, much of it covered in gorse – it's almost as if the hills hav been heaped up to make a golf course. Wit its architecture and setting, it's not hard t see why Kirkcudbright (kirk-**coo**-bree) ha been something of an artists' colony sinc the late 19th century.

Orientation & Information

The town is on the eastern bank of the Rive Dee, at the northern end of Kirkcudbrigh

Bay. Everything in town is within easy walking distance. The TIC (☎ 330494), Harbour Square, opens daily Easter to October. There are some useful brochures detailing walks and road tours in the surrounding district. You'll find a bank with an ATM on St Mary St.

Things to See

The charming sights in Kirkcudbright are all well worth a visit.

McLellan's Castle *(HS;* ☎ *331856, Castle St; adult/child £1.80/75p; open 9.30am-5.30pm daily Apr-Sept)*, near the harbour and TIC, is a large ruin built in 1577 by Thomas MacLellan, then provost of Kirkcudbright, as his town residence.

Nearby, the 18th-century **Broughton House** *(☎ 330437, 12 High St; adult/child £3.50/2.50; open 1pm-5.30pm daily Apr-Oct, 11am-5.30pm daily July-Aug)* contains paintings by EA Hornel, one of the 'Glasgow Boys' group of painters, a reminder of the town's role as a 19th-century artists' colony. Look out for the excellent plaster casts of the **Elgin Marbles** (the original friezes were stolen by the earl of Elgin from the Parthenon in Athens). Behind the house is a beautiful Japanese-style garden.

Tolbooth Arts Centre *(☎ 331556, High St; adult/child £1.50/free; open 11am-4pm Mon-Sat year-round, 2pm-5pm Sun June-Sept)*, as well as catering for today's local artists, has an exhibition on the town's art history. The **Stewartry Museum** *(☎ 331643, St Mary St; adult/child £1.50/free; open 11am-4pm Mon-Sat year-round, 2pm-5pm Sun June-Sept)* is a particularly interesting local museum, with a wide-ranging collection of exhibits.

Places to Stay & Eat

Silvercraigs Caravan & Camping Site *(☎/fax 01556-503806, Silvercraigs Rd)* Sites £7.95-9.55. There are great views from this camp site. It has good facilities, including showers, toilets and laundry.

Parkview *(☎ 330056, 22 Millburn St)* B&B £17 per person. This is a small blue-painted place with shared bathrooms.

Gladstone House *(☎/fax 331734, 48 High St)* Singles/doubles from £39/60.

Gladstone House offers upmarket B&B to nonsmokers in an attractively decorated Georgian house.

Gordon House Hotel *(☎/fax 330670, 116 High St)* Singles £40-50, doubles £70-80. This small, pleasant, Italian-run hotel also serves up good-value pizza (from £4.25) and pasta (from £7.50) in its restaurant. All rooms are en suite.

Selkirk Arms Hotel *(☎ 330402, fax 331639, High St)* En-suite singles/doubles £62/90. The luxurious Selkirk Arms Hotel also has good bar meals (around £6), plus a more expensive dining room (three-course dinner £21).

Auld Alliance *(☎ 330569, 5 Castle St)* Mains £9.50-15. Open daily for dinner only. The Auld Alliance is the best place to eat in town. The name refers to the former political alliance between Scotland and France, but here it means a combination of local fresh Scots produce (such as small scallops known as queenies) with French cooking and wine. Booking is advised.

There's a decent *chip shop* opposite the *Safeway* supermarket on St Cuthbert St.

The Auld Alliance

The Auld Alliance was the name given to an agreement between Scotland and France, which would become the world's longest-standing political alliance between two countries. It's usually believed to have dated from 1295, with the treaty between John Balliol and Philip IV, and was renewed regularly over the next three centuries. As part of the alliance, an army of 6000 Scots fought for Joan of Arc against the English at the Siege of Orleans in 1429.

Support in Scotland for the alliance began to wane when backers of the Scottish Reformation looked to England for guidance and it declined further when James VI, king of Scots, became James I of England.

The alliance allowed Scottish and French people dual nationality and this was recognised in French law until 1908.

Getting There & Away

Kirkcudbright is 28 miles (45km) west of Dumfries. Bus Nos 501 and 76 run hourly to Dumfries (£2.50, one hour) via Castle Douglas. To get to Stranraer (£5), take bus No 501 to Gatehouse of Fleet (two to five daily) and change to bus Nos 500 or X75.

GATEHOUSE OF FLEET
☎ 01557 • pop 919

Completely off the beaten track, Gatehouse of Fleet is an attractive little town on the banks of the Water of Fleet, surrounded by partly wooded hills. The TIC (☎ 814212), High St, opens daily Easter to October (closed Sunday, Easter to mid-June).

One mile (1.6km) south-west on the A75, the well-preserved **Cardoness Castle** *(HS; ☎ 814427; adult/child £1.80/75p; open 9.30am-6.30pm daily Apr-Oct, 9.30am-4.30pm Sat & 2pm-4.30pm Sun Nov-Mar)* was the home of the McCulloch clan. It's a classic 15th-century tower house with great views from the top. **Mill on the Fleet Museum** *(☎ 814099, High St; adult/child £1.50/50p; open 10am-4.30pm daily Apr-Oct)*, in a converted 18th-century cotton mill with a working water wheel, traces the history of the local industry. The town was originally planned as workers' accommodation.

Bobbin Guest House *(☎ 814229, 36 High St)* En-suite singles/doubles £35/50. This is a well-appointed and comfortable B&B.

Bank O' Fleet Hotel *(☎/fax 814302, 47 High St)* En-suite singles/doubles from £30/47. Mains £5.75-14.25 (most under £8). Pleasantly decorated rooms and a hearty breakfast await visitors to this recommended hotel. Live entertainment and good bar meals are on offer here; a ploughman's lunch costs £3.80.

Bus Nos X75 and 500 between Dumfries (£3.50, one hour) and Stranraer (£3.40, one hour 10 minutes) stop here three to seven times daily; service No 501 from Dumfries (via Kirkcudbright; £3.50, 1¼ hours, two to four daily) terminates in the village.

NEW GALLOWAY & AROUND
☎ 01644 • pop 290

New Galloway lies in the Glenkens district, north of Loch Ken. There's nothing much in the village itself, but it's surrounded by beautiful countryside in which you feel as if you're on a high plateau, surrounded by tumbling short-pitched hills.

Galloway Forest Park

South and west of town is the 300-sq-mile (770-sq-km) Galloway Forest Park with numerous lochs and great whale-backed heather and pine-covered mountains. The highest point is **Merrick** (843m). The park is criss-crossed by some superb signposted walking trails, from gentle strolls to long distance paths, including the Southern Upland Way.

The 19-mile (30km) A712 (Queen's Way) between New Galloway and Newton Stewart slices through the southern section of the park.

On the shore of Clatteringshaws Loch 6 miles (10km) west of New Galloway, is **Clatteringshaws Visitor Centre** *(☎ 420285; admission free, parking £1; open 10am-5pm daily Apr-Sept, 10.30am-4.30pm daily in Oct)*, with an exhibition on the area's flora and fauna. From the centre, you can walk to a replica of a Romano-British homestead, and to **Bruce's Stone**, where Robert the Bruce is said to have rested after defeating the English at the Battle of Raploch Moss (1307).

Walkers and cyclists head for **Glen Trool** in the park's west, accessed by the forest road east from Bargrennan off the A714 north of Newton Stewart. Just over a mile (1.6km) from Bargrennan, there's the **Glen Trool Visitor Centre** *(☎ 01671-402420, Glentrool; admission free; open 10.30am-5.30pm daily Apr-Sept, 10.30am-4.30pm daily in Oct)*, with information about the area. The road then winds and climbs up to Loch Trool, where there are magnificent views. There are trails around the loch south to Kirroughtree Forest, and 3 miles (5km) north up to Merrick. Another Bruce's Stone, beside the loch, commemorates Robert the Bruce's victory at the Battle of Glentrool (1307).

St John's Town of Dalry

St John's Town of Dalry is a charming village, distinctly more pleasant than New

Galloway, hugging the hillside about 3 miles (5km) north on the A713. It's on the Water of Ken and gives access to the Southern Upland Way.

Places to Stay & Eat

Kendoon Youth Hostel (☎ 460680, St John's Town of Dalry) Dorm beds £7.50/6.25. Open Apr-Sept. This is the closest hostel to St John's Town of Dalry, located about 5 miles (8km) north on the B7000. Bus No 520 stops about a mile (1.6km) away.

High Park (☎/fax 420298, Balmaclellan) Singles/doubles £16/32. This is a good B&B located in Balmaclellan village, 2 miles (3km) east of New Galloway, just off the A712.

Leamington Hotel (☎ 420327, fax 420778, High St, New Galloway) Rooms £18.50-22.50 per person. Most rooms have en-suite bathrooms, and bar meals are served.

Kitty's Tearooms (☎ 420246, High St, New Galloway) Mains around £7. This recommended restaurant does home baking and offers an adventurous menu.

Getting There & Away

MacEwan's (☎ 01387-256533) bus No 521 runs once or twice daily (except Sunday) to Dumfries (£2.20, 55 minutes). Bus No 520 connects New Galloway with Castle Douglas (£1.25, 30 minutes) one to eight times daily; one to three continue north to Ayr (£3, 1¼–1¾ hours).

NEWTON STEWART

☎ 01672 • pop 3673

Newton Stewart is surrounded by beautiful wooded countryside, and set on the western bank of the River Cree. On the eastern bank, across the bridge, is the older, smaller settlement of Minnigaff. The TIC (☎ 402431), Dashwood Square, opens daily April to October (open Sunday mid-June to early September only).

Newton Stewart is a centre for **hiking** and **fishing**. Many hikers head for Galloway Forest Park (see earlier). Creebridge House Hotel (see Places to Stay later) rents fishing gear and arranges permits.

Places to Stay & Eat

Creebridge Caravan Park (☎/fax 402324) £5-7 per tent. Open Mar-Oct. This park is located under 300m from the bridge in the centre of town.

Minnigaff Youth Hostel (☎ 402211, Minnigaff) Dorm beds from £8.25/7. Open Apr-Sept. This well-equipped SYHA hostel is a half-mile (800m) north of the bridge on the eastern bank.

Kilwarlin (☎ 403047, 4 Corvisel Rd) B&B £17 per person. Open Apr-Oct. Situated just uphill from the TIC, this friendly B&B includes tea and home baking in the evening.

Creebridge House Hotel (☎ 402121, fax 403258, just across the River Cree from Newton Stewart) Singles £59, doubles £78-98. This is a magnificent, refurbished, 18th-century mansion built for the earl of Galloway. There's a good restaurant (main courses around £8), and huntin', shootin' and fishin'. The rooms are tastefully decorated and all have en-suite bathrooms.

Bruce Hotel (☎ 402294, 88 Queen St) Mains from £5.50. The good-value bar meals here include local beef, venison, salmon and lamb.

Self-caterers will find a *Costcutter* supermarket at 49 Victoria St.

Getting There & Away

Bus Newton Stewart (Dashwood Square) is served by buses that run between Stranraer (£1.95, 45 minutes) and Dumfries (£3.95, 1½ hours), including bus Nos 920/921 (National Express) and bus Nos X75 and 500 (various operators, three to eight daily). Bus No 359 runs to Girvan (£3.55, 1¼–1¾ hours) via Glentrool two to five times daily. Buses also run south to Wigtown (£1.20, 15 minutes) and Whithorn (£1.80, 45 minutes).

THE MACHARS

South of Newton Stewart, the Galloway Hills give way to the serene, rich-green, softly rolling pastures of the triangular peninsula known as The Machars. The south has many early Christian sites and the 25-mile (40km) **Pilgrims Way** (see the Activities chapter).

Stagecoach Western's (☎ 01776-704484) bus No 415 runs every hour or two between Newton Stewart and the Isle of Whithorn (£1.80, one hour) via Wigtown £1.20, 15 minutes).

Wigtown & Around
☎ 01988 • pop 1120

Surrounded by attractive countryside, Wigtown (W www.wigtown-booktown.co.uk) has expansive views overlooking Wigtown Bay and north to the Galloway Hills.

At one time economically run down, the town's revival began with the decision to make it Scotland's first 'booktown'; there are currently 24 bookshops, offering the widest selection of books in the country. You can browse in **The Book Shop** (☎ 402499, 17 North Main St), which claims to be Scotland's largest second-hand bookshop, the **Old Bank Bookshop** (☎ 402688, 7 South Main St) and many other places.

Wigtown Bay is a nature reserve with large areas of mud-flats and salt marsh that attract thousands of birds. There's a bird-watching hide down on the shore by the **Martyr's Stake**. The 'stake' is a pillar commemorating the spot where, in 1685, two female Covenanters were left to drown for their religious beliefs. Four miles (6km) west of Wigtown, off the B733, the well-preserved recumbent **Torhouse Stone Circle** dates from the 2nd millennium BC.

Craigenlee (☎ 402498, 8 Bank St) is a good centrally located place to stay; singles/doubles cost £17.50/£35.

Branoch is a village about a mile southwest of Wigtown. B&B at the *Bladnoch Inn* (☎ 402200, Bladnoch), at the southern end of town, costs £23.50 per person. Bar meals cost between £5.25 and £14.50; vegetarian food is available on request and real ales are served.

Garlieston

You can't get more off the beaten track than Garlieston, which has a neat little harbour with a ring of 18th-century cottages running round behind a bowling green. A coastal path leads south to the ruins of **Cruggleton Castle**.

Harbour Inn (☎ 01988-600685, 18 South Crescent. Mains £3.50-9.45. This is a basic pub with great views and bar meals.

Whithorn
☎ 01988 • pop 950

Whithorn has a broad, attractive main street virtually closed at both ends – designed to enclose a medieval market. Hard hit economically, the town has virtually no facilities – a few shops and pubs – but it's worth visiting because of its fascinating history.

In 397, while the Romans were still in Britain, St Ninian established the first Christian mission beyond Hadrian's Wall in Whithorn (predating St Columba on Iona by 166 years). After his death, Whithorn Priory was built to house his remains, and Whithorn became the focus of an important medieval pilgrimage.

Today, the priory's substantial ruins are the centre-point of the **Whithorn Trust Discovery Centre** (☎ 500508, 45 George St; adult/child £2.70/1.50; open 10.30am-5pm daily Apr-Oct), with exhibitions and an audiovisual display. You'll see some important finds and early Christian sculpture; the Latinus Stone (c. 450) is reputedly Scotland's oldest Christian artefact.

Isle of Whithorn
☎ 01988 • pop 400

The Isle of Whithorn, once an island but now linked to the mainland by a causeway, is a curious, ragged sort of place with an attractive natural harbour. The roofless 13th-century **St Ninian's Chapel**, probably built for pilgrims who landed nearby, is on the windswept, evocative, rocky headland. Around Burrow Head, to the south-west but accessed from a path off the A747 before you enter the Isle of Whithorn, is **St Ninian's Cave**, where the saint went to pray.

Dunbar House (☎ 500336, Tonderghie Rd) B&B singles/doubles £18/30. The 300-year-old Dunbar House, overlooking the harbour, has spacious rooms.

Steam Packet Inn (☎ 500334, fax 500627, Harbour Row) B&B £25-30 per person. Mains £4.50-5.75. On the quayside this particularly nice pub has popular bar meals that are excellent value.

Glenluce
pop 580

From the Isle of Whithorn, the A747 heads north-west along the coastal plain of **Luce Bay**, before turning inland to meet the A75 near Glenluce. It's a pretty, quiet, little village that stretches along steep Main St. A couple of miles (3km) north, signposted off the A75, is **Glenluce Abbey** *(HS; ☎ 01581-300541; adult/child £1.80/75p; open 9.30am-6.30pm daily Apr-Oct, weekends only the rest of the year)*, in a tranquil valley near the Water of Luce. This Cistercian abbey was founded in 1190 by Roland, lord of Galloway; the chapter house and complex water-supply system are the most interesting remains.

Bus Nos 430, 500 and X75 run daily between Glenluce and to Castle Kennedy, Stranraer and Newton Stewart.

STRANRAER & CAIRNRYAN
☎ 01776 • pop 11,348

Although a little run down, Stranraer is rather more pleasant than the average ferry port. There's no pressing reason to stay, unless you're catching a ferry or you want to tour the area and visit Portpatrick. Day trips to Ireland, including the Giant's Causeway (15 hours), can be arranged through the TIC and cost £26/18.

Orientation & Information

In Stranraer, the bus stops, train station, accommodation and TIC are close to the Stena Sealink terminal. The TIC (☎ 702595), 28 Harbour St, opens 10am to 5pm Monday to Saturday and 11am to 4pm Sunday, April to mid-June and mid-September to October; 9.30am to 5.30pm (10am to 4.30pm Sunday) daily, mid-June to mid-September; and 10.30am to 4pm Monday to Saturday, the rest of the year.

There's a Clydesdale Bank ATM on Bridge St.

Things to See

Worth a quick visit, **St John's Castle** *(☎ 705544, George St; adult/child £1.20/60p;*

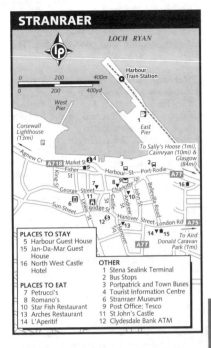

STRANRAER

LOCH RYAN

PLACES TO STAY	OTHER
5 Harbour Guest House	1 Stena Sealink Terminal
15 Jan-Da-Mar Guest House	2 Bus Stops
16 North West Castle Hotel	3 Portpatrick and Town Buses
	4 Tourist Information Centre
PLACES TO EAT	6 Stranraer Museum
7 Petrucci's	9 Post Office; Tesco
8 Romano's	11 St John's Castle
10 Star Fish Restaurant	12 Clydesdale Bank ATM
13 Arches Restaurant	
14 L'Aperitif	

open 10am-1pm & 2pm-5pm Mon-Sat Easter to mid-Sept) was built in 1510 by the Adairs of Kihilt, a powerful local family. Government troops were garrisoned here during the suppression of the Covenanters in the 1680s and it was used as a prison in the 19th century. Displays and a video trace its history.

The two-storey **Stranraer Museum** *(☎ 705088, George St; admission free; open 10am-5pm Mon-Fri, 10am-1pm & 2pm-5pm Sat)* houses exhibits on local history downstairs, including displays on explorers Sir John Ross and his nephew James. Upstairs, there are good temporary exhibitions.

Places to Stay

Aird Donald Caravan Park (☎ 702025, e aird@mimman.u-net.com, London Rd) Sites from £3.90. This is the nearest camp site to town and takes both vans and tents.

Sally's Hoose (☎/fax 703395, e balyet tbb@talk21.com, Balyett, Cairnryan Rd) Hostel beds £10, B&B singles £20-25, B&B

doubles £32-38. A mile (1.6km) north of town on the A77, Sally's Hoose is a five-berth port-a-cabin with good facilities. The B&B is at the nearby ivy-covered farmhouse.

Harbour Guest House (☎ *704626,* e *eharbourguesthouse@callnetuk.com, Market St)* En-suite rooms £19-25 per person. This guesthouse is located on the harbour front, near the town centre.

Jan-Da-Mar Guest House (☎ *706194, 1 Ivy Place, London Rd)* Singles £18-25, doubles £32-40. This conveniently located guesthouse has a range of rooms (some with en suite).

North West Castle Hotel (☎ *704413, fax 702646, Port Rodie)* Singles £55-77, doubles £79.50-109. This is the most luxurious hotel in Stranraer and was formerly the home of Arctic explorer Sir John Ross.

Corsewall Lighthouse Hotel (☎ *853220, fax 854231, Kirkcolm)* B&B £70-200 per person. If you fancy a night in a lighthouse, this unusual place to stay is 13 miles (21km) north-west of Stranraer at Corsewall Point. All rooms have attached bathroom; one room is specially equipped for disabled travellers. The five-course dinner served here costs £29.50.

Places to Eat

L'Aperitif (☎ *702991, London Rd)* Set 3-course dinner £10, available 5.30pm-7pm. L'Aperitif is the best restaurant in town.

Arches Restaurant (☎ *702196, 77 Hanover St)* Mains from £3.95. Arches is a bright, popular cafe.

Romano's (☎ *703102, 36 Charlotte St)* Mains around £5. Romano's does a special of fish, chips, peas and tea for £5.25.

Star Fish Restaurant (☎ *707235, 13 Charlotte St)* Takeaways around £2-4. Open until midnight. This is the best takeaway in town and serves the likes of Scotch pie and chips for £1.80.

There are reasonable pizzas and other fast food at three places on George and Charlotte Sts, including *Petrucci's* (☎ *705837, 2-6 George St),* where pizza costs from £2.50.

If you're after a supermarket there's *Tesco* on Charlotte St.

Getting There & Away

Boat See the Getting There & Away chapter for full details on services to Northern Ireland. There are two alternatives: P&O (☎ 0870 242 4777, W www.poirishsea.com) ferries from Cairnryan to Larne, and Stena Line (☎ 0870 570 7070, W www.stenaline .co.uk) HSS/Superferries from Stranraer to Belfast.

The Cairnryan to Larne service is used mainly by motorists and hauliers. Cairnryan is 5 miles (8km) north of Stranraer on the eastern side of Loch Ryan. Bus Nos 58, 58A and 60 run there from Stranraer four to nine times daily. For a taxi (around £4) phone Central Taxis (☎ 704999).

Stena Line ferries for Belfast connect directly with rail and bus services. The train station is on the ferry pier.

Bus National Express bus Nos 920/921 run twice daily between London and Belfast, via Birmingham, Manchester, Carlisle, Dumfries, the towns along the A75 and Stranraer. Stagecoach Western buses run to Glasgow (change at Ayr) four to 10 times daily (£7, three hours). There are also several daily local buses to Kirkcudbright and the towns along the A75, such as Newton Stewart (£1.95, 45 minutes) and Dumfries (£5, 2¼ hours).

Train Scotrail (☎ 0845 748 4950) runs two to seven trains daily to Glasgow (£15, 2½ hours); it may be necessary to change at Ayr.

Car & Motorcycle It's 126 miles (203km) to Edinburgh; take the A75 east to Dumfries (68 miles; 109km), then the A701 north. Glasgow is 84 miles (135km) north on the coastal A77.

AROUND STRANRAER
Castle Kennedy Gardens

Magnificent Castle Kennedy Gardens (☎ *01776-702024, Rephad; adult/child £3/1; open 10am-5pm daily Apr-Sept),* 3 miles (5km) east of Stranraer, are among the most famous in Scotland. They cover 30 hectares and are set on an isthmus between two lochs and two castles (Castle Kennedy, burned in 1716, and Lochinch Castle, built in 1864).

The landscaping was undertaken in 1730 by the earl of Stair, who used unoccupied soldiers to do the work. Bus Nos 430 (hourly) and 500 stop here.

Loch Ryan

Loch Ryan isn't a lake, but a large narrow inlet that provides a natural shelter from the rough waters of the North Channel. It's especially noted for its **bird-watching** opportunities (October and November is the best time) at the mud-flats of Wig Bay on the western shore, and at rocky Corsewall Point on the northern tip of the peninsula.

PORTPATRICK

☎ 01776 • pop 535

Portpatrick is a charming port on the rugged west coast of the Rhinns (or Rhins) of the Galloway peninsula. Until the mid-19th century it was the main port for Northern Ireland, so it's quite substantial. It's now a coastguard station and a quiet holiday resort.

This is also a good base from which to explore the south of the peninsula, and it's the starting point for the **Southern Upland Way** (see the Activities chapter). You can follow part of the Way to Stranraer (9 miles; 14.5km). It's a cliff-top walk, followed by sections of farmland and heather moor. Start at the Way's information shelter at the northern end of the harbour. The walk is waymarked until a half-mile (800m) south of Stranraer, where you get the first good views of the village.

Onyer Marks Charters (☎ 840346) runs six-hour **fishing trips** from Portpatrick or Drummore for £70 (one or two people) and £140 (three to four people). Equipment can be supplied.

Places to Stay & Eat

On the hillside above the village there are several caravan and camping parks and there's a good variety of places to stay on North Crescent, which curves around the harbour.

Castle Bay Caravan Park (☎ 810462) Car & tent £6. This is an enormous site, one mile (1.6km) from the village.

Knowe Guest House (☎ 810441, fax 810307, 1 North Crescent) Singles £20-30,

doubles £34-38. This charming place overlooks the harbour.

Ard Choille House (☎ 810313, 1 Blair Terrace) Rooms £17.50-25 per person. There are two rooms here, one with en-suite bathroom.

Harbour House Hotel (☎ 810456, fax 810488, 53 Main St) Rooms £28 per person. The Harbour House was formerly the customs house; all rooms are en suite. It's also a popular pub; bar meals range from £5.25 to £12.95.

Port Pantry (Main St) At the bottom of Main St is the friendly Port Pantry, which offers sandwiches (£1.50), cakes (from 75p) and freshly ground Colombian coffee.

Most of the pubs in Portpatrick, such as **The Crown**, serve meals.

Getting There & Away

McCulloch's/King's bus No 367 runs to Stranraer (£1.20, 20 minutes, roughly hourly, three Sunday).

SOUTH OF PORTPATRICK

From Portpatrick, the road south to the Mull of Galloway passes through prime agricultural land, where cattle and sheep graze on a thick carpet of grass (average annual rainfall is about 40 inches/102cm). The coastal scenery includes rugged cliffs, tiny harbours and sandy beaches. The warm waters of the Gulf Stream give the peninsula the mildest climate in Scotland, and frosts on the coast are rare.

This mildness is demonstrated at **Logan Botanic Garden** (☎ 01776-860231, a mile/1.6km north of Port Logan; adult/child £3/1; open 9.30am-6pm daily Mar-Oct), where an array of subtropical flora includes tree ferns and cabbage palms. The garden is an outpost of the Royal Botanic Garden in Edinburgh; there's a free self-guided audio tour.

Farther south, **Drummore** is a fishing village on the east coast. From here it's another 5 miles (8km) to the **Mull of Galloway**, a narrow, rocky, bleak and windy headland, Scotland's most southerly point. The 26m-high lighthouse here was built by Robert Stevenson in 1826; in 1944, a plane crashed into one of the stores buildings and two people were killed. The Mull of Galloway RSPB nature reserve, home to thousands of seabirds, now has a fully staffed **visitor centre** (☎ *01671-402861; admission free; open 10.30am-5pm Tues-Sun, mid-May–mid-July*).

ANNANDALE & ESKDALE

These valleys, in Dumfries & Galloway's east, form part of two major routes that cut across Scotland's south. From Carlisle in England, the traffic-packed M74 heads north-westwards to Glasgow, while the A7 runs north-eastwards to Edinburgh. Most people rush through but, away from the highways, the roads are quiet and there are a few places worth visiting. Placid enough now, this area saw frequent bloody fighting between the Scots and English, but most of it related to thieving of livestock by unruly clans and families on both sides of the border.

Gretna & Gretna Green
☎ 01461 • pop 3149

Many people are drawn to Gretna and Gretna Green by its romantic associations – differences in Scottish and English law once meant that it was easier to marry in Scotland and many young runaway couples from the south came here to wed (see the boxed text opposite).

Today's Gretna Green, on the north-western edge of Gretna, is fairly touristy, but such is the power of the name that about 5000 weddings are performed here annually.

Britain's worst ever rail disaster occurred nearby at Quintinshill in 1915, when a distracted signalman forgot about a local passenger train and a packed troop train crashed into it at full speed. In the crash and resulting fire, 227 people died, most of them soldiers.

The helpful TIC (☎ 337834), Old Headless Cross, Gretna Green, opens 10am to 6pm (to 5pm Sunday) daily mid-June to early September; 10am to 5pm (11am to 4.30pm Sunday) April to mid-June, and the rest of September; and 10am to 4.30pm (11am to 4pm Sunday) daily in October.

Opposite the TIC, the **Old Blacksmith's Shop** (☎ *338441, Gretna Green; adult/child £2/1.50; open 9am-5pm Nov-Mar, 9am-6pm Apr-May & Oct, 9am-7pm Jun & Sept, 9am-*

8pm July & Aug) has an exhibition on Gretna Green's history, a sculpture park and an arts centre, but it's all fairly commercial, with a large gift shop and crowds of tourists.

Hazeldene Hotel (☎ *338292, fax 337222, Gretna Green)* Singles/doubles £35/55, honeymoon suite £95. In this pleasant small hotel, near the Old Blacksmith's Shop, all rooms are en suite.

Old Smithy Restaurant (☎ *338365, Gretna Green)* Mains £3.80-4.35. Right in the centre of things, at the touristy shopping and eating complex, the Smithy Restaurant serves basic but filling meals.

Stagecoach Western bus No 79 runs between Gretna and Dumfries (£2.90, one hour, hourly Monday to Saturday, every two hours Sunday). Trains run from Gretna Green to Dumfries (£5.20, £3 at weekends, 25 minutes, every hour or two, five Sunday) and Carlisle (£3, 13 minutes).

Ecclefechan
☎ 01576 • pop 880

Nearly 10 miles (16km) north of Gretna Green, Ecclefechan – a quiet village in spite of being close to the M74 – was the birthplace of Thomas Carlyle (1795–1881), writer, historian, social reformer and one of the great thinkers of Victorian Britain. The artisan's house where he was born is now a museum. **Thomas Carlyle's Birthplace** (*NTS;* ☎ *300666; adult/child £2.50/1.70; open 1.30pm-5.30pm Fri-Mon Apr-Sept)* is set up to reflect 19th-century domestic life and contains a collection of portraits and Carlyle memorabilia.

Cressfield Caravan Park (☎/*fax 300702)* Tent pitches £5, with car £6-7. Cressfield Caravan Park is close to the village.

Carlyle House (☎/*fax 300322, opposite Thomas Carlyle's Birthplace)* B&B £14. This no-frills B&B has large rooms with shared bathrooms.

Cressfield Country House Hotel (☎ *300281, fax 204218, Townfoot)* Singles £41-46, doubles £51.50-65. Beside the caravan park, this sandstone hotel has good views over Annandale, and comfortable rooms. It also does good substantial meals, including vegetarian; mains cost around £6.

Gretna Green Weddings

ASA ANDERSSON

The 1754 Marriage Act in England and Wales stipulated that couples could only get married if they were both aged over 21, or the parents had given them their permission. However, couples soon discovered that they could legally marry in Scotland because, under Scottish law, people could (and still can) tie the knot at the age of 16 without parental consent. Furthermore, until 1940, they only needed to declare their mutual commitment in front of two witnesses to be considered married. Gretna Green's location, on a major thoroughfare close to the border, made it the most popular venue.

At one time, anyone could perform a legal marriage ceremony but, in Gretna Green, it was usually the local blacksmith, who became known as the 'Anvil Priest'. Scandals associated with tiny Gretna Green were frequent, and church pressure led to a law being passed in 1857, which stated that couples had to be resident in Scotland for 21 days before they could get married. In 1940, the 'anvil weddings' were outlawed, but eloping couples still got married in the church or registry office.

Nowadays, many people make or reaffirm their marriage vows in the village. If you want to get married over the famous anvil in the Old Blacksmith's Shop at Gretna Green, check out the Internet at **W** www.gretnaweddings.com or call ☎ 01461-337961.

Ecclefechan is served by bus No 382 from Carlisle to Moffat (via Gretna Green and Lockerbie).

Lockerbie
☎ 01576 • pop 3982

Red sandstone buildings line the main street of this small country town. Its peace was shattered in 1988 when pieces from a Pan-Am passenger jet fell on the town after a bomb blew up the aircraft; 207 people were killed, including 11 townsfolk. In 2001, a show trial of two Libyans resulted in one being found not guilty; at the time of writing the convicted man had yet to appeal.

Little evidence of the event remains, but the townspeople have created a small garden of remembrance in Dryfesdale Cemetery, about a mile (1.6km) west on the Dumfries road.

Bus No 81 runs to Dumfries (£1.80, 30 minutes, roughly hourly) bus No 382 to Moffat (£1.40, 40 minutes, hourly). There are also numerous trains to Edinburgh, Glasgow, Dundee, Aberdeen and south to England.

Moffat & Around
☎ 01683 • pop 2342

Moffat lies in wild, hilly country near the upper reaches of Annandale. The former spa town is now a centre for the local woollen industry, symbolised by the bronze ram statue on High St. If you have your own transport, it's a good base from which to explore the Lowther Hills and the western Borders.

Information The TIC (☎ 220620), Ladyknowe, opens daily from April to October. The post office and bus stop are on High St.

Things to See & Do The town has a couple of small attractions. At **Moffat Woollen Mill** (☎ 220134, Ladyknowe; admission free; open 9am-5.30pm daily Mar-Oct, 9.30am-5pm daily Nov-Feb), near the TIC, you can see a working weaving exhibition, and trace your Scottish ancestry. Nearby, **Moffat Museum** (☎ 220868, Church Gate; adult/child £1/20p; open 10.30am-1pm & 2.30pm-4.30pm Thur-Tues, plus Sun afternoon only June-Sept), in a former bakery, tells the town's history.

There are short **walks** down by the River Annan; follow the 'Waterside Walks' sign from High St. About 5 miles (8km) north of Moffat, off the A701, you can walk into the **Devil's Beef Tub**, a deep, dark and mist-shrouded valley once used by Border reivers (raiders) to hide their stolen cattle. It was also used as a hide-out by Covenanters, as were the hills around the **Grey Mare's Tail** (NTS), a 60m waterfall 10 miles (16km) north-east of Moffat on the A708. There's a trail to the waterfall, which continues to Loch Skeen and up to the summit of White Coomb (822m). This is also a popular **bird-watching** spot.

Places to Stay & Eat There are plenty of accommodation choices in Moffat.

Hammerland's Farm Camping Ground (☎ 220436, fax 024-7669 4886, Hammerland's Farm) Sites £7.95. Open Mar-Oct. This large camp site, off the A708 just east of town, has a laundry and showers.

Arden House (☎ 220220, High St) Singles £17.50-19.50, doubles £35-39. Arden House, a former bank, is a good centrally located choice, with a good breakfast (vegetarian meal on request).

Buchan Guest House (☎ 220378, Beechgrove) B&B £20-25 per person. You'll find this flower-decked B&B just a short walk north of the centre.

There are several good bakeries on High St and Well St, a couple of good cafes on High St, and all the pubs provide bar meals.

Moffat House Hotel (☎ 220039, High St) 3-course dinners £22. You need to pre-book if you wish to dine at this recommended restaurant.

Adamson's Coffee House (☎ 221429, High St) This cafe serves sandwiches (£2.10-3.10), pizzas and baked potatoes.

Rumblin' Tum (☎ 220026, High St) You can get jacket potatoes from £2.75 from this place.

Moffat Toffee Shop (High St) For pure indulgence, try the home-made fudge with malt whisky.

Getting There & Away There are several daily buses to Edinburgh (bus Nos 100, X100 and 199), Glasgow (Scottish Citylink bus No X74) and Dumfries (bus Nos X74, 100, X100 and 199). Bus No 382 runs regularly to Lockerbie, Gretna Green and Carlisle. Travelling north-east to Selkirk, in the Borders, by bus is limited to the Lowland (☎ 01573-224141) 'Harrier', which runs Tuesday and Thursday between July and September.

There are several scenic roads out of Moffat: the A701 south-west to Dumfries, the A701 north to Edinburgh and the A708 north-east to Selkirk.

Langholm
☎ 013873 • pop 2500

The waters of three rivers – the Esk, Ewes and Wauchope – meet at Langholm, which, with its solid, granite streets, is the centre of Scotland's tweed industry. Hugh MacDiarmid (1892–1978), poet, co-founder of the SNP and sometime member of the Communist Party, was born (and is buried) here

This is clan Armstrong country. Several years after he landed on the moon (1969), US astronaut Neil Armstrong came to Langholm and received the freedom of the town. The **Clan Armstrong Museum and Centre** (☎ 80610, Lodge Walk, Castleholm; adult/child £1.50/1; open 2pm-5pm Tues-Sun mid-Apr–mid-Oct) is probably only of real interest to those bearing that surname.

Most people come for **fishing** and low-key **walking** in the surrounding moors and woodlands.

Places to Stay & Eat *Ewes Water Caravan & Camping Park* (☎ 80386) Tent sites £4. Open Apr-Sept. For camping close to Langholm, try this small, quiet camp site about 1km north of town, just off the A7.

Border House (☎ 80376, 28 High St) B&B £20-25 per person. At this central B&B all rooms are en suite.

Reivers Rest Hotel (☎ 81343, 81 High St) En-suite singles £32-34, doubles £52-56. This white-painted inn serves real ales and bar meals.

Getting There & Away Langholm is on the bus No 195 route between Carlisle and Galashiels (four to nine daily), while bus No A1/112 has up to five daily connections with Eskdalemuir and Lockerbie (no Sunday service).

From Langholm, the A7 heads north to Edinburgh and south to Carlisle. If you're driving to the Borders, an interesting route is the minor road off the A7, just north of town, that runs across empty moorland to Liddlesdale and Newcastleton.

Eskdalemuir

Surrounded by wooded hills, Eskdalemuir is a remote settlement 14 miles (22km) north-west of Langholm. About 1½ miles (2km) farther north is the **Samye Ling Tibetan Centre** (☎ 013873-73232), the first Tibetan Buddhist monastery in the west (1968). The colourful prayer flags, and the red and gold of the Samye Temple, contrast strikingly with the stark grey and green landscape. The temple was built in 1988. The centre offers meditation courses, including weekend workshops for which basic food and board is available (dorm beds £15.50, breakfast £1 and lunch £3).

Those staying here are asked to give two hours a day to help in the kitchen, garden, farm etc. The temple opens to casual visitors (1pm to 5pm daily), for whom there's also a small cafe.

Bus No A1/112 from Langholm/Lockerbie stop at the centre.

Central & North-Eastern Scotland

The Highland line, the massive geological fault that divides the Highlands from the Lowlands, runs across the central section of Scotland, making this possibly the most scenically varied region in the country. To the south are undulating hills and agricultural plains; to the north, the wild, treeless Highland peaks.

The town of Stirling, 26 miles (42km) north-east of Glasgow, has witnessed many of the great battles in the Scottish struggle against English domination. Stirling's spectacular castle, dramatically perched on a rock as is Edinburgh's castle, was for centuries of paramount strategic importance, controlling the main routes in the area.

On the western side of central Scotland, less than 20 miles (32km) north of Glasgow, are the famous 'bonnie, bonnie banks' of Loch Lomond, straddling the Highland line (see also The Highlands chapter). Tourists have been visiting the Trossachs (the lochs and hills just east of Loch Lomond) for over 150 years – Queen Victoria among them. Having set her heart on adding a Highland residence to her list of royal properties, her husband Prince Albert eventually purchased the Balmoral estate in Aberdeenshire.

In the south-east of this area, Fife lies between the Firths (estuaries) of Forth and Tay. The attractive seaside town of St Andrews was once the ecclesiastical centre of the country, but is now better known for its university and as the home of golf. Near the eastern extremity of Fife, Crail is the most beautiful of a series of fishing villages.

Perth is on the direct routes from Edinburgh and Glasgow to Inverness. It was once the capital of Scotland, but it's now just a busy town. Both Dunkeld and Pitlochry, to the north, are appealing (though touristy) places which are useful as walking bases. Frequent buses and trains service this route.

HIGHLIGHTS

- Visiting Scotland's grandest castle at Stirling
- Strolling down the hallowed fairways of St Andrews' Old Course
- Surrounding yourself with the finery of upper-class Highland life at Blair Castle
- Treating yourself to an Antarctic experience at Discovery Point, Dundee
- Exploring Glamis Castle, with its haunted crypt and chapel
- Sampling the spirituous delights of the Malt Whisky Trail

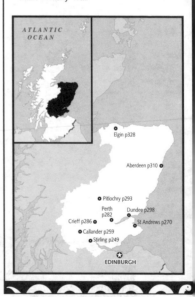

ATLANTIC OCEAN

Elgin p328

Aberdeen p310

Pitlochry p293

Perth p282

Dundee p298

Crieff p286

St Andrews p270

Callander p259

Stirling p249

EDINBURGH

Following the road to Aberdeen from Perth or St Andrews, you quickly reach Dundee one of Scotland's largest cities. Despite its excellent location, it has suffered from modern development and the loss of its jute and shipbuilding industries. It's worth pausing in Dundee to visit Captain Scott's Antarctic ship, *Discovery*, moored near the Tay Bridge.

The eastern Highlands is a great elbow of land that juts into the North Sea between Perth and the Firth of Tay in the south, and Inverness and the Moray Firth in the north. There are excellent hill walks in the Grampians, and the sub-arctic Cairngorm plateaus are as bleak and demanding as any Scottish mountains. The coastline, especially from Stonehaven to Buckie, is particularly attractive. The valley of the Dee – Royal Deeside, thanks to the Queen's residence at Balmoral – has sublime scenery. Braemar, in upper Deeside, is surrounded by good walking country and every September hosts Scotland's most important Highland Games, the Braemar Gathering.

The largest city in the north-east is prosperous Aberdeen, a lively and attractive place fattened on the proceeds of a long history of sea trade and currently through the North Sea oil industry, for which it's the main onshore base.

The small fishing villages of the north coast are little visited, but some are very pretty. Gardenstown is built on steep slopes, which plunge dramatically into the sea. Farther west along this coast, experiments with alternative lifestyles continue at the Findhorn Foundation, an international spiritual community that welcomes outsiders with a range of eclectic courses. Further spiritual guidance is provided in neighbouring Speyside, where whisky distilleries welcome visitors with tours and drams.

Although the larger towns are easy to reach by bus and train, travel into the Grampians, and other interesting walking areas, is often difficult without your own transport. Furthermore, the division between the eastern and western Highlands reflects the transport realities – there are few coast-to-coast links across central Scotland.

WALKING & CYCLING

The West Highland Way, possibly the finest long-distance walk in Scotland, follows the eastern bank of Loch Lomond from Milngavie (near Glasgow) to Crianlarich, and on to Fort William in the western Highlands. See the Activities chapter.

There's some superb hill-walking in the Highland areas of central and north-eastern Scotland, with many hills over the magic figure of 3000 feet (914m), making them Munros (see the boxed text Munros & Munro Bagging in the Activities chapter).

The northern part of the Stirling region, most of Perth & Kinross, and the Angus glens are mountainous areas that boast several excellent centres for walking holidays, including Killin (in the Stirling district), Pitlochry (in Perth & Kinross) and Kirriemuir (in Angus). Braemar is an excellent base in Aberdeenshire for challenging walks through the Cairngorms to Aviemore, via the Lairig Ghru or the less-frequented Lairig an Laoigh.

The Fife Coastal Path runs for over 50 miles (80km) between the Forth Bridges and Crail in the East Neuk. TICs provide leaflets on sections of the walk.

Aside from the busy A9, which roars up the middle of Scotland, the side roads are refreshingly free of traffic and excellent for cycling. There's a National Cycle Network route (NN7C) from Glasgow to Pitlochry via Loch Lomond, the Trossachs, Callander and Killin, which follows forest trails, small roads and disused rail routes. It continues to Inverness via the Drumochter Pass and Aviemore, bringing the total distance from Glasgow to Inverness to 214 miles (345km). For details, contact Sustrans on ☎ 0117-929 0888.

Stirling Region

The Stirling administrative district includes countryside on both sides of the Highland line: the agricultural and industrial Lowlands to the south and the bare peaks of the Highlands to the north. Stirling and Clackmannanshire were formerly known as Central region, a name appropriate not only for the region's location, but for the fact that this area has played a pivotal role in Scotland's history. More than any other part of

Scotland, this area has had the closest association with Scotland's struggle to maintain its freedom from England.

Stirling's administrative capital, also called Stirling, has a superb castle placed on a high rock at the most strategically important spot in the country – at the head of the Firth of Forth and by the main route into the Highlands.

Loch Lomond lies on the western edge of the region (see Argyll & Bute in The Highlands chapter). The Trossachs, Rob Roy country, is another busy tourist destination, currently receiving even more attention following the success of the movie about this Scottish hero. Scotland's first national park, Loch Lomond and the Trossachs, should be open by 2002. The final decision still has to be made by the Scottish parliament; see **W** www.lomondshores.com or call ☎ 01389-758216. The mountainous north of the region sees far fewer visitors as public transport is patchy in parts, nonexistent in others.

GETTING AROUND

For local transport information in the Stirling administrative district, phone Stirling Council's public transport unit on ☎ 01786-442707. First Edinburgh (☎ 01324-613777) is the main operator. Its Heart of Scotland Explorer ticket (adult/child £7.30/5.20) gives you one day's travel on all its services in the Stirling administrative district, Falkirk, Clackmannanshire and West Lothian, and half-price travel to St Andrews, Edinburgh and Glasgow.

The Trossachs Trundler (☎ 01786-442707) is a useful summer bus service circling Aberfoyle, Callander and the pier on Loch Katrine. Some Day Rover tickets (for example, from Glasgow) are valid on this bus; connecting fares from Stirling (with First Edinburgh and Morrison's) are available.

Stirling town is the rail hub but the lines skirt around the edge of this region, so you'll be relying on buses if you don't have your own transport. For train enquiries, phone ☎ 0845 748 4950.

The West Highland Way runs along the western edge of the region, from Glasgow to Fort William (see the Activities chapter).

There are numerous other walks in the area. *Walk Loch Lomond & the Trossachs,* a useful guide published by Collins, is available from TICs (£5.99).

The 60-mile (96km) Glasgow to Killin Cycle Way crosses the region from Glasgow to Killin and Loch Tay, via Balloch on the southern tip of Loch Lomond, Aberfoyle and Callander in the Trossachs, and Loch Earn. There are detours through Queen Elizabeth Forest Park and round Loch Katrine. It's a good route for walkers as well as cyclists because it follows forest trails, old railway routes and canal towpaths. A free brochure showing the route is available from TICs.

STIRLING
☎ 01786 • pop 37,000

The royal *burgh* (Scottish town) of Stirling is such a strategic site that there has been a fortress here since prehistoric times. It was said that whoever held the town controlled the country, and Stirling has witnessed many of the struggles of the Scots against the English.

The castle is perched high on a rock and dominates the town. It's one of the most interesting castles in the country to visit, better even than Edinburgh Castle.

Two miles (3km) north of Stirling, and visible for miles around, the Wallace Monument commemorates William Wallace. Mel Gibson's movie *Braveheart* revived interest in the hero of the wars of independence against England. You can climb this Victorian tower for a panoramic view of no less than seven battlegrounds – one of them at Stirling Bridge, where Wallace defeated the English in 1297.

There is a more famous battlefield 2 miles (3km) south-east of Stirling at Bannockburn, where, in 1314, Robert the Bruce and his small army of determined Scots (outnumbered four to one) routed Edward II's English force and reclaimed Stirling Castle. This victory turned the tide of fortune sufficiently in favour of the Scots for the following 400 years, in the long and bitter struggle against the threat of English domination.

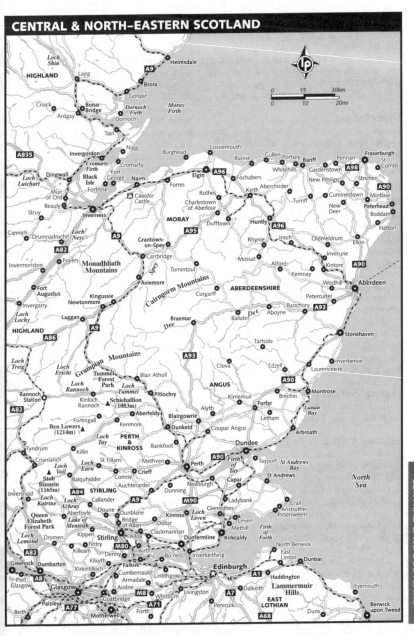

CENTRAL & NORTH-EASTERN SCOTLAND

0   15   30km
0   10   20mi

HIGHLAND

Loch Shin
Lairg
Helmsdale
A9
Brora
Golspie
Croick
Bonar Bridge
Dornoch Firth
Moray Firth
Ardgay
Dornoch
Tain
Nigg
Lossiemouth
Burghead
Cullen Portsoy Banff
A835
Invergordon
Cromarty Firth
Cromarty
Buckie
Whitehills
Gardenstown
Pennan
Fraserburgh
St Combs
A98
Dingwall
Black Isle
Fort George
Nairn
Elgin
A96
Fochabers
Aberchirder
New Pitsligo
Strichen
Loch Luichart
Muir of Ord
Fortrose
Forres
Rothes
Keith
Turriff
Cumineston
Mintlaw
A90
Beauly
Inverness
Cawdor Castle
Charlestown of Aberlour
Dufftown
New Deer
Peterhead
Boddam
Cannich
Drumnadrochit
MORAY
Huntly
A96
Oldmeldrum
Hatton
Struy
Loch Ness
A9
Grantown-on-Spey
A95
Rhynie
Insch
Ellon
A82
Carrbridge
Mossat
Alford
Inverurie
Invermoriston
Foyers
Monadhliath Mountains
Spey
Tomintoul
Kemnay
Kintore
A90
Fort Augustus
Aviemore
Cairngorm Mountains
Corgarff
ABERDEENSHIRE
Westhill
Aberdeen
Invergarry
Kingussie
Newtonmore
Peterculter
Banchory
A93
Loch Lochy
Laggan
A9
Dee
Braemar
Aboyne
HIGHLAND
A86
Dee
Ballater
Stonehaven
Loch Treig
Loch Ericht
Grampian Mountains
Tarfside
Loch Rannoch
Tummel Forest Park
Blair Atholl
A93
Clova
Edzell
Inverbervie
Laurencekirk
Rannoch Station
Kinloch Rannoch
Loch Tummel
Pitlochry
ANGUS
Kirriemuir
Brechin
Montrose
A82
Schiehallion (1083m)
Aberfeldy
Alyth
Forfar
A90
Lunan Bay
Ben Lawers (1214m)
Fortingall
Kenmore
Blairgowrie
Dunkeld
Coupar Angus
Letham
Loch Tay
PERTH & KINROSS
Arbroath
Tyndrum
Killin
Bankfoot
Dundee
Crianlarich
Loch Voil
St Fillans
Methven
A90
Firth of Tay
Tayport
St Andrews
Stob Binnein (1165m)
Loch Earn
Crieff
Perth
Cupar
Inversnaid
Balquhidder
Comrie
Auchterarder
Dunning
Newburgh
North Sea
A84
STIRLING
Callander
Loch Katrine
Loch Achray
Doune
A9
M90
Ladybank
Crail
Anstruther
Pittenweem
Aberfoyle
Lake of Menteith
Dunblane
Bridge of Allan
Dollar
Kinross
Loch Leven
Glenrothes
Queen Elizabeth Forest Park
Kippen
Stirling
Alloa
Clackmannan
Leven
Methil
Firth of Forth
Loch Lomond
Drymen
Killearn
Fintry
Airth
Dunfermline
Kirkcaldy
Greenock
Dumbarton
Kilsyth
Bo'ness
Inverkeithing
North Berwick
A82
Kirkintilloch
Falkirk
East Linton
Dunbar
Port Glasgow
A8
Glasgow
Cumbernauld
Linlithgow
Edinburgh
A1
Haddington
Lammermuir Hills
Eyemouth
Paisley
A77
Coatbridge
M8
Whitburn
Livingston
A7
Dalkeith
EAST LOTHIAN
Beith
Motherwell
Forth
A71
Penicuik
A68
Duns
Berwick upon Tweed

CENTRAL & NE SCOTLAND

Although you can fit the main sights of Stirling into a day trip from Edinburgh or Glasgow, it's a very pleasant place to stay. There are two excellent hostels, including one near the castle, and the town lays on Highland games, a military parade, and numerous other activities in the summer.

Orientation
The old town slopes up from the train and bus stations to the castle, which sits 250 feet (76m) above the plain atop the plug of an extinct volcano.

Information
The TIC (☎ 475019), 41 Dumbarton Rd, opens 9am to 7.30pm Monday to Saturday in July and August (9.30am to 6.30pm Sunday), and shorter hours for the rest of the year. It's closed Sunday, October to May. The TIC has details of the popular ghost walks (£5/3) that take place at 8.30pm daily except Tuesday and Sunday in July and August. Ask about the visitor attraction 10% discount scheme.

The main post office, and banks with ATMs, can be found on Barnton St and Murray Place respectively. Networx, 68 Murray Place, opens daily and charges only £1 per hour for Internet access.

Medical Services The general hospital is Stirling Royal Infirmary (☎ 434000), Livilands Rd, south of the town centre.

Stirling Castle & Argyll's Lodging
The location, architecture and historical significance of Stirling Castle *(HS; ☎ 450000; adult/concession/child £6.50/5/2, including Argyll's Lodging & the Argyll and Sutherland Highlanders Museum; open 9.30am-5.15pm daily Apr-Sept, 9.30am-4.15pm Oct-Mar)* combine to make it one of the grandest of all Scottish castles. It commands superb views across the surrounding plains.

There has been a fortress of some kind here for several thousand years, but the current building dates from the late 14th to the 16th centuries, when it was a residence of the Stuart monarchs. James II murdered the earl of Douglas in the castle and threw his body from a window (1452). The Great Hall and Gatehouse were built by James IV. The spectacular palace was constructed in the reign of James V (1540–42). French masons were responsible for the stonework. James VI remodelled the Chapel Royal and was the last king of Scots to live here.

A £20-million programme of improvements has now been completed; during the work, a skeleton was discovered hidden in a wall of the castle. The castle's 16th-century kitchens, with a reconstruction of medieval conditions, are also very interesting. The magnificent Great Hall, restored to look as it would have done around 1500 and re-opened by the Queen in 1999, has a new roof and lime-washed walls.

In the King's Old Building is the museum of the Argyll and Sutherland Highlanders, which traces the history of this famous regiment from 1794 to the present day.

Argyll's Lodging is the most impressive 17th-century town house in Scotland and you'll find it by the castle, at the top of Castle Wynd. Parts of the lodging date from the early 16th century. This spectacular mansion, complete with turrets, has been restored to look as it did around 1680.

The Royal Burgh of Stirling Visitor Centre *(☎ 462517, Castle Esplanade; admission free; open 9.30am-5pm daily, 9.30am-6.30pm July & Aug, 9.30am-6pm Sept & Oct)* has an audiovisual introduction to Stirling, including the history and architecture of the castle. There's a car park next to the castle (£2 for two hours).

Old Town
Below the castle is the old town, whose growth began when Stirling became a royal burgh, around 1124. In the 15th and 16th centuries, when the Stuart monarchs held court in Stirling, rich merchants built their houses here.

Stirling has the best surviving town wall in Scotland and it can be followed on the **Back Walk**. It was built around 1547 when Henry VIII of England began what became known as the 'Rough Wooing' – attacking the town in order to force Mary Queen of Scots to marry his son in order to unite the

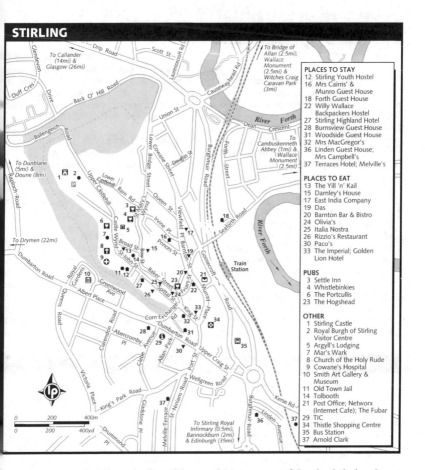

STIRLING

To Callander (14mi) & Glasgow (26mi)

To Bridge of Allan (2.5mi), Wallace Monument (2.5mi) & Witches Craig Caravan Park (3mi)

To Cambuskenneth Abbey (1mi) & Wallace Monument (2.5mi)

To Dunblane (5mi) & Doune (8mi)

To Drymen (22mi)

Train Station

To Stirling Royal Infirmary (0.5mi), Bannockburn (2mi) & Edinburgh (35mi)

PLACES TO STAY
12 Stirling Youth Hostel
16 Mrs Cairns' & Munro Guest House
18 Forth Guest House
22 Willy Wallace Backpackers Hostel
27 Stirling Highland Hotel
28 Burnsview Guest House
31 Woodside Guest House
32 Mrs MacGregor's
36 Linden Guest House; Mrs Campbell's
37 Terraces Hotel; Melville's

PLACES TO EAT
13 The Yill 'n' Kail
15 Darnley's House
17 East India Company
19 Das
20 Barnton Bar & Bistro
24 Olivia's
25 Italia Nostra
26 Rizzio's Restaurant
30 Paco's
33 The Imperial; Golden Lion Hotel

PUBS
3 Settle Inn
4 Whistlebinkies
6 The Portcullis
23 The Hogshead

OTHER
1 Stirling Castle
2 Royal Burgh of Stirling Visitor Centre
5 Argyll's Lodging
7 Mar's Wark
8 Church of the Holy Rude
9 Cowane's Hospital
10 Smith Art Gallery & Museum
11 Old Town Jail
14 Tolbooth
21 Post Office; Networx (Internet Cafe); The Fubar
29 TIC
34 Thistle Shopping Centre
35 Bus Station
37 Arnold Clark

kingdoms. The walk follows the line of the wall from Dumbarton Rd (near the TIC) to the castle, continuing around Castle Rock and back to the old town. There are great views from the path, and you could make a short detour to Gowan Hill to see the **Beheading Stone**, where Murdoch, duke of Albany and former regent of Scotland, was executed in 1425. It's now encased in iron bars to keep ritual axe murderers away.

Mar's Wark, on Castle Wynd at the head of the old town, is the ornate facade of what was once a Renaissance-style townhouse commissioned in 1569 by the wealthy earl

of Mar, regent of Scotland during James VI's minority. During the Jacobite rebellion in 1715, a later earl backed the losing side and his house became the town's barracks, eventually falling into ruin.

The **Church of the Holy Rude** (☎ 475275, *St John St; admission free; open 10am-5pm daily May-Sept*) has been the town's parish church for 500 years and James VI was crowned here in 1567. The nave and tower date from 1456 and the church features one of the few surviving medieval, open-timber roofs. Behind the church is **Cowane's hospital** (☎ 472247, 49 St John St; admission free, *donations welcome; open 9am-5pm Mon-Sat & 1pm-5pm Sun Easter-Sept)*. Incorrectly known as the Guildhall, it was built as an almshouse in 1637 by the merchant John Cowane. It now has multiple uses including hosting *ceilidhs*, banquets and concerts. The curator is extremely knowledgeable about tartan, local genealogy and history.

The **Mercat Cross**, in Broad St, is topped with a unicorn and was once surrounded by a bustling market. Nearby is the **Tolbooth**, built in 1705 as the town's administrative centre. A courthouse and jail were added in the following century and it was renovated in 2001 as a performing arts centre.

The **Old Town Jail** (☎ *450050, St John St; adult/child £3.95/2.75; open 9.30am-6pm daily Apr-Sept, last admission 5.30pm; 9.30am-4pm or 5pm Oct-Mar)* has displays on prison life, excellent 'living history' performances (tours every half hour, from 10am), and a good view from the roof.

At the end of Broad St is **Darnley's House**, where Mary Queen of Scots' second husband, Lord Darnley, is said to have stayed. It has a rare architectural feature: the barrel-vaulted ground floor has no connection with the upper floors.

The floodlit **Thieves Pot** (☎ *470626, This-tle Shopping Centre; admission free; open 9am-5.30pm Mon-Sat, noon-5pm Sun)*, an old dungeon in the town wall, contains two realistic prisoner dummies. Access is down a spiral staircase next to WH Smith.

Smith Art Gallery & Museum

At the Smith Art Gallery & Museum (☎ *471917, Dumbarton Rd; admission free; open 10.30am-5pm Tues-Sat & 2pm-5pm Sun)* you'll find excellent displays covering the history of the town, a fine collection of paintings, and natural history exhibits.

Wallace Monument

Two miles (3km) north of Stirling is Scotland's impressive Victorian monument to Sir William Wallace (☎ *472140, Abbey Craig, Causewayhead; adult/child/family £3.95/2.75/10.75; open 10am-5pm Mar-May & Oct, 10am-6pm June & Sept, 9.30am-6.30pm July & Aug, 10.30am-4pm Nov-Feb)*, who was hanged, drawn and

William Wallace, Scottish Patriot

William Wallace was born in 1270 as the second son of Sir Malcolm Wallace of Elderslie, near Paisley. Little known before 1296, he was then catapulted into fame and a place in history as a highly successful guerrilla commander who harassed the English invaders for many years.

Driven to avenge the barbarous rule of his distant relative, the English king Edward Plantagenet (Edward I, Hammer of the Scots), Wallace secured his first victory in September 1296 by defeating a troop of about 100 English soldiers at the battle of Loudoun Hill in Ayrshire. In May 1297, Wallace summarily executed Sir William de Hazelrigg, the English-imposed sheriff of Lanark, for killing Marion Wallace, his wife. By September, an English army met Wallace and his friends head-on at Stirling Bridge; a large party of English crossed the bridge and were routed after being cut-off by the Scots.

Wallace was knighted by Robert the Bruce and proclaimed Guardian of Scotland in March 1298. However, disaster struck in July, when Edward's superior force defeated the Scots at the Battle of Falkirk. Wallace resigned as guardian, went into hiding, and travelled throughout Europe to drum-up support for the Scottish cause. Many of the Scots nobility were prepared to side with Edward, and Wallace was betrayed after his return to Scotland in 1305.

Sir William Wallace was tried for treason at Westminster (although he had never recognised Edward as his overlord), and he was cruelly hanged, beheaded and disembowelled at Smithfield, London. A memorial plaque is incorporated in the wall of St Bartholomew's Hospital at West Smithfield.

A highly recommended, albeit fictionalised, account of Wallace's exploits is *The Wallace*, by Nigel Tranter.

quartered by the English in 1305. The view from the top is as breathtaking as the 67m (220ft) climb up to it, and the monument contains interesting displays including a parade of other Scottish heroes and Wallace's mighty two-handed sword. Clearly the man was no weakling.

From mid-April to September, an open-top tour bus (see the following Organised Tours section) links the monument with Stirling Castle every 40 minutes, but you could also walk (see Walking & Cycling).

Bannockburn

On 24 June 1314, the greatest victory in the history of Scotland's struggle to remain independent took place at the Battle of Bannockburn.

Run by National Heritage Scotland (NTS), Bannockburn Heritage Centre (☎ 812664, Glasgow Rd; adult/child £2.50/1.70; open 10am-5.30pm Apr-Oct, last audiovisual show 5pm; 10am-4.30pm Mar, Nov, Dec) tells the story with a 12-minute audiovisual display. There are also interesting dioramas about medieval Scotland and the Battle of Stirling Bridge. Outside is the Borestone site, said to have been Robert the Bruce's command post before the battle. There's also his grim-looking statue, dressed in full battle gear and mounted on a charger.

The battle site itself never closes.

Cambuskenneth Abbey

The only substantial remnant of this Augustinian abbey (Cambuskenneth; admission free; always open), founded in 1147, is the belfry. In medieval times, Cambuskenneth became one of the richest abbeys in the country. Its high status is supported by the fact that Robert the Bruce held his parliament here in 1326 and James III and his queen are both buried here. The abbey is a mile from both Stirling Castle and the Wallace Monument.

Walking & Cycling

The best way to reach the Wallace Monument is on foot or by bike; it takes about 45 minutes to walk there. Cross the railway line on Seaforth Place, continue straight ahead onto

Shore Rd and Abbey Rd. There's a footbridge over the River Forth to Cambuskenneth, where you can visit the ruins of the abbey. The Wallace Monument is located just a mile north of here; follow Ladysneuk Rd and turn left at the junction with Alloa Rd.

Organised Tours

From mid-April to September, *Guide Friday* runs an open-top, hop-on hop-off bus tour every 40 minutes, daily, between the castle and the Wallace Monument via Bridge of Allan. A day ticket costs £6.50/5/2 adult/student/child. Check details with the TIC or call ☎ 0131-556 2244.

Places to Stay

Camping *Witches Craig Caravan Park* (☎ 474947, Blairlogie) Tents from £5.25, £5.90 with car. Open Apr-Oct. This is located on the edge of the Ochil Hills in Blairlogie, 3 miles (5km) east of Stirling by the A91.

Hostels Stirling boasts some excellent hostelling options.

Stirling Youth Hostel (☎ 473442, St John St) Dorm beds from £10/8, includes continental breakfast Apr-Oct. Open year-round. The facade of an 18th-century church conceals the hostel, which is in a perfect location in the old part of town. It's a superb modern hostel with 126 beds in small dorms. The less attractive annexe in Union St opens in summer only.

Willy Wallace Backpackers Hostel (☎ 446773, e manager@willywallace.f9 .co.uk, 77 Murray Place) Dorm beds £10. This is an excellent, clean and friendly hostel in the middle of town.

B&Bs & Hotels There are a few typical B&Bs on Linden Ave (just off Burghmuir Rd), which is fairly close to the bus station and less than a half-mile (800m) from the train station.

Linden Guest House (☎/fax 448850, 22 Linden Ave) B&B £19-25 per person. Here there are three rooms with shared bathroom.

Mrs Campbell's (☎ 469017, 24 Linden Ave) B&B £19-25. This place has three en-suite rooms.

The March to Independence

Every year on the Saturday nearest 24 June (the day in 1314 when the Scots inflicted their greatest defeat on the English at Bannockburn), there's a commemorative march from the northern end of Stirling, through the town, and southwards as far as the Bannockburn Heritage Centre. The march ends at Bruce's statue and is followed by an address from the leader of the Scottish National Party (SNP), currently John Swinney, MSP for Tayside North. While some people finish the day with a family picnic on the grass of Bannockburn field, others adjourn to the nearby 1314 Inn, a great place for a pint, a bar meal and heated political discussions.

Woodside Guest House (☎ *475470, 4 Back Walk*) Singles/doubles £20/36. Woodside Guest House is near the TIC.

Burnsview Guest House (☎ *451002, 1 Albert Place*) Double/twin £18-22 per person. Burnsview has three rooms with private facilities. It's close to the TIC.

Mrs MacGregor's (☎/fax *471082, 27 King St*) Singles £20-25, doubles £32-38; add £7 for dinner. This place is conveniently located in the centre of town.

Forth Guest House (☎ *471020, fax 447220, 23 Forth Place*) B&B £19.50-37.50 per person. On the other side of town, a short walk north of the train station, is the excellent Forth Guest House, just off Seaforth Rd. It's a small Georgian terrace house with a tiny rose-filled front garden and five comfortable rooms, all en suite.

Mrs Cairns' (☎ *479228, 12 Princes St*) En-suite B&B from £18 per person. This place is just a short walk north-west of the train station. There are two singles, one double and a twin room here.

Munro Guest House (☎ *472685, 14 Princes St*) Singles £23-30, doubles £40-44. This clean and comfortable place has five rooms, all with attached bathroom.

Terraces Hotel (☎ *472268, fax 450314, 4 Melville Terrace*) Singles £45-69.50, doubles £60-82. Friendly Terraces Hotel is popular

with business people. It's an efficient hotel with good food and real ales too. Vegetarians are catered for.

Stirling Highland Hotel (☎ *272727, fax 272829, Spittal St*) B&B singles/doubles £119.50/169. Stirling Highland Hotel, the smartest hotel in town, is a sympathetic refurbishment of an old high school. Special offers may be available.

Places to Eat

Rizzio's Restaurant (☎ *272727, Spittal St*) Lunch & all-you-can-eat pizza & pasta (served 5.30pm-6.30pm) £4.95. Stylish Rizzio's, in a corner of the Stirling Highland Hotel, has remarkable deals for such an expensive hotel. The restaurant is named after Mary Queen of Scots' Italian secretary, David Rizzio, who was killed on the orders of the earl of Bothwell after he suspected an affair.

Olivia's (☎ *446277, 5 Baker St*) Mains £10-17. Visit Olivia's for a romantic candlelit dinner and fine Scottish cuisine with an international touch.

The Yill 'n' Kail (☎ *473929, 39 Broad St*) Lunch mains from £3.50, dinner mains £7-19. Formerly the town's bathhouse, this restaurant now serves a wide range of contemporary Scottish cuisine. Lunches include pasta and filled baguettes.

Melville's (☎ *472268, 4 Melville Terrace*) Bar meals from £4.75. Melville's, the restaurant at the Terraces Hotel, is popular with locals; haggis, neeps and tatties costs £5.50.

East India Company (☎ *471330, 7 Viewfield Place*) Mains around £6-10. The East India Company is a reasonable Indian restaurant and takeaway, with a cheaper balti bar upstairs.

Das (☎ *472137, 16-18 Barnton St*) Daily buffet £5.99. Das is the best Indian/Punjabi restaurant in Stirling.

Barnton Bar & Bistro (☎ *461698, 3½ Barnton St*) Soup & snacks £1.65-4.95. Open daily until late. Opposite the post office, this is a very popular student and hosteller hang-out serving excellent all-day breakfasts. It's a great place to eat or drink, with large servings of good food, but it can get rather smoky.

The Imperial (☎ *474327, 18 King St*) 2-course business lunch £4.60, buffet dinner Sun-Fri £13.50. The centrally located Imperial offers Cantonese cuisine.

Paco's (☎ *466414, 21-23 Dumbarton Rd*) Fajitas around £8.50. You'll get excellent Tex-Mex food in popular Paco's.

Italia Nostra (☎ *473208, 25 Baker St*) Pizza from £5.20. The Nostra is a busy Italian place that also does takeaways.

Darnley Coffee House (☎ *474468, 18 Bow St*) Just down the hill from the castle, beyond the end of Broad St, Darnley Coffee House is a conveniently located pit stop for home baking and speciality coffees as you walk around the old town.

You'll find shops selling groceries in the Thistle Shopping Centre and surrounding streets.

Entertainment

The town puts on an entertaining programme of events in summer, including Wednesday evening ceilidhs at the Golden Lion Hotel, King St, and pipe bands on the castle esplanade on Tuesday. There are also 'living history' plays performed in and around the castle.

Terraces Hotel (☎ *472268, 4 Melville Terrace*) There's live folk music here every Monday evening.

The Hogshead (☎ *448722, 2 Baker St*) The Hogshead is a traditional pub with great food and real ales.

The Portcullis (☎ *472290, Castle Wynd*) This is the best pub in Stirling. You'll find it just below the castle, and excellent bar meals are served all day. There's a large range of malt whiskies, too.

Whistlebinkies (☎ *451256, 75 St Mary's Wynd*) This pub, farther down the hill, has live folk music every Sunday evening.

Settle Inn (☎ *474609, 91 St Mary's Wynd*) Established in 1733, the Settle Inn is the oldest pub in Stirling and is very popular.

The Fubar (☎ *472619, 6 Maxwell Place*) The Fubar is a pub that transforms into a disco for people aged 17 to 21 on Friday and Saturday evenings.

The *Barnton Bar & Bistro* (see Places to Eat) is another popular place for a drink.

Getting There & Away

Stirling is 26 miles (42km) north-east of Glasgow and 35 miles (56km) from Edinburgh.

Bus Scottish Citylink (☎ 0870 550 5050) runs hourly buses to/from Glasgow (£3.60, 40 minutes). Some buses continue to Aberdeen via Perth and Dundee; others go to Inverness. Stirling to Aberdeen costs £14 and takes 3½ hours; you may need to change at Perth or Dundee. Buses from Stirling to Inverness (£11.80) take 3¾ hours and you'll usually have to change at Perth. A twice-daily service runs from Edinburgh to Fort William via Stirling (with connections to Oban or Skye); fares to Edinburgh, Oban, Fort William, and Portree are £6.20, £12.40, £12.90 and £22 respectively.

First Edinburgh (01324-613777) runs local buses (to Callander, Aberfoyle, and so on) and the hourly buses to Edinburgh (£4.35, two hours).

Train ScotRail (☎ 0845 748 4950) runs services to Edinburgh (£5.10, 50 minutes) twice an hour most of the day from Monday to Saturday, and hourly Sunday. There are twice-hourly services from Glasgow (£4.30, 40 minutes, every two hours or so on Sunday) and regular services to Perth (£4.90 cheap day return, 35 minutes), Dundee (£11.60, one hour) and Aberdeen (£28, 2¼ hours).

Getting Around

It's easy enough to walk around the central part of the town. From the train station to the castle is about three-quarters of a mile (1.2km).

Bus The open-top bus is the best bus for the sights in and around Stirling – see the earlier Organised Tours section for more information. Ask the driver if single fares are available.

Car If you want to drive yourself around, you can hire a car from Arnold Clark (☎ 478686), Kerse Rd. The cheapest deal is for a Fiat Seicento at £18 per day.

AROUND STIRLING
Bridge of Allan
☎ 01786 • pop 4607

This former spa town, just 2½ miles (4km) north of Stirling, is a pleasant place to visit. Stirling University's extensive modern campus is to the west of the town.

Things to See The old **Victorian bath-houses** on Mine Rd, built in 1861, have been turned into an upmarket restaurant. One of the most intriguing structures in the town is the **ornamental clock** in the main thoroughfare, Henderson St. The **Holy Trinity Church** (*☎ 834155, 12 Keir St; admission free; open 10am-4pm Sat June-Sept*) dates from 1860 and is noted for its stained glass windows, unusual roof structure and Charles Rennie Mackintosh designs.

The glass studio **Village Glass** (*☎ 832137, 14 Henderson St; admission free; open 9am-5pm Mon-Fri, 10am-5pm Sat*) sells unusual glassware gifts costing from £2 to £50; realistic-looking glass sweets are £2 each and solid glass writing pens cost £17.95. You can also watch the glassblowers at work on weekdays and on Saturday mornings, so you'll appreciate the skill that goes into making the products.

At the **Bridge of Allan Brewery** (*☎ 834555, Queen's Lane; admission free; open 10am-5pm daily*), just off Henderson St, you can learn about the micro-brewing techniques behind traditional Scottish ales. Free tasting is offered.

Places to Stay & Eat There are plenty of B&Bs in the £15 to £25 price range.

Mrs Skerry's (*☎ 832178, 7 Mayne Avenue*) Singles £15-18, doubles £32-40. This comfortable B&B in a quiet area has some rooms with private bathroom.

Anam Cara (*☎/fax 832030, 107 Henderson St*) Singles/doubles with shared bathroom £20/40. Anam Cara offers pleasant B&B in a converted traditional Victorian home.

Benmore (*☎ 833018, 8 Fountain Rd*) B&B £16-22 per person. There are three rooms (one en suite) at the recommended Benmore. There are vegetarian breakfasts on offer too.

Sunnylaw House (*☎ 833429, 1 Upper Glen Rd*) Singles with bathroom £20-25, doubles £40. Evening meals are available for £12 at this pleasant 19th-century house.

Queen's Hotel (*☎ 833268, 24 Henderson St*) Room rates on application. A superb example of modern design, this hotel will offer overnight accommodation from 2002. Soup and snacks are available in the bar and a la carte prices in the restaurant range from £9.95 to £22.50.

Royal Hotel (*☎ 832284, fax 834377, 55 Henderson St*) Singles/doubles £85/130. This place has pleasant en-suite rooms. Bar meals cost £4.95 to £14.50 and a three course table d'hôte dinner in the recommended restaurant costs £22.50.

Bayne's Bakery (*27 Henderson St*) This is just the place for pastries, buns and pies.

Coffee Pot (*☎ 834998, 33 Henderson St*) Baked potatoes (£3.50 to £4), soup and other snacks are available here.

Allan Water Café (*☎ 833060, 15 Henderson St*) Justifiably famous for its huge portions – home-made soup and a roll is only £1.60 and a large haddock and chips costs £7.90.

Getting There & Away You can walk to Bridge of Allan from Stirling in just over an hour. Local buses stop in Henderson St. Trains to Dunblane, Stirling, Glasgow and Edinburgh depart frequently from the station at the western end of Henderson St. For Stirling, you'll pay £1.10 each way.

Dunblane
☎ 01786 • pop 7200

The name Dunblane will for many years be associated with the horrific massacre that took place in the primary school in March 1996. Five miles (8km) north of Stirling the town straddles the banks of the Allan Water.

It was founded in 602 by St Blane, who lived in a beehive cell at the nearby old *dun* (fort). There's a friendly seasonal TIC (*☎ 824428*) on Stirling Rd.

Things to See The main attraction is **Dunblane Cathedral** (*☎ 823388, Cathedral*

Square; admission free; open 9.30am-6pm Mon-Sat & 1pm-6pm Sun Apr-Sept & 9.30am-4pm Mon-Sat, 2pm-4pm Sun Oct-Mar, possibly closed Thur afternoon and Fri), which is a superb, elegant, sandstone building – a fine example of Gothic style. The lower parts of the walls date from Norman times, the rest is mainly 13th to 15th century. The roof of the nave collapsed in the 16th century; however the cathedral was saved from ruin by a major restoration project in the 1890s.

The fine **cathedral museum** (☎ 823440, Cathedral Square; admission free; open 10am-12.30pm & 2pm-4.30pm Mon-Sat May to early Oct) includes barrel-vaulted rooms dating from 1624 and relates the history of both cathedral and town. Look out for the display of beggar's badges, and the 4000-year-old necklace, found in a nearby Bronze Age grave in 1999.

The **Leighton Library** (☎ 822296, Cathedral Square; admission free; open 10am-noon & 2pm-4pm Tues, Thur & Fri early May to early Oct) is the oldest private library in Scotland and dates from 1684. There are 4500 books in 90 languages.

Places to Stay & Eat Accommodation in Dunblane isn't particularly cheap and you have better choices in Stirling or Bridge of Allan. B&Bs include *Westwood* (☎ 822579, fax 825929, Doune Rd), which has singles/doubles from £30/40, and the luxurious *Rokeby House* (☎ 824447, fax 821399, Doune Rd), with en-suite B&B singles from £65 to £75 and doubles from £90 to £110.

Stirling Arms (☎ 822156, Stirling Rd) Singles/doubles from £40/60. The Stirling Arms has rooms with or without a private bathroom. Its excellent oak-panelled restaurant has a Scottish and international menu (mains £4.35 to £14.95) and serves the best food in town.

Dunblane Hotel (☎ 822178, 10 Stirling Rd) Mains £4.95-8.95. Meals here are fairly reasonable.

Village Bar & Bistro (☎ 825881, 5 Stirling Rd) Mains £4-4.50. This place is just across the street from the Dunblane Hotel.

There's a wide range of takeaway outlets, including Chinese, fish and chips, and a pizzeria. One of the nicest places in town is

the friendly *Choices Delicatessen & Coffee Shop* (☎ 822716, 21 High St), where you can get light meals, soup and snacks.

Shopping Scottish landscape artist Ian McNab sells his work at *Ian McNab* (☎ 0141-638 3072, 62 High St). His excellent paintings cost from £200 to £1200, but cheaper framed prints are available from £15 to £125. McNab's is open between 11am and 5pm daily except Wednesday and Sunday.

Getting There & Away You can walk to Bridge of Allan from Dunblane along Darn Rd, an ancient path used by monks, in about an hour. Alternatively, there are local buses from Stirling. Scottish Citylink buses run to Stirling, Glasgow, Perth and so on, once every hour or two, stopping at the police station on Perth Rd (near the TIC and cathedral). Trains to Stirling (£1.90), and Glasgow or Edinburgh, are more frequent – roughly three per hour, fewer on Sunday.

Doune
☎ 01786 • pop 1212
Seven miles (11km) north-west of Stirling, Doune is now a quiet, rural town. In former times it was known for its drover's market, and was also famous as a centre for the manufacture of sporrans and pistols.

Things to See The main street is dominated by a red sandstone church and tower, and there are some interesting houses in George St, just downhill from the Mercat Cross.

Doune Castle (HS; ☎ 841742, Castle Rd; adult/student/child £2.50/1.90/1; open standard HS hours, although closed Thur afternoon, Fri & Sun morning Oct-Mar) is one of the best preserved 14th-century castles in Scotland, having remained largely unchanged since it was built for the duke of Albany. It was a favourite royal hunting lodge, but was also of great strategic importance because it controlled the route between the Lowlands and Highlands, and Mary Queen of Scots stayed here. The inner hall was restored in 1883. There are great views from

CENTRAL & NE SCOTLAND

the castle walls, and the lofty gatehouse is very impressive, rising nearly 30m. The castle appeared in the film *Monty Python & the Holy Grail*.

Two miles (3km) south of Doune (by the A84, towards Stirling), there's the **Blair Drummond Safari Park** (☎ 841456, Blair Drummond; adult/child £8.50/4.50, covers most attractions; open 10am-5.30pm daily late Mar-early Oct, last admission 4.30pm), with a collection of African and other animals. A safari bus is available for visitors without suitable transport. There's a restaurant in the park.

Places to Stay & Eat *Red Lion Hotel* (☎ 842066, Balkerach St) B&B £18-20 per person. Sleep and eat under the same roof at this place, which dates from 1692 and has three rooms. The bar meals are fairly good (£4.25 to £9.95).

There's a *Life Style* supermarket in Balkerach St.

Getting There & Away First Edinburgh buses run every hour or two to Doune from Stirling (£2.40, 27 minutes), via Blair Drummond (less frequent on Sunday).

THE CAMPSIES & STRATHBLANE

The Campsie Fells, commonly called the Campsies, reach nearly 600m (1968 feet) and lie about 10 miles (16km) north of Glasgow. The plain of the River Forth lies to the north; Strathblane and Loch Lomond lie to the west.

One of several villages around the Campsies, attractive **Killearn** is known for its 31m-high obelisk, raised in honour of George Buchanan, James VI's tutor. Eight miles (13km) to the east, **Fintry** is another pretty village, on the banks of the Endrick Water, which has an impressive 28m waterfall, the **Loup of Fintry**. Six miles (10km) north of Fintry, **Kippen** has a very attractive **parish church** (admission free; open 9.30am-5pm daily). In the west, nearer to Loch Lomond and lying on the West Highland Way, is **Drymen**, also with lots of character. The TIC in Drymen Library (☎ 01360-660068), The Square, opens May to September.

Walking

One of the best walks in the area is the ascent of spectacular Dumgoyne hill (427m), from Glengoyne distillery, about 2 miles (3km) south of Killearn. Walk up the track that heads uphill from the A81, about 100m north of the distillery. You'll pass through trees; go through the gate on the right and head through the field for the gap between two blocks of trees. A steep path beyond this leads up towards the rocky summit of this eroded volcanic remnant (easier on its north and west sides). It's possible to continue, with easier walking, to the highest point on the Campsies, Earl's Seat (578m). Allow at least one hour for the ascent of Dumgoyne. It will take another hour to Earl's Seat, and 1½ hours to return from there to the distillery.

Just on the other side of Strathblane there's The Whangie, an impressive rock formation on the side of Auchineden Hill. A good path leads to the rocks from Queen's View car park on the A809 Glasgow (Bearsden) to Drymen road; it takes about 45 minutes to hike each way.

Places to Stay & Eat

Jaw Farm (☎ 01360-860498, Denny Rd) B&B singles £25, doubles £40-45. Located about a mile (1.6km) east of Fintry, this excellent B&B has three en-suite rooms.

Clachan Hotel (☎ 01360-860237, Denny Rd) Doubles £48-52. This 17th-century former drovers' hostel, situated by Fintry church on the Lennoxtown road, serves bar meals.

Coffee Pot (☎ 01360-860226, 30 Main St) In Fintry village, you'll find the Coffee Pot which serves home baking and lunches daily.

In Drymen, there's a good choice of B&Bs and hotels.

Mrs Lander's (☎ 01360-660273, 17 Stirling Rd) Singles £18-25, doubles £32-40. This reasonable Drymen B&B will be quite secure as Mrs Lander's husband is an inventor of burglar alarms!

Mrs Crooks (☎ 01360-660793, 13 Stirling Rd) Doubles £20-25 per person. Believe it or not, Mrs Crooks also does B&B. There are two comfortable bedrooms and a welcoming open fire in the lounge.

Buchanan Arms (☎ *01360-660588, fax 660943, Main St, Drymen)* Singles from £38, doubles £38-65. The top hotel in the village is the Buchanan Arms with en-suite rooms, and a sport and leisure club with swimming pool, sauna and so on.

Clachan Inn (☎ *01360-660824, The Square)* Mains £4.50-14.25. The best place to eat in the area is the Clachan Inn, Scotland's oldest registered inn (opened in 1734). The extensive menu includes steaks, burgers, salads and vegetarian choices. Try the fillet steak stuffed with haggis for £14.25.

You'll find a *Spar* supermarket and the *Drymen Tandoori* on The Square.

Getting There & Away

First Edinburgh runs up to five buses daily from Glasgow to Drymen (£3) via Queen's View (The Whangie). The No 10 bus from Glasgow to Stirling goes via Dumgoyne and Balfron every hour or two; connect for Aberfoyle (£4.60 from Glasgow) at Balfron. A postbus (☎ 01246-546329) runs twice on weekdays between Balfron and Fintry, once on Saturday.

THE TROSSACHS

The narrow glen between Loch Katrine and Loch Achray is named the Trossachs, but it's now used to describe a wider scenic area round the southern border of the Highlands. The Loch Lomond and the Trossachs National Park should be open by the time you read this.

As all the tourist literature repeatedly informs you, this is Rob Roy country. Rob Roy Macgregor (1671–1734) was the wild leader of one of the wildest of Scotland's clans, Clan Gregor. Although he claimed direct descent from a 10th-century king of Scots and rights to the lands the clan occupied, these Macgregor lands stood between powerful neighbours. Rob Roy became notorious for his daring raids into the Lowlands to carry off cattle and sheep, but these escapades led to the outlawing of the clan – hence his sobriquet, 'Children of the Mist'. He also achieved a reputation as a champion of the poor. Rob Roy is buried in the churchyard at Balquhidder, by Loch Voil.

Actor Liam Neeson was just the most recent of Rob Roy's popularists – Sir Walter Scott's historical novel *Rob Roy* brought tourists to the region in the 19th century. Loch Katrine was the inspiration for Scott's *Lady of the Lake* and, since the early 20th century, the SS *Sir Walter Scott* has been taking visitors cruising on the loch. The main centres in the area are Aberfoyle and Callander. During the summer months, the Trossachs Trundler bus links these two places with Loch Katrine.

Aberfoyle
☎ 01877 • pop 600

Known as the southern gateway to the Trossachs, Aberfoyle is on the eastern edge of the Queen Elizabeth Forest Park (part of the proposed Loch Lomond and the Trossachs National Park), which stretches across to the hills beside Loch Lomond. The village makes a good base for walks and cycle rides in the area, but it can be very busy with tourists in summer.

Three miles (5km) east is one of Scotland's two lakes, the Lake of Menteith. A ferry takes visitors from Port of Menteith village (on the lake) to the substantial ruins of **Inchmahome Priory** (☎ *385294, Inchmahome Island; adult/child £3.30/1.20, including ferry; open 9.30am-5.15pm daily Apr-Sept).* Mary Queen of Scots was kept safe here as a child, during Henry VIII's 'Rough Wooing'.

The TIC (☎ 382352), Main St, opens April to October. About half a mile (800m) north of Aberfoyle, on the A821, is the **Queen Elizabeth Forest Park Visitors Centre** (☎ *382258; admission free, car parking £1; open 10am-6pm Mar-Christmas),* which has audio-visual displays, exhibitions, and information about the numerous walks and cycle routes in and around the park.

Walking & Cycling Waymarked trails start from the visitor centre on the hills above the town; the TIC has a booklet for £1.

There's an excellent 20-mile (32km) circular cycle route that links with the ferry (☎ 376316) along Loch Katrine. From Aberfoyle, join the Glasgow–Killin Cycle Way on the forest trail, or take the A821 over Duke's Pass.

Following the southern shore of Loch Achray, you reach the pier on Loch Katrine; departures are at 11am Thursday to Tuesday from April to October. The ferry should drop you at Stronachlachar (£4/2.30 single), at the western end (note that afternoon sailings do not stop here). From Stronachlachar, follow the B829 via Loch Ard to Aberfoyle.

Places to Stay & Eat If you're keen to camp try *Cobleland Campsite (☎ 382392, Cobleland),* located off the A81, 2 miles (3km) south of Aberfoyle. It charges between £3.75 and £4.70, depending on the time of year.

In Aberfoyle there are very few B&Bs, but that may change when the national park opens.

Forth Inn (☎ 382372, fax 382488, Main St) Singles/doubles with attached bath £27.50/46. In the middle of the village, the Forth Inn has good bar meals (£4.95 to £5.95) available all day.

Old Coach House Inn (☎ 382822, Main St) B&B from £17.50 per person. There also fairly good bar meals and specials (from £4.75) available at this inn.

Covenanters Inn (☎ 382347, fax 382785) B&B £30-35 per person, dinner £13-15 extra. The pleasant Covenanters Inn has a great location on a hillock just south of the River Forth, only a short walk from Main St. Bar meals are available and there's regular live music.

For cheaper coffee and snacks on or just off Main St, try the *Coffee Shop (Main St),* with baked potatoes from £2.50 and a range of meals, or the *Scottish Wool Centre coffee shop.*

Getting There & Away First Edinburgh has up to four daily buses from Stirling (£3.40) and up to five connecting services per day from Glasgow (£4.60) via Balfron.

Royal Mail runs a postbus (☎ 01246-546329) on weekday afternoons from Aberfoyle to Callander via Port of Menteith (30 minutes). Another postbus does a round trip, Monday to Saturday, from Aberfoyle to

Inversnaid on Loch Lomond, giving access to the West Highland Way. The Trossachs Trundler (☎ 01786-442707) has a day ticket that includes Aberfoyle, Callander, Port of Menteith and Stirling for £8/5 adult/child.

Getting Around Bicycles can be hired from Trossachs Cycle Hire (☎ 382614) at the Trossachs Holiday Park for £7.50/12 for a half/full day.

Callander
☎ 01877 • pop 3000

Fourteen miles (22km) north-west of Stirling, Callander is a tourist town that bills itself as the eastern gateway to the Trossachs. It has been pulling in the tourists for over 150 years, and tartan and fudge shops now line the long high street.

Callander is on the eastern edge of the proposed Loch Lomond and the Trossachs National Park.

There are two post offices, one just off the western end of the main street, the other about half a mile to the east. The police station is at the end of Church St, by the River Teith.

The **Rob Roy and Trossachs Visitor Centre** *(☎ 330342, Ancaster Square; free admission to TIC, adult/child £3.25/2.25 for the audiovisual Rob Roy show; open 10am-4.15pm daily Mar-Dec),* in an old church contains the helpful TIC, which is also open at weekends in January and February.

There's a **swimming pool** (£2/1) and **climbing wall** (£3/2) in the **McLaren Community Leisure Centre** (☎ 330000).

You'll find two banks near the TIC and the Health Clinic (☎ 331001) is at 4 Bracklinn Rd.

Walking The impressive Bracklinn Falls are reached by track and footpath from Bracklinn Rd (30 minutes each way from the car park). Also off Bracklinn Rd, a woodland trail leads up to Callander Crag, with great views over the surroundings; round trip takes 1½ hours.

Places to Stay & Eat *Keltie Bridge Caravan Park (☎ 330606, fax 330075)* Tent

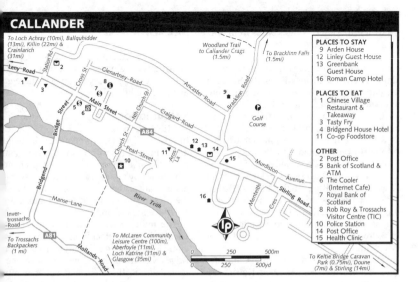

CALLANDER

To Loch Achray (10mi), Balquhidder (13mi), Killin (22mi) & Crainlarich (31mi)

Leny Road

Station Rd

Cross St

Glenartney Road

Main Street

Bridge Street

Church St.

Pearl Street

Bridgend

Manse Lane

River Teith

Invertrossachs Road

To Trossachs Backpackers (1 mi)

A81

Mollands Road

To McLaren Community Leisure Centre (100m), Aberfoyle (11mi), Loch Katrine (31mi) & Glasgow (35mi)

Woodland Trail to Callander Crags (1.5mi)

Ancaster Road

Craigard Road

Bracklinn Road

To Bracklinn Falls (1.5mi)

Golf Course

A84

Aros La.

Murdiston Avenue

Menteith Cres

Stirling Road

To Keltie Bridge Caravan Park (0.75mi), Doune (7mi) & Stirling (14mi)

0   250   500m
0   250   500yd

PLACES TO STAY
9 Arden House
12 Linley Guest House
13 Greenbank Guest House
16 Roman Camp Hotel

PLACES TO EAT
1 Chinese Village Restaurant & Takeaway
3 Tasty Fry
4 Bridgend House Hotel
11 Co-op Foodstore

OTHER
2 Post Office
5 Bank of Scotland & ATM
6 The Cooler (Internet Cafe)
7 Royal Bank of Scotland
8 Rob Roy & Trossachs Visitor Centre (TIC)
10 Police Station
14 Post Office
15 Health Clinic

from £6. Open Apr-Oct. This camp site, at the eastern end of Callander and just off the A84, has good facilities.

Trossachs Backpackers (☎/fax 331200, e mark@scottish-hostel.co.uk, Invertrossachs Rd) Dorm beds £10-15, including breakfast. Trossachs Backpackers is about a mile along Invertrossachs Rd, which runs on the southern side of the river draining Loch Vennachar. Bike rental is available.

Greenbank Guest House (☎ 330296, 143 Main St) Singles/doubles £15/30. This is a good-value B&B.

Linley Guest House (☎ 330087, 139 Main St) B&B from £16-19.50 per person. The Linley is a comfortable well-equipped guesthouse.

Arden House (☎/fax 330235, Bracklinn Rd) B&B £25-30 per person. Arden House is just north of Main St. It's an excellent place to stay and it was used as the setting for the TV series *Doctor Finlay's Casebook*.

Roman Camp Hotel (☎ 330003, fax 331533) B&B £55-135 per person. In a beautiful location by the River Teith, the Roman Camp Hotel dates from 1625. There's an excellent restaurant (reservations required; five-course dinner £35, a la carte

mains £20) and even a tiny chapel for weddings.

Bridgend House Hotel (☎ 330130, fax 331512, Bridgend) B&B £19.50-37.50 per person. Mock-Tudor Bridgend House Hotel, across the river and by the A81 Aberfoyle road, serves good Scottish-style bar meals (£4.95 to £13.45) and has four rooms with attached bathrooms.

Tasty Fry (6 Main St) This is Callander's best fish and chip shop (£3.50).

Chinese Village Restaurant & Takeaway (☎ 331221, 10 Leny Rd) Takeaways £4.70-11.80. You'll get a good meal at this recommended Chinese restaurant.

Along Main St, you'll find a *Co-op* foodstore and lots of places offering meals and snacks for under £5.

Entertainment On Monday, Wednesday and Friday evenings in July and August, the TIC (☎ 330342) organises Scottish evenings, with fiddlers (£3.50/3). The Callander Pipe Band plays outside the TIC from 8pm on Wednesday, late-June to early September (free). The cinema at the TIC shows classic and recent Scottish films on Thursday in summer (£2/1.50).

Getting There & Away First Edinburgh (☎ 01324-613777) operates buses from Stirling (£2.90, 45 minutes, hourly Monday to Saturday) and Killin (£3.40, 45 minutes, six daily Monday to Friday, three daily Saturday). There's also a twice-daily Scottish Citylink bus (☎ 0870 550 5050) from Callander to Edinburgh (£8.10) and Fort William (£11.80) via Crianlarich, with connections to Oban and Skye.

Royal Mail runs a postbus (☎ 01246-546329) from Callander to Trossachs Pier. It departs at 9.15am Monday to Saturday, and links with the 11am weekday (except Wednesday) sailing of the SS *Sir Walter Scott* on Loch Katrine (see the following Loch Katrine section). On weekday afternoons, the postbus runs from Callander to Aberfoyle (one hour) and returns via Port of Menteith.

The Trossachs Trundler calls at Callander and reaches the pier on Loch Katrine 26 minutes later.

Loch Katrine & Loch Achray

This rugged area, 6 miles (10km) north of Aberfoyle and 10 miles (16km) west of Callander, is the heart of the Trossachs and the proposed national park. From April to October, the SS *Sir Walter Scott* (☎ 01877-376316) sails along Loch Katrine from Trossachs Pier at the eastern tip of the loch (return tickets from £6/3.80).

Walking There are two good walks starting from Loch Achray. The path to the rocky cone called Ben A'an (460m) begins at a car park near the old Trossachs Hotel (now a timeshare development). It's easy to follow but you'll need over an hour to get to the top.

On the other side of the Trossachs lies rugged Ben Venue (727m); there's a path all the way to the summit. Start walking from Loch Achray Hotel, follow the Achray Water westwards to Loch Katrine, then turn left and ascend the steep flanks of Ben Venue. There are great views of both the Highlands and the Lowlands from the top. Allow four to five hours for the round trip.

BALQUHIDDER & BREADALBANE

This mountainous and sparsely populated area in the northern part of the Stirling administrative region has only a few villages but it's steeped in clan history and there are lots of good hillwalks.

Balquhidder

☎ 01567 • pop 50

In this small village (pronounced balwhidder), 2 miles (3km) off the main A84 Callander to Crianlarich road, there's a churchyard with **Rob Roy's grave**. His wife and two of his sons are also interred here. In the church there's the 8th-century **St Angus' stone** and a 17th-century church bell.

The minor road continues along pretty **Loch Voil** to Inverlochlarig, where you can climb **Stob Binnein** (1165m) by its southern ridge. Stob Binnein is one of the highest mountains in the area, and it has a most unusual shape: like a cone with its top chopped off.

Places to Stay & Eat *Balquhidder Brae Caravan Park* (☎ 01567-830293, Balquhidder Station) Tents £8-10. There are good facilities here but it's a little overpriced.

Kings House Hotel (☎ 01877-384646, fax 384716, Balquhidder) Singles/doubles £25/50, dinner £12. At the junction with the A84, this hotel was built in 1779 for £40, at the request of the drovers. Nowadays, it offers B&B in more salubrious surroundings. There are bar meals (£3.25 to £8.60) available, with some good vegetarian choices plus dinner for £12.

Golden Larches (☎ 01567-830262, Balquhidder Station) Mains £6-11.35. About a mile (1.6km) north on the A84 at the old Balquhidder train station, this pleasant restaurant has a cheery atmosphere and good Scottish menu.

Getting There & Away First Edinburgh buses between Callander and Killin stop at the Kings House Hotel. On weekdays, postbus (☎ 01246-546329) operates from Killin to Callander (running from Crianlarich and Tyndrum, via Killin, on Saturday); it also stops at the Kings House Hotel. The twice daily Scottish Citylink bus from Edinburgh to Fort William also stops here.

Crianlarich & Tyndrum
☎ 01838 • combined pop 350

These villages are little more than service junctions on the main A82 road, although they're both in good hiking country and on the West Highland Way, just north of the proposed Loch Lomond and the Trossachs National Park. At Crianlarich, there's a train station; tiny Tyndrum, just 5 miles (8km) along the road, is blessed with two stations and a useful new TIC (☎ 400246), open daily April to November.

Tyndrum attracted attention some years ago after the discovery of gold-bearing rock in the hills, but commercial exploitation was not deemed worthwhile.

Walking The West Highland Way can be walked at any time of year.

In summer, hillwalkers can climb the popular An Caisteal (995m). Start at the lay-by near Keilator farm, 1½ miles (2.5km) south of Crianlarich on the A82; a boggy path leads through a tunnel under the railway to a footbridge over the River Falloch. Follow the track towards Coire Earb for about 10 minutes, then head uphill on your right (no path). After 1½ hours uphill, you'll join the northern ridge (Sròn Gharbh), which gives an easy and pleasant route to the top. Return the same way, or more easily via Stob Glas and Derrydarroch farm. Allow around five hours return and carry OS map No 50, a compass, and all appropriate high-level walking gear, food and drink.

Another popular climb is to the top of Ben More (1174m). This unrelenting ascent starts at Benmore Farm, 2 miles (3km) east of Crianlarich on the A85. A track zig-zags up the first 150m, then you should head directly up the north-west shoulder. There are wonderful views from the summit. The authors have had some interesting days up here, including a near miss from lightning! You'll need OS map No 51. Six hours should see you up and down, returning the same way.

The best walk in the Tyndrum area is to the top of magnificent Ben Lui (1130m). If you're fit, you can include Beinn Dubhchraig (978m) and Ben Oss (1029m). Use OS map No 50 to plan your route.

Start from Tyndrum Lower station, follow the track to Cononish farm, then keep to the riverbank as far as Coire Laoigh, between Ben Lui and Ben Oss. The southeastern ridge is straightforward all the way to the top. Descend the same way, and allow seven hours (for Ben Lui alone). There are several other routes on the mountain, including the excellent north-eastern ridge, which, in hard winter conditions, should be climbed with ice-axe and crampons.

Places to Stay & Eat *Crianlarich Youth Hostel (☎ 300260, Station Rd)* Dorm beds from £9.25/6. Open mid-Feb to Oct. This well-equipped hostel, located near Crianlarich Station, is the best budget option (B&BS tend to be expensive in Crianlarich).

Craigbank Guest House (☎ 300279, Crianlarich) Singles/doubles £20/36. Craigbank is by the A85 and is reasonably priced and friendly.

Ben More Lodge Hotel (☎ 300210, fax 300218, Crianlarich) Singles £31-40, doubles £52-64. A little farther east on the Glen Dochart road (A85), this place has snacks and sandwiches starting from £2.10, bar meals (from £4.95) and a full-blown three-course table d'hôte dinner for £16.

Rod & Reel (☎ 300271, Crianlarich) Bar meals £5.10-11.20. The Rod & Reel, by the A85 towards Killin, also serves snacks and baked potatoes (from £3.70). It has a cheaper takeaway service with fish and chips for £3.10 and burgers for £2.85. Packed lunches for hungry walkers cost £2.75.

The *Mace* supermarket, on Station Rd, is home to Crianlarich's post office

Auchtertyre Farm (☎ 400251, fax 400248, Tyndrum) Wigwam £9 per person, camping £3 per person. This place, 3 miles (5km) from Crianlarich (and 2 miles/3km from Tyndrum), is off the A82 and has 16 five-bed heated wigwams. It also has camping with access to all facilities.

CENTRAL & NE SCOTLAND

Pine Trees Leisure Park (☎ *400243, Tyndrum*) Camping £3.50 per person, bunkhouse £8.50 per person. The bunkhouse here doesn't have kitchen facilities. You can also go swimming on in the park (£2 per hour).

West Highlander Restaurant (☎ *400314, Tyndrum*) Breakfast from £2.75. Mains £4.25-6.50. The food at this place, attached to Pine Trees Leisure Park, is rather good; soup and a roll is £1.95.

Self-caterers can stock-up at *Brodie's*, Tyndrum's grocer's and post office.

Getting There & Away Scottish Citylink runs several buses daily to Glasgow, Oban, Fort William and Skye from both villages.

A postbus service (☎ 01246-546329) links Crianlarich, Tyndrum and Killin twice on each weekday (with connections to Callander) and once on Saturday. On Saturday, the postbus makes a return trip to Callander (1½ hours).

ScotRail (☎ 0845 748 4950) runs train services from both villages to Fort William, Oban and Glasgow. Journey times and fares from Crianlarich are 1¾ hours (£12.50), one hour (£7.40), and 1¾ hours (£11.40) respectively.

Killin
☎ 01567 • pop 700

At the western end of Loch Tay, Killin is a pleasant albeit rather touristy village. It makes a good base for exploring the spectacular hills and glens of the surrounding area.

Information The TIC (☎ 820254) is in the Breadalbane Folklore Centre (see the following Things to See section), by the River Dochart. It opens 10am to 5pm daily March to October (with longer hours from June to September).

Killin hosts an annual Highland games (entry £3), usually in early August. There's also a folk festival, in mid-June, with free session bands in pubs. Phone ☎ 820224 for details of these events.

The Outdoor Centre (☎ 820652), Main St, is a shop that sells and hires all sorts of equipment, including canoes (£30 per day) and mountain bikes (£15/11 per day/ha day).

The village has a post office and a Bank of Scotland ATM, both on Main St.

Things to See Killin is a popular destination for tourists who come to see the pretty **Falls of Dochart**, in the centre of the village. The **Clan MacNab burial ground** lies on an island in the river, crossed by the main road and just downstream from the falls; ask the TIC for the gate key. The **Breadalbane Folklore Centre** (☎ *820254; adult/child £1.55/1.05; open 10am-5pm Mar-Oct, 10am-6pm daily June & Sept, 9.30am-6.30pm July & Aug*) is in an old watermill overlooking the falls. St Fillan, a 7th-century missionary preached on this site and his sacred healing stones are kept in the centre. There are also displays about local and clan history, including the MacGregors and MacNabs.

Nearly half a mile (800m) along the main street from the falls, by the Killin Hotel there's an unusual-looking **church** dating from 1744. Inside, there's a remarkable seven-sided font which is over 2000 years old.

One mile (1.6km) from Killin on the Glen Lochay road, **Moirlanich Longhouse** (*NTS; ☎ 820988, Glen Lochay; adult/child £1.50/1; open 2pm-5pm Wed & Sun May-Sept*) is an excellently restored example of a mid-19th century byre.

Walking & Cycling Killin is at the northern end of the cycle way from Glasgow (see Getting Around at the start of the Stirling section).

Seven miles (11km) north-east of Killin Ben Lawers (1214m) rises above Loch Tay. There's an NTS Visitor Centre here and trails lead to the summit (see West Perthshire in the Perth & Kinross section).

Glen Lochay runs westwards from Killin into the hills of Mamlorn. You can take a mountain bike for about 11 miles (18km) up the glen to just beyond Batavaime. The scenery is impressive and the hills aren't too difficult to climb. It's possible, on a nice summer day, to backpack over the top of Ben Challum (1025m) and descend to

Crianlarich, but it's very hard work. The passes on either side of this hill provide low-level alternatives. You'll need OS maps Nos 50 and 51, and allow two days from Killin to Crianlarich (wild camping is possible in upper Glen Lochay from 20 October to 12 August, if you're discreet).

Places to Stay & Eat *Shieling Accommodation* (*☎/fax 820334, Aberfeldy Rd*) Camping £3.50 (Apr-Oct), year-round chalets £150-550 per week. You'll find camping and luxurious wooden chalets in this pleasant woodland location just outside Killin.

Killin Youth Hostel (*☎ 820546, Lochay Rd*) Dorm beds from £8.75/6. Open Mar-Oct & winter weekends. The SYHA (Scottish Youth Hostel Association) hostel is at the northern end of the village. It's a large traditional building, but it has been modernised and is well equipped.

Falls O'Dochart Cottage (*☎ 820363, 1 Grey St*) B&B £16 per person. This B&B is by the falls. Dinner is available.

Fairview House (*☎ 820667, Main St*) En-suite singles £20-24, doubles £40-48. Fairview House is a large traditional villa with dinner for £14.

Coach House (*☎ 820349, Lochay Rd*) Rooms from £18 per person. Pub meals from £3.50. The Coach House serves great pub food, including curry and chilli dishes. Scottish folk bands play here in summer.

Falls of Dochart Inn (*☎ 820270, fax 820159, Falls of Dochart*) Rooms £20-25 per person. Bistro meals £4.95-10.75. This hotel overlooks the falls, and all rooms have attached bath. It's also a good place for a meal or a drink, with bistro/bar meals all day.

Tarmachan Teashop (*☎ 820387, Main St*) The Tarmachan Teashop does snacks, sandwiches and salads from £1.50 to £4.

You'll find supermarkets along Main St, including *Costcutter* and *Co-op*.

In the car park at the village hall, there's a van selling chicken and chips, burgers and so on.

Getting There & Away First Edinburgh runs buses Monday to Saturday from Stirling

(£4.75, 1¾ hours, six daily Monday to Friday, three Saturday) via Callander.

There's a postbus (*☎ 01246-546329*) between Killin and Callander on Saturday (one hour). This bus also runs to Crianlarich and Tyndrum, twice on weekdays and once on Saturday. A postbus runs along the pretty south Loch Tay road, as far as Ardtalnaig, then back to Killin (Monday to Saturday). There's no bus from Pitlochry to Killin, but there's a daily (except Sunday) postbus service between Aberfeldy and Killin (three hours to Killin, 1¾ hours to Aberfeldy).

Clackmannanshire

Although it's one of the smallest administrative districts in Scotland, Clackmannanshire has some significant places of interest.

DOLLAR
☎ 01259 • pop 4199

About 11 miles (18km) east of Stirling, in the foothills of the Ochil Hills that run north-east into Perth & Kinross, is the small town of Dollar. **Castle Campbell** (*HS; ☎ 742408, Dollar Glen; adult/student/child £2.80/2/1; open standard HS hours, although closed Thur afternoon, Fri & Sun mornings Oct-Mar*) is a 20-minute walk up **Dollar Glen**, into the wooded hills above the town. It's a spooky, old stronghold of the dukes of Argyll and stands between two ravines; you can clearly see why it was known as Castle Gloom. There's been a fortress of some kind on this site from the 11th century, but the present structure dates from the 15th century. The castle was sacked by Cromwell in 1654, but the tower is well preserved. You'll find a tearoom at the castle.

There are regular First Edinburgh (*☎ 01324-613777*) buses to Dollar from Stirling; other services run from Alloa (£1.30, every two hours Monday to Friday). From Kinross, the First Edinburgh bus No 204 runs three times daily on Wednesday and Friday only.

ALLOA
☎ 01259 • pop 11,384
Alloa is a large town 6 miles (10km) east of
Stirling. **Alloa Tower** *(☎ 211701, Alloa Park;*
adult/child £3/2; open 1.30pm-5.30pm daily
Apr-Sept & weekends in Oct, last admission
5pm) is a short, clearly signposted walk from
the town centre. The 24m-high tower dates
from before 1497 and it's one of the most
interesting NTS properties. The Italianate
staircase and dome are superb. There are also
a well and pit dungeon, furnishings and
paintings belonging to the Mar family. Views
from the parapet walk are spectacular.

First Edinburgh (☎ 01324-613777) runs
buses to Clackmannan, Dollar, Stirling and
Glasgow.

CLACKMANNAN
☎ 01259 • pop 3410
This village lies 2 miles (3km) south-east of
Alloa and has several interesting sights. In
Main St, the **Clackmannan stone** sits on top
of a large shaft – it's sacred to the pagan
deity Mannan and it clearly predates Christian times.

The adjacent 17th-century **Cross** is engraved with the Bruce coat of arms; the
lower part is heavily worn due to prisoners'
chains. Also adjacent is the **Tolbooth**, built
in 1592 for £284, which served as a court
and prison. **Clackmannan Tower**, uphill
from the church and about 450m from Main
St, was a residence of the Bruce family
from 1365 to 1772. The widow of the last
laird knighted Robert Burns in the tower,
with the sword of Robert the Bruce, in
1787. The five-storey tower has structural
problems due to subsidence and it isn't
open to the public, but it's well worth a
look.

First Edinburgh (☎ 01324-613777) bus
No 15 runs daily to Falkirk and Alloa from
Main St.

Falkirk Region

The little administrative district of Falkirk
covers the town of the same name, the heavily industrial town of Grangemouth, and
some interesting areas to the east, including
Bo'ness.

FALKIRK
☎ 01324 • pop 33,351
Downstream from Stirling, the southern
side of the River Forth is a heavily indus-
trialised, built-up area not exactly noted for
its scenic beauty, but there are interesting
historical buildings in the vicinity.

Falkirk is a large town about 10 miles
(16km) south-east of Stirling. The main
shopping street, High St, is pedestrianised.
There's a TIC (☎ 620244) nearby, at 2
Glebe St.

A mile (1.6km) east of the centre, and
only a 10-minute walk from the bus and
train stations, is the vast mansion **Callendar
House** *(☎ 503770, Callendar Park;*
adult/child £3/1; open 10am-5pm Mon-Sat
year-round & 2pm-5pm Sun Apr-Sept)
complete with turrets and extensive
grounds. Originally a 14th-century keep,
the building was greatly extended by a rich
18th-century merchant, William Forbes,
and his descendants. There are several exhibitions, galleries, a working Georgian
kitchen (where food is prepared) and a tea
shop.

First Edinburgh (☎ 613777) runs regular
buses to Stirling (£2.50) and Edinburgh
(£3.40). ScotRail (☎ 0845 748 4950) services go to Stirling, Dunblane, Perth, Glasgow (£4.40) and Edinburgh (£3.90) from
Falkirk Grahamston station. Glasgow-
Edinburgh express trains stop at Falkirk
High every 15 minutes.

DUNMORE PINEAPPLE
Built in 1761 and restored in the 1970s,
the Dunmore Pineapple *(☎ 01324-831137,*
Airth; admission free, view exterior only,
grounds open 9.30am-sunset) is surely one
of the oddest buildings you'll ever see. The
wacky story about the building is covered
by information plaques. It's located one
mile (1.6km) west of Airth village. First
Edinburgh (☎ 01324-613777) run hourly
buses (every two hours on Sunday) to Airth
from Falkirk (£2.05). Buses from Airth to
Stirling (£2.05) run on the same frequency.

BO'NESS & KINNEIL RAILWAY

The town of Bo'ness on the Firth of Forth is best known for the steam train that shuttles to-and-fro on the Bo'ness & Kinneil Railway (☎ 01506-822298, Bo'ness Station, Union St; £4.50/2 return; four departures weekends only Apr-Oct & Tues-Sun July & Aug). Tickets costing £7/3.50 include admission to the **Birkhill Fireclay Mine**, 130 steps down in the Avon gorge; guided tours run in conjunction with train arrivals. There's also a free **railway exhibition** at the station in Bo'ness.

Direct buses to Bo'ness from Glasgow, Edinburgh, Falkirk, Stirling and Linlithgow are run by First Edinburgh (☎ 01324-513777).

Fife

The Kingdom of Fife, as it calls itself – it was home to Scottish kings for 500 years – lies between the Firths of Forth and Tay. Despite its integration with the rest of Scotland, it has managed to maintain an individual Lowland identity quite separate from the rest of the country.

In the west, the Lomond Hills rise to over 500m; the eastern section is much flatter. Apart from a few exceptions inland, notably Falkland Palace, most attractions in Fife are around the coast. As far as visitors are concerned, the focus of the region is undoubtedly St Andrews – an ancient ecclesiastical centre and university town that's also world famous as the home of golf. To the south, along the coastline of the East Neuk, are picturesque fishing villages. This coast is pleasant walking country, and at Anstruther there's the interesting Scottish Fisheries Museum.

If you're driving from the Forth Road Bridge to St Andrews, a slower but much more scenic route than the M90/A91 is along the signposted Fife Tourist Route, via the coast. Fife Council has a public transport information line (☎ 01592-416000), open 9am to 4pm Monday to Friday, and produces a useful map-guide, *Getting Around Fife*, available from TICs. Trains are less useful in Fife than in some regions,

as the rails run inland away from the main attractions, and no longer reach as far as St Andrews; the nearest station is at Leuchars, 5 miles (8km) north of the town.

CULROSS

☎ 01383 • pop 460

Around the 17th century, Culross (koo-ross) was a busy little community trading in salt and coal. Now it's the best-preserved example of a Scottish burgh, and the NTS owns 20 of the buildings, including the palace, which it bought in 1932. It's a picturesque village with small red-tiled, white-washed buildings lining the cobbled streets, 12 miles (19km) west of the Forth Road Bridge.

Culross has a long history. As the birthplace of St Mungo, the patron saint of Glasgow, it was an important religious centre from the 6th century. The burgh developed as a trading centre under the businesslike laird George Bruce (a descendant of Robert the Bruce), whose mining techniques involved digging long tunnels under the sea to reach coal. A vigorous sea trade developed between Culross and the Forth ports and Holland. From the proceeds, Bruce built the palace, completed in 1611. When a storm flooded the tunnels and mining became impossible, the town switched to making linen and shoes.

You can visit **Culross Palace** (NTS; ☎ 880359; adult/child £5/4; open 10am-5pm daily June-Aug; 12.30pm-4.30pm daily Apr, May & Sept; 12.30pm-4.30pm Sat & Sun Oct), more a large house than a palace, which features extraordinary decorative, painted woodwork, barrel-vaulted ceilings, and an interior largely unchanged since the early 17th century. The **Town House** and the **Study** (same details as palace, admission included in palace ticket), also early 17th century, are open to the public but the other NTS properties can only be viewed from the outside. The NTS Visitor Centre, in the lower part of the Town House, has an exhibition on the history of Culross.

Ruined **Culross Abbey**, founded by the Cistercians in 1217, is on the hill; the choir of the abbey church is now the parish church. The pulpit is 17th century and originally had two levels. In the north-eastern corner of the north transept there's an unusual sight – statues of eight children kneeling in front of their parents' memorial.

St Mungo's Cottage (☎ *882102,* e *martin pjackson@hotmail.com, Low Causeway)* B&B £16-22 per person. If you need a place to stay, this 17th-century cottage has three attractive rooms.

The *NTS tearoom* is a good place for soup and a snack.

First Edinburgh (☎ 01324 613777) buses Nos 14 and 14A run hourly between Stirling and Dunfermline, stopping at Culross.

DUNFERMLINE
☎ 01383 • pop 52,000

Six Scottish kings, including Robert the Bruce, are buried at Dunfermline Abbey. Once the country's capital, Dunfermline is now a large regional centre surrounded by suburbs that are not particularly attractive, but the abbey is worth a visit and the pedestrianised High St has some interesting old buildings.

Information
The TIC (☎ 720999), 13 Maygate, is close to High St and the abbey, and opens 9.30am to 5.30pm Monday to Saturday year-round, plus 11am to 4pm Sunday April to October. There's also an all-year TIC (☎ 417759) about 5 miles (8km) from Dunfermline, in the Queensferry Lodge Hotel at the northern end of the Forth Road Bridge.

The post office is on Pilmuir St, and the bus station is nearby. You'll find banks with ATMs on High St.

Things to See
Queen Margaret founded a Benedictine priory on the hill here in the 11th century, and later her son King David I built **Dunfermline Abbey** *(HS;* ☎ *739026, St Margaret St; adult/child £2/75p; open 9.30am-6.30pm daily Apr-Sept; 9.30am-4.30pm Mon-Wed & Sat, 9.30am-1pm Thur & 2pm-4.30pm Sun Oct-Mar)* on the site. After Margaret's canonisation in 1250, the abbey grew into a major pilgrimage centre, eclipsing the island of Iona (off Mull) as the favourite royal burial ground. Most of the abbey, having fallen into ruins, has now been absorbed into the parish church, but the wonderful Norman nave, with its ornate columns, remains. Robert the Bruce is buried in the choir.

Next to the abbey are the ruins of **Dunfermline Palace** *(same details as abbey),* rebuilt from the abbey guesthouse in the 16th century for James VI. It was the birthplace of Charles I, the last Scottish king born on Scottish soil. The buildings are within walking distance of the train and bus stations.

The award-winning **Abbot House Heritage Centre** *(☎ 733266, Maygate; adult/ child £3/free; open 10am-5pm daily),* near the abbey, dates from the 15th century. Now restored, it has interesting displays about the history of Scotland, the abbey, and Dunfermline. There's also a coffee shop serving excellent home baking and snacks.

St Margaret's Cave *(☎ 313838, Chalmers St Car Park; admission free; open 11am-4pm daily Easter-Sept),* not far from the abbey and 80 steps down from the Bruce St car park, was used by Queen Margaret for prayer and meditation. It later became a shrine in her memory.

The most famous former inhabitant of Dunfermline is Andrew Carnegie, who was born in a weaver's cottage in 1835, now the **Andrew Carnegie Museum** *(☎ 724302, Moodie St; adult/child £2/free; open 11am-5pm Mon-Sat, 2pm-5pm Sun Apr-Oct).* He emigrated to America in 1848 and by the late 19th century had accumulated enormous wealth, $350 million of which he gave away. Dunfermline benefited by his purchase of Pittencrieff Park, beside the palace.

Four miles (8km) north of the town centre, just off the A823, the **Knockhill Racing Circuit** *(☎ 723337)* stages major car and motorcycle racing events between April and December, usually on Sunday. Admission prices are in the range £5 to £25.

Places to Stay & Eat
The Learig (☎ *729676, 2a Victoria St)* B&B £17-19 per person. This solid Victorian town house has two twin rooms and a family room; it's 500m north of High St, along Pilmuir St

Davaar House Hotel (☎ 721886, fax 23633, 126 Grieve St) B&B £35-50 per person. The Davaar is a Victorian villa, around 00m north-west of the abbey. The restaurant (closed Sunday) has good Scottish cuisine (a three-course meal costs around £15).

There's a *Safeway* supermarket and a *Bakers Oven* in the central Kingsgate shopping centre. The *snack bar* in the bus station has baked potatoes and toasties from £1.20. Nearby, on Carnegie Drive, there are several restaurants, a cafe, a fish and chip shop and a nightclub.

Getting There & Away
Dunfermline is a major transport hub, with frequent buses to Edinburgh (£6.10 return, 40 minutes), Dundee (£9.70, 1½ hours), Stirling, Perth and Kirkcaldy. There are half-hourly trains to Edinburgh (£6, 30 minutes) and Leuchars (for St Andrews; £7.40, one hour).

ABERDOUR
☎ 01383 • pop 1800
It's worth stopping in this popular seaside town to see *Aberdour Castle (HS; ☎ 860519; adult/child £2/75p, open 9.30am-6.30pm daily Apr-Sept, 9.30am-4.30pm Mon-Sat & 2pm-4.30pm Sun Oct-Mar)*. It was built by the Douglas family in 1342 and the original tower was extended by the Morton family in the 16th and 17th centuries. They abandoned the castle in 1725 after it was gutted by fire, but the eastern wing was rebuilt and is still in use. An impressive feature of the castle is its attractive walled garden, where there's a fine beehive-shaped 16th-century dovecote (pronounced doo-cot in Scotland). **St Fillan's Church**, by the castle, was founded in 1123 but the current building is mostly 17th century (restored in 1920).

Aberdour Hotel (☎ 860325, fax 860808, High St) B&B £25-29 per person. With real ales and good vegetarian choices on the menu, this is not only a good place to stay but the best place to eat in town (mains from £4.95).

The *Beach House Restaurant*, at the lovely Silver Sands beach, serves two-course lunches and coffee for £5.95.

Bus Nos 7, 7A and 79 leave every 30 minutes for Dunfermline and Kirkcaldy. Bus

No X59 runs once a day to Edinburgh. There are hourly trains for Kirkcaldy and Edinburgh.

KIRKCALDY
☎ 01592 • pop 49,570
Kirkcaldy (kir-kod-ay) sprawls along the edge of the sea for several miles. The political economist, Adam Smith, was born here and, in the second half of the 19th century, Kirkcaldy was the world's largest manufacturer of linoleum. It has an attractive promenade with spectacular pounding surf on windy days, and an interesting museum and art gallery.

The TIC (☎ 267775), just off High St at 19 Whytecauseway, opens year-round. The pedestrianised part of High St has the Mercat Cross Shopping Centre and banks with ATMs.

Things to See
Just a short walk from the train and bus stations, in the War Memorial Gardens, you'll find the **Kirkcaldy Museum and Art Gallery** *(☎ 412860, 50m east of the train station; admission free; open 10.30am-5pm Mon-Sat & 2pm-5pm Sun)*. As well as covering the town's history, there's an impressive collection of Scottish paintings from the 18th to 20th centuries and temporary exhibitions on a wide range of topics.

After looking round the museum, take a walk along the Esplanade to Ravenscraig Park, where ruinous **Ravenscraig Castle**, built in 1460 and one of the earliest castles to be defended by artillery, stands on a plinth of coloured sandstone.

Two miles (3km) north of Kirkcaldy, in Dysart, is the **John McDouall Stuart Museum** *(☎ 260732, Rectory Lane; admission free; open 2pm-5pm daily June-Aug)* the birthplace of the engineer and explorer who, in 1862, became the first person to cross Australia from the south to the north coast. Bus Nos K7 and K8 from Kirkcaldy centre pass this way twice every hour.

Places to Stay & Eat
The Bennochy Bank Guest House (☎ 200733, 26 Carlyle Rd) B&B £18-25 per

person. This comfortable B&B is close to the train station and museum.

Mintella *(☎ 593446, 38 Bennochy Rd)* B&B £16-18 per person. Mintella has four single and two twin rooms, and is only five minutes' walk from the train station.

Wheatsheaf Inn *(☎ 263564, 5 Tolbooth St)* Mains £2.95-4.95. Lunch noon-2.30pm. This pleasant pub, just off High St, does good value bar lunches. It's housed in the second oldest building in town.

Dunnikier House Hotel *(☎ 268393, Dunnikier Way)* Mains £5.95-14.95. Open noon-10pm. This refined hotel restaurant, which has won several awards, is the best place to eat in town.

There are also lots of places to eat, including the usual local bakers and Chinese and Indian takeaways, on High St.

Getting There & Away

Numerous buses run from Hill St bus station (☎ 642394), two blocks inland from the Esplanade. Destinations include St Andrews (one hour), Anstruther (one hour 10 minutes), Dunfermline (30 minutes) and Edinburgh (one hour).

Kirkcaldy is on the main railway line between Edinburgh (£4.80, 30 minutes) and Dundee (£8, 40 minutes); there are two to four trains an hour.

FALKLAND
☎ 01337 • pop 1120

Below the soft ridges of the Lomond Hills in the centre of Fife is the Royal Burgh of Falkland, an attractive conservation village surrounded by rich farmland. It's a very pleasant place to stay and it's famous for the superb 16th-century **Falkland Palace** *(NTS; ☎ 857397; adult/child £5/4; open 10am-5.30pm Mon-Sat & 1.30pm-5.30pm Sun Apr-Oct, last admission 4.30pm)*, a country residence of the Stuart monarchs.

Mary Queen of Scots is said to have spent the happiest days of her life 'playing the country girl in the woods and parks' at Falkland. Built between 1501 and 1541 to replace a castle dating from the 12th century, French and Scottish craftspeople were employed to create a masterpiece of Scottish

Gothic architecture. The king's bedchamber and the chapel, which has a beautiful painted ceiling, have both been restored; you can also look around the gardens and the keeper's apartments in the gatehouse.

The wild boar that the royals hunted, and the Fife forest that was their hunting ground, have now disappeared. One feature of this royal leisure centre still exists: the oldest royal tennis court in Britain, built in 1539 for James V, is in the grounds and still in use. Although the palace still belongs to the reigning monarch, it's administered by the NTS.

Walking

A narrow road runs from Falkland to Leslie over the pass between East and West Lomond. It takes about one hour to walk from Falkland to the pass, then a further 45 minutes or so on a good path to the 522m (1712 feet) summit of West Lomond. East Lomond (420m) is also accessible from the pass; the 2000-year-old hill fort at the top is now reduced to a series of ramparts. The views from the tops are wonderful on a clear day.

Places to Stay & Eat

Falkland Backpackers *(☎ 857710, Back Wynd)* Dorm beds £9-10. Open mid-Mar to early-Oct. This 30-bed independent hostel is basic but clean, comfy and friendly.

Templelands Farm *(☎ 857383)* B&B £15 per person. If the hostel is full, then you might find a room at this farm, ten minutes' walk south-east of the village on the lower slopes of East Lomond Hill.

Covenanter Hotel *(☎ 857224, fax 857163, The Square)* Singles/doubles £39/48. This 18th-century coaching inn, on the square opposite the palace, also has a good information bistro.

Kind Kyttock's Kitchen, just off the square on Cross Wynd, is a delightful tea room in a quaint 17th-century cottage, with excellent home-baked scones and cakes. It's closed on Mondays.

Getting There & Away

Falkland is 11 miles (18km) north of Kirkcaldy and 11 miles (18km) south-west of

Cupar. There are buses roughly every two hours (daily) from Perth, Kirkcaldy and Cupar. The nearest train station is 5 miles (8km) away, at Markinch on the Edinburgh to Dundee line, with an hourly service.

CUPAR & CERES
☎ 01334 • 7610

Cupar is a pleasant market town and the 'capital' of Fife. There are banks with ATMs in St Catherine's St, but there's little of interest to the visitor.

Ceres, 3 miles (5km) south-east of Cupar, is a pretty village with pantiled roofs, a Georgian church and the shortest High St in Scotland. On the High St you'll find the **Fife Folk Museum** *(☎ 828180, High St; adult/child £2.50/free; open 2pm-5pm daily Easter & mid-May to Sept)*, in the historic 17th-century weigh-house and other buildings. There's a wide-ranging collection of folk history exhibits, agricultural tools and a heritage trail.

The **Hill of Tarvit Mansion House**, *(NTS; ☎ 653127; adult/child £5/4; open 1.30pm-5.30pm Easter, May-Sept & Oct weekends, last admission 4.45pm)*, 2½ miles (4km) south of Cupar and a mile from Ceres, was rebuilt for Frederick Sharp in 1906 by Scottish architect Sir Robert Lorimer. Sharp was a wealthy Dundee jute manufacturer who bought the house as a showcase for his valuable collection of furniture, Dutch paintings, Flemish tapestries and Chinese porcelain. There's also an on-site tearoom. A 15-minute walk takes you to the top of the Hill of Tarvit, which has an excellent panoramic view.

Places to Stay & Eat
Arisaig (☎/fax 654529, Arisaig, Westfield Rd, Cupar) B&B £23-28 per person. Arisaig is a spacious modern bungalow a few minutes' walk from Cupar town centre. Veggies are catered for, and the breakfast porridge here won a Fife Tourist Board award.

Ostler's Close Restaurant (☎ 655574, 25 Bonnygate, Cupar) 3-course dinner around £25. Open noon-2.30pm Tues, Fri & Sat, 6.30pm-10pm Tues-Sat. Cupar's top restaurant is a bit expensive but the food – Scottish produce with a French or Mediterranean twist – is superb.

You can get bar meals at *The Drookit Dug* in High St, Cupar, and the *Ceres Inn* in Ceres. In Cupar town centre, you'll find supermarkets, bakeries, fish and chip shops, and the obligatory Asian restaurants and takeaways.

Getting There & Away
Cupar is a busy transport centre with direct bus services to St Andrews, Dundee and Edinburgh. Stagecoach Fife (☎ 474238) bus Nos X59 and X60 from Edinburgh to St Andrews pass through Cupar

Bus No 23 plies the St Andrews–Cupar–Kinross–Stirling route every two hours (twice a day on Sunday). The hourly bus Nos 41 and 41A run from Kirkcaldy to Cupar via Ceres. Bus No 64 runs from Cupar to St Andrews via Ceres, every two hours (not Sunday). There's also a twice daily (once on Saturday, no service on Sunday) Royal Mail postbus linking Cupar, Ceres and Peat Inn.

Cupar is on the rail line between Edinburgh and Dundee; there's roughly one train an hour in each direction (every two hours on Sunday).

ST ANDREWS
☎ 01334 • pop 13,900

St Andrews is a beautiful and unusual seaside town – a concoction of medieval ruins, obsessive golfers, windy coastal scenery, tourist glitz and a university that sees wealthy English undergraduates rubbing shoulders with Scottish theology students. Prince William, son of Prince Charles and the late Diana, Princess of Wales, started studying History of Art here in 2001.

Although St Andrews was once the ecclesiastical capital of Scotland, both its cathedral and castle are now in ruins. For most people, the town is the home of golf and a mecca for the sport's aficionados. It's the headquarters of the game's governing body, the Royal and Ancient Golf Club, and the location of the world's most famous golf course, the Old Course.

History

St Andrews is said to have been founded by St Regulus, who arrived from Greece in the 4th century bringing important relics, including some of the bones of St Andrew – Scotland's patron saint.

The town soon grew into a major pilgrimage centre. The Augustinian Church of St Rule was built in 1127 (only the tower remains); the adjacent cathedral was built in 1160. St Andrews developed into the ecclesiastical capital of the country and, around 1200, the castle was constructed – part fortress, part residence for the bishop.

The university was founded in 1410, the first in Scotland. James I received part of his education here, as did James III. By the mid-16th century there were three colleges: St Salvator's, St Leonard's and St Mary's.

Although golf was being played here by the 15th century, the Old Course dates from the following century. The Royal and Ancient Golf Club was founded in 1754, and the imposing clubhouse was built a hundred years later. The British Open Championship, which was first held in 1860 in Prestwick on the west coast near Glasgow, has taken place regularly at St Andrews since 1873.

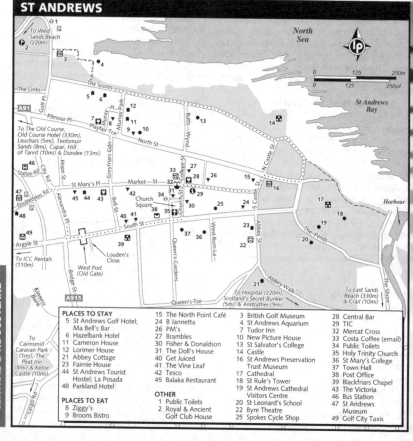

ST ANDREWS

PLACES TO STAY	15 The North Point Café	3 British Golf Museum	28 Central Bar
5 St Andrews Golf Hotel;	24 B Jannetta	4 St Andrews Aquarium	29 TIC
Ma Bell's Bar	26 PM's	7 Tudor Inn	32 Mercat Cross
6 Hazelbank Hotel	27 Brambles	10 New Picture House	33 Costa Coffee (email)
11 Cameron House	30 Fisher & Donaldson	13 St Salvator's College	34 Public Toilets
12 Lorimer House	31 The Doll's House	14 Castle	35 Holy Trinity Church
21 Abbey Cottage	40 Get Juiced	16 St Andrews Preservation	36 St Mary's College
23 Fairnie House	41 The Vine Leaf	Trust Museum	37 Town Hall
44 St Andrews Tourist	42 Tesco	17 Cathedral	38 Post Office
Hostel; La Posada	45 Balaka Restaurant	18 St Rule's Tower	39 Blackfriars Chapel
48 Parkland Hotel		19 St Andrews Cathedral	43 The Victoria
	OTHER	Visitors Centre	46 Bus Station
PLACES TO EAT	1 Public Toilets	20 St Leonard's School	47 St Andrews
8 Ziggy's	2 Royal & Ancient	22 Byre Theatre	Museum
9 Broons Bistro	Golf Club House	25 Spokes Cycle Shop	49 Golf City Taxis

Orientation

St Andrews preserves its medieval plan of parallel streets with small closes leading off them. The most important parts of the old town, lying to the east of the bus station, are easily explored on foot. The main streets for shops are Market and South Sts, running east–west. Like Cambridge and Oxford, St Andrews has no campus – most university buildings are integrated into the central part of the town. There's a small harbour near the cathedral, and two sandy beaches: East Sands extends south from the harbour and the wider West Sands is north of the town.

Information

The TIC (☎ 472021, W www.visit-standrews .co.uk), 70 Market St, opens 9.30am to 5pm Monday to Saturday year-round (closes 5.30pm in May and June, 7pm in July and August, and 6pm in September). From April to September it's also open Sundays from 11am to 4pm (10am to 5pm in July and August). It makes bookings for the theatre and the Edinburgh Tattoo, and sells NTS passes.

The post office is on South St. You can check email at Costa Coffee on Market St, not far from the TIC (£1 for 20 minutes); it's open 8am to 6pm Monday to Saturday, 10am to 6pm Sunday.

You'll find banks with ATMs near the Holy Trinity Church, South St. Shops have half-day closing on Thursday, but in summer many stay open. Parking in the central area requires a voucher, which is on sale in many shops.

The St Andrews Memorial Hospital (☎ 472327) is on Abbey Walk, south of Abbey St.

Walking Tour

The best place to start a walking tour is **St Andrews Museum** (☎ 412690, Kinburn Park, Doubledykes Rd; admission free; open 10am-5pm daily Apr-Sept, 10.30am-4pm Mon-Fri & 12.30pm-5pm Sat & Sun Oct-Mar), near the bus station. Displays chart the history of the town from its founding by St Regulus to its growth as an ecclesiastical, academic and sporting centre. It's much more interesting than some local history museums.

Turn left out of the museum driveway and follow Doubledykes Rd back to the roundabout on City Rd. Turn right, then left onto South St. You'll pass through **West Port**, formerly Southgait Port, the main entrance to the old town. It was built in 1589 and based on Netherbow Port in Edinburgh. Walking east along South St, you pass **Louden's Close** on the right, a good example of the closes built according to the city's medieval street plan. Continuing along South St, the apse of the 16th-century **Blackfriars Chapel** stands in front of Madras College.

Opposite the Victorian town hall is **Holy Trinity**, the town's parish church, built in 1410. On the same side of the street as the town hall is **St Mary's College**, founded in 1537; beside it is the university library. The oak tree in the courtyard is over 250 years old.

Go left along Church St to cobbled Market St. Street markets are held around the **Mercat Cross**, although the cross is now a fountain. The TIC is nearby, at No 70. Follow Market St east to the junction with South Castle St, turn left, and then right into North St.

On the right is **St Andrews Preservation Trust Museum** (☎ 477629, 12 North St; admission free; open 2pm-5pm daily Easter, June-Sept & 30 November), an old merchant's house and a museum of local social and commercial history. It's interesting to note that St Andrews did not retain its medieval character by accident. In the mid-19th century, the provost (mayor) Hugh Lyon Playfair implemented plans for sympathetic civic improvements making sure that they didn't involve the destruction of old buildings.

At the eastern end of North St is the ruined west end of **St Andrews Cathedral** (HS; ☎ 472563, The Pends; adult/child £4/1.25 including St Andrews Castle, cathedral only £2/75p; open 9.30am-6.30pm daily Apr-Sept, 9.30am-4.30pm daily Oct-Mar), once the largest and one of the most magnificent cathedrals in Britain. Although it was founded in 1160, it wasn't consecrated until 1318. It was a focus of pilgrimage until the Reformation, when it was pillaged in 1559. Many of the town's buildings were constructed using stones from the cathedral.

St Andrew's bones lay under the high altar; until the cathedral was built, they had been enshrined in the nearby Church of St Rule. All that remains is the church tower, well worth the climb for the view across St Andrews and a really great place for taking photographs. In the same area are parts of the ruined 13th-century priory. The Visitors Centre includes the calefactory, the only room where the monks could warm themselves by a fire; masons' marks on the red sandstone blocks, identifying who shaped each block, can still be clearly seen. There's also a collection of Celtic crosses and gravestones found on the site.

Not far from the cathedral, with a spectacular cliff-top location, **St Andrews Castle** (☎ 477196, The Scores; adult/child £2.80/1; open 9.30am-6pm daily Apr-Sept, 9.30am-4pm daily Oct-Mar) was founded around 1200 as the fortified home of the bishop. In the 1450s the young King James II often stayed here. A visitor centre gives a good audiovisual introduction and also has a small collection of Pictish stones.

In 1654, part of the castle was pulled down to provide building materials for rebuilding the harbour wall and pier. Enough survives to give you an idea of what each of the chambers was used for. After the execution of Protestant reformers in 1545, other reformers retaliated by murdering Cardinal Beaton and taking over the castle. The cardinal's body was hung from a window in the Fore Tower before being tossed into the bottle-shaped dungeon. The reformers then spent almost a year besieged in the castle; one of the most interesting things to see here is the complex of siege tunnels, said to be the best surviving example of siege engineering in Europe. You can walk along the damp, mossy tunnels, now lit by electric light.

From the castle, follow **The Scores** west past St Salvator's College. At the western end is **St Andrews Aquarium** (☎ 474786, The Scores; adult/child £4.75/3.75; open 10am-6pm daily), which has the usual displays of marine life and an interesting sea-horse exhibition. In league with the Sea Mammal Research Unit at St Andrews University, the aquarium also runs a seal sanctuary.

Nearby is the **British Golf Museum** (☎ 460046, Bruce Embankment; adult/child £3.75/1.50; open 9.30am-5.30pm Apr-Oct, in winter reduced hours & closed Tues & Wed). This is a surprisingly interesting modern museum, equipped with audiovisual displays and touch screens, as well as golf memorabilia.

Opposite the museum is the clubhouse of the Royal and Ancient Golf Club. Outside the club is the Old Course, and beside it stretch the West Sands, the beach made famous by the film Chariots of Fire.

Walking & Cycling

The TIC has a list of local walks and sells OS maps. You can walk from St Andrews to Crail along the coast (15 miles; 24km) but the path is steep and slippery in places, and you have to take care not to get caught by the tide; this section of the Fife Coastal Path is not yet completed. A good shorter walk follows the coast east to Boarhills (4 miles; 6km), from where you can return by bus or by retracing your steps.

Since there are few steep hills in eastern Fife, cycling is pleasant in the area and there are some good rides along quiet side roads. Kellie Castle (see Around Anstruther in the East Neuk section later) and the Hill of Tarvit mansion house (see the Cupar & Ceres section earlier) are within easy cycling distance. You can also cycle north to the forest, beach and nature trail at Tentsmuirs Sands (8 miles; 13km). It's not advisable to cycle the narrow and busy coast road from St Andrews to Crail as it has dangerous bends and no verges in places.

Organised Tours

St Andrews Guided Walks (☎ 850638, e june.riches@virgin.net) has qualified guides who will explain the history of the castle, cathedral and university. The 1½-hour walks depart from Church Square every Wednesday at 11am, and cost £4 (children under 12 free).

The Witches Tour (☎ *655057*) starts at 8pm on Thursday, Friday and Sunday in July and August, Friday and Sunday in June, and Friday only the rest of the year (starts 7.30pm October to March), and at other times by arrangement (minimum of 10 people needed). Meet outside the Tudor Inn on North St. This 1¼-hour tour (£6/4 for adults/children and students) recounts the history and folklore of the town in an unusual fashion, with tales of ghosts and witches enlivened by theatrical stunts.

Places to Stay

Bear in mind that all St Andrews accommodation gets booked solid well in advance whenever a major golf tournament is being held.

Camping & Hostels Note that the attractive Kinkell Braes Caravan Park overlooking East Sands beach doesn't accept tents.

Cairnsmill Caravan Park (☎ *473604, fax 474410,* e *cairnsmill@aol.com, Largo Rd*) Tent pitches for 1/2/4 persons £4/8.50/12.50. This camp site is about a mile west of St Andrews on the A915. It also has bunkhouse accommodation with 12 beds at £8 per person.

St Andrews Tourist Hostel (☎ *479911, fax 479988,* e *info@eastgatehostel.com; Inchcape House, St Mary's Place*) Dorm beds £12. Open 7am-11pm year-round. This 44-bed hostel (6 or 8 bed dorms), only five minutes' walk from the bus station, is the only backpacker accommodation in town; you'll have to book at least two or three weeks ahead in summer.

B&Bs & Guesthouses The cheapest B&Bs in St Andrews (from £15 per person) are a five- to 15-minute walk south of the centre on Largo Rd and the streets to its east. The following are more central but still reasonably priced.

Abbey Cottage (☎ *473727,* e *coull@lineone.net, Abbey Walk*) B&B £19-24 per person. This pretty 18th-century cottage, just south of Abbey St, has a walled garden with pet hens and fantail doves.

Fairnie House (☎ *474094,* e *kate@fairniehouse.freeserve.co.uk, 10 Abbey St*) B&B £16-30 per person. This relaxed and friendly B&B in a Georgian townhouse near the Byre Theatre has one double and two twin rooms.

Almost every house on Murray Park and Murray Place is a guest house. The area couldn't be more convenient but prices are on the high side – most places charge around £25 per person. Most rooms have en-suite bathrooms. During summer, you'll need to book in advance. Two places worth trying are *Lorimer House* (☎/fax *476599,* e *lorimersta@talk21.com, 19 Murray Park*) with B&B for £20 to £30 per person; and *Cameron House* (☎ *472306, fax 479529,* e *elizabeth@cameronhousesta.co.uk, 11 Murray Park*) with B&B for £24 to £30 per person.

Hotels The Scores, a street overlooking the bay, is lined with expensive hotels.

Hazelbank Hotel (☎/fax *472466,* e *michael@hazelbank.com, 28 The Scores*) Singles £47.50-65, doubles £65-104. The Hazelbank is a small (10 rooms) but comfortable, family-run hotel in a fine 1898 Victorian townhouse.

St Andrews Golf Hotel (☎ *472611, fax 472188, 40 The Scores*) B&B £77.50-100 per person. This is an excellent upmarket hotel less than 200m from the Old Course. There are cheaper two-night deals, and the hotel has a golfers bar and an elegant, oak-panelled restaurant.

Parkland Hotel (☎ *473620, fax 653457,* e *parkland@aol.com, Doubledykes Rd*) B&B £75-100 per person, but cheaper deals available. Housed in Kinburn Castle, a 19th-century stately home, the six-room Parkland is a great romantic hideaway only a few minutes' walk from the town centre.

Old Course Hotel (☎ *474371, fax 477668,* e *reservations@oldcoursehotel.co.uk*) Singles £180-339, doubles £199-369. If money's really no object, stay at this imposing, 114-room resort hotel and spa overlooking the Old Course at the western end of town. There are resident golf pros and a team of therapists and beauticians providing massage for both body and ego. If you're planning to drop in out of the sky, it's worth noting that you need prior permission to use the helipad.

Places to Eat

Get Juiced (☎ 472927, 149 South St) Juices from £2.50, sandwiches from £2.70. Open 8am-6pm Mon-Fri, 9am-5pm Sat & 11am-4pm Sun, later hours in summer. Get Juiced is a cafe-bar that serves good sandwiches, paninis and wraps (mostly organic) along with fruit and vegetable juices. It also has great coffee, and there's Internet access at 5p/minute (minimum 50p).

Brambles (☎ 475380, 5 College St) Mains £5.95-12.95. Open 9am-10pm Mon-Sat & 11am-10pm Sun. One of the town's busiest lunchtime spots, this place has excellent soups, salads, burgers, baguettes and vegetarian dishes.

Broons Bistro (☎ 478479, 119 North St) Mains £7.50-14.50. Bar open 10am-1am Mon-Sat & noon-1am Sun. Food served 10am-2.30pm & 5.30pm-9.30pm Mon-Sat & 10am-3pm Sun. Housed in part of an old cinema, Broons is a friendly bar-bistro serving big portions of lamb, duck, steak and so on (plus one veggie option).

Balaka Restaurant (☎ 474825, 3 Alexandra Place) Mains £4.95-11.50. Open 5.30pm-1am Sun-Thur, noon-1am Fri & Sat. The Balaka is a Bangladeshi restaurant that pre-

---

Playing the Old Course

Golf has been played at St Andrews since the 15th century and by 1457 was apparently so popular that James II had to ban it because it was interfering with his troops' archery practice. Everyone knows that St Andrews is the home of golf, but few people realise that anyone can play the Old Course, the world's most famous golf course. Although it lies beside the exclusive, all-male Royal and Ancient Golf Club, the Old Course is a public course, and is not owned by the club.

The Open Championship was first played at the Old Course in 1873.

However, getting a tee-off time is – literally – something of a lottery. Unless you book a year or two in advance, the only chance you have of playing here is by entering the daily ballot. You must enter a minimum of two players by 2pm on the day before you wish to play; the results are shown by 4pm at the clubhouse, the starters' box, and on the Web at ⓦ www.golfagent.com/ballot. You can enter names in the ballot in person or by phone. Be warned that applications by ballot are normally heavily oversubscribed, and green fees are a mere £85 (£40 in winter). There's no play on Sundays.

Single golfers can sometimes get lucky by turning up at the starter's box as early as possible in the morning – the starter will try to join you up with the first available two- or three-ball.

If your number doesn't come up, there are five other public courses in the area, none with quite the cachet of the Old Course, but all of them significantly cheaper.

Advance bookings for the Old Course can be made by letter, phone, fax or email to the Reservations Office, St Andrews Links Trust (☎ 01334-466666, fax 477036, ⓔ reservations@standrews .org.uk), Pilmour House, St Andrews KY16 9SF. It's advisable to book at least a year in advance, and you must present a handicap certificate or letter of introduction from your club.

pares excellent curries flavoured with home-grown herbs; Sean Connery has eaten here. Their three-course set lunch costs from £5.95.

Ziggy's (☎ *473686, 6 Murray Place*) Mains £6.95-10.95, steaks £11.95-15.95. Open noon-10pm daily. Popular with students, Ziggy's serves good burgers, plus a range of steaks, Mexican, seafood and veggie dishes.

La Posada (☎ *470500, Inchcape House, St Mary's Place*) Mains £5.25-8.95. Open 11am-11pm daily. La Posada, in the same building as St Andrews Tourist Hostel, is a funky Mexican place with decor designed by Glasgow artist Jan Nimmo. It serves great fajitas and a mean *mole poblano* (char-grilled chicken in a chilli and bitter chocolate sauce).

The Vine Leaf (☎ *477497, 131 South St*) 2-course dinner £19.95. Open from 7pm Tues-Sat. The Vine Leaf is one of St Andrews' finest eating places, offering a gourmet menu of seafood, game, Scottish beef and vegetarian dishes.

The Doll's House (☎ *477422, 3 Church Sq*) Mains £8.50-12.45. Open noon-2.30pm & 6.30pm-9.30pm daily. The Doll's House vies with the Vine Leaf for the title of best restaurant in town, but certainly pips it on price – the two-course lunch at £6.95 is unbeatable value. The changing menu makes the most of fresh local fish and other Scottish produce.

The North Point Café (*24 North St*) is a good place for coffee, cream tea or a light lunch, while *PM's* (*1-3 Union St*) does breakfast, burgers and fish and chips.

For more upmarket snacks, head for *Fisher & Donaldson* on Church St, which sells Selkirk *bannocks* (rich fruit bread), cream cakes and a wonderful range of pastries. *Tesco* at 138 Market St is a good centrally located supermarket.

Don't leave town without sampling one of the 52 varieties of ice cream at *B Jannetta* (*31 South St*), a St Andrews institution. Most popular flavour? Vanilla. Weirdest? Irn Bru!

The Peat Inn (☎ *840206,* W *www .thepeatinn.co.uk, by Cupar*) 3-course lunch £19.50, 3-course dinner £28. Open noon-2pm & 7pm-10pm Tues-Sat. Run by master chef and wine expert David Wilson, the Peat Inn is one of the best restaurants in Scotland. Housed in a rustic country inn about 6 miles (10km) west of St Andrews, its Michelin Rosette-winning menu includes such delights as roast saddle of venison with a mushroom and truffle crust. If you want to stay the night, there are eight double or twin suites available at £145 (£95 for single occupancy). To get there, head west for 5 miles (8km) on the A915 then turn right on the B940 for another 1½ miles (2.5km).

Entertainment

Check the local *What's On* guide, published weekly and available from the TIC, or the TIC Web site (W www.visit-standrews.co.uk).

The St Andrews Living History Programme presents free medieval plays at weekends in July and August. They're usually held in Church Square, at the cathedral or the castle. Contact the TIC for details.

In July and August, the Royal Scottish Country Dance Society (RSCDS; ☎ 0131-225 3854, @ info@rscdshq.freeserve.co.uk) holds a summer school in St Andrews. Classes are available for students of all levels from complete beginners upwards; course fees begin at £103 for a week. For details send a stamped, self-addressed envelope to The Secretary, RSCDS 12 Coates Crescent, Edinburgh EH3 7AF, or check their Web site at W www.scottishdance.org.

The Byre Theatre (☎ *475000,* W *www .byretheatre.com, Abbey St*) This theatre company started life in a converted cow byre in the 1930s, and moved into new, purpose-built premises in 2000. Contact the TIC or check the Web site for details of performances.

The two-screen *New Picture House* (☎ *473509*) on North St shows current films; tickets cost from £3.50.

Pubs St Andrews has a good range of pubs, representing its varied population. The *Central Bar* on Market St is all polished brass and polished accents, full of rich students from south of the border. *Ma Bell's Bar* at the St Andrews Golf Hotel (see Places to Stay earlier) is a favourite meeting place for golfers. *The Victoria* on St Mary's Place is popular with all types of students and serves good bar meals from £3.50.

Special Events
The Royal and Ancient Golf Club is the body that organises the annual **Open Golf Championship**, which takes place in July. However, the tournament venue changes from year to year, and the Open only comes to St Andrews itself every five or six years – the venue for future championships can be found on the Information section of the Open's official Web site (**W** www.opengolf .com). The 2002 Open will be held at Muirfield, in Gullane, near Edinburgh.

St Andrews Highland Games (☎ 476305) are held on the North Haugh on the last Sunday in July.

During the **Lammas Fair**, held over four days preceding the second Tuesday in August, South St and part of Market St are taken over by carnival rides, craft stalls and street theatre.

St Andrews Week is a week of festivities held around St Andrew's Day (30 November), the feast day of Scotland's patron saint. The celebrations include a festival of Scottish food and drink, and various arts events. Contact the TIC for details.

Getting There & Away
St Andrews is 55 miles (89km) north of Edinburgh and 13 miles (21km) south of Dundee.

Bus Stagecoach Fife (☎ 474328) operates a half-hourly bus service from Edinburgh to St Andrews via Kirkcaldy (£5.70, two hours). Buses to Dundee (30 minutes) and Cupar (20 minutes) also have a half-hourly frequency. Bus No 23 to Stirling runs six times daily, except Sunday. Other destinations include Crail (30 minutes) and Anstruther (40 minutes).

Train There is no train station in St Andrews itself, but you can take a train from Edinburgh to Leuchars, 5 miles (8km) to the north-west (£12.90 return, one hour), and then a bus or taxi (see later) into town. The

St Andrews Railbus scheme is a combined ticket (£15.80 return) that covers both train and bus.

Bus Nos 93, 94, 95 and 96 run frequently (two to four times an hour) between Leuchars train station and St Andrews (£1.20, 15 minutes).

Getting Around
Bus Stagecoach Fife (☎ 474238) operates a hop-on hop-off, open-top bus service that makes a circuit of the main sights once an hour between 9.30am and 4.30pm Friday to Monday, late May to September, and daily in July and August. Tickets valid for one day cost £5.50/2.75 for adults/children.

Car ICC Rentals (Ian Cowe Coachworks; ☎ 472543), 76 Argyle St, rents small cars for £27 per day, unlimited mileage.

Taxi There are taxi ranks at the bus station and at Holy Trinity Church on South St. To order a cab, call Golf City Taxis (☎ 477788) or Williamsons Taxis (☎ 476787). A taxi between Leuchars train station and the town centre costs around £7.

Bicycle You can rent bikes at Spokes (☎ 477835), 77 South St; mountain bikes cost £3/10.50 per hour/day.

EAST NEUK
The section of the southern Fife coast that stretches from Crail westwards to Largo Bay is known as the East Neuk ('neuk' means 'corner' in Scots). There are several picturesque fishing villages and some good coastal walks in the area.

Crail
☎ 01333 • pop 1290
One of the prettiest of the East Neuk villages and a favourite with artists, Crail has a much-photographed and painted harbour ringed by stone cottages with red pantiled roofs. There are far fewer fishing boats here now than there once were, but you can still buy fresh lobster and crab at the harbour. There are a couple of interesting antique and craft shops and art galleries too.

The TIC (☎ 450869), 62 Marketgait (at the museum), opens from 10am to 5pm Monday to Saturday and noon to 5pm Sunday, closed 1pm to 2pm on Monday, Friday and Saturday, April to September. The Royal Bank, on High St, has an ATM.

Guided walks begin at 2.30pm on Sundays in July and August; phone the TIC for details.

Things to See The village's history and involvement with the fishing industry are outlined in the **Crail Museum** (☎ 450310, 62 Marketgait; admission free; open 10am-1pm & 2pm-5pm Mon-Sat & 2pm-5pm Sun June-Sept; 2pm-5pm Sat & Sun Apr & May).

The 16th-century **tolbooth**, also in Marketgait, is now the library and town hall. Also worth looking for are the 13th-century **collegiate church** and the **Mercat Cross**, topped with a unicorn. Follow **Castle Walk** for the best views of the harbour.

Places to Stay & Eat Crail has a couple of B&Bs.

Caiplie Guest House (☎/fax 450564, [e] caipliehouse@talk21.com, 53 High St) B&B £17-25 per person. Open Mar-Nov. This friendly and centrally located Victorian town house has six bedrooms, some en suite and some with sea views. Evening meals are available too.

Marine Hotel (☎ 450207, fax 450272, 54 Nethergate) B&B £20-35 per person. Bar meals £5.25-8.75. All rooms at the Marine are en suite, and the lucky ones at the front have a grand view to the Isle of May.

The *East Neuk Hotel* (67 High St) does good bar meals, including cullen skink and Crail crab salad, for £5.05 to £6.25, and the *Honeypot Tearoom* (High St) has soup, sandwiches and cakes. There are also a couple of coffee shops, a baker and an **Alldays** supermarket on High St.

Getting There & Away Crail is 10 miles (16km) south-east of St Andrews. The Stagecoach Fife (☎ 01334-474238) bus No 95 between Leven, Anstruther, Crail, St Andrews and Dundee passes through Crail hourly every day (30 minutes to St Andrews).

Anstruther
☎ 01333 • pop 3270

A sizeable former fishing village, 9 miles (14km) south of St Andrews, Anstruther (often pronounced en-ster) has grown to become the main tourist centre of the East Neuk. It's worth visiting for the Scottish Fisheries Museum, for boat trips to the Isle of May and for walks along the coast.

The helpful TIC (☎ 311073) is in the Fisheries Museum. It opens 10am to 5pm daily April to October (noon to 5pm on Sunday). There are banks with ATMs in the town centre.

Scottish Fisheries Museum The displays at this excellent museum (☎ 310628, [w] www.scottish-fisheries-museum.org, St Ayles, Harbourhead; adult/child £3.50/2.50; open 10am-5.30pm Mon-Sat & 11am-5pm Sun Apr-Oct, till 4.30pm Oct-Mar) include a cottage belonging to a fishing family, and the history of the herring and whaling industries that were once the mainstay of the local economy, but the centrepiece is the Zulu Gallery housing the huge, part-restored hull of a traditional Zulu-class fishing boat, redolent with the scents of tar and timber. Afloat in the harbour outside the museum lies *The Reaper*, a fully restored Fifie-class fishing boat, built in 1902. The museum has a good *tearoom*.

Isle of May The mile-long **Isle of May**, 6 miles (10km) south-east of Anstruther, is a nature reserve. Between April and July, the cliffs are packed with breeding kittiwakes, razorbills, guillemots, shags and around 40,000 puffins. Inland, there are remains of the 12th-century **St Adrian's Chapel**, dedicated to a monk who was murdered on the island by the Danes in 875.

The five-hour excursion to the island on the *May Princess*, including two to three hours ashore, sails daily except Friday (weather permitting) from May to October; tickets cost £13/6 for adults/children. You can make reservations and buy tickets at the harbour kiosk near the museum at least an hour before departure. Departure times vary depending on the tide – check times for the next week or so by calling ☎ 310103.

Places to Stay & Eat Unfortunately there's no real budget accommodation in Anstruther.

Mrs Smith (☎ 310042, 2 Union Place) B&B £15-17 per person. This B&B is just uphill from the museum.

Beaumont Lodge (☎/fax 310315, e *reservations@beau-lodge.demon.co.uk, 43 Pittenweem Rd)* B&B £22-28 per person. Many travellers have recommended the warm welcome at the Beaumont, a lovely Victorian villa 10 minutes' walk west of the harbour.

Spindrift (☎/fax 310573, e *info@ thespindrift.co.uk, Pittenweem Rd)* B&B £26.50-31 per person. The Spindrift is a very comfortable guesthouse in a 19th-century sea-captain's house, just across the street from the Beaumont. All rooms have en-suite bathrooms and dinner is available from £13.50.

Dreel Tavern (☎ 310727, 16 High St West) 2-course lunch £5.50, 2-course dinner £7.50. Food served noon-2pm & 5.30pm-9pm. This charming old pub on the banks of the Dreel Burn serves excellent bar meals and has an outdoor beer garden in summer.

Cellar Restaurant (☎ 310378, 24 East Green) 3-course set dinner £28.50. Tucked away in an alley behind the museum, the Cellar is famous for its seafood – crab, lobster, scallops, langoustine, monkfish, turbot and so on – and fine wines. Advance bookings are essential.

The *Craw's Nest* on Bankwell Rd, a 15-minute walk west on Pittenweem Rd, overlooks the sea and is another good place for bar meals. The *Anstruther Fish Restaurant*, on the harbour front, is one of Fife's best fish and chip shops, often with queues stretching out the door. Nearby is the *Caspian Fast Food* kebab shop and the *Co-op* foodstore.

Getting There & Away The hourly Stagecoach Fife (☎ 01334-474238) bus No 61/61A/61B runs daily between St Andrews and Earlsferry, stopping at Crail, Anstruther (harbour), St Monans and Elie; No 61B goes via Arncroach, near Kellie Castle. Bus No 62 makes four trips a day between Anstruther and Crail. The hourly (two hourly on Sunday)

X27 service connects Anstruther with Kirkcaldy (one hour 10 minutes), Dunfermline and Glasgow (three hours).

Around Anstruther

Kellie Castle & Gardens *(NTS; ☎ 01333-720271; adult/child £5/4; castle open 1.30pm-5.30pm daily Easter-Sept, 1.30pm-5.30pm Sat & Sun Oct; garden open 9.30am-sunset daily)* are 3 miles (5km) west of Anstruther on the B9171 road. The castle is a magnificent example of Lowland Scottish domestic architecture and is well worth a visit. It's set in a beautiful garden, and many of the rooms contain superb plasterwork. The original part of the building dates from 1360; it was enlarged to its present dimensions around 1606. Robert Lorimer worked on the castle in the 1870s, when it was not in good shape, and it was bought by the NTS in 1970.

Bus No 61B from St Andrews to Earlsferry via Crail and Anstruther passes the castle gates four times daily (except Sunday), or you can walk there from Anstruther in just over an hour.

Three miles (5km) north of Anstruther off the B9131 road to St Andrews is **Scotland's Secret Bunker** *(☎ 01333-310301, Troy Wood; adult/child £6.95/3.75; 10am-5pm daily Apr-Oct)*. This fascinating labyrinth would have been one of Britain's underground command centres and a home for Scottish leaders if nuclear or civil war had ever broken out. Hidden 30m underground, and surrounded by nearly 5m of reinforced concrete, are operations rooms, a communication centre, a cafe and dormitories. A 25-minute audiovisual display, shown at 11.30am and 2.30pm, explains how it would have been used.

Nine buses a day (except Sunday) run between St Andrews and Anstruther via Troy Wood.

Pittenweem

☎ 01333 • pop 1640

This is now the main fishing port on the East Neuk coast, and there are lively fish sales at the harbour from 8am. The village name means 'place of the cave', referring to

St Fillan's cave in Cove Wynd, which was used as a chapel by a 7th-century missionary. The saint reputedly possessed miraculous powers – apparently, when he wrote his sermons in the dark cave, his arm would illuminate his work by emitting a luminous glow. The cave is protected by a locked gate, but a key is available from The Gingerbread Horse cafe (☎ 311495), 9 High St (usually open 10am to 5pm).

Kellie Lodging, High St, is a small and intriguing, restored 16th-century townhouse.

Harbour Guest House (☎ *311273, 14 Mid Shore*) does B&B for £25 to £30 per person and has en-suite rooms overlooking the harbour. The *Anchor Inn (42 Charles St)* does bar meals and high teas.

Bus details are as for Anstruther.

St Monans
☎ 01333 • pop 1360
This ancient fishing village is situated just over a mile west of Pittenweem and is named after a local cave-dwelling saint who was most probably killed by pirates.

Things to See In streets near the attractive **harbour** there are lots of houses with crow-stepped gables, forestairs and red pantiled roofs.

The **parish church**, at the western end of the village, was built in 1362 on orders from a grateful King David II, who was rescued by villagers from shipwreck in the Firth of Forth. A model of a full-rigged ship, dating from 1800, hangs above the altar.

From the church, you can follow the coastal path westwards for half a mile to the ruins of 15th-century **Newark Castle**. Nearby is a 16th-century **beehive dovecot**, which housed pigeons that were intended for human consumption in winter. The path continues to Elie, 2 miles (3km) away.

Just east of the village, by the coastal path to Pittenweem, there's a renovated 18th-century **windmill** *(admission free; open 11am-4pm daily Jul & Aug)*, with displays about the 18th-century salt industry.

Places to Stay & Eat There are several B&Bs along Braehead, above the harbour.

Newark House (☎ *730027*) B&B £18-25 per person. Open Apr-Oct. This attractive farmhouse B&B is 300m west of the village, overlooking the sea.

Itches – The Seafood Restaurant (☎ *730327, 16 West End*) 3-course dinner around £25. Ichthys (the Greek word for fish) is a superb seafood restaurant within salt-spray distance of the sea just west of the harbour.

Getting There & Away Bus details for St Monans are as for Anstruther.

Elie & Earlsferry
☎ 01333 • pop 1500
These two attractive villages mark the south-western end of the East Neuk. There's not a lot of historical interest, except for Elie's 16th-century harbour and the old granary on the pier, but there are great sandy beaches, a top golf course and good walks along the coast.

Elie Watersports (☎ *330962*), on the harbour at Elie, rents out windsurfers (£16 for two hours), sailing dinghies (Lasers £10 an hour, Wayfarers £15 an hour), canoes (£5 an hour) and mountain bikes (£9 a day), and provides instruction as well.

Places to Stay & Eat There's not a lot of B&B accommodation in Elie and Earlsferry, so book ahead.

The Elms Guest House (☎/fax *330404*, ⓔ *lindseyterras@lineone.net, 14 Park Place, Elie*) B&B £16-24.50 per person. The Elms is a very relaxed and comfortable, family-run guest house. A three-course dinner adds £12.50 to the price.

The Bouquet Garni (☎ *330374, 51 High St, Elie*) 2-course lunch £8.50, 3-course dinner £16.50. Open noon-2pm & 7pm-10pm Mon-Sat. The candle-lit Bouquet Garni is another of the East Neuk's excellent restaurants, specialising in seafood, game and Scottish beef. Booking is recommended.

Ship Inn (☎ *330246, The Toft, Elie*) Mains £6.25-7.95. The Ship Inn, down by Elie harbour, is a pleasant and popular place for a bar lunch.

Perth & Kinross

This area includes most of the former region of Tayside – the area covered by the River Tay and its tributaries. It contains, in miniature, as many variations in terrain as Scotland itself, from the bleak expanse of Rannoch Moor in the west to the rich farmland of the Carse of Gowrie between Perth and Dundee.

From 838, Scotland's monarchs were crowned at Scone, just outside Perth. Mary Queen of Scots was imprisoned in Loch Leven Castle, and at Killiecrankie the Jacobites defeated the government forces.

The county town of Perth, built on the banks of the Tay, has a medieval church and many fine Georgian buildings. West of Perth there's attractive Strath Earn, with small towns and villages including the wealthy former resort of Crieff. Blairgowrie lies north of Perth, in an area known for fruit growing.

The Highland line cuts across this region – in the north and north-west are the rounded, heathery Grampians. North of Blairgowrie, the twisty road to Braemar follows Glen Shee and crosses the Cairnwell, Britain's highest main-road pass.

Flowing out of Loch Tay, in West Perthshire, the River Tay runs eastwards through hills and woods towards Dunkeld, where there's a cathedral on the riverbank. Queen Victoria, when looking for a place to buy, was quite taken by the Pitlochry area, particularly the view over Loch Tummel. North of Pitlochry, at Blair Atholl, is Blair Castle, ancestral seat of the dukes of Atholl.

GETTING AROUND

The busy A9 highway cuts across the centre of this region via Perth and Pitlochry. It's the fast route into the Highlands and to Inverness – watch out for speed traps.

Perth is the main public transport hub. Phone Perth & Kinross Council's Public Transport Traveline on ☎ 0845 301 1130, 8.30am to 5pm weekdays. Bus operators include: Scottish Citylink (☎ 0870 550 5050), Stagecoach (☎ 01738-629339), Strathtay

Scottish (☎ 01382- 228345) and Stagecoach Fife (☎ 01592-416060). For detailed rail information phone ☎ 0845 748 4950.

Trains run alongside the A9, destined for Inverness. The other main line connects Perth with Stirling (in the south) and Dundee (in the east).

KINROSS & LOCH LEVEN
☎ 01577 • pop 4032

Kinross lies in the extreme south of the Perth & Kinross region, on the western shore of Loch Leven. It's the largest loch in the Lowlands, known for its extensive bird life.

Helpful Kinross Services TIC (☎ 863680), by Junction 6 of the M90, may be closed from November to Easter. Three banks in town have ATMs.

Things to See

Loch Leven Castle *(mobile ☎ 0777 804 0483; adult/child £3.30/1.20, including ferry from Kinross; open 9.30am-5.15pm daily Apr-Oct)*, on an island in the loch, served as a fortress and prison from the late 14th century. Its most famous captive was Mary Queen of Scots, who spent almost a year incarcerated here from 1567. Her infamous charms bewitched Willie Douglas, who managed to get hold of the cell keys to release her, then row her across to the shore. The castle is now roofless but basically intact.

About 2 miles (3km) from Kinross, just outside Milnathort on the A911 to Leslie, there's the intriguing **Burleigh Castle** *(☎ 862408, Burleigh Rd; admission free; open by arrangement with keyholder)*. This red-sandstone tower house, built around 1450, has an extraordinarily shaped and still-roofed tower. King James IV was a frequent guest here. You can get the key from Mrs Cubitt (☎ 862408), 16 Burleigh Rd, Milnathort.

Places to Stay & Eat

Gallowhill Farm Caravan Park *(☎ 862364, Gallowhill Farm)* Camping from £5. Open Apr-Oct. This place is 2 miles (3km) from Kinross, near the A91.

Roxburghe Guest House *(☎ 862498, 126 High St, Kinross)* Singles £18-20, doubles

£32-36. Evening meals are also available in this fairly standard guesthouse.

Warroch Lodge (☎ *863779, Milnathort*). B&B £22-25 per person. This comfortable place is 4 miles (6km) from the M90 (Junction 6), near Milnathort. Rooms have en-suite facilities, and you can get evening meals for £9.

Carlin Maggie's (☎ *863652, 191 High St, Kinross*) 2-course lunch £9.95, dinner mains £8.95-14.95. This is a highly recommended restaurant, specialising in seafood and vegetarian dishes.

Cafe 98 (☎ *862870, 98 High St, Kinross*) You'll get soup and snacks here; homemade soup and a roll costs £1.40.

Central Café (☎ *863234, 124 High St*) does takeaway fish and chips for £3.80, but there's a better 'chippy' in Milnathort.

Getting There & Away

Scottish Citylink has an hourly service between Perth (£3.10, 25 minutes) and Edinburgh (£4.50, one hour) via Kinross, also stopping at Milnathort and Dunfermline. There are two to six buses daily to Falkland and a twice-weekly service to Dollar.

PERTH

☎ 01738 • pop 42,086

In *The Fair Maid of Perth*, Sir Walter Scott extolled the virtues of this county town. 'Perth, so eminent for the beauty of its situation, is a place of great antiquity,' he wrote. This is all still true and (in the 1990s) the town was voted the best place to live in Britain for quality of life.

Perth's rise in importance derives from Scone (pronounced scoon), 2 miles (3km) north of the town. In 838, Kenneth MacAlpin became the first king of a united Scotland and brought the Stone of Destiny, on which all kings were ceremonially invested, to Scone. An important abbey grew up on the site. From this time on, all Scottish kings were invested here, even after Edward I of England stole the sacred talisman, carting it off to London's Westminster Abbey in 1296. In 1996 Prime Minister John Major persuaded the Queen to promise to return it to Scotland, but it went to Edinburgh Castle rather than Scone. There's actually some doubt about whether Edward I stole the real stone – there have been suggestions that he stole a fake.

Built on the banks of the River Tay, Perth grew into a major trading centre, known for weaving, dyeing and glove-making. It was originally called St John's Toun, hence the name of the local football team, St Johnstone. From the 12th century, Perth was Scotland's capital, and in 1437 James I was murdered here. There were four important monasteries in the area and the town was a target for the Reformation movement in Scotland.

Perth is now a busy market town and a centre for service industries. It's the focal point for this agricultural region and there are world-famous cattle auctions of the valuable Aberdeen Angus breed. The bull sales in February draw international buyers.

The top attraction in the area is Scone Palace, but the town itself has a number of interesting things to see, including an excellent art gallery, housing the work of local artist JD Fergusson.

Orientation & Information

Most of the town lies on the western bank of the Tay; Scone Palace and some of the B&Bs are on the eastern bank. There are two large parks: North Inch, the scene of the infamous 'Battle of the Clans' in 1396, and South Inch. The bus and train stations are close to each other, near the north-western corner of South Inch.

The TIC (☎ 638481), Lower City Mills, West Mill St, opens daily from April to October (otherwise closed Sundays November to March). In July and August, the TIC opens 9am to 6.30pm Monday to Saturday, and 11am to 5pm Sunday. Opening hours are shorter at other times. Buy tickets here for the Guide Friday hop-on hop-off bus service (£5.50/4/2 adult/concession/child) that takes you to Scone Palace daily from late May to early September. Ask for details about the walk up Kinnoull Hill.

Lloyds TSB has an ATM on King Edward St. For outdoor equipment visit Mountain Man Supplies (☎ 632368) at 133 South St.

Perth Royal Infirmary (☎ 623311), Taymount Terrace, is west of the town centre.

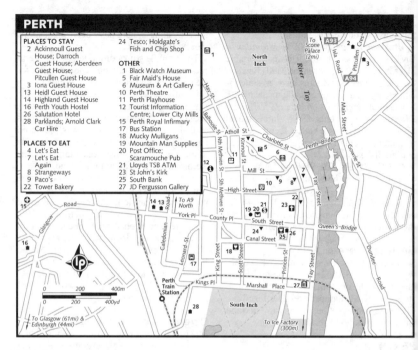

PERTH

PLACES TO STAY	24 Tesco; Holdgate's
2 Ackinnoull Guest	Fish and Chip Shop
House; Darroch	
Guest House; Aberdeen	**OTHER**
Guest House;	1 Black Watch Museum
Pitcullen Guest House	5 Fair Maid's House
3 Iona Guest House	6 Museum & Art Gallery
13 Heidl Guest House	10 Perth Theatre
14 Highland Guest House	11 Perth Playhouse
16 Perth Youth Hostel	12 Tourist Information
26 Salutation Hotel	Centre; Lower City Mills
28 Parklands; Arnold Clark	15 Perth Royal Infirmary
Car Hire	17 Bus Station
	18 Mucky Mulligans
PLACES TO EAT	19 Mountain Man Supplies
4 Let's Eat	20 Post Office;
7 Let's Eat	Scaramouche Pub
Again	21 Lloyds TSB ATM
8 Strangeways	23 St John's Kirk
9 Paco's	25 South Bank
22 Tower Bakery	27 JD Fergusson Gallery

Things to See

St John's Kirk *(admission free; open 10am-4pm Mon-Sat May-Sept, plus noon-2pm Sun Jun-Sept),* founded in 1126, is surrounded by cobbled streets and is still the centrepiece of the town. In 1559, John Knox preached a powerful sermon here that helped begin the Reformation, resulting in the destruction of monasteries, including the one at Scone. The kirk was restored in the 1920s.

Three blocks south of St John's Kirk is the Round House, the old waterworks building on the edge of South Inch that now houses the **JD Fergusson Gallery** *(☎ 441944, Marshall Place; admission free; open 10am-5pm Mon-Sat).* This artist, one of the group known as the Scottish colourists, was noticeably influenced by French styles after spending much of his life in France in the early part of the 20th century. The gallery is well worth seeing.

Two blocks north of the High St is the **Museum and Art Gallery** *(☎ 632488, 78 George St; admission free; open 10am-5pm Mon-Sat),* which charts local history. There are displays of Perth art glass, an impressive silver collection and natural history displays.

Nearby, is the **Fair Maid's House** *(Curfew Row; not open to the public),* the house chosen by Sir Walter Scott as home for Catherine Glover, the romantic heroine in his novel *The Fair Maid of Perth.* The novel was set in the 14th century, but this house dates from the 16th, when it was a meeting hall for the town's glove manufacturers.

South-west of the Fair Maid's House, **Lower City Mills** *(☎ 627958, West Mill St; adult/child £2/90p; open 10am-5pm Mon-Sat Apr-Nov)* is a restored and working Victorian oatmeal mill which now contains the TIC. In the north of the town, Balhousie Castle houses the **Black Watch Museum** *(☎ 0131-310 8530, Hay St; admission free; open 10am-4.30pm Mon-Sat May-Sept but closed last Sat in June, 10am-3.30pm Mon-Fri the rest of the year),* charting the military campaigns of Scotland's foremost regiment since 1740.

Scone Palace

Two miles (3km) north of Perth and just off the A93 near Old Scone, Scone Palace (☎ *552300, Old Scone; adult/child £5.90/3.40 for the house and grounds, £2.90/1.70 for the grounds only; open 9.30am-5.15pm daily Apr-Oct, last entry 4.45pm)*, the home of the earl and countess of Mansfield, should not be missed. It was built in 1580 in the grounds of a former abbey; the abbey was destroyed in 1559 by a crowd inflamed by John Knox's sermon in St John's Kirk. With the destruction of the abbey buildings, the land passed to the Gowrie family and then to the Murrays.

From 1803 to 1808, the palace was enlarged, and it now houses a superb collection of French furniture, including Marie Antoinette's writing table. Displays of 16th-century needle work include bed hangings worked by Mary Queen of Scots. In the library is a valuable collection of 18th- and 19th-century porcelain. The palace is surrounded by parkland, which includes rare pine trees.

The hop-on hop-off bus (contact the TIC for tickets) goes this way, as does bus No 58 (not Sunday).

Places to Stay

Perth Youth Hostel (☎ 623658, 107 Glasgow Rd) Dorm beds £8.75/7.50. Open Mar-Oct. This is an excellent hostel.

The main B&B areas are along Glasgow Rd, Dunkeld Rd, Dundee Rd and Pitcullen Crescent.

Iona Guest House (☎/fax 627261, 2 Pitcullen Crescent) Singles £18-21, doubles £36-42. All rooms in this clean and friendly establishment are en suite; vegetarian breakfast is available on request.

Ackinnoull Guest House (☎ 634165, 5 Pitcullen Crescent) Singles £20-30, doubles £36-50. This is a grand villa with four en-suite rooms.

Darroch Guest House (☎/fax 636893, 9 Pitcullen Crescent) Singles £16-18, doubles £32-42. This villa offers acceptable B&B.

Some rooms have shared facilities; dinner is available at £8.50 extra.

Aberdeen Guest House (☎/fax 633183, 13 Pitcullen Crescent) B&B from £17 per person. Only one room is en suite. The Aberdeen can do a vegetarian breakfasts.

Pitcullen Guest House (☎ 626506, 17 Pitcullen Crescent) Singles £26-35, doubles £36-48. All rooms have private facilities in this comfortable establishment.

Closer to the centre, there are B&Bs along York Place, including the following two.

Heidl Guest House (☎ 635031, fax 643710, 43 York Place) Singles £18-26, doubles £32-48. At Heidl Guest House, the place with the bizarre colour scheme, only two of the eight rooms are en suite.

Highland Guest House (☎/fax 638364, 47 York Place) B&B £16-22 per person. All rooms have private facilities in this traditional villa.

Salutation Hotel (☎ 630066, fax 633598, 34 South St) Singles £67-79, doubles £86-100. This hotel was first opened in 1699 and was reputedly used as a headquarters by Bonnie Prince Charlie during the Jacobite rebellion of 1745. If business is slack at the weekend the hotel sometimes offers special deals.

Parklands (☎ 622451, fax 622046, 2 St Leonard's Bank) En-suite B&B singles £69-85, doubles £80-116. Parklands, the former home of lord provosts (mayors), is one of the most luxurious places to stay in Perth. It's a small hotel with 14 rooms and a restaurant.

Places to Eat

Let's Eat (☎ 643377, 77 Kinnoul St) Lunch mains £8.25-10.25, evening mains around £9-15. This award-winning and very pleasant bistro is the best place in town for a special meal.

Let's Eat Again (☎ 633771, 33 George St) 3-course lunch/dinner around £15/20. Let's Eat Again serves light meals and desserts in a laid-back atmosphere. Popular menu items include sticky toffee pudding with toffee sauce and whipped cream (£3.95).

Paco's (☎ 622290, 16 St John's Place) Mains £5.45-14.45. Paco's has a huge menu, including pizzas, Tex-Mex, vegetarian, burgers and steaks. There's some outdoor seating.

Strangeways (☎ 560704, 24 George St) 2-course bar lunches £4. Strangeways is a friendly bistro that's open daily, but stops serving food at 5pm. It's a good place to have a drink in the evening.

Scaramouche (☎ 637479, 103 South St) Lunch specials £2. This is a great pub, serving a wide range of bar meals, including vegetarian dishes.

Holdgate's fish and chip shop (146 South St) Next to Tesco, this place does excellent takeaway fish suppers for £3.60. You can also sit-in.

In County Place and South St there are about a dozen Italian, Chinese, Thai, Turkish and Indian restaurants. Some pubs do bar meals – see the following Entertainment section. There's a *Tesco* supermarket in the town centre on South St. The *Tower Bakery (30 St John St)* does filled rolls and baked goods.

Outside of Perth, *Scone Palace* has a good coffee shop and restaurant.

Entertainment

South Bank (☎ 444094, 38 South St) All mains £3.50. South Bank is another pub with a pleasant atmosphere.

Mucky Mulligans (☎ 636705, 97 Canal St) Mucky Mulligans is an authentic Irish pub, with live music every Wednesday evening and bar meals daily.

The Ice Factory (☎ 630011, 6 Shore Rd) Nominated nightclub of the year 2000, this place is the hotspot for clubbers.

Perth Theatre (☎ 621031, 185 High St) The renovated Art Deco theatre hosts arty dramatic productions.

Perth Playhouse (☎ 623126, 6 Murray St) The seven-screen cinema concentrates on Hollywood fare.

Getting There & Away

Bus Scottish Citylink operates regular buses from Perth to Glasgow (£7.50, 1½ hours), Edinburgh (£5.50, one to 1½ hours), Dundee (£3.60, 35 minutes), Aberdeen (£11.50, 2¼ hours) and Inverness (£10.30, 2¾ hours).

Stagecoach buses serve Dunkeld (£1.90, 40 minutes, three to seven daily), Pitlochry (£3, one hour, three to seven Monday to Saturday) and Aberfeldy (£3, 1¼ hours, up to five daily except Sunday); Crieff (£2.30, 45 minutes, every hour or two); St Fillans (£3, 1¼ hours, five daily except Sunday) via Crieff and Comrie; and Dunning (£1.80, 40 minutes, seven daily except Sunday) via Forteviot. Strathtay Scottish (☎ 01382-228345) buses travel from Perth to Blairgowrie (£2.20, 47 minutes, five to seven Monday to Saturday) and Dundee (£2.15, 1¾ hours, every hour or two).

Ask at the TIC whether Stagecoach has reinstated the summer 'Heatherhopper' bus service to Braemar via Dunkeld and Pitlochry.

Train There's an hourly train service from Glasgow Queen St (£9.40, one hour), two hourly on Sunday, and less frequent trains from Edinburgh (£9.40, around one hour 20 minutes). Other rail destinations include Stirling (£4.90 cheap day return), Dundee (£4.60), Pitlochry (£4.90 cheap day return) and Inverness via Aviemore (£15.80).

Getting Around

Local buses are operated by Stagecoach. For a taxi, call Ace Taxis on ☎ 633033.

Hiring a car will cost from £18 per day with Arnold Clark (☎ 442202), St Leonards Bank.

STRATHEARN

West of Perth, the wide *strath* (valley) of the River Earn was once a great forest where medieval kings hunted. The Earn, named after a Celtic goddess, runs from St Fillans (named after the mystic who lived on an island in Loch Earn), through Comrie and Crieff and eventually into the Tay near Bridge of Earn. The whole area is known as Strathearn, a very attractive region of undulating farmland, hills and lochs. The Highlands begin in the western section of Strathearn and the so-called Highland line runs through Comrie and Crieff, and on through Angus (via Kirriemuir and Edzell) to Stonehaven.

Dunning
☎ 01764 • pop 1000

Historic Dunning nestles at the foot of the Ochil Hills on the southern side of Strathearn, about 8 miles (13km) south-west of Perth. The area was always of strategic importance. The Battle of Duncrub was fought nearby in 965 and, in 1716, retreating Jacobites burned the village after their defeat at Sheriffmuir. Dunning is dominated by the 12th-century Norman tower of **St Serfs church**, but most of the building dates from 1810. The 9th-century **Dupplin Cross**, one of the earliest Christian stone crosses in Scotland, was originally located near Forteviot (3 miles; 5km, from Dunning). It's currently in the National Museum of Scotland in Edinburgh, but will return to St Serfs church by 2003. About a mile (1.6km) west of Dunning, by the B8062, there's a strange **cross** commemorating the burning of a witch in 1657.

Kirkstyle Inn *(☎ 684248, Kirkstyle Square)* Mains £4.50-12.95. The Kirkstyle Inn serves excellent bar and restaurant meals, including a vegetarian dish.

Pan Haggerty *(☎ 684604, Tron Square)* Mains around £5. This place is popular with locals and serves home baking, bistro meals and takeaway fish and chips.

Stagecoach bus No 17 runs from Perth to Forteviot and Dunning seven times daily, except Sunday (£1.80, 40 minutes). Docherty's Midland Coaches (☎ 662218) No 18 bus departs for Auchterarder (£1.30, eight minutes, two to six times each weekday) and Crieff (£2.20, 50 minutes, two or three times each weekday). Bus No 20 runs from Dunning to Auchterarder twice daily (except Sunday).

Auchterarder
☎ 01764 • pop 2932

Four miles (6km) west of Dunning and overlooked by the Ochil Hills, Auchterarder is a small town in a rich agricultural area. There's a TIC (☎ 663450), 90 High St, open year-round, with an interesting **heritage centre** (free) detailing wide-ranging aspects of local history. **Whitelaw's antique shop** *(118 High St)* almost doubles-up as a museum of 18th- and 19th-century furniture.

The town is probably best known for the internationally famous hotel on its outskirts.

Gleneagles Hotel *(☎ 662231, fax 662134, Auchterarder)* Singles/doubles from £165/260. Gleneagles Hotel, just over 2 miles (3km) west of Auchterarder, is a splendid place with three championship golf courses, three swimming pools, a Jacuzzi, sauna, gym, and tennis and squash courts. Room charges include full use of the leisure facilities. The most expensive room is the £1400 Royal Lochnagar Suite, complete with antiques, silk-lined walls and hand-woven carpets. The hotel even has its own train station, 50 minutes (£9.30) from Glasgow, and there's complimentary transport between the station and hotel. However, if you can afford to stay here, you can afford the limousine from Glasgow airport (£130).

Auld Nick *(☎ 662916, 89 Feus)* Singles £15-18, doubles £36-44. A cheaper alternative to the Gleneagles Hotel is B&B at the curiously named Auld Nick.

Cafe Cento *(☎ 664907, 100 High St)* Mains around £5-8. Cafe Cento serves excellent pizza and pasta. Takeaway fish and chips are available.

Sheray Punjab *(☎ 664277, 97 High St)* Mains £6-9. This Indian restaurant does good, large portions and has a takeaway service.

Gleneagles Bakery *(162 High St)* This bakery is good for bread and pastries.

Docherty's Midland Coaches (☎ 662218) runs buses two or three times daily, Monday to Saturday, from Auchterarder to Dunning (£1.30, eight minutes), Crieff (£1.70, 30 minutes) and Stirling (£1.80, 40 minutes), and three to 14 buses daily to Perth (£1.90, 40 minutes).

Crieff & Around
☎ 01764 • pop 6359

Attractively located on the edge of the Highlands, Crieff has been a popular resort town since Victorian times. Until 1770 it was the scene of a large cattle fair; some vendors would come from as far away as Skye – swimming the cattle across to the mainland.

Information The all-year TIC (☎ 652578) is in the High St clock tower, part of the

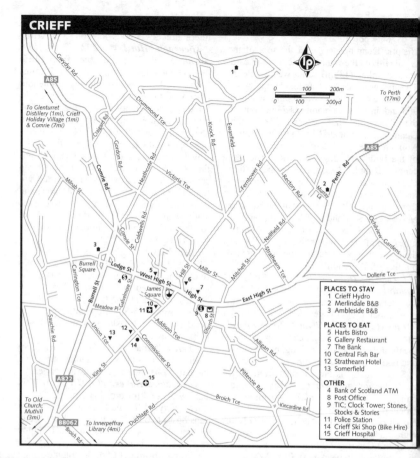

CRIEFF

PLACES TO STAY
1 Crieff Hydro
2 Merlindale B&B
3 Ambleside B&B

PLACES TO EAT
5 Harts Bistro
6 Gallery Restaurant
7 The Bank
10 Central Fish Bar
12 Strathearn Hotel
13 Somerfield

OTHER
4 Bank of Scotland ATM
8 Post Office
9 TIC; Clock Tower; Stones,
  Stocks & Stories
11 Police Station
14 Crieff Ski Shop (Bike Hire)
15 Crieff Hospital

town hall. The four banks all have ATMs. The post office is on High St. The police station is on King St and Crieff Hospital (☎ 653173) is just off it. Needy travellers should note that the public toilets on James Square charge 30p.

Things to See In the basement at the TIC, **Stones, Stocks & Stories** (☎ 652578, *High St; admission free; open variable times daily Apr-Oct, Mon-Sat Nov-Mar*) is an interesting exhibition of the town stocks, the Mercat Cross and a 9th-century Pictish cross slab.

There are several interesting things around Crieff. **Glenturret Distillery** (☎ 656565, *The Hosh; adult/child £3.50/2.30; visitor centre open 9.30am-6pm, afternoon only Sunday, last tour 4.30pm*) is about a mile (1.6km) from the centre of town. Opening hours are shorter in January. It's all fairly touristy but a free dram is included in the price. See Places to Eat later for details of the Glenturret restaurant.

Innerpeffray Library (☎ 652819, *Innerpeffray; adult/child £2.50/50p, includes guided tour; open 10am-12.45pm & 2pm-4.45pm daily except Thur & 2pm-4pm Sun Apr-Sept,* *losing 4pm in winter, open Jan & Dec by ppointment)*, about 4 miles (6km) south-ast of Crieff on the B8062, is Scotland's irst lending library (founded in 1680). "here's a huge collection of rare, interesting nd ancient books, some of them 500 years ld. The library building (from 1762), and e early **16th-century chapel and graveyard** ext door are very interesting too. A **Roman** bad runs nearby.

At Muthill, 3 miles (5km) south of Crieff, ou'll find the excellent **Old Church** *Muthill; admission free; key from key-older, information posted by gate)*. The hurch is now just a series of ruined arches, ut the attached **bell tower** (originally free tanding) is still roofed. This extraordinary ower, with unusual arched belfry windows, s one of the oldest complete structures n Scotland: it dates from around 1225 to 250.

Places to Stay Crieff has a large selection f B&Bs and hotels. The nearest budget ccommodation is 5 miles (8km) away, near Comrie (see the upcoming Upper Strathearn ection). Most of the hotels are on Perth Rd r Comrie Rd.

Crieff Holiday Village (☎ 653513, fax 55028, Turret Bank) Tents £6. There's ear-round camping here, by the A85 just vest of Crieff.

Ambleside (☎ 652798, 3 Burrell Square) Singles/doubles £16/32. This is a centrally ocated, pleasant B&B.

Merlindale (☎/fax 655205, Perth Rd) B&B £22.50-35 per person. Merlindale, ne of the best places in town, is a luxuri-us Georgian house with three en-suite ooms and a Jacuzzi.

Crieff Hydro (☎ 655555, fax 653087, Ferntower Rd) Dinner B&B £31-95 per erson. The Hydro is the best-known hotel n Crieff. It's on the hill at the northern side f town and has one of the highest occu-ancy rates in Scotland. There's a wide range of leisure facilities and good food is served (see Places to Eat below).

Places to Eat There's a good restaurant at he *Glenturret Distillery (☎ 656565, The*

Hosh), which serves traditional Scottish lunches and home baking.

Crieff Hydro (☎ 655555, fax 653037, Ferntower Rd) 3-course set dinner £19, brasserie dinner mains £6.25-16.95. The stylish new brasserie at the Hydro has an adventurous menu; cheaper snacks are served throughout the day.

There are lots of places to eat on or near both King St and High St.

The Bank (☎ 656575, 32 High St) 2-course lunch from £8.05, dinner mains £8.95-15.50. Scottish food with an international twist is served here.

Gallery Restaurant (☎ 653249, 13 Hill St) Mains £8.50-11.95. Scottish and inter-national-style meals are available in this pleasant bistro.

Harts Bistro (☎ 654407, 1 West High St) Mains £5.45-9.95. Harts Bistro also does pasta, bread and salad for £4.49.

Strathearn Hotel (☎ 652089, 57 King St) Bar snacks from £1.35, meals £4.15-10.50. This place offers ordinary but acceptable bar meals.

Central Fish Bar (☎ 652890, 15 King St) Most takeaways £2-3.15. Unusual salmon suppers in this traditional fish and chip shop cost £3.15.

For self-catering, there's a *Somerfield* supermarket *(Union Terrace)*.

Getting There & Away Hourly Stage-coach buses link Crieff with Perth, less fre-quently on Sunday (£2.30, 45 minutes). Other buses run to Comrie (£1.40, 20 min-utes, roughly hourly Monday to Saturday, every two hours Sunday) and St Fillans (£2.10, 35 minutes, five daily except Sun-day), and Stirling (£2.65, 50 minutes, four to six daily). Docherty's Midland Coaches (☎ 662218) runs between Crieff, Auchter-arder (£1.70, 30 minutes, three to five on weekdays) and Dunning (£2.10, 50 minutes, two or three direct buses on weekdays).

Ask Stagecoach if the Perthshire 'Tourist Trail' vintage bus has been reinstated.

Getting Around Most of the weekday Stagecoach buses to Auchterarder run via Muthill; others go via Innerpeffray (once on Tuesday and Thursday only). The Crieff to Stirling bus goes via Muthill. Bikes can be hired from Crieff Ski Shop (☎ 654667), 66 Commissioner St, for £10 per day.

Upper Strathearn
☎ 01764 • pop 1900

The Highland villages of **Comrie** (pop 1430) and **St Fillans** (pop 350), in upper Strathearn, are surrounded by craggy scenery, forests and bare mountain-tops where deer and mountain hares live in abundance. Comrie is 24 miles (38km) west of Perth and St Fillans is about 5 miles (8km) farther west.

Things to See Comrie is near several geological faults and small earthquakes occur frequently. In the 19th century, the world's first seismometers were set up here; replicas are currently on view in tiny **earthquake house** *(The Ross; admission free; open 24 hours daily Apr-Oct)*, just west of the village. **Glen Lednock** extends for 6 miles (10km) into the hills north-west of Comrie; at the head of the glen there's a reservoir and the highest hill in Strathearn, Ben Chonzie (931m). Near the village, at the foot of the glen, there's the 22m-high **Melville monument** on top of Dunmore hill (256m), and the **Devil's Cauldron**, a spectacular waterfall on the River Lednock.

St Fillans is at the eastern end of **Loch Earn**. It's a peaceful place now, but it wasn't always so. The ancient **crannog** (man-made island) just offshore was the site of a gruesome massacre in 1612, when the McNabs from Killin carried a boat 8 miles (13km) over the hills, then rowed out and surprised and slaughtered the bandit McNeishes. One McNeish escaped, and all with this name today are descended from him.

Walking The pleasant mile-long woodland hike to the Deil's Cauldron starts from a car park about 50m up the Glen Lednock road. A steep path from the waterfall goes up to the road; follow it up the glen for a short way then turn left onto a steep trail leading to the Melville monument, an excellent viewpoint. You can return to Comrie on the road.

Places to Stay & Eat *Braincroft Bunkhouse (☎ 670140, fax 679691, Comrie Rd)* Dorm beds £9-10. Open year-round. This place is 2 miles (3km) from Comrie toward Crieff and is the best budget option.

St Margaret's (☎ 670413, Braco Rd, Comrie) Singles £17-19, doubles £34-38. Vegetarians are catered for at this B&B; two out of the three rooms have shared bathroom.

Comrie Hotel (☎ 670239, Drummond St, Comrie) From £25 per person. Bar meals are available at this comfortable place (£5.50 to £14; jacket potatoes start at £2.95).

Achray House Hotel (☎ 685231, fax 685320, St Fillans) Singles/doubles £34.50/69. At the friendly Achray House Hotel, rooms may be heavily discounted in winter. The bar meals (£7-£12.95) are tasty and a three-course table d'hôte dinner costs £19.50.

Ancaster Arms (☎ 670722, 26 Drummond St, Comrie) 2-courses/3-courses £4/5. The home-cooked bar meals here are great value but are served only from 11am to 2pm and 5pm to 7pm Wednesday to Sunday.

Getting There & Away Stagecoach (☎ 01738-629339) operates daily buses from Perth, via Crieff, to Comrie (£3, one hour, hourly) and St Fillans (£3, 1¼ hours, five daily except Sunday).

There's no bus service between St Fillans and Lochearnhead.

WEST PERTHSHIRE

The lochs and hills of this remote area are possible to reach by public transport but buses are usually once-daily postal services.

From the A9, north of Dunkeld, the A82 heads west to Aberfeldy, Loch Tay and Killin. West of Aberfeldy, the village of Fortingall, at the foot of beautiful Glen Lyon, is famous as the birthplace of Pontius Pilate. A little farther north, the Rannoch area is renowned for its beauty and the almost perfectly shaped hill, Schiehallion (see under Strathtummel & Loch Rannoch).

Aberfeldy
☎ 01887 • pop 1956

This slightly shabby small town has the unique distinction of sitting at the exact

The exclusive Royal and Ancient Golf Club's clubhouse, St Andrews, viewed from West Sands beach

An old cannon and a great view at Stirling's grand castle

Snowed under in Dunkeld

Remnants of the ancient Caledonian pine forest that once covered most of Scotland

Autumn colours frame the glassy River Tummel, near Killiecrankie

Provost Ross' House, Aberdeen

A Castlegate pub, Aberdeen

Statue of Peter Pan, Kirriemuir

The Braemar Gathering, Scotland's best-known Highland Games

geographic centre of Scotland. Aberfeldy can be a bit rough, especially late in the evening.

The TIC (☎ 820276), in an old church on The Square, opens year-round; there's a plan of the town on the wall. Two banks have ATMs. The cottage hospital (☎ 820314) is on Old Crieff Rd.

Things to See The B846 to Tummel Bridge crosses the River Tay in Aberfeldy by a fine **Wade bridge**; construction began in 1733 by General Wade as part of his pacification of the Highlands project. Nearby stands the **Black Watch monument**, which commemorates the first muster in 1740.

The **Aberfeldy water mill** (☎ 820803, Mill St; adult/child £2.50/1; open 10am-4.30pm Mon-Sat & noon-4.30pm Sun Easter to mid-Oct) was built in 1825 and restored in 1983. Stone-ground oatmeal is produced here by water power and two stones, each weighing ½ tonnes.

Castle Menzies (☎ 820982, Weem; adult/child £3/2; open 10.30am-5pm Mon-Sat & 2pm-5pm Sun Apr to mid-Oct, last admission 4.30pm), 1½ miles (2.5km) west of town by the B846 at Weem, is the impressive restored 16th-century seat of the Chief of the Clan Menzies. There's a small clan museum and a tearoom at the castle.

Places to Stay & Eat Aberfeldy is not short of places to stay.

Aberfeldy Caravan Park (☎ 820662, Dunkeld Rd) Camping £8-9.75. Open Apr-Oct. The park is located on the eastern side of town.

Dunollie House (☎ 820298, Taybridge Drive) Dorm beds £7.50-13. This hostel is at the western end of town, by the A827 and the river.

Tighnabruaich (☎ 820456, fax 829254, Taybridge Terrace) Singles £18-20, doubles £36-40. Tighnabruaich is a friendly homely Victorian place with delicious home baking. There are three rooms with shared bathroom.

Tigh'n Eilean Guest House (☎/fax 820109, Taybridge Drive) Singles £18-24, doubles £38-48. Another fine and superbly decorated Victorian house with good food,

en-suite rooms, and a wonderful lounge with an open fire. Dinner costs £13.

Khanam Tandoori (☎ 829200, 48 Dunkeld St) Mains £5.95-12.95. You'll find a huge range of Indian dishes on the menu at Khanam.

Black Watch Inn (☎ 820699, Bank St) Mains from £3.75. Enjoy a good home-cooked bar meal in either the public bar or the quieter lounge.

Country Fare (Bridge End) Snacks from £1.45. Country Fare serves home baking, baked potatoes and filled baguettes.

Plaice in The Square (The Square) This is a clean fish and chip shop – haddock and chips costs £3.40.

Self-caterers can visit the *Co-op* in The Square.

Getting There & Away Stagecoach runs buses from Aberfeldy to Pitlochry (£2.10, 45 minutes), Dunkeld (£3, 1¼ hours) and Perth (£3, around 1¾ hours) up to 10 times daily (except Sunday). Strathtay Scottish has a twice daily service (schooldays only) between Aberfeldy and Blairgowrie (£3, 1¼ hours), via Dunkeld (£2.15, 40 minutes). A postbus service (☎ 01246-546329) goes to Killin (three hours) via Kenmore, and another goes to the top of Glen Lyon, at Lubreoch, via Fortingall (both once daily except Sunday). Elizabeth Yule Transport (☎ 01796-472290) operates from Aberfeldy to Kinloch Rannoch (£2.40, one hour 10 minutes, once daily) on schooldays.

The central bus stop is at Chapel St, just off The Square.

Loch Tay

The greater part of Ben Lawers (1214m), Scotland's ninth tallest peak, crouches like a lion over Loch Tay. It's in the care of the NTS and there's a visitor centre (admission £1) high on the slopes of the mountain; the access road continues over a wild pass to Glen Lyon. A trail leads to the summit from the centre, but you should take a good map (OS map No 51).

Attractive **Kenmore**, at the eastern end and outlet of Loch Tay, is about 6 miles (10km) west of Aberfeldy. The short main street is dominated by a church with a clock tower, and a spectacular archway – the entrance to privately owned Taymouth Castle. The opening of the salmon-fishing season is always celebrated with style on 15 January in Kenmore. Just a quarter of a mile (400m) along the south Loch Tay road from the village, the **Scottish Crannog Centre** (☎ 01887-830583, adult/child £3.50/2.50; open 10am-4.30pm daily Apr-Oct) has a reconstruction of an artificial Iron Age island-house. There are interesting demonstrations of Iron Age skills, including starting a fire using only two pieces of wood and dry kindling.

Kenmore Hotel (☎ 01887-830205, fax 830262, The Square) B&B singles £45-50, doubles £70-80, double suites £110. The Kenmore Hotel claims to be Scotland's oldest inn and dates from 1572. Look out for the Burns poem on the wall, written here in 1787. The gents toilets are distinctly unusual! Top-floor rooms, such as 'The Square', also have great character. In the bar, filled baguettes start at £3.50 and meals cost £5.95 to £15.95.

The Aberfeldy to Killin postbus passes through Kenmore and Lawers once daily, except Sunday.

Fortingall & Glen Lyon

Fortingall is one of the prettiest villages in Scotland, with 19th-century thatched cottages in a very tranquil setting. It was designed by James Marjorybanks McLaren, who taught Charles Rennie Mackintosh. The

Crannogs

Usually built in a loch for defensive purposes, a crannog (from the Gaelic word crann, meaning tree) consists of an artificial rock island with timber posts and struts supporting a hut above high-water level. Crannogs were used on many lochs, including Lochs Awe, Earn and Tay, from prehistoric times up to the 18th century. Some crannogs had curious underwater causeways that could zigzag or have traps, making night-time assaults without a boat extremely difficult.

church (admission free; open 10am-4pm daily Easter-Sept) has impressive wooden beams and a 7th-century **monk's bell**. In the churchyard, there's a **5000-year-old yew**, probably the oldest tree in Europe. This tree was already ancient when the Romans camped on the meadows by the River Lyon.

Glen Lyon is one of Scotland's most wonderful glens. The long single-track road ensures few visitors penetrate its remote upper reaches, where capercaillie live in patches of Scots pine forest. Just 3 miles (5km) upstream from Fortingall, opposite Chesthill, there's a **Roman bridge** crossing the Allt Dà-ghob, where there's a waterfall. You can see the bridge from the Glen Lyon road.

Fendoch (☎ 01887-830322, e fendoch@ eidosnet.co.uk, Fortingall) Singles £16-18, doubles £32-36. Fendoch is highly recommended for B&B. All rooms have private bath; evening meals are available.

Fortingall Hotel (☎/fax 01887-830367, Fortingall) B&B £25-35 per person. Part of the hotel dates from 1300; there are some very nice rooms on the first floor – for example, room No 8. The bar meals (from £6) here are recommended. Try the local venison braised in red wine and juniper berries (£7.50).

The Aberfeldy to Glenlyon postbus (☎ 01246-546329) runs via Fortingall once daily, except Sunday.

Strathtummel & Loch Rannoch

There are comparatively few 'visitor attractions' but there's lots of great scenery in this area. A visit in autumn is recommended, when the birch trees are at their finest. In winter, Tummel Bridge is often one of the coldest places in Scotland.

Queen's View Visitor Centre (☎ 01796-473123, Strathtummel; £1 parking charge; open 10am-6pm daily Apr-Oct), at the eastern end and outlet of Loch Tummel, has a magnificent outlook towards Schiehallion and displays and audiovisual programme about the area. Although Queen Victoria probably visited in 1866, it's thought that the viewpoint is named after Queen Isabella, wife of Robert the Bruce.

Kinloch Rannoch is a pleasant village with a grocer's shop and post office. It's a good base for local walks or a cycle trip around **Loch Rannoch**. There's an interesting **clan trail** around the loch, with roadside notice boards about local clans. Beyond the western end of the loch, you enter bleak Rannoch Moor, which extends all the way to Glen Coe. The rivers and lochs on the moor are good for fishing.

Schiehallion You can walk up the popular peak Schiehallion (1083m) from Braes of Foss (five hours return). There's a path up to the summit ridge, then it's very rocky and can be unpleasant in bad weather. Take all the usual precautions: map (OS map No 51), compass, food, water, good boots and waterproofs. The near-perfect shape of this hill allowed physicists to use its gravitational attraction on a pendulum to estimate the gravitational constant, G, and hence calculate the mass of the earth.

Places to Stay & Eat *Kilvrecht (☎ 01350-727284, Kinloch Rannoch)* Camping £3/6 without/with car. Open Apr-Oct. This basic camp site is secluded and situated 3½ miles (6km) from Kinloch Rannoch on the south Loch Rannoch road.

Glenrannoch House (☎ 01882-632307, Kinloch Rannoch) En-suite singles/doubles £22/44. Vegetarian B&B is available here, just off the south Loch Rannoch road. Dinner is available for £15 extra.

Bunrannoch House (☎/fax 01882-632407, Kinloch Rannoch) Singles/doubles £22/44. Grand Bunrannoch House is a former shooting-lodge.

Moor of Rannoch Hotel (☎/fax 01882-633238) Mains around £6. If you get as far as Rannoch Station (16 miles/26km west of Kinloch Rannoch), try the excellent food at the Moor of Rannoch Hotel. B&B is also available for £40 per person.

Getting There & Away On schooldays only, Elizabeth Yule Transport (☎ 01796-472290) operates from Kinloch Rannoch to Aberfeldy (£2.40, one hour 10 minutes, once daily in each direction), passing within 2½

miles (4km) of Braes of Foss. The Kinloch Rannoch to Pitlochry service runs one to three times daily, except Sunday (£2.40, 50 minutes).

The Pitlochry to Rannoch Station postbus (☎ 01246-546329) has a once daily service (except Sunday and public holidays) via Kinloch Rannoch and both sides of the loch.

ScotRail runs trains from Rannoch Station, north to Fort William and Mallaig, and south to Glasgow.

PERTH TO AVIEMORE
There are a number of major sights strung out along the A9, the main route north to Aviemore in the Highlands. Frequent buses and trains run along this route; most stop at the places described in this section.

Dunkeld & Birnam
☎ 01350 • pop 1050
Fifteen miles (24km) north of Perth, Dunkeld is an attractive village on the Highland line with some excellent walks in the surrounding wooded area. Dunkeld TIC (☎ 727688), The Cross, opens April to December.

Things to See & Do Dunkeld Cathedral *(☎ 0131-668 6800, High St; admission free; open standard HS hours Apr-Sept, otherwise 9.30am-4pm Mon-Sat & 2pm-4pm Sun)* must be among the most beautifully sited cathedrals in the country. Half of it is still in use as a church, the rest is in ruins. The oldest part of the original church is the choir, completed in 1350. The 15th-century tower is also still standing. The cathedral was damaged during the Reformation and burnt during the Battle of Dunkeld in 1689.

On High and Cathedral Sts is a collection of 20 artisans' houses restored by the NTS. Across the bridge is Birnam, made famous by *Macbeth*, but there's not much left of Birnam Wood.

Good local **walks** include the Hermitage Woodland Walk, starting from a car park by the A9, a mile (1.6km) west of Dunkeld. The well-marked trail follows the River Braan to the Black Linn Falls, where the duke of Atholl built a folly, **Ossian's Hall**, in 1758.

CENTRAL & NE SCOTLAND

The **Loch of the Lowes Visitor Centre** (☎ 727337, Loch of the Lowes; admission free, donation advised; open 10am-5pm Apr-Sept), 2 miles (3km) east of Dunkeld off the A923, has wildlife displays and an excellent birdwatching hide with binoculars provided. A pair of ospreys breeds here.

Places to Stay & Eat *Wester Caputh Independent Hostel* (☎/fax 01738-710617, Caputh) Dorm beds £10. This lively 18-bed hostel is by the A984 Coupar Angus road (5 miles/8km east of Dunkeld); free pick-up at Birnam or Dunkeld is available. Guests frequently attend traditional music sessions in Dunkeld at *MacLean's Real Music Bar* (☎ 727340, Tay Terrace).

Elwood Villa (☎ 727330, Perth Rd, Dunkeld) Singles £16-17.50, doubles £32-35. All rooms have shared bath and vegetarians are catered for at this B&B.

Birnam House Hotel (☎ 727462, fax 728979, Perth Rd, Birnam) Singles £26-55, doubles £40-84. The Birnam House Hotel is a grand-looking place with crow-stepped gables and four-poster beds; most rooms have private bathroom. The bar meals are recommended.

The Dunkeld Restaurant (☎ 727427, 5 Atholl St) 3-course lunch £7.50, mains around £6. The food here is quite good.

Tappit Hen (☎ 727472, 7 Atholl St) The Tappit Hen serves coffee, cakes, sandwiches (around £1.50) and soup and a roll (£1.70).

You can get fish and chips for £3.50 at the *Osprey* (12 Atholl St).

Getting There & Away
Scottish Citylink buses between Glasgow/Edinburgh and Inverness stop at the train station (by Birnam) two or three times daily. Birnam to Perth or Pitlochry takes 20 minutes (£4.30 and £4, respectively). Trains to Inverness (£15.80, two hours) or Perth (£4.50, 18 minutes) run three to eight times daily.

Stagecoach buses from Perth to Pitlochry and Aberfeldy all stop in Dunkeld. Strathtay Scottish (☎ 01382-228345) have a twice daily service (except Sunday) between Blairgowrie and Aberfeldy, via Dunkeld (no bus to Aberfeldy on Saturday and school holidays).

Ask the TIC or Stagecoach if the summer 'Heatherhopper' service from Perth to Braemar via Dunkeld and Pitlochry has been reinstated.

Pitlochry
☎ 01796 • pop 2439
Despite the tourist shops, Pitlochry is a pleasant town and makes a useful base for exploring the area; there are good transport connections if you don't have your own wheels.

The TIC (☎ 472215), 22 Atholl Rd, opens daily (except Sunday in winter). From late May to mid-September, its opening hours are from 9am to 7pm. You'll find an ATM at the Royal Bank of Scotland, Atholl Rd, by the post office.

Things to See If you haven't yet been on a tour of a whisky distillery, Pitlochry has two. **Bell's Blair Atholl Distillery** (☎ 482003, Perth Rd; admission £3, includes voucher redeemable against purchases; open 9am-5pm Mon-Sat & noon-5pm Sun Easter-Sept, otherwise reduced hours Mon-Fri only) is at the southern end of the town. **The Edradour** (☎ 472095, by A924; admission free; open 9.30am-5pm Mon-Sat & noon-5pm Sun Mar-Oct, phone to confirm times in winter) is Scotland's smallest distillery, 2½ miles (4km) east of Pitlochry on the A924.

When the power station was built on the River Tummel, a **fish ladder** was constructed to allow salmon to swim up to their spawning grounds. It's in the **Scottish & Southern Energy Visitor Centre** (☎ 473152, Pitlochry Power Station; adult/child £2/1; open 10am-5.30pm daily Mar-Oct), where there are high-tech interactive displays on hydroelectric power and a salmon video; entry to the observation chamber for the fish ladder is free. May and June are the best months to watch the fish.

Nearby, at the Pitlochry Festival Theatre, the **Scottish Plant Collector's Garden** commemorates 300 years of plant collecting and is due to open in summer 2002. For details, call ☎ 484600.

Walking The TIC sells the useful publication *Pitlochry Walks* (50p), which lists four short and four long local walks.

The Edradour walk (2 miles; 3km) goes past the distillery and the Black Spout waterfall. An 8½-mile (14km) hike goes around Loch Faskally, past the theatre and fish ladder, and up to the Pass of Killiecrankie (see that section later). A 7-mile (11km) hike takes you to Blair Castle; you could catch the bus back, but check times with the TIC before you go. There's a steep 3-mile (5km) round trip to 400m-high Craigower, a viewpoint above Pitlochry. For a more spectacular view,

tackle Ben Vrackie (841m), a steep 6-mile (10km) walk from Moulin (on the A924).

Places to Stay Pitlochry is packed with places to stay, but anything central tends to be a bit pricey.

Pitlochry Youth Hostel (☎ 472308, Knockard Rd) Dorm beds £8/6. Open year-round. The SYHA hostel overlooks the town centre and has great views. Laundry facilities are available.

Pitlochry Backpackers (☎ 470044, fax 470055, 134 Atholl Rd) £11 per person. Open Mar-Oct. This place has double or twin

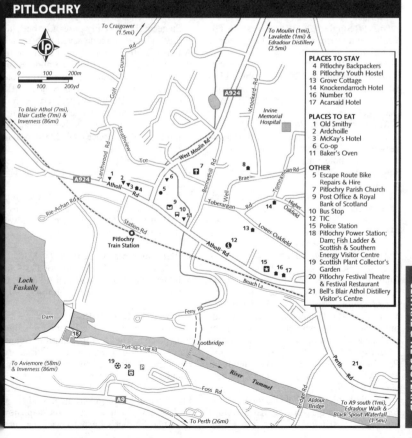

PITLOCHRY

PLACES TO STAY
4 Pitlochry Backpackers
8 Pitlochry Youth Hostel
13 Grove Cottage
14 Knockendarroch Hotel
16 Number 10
17 Acarsaid Hotel

PLACES TO EAT
1 Old Smithy
2 Ardchoille
3 McKay's Hotel
6 Co-op
11 Baker's Oven

OTHER
5 Escape Route Bike
   Repairs & Hire
7 Pitlochry Parish Church
9 Post Office & Royal
   Bank of Scotland
10 Bus Stop
12 TIC
15 Police Station
18 Pitlochry Power Station;
   Dam; Fish Ladder &
   Scottish & Southern
   Energy Visitor Centre
19 Scottish Plant Collector's
   Garden
20 Pitlochry Festival Theatre
   & Festival Restaurant
21 Bell's Blair Athol Distillery
   Visitor's Centre

CENTRAL & NE SCOTLAND

rooms. It offers fairly standard backpacker accommodation.

Grove Cottage *(☎/fax 472374, 10 Lower Oakfield)* Singles £15-17, doubles £30-34. Open year-round. Grove Cottage is pleasantly located and offers good-value B&B. The cheaper rooms have a shared bathroom. Dinner is available for £9.50 extra.

Lavalette *(☎ 472364, Manse Rd, Moulin)* Singles/doubles £15/32. Open Mar-Oct. This is a pleasant modern cottage about a mile north on the A924; vegetarians are catered for at this B&B.

There are plenty of places to stay along Atholl Rd, which runs through the centre of town.

Number 10 *(☎ 472346, fax 473519, 10 Atholl Rd)* Singles £20-30, doubles £40-66. You'll get a warm welcome at this pleasant Victorian villa.

Acarsaid Hotel *(☎ 472389, fax 473952, 8 Atholl Rd)* Singles £29-40, doubles £58-80. Open Mar-Dec. This luxurious hotel has 19 rooms, all with attached bath. There's also a good restaurant here.

Knockendarroch Hotel *(☎ 473473, fax 474068, Higher Oakfield)* B&B £48-63 per person. The Knockendarroch Hotel is one of the nicest hotels in Pitlochry. Traditional Scottish dinners are included in the price, and are also available to nonresidents for £21, but you'll need to book at least a week in advance.

Places to Eat There's a reasonable range of places to eat in Pitlochry.

Festival Restaurant *(☎ 484626, Foss Rd)* 2-course/3-course set dinner £18/21. Booking is advised for the recommended restaurant at the Pitlochry Festival Theatre.

Old Smithy *(☎ 472356, 154 Atholl Rd)* Mains £5.25-11.75. This worthwhile restaurant boasts roast haunch of venison for £9.25, and vegetarian choices are available.

McKay's Hotel *(☎ 473888, 138 Atholl Rd)* Mains around £5-8. Bar meals at McKay's Hotel include beef and Guinness pie (£6.95).

On Atholl Rd, try the hot pies for 57p at the ***Baker's Oven***, or the takeaway fish and chips for £3.20 at ***Ardchoille***. There's a ***Co-op***

supermarket *(West Moulin Rd)* if you're self catering.

Entertainment The well-known *Pitlochry Festival Theatre (☎ 472680, Foss Rd; tickets £4-25)* stages a different play six nights out of seven during its season from May to mid-October.

Getting There & Away Scottish Citylink runs approximately hourly buses between Inverness and Glasgow/Edinburgh via Pitlochry. Prices and journey times to destinations from Pitlochry are: Inverness (£8.10, two hours), Aviemore (£6.40, 1¼ hours), Perth (£5, 40 minutes), Edinburgh (£8, two hours) and Glasgow (£8, 2¼ hours).

Stagecoach runs daily buses to Aberfeldy (£2, 30 minutes, three to seven daily), Blair Atholl (£1.30, 25 minutes, once daily on weekdays), Dunkeld (£1.90, 25 minutes, up to 12 daily except Sunday) and Perth (£3, one hour, up to seven daily except Sunday). Ask if the summer 'Heatherhopper' service from Perth to Braemar via Dunkeld and Pitlochry has been reinstated. There's also a Monday to Saturday postbus service (☎ 472386) to Blair Atholl (30 to 45 minutes).

See the earlier Strathtummel & Loch Rannoch section for details of buses to Kinloch Rannoch.

Pitlochry is on the main rail line from Perth to Inverness. There are seven trains a day from Perth (£8.20, 30 minutes), fewer on Sunday.

Getting Around Escape Route (☎ 473859), 8 West Moulin Rd, hires bikes for £15/9 for a full/half-day. It also does repairs. For a taxi call Elizabeth Yule Transport on ☎ 472290.

Pass of Killiecrankie

The first skirmish of the Jacobite rebellion took place in 1689 in this beautiful, rugged gorge, 3½ miles (6km) north of Pitlochry. Highland soldiers led by Jacobite Bonnie Dundee routed government troops led by General Mackay, but Bonnie Dundee was killed. One of the government soldiers is said to have jumped across the gap, now known as Soldier's Leap, to evade capture.

The **NTS Visitors Centre** (☎ *01796-473233, Killiecrankie; admission free, car parking £1; open 10am-5.30pm daily Apr-Oct)* has a display on the battle and local natural history.

Elizabeth Yule Transport (☎ 01796-472290) runs between Pitlochry and Blair Atholl/Calvine via Killiecrankie four or five times daily (except Sunday).

Blair Castle & Blair Atholl
☎ 01796

One of the most popular tourist attractions in Scotland, Blair Castle (☎ *481207, Blair Atholl; adult/child/family grounds only £6.25/ 4/18, £2/1/5; open 10am-6pm daily Apr-Oct, last entry 5pm)* is the seat of the duke of Atholl, but the castle and its 70,000 acres are now managed by a charitable trust. Outside this impressive whitewashed castle, set beneath forested slopes above the River Garry, a piper pipes in the crowds each day. In May, there's the parade of the Atholl Highlanders, the only private army in Europe.

The original tower was built in 1269, but the castle has undergone significant remodelling since then. In 1746 it was besieged by the Jacobites, the last castle in Britain to be subject to siege.

Thirty rooms are open to the public, and they're packed with paintings, arms and armour, china, lace and embroidery, presenting a wonderful picture of upper-class Highland life from the 16th century to the present. One of the most impressive rooms is the ballroom, with a wooden roof and walls covered in antlers.

Blair Castle is 7 miles (11km) north of Pitlochry, and a mile (1.6km) from Blair Atholl village. There's a restaurant and a giftshop on site.

The other attractions in Blair Atholl village include the **Atholl Country Collection** (☎ *481232, Blair Atholl; adult/child £2/1; open 1.30pm-5pm daily June-Oct, 10am-5pm July to mid-Sept)*, a folk museum with a stuffed highland cow! You can hire bikes from **Atholl Mountain Bikes** (☎ *473553)* for £12/8 for a full/half-day. It has a leaflet listing cycle routes in the area, including a 16-mile (26km) ride along an estate road up

Glen Tilt, a 12-mile (19km) ride around Bruar Falls and Old Struan, or a 6-mile (10km) ride to Killiecrankie Pass and back.

Dalgreine (☎ *481276, off St Andrew's Crescent)* Singles £17-18, doubles £34-40. Dalgreine is an excellent guesthouse. Some rooms are en suite; dinner is £10 extra.

Elizabeth Yule Transport (☎ 01796-472290) runs a service four or five times daily except Sunday between Pitlochry and Blair Atholl (£1.30, 20 minutes). Some buses go directly to the castle. There's a train station in the village, but not all trains stop here.

For a continuation of this route, see The Cairngorms section in The Highlands chapter.

BLAIRGOWRIE & GLENSHEE
☎ 01250 • pop 8500

Blairgowrie and Braemar are the main accommodation centres for the Glenshee ski resort, although there's a small settlement 5 miles (8km) south of the ski runs at Spittal of Glenshee.

There's a TIC (☎ 872960), 26 Wellmeadow (the central square), Blairgowrie, which opens year-round; ask for a leaflet about the Cateran Trail. You'll find two banks with ATMs in Allan St, just off Wellmeadow.

Glenshee Ski Resort Glenshee ski resort (☎ *01339-741320,* e *glenshee@sol.co.uk,* w *www.ski-glenshee.co.uk)*, on the border of Perthshire and Aberdeenshire, has 38 pistes and is one of Scotland's largest skiing areas. The chair lift can whisk you up to 910m, near the top of The Cairnwell (933m). Whenever there's enough snow in winter it opens daily (it's currently closed in summer, but check with the TIC). A one-day lift pass and ski hire costs from £26; two-hour class instruction costs £12.

Other Things to See There's not much to see in Blairgowrie, but **Keathbank Mill & Heraldry Centre** (☎ *872025, Balmoral Rd; adult/child £4/2; open 10.30am-5pm daily Easter-Sept)*, off the A93 Braemar road, is worth a look. You'll see Scotland's largest working water wheel, a steam engine dating from 1862, two model railways, a heraldry museum and woodcarving displays.

About 3 miles (5km) south of Blairgowrie, by the A93 to Perth, there's a curious attraction – the **Meikleour beech hedge**, planted in 1746. At 30m, it's the world's highest hedge. It must be difficult to trim.

Alyth is an interesting village about 5 miles (8km) east of Blairgowrie. Ask the TIC for the three *Walk Old Alyth* leaflets; there are lots of old buildings to see, including church ruins dating from 1296. **Alyth Museum** *(☎ 01738-632488, Commercial St; admission free; open 1pm-5pm Wed-Sun May-Sept)* covers local history.

Places to Stay & Eat There are a number of good places in Blairgowrie.

Dunmore (☎ 874451, Newton St) Singles £17-19, doubles £34-38. For year-round B&B, try friendly Dunmore. It has a TV lounge and rooms with shared bathroom.

Angus Hotel (☎ 872455, fax 375615, 46 Wellmeadow) Singles £30-50, doubles £60-100. Bar meals £4.50-8.95. The Angus Hotel offers special winter rates for dinner and B&B. The bar meals here are good.

Cargill's Bistro (☎ 876735, Lower Mill St) Mains £5.50-14.95. In a pleasant riverside area, Cargill's Bistro also does excellent snacks such as soup and a roll (£1.75).

Blue Jays (☎ 870088, Boat Brae) Mains £6.50-14.95. In this pleasant restaurant/wine bar, you can get baked potatoes from £3.45.

There are several supermarkets in Blairgowrie, such as *Somerfield* by Wellmeadow.

There are also several good places in Alyth.

Drumnacree House (☎/fax 01828-632194, St Ninian's Rd) Singles £48.50-53.50, doubles £80-90. All rooms have private facilities. The recommended arty bistro here (mains £4.80 to £13.90) is the only oven bistro north of Edinburgh.

Alyth Fish & Chip Shop (☎ 01828-632538, Airlie St) The best takeaway in the area is this one in Alyth, where a tasty haddock and chips costs £2.95.

Blackbird Inn (☎ 01828-632293, by Alyth) Bar meals £3.25-3.75. The Blackbird Inn, by the A926 just west of Alyth, dates from 1869 and serves home-made bar meals.

Spittal of Glenshee Hotel (☎ 885215, Spittal of Glenshee) Singles/doubles £28/56, B&B in bunkhouse £13.50. This is a large place closer to the ski slopes offering B&B in rooms with attached bath. There's also a good bar and a bunkhouse (without cooking facilities).

Dalmunzie House Hotel (☎ 885224, fax 885225, Spittal of Glenshee) Singles £37-62, doubles £60-112. This grand hotel, also near the slopes, boasts the highest nine-hole golf course in Britain and is set in a 6000-acre estate, 1½ miles (2.5km) off the main road. Fine restaurant meals cost around £25 extra.

Getting There & Away Strathtay Scottish operates a service from Perth to Blairgowrie (£2.20, 50 minutes, six or seven daily except Sunday). There's also a bus from Blairgowrie to Dundee (£2.40, 50 minutes, six to eight daily, except Sunday).

The only service from Blairgowrie to the Glenshee area is the postbus (☎ 872766) to Spittal of Glenshee (no Sunday service).

Dundee & Angus

Dundee – the fourth-largest city in Scotland – was once a whaling port and the centre of the thriving jute industry. Having suffered from industrial decline and chronic unemployment in the late 20th-century, it is now on the rise again. The city has several interesting attractions for visitors, including Scott of the Antarctic's research ship *Discovery* and the Verdant Works museum.

Angus is the region of fertile farmland to the north and east of Dundee, an attractive area of peaceful glens and wide straths running down to the sea. It was part of the Pictish kingdom in the 7th and 8th centuries, and there are many interesting Pictish symbol stones, notably at Aberlemno. Robert the Bruce signed a declaration of independence from England at Arbroath Abbey in Angus in 1320. Although a ruin, much of the abbey still stands. The main draw in Angus is Glamis Castle of *Macbeth* fame.

DUNDEE
☎ 01382 • pop 142,700

Dundee enjoys perhaps the finest location of any Scottish city, spreading along the northern shore of the Firth of Tay. In the late 19th and early 20th centuries it was one of the richest cities in the country – there were more millionaires per head in Dundee than anywhere else in Britain. The processing of jute (a natural fibre used in making ropes and sacking) and the textile and engineering industries declined in the second half of the 20th century, leading to high unemployment and urban decay. In the 1960s and '70s Dundee was scarred by ugly blocks of flats and office buildings joined by unsightly concrete walkways – the view as you approach across the Tay Bridge does not look promising.

But since the mid-1990s the city has begun to pull itself up by the bootstraps, reinventing itself as a tourist destination and a centre for banking, insurance and new industries such as biotechnology. Captain Scott's polar research ship *Discovery*, which was built in Dundee, returned as a tourist attraction in 1993, and has been joined by the Verdant Works museum and modern developments such as the Dundee Contemporary Arts centre. Dundee's hotels and restaurants are good value, and 4 miles (6km) east of the city is the attractive seaside suburb of Broughty Ferry.

Despite the feeling of desolation in parts of the town, there's a new feeling of optimism here. The vigour that remains in the city is in the hearts of the Dundonians, who are among the friendliest, most welcoming and most entertaining people you'll meet anywhere in the country.

History
Dundee first began to grow in importance as a result of trade links with Flanders and the Baltic ports. It was awarded the first of its royal charters by King William in the late 12th century.

In its chequered history, Dundee was captured by Edward I, besieged by Henry VIII and destroyed by Cromwellian forces in the 17th century. It became the second most important trading city in Scotland after Edinburgh.

In the 19th century, Dundee was a major player in the shipbuilding and railway engineering industries. Linen and wool gave way to jute, and since whale oil was used in the production of jute, whaling developed alongside. At one time, there were as many as 43,000 people employed in the textile industry, but as the jute workers became redundant, light engineering, electronics and food processing provided employment.

Dundee is often called the city of the three 'J's – jute, jam and journalism. No jute is produced here anymore, and when the famous Keiller jam factory was taken over in 1988, production was transferred to England. Journalism still thrives, however, led by the family firm of DC Thomson. Best known for children's comics such as *The Beano*, Thomson is the city's largest employer.

Orientation
Most people approach the city from the Tay Road Bridge or along the A90 from Perth. From the A90, turn onto Riverside Drive for the city centre. The train station and *Discovery* are just west of the bridge; the bus station is a short walk to the north, just off Seagate.

Immediately north of the city centre is the prominent hill of Dundee Law (174m). Four miles to the east of Dundee is Broughty Ferry, Dundee's seaside resort. Regular buses run to the resort and it's a very pleasant place to stay.

Information
The very helpful TIC (☎ 527527), 21 Castle St, opens 9am to 5pm Monday to Saturday October to April, and 9am to 6pm Monday to Saturday and noon to 4pm Sunday May to September. As well as the usual accommodation booking service, it sells maps, guidebooks and Scottish Citylink and National Express bus tickets.

Guided walks are available with a minimum charge of £10 per hour per group (minimum four people) – a heritage and industrial walk, a maritime walk, and other possibilities can be catered for. For details, call ☎ 532754.

CENTRAL & NE SCOTLAND

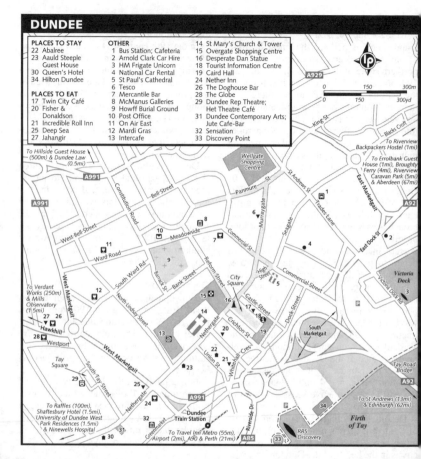

DUNDEE

PLACES TO STAY
22 Abalree
23 Aauld Steeple
   Guest House
30 Queen's Hotel
34 Hilton Dundee

PLACES TO EAT
17 Twin City Café
20 Fisher &
   Donaldson
21 Incredible Roll Inn
25 Deep Sea
27 Jahangir

OTHER
1 Bus Station; Cafeteria
2 Arnold Clark Car Hire
3 HM Frigate Unicorn
4 National Car Rental
5 St Paul's Cathedral
6 Tesco
7 Mercantile Bar
8 McManus Galleries
9 Howff Burial Ground
10 Post Office
11 On Air East
12 Mardi Gras
13 Intercafe

14 St Mary's Church & Tower
15 Overgate Shopping Centre
16 Desperate Dan Statue
18 Tourist Information Centre
19 Caird Hall
24 Nether Inn
26 The Doghouse Bar
28 The Globe
29 Dundee Rep Theatre;
   Het Theatre Café
31 Dundee Contemporary Arts;
   Jute Cafe-Bar
32 Sensation
33 Discovery Point

You'll find banks with ATMs on High St and Murraygate. The main post office is on Meadowside, a block north of the Overgate Shopping Centre. You can check email at Intercafe, on the 1st floor of Debenhams department store in the Overgate Shopping Centre (£1.50 for 30 minutes); it opens 9am to 5.30pm Monday to Saturday (7pm Thursday) and till 4.30pm Sunday.

Medical Services There's a 24-hour casualty department at Ninewells Hospital (☎ 660111) at Menzieshill, west of the city centre.

Town Centre

The heart of the city is **City Square**, flanked to the south by the 1930s facade of **Caird Hall** (the City Chambers). A new addition to the square, unveiled in 2001, is a bronze statue of **Desperate Dan**, one of the best-loved cartoon characters from the children's comic *The Dandy*, published by Dundee firm DC Thomson since the 1930s.

Pedestrianised High St leads west into Nethergate, flanked to the north by **St Mary's Parish Church**; although most of the present building dates from the 19th century, there has been a church here since

1190. The oldest part of the church is the **Old Steeple** (☎ *206790, Nethergate; adult/child £2/1.75; open 10am-5pm Mon-Sat & noon-4pm Sun Apr-Sept, 11am-4pm Mon-Sat & noon-4pm Sun Oct-Mar)*, built around 1460. A guided tour takes you through the bell-ringers' chamber and up to the belfry for a grand view over the city.

Discovery Point

Make an effort to see Dundee's much-publicised visitor attraction, centred on Captain Scott's famous polar expedition vessel, the **RRS** *Discovery* (☎ *201245,* **W** *www .rrsdiscovery.com, Discovery Quay; adult/ child £5.95/3.85; open 10am-5pm Mon-Sat & 11am-5pm Sun Apr-Oct, 10am-4pm Mon-Sat & 11am-4pm Sun Nov-Mar)*. The ship was built in Dundee in 1900, with a hull at least two feet thick to survive the Antarctic pack ice. Scott sailed for the Antarctic in 1901 and, in a not uneventful voyage, spent two winters trapped in the ice.

After viewing the interesting exhibitions and audiovisual displays in the main building, you board the ship – afloat in a protected dock – to see the cabins used by Scott and his crew. The complex is on the bank of the Firth of Tay, near the northern end of the Tay Road Bridge. A joint ticket that gives entry to the Verdant Works costs £10.15/7.

HM Frigate *Unicorn*

Unlike the polished and much-restored *Discovery*, Dundee's other floating tourist attraction retains more of the atmosphere of a salty old ship. Built in 1824, the 46-gun **HM Frigate** *Unicorn* (☎ *200893, Victoria Dock; adult/child £3.50/2.50; open 10am-5pm Wed-Mon Apr-Oct, 10am-4pm Wed-Sun Oct-Mar)* is the oldest British-built warship still afloat – perhaps because it never saw action. By the mid-19th century, sailing ships were outclassed by steam and the *Unicorn* served as storage for gunpowder, then later as a training vessel. When it was proposed to break up the historic ship for scrap in the 1960s, a preservation society was formed.

Wandering around the four decks gives you an excellent impression of what it must have been like for the crew forced to live in such cramped conditions. The *Unicorn* is berthed in Victoria Dock, just north-east of the Tay Bridge. The entry price includes a guided tour (also available in French and German).

Verdant Works

One of Europe's best industrial museums, the **Verdant Works** (☎ *225282,* **W** *www .verdantworks.com, West Henderson's Wynd; adult/child £5.95/3.85; open 10am-5pm Mon-Sat & 11am-5pm Sun Apr-Oct, 10am-4pm Mon-Sat & 11am-4pm Sun Nov-Mar)* is housed in a restored jute mill. Original machinery in working condition is complemented by interactive exhibits and computer displays that detail the history of the jute industry. Funding problems at the time of writing meant that the future of the museum was in doubt; check with the TIC or the museum Web site for the latest situation.

Other Things to See

The **McManus Galleries** (☎ *432084, Albert Square; admission free; open 10.30am-5pm Mon-Sat, 10.30am-7pm Thur, 12.30pm-4pm Sun)* is a solid Victorian Gothic building, designed by Gilbert Scott, containing the city's museum and art collection. The exhibits are well displayed and interesting, and include the history of the city from the Iron Age to the present day. There's an impressive display of Scottish Victorian paintings, furniture and silver. Look out for the display on William McGonagall, Scotland's worst poet, whose lines about the Tay Rail Bridge disaster are memorably awful.

Over the road is the **Howff Burial Ground**, a historic graveyard given to the people of Dundee by Mary Queen of Scots. The carved gravestones feature the signs and symbols of the old craft guilds and date back to the 16th century.

Just west of the town centre is **Dundee Contemporary Arts** (☎ *606220,* **W** *www.dca .org.uk, Nethergate; admission free; galleries open 10.30am-5.30pm Tues, Wed, Sat & Sun, 10.30am-8pm Thur & Fri)*, a new centre for modern art, design and cinema. The galleries exhibit work by contemporary UK and international artists, and there are

CENTRAL & NE SCOTLAND

studios where you can watch artists at work, or take part in workshops.

Sensation (*☎ 228800, Greenmarket; adult/child £5/3.50; open 10am-5pm daily*) is an interactive science centre for kids, based around the five senses, and includes a cafe and shop.

It's worth making the climb up to the **Dundee Law**, at 174m the highest point in the city. The Law is the remains of an ancient volcanic plug and provides great views of the city, the two Tay bridges, and across to Fife. The 1½-mile Tay Road Bridge was opened in 1966. The **railway bridge** is just over 2 miles (3km) long, still the longest in Europe. The part nearest Dundee was completed in 1887, replacing a section destroyed by a storm one dark night in 1879. Moments after the collapse, a train attempted to cross, and plunged into the firth, killing 75 people.

Mills Observatory (*☎ 435846, Balgay Hill; admission free; open 11am-5pm Tues-Fri, 12.30pm-4pm Sat & Sun Apr-Sept; 4pm-10pm Mon-Fri, 12.30pm-4pm Sat & Sun Oct-Mar*), on nearby Balgay Hill, has displays on astronomy and space exploration, and a 10-inch telescope for public use.

Places to Stay

Camping The nearest camp site is at Monifieth, 5 miles (8km) east of the city centre.

Riverview Caravan Park (*☎ 535471, fax 535375, Marine Drive, Monifieth*) Tent pitches £8-10. This five-star site has an attractive location near the beach, and is only five minutes walk from a supermarket.

Hostels & Colleges There's not much choice for budget travellers in Dundee.

Riverview Backpackers Hostel (*☎ 450565, 127 Broughty Ferry Rd*) Beds £10 per person including breakfast. Open year-round. This 10-bed hostel – a little run down and seedy-looking – is a 15-minute walk east of the bus station on the main road towards Broughty Ferry. You can camp here for £2.50.

University of Dundee (*☎ 344038, e hol idays@dundee.ac.uk, University of Dundee*) Singles/doubles from £22/32. During the Easter and summer vacations, you can stay

in the university residences in West Park Hall and West Park Villas, 1½ miles (2.5km) west of the centre.

B&Bs & Guesthouses There are plenty of centrally located, good-value B&Bs.

Abalree (*☎ 223867, 20 Union St*) B&B singles/doubles £18/30. This is a basic guesthouse but you couldn't be more central.

Aauld Steeple Guest House (*☎ 200302, 94 Nethergate*) Singles £21-23, doubles £36-38. Just around the corner from the Abalree, this place is a bit more upmarket.

Hillside Guest House (*☎/fax 223443, e info@tildab.co.uk, 43 Constitution St*) B&B singles/doubles £24/42. Hillside is a spacious Victorian villa off Constitution Rd, 500m north of the city centre.

Errolbank Guest House (*☎ 462118, 9 Dalgleish Rd*) B&B £22-30 per person. This guesthouse is a mile east of the city centre, just north of the road to Broughty Ferry.

Hotels Many of Dundee's hotels are business oriented.

Hilton Dundee (*☎ 229271, fax 200072, Earl Gray Place*) Singles/doubles from £54/86. The Hilton is on the waterfront, right beside the Tay Bridge, and has a leisure club and swimming pool. The lowest rates apply at the weekend.

Travel Inn Metro Dundee (*☎ 203240, fax 203237, Discovery Quay, Riverside Drive*) Rooms £49.95. This place is just west of Discovery Point – the room rate includes up to two adults and two children under 16.

Queen's Hotel (*☎ 322515, fax 202668, e enquiries@queenshotel-dundee.com, 160 Nethergate*) Singles/doubles £40/60. This grand Victorian hotel in the lively West End is one of Dundee's finest places to stay.

Shaftesbury Hotel (*☎ 669216, fax 641598, e reservations@shaftesbury-hotel.co.uk, 1 Hyndford St*) Singles/doubles £49.50/72. The Shaftesbury is on the western side of Dundee, just off the Perth road and about 1½ miles (2.5km) from the city centre. It's a former jute baron's mansion, and is popular with businesspeople. There are bargain midweek and weekend rates available.

Places to Eat

There's an increasing number of good places to eat in Dundee, especially in the West End, and prices are often very competitive.

Twin City Café *(☎ 223662, 4 City Square)* Mains £3.95-5.95. Open 7.30am-7pm Mon-Thur, 7.30am-9pm Fri & Sat, 10.30am-5.30pm Sun. Twin City is a pleasant cafe on the main square, with outdoor tables in summer. It has good salads and sandwiches, including tasty veggie stuff such as falafel and hummus wraps.

Jute Cafe-Bar *(☎ 606220, Nethergate)* Mains £4.95-8.95. Open 10.30am-midnight daily. The stylish cafe in the Dundee Contemporary Arts Centre serves good pastas and salads, as well as more adventurous fusion cuisine.

Het Theatre Café *(☎ 206699, Tay Square)* Open noon-3pm & 5pm-7.30pm Sun & Mon, noon-3pm & 5pm-9pm Tues-Thur, noon-3pm & 5pm-10.30pm Fri & Sat. Sandwiches from £2.20, mains £6.50-9.90. This place is at the Dundee Rep Theatre. It's a European-style coffee-bar, and a great place for coffee, a drink or a meal.

Jahangir *(☎ 202022, 1 Session St)* Mains £4.25-6.95. Open noon-midnight Sun-Thur, noon-1am Sat & Sun. It's worth going to this place for the decor alone – pure Hollywood Moghul, with an over-the-top tent, and a fountain with goldfish and carp (they're not on the menu). The food's good and it also does takeaways.

Raffles Restaurant *(☎ 226344, 18 Perth Rd)* Mains £5.50-12.75. Food served noon-3pm & 5pm-8pm Mon-Sat, 11am-4pm Sun. Raffles is a lively bar and bistro, close to the university and not too far from the city centre.

Deep Sea *(81 Nethergate)* Open 9.30am to 6.30pm Monday to Saturday. This is the oldest fish and chip shop in Dundee; haddock and chips costs £4.30.

Fisher & Donaldson *(12 Whitehall St)* is rather more upmarket, an excellent bakery and patisserie with a cafe attached.

The ***Incredible Roll Inn*** *(Whitehall Crescent)* is a popular place for a snack, with 100 different types of hot and cold filled rolls starting at 80p.

The ***bus station cafeteria*** *(on Seagate)* is basic but very cheap.

Self-caterers should head for the ***Tesco*** supermarket on Murraygate; it opens 7.30am to 7pm Monday to Saturday (8pm on Thursday) and 9am to 6pm Sunday.

Entertainment

Dundee's nightlife may not be as hot as Glasgow's, but there are plenty of places to go. Pick up a copy of *The Accent* what's-on guide from the TIC. For music gigs in the Dundee area, check the Web site at W www.gigged .co.uk. Tickets for most events can be bought at the Dundee Contemporary Arts centre.

If you're around in July, look out for the Dundee Blues Bonanza, a day-long festival of free blues and rock (second Saturday in July).

Caird Hall *(☎ 434940, W www.cairdhall .co.uk, City Square)* Tickets for orchestral concerts £15. The Caird Hall hosts regular concerts of classical music, as well as rock bands, dances, fetes and fairs. Check their Web site for details of coming events.

Dundee Rep Theatre *(☎ 223530, Tay Square)* Dundee's main venue for the performing arts, this theatre hosts touring companies and also stages its own performances.

The Doghouse Bar *(☎ 227080, 13 Brown St)* This pub is housed in a converted school building and has outdoor seating in summer. It has live rock and blues bands on Monday, Thursday and Saturday (tickets £4-6, free on Saturday) and stand-up comedy on Friday nights (admission £5).

On Air East *(☎ 203226, 15 Ward Rd)* Tickets £8-10. This is one of Dundee's main club venues for dance music, drum 'n' bass, hip hop, house and reggae.

There are many lively bars, especially in the West End and along West Port. The ***Nether Inn*** *(134 Nethergate)* is a large, stylish pub popular with students, with live jazz on Saturday afternoon. ***The Globe*** *(3-57 West Port)* serves good bar meals from noon to 7.30pm (6pm Sundays) and often has live music. The ***Mercantile Bar*** *(100 Commercial St)* is another lively city centre pub.

The biggest nightclub in Dundee is ***Mardi Gras*** *(☎ 205551, South Ward Rd)*,

CENTRAL & NE SCOTLAND

where the cover charge on Friday nights is £2.50 before midnight, rising to £6 after.

Getting There & Away

Dundee is 445 miles (712km) from London, 84 miles (93km) from Glasgow, 62 miles (99km) from Edinburgh, 67 miles (107km) from Aberdeen and 21 miles (34km) from Perth. If you're driving over the Tay Road Bridge from Fife, it's toll-free in that direction.

Air The airport (☎ 643242), in Riverside Drive, close to the centre, has daily scheduled services to London City airport, and flights to Aberdeen, Edinburgh and Manchester.

Bus No 100 runs from the bus station to the airport (10 minutes, seven or eight daily except Sunday). A taxi to the airport takes five minutes and costs £2.

Bus National Express operates four services a day (two direct) to Dundee from London (10 hours direct), including one night service.

Scottish Citylink has hourly buses from Edinburgh (£6.50, two hours) and Glasgow (£7, 2¼ hours) via Perth. On some services you may have to change in Perth (£3.20, 35 minutes).

There are also hourly services to Aberdeen (£6.70, two hours). Some buses to Aberdeen go via Arbroath, others via Forfar. However, getting to the west coast is a major pain – you must go via Glasgow to reach either Fort William or Oban.

Strathtay Scottish runs buses to Perth (one hour, hourly), Blairgowrie (one hour, hourly), Forfar (40 minutes, once or twice an hour), Kirriemuir (70 minutes, hourly), Brechin (1¼ hours, 10 daily, change at Forfar) and Arbroath (one hour, every 30 minutes).

Stagecoach Fife bus No 95 runs twice an hour to St Andrews (30 minutes) and hourly to the East Neuk fishing villages of Crail (one hour), Anstruther, Pittenweem, St Monans and Elie (1½ hours).

Train Trains run to Dundee from Edinburgh (£14.90, 1¼ hours) and Glasgow (£19.70, 1½ hours) at least once an hour, Monday to Saturday; hourly on Sunday from Edinburgh, every two hours on Sunday from Glasgow.

Trains from Dundee to Aberdeen (£17.40, 1¼ hours) run via Arbroath and Stonehaven. There are around two trains an hour, fewer on Sunday.

Getting Around

The city centre is compact, and is easy to get around on foot.

For information on local public transport, call Travel Dundee (☎ 201121). It's possible to catch a train to Broughty Ferry, but the buses (80p, 15 minutes) are much more frequent.

Phone Discovery Taxis (☎ 732111) if you need a cab.

Alternatively, if you'd like to drive yourself, rental companies in Dundee include Arnold Clark (☎ 225382), East Dock St, and National Car Rental (☎ 224037), 45-53 Gellatly St.

BROUGHTY FERRY
☎ 01382

This attractive suburb is 4 miles (6km) east of Dundee city centre. There's a long, sandy beach east of Broughty Castle and a number of good places to eat and drink.

Broughty Castle Museum (☎ 436916, Castle Green; admission free; open 10am-4pm Mon-Sat & 12.30pm-4pm Sun Apr-Sept, 10am-4pm Tues-Sat & 12.30pm-4pm Sun Oct-Mar) is in a reconstructed 16th-century tower that looms imposingly over the harbour, guarding the entrance to the Firth of Tay. It has an interesting display on the local whaling industry.

Claypotts Castle (HS; ☎ 01786-431324, Arbroath Rd; adult/child £1.50/50p; limited opening, phone to check), built in the late 16th century, was once in the country but has now been absorbed by suburbia. Looking like a house perched on top of a tower, it's actually one of the most complete Z-plan tower houses in the country.

Places to Stay

Broughty Ferry is a more attractive place to stay than Dundee city centre.

Auchenean (☎ 774782, 177 Hamilton St) B&B £19 per person. This is a pleasant place five minutes' walk from the beach in the eastern part of Broughty Ferry.

Homebank (☎/fax 477481, 9 Ellieslea Rd) B&B £22.50-25 per person. Close to the yacht club in the western part of Broughty Ferry, Homebank is a Victorian mansion set in a lovely walled garden.

Beach House Hotel (☎ 776614, fax 480241, 22 Esplanade) Singles/doubles £38/48. Right on the seafront, five minutes' walk east of the harbour, this friendly hotel has eight rooms, five of them en suite.

Premier Lodge Dundee East (☎ 0870 700 1360, fax 0870 700 1361, 115-117 Lawers Drive, Panmurefield) Rooms £42. This modern budget hotel is just off the A92 road to Aberdeen, 4½ miles (7km) east of Dundee city centre and 20 minutes' walk from Broughty Ferry beach. Room rate includes up to two adults and two children under 16.

Places to Eat

There are lots of good pubs and cafes.

Fisherman's Tavern (☎ 775941, 10-16 Fort St) Mains £5.25-6.25. Lunch noon-3pm, dinner 6pm-9pm. The Fisherman's is a lively pub with good beer and excellent bar meals. It also has accommodation, at £39 to £56 for a double room with B&B.

Ship Inn (☎ 779176, 121 Fisher St) Mains £5.75-12. Meals served noon-2pm & 5pm-10.30pm Mon-Fri, noon-10.30pm Sat & Sun. On the seafront around the corner from the Fisherman's is the cosy, 19th-century Ship Inn, which serves top-notch bar meals such as venison steaks or haddock and chips.

Visocchi's (☎ 779297, 40 Gray St) Visocchi's – a 70-year-old institution – is an Italian cafe that sells delicious home-made ice cream in a wide range of flavours.

GLAMIS CASTLE & VILLAGE

Looking every bit the Scottish castle, with its forest of pointed turrets and battlements, Glamis (pronounced glams) Castle (☎ 01307-840393, adult/child £6.20/3.10; open 10.30am-5.30pm Apr-Oct, last entry 4.45pm) was the legendary setting for Shakespeare's *Macbeth*. The Grampians and an extensive park

provide a spectacular backdrop for this family home of the earls of Strathmore and Kinghorne. A royal residence since 1372, the Queen Mother (née Elizabeth Bowes-Lyon) spent her childhood here and Princess Margaret (the Queen's sister) was born at Glamis.

The five-storey, L-shaped castle was given to the Lyon family in 1372, but was significantly altered in the 17th century. Inside, the most impressive room is the drawing room, with its arched plasterwork ceiling. There's a display of armour and weaponry in the crypt (haunted) and frescoes in the chapel (also haunted). Duncan's Hall is where King Duncan was murdered in *Macbeth*. You can also look round the royal apartments, including the Queen Mother's bedroom.

Glamis Castle is 12 miles (19km) north of Dundee, and there's a restaurant on site. You're escorted round in a guided tour, which takes an hour and leaves every 15 minutes.

The **Angus Folk Museum** (NTS; ☎ 01307-840288, Kirkwynd, Glamis; adult/child £3/2; open 11am-5pm May-Sept & weekends Oct) is just off The Square in Glamis village. In a row of 18th-century cottages, you'll find a fine collection of domestic and agricultural relics.

There are two to five buses a day from Dundee (35 minutes) to Glamis, operated by Strathtay Buses; some continue to Kirriemuir.

ARBROATH
☎ 01241 • pop 23,528

This fishing port – source of the famous Arbroath smokies (smoked haddock) – was established in the 12th century. Nowadays, the town is a busy seaside resort, but some fishing still continues. There's an all-year TIC (☎ 872609) in Market Place, open 9.30am to 5.30pm Monday to Saturday and 10am to 3pm Sunday, June to August; 9am to 5pm Monday to Friday, 10am to 5pm Saturday, April, May and September; 9am to 5pm Monday to Friday and 10am to 3pm Saturday, October to March.

Things to See King William the Lion founded **Arbroath Abbey** (HS; ☎ 878756,

Abbey St; adult/child £2.50/1; open 9.30am-6.30pm daily Apr-Sept, 9.30am-4.30pm Mon-Sat & 2pm-4.30pm Sun Oct-Mar) in 1178, and is buried here. It is thought that the abbot of Arbroath wrote the famous Declaration of Arbroath in 1320 (see 'The Declaration of Arbroath' boxed text in the Facts about Scotland chapter) that asserted Scotland's right to independence from England. Closed following the Dissolution, the fortified abbey fell into ruin, but enough survives to make this an impressive sight. There's a tall gable in the southern transept, with a circular window that once held a shipping beacon, and parts of the nave and sacristy are intact. The abbey is near the top of High St, near the TIC and bus and rail stations. There's a good booklet available for £1.95.

The **Arbroath Museum** *(☎ 875598, Ladyloan; admission free; open 10am-5pm Mon-Sat year-round, also 2pm-5pm Sun in July-Aug)*, housed in elegant Signal Tower, covers local history including the textile and fishing industries. The tower was once used to send signals to the construction team working on the Bell Rock Lighthouse, built between 1807 and 1811, 12 miles (19km) offshore.

At **St Vigeans**, about a mile north of the town centre, there's an interesting red sandstone **church** perched on top of a conical hill. At the foot of the hill, you'll find an excellent **museum of Pictish & medieval sculptured stones** *(admission free; key available 9.30am-6.30pm daily Apr-Sept, 9.30am-4.30pm Mon-Sat & 2pm-4.30pm Sun Oct-Mar)*, which includes crosses and human and animal carvings. The museum is unmanned – the key's kept at cottage No 7, and is available during the stated opening times.

An excellent walk follows a path along the top of the Seaton sea cliffs north-east of Arbroath for 3 miles (5km) to the quaint fishing village of **Auchmithie**, where there are several caves and a good tearoom.

Places to Stay & Eat There are central B&Bs in Marketgate and Ladybridge St.

Scurdy House (☎ 872417, fax 874603, 33 Marketgate) B&B £16-23. This warm and friendly B&B is conveniently located close to the TIC.

Seaton (☎ 430424, 2 Seaton Rd) B&B £20 per person. Seaton is an attractive Victorian villa close to the start of the cliff-top walk to Auchmithie.

Café Rendezvous (1B Millgate) Mains under £2.30. This place, behind the Arbroath Herald building near the bus station, is incredibly cheap: soup and bread is just £1.10 and *stovies* (slow-cooked potatoes, onion and meat – usually bacon, sausage or beef) and bread are £1.20.

Corn Exchange (☎ 879945, 34 Reform St) Mains £2-7. A Wetherspoons pub, but quite pleasant nonetheless, the Corn Exchange place serves good-value pub grub; you can get two meals for £5 from 2pm to 10pm Monday to Thursday, and 2pm to 8pm Friday and Saturday.

The *Golden Haddock* chip shop near the harbour, open daily from noon to 10.30pm, does smokie and chips for £4.35. You can buy smokies, kippers, fresh fish and shellfish from various stalls east of the harbour.

Getting There & Away Scottish Citylink buses run every two hours to Aberdeen (1½ hours) via Montrose and Stonehaven. Strathtay Scottish operates buses to Brechin, changing at Montrose. Bus No 140 runs from Arbroath to Auchmithie roughly every two hours (but only twice on Sunday).

There are frequent buses to Dundee, but it's better to go by train along the scenic coastline (£3.25, 20 minutes, two an hour).

FORFAR & AROUND
☎ 01307 • pop 12,652

Forfar, the county town of Angus, isn't terribly exciting, but there are some excellent historical sites nearby. The TIC (☎ 467876, 40 East High St, opens 10am to 5pm Monday to Saturday April to September (closes 5.30pm in July and August); ask for the *Town Trail* leaflet. Buses stop in East High St, by the Royal Bank.

Things to See The ruins and early Romanesque square tower of **Restenneth Priory**, probably founded by David I, are 1½ miles (2.5km) east of Forfar (on the B9113). About 4 miles (6km) east of Forfar is the site of the **Battle of Nechtansmere** (also called Dunnichen), where the Picts defeated invading Northumbrians in AD 685.

Five miles (8km) north-east of Forfar, on the B9134, are the **Aberlemno Pictish stones**, some of Scotland's best; these are well worth going to see. There are three 7th- to 9th-century stones by the roadside with various symbols, including the z-rod and double disc. In the churchyard at the bottom of the hill, there's a magnificent 8th-century cross-slab displaying a Celtic cross, interlace decoration, entwined beasts and, on the reverse, scenes of the Battle of Nechtansmere. See the boxed text 'Pictish Symbol Stones' under Pictavia in the Brechin section later. The stones are covered up from November to March; otherwise there's open access (admission is free). The adjacent **Aberlemno parish church** has a 12th- or 13th-century stone baptismal font.

Places to Stay & Eat Nearby Kirriemuir (see the next section) is a nicer place to stay but there is B&B in Forfar.

Mrs Horsburgh's (☎ 468285, 34 Canmore St) B&B £16-18 per person. Just off Castle St, this place is close to the town centre and opens year-round.

Cheap places to eat include the *bakeries* on East High St and Castle St; try a Forfar *bridie* (a pie filled with meat, potatoes, onions and sometimes other vegetables) at *Saddler's*. For bar lunches, head for *Raffters Bar* on Castle St.

Getting There & Away Scottish Citylink buses run three or four times daily to Dundee (30 minutes), Brechin (20 minutes) and Aberdeen (£6.45, 1½ hours).

Strathtay Scottish operates buses to Dundee (40 minutes, once or twice an hour), Kirriemuir (25 minutes, hourly), and Aberlemno and Brechin (15 and 30 minutes respectively, once every hour or two).

KIRRIEMUIR
☎ 01575 • pop 5306
The highly recommended conservation town of Kirriemuir is a very attractive place, with narrow winding streets and a great feeling of times past. Kirriemuir is a good base for exploring the Angus Glens (see the next section), and it's one of the cheapest places to eat in the country. The TIC (☎ 574097), Cumberland Close, opens 10am to 5pm Monday to Saturday April to September (closes 5.30pm in July and August).

Things to See
Barrie's Birthplace *(NTS; ☎ 572646, 9 Brechin Rd; adult/child £2.50/1.80; open 10am-5.30pm Mon-Sat & 1.30pm-5.30pm Sun May-Sept, also weekends Oct)* is a two-storey house where JM Barrie, author of *Peter Pan*, was born in 1860. The upper floors are furnished in traditional style. There's also an outside wash-house and an exhibition about Barrie's work.

By the town square there's **The Tolbooth**, dating from 1604, and previously used as a jail. The **Aviation Museum** *(☎ 573233, Bellies Brae; donations welcome; open 10am-5pm)* has a large collection of WWII relics, both Allied and German.

Places to Stay & Eat
Airlie Arms Hotel (☎ 572847, fax 573055, ⓔ info@airliearms-hotel.co.uk, St Malcolm's Wynd) Singles/doubles £28.50/56. This place is in a medieval monastery which was converted into an inn after the Dissolution. The original arch-roofed refectory is now the function suite.

Cheaper B&B is available at *Crepto (☎ 572746, Kinnordy Place)* and *Woodlands (☎ 572582, 2 Lisden Gardens)*, which both charge £22 per person.

Kirrie Food Bazaar (Reform St) does cheap takeaways for around £1 to £1.80, and the Chinese restaurant *Tin On (30 Roods)* does chicken chow mein for £3.80. There's a large *Tesco* supermarket across the street.

Getting There & Away
Strathtay Scottish operates bus services to Dundee (one hour 10 minutes, hourly, every two hours on Sunday), Forfar (25 minutes, hourly) and Glamis (20 minutes, twice daily except Sunday).

CENTRAL & NE SCOTLAND

A Royal Mail postbus (☎ 0845 774 0740) runs from Kirriemuir to Glen Prosen (once daily except Sunday); another runs to Glen Clova (twice on weekdays, once on Saturday).

ANGUS GLENS

There are five major glens in the north of Angus: Glens Isla, Prosen, Clova, Lethnot and Esk.

All have attractive scenery, though each glen has its own peculiar character. Glen Clova and Glen Esk are clearly the most beautiful while Glen Lethnot is the least frequented.

Glen Isla

This glen, which runs roughly parallel with Glen Shee, has a number of scattered communities. At the foot of the glen, by Bridge of Craigisla, there's a pleasant waterfall, **Reekie Linn**.

The wild and mountainous upper reaches of Glen Isla include the **Caenlochan National Nature Reserve**.

A Royal Mail postbus (☎ 0845 774 0740) operates from Blairgowrie to Auchavan at the head of the glen, once daily except Sunday.

Glen Prosen

Near the foot of the glen, 6 miles (10km) north of Kirriemuir, there's a good forest walk up to the **Airlie monument** on Tulloch Hill (380m); start from the eastern road, about a mile beyond Dykehead.

From Glenprosen Lodge, at the top of the glen, the **Kilbo Path** leads over a pass between Mayar (928m) and Driesh (947m), descending to Glendoll Youth Hostel at the head of Glen Clova. Allow at least five hours, and wear appropriate mountain gear.

The Kirriemuir to Glen Prosen postbus (☎ 0845 774 0740) runs once daily except Sunday.

Glen Clova

This long and beautiful glen stretches north from Kirriemuir and is dominated by craggy mountains at its head. Look out for the waterwheel by the Clova Hotel, and picturesque **Cortachy Castle** in the lower part of the glen, where Charles II stayed in the 17th century.

There are great hikes in the glen, including the **Loch Brandy** circuit from the hotel (four hours) and Mayar and Driesh from Glendoll Youth Hostel (six to seven hours); use OS map No 44.

You can also walk **Jock's Road** from the hostel to Braemar (five to seven hours), but this route climbs above 900m and it's not an easy option. The descent to Glen Callater is very steep and may require an ice axe and crampons in winter. You'll need OS maps Nos 43 and 44.

There's a *camp site* (☎ 01575-550233) with basic facilities (April to September) by the bridge at Acharn (near the end of the road); a pitch costs £3.

Glendoll Youth Hostel (☎ 01575-550236, Glen Clova) Dorm beds £8.25/7. Open Apr-Sept. This hostel is at the end of the Glen Clova public road, well-situated for exploring the surrounding hills.

Clova Hotel (☎ 01575-550350, fax 550292, Glen Clova) B&B £35-39 per person. Bunkhouse bed £9.50. This hotel is 3½ miles (5.5km) down the road from the hostel. Bar meals are available here (£4.75 to £5.50). There's also a year-round 30-bed bunkhouse with a fully fitted kitchen.

The Kirriemuir to Glen Clova postbus (☎ 0845 774 0740) runs services twice on weekdays and once on Saturday. The 8.30am departure from Kirriemuir goes to the hostel, but the 3.05pm departure from Kirriemuir (not Saturday) only goes as far as Clova Hotel.

Glen Lethnot

At the foot of this glen, about 5 miles (8km) north-west of Brechin, there are the **Brown and White Caterthuns**. These two extraordinary Iron Age hill forts, defended by ramparts and ditches, are at 287m and 298m respectively. From the road between them it's an easy walk to either fort, and they're both great viewpoints. If you don't have your own car, you'll have to walk from Brechin, or from Edzell (4 miles; 6km).

The *Post House* (☎ 01356-660277), 2 miles (3km) north of the forts at Bridgend offers B&B for £14 per person, and dinner for £6 extra.

Glen Esk & Edzell

A pleasant planned village at the foot of Glen Esk and 6 miles (10km) north of Brechin, Edzell has an arched stone gateway over the public road, the **Dalhousie Arch**. One mile to the west, there's **Edzell Castle** *(HS; ☎ 01356-648631; adult/child £2.80/1; open 9.30am-6.30pm daily Apr-Sept, 9.30am-4.30pm Mon-Wed & Sat, 9.30am-1pm Thur & 2pm-4.30pm Sun Oct-Mar)*, a 16th-century L-plan tower house. It has an excellent garden, the pleasance, with sculptured wall panels. The castle's now roofless, but it's worth a visit.

Ten miles (16km) up the glen from Edzell, **Glenesk Folk Museum** *(The Retreat; ☎ 01356-670254; adult/child £2/1; open noon-6pm daily June-Oct, noon-6pm Sat-Mon Easter-May)* has an extensive local folk history collection and a tearoom. Tarfside village, 1½ miles (2.5km) beyond The Retreat, has a general store.

Four miles (6.5km) farther on, the public road ends at **Invermark Castle**, an impressive ruined tower guarding the southern approach to The Mounth, a hill track to Deeside. About three-quarters of a mile west of the castle, there's an old church by **Loch Lee**. Beyond the loch, there are lots of beetling cliffs and waterfalls.

Inchcape (☎ 01356-647266, High St) B&B £16-18 per person. This is an attractive Victorian house with comfortable en-suite rooms.

Glenesk Hotel (☎ 01356-648319, fax 647333, High St) Singles/doubles £58/95. The Glenesk is a plush hotel adjoining the golf course, and boasts a pool, spa and sauna.

Doune House (☎ 01356-648201, High St) B&B £16-20 per person. The Victorian Doune House is next to the TIC and post office in the middle of the village, and serves delicious home baking.

Strathtay Scottish runs two to six buses daily from Brechin to Edzell (20 minutes). There's no public transport from Edzell into the glen.

BRECHIN
☎ 01356 • pop 7593

Brechin, on the River South Esk, is an interesting town with several things to see. There's a small TIC (☎ 623050), in St Ninian's Place, east of High St, and another one at the Brechin Castle Centre (☎ 623050) on the edge of town. You'll find a bank with an ATM on Clerk St.

Pictavia

Adjoining Brechin Castle Centre, a gardening and horse-riding centre on the A90 just west of Brechin, is Pictavia *(☎ 626241, W www.pictavia.org.uk; adult/child £3.25/ 2.25; open 9am-5.30pm Mon-Sat & 10.30am-5.30pm Sun)*, an interpretive centre telling the story of the Picts, and explaining current theories about the mysterious carved symbol stones they left behind. It's worth making a trip here before going to see the Pictish stones at Aberlemno.

Other Things to See & Do

There's been a church in Brechin since the 9th century, and a 32m-high free-standing **round tower** (one of only three in Scotland) was built around 1000. Its elevated doorway, 2m above the ground, has carvings of animals, saints, and a crucifix. The adjacent **Brechin Cathedral**, Church Square, has been much altered throughout history. Nearby, there are several interesting buildings on High St, which is on a steep hill.

Farther east, near the TIC, the **Brechin Museum** *(☎ 622687, St Ninian's Square; admission free; open 9.30am-8pm Mon & Wed, 10am-6pm Tues, 9.30am-6pm Thur, 9.30am-5pm Fri & Sat)* has local historical relics.

On Sundays from June to early September, the **Caledonian Railway** *(☎ 377760, 2 Park Rd)* runs steam trains between Brechin and Bridge of Dun, 3½ miles (5.5km) to the east. There are six journeys between 11.25am and 5.05pm; tickets cost adult/ child £4.50/2.50 return.

From Bridge of Dun it's a 15-minute walk to **House of Dun** *(NTS; ☎ 810264; adult/child £3.70/2.50; open 1.30pm-5.30pm May-Sept, also open Easter & Oct weekends)*, a well-appointed Georgian mansion built in 1730.

CENTRAL & NE SCOTLAND

Pictish Symbol Stones

The Romans permanently occupied only the southern half of Britain up to 410. Caledonia, the section north of Edinburgh and Glasgow, was mostly left alone, especially after the mysterious disappearance of the Ninth Legion.

Caledonia was the homeland of the Picts, about whom little is known. In the 9th century they were culturally absorbed by the Scots, leaving a few archaeological remains and a scattering of Pictish place names beginning with 'Pit'. However, there are hundreds of mysterious standing stones decorated with intricate symbols, mainly in the north-east. The capital of the ancient Southern Pictish kingdom is said to have been at Forteviot in Strathearn, and Pictish symbol stones are to be found throughout this area and all the way up the eastern coast of Scotland into Sutherland and Caithness.

It's believed that the stones were set up to record Pictish lineages and alliances, but no-one is yet quite sure exactly how the system worked. The stones fall into three groups: Class I, the earliest, are rough blocks of stone, carved with any combination from a basic set of 28 symbols; Class II are decorated with a Celtic cross as well as with symbols; and Class III, dating from the end of the Pictish era (790-840), have only figures and a cross.

With your own transport, it's possible to follow a number of symbol-stone trails in the area. Starting at Dundee (visit the McManus Galleries first), drive north-east to Arbroath. On the outskirts of Arbroath is St Vigeans Museum which contains several interesting stones. Continue north along the A92 to Montrose, where there are more stones in the local museum. Along the A935, in Brechin Cathedral, is a good example of a Class III stone. From Brechin, take the B9134 to Aberlemno, where there are excellent examples of all three classes. Along the A94, at Meigle, there's the **Meigle Sculptured Stone Museum** (☎ 01828-640612; adult/child £2/75p; open 9.30am-6.30pm daily Apr-Sept only), with one of the best collections of stones in the country.

For more information, it's worth getting a copy of The Pictish Trail, by Anthony Jackson (Orkney Press), which lists 11 driving tours, or his more detailed Symbol Stones of Scotland, both available in TICs.

Places to Stay & Eat

Doniford (☎ 622361, 26 Airlie St) B&B £18.50-20 per person. Centrally located Doniford is quiet and comfortable, with a TV and coffee-making kit in your room.

Northern Hotel (☎ 625505, fax 622714, 2 Clerk St) Singles/doubles £42.50/65. The family-run Northern, an early 19th-century coaching inn, has a good restaurant and cafe-bar.

The ***Coffee Shop*** (St James Place) has a huge snack menu with all meals under £4.50, and there's takeaway service. On High St, there are the usual Chinese and Indian takeaways.

Getting There & Away

Scottish Citylink runs buses three or four times daily to Dundee (50 minutes), Forfar (20 minutes) and Aberdeen (one hour). The bus stop is on Clerk St.

Strathtay Scottish operates buses from South Esk St to Forfar (30 minutes, roughly once an hour), Edzell (20 minutes, two to six daily) and Aberlemno (15 minutes, once every hour or two).

MW Nicoll's (☎ 01561-377262) bus service from South Esk St to Stonehaven runs two to five times daily (55 minutes).

Aberdeenshire & Moray

This area is bound to the west and south by the Grampian mountains. The largest place is the prosperous city of Aberdeen – a tidy city of impressive and renowned granite architecture – which is still reaping the rewards of the North Sea oil industry.

Aberdeenshire incorporates Royal Deeside – the valley of the grand River Dee – royal because Queen Victoria liked it so much that she bought Balmoral here. The royal family still spends part of every summer here, appearing at the well-known Braemar Gathering.

Around the coast are the fertile plains immortalised by Lewis Grassic Gibbon in his trilogy, *A Scots Quair*, which was based on the life of a farming community in the 1920s. The east coasters, and particularly the Aberdonians, have always had a reputation for being hard-working and thrifty. Certainly anyone living near, or making a living from, the North Sea would have to be tough.

There's a strong indigenous culture in the north-east, quite separate from the rest of Scotland. Much of it is expressed in lively anecdotal or poetic form (in dialect). The bothy ballads and bands, which provided home entertainment among the workers on the big farms, still get high billing on local radio and TV.

Along the north coast of Banff and Moray are small fishing harbours with neat little streets looking out to sea. This coastline gets a lot of sun and not much rainfall, and the small nontouristy towns have a brisk, no-nonsense feel.

There are many castles in the characteristic Scottish baronial style in this area. Along the River Spey, in the north-west of the region, and across the border in the Highlands, the biggest industry is the distilling of whisky – many distilleries offer tours followed by drams.

If you plan to do a lot of travelling by bus, Stagecoach Bluebird (☎ 01224-212266) offers a Bluebird Rover ticket (£7) that gives unlimited bus travel for a day on all of its services.

ABERDEEN
☎ 01224 • pop 211,250

Aberdeen is an extraordinary symphony in grey. Almost everything is built of grey granite, including the roads, which are paved with crushed granite. In the sunlight, especially after a shower of rain, the stone turns silver and shines as if in a fairytale, but with low, grey clouds and rain scudding in off the North Sea, it can be a bit depressing.

Aberdeen was a prosperous North Sea trading and fishing port centuries before oil was considered a valuable commodity. After the townspeople supported Robert the Bruce against the English at the Battle of Bannockburn in 1314, the king rewarded the town with land for which he had previously received rent. The money was diverted into the Common Good Fund, to be spent on town amenities, as it still is today. It finances the regimented floral ranks that have won the city numerous awards, and helps keep the place spotless. As a result, the inhabitants have been inculcated with an almost overbearing civic pride.

The name Aberdeen is a combination of two Pictish-Gaelic words, 'aber' and 'devana', meaning the meeting of two waters. The area was known to the Romans, and was raided by the Vikings when it was an increasingly important port, with trade conducted in wool, fish, hides and fur. By the 18th century, paper and rope-making, whaling and textile manufacture were the main industries; in the following century it was a major herring port.

Since the 1970s, Aberdeen has become the main onshore service port for one of the largest oilfields in the world. Unemployment rates, once among the highest in the country, dropped dramatically, but have since fluctuated with the rise and fall of the price of oil.

CENTRAL & NE SCOTLAND

ABERDEEN

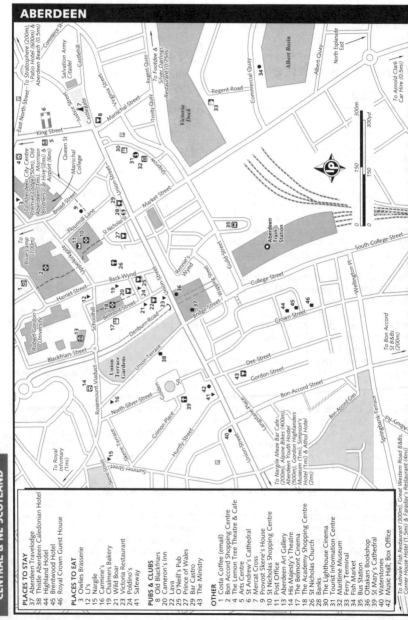

PLACES TO STAY
37 Aberdeen Travelodge
38 Thistle Aberdeen Caledonian Hotel
44 Highland Hotel
45 Brentwood Hotel
46 Royal Crown Guest House

PLACES TO EAT
3 Owlies Brasserie
12 LJ's
15 Nargile
16 Carmine's
19 Chalmers Bakery
21 Wild Boar
23 Victoria Restaurant
24 Poldino's
41 Safeway

PUBS & CLUBS
8 Old Blackfriars
20 Cameron's Inn
22 Lava
25 O'Neill's Pub
27 Prince of Wales
29 Bar Castro
43 The Ministry

OTHER
1 Costa Coffee (email)
2 Bon Accord Shopping Centre
4 The Lemon Tree Theatre & Cafe
5 Arts Centre
6 St Andrew's Cathedral
7 Mercat Cross
9 Provost Skene's House
10 St Nicholas Shopping Centre
11 Post Office
13 Aberdeen Art Gallery
14 His Majesty's Theatre
17 The Belmont Cinema
18 The Academy Shopping Centre
26 St Nicholas Church
28 Banks
30 The Lighthouse Cinema
31 Tourist Information Centre
32 Maritime Museum
33 Ferry Terminal
34 Fish Market
35 Bus Station
36 Ottakars Bookshop
39 St Mary's Cathedral
40 Waterstones
42 Music Hall; Box Office

Aberdeen is certainly worth a visit. It's a very lively city – there are more bars than would seem even remotely viable. Start with over 200,000 Scots, add multinational oil workers and a large student population – the result: thriving nightlife.

Orientation

Central Aberdeen is built on a ridge that runs east–west to the north of the River Dee. Union St, the main shopping street, runs along the crest of this ridge between Holborn Junction in the west and Castlegate in the east. The bus and train stations are next to each other, between Union St and the river. A half-mile east of the centre lies Aberdeen Beach. Old Aberdeen is just over a mile to the north of the centre.

Information

The TIC (☎ 288828) is next door to the Maritime Museum on Shiprow. It opens daily May to September, at least 9am to 5pm (with extended weekday opening to 7pm in July and August; shorter hours on Sunday). It's closed on Sunday between October and May. Note that the location and opening times of Aberdeen's TIC have changed several times, and may have changed again by the time you read this.

There are two handy banks with ATMs on Union St and St Nicholas St. The main post office is in the St Nicholas Shopping Centre on Upperkirkgate. You can check email at Costa Coffee on Loch St, on the north side of the Bon Accord Shopping Centre; it opens 8am to 6pm Monday to Saturday (7.30pm Thursday), 10am to 5pm Sunday, and charges 50p for 15 minutes.

For books and maps, head for Ottakars Bookshop (☎ 592440), 3-7 Union Bridge, or Waterstone's (☎ 571655), 236 Union St.

Medical Services Aberdeen Royal Infirmary (☎ 681818), Foresterhill, is about a mile north-west of the western end of Union St.

The Harbour

The harbour has always been a busy place. From dawn until about 8am, the fish market operates as it has for centuries.

Maritime Museum Situated in Provost Ross's House, the oldest building in the city, the Maritime Museum (☎ 337700, Shiprow; admission free; open 10am-5pm Mon-Sat, noon-5pm Sun) explains Aberdeen's relationship (almost exclusively commercial) with the sea. There are some interesting displays about shipbuilding and the whaling and fishing industries. Speedy Aberdeen clippers were a 19th-century shipyard speciality that were attractive to British tea merchants for the transportation of emigrants to Australia and, on return, the import of tea, wool and exotic goods (opium, for instance).

The City

Union St is the main thoroughfare, lined with solid granite buildings, many of them Victorian. The oldest area is **Castlegate**, at the eastern end, where the castle once stood. When it was captured from the English for Robert the Bruce, the password used by the townspeople was 'Bon Accord'. A street and shopping centre commemorate the password, which is now the city's motto.

In the centre of Castlegate stands the 17th-century **Mercat Cross**, bearing a sculpted frieze of portraits of Stuart monarchs. The baronial heap towering over the eastern end of Castlegate is the **Salvation Army Citadel**, which was modelled on Balmoral Castle.

On the northern side of Union St, 300m west of Castlegate, is **St Nicholas Church**, the so-called 'Mither Kirk' (Mother Church) of Aberdeen. The granite spire dates from the 19th century, but there has been a church on this site since the 12th century; the early 15th-century St Mary's Chapel survives in the eastern part of the church.

Provost Skene's House Surrounded by concrete and glass office blocks in what was once the worst slum in Aberdeen, is a late-medieval, turreted townhouse (☎ 641086, Guestrow; admission free; open 10am-5pm Mon-Sat, 1pm-4pm Sun) occupied in the 17th century by the provost (the Scots equivalent of a mayor) Sir George Skene. It was commandeered for a short time by the duke of Cumberland and his English redcoat soldiers, and later it became a dosshouse. It would have been demolished in the 1940s, but a long-running campaign to save it, supported by the present-day Queen Mother, led to its opening as a museum in 1953.

Typical of its period, it has intimate, panelled rooms. The 1622 tempera-painted ceiling, with its religious symbolism, is unusual for having survived the depredations of the Reformation. It's a gem of its time, featuring earnest-looking angels, St Peter with cockerels crowing, and period-type soldiers. At the top of the house is an archaeology display and a gallery of local domestic artefacts.

Marischal College Across Broad St from Provost Skene's House, this huge building used to house the science faculty of the University of Aberdeen. Marischal College was founded in 1593 by the 5th Earl Marischal, and merged with King's College (founded 1495) in 1860 to create the modern University of Aberdeen. The present building is late Victorian Gothic, made peculiar by the use of granite. It's the kind of building you either love or hate, but cannot avoid being impressed by.

Marischal Museum (☎ 274301, Marischal College, Broad St; admission free; open 10am-5pm Mon-Fri, 2pm-5pm Sun) is straight ahead through the main quadrangle and up the stairs, and is well worth visiting. In one room, there's a lively depiction of north-east Scotland through its famous people, customs, architecture, trade and myths. The displays are organised thematically, so visitors can easily get a good picture of the rich and complex local culture.

The other gallery is set up as an anthropological overview of the world, incorporating objects from vastly different cultures. It's also arranged thematically (Polynesian wooden masks alongside gasmasks etc). There are the usual bizarre Victorian curios, an Indian kayak found in the local river estuary and some Inuit objects collected by whalers.

Aberdeen Art Gallery Behind the grand facade of the art gallery (☎ 523700, Schoolhill; admission free; open 10am-5pm Mon-

Sat, 2pm-5pm Sun) is a cool, white space exhibiting the work of young contemporary Scottish and English painters, such as Gwen Hardie, Stephen Conroy, Trevor Sutton and Tim Ollivier. There's also a Francis Bacon and a selection of modern textiles, ceramics and jewellery. There's evidently a vigorous school of applied arts in Aberdeen. There are also several Joan Eardley landscapes; she lived in a cottage on the cliffs near Stonehaven in the 1950s and '60s, and painted tempestuous oils of the North Sea and poignant portraits of slum children.

Among the Pre-Raphaelites upstairs is a collection of 92 small portraits of artists, many of them self-portraits of now forgotten painters. The collection was begun around 1880 by Alexander Macdonald, and the first portrait painted was of Millais.

Downstairs, a large, empty, white, circular room, with fish-scaled balustrades evoking the briny origins of Aberdeen's wealth, commemorates the 165 people who lost their lives in the Piper Alpha oil rig disaster in 1988.

Aberdeen Beach

Just half a mile east of Castlegate is a spectacular two-mile sweep of clean, golden sands, stretching between the mouths of the Rivers Dee and Don. At one time Aberdeen Beach was a good, old-fashioned British seaside resort, but the availability of cheap package holidays has lured Scottish holidaymakers away from its somewhat chilly delights. On a warm summer's day though it's still an excellent beach.

The Esplanade still sports several traditional seaside attractions, including **Codona's Amusement Park** (☎ 595910, Beach Boulevard; admission free, pay per ride; open from 1pm daily June-Aug, from 1pm Fri-Sun Mar-May & Sept-Nov), complete with lunch-churning waltzers, dodgems, a roller-coaster log flume and haunted house. The adjacent **Sunset Boulevard** (☎ 595910; admission free, ten-pin bowling £2.15-3 per game; open 10am-midnight daily) is the indoor alternative, with ten-pin bowling, arcade games dodgems and pool tables.

Halfway between the beach and the city centre is **Stratosphere** (☎ 640340, 179

Constitution St; adult/child £5/3; open 10am-5pm Mon-Sat, 11.30am-5pm Sun), a hands-on, interactive science centre.

You can get away from the fun fair atmosphere by walking north towards the more secluded part of the beach. There's a **bird-watching hide** on the south bank of the River Don, between the beach and King St, which leads back south towards Old Aberdeen.

Bus Nos 14 and 15 (eastbound) from Union St go to the beach; or you can walk from Castlegate in 10 minutes.

Old Aberdeen

Just over a mile north of the city centre is the separate suburb of Old Aberdeen. The name is somewhat misleading – although Old Aberdeen is certainly old, the area around Castlegate is actually older. Old Aberdeen was once called Aulton, from the Gaelic for 'village by the pool', and this was anglicised in the 17th century to Old Town. The university buildings and St Machar's Cathedral are at the centre of this peaceful suburb.

It was here that Bishop Elphinstone established King's College, Aberdeen's first university, in 1495. The 16th-century **King's College Chapel** *(☎ 272137, College Bounds; admission free; open 9am-4.30pm Mon-Fri)* is easily recognisable by its crown spire. The interior is largely unchanged – the stained-glass windows and choir stalls are most impressive.

The **King's College Visitor Centre** *(☎ 273702, College Bounds; admission free; open 10am-5pm Mon-Sat, 2pm-5pm Sun)* houses a multimedia display on the university's history. There's also a pleasant coffee shop.

The 15th-century **St Machar's Cathedral** *(☎ 485988, The Chanonry; admission free; open 9am-5pm daily)*, with its massive twin towers, is one of the few examples in the country of a fortified cathedral. According to legend, St Machar was ordered to establish a church where the river takes the shape of a bishop's crook, which it does just here. The cathedral is best known for its impressive heraldic ceiling, dating from 1520,

which has 48 shields of kings, nobles, archbishops and bishops. Services on Sunday are at 11am and 6pm.

Bus No 20 from Littlejohn St (just north of Marischal College) runs to Old Aberdeen.

Gordon Highlanders Museum

This excellent military museum *(☎ 311200, St Lukes Viewfield Rd; adult/child £2.50/1; open 10.30am-4.30pm Tues-Sat & 1.30pm-4.30pm Sun Apr-Oct)* lies about a mile west of the western end of Union St. It records the history of one of the British Army's most famous fighting units, described by Winston Churchill as 'the finest regiment in the world'. The regiment was originally raised in the north-east of Scotland. Take bus No 14 or 15 from Union St.

Organised Tours

First Aberdeen (☎ 650065) operates tours of the city on an open top bus from July to September. There are departures every 40 minutes from 10am to 4pm from Castle St, and the route takes in King's College (Old Aberdeen), the Espalanade (Aberdeen Beach) and Duthie Park on the River Dee, south of the centre. Tickets cost £4/2 and are valid for the whole day.

Places to Stay

Camping Since Hazlehead Caravan Park closed down, the nearest camp site to Aberdeen is *Craighill Holiday Park (☎/fax 781973, Craighill)*, 2½ miles (4km) south of the city centre, on the main A92 road to Stonehaven. Pitches at this year-round site cost £5; it has rather basic shower and toilet facilities.

Hostels & Colleges *Aberdeen Youth Hostel (☎ 646988, 8 Queen's Rd)* Dorm beds £12.25/10.75 including breakfast Apr-Oct, £1 surcharge Jul & Aug, £9/6 Nov-Feb. Open year-round. This hostel is a mile west of the train station. Walk west along Union St and take the right fork along Albyn Place until you reach a roundabout; Queen's Rd continues on the western side.

During the university holidays, some colleges let rooms to visitors. The list of colleges offering accommodation changes from year to year – check with the TIC.

Robert Gordon University *(☎ 262134, fax 262144, Business and Vacation Accommodation Service, Schoolhill, Aberdeen AB10 1FR)* 6-8 bed flats £23-44 per week. Open Jun-Aug. Robert Gordon's lets self-catering apartments in the city centre and surrounding areas.

University of Aberdeen *(☎ 272664, fax 276246, Conference Office, King's College, Old Aberdeen AB24 3FX)* 4-7 bed flats £230-280 per week. The university has self-catering apartments overlooking Seaton Park and the River Don in Old Aberdeen.

B&Bs & Guest Houses There are clusters of B&Bs on Bon Accord St and Springbank Terrace (both 400m south-west of the train station), and along Great Western Rd (the A93, a 25-minute walk south-west of the centre). They're usually more expensive than the Scottish average and, with all the oil industry workers here, single rooms are at a premium. Prices tend to be lower at the weekend.

Royal Crown Guest House *(☎ 586461, fax 575485, 111 Crown St)* B&B £17-35 per person. The eight-room Royal Crown is only five minutes' walk from the train station (though up a steep flight of stairs), and is handy for the city centre.

There are several comfortable, semi-detached guest houses in Bon Accord St.

Dunrovin Guest House *(☎/fax 586081, 168 Bon Accord St)* B&B £17.50-30. Dunrovin is a typical, granite Victorian house, with eight rooms. The friendly owners will provide a veggie breakfast if you wish.

Other places worth trying here are just next door. ***Crynoch Guest House*** *(☎ 582743, 164 Bon Accord St)*, with B&B from £17 to £30 per person; and ***Denmore Guest House*** *(☎/fax 587751, 166 Bon Accord St)*, with B&B for £16 to £25 per person.

There are numerous places to stay along Great Western Rd.

Penny Meadow Private Hotel *(☎ 588037, fax 573639, 189 Great Western Rd)* B&B £25-46 per person. This is a small, friendly place with two twin rooms and one family room, all en suite.

Strathisla Guest House *(☎ 321026, 408 Great Western Rd)* B&B £20-32 per person. For nonsmokers only, the comfortable Strathisla Guest House has five rooms, all en suite.

Aurora Guest House *(☎ 311602, 429 Great Western Rd)* Singles/doubles from £20/34. This is another small, family-run B&B. There are six rooms, all with shared bathroom.

Hotels The comings and goings of oil industry personnel mean that Aberdeen hotels are not cheap, and often busy – book ahead, especially on weekdays; weekends are often quieter. The lower end of the quoted price ranges apply at weekends.

There are two budget chain hotels right in the city centre. ***Aberdeen Travelodge*** *(☎ 584555, 🅦 www.travelodge.co.uk, 9 Bridge St)* Rooms £49.95. The Travelodge is right between the train station and Union St, and the room rate includes up to two adults and two children under 16.

Aberdeen City Centre Premier Lodge *(☎ 0870 700 1304, fax 0870 700 1305, 🅦 www.premierlodge.co.uk, Inverlair House, West North St)* Rooms £46. The Premier Lodge, just east of Marischal College, is also very central – the room rate includes up to two adults and two children under 16.

There are many hotels and guest houses clustered around Crown St, just south of Union St.

Brentwood Hotel *(☎ 595440, fax 571593, 🅔 reservations@brentwood-hotel.demon.co .uk, 101 Crown St)* Singles £35-70, doubles £50-90. The friendly Brentwood is one of the best hotels in this area, comfortable and conveniently located, but often full during the week.

Highland Hotel *(☎ 583685, fax 572551, 🅔 coffeyanne@aol.com, 93-95 Crown St)* Singles £35-60, doubles £45-75. The family-run, 30-room Highland is also worth trying. There's a good bar and restaurant here.

Thistle Aberdeen Caledonian Hotel *(☎ 640233, fax 641627, 🅔 aberdeen.caledonian@thistle.co.uk, 10-14 Union Terrace)* Singles £30-130, doubles £60-150. This is a fine old hotel with much character on the northern side of Union St. It has several restaurants, and is renowned for its fine Scottish food.

Patio Hotel (☎ 633339, fax 638833, e patioab@globalnet.co.uk, Beach Boulevard) B&B from £75 per person mid-week, £26 per person at weekends. Part of a Norwegian hotel chain, the attractively modern Patio is a ten-minute walk north-east of Castlegate, and only a few minutes' stroll from the beach. It has a pool, sauna, gym and solarium.

Atholl Hotel (☎ 323505, fax 321555, e info@atholl-aberdeen.co.uk, 54 Kings Gate) Singles £50-85, doubles £65-110. Two miles (3km) west of the city centre, the refined Atholl Hotel is an elegant granite building, and one of the nicest places to stay in Aberdeen. It has an excellent restaurant, and also does good bar meals.

Simpson's Hotel (☎ 327777, fax 327700, e bookings@simpsonshotel.co.uk, 59 Queen's Rd) Singles £70-115, doubles £80-125. Simpson's, a mile west of Union St, is a trendy boutique hotel with a Mediterranean theme, all terracotta and aqua. It's aimed at both business and private guests, and is totally wheelchair-accessible.

Corner House Hotel (☎/fax 313063, e cornerhouse@virgin.net, 385 Great Western Rd) Singles £38-50, doubles £50-60. The Corner House is a solid, turreted building with private parking, and evening meals if required. It's a mile and a half south-west of Union St.

Places to Eat

Aberdeen has an excellent range of places to eat, from fast-food chains to expensive gourmet restaurants.

Bistros & Cafes *Carmine's (☎ 624145, 32 Union Terrace)* 3-course lunch £3.99, pizza from £3. Open noon-5.30pm Mon-Sat. Carmine's does good, inexpensive Italian food (including the best pizzas in town); the lunch deal is available noon to 2pm Monday to Friday.

Lemon Tree Cafe (☎ 621610, 5 West North St) Mains £4.25-6.45. Open noon-3pm Wed-Sun. The lively cafe-bar at the theatre

does excellent coffee, cakes and light meals, and great tortilla wraps (from £3.45) with fillings such as brie, grape and apple, or duck with hoisin sauce.

Nargile Meze Bar Cafe (☎ 454203, 3-5 Rose St) Dishes from £3.25. Open noon-3pm & 5.30pm-10.30pm Mon-Thur, noon-3pm & 5.30pm-11pm Fri & Sat. If you don't want the full, sit-down, linen-tablecloth treatment at Nargile (see under Restaurants below), you can sample the delights of Turkish cuisine at Nargile's cafe and takeaway outlet, just off Union St.

Victoria Restaurant (☎ 621381, 140 Union St) Mains £4.95-6.25. 2-course lunch £5.95. Open 9am-5pm Fri-Weds, 9am-6.30pm Thur. The Victoria, above the Carry & Jamieson jewellery shop, is a traditional tearoom with delicious fresh soups, salads and sandwiches.

Wild Boar (☎ 625357, 19 Belmont St) Mains £4.50-9.95. The Wild Boar is a popular, stylish bistro, with good vegetarian choices; couscous costs £5.75. Cake fanatics will have a great time here.

Restaurants *LJ's (☎ 635666, 46 School Hill)* Mains £4.50-10.95. Open 10am-late Mon-Sat, 11am-late Sun. This branch of the Littlejohn's chain has all the usual diversions, including a toy train. There are burgers from £4.50, other main dishes (such as char-grilled chicken) from around £8.

Owlies Brasserie (☎ 649267, Littlejohn St) Mains £8.75-12.65. Open 5,30pm-11pm Mon-Sat, noon-2.30pm Fri & Sat. Owlies Brasserie place is highly recommended, good value and, consequently, very popular. There's a tapas bar downstairs (tapas around £3.50) and full restaurant upstairs, with a good range of vegetarian and vegan dishes.

Nargile (☎ 636093, 77-79 Skene St) Lunch £7.50, dinner £13.50. Open noon-3pm & 5.30pm-10.30pm Mon-Thur, noon-3pm & 5.30pm-11pm Fri & Sat. An Aberdeen institution for more than a decade, and probably the best Turkish restaurant in Scotland – delicious, melt-in-the-mouth kebabs and marinated meats, and tasty spreads of *mezes* (starters).

Poldino's (☎ 647777, 7 Little Belmont St) Pizza & pasta £6.60-7.95. Open noon-2.30pm & 6pm-10.45pm Mon-Sat. Poldino's is a good, upmarket Italian restaurant.

For a splurge or a special meal, there are a number of choices.

Silver Darlings (☎ 576229, Pocra Quay, North Pier) 3-course dinner from £20. This restaurant is at the southern end of The Esplanade, overlooking the entrance to Aberdeen Harbour. It's renowned for fresh Scottish seafood prepared in the French style; reservations are recommended.

Faradays Restaurant (☎ 869666, 2 Kirk Brae, Cults) 3-course dinner £14.95-25.50. Open noon-2pm & 6pm-9.30pm Tues-Sat. Faradays is 4 miles (6km) from the city centre, just off the A93 in the south-western suburb of Cults. It's housed in a refurbished electricity station and has interesting and intimate decor. The cuisine is a combination of traditional Scottish and French, with lots of fresh local ingredients.

Fast Food & Takeaways Aberdeen harbour's fish market means that the fish in fish and chip shops is usually fresh and delicious.

Ashvale Fish Restaurant (42-48 Great Western Rd) Takeaways from £1.50. Open 11.45am-11pm daily. This fish and chip shop is well known outside the city, having won several awards. Ask for mushy peas with your haddock and chips (from £3.30 to take away) – they taste much better than they sound.

New Dolphin (3 Chapel St) Mains from £2.50. Open noon to 3am Thur-Sun. New Dolphin, just off Union St, is an excellent fish and chip shop with a sit-in section. Haddock and chips costs £3.30.

Chalmers Bakery (14 Back Wynd) Open 7am-5.30pm Mon-Fri, 7am-5pm Sat. This bakery, close to Union St, does excellent and inexpensive takeaway grub such as soup (55p), stovies (£1), sandwiches, pastries and pasta dishes.

Self-Catering You'll find large **supermarkets** at Bridge of Dee and Bridge of Don. There's also a convenient **Safeway** supermarket on Union St near the Music Hall, open 7.30am to 8pm Monday to Friday, 7.30am to 7pm Saturday and 10am to 5pm Sunday.

Entertainment

For info on pubs and clubs with live music, check the Gigs section of the W www .whatsonaberdeen.co.uk Web site.

Pubs Aberdeen is a great city for a pub crawl – it's more of a question of knowing when to stop than where to start. There are lots of style bars in Belmont St and The Academy shopping centre. Most bars are open from 11am to midnight Monday to Saturday and 12.30pm to 11pm on Sunday.

Prince of Wales (☎ 640597, 7 St Nicholas Lane) This is possibly the best-known Aberdeen pub. Down an alley off Union St, it boasts the longest counter in the city, a great range of real ales and good-value pub grub at lunchtime. It can get very crowded.

Bar Castro (☎ 639920, 47 Netherkirkgate) Aberdeen's only gay bar, Castro's opens till 2am every night except Monday; there's free admission before 11pm and a cover charge after.

The Blue Lamp (☎ 647472, 121 Gallowgate) A long-standing feature of the Aberdeen pub scene, the Blue Lamp has real ale, a great jukebox and occasional live bands; it's a popular student hang-out.

Cameron's Inn (☎ 644487, 6 Little Belmont St) Known as Ma Cameron's, this is Aberdeen's oldest pub, established in 1789. It has a pleasant old-fashioned ambience, and a range of excellent real ales and malt whiskies.

Old Blackfriars (☎ 581922, 52 Castlegate) This is one of the most attractive traditional pubs in the city, with a lovely stone and timber interior and a relaxed atmosphere – a great place for an afternoon pint.

O'Neill's Pub (☎ 621456, 9 Back Wynd) This pub has a good selection of Irish beers, stout, whiskeys and *poitín* (poteen). It serves food all day and there's live music (mainly Celtic) on evenings from Thursday to Saturday (see under Clubs later for more entertainment options at O'Neill's Pub).

Clubs Aberdeen has a pretty lively club scene – find out what's happening in *The Guide* (free; quarterly), available in clubs, bars and student unions, or check out **W** www .theguide-online.com.

The Ministry (☎ *211661, 16 Dee St*) Cover charge £3-7. Housed in a deconsecrated church, this has been the city's top club for a few years now. It has student nights with drinks promos on Monday and Wednesday, DJs on Friday and Saturday and a monthly Wicked club night with top UK DJs on Sunday.

Lava (☎ *648000, 9 Belmont St*) Cover charge £3-7. Probably Aberdeen's coolest club, Lava hosts lots of regular club nights, from disco to dance to hard house to funk. Crank it up beforehand in *Siberia*, a vodka bar in the same venue.

The Lemon Tree (☎ *642230, 5 West North St*) Cover charge £1-5. The Lemon Tree has regular Wednesday and Saturday club nights – jazz-funk, hip hop, drum 'n' bass – plus occasional live rock gigs.

O'Neill's Pub (☎ *621456, 9 Back Wynd*) Open till 2am. Admission £1-2.50. Upstairs at O'Neill's you're guaranteed a wild night of pounding Irish rock, indie and alternative music.

Concerts, Theatre & Film You can book tickets for most concerts and other events at the Box Office (booking line ☎ 641122), next to the Music Hall in Union St, open 9.30am to 6pm Monday to Saturday. A free listings guide, *What's On in Aberdeen*, is available from the TIC and the Box Office.

His Majesty's (☎ *637788, Rosemount Viaduct*) The city's main theatre is His Majesty's, which hosts everything from ballet and opera to musicals and pantomimes.

Music Hall (☎ *632080, Union St*) This is the main venue for classical music concerts.

Arts Centre (☎ *635208, King St*) Tickets £5-7.50. The Arts Centre stages regular drama productions in its theatre, and changing exhibitions in its gallery.

The Lemon Tree (☎ *642230,* **W** *www .lemontree.org, 5 West North St*) The Lemon Tree theatre has an interesting programme of dance, music and drama, and often has rock, jazz and folk bands playing. It also has an excellent cafe (see Places to Eat earlier).

Lighthouse Cinema (☎ *0845 602 0266, 10 Shiprow*) Adult/child £5.50/3. The Lighthouse is a seven-screen multiplex that shows mainstream, first-run films, conveniently located just off Union St.

The Belmont (listings ☎ *343534, bookings* ☎ *343536, 49 Belmont St*) Adult/child £5.50/3. The Belmont is a great little arthouse cinema, with a lively programme of cult classics, director's seasons, foreign films and mainstream movies. There's also a Saturday morning kid's club, with a children's movie screened at 11.30am.

Getting There & Away

Air Aberdeen airport is at Dyce, 6 miles (10km) north-west of the city centre. The presence of the oil industry ensures there are regular flights to numerous Scottish and UK destinations, including Orkney and Shetland, and international flights to the Netherlands and Norway.

For airport information, phone ☎ 722331. Bus Nos 27 and 27A run from the city centre to the airport (35 minutes). A taxi from the airport costs £10 to £12.

Bus National Express has daily buses from London, but it's a tedious 12-hour trip. Scottish Citylink runs direct services to Dundee (£6.50, two hours), Perth (£9.75, 2½ hours), Edinburgh (£13, four hours), Glasgow (£13.30, 4¼ hours) and Stirling (3½ hours).

Stagecoach Bluebird is the main local bus operator. Bus No 10 runs hourly to Huntly, Keith, Elgin, Nairn and Inverness. Service No 201 runs every half-hour to Banchory (hourly on Sunday), every hour to Ballater (less frequently on Sunday) and five to eight times daily to Braemar. You can also get to Ballater on bus No 210 (one to five daily runs).

Other local bus routes serve Stonehaven, Peterhead, Fraserburgh, Banff and Buckie. From Aberdeen, you can travel around the coast to Elgin (possible in one day, better in two), then continue on bus No 10 to Inverness.

CENTRAL & NE SCOTLAND

Train There are numerous trains from London's King's Cross (usually requiring a change of train in Edinburgh). Direct trains (three per day) take an acceptable seven hours, although they're considerably more expensive than buses.

Other destinations served from Aberdeen by rail include Edinburgh (2½ hours), Glasgow (2¾ hours), Stirling (2¼ hours), Perth (1¾ hours), Dundee (1¼ hours) and Inverness (2¼ hours).

Boat The ferry terminal is a short walk east of the train and bus stations. P&O Scottish Ferries (☎ 572615, fax 574411, W www.posf .co.uk) has ferries from Aberdeen to Orkney and Shetland; for details, see the relevant Getting There & Away sections in the Orkney & Shetland Islands chapter.

Getting Around

Bus First Aberdeen (☎ 650065) is the main city bus operator. Their free leaflet gives details of all the main routes and bus stops. Fares range from 35p to £1.25; pay the driver as you board the bus.

The most useful services are Nos 18, 19 and 24 from Union St to Great Western Rd (the latter two continue to Cults), No 27 from the bus station to the youth hostel and No 20 for Old Aberdeen. If you're using the buses frequently, you can buy a prepaid farecard (like a phonecard), in denominations of £2, £5, £10 and £20; you can buy them at post offices, and from the First Aberdeen information kiosk in St Nicholas St.

An Explorer ticket (£6/3) allows unlimited travel for one day on all First Aberdeen buses including the open top tour bus (see Organised Tours earlier in this section).

Car Try Arnold Clark (☎ 249159), Girdleness Rd, with Nissan Micras for £18 per day or £90 per week. There's also Morrison Brothers (☎ 826300), Broadfield Rd, Bridge of Don.

Taxi For a taxi, phone Mair's (☎ 724040).

Bicycle Mountain bikes can be rented from Alpine Bikes (☎ 211455), 64 Holburn St. It

opens every day and charges £15 a day during the week and £30 for a weekend (Friday evening to Monday morning).

DEESIDE & DONSIDE

The region around the rivers Dee and Don from Aberdeen westwards to Braemar, is castle country, and includes the Queen's residence at Balmoral. There are more examples of fanciful Scottish baronial architecture here than anywhere else in Scotland. The TICs have information on a Castle Trail, but you really need private transport to follow it.

The River Dee, flowing through the southern part of this area, has its source in the Cairngorm mountains, to the west. The River Don follows a shorter, but almost parallel course. The best walking country in the region is around Braemar and Ballater, in upper Deeside.

Crathes Castle

By the A93, 16 miles (25.5km) west of Aberdeen, this excellent 16th-century castle (NTS; ☎ 01330-844525; adult/child £7/1, open 10.30am-5.30pm daily Apr-Sept with last admission 4.45pm; 10.30am-4.30pm daily Oct) contains painted ceilings and original furnishings. The gardens include 300-year-old yew hedges that will interest topiarists. There's an on-site restaurant.

The castle is on the main Aberdeen Banchory-Ballater bus route.

Ballater
☎ 013397 • pop 1260
This small town supplies nearby Balmoral Castle with provisions, hence the many shops sporting 'By Royal Appointment' crests. Ballater is a pleasant place, but accommodation is fairly expensive and budget travellers usually head for Braemar.

The TIC (☎ 55306), Station Square, opens from Easter to October. There's a supermarket and a bank with an ATM on Bridge St.

Things to See There's a **parish church** and **clock tower** (1798) in the central square. In **Dee Valley Confectioners** (☎ 55499, Station Square; admission free; open 9am-noon &

2pm-4.30pm Mon-Thur Apr-Oct) hungry travellers can drool over the manufacture of Scottish 'sweeties'. There are free samples too.

Walking There are a few pleasant walks in the hills around Ballater. The woodland walk up Craigendarroch (400m) takes just over an hour, but it's quite steep. Morven (871m) is a more serious prospect, taking around six hours, but has good views from the top.

The best walk in the area goes to the summit of Lochnagar (1155m) from Spittal of Glenmuick car park. It's not a difficult route, but care should be taken on the summit plateau – there are huge cliffs on the northern side. Follow the track westwards from the car park; after 2½ miles (4.5km), a steep path leads up to the plateau. Allow at least six hours, and carry OS map No 44 along with a compass, food, water and appropriate equipment.

Places to Stay & Eat B&Bs include *Celicall* (☎ 55699, 3 Braemar Rd), with B&B for £17 to £25 per person; and the elegant *Coyles Hotel* (☎ 55064, fax 55212, e coyleshotel@sol.co.uk, 43 Golf Rd), with B&B for £18 to £26 per person.

Alexandra Hotel (☎ 55376, fax 55466, 12 Bridge Square) B&B £24-30 per person. This is a friendly and comfortable hotel.

Station Restaurant (☎ 755805, Station Square) Mains from £2. This a cheaper alternative, with home baking from £1.80 and inexpensive burgers for around £2.

Getting There & Away Stagecoach Bluebird buses run almost every hour from Aberdeen (1¾ hours); every two hours on Sunday. The service continues to Braemar.

Balmoral Castle

Eight miles (13km) west of Ballater, Balmoral (☎ 013397-42334; adult/child £4.50/1; open 10am-5pm daily mid Apr-end July) was built for Queen Victoria in 1855 as a private residence for the royal family. The grounds and an exhibition of paintings, artwork and royal tartans in the ballroom are open; the rest of the castle is closed to the prying eyes of the public. On the edge of the estate is Crathie Church, which the royals visit when they're here.

Balmoral Castle attracts large numbers of visitors. It's beside the A93 and can be reached on the Aberdeen–Braemar bus (see Getting There & Away under Braemar later).

Braemar

☎ 013397 • pop 410

Braemar is an attractive village surrounded by mountains. It makes an excellent walking base and there's winter skiing at Glenshee (see the earlier Blairgowrie & Glenshee section). In winter, Braemar is one of the coldest places in the country, and temperatures as low as minus 29°C have been recorded. During spells of severe cold, hungry deer wander the streets looking for a bite to eat.

There's a very helpful TIC (☎ 41600), The Mews, Mar Rd, open year-round. It has lots of useful information on walks in the area. There's a bank with an ATM at the junction in the centre.

Things to See Just north of the village, turreted **Braemar Castle** (☎ 41219; adult/child £3/1; open 10am-6pm Sat-Thur Apr-Oct, same hours Sat-Fri July, same hours daily Aug) dates from 1628 and it's well worth a visit. It was a government garrison after the 1745 Jacobite rebellion, then it became the home of the Farquharson family.

The **Braemar Highland Heritage Centre** (☎ 41944, Mar Rd; admission free; open 9am-6pm daily May-Sept, 9am-5pm Mon-Fri, 10am-5pm Sat & Sun), beside the TIC, tells the story of the area with displays and video.

Walking An easy walk from Braemar is up Creag Choinnich (538m), a hill to the east of the town, above the A93. There are route markers and the walk takes about 1½ hours. For a longer walk (three hours) and superb views of the Cairngorms, climb Morrone (859m), the mountain south-west of Braemar.

Special Events On the first Saturday in September, Braemar is invaded by 20,000 people, including the royal family, for the

Braemar Gathering

There are Highland games in many towns and villages throughout the summer, but the best known is the Braemar Gathering, which takes place on a 12-acre site on the first Saturday in September. It's a major occasion, annually organised by the Braemar Royal Highland Society since 1817. Events include highland dancing, pipers, tug-of-war, a hill race up Morrone, tossing the caber, hammer- and stone-throwing and the long jump. International athletes are among those who take part.

These types of events took place informally in the Highlands for many centuries as tests of skill and strength, but they were formalised around 1820 due to rising pseudo-Highland romanticism caused by people such as King George IV and Sir Walter Scott. Queen Victoria attended the Braemar Gathering in 1848, starting the tradition of royal patronage that continues to this day.

ASA ANDERSSON

annual **Braemar Gathering** (Highland games). Bookings are essential and tickets cost from £6/2 for entry to the field and £10-12 for the uncovered stand, to £18.50 for the grandstand; car parking costs £6. Contact the TIC for current details.

Places to Stay & Eat *Braemar Youth Hostel* (☎ 41659, 21 Glenshee Rd) Dorm beds £9.25/8. Open year-round. The hostel is south of the village centre on the A93 to Perth.

Braemar Bunkhouse (☎ 41517, 15 Mar Rd) Beds £7-8.50. This place near the newsagent/chemist has six-, eight-, and 10-bed dorms, plus a chalet and some bedrooms.

Good B&Bs include *Craiglea* (☎ 41641, Hillside Drive), with B&B for £17 to £19 per person; *Wilderbank* (☎ 41651, Kindrochit Drive), with B&B for £18.50 to £20 per person; and *Schiehallion House* (☎ 41679, 10 Glenshee Rd), with B&B for £19 to £21 per person.

Callater Lodge Hotel (☎ 41275, fax 41345, [e] maria@hotel-braemar.co.uk, 9 Glenshee Rd) B&B £24-29 per person. Evening meals for £13. This is a small hotel set in its own grounds; most rooms have en-suite bathrooms.

Braemar Lodge (☎/fax 41627, Glenshee Rd) B&B from £20-40 per person. The best place to stay in Braemar is this restored Victorian shooting lodge on the outskirts of the village.

Fife Arms Hotel (☎ 741644, Mar Rd) Bar meals £4.95-9.95. This is a great place for lunch or dinner, with bar meals and a daily carvery. There's a roaring log fire in winter.

Cheaper alternatives include the *Braemar Takeaway* (14 Invercauld Rd) with fish and chips for £3.10. There's also an *Alldays* supermarket on Mar Rd.

Getting There & Away The drive from Perth to Braemar is beautiful, but public transport is limited to one bus daily – Stagecoach Bluebird bus No 200 – which departs Perth at 4.45pm (£6, 2¼ hours). From Aberdeen to Braemar (£6, 2¼ hours), there are several buses a day operated by Stagecoach Bluebird.

Inverey

Five miles (8km) west of Braemar is the tiny settlement of Inverey. Numerous mountain walks start from here, including the adventurous Lairig Ghru walk – 21 miles (34km) over

Sea stacks at Duncansby Head nr John 'o Groats

A wintry outlook from Stob Coire nan Lochan

Climber atop Beinn Mheadhoin, near Cairn Gorm

Boats harboured in Loch Broom, Ullapool

GRAEME CORNWALLIS

GRAEME CORNWALLIS

Gairloch's curvaceous coastline

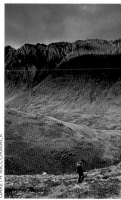

GARETH MCCORMACK

Mind how you go on Glen Coe

Conquering the Old Man of Stoer

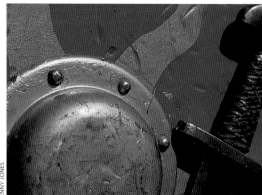

JENNY JONES

Shield & sword: Celtic battles are re-enacted at Highland Games

GARETH MCCORMACK

The haunting view across the Mamores summits from the steep slopes of Ben Nevis

the pass to Aviemore. The Cairngorm peaks of Cairn Gorm and Ben Macdui (see Aviemore in The Highlands chapter) are actually on or just this side of the regional border.

The Glen Luibeg circuit is a good day hike. Start from the **Linn of Dee**, a narrow gorge about 1½ miles (2.5km) west of Inverey. From the woodland car park less than 300m beyond the linn, follow the footpath and track to Derry Lodge and **Glen Luibeg**, where there are wonderful remnants of the ancient Caledonian pine forest. Continue westwards on a pleasant path, over a pass into Glen Dee, then follow the River Dee back to the linn. It's an easy 15-mile route from the linn (six hours). Another interesting circuit includes Glen Lui and Glen Quoich. The **Linn of Quoich** is a narrow slot that the river thunders through; don't try to jump it. Use OS map No 43 for both routes.

Inverey Youth Hostel (013397-41969) Dorm beds £6.50/5.75. Open mid-May to early-Oct. There's an afternoon postbus (daily except Sundays) from Braemar to this hostel, Linn of Dee and Linn of Quoich.

Strathdon

The A944, A97 and A939 run through Strathdon valley, and many of the best castles in Aberdeenshire are near these roads. Beyond Inverurie, Kemnay and Alford (ah-ford) are the main villages.

Alford, 27 miles (43km) west of Aberdeen, is well worth a visit and makes a good day trip from the city. It has a TIC (☎ 01975-562052), open April to October, banks with ATMs, and a supermarket. Avoid detouring along a minor road from tiny Strathdon village: the sign indicates 'Lost'!

Castle Fraser This superb 16th-century castle *(NTS; ☎ 01330-833463; adult/child £6/1; open 11am-5.30pm daily June-Aug, 1.30pm-5.30pm daily May & Sept, 1.30pm-5.30pm Sat & Sun Oct)*, 3 miles (5km) south of Kemnay, looks rather like a French chateau and is reputedly the most photographed castle in Scotland.

Alford The **Grampian Transport Museum** *(☎ 019755-62292; adult/child £3.50/2.50;* *open 10am-5pm Apr-Oct)* is a fascinating place with lots of cars, buses, steam engines, trams and some unique exhibits. There's also a small **railway museum** at the TIC; the narrow-gauge **Alford Valley steam railway** runs daily from here in afternoons from June to August (£2).

Craigievar Castle The most spectacular of local castles, Craigievar *(NTS; ☎ 01339-883280; adult/child £7/5; open 1.30pm-5.30pm daily mid Apr-Sept)*, 9 miles (14.5km) south of Alford, has remained unchanged since completion in 1626. Turret fans will enjoy it.

Kildrummy Castle Nine miles (14.5km) west of Alford, this interesting and extensive 13th-century ruin *(HS; ☎ 019755-71331; adult/child £2/75p; open 9.30am-6.30pm daily Apr-Sept, 9.30am-4.30pm Mon-Sat & 2pm-4.30pm Sun Oct-Mar)* was attacked and treacherously captured in 1306 while being defended by Sir Neil Bruce, a brother of Robert the Bruce. After the 1715 Jacobite rebellion, the earl of Mar was exiled in France and his castle fell into ruin.

Corgarff Castle In the wild upper reaches of Strathdon, by the A939 to Tomintoul, you'll find this impressive tower house and star-shaped defensive curtain wall. Most of the castle *(HS; ☎ 01975-651460; adult/child £2.80/1; open 9.30am-6.30pm daily Apr-Sept, 9.30am-4.30pm Sat & 2pm-4.30pm Sun Oct-Mar)* dates from 1750 and it was a redcoat's barracks after the 1745 rebellion.

Lecht Ski Resort At the head of Strathdon valley, the A939 crosses the Lecht pass (637m), where there's a small skiing and snowboarding area with lots of easy and intermediate runs. You can hire skis, boots and poles from the **Good Brand** knitwear shop *(☎ 01975-651433)*, Corgarff, for £11 a day. At the slopes, equipment hire is £12.50 and a day pass is £15. A two-day package including ski hire, lift pass and instruction costs £70 with **Lecht Ski Company** *(☎ 01975-651440)*.

The ski centre opens in summer too, when you can ski or board on the dry ski slope

CENTRAL & NE SCOTLAND

(£10 for two hours, including equipment hire), or rent go-karts and quad bikes (£7.50 a session) or just take a trip up on the chair-lift (£3.50 return).

Places to Stay & Eat – Alford For B&B, try *Bydland* (☎ *019755-63613, 18 Balfour Rd)*, with B&B for £19 to £20 per person.

Forbes Arms Hotel (☎ *019755-62108, fax 63467, Bridge of Alford)* B&B £27.50-36 per person. Bar meals £5.25-9. A mile away at Bridge of Alford, the pleasant Forbes Arms Hotel has en-suite rooms and bar meals.

Salad Days (Main St) serves takeaways, including filled rolls from £1.75.

Places to Stay & Eat – Kildrummy If you're after a bit of luxury try *Kildrummy Castle Hotel* (☎ *019755-71288, fax 71345,* ℮ *bookings@kildrummycastlehotel.co.uk)* Singles £80-90, doubles £135-170. The Kildrummy Castle Hotel, across the river from the castle, is the top place to stay in Donside. It also offers a three-course dinner (£17), except on Sundays.

Mossat Restaurant (☎ *019755-71355)* Mains £4.50. Open to 5.30pm. At the A944/A97 junction, the popular Mossat Restaurant has baked potatoes (from £2.25) and main courses.

Places to Stay & Eat – Corgarff *Jenny's Bothy* (☎ *01975-651449,* ℮ *jenboth@talk21 .com)* Beds £8. This is an excellent all-year bunkhouse, with ten beds. Look out for the sign by the main road, then follow the old military road (drivable) for 1200m.

Good Brand Tearoom Open 9am-6pm Apr-Sept, 9am-5pm Oct to Mar. This place has toasties for £1.45, soup and a roll for £1.55, and baked potatoes from £2.95.

Getting There & Away Stagecoach Blue-bird bus No 220 runs from Aberdeen to Strathdon village (via Alford) twice daily except Sunday. Buses from Aberdeen to Alford (1¼ hours) run around once an hour, but there are only five runs on Sunday. You'll need your own transport to reach Craigievar or Corgarff castles and the Lecht.

NORTHERN ABERDEENSHIRE & INLAND MORAY

The direct rail and road route from Aberdeen to Inverness cuts across rolling agricultural country that, thanks to a mild climate, produces everything from grain to flower bulbs. The grain is turned into that magical liquid known as malt whisky. You may be tempted by the **Malt Whisky Trail**, a 70-mile signposted tour which gives you an inside look and tastings at a number of famous distilleries (including Cardhu, Glenfiddich and Glenlivet). TICs stock a leaflet covering the tour.

Haddo House

Haddo House *(NTS;* ☎ *01651-851440, Tarves, by Ellon; adult/child £6/1; open 1.30pm-5.30pm daily Easter-Sept, 1.30pm-5.30pm Sat & Sun Oct)*, 19 miles (30km) north of Aberdeen, was designed by William Adam in 1732. It's best described as a classic English stately home transplanted to Scotland. Stagecoach Bluebird bus No 290/291 runs hourly (infrequent on Sunday) from Aberdeen to Tarves/Methlick via the end of the Haddo House driveway (a mile-long walk).

Fyvie Castle

This is also castle country, and there's a *Castle Trail* leaflet available from TICs to guide you around. Fyvie Castle *(NTS;* ☎ *01651-891266, Fyvie, by Turriff; adult/child £6/4; open 11am-5.30pm June-Aug, 1.30pm-5.30pm Easter May & Sept, 1.30pm-5.30pm Sat & Sun Oct)*, 8 miles (13km) south of Turriff, is a magnificent example of Scottish baronial architecture; there's a tearoom here.

Bus No 305 runs hourly every day from Aberdeen to Banff and Elgin via Fyvie village, a mile from the castle. There are numerous other castles in the area, in various states of preservation.

Huntly
☎ 01466 • pop 4150

This small town, with an impressive ruined castle and an attractive main square, is located in a strategically important position on a low-lying plain, along the main route from Aberdeen to Moray and Strathspey.

The TIC (☎ 792255), The Square, opens 9.30am to 6pm Monday to Saturday and 10am to 3pm Sunday from Easter to October. There's a bank with an ATM next to the TIC.

On the northern edge of town, 16th-century **Huntly Castle** (☎ 793191; adult/child £2.80/1; open 9.30am-6.30pm daily Apr-Sept; 9.30am-4.30pm Mon-Wed & Sat, 9.30am-1pm Thur & 2pm-4.30pm Sun Oct-Mar), the former stronghold of the Gordons, is in a park on the banks of the River Deveron. Over the main door is a superb carving that includes the royal arms and the figures of Christ and St Michael.

Places to Stay & Eat There are a couple of hotels on the main square, and a handful of B&Bs in the surrounding streets.

Hillview (☎ 794870, Provost St) B&B £15-18 per person. Travellers have recommended the Hillview, which has three rooms, one of them with en-suite bathroom.

Huntly Hotel (☎/fax 792703, 18 The Square) Singles £25-35, doubles £40-50. Bar meals £2.95-5.95. The hotel on the western side of the square does good bar meals.

The *Huntly Tandoori* (☎ 792667, 109 Gordon St) serves curries from £4.95, 10% less for takeaways.

The Stagecoach Bluebird Aberdeen to Inverness bus (No 10) passes through Huntly hourly (1¼ hours in each direction), and the town is also on the Aberdeen-Inverness rail line.

Dufftown
☎ 01340 • pop 1700
Founded only in 1817 by James Duff, 4th earl of Fife, Dufftown is 14 miles (22km) west of Huntly. It's a good place to start the Malt Whisky Trail; there are seven working distilleries in Dufftown alone. Locals claim that 'Rome may be built on seven hills, but Dufftown's built on seven stills'.

The TIC (☎ 01340-820501), in the clocktower in the square, opens 10am to 1pm and 2pm to 6pm Monday to Saturday and 1pm to 6pm Sunday Easter to October; the attached **museum** has some interesting local items.

At the northern edge of town there's the **Glenfiddich Distillery Visitor Centre**

(☎ 820373; admission free; open 9.30am-4.30pm Mon-Sat, noon-4.30pm Sun Easter-mid-Oct, 9.30am-4.30pm Mon-Fri mid-Oct-Easter). Visitors are guided through the process of distilling and can see the whisky being bottled here – the only Highland distillery where this is done on the premises. There's no entry charge – your free dram really is free.

The nearby 13th-century **Balvenie Castle** (HS; ☎ 820121; adult/child £1.50/50p; open 9.30am-6.30pm daily Apr-Sept) was built by Alexander 'the Black' Comyn. It was transformed into a stately home after 1550 and was visited by Mary Queen of Scots in 1562. Note the moat and external latrine chutes.

Places to Stay & Eat *Davaar* (☎ 820464, 17 Church St) B&B £16-18 per person. This central B&B is just across the street from the TIC.

Commercial Hotel (☎ 820313, 4 Church St) B&B £17 per person. At the Commercial Hotel there are ceilidhs on Thursdays at 8.30pm from June to September; there's also a whisky-tasting session at 8pm on Tuesdays.

Fife Arms Hotel (☎ 820220, fax 821137, 2 The Square) Bar snacks from £1.40, mains from £5. Lunch noon-2.30pm, dinner 6pm-8pm. The bar meals at the Fife Arms include locally farmed ostrich steaks. Single rooms are available from £25 to £27, and doubles from £40 to £44.

A Taste of Speyside (☎ 820860, 10 Balvenie St) Mains £9.90-11.90. Open 12.30pm-9pm Mon-Sat. Just downhill from the TIC, this upmarket eating place offers traditional Scottish dishes using fresh local produce.

Stagecoach Bluebird bus No 10 links Dufftown to Elgin (£3.25, 50 minutes), Huntly, Aberdeen and Inverness.

Tomintoul
☎ 01807 • pop 320
This high-altitude village (345m) lies on the A939, roughly midway between Strathdon and Grantown-on-Spey, and 6 miles (10km) from the Lecht Ski Resort (see Strathdon earlier). There's a TIC (☎ 580285), on The Square, open Easter to October.

CENTRAL & NE SCOTLAND

Tomintoul Museum & Visitor Centre *(☎ 673701, The Square; admission free; open 10am-4pm Mon-Sat June-Sept, 10am-4pm Mon-Fri May & Oct)* has displays on a range of local topics. Glenlivet Estate has an **information centre** *(☎ 580283, Main St)* which distributes free maps of walking and cycling trails.

A spur of the Speyside Way long-distance footpath (see Walking in the Activities section), which runs from Aviemore to Spey Bay on the coast, runs from Tomintoul to Ballindalloch, 15 miles (24km) to the north. For information about the route, contact the Ranger Service on ☎ 01340-881266, or check the Web site at **W** www.speysideway.org.

Places to Stay & Eat There's some accommodation for walkers, including the ***Tomintoul Youth Hostel*** *(☎ 580282, Main St)* with dorm beds at £6.75/6 (open mid-May to Oct), and the ***Tomintoul Bunkhouse*** *(☎ 01343-548105, The Square)* with beds at £8 (open year-round).

The ***Glenavon Hotel*** *(☎ 580218, fax 580733, The Square)* is a more comfortable alternative, with B&B for £15 to £26 per person.

There are various places to eat, including the ***Clockhouse*** on The Square. Two shops sell groceries (including the post office).

Infrequent buses connect Tomintoul with Aberlour (on schooldays, with a connection to Elgin), Elgin (Thursday only, 1¼ hours) and Keith via Dufftown (Tuesday only, 1¼ hours). For details phone Roberts of Rothiemay on ☎ 01466-711213.

THE COAST

The Grampians meet the sea at Stonehaven, close to spectacular Dunnottar Castle. Continuing around the coast from Aberdeen, there are long stretches of sand and, on the north coast, some magical fishing villages, such as Pennan, where parts of the film *Local Hero* were shot.

Stonehaven

☎ 01569 • pop 9310

Originally a small fishing village, 'Stane-hyve' became the county town of Kincardineshire in 1600. There's a TIC (☎ 762806), 66 Allardice St, which opens 10am to 7pm Monday to Saturday and 1pm to 6pm Sunday, April to October. On Market Square, there's a supermarket and banks with ATMs. Stonehaven is situated on the busy bus and rail routes between Dundee and Aberdeen.

Dunnottar Castle The principal attraction at Stonehaven is definitely Dunnottar Castle *(☎ 762173; adult/child £3.50/1; open 9am-6pm Mon-Sat, 2pm-5pm Sun Easter-Oct, 9am-sunset Mon-Sat Nov-Mar, last admission 30 mins before closing)* on the coast 1½ miles (3km) south of the town. It's a pleasant walk to the castle from town; the TIC has a walking leaflet. The castle ruins are spread out across a grassy promontory rising 150 feet above the sea – as dramatic a film set as any director could wish for. It was last used for Zeffirelli's *Hamlet*, starring Mel Gibson. The original fortress was built in the 9th century; the keep is the most substantial remnant, but the drawing room (restored in 1926) is more interesting. The castle must have supported quite a large community, judging by the extent of the ruins.

Other Things to See Just west of the A90 bypass and only a mile from the town centre, is the pretty hamlet of **Kirkton of Fetteresso**, where the cottages cluster around the ruin of a 17th-century church.

The harbour is the most attractive part of town. **The Tolbooth**, built around 1600 by the Earl Marischal, is Stonehaven's oldest building. It now houses a pricey restaurant and museum (open June to September). Nearby, parts of the **Mercat Cross** date from 1645.

Places to Eat *Marine Hotel* (☎ 762155, 9-10 The Shore) Mains £5.95-12.95. Lunch noon-2pm, dinner 5pm-9pm. The Marine is an excellent real-ale pub overlooking the harbour, with a great 1970s jukebox and good but pricey bar meals, including fresh seafood.

The Tolbooth Restaurant (☎ 762287, Old Pier) Mains £8.95-16.95. Open 6.30pm-

10.30pm Thur-Sun. The Tolbooth is one of the best seafood restaurants in the region – reservations are recommended.

Sandy's on Market Square in the town centre is the place to go for takeaway fish and chips. *Robertson's bakery and tearoom (68 Allardice St)* has soup and snacks from 50p (including the local favourite, hot butteries – butter-rich bread rolls).

Peterhead
☎ 01779 • pop 18,500

The remains of a once-great fishing industry are still based in this fairly dreary town. Only a decade or so ago, the high-tech trawlers operating from here were so productive that they supported a local Ferrari-driving fishing community with a high disposable income. Overfishing and EU quotas have now led to a point where the entire industry is in danger of disappearing.

Peterhead Maritime Heritage *(☎ 473000, The Lido, South Rd; adult/child £3/2; open 11am-4pm Mon-Sat, noon-4pm Sun Apr-Oct)* is worth a visit. There's an audiovisual presentation on sealife and displays on whaling, fishing and the oil industry. The central **Arbuthnot Museum** *(☎ 477778, St Peter St; admission free; open 11am-1pm & 2pm-4.30pm Mon-Sat, closes 1pm Weds)* has wide-ranging displays of local and Arctic interest.

Carrick Guest House (☎/fax 470610, 16 Merchant St) has B&B from £20 per person. *Palace Hotel (☎ 474821, fax 476119,* e *info@palacehotel.co.uk, Prince St)* Singles £35-50, doubles £60-70. This is a good hotel with en-suite rooms that are cheaper at weekends. Meals (mains from £4.95) are available too.

Stagecoach Bluebird buses run every half-hour from Aberdeen (hourly on Sunday).

Fraserburgh
☎ 01346 • pop 13,000

Fraserburgh, affectionately known to local people as 'The Broch', achieved burgh status in 1546, but prosperity has clearly moved elsewhere. However, the harbour can be interesting when crowded with boats, and there are good sandy beaches east of the town. There's a TIC (☎ 518315), open April

to September, and a supermarket on Saltoun Square, and you'll find banks with ATMs on Broad St.

The interesting **Museum of Scottish Lighthouses** *(☎ 511022, Kinnaird Head; adult/child £3.50/1.95; open 10am-6pm Mon-Sat & noon-6pm Sun Apr-Oct, 10am-4pm Mon-Sat & noon-4pm Sun Nov-Mar)* is a recommended attraction with guided tours to the top of bizarre-looking Kinnaird Head lighthouse, a converted 16th-century castle.

Maggie's Hoosie *(26 Shore St, Inverallochy; admission free; open 10am-noon Mon & Weds-Fri & 2pm-4.30pm Weds-Mon Apr-Sept)* Maggie's Hoosie is 4 miles (6km) east of Fraserburgh. It's a traditional 'fishwife's' cottage, with earth floor and original furnishings.

Saltoun Arms Hotel (☎ 518282, fax 515882, Saltoun Square) Singles/doubles £38/55. The pleasant Saltoun Arms Hotel has en-suite rooms and offers cheap weekend breaks.

For something cheaper, try *Clifton House (☎ 518365, 131 Charlotte St)* where B&B costs £17 to £21 per person. Fraserburgh is no gourmet's delight; the *Fisherman's Mission (Shore St)* is the cheapest place to eat, with dishes from £1.70.

Stagecoach Bluebird buses run regularly from Aberdeen, and hourly from Peterhead. Buses to Banff are infrequent.

Pennan

Nestling under red sandstone cliffs, Pennan is a very attractive village with a small harbour. Whitewashed houses are built gable-end-on to the sea here – the waves break just metres away, on the other side of the road.

The *Pennan Inn (☎ 01346-561201)* featured in the film *Local Hero*, as did the red telephone box outside, though one of the houses further along to the east doubled for the exterior of the hotel. B&B costs £40 a double – the rooms are a bit on the small side – and there's a good restaurant.

Stagecoach Bluebird buses run twice to Banff on Saturday only; they pick up and drop off past the junction with the main road, 350m south of (and a steep climb uphill from) the village.

CENTRAL & NE SCOTLAND

Gardenstown

Gardenstown (or Gamrie, pronounced game-ree) was founded by Alexander Garden in 1720. It's another fishing village, but it's unique in Scotland as it was built on cliff ledges. Drivers should beware of severe gradients and hairpin bends in the village. Parts of the village can only be reached on foot.

Banff & Macduff
☎ 01261 • combined pop 8170

A popular seaside resort, the twin towns of Banff and Macduff are separated by Banff Bay at the mouth of the River Deveron. Interesting Banff could be an attractive little town, but there's vandalism and neglect here. Nearby Macduff is still a busy fishing port.

The TIC (☎ 812419) is beside St Mary's car park (at the southern end of High St), Banff. It opens 9am to 5.30pm Monday to Saturday, April to October (and Sunday afternoons in July and August), and has an hour-long free audio tour (£1 deposit) to encourage you to look around the town. You'll find banks with ATMs in Castle St, Banff, and in Shore St, Macduff. There's a large supermarket near Banff Bridge.

Duff House This impressive Georgian baroque mansion (☎ 818181; adult/child £4/3; open 11am-5pm daily Apr-Oct, 11am-4pm Thur-Sun Oct-Mar) is on the southern edge of Banff. It was designed by William Adam and completed in 1737. It's been a hotel, a hospital and a POW camp, but after extensive refurbishment it opened as an art gallery housing a collection of paintings from the National Gallery of Scotland.

Macduff Marine Aquarium The aquarium (☎ 833369, 11 High Shore; adult/child £2.75/2; open 10am-5pm daily) is in a 400,000L open-air tank, complete with kelp reef and wave machine. Oddities include the local cuckoo wrasse – it looks more like a tropical fish.

Other Things to See The Banff Museum (☎ 622906, High St; admission free; open 2pm-4.30pm Mon-Sat June-Sept) has an award-winning display on local wildlife, geology and history, and Banff silver. Just off Carmelite St, Banff, there's the medieval ruin of **St Mary's Kirk** and an interesting graveyard, sadly vandalised. Nearby, the **Market Arms Bar**, built in 1585, is the oldest continuously occupied building in Banff. In Low St, Banff, the **Townhouse** dates from 1797; the adjacent cannon was captured at Sebastopol.

Two miles (3km) west of Banff, the quiet, picturesque fishing village of **Whitehills** has narrow lanes and rows of neatly painted cottages gable-end-on to the sea. The village church has an excellent **clock tower**.

Places to Stay & Eat Banff has a bigger and better range of accommodation than Macduff.

Banff Links Caravan Park (☎ 812228, Banff) Tent pitches £3.60-9.50. Open Apr-Oct. This site is beside the beach, a half-mile west of town.

Bryvard Guest House (☎/fax 818090, e bryvard@hotmail.com, Seafield St, Banff) B&B £22.50 per person. This place has good B&B. It is on the A98 heading west.

County Hotel (☎ 815353, fax 818335, e countyhotel@yahoo.co.uk, 32 High St, Banff) Singles £35, doubles £48-65. The County Hotel also offers meals (bar meals around £6, lunch specials £4.95).

For something to eat, try the *Broken Fiddle* (9 Strait Path, Banff).

Getting There & Away Stagecoach Bluebird runs hourly buses to Elgin via Whitehills (£7, one hour) and Aberdeen, and an infrequent service to Fraserburgh (once on school days, twice on Saturday).

Portsoy
☎ 01261 • pop 1800

In Portsoy there's an attractive 17th-century harbour, two churches and lots of narrow streets with interesting architecture. The town is now a conservation area; it's well worth stopping here to soak up its atmosphere. Beautiful Portsoy marble was quarried near the harbour, and there's some in the Palace of Versailles.

Each year on the last weekend in June, Portsoy harbour is home to the Scottish

Traditional Boat Festival (☎ 842951), a gathering of historic wooden sailing boats, accompanied by sailing races, music, street theatre and a food festival.

The **Boyne Hotel** *(☎/fax 842242, 2 North High St)* offers B&B for £20 to £25 per person, while the **Shore Inn** on the harbour is a great place for lunch or just a couple of beers.

The hourly bus No 305 between Elgin and Banff stops in Portsoy.

Fordyce

This well-preserved historic village lies 1½ miles (3km) south of the A98 and about 3 miles south-west of Portsoy. **St Tarquin's Church** dates back to at least 1272 and has extraordinary canopied tombs. There's also the four-storey 16th-century **Fordyce Castle** (not open to the public). The **Joiner's Workshop & Visitor Centre** *(☎ 01771-622906; admission free; open 10am-6pm Thur-Mon)* has a collection of woodworking tools and machinery, and demonstrations by a master joiner.

Fochabers & Around
☎ 01343 • pop 1500

The last bridge over the River Spey before it enters the sea is in Fochabers. The town has a pleasant square with a church and clock tower dated 1798.

In a converted church, the **Fochabers Folk Museum** *(☎ 821204, High St; admission by donation; open 9.30am-6pm, closes 5pm winter)* has over 4000 exhibits, covering a wide range of subjects. It's worth a visit, but you'll need plenty of time!

West of the bridge over the Spey, by the A96, **Baxters Highland Village** *(☎ 820666; admission free; open 9am-5.30pm daily Apr-Dec, 10am-4pm Jan-Mar)* tells the story of this famous food-producing family. The history begins in 1868, when they opened their first shop in Fochabers. You get a factory tour with cookery demonstrations on weekdays.

Four miles (6.5km) north of Fochabers, at the mouth of the River Spey, is the tiny village of **Spey Bay**. It's the starting point for the Speyside Way long-distance footpath to Aviemore, and home to **Tugnet Ice House** *(☎ 01309-673701; admission free; open 11am-4pm daily May-Sept)*, a salmon-

fishing museum, and the **Moray Firth Wildlife Centre** *(☎ 820339; adult/child £1.50/75p; open 10.30am-5pm Apr-Oct, 10.30am-7pm Jul & Aug)*, which has an exhibition on the Moray Firth dolphins.

Bluebird Stagecoach runs frequent buses from Aberdeen to Elgin and Inverness via Fochabers.

Elgin
☎ 01343 • pop 20,000

At the heart of Moray, Elgin has been the provincial capital for the past eight centuries, but in medieval times it was much more important than it is now. The town is dominated by a monument to the fifth duke of Gordon, erected in 1839, which crowns Lady Hill west of the centre.

The TIC (☎ 542666), 17 High St, opens 9am to 6pm Monday to Saturday and 11am to 4pm Sunday April to October, and 9am to 5pm Monday to Saturday from November to March. The central part of High St is pedestrianised and quite pleasant; it has a good range of shops and banks with ATMs. The bus station on Alexandra Rd is central, but the train station is 900m south of the centre.

The post office is in the Tesco supermarket on Batchen Lane, just south of High St. The police station (☎ 543101) is on Moray St.

Elgin Cathedral This great cathedral *(HS; ☎ 547171; adult/child £2.80/1, joint ticket with Spynie Palace £3.30/1.20; open 9.30am-6.30pm daily Apr-Sept, 9.30am-4.30pm Mon-Wed & Sat, 9.30am-1pm Thur & 2pm-4.30pm Sun Oct-Mar)*, known as the 'lantern of the north', was consecrated in 1224. In 1390 it was burnt down by the infamous Wolf of Badenoch, the illegitimate son of Robert II, following his excommunication by the bishop.

It was rebuilt, but ruined once more after the Reformation. Among the ruins there's a particularly fine octagonal chapter house and a Pictish cross-slab.

Spynie Palace The palace *(HS; ☎ 546358; adult/child £2/75p, joint ticket with Elgin Cathedral £3.30/1.20; open 9.30am-6.30pm daily Apr-Sept, 9.30am-4.30pm Sat & 2pm-*

CENTRAL & NE SCOTLAND

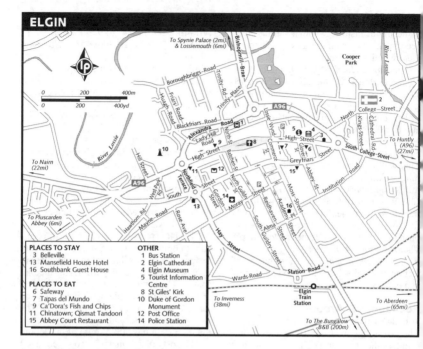

ELGIN

To Spynie Palace (2mi)
& Lossiemouth (6mi)

Cooper
Park

River Lossie

0   200   400m
0   200   400yd

To Nairn
(22mi)

River Lossie

To Huntly
(A96)
(27mi)

To Pluscarden
Abbey (6mi)

To Inverness
(38mi)

To Aberdeen
(65mi)

To The Bungalow
B&B (200m)

Elgin
Train
Station

PLACES TO STAY	OTHER
3 Belleville	1 Bus Station
13 Mansefield House Hotel	2 Elgin Cathedral
16 Southbank Guest House	4 Elgin Museum
	5 Tourist Information
PLACES TO EAT	Centre
6 Safeway	8 St Giles' Kirk
7 Tapas del Mundo	10 Duke of Gordon
9 Ca'Dora's Fish and Chips	Monument
11 Chinatown; Qismat Tandoori	12 Post Office
15 Abbey Court Restaurant	14 Police Station

4.30pm Sun Oct-Mar), 2 miles (3km) north of Elgin, was the residence of the medieval bishops of Moray until 1686. It's now a ruin, with good views over Spynie Loch.

Other Things to See The **Elgin Museum** (☎ 543675, 1 High St; adult/child £2/50p; open 10am-5pm Mon-Fri, 11am-4pm Sat & 2pm-5pm Sun Apr-Oct) has excellent collections of fossil fish and Pictish carved stones. There are also displays on archaeology and natural and social history.

Pluscarden Abbey (☎ 890257; admission free; open 4.45am-8.45pm daily), 6 miles (10km) south-west of Elgin, was restored in 1948 by Benedictine monks, who still run it today. There are guided tours, and the church services are open to the public.

Places to Stay & Eat There are lots of B&Bs and some good restaurants in Elgin.
Belleville (☎/fax 541515, e belleville@ talk21.com, 14 South College St) B&B

£17-25 per person. Mrs McMillan's friendly B&B, with two en-suite double rooms, is only two minutes' walk from the TIC.

Southbank Guest House (☎/fax 547132, 36 Academy St) B&B £19-26 per person. Evening meals around £6. The family-run, 11-room Southbank is set in a spacious Georgian townhouse in a quiet street south of the centre.

The Bungalow (☎ 542035, 7 New Elgin Rd) B&B £16 per person. Just south of the train station, The Bungalow is run by the friendly Mr Ross.

Mansefield House Hotel (☎ 540883, fax 552491, e reception@mansefieldhousehotel .com, Mayne Rd) Singles £55-68, doubles £80-110. Set in a former manse (minister's house), this elegant hotel boasts an excellent seafood restaurant.

Abbey Court Restaurant (☎ 542849, 15 Greyfriars St) Mains £5.65-16.85, 2-course lunch £5. Open 11am-2pm Mon-Sat, 6pm-11pm Mon-Thur, 6pm-11.45pm Fri & Sat.

This restaurant has an international menu with vegetarian and pasta dishes, but it also serves traditional Scottish meals, including seafood.

Tapas del Mundo *(☎ 549737, High St)* Mains £3.30-5.95. Open 5pm-10pm daily. Part of Flanagan's Bar, tucked up a narrow wynd on the southern side of High St near the TIC, this place has great Spanish food – they do an all-you-can-eat deal for £10 on Wednesday and Sunday.

For takeaways, try ***Ca'Dora's*** *(181 High St)* fish and chip shop, ***Chinatown*** *(☎ 552332, 210 High St)* or ***Qismat Tandoori*** *(☎ 541461, 204 High St)*; the latter has a set lunch for £3.95 Monday to Saturday.

Getting There & Away Stagecoach Bluebird runs buses along the coast to Banff and Macduff (£7, one hour), south to Dufftown (£3.25, 30 minutes), west to Inverness (£6.50, one hour), and south-east to Aberdeen (£7.50, 2¼ hours).

Trains run five to ten times daily from Elgin to Aberdeen and Inverness.

Findhorn
☎ 01309

The attractive village of Findhorn lies at the mouth of the River Findhorn, just east of the Findhorn Bay nature reserve. It's a great place for bird-watching, seal-spotting and coastal walks.

Findhorn Heritage Centre *(☎ 630349; admission free; open 2pm-5pm Wed-Mon June-Aug, 2pm-5pm Sat & Sun May & Sept)*, housed in a former salmon-fisher's *bothy* (hut) at the northern end of the village, records the history of the settlement. The beach is just over the dunes north of the centre. At low tide, you can see seals hauled out on the sandbanks off the mouth of the River Findhorn.

Places to Stay & Eat There's plenty of accommodation and some good eating places in Findhorn.

Findhorn Bay Caravan Park *(☎ 690203)* Tent pitches £6.50-10. Open Apr-Oct. This site, at the southern end of the village, is where the Findhorn Foundation was born.

Findhorn Sands Caravan Park *(☎ 690324)* Tent pitches £8-10. Open Apr-Oct. Find-

horn's other camping ground is at the northern end of the village, near the beach.

Crown & Anchor *(☎ 690243)* Mains £5.25-11.95. Food served noon-9pm. The Crown and Anchor is a friendly hotel (B&B £25 per person) and pub that serves excellent bar meals, including fresh seafood. Kids love the toy train that carries meal orders from the bar to the kitchen.

Kimberley Inn *(☎ 690492)* Mains from £5.95-12. Food served noon-10pm. Findhorn's other pub also does good bar meals.

Around Findhorn On the western side of Findhorn Bay is **Culbin Forest**, a vast swathe of Scots and Corsican pine that was planted in the 1940s to stabilise the shifting sand dunes that buried the Culbin Estate in the 17th century. The forest is a unique wildlife habitat, and is criss-crossed by a maze of walking trails.

The tidy town of Forres, 4 miles (6km) south of Findhorn, is famous for **Sueno's Stone**, a remarkable, 6.5m-tall Pictish stone. It is the tallest and most elaborately carved Pictish stone in Scotland, dating from the 9th or 10th century, and is thought to depict a battle between the Picts and invading Scots or Vikings. It's protected from the elements by a huge plate-glass box.

Hippies old and new should check out the **Findhorn Foundation** *(☎ 01309-690311, **W** www.findhorn.org, Forres, IV36 0TZ; open 9am-12.30pm & 2pm-5pm Mon-Fri, 2pm-5pm Sat & Sun May-Aug; Mon-Fri only Mar, Apr, Sept & Oct; 9am-12.30pm Mon-Fri Nov-Feb)*. The Foundation is an international spiritual community, founded in 1962. There are about 150 members and many more sympathetic souls who have moved into the vicinity.

With no formal creed, the community is dedicated to cooperation with nature, 'dealing with work, relationships and our environment in new and more fulfilling ways' and fostering 'a deeper sense of the sacred in everyday life'. Projects include ecofriendly houses, a biological sewage-treatment plant and a wind-powered generator. Guided tours (£1) are available at 2pm Monday, Wednesday and Friday March to October, and on Saturday and Sunday June to August.

CENTRAL & NE SCOTLAND

The Highlands

Forget the castles, forget the towns and villages. The spectacular Highlands are all about mountains, sea, heather, moors, lochs – and wide, empty, exhilarating space. This is one of Europe's last great wildernesses, and it's more beautiful than you can imagine.

The Highlands is an imprecise term for the upland area which covers the far western and northern parts of mainland Scotland. This chapter covers the administrative regions known as Argyll & Bute, and Highland, excluding the Isle of Skye and the islands of the Inner Hebrides.

Although pleasant, the east coast can't compete with the dramatic north and west, where the mountains and sea collide, and superlatives get exhausted. Some of the most beautiful areas can only be reached by many miles of single track road, either by boat or on foot. Make the effort and you'll be rewarded!

WALKING

The Highlands offer some of Scotland's finest walking country, whether it's along the coast, or on inland peaks and ridges such as the Aonach Eagach, the Five Sisters of Kintail, An Teallach, Stac Pollaidh, Suilven (the Sugar Loaf) or Ben Hope (Scotland's most northerly Munro).

The West Highland Way is the main long-distance footpath and runs for 95 miles (152km) from Milngavie (just north of Glasgow) to Fort William. The route falls almost entirely within this chapter.

The mountains can be treacherous and some walkers come to grief every year. There are weather forecast phone lines, which cost from 60p to an extortionate £1.50 per minute, but they are rarely used; forecasts on Radio Scotland (5.55pm daily) or in *The Scotsman* and *The Herald* newspapers provide enough information. There's also a mountain weather forecast Web site at W www.onlineweather .com. A handy leaflet, *Enjoy the Scottish Hills in Safety*, offers basic safety advice. Campers should read the Mountaineering Council of Scotland's *Wild Camping* leaflet.

OTHER ACTIVITIES

Fishing is a popular Highland activity, but it's strictly regulated and some of the famous salmon fishing beats can be very expensive. Fishing for brown trout in lochs is more affordable. Local tourist offices can advise on permits and equipment as well as suggest the best locations.

For **skiing** and **snowboarding**, try Cairngorm (Aviemore), Glencoe Ski Centre or Nevis Range (Fort William). Thurso has good surf, but the Isle of Lewis is better (see The Hebrides chapter). **Pony trekking**, **deer stalking**, **cycling** and **golf** are other popular Highland activities.

Argyll & Bute

Argyll & Bute stretches from the tip of the Kintyre peninsula (subject of Paul McCartney's song *Mull of Kintyre*) almost to Glen Coe, and east to Loch Lomond. The region includes the Isle of Bute, parts of the West Highlands, and the islands of the Inner Hebrides – Islay, Jura, Colonsay, Mull, Coll and Tiree (see The Hebrides chapter).

This area is centred on the ancient kingdom of Dalriada, named by Irish settlers (known as the Scotti) who claimed it in the 6th century. From their headquarters at Dunadd, in the Moine Mhor (meaning 'great bog') near Kilmartin, they gained ascendancy over the Picts and established the kingdom of Alba, which eventually became Scotland.

Just 20 miles (32km) from Glasgow, Loch Lomond is a very popular destination. Its western bank, where most of the tourist activity takes place, lies in Argyll & Bute; the eastern bank in Stirling.

The Firth of Clyde, to the south, is a complex system of long, deep fjords, or sea lochs, such as Loch Long and Loch Fyne. This pattern of glacial valleys, drowned by the incoming sea, continues all the way up the west coast of Scotland, creating a great length of indented coastline. It's an area that records some of the highest rainfall in Britain.

Most people heading for the islands pass through the pleasant town of Oban, the only place of any size in the area, at least once.

ISLE OF BUTE
☎ 01700 • pop 7354

The slightly dilapidated resort of **Rothesay** is Bute's only town, with all the usual facilities. The island sees around a million visitors a year and Rothesay itself is very busy in summer with crowds (mostly on day trips) from Glasgow and Ayrshire.

The friendly TIC (☎ 502151), in the Isle of Bute Discovery Centre, Victoria St, has long lists of B&Bs and hotels, but there's no youth hostel on the island. In late July there's a popular folk festival (☎ 831614) and there's a jazz festival (☎ 502800) during the first weekend of May.

Things to See
Owned by Historic Scotland (HS), **Rothesay Castle** *(☎ 502691, King St; adult/child £2/75p; open standard HS hours but closed Thur afternoon, Fri & Sun morning in winter)* is a considerable ruin with a wonderful water-filled moat. **Bute Museum** *(☎ 505067, Stuart St; adult/child £1.20/70p; open 10.30am-4.30pm Mon-Sat, 2.30pm-4.30pm Sun Apr-Sept, 2.30pm-4.30pm Tues-Sat Oct-Mar)* has a good collection covering the natural history, archaeology and geology of the island. It has an unusual 3500-year-old lignite necklace. Botanists should enjoy the **Victorian Fernery** *(☎ 504555, Ascog Hall, Ascog; adult/child £2.50/free; open 10am-5pm Wed-Sun mid-Apr–mid-Oct)*.

Britain's most spectacular mock-Gothic mansion, **Mount Stuart House** *(☎ 503877, Mount Stuart; adult/child/family £6.50/2.50/15; open 11am-5pm Fri-Mon & Wed May–mid-Sept)*, belongs to the marquess of Bute. It has a magnificent marble interior, a chapel, and the distinctly unusual horoscope room.

In the southern part of Bute, you'll find the 12th-century ruin of **St Blane's Chapel**, with a 10th-century tombstone in the graveyard. There's a good walk from Kilchattan via the coast (1½ hours) and there's a beach with red sand at **Kilchattan Bay**.

On the west coast, there's a fine beach at **Scalpsie Bay** and you can spot seals at nearby **Ardscalpsie Point**.

Places to Stay & Eat
Roseland Caravan Park (☎ 504529, Canada Hill, Rothesay) Pitches £6-8. Open Mar-Oct. This is a pleasant site above the town.

THE HIGHLANDS

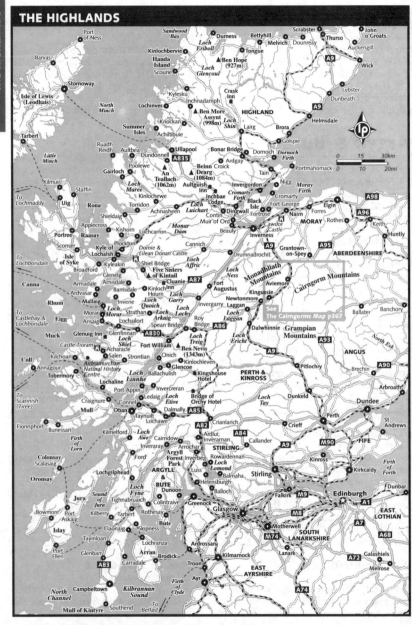

Ascog Farm (☎ *503372, Ascog)* Singles/doubles with shared bathroom £17/34. On the southern edge of town, towards Mount Stuart, this is an excellent B&B.

Ardyne-St Ebba Hotel (☎ *502052, fax 505129, 37/38 Mount Stuart Rd, Rothesay)* En-suite singles/doubles from £30/55. This comfortable hotel offers a good Scottish menu (three-course dinner £16.50, or £14.50 for residents).

Black Bull (☎ *502366, Albert Place, Rothesay)* Snacks & meals £1.50-11.50. The Black Bull does good-quality bar snacks and meals. The latter aren't available on Sunday.

Kettledrum (☎ *505324, 32 East Princes St, Rothesay)* Mains £4.75-7.75. Kettledrum is the most pleasant of Rothesay's cafes, offering cheaper snacks such as soup and a roll (£1.25).

St Blane's Hotel (☎/fax 831224, Kilchattan Bay) B&B £23-28.50 per person. This popular place is in an unusual building with a pleasant shorefront location at Kilchattan Bay. Bar meals are available for £2.95 to £5.50.

Getting There & Away
Frequent CalMac ferries ply between Wemyss Bay and Rothesay (£3.25/13.15 foot passenger/car, 35 minutes). Another regular ferry crosses the short stretch of water between Rhubodach in the north of the island and Colintraive (£1/6.60 foot passenger/car, five minutes).

Stagecoach Western (☎ 502076) runs several times weekly from Rothesay, west to Tighnabruaich, and east to Dunoon.

Getting Around
The Stagecoach Western service around Bute is fairly good, but limited on Sunday. Buses link with ferries at Rothesay and run roughly hourly (except Tuesday and Thursday) to Mount Stuart House (£2.50 return).

Cycling on Bute is excellent – the roads are well surfaced and fairly quiet. Hire a bike at the Mountain Bike Centre (☎ 502333, 24 East Princes St, Rothesay) for £6/10 per half/full day (£10 deposit).

COWAL
Located north of Bute and between Loch Fyne and Loch Long, the Cowal peninsula has extensive forests and mountains almost 800m high. The northern section of the area is part of the Argyll Forest Park.

The area is traversed by several roads, some of them fairly narrow. The scenery around Loch Riddon, on the way to the village of Tighnabruaich, is particularly enchanting. The only town in the area is the uninviting Dunoon, on the Firth of Clyde, opposite Gourock.

Tighnabruaich
☎ 01700 • pop 196
Pleasant Tighnabruaich, a popular sailing centre, has an excellent location by the Kyles of Bute and is well worth a visit. Ask at Kames Cabin, half a mile (1km) towards Kames, for local information, including forest walks. Tighnabruaich has a bank (without ATM), two shops (the Spar has an ATM) and a post office.

Ferguslie (☎ *811414, Seafront, Tighna bruaich)* Singles/doubles £18/34. Open Apr-Sept. A light supper is included in the room rates at Ferguslie.

Royal Hotel (☎ *811239, fax 811300, Tighnabruaich)* B&B £37-77 per head. You'll get an excellent, freshly prepared meal (brasserie meals £5.45 to £20.95, three-course set dinner £26.95) in this seafront hotel.

Burnside Cafe-Bistro (☎ *811739, Tighnabruaich)* Mains from £5.50. This is a fairly basic option.

Stagecoach Western (☎ 502076) runs several times a week to Rothesay, with possible connections at Auchenbreck for Dunoon. There's also a postbus (☎ 01246-546329) to Dunoon Monday to Saturday.

Dunoon
☎ 01369 • pop 8726
If you stay in Dunoon, be careful after dark. The local economy took a downturn after the Americans pulled out of the nearby Holy Loch naval base, and there's still no sign of improvement.

Dunoon is served by two frequent ferry routes from Gourock. The CalMac sailing is best if you want to arrive in the town centre. See the Gourock section in the Glasgow chapter for details.

Holy Loch's Hidden Legacy

The sheltered, deep-water inlet of Holy Loch, just north of Dunoon, was used as a base for US Navy nuclear submarines from the early 1960s until 1992. When the Americans departed, they took with them fond memories, not a few Scottish wives and husbands, and a huge chunk of the local economy.

But what they left behind has only recently been discovered. A survey of the sea bed in the Holy Loch revealed that the US Navy had been a little untidy. A three-year clean-up programme, completed in 2001, used electromagnetic and mechanical grabs to recover more than 2700 tonnes of debris from the sea floor. The haul included steel, concrete, wooden piles, scaffolding, hoses, pipes, gas cylinders, ammunition, a barge, an entire landing craft, 30 ID cards... and two sets of human bones.

The US Navy is fairly certain that one of the skeletons belongs to a seaman from Alabama who disappeared overboard many years ago, but the identity of the second set of bones remains a mystery.

The town has all the essential facilities, including banks with ATMs on Argyll St, which runs parallel with the shore. There's a big Safeway supermarket on John St, just off Argyll St. The TIC (☎ 703785), 7 Alexandra Parade, opens year-round. Dunoon hosts the annual Cowal Highland Gathering (☎ 703206, W www.cowalgathering.com) in mid-August; there are usually over 150 pipe bands.

Pitcairlie House *(☎ 704122, Alexandra Parade)* B&B with shared bathroom £16-20. This recommended B&B is 10 minutes' walk north of the CalMac ferry terminal.

Argyll Hotel *(☎ 702059, fax 704483, Argyll St)* Singles/doubles from £45/65. All rooms are en suite at the prominent Argyll Hotel. Bar meals are available (£3.95 to £16.95).

Chatters *(☎ 706402, 58 John St)* Mains £5.75-14.50. Closed Sun. Chatters does good evening meals.

There's a ***fish and chip shop*** (£3.10) on Church St and several cheap eateries and takeaways on Argyll St.

Stagecoach Western (☎ 707701) runs several times a week to Rothesay and Tighnabruaich; three buses daily except Sunday run to Inverary. On Saturday, a postbus (☎ 01246-546329) goes to Colintraive and there's a once or twice daily service to Tighnabruaich (except Sunday).

Highland Stores *(☎ 702007, 156 Argyll St)* charges £13 per day for bicycle hire.

HELENSBURGH
☎ 01436 • pop 16,000

For such a large place, there's comparatively little of interest here apart from **Hill House** *(☎ 673900, Upper Colquhoun St; adult/child £6/4.50; open 1.30pm-5pm daily Apr-Oct)*. This property, cared for by the National Trust for Scotland (NTS), is one of the finest houses Charles Rennie Mackintosh designed; the bathroom has an intriguing Edwardian shower and there's a tearoom in the excellent kitchen.

The TIC (☎ 672642), in the Clock Tower on the waterfront, opens April to October; there are supermarkets and banks (with ATMs) in the same area.

In Helensburgh, most of the B&Bs are fairly expensive.

Eastbank *(☎ 673665, 10 Hanover St)* Singles £18-20, doubles £36-46. There are two rooms, one of which is en suite, in this reasonably priced B&B.

Upper Crust *(☎ 678035, 88a West Clyde St)* Mains £6.95-10.20. The Upper Crust has an adventurous Scottish menu and a lovely courtyard garden.

Bar Budda *(☎ 674252, 41-42 West Clyde St)* Pasta £3.75-3.95. Bar Budda is a pleasant place; it also offers Mexican dishes from £4.65.

Lido *(7 West Clyde St)* is the best place for fish and chips (£3.60).

Helensburgh has ferry connections with Gourock (see the Glasgow chapter for details) and good train connections with Dumbarton and Glasgow (£3.80, 45 minutes, two trains per hour).

LOCH LOMOND
After Loch Ness, this is perhaps the most famous of Scotland's lochs. Measuring 27½ sq

miles (70 sq km), it's the largest lake in mainland Britain. Its proximity to Glasgow (only 20 miles/32km north-west) means that parts of the loch get quite crowded in summer. The main tourist focus is on the western shore of the loch, along the A82, and at the southern end, around Balloch, which can be a nightmare of jet skis and motorboats. The eastern shore north of Rowardennan, which the West Highland Way follows, sees few visitors. Things may change significantly when the Loch Lomond & the Trossachs National Park opens in 2002.

The loch was formed during the Ice Age by the action of glaciers, and later lay at the junction of the three ancient Scottish kingdoms of Strathclyde, Dalriada and Pictland. Some of the 37 islands in the loch made perfect retreats for early Christians. The missionary St Mirrin spent some time on Inchmurrin, the largest island, which is named after him.

Loch Lomond crosses the Highland line and its character changes quite obviously as you move from south to north, with the most dramatic scenery in the north. The highest mountain in the area is Ben Lomond (974m), on the eastern shore.

Orientation & Information

The loch is 22 miles (35km) long and up to 5 miles (8km) wide. The A82 is a major route north and sticks to the western shore through Tarbet and on to Crianlarich. The main thoroughfare on the eastern shore is just a walking trail, the West Highland Way, but it's reached by road from Drymen and Aberfoyle.

There are TICs at: Balloch (☎ 01389-753533), Balloch Rd, open April to October; Drymen (☎ 01360-660068), in the library on the square, open May to September; and Tarbet (☎ 01301-702260), at the A82/A83 junction, open April to October.

A new national park visitor centre, Lomond Shores, will open in spring 2002 with a large-format cinema showing films about Loch Lomond. The proposed site is on Old Luss Rd, Balloch; see the Web site at Ⓦ www.lomondshores.com or call ☎ 01389-758216 for the latest details.

Walking & Cycling

The big walk around here is the **West Highland Way**, portions of which are accessible for shorter walks. See the Activities chapter for details.

From Rowardennan, you can tackle **Ben Lomond**, a popular five- to six-hour round trip. The route starts at the car park by the Rowardennan Hotel, and you can return via the Ptarmigan (731m) for good views of the loch.

Another good walk is **Ben Vorlich** (943m), a good five- to six-hour return trip from Ardlui station. From the underpass just south of the station, head uphill into Coire Creagach and bear right up to the ridge at 580m. Then follow the ridge to the double summit of the hill.

The main cycle route in the area is the **Glasgow-Killin Cycle Way**, which reaches the loch at Balloch. Most of the route is set back to the east of the loch, through the Queen Elizabeth Forest Park. Along the western shore, the A82 is very busy in summer, but there are short sections of the old road beside it that are quieter.

Boat Trips

The main centre for boat trips is Balloch, where two outfits, *Sweeney's Cruises* (☎ 01389-752376) and *Mullen's Cruises* (☎ 01389-751481), offer a wide range of trips from £4.50/2.50 an hour per adult/child. There's a daily 2½-hour cruise (£7.50/3.50) to Luss village, allowing 30 minutes ashore, departing at 2.30pm from Balloch. If this twee place looks like a film set, that's because it was. When the TV soap *High Road* was running, the village was popular with Scottish visitors hoping to catch a glimpse of its stars.

Cruise Loch Lomond (☎ 01301-702356) operates from Tarbet – its trips go to Inversnaid and Rob Roy MacGregor's cave (see The Trossachs in the Central & North-Eastern Scotland chapter for details on Roy MacGregor).

Balloch Castle Country Park

Balloch Castle Visitor Centre (☎ 01389-758216, Mollanbowie Rd; admission free; open 10am-6pm daily Easter-Oct) has displays about the Loch Lomond Park (which will be part of the new Loch Lomond & the Trossachs National Park by 2002) and the popular Balloch Castle Country Park.

Balloch Castle, originally built around 1238, has long since disappeared. The current castle is actually a grand crenellated mansion dating from 1808 and constructed by the rich financier John Buchanan. Buchanan also ordered the layout of the 81 hectares of ornamental gardens and parkland which surround the castle. There are several other buildings in the park, plus an attractive walled garden. Unfortunately, reports of lots of rubbish in the area have some foundation.

Access is easy – from Balloch train station, walk a quarter mile (500m) east on Balloch Rd to the southern pedestrian entrance, then it's a half mile (800m) north to the castle.

Places to Stay
Camping There are several recommended camp sites around Loch Lomond.

Lomond Woods (☎ 01389-755000, fax 755563, Tullichewan, Balloch) From £7 per tent. This is the finest camping and caravan park in the area.

Forestry Commission Cashel Campsite (☎ 01360-870234, Rowardennan) Pitches from £7.50. Open late-Mar–Oct. This popular and well-located camp site is on the eastern shore, 3 miles (5km) north of Balmaha. It has a cafe.

Ardlui Holiday Home Park (☎ 01301-704243, fax 704268, Ardlui) Pitches from £8.50. You can also rent boats at this site.

Backpacker's Camp Site (☎ 01301-704244, Ardlui) Pitches £5. Near the station in Ardlui, there's this tiny backpacker's camp site with basic facilities.

Hostels There are three hostels by the loch.
Loch Lomond Youth Hostel (☎ 01389-850226, fax 850623, Arden) Beds from £11.75/10.50. Open Mar-Oct. Loch Lomond Youth Hostel is an imposing building and one of the most impressive hostels in the country. It's set in beautiful grounds, 2 miles (3km) north of Balloch. Book in advance in summer. And yes, it is haunted.

Rowardennan Youth Hostel (☎ 01360-870259, fax 870256, Rowardennan) Beds

from £9/6. Open Mar-Oct. Rowardennan Youth Hostel is halfway up the eastern shore of the loch. It's also an activity centre and is the perfect base for climbing Ben Lomond.

Beinn Ghlas Farm Wigwams (☎/fax 01301-704281, Inverarnan) Beds £9, sheets £2, breakfast £5 extra. Accommodation is in weird-looking beehive-shaped huts at this place on the West Highland Way.

B&Bs & Hotels The numerous B&Bs, centred on Balloch, Luss, Inverbeg and Tarbet, tend to be rather expensive.

Argyll Lodge (☎ 01389-759020, 16 Luss Rd, Balloch) Singles £20-24, doubles £36-44. Argyll Lodge is a friendly B&B; all rooms have private bathroom.

Inverbeg Inn (☎ 01436-860678, fax 860686, Inverbeg) Singles £45-65, doubles £76-98. All rooms are en suite and the food here is good (bar meals £6.50 to £8.50; three-course dinner £20 to £25).

Ardlui Hotel (☎ 01301-704243, fax 704268, Ardlui) Singles £40-50, doubles £60-80. Most of the nicely decorated rooms are en suite but some share a bathroom at the popular and refurbished Ardlui Hotel. Most meals cost under £8.

Drover's Inn (☎ 01301-704234, e the droversinn@aol.com, Inverarnan) B&B from £23 per person. At the northern end of the loch, this is one pub you shouldn't miss. It has smoke-blackened walls, bare wooden floors, a grand hall filled with moth-eaten stuffed animals, and wee drams served by barmen in kilts. It's a great place for a serious drinking binge. Accommodation varies from basic rooms with shared bath in the old building to plush, modern, newly built en-suite rooms in an annexe. Meals are available for £1.95 to £11.25.

Places to Eat You'll not go hungry around Loch Lomond – there are plenty of places to eat.

Stagger Inn (☎ 01301-704274, Inverarnan) Mains £4.25-13.95, 3-course dinner £19.50. Across the road from the Drover's Inn, the cheery Stagger Inn serves good food.

Rowardennan Hotel (☎ 01360-870273, Rowardennan) Bar meals £5.95-13.95. Daily specials are available at this hotel near the Rowardennan Youth Hostel.

***Balloch Hotel** (☎ 01389-752579, Balloch)* Mains around £7. This hotel does good bar meals.

***Princess Rose** (☎ 01389-755873, Luss Rd, Balloch)* Mains around £6-9. Princess Rose is a good Chinese restaurant; takeaways are available.

In Luss, you'll find a popular *milk bar* and a *coffee shop* that does home baking and snacks.

Getting There & Away

Scottish Citylink (☎ 0870 550 5050) runs regular daily buses from Glasgow to Balloch (£3.60, 40 minutes), but the bus stops are at lay-bys nearly a mile (1.6km) from Balloch town centre; the buses then continue up the A82 to Luss (55 minutes) and Tarbet (one hour 5 minutes). Most of the buses go to Ardlui (£7.40, 1¼ hours) and, north of the loch, Crianlarich.

There are two railway lines from Glasgow. One serves Balloch twice an hour (£3.20, 35 minutes); the other is the West Highland line to Oban and Fort William (two to five daily), which follows the loch from Tarbet to Ardlui.

Getting Around

The island's hotel runs ferry services between Mid-Ross (1 mile/1.6km north of Arden) and Inchmurrin Island. Other services link: Inveruglas and Inversnaid (☎ 01877-386223); Tarbet and Inversnaid (☎ 01301-702356); and Inverbeg and Rowardennan (☎ 01301-702356, £3, three daily). The mail boat, run by MacFarlane & Son (☎ 01360-870214), sails from Balmaha, visiting Inchcailloch Island nature reserve and the inhabited islands Monday to Saturday.

ARROCHAR
☎ 01301 • pop 635

The village of Arrochar has a wonderful location, dominated by sharp peaks. Situated at the inner end of Loch Long, it's a starting point for great walks in the **Argyll Forest Park**. Forest Enterprise has a **visitor centre** (☎ 702432, Ardgartan; admission free; open

10am-5pm daily Apr-Oct) with displays about the area.

The village has several hotels, shops, a bank and a post office. You can hire a bike from **South Peak** *(☎ 702288, Glen Croe; £11.50/8 per full/half day).*

Walking

To reach **The Cobbler**, start from the roadside car park at Succoth, just round the top of the loch. It's a steep uphill hike beside the woods, then it's easier as you trend leftwards towards the triple peaks. Once you pass the Shelter Stone, it's steep uphill again to the pass between the north and central peaks. Turn left for the central peak – scramble through the hole and along the ledge to reach the airy summit. This is a serious hill walk and you must be properly equipped. Allow five to six hours for the return trip.

The **Arrochar Caves** are about a mile (1.6km) north of Succoth. Follow the track past the houses and into the forest. Bear left on a rough path and head uphill to the caves. Take a torch, but don't venture too far in or you might not get out. The walk to the caves from the village takes under an hour.

Forest Enterprise has marked a 2½-mile (4km) forest walk on the flanks of Cruach Tairbeirt. It starts at Arrochar & Tarbet train station and climbs fairly easily to a couple of good viewpoints. Follow the red markers and allow two hours.

Places to Stay & Eat

***Loch Long Youth Hostel** (☎ 702362, fax 450198, Ardgartan)* Beds £7.50/6.25. Open Apr-Oct. Most budget travellers head for this hostel, 2 miles (3km) west of Arrochar at the foot of Glen Croe.

***Ardgartan Caravan & Campsite** (☎ 702293, Ardgartan)* Camping from £5.80. Open Apr-Oct. This site has a grocery store.

***Cobbler Hotel** (☎ 702238, fax 702353, Arrochar)* Singles £25-30, doubles £50-56. The Cobbler puts on regular live entertainment and has bar meals for £3.85 to £8.95.

***Pit Stop Diner** (Arrochar)* Here you'll get fish and chips (£3.20) and cheap burgers (from £1.80).

***Arrochar Hotel** (☎ 702484)* Bar meals £4-5.95. Vegetarian dishes are available.

***Road Man's Cottage** (☎ 702557, Glen Croe)* B&B singles £15-16, doubles £30-32. This is an interesting remote option in Glen Croe, with good dinners (£8.50).

Getting There & Away

Scottish Citylink (☎ 0870 550 5050) buses from Glasgow call at Arrochar and Ardgartan three times daily (£5.30, 1¼ hours); they continue to Inverary and Campbeltown. Scot Rail (☎ 0845 748 4950) runs two to five trains daily from Glasgow to Arrochar & Tarbet station (£7.30, 1¼ hours), and on to Oban and Fort William.

INVERARAY
☎ 01499 • pop 704

On the shores of Loch Fyne, Inveraray is a picturesque, small town with some interesting attractions. It's an early planned town, built by the duke of Argyll when he revamped his nearby castle in the 18th century. The TIC (☎ 302063) is on the street that runs along the loch and it opens year-round. There's a Spar shop and two banks with ATMs. The Inverary Highland Games take place in mid-July.

Inveraray Castle

On the edge of the town, Inveraray Castle *(☎ 302203; adult/child £5.50/3.50; open 10am-5.45pm Mon-Sat & 1pm-5.45pm Sun July & Aug, closed 1pm-2pm Mon-Thur & Sat & all day Fri Apr-June, Sept & Oct)* has been the seat of the dukes of Argyll (the chiefs of Clan Campbell) since the 15th century. The current 18th-century building includes whimsical turrets and fake battlements. Inside is the impressive armoury hall, which has walls patterned with an extensive collection of more than 1000 pole arms, dirks, muskets and Lochaber axes. The dining and drawing rooms have ornate ceilings and there's a large collection of porcelain.

Inveraray Jail

The Georgian jail and courthouse *(☎ 302381, Church Square; adult/child £4.90/2.40; open 9.30am-6pm daily Apr-Oct, 10am-5pm Nov-*

Mar), in the centre of the town, have been converted into an entertaining tourist attraction. You sit in on a trial, try out a cell and discover the meaning of 'picking oakum'. Chatty warders and attendants in 19th century costume accost visitors. Last entry is one hour before closing.

Inverary Maritime Museum

The *Arctic Penguin*, a three-masted schooner built in 1911 and one of the world's last surviving iron sailing ships, is now a 'unique maritime experience' *(☎ 302213, The Pier, adult/child £3/1.50; open 10am-6pm daily Apr-Sept, 10am-5pm Oct-Mar)*. There are displays on the maritime history of the Clyde, piracy and the Highland Clearances as well as archive videos to watch and activities for children.

Places to Stay & Eat

***Inveraray Youth Hostel** (☎ 302454, Dalmally Rd)* Beds £8.50/7.25. Open Apr-Sept. This SYHA hostel is a modern bungalow on the left just through the arched entrance to Dalmally Rd.

***Newton Hall** (☎ 302484, Shore Rd)* B&B £18-22 per person. Open Mar-Dec. This friendly B&B is housed in a converted church overlooking Loch Fyne.

***Claonairigh House** (☎ 302160, Bridge of Douglas)* B&B £16-24 per person. Set in a grand house dating from 1745, this B&B has three hectares of garden on the bank of a salmon river (fishing available). It's 4 miles (7km) south of town on the A83.

***Argyll Hotel** (☎ 302466, fax 302389, Front St)* Singles £40-60, doubles £72-90, dinner B&B £59-68 per person. The four-star Argyll is a fully modernised 18th-century inn with excellent Scottish cuisine and a great location overlooking the loch.

***George Hotel** (☎ 302111, Main St East)* B&B £20-30 per person. This hotel has a pleasant pub with stone walls, a flagstone floor, peat fires and meals for £2.95 to £11.75.

***Loch Fyne Oyster Bar** (☎ 600236, Clachan, Cairndow)* Mains £7.25-19.95. Open 9am-9pm daily. The best place to eat in the area is the Loch Fyne Oyster Bar, 6 miles (10km) north of Inveraray. The menu includes local mussels and oysters, and there's a good range of fresh and smoked fish and shellfish. The neighbouring shop sells packaged seafood to take away.

Getting There & Away
There are five daily Citylink buses (four on Sunday) to Inveraray from Glasgow (£6.90, ¾ hours). Three of these buses continue to Lochgilphead and Campbeltown (£7.60, 2½ hours); the others continue to Oban (£4.90, ¼ hours).

LOCHGILPHEAD
☎ 01546 • pop 2600
There's not much to see in Lochgilphead itself, but there's plenty of interest in the surrounding area.

The TIC (☎ 602344), Lochnell St, opens April to October. On Argyll St, there's a post office, Spar and Co-op. There are two banks with ATMs on Poltalloch St. There are various places to eat, including *The Stables* cafe on Argyll St, and an Indian restaurant and a Chinese takeaway on Lochnell St.

Lochgilphead Caravan Park (☎ 602003, fax 603699, Bank Park) Pitches £7.50. Open Apr-Oct. This place is a short walk west of the town centre. It has bikes for rent – useful for getting to Dunadd and around Kilmartin.

Argyll Hotel (☎ 602221, fax 603576, e argyllhotel@btclick.com, 69 Lochnell St) Singles £19-25, doubles £36-44. The best place to stay in town is the refurbished Argyll, with a lively bar (meals £6) and steakhouse restaurant.

Empire Travel Lodge (☎ 602381, fax 606606, Union St) B&B £22-24 per person. This comfortable, nine-room lodge is in a converted cinema.

There are three daily Citylink buses from Glasgow to Lochgilphead (£7.65, 2½ hours), continuing to Campbeltown. There's also a daily (except Sunday) bus to Oban (£3.50, ½ hours).

CRINAN CANAL
☎ 01546
The scenic Crinan Canal runs 9 miles (13km) from Ardrishaig, 2 miles (3km) south of Lochgilphead, to Crinan, 7 miles (11km) north-west of Lochgilphead. Completed in 1801, the canal allows sea-going vessels – mostly yachts these days – to take a short-cut from the Firth of Clyde and Loch Fyne to the west coast of Scotland, avoiding the long passage around the Mull of Kintyre. You can easily walk or cycle the full length of the canal towpath in a day.

Gemini Cruises (☎ 830238, W www.gemini-crinan.co.uk; adult/child £11/7.50), at Kilmahuaig, a half-mile (800m) west of the Crinan Hotel at the north-western end of the canal, runs two-hour boat trips to the spectacular Gulf of Corryvreckan, where strong tidal currents create Britain's biggest whirlpool. They will also ferry groups across to the northern end of Jura (£40 for up to 12 passengers and bicycles, 30 minutes).

Cairnbaan Hotel (☎ 603668, fax 606045, e cairnbaan.hotel@virgin.net, Cairnbaan) Singles £55-65, doubles £75-110. Set halfway along the canal, the Cairnbaan Hotel's restaurant serves delicious bar meals, including haddock and chips, venison burgers, and roast veggies with tagliatelle (meals £6.95 to £12.95).

Crinan Hotel (☎ 830261, fax 830292, e nryan@crinanhotel.com, Crinan) Dinner B&B £95-120 per person. The luxurious Crinan Hotel, overlooking Loch Crinan at the north-western end of the canal, has one of Scotland's finest (and most expensive) seafood restaurants.

There are several B&Bs in and around Crinan, and the *Coffee Shop* on the western side of the canal basin at Crinan has great home-baked cakes and scones.

KILMARTIN GLEN
☎ 01546
This magical glen is at the centre of one of the most concentrated areas of prehistoric sites in Scotland. This is where Irish settlers founded the kingdom of Dalriada in the 6th century, which eventually united with the Picts in 843 to create the first Scottish kingdom.

The nearest TIC is at Lochgilphead, 8 miles (13km) south of Kilmartin (see the previous Lochgilphead section). There's a shop and post office in Kilmartin village.

Things to See

The oldest monuments at Kilmarten date from 5000 years ago and comprise a linear cemetery of **burial cairns** that run south of Kilmartin village for 1½ miles (2.5km). There are also ritual monuments (two stone circles) at **Temple Wood**, three-quarters of a mile (1.2km) south-west of Kilmartin.

There are some 10th-century Celtic crosses in **Kilmartin Church** and lots of medieval grave slabs in the churchyard. Apart from the church, **Kilmartin House** (☎ 510278, ⓦ www.kilmartin.org; adult/child £3.90/1.20; open 10am-5.30pm daily) is an interesting centre for archaeology and landscape interpretation with artefacts from local sites, reconstructions, prehistoric music, interactive displays, guided tours and a tearoom. The project was partly funded by midges – the curator exposed himself in Temple Wood on a warm summer's evening and was sponsored per midge bite!

The hill fort of **Dunadd**, 3½ miles (5km) south of Kilmartin village, overlooks the boggy plain that's now the Moine Mhór Nature Reserve. It was chosen as the royal residence of the first kings of Dalriada, and this was probably where the Stone of Destiny, used in investiture ceremonies, was originally located. The faint rock carvings of a wild boar and two footprints with an ogham inscription – from an ancient alphabet – were probably used in some kind of inauguration ceremony.

At **Kilmichael Glassary**, a mile (1.6km) east of Dunadd, elaborate designs – so-called cup and ring marks – are cut into rock faces; their purpose is unknown.

Just over a mile (1.6km) north of Kilmartin are the extensive remains of the 16th-century tower house **Carnassarie Castle**, built by the bishop of the Isles. There's some excellent carved stonework and other architectural detail here.

Places to Stay & Eat

There are several places to stay and eat in and around Kilmartin. The nearest camp site is at Lochgilphead, 8 miles (13km) to the south.

Burndale (☎ 510235, ⓔ alan-hawkins@ burndale-kilmartin.freeserve.co.uk) B&B £21 per person. This B&B, set in an old manse (minister's house), is just three minutes' walk from Kilmartin House.

Kilmartin Hotel (☎/fax 510250 ⓔ kilmartinhotel@aol.com) B&B from £18 per person, with bathroom £25. This hotel also has a restaurant and bar; there's folk music here some weekends.

The Cairn Restaurant (☎ 510254) Mains £11.25-15.45. Open 5pm-10pm Wed-Mon. This place, close to the Kilmartin Hotel, does good bar meals and restaurant dinners.

The **Horseshoe Inn** (☎ 606369) at Bridg end, 4 miles (6.5km) south of Kilmartin serves bar meals from noon to 8pm.

Getting There & Away

The daily (except Sunday) Lochgilphead to Oban bus, leaving at 9.10am, stops at Kilmartin (£1.55, 15 minutes). The return bus from Oban to Kilmartin (£3.40, 1¼ hours) and Lochgilphead leaves Oban at 1.45pm.

KINTYRE

Forty miles (65km) long and 8 miles (13km) wide, the Kintyre peninsula is almost an island, with only a narrow isthmus connecting it to the wooded hills of Knapdale at Tarbert. The Viking Magnus Barefoot, who was allowed to claim as his own any island he had circumnavigated, made his men drag their longship across this strand to validate his claim to Kintyre in 1098.

Tarbert
☎ 01880 • pop 1500

Tarbert, the gateway to Kintyre, is an attractive fishing village that also attracts the yachting crowd. The TIC (☎ 820429) is on Harbour St and opens April to October. There's a Co-op supermarket and two banks near the head of the harbour.

Things to See The **An Tairbeart Arts Centre** (☎ 821116, Campbeltown Rd; admission free; open 10am-5pm daily) is at the southern edge of the village and has galleries of crafts and contemporary arts, as well as displays about local natural history and human interaction with the environment. You may see various wild birds, including peregrine falcons, hen harriers and owls, on a mile-long (1.6km) woodland trail.

The crumbling, ivy-covered ruins of **Tarbert Castle**, built by Robert the Bruce in the 14th century, overlook the harbour – there's a signposted footpath beside the Ann R Thomas Gallery on Harbour St.

Special Events Tarbert is a lively little place, and never more so than during the annual Scottish Series Yacht Race, held over five days around the last weekend in May, when the harbour is crammed with hundreds of visiting yachts. The Tarbert Seafood Festival is held on the first weekend in July, and the Tarbert Music Festival on the third weekend in September.

Places to Stay & Eat There are plenty of B&Bs and hotels, but book ahead during the yacht-race season mentioned above.

West Loch Tarbert Holiday Park (☎ 820873, *Escart Bay*) Tent pitches £5-7. Open Apr-Oct. This site is 2 miles (3km) south-west of Tarbert on the road to Campbeltown.

Anchor Hotel (☎ 820577, e *anchorhotel@lochfyne-scotland.co.uk, Harbour St*) Rooms from £28 per person. The recently refurbished Anchor has a perfect location overlooking the harbour and serves excellent meals, both in the bar and the restaurant (mains £6.95 to £14.50).

Columba Hotel (☎/fax 820808, e *columbahotel@fsbdial.co.uk, East Pier Rd*) Rooms from £36 per person. The peaceful Columba is a 10-minute walk from the village centre along the southern side of the harbour. Its restaurant serves top Scottish cuisine (three-course dinner £20.50, bar meals £5.25 to £8.50).

Victoria Hotel (☎ 820236, *Barmore Rd*) Bar meals served noon-2pm & 6pm-9.30pm. The bright yellow Vic, overlooking the head of the harbour, is a lively pub popular with yachties. It serves good bar meals and also has accommodation (B&B £29 per person).

The Anchorage (☎ 820881, *Harbour St*) Mains £11.95-15.95. Open for dinner daily, closed Sun & Mon Nov-Mar. The Anchorage serves excellent local seafood, game and meat dishes with a Mediterranean flavour.

Ca' Dora Cafe, on Harbour St, serves inexpensive cafe grub, including good ice cream; *An Tairbeart Arts Centre* has a cafe serving vegetarian and vegan food.

Getting There & Away Tarbert is served by the four daily Citylink buses that link Campbeltown with Glasgow and Oban.

CalMac runs a small car ferry from Tarbert to Portavadie on the Cowal Peninsula (passenger £2.70, bicycle £1, car £12.65, 25 minutes, hourly); it runs daily from Easter to September.

The Kennacraig ferry terminal on West Loch Tarbert, 5 miles (8km) south of Tarbert, has ferries to the islands of Islay and Colonsay (see The Hebrides chapter for details).

Skipness
☎ 01880 • pop 100

The tiny village of Skipness is about 13 miles (20km) south of Tarbert by road, on the east coast of Kintyre. It's a pleasant and quiet spot with great views of Arran. There is a post office and general store in the village.

The 13th-century **Skipness Castle** and 16th-century tower house are still in good condition and far more impressive than Tarbert's castle. **St Brendan's Chapel**, less than 300m from the castle, has some excellent carved grave slabs.

Skipness Seafood Cabin (☎ 760207) Mains £4.95-7.95. Open 11am-6pm daily late May-Sept. This place serves teas, coffees and home baking, as well as local fish and shellfish dishes to eat in or take away.

There's a route-marked **forest walk** through the remote hills from Tarbert to Skipness (9 miles/14km, four to five hours); pick up a free map from the TIC at Tarbert.

Henderson Hiring (☎ 820220) runs three buses a day between Tarbert and Skipness (35 minutes).

At Claonaig, 2 miles (3km) west of Skipness, there's a daily car ferry to Lochranza on the Isle of Arran (passenger £4, bicycle £1, car £18.05, seven to nine daily, 30 minutes).

Isle of Gigha
☎ 01583 • pop 120

Gigha (pronounced **ghee**-a, with a hard 'g') is a low-lying island 6 miles (10km) long by about a mile (1.5km) wide. It's famous for the subtropical **Achamore Gardens** (☎ 505254, Achamore House; admission by donation; open 9am-dusk daily). Gigha cheese is sold in many parts of Argyll and is recommended, though not cheap.

There's a range of self-catering cottages available – check W www.isle-ofgigha.co.uk. Camping is not allowed on the island.

Post Office House (☎ 505251), at the top of the hill above the ferry slip, offers B&B for £20 per person.

Gigha Hotel (☎ 505254, fax 505244, e hotel@isle-of-gigha.co.uk) Singles/doubles £51/90. The island's only hotel, 100m south of the post office, has a good restaurant (four-course dinner £25) and a lively bar.

CalMac runs a daily ferry from Tayinloan in Kintyre to Gigha (passenger £4.75, bicycle £2, car £17.90, 20 minutes, hourly, six on Sunday). Only return tickets are available.

There are island walks, and bikes can be rented from either Post Office House or the Gigha Hotel (£5/10 for a half/full day).

Mid-Kintyre
At Glenbarr, 6 miles (10km) south of Tayinloan, is the **Glenbarr Abbey Visitor Centre** (☎ 01583-421247; adult/child £2.50/2; open 10am-5.30pm Wed-Mon Easter-Oct). This 18th-century house has a large collection of clothes, thimbles and china, and even a pair of gloves worn by Mary Queen of Scots. It is a centre for the Clan Macalister. The Laird of Glenbarr himself will take you on an entertaining guided tour.

On the east coast of Kintyre is the pretty village of **Carradale**, with a shop and post office. The **Network Heritage Centre** (☎ 01586-431296; admission free; open 10am-5pm Mon-Sat & 12.30pm-5pm Sun July & Aug; 10am-5pm Tues, Wed, Fri & Sa & 12.30pm-4pm Sun Easter-June & Sept–mid-Oct) in Carradale is housed in an old school house, and has fishing, farming and forestry displays. There are several interesting ruins in the area including the 12th-century **Saddell Abbey** (5 miles/8km south), founded by Somerled, lord of the Isles, and a vitrified Iron Age fort on the eastern point of Carradale Bay.

Carradale Bay Caravan Park (☎ 01583-431665) Pitches £7.50-12.80. Open Easter-Sept. This site has a lovely location beside the broad, sandy beach of Carradale Bay.

Carradale Hotel (☎/fax 01583-431223) Singles £25-40, doubles £50-70. The comfortable Carradale Hotel offers excellent cooking, a sauna, a golf course and beautiful views over the sea to Arran.

Mains Farm (☎ 01583-431216) in Carradale offers B&B for £17 per person.

Campbeltown
☎ 01586 • pop 6000
Campbeltown, with its grey houses, seems like a mining town that's been plucked from the coalfields of central Scotland and dumped incongruously in the wilds of Argyll. Once a thriving fishing port and whisky-making centre, industrial decline and the closure of the former air force base at nearby Machrihanish has seen the town slip into decline. It's now a low-key holiday resort and feels a very long way away from anywhere else.

The TIC (☎ 552056), open year-round, is beside the harbour. There are plenty of shops and banks in the nearby town centre.

Things to See There were once no fewer than 32 distilleries in the Campbeltown area, but most closed down in the 1920s. Today, **Springbank Distillery** (☎ 552085; phone to make an appointment) is the only survivor. It is also the only distillery in Scotland that still distills, matures and bottles all its whisky on the one site.

Campbeltown Heritage Centre (☎ 07783-485387, Big Kiln; adult/child £2/1.25; open 11am-5pm Mon-Sat & 2pm-5pm Sun Apr-Oct) covers most aspects of local life and is worth a visit. **Campbeltown Museum** (☎ 552367, Hall St; admission free; open 10am-1pm & 2pm-5pm Tues & Thur-Sat, 5.30pm-7.30pm Wed) houses displays of geological, cultural and archaeological interest. The **Picture House** (☎ 553657, 26 Hall St), opened in 1913, is the oldest purpose-built cinema still in operation in Scotland.

One of the most unusual sights in Argyll is an eerie **cave-painting of the Crucifixion** by local artist Archibald MacKinnon, which he painted in 1887. The cave is on the southern side of the island of Davaar, at the mouth of Campbeltown Loch, 2 miles (3km) east of town. You can walk to the island at low water across a shingle bar called The Dhorlinn (allow at least 1½ hours for the return trip), but make sure you're not caught by a rising tide (check tide times with the TIC before you set off).

The **Mull of Kintyre Music Festival** (☎ 551053, **W** www.mokmf.com), held in Campbeltown annually in late August, is a popular event featuring traditional Scottish and Irish music; pub gigs are free.

Places to Stay & Eat There are plenty of B&Bs in town, including the quiet and friendly *Eagle Lodge (☎ 551359, 56 High St)*, which charges £15 to £16 per person.

Ardshiel Hotel (☎ 552133, fax 551422, Kilkerran Rd) Singles £30-40, doubles £60-70. The central, family-run Ardshiel has a garden restaurant serving good home cooking (mains from £5.25).

For bar meals, try the *White Hart Hotel (☎ 552440, Main St)*. The *Dhorlinn Cafe* in Longrow is good for fish and chips.

Getting There & Away British Airways flies twice every weekday from Glasgow to Machrihanish airport, 4 miles (6.5km) west of Campbeltown (£76, 40 minutes).

Scottish Citylink runs three buses daily (two on Sunday) from Campbeltown to Glasgow (£11.80, 4½ hours) via Tayinloan, Kennacraig, Tarbert, Lochgilphead (£5.70, 1¾ hours) and Inveraray (£7.60, 2½ hours).

At the time of writing, the ferry service between Campbeltown and Ballycastle in Northern Ireland was not operating, but it may resume in the near future. You can visit **W** www.campbeltownferry.com on the Web to find out the latest situation.

Mull of Kintyre

A narrow winding road, about 18 miles (30km) long, leads south from Campbeltown to the Mull of Kintyre, passing some good sandy beaches near Southend. The name of this remote headland has been immortalised by Paul McCartney's famous song – the former Beatle owns a farmhouse in the area. A lighthouse marks the spot closest to Ireland, the coastline of which is often visible (only 12 miles/19km away across the North Channel).

OBAN
☎ 01631 • pop 8517

Oban can be overrun by visitors in high summer, but as the most important ferry port on the west coast, it manages to hold its own. By Highlands standards it's quite a large town, but you can easily get around on foot. There isn't a great deal to see or do, but the bay is beautiful, the harbour is interesting and there are some good coastal and hill walks in the vicinity.

Orientation

The bus, train and ferry terminals are all grouped conveniently together next to the harbour on the southern edge of the bay. Argyll Square is one block east of the train station, and George St, the main drag, runs north along the promenade to North Pier. From the pier, Corran Esplanade runs round the northern edge of the bay.

Information

Oban TIC (☎ 563122, **e** info@oban.org.uk) is in an old church on Argyll Square. It opens 9am to 9pm Monday to Saturday and 9am to 7pm Sunday, July and August; 9am to 5.30pm Monday to Saturday and 9am to 5pm Sunday, May, June and September; and 9am to 5.30pm Monday to Saturday the rest of the year.

The main post office is in the Tesco supermarket on Lochside St. You can check your email at the TIC (£1 for 10 minutes) and at Oban Backpackers Lodge (£2 for 15 minutes or £5 an hour).

The Lorn and Islands District General Hospital (☎ 567500) is at the southern end of Oban, on Glengallan Rd.

Things to See & Do

Crowning the hill above the town centre is **McCaig's Tower**, built at the end of the 19th century. It was intended to be an art gallery but was never completed, and now looks like a miniature version of Rome's colosseum; it

THE HIGHLANDS

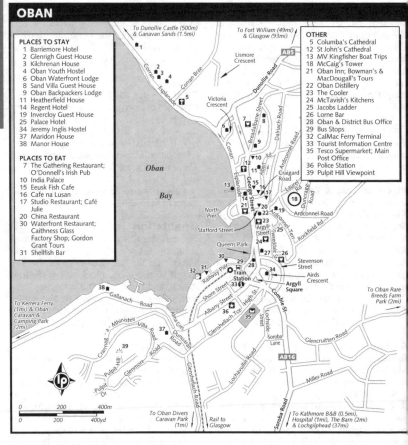

OBAN

PLACES TO STAY
1 Barriemore Hotel
2 Glenrigh Guest House
3 Kilchrenan House
4 Oban Youth Hostel
6 Oban Waterfront Lodge
8 Sand Villa Guest House
9 Oban Backpackers Lodge
11 Heatherfield House
14 Regent Hotel
19 Invercloy Guest House
25 Palace Hotel
34 Jeremy Inglis Hostel
37 Maridon House
38 Manor House

PLACES TO EAT
7 The Gathering Restaurant;
   O'Donnell's Irish Pub
10 India Palace
15 Eeusk Fish Cafe
16 Cafe na Lusan
17 Studio Restaurant; Café
   Julie
20 China Restaurant
30 Waterfront Restaurant;
   Caithness Glass
   Factory Shop; Gordon
   Grant Tours
31 Shellfish Bar

OTHER
5 Columba's Cathedral
12 St John's Cathedral
13 MV Kingfisher Boat Trips
18 McCaig's Tower
21 Oban Inn; Bowman's &
   MacDougall's Tours
22 Oban Distillery
23 The Cooler
24 McTavish's Kitchens
25 Jacobs Ladder
26 Lorne Bar
28 Oban & District Bus Office
29 Bus Stops
32 CalMac Ferry Terminal
33 Tourist Information Centre
35 Tesco Supermarket; Main
   Post Office
36 Police Station
39 Pulpit Hill Viewpoint

looks spectacular when floodlit at night. Take the steep climb up 'Jacob's Ladder' from Argyll St (follow the signs) for amazing views over the bay. The tower is always open and there's no admission charge. There's an even better view from **Pulpit Hill**, to the south of the bay.

Oban Distillery (☎ 572004, Stafford St; adult £3.50; open 9.30am-8.30pm Mon-Fri, 9.30am-5pm Sat & noon-5pm Sun July-Sept; 9.30am-5pm Mon-Sat Easter-June & Oct; 9.30am-5pm Mon-Fri Nov-Easter), in the centre of the town, has been producing Oban single malt whisky since 1794. There

are guided tours available year-round (last tour begins one hour before closing time) but even without a tour it's still worth visiting the small exhibition in the foyer.

You can watch glass-makers in action at the **Caithness Glass Factory Shop** (☎ 563386, The Waterfront Centre, Railway Pier; admission free; open 9am-5pm Mon-Sat & 11am-5pm Sun Apr-Oct, 10am-5pm Mon-Sat Nov-Mar) beside the train station.

The **Oban Rare Breeds Farm Park** (☎ 770608, New Barran Farm, Glencruitten; adult/child £5/3.50; open 10am-5.30pm late Mar-Oct, with extended hours mid-June-Aug is 2 miles (3km) east of the town centre. It keeps rare breeds of farm animals.

The *MV Kingfisher* (☎ 563138) offers boat trips to spot seals and other marine wildlife from Corran Esplanade, 200m north of North Pier. Trips depart at 10am and 2pm daily from April to September, and cost £7.50 a head.

Walking & Cycling

It's a pleasant 20-minute walk north from Oban Youth Hostel along the coast road to **Dunollie Castle**, built by the MacDougalls of Lorn in the 13th century. The castle was unsuccessfully besieged for a year during the 1715 Jacobite rebellion. It's always open and very much a ruin. You can continue along this road to the beach at Ganavan Sands, 2½ miles (4km) from Oban.

A TIC leaflet lists local bike rides. They include a 7-mile (11km) Gallanach circular tour, a 16-mile (26km) route to the Isle of Seil and routes to Connel, Glenlonan and Kilmore.

Special Events

During West Highland Yachting Week ☎ 563309, W www.whyw.co.uk), at the end of July/beginning of August, Oban becomes the focus of one of Scotland's biggest yachting events. Hundreds of yachts cram into the harbour and the town's bars become jammed with thirsty sailors.

The Argyllshire Gathering (☎ 562671), held over two days in Oban in late August, is one of the most important events on the Scottish Highland games calendar. The event includes a prestigious pipe band competition. The main games are held at Mossfield Park on the eastern edge of town.

Organised Tours

From April to October, *Bowman's & Mac-Dougall's Tours* (☎ 563221, 3 Stafford St) offers a 'Three Isles' day-trip from Oban to Mull, Iona and Staffa (adult/child £32/17, 10 hours, Sun-Thur). A shorter day trip visits Mull and Iona only (adult/child £21/12, 8 hours, daily).

Gordon Grant Tours (☎ 562842), opposite the train station on Railway Pier, also offers combined coach and boat excursions to Mull, Iona and Staffa from March to October.

McCaig's Folly

McCaig's Tower – a bizarre landmark on top of a hill overlooking Oban harbour – is vaguely reminiscent of Rome's Colosseum. Its construction was commissioned in 1890 by local worthy John Stuart McCaig, an art critic, philosophical essayist and banker, who had a philanthropic intention of providing work for unemployed stonemasons during construction.

However, work was abandoned in 1900 when over £5000 had been spent. A planned 29m-high central tower was never built and the bronze statues of family members stipulated by McCaig's will were never installed. As a result, the unfinished monument came to be known as McCaig's Folly. Its best feature is the stunning view of Mull from the seaward arches.

Places to Stay

Camping There are several camping grounds in the Oban area.

Oban Divers Caravan Park (☎/fax 562755, Glenshellach Rd) Pitches £6-8.50. Open Mar-Oct. The nearest camp site to the train station is 1½ miles (2.5km) south of town in pleasant Glenshellach.

Ganavan Sands Caravan Park (☎ 562179, Ganavan Rd) Tent pitch £4 per person. Bunkhouse bed £8.50. Open Mar-Oct. This site is beside a sandy beach, 2 miles (3km) north of the town centre (keep going past the youth hostel). There's also a six-bed bunkhouse.

Oban Caravan & Camping Park (☎ 562425, fax 566624, Gallanachmore Farm) Pitches £8-9. Open Apr–mid-Oct. This site has a great hill-top location overlooking Kerrera, 2½ miles (4km) south of Oban.

Hostels All of Oban's hostel accommodation opens year-round.

Oban Backpackers Lodge (☎ 562107, e oban@scotlands-top-hostels.com, Breadalbane St) Beds £9.50-11.50. This is a friendly place with a communal kitchen; breakfast costs £1.50. From the train station, walk 800m north along George St, past the cinema, and veer right into Breadalbane St.

Oban Waterfront Lodge *(☎ 566040, fax 566940, 1 Victoria Crescent)* Beds £10-20. This place, also 800m north of the train station, has big comfy beds and a good waterfront location. It accepts credit cards.

Jeremy Inglis Hostel *(☎ 565065, fax 565933, 21 Airds Crescent)* Dorm beds £6.50, singles £11-12, doubles £13-15. This is more of a basic B&B than a hostel, but is more central than the other budget options. The price includes a continental breakfast.

Oban Youth Hostel *(☎ 562025, Corran Esplanade)* Beds £12.25/10.75, plus £1 July & Aug. Oban's SYHA hostel is on the Esplanade, 1000m north of the train station. Prices drop to £9/6 from November to March.

B&Bs & Guesthouses Oban has dozens of B&Bs and guesthouses. The principal areas are around the northern end of George St, on Soroba Rd, and along Corran Esplanade.

Maridon House *(☎ 562670,* e *maridon hse@aol.com, Dunuaran Rd)* B&B £16-20 per person. Maridon House has eight rooms, all en suite, and is convenient for the ferry terminal.

Sand Villa Guest House *(☎ 562803, Breadalbane St)* B&B £15-20 per person. This is an efficient place with 15 rooms (three with en-suite bathroom).

Invercloy Guest House *(☎ 562058, Ardconnel Terrace)*. B&B £15-22 per person. This place is on a quiet street high above town, with great views over the bay.

There are a number of other B&Bs around McCaig's Tower too.

North of the town, Corran Esplanade is lined with more expensive guesthouses and small hotels, all facing seaward and most offering rooms with bathrooms attached. ***Glenrigh Guest House*** *(☎/fax 562991, Corran Esplanade)* and ***Kilchrenan House*** *(☎ 562663, Corran Esplanade)* both offer B&B from £23 to £32 per person.

You'll find plenty more B&Bs along Soroba Rd and Glencruitten Rd.

Kathmore *(☎ 562104, Soroba Rd)* B&B £15-22.50 per person. Friendly Kathmore is a 10-minute walk south of the train station and does an excellent breakfast.

Hotels There are several big hotels in the town centre and many smaller ones scattered around the rest of the town.

Palace Hotel *(☎ 562294, George St)* Singles £17.50-25, doubles £32-50. This small friendly, family-run place is right in the centre of town.

Regent Hotel *(☎ 562341, fax 565816 Corran Esplanade)* Singles £30-50, doubles £50-96. Just north of the North Pier, the Art Deco Regent has a good waterfront location

Barriemore Hotel *(☎/fax 566356, Corran Esplanade)* Singles £25-32, doubles £50-60 Open Mar-Nov. At the far end of the Esplanade, this recommended hotel offers excellent accommodation and dinner.

Heatherfield House *(☎ 562681, fax 570340,* e *heatherfield@dial.pipex.com, Albert Rd)* B&B £25-35 per person. Also highly recommended is the homely, five-room Heatherfield House, a converted 1870s manse with, of all things, an observatory for amateur astronomers. It also has a fine restaurant.

Manor House *(☎ 562087, fax 563053 Gallanach Rd)* Doubles £60-124. The Manor House, on the southern edge of the bay, is one of Oban's top hotels. Built in 1780, it was originally part of the estate of the duke of Argyll. The restaurant serves Scottish and French cuisine.

Places to Eat

There's no shortage of places to eat in Oban Most are along the bay between the train station and the North Pier, and along George St

Cafe na Lusan *(☎ 567268, 9 Craigard Rd)* Snacks £1.90-5, mains £5.95-7.50. Open 11.30am-9.30pm Wed-Sat, 3.30pm-9.30pm Sun-Tues. This is a great little cafe with good coffee, sandwiches and veggie meals. It has Internet access to boot.

Café Julie *(☎ 565952, 37 Stafford St)* Sandwiches £2.10-3.20. Open 10.30am-5pm Mon-Sat & noon-4pm Sun May-Sept. Nip into Julie's (opposite the distillery) for coffee and cake, tea and a scone, or some delicious Luca's ice cream.

Eeusk Fish Cafe *(☎ 565666)* Lunch £4.50-6.95, mains £9.50-14.95. Open noon-3pm & 6pm-10pm daily. This stylish bistro, set in converted bank, serves sophisticated seafood

– try the mussel and langoustine sandwich for lunch, or Thai fish steaks for dinner.

Waterfront Restaurant (☎ 563110, The Waterfront Centre, Railway Pier) Lunch mains £6.95, dinner mains £10.50-16.50. Open noon-2.15pm & 5.30pm-9.30pm daily. The cool blue Waterfront, housed in the converted seaman's mission, is a great restaurant which serves seafood freshly landed at the quay just a few metres away.

Shellfish Bar (Railway Pier) Sandwiches £2.20-2.50. Open 9am-6pm daily. At Oban's famous seafood stall, you can buy fresh and cooked fish and seafood to take away – try a prawn sandwich at £2.50 or fresh oysters at 45p each.

Studio Restaurant (☎ 562030, Craigard Rd) Mains £8.95-14.25. Open 5pm-10pm daily. This snug little place, up the hill off George St, continues to deserve its good reputation. Local cuisine includes paté and oatcakes, crab claws with garlic butter, roast Angus beef and Scottish cheeses. The set three-course dinner costs £13.25 (£11.50 before 6.30pm).

The Gathering Restaurant (☎ 565421, Breadalbane St) Restaurant mains £8-15. Bar meals £4-5. Established in 1882, The Gathering is a bit on the touristy side, but the food – mostly steak and seafood – is tasty and good value.

India Palace (☎ 566400, 146 George St) 3-course lunch £4.95. Open noon-2pm & 5pm-midnight daily. This is Oban's best tandoori restaurant, with an all-you-can-eat buffet for £8.95 every night.

China Restaurant (☎ 563575, 39 Stafford St) Mains £6.90-9.50. Open noon-2pm & 5pm-10.30pm daily. Opposite the Oban Distillery, this Chinese restaurant does takeaways as well as table-service.

Entertainment

Oban Inn (☎ 562484, Stafford St) The lively Oban Inn, overlooking the harbour by the North Pier, is the best pub in town. It's a traditional bar with wood panelling, brass and stained glass, and has a wide range of single malt whiskies and good bar food.

O'Donnells Irish Pub (☎ 656421, Breadalbane St) Open 2pm-1am Sun-Thur,

2pm-2am Fri & Sat. This Irish bar, opposite Oban Backpackers and downstairs from The Gathering Restaurant, has live entertainment, usually Celtic music, most nights.

McTavish's Kitchens (☎ 563064, George St) Adult/child £4/2 for show only, £2/1 if dining as well. 3-course dinner £10.25. Shows 8.30pm-10pm May-Sept. The nightly 'Scottish show' at McTavish's Kitchens caters to the kilts-and-tartan tourist market. There's Scottish country dancing with a live band, a piper, fiddle music and Gaelic songs.

The Barn (☎ 564618, Lerags) Open 11am-11pm Mon-Sat year-round, plus noon-11pm Sun Apr-Oct. This family-friendly pub, with an outdoor beer garden and children's play area, is in a lovely country setting 2 miles (3km) south of Oban. It does bar meals, with a special children's menu and some good veggie options.

The renovated *Lorne Bar* on Stevenson St is popular with Oban's late teens and twenty-somethings, and stays open till 2am Thursday to Saturday. The newly opened *Cooler*, a cellar wine-bar at 60 George St, claims to be the coolest nightspot in the Highlands; it opens till 10pm Thursday to Saturday.

Getting There & Away

Bus Scottish Citylink runs two to four buses a day to Oban from Glasgow (£11.20, three hours) and Edinburgh (£14.10, 4½ hours) via Inveraray. Four buses a day (except Sunday) follow the coast north via Appin to Fort William (£7, 1½ hours), with connections to Inverness.

Train Oban is at the end of a scenic route that branches off the West Highland line at Crianlarich. There are up to three trains a day from Glasgow to Oban (£15.50, three hours). There's a free *Window Gazer's Guide* available on the train.

The train's not much use for getting from Oban to other parts of Scotland. To reach Fort William requires a trip via Crianlarich round three sides of a rectangle – take the bus instead.

Boat Numerous CalMac ferries link Oban with the Inner and Outer Hebrides. There are services to Mull (five to seven daily), Colonsay (three times a week), Coll and Tiree (daily except Thursday and Sunday), Barra and South Uist (five sailings per week) and Lismore (two to four daily, except Sunday). See each island's entry for details.

Getting Around

Bus Oban & District (☎ 562856) is the local bus company and has services up to McCaig's Tower and to the beach at Ganavan Sands.

Taxi There's a taxi rank outside the train station. Otherwise call Oban Taxis (☎ 0800 123 444) or Kennedy's Taxis (☎ 564172).

Car Hazelbank Motors (☎ 566476) rents small cars from £35/195 a day/week including VAT, insurance and CDW.

Bicycle You can rent bicycles from Oban Cycles (☎ 566996, Craigard Rd), for £10 a day, and Hazelbank Motors (☎ 566476, Lynn Rd) for £14 a day or £60 a week.

AROUND OBAN
Isle of Kerrera

Some of the best walking in the area is on the beautiful **Isle of Kerrera**, which faces Oban across the bay. There's a 6-mile (11km) circuit of the island (two to three hours) which follows tracks or paths (use OS map No 49) and you'll have the chance to spot wildlife such as Soay sheep, wild goats, otters, golden eagles, peregrine falcons, seals and porpoises. At Lower Gylen, at the southern end of the island, there's a ruined castle.

Kerrera Bunkhouse & Tea Garden (☎ 570223 from 9am to 5pm, e kerrerabunk house@talk21.com, Lower Gylen) Beds £7.50. Open year-round. This six-bed bothy is at Lower Gylen, a 40-minute walk south from the ferry (keep left at the fork just past the telephone box). Booking is recommended, especially in winter. You can get snacks and light meals at the nearby Tea Garden (open April to September only).

Ardentrive Farm Hostel (☎ 567180, Ardentrive Farm) Beds £8. Open year-round. This place is on a working farm at the northern end of the island, just south of the yacht marina.

There's a daily passenger ferry (☎ 563665) to Kerrera from Gallanach, about 2 miles (3km) south-west of Oban town centre, along Gallanach Rd (adult/child £3/1.50 return, bicycle 50p, 10 minutes). From April to September it runs every half-hour from 10.30am to 12.30pm and 2pm to 6pm, and at 8.45pm Monday to Saturday. Call to check winter ferry times.

Isle of Seil
☎ 01852 • pop 506

The small island of Seil, 10 miles (16km) south of Oban, is best known for its connection to the mainland – the so-called **Bridge over the Atlantic**, designed by Thomas Telford and opened in 1793. The bridge has a single stone arch and spans the narrowest part of the tidal Clachan Sound.

On the west coast of the island is the pretty conservation village of **Ellanbeich** with its whitewashed cottages, 4 mile (6.5km) from the Clachan bridge; it has a post office and grocery store. The village was built for slate quarrying, but the industry collapsed in 1881 when the sea flooded the main quarry pit, which can still be seen.

Coach tours flock to the **Highland Arts Studio** (☎ 300273, Easdale; open 9am-9pm daily Apr-Sept, 10am-6pm daily Oct-Mar), a crafts shop and shrine to the eccentric output of the late 'poet, artist and composer' C John Taylor. Try to keep a straight face.

Just offshore from Ellanbeich is the small island of Easdale, which has more old slate workers' cottages and the interesting **Easdale Folk Museum** (☎ 300370; adult/child £2/50p; open 10.30am-5.30pm daily Apr-Oct). The museum has displays about the slate industry and life on the islands in the 18th and 19th centuries. Climb to the top of Easdale island (a 38m peak!) for a great view of the surrounding area.

Sea.fari Adventures (☎ 300003), at Easdale Harbour, runs a series of exciting two-hour boat trips in high-speed RIBs (semi-rigid inflatable boats) to the Corryvreckan whirlpool, the slate island of Belnahua (see the Isle of Luing section later and the remote Garvellach Islands (adult/child £22/16.50). A 15-minute spin around Easdale Island costs £4.50/3.

Places to Stay & Eat There's a handful of B&Bs and hotels on the island.

Inshaig Park Hotel (☎/fax 300256, Easdale) Singles £29-39, doubles £54-66. The friendly, six-room Inshaig Park is a big villa with fine sea views.

Willowburn Hotel (☎ 300276, fax 300579, e willowburn.hotel@virgin.net, Clachan Seil) Dinner B&B £53-58 per person. The Willowburn is an attractive countryside hotel with a good restaurant and a roaring log fire in winter.

For something to eat, try the *Harbour Seafood & Oyster Bar* in Ellanbeich village. The *Tigh an Truish* pub next to the Bridge Over the Atlantic serves real ales and does good bar meals for £3.95 to £5.15.

Getting There & Around Oban & District (☎ 01631-562856) runs buses at least twice daily, except Sunday, from Oban to Ellanbeich and on to North Cuan for the ferry to Luing (see the Isle of Luing below for details).

Argyll and Bute Council (☎ 01631-62125) operates the daily passenger-only ferry service from Ellanbeich to Easdale (£1 return, bicycles free, five minutes). Most runs are on request, at the times displayed on the pier. To call the boat to Ellanbeich pier, sound the hooter during daylight, or switch on the light at night.

Isle of Luing
☎ 01852 • pop 180

Luing (pronounced ling) is about 6 miles (10km) long and 1½ miles (3km) wide and has a rugged west coast. It's separated from the southern end of Seil by the narrow Cuan Sound. There are two pleasant villages – Cullipool at the northern end (2 miles/3km from the ferry), which has a well-stocked shop and post office; and Toberonochy in the east – but Luing's main pleasures are scenic. The slate quarries of Cullipool were abandoned in 1965. About 1½ miles (2.5km) out to sea you'll see the remains of the extensively quarried slate islet of Belnahua. There are two

Iron Age forts, the best being Dun Leccamore, about a mile (1.6km) north of Toberonochy.

In Toberonochy are the ruins of the late medieval Kilchatton Church and an unusual graveyard with slate gravestones.

You can visit both villages, the fort, the ruined chapel and the scenic west coast on a pleasant 8-mile (13km) circular walk.

The small car ferry (☎ 01631-562125) from Cuan (on Seil) to Luing runs daily, roughly twice an hour (£1 return, £5.20 for a car, free for bicycles, five minutes).

There's a Monday to Saturday postbus (☎ 01463-256200) service around Luing which connects to Ellanbeich on Seil.

Isle of Luing Bike Hire (☎ 314256) in Cullipool rents bikes for £10/6 a day/half-day.

LOCH ETIVE
Loch Etive is one of Scotland's most beautiful sea lochs, extending for 17 miles (27km) from Connel to Kinlochetive and flanked by some impressive mountains, including Ben Cruachan (1126m) and Ben Starav (1078m).

Connel
☎ 01631 • pop 500

Connel, 4 miles (6km) from Oban, has a store and several places to stay. Where Loch Etive exits into the sea (under the Connel bridge), there's an underwater rock ledge; at certain times of the tide, this causes The Falls of Lora.

Dunstaffnage Castle (☎ 01631-562465, Dunstaffnage; adult/child £2/75p; open 9.30am-6.30pm daily Apr-Sept & 9-30am-4.30pm daily except Thur afternoon, Fri and Sun morning Oct-Mar) is 2 miles (3km) west of Connel and easily reached by bus from Oban. It was built on a rock plinth, around 1260, and captured by Robert the Bruce during the Wars of Independence in 1309. The nearby ruins of the 13th-century chapel are slightly creepy – perhaps the skulls carved in the stonework are watching you.

Dunstaffnage Arms Hotel (☎ 01631-710666, Connel) Mains £5.95-15.95. This friendly place does home-made bar meals and specialises in local seafood.

Trains between Oban and Glasgow, and buses between Oban and Fort William or Glasgow, all stop in Connel.

Taynuilt

☎ 01866 • pop 700

Taynuilt, 6 miles (10km) east of Connel, has the **Bonawe Iron Furnace** *(☎ 822432, by Taynuilt; adult/child £2.30/1.75; open 9.30am-6.30pm daily Apr-Sept & 9.30am-4pm Mon-Wed & Sat, 9.30am-noon Thur & 2pm-4pm Sun Oct-Nov)*. It's the best-preserved charcoal-burning ironworks in Scotland, dating from 1753, and there's a good exhibition.

Loch Etive Cruises (☎ 822430), in Taynuilt, sails to the head of the loch and back between one and three times a day from April to October. There are 1½-hour and three-hour cruises (£5 and £8 respectively); you may see eagles, otters, seals, deer and the famous Etive slabs.

Polfearn Hotel (☎/fax 822251, by Taynuilt) Singles/doubles £25/50. The Polfearn Hotel, 1½ miles (2.5km) north of Taynuilt, has 14 rooms and an extensive bar menu (£6.75 to £12.50), including meals such as pigeon breast and scallops.

Taynuilt has a couple of shops for groceries and the *Robin's Nest* tearoom for snacks and lunches.

Scottish Citylink buses and trains to and from Oban stop here.

BENDERLOCH & APPIN

North of Loch Etive, you'll find the 16th-century **Barcaldine Castle** *(☎ 01631-720598, Benderloch; adult/child £3.25/1.70; open 11am-5pm July-Aug, or by appointment)*. It's 2 miles (3km) north of Ledaig, just off the main road. The castle is reputedly haunted by the ghost of the Blue Lady; there are secret stairways and a bottle dungeon.

The **Scottish Sea Life & Marine Sanctuary** *(☎ 720386, Barcaldine; adult/child £6.50/4.50; open 9am-6pm daily Apr-Sept, 10am-5pm daily Nov-Mar)*, 8 miles (13km) north of Oban on the shores of Loch Creran, provides a haven for orphaned seal pups. As well as the seal pools, there are tanks of herring, rays and flatfish, touch pools and displays on Scotland's marine environment.

Glen Creran, at the head of Loch Creran, is a pleasant glen with several walks. North of Loch Creran, you come to **Appin** (pop 100), with the villages of Portnacroish and Port Appin. At Portnacroish, there's a wonderful view of **Castle Stalker** on a tiny offshore island. Port Appin, a couple of miles (3km) of the main road, is a pleasant spot with a passenger ferry to the island of Lismore.

Pierhouse Hotel (☎ 01631-730302, fax 730400, Port Appin) B&B from £30 per person. The Pierhouse Hotel has an excellent seafood restaurant (mains £7.95 to £16.95).

Scottish Citylink buses run two to four times daily (except Sunday) from Oban to Portnacroish (30 minutes, £4.50) and on to Fort William.

LISMORE

☎ 01631 • pop 146

Lismore is a quiet and very fertile island in the Firth of Lorn, 4 miles (6km) north of Oban. It's about 9½ miles (15km) long and just over a mile (1.6km) wide, with a road running almost its full length. There are few scattered communities and two ferry terminals, one half way up the east coast, at Achnacroish, the other at Point, the island's northernmost tip. Lismore Stores is the main shop and post office, north of Achnacroish towards Clachan.

Things to See & Do

Castle Coeffin, 13th-century ruins with a lovely coastal location, and **Tirefour Broch** where double walls reach 3m in height, are both only half a mile (800m) from Clachan. Ask in Achnacroish for details about the **Lismore Historical Society Museum**.

Lismore is a place to relax and enjoy the scenery. However, if you're feeling energetic, the best **walk** on the island runs from Kilcheran, in the south, up to the top of **Barr Mór** (127m), then south-west along the ridge to the southern end of the island, returning to Kilcheran by track. It's about 6 miles (10km) for the round trip. Allow three to four hours to fully appreciate the fantastic views of the surrounding mountains.

Places to Stay

There are currently no B&Bs on Lismore. However, there are several self-catering options advertised on the Web at **W** www.isleoflismore.com.

Pier Cottage (☎ 760221, e janette.stew rt@talk21.com, Achnacroish) £180-240 per week. Open Mar-Oct. This accommodation takes up to six persons and is located in the former post office.

Getting There & Around

CalMac (☎ 566688) runs ferries from Oban to Achnacroish, with two to four sailings Monday to Saturday (£2.45/£21 foot passenger/car, 50 minutes). Argyll and Bute Council (☎ 01546-604695) sails from Port Appin to Point eight to 12 times daily. This 10-minute ferry takes passengers and bicycles only (£1 for foot passengers, bikes free).

The postbus (☎ 01246 546329) does several runs Monday to Saturday, but only calls at Point at 12.40pm. Lismore is great for cycling; contact Peter McDougall (☎ 760213) to hire bikes from the Point ferry terminal for £10/6 per day/half day).

LOCH AWE & GLEN ORCHY
Loch Awe

Loch Awe is one of Scotland's most beautiful lochs, with rolling forested hills around its southern end and spectacular mountains in the north. The loch lies between Oban and Inverary and it's the longest in Scotland at a stretch of about 24 miles (38km) – but it averages less than a mile (1.6km) wide.

At its northern end, the loch widens out and there are several interior islands you can visit: Inishail has a ruined church and Fraoch Eilean has a broken-down castle. For details of boat hire, contact Oban TIC (☎ 01631-63122).

Loch Awe escapes to the sea through the narrow Pass of Brander, where Robert the Bruce defeated the MacDougalls. In the pass, by the A85, you can visit Cruachan Power station (☎ 01866-822618, Lochawe; adult/child £3/1.50; open 9.30am-5pm daily Apr-June & Sept-Nov, 9.30am-6pm daily July & Aug). Electric buses take you more than half a mile (800m) inside Ben Cruachan allowing you to see the pump-storage hydro-electric scheme in action.

Tight Line (☎ 01838-200215, Lochawe village) is the village pub where you can get reasonable bar meals for £3.95 to £5.50.

At the northern end of Loch Awe stands the scenic ruin of Kilchurn Castle (by Dalmally; admission free; closed winter), built in 1440 and one of Scotland's finest. It's accessible by foot up a rough track from the A85. Otherwise, Loch Awe Steam Packet Company (☎ 01866-833333) sails hourly steamboats from Lochawe village pier to the castle, between 10am and 5pm daily from April to November (£4/3 adult/child return), allowing 40 minutes at the castle.

Nearby Dalmally (pop 300), popular with anglers, has a train station, post office, shop and hotel.

Glenorchy Lodge Hotel (☎ 01838-200312, Dalmally) En-suite singles £30-35, doubles £50-60. There's a good choice of main courses (£5.95 to £8.95), including vegetarian options.

Ben Cruachan Walk

Ben Cruachan can be climbed from the power station. A complete traverse of the ridge, mostly a walk with some scrambling, could take as long as nine hours. The quickest route – of about six hours – follows the path from the power station steeply uphill to the dam, then left around the reservoir to its head. From there, go westwards up to the pass below Meall Cuanail, then northwards up a steep boulderfield to the summit (return by the same route). This is no mere ramble – you must be well equipped with boots, food and water.

Glen Orchy

The A85 goes east from Dalmally, up bleak Glen Lochy to Tyndrum, but it's much better to follow beautiful Glen Orchy to Bridge of Orchy and Loch Tulla, where there are lots of Munros. The A82 Glasgow to Fort William road passes Loch Tulla, but the western side is quiet, and you'll see remnants of the ancient Caledonian pine forest here.

Bridge of Orchy Hotel (☎ 01838-400208, fax 400313, Bridge of Orchy) Singles £25-45, doubles £40-90 By the A82, this hotel also has a large bunkhouse without a kitchen (beds from £9); breakfast is available for £5 and bar meals for £6 to £12.

Getting There & Around

Trains from Glasgow to Oban stop at Dalmally and Lochawe village, while trains from Glasgow to Fort William stop at Bridge of Orchy. Scottish Citylink buses from Glasgow to Oban go via Dalmally, Lochawe village and Cruachan Power Station. Bridge of Orchy is served by the Glasgow to Fort William Citylink bus.

Daily, except Sunday, there's a postbus run around the area; ring ☎ 01246-546329 for details.

Central West Highlands

This area extends northwards from Rannoch Moor and Appin, beyond Glen Coe and Fort William, and includes the southern reaches of the Great Glen. Its scenery is grand throughout, with high and wild mountains dominating the glens. Great expanses of moor alternate with lochs and patches of planted forest. Fort William, at the inner end of Loch Linnhe, is the only town in the area, but there's a fair number of villages. Roads follow the coast and run through the main glens, and the railway from Glasgow cuts across Rannoch Moor to Lochaber district, the town of Fort William and the west coast village of Mallaig.

GLEN COE

Scotland's most famous glen was written into the history books in 1692 when MacDonalds were murdered by Campbells in what became known as the Massacre of Glen Coe. However, it's also one of the most beautiful glens, with steeply sloping sides and narrow-sided valleys that provided any cattle-rustling Highlanders with the perfect place to hide their stock. The glen is dominated by three massive, brooding spurs, known as the Three Sisters of Glencoe.

There are wonderful walks in this highly atmospheric glen, much of which is owned by the NTS, and there's also some excellent accommodation.

Glencoe Village

☎ 01855 • pop 360

Standing by Loch Leven, at the entrance to the glen, the village is 16 miles (26km) from Fort William on the main Glasgow road. There's little to see in the village itself apart from the thatched **Glencoe Folk Museum** (☎ 811664 Glencoe; adult/child £2/free; open 10am-5.30pm Mon-Sat mid-May–Sept), which has a varied collection on display, from costume and military memorabilia to domestic items and dairy equipment, as well as tools of the woodworking, blacksmithing and slate quarrying trades.

McCubbin's store is useful if you need provisions, and there's a post office.

Glen Coe Visitor Centre (NTS; ☎ 811307 Inverigan; fee to be determined; open 9.30am-5.30pm daily May-Aug, shorter hours Sept-Apr), by the A82 about a mile (1.6km) south of the village, should be open by the time you read this. Exhibitions will include videos and interactive displays about the massacre, local natural history, the NTS and its work in the glen, and mountaineering

You can learn basic summer and winter mountaineering skills with Paul Moore's **Glencoe Guides** (☎ 811402), from £125 per day (one to four people). Paul also offers rock climbing and guiding on hard winter climbs (maximum two clients per trip) for more advanced parties.

Places to Stay & Eat There's a good selection of accommodation and eating choice in the glen.

Invercoe Caravans (☎/fax 811210, Glencoe) Sites £9-14. Chalets/cottages £200-510 per week. Here you can camp, or rent a chalet or cottage by the week. The view down Loch Leven is stunning.

Glencoe Youth Hostel (☎ 811219, Glencoe) Beds from £8.50/5. Open year-round. The SYHA hostel is 1½ miles (2.5km) from the village, on the old Glencoe road. It's very popular, so you'll need to book ahead.

Leacantuim Farm Bunkhouse (☎ 811256 Glencoe) Beds £6.50-7.50. Nearby, Leacantuim Farm has bunkhouse accommodation. It also runs **Red Squirrel Campsite**, farther along the Glencoe road, charging campers £4 each

GLEN COE

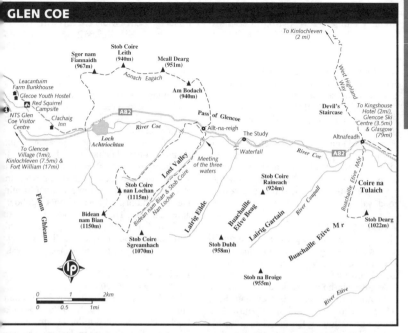

Clachaig Inn (☎ 811252, fax 811679, Glencoe) Singles £22-35, doubles £44-70. The Clachaig Inn, 2½ miles (4km) south-east of the village, is popular with climbers. The ice-axe door handle is decidedly quirky; the sign at reception – 'No Hawkers or Camp-bells' – even more so. There's good food (£5.75 to £13.95) and live Scottish, Irish and blues music several times a week. From January to March, slide lectures on mountain topics are held fortnightly (from £5).

Glencoe Guest House (☎ 811244, fax 811873, Strathlachan) Rooms £14-19 per person. On the village outskirts, in Strathlachan, is Glencoe Guest House.

An Darag (☎ 811643, Upper Carnoch) B&B £17-20 per person. Open Jan-Oct. All rooms have en-suite bathrooms.

You can get B&B in several other places on the main street too.

Getting There & Away Highland Country Buses (☎ 01397-702373) runs up to seven buses daily, except Sunday, from Fort William to Glencoe (35 minutes). Scottish Citylink buses run four times daily to Glasgow (£10.30, 2½ hours) and Fort William (£3.40).

Kingshouse Hotel & Glen Etive
Kingshouse Hotel (☎/fax 01855-851259, Glencoe) Singles/doubles from £23.50/54, breakfast £7 extra. Bar meals £6-9. This isolated place on the West Highland Way at the eastern end of the glen is Scotland's oldest established inn. It attracts hikers, who stop to tuck into a plate of haggis, neeps and tatties (haggis, mashed turnip and mashed potato; £5.95) and a refreshing drink in the bar. It's also a good place to stay.

Quiet **Glen Etive** runs south-west from the hotel and is worth visiting for the beautiful scenery en route. Wild camping is possible in the area. If you don't have your own wheels, there's a Monday to Saturday post-bus (☎ 01246-546329) from Fort William to Glen Etive via Kingshouse Hotel.

Glencoe Ski Centre

About 1½ miles (2.5km) from the Kings-house Hotel, on the other side of the A82, is the car park and base station for this ski centre, where commercial skiing in Scotland first started in 1956. There's an inexpensive cafe here, with snacks from £1.50 and main courses (in winter) around £4.50.

The chair lift (☎ 01855-851226, W www .ski-glencoe.co.uk) operates daily in summer (July and August), from 9.30am to 4.15pm; adult/child/family £4/2.50/11 return. In winter, a full day-pass including ski-tows costs £17.50/9.50 adult/child, and the skiing is generally good. The chair lift is the easiest way to get to the 640m-high viewpoint and several good walks.

Walking

This is serious walking country and you'll need maps, warm clothes, food and water. The Glen Coe Visitor Centre stocks lots of useful information.

A great six-hour hike leads through the Lost Valley to the top of **Bidean nam Bian** (1150m). Cross the footbridge below Allt-na-reigh and follow the gorge up into the Lost Valley, continuing up to the rim, then along it, to the right, to the summit. You need to be very careful crossing to Stob Coire Nan Lochan as there are steep scree slopes. Descend the western side of this ridge and round into Coire nan Lochan, where a path heads back to the road.

For something less strenuous, hike this route only as far as the **Lost Valley**, a hidden mountain sanctuary still haunted by the ghosts of murdered MacDonalds. Allow three hours for this route.

The **Aonach Eagach**, the glen's northern wall, is said to be the best ridge walk on the Scottish mainland, but it's difficult in places and you need a good head for heights. Some parts could almost be graded a rock climb. It's best done from east to west, and there's a path up the hillside north of Allt-na-reigh and down from Sgor nam Fiannaidh at the western end, towards Loch Achtriochtan. The more direct gully that leads to Clachaig Inn isn't a safe way down. It takes six to eight hours to complete this hike.

From Kingshouse Hotel, the view of **Buachaille Etive Mór** (1022m) will give you a sense of déjà vu, as it appears in photographs and adverts all over the world. The walking route to the top starts at Altnafeadh, 2½ miles (4km) west of the hotel. It takes only four hours, but it's not for casual hikers, as the higher part of the route leads up steep scree slopes in Coire na Tulaich. There's also a Munro at the far southwestern end of the summit ridge.

There are several short, pleasant walks around **Glencoe Lochan**, near the village. To get there, turn left off the minor road to the youth hostel, just beyond the bridge over the River Coe. There are three walks (40 minutes to an hour), all detailed on a signboard at the car park. The artificial lochan was created by Lord Strathcona in 1895 for his homesick Canadian wife Isabella and is surrounded by a North American-style forest.

KINLOCHLEVEN
☎ 01855 • pop 1100

Kinlochleven is hemmed in by high mountains at the head of the beautiful fjord-like Loch Leven, about 7 miles (11km) east of Glencoe. The aluminium factory has now closed and there's not much work in the area, so the villagers are developing new ideas and there are plans to turn Kinlochleven into Scotland's premier mountaineering centre. The multi-million pound redevelopment scheme will include Scotland's first artificial **ice-climbing wall**.

Things to See & Do

Kinlochleven Visitor Centre (☎ 831663, Linnhe Rd; admission free; open 10am-1pm & 2pm-5pm weekdays year-round, plus 6pm-8pm Tues Apr-Oct), by the factory, tells the interesting story of the British Aluminium Company, the smelter (which opened in 1908), the Blackwater Reservoir and the hydro-electric scheme. It's in the same building as the public library.

The **West Highland Way** passes through Kinlochleven. Most walkers decide to stay in the village before walking the last 14-mile (22km) section to Fort William. Other hikes in the area include moderate walks up the glen of the River Leven, with pleasant woods and the Grey Mares Tail waterfall, and harder mountain trips on the Mamores. Paths give access to the Mamores from the Mamore Lodge road.

Once you're up there, you can walk fairly easily around the ridges of **Na Gruagaichean** (1055m), **Stob Coire a'Chairn** (981m) and **Am Bodach** (1032m). You must be well equipped though, and you'll need OS map No 41 and a compass.

Places to Stay & Eat

The village has a *Co-op* supermarket and a *general store*. There are several places to eat, including a cheap bakery and a fish and chip shop.

The *camp site* (☎ 831539, fax 831416, Fort William Rd), behind the MacDonald Hotel, charges £4 per person, including shower.

Blackwater Hostel (☎ 831253, fax 831402, Lab Rd) Dorm beds £10. Breakfast is available and bike hire can be arranged.

MacDonald Hotel (☎ 831539, fax 831416, Fort William Rd) E-suite B&B £28-34 per person. The bar here offers great views down the loch (pub meals cost £4.95 to £10.90).

Mamore Lodge (☎/fax 831213, Kinlochleven) B&B singles £21-45, doubles £39-70 per head. This distinctly wacky hotel is high on the hillside, 200m above Kinlochleven. The pine-panelled rooms and strange beds have an air of decrepitude about them. The meals are also a bit odd. It's an interesting experience you will not forget in a hurry.

Tailrace Inn (☎ 831777, Riverside Rd) Snacks from £1.70, bar meals from £4.75. The bar at the Tailrace Inn has loud music and there are occasional ceilidhs so you might prefer somewhere else if you're after peace and quiet.

Getting There & Away

Highland Country Buses (☎ 01397-702373) has services from Fort William/Glencoe village to Kinlochleven up to seven/ten times daily, except Sunday (£2.65/£1.05, 50/15 minutes).

GLEN COE TO FORT WILLIAM

From Glencoe, the B863 goes east to Kinlochleven and the A82 heads westwards to the old slate quarrying village of Ballachulish.

The Glen Coe Massacre

The brutal murders that took place here in 1692 were particularly shameful, perpetrated as they were by one Highland clan on another (with whom they were lodging as guests).

In an attempt to quash remaining Jacobite loyalties among the Highland clans, King William III had ordered that all chiefs take an oath of loyalty to him by the end of the year (1691). Maclain, the elderly chief of the MacDonalds of Glen Coe, was late in setting out to fulfil the king's demand and going first to Fort William rather than Inverary made him later still.

The secretary of state for Scotland, Sir John Dalrymple, declared that the MacDonalds should be punished as an example to other Highland clans, some of whom had not bothered to even take the oath. A company of 120 soldiers, mainly of the Campbell clan, were sent to the glen. Since their leader was related to Maclain by marriage, the troops were billeted in MacDonald homes. It was a long-standing tradition for clans to provide hospitality to passing travellers.

After they'd been guests for 12 days, the order came for the soldiers to put to death all MacDonalds aged under 70. Some Campbells alerted the MacDonalds to their intended fate, while others turned on their hosts at 5am on 13 February, shooting Maclain and 37 other men, women and children. Some died before they knew what was happening, while others fled into the snow, only to die of exposure.

The ruthless brutality of the incident caused a public uproar and after an enquiry several years later, Dalrymple lost his job. There's a monument to Maclain in Glencoe village and members of the MacDonald clan still gather here on 13 February each year.

There's a seasonal TIC situated here (☎ 01855-811296), with displays about the quarries.

Strathassynt *(☎ 01855-811261, fax 0870 056 9202, Loan Fern)* Singles £20-25, doubles £36-44. This is a well appointed, clean and friendly B&B in a large modern villa near the TIC. Dinner is available for £9.

Two miles (3km) farther west, at South Ballachulish, the A828 goes west then south to Oban, while the A82 goes north over the **Ballachulish Bridge** to meet the B863 after its circuit of Loch Leven. There are great views of the mountains from the bridge. Just north of the bridge, at the **Confectionery Factory Visitor Centre** *(☎ 01855-821277, North Ballachulish; admission free; open 9am-5.30pm Mon-Sat Nov-Easter, 10.30am-5.30pm Mon-Sat the rest of the year)*, you can see production of traditional confections and chat to the workers (although not on Saturday). The speciality food shop sells coconut ice, 24 varieties of tablet and lots of other things.

North Ballachulish merges with **Onich** and there are a number of hotels here with lovely lochside locations, but not all are recommended.

Lodge on the Loch *(☎ 01855-821237, fax 821463, Onich)* Dinner B&B from £46.50 per person, 4-course dinner £29.50. The stylish Lodge on the Loch has luxurious rooms and a good restaurant with contemporary Scottish cuisine.

Beyond Onich, you'll reach **Inchree**, easily reached by bus as it's on the main route between Fort William and Glasgow or Oban.

Inchree Centre *(☎/fax 01855-821287, Inchree)* Beds from £9. There's excellent Scandinavian-style accommodation here.

Inchree pub/restaurant *(☎ 01855-821287, Inchree)* Mains £5.95-8.50. 3-course meals from £12. The food here is recommended.

Less than a mile (1.6km) to the north, there's the Corran ferry to Ardgour. Boats run at least twice hourly across Loch Linnhe (foot passengers free, cars £4.20, five minutes).

Nether Lochaber Hotel *(☎ 01855-821235, fax 821545, next to the Corran ferry)* Pub food £5.25-13.95. This inn is another good place to eat or stay (£25 to £24 per person).

North of Corran, the A82 twists its way along Loch Linnhe to Fort William.

FORT WILLIAM
☎ 01397 • pop 10,774

Fort William, which lies beside Loch Linnhe amid some of Scotland's most magnificent mountain landscapes, has one of the finest settings in the country. Although insensitive civic planning compromised its appeal for many years, the pedestrianisation of the High St and the determination of its people have turned it into a rather pleasant little town. As a major tourist centre, it's easily accessed by rail and bus lines, and makes a great place to base yourself for exploring the mountains and glens of Lochaber. Magical Glen Nevis begins near the northern end of the town and extends south and east below the slopes of Ben Nevis. 'The Ben' – Britain's highest mountain at 1344m – and neighbouring mountains are a magnet for hikers and climbers. The glen is also popular with movie-makers – part of Mel Gibson's Oscar-winning *Braveheart* was filmed here.

Orientation & Information

The town meanders along the edge of Loch Linnhe for around 3 miles (5km). The centre, with its small selection of shops, takeaways and pubs, is easy to get around on foot. Some B&Bs can be fairly distant, however.

The busy TIC (☎ 703781, e fortwilliam@ host.co.uk), in Cameron Square, has a good range of books and maps. For local walks, get a copy of the handy *Best Walks Around Fort William* (£1.99), which incorporates maps and basic information on 15 routes, but you'll need an OS map for more adventurous hikes, such as Ben Nevis. More information is available from the Glen Nevis Visitor Centre, Ionad Nibheis (admission free), 1½ miles (2.5km) up the glen from town.

There are banks with ATMs in the High St. As you might expect, Fort William has well-stocked outdoor-equipment shops. Nevisport (☎ 704921), near the train station at Airds Crossing, has a marvellous range of books and maps for mountaineers. The downstairs bar has an Internet terminal and charges an extortionate £1 for ten minutes.

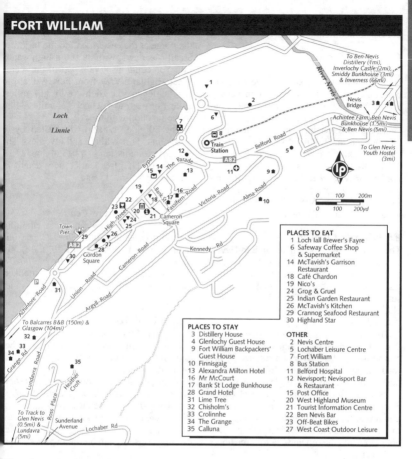

FORT WILLIAM

PLACES TO EAT
1 Loch Iall Brewer's Fayre
6 Safeway Coffee Shop
  & Supermarket
14 McTavish's Garrison
   Restaurant
18 Café Chardon
19 Nico's
24 Grog & Gruel
25 Indian Garden Restaurant
26 McTavish's Kitchen
29 Crannog Seafood Restaurant
30 Highland Star

PLACES TO STAY
3 Distillery House
4 Glenlochy Guest House
9 Fort William Backpackers'
  Guest House
10 Finnisgaig
13 Alexandra Milton Hotel
16 Mr McCourt
17 Bank St Lodge Bunkhouse
28 Grand Hotel
31 Lime Tree
32 Chisholm's
33 Crolinnhe
34 The Grange
35 Calluna

OTHER
2 Nevis Centre
5 Lochaber Leisure Centre
7 Fort William
8 Bus Station
11 Belford Hospital
12 Nevisport; Nevisport Bar
   & Restaurant
15 Post Office
20 West Highland Museum
21 Tourist Information Centre
22 Ben Nevis Bar
23 Off-Beat Bikes
27 West Coast Outdoor Leisure

West Coast Outdoor Leisure (☎ 705777) is at 102 High St.

The Belford Hospital (☎ 702481), on Belford Rd, lies opposite the train station.

West Highland Museum

Beside the TIC, this museum (☎ 702169, Cameron Square; adult/child £2/50p; open 10am-4pm Mon-Sat Oct-May, 10am-5pm Mon-Sat June-Sept, plus 2pm-5pm Sun July & Aug) is packed with Highland memorabilia. Of particular interest is the secret portrait of Bonnie Prince Charlie. After the Jacobite rebellions, all things Highland were

banned, including pictures of the exiled leader. This picture looks like nothing more than a smear of paint until placed next to a curved mirror, when it reflects a credible likeness of the prince.

Steam Train

The Jacobite (☎ 01524-732100, 🖵 www .westcoastrailway.co.uk) steam train runs from Fort William to Mallaig at 10.20am weekdays from mid-June to late September (and Sunday in August), returning at 2.10pm. The journey crosses the historic Glenfinnan viaduct, with great views down

Loch Shiel. A 2nd-class day return costs £22/12.50 adult/child.

Other Things to See

There's little left of the original **Fort William** from which the town takes its name, as it was pulled down in the 19th century to make way for the railway. The fort was originally built by General Monk in 1635 to control the Highlands, but the surviving ruins are of the structure built in the 1690s by General MacKay and named after the king, William III.

The **Ben Nevis Distillery** (*☎ 702476, Lochy Bridge; tour & tasting £2; open 9am-5pm Mon-Fri Sept-June, 9am-7.30pm Mon-Fri & 10am-4pm Sat July & Aug*) has a visitor centre and sales outlet.

Walking & Cycling

The most obvious local hike, up **Ben Nevis**, shouldn't be undertaken lightly. The weather at the top is more often bad (thick mist) than good, so go prepared for the worst even if it's sunny when you set off. You'll need warm clothes, food and something to drink, and a detailed map.

The path begins in Glen Nevis, either from the car park by Achintee Farm (on the northern side of the river and reached by the road through Claggan), or from the youth hostel on the road up the glen – these two trails join after less than a mile (1.6km). Then follow the Red Burn before zigzagging up to the summit and the old observatory ruins. It can take between four and five hours to reach the top and 2½ to three hours to descend.

You can walk for miles on the ridges of the **Mamores**. One of the best hill walks in the area starts at the Lower Falls in Glen Nevis (at Achriabhach) and heads southwards up the glen between **Sgurr a'Mhaim** and **Stob Ban**. A good path takes you to the tiny loch below the **Devil's Ridge**; zigzag up the steep slope north-east of the loch and turn left along the spectacular ridge for Sgurr a'Mhaim (1099m). It's narrow in places but there's little real scrambling. From the top of Sgurr a'Mhaim you can easily descend to the car park at Achriabhach. The round trip takes about six hours.

There are very pleasant (and far les strenuous) walks along Glen Nevis through the gorge at the eastern end to the beautifu **Steall Meadows**, with its 100m-high water-fall. You could also walk part of the scenic **West Highland Way** from Fort William to Kinlochleven via Glen Nevis (14 miles 22km) or even to Glencoe (21 miles/34km to the junction with the A82).

The 80-mile (128km) **Great Glen Cycle Route** links Fort William and Inverness. The Forestry Commission's (☎ 01320-366322, o contact the TIC) free leaflet gives details o this mainly off-road route.

Activities

The **Lochaber Leisure Centre** (*☎ 704359, Belford Rd*) offers **swimming**, a **climbing wall** and other activities. For at least one hour, swimming costs £2.20/1.20, and climbing costs £2.50. The **Nevis Centre** (*☎ 700707, An Aird*), near the bus station, offers **snooker, 10-pin bowling** (from £2.50) and othe activities.

Organised Tours

Glengarry Mini Tours (*☎ 01809-501297* does half- or full-day tours around Lochabe and Glencoe, starting at £7.50 for a four-hour afternoon tour.

There are also 1½-hour boat trips (£6/3 on the loch with *Seal Island Cruises* (*☎ 703919*), who operates from the Tow Pier where there's a booking kiosk. There are four trips during the day, plus a buffe evening cruise at 7pm on summer weekdays

Places to Stay

Although Fort William has numerous accommodation options, book well ahead in summer, even for hostels.

Camping The best camping option is up scenic Glen Nevis, 3 miles (5km) from town.

Glen Nevis Caravan & Camping Park (*☎ 702191, fax 703904, Glen Nevis*) One person £4.30-6.30, two people £5-7.30 Open mid-March–Oct. This camp site, near Glen Nevis Youth Hostel, charges extra i you bring a car (£1.70 to £3.30).

Hostels Fort William has a good range of hostel and backpacker accommodation.

Fort William Backpackers' Guest House *(☎ 700711, ⓔ fortwilliam@scotlands-top -hostels.com, Alma Rd)* Beds from £10. This is a popular hostel, just a short walk from the bus stops and train stations.

Glen Nevis Youth Hostel *(☎ 702336, Glen Nevis)* Beds from £9/6. Open year-round. Three miles (5km) from Fort William, by the start of one of the paths up Ben Nevis, you'll find the large, impersonal SYHA Glen Nevis Youth Hostel.

Ben Nevis Bunkhouse *(☎ 702240, ⓔ achintee.accom@glennevis.com, Glen Nevis)* Beds £9.50. A good alternative is the Ben Nevis Bunkhouse at Achintee Farm, over the river from the Glen Nevis Visitor Centre. Upstairs there's a cafe with live music and Internet access.

Calluna *(☎ 700451, fax 700489, ⓔ moun tain@guide.u-net.com, Heathercroft)* Dorm beds £9-10. A 15-minute walk from the town centre lies Calluna, a hostel run by well-known mountain guide Alan Kimber. Phone for a free pick-up from town.

Bank Street Lodge Bunkhouse *(☎ 700070, fax 705569, ⓔ info@stablesrooms.fsnet.co .uk, Bank St)* Beds £10 (£12 en suite). Doubles without/with breakfast £35/46. This is a centrally located choice.

Smiddy Bunkhouse *(☎ 772467, fax 772411, ⓔ bunks@bunksville.com, Station Rd)* Beds £6-10. This is another independent hostel, this time in Corpach, 4 miles (6km) along the Mallaig road and north-west of Fort William. The attached activity centre organises mountaineering, kayaking and sailing trips.

B&Bs & Hotels Several B&Bs in and around Alma and Fassifern Rds are close to the train and bus stations.

Finnisgaig *(☎ 702453, Alma Rd)* Doubles £32-37. There are two rooms with shared bathroom at this place.

Mr McCourt *(☎ 703756, 6 Caberfeidh, Fassifern Rd)* En-suite singles £18-30, doubles £36-50. Vegetarian breakfast is provided on request here.

Achintore Rd, which runs south along the loch, is packed with B&Bs and hotels, but some seem large and characterless and are best avoided.

Lime Tree *(☎ 701806, ⓔ info@lime treestudio.co.uk, Achintore Rd)* B&B £15-22.50 per person. More interesting than most is this friendly B&B-cum-art gallery.

Chisholm's *(☎ 705548, 5 Grange Rd)* Singles £20-25, doubles £28-33. Chisholm's is nearby with two rooms with shared bathroom.

Several B&Bs just off Achintore Rd offer pleasant loch views, including the excellent ***Balcarres*** *(☎ 702377, Seafield Gardens)* where there are four en-suite rooms. Singles cost from £20 to £25, doubles from £38 to £50.

On Grange Rd, parallel to Achintore Rd, there are two very comfortable guesthouses whose owners' attention to detail has earned them the top tourist-board rating.

The Grange *(☎ 705516, fax 701595, Grange Rd)* En-suite doubles £38-46 per person. Open Mar-Nov. This is an excellent four-room guesthouse.

Crolinnhe *(☎ 702709, fax 700506, Grange Rd)* Singles £76-80, doubles £76-110. Open Mar-Nov. All rooms here are en suite and vegetarian breakfast is provided on request.

Glen Nevis offers several more places to stay including ***Achintee Farm*** *(☎ 702240, fax 705899, Glen Nevis)* with B&B accommodation as well as the bunkhouse. Singles cost between £22 and £28, doubles £44 to £56.

There are several more upmarket options in and around town.

Alexandra Milton Hotel *(☎ 702241, fax 705554, The Parade)* Singles £30-45, doubles £60-90. This large, traditional hotel has comfortable rooms with bathroom.

Grand Hotel *(☎/fax 702928, Gordon Square)* Singles £25-42.50, doubles £44-65. The large, central Grand Hotel has a fairly good restaurant.

Distillery House *(☎ 700103, fax 702980, Nevisbridge)* En-suite singles £25-45, doubles £40-70. Located at the old Glenlochy Distillery and near the road into Glen Nevis, Distillery House is thoroughly recommended.

Glenlochy Guest House *(☎ 702909, Nevisbridge)* Singles £18-26, doubles £32-54. Just across the road from Distillery House, this clean and comfortable place is also recommended. Most rooms are en suite.

Inverlochy Castle (☎ 702177, fax 702953, Torlundy) Singles £180-255, doubles £250-480. The wonderfully grand, five-star Inverlochy Castle, set in 200 hectare grounds 3 miles (5km) north of Fort William, is an opulent Victorian creation completed in 1865. It has everything you'd expect to find in a castle – crenellated battlements, stags' heads, log fires and a wide staircase. Reservations are requisite.

Places to Eat

With the honourable exception of the popular Crannog Seafood Restaurant (see later), Fort William is pretty much a culinary desert.

Loch Iall Brewer's Fayre (☎ 703707, An Aird) Mains from £5.20. Just across the road from Safeway, this place does a range of main courses, including some vegetarian options.

Nevisport Bar & Restaurant (☎ 704921, Airds Crossing) Bar meals from £4.75. Downstairs at the outdoor-equipment shop, you can get bar meals, including vegetarian options, but they're fairly average. The upstairs restaurant-cum-cafeteria isn't great value.

Most other places to eat line the High St.

Nico's (37 High St) Nico's fish and chip shop charges £3.40 for cod and chips and is recommended.

Café Chardon (☎ 702116, 28 High St) Café Chardon, upstairs in P Maclennan's store, has soup for £1.95, filled ciabatta sandwiches for £3.55 and quiche for £2.55.

McTavish's Kitchen (☎ 702406, 100 High St) This has the same menu and floor show (see Entertainment later) as the Oban branch. There's a self-service cafe downstairs.

McTavish's Garrison Restaurant (☎ 702406, High St) The popular McTavish's Garrison Restaurant offers food only (no floor show).

Indian Garden Restaurant (☎ 705011, 88 High St) 2-course weekday lunches £5.95. This place isn't too pricey. It does takeaways for around £5 to £8, and stays open late.

Highland Star (☎ 703905, 155 High St) Takeaways from £5.30, mains from £6. You can also get takeaways from the town's only Chinese restaurant, the Highland Star.

Grog & Gruel (☎ 705078, 66 High St) Mains £5.60-11.95. Another ethnic option is the Tex-Mex-oriented Grog & Gruel. It has enchiladas, burritos, fajitas, burgers, steaks, pizza and pasta.

Crannog Seafood Restaurant (☎ 705589, The Pier) Mains £11.50-15.50. The best restaurant in town also has the best location. It's on the pier, giving diners an uninterrupted view over the loch. Cullen skink (fish soup with smoked haddock) costs £4.25.

Glen Nevis Restaurant (☎ 705459, Glen Nevis) Mains £4.90-12.90. Up in Glen Nevis, near the SYHA hostel, you can get a good meal at this pleasant restaurant. It has home baking and snacks during the day and main courses in the evening.

Safeway Coffee Shop (☎ 700333, An Aird) Open 8am-8pm Mon-Sat, 9am-6pm Sun. For those on a tight budget, the Safeway Coffee Shop sells good value light meals, such as filled jacket potatoes from £2 and an all-day breakfast (£1.99 to £3.09).

Entertainment

McTavish's Kitchen (☎ 702406, 100 High St) McTavish's Kitchen takes the pile 'em high, sell 'em cheap approach to Scottish cuisine and culture, but the music's good and if you get into the spirit of things, it can be a lot of fun. Shows are staged nightly, from 8pm, with dancing, a live band and a piper. The standard charge is £4/2 for an adult/child, £2/1 if eating a meal as well. Better value is the set meal (£8.95) which includes the show. A disco operates on Saturday from 10.30pm (cover charge £3).

Ben Nevis Bar (☎ 702295, 105 High St) The Ben Nevis Bar is a popular Thursday and Friday night music venue and a good place for a drink or inexpensive meal (mains £3.50 to £5.95).

Nevisport Bar (☎ 704921, Airds Crossing) Downstairs at the Nevisport complex, the Nevisport Bar beckons walkers and climbers with real ales and, on the second Saturday of each month, free blues, folk and jazz performances.

Getting There & Away

Fort William lies 146 miles (234km) from Edinburgh, 104 miles (166km) from Glasgow and 66 miles (106km) from Inverness.

If you have a spare week, you may want to trek here on the 95-mile (152km) West Highland Way from just north of Glasgow (see the Activities chapter).

Bus Scottish Citylink (☎ 0870 550 5050) has four daily buses to Glasgow (£11.80, three hours) and two daily buses to Edinburgh (£16.50, 3¾ hours), both via Glencoe and Crianlarich. There are three direct daily Scottish Citylink buses between Fort William and Kyle of Lochalsh (£10.70, two hours). There are also two to four buses Monday to Saturday between Fort William and Oban (£6.90, 1½ hours). Five or six daily services run from Fort William along Loch Ness to Inverness (£7.40, two hours).

Shiel Buses/Scottish Citylink run one bus daily, except Sunday, to/from Mallaig (£4, 1¼ hours), via Glenfinnan (£2, 35 minutes).

Highland Country Buses (☎ 702373) runs six daily services to Kinlochleven (£2.65, 50 minutes) via Inchree, Onich, Ballachulish and Glencoe (£2.05, 40 minutes). Two buses daily (June to September) run from Fort William to Cairngorm via Laggan, Netonmore and Aviemore.

Train For rail enquiries, phone ☎ 0845 748 4950. The spectacular West Highland line runs from Glasgow via Fort William to Mallaig. There's a particularly wonderful wild section across the bleak Rannoch Moor. There's no direct rail connection between Oban and Fort William; use the Citylink bus services to avoid backtracking to Crianlarich.

There are two or three trains daily from Glasgow to Fort William (£18, 3¾ hours), and one to five trains between Fort William and Mallaig (£7.40, 1½ hours). The Highland Rover ticket allows unlimited travel on four days in eight consecutive days (see the Getting Around chapter).

An overnight train connects Fort William and London Euston (from £69, including the sleeper), but you'll miss the views.

Car The TIC has a leaflet listing car hire companies. It's worth trying Nevis Garage (☎ 702432, **W** www.nevis-garage.co.uk), Ardgour Rd, Caol.

Getting Around

Bus Highland Country Buses (☎ 702473) does the 10-minute run from the bus station up Glen Nevis to the youth hostel. They leave roughly hourly (every two hours in the evening) between 8.25am and 10.10pm, Monday to Saturday, June to September (and there is a reduced Sunday service). The fare is £1.10. Buses to Corpach (85p, 15 minutes) run as frequently as four per hour.

Taxi You'll find taxis waiting in the High St opposite McTavish's Garrison Restaurant; to book, call ☎ 702545 or ☎ 773030.

Bicycle At the Nevis Range base station, Off-Beat Bikes (☎ 704008, 117 High St) has mountain bikes for £8.50/12.50 for a half/full day.

ARDGOUR & ARDNAMURCHAN

West of Fort William lies Scotland's Empty Quarter, a rugged landscape of wild mountains, lonely coastlines and few roads. The area has a turbulent history. Nowadays, it's home to few people, mainly due to the 19th-century Highland Clearances, in which entire villages were evicted by zealous landlords who preferred sheep to tenants. As a result, the Gaelic culture was undermined in the region.

This part of the country is noted for its wildlife; the name Ardgour means 'height of the goats', but you can also see deer, pine martens, wildcats and eagles.

Ardnamurchan Natural History Centre

The recommended Ardnamurchan Natural History Centre (☎ 01972-500209, Glenmore; adult/child £2.50/1.50; open 10.30am-5.30pm Mon-Sat & noon-5.30pm Sun Easter-Oct) is midway between Salen and Kilchoan. Devised by local photographer Michael MacGregor, it displays some of his finer work and brings you face-to-face with the flora and fauna of the Ardnamurchan peninsula. The Living Building is designed to attract local wildlife and you'll have a decent chance of observing pine martens, eel-like butterfish and local birdlife. Snacks and lunches are available in the tearoom. The bus that runs between Fort William and Kilchoan stops here.

At the time of writing there was some uncertainty over future plans for the centre; call ahead to check it's open before visiting.

Ardnamurchan Lighthouse

The lighthouse (☎ 01972-510210, by Kilchoan; adult/child/family £2.50/1.50/7; open 10am-5pm daily Apr-Oct) at stark Ardnamurchan Point, the westernmost point of the British mainland, boasts a cluster of related attractions. The imposing 36m-high lighthouse dates from 1849, and the adjacent engine room and head keeper's house are all open to the public. Light meals are available at the attached cafe. Soup and a roll will set you back £1.80.

Corran (Chorrain) & Clovullin (Clo Mhuillin)

These two lochside villages sit at the bottom end of wild Glen Gour on a large glacial outwash deposit which nearly cuts Loch Linnhe in two. Several nearby tracks are good for afternoon strolls. Between them, the villages have a general store, tearoom and a hotel.

The Inn at Ardgour (☎ 01855-841225, fax 841214, Corran) B&B singles/doubles from £30/40. The Inn at Ardgour was for sale at the time of research. The hotel is a traditional villa with annexes, modernised inside as recently as 1998. Bar meals are available for around £6 to £12.

Access is by the Corran ferry, or along a long single-track road from Kinlocheil.

Strontian (Sron an t-Sithean)
☎ 01967

This attractive little village's greatest claim to fame is the fact that it lent its name to the element strontium, which was discovered in ore from the nearby lead mines in 1790. The **Ariundle Nature Reserve**, about 2 miles (3km) north of the village, offers a pleasant nature trail through the glen. In Strontian, you'll find two shops, a post office, a snack bar and a TIC (☎ 402381), which is open from April to October.

Glenview Caravan Park (☎ 402123) Camping £3.50 per person. Glenview Caravan Park is about a quarter of a mile (400m) from the TIC.

Strontian Hotel (☎ 402029, fax 402314, Strontian) Singles £25-35, doubles £40-62.50. The Strontian Hotel dates back to 1808. You'll get a home-cooked bar meal here (£3.95 to £9.50).

Salen (An Sailean)
☎ 01967

Walkers wishing to explore the appealing surroundings of Salen, at the head of constricted Salen Bay, will find information on hikes at the Salen Inn.

Resipole Caravan Park (☎ 431235, fax 431777, Resipole) Tent pitches from £7. Camping and meals are available at Resipole Caravan Park, 2 miles (3km) east of the village.

Salen Inn (☎/fax 431661, Salen) B&B singles/doubles from £28/46. The Salen Inn does bar meals, including seafood, venison and other game dishes (£5 to £12).

Acharacle (Ath-Tharracaill) & Castle Tioram

At one time, the village of Acharacle seemed destined for greatness as the western sea outlet of the Caledonian Canal, but the proposed extension via Glenfinnan and Loch Shiel was never completed. Today, the main reason to visit this traditional crofting community is the picturesque roofless ruin of 13th-century **Castle Tioram** (admission free; open at all times), just 2½ miles (4km) to the north. The castle sits on a lovely island in Loch Moidart, connected to the mainland by a narrow strand which is submerged at high tide (the castle's name means 'dry land'). It served as the headquarters of the chief of Clanranald MacDonald (sorry kids, no burgers here) but was severely damaged by the Jacobites after the failed rebellion in 1715, in hopes of discouraging a takeover by enemy Hanoverian troops. A five-year restoration project hopes to return it to its former condition and once complete, around 2006, it will be open to the public for 49 days of the year.

The village has a small shop, a post office, a *tearoom* and the reasonable *Stacks of Snacks* takeaway.

Loch Shiel House Hotel (☎ *01967-431224, fax 431200, Acharacle*) En-suite singles/doubles £37.50/65. The Loch Shiel House Hotel is a centrally located traditional villa. Bar meals are available for £.3.95 to £12.95.

Clanranald Hotel (☎ *01967-431202, Mingarry*) En-suite singles £19.50-25, doubles £39-50. The meals (£6) are recommended at the modern Clanranald Hotel, 2 miles (3km) north of Acharacle.

Glenuig Inn (☎ *01687-470219, Glenuig*) B&B bunkhouse £12.50, doubles £18.50. The isolated Glenuig Inn, about 12 miles (19km) north of Acharacle and by the A861 to Lochailort, is a great pub (bar meals £4.25 to £6.25; vegetarian choices are available).

Kilchoan (Cille Chomhghain)
☎ 01972

This scattered crofting village is best known for the scenic fortified tower of the ruined **Mingary Castle**, which serves as a stark reminder of medieval clan warfare. For information, visit the TIC (☎ 510222), Pier Rd, which opens Easter to October.

You'll find provisions at the incongruously named Ferry Stores, which is actually in the village, a mile (1.6km) from the pier.

Kilchoan House Hotel (☎/fax 510200, Kilchoan*) B&B £25 per person. Open Mar-Oct. You can camp or get B&B at the Kilchoan House Hotel.

Getting There & Away
Shiel Buses (☎ 01967-431272) has one daily service (except Sunday) between Fort William and Kilchoan (£6), via Corran (£1.25), Strontian (£2.50) and Acharacle (£4). It also runs buses from Fort William to Acharacle via Lochailort (£4.25) and Glenuig (£3.50), once or twice daily except Sunday.

For details on ferries between Kilchoan and Tobermory, see Getting There & Away under the Isle of Mull in The Hebrides chapter.

MORVERN PENINSULA
Although the east coast of the Morvern Peninsula has been spoiled by the Glensanda Superquarry, the inland route to Loch Aline passes through some very pleasant hillscapes.

Ardtornish is known as the home of Patrick Sellers, the rather unsavoury factor and landlord who cleared large numbers of clanspeople from the region in the early 19th century. (This was the sort of bloke who'd now greet hillwalkers with a shotgun.) The substantial stone keep at **Kinlochaline Castle**, Ardtornish, has been renovated and is no longer open to the public.

For supplies, go to Lochaline village (Loch Alainn), which has a store, post office and art gallery. In the late 1980s, the CalMac ferry to Mull ploughed into the fish farm cages at Lochaline, allowing the salmon to escape. For the local people, it seemed as if Christmas had come early, and their freezers were full for months. Alas, such luck is rare, so you'll probably have to buy yours in Fort William.

Lochaline Hotel (☎ *01967-421657, fax 421350, Lochaline*) B&B singles/doubles with shared bathroom £23/35. The Lochaline has fairly standard accommodation in a traditional villa, ½ mile from the Mull ferry pier. You can get bar meals for £5 to £10.95.

Getting There & Away
Shiel Buses (☎ 01967-431272) runs on schooldays to Fort William on Monday at 7.20am and returns on Friday at 3.45pm; other runs depart Lochaline at 9am on Tuesday, Thursday and Saturday (£3.50), returning from Fort William at 2.50pm. For information on ferries to Fishnish on the Isle of Mull, see The Hebrides chapter.

ROAD TO THE ISLES
The scenic, 46-mile (74km) Road to the Isles (the A830) takes you from Fort William via Glenfinnan to Arisaig and Mallaig. Details on the area can be found on the Web site at **W** www.road-to-the-isles.org.uk.

It's worth taking a half-mile (800m) detour from the main route at Banavie to see **Neptune's Staircase**, a flight of eight locks which raises the water in the Caledonian Canal by 20m. Thomas Telford's canal was built from 1803 to 1822 to connect the east and west coasts of Scotland, from Inverness to Fort William. Three lochs make up 38 miles (61km) of the canal's total 60 miles (96km) and there are 29 locks.

Corpach

Rock enthusiasts shouldn't miss the award-winning **Treasures of the Earth** (☎ 01397-772283, Corpach; adult/child £3/2.75; open 10am-5pm daily Oct-June & 9.30am-7pm daily July-Sept, closed most of Jan) exhibition. Particularly impressive are the large amethyst samples, the baby **diapsid** (a kind of dinosaur) from China, and the grossular garnet that looks good enough to eat.

Glenfinnan

The **NTS Visitor Centre** (☎ 01397-722250, Glenfinnan; adult/child £1.50/1; open 10am-5pm daily Apr-Oct, 9.30am-6pm daily mid-May–Augt) recounts the story of Prince Charles Edward Stuart, or Bonnie Prince Charlie, whose 1745 rising started here and ended 14 months later when he fled to France. The nearby **Glenfinnan Monument** offers fine views over Loch Shiel. There's a *cafe* in the visitor centre.

Another item of interest is the **Station Museum** (☎ 01397-722295, Glenfinnan Station; adult/child 50/25p; open 9.30am-4.30pm daily June-Sept), which contains relics of the West Highland line from the opening of the Glenfinnan section in 1901 until the present day.

Loch Shiel Cruises (☎ 01397-722235) sails on Loch Shiel four to six times weekly from April to October; cruises vary from one to 5½ hours and cost from £5 to £15. Departures are from Glenfinnan House Hotel, Glenfinnan.

The particularly good **Glenfinnan Highland Games** (☎ 722324) are held on a Saturday in mid-August.

Arisaig & Morar

Arisaig is the only place between Mallaig and Fort William where you'll find a decent range of supplies; there's also a ferry to the Small Isles from here (see The Hebrides chapter). The **Land, Sea & Islands Heritage Centre** (Arisaig; adult/child £1.50/1; open 10am-4pm daily Apr-Oct) has exhibits covering local culture and natural history.

Between Arisaig and Morar, the road winds around attractive bays, as well as the wonderful beaches known as the **Silver Sands of Morar**. Morar village lies at the outlet of 330m-deep **Loch Morar**, which is Britain's deepest body of fresh water. It's thought to contain its own monster, known as Morag.

Mallaig

☎ 01687 • pop 900

The lively fishing village of Mallaig makes a nice stopover between Fort William and Skye or the Small Isles. The TIC (☎ 462170) opens year-round. For medical services, contact the doctor (☎ 462202).

In addition to its lively pub life, the main attraction is **Mallaig Marine World** (☎ 462292, The Harbour; adult/child £2.75/1.50; open 9am-9pm Mon-Sat & 10am-6pm Sun June-Sept, 9am-5.30pm Mon-Sat & 10am-5pm Sun Oct-May, closed Sun Nov-Mar), an aquarium which keeps local aquatic species. Many are surprisingly colourful and you can touch the skates and rays.

The **Mallaig Heritage Centre** (☎ 462085, Station Rd; adult/child £1.80/90p; open 1pm-4pm Mon-Fri) provides insight into the archaeology and history of the region, including disturbing details on the Clearance of Knoydart, as well as information on steam trains and the ongoing fishing industry.

For details of **sea-fishing trips** and **seal-watching tours** on the MV *Grimsay Isle*, ring ☎ 462652.

Highland Cattle

Bred for their quality beef, Highland cattle are Scotland's most distinctive bovine breed. They're fierce-looking (with their horns) but docile-natured, with long reddish-brown coats.

Highland cattle were popular with 18th-century drovers who took them from their mountain habitats to the Lowland markets. Nowadays, they're popular with tourist photographers looking for interesting foreground!

PATRICK WATSON

Places to Stay & Eat

Glenfinnan There are a few good options in Glenfinnan.

Sleeping Car Bunkhouse (☎ 01397-722295, fax 701292, Glenfinnan Station) Beds £8-10 per person. This excellent hostel is housed in a railway carriage at the station.

Railway Carriage Restaurant (☎ 01397-722295, Glenfinnan Station) Meals £5-10. Open Fri-Sun. Another railway theme item is the Railway Carriage Restaurant, which serves snacks during the day and full meals in the evening.

Prince's House Hotel (☎ 01397-722246, fax 722307, Glenfinnan) Singles/doubles £35/70, lower off-season rates. It isn't known whether Bonnie Prince Charlie actually stayed at the historic Prince's House Hotel in 1745, but the building dates from 1658, so he was definitely aware of it. The public bar, in an extension previously built to house railway workers, had a hatch in the floor through which locals could fish while enjoying a pint. Unfortunately, the hatch ceased to exist in 1980 when the public bar was demolished. Food is available (£7 to £15).

The hotel has new owners and should have been redecorated by the time you read this. They currently offer light lunches, an extensive menu of evening bar meals, and a four-course table d'hote dinner for £25.

Lochailort Tiny Lochailort only has one option.

Lochailort Inn (☎ 01687-470208, Lochailort) B&B singles/doubles from £30/60. Mains £4.50-10.95. The rebuilt Lochailort Inn has en-suite rooms, and a bar with good value main courses.

Arisaig There are two choices in Arisaig.

Arisaig Hotel (☎ 01687-450210, fax 450310, Arisaig) Singles £28-40, doubles £56-80. All rooms in this Jacobean-era hotel are en suite. Bar meals cost from £3.80.

The Old Library (☎ 01687-450651, fax 450219, Arisaig) En-suite singles £40-48, doubles £68-96. The well-appointed Old Library hotel also has a recommended restaurant serving snacks (from £2.10), lunches and dinners.

You'll find a number of seasonal *camping grounds* scattered north along the coast; most are open only in the summer months.

Mallaig You'll find some surprisingly good places to stay and eat in Mallaig.

Sheena's Backpacker's Lodge (☎ 462764, fax 462708, Harbour View) Dorm beds £10. This is a very nice, clean and friendly hostel; the attached daytime cafe does baked potatoes from £3.60 and a pint/half pint of prawns costs £8.50/5.

Marine Hotel (☎ 462217, fax 462821, Station Rd) Singles/doubles £30-38/56-72. The Marine Hotel's highly recommended restaurant (meals £5.95 to £11.95) serves a la carte chicken, venison, seafood and vegetarian meals, as well as such specialities as pan-fried Minch scallops in cream and wine sauce for £10.95. All rooms are comfortable and modern and are either en suite or have a private bathroom.

Cornerstone Cafe (☎ 462306, Main St) Light meals & snacks £3-5, mains from £5. The Cornerstone Cafe, at the harbour, does light meals, snacks and main courses.

Cabin Seafood Restaurant (☎ 462207, Main St) Mains £5-10. This restaurant cooks up seafood specialities (and what else would you want in a fishing community?).

Getting There & Away

Shiel Buses/Scottish Citylink (☎ 01967-431272) operates one bus daily, except Sunday, to/from Fort William (£4, 1¼ hours), via Glenfinnan (£3, 35 minutes).

The beautiful West Highland railway to and from Fort William (£7.40, 1½ hours) operates one to five times daily, with connections through to Glasgow. In summer, there are steam trains on this route; see under Steam Train in the Fort William section earlier.

Ferries run from Mallaig to the Small Isles and Skye year-round (Skye ferries now take vehicles all year). From July to early September, a car ferry runs between Mallaig and Castlebay (Barra) and Lochboisdale (South Uist). Arisaig Marine's MV *Shearwater* (☎ 01687-450224) connects Arisaig to the islands of Rum, Eigg and Muck. For details, see The Hebrides chapter.

A ferry service run by Bruce Watt Cruises (☎ 01687-462320) has two return trips from Mallaig to Inverie in Knoydart (£5/7 single/day return) on Monday, Wednesday and Friday at 10.15am and 2.15pm (the afternoon trip also includes a quick visit to Tarbet in upper Loch Nevis). There are also Tuesday and Thursday sailings from June to mid-September.

KNOYDART PENINSULA
☎ 01687

Stuck solidly between heaven and hell (actually, the Lochs of Nevis, or 'heaven' and Hourn, or 'hell'), the Knoydart Peninsula is now a wilderness region thanks to depopulation in the 19th-century Highland Clearances. As a result, walkers can tramp for days through wild country.

Inverie, with just 60 inhabitants, is the peninsula's only population centre, and is the only village in Scotland without access to the road system. If you want to try out the local tracks, you can hire a **bike** from **The Pier House** (☎ 462347).

A favoured two-day hiking route leads from Kinloch Hourn to Inverie via Barrisdale. You may also enjoy spending an additional day at Barrisdale to climb the dramatic 1020m peak **Ladhar Bheinn** (pronounced lar ven), which affords some of the west coast's finest views.

Places to Stay & Eat
Knoydart Hostel (☎ 462242, fax 462272, *Inverie*) Beds £7.50. Knoydart Hostel is near Inverie House, a half-mile (800m) east from the ferry landing.

The Shieling Hostel (☎/fax 462669) Dorm beds £15. Open year-round. The atmospheric Shieling Hostel, three-quarters of a mile (1.2km) west from the pier in Inverie, is a tad overpriced. It has gas cooking and a wood-burning stove in the sitting room.

Barrisdale Bothy (☎ 01599-522302, *Barrisdale*) Sleeping-bag space £2.50. This very basic hostel in Barrisdale has sleeping platforms without mattresses. You can also camp outside.

Skiary (☎ 01809-511214, *by Kinloch Hourn*) Full board £70 per person. A highly

recommended place for dinner, lunch and B&B is the rustic Skiary, a mile (1.6km) from the road's end at Kinloch Hourn. You can either walk in on the Barrisdale track or arrange to be picked up by boat from Kinloch Hourn.

The Old Forge (☎ 462267, *Inverie*) 2-course meals from £10. This pub in Inverie, by the pier, also sells bread and milk.

Getting There & Away
For ferry information see Mallaig earlier in this chapter. Len Morrison (☎ 01599-522352), Croftfoot, Arnisdale, runs a fair-weather open boat from Arnisdale to Barrisdale (and other places) by arrangement. Mr Morrison can take up to five passengers at a cost of £13 plus £3 per person, each way.

There's a postbus (☎ 01246-546329) between Invergarry and Kinloch Hourn on Monday, Wednesday and Friday. It arrives/departs Kinloch Hourn at around 1pm, but you should confirm in advance. This bus can only take two or three people with luggage.

The Cairngorms

The magnificent Cairngorms, Britain's second highest mountain range and its most popular skiing area, soar above forests of regenerating native Caledonian pine in the upper reaches of Strathspey (Speyside).

Far more attractive than the regimented Forestry Commission conifer plantations, these native woodlands are home to rare animals such as pine martens and wildcats. Red squirrels, ospreys and capercaillie also survive here, as does Scotland's only herd of reindeer.

The Cairngorm summits provide Scotland's only example of alpine tundra vegetation and are therefore inhabited by high-altitude species otherwise found farther north, such as snow buntings, ptarmigans and dotterels. What's more, even non-hikers can reach the high peaks as the Cairngorm funicular railway operates year-round.

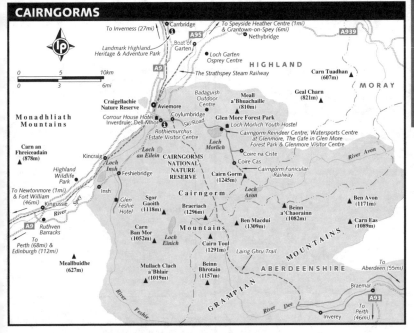

The Cairngorms have been proposed as a national park, but the decision (and the park's possible boundary) has yet to be confirmed.

Aviemore, which is popular with flocks of skiers, hikers and cyclists, is the main resort town. The top hiking routes include the 24-mile (38km) Lairig Ghru tramp through the peaks and right down to Braemar in the Grampians. If you prefer to avoid the crowds, the lovely but less dramatic Monadhliath (pronounced mona-lee-a) Range, west of the Spey, sees fewer tourists.

The 100-mile-long (160km-long) Spey, one of Scotland's top salmon rivers, attracts anglers from around the world. Pure mountain water from its tributaries provides a basic ingredient for whisky production – some of the distilleries are open to the public. North of Grantown-on-Spey, the Spey meets the River Avon (pronounced ahn) and continues out of the Cairngorms into Moray. For information, including details

on the popular Speyside whisky distilleries, see Aberdeenshire & Moray in the Central & North-Eastern Scotland chapter.

AVIEMORE
☎ 01479 • pop 2421

In the early 1960s, Aviemore was still a sleepy Highland village of 200 inhabitants, but today it looks more like a downmarket resort in the Rockies that can't quite live up to its swanky aspirations. Fortunately, visitors can avoid the appalling kitsch that reigns through the summer by heading for the hills.

Orientation

Aviemore is just off the A9 bypass. With all the tat lined up along Grampian Rd you can hardly get lost.

The train station, banks and eateries are found along this road. The Cairngorm skiing/hiking area lies 8 miles (13km) east of Aviemore at the end of Ski Rd, which passes

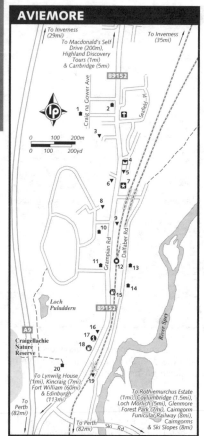

AVIEMORE

PLACES TO STAY
1 Craig na Gower Ave B&Bs
2 Mackenzie's Inn
10 Kila
11 Cairngorm Hotel
13 Kinapol Guest House
14 Ardlogie Guest House
20 Aviemore Youth Hostel

PLACES TO EAT
3 Winking Owl
5 Ski-ing Doo
6 Littlejohn's
8 Tesco
9 Smiffy's Fish & Chip Restaurant; Ellis Brigham
16 Royal Tandoori
19 Old Bridge Inn

OTHER
4 Post Office
7 Police Station
12 Train Station; Strathspey Steam Railway; No 1 Licensed Restaurant
15 Petrol Station
17 Tourist Information Centre
18 Petrol Station

the Cairngorms, which covers the whole area. Ernest Cross' *Walks in the Cairngorms* describes the main hikes.

Money You'll find a cluster of ATMs outside the Tesco supermarket on Grampian Rd. There's also a bureau de change at the post office (on Grampian Rd) and another at the TIC.

Outdoor Equipment Of the outdoor-equipment shops along Grampian Rd, try *Ellis Brigham* (☎ 810175), at No 9, which can organise both equipment hire and ski lessons.

Craigellachie Nature Reserve
Over the A9 from Aviemore, the Craigellachie Nature Reserve makes a great place for day hikes over steep hills and through natural birch forest.

Look out for birds and other wildlife that shelter here, including finches, jackdaws and peregrine falcons (which nest from April to July). If you're lucky, you may even spot a capercaillie.

through two large forest estates: Rothiemurchus and Glenmore.

Information
The busy TIC (☎ 810363), 500m south of the centre on Grampian Rd, opens year-round, with extended hours mid-July to mid-August (until 7pm weekdays, until 6pm Saturday and until 5pm Sunday). It's closed Sunday in winter. The local accommodation guide is distributed free, but you'll pay £3 for bookings through the TIC. The centre sells a good range of books and maps, including the yellow OS Outdoor Leisure Map *Aviemore &*

Rothiemurchus Estate

The **Rothiemurchus Estate Visitor Centre** (☎ 810858, Ski Rd; admission free; open 9am-5.30pm daily), a mile (1.6km) from Aviemore along Ski Rd, organises lots of activities; pick up the free Visitor Guide and Footpath Map. The estate, taking in the villages of Inverdruie and Coylumbridge, extends from near Aviemore to the Cairngorm tops.

It's owned by a single family, the Grants (no connection with the whisky family), who manage the extensive Caledonian pine forest here and lay on facilities for visitors. There's free access to 50 miles (80km) of footpaths, including some particularly attractive trails through the forests around Loch an Eilein. Visitors can also opt for ranger-guided walks, clay-pigeon shooting instruction, Land Rover tours and fishing for rainbow trout at the estate's fish farm or in the Spey.

Glen More Forest Park

Around Loch Morlich, 7 miles (11km) from Aviemore, Ski Rd passes through 2000 hectares of pine and spruce that make up Glen More Forest Park.

Attractions include a pleasant sandy beach and a popular **watersports centre** (☎ 861221, Glenmore; charges vary; open daily May-Oct) offering canoeing, windsurfing, sailing and fishing. At the **Cairngorm Reindeer Centre** (☎ 861228, Glenmore; adult/child £5/3; walks at 11am, plus 2.30pm in summer) the warden will take you to see and feed the reindeer.

The **Glenmore Visitor Centre** (☎ 861220, Glenmore; admission free; open daily), near the loch, is run by Forest Enterprise and sells a Glen More Forest Guide Map detailing local walks (£1.50).

Cairngorm Funicular Railway

To get straight to the best views, take the **funicular** (☎ 861261, Cairngorm; adult/child £7.50/5; open 10am-5pm daily May-Nov, late closing July & Aug) to the Cairngorm plateau. It starts from the car park at the end of Ski Rd and climbs to the 1085m level where you'll find Britain's highest cafe (serving Scottish food), with a free **mountain exhibition**. Unfortunately, for environmental

and safety reasons, you're not allowed out of the top station and you must return with the funicular to the car park.

Activities

Walking Since the opening of the funicular in 2002, hikers no longer have easy access to the Cairngorm plateau. However, hiking from the car park at the end of Ski Rd to the **summit of Cairn Gorm** (1245m) takes only about two hours one way. From there, you can continue south to climb Ben Macdui (Britain's second highest peak at 1309m), but this can take eight to ten hours return from the car park and it's a serious proposition for most people.

The **Lairig Ghru trail**, which can take up to eight hours, is a demanding 24-mile (38km) route from Aviemore over the Lairig Ghru Pass to Braemar. If you're not doing the full route, it's still worth taking the six-hour return hike up to the pass and back to Aviemore.

Hikers will need a lunch, plenty of liquids, a map, a compass, plus a wind and waterproof jacket. The weather can change almost instantly and snow, even in mid-summer, isn't unknown.

Skiing Aviemore isn't Aspen or Val d'Isere, but with 19 runs and 37km of piste, it's Britain's biggest ski area. When the snow is at its optimum and the sun is shining, you can close your eyes and imagine you're in the Alps. The season usually runs from January until the snow melts, which may be as late as the end of April; but some years have poor snowfall. There are also several cross-country routes around Loch Morlich.

The ski area is about 9 miles (14km) from Aviemore centre. The ski tows and funicular start at the main Coire Cas car park, connected to the more distant Coire na Ciste car park by free shuttle bus. A Cairngorm Day Ticket for lifts costs £21 for adults and £12 for under-16s. Ski or snowboard rental costs £14.50 per day. The Cairngorm Combi includes equipment hire and lift tickets and costs £32/21 per adult/child per day. The TIC distributes a free Cairngorm Piste Map & Ride Guide leaflet.

During the season the TIC displays relevant avalanche warnings. For reports on

snow conditions, see the Internet at **W** www
.cairngormmountain.com or **W** www.born2
ski.com, or tune into Cairngorm Radio Ski
FM on 96.6MHz.

Fishing This is a major sport, both on the
Spey and in most of the lochs. Ask at the TIC
for information on beats (areas) and permits.
At local shops, salmon and trout fishing permits cost £25 and approximately £11 per day
respectively. **Alvie Estate** (*☎ 01540-651255*)
rents out rods for £5 per day.

Organised Tours
Highland Discovery Tours (*☎ 811478, 27
Corrour Rd*) runs 16-seat mini-bus day trips
to Loch Ness and Skye for £18 and £29
respectively.

Places to Stay
Camping There are a couple of decent
camp sites in the area.

Rothiemurchus Caravan Park (*☎/fax
812800, Coylumbridge*) Pitches from £3.50
per person. This is the nearest camping
ground to Aviemore, at Coylumbridge, 1½
miles (2.5km) along the Ski Rd. It has a
high standard of facilities and is highly
recommended.

Glenmore Camping & Caravan Park
(*☎ 861271, Glenmore*) Camping from £4.60.
Closed Nov–mid-Dec. The Forestry Commission's Glenmore Camping & Caravan
Park is 5 miles (8km) farther along the road
from Rothiemurchus, near Loch Morlich. It's
another good and well-organised site.

Hostels There's only one hostel in Aviemore,
but there are two near Loch Morlich.

Aviemore Youth Hostel (*☎ 810345, 25
Grampian Rd*) Beds from £9/6, including
breakfast in summer. Open year-round.
Aviemore Youth Hostel offers upmarket
hostelling in a well-equipped building near
the TIC and the start of Ski Rd.

Loch Morlich Youth Hostel (*☎ 861238,
Glenmore*) Dorm beds from £9.25/6. Open
year-round. This popular, clean and well-
run hostel has a great location in Glen
More Forest Park, 7 miles (11km) from
Aviemore; pre-booking is essential.

Badaguish Outdoor Centre (*☎ 861285,
fax 861258, Glenmore*) Dorm beds £5-10.
Badaguish Outdoor Centre is north of Loch
Morlich and a mile (1.6km) from Ski Rd.

B&Bs & Hotels – Centre Off Grampian
Rd on Craig na Gower Ave, 400m north of
the train station, there's an enclave of B&Bs.
Most offer accommodation year-round.

Ardenlea (*☎ 811738, 13 Craig na Gower
Ave*) En-suite singles £18-22, doubles £30-
36. Ardenlea has a no-smoking policy. It's
particularly recommended and a hearty
breakfast is served.

Dunroamin (*☎ 810698, Craig na Gower
Ave*) En-suite singles £20-40, doubles £32-
50. Dunroamin offers pleasant B&B accommodation. There's a communal lounge but
there are TVs in each of the three bedrooms.

Karn House (*☎ 810849, Craig na Gower
Ave*) En-suite singles £18-20, doubles £33-
36. This is a very comfortable B&B in an intriguingly designed modern house.

On Dalfaber Rd are two larger guesthouses.

Kinapol Guest House (*☎/fax 810513,
Dalfaber Rd*) Singles £16-32, doubles £32-
36. All the rooms at Kinapol have a shared
bathroom.

Ardlogie Guest House (*☎/fax 810747,
Dalfaber Rd*) B&B doubles £36-40. This
place has five en-suite rooms, each with a
TV; there's also a resident's lounge.

There are plenty of other places on
Grampian Rd.

Kila (*☎ 810573,* **e** *dave@kila.fsnet.co
.uk, Grampian Rd*) En-suite singles/doubles
from £16/32. Open year-round. Centrally
located Kila is opposite the train station.
It's a friendly place and the breakfast is
good.

Mackenzie's Inn (*☎ 810672, fax 810595,
125 Grampian Rd*) En-suite doubles £36-
50. The highly commended Mackenzie's Inn
has eight well-equipped doubles. It's a traditional villa which has been modernised
and extended.

Cairngorm Hotel (*☎ 810233, fax 810791,
Grampian Rd*) En-suite singles/doubles
£25/50. The recommended Cairngorm
Hotel, otherwise known as the Cairn, ha

good facilities, including room service, laundry service and satellite TV.

Lynwilg House (☎/fax 811685, Lynwilg). B&B with attached bathroom £28-35 per person, or £45-60 including dinner. Open Jan-Oct. A mile (1.6km) out of town, this excellent country-house hotel is a B&B to write home about.

B&Bs & Hotels – Ski Rd
There are several recommended options along Ski Rd.

Corrour House Hotel (☎ 810220, fax 811500, Inverdruie) Rooms with attached bathroom £30-40 per person. Open Dec-Oct. This excellent hotel, 1½ miles (2.5km) from Aviemore, has splendid views of the Lairig Ghru Pass.

Riverside Lodge (☎ 810153, fax 810143, Inverdruie) En-suite singles £25-30, doubles £40-50. Riverside Lodge is a modern B&B in a fine woodland setting.

Mrs Bruce (☎ 810230, 2 Dell Mhor) B&B singles/doubles £16/32. This is a good-value B&B, just beyond Inverdruie on Dell Mhor.

Junipers (☎ 810405, fax 812850, 5 Dell Mhor) B&B singles £18-20, doubles £32-36. Also on Dell Mhor, Juniper's is a pleasant place with a lovely garden.

Hilton Coylumbridge (☎ 811811, fax 811309, Coylumbridge) Singles £55-110, doubles £70-130. The Hilton Coylumbridge is perhaps the finest of the resort hotels with room service, indoor swimming pool and leisure facilities; it enjoys an excellent location just outside Aviemore.

Places to Eat
There's no shortage of places to eat, but only a few are particularly inviting.

Royal Tandoori (☎ 811199, 43 Grampian Rd) Mains from £5.50-10.95, vegetarian mains £8. Near the TIC, the Royal Tandoori offers five vegetarian choices as well as the normal Indian dishes; takeaways are available at a 10% discount.

Smiffy's Fish & Chip Restaurant (Grampian Rd) Smiffy's, near the station, does takeaways and a reasonable fry-up, with cod and chips at £2.40.

No 1 Licensed Restaurant (☎ 811161, Station Square) Breakfast from £3.95, mains

from £5.25. This friendly restaurant has an extensive menu.

Littlejohn's (☎ 811633, 113 Grampian Rd) Mains from £4.25. Farther north along Grampian Rd, opposite the police station, there's a branch of Littlejohn's that serves steaks, pizzas, burgers, ribs, potato skins, burritos etc.

Ski-ing Doo (☎ 810392, 9 Grampian Rd) Steaks up to £13. Ski-ing Doo, across the road from Littlejohn's, conjures up images of schussing pigeons. It serves a range of steaks, including 10-ounce sirloins (£11.99) and 16-ounce T-bones (£12.99).

Winking Owl (☎ 810646, 123 Grampian Rd) Mains £4.80-12.25. Another avian type (albeit less active than Ski-ing Doo), the Winking Owl has a choice of pub food and great outdoor seating.

Old Bridge Inn (☎ 811137, 23 Dalfaber Rd) Mains £8.95-14.50. The highly recommended Old Bridge Inn, near the youth hostel, does excellent innovative dishes.

There's a small *cafe* along Ski Rd in Glen More Forest Park. The *snack bar and restaurant* at the ski resort day lodge in Coire Cas serves snacks, meals and drinks until 4.30pm or 5pm in winter and until 11pm in July and August.

If you prefer to self-cater, Aviemore has an enormous *Tesco* (☎ 887400, Grampian Rd) supermarket. For smoked trout, venison, paté and other delicacies visit *Rothiemurchus Larder* (☎ 810858, Rothiemurchus Estate Visitor Centre), a mile (1.6km) along Ski Rd.

Entertainment
There's occasional live music at both *Mackenzie's Inn* (☎ 810672, 125 Grampian Rd) and the *Cairngorm Hotel* (☎ 810233, Grampian Rd).

Getting There & Away
Aviemore is 33 miles (53km) from Inverness, 62 miles (99km) from Fort William and 127 miles (203km) from Edinburgh.

Bus Buses stop on Grampian Rd; buy tickets at the TIC. Scottish Citylink (☎ 0870 550 5050) connects Aviemore with Inverness (£4.70, 45 minutes), Kincraig (£2.50,

10 minutes), Kingussie (£3.60, 18 minutes), Newtonmore (£4.20, 25 minutes), Dalwhinnie (£5.30, 40 minutes), Pitlochry (£6.40, 1¼ hours), Perth (£9, two hours), Glasgow (£12.50, 3¼ hours) and Edinburgh (£12.50, 3¼ hours). For Aberdeen, you must change at Inverness.

There's a daily overnight bus service to London's Victoria coach station (12 hours). For details, call National Express (☎ 0870 550 5050).

Highland Country Buses (☎ 811211) runs two buses daily (June to September) from Aviemore to Fort William (£6.30) via Kingussie, Newtonmore and Laggan. There are also various weekday or schoolday runs from Aviemore to Kingussie (£3.20).

Train There are direct train services to London (from £63.60, 10½ hours), Glasgow/Edinburgh (£28.70, 3 hours) and Inverness (£9.30, four to nine daily, 40 minutes). For details phone ☎ 0845 748 4950.

Strathspey Steam Railway (☎ 810725) operates between Aviemore train station, Boat of Garten and Nethy Bridge. At the time of writing, work was ccontinuing on an extension to Grantown.

Getting Around

Highland Country Buses (☎ 811211) links Aviemore and Cairngorm seven times daily from June to September and from late October to April (£2.50). Buses run twice hourly (except Sunday) between Aviemore and Coylumbridge.

Several places in central Aviemore hire out mountain bikes; most charge £9 to £11 per day. You can also hire bikes in Rothiemurchus Estate and Glen More Forest Park.

You can rent cars from MacDonald's Self Drive (☎ 811444), 13 Muirton, from £34 a day. The company will deliver/collect from your hotel.

AROUND AVIEMORE
Kincraig & Glen Feshie

Kincraig, 6 miles (10km) south-west of Aviemore, makes another good Cairngorm base.

Run by the Royal Zoological Society of Scotland, the **Highland Wildlife Park** (☎ 01540-651270, Kincraig; adult/child £6.50/4.35; open 10am-6pm daily Apr-May & Sept-Nov; 10am-7pm daily June-Aug; 10am-4pm daily Dec-Mar; last entry two hours before closing), just outside the village, features breeding stocks of local wildlife past and present. There's a drive-through safari park and several woodland walks offering most people their best opportunity to come face-to-face with an elusive wildcat or a furiously displaying male capercaillie. Visitors without cars are driven around by staff (at no extra cost).

At Kincraig, the Spey widens into **Loch Insh**, home of the **Loch Insh Watersports Centre** (☎ 01540-651272, Kincraig), which offers canoeing, windsurfing, sailing, bike hire and fishing, as well as B&B accommodation from £18.50 per person in comfortable rooms with attached bathrooms. The food here is good, especially after 6.30pm when the lochside cafe metamorphoses into a restaurant.

Glen Feshie extends east into the Cairngorms. It's a lovely quiet glen with lots of pine woods and heathery hills soaring up to their baldy summits. There's also a good hostel here.

Glen Feshie Hostel (☎ 01540-651323, e glenfeshiehostel@totalise.co.uk, Glen Feshie) Beds £8. About 5 miles (8km) from Kincraig, this friendly, independent 14-bed hostel is popular with hikers. The overnight charge includes linen and a steaming bowl of porridge to start the day.

Carrbridge
☎ 01479 • pop 543

At Carrbridge, 7 miles (11km) north-east of Aviemore, the **Landmark Highland Heritage & Adventure Park** (☎ 01479-841613, Carrbridge; adult/child £5.95/4.20; open 10am-6pm daily Apr-mid-July, 10am-7pm daily mid-July-Aug, 10am-5pm daily Sept-Mar), set in a forest of Scots pines, offers a few novel and worthwhile concepts, such as the raised Treetop Trail which allows you to view red squirrels, crossbills and crested tits, and the steam-powered sawmill. Most of it, however, seems rather tacky.

You'll find the ultimate in humpback bridges in the centre of the village. Built in 1717, it now looks decidedly unsafe but remains impressive with the thundering rapids below.

Ask locally if the September music week is running, or contact the TIC in Aviemore.

Places to Stay & Eat Carrbridge has a *Spar* store, an inexpensive *coffee shop*, and a couple of hotels.

Cairn Hotel (☎ 841212, fax 841362, Main Rd) Singles with shared bathroom £19, singles/doubles with bathroom £26/44. This is a comfortable and friendly place to stay, with snacks available from £1.50 and bar meals from £4.50.

Carrbridge Bunkhouse Hostel (☎/fax 841250, Carrbridge) Beds £6.50-7.50. This hostel is situated on the left when heading west on the A938 to Inverness.

Getting There & Away Highland Country Buses (☎ 01463-222244) runs several buses daily (except Sunday) from Inverness to Carrbridge (£3.15, 45 minutes) and onwards to Grantown-on-Spey (£2.05, 17 minutes).

Boat of Garten
☎ 01479 • pop 571

Eight miles (13km) north-east of Aviemore, Boat of Garten is known as the Osprey Village since these rare birds of prey nest at the RSPB's **Loch Garten Osprey Centre** *(☎ 831694, Grianan, Tulloch, Nethybridge; admission for nonmembers £2.50/50p; open 10am-6pm daily Apr-Aug)* in Abernethy Forest, 2 miles (3km) east of the village. RSPB volunteers guard the site throughout the nesting season to deter egg collectors.

Boat of Garten has a general store and post office, plus a few accommodation options.

Loch Garten Lodges (☎ 831769, fax 831708, Loch Garten Rd) Pitches £4-9. You can stick up a tent at this caravan park. Caravans and a cottage are also available for £200-370 per week year-round.

Fraoch Lodge (☎/fax 831331, Deshar Rd) Beds £7.50-12. This independent hostel opens year-round. The cheaper beds are available if you bring your own sleeping bag. Breakfast, dinner and transport to/from the hostel can be arranged in advance.

Boat Hotel (☎ 831258, fax 831414, Boat of Garten) En-suite B&B £22.50-60 per person. The Boat Hotel has very pleasant rooms and the meals are recommended (bar meals £6.95 to £12.95; three-course dinner £29.50). Pan-fried fillet of Scottish salmon with grape risotto costs £8.05.

The best way to get to Boat of Garten is on the Strathspey Steam Railway (☎ 810725) which runs five times daily from Aviemore – a ticket in 3rd class costs £6 return.

Dulnain Bridge & Skye of Curr

At the **Speyside Heather Centre** *(☎ 01479-851359, Skye of Curr; garden centre free, exhibition 75p; open daily year-round)*, 2 miles (3km) south-west of Dulnain Bridge, there's an indoor exhibition about the innumerable uses of heather over the centuries.

After taking a pleasant stroll around the garden centre and antique shop, you may wish to sample one of 21 ways to enjoy Scottish dumpling (rich fruit cake steamed in a *cloot*, or linen cloth) in the adjacent *Clootie Dumpling Restaurant*; the Heather Centre Special comes with cream, ice cream, heather cream liqueur, chopped nuts and blackberry preserve for £3.65.

Nethybridge
☎ 01479 • pop 675

This quiet village isn't particularly exciting, but it's a very inviting place to simply sit and soak up the clean air and woodland atmosphere.

There's year-round hostel accommodation at *Nethy House (☎/fax 821370, Nethybridge)* where dorm beds cost between £6 and £9.50.

Aspen Lodge (☎ 01479-821042, fax 821131, Nethybridge) B&B singles/doubles from £25/39. Good for novelty value, Aspen Lodge is a former police station.

Highland Country Buses (☎ 01463-222244) runs four times daily Monday to Friday from Grantown-on-Spey to Nethybridge; two of these buses continue to Inverness.

GRANTOWN-ON-SPEY
☎ 01479 • pop 3241

This Georgian town (pronounced granton) on the Spey, which attracts throngs of coach tourists in the summer, lies amid an angler's paradise. Most hotels can kit you up for a day of fishing or put you in touch with someone who can. The TIC (☎ 872773), at 54 High St, opens daily from March to October. Other amenities include a bank, ATMs, food shops and post office.

Places to Stay
Grantown's accommodation reflects its senior clientele, with plenty of comfortable upmarket hotels noted for their food. However, there are some budget options.

Grantown-on-Spey Caravan Park (☎ 872474, fax 873696, Seafield Avenue) From £5 per tent. Located half a mile (800m) from the centre. From April to October, caravans are also available for £150-250 per week.

Speyside Backpackers (☎/fax 873514, 16 The Square) Dorm beds £9.50-11. Speyside Backpackers is also known as the Stop-Over. Breakfast and double or twin rooms are available at this fairly average hostel.

Crann-Tara Guest House (☎ 872197, High St) Singles £17-19, doubles £34-36, all with shared bath. Dinner is available for £10 at this guesthouse.

Bank House (☎ 873256, 1 The Square) B&B £15-20 per person. Basic B&B is available at the Bank House, in the former Bank of Scotland.

Firhall Guest House (☎/fax 873097, Grant Rd) Singles £17-19, doubles £34-50. The recommended Firhall Guest House, in a traditional villa, charges £10 extra for dinner. There's a TV in each of the bedrooms and in a separate guests lounge.

Culdearn House Hotel (☎ 872106, fax 873641, Woodlands Terrace) Dinner B&B singles/doubles £75/150. This nicely decorated and friendly four-star hotel is noted for its food. See the following Places to Eat section. All rooms are en suite.

Places to Eat
On the High St, you'll find huge portions of fish and chips (£2.60) at the *Royal Fish*

Bar. Also on High St, the *Coffee House & Ice Cream Parlour* does soup and snacks and the *Golden Grantown* (☎ 873421, 58 High St) Chinese takeaway is just two doors from the TIC.

Ben Mhor Hotel (☎ 872056, High St) Mains £4.15-8.95. This hotel, opposite the TIC, offers a pleasant atmosphere and bistro meals.

Culdearn House Hotel (☎ 872106, fax 873641, Woodlands Terrace) 4-course dinner £25. You can treat yourself to an excellent meal here, where the traditional Scottish menu is also quite adventurous. Bookings are essential.

Getting There & Away
Highland Country Buses (☎ 01463-222244) runs six to nine buses daily, except Sunday, between Grantown-on-Spey and Aviemore (£3.70, 35 minutes). To/from Inverness via Carrbridge, buses run two or three times daily, except Sunday (£4.20, one hour). Also, work is continuing to extend the Strathspey Steam Railway to Grantown-on-Spey.

KINGUSSIE
☎ 01540 • pop 1461

The tranquil Speyside town of Kingussie (pronounced kin-yewsie) is best known as the home of one of Scotland's finest folk museums. The unstaffed TIC (☎ 661297), at the Highland Folk Museum, Duke St, opens 9.30am to 5.30pm Monday to Saturday from April to September, and 9.30am to 4.30pm from Monday to Saturday in October.

Parts of the BBC TV series *Monarch of the Glen* have been filmed in Kingussie.

Highland Folk Museum
The Highland Folk Museum (☎ 661307, Duke St; adult/child £1/50p; open 9.30am-5.30pm Mon-Sat Apr-Sept) comprises a collection of historical buildings and relics revealing all facets of Highland culture and lifestyles. The 18th-century Pitmain Lodge holds displays of ceilidh musical instruments, costumes and old washing utensils.

The village-like grounds also include a traditional thatch-roofed Isle of Lewis blackhouse, a water mill, a 19th-century corrugated iron shed for smoking salmon and assorted farm implements.

You'll find another section of this museum in nearby Newtonmore.

Ruthven Barracks

Built in 1719 on the site of an earlier 13th-century castle, Ruthven Barracks *(1 mile/1.6km south of Kingussie, across the A9; admission free; open at all times)* was one of four fortresses constructed after the first Jacobite rebellion of 1715 as part of a Hanoverian scheme to take control of the Highlands. Given the long-range views, the location is perfect. The barracks were last occupied by Jacobite troops awaiting the return of Bonnie Prince Charlie after the Battle of Culloden. Learning of his defeat and subsequent flight, they destroyed the barracks before taking to the glens. The ruins are floodlit at night.

Walking

The Monadhliath Range, north-west of Kingussie, attracts fewer hikers than the nearby Cairngorms, and makes an ideal destination for walkers seeking peace and solitude. However, during the deer-stalking season (August to October), you'll need to check with the TIC before setting out.

The recommended six-hour circular walk to the 878m summit of Carn an Fhreiceadain, above Kingussie, begins north of the village. It continues to Pitmain Lodge and along the Allt Mór river before climbing to the cairn on the summit. You can then follow the ridge east to the twin summits of Beinn Bhreac before returning to Kingussie via a more easterly track.

Places to Stay & Eat

Kingussie Golf Club (☎ 661600, fax 662066, Gynack Rd) Pitches from £6. You can camp alongside the golf course here.

Lairds Bothy Hostel (☎ 661334, fax 662063, 68 High St) Dorm beds £9. The Lairds Bothy Hostel lies behind the Tipsy Laird pub. There are four family rooms (£9 per person) and several eight-bed dorms.

St Helens (☎ 661430, Ardbroilach Rd) Doubles £40-44. All rooms are en suite at this particularly good B&B, and there's a TV lounge for guests.

Homewood Lodge (☎ 661507, Newtonmore Rd) Singles £15-20, doubles £30-40. On the western outskirts of Kingussie, friendly Homewood Lodge does four-star B&B and dinner for £10 extra.

Osprey Hotel (☎/fax 661510, Ruthven Rd) Singles £25-39, doubles £50-68. The Osprey Hotel, a comfortable Victorian townhouse, does good home cooking (four-course table d'hôte dinner £22).

The Cross (☎ 661166, fax 661080, Tweed Mill Brae, Ardbroilach Rd) Dinner B&B £95-115 per person, dinner £37.50 for nonresidents. Closed Tues & Dec-Mar. If you're feeling flush, visit The Cross, one of the best hotel-restaurants in the Highlands. It's in a converted water mill.

Tipsy Laird (☎ 661334, High St) Mains £6.50-9.95. The quality and portions of the pub meals at the Tipsy Laird are great, in keeping with the friendliness of the staff.

La Cafetière (☎ 661020, 54 High St) The most promising of the High St cafes does speciality coffees from 90p, soup and a roll for £1.50, and toasties from £2.20.

Getting There & Away

Kingussie is 115 miles (185km) from Edinburgh, 71 miles (114km) from Perth and 43 miles (69km) from Inverness. Just to the north of town, the A9 heads south to Perth, leaving the Highland region via the bleak Pass of Drumochter.

Kingussie is also on the main Edinburgh/Glasgow to Inverness rail and bus routes; all trains stop here but only some Citylink buses do. Highland Country Buses (☎ 01479-811211) runs a twice-daily service (June to September) between Aviemore, Kingussie, Newtonmore and Fort William; for other buses to Aviemore, see the earlier Aviemore section. For rail information, phone ☎ 0845 748 4950.

NEWTONMORE
☎ 01540 • pop 1172

It's hard to imagine a more relaxed place than Newtonmore, which is strung out along its main street. The only time it has ever hit the news was during the severe winter of 1995/96 when the boiler at the Braeriach Hotel exploded, causing extensive damage.

In the main street, you'll find hotels, the post office, an ATM, a TIC and a Co-op supermarket. The TIC (☎ 673253), at Ralia, 1½ miles (2.5km) south of Newtonmore along the A9, opens daily Easter to October.

Highland Folk Museum
The Highland Folk Museum (☎ 661307, Newtonmore; adult/child £5/3; open 10.30am-5.30pm daily Apr-Aug) in Newtonmore, located at the northern end of the village, includes a reconstructed village with wattle and daub cottages, a school and a farm. On-site demonstrations include woodcarving, spinning and peat-fire baking.

Clan MacPherson Museum
At the junction of the A86 and B9150 you'll find the Clan MacPherson Museum (☎ 673332, Main St; admission free; open 10am-5pm Mon-Sat & 2.30pm-5.30pm Sun May-Sept), which reveals the histories of Clan MacPherson and Badenoch district.

Dalwhinnie Distillery
A short day-excursion from Newtonmore will take you to the Dalwhinnie Distillery (☎ 672219, Dalwhinnie; tours £3, includes £3 discount voucher; open 9.30am-4.30pm Mon-Fri Mar-Dec, plus 9.30am-4.30pm Sat June-Oct & 12.30pm-4.30pm Sun July & Aug), 12 miles (19km) south down the A9, which claims to be Scotland's highest distillery.

Places to Stay & Eat
Newtonmore Hostel (☎/fax 673360, Main St) Beds without linen £8.50. The main budget place is the Newtonmore Hostel, in the heart of town. Breakfast is available on request and there's a TV lounge.

Strathspey Mountain Hostel (☎ 673694, Main St) Beds without linen £9. You'll find this just along from Newtonmore Hostel. It has a TV lounge and offers various discounts for long stays.

Craigerne House Hotel (☎/fax 673281, Golf Course Rd) Singles £24-26.50, doubles £48-68. The grand Craigerne House Hotel offers dinner for £16.50 extra.

Glen Hotel (☎ 673203, Main St) Snack from £2.25, bar meals £4.50-10.95. The bar in the Glen Hotel, at the main road junction, serves snacks and bar meals (most under £5.25) in a cosy setting.

Mains Hotel (☎ 673206, Main St) Main around £6-10. The Mains Hotel, over the road from the Glen Hotel, exudes a similar ambience and puts on entertainment regularly.

Getting There & Away
From Kingussie, the A86 to Fort William leaves the A9 and follows a lovely route through Newtonmore to skirt Loch Laggan and Loch Moy, providing fine views of Ben Nevis.

A postbus (☎ 01246-546329) runs daily (except Sunday) between Newtonmore, Kinlochlaggan and Ardverikie House (where parts of the BBC TV series *Monarch of the Glen* have been filmed).

Highland Country Buses (☎ 01479-811211) runs a twice-daily service (June to September) between Aviemore, Kingussie, Newtonmore and Fort William.

Only four or five trains and six or seven Citylink buses between Inverness and Edinburgh/Glasgow stop in Newtonmore. The rest pass without stopping.

Inverness & the Great Glen

Inverness – which was officially declared a city in December 2000 – is the 'capital' of the Highlands and one of the fastest growing towns in Britain. It's a major transport hub and jumping-off point for exploring the northern and western Highlands, the Moray Firth coast and the Great Glen, and a lively town that's well worth visiting in its own right.

The Great Glen is a geological fault line running across Scotland from Fort William to Inverness. The glaciers of the last Ice Age eroded a deep valley along the fault that is now largely filled by a series of lochs

– Linnhe, Lochy, Oich and Ness. The glen has always been an important communication route – General George Wade built a military road along the southern side of Loch Ness in the early 18th century, and in 1822 the various lochs were linked by the Caledonian Canal to create a cross-country waterway. The modern A82 road was completed in 1933.

The 80-mile (128km) Great Glen Cycle Route from Fort William to Inverness, via Fort Augustus, follows canal tow-paths and gravel tracks through forests to avoid the busy roads, where possible. The *Cycling in the Forest* leaflet, available from TICs and the Forestry Commission, gives details.

INVERNESS
☎ 01463 • pop 41,800

Inverness has a great location on the Moray Firth at the northern end of the Great Glen. The town was probably founded by King David in the 12th century and is now the main urban centre in the Highlands. In summer it overflows with visitors intent on monster-hunting at nearby Loch Ness. However, it's worth spending some time strolling and bird-watching along the picturesque River Ness or cruising on the Moray Firth in search of its hundred or so bottlenose dolphins.

Orientation
The broad River Ness, which flows from Loch Ness into the Moray Firth, runs through the heart of town. The town centre lies on the eastern bank, at the foot of the castle hill. The bus and train stations are next to each other just north of the centre.

Information
The TIC (☎ 234353, e inverness@host.co uk, Castle Wynd) is beside Inverness Museum, just off Bridge St. It opens 9am to 8pm Monday to Saturday, 9.30am to 5pm Sunday, and contains a bureau de change, CalMac ferry office and accommodation booking service; it also sells tickets for tours and cruises.

The main post office, on Queensgate, opens 9am to 5.30pm on weekdays and 9am to 6pm on Saturday. You can check your email at the TIC for £2 per 20 minutes.

Leakey's (☎ 239947, Greyfriars Hall, Church St) is an excellent second-hand bookshop with a good cafe; it opens 10 am to 5.30pm Monday to Saturday.

The launderette on Young St charges £3 a load, £1.40 to dry, and opens 8am to 8pm Monday to Friday, 8am to 6pm Saturday.

Things to See
The **Inverness Museum and Art Gallery** (☎ 237114, Castle Wynd; admission free; open 9am-5pm Mon-Sat) contains wildlife dioramas, geological displays, period rooms with historic weapons, Pictish stones and a missable art gallery, along with a variety of short-term events and displays. The entrance is immediately uphill from the TIC.

The hill above the museum is topped by the baronial turrets of **Inverness Castle**. In the 11th century, a timber castle probably stood to the east of the present castle site. In the 12th century it was replaced with a stone castle, which was then rebuilt in the 15th century. It was repaired in 1718 and expanded in 1725, only to be taken over by the Jacobites in 1746 and blown up. The present rose-coloured structure was constructed between 1837 and 1847, and today it serves as the local Sheriff's Court.

The only part of the castle open to the public is the Drum Tower, which houses the **Castle Garrison Encounter** (☎ 243363, Inverness Castle; adult/child £3/2; open 10.30am-5.30pm daily Easter–late-Nov). For the entry fee you meet actors representing characters from the Hanoverian army of 1746. In front stands a statue of Highland heroine Flora McDonald, who helped the escaping Bonnie Prince Charlie.

Thanks to Inverness' often violent history, few buildings of real age or historical significance have survived and much of the town dates from the completion of Telford's Caledonian Canal in 1822. Older structures include the 1593 **Abertarff House** and the 1668 **Dunbar's Hospital**, both in Church St. Inverness' **Mercat Cross** stands in front of the ornate **Town House**, the Gothic-style town hall. Across the river and south along the bank lie **St Andrew's Cathedral**, dating from 1866 to 1869, and the **Eden Court Theatre**,

THE HIGHLANDS

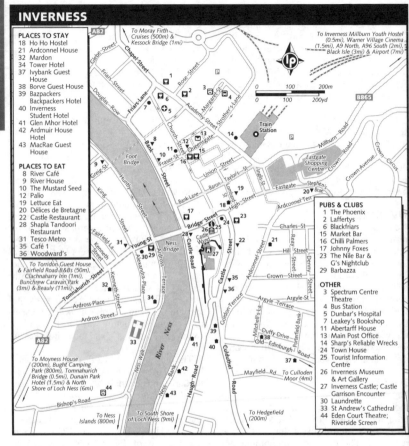

INVERNESS

PLACES TO STAY
18 Ho Ho Hostel
21 Ardconnel House
32 Mardon
34 Tower Hotel
37 Ivybank Guest House
38 Borve Guest House
39 Bazpackers Backpackers Hotel
40 Inverness Student Hotel
41 Glen Mhor Hotel
42 Ardmuir House Hotel
43 MacRae Guest House

PLACES TO EAT
8 River Café
9 River House
10 The Mustard Seed
12 Palio
17 Lettuce Eat
20 Délices de Bretagne
22 Castle Restaurant
28 Shapla Tandoori Restaurant
31 Tesco Metro
35 Café 1
36 Woodward's

PUBS & CLUBS
1 The Phoenix
2 Laffertys
6 Blackfriars
15 Market Bar
16 Chilli Palmers
17 Johnny Foxes
23 The Nile Bar & G's Nightclub
29 Barbazza

OTHER
3 Spectrum Centre Theatre
4 Bus Station
5 Dunbar's Hospital
7 Leakey's Bookshop
11 Abertarff House
13 Main Post Office
14 Sharp's Reliable Wrecks
24 Town House
25 Tourist Information Centre
26 Inverness Museum & Art Gallery
27 Inverness Castle; Castle Garrison Encounter
30 Laundrette
33 St Andrew's Cathedral
44 Eden Court Theatre; Riverside Screen

which hosts regular art exhibits. It's also worth strolling to the **Ness Islands**, connected to the river banks by footbridges.

Organised Tours
Walking Tours Guided walking tours of the town (£4/2) leave from outside the TIC and last 1¼ hours; check with the TIC for details.

Davy the Ghost Tours (mobile ☎ 07730 831069) offers 1¼-hour tours (adult/child £6/3) at 7pm nightly. Visitors will be treated to tales of Inverness' horrific past, including ghosts, torture, witches, murders and hangings. They're led by an '18th-century ghost'

in period costume. Tours depart from the blackboard outside the TIC.

Bus & Taxi Tours Over Easter and from May to September, *Guide Friday (☎ 224000)* runs hop-on hop-off bus tours of Inverness and the Culloden battlefield. An all-day ticket for the Culloden tour (one hour 20 minutes) costs £7.50/2.50; for the city only (30 minutes) it's £5.50/2.50.

Guide Friday also offers bus tours to Loch Ness and Urquart Castle that include admission to the Loch Ness 2000 exhibition and a half-hour cruise on the loch from

Drumnadrochit. Tickets cost £14.50/6.50 and the tours, which last three hours, depart from the TIC twice daily at 10.30am and 2.30pm.

From June to early September, *John o'Groats Ferries* (☎ 01955-611353) runs daily tours (13½ hours) by bus and passenger ferry from Inverness to Orkney for £44/22.

Highland Taxi Tours (☎ 220222) has a wide range of day tours to places as far afield as Skye and Deeside. Fares per car (with up to four people) include £40 for a three-hour trip to Fort George and Culloden, and £50 for a four-hour circular tour around Loch Ness.

Cruises From Tomnahurich Bridge, the *Jacobite Queen* (☎ 233999) departs for 3½-hour cruises on Loch Ness for £10/8. A one-way trip to Urquhart Castle (see the Loch Ness section), including entry, costs £10.50/8.50.

Moray Firth Cruises (☎ 717900) offers 1½-hour wildlife cruises (adult/child £10/7.50) to look for dolphins, seals and birdlife. Sightings aren't guaranteed but it's still enjoyable, especially on fine days. The cruises run between 10.30am to 4.50pm daily March to October and 10.30am to 6pm July and August. Follow the signs to Shore St Quay from the far end of Chapel St. A shuttle bus leaves from the TIC 15 minutes before sailings.

Places to Stay

In peak season, either pre-book your accommodation or get an early start looking for something. The TIC charges £1.50 for local bookings.

Camping There's a basic camp site close to the centre of town, and a more pleasant one further out.

Bught Camping Park (☎ 236920, fax 712850, The Bught) Tent pitch £4.30, plus £2 for a car. Open Apr-Sept. This site is a mile (1.6km) south-west of the city centre, near Tomnahurich Bridge.

Bunchrew Caravan Park (☎ 237802) Tent with two people £5. Open Apr-Oct. Bunchrew is an attractive, grassy site among trees, on the shore of the Beauly Firth, 3 miles (5km) west of the city centre.

Hostels & College Accommodation

Inverness has a good range of backpacker accommodation.

Inverness Millburn Youth Hostel (☎ 231771, Victoria Drive) Dorm beds £11.75/10.75 including continental breakfast, add £2/1 in July & Aug. Inverness' flashy 166-bed SYHA hostel is 10 minutes' walk north-east of the town centre. Some reckon it's the best hostel in the country. Booking is essential, especially over the Easter break, July and August.

Inverness Student Hotel (☎ 236556, 8 Culduthel Rd) Dorm beds £10. This place has the same owner as Edinburgh's High St Hostel – you can make phone bookings from there. It's friendly and homely with a great view, and just a 10-minute walk from the train station, just past the castle.

Bazpackers Backpackers Hotel (☎ 717663, 4 Culduthel Rd) Dorm beds £10, twins or doubles £14 per person. This is a friendly place with a wood-burning stove, a small garden and more great views, though the dorms are a bit cramped.

Ho Ho Hostel (☎ 221225, 23a High St) Dorm beds £8.90-9.90, twin room £12 per person including breakfast. The entrance to the Ho Ho Hostel, which occupies a fine old Victorian building, is in an alley between High St and Baron Taylor St.

Hedgefield (☎ 713430, 23 Culduthel Rd) Family rooms and twin rooms £11 per person. Open July & Aug only. Hedgefield – Inverness College's student residence – is a great place to stay. It's a big old mansion in country-house grounds, just 10 minutes' walk south of the castle. Booking is recommended; call the number provided between 9am and 5am Monday to Friday.

B&Bs & Hotels There are lots of guesthouses and B&Bs along Old Edinburgh Rd and Ardconnel St, south of the centre, including *Ardconnel House* (☎/fax 240455, 21 Ardconnel St), where B&B costs from £20 to £38 per person, and *Borve Guest House* (☎/fax 234728, 9 Old Edinburgh Rd), where B&B is £25 to £35 per person.

Ivybank Guest House (☎/fax 232796, e ivybank@talk21.com, 28 Old Edinburgh

Rd) B&B doubles or twins £20-27.50 per person. This guesthouse, in a lovely old listed building, is highly recommended.

West of the river, on Kenneth St and adjoining Fairfield Rd, you'll find many B&Bs in the £15 to £22 price range, including *Mardon* (☎ *231005, 37 Kenneth St)*, *Torridon Guest House* (☎*/fax 236449, 59 Kenneth St)*, *Strome Lodge* (☎ *221553, 41 Fairfield Rd)* and *Amulree* (☎ *224822, 40 Fairfield Rd)*.

For a few pounds more, it's possible to have a river view.

MacRae Guest House (☎*/fax 243658, 24 Ness Bank)* B&B doubles or twins £22-26 per person. Travellers have recommended this Victorian house on the eastern bank of the river.

Ardmuir House Hotel (☎*/fax 231151, 16 Ness Bank)* Singles £34.50-37, doubles £57-68. The family-run Ardmuir House, part of a Georgian terrace, is quiet and mostly non-smoking.

Glen Mhor Hotel (☎ *234308, fax 713170,* e *glenmhor@ukonline.co.uk, 9-12 Ness Bank)* Singles £49-69, doubles £70-118. The large and elegant Glen Mhor has two excellent restaurants serving Scottish and international cuisine.

Tower Hotel (☎ *232765, fax 232970, 4 Ardross Terrace)* Singles £36-48, doubles £56-72. Recognisable by its Addams family-style tower, this hotel has a great setting overlooking the river, just a few minutes' walk from the centre.

Moyness House (☎*/fax 233836, 6 Bruce Gardens)* B&B £31-35 per person. This attractive seven-room guest house is west of the river, just off the A82, and has exceptional breakfasts.

Dunain Park Hotel (☎ *230512, fax 224532,* e *info@dunainparkhotel.co.uk, Dunain Park)* Doubles £69-99 per person. This luxury hotel, on the A82 Fort William road a mile (1.6km) south-west of Inverness, is the place to head if you want to spoil yourself. It's a country mansion set in beautiful wooded grounds, five minutes' stroll from the Caledonian Canal and River Ness. The more expensive rooms have Victorian four-poster beds. The hotel restaurant is exceptional.

Places to Eat

The Inverness Museum has a small *coffee shop*, but the *River Cafe* (☎ *714884, 10 Bank St)* is a nicer place to drop in for a pot of tea and a scone (£1.75); there's a restaurant upstairs with more filling fare such as casseroles and lasagne (£5.50 to £6.50).

Lettuce Eat (☎ *715064, 7 Lombard St)* Sandwiches £1.20-2.50. Open 8.30am-4pm Mon-Sat. This is a good place for inexpensive sandwiches, baguettes, salads and the like.

Castle Restaurant (☎ *230925, 41 Castle St)* Mains £4-8. This place, close to the TIC, is a traditional cafe that prides itself on plentiful portions and low prices.

Shapla Tandoori Restaurant (☎ *241919, 2 Castle Rd)* 3-course lunch £5.95. Open noon-2.30pm & 6pm-11pm daily. This restaurant dishes up average curries, in an attractive dining room, with above-average views over the river.

Inverness has an increasing number of top-quality restaurants to choose from. Here are the best places in the town centre.

Café 1 (☎ *226200, 75 Castle St)* Mains £7.50-14.50. Lunch noon-2pm, dinner 6pm-9pm Mon-Sat. Café 1 is a stylish bistro with dishes such as prime Aberdeen Angus fillet steak on *skirlie* (fried oatmeal and onion) with a red onion jam.

Woodward's (☎ *709809, 99 Castle St)* Mains £6.85-10.25. Open 5.30pm-late daily. Set in an attractively renovated old house, this place dishes up imaginative 'Scottish fusion' cuisine – try seared salmon fillet in a Thai green curry sauce with mussels.

The Mustard Seed (☎ *220220, 16 Fraser St)* Mains £6.45-11.65. Open 11am-10pm daily. This cheerfully yellow-painted bistro has some good vegetarian choices, and does a two-course lunch (noon-3pm) for £4.95.

River House (☎ *222033, 1 Greig St)* 2-course/3-course dinner £22.95/26.95. Open 12.15pm-10.30pm Thur-Sat, 6.30pm-10.30pm Mon-Wed. The River House is an elegant eating place of the polished-wood and crisp-linen variety, serving carefully prepared venison, beef, lamb, duck and seafood.

Other places worth trying include the *très français Délices de Bretagne* (☎ *712422, 6 Stephen's Brae)* at the eastern end of High

St, which does excellent coffee and Breton galettes (£2.40-5.30), and *Palio* (☎ *711950, 26 Queensgate*), a stylish Italian restaurant that has pizzas for £4 to £6, and a two-course lunch for £4.95.

For a real splurge, book a table at the restaurant in the *Glen Mhor Hotel* or the *Dunain Park Hotel* (see Places to Stay earlier) but be prepared to fork out up to £30 a head.

The *Tesco Metro* supermarket on King St opens 8.30am to 8pm daily (to 9pm Thursday and Friday) and 9am-6pm Sunday.

Entertainment

Pubs & Clubs There's a good online guide to Inverness' pubs, clubs and events at W www.nessweb.co.uk.

The Phoenix (☎ *233685,108 Academy St*) Open 11am-midnight Mon-Sat, 12.30pm-11pm Sun. This is the best of the traditional pubs in the city centre, with an island bar, a comfortable, family-friendly lounge and good food at both lunchtime and in the evenings. Real ales on tap include the rich and fruity Orkney Dark Island.

Blackfriars (☎ *233881, 93-95 Academy St*) Open 11am-midnight Mon-Sat, 12.30pm-11pm Sun. Food served noon-3pm & 6pm-9pm daily. Just along the street from the Phoenix, Blackfriars is a friendly place with good bar meals from £4.95 and live music most nights.

Lafferty's (☎ *712270, Academy St*) Open 11am-midnight Mon-Sat, 12.30pm-11pm Sun. A big and bustling Irish theme pub, Lafferty's has live sport on a big-screen TV and karaoke on Friday nights.

Johnny Foxes (☎ *236577, 26 Bank St*) Open 11am-midnight Mon-Sat, 12.30pm-11pm Sun. Overlooking the river, Johnny Foxes is another big and boisterous Irish bar, with a wide range of food served all day and live music every night.

Barbazza (☎ *243342, 5-9 Young St*) Open 11.30am-1am Mon-Thur, 11.30am-1.30am Fri & Sat, 12.30pm-11pm Sun. Cool Barbazza probably has the highest pierced belly-button count in Inverness. It serves booze-absorbing grub such as baked potatoes, burgers and nachos. There are regular DJs, and drinks promos from 8pm to 11pm Wednesday and Sunday.

The Nile Bar & G's Nightclub (☎ *233322, 9-21 Castle St*) Open 9.30pm-1.30am Wed-Mon, last admission midnight Fri, 11.15pm Sat, 10.30pm Sun, 12.30am Mon, Wed & Thur. The Nile is a theme bar, this time with an Egyptian style. It feeds into G's nightclub, which is in the same building – cheap drinks on Monday (student night) and Thursday, no cover charge on Sunday. They also host a club night for 12-17 year-olds, 6pm to 9.30pm Fridays.

The small and cosy *Market Bar*, upstairs in the Old Market Inn, tucked up an alley behind the Victorian Market off Church St, is a good, old-fashioned bar, with live folk music most evenings. *Chilli Palmers*, at 73 Queensgate, is a modern cafe-bar, which is a pleasant place to hang out.

Just over a mile (1.6km) north-west of the centre, on the A862 towards Beauly, the *Clachnaharry Inn* (☎ *239806, 17-19 High St, Clachnaharry*) is a delightful old coaching inn with excellent real ale and good food.

Music & Theatre Inverness' main cultural venue is the *Eden Court Theatre* (☎ *221718, Ness Walk*), on the western bank of the river. It has a busy programme of drama, dance and music, and an excellent cinema (see Cinema below). There's also a good bar and restaurant. Pick up a listing from the foyer or check the Web site at W www.eden-court.co.uk.

From mid-June to mid-September, the *Spectrum Centre Theatre* (☎ *0800 015 8001, Margaret St*) stages 'Scottish Showtime', an evening of traditional Scottish music, song and dance. Doors open at 8pm Monday to Thursday up to mid-July, and Friday for the second half of the summer.

Cinema The *Riverside Screen* (☎ *221718, Ness Walk*), in the Eden Court Theatre complex, is Inverness' art-house cinema, showing both recent films and old classics; tickets cost £4.50/3.

There's a multiplex cinema – the seven-screen *Warner Village* (☎ *711147, Eastfield Way*) – way out on the eastern edge of town, just south of the A96 road to Nairn.

Getting There & Away

Inverness is 155 miles (248km) from Edinburgh, 110 miles (176km) from Aberdeen and 135 miles (216km) from Dundee.

Air Inverness airport (☎ 232471) is at Dalcross, 8 miles (13km) east of town on the A96 road to Nairn. There are flights to Glasgow, Edinburgh, Stornoway, Orkney, London and Amsterdam.

Bus For Inverness bus station, phone ☎ 233371. Scottish Citylink has connections with lots of major centres in England, including London (£28, 13 hours) via Perth and Glasgow. There are numerous buses to Glasgow (£14, 3½ hours), and Edinburgh (£14, four hours) via Perth. Buses to Aberdeen (£10, three hours) are run by Stagecoach Bluebird.

In summer, there are two or three Citylink buses daily to Ullapool (£6, 1½ hours) via Dingwall and Strathpeffer, connecting with the CalMac ferry to Stornoway on Lewis (not Sunday).

There are three to five daily Citylink services to Thurso and Scrabster (£10, three hours) via Dornoch, Helmsdale and Wick, connecting twice a day (not Sunday) with the ferry to Orkney. There are also regular daily services along Loch Ness to Fort William (£7.40, two hours).

Citylink/Skye-Ways (☎ 01599-534328) runs three buses a day (two Sunday) from Inverness to Kyle of Lochalsh and Portree, on Skye (£12.40, three hours).

It's possible to head towards the northwest via Lairg. Stagecoach Inverness has a Monday to Saturday service to Lairg (Sunday too in summer). In summer, daily buses run through to Durness. There's also a Monday to Saturday postbus service (☎ 01246-546329), travelling the Lairg-Tongue-Durness route.

Train The standard one-way fare from London to Inverness costs £90.50 and the journey takes about eight hours. There are direct trains from Aberdeen (£17.80, 2¼ hours), Edinburgh (£30.60, four hours) and Glasgow (£29.90, four hours).

The line from Inverness to Kyle of Lochalsh (£14.70, 2½ hours) offers one of the greatest scenic journeys in Britain; there are three trains a day (none Sunday). Train to Thurso (£12.50, 3½ hours) have the same frequency.

Getting Around

To/From the Airport The twice-daily airport bus connects with Stornoway and London flights (£2.50, 20 minutes). A taxi cost around £10.

Bus Stagecoach Inverness (☎ 239292) and Highland Country (☎ 222244) have service to places around Inverness, including Nairn, Forres, the Culloden battlefield, Beauly, Dingwall and Lairg.

A Stagecoach Inverness Day Rover Highland ticket costs £6.50/3.25, while a Highland Bus Day Rover ticket costs £9/4.50. The Highland Country return fare to Culloden i £2.10; to Cawdor it's £8.50.

Car The TIC has a handy *Car Hire* leaflet. The big boys charge from £35 per day, o you could try Sharp's Reliable Wreck (☎ 236694), 1st Floor, Highland Rail House, Station Square, for cheaper cars and van from £24 per day.

Taxi Call Central Taxis on ☎ 222222.

Bicycle There are some great cycling opportunities out of Inverness, and severa rental outlets, including Wilder Ness (ask a Bazpackers Hostel) charging £7.50/10 for half/full day, and the accommodation des in the train station, which charges £12 a day.

AROUND INVERNESS

The area around Inverness and the Moray Firth has farmland along the coast, with for est and rolling heather-clad hills inland. I the more mountainous western part of the district, there are several wild and beautiful glens, with plenty of wildlife to look out for An autumn visit reveals the forest colours a their very best.

Culloden

Culloden is about 6 miles (10km) east of Inverness. The Battle of Culloden in 1746, the ast fought on British soil, saw the defeat of Bonnie Prince Charlie and the slaughter of 1200 Highlanders in a 68-minute rout. The Duke of Cumberland won the label Butcher Cumberland for his brutal treatment of the defeated Scottish forces. The battle sounded the death knell of the old clan system, and the horrors of the Clearances (see the Dunrobin Castle section later in this chapter) soon followed. The sombre 49-hectare moor where the conflict took place has scarcely changed in the ensuing 250 years. The battlefield, with its many markers and memorials, is always open.

The **visitor centre** *(NTS;* ☎ *01463-790607, Culloden; adult/child £4/3; open 9am-5.30pm daily Apr-Oct, 10am-4pm daily Nov-Mar)* offers a 15-minute audiovisual presentation on the battle. Guided tours of the battlefield (£3/2) depart daily at 10.30am, noon, 1.30pm and 3pm.

Clearly signposted 1½ miles (2.5km) east of Culloden, the **Clava Cairns** are a picturesque group of cairns and stone circles dating from the late Neolithic period (around 4000 to 2000 BC). There's a superb railway viaduct nearby.

Fort George

Off the A96, about 11 miles (18km) north-east of Inverness, is the magnificent and virtually unaltered 18th-century artillery fortification of Fort George *(HS;* ☎ *01667-462777; adult/child £4/1.50; open 9.30am-6.30pm daily Apr-Sept, 9.30am-4.30pm Mon-Sat & 2pm-4.30pm Sun Oct-Mar)*, one of the best examples of its kind in Europe. It was completed in 1769 as a base for George II's army. The mile-plus (1.75km) walk around the ramparts offers fine views out to sea and back to the Great Glen. Given its size, you'll need several hours to look around.

Nairn

☎ 01667 • pop 11,190

This pleasant town is a popular seaside resort with a good sandy beach, but there's not a great deal to see. In the rather compact centre, it's easy to find your way around and there's a good selection of shops, hotels and restaurants.

The TIC (☎ 452763), 62 King St, opens 10am to 6pm Monday to Friday, 10am to 5pm Saturday and 1.30pm to 4pm Sunday, April to October. You'll find banks with ATMs in the High St, and the post office in Cawdor St. Nairn has a swimming pool on Marine Rd.

The most pleasant part of Nairn is the old fishing village of Fishertown, down by the harbour. **Nairn Museum** *(☎ 458531, Viewfield House; adult/child £1/50p; open 10am-4.30pm Mon-Sat May-Sept)*, a few minutes' walk from the TIC, has displays on the history of **Fishertown**, as well as on local archaeology, geology and natural history.

You can spend many pleasant hours wandering along the **East Beach**, which is one of the finest in Scotland.

In August, the Nairn Highland Games are a major event held on The Links. Admission is free. The Nairn International Jazz Festival is also held in August. Contact the TIC for details of both events.

Places to Stay & Eat There's no hostel, but you can camp at *Spindrift Caravan Park (☎ 453992, Little Kildrummie)*, 2 miles (3km) south-west of town, on the B9090 road towards Cawdor. Pitches cost £4.50-8.50.

For B&B for around £16 per person, try *Braighe (☎ 453285, Albert St)*, or rural *Brightmony Farm House (☎ 455550)* in Auldearn, 2 miles (3km) east of town.

Havelock House Hotel (☎/fax 455500, Crescent Rd) Singles £20-30, doubles £30-50. This hotel was built by the emir of Jaipur as his summer residence after he was exiled from India in 1757. You can still get a good curry in the restaurant for just £5.95.

Windsor Hotel (☎ 453108, fax 456108, e windsornairnscotland@btinternet.com, 16 Albert St) Singles £42.50, doubles £80. The elegant Windsor does good bar meals for between £4.95 and £12.95 and a la carte restaurant meals (mains £10 to £18).

The *Links Hotel (☎ 453321, 1 Seafield St)* serves excellent bar meals in its attractive conservatory, while *Friar Tucks (30 Harbour St)* is the best place for a fish supper. *Asher's Bakery (2 Bridge St)* is recommended for cakes and snacks.

THE HIGHLANDS

Getting There & Around Stagecoach Bluebird runs buses hourly (less frequently on Sunday) from Inverness to Aberdeen via Nairn.

Nairn lies on the Inverness to Aberdeen railway line; there are five to seven trains daily from Inverness (£3.30, 20 minutes).

Bike hire is available at The Bike Shop (☎ 455416), 178 Harbour St.

Cawdor

Cawdor Castle (☎ 01667-404615; adult/ child £5.60/3; open 10am-5pm daily May-Oct) is 5 miles (8km) south-west of Nairn. Originally the home of the Thanes of Cawdor, its name is often linked with Macbeth's castle and is the scene of Duncan's murder in Shakespeare's play – hardly likely in real life, since the central tower dates from the 14th century (the wings were 17th-century additions) and Macbeth died in 1057.

It's worth stopping at the *Cawdor Tavern* (☎ 01667-404777, Cawdor), in the nearby village. Deciding what to drink can be difficult as it stocks over 100 varieties of whisky. There's also reasonable pub grub; mains cost between £5 and £8.

Brodie Castle

Brodie Castle (NTS; ☎ 01309-641371; adult/ child £5/free; open 11am-5.30pm Mon-Sat & 1.30pm-5.30pm Sun Apr-Sept) is set in 70 hectares of parkland, 8 miles (13km) east of Nairn. Although the Brodies have been living here since 1160, the present structure dates from the 16th century. You can look round several rooms, some of which have wildly extravagant ceilings, and there's a large collection of paintings and furniture. Don't miss the huge Victorian kitchen beyond the small cafe. There are also woodland walks and an observation hide by the pond.

The half-hourly Stagecoach Bluebird bus No 10 runs from Inverness to Elgin and Aberdeen via Culloden, Nairn and Brodie.

LOCH NESS

Dark, deep and narrow Loch Ness stretches 23 miles (37km), from 5 miles (8km) southwest of Inverness to Fort Augustus at its southern tip. Its bitterly cold waters have been extensively explored for Nessie, the elusive Loch Ness monster, and although some visitors get lucky, most see only her cardboard cut-out form at monster exhibitions. Along the north-western shore runs the congested A82, while the more tranquil but extremely picturesque B862 follows the south-eastern shore. A complete circuit of the loch is about 70 miles (112km) – travel anti-clockwise for the best views.

Drumnadrochit
☎ 01456 • pop 600

Exploitation of poor Nessie reaches fever pitch at Drumnadrochit, where two Monster exhibitions battle for your money. The villages of Milton, Lewiston and Strone virtually touch Drumnadrochit, while Urquhart Castle lies immediately to the south.

One-hour **monster-hunting cruises**, complete with sonar and underwater cameras aboard the *Nessie Hunter* (☎ 450395), operate from Drumnadrochit. They run from 10.30am to 5pm daily, April to October, and cost £8/5.

Monster Exhibitions

The prominent **Official Loch Ness Exhibition Centre** (☎ 450573, W www.loch-ness-scotland.com, Drumnadrochit; adult/child £5.95/3.50; open 9am-8pm daily Jul & Aug; 9am-6pm daily June & Sept; 9am-5.30pm daily Oct; 9.30am-5pm daily Easter-May; 10am-3.30pm daily Nov-Easter) is the better of the two Nessie-theme exhibitions, featuring a 40-minute audiovisual presentation plus exhibits of equipment used in the various underwater monster hunts. Students must have ID.

The nearby **Original Loch Ness Monster Centre** (☎ 450342, Drumnadrochit; adult/ child £3.50/2.75; open 9am-8pm daily Jul & Aug; 10am-5.30pm daily Apr-June & Sept & Oct; 10am-4pm daily Nov-Mar) shows a superficial 30-minute Loch Ness video (with multilingual headsets), but its main function is to sell you tacky Loch Ness Monster souvenirs.

Urquhart Castle

Urquhart Castle (HS; ☎ 450551, west bank

Nessie

There's a tale of St Columba meeting 'Nessie' (the Loch Ness Monster) in the 6th century, but the craze only really developed after 1933, when the A82 road was completed along the northern banks of the loch.

The classic photograph of a dinosaur-like creature's long neck emerging from the water was taken in 1934, from which time the monster hunt gathered pace. In recent years there have been sonar hunts, underwater cameras and computer studies, but no monster has yet been spotted. The loch is very deep and very murky, so the Nessie tourist business has to pedal hard to make a go of it. Keep your camera handy though, you might be the one to prove incontrovertibly that Nessie exists.

If you want to find out more before you leave, check out the official Nessie Web site at w www.lochness.co.uk.

JANE SMITH

of Loch Ness; adult/child £3.80/1.20; open 9.30am-6.30pm daily Apr-Sept, 9.30am-4.30pm Mon-Sat & 2pm-4.30pm Sun Oct-Mar), one of Scotland's best-known castles, was taken and lost by Edward I, held for David II against Edward III and fought over by everyone who passed this way. Not only was it repeatedly sacked, damaged and rebuilt over the centuries, but the unfortunate inhabitants of the Great Glen were also regularly pillaged and robbed in the process.

Destruction and reconstruction followed so regularly that it's hard to trace the full story of the castle's development. By the 1600s, it had become redundant, superseded by more palatial residences and more powerful fortresses at Fort William and Inverness. It was finally blown up in 1692 to prevent Jacobites using it, and its remains perch dramatically on the edge of the loch, approached by a steep path from the roadside car park.

The castle was entered by a drawbridge which led into the gatehouse. The summit of the upper bailey at the southern end was probably used as a hill-fort over 1000 years ago, but by the 15th century the lower bailey at the northern end had become the focus of fortifications. The five-storey tower house at the most northerly point is the most impressive remaining fragment and offers wonderful loch views.

Places to Stay & Eat

You can camp at **Borlum Farm Caravan & Camping Park** (☎ 450220), a half-mile (800m) south-east of Drumnadrochit, for £3 to £4 per person.

Loch Ness Backpackers Lodge (☎ 450807, e hostel@lochness-backpackers .com, Coiltie Farmhouse, East Lewiston) Dorm beds £9-9.50. This smart hostel lies within easy walking distance of both Drumnadrochit and Urquhart Castle.

Loch Ness Youth Hostel (☎ 01320-51274) Beds £8.25-7.25. This is the nearest SYHA hostel to Drumnadrochit, at Glenmoriston, 13 miles (21km) down the loch towards Fort Augustus.

In addition, Drumnadrochit boasts numerous B&Bs in the £16 to £20 per person price range, but single rooms are in short supply.

Drumbuie Farm (☎ 450634, Drumnadrochit) B&B £18-22 per person. Welcoming and comfortable Drumbuie Farm is on the right as you enter Drumnadrochit from Inverness. Dinner is available at a cost of £12.

Gillyflowers (☎/fax 450641, Drumnadrochit) B&B doubles £14-21 per person. This pleasant place is in a renovated 18th-century farmhouse.

Drumnadrochit Hotel (☎ 450202, fax 450793, Drumnadrochit) B&B £17.50-40 per person. The restaurant at the Drumnadrochit

Hotel is noted for its fine cuisine and service. They have well-appointed rooms too.

Near the Drumnadrochit village green are the *Glen Café Bar* (☎ *450282*) and the more expensive, nonsmoking *Fiddler's Café Bar* (☎ *450678*), which serves traditional Scottish fare and has a non-GM food policy.

Getting There & Away

Citylink runs five or six buses daily between Fort William (1½ hours) and Inverness (30 minutes) via Drumnadrochit; the one-way fare from Inverness to Urquhart Castle costs £4.50. From July to September, there are four additional daily services between Urquhart Castle and Inverness. Highland Country operates four to six weekday bus services from Inverness to Cannich and Tomich via Drumnadrochit.

FORT AUGUSTUS

☎ 01320 • pop 600

Fort Augustus, at the junction of four of General Wade's military roads, was the headquarters for his road-building operations in the early 18th century. Today it's overrun by tourists, but somehow still manages to convey a rather haunting medieval ambience. Look out for the bizarre Loch Ness Monster bush by the canal!

The TIC (☎ 366367), in the village car park, opens Easter to October. There's an ATM and a bureau de change (in the post office) beside the canal.

Cruises on Loch Ness on the *Royal Scot* (☎ *366277*) operate hourly between 10am and 7pm April to October. The 50-minute trip costs £6/3.

Fort Augustus Abbey

Between 1729 and 1742, as part of his plan to pacify the Highlands, General George Wade built a fort at the point where the River Tarff joined Loch Ness. Although it was captured, and later damaged, by the retreating Jacobites, it remained occupied until 1854. In 1876, Benedictine monks took over the building and founded Fort Augustus Abbey. The abbey closed down late in 1998, but in 2001 the **Abbey Cloisters & Gardens** *(Fort Augustus; adult/child £3/2;*

open 10am-5pm daily) were opened to the public. You can visit the monks' burial ground and there are great views along Loch Ness.

Caledonian Canal Locks

At Fort Augustus, boats using the Caledonian Canal are raised and lowered 13m by **five locks**. When the swing bridge is opened it can cause long delays on the busy A82. The promontory between the canal and the River Oich affords a fine view over Loch Ness.

Tiny **Cherry Island**, on the Inverness side of Fort Augustus, was originally a crannog (artificial island settlement).

The **Caledonian Canal Heritage Centre** (☎ *366493, admission free; open 10am-5pm daily)*, beside the lowest lock, showcases the history of the canal.

Places to Stay & Eat

Fort Augustus Caravan & Camping Park (☎ *366618*) is just south of the village, on the western side of the road to Fort William. It costs £4/2.50 per adult/child per night to camp here.

There's a wide choice of B&Bs in Fort Augustus in the £15-to-£20-per-person price bracket. These include *Appin* (☎ *366541, Inverness Rd)*, *Greystone's* (☎ *366736, Station Rd)*, *Kettle House* (☎ *366408, Golf Course Rd)* and *Caledonian House* (☎ *366236, Station Rd)*.

Lovat Arms Hotel (☎ *366206, Fort Augustus)* B&B from £35 per person. You'll find more upmarket accommodation at the three-star Lovat Arms Hotel.

The *Scots Kitchen* (☎ *366361*), opposite the village car park, offers cafe-style food, plus dishes such as steak and ale pie (£5.95). The *Bothy Restaurant* (☎ *366710*) does soups and steaks, with main courses ranging from £5.95 to £14.50.

Getting There & Away

Scottish Citylink runs five or six buses daily in each direction between Inverness and Fort William, stopping at Fort Augustus en route. The trip to either town takes an hour and costs £6.

FORT AUGUSTUS TO FORT WILLIAM

For 33 miles (53km), between Fort Augustus and Fort William, the A82 provides access to some of the forested glens and narrow lochs of the Lochaber region.

Achnacarry & Loch Arkaig

The B8004, between Banavie and Gairlochy, follows the western side of the Great Glen, with wonderful views of Ben Nevis. From Gairlochy, the B8005 turns north and follows the shore of Loch Lochy to the **Clan Cameron Museum** (☎ 01397-712480, Achnacarry; adult/child £3/free; open 1.30pm-5pm daily Easter, June, Sept & Oct, 11am-5pm Jul & Aug), which displays the history of the clan and its involvement with the Jacobite rebellions. Just to the west lies the lovely Loch Arkaig. By the road, at the mouth of Gleann Cia-aig, there's a series of spectacular waterfalls. From the road end, at the western end of the loch, it's possible to hike through the glens to Loch Nevis and Knoydart (it takes two days so you'll need a tent). There's no public transport beyond Achnacarry and hitching along the loch is difficult.

Glen Spean & Glen Roy

East of the **Commando Memorial** at Spean Bridge, which commemorates the WWII forces who trained in this area, lie these two valleys. They are noted for their intriguing 'parallel roads' – ancient terraced shorelines formed by the waters of an ice-dammed glacial lake during the last Ice Age. Whenever the dam burst, or otherwise allowed water to spill out, the level dropped and formed a new terrace. The best viewpoint is 3 miles (5km) up Glen Roy – drive, cycle or walk up the road.

The two main villages are Spean Bridge and Roybridge, both of which have post offices and shops.

Nevis Range

The Nevis Range **ski area** (☎ 01397-705825), 6 miles (10km) north of Fort William, skirts the upper slopes of Aonach Mór (1221m). The gondola to the top station

at 655m operates year-round, except November to Christmas, and costs £6.90/4.25 return (15 minutes each way). The **Snowgoose Restaurant**, at the top station, serves hearty inexpensive meals. There are walking routes from the Snowgoose and through nearby Leanachan Forest.

During the ski season, passes for the lift from the top station of the gondola cost £19.75/11 per day.

A new downhill **mountain bike trail** (mid-May to mid-September) – for experienced riders only – runs from the Snowgoose restaurant to the base station; bikes are carried on a rack on the gondola cabin. A single trip costs £9.25/6.75; a one-day pass is £15/11.50. You can hire bikes for £17.50/35 for a single trip/all day.

Places to Stay & Eat

Invergarry Hotel (☎ 01809-501206, fax 501400, Invergarry) Singles/doubles £40/70. This well-appointed Victorian coaching inn at Invergarry, on the western side of Loch Oich, has a good restaurant (dinner £18).

Lundie View Guest House (☎/fax 01809-501291, Invergarry) B&B £20-30 per person. Set in a former gamekeeper's cottage, this charming B&B offers excellent cooked breakfasts, including vegetarian options.

Loch Lochy Youth Hostel (☎ 01809-501239, South Laggan) Beds £8.50/7.25. Open Apr-Oct. This SYHA hostel is at South Laggan, at the northern end of Loch Lochy. There's a grocery shop a mile (1.6km) north at The Well of the Seven Heads.

Smiddy House Guest House (☎ 01397-712335, fax 712043, Spean Bridge) B&B £22.50 per person. One of the best places in Spean Bridge is this guesthouse and bistro, next to the old village blacksmith's workshop. The bistro menu includes ample vegetarian choices (all meals around £8).

Roybridge Inn Hostel (☎ 01397-712236, Roybridge) Beds £9-10. This independent hostel (with bar), also known as the Grey Corrie Lodge, is in Roybridge, 4 miles (6.5km) east of Spean Bridge.

Àite Cruinnichidh (☎ 01397-712315, Achluachrach) Beds £8-12. Two miles

(3km) east of Roybridge at Achluachrach is this recommended hostel, with beds in a converted barn. Phone for free pick-up from Roybridge train station.

Station Lodge Bunkhouse (☎ *01397-732333)* Beds £10, including linen. Five miles (8km) east of Roybridge is the Station Lodge Bunkhouse, at Tulloch Station – it's in the original station building, dating from 1894. There's a kitchen, but meals (including vegetarian dishes) are available.

Getting There & Away
Highland Country (☎ 01397-702373) has services from Fort William to Achnacarry, Nevis Range, Spean Bridge and Roybridge. Scottish Citylink buses connect Fort William with Spean Bridge, Invergarry, Skye and Inverness. The railway from Fort William to Glasgow has stops at Spean Bridge and Roybridge.

WEST OF INVERNESS
Beauly
☎ 01463 • pop 1800
In 1584, Mary Queen of Scots is said to have given this village its name when she exclaimed, in French, '*quel beau lieu*' (what a beautiful place).

Beauly has supermarkets, banks with ATMs, and a couple of camping grounds.

The red sandstone **Beauly Priory** (☎ *01667-460232; adult/child £1.20/50p; open 9.30am-6.30pm daily mid-June–Sept)* was founded in 1230 and is now an impressive ruin; for access, you'll need to get the key from the Priory Hotel.

Priory Hotel (☎ *782309, fax 782531,* e *reservations@priory-hotel.com, The Square)* Singles £39.50-47.50, doubles £59-90. The attractive and centrally located Priory has an excellent restaurant.

For B&B, try *Ellangowan* (☎ *782273, Croyard Rd)*, which charges £14-16 per person in a double or twin room.

The aptly named *Friary* does fish and chips, and *Beauly Tandoori* on the other side of The Square does curries.

Stagecoach Inverness runs hourly services daily (four on Sunday) from Dingwall and Inverness (£2.90).

Strathglass & Glen Affric
Strathglass (a broad valley) extends about 18 miles (29km) inland from Beauly. Several long and narrow glens lead into the hills from Strathglass, including **Glen Affric**, one of the most beautiful glens in Scotland. All the glens have hydro-electric schemes, but Loch Affric is unaffected. The upper reaches of Glen Affric, owned by the NTS, offer lots of great walking, both in the glens and on the mountain ridges.

The only village in the area is **Cannich**, where there's a Spar shop and a post office.

Things to See & Do About 5 miles (8km) west of Beauly, at the Aigas Dam on the River Beauly, there's a **fish lift** *(open 10am-3pm Mon-Fri mid-June–early-Oct)* where you can watch migrating salmon take advantage of a dam bypass.

There's a parking area and picnic site at the eastern end of **Loch Affric**, from which there are several short **walks** down the river and the loch. You can make a superb circular walk (10 miles/16km, allow five hours) right around the loch on good paths, taking you into the heart of some very wild scenery

It's possible to walk all the way from Cannich to Loch Duich on the west coast (35 miles/56km in total) in two days, spending the night at the remote Glen Affric Youth Hostel (see Places to Stay & Eat).

Places to Stay & Eat You can camp at *Cannich Caravan Park* (☎ *01456-415364, Cannich)* for £6 per tent.

There are also several hostels serving the many hikers who visit this area, including the SYHA's *Cannich Youth Hostel* (☎ *01456-415244, Cannich)* with beds for £8.25/7.25 (open May-Oct), and the independent *Glen Affric Backpackers* (☎ *01456-415263, Cannich)*, with beds for £6.

Glen Affric Youth Hostel (0870 155 3255) Dorm beds £8.75/7.50. Open May-Oct. The remote Glen Affric Youth Hostel is set among magnificent scenery and is the halfway point on a cross-country walk from Cannich to Ratagan hostel on the west coast Booking is recommended; call the SYHA reservations number provided.

Cougie Lodge (☎ 01320-351354) Beds £8. This remote lodge is 9 miles (14km) south-west of Cannich and would make a good overnight stop between Cannich and Glen Affric Youth Hostel. You can also camp here for £5.

The *Slaters Arms* (☎ 01456-415215, *Crannich*) does good bar meals, with mains & vegetarian options from £4.

Tomich Hotel (☎ 01456-415399, fax 415469) Singles £42-53, doubles £54-74. The Tomich Hotel, a Victorian hunting lodge about 3 miles (5km) south-west of Cannich on the southern side of the river, is a good place to eat. It has eight comfortable, en-suite rooms, and a small, heated, indoor swimming pool.

Getting There & Away Ross's Minibuses (☎ 01463-761250) runs two buses a day on Tuesday, Friday and Saturday from Inverness and Beauly to Cannich (1¼ hours). Some runs extend as far as Tomich.

Black Isle

A peninsula rather than an island, the Black Isle is linked to Inverness by the modern **Kessock Bridge**.

Fortrose & Rosemarkie At **Fortrose Cathedral**, you'll find the vaulted crypt of a 13th-century chapter house and sacristy, plus ruinous 14th-century southern aisle and chapel. Chanonry Point, a mile (1.6km) and a half to the east, is a favourite dolphin-spotting vantage point.

In Rosemarkie, the **Groam House Museum** (☎ 01381-620961; *adult/child £1.50/ 50p; open 10am-5pm Mon-Sat & 2pm-4.30pm Sun Easter & May-Sept, 2pm-4pm Sat & Sun in winter*) has a superb collection of Pictish stones engraved with designs similar to those on Celtic Irish stones.

The short but pleasant **Fairy Glen walk** starts at the northern end of High St, in Rosemarkie. The signposted trail leads you through gorges with waterfalls.

Both Fortrose and Rosemarkie have shops and post offices. Fortrose also has a bank with an ATM and the *Royal Hotel* (☎/fax 01381-620236, *Union St*), which offers B&B for £37.50 to £50 per person.

Crofters (☎ 01381-620844), on the waterfront in Rosemarkie, has bar meals from around £4.50.

Cromarty The Cromarty Firth, north of the Black Isle, is famous for the huge offshore oil rigs which are built or repaired at Nigg before being towed out to the North Sea.

At the Black Isle's north-eastern end, the pretty village of Cromarty has many fascinating 18th-century stone houses, with several offering B&B. The village has two stores, a post office and a bank (without ATM).

The 18th-century **Cromarty Courthouse** (☎ 01381-600418, *Church St; adult/child £3/2; open 10am-5pm daily Apr-Oct & noon-4pm daily Nov, Dec & March, closed Jan & Feb*) has a thoroughly interesting local history museum. The admission cost includes an audio tour of Cromarty's other historic buildings (also available in French).

Next to the Courthouse is **Hugh Miller's Cottage** (*NTS;* ☎ 01381-600245, *Cromarty; adult/child £2.50/1; open 11am-1pm & 2pm-5pm Mon-Sat & 2pm-5pm Sun May-Sept*). Miller (1802–56) was a local stonemason and amateur geologist who later moved to Edinburgh and became a famous journalist and newspaper editor.

From Cromarty Harbour, *Dolphin Ecosse* (☎ 01381-600323) runs boat trips to see bottlenose dolphins and other wildlife. The 2½ hour trips cost £15 per person, a full-day cruise (four to five hours) is £50.

Several places offer B&B from £16 a head, including *Mrs Robertson* (☎ 01381-600488, *7 Church St*). For something to eat, try the pleasant *Country Kitchen* tearoom on the corner of Church St and Forsyth Place (closed Monday), or the *Cromarty Arms* (☎ 01381-600230, *Church St*), a good pub with bar meals and live music; it's opposite the court house.

Getting There & Away Highland Country (☎ 01463-233371) runs a daily bus service (except Sunday) from Inverness to Fortrose and Rosemarkie. Some buses continue to Cromarty (£4.70, 55 minutes).

East Coast

The east coast starts to get interesting once you leave behind the industrial tow of Invergordon. Beyond this, great heather-covered hills heave themselves out of the wild North Sea, with pleasant little towns moored precariously at their edge. The scenery is particularly lovely around the Dornoch Firth and Kyle of Sutherland.

STRATHPEFFER
☎ 01997 • pop 1385

Eighteen miles (29km) north-west of Inverness is the charming village of Strathpeffer. The village was a fashionable spa in Victorian and Edwardian times – it was advertised as the 'Harrogate of the North' – and many grand houses and hotels survive. The spa slipped into decline after WWII and the spa baths were demolished in 1950. There are plans to renovate the concert pavilion, opposite the TIC.

The TIC (☎ 421415), on The Square, opens 9am to 5pm Monday to Saturday and 10am to 4pm Sunday Easter to October. You'll find a Spar shop and a post office nearby. In summer, there's Highland dancing and bagpipe playing in the square.

The newly renovated **Pump Room** (☎ 420124, Strathpeffer; adult/child £2.50/1; open 10am-5pm Mon-Fri Apr-Oct), just across the main road from the TIC, is where the spa visitors gathered in the mornings to sample the waters. There's an interesting exhibition on the various spa treatments and a chance to taste the waters yourself. The chalybeate (iron-rich) spring water is delicious, but the sulphurous Morrison Well is pretty whiffy – imagine swigging a pint of this stuff every morning!

About half a mile (800m) downhill from the TIC, at the old Victorian train station, is the **Highland Museum of Childhood** (☎ 421031; adult/child £1.50/free; open 10am-5pm Mon-Sat, 1pm-5pm Sun Mar-Oct, plus 7pm-9pm July & Aug). It has a wide range of social history displays about childhood in the Highlands, from birth to school and child labour. It has a collection of dolls, toys, games and train sets.

Walking

There are many good **walking trails** around Strathpeffer, a legacy of the days when brisk exercise was prescribed as part of the treatment for spa patients. One of the best of these follows the old carriage drive up to the remains of an Iron Age fort on Knock Farril (4½ miles/7km, two hours).

Ben Wyvis (1046m), a bulky Munro which looms to the north-west, is usually climbed from Garbat, about 15 miles (24km) west of Strathpeffer on the A835 road to Ullapool.

Places to Stay & Eat

Strathpeffer Youth Hostel (☎ 421532) Dorm beds £9/7.75. Open May-Sept. This SYHA hostel is at the southern end of the village, five minutes' walk uphill from the TIC.

Craigvar (☎ 421622, The Square) B&B £25-30 per person. This is a deluxe B&B in a delightful Georgian town house.

Scoraig (☎ 421847, 8 Kinnettas Square) £15-25 per person. For somewhere cheaper try Scoraig.

Highland Hotel (☎ 421457, fax 421033) Two night breaks for £50 per person. Many of the old spa hotels have fallen into neglect, but this one has been taken over and renovated. It's a magnificent, European chateau-style building overlooking the TIC, with a wood-panelled lobby and lounge, plus lovely wooded grounds.

The **Museum Tearoom**, housed in the Victorian train station building next to the Highland Museum of Childhood, has tables out on the platform (there are no rails now, just flowers!). It is a pleasant place for tea and shortbread (£1.05).

Getting There & Away

Stagecoach Inverness operates an hourly service Monday to Saturday from Inverness to Strathpeffer.

The Inverness to Gairloch and Durness buses, plus some Inverness to Ullapool buses, run via Strathpeffer.

CROMARTY FIRTH

Sir Hector Munro, a military hero, commemorated his most notable victory, the capture of the Indian town of Negapatam in 1781, by erecting the **Fyrish Monument**, a replica of the Indian town's gateway, high above nearby Evanton. Turn towards Boath off the B9176; from the car park, the monument is a 45-minute walk along the Jubilee Path.

From Evanton, you can walk a mile (1.6km) west to the **Black Rock of Novar**, an amazingly narrow gorge, rarely more than 3.5m wide but up to 30m deep (2½ miles/4km, one hour).

Invergordon, near the mouth of the firth, is the main Scottish centre for repairing North Sea oil rigs.

The church in **Nigg** village contains a fine Pictish carved stone. It opens 10am to 4.30pm (to 5pm Sunday) Easter to October.

TAIN
☎ 01862 • pop 4119

Tain's High St has the usual shops, a post office and banks (the Royal Bank of Scotland has an ATM). Turn down Castle Brae for the train station.

Things to See

Tain was a centre for the management of the Highland Clearances and has a curious 17th-century **tolbooth**, which was originally court offices and a jail. St Duthac was born in Tain, died in Armagh (Ireland) in 1065, and is commemorated by the 12th-century ruins of **St Duthac's Chapel**, as well as by St Duthus Church.

The church is now part of the **Tain Through Time** (☎ 894089; adult/child £3.50/2.50; open 10am-6pm daily Apr-Oct, phone to find out winter opening hours) heritage centre, which describes the history of Tain as a place of pilgrimage.

On the northern edge of town is the **Glenmorangie Distillery and Visitor Centre** (☎ 892477; adult/child £2/free; open 9am-5pm Mon-Fri year-round, plus 10am-4pm Sat & noon-4pm Sun June-Aug); there are regular guided tours of the distillery from 10.30am to 3.30pm.

Places to Stay

St Duthus Hotel (☎ 894007, Tower St), at the western end of High St, does B&B for £20 per person. The *Morangie House Hotel*

(☎ 892281, fax 892872, Morangie Rd) is posher, with singles/doubles from £60/90. There are cheaper B&Bs all along Morangie Rd.

Getting There & Away

Citylink buses from Inverness to Thurso pass through Tain. There are three trains daily (two on summer Sundays) to Inverness (£8.30, one hour) and Thurso (£10.60, 2½ hours).

PORTMAHOMACK
☎ 01862 • pop 608

This small place used to be a busy fishing village, but it's now a quiet and relaxing place with a shop, post office and two hotels for bar meals.

The **Tarbat Discovery Centre** (☎ 871351, Tarbatness Rd; adult/child 3.50/1; open 10am-5.30pm daily May-Sept, 2pm-5pm daily Mar, Apr & Oct-Dec), in Tarbat Church, covers Pictish and early Christian archaeological finds. Nearby **Fearn Abbey** looks great when floodlit at night.

There are good coastal walks at **Tarbat Ness**, 3 miles (4.5km) north-east of the village; the headland is marked by a tall, red-and-white striped lighthouse.

Caledonian Hotel (☎ 872345, fax 871757, Main St) Singles £29-35, doubles £45-59. The friendly and comfortable Caley overlooks the village's sandy beach and has a good restaurant.

Oyster Catcher Restaurant (☎ 871560, Main St) Snacks from £2, mains £6-10. Open 11am-6pm & 7pm-8.30pm daily Mar-Jan. This bright and cheerful restaurant does inexpensive snacks during the day and bistro meals in the evening.

Local buses run from Tain to Portmahomack (seven daily Monday to Friday).

BONAR BRIDGE & AROUND

The A9 crosses the Dornoch Firth, on a bridge and causeway, near Tain. An alternative route goes around the inner end of the firth via the tiny settlements of **Ardgay**, where you'll find a train station, shop and a hotel, and **Bonar Bridge**, where the A836 road to Lairg branches west.

From Ardgay, a single-track road leads 10 miles (16km) up Strathcarron to **Croick**, the scene of notorious evictions during the 1845 Clearances. You can still see the sad messages scratched by refugee crofters from Glencalvie on the eastern windows of Croick Church.

Carbisdale Castle Youth Hostel (☎ 01549-421232, Culrain) Beds £13.50/11.25, plus £50p/£1.25 in July & Aug. Open Mar-Oct. Carbisdale Castle was built in 1914 for the Dowager Duchess of Sutherland and given to the SYHA in 1943. It is now Scotland's biggest and most opulent youth hostel, its halls studded with statues. It's 10 minutes' walk north of Culrain train station. Advance bookings are recommended.

There are three buses daily (not Sunday) from Inverness to Lairg via Ardgay and Bonar Bridge. Trains between Inverness and Thurso stop at Ardgay and Culrain (half a mile/800m from Carbisdale Castle) two or three times daily.

LAIRG
☎ 01549 • pop 904

Lairg, at the southern end of Loch Shin, is the gateway to the remote mountains and lochan-speckled bogs of central Sutherland. From here, single-track roads run north to Tongue, Laxford Bridge (between Durness and Kylesku) and Ledmore (between Kylesku and Ullapool). The A836 from Lairg to Tongue passes Ben Klibreck (961m) and Ben Loyal (764m). Ben Hope (927m) lies just to the west, at the head of Loch Hope.

From June to September, just south of Lairg, you can watch salmon leaping the **Falls of Shin** on their way upstream to spawn.

Lairg has a seasonal (April to September) TIC (☎ 402160) at Ferrycroft Countryside Centre (on the far side of the river from the village), shops, a bank (with ATM), a post office and a camp site.

Crask Inn (☎ 411241, Crask) B&B £20 per person. The small (three rooms) and remote Crask Inn, 13 miles (21km) north of Lairg on the A836, is notorious for being the coldest place in Scotland. In December 1995 a record low of –30°C was recorded here, but peat-burning stoves and central heating keep it cosy. Roast venison is often on the menu (dinner £8.50).

Sleeperzzz (☎ 01408-641343, ⓦ www.sleeperzzz.com, Rogart Station) Beds £9, 10% discount for cyclists and train travellers. Open Mar-Nov. Nine miles (14.5km) east of Lairg, at Rogart train station, is this charming and unique hostel. Ten compartments in two first-class railway carriages have been fitted with two comfortable bunks each; there's also an old two-bed gypsy caravan to let. Bike hire is free to guests.

The *Nip Inn (☎ 402243, Main St)* does B&B for £22 to £27 per person and bar meals from £5.50. The *Shin Fry*, also on Main St, is a fish and chip shop.

Getting There & Around

Trains from Inverness to Thurso stop at Lairg (£10,40, 1½ hours) and Rogart (£10.40, 1¾ hours) two or three times daily in each direction.

Stagecoach Inverness buses run from Inverness to Lairg (£7, two hours) via Tain from Monday to Saturday. Postbus services (☎ 01463-256228) connect Lairg with Rogart once daily Monday to Saturday.

DORNOCH
☎ 01862 • pop 1000

On the coast, 2 miles (3km) off the A9, Dornoch is a pleasant seaside town and golfing resort.

The TIC (☎ 810400), in the main square, opens 9am to 5pm Monday to Saturday (till 6pm July and August), 11am to 4pm Sunday (from 10am July and August) April to October, plus Monday to Friday only from December to March.

The town is clustered around the 13th-century **Dornoch Cathedral**. The original building was destroyed in 1570 during a clan feud. Despite some patching up, it wasn't completely rebuilt until 1837. The last witch to be burned in Scotland was set alight in Dornoch in 1722. Nowadays, the town is famous for its **championship golf course** (☎ 810283), which lies immediately south of the town on Golf Rd.

South of Dornoch, seals are often visible on the sand bars of **Dornoch Firth**. North of

Dornoch, the A9 crosses the head of **Loch Fleet** on the Mound, an embankment built by Thomas Telford between 1815 and 1816. Look out for seals and wading birds here.

Dornoch has several camping grounds and plenty of B&Bs.

Dornoch Castle Hotel (☎ *810216, fax 810981, Castle St*) B&B £25-50 per person. You can dine in style at the restaurant (dinner £22) in this grand 16th-century former Bishop's Palace.

Mallin House (☎ *810335, Church St*) B&B £29-35 per person. This place, five minutes' walk south of High St past the Dornoch Inn, has a superb restaurant (mains £16.95 to £19.95; bar meals £5.95-10.90). It is only open for dinner, except on Sundays when it lays on a traditional Sunday lunch for £5.95.

The *Sutherland House* (☎ *811023, High St*) pub, just off the square, has good bar meals from £4.95 to £7.50.

Citylink buses between Inverness and Thurso stop in Dornoch three to five times daily.

GOLSPIE
☎ 01408 • pop 1647
Golspie is basically one street and a beach, with a couple of supermarkets, banks and a post office. It's the starting point for a couple of good walks. One leads north along the coast for 5 miles (8km) to Brora, passing the remains of the Iron Age *broch* (circular fortified tower) of **Carn Liath** about half way. The other climbs steeply above the village to the summit of **Ben Bhraggie** (394m), which is crowned by a massive monument to the duke of Sutherland, erected in 1834 and visible for miles around.

Dunrobin Castle
One mile (1.6km) north of Golspie is Dunrobin Castle (☎ *01408-633177; adult/child £6/4.50; open 10.30am-4.30pm Mon-Sat & noon-4.30pm Sun Apr, May & Oct, 10.30am-5.30pm daily June-Sept*), the largest house in the Highlands (187 rooms). Although it dates back to around 1275 and additions were made in the mid-1600s and late 1700s, most of what you see today was built in French style between 1845 and 1850. One of the

homes of the earls and dukes of Sutherland, it's richly furnished and offers an intriguing insight into their opulent lifestyle.

Judging by the numerous hunting trophies and animal skins, much of the family's energy seems to have gone into shooting things. The house also displays innumerable gifts from farm tenants (probably grateful that they hadn't been asked to join in the Sutherlands' Clearance activities). Behind the house, magnificent formal gardens slope down to the sea, and a summer house offers an eclectic museum of archaeological finds, natural-history exhibits and more big-game trophies.

Getting There & Away
Buses and trains between Inverness and Thurso stop in Golspie (£11.40, two hours, three Monday to Saturday, two Sunday).

BRORA
☎ 01408 • pop 1860
Located at the mouth of a river famed for its salmon, Brora has a fine beach, but parts of the village could do with improvement. The village has two small supermarkets, a bank and a post office. The golf course has a good reputation.

On the northern edge of town is **Clynelish Distillery** (☎ *623000, Brora; tours £3; open 9.30am-4.30pm Mon-Fri Mar-Oct, by arrangement Nov-Feb*), the most northerly distillery in mainland Scotland.

There are camp sites nearby and plenty of B&Bs in town; contact the TIC at Durnoch for details.

Royal Marine Hotel (☎ *621252, fax 621181, Golf Rd*) Singles £85-105, doubles £98-138. Leisure facilities at the plush Royal Marine include an excellent restaurant, a swimming pool and a curling rink. Salmon fishing is available for residents for £10 per day.

Cheaper snacks and meals can be found at the *Fountain Café* and the *Golden Fry* in the village centre.

Helmsdale
☎ 01431 • pop 861
Helmsdale, with its pretty harbour and salmon river, is a busy place in summer.

THE HIGHLANDS

Crofting & the Clearances

Many Highland settlements are described as crofting communities. The word croft comes from the Gaelic *croitean*, meaning a small enclosed field.

Highland land was generally owned by clan chiefs until the early 19th century, and their tenants farmed land on the 'run-rig' system – in other words, the land was divided into strips which were shared among the tenants. The strips were periodically shuffled around so no tenant was stuck with bad land or always enjoyed the good land. Unfortunately, it also meant they might end up with several widely scattered strips and there was no incentive to improve them because tenants knew they would soon lose them. Accordingly, the system was changed and the land rented out to the tenants as small 'crofts', averaging about 1.2 hectares. Each tenant then built their own house on their croft and the former tight cluster of homes spread out. Crofters could also pasture their animals on the common grazings, land which was jointly held by all the local crofters.

Crofting remained a precarious lifestyle. The small patch of land each crofter rented barely provided a living and each year the tenancy could be terminated with the crofter losing not only the croft but the house they had built on it. During the Highland Clearances, that was precisely what happened. Following the ban on private armies, clan chiefs no longer needed large numbers of tenants and many decided sheep farming was more profitable than collecting rent from poverty-stricken crofters. The guidebook to Dunrobin Castle, seat of the Sutherland family, blithely notes that they 'proceeded to make large-scale improvements to Sutherland's communications, land and townships which involved the clearance of some 5000 people from their ancestral dwellings'.

Despite the Clearances, a number of crofters remained and when the economic depression of the late 19th century hit, many couldn't pay their rent. This time, however, they resisted expulsion, instead forming the Highland Land Reform Association and their own political party. The resistance led to several of the crofters' demands being acceded to by the government, including security of tenure, fair rents and eventually the supply of land for new crofts. Crofting tenancies still exist today and complex regulations now protect the crofters.

There are three stores, a bank and a post office. For tourist information, go to the Timespan Heritage Centre.

The excellent **Timespan Heritage Centre** (☎ 821327, Dunrobin St; adult/child £3.50/1.75; open 9.30am-5pm Mon-Sat & 2pm-5pm Sun Easter-June & Sept–mid-Oct, 9.30am-6pm daily July & Aug) has details of the 1869 Strath of Kildonan gold rush and a model of Barbara Cartland, the late queen of pulp romance novels (she holidayed here for over 60 years).

Strathullie Crafts & Fishing Tackle (☎ 821343), Dunrobin St, can organise **fishing** on the river for around £20 per day, plus rod hire is available at £15 per day. The shop also rents out **gold-panning** kits (trowel, riddle and pan) for £2.50 per day, but you'll also need rubber boots, a shovel and lots of determination. Licences are free. Small quantities of gold are still found in the Kildonan Burn at Baile an Or ('town of gold'), about a mile (1.6km) from Kildonan train station.

There are several B&Bs and a hostel in town.

Helmsdale Youth Hostel (☎ 821577, On the corner of the A9 and Old Caithness Rd) Beds £7.50/6.25. Open mid-May–Sept. This place, at the northern end of the village, gets busy; book well ahead for July and August.

Nancy Sinclair, proprietor of **La Mirage** fish and chip restaurant on Dunrobin St, is a huge fan of Barbara Cartland, and the chip shop is a shrine to all things pink and fluffy. Haddock and chips costs £5.95 here.

Bunillidh Restaurant (☎ 821457, Dunrobin St) £6.50-12. Across the street from La Mirage, this restaurant serves seafood, venison and vegetarian dishes.

The **Belgrave Arms Hotel** (☎ 821242), on the corner of Dunrobin St and the A9 does B&B from £17 per person.

Buses and trains between Inverness and Thurso stop in Helmsdale (£11.40, 2½ hours, three Monday to Saturday, two Sunday).

HELMSDALE TO LATHERON
North of Helmsdale, the road climbs to a fine viewpoint at the **Ord of Caithness**. About 7 miles (11km) north of Helmsdale a 15-minute walk east from the A9 (signposted) takes you to **Badbea**, where the ruins of crofts are perched on the cliff top. The **Berriedale Braes**, 2½ miles (4km) beyond the Badbea parking area, is a difficult section of the A9, with steep gradients and hairpin bends.

Dunbeath, a pleasant village in a deep glen, has a couple of shops and a **heritage centre** (☎ 01593-731233, The Old School; adult/child £1.50/50p; open 11am-5pm daily Apr-Sept), with displays about the history of Caithness, including crofting and fisheries.

The **Dunbeath Hotel** (☎ 01593-731208, fax 731242) has singles/doubles for £42/68. The bar meals here are excellent.

Just north of Dunbeath, the **Laidhay Croft Museum** (☎ 01593-731244, ¾ mile/1.2km north of Dunbeath on the A9; adult/child £1/50p; open 10am-5pm daily Apr-Oct), in a restored traditional long-house, recreates crofting life from the mid-1800s to WWII. Its tearoom serves good home baking and soup.

At the **Clan Gunn Heritage Centre & Museum** (☎ 015932-731370, Latheron; adult/child £1.50/75p; open 11am-5pm Mon-Sat June-Sept, plus 2pm-5pm Sun July & Aug), in Latheron, 3 miles (4.5km) north of Dunbeath on the A9, you learn that it was really a Scot, not Christopher Columbus, who discovered America.

LYBSTER & AROUND
☎ 01593
Lybster is a purpose-built fishing village and harbour dating from 1810. Its herring fishing days are long since gone, but the harbour is still home to some working fishing boats. Overlooking the harbour is the **Waterlines Visitor Centre** (☎ 721520, Lybster; admission free; open 11am-5pm daily May-Sept), with a heritage exhibition, a boat-builder's workshop, and CCTV beaming live pictures of nesting seabirds from nearby cliffs.

At Ulbster, 5 miles (8km) north of Lybster on the A9, is **Whaligoe Steps**, a spectacular staircase cut into the cliff face giving access to a tiny natural harbour ringed by vertical cliffs and echoing with the cackle of nesting fulmars. The path begins at the end of the minor road beside the telephone box, opposite the road signposted 'Cairn of Get'.

There are several interesting prehistoric sites near Lybster. Five miles (8km) to the north-west of Lybster, on the minor road to Achavanich, just south of Loch Stemster, are the 40 or so **Achavanich Standing Stones**.

A mile (1.6km) east of Lybster on the A9, a turn-off leads north to the **Grey Cairns of Camster**. Dating from between 4000 and 2500 BC, these burial chambers are hidden in long, low mounds rising from an evocatively desolate stretch of moor. The Long Cairn measures 200 feet by 70 feet (61m by 21m). You can enter the main chamber, but must first crawl into the well-preserved **Round Cairn**. The Round Cairn has a corbelled ceiling. Afterwards, you can continue 7 miles (11km) north on this remote road to approach Wick on the A882.

Back on the A9, the **Hill o'Many Stanes**, another 2 miles (3.5km) beyond the Camster turn-off, is a curious, fan-shaped arrangement of 22 rows of small stones probably dating from around 2000 BC. Nearer to Wick, at Ulbster, the **Cairn o'Get**, a prehistoric burial cairn, lies 1 mile (1.6km) northwest of Ulbster.

Portland Arms Hotel (☎ 721721, fax 721722, e portland.arms@btconnect.com, Lybster) Singles £45-55, doubles £58-80. The warm and welcoming Portland Arms, on the A9 main road in Lybster, has stylish, snug rooms and an excellent restaurant.

Getting There & Away
Citylink buses between Inverness and Thurso run via Dunbeath, Latheron and Lybster three to five times daily. Highland Country Buses run three or four times daily from Wick to Ulbster, Lybster, Dunbeath and Berriedale.

WICK
☎ 01955 • pop 8000

Wick, with its boarded-up buildings, hasn't always been so dismal. A century ago, it was the world's largest herring fishing port, its harbour crammed with fishing boats as well as larger ships to carry barrels of salted herring abroad, and thousands of seasonal workers streaming into town to pack the catch. After WWI, the herring began to disappear, and by WWII the industry had died.

Wick's massive harbour was the work of the engineer and canal pioneer Thomas Telford, who also designed Pulteneytown, the model town commissioned by the engagingly named British Society for Extending the Fisheries and Improving the Sea Coasts of the Kingdom. A failed attempt to add a breakwater was the work of Thomas Stevenson, father of author Robert Louis Stevenson.

Information
The TIC (☎ 602596) is on Whitechapel Rd, the road leading to the Safeway supermarket car park off High St. It opens 9.30am to 5pm Monday to Saturday and 11am to 4pm Sunday in July and August; 10am to 4pm Monday to Saturday April to June and September (till 5pm Monday to Saturday plus noon to 4pm Sunday in June); and 11am to 4.30pm Monday to Friday October to March.

Wick Heritage Centre
The town's award-winning local museum (☎ 605393, Bank Row; adult/child £2/50p; open 10am-5pm Mon-Sat May-Sept) deserves all the praise heaped upon it. It tracks the rise and fall of the herring industry, and displays everything from fishing equipment to complete herring fishing boats.

The Johnston photographic collection is the museum's star exhibit. From 1863 to 1977, three generations of Johnstons photographed everything that happened around Wick, and the 70,000 photographs are an amazing portrait of the town's life. The museum even displays the Johnstons' photo studio. Prints of their superb early photos are for sale.

Other Things to See
A path leads a mile (1.6km) south of town to the ruins of 12th-century Old Wick Castle, with the spectacular sea cliffs of the Brough and the Brig, as well as Gote o'Trams, a little farther south. In good weather, it's a fine coastal walk to the castle, but take care on the final approach. Three miles (4.5km) north-east of Wick is the magnificently located cliff-top ruin of Castle Sinclair.

Just past Wick airport, on the northern side of town, you can watch the glass-blowing operations at the Caithness Glass Visitors Centre (☎ 602286, Wick; admission free; open 9am-4.30pm Mon-Fri year-round). The shop opens 9am to 5pm Monday to Saturday year-round plus 11am to 5pm Sunday Easter to December.

Places to Stay
Riverside Caravan Club Site (☎ 605420, Riverside Drive) Pitches £4-11. This site is a half-mile (800m) west of the town centre, on the road to Thurso.

Wellington Guest House (☎ 603287, 41 High St) B&B £19-25 per person. This place has rooms with en-suite bathroom and is just around the corner from the TIC.

Quayside (☎ 603229, 25 Harbour Quay) B&B £16-22 per person. This B&B is down by the harbour. Dinner is available for an extra £6.95.

Clachan (☎ 605384, South Rd) Singles/ doubles from £25/40. The Clachan, on the A9 at the southern edge of town, is recommended.

MacKays Hotel (☎ 602323, fax 605930, Union St) Singles/doubles £45/70. The recently renovated MacKays is the best hotel in Wick. The 2.75m-long Ebenezer Place, the shortest street in Britain, runs past one end of the hotel. A four-course dinner is available for £18.50.

Places to Eat
Wick is hardly a gourmet's paradise, but there is at least one restaurant worth seeking out – the Bord de L'Eau.

Bord de L'Eau (☎ 604400, 2 Market St) Mains £5.75-11.95. Open noon-2.30pm & 6pm-10.30pm Tues-Sun. This new and up-market French restaurant, overlooking the

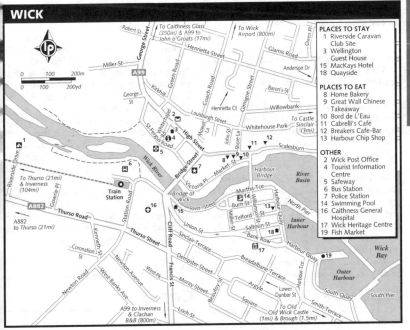

WICK

PLACES TO STAY
1 Riverside Caravan Club Site
3 Wellington Guest House
15 MacKays Hotel
18 Quayside

PLACES TO EAT
8 Home Bakery
9 Great Wall Chinese Takeaway
10 Bord de L'Eau
11 Cabrelli's Café
12 Breakers Cafe-Bar
13 Harbour Chip Shop

OTHER
2 Wick Post Office
4 Tourist Information Centre
5 Safeway
6 Bus Station
7 Police Station
14 Swimming Pool
16 Caithness General Hospital
17 Wick Heritage Centre
19 Fish Market

river, serves dishes such as *escargots*, and red snapper with a chive and shallot butter sauce.

Cabrelli's Café (☎ 603155, 134 High St) Mains from £2.60. They do good burgers and pasta dishes here, as well as fish teas (fish, chips, bread and butter, a cup of tea) for £4.99.

The *Harbour Chip Shop* (Harbour Quay) does a fish supper for £3, and the *Home Bakery* (High St) has snacks and baked potatoes from £1; it opens 9am to 4pm Monday to Saturday (to 1.30pm Wednesday). Just along the street, you'll find the *Great Wall Chinese Takeaway*. *Breakers Cafe-Bar*, down on The Shore, is another place worth trying for lunch.

Getting There & Away
Wick airport is served by direct flights from Aberdeen, Edinburgh and Shetland.

There are regular bus and train services from Inverness to Wick and on to Thurso; see the Inverness section earlier in this chapter for details. Highland Country Buses

(☎ 01847-893123) runs the connecting service to John o'Groats for the passenger ferry to Burwick, Orkney.

JOHN O'GROATS
☎ 01955 • pop 512
Sadly, the coastline most people see at the country's far north-eastern tip is not particularly dramatic, and modern John o'Groats is little more than a big car park and tourist trap. Its name comes from Jan de Groot, one of three brothers commissioned by James IV to operate a ferry service to Orkney in 1496.

The TIC (☎ 611373), beside the car park, opens 10am to 5pm Monday to Saturday and 10am to 5pm Sunday, April to October. There are also souvenir shops, a post office, a fish and chip shop and a crafts complex.

Two miles (3km) east of John o'Groats is **Duncansby Head**, home to many seabirds at the start of summer. A path leads to **Duncansby Stacks**, spectacular natural rock formations soaring over 60m above the sea.

There is a series of narrow inlets and deep coves on this wonderful stretch of coast.

Places to Stay & Eat

John o'Groats Caravan & Camping Site (☎ 611329) £7.50 for a car and tent. Open Apr-Oct. This site is right beside the car park and ferry pier.

John o'Groats Youth Hostel (☎ 611424, Canisbay) Beds £8.50/7.25. Open May-Sept. This SYHA hostel is 3 miles (5km) west of John o'Groats at Canisbay.

There are several B&Bs in John o'Groats itself and at nearby Canisbay. The **Caberfeidh Guest House** (☎ 611219), at the road junction in John o'Groats, does B&B for £15 per person; the **Seaview Hotel** (☎ 611220), across the road, charges £14.50 and does breakfast, lunch and dinner for nonresidents.

Groats Inn, adjacent to John o'Groats House Hotel, serves pizzas. The dilapidated **John o'Groats House Hotel** was closed for renovation at the time of research.

Getting There & Away

Bus Highland Country Buses runs up to seven buses daily (Monday to Saturday year-round plus Sunday from mid-May to September) between John o'Groats and Wick (£2.50, one hour) via the youth hostel at Canisbay. Harrold Coaches (☎ 01955-631295) runs a bus from Thurso train station to John o'Groats several times daily, except Sunday.

Boat From May to September, the passenger ferry MV *Pentland Venture*, operated by John O'Groats Ferries (☎ 01955-611353), shuttles across to Burwick in Orkney. The single fare to Burwick is £16/8 adult/child, a return is £26/13, and a coach tour of Orkney mainland, including the ferry fare, is £33/16.50. Ninety-minute wildlife cruises to the island of Stroma or Duncansby Head cost £12.

See the Inverness section earlier in this chapter for details of the John o'Groats Ferries bus-ferry-bus service, which takes you all the way from Inverness to Kirkwall on Orkney.

DUNNET HEAD

Let's put a common misconception to rest. Contrary to popular belief, John o'Groats is not the British mainland's most northerly point; that honour goes to Dunnet Head, 10 miles (16km) to the west. The head is marked by a lighthouse that dates from 1832.

The Pentland Firth, which separates Orkney and the mainland, is one of the most dangerous stretches of water around the British coast, with tidal streams that rip through at up to eight knots.

Just south-west of Dunnet Head is a magnificent stretch of sandy beach, at the southern end of which lies the tiny harbour of **Castlehill**, where a heritage trail explains the evolution of the local flagstone industry.

Dunnet Head Tearoom (☎ 01847-851774) Open noon-3pm & 6pm-9pm daily. Situated on the minor road that leads to Dunnet Head, this place offers good, inexpensive food, including meals for vegetarians, and does B&B for £17 to £20 per person.

North & West Coast

From just beyond Thurso, the coast round to Ullapool is mind-blowing. Everything is massive – vast, empty spaces, enormous lochs and snow-capped mountains. Ullapool is the most northerly village of any significance and there's more brilliant scenery round to Gairloch, along the incomparable Loch Maree and down to Kyle of Lochalsh (a short hop from Skye). From here you're back in the land of the tour bus; civilisation (and main roads) can be quite a shock after all that empty space.

Local tourist offices have good information leaflets about the coast route. Look for *Caithness & North Coast Sutherland* (including Thurso to Bettyhill), *North West Sutherland* (Tongue to Ullapool) and *Wester Ross* (Inverpolly to Lochcarron).

Banks and petrol stations are few and far between in this corner of Scotland, so check your funds and fuel before setting out.

GETTING AROUND

Public transport in the north-west is rather patchy. Getting to Thurso or Kyle of Lochalsh by bus or train is easy, but it can be difficult to follow the coast between these places, especially from October to May. All postbuses run year-round; fares vary, but long journeys are usually good-value at around £4 or £5.

From June to September, Highland Country Buses (☎ 01847-893123) runs the Northern Explorer bus once daily (except Sunday) from Thurso to Durness, leaving Thurso at 11.30am (£7.25, 2½ hours). The rest of the year, there are Monday to Saturday services from Thurso to Bettyhill; the Saturday service (departing Thurso at 11.35pm) reaches Melvich at 12.15pm, where you can change to the postbus (☎ 01246-546329), departing Melvich at 12.56pm and arriving at Tongue at 4.20pm. Much simpler is the Thurso-Tongue postbus, which departs Thurso at 9.40am and arrives at Tongue at 11.15am, Monday to Saturday. At 10am, Monday to Saturday, a postbus runs from Tongue to Durness.

From 28 May to 19 September, Tim Dearman Coaches (☎ 01349-883585) runs buses once daily (except Sunday) from Inverness to Durness (£13.50) via Ullapool.

An alternative is to come up from Inverness via Lairg. There are trains (daily, except Sunday in winter) and Inverness Traction buses (☎ 01463-239292; three daily except Sunday, change at Tain) to Lairg. Monday to Saturday, postbus services operate the Lairg-Tongue and Lairg-Kinlochbervie-Durness routes and from Lairg to Lochinver. There are also services around the coast from Elphin to Scourie, Drumbeg to Lochinver, Applecross to Torridon via Shieldaig, and Shieldaig to Torridon and Strathcarron, but always with gaps between villages.

There are regular Scottish Citylink buses between Inverness and Ullapool. Westerbus (☎ 01445-712255) runs every Thursday year-round between Ullapool and Gairloch. The once daily (except Sunday) Westerbus service from Inverness to Gairloch, runs via Kinlochewe and Achnasheen on Tuesday, Thursday and Friday, or via Dundonnell on Monday, Wednesday and Saturday. The route via Dundonnell provides a link between Ullapool and Gairloch (via Braemore Junction). The Achnasheen-Kinlochewe-Torridon postbus can be used in conjunction with the Westerbus, taking you from Gairloch to Kinlochewe and Torridon (at least one day after the Ullapool to Gairloch leg).

From Torridon, the MacLennan bus service (☎ 01520-755239) goes to Strathcarron once daily (except Sunday) from June to September, otherwise Monday, Wednesday and Friday only. Now you can return to sanity and bin all your bus timetables! From Strathcarron, trains run two to four times daily to Inverness (£12) and Kyle of Lochalsh (£3.60).

Renting a car or hitching are more viable options.

THURSO & SCRABSTER
☎ 01847 • pop 9233

The most northerly town on the British mainland, Thurso is a fairly large, fairly bleak place looking across the Pentland Firth to Hoy in Orkney. Medieval Thurso was Scotland's major port for trade with Scandinavia. Today, ferries cross from Scrabster, 2½ miles (4km) west of Thurso, to Orkney. The ferry aside, Scrabster is little more than a collection of BP oil storage containers.

Information

The TIC (☎ 892371), Riverside Rd, opens daily April to October. The medical centre is in Janet St (☎ 892027).

Things to See & Do

Thurso Heritage Museum (☎ 892459, High St; adult/child £1/25p; open 10am-1pm & 2pm-5pm Mon-Sat June-Sept), in Thurso Town Hall (☎ 892692), displays Pictish and Christian carved stones, fossils and a reconstruction of a croft interior. There's also a display on Sir John Sinclair, who planned the 'new town' of Thurso at the end of the 18th century.

The ruins of **Old St Peter's Kirk** date mainly from the 17th century, but the original church on the site was founded around 1220 by Gilbert Murray, the bishop of Caithness. The small round building over the **Meadow Well** marks the site of a former well.

The **Swanson Art Gallery** (☎ 896357, Thurso Library, Davidson's Lane; admission free; open 1pm-6pm Mon-Wed, 1pm-8pm Fri & 10am-1pm Sat) features monthly exhibitions, from crafts to fine art.

THE HIGHLANDS

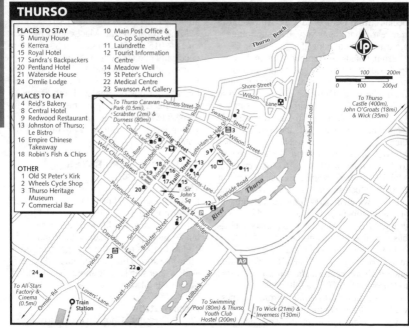

THURSO

PLACES TO STAY
5 Murray House
6 Kerrera
15 Royal Hotel
17 Sandra's Backpackers
20 Pentland Hotel
21 Waterside House
24 Ormlie Lodge

PLACES TO EAT
4 Reid's Bakery
8 Central Hotel
9 Redwood Restaurant
13 Johnston of Thurso;
   Le Bistro
16 Empire Chinese
   Takeaway
18 Robin's Fish & Chips

OTHER
1 Old St Peter's Kirk
2 Wheels Cycle Shop
3 Thurso Heritage
   Museum
7 Commercial Bar

10 Main Post Office &
   Co-op Supermarket
11 Laundrette
12 Tourist Information
   Centre
14 Meadow Well
19 St Peter's Church
22 Medical Centre
23 Swanson Art Gallery

Thurso is an unlikely **surfing** centre, but the nearby coast has arguably the best and most regular surf on mainland Britain. There's an excellent right-hand reef break on the eastern side of town, directly in front of Lord Thurso's castle (closed to the public), and another shallow reef break 5 miles (8km) west at Brimms Ness.

If the weather's bad, there's **All Stars Factory** (☎ 895050, Ormlie Rd; open daily), a six-lane bowling alley, cinema, restaurant and bar. Prices for bowling start at £1.70/1.40. The **swimming pool** (☎ 893260, Millbank Rd; open daily, variable hours) charges £2.20/1.10 for a dip.

North of Scrabster harbour, there's a fine **cliff walk** along Holborn Head. Take care in windy weather.

Places to Stay

Thurso Caravan Park (☎ 805503, fax 01955-604524, Scrabster Rd) Pitches from £7. Open May-Sept. By the coast, this camp site is on the edge of Thurso towards Scrabster.

Ormlie Lodge (☎/fax 896888, Ormlie Rd) Dorm beds without/with sheets £6.50/9.50. Open year-round. Scruffy Ormlie Lodge offers basic hostel accommodation.

Thurso Youth Club Hostel (☎ 892964, e t.y.c.hostel@btinternet.com, Millbank) Dorm beds £8, including breakfast. Open July & Aug. This is another fairly basic hostel.

Sandra's Backpackers (☎/fax 894575, 24-26 Princes St) En-suite dorms from £7. This excellent hostel has great facilities and charges 75p for 15 minutes' Internet access.

Thurso has many moderately priced B&Bs. The TIC charges £3 for local bookings.

Waterside House (☎ 894751, 3 Janet St) Singles £16-19, doubles £32-40. Vegetarian breakfast is available on request here.

Kerrera (☎ 895127, 12 Rose St) Doubles £16-18 per person. Open Feb-Nov. Kerrera is a reasonable B&B.

Murray House (☎ 895759, 1 Campbell St) B&B singles £16-22, doubles £30-40. At this pleasant B&B, all rooms have private bathrooms.

Pentland Hotel (☎ 893202, fax 892761, Princes St) En-suite singles/doubles £35/60. The large centrally located Pentland Hotel has an attached restaurant with an adventurous menu (mains £7.95 to £15.50, set dinner £17.50).

Royal Hotel (☎ 893191, fax 895338, Traill St) En-suite B&B £35 per person. Dinner £12. You'll get good service at the comfortable Royal Hotel.

Places to Eat

Le Bistro (☎ 893737, 2 Traill St) Snacks and meals from £1.80. New Le Bistro is a nice place, noted for its fish dishes.

Central Hotel (☎ 893129, Traill St) Snacks from £1.45, mains £4-5.80. For a cheap bar meal, try the Central Hotel.

Redwood Restaurant (☎ 894588, Grove Lane) Bar meals £4-5.30. Opposite the Co-op supermarket, the Redwood Restaurant has entertainment for the older set at weekends.

Fisherman's Mission (☎ 892402, West Quay, Scrabster) Light meals and snacks from around £2. You can eat at the very cheap Fisherman's Mission. It's a Christian organisation, so it's closed on Sunday.

Basic cafes include *Reid's Bakery (3 High St)* in the pedestrian mall and *Johnston of Thurso (10 Traill St)*. For takeaways, try *Robin's Fish & Chips (15a Princes St)*, where reasonable fish and chips costs £2.95. Or just across the road there's the *Empire Chinese Takeaway (☎ 896332, 20 Princes St)*, where sweet and sour pork with rice goes for £5.80.

Entertainment

The free jamming sessions at the *Commercial Bar (☎ 893366, 1 Princes St)* after 10pm every Wednesday are popular with most age groups. It's also a good place for a drink.

Getting There & Away

Thurso is 290 miles (464km) from Edinburgh, 130 miles (208km) from Inverness and 21 miles (34km) from Wick. From Inverness, Citylink buses operate four to five times daily via Wick to Thurso (£10, 3½ hours); they stop in Sir George's St. Highland Country Buses (☎ 893123) operates the daily Wick-Thurso route.

There are two or three daily train services from Inverness in summer (£12.50, 3½ hours), but space for bicycles is limited so book ahead.

Getting Around

It's a 2-mile (3km) walk from Thurso train station to the ferry port at Scrabster, or there are buses from Olrig St (80p). Wheels Cycle Shop (☎ 896124), The Arcade, 35 High St, hires out mountain bikes from £5 per day. William Dunnet & Co (☎ 893101) rents cars.

THURSO TO DURNESS

It's 80 winding and often spectacular coastal miles (128km) from Thurso to Durness.

Dounreay & Melvich

On the coast 10 miles (16km) west of Thurso, there's the **Dounreay Nuclear Power Station Visitor Centre** (☎ 01847-802572, Dounreay; admission free; open 10am-4pm daily May-Oct), which tells the interesting story of the Dounreay experimental reactor and its de-commissioning. Just beyond Dounreay, **Reay** has a shop and an interesting little harbour dating from 1830. Melvich (pop 541) overlooks a fine beach and there are great views from **Strathy Point** – from the coast road, it's a 2-mile (3km) drive, then a 15-minute walk.

Melvich Hotel (☎ 01641-531206, Melvich) Bar meals £5.95-12.95. Meals include venison, shellfish and beef dishes. B&B is also available (£20 to £35 per person).

Bettyhill (Am Blaran Odhar)
☎ 01641 • pop 553
Bettyhill is a crofting community named after Elizabeth, countess of Sutherland, who kicked her tenants off their land at Strathnaver to make way for more profitable sheep, then resettled the tenants here. There are fine sandy beaches at both **Farr Bay** and **Torrisdale Bay**.

Bettyhill TIC (☎ 521342) opens April to October. There's also a shop and post office.

The **Strathnaver Museum** (☎ *521418, Farr Bay; adult/child £1.90/50p; open 10am-1pm & 2pm-5pm Mon-Sat Apr-Oct, by arrangement at other times)*, in an old church, tells the sad story of the Strathnaver Clearances. The museum contains memorabilia of Clan Mackay, various items of crofting equipment and a 4000-year-old beaker. There's a late 8th-century Pictish cross-slab in the graveyard behind the museum.

Dunveaden (☎ *521273, Bettyhill)* B&B £16-18 per person, camping £2-10 per person. This is a friendly B&B and camp site by the main road.

Bettyhill Hotel (☎/*fax 521352, Bettyhill)* B&B £15 per person. Some rooms are en suite here. Bar meals are available (£4 to £5.50).

From Bettyhill, the B871 turns south for Helmsdale, through **Strathnaver**, where the Clearances took place.

Coldbackie & Tongue
☎ 01847 • pop 445

The wonderful beach at Coldbackie is overlooked by the Watch Hill viewpoint. Only 2 miles (3km) farther on is Tongue, with the 14th-century ruins of Castle Varrich, once a Mackay stronghold. Tongue has a shop, post office, bank and BP petrol station.

Tongue Youth Hostel (☎ *611301, Tongue)* Dorm beds from £8.25/7. Open Apr-Sept. Down by the causeway, across the Kyle of Tongue, the SYHA hostel has a spectacular location looking up and down the kyle (a kyle is a narrow strait).

Mrs MacIntosh (☎ *611251, 77 Dalcharn)* Singles/doubles £15/26. This is one of several B&Bs in the area, located just east of Coldbackie. Dinner costs £7 extra.

Ben Loyal Hotel (☎ *611216, fax 611212, Tongue)* Singles £25-45, doubles £50-90. The recommended meals in this excellent hotel are mostly under £9 (bar meals £4 to £5.50).

Tongue to Durness

From Tongue it's 37 miles (59km) to Durness – you can take the causeway across the **Kyle of Tongue** or the beautiful old road which goes around the head of the kyle. A detour to **Melness** (Mealainis) and **Port Vasgo** may be rewarded with the sight of seals on the beach.

Craggan Hotel (☎/*fax 01847-601278, Melness)* B&B from £17.50 per person. The atmospheric Craggan Hotel does great bar meals, with an adventurous menu (mains £5.50 to £16). There are four en-suite rooms.

Continuing west, the road crosses a desolate moor past **Moine House** (built as a shelter for travellers in 1830, but now a ruin) to the northern end of **Loch Hope**. A 10-mile (16km) detour south along the loch leads to **Dun Dornaigil**, a well-preserved broch in the shadow of **Ben Hope** (927m). If you'd like to bag this Munro, it's a three- to four-hour round trip along the route from the car park, which is 2 miles (3km) before the broch, near a large barn.

Beyond Loch Hope, on the main road, **Heilam** has stunning views out over **Loch Eriboll**, Britain's deepest sea inlet and a shelter for ships during WWII.

DURNESS (DIURANAIS)
☎ 01971 • pop 353

Durness has one of the finest locations in Scotland. When the sun shines, the effects of blinding white sand, the call of sea birds and the lime-coloured seas combine in a magical way. Perhaps this magic inspired John Lennon, who had many happy holidays here.

Orientation & Information

What's known as Durness is really two villages strung along the main road: Durness, in the west, and Smoo, a mile (1.6km) to the east.

The friendly TIC and visitor centre (☎ 511259) opens daily May to August, weekdays only the rest of the year. It organises guided walks in summer. The visitor centre (admission free) has folk history, and natural history and geological displays.

Durness has two stores (Mace, with the post office, is recommended), a petrol station, a health centre (☎ 511273) and a travelling bank (10.45am to 12.45pm every Tuesday).

The annual Highland Gathering takes place on the last weekend in July; contact the TIC for details.

The village has a Web site at **W** www .durness.org.

Things to See & Do

A mile (1.6km) east of the village centre there's a path down to **Smoo Cave** from near the SYHA hostel. The vast cave entrance stands at the end of an inlet, or *geo*, and a river cascades through its roof into a flooded cavern, then flows out to sea. There's evidence the cave was inhabited around 6000 years ago. You can take a **boat trip** (£2.50/1) into the floodlit cave, although after heavy rain the waterfall can make it impossible to get past.

Durness has several beautiful beaches, starting at Rispond to the east. One of the best is Sangobeg, but there's also a 'secret beach' just to the east, which can't be seen from the road. The sea offers great windsurfing. Around the coast, there are wrecks, caves, seals and whales. Enquire at the TIC for **trout-fishing** permits.

The disused radar station at **Balnakeil**, less than a mile (1.6km) up a minor road from Durness, has been turned into a hippy craft village, with a bookshop and a restaurant. At the end of the road, there's the interesting ruins of **Balnakeil Church**, dating from 1619. Have a look for the gravestone with carved skull and crossbones. There's also a mass grave with the remains of people from a ship which sank, with all hands, off **Faraid Head** in 1849. The austere **Balnakeil Farm**, overlooking the church, has a room panelled with wood salvaged from a 1688 Spanish Armada wreck (not open to the public). Walk north along the beach to reach Faraid Head, where puffin colonies can be seen in early summer.

Places to Stay & Eat

Lazy Crofter Bunkhouse (☎ *511209, fax 511321, Durness)* Dorm beds and doubles £9 per person. This hostel is located near the Mace supermarket.

Durness Youth Hostel (☎ *511244, Smoo)* Beds from £7.50/6.25. Open Apr-Sept. This SYHA hostel is at Smoo, on the eastern side of the village.

Sango Sands Oasis (☎ *511222, fax 511205, Durness)* Pitches from £4.20. This camp site has gas cookers but there's also an attached restaurant (mains £5 to £11.20).

Puffin Cottage (☎/fax *511208, Durness)* Doubles from £17-20 per person. Open Apr-Sept. Puffin Cottage is a particularly good B&B.

Smoo Falls (☎ *511228, Smoo)* Doubles £18-20 per person. Open Mar-Oct. Friendly Smoo Falls is opposite Durness Youth Hostel.

Smoo Cave Hotel (☎/fax *511227, Smoo)* En-suite doubles £16.50-19.50 per person. The great pub grub here (bar meals £5.50 to £9.50) includes a two-choice vegetarian selection.

Loch Croispol Bookshop & Restaurant (☎ *511777, 17c Balnakeil Craft Village)* Lunch & snacks £1.95-3.90, 2-course/3-course dinner £9.50/12.50. The food is excellent in this recommended restaurant.

DURNESS TO ULLAPOOL

It's 69 miles (110km) from Durness to Ullapool, with plenty of side trips and diversions to make along the way.

Cape Wrath

The cape is crowned by a lighthouse (dating from 1827) and stands close to the seabird colonies on Clo Mor Cliffs, the highest sea cliffs on the mainland. Getting to Cape Wrath involves a ferry ride (☎ 01971-511376) across the Kyle of Durness (£3.80 return) and a connecting minibus (☎ 01971-511287) for the 11 miles (18km) to the cape (£6.50 return, 40 minutes one way). The services usually operate daily May to September and up to eight times daily in July and August, but this is weather-dependent, plus the road can be closed for Ministry of Defence training.

South of Cape Wrath, **Sandwood Bay** boasts one of Scotland's best and most isolated beaches, guarded at one end by the spectacular rock pinnacle **Am Buachaille**. Sandwood Bay is about 2 miles (3km) north of the end of a track from Blairmore (approach from Kinlochbervie), or you could walk south from the cape (allow eight hours) and on to Blairmore. **Sandwood House** is a creepy ruin reputedly haunted by the ghost of a 17th-century shipwrecked sailor.

Kinlochbervie
☎ 01971 • pop 464

For such a small place, you'll be amazed to learn that, until the mid-1990s, Kinlochbervie was one of Scotland's premier fish-landing ports. Fish is sold on the quayside in the evening and it's possible to get incredible bargains if there are a few spares lying about. However, it can be difficult trying to eat a gigantic cod before it goes bad.

There's a lovely beach at **Oldshoremore**, a crofting settlement about 2 miles (3km) north-west of Kinlochbervie.

Braeside (☎ *521325, Kinlochbervie*) B&B £18-20 per person. Here you'll find a friendly B&B in a modern bungalow.

Kinlochbervie Hotel (☎ *521275, fax 521438, Kinlochbervie*) En-suite B&B £45-55 per person. Bar meals £5.50-10.95. The well-appointed Kinlochbervie Hotel is popular with both locals and tourists.

Kinlochbervie also has a well-stocked *Mace* supermarket.

Scourie
☎ 01971 • pop 150

Ferries (☎ 502340) go out to the important **Handa Island** seabird sanctuary from Scouriemore, one mile (1.6km) west of Scourie, on request Monday to Saturday, April to September (£7 return). You may see skuas and puffins as well as seals. The **Old Man of Stoer** (see later) can be seen across Eddrachillis Bay and there are impressive stacks (towers of rock rising from the sea) on Handa Island.

Scourie is a pretty crofting community with several well-known herds of Highland cattle. The village has a *Mace* supermarket and post office, a petrol station, a *camp site (Harbour Rd)* and several B&Bs.

Scourie Hotel (☎ *502396, fax 502423, Scourie*) Singles £34-46, doubles £58-80. The nicely decorated Scourie Hotel attracts anglers. Dinner is available for £12 extra and there are bar meals for £4.50 to £10.95.

Eddrachilles Hotel (☎ *01971-502080, fax 502477, Badcall Bay*) B&B £40-55 per person. The attractive Eddrachilles Hotel, in lovely surroundings, just south of Scourie, has an excellent restaurant (lunchtime bar snacks from £2, three-course table d'hôte dinner £12.75).

Kylesku & Loch Glencoul
☎ 01971

Kylesku is known for its sweeping modern bridge over Loch a'Chàirn Bhàin. Cruises on Loch Glencoul pass seal colonies and you'll see the 213m drop of **Eas a'Chual Aluinn**, Britain's highest waterfall. In summer, the MV *Statesman* (☎ 01571-844446) runs two-hour trips twice daily from Kylesku Old Ferry Pier for £10/5.

Kylesku Hotel (☎ *502231, fax 502313, Kylesku*) Singles/doubles £35/65. While you wait, you can enjoy a pint and a snack or a meal (mains £5.75 to £9.95) in the Kylesku Hotel, overlooking the pier. The squat lobsters are recommended.

Kylesku Lodges (☎ *502003, Kylesku*) Beds £10-11, chalets £150-450 per week. Open year-round. There's a small 12-bed hostel at Kylesku Lodges. There are also three fairly basic self-catering chalets, each with three bedrooms.

It's a fine three-hour, 6-mile (10km) round-trip walk to the top of the falls, starting from beside Loch na Gainmhich at the top of the climb out of Kylesku towards Ullapool. OS Landranger map No 15 shows the route.

The Old Man of Stoer
It's roughly a 30-mile (48km) detour off the main A894 to the Point of Stoer and the Rhu Stoer Lighthouse (1870) and back to the main road again. Along the coast road you need to be prepared for single-track roads, blind bends, summits… and sheep. The rewards are spectacular views, pretty villages and excellent beaches. From the lighthouse, it's a good one-hour cliff walk to the Old Man of Stoer, a spectacular sea stack.

There are more good beaches between Stoer and Lochinver, including one at Achmelvich, where there's a camp site and hostel.

Shore Caravan Site (☎ *01571-844393, fax 844782, 106 Achmelvich*) Pitches from £4, caravans £150-250 per week. This camp site also has three caravans to let, sleeping one to six people.

Achmelvich Youth Hostel (☎ *01571-844480, Achmelvich*) Beds £7.50/6.25. Opens Apr-Sept. This is a SYHA hostel about 1½ miles (2.5km) from the Lochinver-Drumbeg postbus route, and 4 miles (6km) from Lochinver.

Lochinver & Assynt
☎ 01571

Lochinver The popular little fishing port of Lochinver (pop 639) is no budget traveller's paradise.

The TIC and award-winning visitor centre (☎ 844330), Main St, opens April to October. There's an interpretive display and an exhibit of bear and lynx bones. Lochinver Stores stocks groceries. There's also a post office, bank (with an ATM), an Esso petrol station and a doctor (☎ 844755). **Highland Stoneware Pottery** (☎ *844376, Baddidarrach; admission free; open 9am-6pm Mon-Fri year-round & 9am-5pm Sat Easter-Oct*) sells distinctive hand-painted ceramics and you can see the potters at work.

Places to stay and eat including the comfortable *Ardglas* (☎ *844257, fax 844632, Inver*), where singles cost between £15 and £17, doubles between £30 and £34.

The Albannach (☎ *844407, fax 844285, Lochinver*) Dinner B&B singles £75-105, doubles £150-170. This is the finest hotel in the village, with five en-suite rooms.

Culag Hotel (☎ *844270, Lochinver*) Bar meals £5.80-7.10. On the sprawling waterfront, the Culag Hotel serves reasonable food.

Lochinver Larder & Riverside Bistro (☎ *844356, 3 Main St*) Mains £5.45-16.95. This place has interesting local food, especially fish, to eat in or take away.

Caberfeidh Restaurant (☎ *844321, 5 Main St*) Snacks from £1.50, mains £7.60-11.95. The lively Caberfeidh Restaurant serves snacks and main courses (including seafood and vegetarian dishes).

Inverkirkaig Two miles (3km) south of Lochinver, on the narrow road to Achiltibuie, there's a pleasant bay and a great walk along the river for 2 miles (3km) to the Falls of Kirkaig.

Achins Bookshop & Coffee Shop (☎ *844262, Inverkirkaig*) is at the start of the trail and is good for a snack or a quick browse.

Loch Assynt The Lochinver-Lairg road (A837) meets the Durness road (A894) at **Skiag Bridge**, by Loch Assynt, about 10 miles (16km) east of Lochinver. Half a mile (800m) south of here, by the loch, there's the ruin of the late 15th-century MacLeod stronghold, **Ardvreck Castle**. The marquis of Montrose was betrayed here in 1650 after fleeing the disastrous battle at Culrain near Bonar Bridge. There are wonderful summer sunsets over the castle and the loch.

Hills of Assynt The spectacularly shaped hills of Assynt are popular with walkers and include peaks such as Suilven (731m), Quinag (808m), Ben More Assynt (998m) and Canisp (846m). Remember to check locally about access during the deer-stalking season, from August to October. The Inchnadamph National Nature Reserve has a network of **caves**; the ones in Gleann Dubh, 1½ miles (2.5km) from Inchnadamph, are easily visited but you'll need to be an experienced caver to venture in.

Inchnadamph Lodge (☎ *822218, fax 822232, Inchnadamph*) Dorm beds £10-10.50, doubles £16-16.50. By the Lochinver-Lairg road, the excellent and friendly 50-bed Inchnadamph Lodge charges £2 for 30 minutes' Internet access and has a basic licensed grocery shop. It's an ideal base for climbing Ben More Assynt, a seven-hour round trip via Gleann Dubh and the northern ridge of Conival (988m). Prices include breakfast.

Knockan & Inverpolly Nature Reserve

There's a new SNH (Scottish Natural Heritage) **Interpretation Centre** (☎ *01854-613418)*, as well as trails with sculptures at Knockan Crag, on the A835 Ledmore Junction to Ullapool road, beside Inverpolly Nature Reserve. It describes the geological processes that shaped the surrounding area.

The **Inverpolly Nature Reserve** has numerous glacial lochs and the three peaks of Cul Mor (849m), Stac Pollaidh (613m) and

Cul Beag (769m). **Stac Pollaidh** is one of the most exciting walks in the area, with some good scrambling on its narrow sandstone crest. It takes just three hours on a round trip from the car park on Loch Lurgainn.

Farther south along the A835, there are good views of Isle Martin from just before Ardmair and then of the Summer Isles, Loch Broom and Ullapool.

Achiltibuie
☎ 01854 • pop 290

Reached by a circuitous route around Loch Lurgainn or south from Lochinver via Inverkirkaig, Achiltibuie has a great situation, sheltered from the west by the wonderfully named Summer Isles. In the village, there's a post office and general store.

Things to See & Do The **Hydroponicum** *(☎ 622202, Achiltibuie; adult/child £4.75/ 2.75; hourly tours 10am-5pm daily Apr-Sept, noon & 2pm Mon-Fri Oct)* grows tropical fruit, vegetables and flowers, without soil. It also has an attached cafe, where soup made from hydroponic ingredients (and a home-baked roll) costs £2.

About 5 miles (8km) north-west of Achiltibuie, the **Smokehouse** *(☎ 622353, Altandhu; admission free; open 9.30am-5pm Mon-Sat Easter-Oct)* smokes all sorts of things, from cheese to eel and salmon. You can watch the processing and buy the results in the shop.

Summer Isles Cruises *(☎ 622200)* operates boat trips to the Summer Isles from Achiltibuie. The 3½-hour trips cost £15/7.50, and you get one hour ashore on **Tanera Mor**, where the post office issues its own stamps.

The coastal path from Achiltibuie to Strath Kanaird isn't an easy route and is best avoided.

Places to Stay & Eat *Achininver Youth Hostel (☎ 622254, Achininver, Achiltibuie)* Beds £7.50/6.25. Open mid-May–Sept. This basic 20-bed hostel is at the southern end of Achiltibuie.

Summer Isles Hotel (☎ 622282, fax 622251, Achiltibuie) Bar meals £6.95-12, 5-course dinner £40. Open Apr-Oct. Snacks

and bar meals are available all day, but the hotel is better known for its excellent, though expensive, evening meals and wine list. Single rooms cost £69 to £106, doubles £104 to £130).

Getting There & Away Spa Coaches *(☎ 01997-421311)* operates Monday to Saturday buses from Reiff, Badenscallie (half a mile, 800m, from the hostel) and Achiltibuie to Ullapool, once or twice daily.

ULLAPOOL
☎ 01854 • pop 1558

Ullapool is a pretty fishing village from where ferries sail to Stornoway on the Isle of Lewis. Small though it is, Ullapool is the biggest settlement in Wester Ross. Although it's a long way around the coast in either direction, Ullapool is only 59 miles (94km) from Inverness via the A835 along beautiful Loch Broom.

Information
The helpful TIC *(☎ 612135)* is at 6 Argyle St (call for opening hours). The only bank is the Royal Bank of Scotland (with ATM) in Ladysmith St. The *Ullapool Bookshop (Quay St)*, opposite the Seaforth Inn, is excellent and has lots of books on Scottish topics. For outdoor equipment, try the *Mountain Man Supplies* shop, opposite the Ullapool Museum.

Things to See
The **Ullapool Museum and Visitor Centre** *(☎ 612987, 7-8 West Argyle St; adult/child £2/1.50; open 9.30am-5.30pm Mon-Sat Apr-Oct, 11am-3pm Wed, Thur & Sat Nov-Feb, 11am-3pm Mon-Sat Mar)* is in a converted Telford Parliamentary church. An audiovisual presentation, interactive exhibits and various other displays chart the history of the area and its people.

The curious and ornate **Ullapool Clock**, at the junction of Quay St and Argyle St, dates from 1899 and was erected in memory of the sons and grandsons of Sir John Fowler of Braemore. The clock was put in its current location in the 1960s; it was wound-up by hand until 1995, but is now electrically powered.

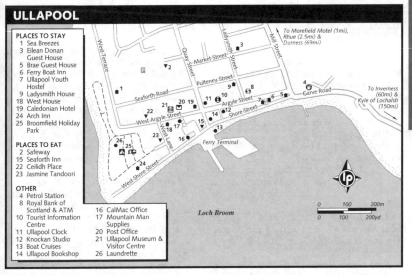

ULLAPOOL

PLACES TO STAY
1 Sea Breezes
3 Eilean Donan
  Guest House
5 Brae Guest House
6 Ferry Boat Inn
7 Ullapool Youth
  Hostel
9 Ladysmith House
18 West House
19 Caledonian Hotel
24 Arch Inn
25 Broomfield Holiday
   Park

PLACES TO EAT
2 Safeway
15 Seaforth Inn
22 Ceilidh Place
23 Jasmine Tandoori

OTHER
4 Petrol Station
8 Royal Bank of
  Scotland & ATM
10 Tourist Information
   Centre
11 Ullapool Clock
12 Knockan Studio
13 Boat Cruises
14 Ullapool Bookshop
16 CalMac Office
17 Mountain Man
   Supplies
20 Post Office
21 Ullapool Museum &
   Visitor Centre
26 Laundrette

To Morefield Motel (1mi),
Rhue (2.5mi) &
Durness (69mi)

To Inverness
(60mi) &
Kyle of Lochalsh
(150mi)

Ferry Terminal

Loch Broom

Rhue Studio (☎ 612460, Rhue; admission free; open 10am-6pm Mon-Sat Apr-Sept, call for details Oct-Mar), 2½ miles (4km) north-west of Ullapool, displays and sells the excellent art of contemporary landscape painter James Hawkins.

Walking

There's a good low-level walk up the track beside the Ullapool River to Loch Achall (two hours return); or go farther, to East Rhidorroch Lodge, a round trip of 16 miles (26km, six hours).

Ullapool is a great centre for hillwalking. If you don't have a car, the regular buses to Inverness on the A835 can be used, giving access to Beinn Dearg (1084m) and The Fannichs, a range south of the road.

There are only a few paths in the area – the good one up Gleann na Sguaib heads for the top of Beinn Dearg from Inverlael, at the inner end of Loch Broom. Another way of approaching this rough and wild mountain is from the south, at the head of Loch Glascarnoch (no path). The walk will take about eight hours, whichever route you take. Make sure that you're well equipped, and remember to carry OS map No 20.

Ridge-walking on The Fannichs is relatively straightforward and many different routes are possible. The western Fannichs are best reached from the A832 road from Braemore to Dundonnell at Loch a'Bhraoin. From the eastern end of the loch, a path goes southwards to a pass at 560m, giving access to Sgurr Breac (1000m) to the west. A ridge extends farther west, giving pleasant walking to A'Chailleach (999m). Return to Loch a'Bhraoin via Loch Toll an Lochain. You'll need OS map Nos 19 and 20.

Organised Tours

The *MV Summer Queen* (☎ 612472) operates four-hour trips to the Summer Isles departing from Ullapool ferry terminal, landing on Tanera Mor, daily at 10am in summer (adult/child £16/9). There's also a daily two-hour nature cruise at 2.15pm (and 11am Sunday) for £9/5.

Places to Stay

Broomfield Holiday Park (☎ 612664, fax 613151, West Lane) Hiker & tent £5, car & tent £9. Open May-Oct. There's not much shelter at this exposed site.

Ullapool Youth Hostel (☎ *612254, fax 613254, 22 Shore St*) Dorm beds from £8.50/7.25. Closed most of January. At this friendly harbourside hostel, booking is advisable at New Year, Easter and in summer. Internet access here costs £1 for 12 minutes.

West House (☎/*fax 613126, West Argyle St*) Bunks £8.50, doubles £25. Open year-round. Free Internet access for guests and day tours by bus to Lochinver and Achiltibuie (£10 to £15) are available.

There are lots of B&Bs and guesthouses along Seaforth Rd and Pulteney St, and on Argyle St near the Quay St junction. There are also a few places in the Morefield estate, just off the A835 at the northern end of the village.

Arch Inn (☎ *612454, fax 612012, 11 West Shore St*) Rooms £20-25 per person. The pub at the waterfront Arch Inn is popular with locals.

Brae Guest House (☎ *612421, Shore St*) Rooms £20-25 per person. Open May-Oct. Brae Guest House is also right on the waterfront.

Eilean Donan Guest House (☎ *612524, 14 Market St*) Rooms £18-24 per person. This friendly place has a pleasant restaurant (mains £7.50 to £12.50; closed Sunday).

Ladysmith House (☎ *613286, 24 Pulteney St*) Rooms £15-20 per person. Another centrally located and pleasant B&B.

Sea Breezes (☎ *612148, 2 West Terrace)* Singles/doubles from £15/30. Recommended Sea Breezes is a particularly friendly B&B.

Ferry Boat Inn (☎ *612366, fax 613266, Shore St*) Singles/doubles from £31/58. Here you'll get pleasant hotel rooms with views up the loch.

Caledonian Hotel (☎ *612306, fax 612679, Quay St*) En-suite singles £30-47, doubles £50-84. Open Mar-Oct. The large Caledonian Hotel has a restaurant. Accommodation is modern and comfortable; room service and laundry service are available.

Morefield Motel (☎ *612161, fax 612171, North Rd*) En-suite B&B £20-25 per person. The Morefield Motel is located in the Morefield estate, at the northern end of the village.

Places to Eat

Morefield Motel (☎ *612161, North Rd*) Mains £8.25-18.75. At the Morefield Motel, the excellent but pricey bar and restaurant meals have an emphasis on fish dishes.

Ceilidh Place (☎ *612103, 14 West Argyle St*) Mains £8.50-17. The Ceilidh Place has a daytime cafe (open from 8am) with soup and snacks from £1.95, but the touristy evening restaurant is fairly expensive. It's also Ullapool's main entertainment centre, with live folk, jazz, contemporary or classical music most nights in summer (admission £5).

Ferry Boat Inn (☎ *612366, Shore St*) Bar lunch £5.25-7.25. 2-course/3-course set dinner £15.75/18.75. The home-made food is excellent at the Ferry Boat Inn.

Arch Inn (☎ *612454, 11 West Shore St*) Mains £5.50-6.50. You'll get a good pub lunch or dinner here.

Jasmine Tandoori (☎ *613331, West Lane*) Takeaway mains £5-10.95. You can also eat in at this good Indian restaurant, but prices are a little dearer.

Seaforth Inn (☎ *612122, Quay St*) Mains from £6. Upstairs at the Seaforth Inn, there's good fish and chips and other seafood; takeaways from the hatch downstairs (not the Quayplaice!) are £3.30.

For self catering, the large *Safeway* supermarket is next to the car park north of Seaforth Rd.

Shopping

Check out the *Knockan Studio* (☎ *01854-613365, Argyle St)*, an excellent and unique craft and jewellery centre which uses Scottish gold and gemstones.

Getting There & Away

Ullapool is 215 miles (344km) from Edinburgh and 60 miles (96km) from Inverness. See Inverness earlier in this chapter for bus information. See The Hebrides chapter for details of the ferry to Stornoway on the Isle of Lewis.

Getting Around

Bikes can be hired from the West House hostel for £10/6 per day/half-day.

ULLAPOOL TO THE EAST COAST

The A835 goes south from Ullapool to Braemore Junction, then continues over the wild Dirrie More to the Glascarnoch dam, with great views of Beinn Dearg on the way. This section is sometimes closed by snow in winter.

Aultguish Inn Bunkhouse (☎/fax 01997-455254, e richard@aultguish.co .uk, by Garve) Bunkhouse beds £6 (no kitchen), en-suite B&B £16 per person. Breakfast £4, bar meals from £4.50. Just below the dam, the friendly Aultguish Inn Bunkhouse serves traditional Scottish bar meals.

There's also a hotel farther down the road, below the bulk of **Ben Wyvis** (1046m).

Inchbae Lodge Hotel (☎ 01997-455269, fax 455207, Inchbae, by Garve) B&B from £33 per person. Bar meals £6, 3-course/ 5-course set dinner £19.95/26.95. The Inchbae Lodge Hotel serves excellent bar meals, including vegetarian dishes; the five-course set dinner changes daily. There's also a selection of real ales in the bar.

Hiking opportunities from the lodge include Ben Wyvis, but some of the tracks through the forestry can be extremely wet. Allow five hours return from Garbat, just a mile (1.6km) down the road from the lodge. Use OS map No 20 and carry plenty of food and water (there's no water on the hill).

Five miles (8km) south of Inchbae, there's a junction where the A832 goes west to Gairloch through pleasant **Strath Braan**. The A835 continues south-east, past **Garve** village and Loch Garve to **Contin**, where there's a Spar shop, a camp site, B&Bs and a couple of good hotels.

Achilty Hotel (☎ 01997-421355, fax 421923, Achilty, Contin) En-suite B&B singles £32-54, doubles £49-74. You can get good bar meals at this former 18th-century coaching inn.

Coul House Hotel (☎ 01997-421487, fax 421945, Contin) Singles £53-70, doubles £76-110. Bar meals £3.25-7.95, restaurant mains £14.90-16.75. This very fine country mansion dates from 1821 and lies up a half-mile (800m) private drive from Contin. The meals are excellent.

From Contin, it's only 2 miles (3km) to Strathpeffer (see the Dingwall & Strathpeffer section earlier in this chapter).

Ullapool to Inverness buses follow this route and stop off at Contin, Garve and Aultguish; ask Scottish Citylink (☎ 0870 550 5050) if other stops are possible . Trains from Inverness to Kyle of Lochalsh stop at Garve.

ULLAPOOL TO KYLE OF LOCHALSH

Although it's less than 50 miles (80km) as the crow flies from Ullapool to Kyle of Lochalsh, it's more like 150 miles (240km) along the circuitous coastal road, with fine views of beaches and bays backed by mountains all along the way.

Falls of Measach

The A832 doubles back to the coast from the A835, 12 miles (19km) from Ullapool. Just before the junction, the Falls of Measach ('ugly' in Gaelic) spill 45m into the spectacularly deep and narrow Corrieshalloch Gorge.

You can cross from side to side on a wobbly suspension bridge, built by Sir John Fowler of Braemore. The gorge is of great botanical and geological interest and there's an informative noticeboard giving details. The NTS expects visitors to pay £1 to see the falls, but the justification for this isn't entirely clear.

Dundonnell & Around

☎ 01854 • pop 169

Between Braemore and Poolewe, there are relatively few houses but lots of great scenery. **An Teallach** (1062m), at Dundonnell, is a magnificent mountain – the highest summit can be reached by a path starting less than 500m south-east of the Dundonnell Hotel (six hours return). The traverse of the ridge to Sail Liath is a more serious proposition, with lots of scrambling in precarious places and difficult route finding. Carry OS map No 19, food and water. Make sure you're well equipped; it's amazing how quickly the weather can turn foul here.

Badrallach Bothy (☎ 633281, e michael .stott2@virgin.net, 9 Badrallach) Sleeping bag space £3-4.50, camping £3-10, B&B £15 per person. Badrallach Bothy, 7 miles (11km) from the A832, at Badrallach, has varied accommodation and serves food (dinner £10).

Sail Mhor Croft Hostel (☎/fax 633224, Camasnagaul) Dorm beds £9. Bring your own sleeping bag or hire sheets at this roadside hostel 1½ miles (2.5km) west of Dundonnell.

Dundonnell Hotel (☎ 633204, fax 633366, Dundonnell) En-suite B&B £35-72.50 per person. The highly regarded Dundonnell Hotel has adventurous menus (bar meals £6 to £11, three-course dinner around £25).

There's also the small, basic *Northern Lights Campsite* (from £5) just before Badcaul. You'll find a well-stocked shop and post office at Badcaul, just off the main road.

Gruinard Island, in the large Gruinard Bay west of Dundonnell, was contaminated with anthrax spores after testing of biological weapons in WWII. In the 1990s, after extensive treatment with formaldehyde, the island was declared safe.

Inverewe Gardens

At Poolewe on Loch Ewe, the subtropical Inverewe Gardens *(NTS; ☎ 01445-781200, Poolewe; adult/child £5/4; open 9.30am-sunset daily)* are a testament to the warming influence of the Gulf Stream. The gardens were founded by Osgood Mackenzie in 1862 – a barren, windswept peninsula was gradually transformed into a luxuriant, colourful 26-hectare garden. There's a pleasant restaurant for soup and sandwich lunches.

Gairloch & Around
☎ 01445 • pop 1061

Gairloch is a group of villages (comprising Auchtercairn, Strath and Charlestown) around the inner end of a loch of the same name. The surrounding area is noted for its sandy beaches, good trout-fishing and birdwatching. Hill walkers also use Gairloch as a base for the Torridon hills and An Teallach.

The TIC (☎ 712130) is at the car park in Auchtercairn, where a road branches off to the main centre at Strath. It opens April to October (daily from May). There are shops and takeaways in Strath and Auchtercairn, a petrol station in Auchtercairn and a bank (with an ATM) between Auchtercairn and

Charlestown. For a doctor, call the Auchtercairn health centre on ☎ 712229.

Things to See The excellent **Heritage Museum** *(☎ 712287, Auchtercairn; adult/child £2.50/50p; open 10am-5pm Mon-Sat Apr-Sept, 10am-1.30pm Mon-Sat Oct)*, near the TIC, tells of life in the West Highlands from the Picts to the present. You can see a typical crofting cottage, schoolroom and shop. Arranged activities include butter-making and corn-grinding. There's a coffee shop and restaurant on site.

The **Gairloch Marine Life Centre** *(☎ 712636, Pier Rd, Charlestown; admission free; typically open 9.30am-4pm Mon-Fri & noon-3.30pm Sat-Sun Easter-Sept)* has audiovisual and interactive displays, lots of charts and photos, and knowledgeable staff.

Organised Tours An experienced hiker and fisherman, *John Heath (mobile ☎ 0786 772 0451, Aultbea)* offers guided hillwalking (£40 per group per day, maximum six persons) and trout, salmon and sea-trout fishing (£50 per group per day, maximum two persons). Fishing permits (£2.50 to £15 per day) and boat hire (£5 to £20 per day) cost extra; rod and tackle hire costs around £5 per day.

Sea fishing can be arranged by *Barry Davies* (☎ 712458).

Gairloch Marine Cruises (☎ 712636) sail three times daily, Easter to September (£14/12), from The Pier, Charlestown; during the two-hour trip you may see basking sharks, porpoises and Minke whales.

Places to Stay & Eat There are several camp sites and hostels in and around Gairloch.

Gairloch Holiday Park (☎ 712373, Strath) Pitches from £6.50. This is a centrally located site.

The Old Inn (☎ 712006, fax 712445, Charlestown) Bunkhouse beds from £10, en-suite B&B from £20. The Walkers Lodge bunkhouse at The Old Inn has a wonderful riverside location and recommended bar meals (£5 to £8).

Carn Dearg Youth Hostel (☎ 712219, by Gairloch) Beds from £8.75/7.50. Open mid-May–Sept. This is a SYHA hostel, 3

miles (5km) west of Gairloch, on the road to Melvaig.

Ruadh Reidh Lighthouse Hostel (☎ 771263, ⓔ ruareidh@netcomuk.co.uk, by Melvaig) Beds £8, B&B from £15.50. At the end of the road, 13 miles (21km) from Gairloch, you can stay at this excellent hostel. It also does good meals for £12, by reservation. Buses (Westerbus, ☎ 712255) from Gairloch run as far as Melvaig once on weekdays, then it's a 3-mile (5km) hike along the road to the lighthouse. Many people find hitching a better bet.

B&B accommodation is available throughout Gairloch from £14 to £25 per person.

Mrs Gibson (☎/fax 712085, 13 Strath) Singles £14-16, doubles £28-35. Open Apr-Sept. There's one single and one en-suite double.

Duisary (☎/fax 712252, Strath) B&B £16-20. Open Apr-Oct. Duisary is a good B&B, but only one room is en suite.

Myrtle Bank Hotel (☎ 712004, fax 712214, Low Rd) En-suite singles £35-44, doubles £70-88. You'll get an excellent bar or restaurant meal here (bar meals £6.10 to £12.95).

Millcroft Hotel (☎ 712376, fax 712091, Strath) En-suite singles £22-39, doubles £44-72. The Italian-run Millcroft Hotel also serves great meals (pizzas from £4.85, Italian mains from £6.75).

Loch Maree & Victoria Falls

The A832 runs alongside craggy Loch Maree, sprinkled with islands and a series of peaks along the northern shore, culminating in 980m-high Slioch.

The Victoria Falls (commemorating Queen Victoria's 1877 visit) tumble down to the loch between Slattadale and Talladale. Look for the 'Hydro Power' signs to find it.

Kinlochewe to Torridon

Kinlochewe & Around Check out the SNH **Beinn Eighe Visitor Centre** (☎ 01445-760258, Kinlochewe; admission free; open 10am-5pm daily Easter-Oct), a mile north of Kinlochewe, with details on local geography, geology, ecology and walking routes.

Kinlochewe (pop 107) is a good base for outdoor activities. You'll find an outdoor-equipment shop, a petrol station and a

shop/post office which runs a cafe in summer. There's a basic free *camp site* (☎ 01445-760254) 1½ miles (2.5km) north of the village. It opens year-round.

Hillhaven (☎ 01445-760204, Kinlochewe) En-suite B&B £20 per person. This excellent friendly B&B organises hawk-flying displays.

Kinlochewe Hotel (☎ 01445-760253, ⓔ kinlochewehotel@tinyworld.co.uk, Kinlochewe) Bunkhouse £8, B&B without/with bath £22.50/25 per person. The traditional bar meals (£4.95 to £9.75) here include baked salmon (£6.95).

East of Kinlochewe, the single-track A832 continues to Achnasheen, where there's a train station.

Ledgowan Lodge Hotel (☎ 01445-720252, fax 720240, Achnasheen) En-suite singles £34-39, doubles £68-78. Open Apr-Oct. This friendly olde-worlde hunting lodge has an aquarium. Dinner is available for £15 and bar meals for around £6 to £9.

Torridon & Around Westwards, the A896 follows Glen Torridon, overlooked by the multiple peaks of Beinn Eighe (1010m) and Liathach (1055m). The road reaches the sea at Torridon, where an NTS **Countryside Centre** (☎ 01445-791221, Torridon Mains; adult/child £1.50/1; open 10am-5pm Mon-Sat & 2pm-5pm Sun May-Sept) offers information on walks in the rugged area. There's an unstaffed **Deer Museum** (open daylight hours year-round) nearby.

Torridon village (pop 198) has a shop and several B&Bs.

Camp Site (☎ 01445-791313, Torridon) Pitches £2.50. The fee includes use of the shower.

Torridon Youth Hostel (☎ 01445-791284, Torridon) Beds £8.75/6. Open Mar-Oct & New Year. The modern 60-bed SYHA hostel is near the countryside centre.

Loch Torridon Hotel (☎ 01445-791242, fax 791296, Torridon) B&B en-suite singles £50-90, doubles £80-260. The beautiful Loch Torridon Hotel, complete with clock tower, is one of the nicest places to stay in Scotland. A superb four-course table d'hôte dinner will set you back £38, but there's bar food at the nearby Ben Damph Lodge from

£4.95 (April to October only). Activities, including hill-walking, clay-pigeon-shooting, sea-kayaking, fly-fishing and archery, are also available to nonresidents.

The A896 continues westwards to lovely **Shieldaig**, which boasts an attractive main street of whitewashed houses. In Shieldaig there's a shop, a post office, a free basic camp site and a hotel.

Tigh an Eilean Hotel (☎ 755251, Shieldaig) Bar meals £5.75-7.25. The bar meals here are reasonable.

Applecross & Lochcarron

Applecross A long side trip abandons the A896 to follow the coast road to the remote seaside village of Applecross (pop 222), which has a good grocery store and a petrol station. The scenery around here is fantastic.

Applecross Inn (☎ 01520-744262, fax 744400, Shore St) Singles £26-30, doubles £52-70. The Applecross Inn reputedly does the best pub grub (mains £4.95 to £10.95) in the West Highlands. Specials change daily.

There's also a garden centre (☎ 01520-744268) with a tearoom and camp site. Turning inland from Applecross, the road climbs to the Bealach na Ba pass (626m), then drops steeply to rejoin the A896. This winding, precipitous road can be closed in winter. There's a once-daily (except Sunday) post-bus service from Applecross to Torridon.

The A896 runs south from Shieldaig to **Kishorn**, where there's a general store and post office, and spectacular views westwards to the steep sandstone Applecross hills.

Kishorn Seafood & Snack Bar (☎ 01520-733240, Kishorn) Open daily Apr–mid-Oct. You can eat well here; the queen scallops (45p each) and home-made soup (£1.50) are rather good. A half-pound of squat lobster with a garlic butter side order costs £5 and is worth every penny.

Lochcarron The next place is the village of Lochcarron (pop 871), a veritable metropolis with two supermarkets, a bank (with an ATM!), a post office, two hotels, a petrol station and a nine-hole golf course. The TIC (☎ 01520-722357) opens Monday to Friday year-round, plus Saturday from April to October and Sunday in July and August.

Two miles (3km) along the road to Strome, you'll find **Lochcarron Weavers** (☎ 01520-722212, Lochcarron; admission free; open 9am-5pm Mon-Fri mid-Oct–Easter, plus 9am-5pm Sat Easter–mid-Oct), where you can watch tartan being made (weekdays only).

Lochcarron is a good base for hill-walking, with lots of spectacular peaks and good trails in the area. Ask at the TIC or any of the hotels for details.

There are lots of B&Bs in Lochcarron.

Bank House (☎ 01520-722332, fax 722780, Main St) Singles £23-29, doubles £32-44, all with shared bathroom. This B&B is in the same building as the Bank of Scotland and was the former manager's home.

Castle Cottage (☎ 01520-722564, Main St) Singles £17-25, doubles £34-42. Two rooms in this place share a bathroom, the other one is en suite.

Rockvilla Hotel (☎ 01520-722379, fax 722844, Main St) Bar meals £5.50-11. If you like fresh seafood, visit the Rockvilla Hotel, which is renowned for its scallops. You can eat in the restaurant where Scallops Thermidor costs £12.50. Single rooms cost £34 to £40, doubles £48 to £60.

Three miles (5km) away, at the top of Loch Carron, you'll reach the A890; southwards leads to Plockton, Kyle of Lochalsh and the Isle of Skye.

At **Strathcarron**, you'll find a train station and the cosy, friendly Strathcarron Hotel.

Strathcarron Hotel (☎ 01520-722227, Strathcarron), Singles/doubles £35/60. Free camping is also available here, and you can use the hotel facilities. Good pub grub starts at £2.35 for home-made soup and a roll. Mains cost £5.95 to £13.95.

PLOCKTON
☎ 01599 • pop 428

From Stromeferry (no ferry!), there are two routes to Kyle of Lochalsh, from where ferries once crossed to the Isle of Skye. The coastal route detours via idyllic Plockton once a clearing centre for those displaced in the Clearances. It's now a really delightful place to stay, with a main street lined with palms and whitewashed houses, each with a seagull gazing out to sea perched on its chimney-stack.

The steady flow of visitors has been augmented by viewers of the popular TV series *Hamish MacBeth* coming in search of locations from the stories.

Plockton has a grocery store, a post office and a train station.

Organised Tours

From May to September, *Leisure Marine* (*☎ 544306)* runs one-hour seal- and otterwatching cruises for £5/3. *Sea Trek Marine* (*☎ 544356)* operates similar tours, with hourly departures through the day; it also offers guided hill-walks.

Places to Stay & Eat

Plockton Station Bunkhouse (*☎ 544235,* e *gill@ecosse.net, Nessun Dorma, Plockton)* Beds £8.50-10. Open year-round. This bunkhouse is located in the former station building.

An Caladh (*☎ 544356, 25 Harbour St)* B&B £16-22.50. There are good harbour views from this pleasant B&B.

Sheiling (*☎ 544282)* B&B £18-22. The Sheiling is right by the sea, next to the lone thatched cottage.

Craig Highland Farm (*☎/fax 544205, Plockton)* B&B £15 per person, cottages for 2-6 persons £100-400 per week. This is a delightful conservation centre about 2 miles (3km) east of Plockton. It has excellent self-catering cottages. There are lots of animals around (including llamas). If you don't want to stay, you can still visit for £1.50/1.

Off The Rails (*☎ 544423, Plockton Station)* Meals around £4-8. Good home-made food is available at Off The Rails. During the day you can get things like baked potatoes from £2.75; in the evening, meals such as 'haggis and clapshot'.

Plockton Hotel (*☎ 544274, fax 544475, Harbour St)* Mains from £5.25. The black-painted Plockton serves popular pub food; fish dishes start at £5.75. En-suite singles are available for £35, doubles for £55 to £70.

Haven Hotel (*☎ 544223, fax 544467, Innes St)* 4-course meals £24.80. The best food in Plockton is to be had at the Haven Hotel. B&B costs £38 to £41 per person.

KYLE OF LOCHALSH
☎ 01599 • pop 1000

Before the Skye Bridge opened, Kyle of Lochalsh (normally just called Kyle) was the main jumping-off point for trips to the Isle of Skye. Now, however, its many B&B owners have to watch most of their trade whizzing past without stopping.

The TIC (☎ 534276), beside the main seafront car park, opens April to October and stocks information on Skye. In the village, you'll find two supermarkets, two banks with ATMs, a post office and a swimming pool (£2.20).

Organised Tours

Sea Probe Atlantis (*☎ 0800 980 4846)* is a glass-bottomed boat that sails four or five times daily from the old ferry quay near the traffic lights in Kyle. Cruises last from 30 minutes to 2½ hours and prices start from £6.50/3.50. Depending on the tour, you may see a WWII shipwreck, kelp forests, seals or other marine life.

Places to Stay & Eat

Cuchulainn's (*☎ 534492, Station Rd)* Beds £9.50. For dormitory accommodation, try the recommended Cuchulainn's.

Old Schoolhouse (*☎/fax 534369, Erbusaig)* En-suite singles £40-45, doubles £54-60. You'll find this luxurious B&B 2 miles (3km) north of the village.

Seagreen Restaurant & Bookshop (*☎ 534388, Plockton Rd)* Mains around £5-10. Less than a mile (1.6km) north of Kyle, this restaurant has wonderful wholefood, such as broccoli, wild mushroom and local cheese quiche. Oysters baked with butter and lemon are 75-95p each, and the oak-smoked seafood platter is £7.25.

Seafood Restaurant (*☎ 534813, Kyle Station)* Lunch mains from £6.25, dinner mains £9.50-13.99. This is an alternative, pricier seafood restaurant in Kyle Station.

Gateway Café (*☎ 534030, Station Rd)* Takeaways around £3. This place does good takeaway fish and chips (£3.45).

Getting There & Away

Kyle can be reached by bus and train from Inverness (see Getting There & Away under Inverness earlier in this chapter), and by direct Scottish Citylink buses from Glasgow (£17.50, 5½ hours). Citylink continues across the bridge to Kyleakin (£1.60, 10 minutes) and on to Portree (£7.40, one hour) and Uig (£7.90, 1½ hours), for ferries to Tarbert on Harris and Lochmaddy on North Uist. Highland Country Buses runs to/from Kyleakin twice an hour.

The 82-mile (131km) train ride between Inverness and Kyle of Lochalsh (£14, 2½ hours) is one of Scotland's most scenic rail routes.

KYLE TO THE GREAT GLEN

It's 55 miles (88km) via the A87 from Kyle to Invergarry, which lies between Fort William and Fort Augustus, on Loch Oich (see The Great Glen section earlier in this chapter).

Dornie

☎ 01599 • pop 256

This quiet village at the junction of Loch Long, Loch Duich and Loch Alsh has a general store, a post office and the magnificent Eilean Donan Castle, which is on an offshore islet, magically linked to the mainland with a stone-arched bridge.

Eilean Donan Castle Photogenically sited at the entrance to Loch Duich, Eilean Donan Castle (☎ 555202, Dornie; adult/child £3.95/3.20; open 10am-6pm daily mid-Mar–Nov) is Scotland's best-looking castle, with an excellent exhibition and history display panels, spiral staircases, vaulted ceilings, tower bedrooms, impressive interiors (furniture from the 1650s) and a recreation of the kitchen as it was in 1932. It was ruined in 1719 after Spanish Jacobite forces were defeated at the Battle of Glenshiel and was rebuilt between 1912 and 1932.

Places to Stay & Eat There are several acceptable places to stay and eat in the area.

Dornie Bunkhouse (☎ 555264, Carndubh) Beds £9. Accommodation is available at this four-bed hostel, half a mile (800m) along the eastern side of Loch Long. Breakfast is included in the price.

There are several B&Bs in and around the village.

Rockhouse (☎ 555387, Dornie) Beds from £10. Rockhouse is a typical modern bungalow, directly opposite the castle.

Dornie Hotel (☎ 555205, fax 555429, Francis St) Singles £25-35, doubles £50-70. The recommended Dornie Hotel has good bar meals (£6.95 to £16.95), with vegetarian choices.

Jenny J's (☎ 555362, Dornie) Mains from £6.25. Jenny J's is located half a mile (800m) towards Kyle; vegetarian soup costs £1.95.

Getting There & Away Citylink buses from Fort William and Inverness to Portree stop opposite the castle and by the bridge at Dornie.

Glen Shiel & Glenelg

From Eilean Donan Castle, the A87 follows Loch Duich into spectacular Glen Shiel, with 1000m-high peaks soaring up on both sides of the road. At Shiel Bridge, a narrow side road goes over the **Bealach Ratagain** (pass) to Glenelg, where there's still a ferry to Skye.

Things to See & Do There are several good walks in the area, including the low-level route from Morvich to Glen Affric Youth Hostel, via spectacular Gleann Lichd (four hours each way). A traverse of the **Five Sisters of Kintail** is a classic and none-too-easy expedition; start a mile (1.6km) east of the Glen Shiel battle site and finish at Shiel Bridge (eight to 10 hours).

From the Bealach Ratagain, there are great views of the Five Sisters. Continue past Glenelg to the two fine ruined Iron Age **brochs**, Dun Telve and Dun Troddan. Dun Telve still stands to a height of 10m, making it the second best-preserved broch in Scotland, after Mousa in Shetland.

From Glenelg round to the road-end at **Arnisdale**, the scenery becomes even more spectacular, with great views across Loch Hourn to Knoydart. Gavin Maxwell wrote his famous book *Ring of Bright Water* while living at Sandaig, on the coast south of Glenelg.

Places to Stay & Eat There are a few decent options around Shiel Bridge and in Glenelg.

Shiel Bridge Campsite (☎ 01599-511211, Shiel Bridge) Pitches for 1/2 people £4/7. Enquire at the Five Sisters Restaurant if you'd like to stay here.

Ratagan Youth Hostel (☎ 01599-511243, Shiel Bridge) Beds from £9.25/6. This is a particularly good SYHA hostel, by Loch Duich at Ratagan.

Five Sisters Restaurant (☎ 01599-511307, Shiel Bridge) Mains £5.95-7.50, including vegetarian dishes. There's a shop and the Five Sisters Restaurant at the BP petrol station in Shiel Bridge.

Kintail Lodge Hotel (☎ 01599-511275, fax 511226, Shiel Bridge) Bunkhouse beds £10. Singles £30-40, doubles £56-76. At the fine Kintail Lodge Hotel, meals (£7 to £12.50) include local venison and salmon. The bunkhouse has a kitchen.

Glenelg Inn (☎ 01599-522273, fax 522283, Glenelg) Dinner B&B from £50 per person. Don't miss the wacky Glenelg Inn with its kilt-clad proprietor, excellent accommodation and delicious meals (bar meals around £7 to £10).

Getting There & Away Citylink buses between Fort William, Inverness and Skye operate along the A87. There's a postbus (☎ 01246-546329) operating once daily, except Sunday, from Kyle to Arnisdale via Shiel Bridge and Glenelg. For details of the ferry from Glenelg to Skye, see The Hebrides chapter. For details of the ferry service between Arnisdale and Barrisdale (in Knoydart), see Knoydart Peninsula earlier in this chapter.

Cluanie Inn

Beyond the top of Glen Shiel, the A87 passes the remote, but welcoming, Cluanie Inn, which now has a TIC at reception.

Cluanie Inn (☎ 01320-340238, fax 340293, Glenmoriston). B&B £25.50-49.50 per person. There's even a four-poster bed, Jacuzzi and sauna in here. Bar meals (£5.95 to £9.50) for hungry walkers include freshly shot haggis for £5.95.

From the inn, you can walk along several mountain ridges, bagging Munros to your heart's content (check locally about the deer stalking, August to October). There's a low-level route through to Glen Affric Youth Hostel (see West of Inverness earlier in this chapter), which takes three hours, but it gets very wet at certain times of year.

The Hebrides

The islands of western Scotland offer some of the best scenery in the world. From beautiful silver-sand beaches to craggy mountain tops, there's a huge range of spectacular vistas. Soft light is the most attractive feature and the seemingly endless summer sunsets appeal to all. The best time for a visit is from spring to early summer, when the weather's usually at its best, the midges haven't hatched and a pleasing freshness pervades the air.

The Isle of Islay is famous for its distilleries, while Jura is best known for its 'Paps' (breast-shaped hills). Accessible from the town of Oban, the Isle of Mull has virtually everything, from picturesque villages and castles to whale-watching and mountain-walking. Just off Mull's west coast is beautiful Iona, where St Columba founded his monastery in the 6th century. Nearby Staffa has incredible rock architecture and, farther west, the rather flat Isles of Coll and Tiree beckon with their miles of unspoilt beaches.

The Small Isles are reached from Mallaig. Each is different – Muck is flat and sandy, Eigg is hilly with one rock peak, Rum (Rhum) has a high mountain ridge, and Canna has an interesting history and a great position near the Cuillin of Skye.

The Isle of Skye is great for walking and climbing; there are also castles, lots of wildlife and an attractive capital, Portree. Raasay is much quieter and good for walking.

Scenery in the Outer Hebrides includes wonderful beaches, bleak moors on Lewis, rocky mountains in Harris and the maze of lochs on North Uist. Listen for corncrakes and curlews on the machair (grass- and wildflower-covered dunes). From the sea around Mingulay and St Kilda you can look at the bird-cliffs and stacks and, if you are lucky with the weather, you may be able to go ashore.

You'll find many Gaelic speakers on the islands, mainly on Islay, Skye and the Outer Hebrides. In Harris, Lewis and Raasay, the Sabbath is strongly observed. Take care not to upset local sensitivities, whatever your views.

HIGHLIGHTS

- Sampling the local *uisge beatha* at Islay's whisky distilleries
- Taking a boat trip to the Corryvreckan whirlpool at the northern end of Jura
- Exploring the majestic mountain and coastal scenery on Mull
- Hiking among the jagged peaks of the spectacular Black Cuillins on Skye
- Pondering the meaning of the mysterious Standing Stones of Callanish on Lewis

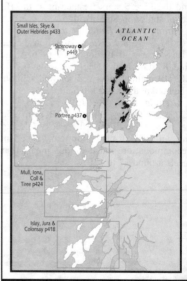

Small Isles, Skye & Outer Hebrides p433

ATLANTIC OCEAN

Stornoway p449

Portree p437

Mull, Iona, Coll & Tiree p424

Islay, Jura & Colonsay p418

Although many areas are still traditional crofting communities without glitzy 'visitor attractions', things are changing, particularly on Skye, where tourism has really taken off in the last 10 years.

WALKING

There are lots of great walks on the islands from easy coastal rambles to ridge

Sunrise over a bare, black Cuillin peak on the mountainous Isle of Skye

Camping at Howmore on South Uist, the second largest island in the Outer Hebrides

GRAEME CORNWALLIS

The walk along the west coast of the Isle of Jura is a gruelling, lonely task. Attempt only if very fit!

ANDREW MARSHALL & LEANNE WALKER

The colourful waterfront at Portree, the Isle of Skye's main town

COLIN HOOD

Feeling a little sheepish: trapped by a loch's high tide on the Isle of Skye

scrambling. The rugged landscapes of Jura, Rum, the Cuillin of Skye and Harris provide challenging ground for even the most serious walker.

Although parts of the Cuillin Ridge involve serious rock climbing (with no easy alternative), there's plenty for the casual rambler to do in the area. See also Walking in The Highlands chapter.

Southern Inner Hebrides

ISLE OF ISLAY
☎ 01496 • pop 3400

The most southerly of the Inner Hebrides, Islay is best known for its single malt whiskies, which have a highly distinctive smoky flavour. There are six distilleries, most of which welcome visitors with guided tours.

With a list of over 250 recorded species, Islay also attracts bird-watchers. It's an important wintering ground for thousands of white-fronted and barnacle geese. As well as the whisky and the wildfowl, there are miles of sandy beaches and some good walks. There's great scenery and pleasant walking around the beach at Machir Bay, Kilchoman.

Since it's farther from the Scottish mainland than Arran or Mull, Islay receives far fewer visitors, but it's definitely worth the trip.

Orientation & Information

There are two ferry terminals on the island, both served by ferries from Kennacraig in West Loch Tarbert – Port Askaig on the east coast, opposite Jura, and Port Ellen in the south. Islay Airport lies midway between Port Ellen and Bowmore, 5 miles (8km) from both.

The island's TIC (☎ 810254) in Bowmore is at The Square and opens March to October.

There are post offices in the main towns and Internet access in Port Ellen; the MacTaggart Community CyberCafe (tucked behind the village hall at the head of the bay – see Places to Stay & Eat in the Port Ellen section later) charges £1 for 15 minutes.

THE HEBRIDES

The MacTaggart Leisure Centre (see the Bowmore section later) has a coin-operated launderette (wash £3, dry £1.50).

There's a camp site and bunkhouse at Kintra, near Port Ellen, and a youth hostel in Port Charlotte. If you want to camp elsewhere, ask permission first. Camping is prohibited on the Ardtalla and Dunlossit estates on the eastern side of Islay.

Port Ellen & Around

Port Ellen is the main point of entry for Islay, with 10 ferries weekly compared to Port Askaig's eight. It has a grocery store, pub,

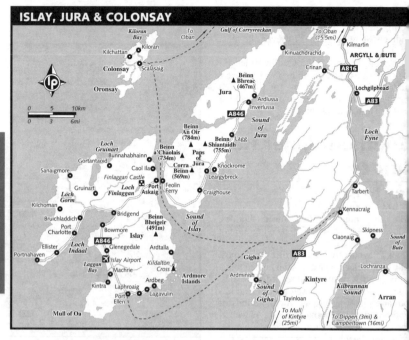

ISLAY, JURA & COLONSAY

hotel and bank (no ATM, closed most afternoons and all day Wednesday), but there's nothing to see in the town.

However, the coast stretching north-east from Port Ellen is one of the loveliest parts of the island. There are three **whisky distilleries** in close succession – **Laphroaig** (☎ 302418), **Lagavulin** (☎ 302400) and **Ardbeg** (☎ 302244) – all of which offer tours by appointment.

Islay was an early focus for Christianity. The exceptional late-8th-century **Kildalton Cross**, at the roofless Kildalton Chapel, 8 miles (13km) north-east of Port Ellen, is the only remaining Celtic High Cross in Scotland. There are carvings of a biblical scene on one side and animals on the other. There are several extraordinary grave slabs at the chapel, some carved with swords and engrailed crosses – symbols of the enigmatic Knights Templar.

The **Ardmore Islands**, off the south-eastern corner of Islay near Kildalton, are a wildlife haven and home to the second largest colony of common seals in Europe.

Laggan Bay, 3 miles (5km) north-west of Port Ellen, has a beautiful, 5-mile long sandy beach.

Places to Stay & Eat The only official camp site and independent hostel on the island is 3 miles (5km) north-west of Port Ellen at Kintra.

Kintra Farm (☎ 302051, Kintra) Pitches £4.80-6.50, dorm beds £6.50, B&B £15 per person. Open Apr-Sept. Kintra Farm, at the southern end of Laggan Bay, offers B&B in the farmhouse and 23 dorm beds (bedding available for £2) in Kintra Bunk Barns; there's also a small camp site close to the beach.

There are a couple of pleasant B&Bs in Port Ellen village, including the *Trout Fly Guest House* (☎ 302204) and *Mrs McGillivray* (☎ 302420). Both charge around £18 per person.

Glenmachrie Farmhouse (☎/fax 305260, e glenmachrie@lineone.net) B&B singles/ doubles £45/60, dinner B&B £53 per person. Glenmachrie is a delightful country guest-house 4 miles (6.5km) north of Port Ellen, near the airport and Machrie Golf Links; the food is superb.

MacTaggart Community CyberCafe (☎ 302693, Mansfield Place) Meals £2.20-4.40. Open 11am-10pm Mon-Sat, noon-9pm Sun. Food served till 5.30pm. Port Ellen's cybercafe does snacks and salads to eat in or takeaway, as well as tea, coffee and cakes. The *Old Kiln Cafe* at the Ardbeg distillery (see Port Ellen & Around earlier) serves good soups, sandwiches and home baking.

Bowmore

The pleasant village of Bowmore is the island's capital. It's on the eastern shore of Loch Indaal, 10 miles (16km) from both Port Askaig and Port Ellen. It has a TIC (☎ 810254), two banks with ATMs, and plenty of shops.

The distinctive **Round Church** at the top of Main St was built in 1767 to ensure that the devil had no corners to hide in. **Bowmore Distillery** (☎ 810441, School St; adult/child £2/1; tours at 10.30am, 11.30am, 2pm & 3pm Mon-Fri & 10.30am Sat May-Sept, 10.30am & 2pm Mon-Fri Oct-Apr) has a friendly visitor centre and offers regular guided tours. The admission charge includes a dram and is redeemable against purchases.

If the weather's bad, there's always the **Mactaggart Leisure Centre** (☎ 810767, School St; pool adult/child £2.20/1.40; open 12.30pm-9.30pm Tues, 2pm-9pm Wed, 12.30pm-9pm Thur & Fri, 10am-6pm Sat, 10.30am-5.30pm Sun). It has a 25m pool, a sauna and a fitness centre.

You can hire **bikes** at the post office, near the church at the top of Main St, for £10 a day.

Places to Stay & Eat There are several places in town offering B&B for £18 to £20 per person, including *Lambeth House* (☎ 810597, Jamieson St) and *Meadowside* (☎ 810497, Birch Drive).

Harbour Inn (☎ 810330, fax 810990, e harbour@harbour-inn.com, The Square)

Singles £42-45, doubles £75-85. The Harbour Inn is a great place to stay and also has a good restaurant (lunch mains £4.75 to £9.10, dinner £11.25 to £16.75) – the whisky-soaked smoked beef is exceptional. They serve breakfast from 9.30am to 11.45am.

Lochside Hotel (☎ 810244, fax 810390, e ask@lochsidehotel.co.uk, 19 Shore St) Singles £39.50, doubles £79. The Lochside's bar has around 400 malts on offer, including a 29-year-old Black Bowmore (50% ABV) for £150 per 35ml! It runs speciality malt whisky weekends from £125 per person; the price includes three nights' B&B (with dinner) and whisky tours.

The *Co-op* (Main St) supermarket opens 8am to 8pm Monday to Saturday.

Port Charlotte & Around

Eleven miles (18km) from Bowmore, on the opposite shore of Loch Indaal, is the attractive village of Port Charlotte. It has a Spar shop, post office, youth hostel, museum and wildlife centre. You can hire bikes from the house opposite the Port Charlotte Hotel.

Islay's long history is recorded in detail at the **Museum of Islay Life** (☎ 850358; adult/child £2/1; open 10am-5pm Mon-Sat & 2pm-5pm Sun Easter-Oct), with around 10,000 items covering just about every feasible topic. The **Islay Wildlife Information Centre** (☎ 850288, next to the youth hostel; adult/child £2/1; open 10am-3pm Mon, Tues, Thur & Fri Apr-Oct) has a useful reference library and displays on the island's natural history.

Seven miles (11km) north of Port Charlotte, there's an interesting **RSPB information centre** (☎ 850505; admission free; open 10am-5pm daily Apr-Oct, 10am-4pm Nov-Mar) at the southern end of Loch Gruinart. Two- to three-hour guided walks around the adjacent nature reserve are available (£2 per person, £1 for RSPB members) at 10am every Thursday and at 6pm on Tuesday in August.

The beach at **Killinallan**, north-east of the reserve, is one of Islay's best. You can walk for miles along the coast, following the **raised beaches** that were caused by the land rising after they were depressed by glacier ice during the last Ice Age.

Six miles (10km) south-west of Port Charlotte the road ends at **Portnahaven**, another pretty village, purpose-built as a fishing harbour in the 19th century. The world's first commercially viable, wave-powered electricity generating station has been built on the sea cliffs, which are open to the Atlantic swell, a mile north of the village. The 500kW plant – known as 'Limpet' (Land-installed, marine-powered energy transformer) – provides enough electricity to supply 200 island homes.

Places to Stay & Eat There are B&Bs, a hotel and a youth hostel in Port Charlotte.

Islay Youth Hostel (☎ 850385) Beds £9/7.75. Open May-Sept. This comfortable and atmospheric Scottish Youth Hostel Association (SYHA) hostel is housed in a former distillery building with good views over the loch.

Port Charlotte Hotel (☎ 850360, fax 850361) Singles £49-59, doubles £56-90. This is a lovely old Victorian hotel overlooking the sea, with a good restaurant serving local seafood, beef and lamb (a three-course evening meal costs around £20).

Mrs Halsall (☎ 850431, Nerabus) and *Mrs Hastie* (☎ 850432, Tigh-na-Greing) offer B&B for around £18 per person.

The *Croft Kitchen* (☎ 850230), opposite the Museum of Island Life, serves excellent snacks and meals, and the *Loch Indaal* (☎ 850202) pub, 50m south of the Port Charlotte Hotel, does good bar meals; last orders for food at both places is 8.30pm.

Port Askaig & Around

Port Askaig is little more than a hamlet and a ferry slip halfway along the Sound of Islay, the strait that separates Islay and Jura. It has a grocery store, post office and hotel.

The **Caol Ila Distillery** (☎ 840207; admission £3; tours by appointment Mon-Fri), opened in 1846, is just a half-mile walk north of Port Askaig. The admission charge is redeemable against any whisky purchased – Caol Ila (pronounced cull ee-la) is a typical smoky Islay malt. The distillery enjoys a wonderful location, with great views across to Jura.

The **Bunnahabhain Distillery** (pronounced boo-na-ha-ven; ☎ 840646; open 10am-4pm Mon-Fri Mar-Oct, by arrangement Nov-Feb) is 3 miles (5km) north of Port Askaig and has a small visitor centre and shop.

Islay was once the seat of secular power for the Hebrides, and the meeting place of the Lords of the Isles during the 14th century. On an island in **Loch Finlaggan**, 3 miles (5km) west of Port Askaig, are the remains of the stronghold from which the powerful Mac Donald Lords of the Isles administered their considerable island territories. The **Finlaggan Visitor Centre** (☎ 810629; open at variable times), in a nearby cottage, explains the site's history and archaeology, which has been inhabited since prehistoric times. Call the TIC at Bowmore for details of opening hours.

Port Askaig Hotel (☎ 840245, fax 840295) Singles £30-42, doubles £36-45. This hotel is situated right beside the ferry slip. Bar meals are available from £4.95.

Special Events

The Islay Festival (Feis Ile; W www.ileach.co.uk/festival), held at the end of May, is a week-long celebration of traditional Scottish music and includes the Islay Whisky Festival (W www.islaywhiskyfestival.com). Events include ceilidhs, pipe bands, distillery tours and whisky tastings. Both festivals are promoted by Distillery Destinations (☎ 0141-429 0762, W www.whisky-tours.com).

The annual three-day Islay Jazz Festival, promoted by Assembly Direct (☎ 0131-553 4000, W www.ileach.co.uk/jazz), takes place over the second weekend in September and sees a varied line-up of international talent playing at various venues across the island.

Getting There & Away

British Airways Express flies from Glasgow to Islay twice on weekdays and once on Saturday (from £95 return, 40 minutes).

CalMac (☎ 302209) runs ferries from Kennacraig in West Loch Tarbert to Port Ellen (passenger/car £7.05/37.50, 2¼ hours) and Port Askaig (same fare, two hours). They operate daily, except Wednesday when there's only a ferry to Port Askaig, and Sunday when there's only a ferry to Port Ellen.

On Wednesday in summer, the ferry continues from Port Askaig to Colonsay (£3.55/8.75, 1¼ hours), and returns in the evening, allowing six hours ashore.

Getting Around

A bus service runs between Ardbeg, Port Ellen, Bowmore, Port Charlotte, Portnahaven and Port Askaig (only one bus on Sunday). The timetable is so complex that there's a danger you'll miss your bus while trying to work it out – get a copy from the TIC.

Taxis are available in both Bowmore (☎ 810449) and Port Ellen (☎ 302155).

You can hire bikes in Bowmore and Port Charlotte (see those sections earlier).

ISLE OF JURA
☎ 01496 • pop 200

Jura is a magnificently wild and lonely island, and one can quite understand why George Orwell chose it as a writer's retreat. In 1948 he spent several months in Barnhill, a house in the north of the island, writing his novel *1984*.

Jura is a wonderful place to walk – in fact there's really nothing else to do here, apart from having a look around **Craighouse**, the island's only village, graced by a shop (Jura Stores) and **The Isle of Jura Distillery** (☎ 820240; admission free; open by appointment only). The mountain scenery is superb – the distinctive shapes of the Paps of Jura are visible from miles around.

At the northern end of the island, between Jura and Scarba, is the great tidal race known as the **Corryvreckan whirlpool** (see the boxed text 'The Scottish Maelstrom'). There's another impressive tidal race, between the islands of Scarba and Lunga, called Bealach a'Choin Ghlais, or the 'Pass of the Grey Dogs', where the water runs like river rapids during the spring tides.

Walking

The **Paps of Jura** provide a tough hill walk that requires good navigational skills and takes around eight hours, although the record for the Paps of Jura fell race is just three hours! Look out for adders – the island is infested with them, but they are shy snakes that will move away as you approach.

The Scottish Maelstrom

It may look innocuous on the map, but the Gulf of Corryvreckan – the 1000m-wide channel between the northern end of Jura and the island of Scarba – is home to one of the three most notorious tidal whirlpools in the world (the others are the Maelstrom in Norway's Lofoten Islands, and the Old Sow in Canada's New Brunswick).

The tide doesn't just rise and fall twice a day, it flows – dragged around the earth by the gravitational attraction of the moon. On the west coast of Scotland, the rising tide – known as the flood tide – flows northwards. As the flood moves up the Sound of Jura, to the east of the island, it is forced into a narrowing bottleneck jammed with islands and builds up to a greater height than the open sea to the west of Jura. As a result, millions of gallons of sea water pour westwards through the Gulf of Corryvreckan at speeds of up to 8 knots – an average sailing yacht is going fast at 6 knots.

The Corryvreckan whirlpool forms where this mass of moving water hits an underwater pinnacle, which rises from the 200m-deep sea bed to within just 38m of the surface, and swirls over and around it. The turbulent waters create a magnificent spectacle, with white-capped breakers, bulging boils and overfalls, and countless miniature maelstroms whirling around the main vortex.

Corryvreckan is at its most violent when a flooding spring tide, flowing west through the gulf, meets a westerly gale blowing in from the Atlantic. In these conditions, standing waves up to 5m high can form and dangerously rough seas extend more than 3 miles (5km) west of Corryvreckan, a phenomenon known as the Great Race.

You can see the whirlpool by making the long hike to the northern end of Jura, or by taking a boat trip from Easdale (see the Around Oban – Isle of Seil section in the Highlands chapter).

A good place to start is by the bridge over the Corran River, north of Leargybreck. The first pap you reach is Beinn a'Chaolais

THE HEBRIDES

(734m), the second is Beinn an Oir (784m) and the third is Beinn Shiantaidh (755m). Most people also climb Corra Bheinn (569m), before joining the path that crosses the island from Glenbatrick to return to the road.

It's possible to follow the west coast from Feolin Ferry all the way to the northern tip of Jura, but it's a gruelling endurance test and only suitable for a very fit, well-equipped and experienced party. It's about 40 miles (64km) one way and takes at least five days. Camping will be necessary. You're likely to encounter raised beaches; unbridged rivers; lots of wildlife, including wild goats; extreme tussocks; caves with rooms, ladders and beds; and a range of other experiences. There's not much chance of seeing anyone else. You'll never forget Jura afterwards.

Remember that much of the island is run as a deer-stalking estate and access to the hills is restricted during the stalking season (July to February); the Jura Hotel can provide details of areas to be avoided (see below).

Places to Stay & Eat
Accommodation on the island is limited, so book ahead – don't rely on just turning up and hoping to find a bed.

There is a small *camp site* (£5 per person) in the field adjoining the Jura Hotel (see later in this section), with showers (£1) and a laundrette. There are also *bunkhouses* (☎ 820332) at Knockrome, 3½ miles (5.5km) north of Craighouse, and Kinuachdrachd (☎ 07899-912116), in the far north of the island, but these are geared mainly to groups rather than individual travellers.

Gwen Boardman (☎ 820379, 7 Woodside, Craighouse) and *Liz Mack* (☎ 820332, Knockrome) offer B&B for around £18 per person.

Ivy Cottage (☎ 820322, Inverlussa) B&B £15-20 per person. This is a delightful cottage with one double and one single room overlooking the bay at Inverlussa, 17 miles (27km) north of Craighouse. Their three-course dinner costs £12.

Jura Hotel (☎ 820243, fax 820249, e jurahotel@aol.com, Craighouse) Rooms £33-49 per person. The 18-room Jura Hotel is a great place to stay and the only place to

drink on Jura. Try to get the rooms at the front for the views; book ahead in summer. It also offers a three-course dinner for £16.95.

Antlers Tearoom (☎ 820395, Craighouse) serves tea, coffee and snacks during the day.

Getting There & Away
You get to Jura via Islay. A small car ferry shuttles between Port Askaig and Feolin (car and driver £10, passenger £1.80, five minutes), roughly hourly Monday to Saturday and less often on Sunday.

Getting Around
Charles MacLean (☎ 820314 or ☎ 820221) runs a bus service five or six days a week between Feolin and Craighouse. One or two of the runs go as far as Inverlussa in the north of the island.

ISLE OF COLONSAY
☎ 01951 • pop 106

Colonsay, to the north of Islay, is one of the remotest islands of the Inner Hebrides. It's an unspoilt island of varied landscapes; it has a good sunshine record and receives only half the rainfall of the Argyll mainland. As well as cliffs and a rocky coastline, there are several beaches of golden sand, the most spectacular being Kiloran Bay. Along the west coast are several stony raised beaches. The island is of particular interest to ornithologists, with more than 150 species of birds recorded, including golden eagles and corn crakes.

Orientation & Information
The ferry pier is at the main village, Scalasaig, where you'll find a grocery shop cum post office (Rutherford's), a restaurant, a telephone box and a hotel. There is no TIC and no banks or ATMs on the island. General information is available at the CalMac waiting room beside the ferry terminal.

There's a tiny *bookshop* (☎ 200232) at the hotel.

Guided walks (£10 an hour) and boat trips (£15 per person) are available from *Kevin and Christa Byrne* (☎ 200320, e byrne@colonsay.org.uk).

For a doctor, call ☎ 200328.

Things to See & Do

Botanists will appreciate the **Woodland Gardens** (☎ 200211; admission free; open dawn-dusk daily) at Colonsay House, 1½ miles (2.5 miles) north of Scalasaig, which is famous for its outstanding collection of hybrid rhododendrons and unusual trees. The formal walled garden around the mansion, which has a terrace cafe, opens Wednesday and Friday only, Easter to September.

There are **standing stones** at various places, such as Kilchattan and Garvard, and the sparse remains of eight Iron Age forts. Some of the caves near Kiloran Bay may have been inhabited 6000 years ago.

At low spring tides (at the time of the full or new moon), you have three to four hours to walk across the half-mile of The Strand and visit **Oronsay**, a small island to the south, where the ruins of an Augustinian priory date from the 14th century. There's a spectacular late-15th-century **stone cross** at the entrance, and a collection of 15th- and 16th-century carved tombstones in the Prior's House.

Places to Stay & Eat

There are few places to stay, none of them cheap, and camping isn't allowed. As beds are limited, all accommodation should be booked before coming to the island.

Keepers Backpackers Lodge (☎ 200312) Beds £8.50-10 per person. This hostel, set in a former gamekeeper's house in the middle of the island near Loch Fada is about 30 minutes' walk from the ferry terminal. It has showers and a fully equipped kitchen. Bikes can be hired for £5 per day.

Seaview (☎/fax 200315) B&B £23 per person. This peaceful farmhouse is in Kilchattan, near the rugged west coast of the island. Dinner/packed lunches are available for an additional £16/3.50.

Isle of Colonsay Chalets (☎ 200320, ☎/fax 200242, ⓔ chalets@colonsay.org.uk) Singles/doubles £25/40. These comfortable modern chalets are just 10 minutes' walk from the ferry pier at Scalasaig. You can check last-minute availability at ⓦ www .colonsay.org.uk/newother/lodges.html.

Isle of Colonsay Hotel (☎ 200316, fax 200353, ⓔ colonsay.hotel@pipemedia.co.uk)

Dinner B&B £69-80 per person, including bicycle hire. This comfortable eight-room hotel dates from the 18th century and has an excellent restaurant, a coffee shop and a gift shop. Bar meals are available from £4 to £6.

The Pantry (☎ 200325, beside the ferry pier) serves meals, snacks and ice creams throughout summer and on the days the ferry calls the rest of the year.

Getting There & Away

CalMac operates ferries to Colonsay from Oban on Sunday, Wednesday and Friday (passenger/car £10.10/48.50, 2¼ hours), and on Wednesday only in summer from Islay's Port Askaig (passenger/car £3.55/ 18.75, 1¼ hours) and Kennacraig on the Kintyre peninsula (passenger/car £10.10/ 48.50, 3½ hours). From April to September, a Wednesday day trip to Colonsay from Kennacraig or Port Askaig allows you about five hours on the island.

Getting Around

Bike hire is available from A McConnel (☎ 200355). On Tuesday, Wednesday and Saturday, there's a postbus service (☎ 01463-256200) around the island – it also goes to Oronsay, with times dependent on the tides.

MULL & IONA
pop 2600

It's easy to see why Mull is so popular with tourists. As well as having superb mountain scenery, two castles, a narrow-gauge railway and being on the route to the holy isle of Iona, it's also a charmingly endearing place.

Where else would you find a police station that used gerbils to shred important documents (really!), or a stately home where notices actually encourage you to sit on the chairs? And there can be few places left in Britain where the locals don't lock their doors at night.

Despite the numbers of visitors who flock to the island, it seems to be large enough to absorb them all; many stick to the well-worn route from Craignure to Iona, returning to Oban in the evening. If you're looking for budget accommodation, there's not much of it on Mull, so you'd be advised to take a tent.

Orientation & Information

About two-thirds of Mull's population is centred on Tobermory, the island's capital, in the north. Craignure, at the south-eastern corner, has the main ferry terminal and is where most people arrive. Fionnphort is at the far western end of the long Ross of Mull peninsula, and is where the ferry to Iona departs.

There are TICs at Craignure and at Tobermory. Tobermory has a bank with an ATM; elsewhere, you'll have to wait for a mobile bank. There are post offices and grocery stores in most villages – the Co-op supermarket in Tobermory is the best place for provisions.

The hospital (☎ 01680-300392) is centrally located at Salen. For a doctor in Tobermory or Bunessan call ☎ 01688-302013 or ☎ 01681-700261 respectively.

Craignure & Around
☎ 01680

Apart from the ferry terminal, there's not much at Craignure other than the hotel, pub

and the TIC (☎ 812377) opposite the quay; it opens 8.30am to 7pm Monday to Thursday, 8.30am to 5.15pm Friday, 9am to 5pm Saturday and 10am to 5pm Sunday, with shorter hours in winter.

The **Mull Railway** (*☎ 812494, Old Pier Station, adult/child £2.50/1.50 one way; open Apr-Oct*) is a miniature steam train that transports passengers some 1½ miles (2.5km) south to Torosay Castle.

Torosay Castle & Gardens (*☎ 812421; adult/child £4.50/1.50, gardens only £3.50/1; house open 10.30am-5.30pm daily Easter-mid-Oct, gardens open 10.30am-dusk daily*) is a Victorian house in the Scottish baronial style. 'Take your time but not our spoons' advises the sign; otherwise you're left to wander at will. The house is set in a beautiful garden that can be visited on its own.

A 30-minute walk beyond Torosay is **Duart Castle** (*☎ 812309; adult/child £3.80/1.90; open 10.30am-6pm May–mid-Oct*), a formidable fortress dominating the Sound of

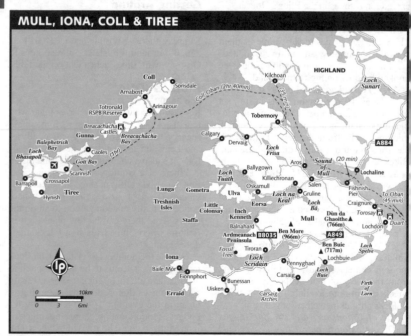

MULL, IONA, COLL & TIRE

Mull. The seat of the Clan Maclean, this is one of the oldest inhabited castles in Scotland – the central keep was built in 1360. In 1911, Sir Fitzroy Maclean bought and restored the castle. It has damp dungeons, vast halls and bathrooms equipped with ancient fittings. If Lady Mac is in residence, she'll take your money at the door.

Places to Stay & Eat There's a camp site and a couple of hotels and B&Bs close to the Craignure ferry terminal.

Shieling Holidays (☎ 812496, Craignure) Tent & two persons £9-10, car £1.50, dorm beds £8. Open Apr-Oct. Less than 10 minutes' walk from the ferry terminal at Craignure, this site has hostel-style beds as well as top-quality camping facilities. It also lets two-person, semi-permanent tents (from £20 a night, minimum two nights).

Chronicle (☎/fax 812364, ℮ chronicle@ isle-of-mull.demon.co.uk, Craignure) B&B from £21 per person. The Chronicle is just 10 minutes' walk from the ferry and offers comfortable, quiet rooms with en-suite bathrooms.

Aon a'Dha (☎ 812318 Kirk Terrace, Craignure) B&B from £16 per person. Aon a'Dha is also close to the ferry, but is cheaper and doesn't have en-suite facilities.

Craignure Inn (☎ 812305, fax 812470, ℮ janice@craignureinn.freeserve.co.uk, Craignure) Singles £40-45, doubles £59-65. The local pub, set in an 18th-century drovers' inn, has three rooms to let.

Isle of Mull Hotel (☎ 812351, fax 812462, Craignure) Singles £30-55, doubles £50-96. Open Mar-Nov. This modern, purpose-built hotel is 800m north of the ferry terminal; most rooms have good sea views.

There are a couple of B&Bs in the hamlet of Lochdon, 3 miles (5km) south of Craignure, including *Redburn* (☎/fax 812370 ℮ weir.c.lochdon@talk21.com), with rooms for £20 to £ 25 per person, and *Old Mill Cottage* (☎/fax 812442, ℮ oldmill@mull .com), which has a good restaurant and charges £25 to £30 per person.

In Craignure, you can get snacks and full meals at *MacGregror's Bistro* (beside the ferry terminal) and bar meals at the nearby *Craignure Inn* and *Isle of Mull Hotel*.

South Mull
☎ 01681

There are some interesting places to visit in the south, but you'll need to hitchhike, walk or bring your own transport. At remote **Lochbuie**, there's an impressive prehistoric stone circle and the Moy Castle ruins.

The road from Craignure to Fionnphort climbs through some wild and desolate scenery before reaching the south-western part of the island, which consists of a long peninsula called the Ross of Mull. The Ross has a spectacular south coast with black basalt cliffs, which give way farther west to pink granite crags and white sandy beaches. The cliffs reach their highest at Malcolm's Point, near the superb **Carsaig Arches** (see Walking later in this section).

The little village of Bunessan has a hotel, tearoom, pub and some shops, and is home to the **Ross of Mull Historical Centre** (☎ 700659; admission £1; open 10am-4.30pm Mon-Fri Apr-Oct, by arrangement Nov-Mar), which covers local history, geology, archaeology, genealogy and wildlife.

At the western end of the Ross, 38 miles (61km) west of Craignure, is **Fionnphort** (pronounced finn-a-fort). The coast here is a beautiful blend of pink granite rocks, white sandy beaches and vivid turquoise seas. The **St Columba Exhibition and Welcome Centre** (☎ 700660; admission free; open 10.30am-1pm & 2pm-5.30pm daily Apr-Oct) has displays about the life of St Columba, the Celts and the history of Iona.

Places to Stay & Eat Places to stay and eat are concentrated in the villages of Bunessan and Fionnphort.

Pennyghael Hotel (☎ 704288, fax 704205, Pennyghael) Singles £31-46, doubles £62-72. Open Mar-Oct. This delightful country hotel, with six rooms and a good restaurant, is near the head of Loch Scridain, about halfway between Craignure and Fionnphort.

Ardness House (☎/fax 700260, Bunessan) En-suite B&B £18-22 per person. This is a modern bungalow with great views over Loch na Lathaich. Dinner is available for £12.

Argyll Arms (☎ 700240, ℮ argyllarms@ isleofmull.co.uk, Bunessan) B&B £25-28 per

THE HEBRIDES

person. The six-room Argyll Arms is in the middle of the village and has a lively bar. The hotel's *MacLeod Lounge* does bar meals from £3.25 to £10.95. Meals are served between noon and 2pm and 6pm and 9pm.

The nearby *Argyll Tearooms* does inexpensive snacks.

At Fionnphort, there's a basic camp site at *Fidden Farm (☎ 700427)*, which charges £2 per person and opens April to September. It's 1¼ miles (2km) south of the village.

Seaview (☎ 700235, fax 700669, Fionnphort) B&B £17-26 per person. Seaview is barely a minute's walk from the Iona ferry and has grand views across to the island.

Staffa House (☎/fax 700677, Fionnphort) B&B from £20 per person. Open Mar-Oct. Readers have recommended Staffa House for its charm and hospitality.

Keel Row (☎ 700458, Fionnphort) Bar meals £6-10. The Keel Row, next door to Seaview, does home-made bar meals and snacks. Specials, mainly local fish dishes, cost up to £15.

There's also a basic *snack bar* down at the ferry slip.

Isle of Iona
☎ 01681 • pop 130

A short ferry trip from Fionnphort takes you to the sacred isle of Iona. St Columba landed here from Ireland in 563, before setting out to convert Scotland. A monastery was established and it was here that the Book of Kells, the prize attraction of Dublin's Trinity College, is believed to have been transcribed. It was taken to Kells, in Ireland, when Viking raids drove the monks from Iona.

The monks returned and the monastery prospered until its destruction during the Reformation. The ruins were given to the Church of Scotland in 1899, and by 1910 Iona Abbey *(☎ 700512; adult/child £2.80/1.20; open 24 hours year-round)* was reconstructed by a group of enthusiasts called the Iona Community. Run by Historic Scotland (HS), it's still a flourishing spiritual community, which holds regular courses and retreats.

Iona is indeed a very special place, with some of the best beaches and coves in the Hebrides, but the stampeding hordes that

pile off the tour buses every day in summer make it difficult to appreciate. The best advice is to spend the night here. After the crowds have gone, you can walk to the top of the hill, go to an evening service or look around the ancient graveyard where 48 of Scotland's early kings, including Macbeth, are buried. The grave of former British Labour leader John Smith is also here.

Iona has a Spar shop and post office, near the pier. You can visit the **Iona Heritage Centre** *(☎ 700576; admission £1.50; open 10.30am-4.30pm Mon-Sat Apr-Oct)* which covers the history of Iona, crofting and lighthouses; home-baking is available in the centre's coffee shop.

The ferry from Fionnphort to Iona (£3.30 return, five minutes) runs frequently between 8.15am and 6.15pm daily. There are also various day trips available from Oban to Iona – see Organised Tours under Oban in the Highlands chapter.

Places to Stay & Eat A shiny new 21-bed hostel opened on Iona in late 2001.

Iona Hostel (☎ 700642, email iinfo@ionahostel.co.uk, at the far northern end of the island) Beds £12, sheets £1.50. This hostel has stunning views out to Staffa and the Treshnish Isles and, on a clear day, as far as the Isle of Skye. Rooms are clean and functional, and the cosy, well-equipped lounge/kitchen area has an open fire and, best of all, duck eggs on sale for 15p each. To get there, turn right off the ferry and follow the road for 1½ miles (2.5km) until it ends.

Argyll Hotel (☎ 700334, fax 700510, e reception@argyllhoteliona.co.uk) Singles £37-46, doubles £36-96. This is the island's most luxurious accommodation and top eaterie (bar lunches £4 to £6, four-course dinner £19.50). Lunch is available from 12.30pm to 2pm, dinner from 7pm to 8.30pm.

For B&B try *Bishop's House (☎ 700800, fax 700801)* near the abbey, which charges £22 to £29.50 per person, or *Cruachan (☎ 700523)*, which is cheaper at £16 to £17.50 per person and is a half-mile walk south of the ferry landing.

Meals are available at the *Martyr's Bay Restaurant (☎ 700382)*, near the ferry pier.

You can hire bikes from Finlay, Ross Ltd (☎ 700357) at the craft shop above the pier.

Isle of Staffa
☎ 01681

This uninhabited island is a truly magnificent sight – it inspired Mendelssohn to compose his *Hebridean Overture*. Immense hexagonal basalt pillars form the walls, roof and floor of the cathedral-like **Fingal's Cave**. You can land on the island and walk into the cave via a causeway.

Boat Cave can be seen from the causeway, but you can't reach it on foot. Staffa also has a sizeable puffin colony, north of the landing place.

During summer, *Gordon Grant Marine* (☎ 700388) runs twice-daily boat trips to Staffa from Fionnphort and Iona (adult/child £12.50/6.50, 2½ hours). Tours on the *MV Iolaire* (☎ 700358) are similar (£12.50/5).

Turus Mara (☎ 0800 085 8786) runs boat trips to Staffa from Ulva Ferry in central Mull (£14.50/8, 3½ hours). It also runs day trips to Staffa by bus and boat from Oban via Craignure (£24/12.50, 10 hours). More expensive tours take in Iona and the Treshnish Isles.

Treshnish Isles
☎ 01681

This chain of deserted islands lies north-west of Staffa; two of them have ruined castles. The two main islands are the curiously shaped **Dutchman's Cap** and **Lunga**. You can land on Lunga, walk to the top of the hill, and visit the shag, puffin and guillemot colonies on the west coast at **Harp Rock**. Camping is possible, but you need to bring all your drinking water.

Gordon Grant Marine (☎ 700388) sails to Staffa and the Treshnish Isles from Fionnphort and Iona on Tuesday, Wednesday, Thursday and Saturday from mid-May to July (£25/12.50, six hours). Turus Mara (☎ 0800 085 8786) sails from Ulva Ferry to the Treshnish Isles and Staffa daily, except Friday, from May to September (£29.50/15, six hours).

Central Mull
☎ 01680

Central Mull lies between the Craignure–Fionnphort road and the narrow isthmus between Salen and Gruline, and contains the island's highest peak, Ben More (see Walking later in this section), and some of its wildest scenery.

At Gruline, near the head of Loch na Keal, is the **MacQuarrie Mausoleum**. Sir Lachlan MacQuarrie (1762–1824) was born on Mull and served as governor of New South Wales in Australia from 1809 to 1821.

The narrow road along the southern shore of Loch na Keal squeezes past some impressive cliffs before cutting south towards Loch Scridain. At the tip of the remote Ardmeanach Peninsula, there is a remarkable, 50-million-year-old **fossil tree**, preserved in the basalt lava flows of the cliffs. It's a very strenuous, 5-mile hike from Tiroran to the tree – check tide times with a TIC before setting off.

Just north of Ulva Ferry, there's more wonderful scenery, and a spectacular waterfall, **Eas Fors**, where a bizarrely shaped tree grows back on itself.

Places to Stay & Eat There's not much accommodation in the centre of the island.

Balmeanach Park Caravan & Camping Site (☎/fax 01680-300342) Adult/child £4/2.50, car 50p extra. Bunkhouse beds £6.50. Open Mar-Oct. This camp site and bunkhouse is 10 minutes' walk from the Fishnish-Lochaline ferry, on the main road between Craignure and Tobermory.

Salen Hotel (☎ 01680-300324, fax 300599, Salen) Singles £21-32, doubles from £52-54. This hotel is centrally located, about halfway between Craignure and Tobermory.

There's also a very basic *camp site* at Killiechronan, a half-mile north of Gruline, which charges £3 per person. Toilets and water are a five-minute walk away.

Isle of Ulva
☎ 01688 • pop 30

Ulva is about 5 miles (8km) long and lies just off the west coast of Mull. It's linked by a bridge to the even more remote island of Gometra. The island has good walking and mountain biking, great scenery, a 9th-century Viking fort, **Dùn Bàn**, and an old chapel with a graveyard, **Cille Mhic Eoghainn**.

THE HEBRIDES

A short walk north of the ferry, **Sheila's Cottage Heritage Centre** (☎ *500241; adult/ child £4/2 including ferry; open 9am–5pm Mon–Fri Easter–Oct, 9am–5pm Sun June–Aug*) is a reconstruction of a traditional thatched crofter's cottage, with displays about the history of the island.

The Boathouse tearoom, beside the ferry landing, serves locally harvested oysters with Guinness, as well as soup, toasties and filled rolls. An interpretative centre upstairs has information on walks and natural history.

There's no accommodation on Ulva, but you can camp if you make arrangements by calling ☎ 500264 beforehand.

The two-minute ferry crossing (☎ 500226; £4/2 return) runs on demand during Heritage Centre opening hours. At other times, phone to make arrangements. The fare includes admission to the Heritage Centre.

Tobermory
☎ 01688 • pop 750

Tobermory, the island's main town and a major yachting centre, is a picturesque little fishing port with brightly painted houses ranged around a sheltered harbour.

The TIC (☎ 302182), beside the ferry terminal, only opens April to October. You can check email at the Spar shop next to the Mishnish Hotel for 95p per 15 minutes.

Mull Museum (☎ *302493, Main St; adult/child £1/20p; open 10am–4pm Mon–Fri & 10am–1pm Sat Easter–Oct*) records the history of the island. The **Tobermory Distillery** (☎ *302645; adult/child £2.50/1; open 10am–5pm Mon–Fri Easter–Oct*) offers guided tours every 30 mins from 10.30am to 4pm. The admission cost includes a dram.

The Hebridean Whale and Dolphin Trust's **Marine Discovery Centre** (☎ *302620, 28 Main St; admission free; open 10am–5pm Mon–Fri & 11am–4pm Sun Apr–Oct, 11am–5pm Mon–Fri Nov–Mar*) has displays, videos and interactive exhibits on whale and dolphin biology and ecology.

Somewhere out in Tobermory Bay is the wreck of a Spanish galleon – part of the Armada fleeing from Sir Walter Raleigh – that sank here in 1588. No one is sure if the ship was the *Florida*, the *San Juan* or the *Santa Maria*, but rumours of a cargo of gold have kept treasure-hunters looking ever since.

Places to Stay Tobermory has the best choice of places to stay on the island. There are dozens of B&Bs, but the place can still be booked solid in July and August, especially at weekends. B&B rates range from £15 to £30 per person. Contact the TIC for details and reservations.

Tobermory Camp Site (☎ *302525 or 302624,* e *angus.williams@icscotland.net, Newdale, Dervaig Rd)* Adult/child £3.50/2 per night. Open Mar–Oct. This quiet, country site is a mile west of town on the road to Dervaig.

Tobermory Youth Hostel (☎ *302481, Main St)* Beds £8.75/7.50. Open Mar–Oct. This renovated hostel has a great location right on the waterfront. Bookings are recommended.

Arle Farm Lodge (☎ *01680-300343, Arle Farm, Aros)* Dorm beds £11 per person. This modern, well-appointed place, 6 miles (10km) south of Tobermory on the road to Craignure, offers 26 hostel-style beds with duvets.

Ulva House Hotel (☎*/fax 302044,* e *info@ulvahousehotel.co.uk)* Dinner B&B £47.50-54.50 per person. The snug, six-room Ulva House overlooks the harbour from above the ferry terminal. The food is top notch, and the log fires in the lounge and bar will warm your weary feet after a day's hike.

Western Isles Hotel (☎ *302012, fax 302297* e *wihotel@aol.com)* Singles £41-180, doubles £82-190. One of the top hotels on Mull, this grand Victorian pile commands the heights above the harbour. It has luxurious rooms and a great conservatory bar/restaurant with panoramic views.

Places to Eat There's also a good range of eateries in Tobermory.

Back Brae Restaurant (☎ *302422, Back Brae)* Mains £7-15. Open 6pm-late daily. The snug and atmospheric Back Brae is the village's oldest restaurant, specialising in Scottish seafood, beef, lamb and venison. There are vegetarian dishes and a children's menu.

MacGochan's (☎ *302350, Ledaig)* Mains £3.50-5.95. Meals served noon-10pm daily. MacGochan's is a new and lively pub beside the car park at the southern end of the waterfront. It does good bar meals and there are outdoor barbecues on summer evenings, a weekend brunch (11am to 2.30pm) and live music in the bar every weekend. It opens 11am to midnight (till 2am Friday and Saturday).

Mishnish Hotel (☎ *302009, Main St*) Mains £4.50-12.50. You can't miss the virulently yellow facade of the 'Mish', a favourite hang-out for visiting yachties. It serves good bar meals, and there's often live music and sometimes a disco.

Posh Nosh (*above the TIC at the CalMac ferry terminal*) Open 10am to 11pm daily. Posh Nosh is a cafe and fish-and-chip shop that does the usual fried food, as well as kebabs and scallops.

For truly posh nosh, try the ***Pisces*** seafood restaurant at the Western Isles Hotel, or the ***Water's Edge*** at the Tobermory Hotel on the harbourfront; expect to pay around £20 a head excluding wine.

North Mull
☎ 01688

Eight miles (13km) west of Tobermory, at Dervaig, is the **Mull Little Theatre** (☎ *400245, Dervaig; adult/child around £12/7; shows at 8.30pm Apr-Sept*). With only 43 seats, this is Scotland's smallest theatre, but it enjoys a reputation for staging excellent productions.

One mile south of Dervaig, you'll find the **Old Byre Heritage Centre** (☎ *400229; adult/child £3/1.50; open 10.30am-6.30pm daily Easter-Oct*), which is highly recommended. Displays comprise six cases of stuffed birds, a 40cm model of a midge, and excellent plasticine models of life on Mull and Iona from the Stone Age to the present. The centre's ***tearoom*** serves good, inexpensive snacks, including delicious soup and 'clootie dumpling' with cream.

Mull's best silver-sand beach is at **Calgary**, about 4 miles (7km) west of Dervaig. It's a wonderful place, flanked by cliffs, with views out to Coll and Tiree.

Places to Stay & Eat There's a very basic ***camp site***, at the southern end of the beach at Calgary Bay, which charges £3 per person.

Dervaig Hall Bunkrooms (☎ *400492, Dervaig*) Beds £8 per person. This place, in the middle of Dervaig village, offers basic bunkhouse accommodation.

Bellachroy Hotel & Pub (☎/*fax 400314, Dervaig*) B&B £20-27.50 per person. The Bellachroy is an atmospheric 17th-century droving inn. The bar is a focus for local social life and serves good-value bar meals. Dinner B&B is available for an extra £10.

Druimard Country House & Restaurant (☎/*fax 400345, Dervaig*) Dinner B&B singles £74-77, doubles £125-153. Near the theatre, the upmarket Druimard offers luxurious but homely accommodation and excellent food. Their four-course dinner costs £28.50 for nonresidents.

Calgary Farmhouse Hotel (☎/*fax 400256,* e *calgary.farmhouse@virgin.net, Calgary*). B&B £33-36 per person. This place provides delightfully rustic accommodation a few minutes' walk from the sandy beach at Calgary Bay. There are also two self-catering loft apartments available for £360 per week (sleeping two to four persons). A three-course dinner is available for £15 to £25.

Walking

Ben More The highest peak on the island, Ben More (966m) has spectacular views across to the surrounding islands when the weather is clear. If it's overcast or misty, wait until the next day because Mull's weather is notoriously changeable. A trail leads up the mountain from Loch na Keal, by the bridge on the B8035 over the Abhainn na h-Uamha – the river 8 miles (13km) south-west of Salen. There's good wild camping by the roadside here (ask permission first). Return the same way or continue down the narrow ridge to the eastern top, A'Chioch, then descend to the road via Gleann na Beinn Fhada. The glen can be rather wet and there's not much of a path. Allow five to six hours for the round trip.

Carsaig Arches One of the best walks on Mull is along the coast west of Carsaig Bay to the Carsaig Arches at Malcolm's Point. There's a good path below the cliffs all the way from Carsaig, but it becomes a bit exposed near the arches – the route climbs, then traverses a steep slope above a vertical drop into the sea. You'll see spectacular rock formations on the way, including one that looks like a giant slice of Christmas cake. The **Nun's Pass** is a gap in the cliffs through which some nuns from Iona fled after the Reformation. The arches are two sea-cut rock formations. One, nicknamed 'the keyhole', is a free-standing rock stack; the other, 'the tunnel', is a huge natural arch. The western entrance is hung with curtains of columnar basalt. It's an impressive place. Allow three to four hours' walking time plus at least an hour at the arches.

Other Walks In the east, there's good walking on **Beinn Talaidh** (762m) and **Dùn da Ghaoithe** (766m). Beinn Talaidh is easiest to reach by its southern ridge; look out for the aircraft wreckage near the top. Allow about four hours for the return trip. Dùn da Ghaoithe can be ascended from various places including Scallastle, about one mile (1.5km) north of Craignure. Allow around five hours.

Organised Tours

See Oban in The Highlands chapter for details of day tours to Mull and Iona by ferry and bus. There are several companies running wildlife and whale-watching tours – booking for these is strongly advised.

Travellers have recommended the 7½-hour Land Rover tours offered by *Mull Wildlife Expeditions (☎ 302044, Ulva House Hotel, Tobermory)*. The cost (adult/child £27.50/19.50) includes a picnic lunch. You'll have a chance to spot golden eagles, peregrine falcons, hen harriers, red deer, seals, otters, and perhaps dolphins and porpoises. Tours leave from Tobermory at 10am and from Craignure an hour later, returning to Craignure for the 5pm ferry so that you can make a day trip from Oban.

Sea Life Surveys (☎ 01688-400223, Tobermory) runs whale-watching trips to the waters north and west of Mull. An 'all-day whale watch' (£45, or £48 in July and August) gives up to six hours at sea and is not recommended for kids under 12. The 4½-hour 'family whale watch' is geared more to

young children and costs £32/28 (£3/2 more in July and August).

Duncan's Island Tours (☎ 302194, 50 Main St, Tobermory) offers day trips by minibus to Iona, and to Ulva and Calgary beach (£18 per person).

Special Events

The annual Mull Music Festival (☎ 01688-302383) takes place on the last weekend of April and includes Celtic music and Irish folk music. The Mull Highland Games and Dance (☎ 01688-302001) is a one-day event in late July. The Tour of Mull Rally (☎ 01688-302133), part of the Scottish Championship, is in early October. More than 100 cars are involved and public roads are closed for parts of the weekend.

Getting There & Away

There are four to seven CalMac (☎ 01631-566688) ferries daily from Oban to Craignure (passenger/car £3.55/24.55, 40 minutes). There's another ferry link between Fishnish, on the east coast of Mull, and Lochaline (£2.15/9.65, 15 minutes); boats run at least hourly every day.

A third CalMac car ferry links Tobermory to Kilchoan on the Ardnamurchan peninsula (£3.40/18.05, 35 minutes); Monday to Saturday there are seven crossings a day, and from June to August there are also five sailings on Sunday. Call ☎ 01688-302017 for details.

Getting Around

Public transport on Mull is limited. Bowman's Buses (☎ 01680-812313) is the main operator, connecting the ferry ports and main villages. The Craignure to Tobermory service (one hour) runs six times a day Monday to Saturday (and twice on Sunday Easter to October). The Craignure to Fionnphort service (1¼ hours) runs five times a day Monday to Saturday (and once Sunday Easter to October). There's also a postbus (☎ 01463-256200) from Salen to Burg (Kilninian) via Ulva Ferry. RN Carmichael (☎ 01688-302220) runs buses from Tobermory to Dervaig (five a day) and Calgary (four a day); there are only two buses Saturday and none Sunday.

For a taxi in Tobermory, call ☎ 01688-302204.

Cycling is a good way to get around and you can hire bikes from a number of places for around £10 to £13 per day. In Salen, try On Yer Bike (☎ 01680-300501); it also has an outlet in the craft shop (☎ 01680-812487) near the ferry terminal in Craignure. In Tobermory, try Mrs MacLean at Tom-A-Mhuillin (☎ 01688-302164) on Salen Rd, or Archibald Brown's hardware shop (☎ 01688-302020) on Main St.

ISLE OF COLL
☎ 01879 • pop 172

This lovely island, about 12 miles (20km) long and 3 miles (5km) wide, has a good sunshine record but can be very windy. On the west coast, the wind has formed sand dunes up to 30m high. Crossapol beach is one of the best spots on Coll. At **Totronald RSPB reserve** *(☎ 230301)*, on the west coast of the island, there's a free information centre (open year-round); listen for the corncrakes on the machair. Two nearby castles, both known as **Breachachadh Castle**, were built by the Macleans. There was a clan battle here in 1593.

Coll Stores and the Corner Shop sell groceries; both are in the island's only village, **Arinagour**, where the ferry docks. There's also a post office, and Coll Ceramics – pottery with art exhibitions.

Places to Stay & Eat
Garden House Camping & Caravan Site *(☎ 230374, Uig)* Pitches £5 per person. Open May-Sept. Located 4½ miles (7km) south of Arinagour, near Breachachadh Castle, this is a basic site with toilets and cold water only. No dogs are allowed.

Coll Hotel *(☎ 230334, fax 230317,* [e] *joliphot@aol.com, Arinagour)* B&B £25-40 per person. The island's only hotel, in Arinagour, has a really good restaurant serving lobster and scallops, the local specialities. Their three-course dinner costs £21.

There are several places offering B&B, including *Taigh Solas* *(☎/fax 230333)* in Arinagour, which charges from £18 to £22 per person, and *Achamore* *(☎ 230430)*, a

mile-and-a-half north of Arinagour, which charges from £19 to £21 per person.

For light meals and snacks, try the *Corner Cafe* in Arinagour.

Getting There & Around
The CalMac ferry (☎ 230347) runs from Oban Monday to Wednesday, Friday and Saturday (passenger/car £11.40/65, 2¾ hours). The same ferry runs between Coll and Tiree (£2.90/16.65, one hour) on the same days.

Mountain bikes can be hired in Arinagour from Tammie Hedderwick (☎ 230382) for £8 per day, and from the B&Bs listed earlier.

ISLE OF TIREE
☎ 01879 • pop 750

Tiree is a low-lying island with some beautiful sandy beaches, and has one of the best sunshine records in Britain, particularly during the early months of summer. Tiree's main attractions are its sandy beaches, windsurfing and gentle walking.

The ferry arrives at Gott Bay, towards the eastern end of the island. The airport is right in the centre. There's a bank (without ATM), post office and Co-op store in Scarinish, the main village, a half-mile south of the ferry pier. There's another shop at Crossapol, just south of the airport. For the island's doctor, call ☎ 220323.

An Iodhlann *(☎ 220793)*, in Scarinish, is a historical and genealogical archive, with exhibitions on island life and history.

At Sandaig, in the far west of the island, is the **Island Life Museum** *(admission free; open 2pm-4pm Mon-Fri June-Sept)*, a terrace of thatched buildings with a reconstruction of a 19th-century crofter's home.

The **Skerryvore Lighthouse Museum** *(admission free; open daylight hours)* is at Hynish, near the southern tip of the island. The signal tower, pier and cottages, built using granite from the Ross of Mull, were used as a base for the construction of the remote Skerryvore Lighthouse (10 miles/16km to the south-west) in 1843.

For the best view on the island, walk up **Ben Hynish** (141m), at the southerly tip of the island, capped by a conspicuous radar station known locally as the Golf Ball.

Reliable wind and big waves have made Tiree one of Scotland's top **windsurfing** venues – there are annual competitions here in October. Wild Diamond Windsurfing (☎ 220399, W www.tireewindsurfing.com) runs courses at Loch Bhasapoll in the northwest of the island; a five-hour beginners course costs £40, including equipment hire.

Places to Stay
Accommodation on the island isn't cheap. There's a very basic *camp site* near the Co-op shop in Scarinish; if you want to camp elsewhere, ask permission from the farmer or crofter who owns the land.

Kirkapol (☎/fax 220729, Gott Bay) B&B £25-27 per person. This place is in a converted 19th-century church overlooking a beautiful sandy beach.

Scarinish Hotel (☎ 220308, fax 220410, Scarinish) Singles £25-28, doubles £46-50. Tiree's main hotel, with six rooms, overlooks the small-boat harbour at Scarinish.

Getting There & Around
British Airways (BA) fly from Glasgow to Tiree Airport (☎ 220309) Monday to Saturday (around £100 return). Ferry connections and fares are the same as for Coll (see Isle of Coll earlier in this chapter).

For car hire, contact Tiree Motor Company (☎ 220469) or McLeannan Motors (☎ 220555). For a taxi, call ☎ 220344. Bikes are available from Mr MacLean (☎ 220428) in Kenovay, just north of the airport. The postbus (☎ 220301) does runs Monday to Saturday, including an airport service.

Small Isles

The Small Isles consist of Muck, Eigg, Rum and Canna. Lying between the Ardnamurchan peninsula and the Isle of Skye, they're reached by ferry from Arisaig or Mallaig. Muck is flat and has great beaches. The tempestuous Isle of Eigg, with a violent blood-soaked history and unfortunate modern-day disputes, has settled down – for the time being. Rum is a nature reserve, entirely owned by Scottish Natural Heritage (SNH),

and the jewel of the Inner Hebrides – peaks soar to over 750m and the glens are noted for their wildlife. Canna is owned by the National Trust for Scotland (NTS); it's an intriguing place, with interesting archaeology and a magnetic hill.

GETTING THERE & AWAY
The main ferry operator is CalMac (☎ 01687-462403). It sails various routes around the islands Monday to Saturday. To land on Rum (Monday, Wednesday, Friday and Saturday), Eigg (Monday, Tuesday and Thursday to Saturday) and Muck (Tuesday, Thursday, Friday and Saturday), you have to transfer to a lighter boat. Single fares to Muck/Eigg/Rum/Canna are £7.25/4.75/7.10/8.10.

Arisaig Marine (☎ 01687-450224) sails from Arisaig from May to September, with six runs per week to Eigg (£14 return), up to four per week to Rum (£18 return), and three per week to Muck (£14 return). The trip includes whale-watching, with up to an hour (in total) for close viewing.

Sailing times range from one to five hours.

MUCK
☎ 01687 • pop 34
Muck is tiny, measuring just 2 miles by a mile (3.2km by 1.6km), but it's got a lot to offer, including corncrakes, a puffin colony, good shell and sand beaches, and porpoises in the bays. Walk to the top of **Beinn Airein** (137m) for the best views. You'll find an interesting limestone pavement below the high water line at Camas Mor, one of the two southern bays. Muck has exceptionally fertile soil, and the island has carpets of wild flowers in spring and early summer.

Ferries call at the southern settlement of **Port Mor**. The *tearoom/craftshop* (☎ 462362), situated in a blackhouse-style building (possibly named after the soot left on the walls by the burning peat fire in the centre), does great snacks and evening meals on request; it also sells fresh bread. Ask here for permission to camp.

Port Mhor Guesthouse (☎ 462365, Port Mor) Dinner B&B with shared bathroom £35 per person. The recommended three-course

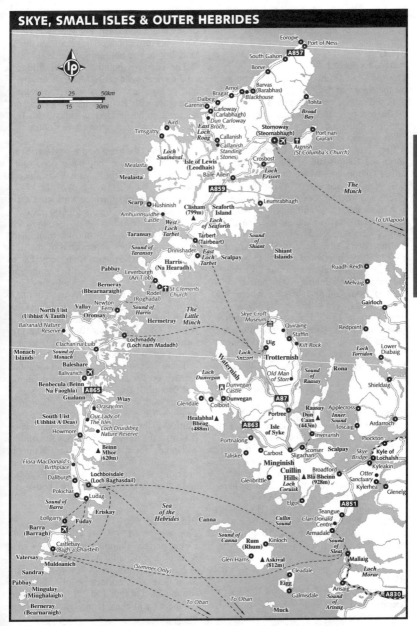

SKYE, SMALL ISLES & OUTER HEBRIDES

THE HEBRIDES

Eoropie
Port of Ness
South Galson A857
Borve
Arnol Barvas
Bragar (Barabhas)
Dalbeg Blackhouse
Garenin Tolsta
Carloway
(Carlabhagh) Broad
Dun Carloway Bay
East Broch
Aird Loch
Timsgatry Roag Callanish Stornoway Port nan
Loch Callanish (Steornabhagh) Giúran
Suainaval Standing Aignish
Isle of Lewis Stones (St Columba's Church)
Mealasta (Leodhais) Crosbost
Mealasta Baile Ailein Loch
Erisort The
A859 Minch
Scarp Hushinish Clisham Seaforth Leumrabhagh To Ullapool
Amhuinnsuidhe (799m) Island
Castle West Loch
Taransay Loch of Seaforth Ruadh Reidh
Tarbet Tarbert Sound
Sound of (Tairbeart) of Melvaig
Taransay Drinishader Shiant
East Scalpay Shiant
Pabbay Loch Islands Gairloch
Harris Tarbert
Leverburgh (Na Hearadh)
Berneray (An T-ob) Ruadh Reidh
(Bbearnaraigh) Rodel St Clements Skye Croft
(Roghadal) Church Museum Redpoint
North Uist Valley Newton Sound of The Quiraing Loch Lower
(Uibhist A Tuath) Oronsay Ferry Harris Little Staffin Torridon Diabaig
Balranald Nature Hermetray Minch Uig Kilt Rock
Reserve Clachan na Luib Trotternish Shieldaig
Monach Lochmaddy Skye
Islands Sound of (Loch nam Madadh) Waternish Snizort Old Man Sound Rona
Monach Loch of Storr of
Baleshare Dunvegan Raasay Applecross
Balivanich Dunvegan A87 Raasay Inner Ardarroch
Benbecula (Beinn Castle Portree Dun Sound Plockton
Na Faoghla) A865 Glendale Dunvegan Caan Toscaig
Gualann Colbost (443m) Skye Kyle of
Wiay Healabhal A863 Inverarish Bridge Lochalsh
Orasay Inn Bheag Isle Sconser Scalpay Kyleakin
South Uist Our Lady of (488m) of Skye Sligachan
(Uibhist A Deas) The Isles Portnalong Broadford Otter
Howmore Loch Druidibeg Talisker Carbost Minginish Sanctuary
Nature Reserve Cuillin Blà Bheinn Kylerhea
Beinn Hills (928m) Glenelg
Flora MacDonald's Mhor Glenbrittle Loch
Birthplace (620m) Coruisk
Daliburgh Lochboisdale Elgol A851
Polochar (Loch Baghasdail) Teangue Clan Donald
Sound of Ludag Sea Cuillin Centre
Barra of the Canna Sound Armadale
Eollgarry Eriskay Hebrides Sound of Rum Kinloch Sound
Barra Fuday Canna (Rhum) of
(Barragh) Glen Harris Askival Sleat Mallaig
Castlebay (812m)
Vatersay (Bagh a'Chaisteil) Cleadale Loch
Muldoanich Eigg Morar
Sandray (Summer Only) Galmisdale Sound A830
Pabbay of
Mingulay To Oban To Oban Muck Arisaig
(Miughalaigh)
Berneray
(Bearnaraigh)

0 25 50km
0 15 30mi

dinners here are available to nonresidents for £15 (reserve by the previous evening).

EIGG
☎ 01687 • pop 78

This small but distinctive island is dominated by the **Sgurr of Eigg**, a 393m-high basalt peak with three vertical sides. The Sgurr is the largest outcrop of columnar pitchstone lava in Britain and it can be climbed easily by its western ridge.

Eigg has two villages, **Cleadale** in the north and **Galmisdale** in the south. Ferries call at Galmisdale, where there's a post office, shop and tearoom (☎ 482487) offering snacks and Internet access, all by the pier.

A monastery was built at Kildonnan, one mile (1.6km) north of Galmisdale, but all 53 monks were murdered by pirates in 617. At the monastery site, there are the ruins of a 14th-century church and a Celtic cross slab.

There are several caves around the coast, including **Uamh Fraing**, only half a mile (800m) from Galmisdale pier, where 395 MacDonalds were killed by the MacLeods from Skye in 1577. The nearby **Cathedral Cave**, used after the 1745 rebellion for banned Catholic services, is still occasionally in use today. The island was sacked in 1588 by pirates, and again in 1746, this time by the government, who didn't think much of the islanders' Jacobite sympathies.

Places to Stay

Camping is allowed near Galmisdale (£3); there are showers and toilets at the pier.

The Glebe Barn (☎/fax 482417, Galmisdale) Beds £9.50-11. Open year-round. You'll find acceptable dorm beds (including sheets), bike hire and kitchen facilities here.

Lageorna (☎ 482405, fax 482432, Cleadale) Singles/doubles £15/30, B&B with dinner £34 per person, 6-bed self-catering cottages £180-380 per week. This friendly B&B is about 3 miles (5km) north of the ferry landing.

RUM
☎ 01687 • pop 30

Nearly all of the people who live on Rum work for SNH; the entire island is a nature reserve. Advise the reserve office (☎ 462026) of any intention to visit. For various reasons, SNH puts restrictions on travel around the island, but they're not prohibitive.

The island is noted for its wildlife, including deer, wild goats, Manx shearwaters, and golden and white-tailed sea eagles. There are also Rum ponies and Highland cattle. Rum has unusual geology, with Torridonian sandstone, gabbro, peridotite and felsite.

Kinloch is the main centre, and ferries arrive here. The Spar shop has a good range of groceries, but check with SNH since it may close; there's also a post office.

The grand and turreted **Kinloch Castle** *(☎ 462037, Kinloch; adult/child £3/1.50; open for guided tours only, in conjunction with boat arrivals)* is the most extraordinary of several buildings constructed by the Bullough family, who owned Rum from 1888 to 1957. It's well worth a visit to see the furnishings, and it's even possible to stay here. There's also the **Bullough Mausoleum** *(admission free; always open)*, a 'folly' in Glen Harris, which wouldn't look out of place in Athens. Glen Harris is a 10-mile (16km) return walk from Kinloch, on a 4WD track – allow four to five hours walking time.

There's some great coastal and mountain scenery on the island, especially at **Guirdil** and **Dibidil**. It takes a couple of hours each way to walk the paths to either place from Kinloch. You can follow the main ridge from Hallival to the island's highest point, **Askival** (812m) – the route involves rock scrambling and takes about six hours from Kinloch. Strong parties may be able to traverse the entire ridge as far as Sgùrr nan Gillean (764m) and return via the ruinous **Papadil Lodge** and the coast.

Places to Stay

Camping (☎ 462026, fax 462805, Kinloch) £3 per person. Camping is only allowed at Kinloch and it's a bit basic.

Farmhouse Hostel (☎/fax 462037, Kinloch) Beds £8. Fourteen people can be accommodated at this hostel. It's fairly basic, but there's a kitchen. Bring your own sleeping bag.

Kinloch Castle (☎/*fax 462037, Kinloch*)
Hostel beds £12 (bedding £1 extra), B&B
£18.50, hotel doubles £71. Hotel rooms in
the castle have a wonderful ambience, with
four-poster beds. Bistro dinners are available
for £10.

CANNA & SANDAY
☎ 01687 • pop 16

These pleasant little roadless islands can
easily be explored in a day. The ferry arrives
at the hamlet of **A'Chill** on Canna, where
tourists have created extensive graffiti on
the rock face south of the harbour. There are
no shops, but you'll find a tiny post office in
a hut, a **Celtic cross**, and the remains of the
7th-century **St Columba's Chapel**. There are
now two churches, surely more per head of
population than anywhere else; the Protestant church has an unusual circular bell
tower. Just east of the ferry pier is **An
Coroghon**, a prison dating from the Middle
Ages. At the north-eastern corner of Canna,
Compass Hill (143m) contains enough iron
to affect compasses in passing ships. Canna
is linked to the adjacent Sanday by bridge.

Contact the NTS warden on ☎ 462466
for permission to camp. Self-catering accommodation may also be available.

Isle of Skye

pop 8847

Skye is a rugged, convoluted island stretching
about 50 miles (80km) from end to end.
It's ringed by a beautiful coastline and dominated by the Cuillin, immensely popular for
Munro bagging. Tourism is a mainstay of the
island economy, so until you get off the main
roads, don't expect to escape the hordes.
Come prepared for changeable weather;
when it's nice it's very nice, but often it isn't!

Portree and Broadford are the main population centres. Getting around the island
midweek is fairly straightforward, with
postbuses supplementing the normal bus
services. But here, as in the Highlands,
transport dwindles to nothing at weekends,
particularly in winter and even more dramatically (so it seems) when it rains.

Gaelic is spoken by some of Skye's residents, and there's a Gaelic college, Sabhal
Mòr Ostaig, at Teangue (An Teanga).

Despite the closing of the old Kyle of
Lochalsh to Kyleakin ferry route when the
Skye Bridge opened in 1995, there are still
two ways to travel over the sea to Skye –
Mallaig to Armadale and Glenelg to Kylerhea
(the latter, mid-April to October only). See
Armadale and Kylerhea later in this section.

The bridge tolls are still being resisted
and there are regular court cases. However,
locals can buy 20 tickets for £26.80 – a huge
saving compared with the extortionate £4.70
(£5.70 in summer) single-crossing fee (per
car) that most motoring tourists pay.

WALKING

Skye is one of the best places in Scotland
for walking. There are many detailed guidebooks available. For the Cuillin Ridge, the
best is *Black Cuillin Ridge – a scrambler's
guide*, by SP Bull (Scottish Mountaineering
Trust). Charles Rhodes has written a series
of four walking guides, available from
Portree TIC for £2.95 to £3.75 each.

You must obtain Ordnance Survey (OS)
map Nos 23 and 32 to appreciate the following
routes. Don't attempt the longer
walks without proper experience, and avoid
these routes in winter or in bad weather.

Easy low-level routes include: Torrin to
Luib (two hours); Sligachan to Kilmarie, via
Camasunary (four hours); and Portnalong to
Talisker, via Fiskavaig (four hours return).

Harder walks, but still on good paths, are:
Kilmarie to Coruisk via the 'Bad Step', an
exposed section of scrambling (at least four
hours return); Glenbrittle camp site to Coire
Lagan (at least three hours return); and The
Quiraing, from the high point on the Staffin
to Uig road – allow at least three hours to
appreciate the pinnacles around The Table.

Longer walks include: from Orbost
(3 miles/5km, south of Dunvegan) to MacLeod's Maidens, Glen Ollisdal, returning
via Healabhal Bheag (488m) – seven hours;
Glenbrittle camp site to Coire Lagan and
Sgurr Alasdair by the Great Stone Chute,
with some airy scrambling near the summit
– five to six hours; and Glenbrittle camp site

to Coir' a'Ghrunnda and Sgurr Dubh Mór – six to seven hours of hard walking, with wet terrain and some difficult rock-scrambling near the top.

ORGANISED TOURS

One of the best ways to see Skye is with *Red Deer Travel* (☎ *01478-612142*), which runs cultural and historical tours in an eight-seat minibus. You can also book at Portree TIC.

John Heath (*mobile* ☎ *0786 772 0451*) is an experienced hiker with a Mountain Leadership Training Board Certificate, and can take small groups walking or scrambling in Skye. Maximum group sizes vary from three to six, depending on the route, and the cost is £55 to £60 per person.

GETTING AROUND

Highland Country Buses (☎ 01478-612622) offers a one-/three-day bus Rover ticket for £6/15.

PORTREE (PORT RIGH)

☎ 01478 • pop 2561

Port Righ is Gaelic for King's Harbour, named after James V called here in 1540 to pacify local clan chieftains. The harbour is very pretty and there are great views of the surrounding hills. Portree is Skye's biggest settlement, with most of the facilities, such as banks with ATMs, petrol stations and a post office with foreign exchange facilities. There are also two supermarkets, including a large Co-op off Dunvegan Rd.

The TIC (☎ 612137), Bayfield Rd, opens year-round, including Sunday from late May to mid-October. It handles foreign exchange. The hospital can be contacted on ☎ 613200.

The annual Isle of Skye Highland Games are held in Portree in early August.

Things to See

On the southern edge of Portree, the **Aros Experience** (☎ *613649, Viewfield Rd; adult/ child £3/2; open 9am-5.15pm daily*) offers a lively introduction to Skye life and includes excellent live CCTV viewing of a sea eagle's nest. There's also a good restaurant.

Castle Keep (☎ *612114, Unit 7BI, Portree Industrial Estate; admission free; open 10am-4.30pm Mon-Fri*), a mile (1.6km) from town on the Dunvegan Rd, features a working bladesmith who hand-forges traditional Scottish swords and dirks. There's an exhibition and a shop on site.

An Tuireann Art Centre (☎ *613306, Strain Rd; admission free; open 10am-5pm Mon-Sat, shorter hours in winter*), out of town on the Struan road (B885), hosts contemporary art exhibitions and has a good cafe.

Organised Tours

Brigadoon Boat Trips (☎ *613718*) runs wildlife tours out to the Sound of Raasay three times daily. A two-hour trip costs £10/6.50. Porpoises, seals and eagles are commonly seen, and you can explore sea caves in the boat. Fishing trips can also be arranged.

Places to Stay

Camping Located on the edge of town on the Staffin road, *Torvaig Camping Site* (☎ *612209, Torvaig*) opens April to October and offers pitches for £7.

Hostels In the old post office, near Somerled Square, *Portree Independent Hostel* (☎*/fax 613737, The Green*) has beds for £9.50 to £10.50. Another option is *Portree Backpackers Hostel* (☎ *613641, fax 613643, Dunvegan Rd*), near the Co-op, about half a mile (800m) from Somerled Square, with beds for £8.50 to £9.50.

B&Bs & Hotels *Seaview* (☎ *611123, 4 Mill Rd*) Singles/doubles £20/32. Recommended by readers, this friendly B&B in a 100-year-old villa offers great views of Raasay.

Mrs Matheson's (☎ *612808, 9 Martin Crescent*) En-suite singles £20-25, doubles £32-36. This modern B&B is in a quiet residential area, just uphill from the town centre.

Bayview House (☎ *613340, Bayfield*) Bed only from £15 per person. This is another friendly place with en-suite facilities.

Easdale (☎ *613244, Bridge Rd*) Doubles £40-50. Open Mar-Oct. Easdale is a standard B&B with en-suite facilities.

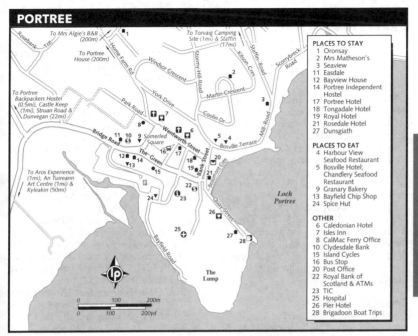

PORTREE

PLACES TO STAY
1 Oronsay
2 Mrs Matheson's
3 Seaview
11 Easdale
12 Bayview House
14 Portree Independent Hostel
17 Portree Hotel
18 Tongadale Hotel
19 Royal Hotel
21 Rosedale Hotel
27 Dunsgiath

PLACES TO EAT
4 Harbour View Seafood Restaurant
5 Bosville Hotel; Chandlery Seafood Restaurant
9 Granary Bakery
13 Bayfield Chip Shop
24 Spice Hut

OTHER
6 Caledonian Hotel
7 Isles Inn
8 CalMac Ferry Office
10 Clydesdale Bank
15 Island Cycles
16 Bus Stop
20 Post Office
22 Royal Bank of Scotland & ATMs
23 TIC
25 Hospital
26 Pier Hotel
28 Brigadoon Boat Trips

THE HEBRIDES

Dunsgiath *(☎ 612851,* e *stay@duns giath.com, The Harbour)* Doubles/twins £34-54. The recommended Dunsgiath B&B has great views across the harbour to Beinn Tianavaig and Raasay.

Mrs Algie's *(☎/fax 613149, 2 Carn Dearg Place)* Singles £20-30, doubles £40-60. Mrs Algie's is located inland and about 600m from the harbour, and is a good B&B with some en-suite rooms.

Oronsay *(☎ 612192, 1 Marsco Place)* Singles £20, doubles £36-40. All rooms at Oronsay have private facilities.

Tongadale Hotel *(☎ 612115, fax 613376, Wentworth St)* B&B £25 per person. Just off Somerled Square, the friendly Tongadale has a lively pub.

Portree Hotel *(☎ 612511, fax 613093, Somerled Square)* Singles £30-43, doubles £60-76. All rooms at the Portree have en-suite bathrooms.

Rosedale Hotel *(☎ 613131, fax 612531, Beaumont Crescent)* En-suite singles £40-46,

doubles £68-98. Open Apr-Nov. The Rosedale Hotel is right on the waterfront and has a fine restaurant.

Royal Hotel *(☎ 612525, fax 613198, Bank St)* Singles £45-55, doubles £75-90. Formerly known as MacNab's Inn, the historic Royal Hotel was visited by James V in 1540. Bonnie Prince Charlie and Flora MacDonald parted company in a room here, shortly before the prince left for Raasay.

Places to Eat
The best places to eat in Portree are the ***Bosville Hotel*** *(☎ 612846, Bosville Terrace)* and ***Portree House*** *(☎ 613713, Home Farm Rd)*; they both do bar meals for around £7 to £12.

There's also pub food from £3.65 at the ***Portree (Somerled Square)*** or ***Tongadale (Wentworth St)*** hotels. For curries and other Indian meals for £5.50 to £8.50, head to the ***Spice Hut*** *(☎ 612681, Bayfield Rd)*. For good takeaway fish and chips (£3.25), head to *Bayfield Chip Shop* *(Bayfield)*.

Chandlery Seafood Restaurant (☎ 612846, Bosville Terrace) Mains £12.95-21.50. 3-course meal around £27. This elegant restaurant, at the Bosville Hotel, serves fine food and wines.

Harbour View Seafood Restaurant (☎ 612069, 7 Bosville Terrace) Mains £9.50-16.50. The food here is reasonable but it seems a bit overpriced.

An Tuireann Art Centre Café (☎ 613306, Struan Rd) Open 10am-5pm Mon-Sat, shorter hours in winter. An Tuireann, out of town on the Struan road (B885), caters exclusively for vegetarians and vegans.

Granary Bakery (☎ 612873, Somerled Square) Meals £2.95-5.25. The Granary Bakery sells fresh bread and pastries. Its coffee shop serves snacks and meals.

The *cafe* next to the Caledonian Hotel in Wentworth St opens from breakfast time; its snacks cost around £2.

Entertainment

Isles Inn (☎ 612129, Somerled Square) The Isles Inn features a Jacobean-theme bar with a flagstone floor and real fires. The bar meals are recommended and B&B singles/doubles are available from £20/40.

Caledonian Hotel (☎ 612641, Wentworth St) The bar here is popular with locals, with varied live music Thursday to Saturday.

Pier Hotel (☎ 612094, Quay St) The Pier Hotel is a popular drinking spot on the waterfront.

Getting There & Away

Somerled Square is the Portree bus stop. Scottish Citylink (☎ 0870 550 5050) operates a Glasgow-Fort-William-Kyle-Kyleakin-Portree-Uig route, three times daily in summer, taking three hours from Fort William to Portree (£14.50). It also runs the Inverness to Portree service twice daily (£12.40, 3¼ hours).

Getting Around

Bikes can be hired at Island Cycles (☎ 613121), The Green, for £10 per day.

KYLEAKIN (CAOL ACAIN)
☎ 01599

Even more than for Kyle of Lochalsh on the mainland, Kyleakin has had the carpet pulled from under it by the opening of the Skye Bridge. It's a pleasant wee place, but it's now backpacker city – there are three hostels and even a backpackers pub.

Seacruise (☎ 534760) charges £5.50/3.50 for its one-hour cruises to see seals, a shipwreck and an otter sanctuary. There's also a two-hour evening cruise to Eilean Donan Castle (£10/5).

Places to Stay & Eat

Kyleakin Youth Hostel (☎ 534585) Dorm beds from £9/6. This fine SYHA hostel, formerly a hotel, faces the central grassy area about halfway along the main street.

Skye Backpackers (☎/fax 534510, Ⓔⓔ skye@scotlands-top-hostels.com, Benmhor) Beds £10-12. Friendly and busy Skye Backpackers offers breakfast for £1.40.

Dun Caan Independent Hostel (☎/fax 534087, Castle View) Dorm beds £10. Near the old ferry quay, the friendly Dun Caan hostel rents out bikes for £10 per day.

Saucy Mary's (☎ 534845) Mains £4.15-6.15. Saucy Mary's is a lively, boozy backpackers pub facing the grassy area about two-thirds of the way along the main street.

Crofter's Cafe (☎ 534134) 2-course/3-course lunch £4.95/5.95. The best place to eat in Portree is the bright and airy Crofter's Kitchen, at the western end of the village.

On the waterfront, you'll find the *Pier Coffee House (☎ 534641)*, with snacks and meals for £1 to £5.95.

Getting There & Away

Highland Country Buses (☎ 01478-612622) runs twice hourly to Kyle of Lochalsh and one to three times Monday to Saturday to Broadford and Portree. Scottish Citylink runs to Inverness (two daily), Fort William and Glasgow (three daily), and Broadford and Portree (four daily).

KYLERHEA (CAOL REITHE)

Kylerhea is about 4 miles (6km) south-east of Kyleakin, and there's a seasonal car ferry from there to Glenelg on the mainland. Before crossing to Glenelg, you can follow a 1½-hour nature trail with the chance to see otters from a shoreline hide (☎ 01320-366322); admission is free. Even if the otters elude you, you should still see basking seals and assorted birds.

The ferry (☎ 01599-511302, **W** www.skye ferry.co.uk), for six cars, operates from 9am to 5.45pm Monday to Saturday mid-April to mid-May; 9am to 7.45pm daily mid-May to August (10am to 5.45pm Sunday); and 9am to 5.45pm daily September and October (first ferry at 10am Sunday). Prices are: car and four passengers £6; motorcycle £3; foot passenger 70p; bicycle 30p.

ARMADALE (ARMADAL)
☎ 01471

You can also arrive on Skye by boat from Mallaig. If you do that, you'll wind up in Armadale, where there's a food store, post office and hostel. CalMac (☎ 844248) runs the ferries (passengers £2.80, cars £15.65, 30 minutes).

The **Museum of the Isles** (☎ *844305, Armadale; adult/child £3.90/2.85; open 9.30am-5pm Apr-Oct)*, in a restored part of the ruined Armadale Castle, tells you all you ever wanted to know about the MacDonald clan. Family research facilities are available. There's a pleasant restaurant serving home-made soup, snacks and meals, but they're not cheap.

Sea.fari (☎ 822361) runs two-hour RIB (rigid inflatable boat) trips around the area for £15 per person. Longer trips to Canna, Rum etc can be arranged (but you'll need cast-iron buttocks).

Places to Stay & Eat
Armadale Youth Hostel (☎ 844260, Ardvasar) Beds from £8.25/7. Open Apr-Sept. This no-frills but well-equipped SYHA/HI hostel lies 900m north of the ferry terminal.

Flora MacDonald Hostel (☎ 844440, The Glebe, Kilmore) Beds £8. The Flora MacDonald Hostel at Kilmore (A'Chille Mhór), 3 miles (5km) north of the ferry, offers reasonable dorm beds, laundry facilities and a basic grocery outlet.

Hotel Eilean Iarmain (☎ 833332, fax 833275, Eilean Iarmain) En-suite doubles £60-75. This hotel is 8 miles (13km) north from the ferry, towards Broadford. The bar and restaurant meals are excellent (bar meals £5.50 to £8, five-course set dinner £31).

Pasta Shed Seafood Takeaway (☎ 844264, The Pier, Armadale) Mains from around £4.50, specials £8.50-9.50. Try the Pasta Shed, where you can also sit in, for snacks and meals, including fish and chips (£4.50) and vegetarian dishes.

Getting There & Away
Highland Country Buses (☎ 01478-612622) does four to six runs (Monday to Saturday) to Broadford and/or Portree. You can hire a bike from the Ferry Filling Station (☎ 844249) for £6/30 per day/week.

BROADFORD (AN T-ATH LEATHANN)
☎ 01471 • pop 1050

Broadford, the main service centre of several scattered communities, is a good base for hillwalkers, who head for Blà Bheinn (928m). The route starts from the head of Loch Slapin, 7 miles (11km) west of Broadford; allow six hours for the return trip.

The TIC (☎ 822361), by the large 24-hour Esso petrol station, opens Easter to October. There's a Co-op supermarket nearby. Also in the village there's a bank (with ATM) and a hospital (☎ 822137).

In the **Serpentarium** (☎ *822209, The Old Mill, Harrapool; adult/child/family £2.50/1.50/7; open 10am-5pm Mon-Sat Easter-Oct & Sun July & Aug)* you can see and touch all sorts of snakes, some of them illegally imported, impounded by Customs and given refuge here.

Places to Stay & Eat
Broadford Youth Hostel (☎ 822442, Broadford) Beds from £8.50/7.25. Open Mar-Oct. The Broadford Youth Hostel is particularly well equipped.

Fossil Bothy (☎ 822297, 13 Lower Breakish) Beds £8. This is a small (eight-bed) but pleasant hostel, located 2½ miles (4km) east of Broadford.

THE HEBRIDES

Tigh-na-Mara (☎/fax 822475, Lower Breakish) Singles £18-20, doubles £36-40. Open Apr-Oct. Tigh-na-Mara, by Broadford Bay and with great views out to sea, has one room with a private bathroom.

Fairwinds (☎/fax 822270, Elgol Rd) Ensuite singles £25, doubles £40-44. Open Mar-Oct. Fairwinds is a pleasant B&B.

Claymore (☎ 822333, Broadford) Soup £1.70, mains £4.35-6.75. The Claymore pub, by the road to Kyle, does good bar meals.

Rendezvous (☎ 822001, Upper Breakish) 2-course meal £12-22. You'll get an excellent meal at Rendezvous.

Getting There & Away

Daily Citylink buses run to Portree, Inverness and Fort William. You can hire a mountain bike from Fairwinds Cycle Hire (☎ 822270), or rent a car from Skye Car Rental (☎ 822225).

ELGOL (EALAGHOL)

On a clear day, Elgol, south of the Cuillin Hills, may well be the most scenic place on Skye. The superb view from the pier towards **Loch Coruisk**, in the heart of the Cuillin, presents a magnificent scene.

A great way to appreciate the Cuillin Hills and Loch Coruisk is on an organised boat trip. The *Bella Jane* (☎ 0800 731 3089) charges £10/13.50 one-way/return (April to mid-October), and the *Kaylee Jane* (☎ 01687-462447) charges £10/6. You sail into **Loch na Cuilce**, an impressive place with acres of rock-slab, and clamber ashore (on a calm day). You might see seals, otters and porpoises here. A short walk from the boat is Loch Coruisk, connected to the sea by River Scavaig.

Rowan Cottage (☎/fax 01471-866287, 9 Glasnakille) Singles/doubles from £35/40. Open mid-Mar–Nov. Located in the scattered crofting community of Glasnakille, 2 miles (3km) east of Elgol, Rowan Cottage specialises in seafood and offers residents excellent meals using fresh local produce. The three-course dinner costs from £15.50 to £20.

Postbuses run from Broadford to Elgol in the morning (Monday to Saturday) and afternoon (Monday to Friday), but you have to stay overnight in Elgol to do a boat trip.

THE CUILLINS & MINGINISH PENINSULA

☎ 01478

The rocky Cuillin Hills, west of Broadford, provide spectacular walking and climbing country. The complete traverse of the Black Cuillin ridge usually requires two days and involves real rock climbing; make sure you're properly equipped. The 986m summit of the **Inaccessible Pinnacle** is a spectacular, but not too difficult, rock climb and abseil. **Sgurr Alasdair**, at 993m, is the highest point and only involves a little scrambling (see Walking earlier in this section for details).

At **Sligachan**, there's a *camp site* (☎ 650333) that charges £4 per head; it's a popular jumping-off point for Cuillin climbers. There's also the *Sligachan Hotel* (☎ 650204, fax 650207, Sligachan) where rooms cost from £20 to £40 per person. The bar serves local real ales and whiskies, as well as meals for £5.95 to £6.75. There's also a restaurant offering mains for £6.95 to £14.95. Internet access here costs £1 for 15 minutes.

In **Carbost**, there's a store, post office and the **Talisker Distillery** (☎ 614306, Carbost; admission £3.50, including dram and discount voucher; open Mon-Sat July-Sept).

Old Inn (☎ 640205, fax 640450, Carbost) Bunkhouse beds £10, hotel B&B £24.50-26.50 per person. The Old Inn, in Carbost, is a favourite with walkers and climbers from Glenbrittle. Food is available (mains £5.50 to £10.95); a chickwich (really!) costs £2.95. The bunkhouse has a self-catering kitchen.

There are two hostels in **Portnalong** (Port nan Long), about 3 miles (5km) from Carbost. Cheap but good bar meals are available close to both hostels.

Croft Bunkhouse (☎/fax 640254, 7 Portnalong) Beds £6.50-8.50, less for campers. The popular Croft Bunkhouse offers acceptable bunk accommodation (including sheets) and cooking facilities. Transport to/from the hostel and bike hire may be arranged.

Skyewalker Independent Hostel (☎ 640250, fax 640420, Fiskavaig Rd, Port-

nalong) Beds £7-8.50. This hostel, at the Old School, has decent dorm beds. There's a kitchen, but meals are available on request.

Taigh Ailean Hotel *(☎ 640271, 11 Portnalong)* This small pleasant hotel also offers snacks (£2.20) and mains (£5.50 to £11.75).

Talisker (Talasgair) is a magnificent place, with a sandy beach, sea stack and waterfall. There are two guesthouses.

Talisker House *(☎ 640245, fax 640214, Talisker)* Singles/doubles £55/86. Open mid-Mar–Oct. Talisker House is a magnificent whitewashed building containing rooms with four-poster beds; dinner is available for £25.

Bay View *(☎/fax 640244, Talisker)* Singles £20-25, doubles £40. Bay View is a pleasant bungalow at the end of the public road; dinner costs an extra £15.

The road to **Glenbrittle** (Gleann Bhreatail) gives great views of the central Cuillin.

Glenbrittle Youth Hostel *(☎ 640278, Glenbrittle)* Beds from £8.25/7. Open Apr-Sept. In the glen, most people head for this pleasant SYHA hostel.

There's also a ***camp site*** *(☎ 640404)* and shop down by the sea, but the midges can be diabolical. It's only £3.50 per person.

Monday to Saturday, Highland Country Buses (☎ 612622) runs twice a day from Portree to Glenbrittle via Sligachan and Carbost (Talisker Distillery). Hitching to Glenbrittle can be slow, especially late in the day, so be prepared to walk. Highland Country Buses from Portree to Portnalong only run on Tuesday and Thursday during the school term, but Nicholson's Coaches (☎ 01470-532240) run twice a day Monday to Friday.

NORTH-WEST SKYE
☎ 01470

Magnificent **Dunvegan Castle** *(☎ 521206, Dunvegan; adult/child £5.50/3; open 10am-5.30pm daily, 11am-4pm in winter)*, at Dunvegan (Dùn Bheagain), dates back to the 13th century, although it was restored in Romantic style in the mid-19th century. Inside, you can see the fairy tower, the dining room (with beautiful silver on display), a decidedly alarming dungeon and, right next door, an excellent drawing room with the famous Fairy Flag. It also runs daily seal cruises for £4/2.50.

There are several other museums in the area, including the **Glendale Toy Museum** *(☎ 511240, Holmisdale House, Glendale; adult/child £2.50/1; open 10am-6pm Mon-Sat)* and the **Colbost Croft Museum** *(☎ 01470-521296, Tigh na Bruaich, Colbost; admission free; open Mon-Sat Apr-Oct)*, about halfway from Dunvegan to Glendale (Gleann Dàil), in a 19th-century black-house.

See Walking earlier in this section for details of the excellent walks in the area. It's also worth taking a drive beyond Glendale, out to Waterstein, for great views of **Neist lighthouse**, **Waterstein Head** and the Outer Hebrides.

There are several possible places to stay.

Mr Stirling's *(☎ 01470-521407, 6 Castle Crescent, Dunvegan)* Singles £18-20, doubles £32-36. Open year-round. There are two rooms with shared bathroom at this recommended B&B.

Tables Hotel *(☎/fax 01470-521404, Dunvegan)* Singles £26-45, doubles £52-76. The bright and cheery Tables Hotel, a mile from the castle, offers vegetarian, vegan and organic cooking (mains £8.80 to £10.50).

MacLeod's Table Bistro *(☎ 01470-521206, Dunvegan Castle)* Lunch mains £5-8, dinner mains £5.75-22.50. The castle has the pleasant MacLeod's Table Bistro for snacks and meals, from baked potatoes to whole lobsters.

Monday to Friday, you can get from Portree to Dunvegan by Nicholson's Coaches (☎ 01470-532240), leaving at 10am and returning from the castle at 12.54pm (allowing two hours at the castle); a bus also leaves for Portree at 4.34pm. Most of these buses operate to/from Colbost and Glendale.

TROTTERNISH PENINSULA
North of Portree, Skye's coastal scenery is at its finest in the Trotternish Peninsula. Look out for the rocky spike of the **Old Man of Storr**, the spectacular **Kilt Rock** and the ruins of **Duntulm Castle**. Near Staffin (Stamhain), the spectacular **Quiraing** also offers dramatic hill walking.

At the northern end of the peninsula, at Kilmuir (Cille Mhoire), the **Skye Museum of**

THE HEBRIDES

Island Life (☎ 01470-552206, Kilmuir; adult/child £1.75/50p; open 9.30am-5.30pm Mon-Sat Apr-Oct) re-creates crofting life in a series of thatched cottages overlooking marvellous scenery.

The largest settlement is **Staffin**, where you can stop for lunch or dinner at the award-winning community centre, Columba 1400, except on Sunday.

Columba 1400 Restaurant (☎ 01478-611400, Staffin) Snacks and mains £2.95-7.95. Open 9am-5pm Mon, 9am-9pm Tues-Sat. This new and recommended restaurant offers Internet access (£1.50 for 20 minutes, £1 to check email).

Glenview Inn (☎ 01470-562248, fax 562211, Culnaknock) B&B doubles £50-70. Open Mar-Oct. The traditional and pleasant Glenview Inn, 3 miles (5km) south of Staffin at Culnaknock (Cùl nan Cnoc), also serves its excellent meals to nonresidents (three-course dinners £12.50).

Three miles (5km) north of Staffin, there's tiny **Flodigarry** (Flodaigearraidh).

Flodigarry Country House Hotel (☎ 01470-552203, fax 552301, Flodigarry) Singles £49-55, doubles £98-160. The restaurant at the award-winning historic Flodigarry Country House Hotel serves good but expensive (dinner around £27) meals. The home of Highland heroine **Flora MacDonald** is now part of the hotel, and her grave at Kilmuir indicates that she was a real victim of tourism – the 1955 memorial states, of the original memorial, that 'every fragment has been removed by tourists'.

Dun Flodigarry Hostel (☎/fax 01470-552212, Flodigarry) Beds £8-10. There are 52 beds at this recommended hostel. Breakfast is available on request.

Just west of Staffin, at Stenscholl (Steinnseal), **Ceol na Mara** (☎ 01470-562242, Stenscholl) offers doubles and twins (£30 to £40).

Monday to Friday, Skyeways Travel (☎ 01599-534328) runs a bus service from Portree to Flodigarry.

UIG (UIGE)
☎ 01470 • pop 300
The TIC (☎ 542404) at Uig (pronounced 'oo-ig') is in the ferry terminal building; it

---

Flora MacDonald

The Isle of Skye was home to Flora MacDonald, who became famous for helping Bonnie Prince Charlie escape his defeat at the Battle of Culloden.

Flora was born in 1722 at Milton in South Uist, where a memorial cairn marks the site of one of her early childhood homes. After her mother's abduction by Hugh MacDonald of Skye, Flora was reared by her brother and educated in the home of the Clanranald chiefs.

In 1746, she helped Bonnie Prince Charlie escape from Benbecula to Skye disguised as her Irish servant. With a price on the Prince's head, their little boat was fired on, but they managed to land safely and Flora escorted the prince to Portree where he gave her a gold locket containing his portrait before setting sail for Raasay.

Waylaid on the way home, the boatmen admitted everything. Flora was arrested and imprisoned in the Tower of London. She never saw or heard from the prince again.

In 1747, she returned home, marrying Allan MacDonald of Skye and going on to have nine children. Dr Johnson stayed with her in 1773 during his journey around the Western Isles, but later poverty forced her family to emigrate to North Carolina. There her husband was captured by rebels. Flora returned to Kingsburgh on Skye where she died in 1790 and was buried in Kilmuir churchyard, wrapped in the sheet in which both Bonnie Prince Charlie and Dr Johnson had slept.

---

opens Easter to October, including Sunday mornings in July and August. Nearby, the **Isle of Skye Brewery** (☎ 542477, The Pier) sells four locally brewed and bottled beers. There's a shop and post office in the village.

Uig Youth Hostel (☎ 542211, Uig) Beds from £8.25/7. Open late-Apr–Sept. This SYHA hostel is in a well-equipped modern building.

There's a cluster of bungalow B&Bs with beds for around £16 to £20. By the bay, about a mile east of the pier, the **Old Ferry Inn** (☎ 542242, fax 542377, Uig) has rooms for £25 to £35 per head and bar meals for £6 to £9. The *Uig Hotel (☎ 542205)* is by the main road but also overlooks the bay; singles/doubles cost £25 to £40.

Both hotels do bar meals, and there's another place down by the pier.

Pub at the Pier (☎ 542212, The Pier) Mains £3.75-7.95. Vegetarian dishes are available here, but there's also a range of typical pub food for carnivores.

From Uig pier, CalMac has daily services to Lochmaddy on North Uist (passenger £8.50, car £40, bike £2, 1¾ hours), and Monday to Saturday services to Tarbert on Harris (same prices, 1½ hours). Uig has once or twice daily Scottish Citylink (☎ 0870 550 5050) bus connections with Portree, Inverness, Fort William and Glasgow. The buses connect with the ferries.

RAASAY
☎ 01478 • pop 163

This is a long, narrow and now very quiet island. There's no petrol on Raasay, but there is a traditional store and post office at Inverarish.

The broken-down remains of **Dùn Borodale** broch are just north of Inverarish. The extraordinary ruin of **Brochel Castle**, perched on a pinnacle at the northern end of Raasay, was home to Calum Garbh MacLeod, an early-16th-century pirate who looted passing ships. At the battle of Culloden in 1746, Raasay supplied around 100 fighting men and 26 pipers, but the people paid dearly for their Jacobite sympathies when victorious government forces arrived and proceeded to murder, rape and pillage their way across the island. The ghastly Raasay clearances of the mid-19th century are well described in verse by the famous Raasay poet, Sorley MacLean. The 1½-mile-long (2.5km) road from Brochel to Arnish was constructed by the local postman over a period of 20 years.

There are several good walks, including one to the odd-looking flat-topped hill, **Dun Caan** (443m), and also around the remote northern end, but you have to cover 10 miles (16km) of road first – there's no bus. Forest Enterprise publishes a free leaflet with suggested walks and forest trails.

Raasay Outdoor Centre (☎ 660266, 660200, Raasay House) Camping from £4. Outdoor activity courses here cost up to £38 per day. The restaurant is quite good; mains cost around £6.

Raasay Youth Hostel (☎ 660240, Creachan Cottage) Beds from £7/5.75. Open mid-May–August. This SYHA hostel is high on the hillside, overlooking Skye, and it's a long hike from the pier; it's also fairly basic but it's a good starting point for exploring the island.

Mrs MacKay (☎ 660207, fax 0870 122 7170, 6 Oskaig Park) Singles/doubles £20/31. Mrs MacKay's B&B is more conveniently located than the youth hostel; it's 3 miles (5km) north of the ferry terminal.

Isle of Raasay Hotel (☎/fax 660222, Borodale House, Inverarish) B&B £25-30 per person. There are 12 en-suite rooms at this hotel, and the traditional Scottish bar meals are reasonable.

Raasay is reached by the CalMac ferry from Sconser, between Portree and Broadford. Monday to Saturday in summer, the ferry operates up to 11 times a day (£2.30/1/9.35, passenger/bicycle/car, 15 minutes).

Outer Hebrides

Synonymous with remoteness, the Outer Hebrides (Western Isles) are a string of islands running in a 130-mile (208km) arc from north to south, shielding the north-west coast of Scotland. Bleak, isolated, treeless and exposed to gales that sweep in from the Atlantic, the Outer Hebrides are irresistibly romantic. They form one of Europe's most isolated frontiers and have a fascinating history, signposted by Neolithic standing stones, Viking place names, empty crofts and folk memories of the Clearances.

Immediate reality can be disappointing, however. The towns are straggly, unattractive and dominated by stern, austere churches. Although the ruins of traditional black-houses can still be seen, they've been supplanted by unattractive (though no doubt more comfortable) concrete block bungalows. Rugged and apparently inhospitable though the islands are, they support a surprisingly large and widely distributed population, and in summer the CalMac ferries disgorge a daily cargo of tourists.

The landscapes can be mournful, but they're also spectacular, with wide horizons of sky and water, dazzling white beaches, azure bays, wide peat moors, and countless lochs, mountains and stony hills. These are islands that reward an extended stay, especially if you travel on foot or by bike; a rushed tour will be less satisfying, and when driving you have to pay too much attention to the road (often single-tracked and sheep-ridden) to appreciate the views.

The local culture is not very accessible to outsiders, but it is distinctive. Of around 18,000 crofts registered in Scotland, some 6000 are on the Outer Hebrides. Of the 66,000 Scottish Gaelic speakers, around 25,000 live on the islands. Religion still plays a central role in island life, especially in the Protestant north, where the Sunday Sabbath is strictly observed – although the swings in Stornoway's playground are no longer padlocked on that day.

These are deeply conservative parts, where a Scot from Glasgow is as much an incomer as someone from London. But the EU is working to reduce the islands' isolation and many roads are being upgraded courtesy of grants from the European Regional Development Fund.

Life moves very slowly here, with supplies dependent on boats and planes. Often newspapers and bread are unavailable before 10am. Bad weather can cause supplies to dry up altogether. Accommodation is in fairly short supply; book ahead in summer.

HISTORY

The first evidence of settlement dates back to around 4000 BC, when Stone-Age farmers settled the islands. They constructed massive stone tombs and the mounds can still be seen (as at Bharpa Langass, North Uist). About 5000 years ago, groups of standing stones were set up, most notably at Callanish on Lewis. Bronze-Age Beaker People, named after their distinctive pottery, arrived around 1800 BC.

Around 1000 BC, the climate deteriorated and the peat that now blankets much of the islands (in places to depths of 6m) began to accumulate.

Acidity increases when soil becomes permanently waterlogged, creating a sterile environment where bacterial activity slows and where the dead grass, sedge, heather and moss build up in layers instead of rotting.

This spongy, nutrient-poor environment was not good for farming and the population was forced onto the coastal fringe. When cut and dried, however, the peat provided the islanders with fuel. Every spring, families still cut it into bricks, which are wind-dried in neat piles before being stacked outside homes.

The Iron-Age, Gaelic-speaking Celts arrived around 500 BC and several defensive brochs remain from this period, the most impressive at Carloway on Lewis.

Vikings settled on the islands by 850, and many island clans, including the Morrisons, Nicolsons, MacAulays and MacLeods, are thought to have Norse backgrounds. The traditional island houses, the black-houses that remained in common use into the 1930s, were essentially Viking long-houses. The Middle Ages saw a new influx of Gaelic-speaking Celts from Scotland and Ireland, and a weakening of the links to Norway, resulting in a Gaelic-speaking Celtic/Norse population.

LANGUAGE

Scottish Gaelic is similar to Irish Gaelic; about 75% of the islanders speak it (as opposed to just 1.5% of the total Scottish population), and recent efforts have ensured its survival. Many Gaelic television and radio programmes are now produced.

All islanders speak English and there's no reluctance to use it when speaking to outsiders. However, some road signs are only in Gaelic, which can cause confusion. When talking to outsiders, islanders use the anglicised version of a name, but this can bear little similarity to the Gaelic on the signs. The CalMac ferry company and the airlines also use anglicised names. One of the first purchases a visitor should make is a bilingual

The Wee Frees & Other Island Creeds

Religion plays a complex and important role in island life, and priests and ministers enjoy powerful positions in the community. The split between the Protestants to the north of Benbecula and the Catholics to the south creates, or perhaps reflects, a different communal atmosphere.

Hebridean Protestants have developed a distinctive fundamentalist approach, with Sunday being devoted to religious services, prayer and Bible reading. On Lewis and Harris, virtually everything closes down. In general, social life is restricted to private homes and, as public drinking is frowned upon, pubs are mostly uninspiring.

The Protestants are further divided into three main sects with convoluted, emotionally charged histories. The Church of Scotland, the main Scottish church, is state-recognised or 'established'. The Free Presbyterian Church of Scotland and the Free Church of Scotland (or Wee Frees) are far more conservative and intolerant, permitting no ornaments, organ music or choirs. Their ministers deliver uncompromising sermons (usually in Gaelic) from central pulpits, and precentors lead the congregation in unaccompanied but fervent psalm-singing. Visitors are welcome to attend services, but due respect is essential.

The most recent split occurred in 1988 when Lord Mackay, then lord chancellor and a prominent Free Presbyterian, committed the awful crime of attending a friend's Catholic requiem Mass. The church elders threatened him with expulsion, so he and his supporters responded by establishing the breakaway Associated Presbyterian Church!

The Catholic Church south of Benbecula survived the Reformation. The priests were expelled early in the 17th century but, despite several missionary attempts, Protestantism failed to take hold. The Sunday Sabbath on South Uist and Barra is more easygoing, and the attitude towards the 'demon drink' distinctly more relaxed.

THE HEBRIDES

road map showing both names; Estate Publication's red-covered *Official Tourist Map – Western Isles* (£4.50) is ideal.

This book uses English names where they are in common usage, while the Gaelic names are given in brackets at the first main reference. See Scottish Gaelic in the Language chapter at the back of this book.

ORIENTATION & INFORMATION

Lewis and Harris are actually one island with a border of high hills between them. The northern half of Lewis is low and flat with miles of peat moors; southern Lewis and Harris are rugged, with some impressive stony mountains and glorious beaches. Berneray, North Uist, Benbecula, South Uist and Eriskay are joined by bridges and causeways. Mostly, these islands are low, flat and green, half drowned by sinuous lochs and open to the sea and sky.

There are several TICs – one in every ferry port, open late for ferry arrivals (up to 10pm April to mid-October).

The main Western Isles Tourist Board (☎ 01851-703088, W www.witb.co.uk), 26 Cromwell St, Stornoway, Lewis HS1 2DD, produces a free brochure, which shows all accommodation possibilities from hotels to B&Bs and self-catering cottages. TICs also stock 13 walking leaflets (50p to 75p each). *The Outer Hebrides Handbook & Guide* (Kittiwake, £7.95), written by local experts, gives lots of data on the islands' history, culture, flora and fauna.

PLACES TO STAY & EAT

Camp sites with facilities are scarce, but free camping is usually allowed, provided you get permission from the nearest house and remove all your rubbish. Some landowners may ask for a small fee.

There are a few basic hostels in old crofts scattered around the islands, but most are difficult to get to without transport or a readiness to hike.

Most are run by the Gatliff Hebridean Hostels Trust (e ghht@peterclarke.com),

30 Francis St, Stornoway, Lewis HS1 2ND, but are marketed by the SYHA. The Gatliff Trust hostels have bunk beds, blankets, cooking equipment, hot and cold running water, showers and coal-burning stoves. Bring a sleeping bag and eating utensils. Local crofters look after the hostels, but no advance bookings are accepted and they prefer people not to arrive or depart on Sunday.

In recent years, several independent hostels have opened. These tend to be very clean, modern and, consequently, more expensive than the Gatliff Trust/SYHA hostels.

B&Bs provide opportunities to meet the islanders, who are famous both for their hospitality and the size of their breakfasts. Few offer private bathrooms, but they're usually comfortable and clean, and offer hearty dinners as well. Most B&B hosts, especially on Lewis and Harris, appreciate guests booking ahead if they are going to stay on a Sunday night.

A few B&Bs are handy for the ferry ports, but most are scattered around the countryside. The ports themselves are generally uninspiring, but always have at least one pub where meals are available. If you do stay in the countryside – which is recommended – check whether there's a convenient pub, make arrangements to eat at your B&B, or take your own provisions to a hostel.

Self-catering cottages must be booked in advance.

Options for eating out centre on hotels and pubs, which are few and far between and not particularly cheap. The picture for vegetarians isn't unreasonable; most hotels with pubs manage at least one suitable dish.

GETTING THERE & AWAY
Air
British Regional Airlines/Loganair (☎ 0845 773 3377, from outside the UK ☎ 44-141 222 2222) flies to the islands, and there are airports at Stornoway on Lewis, and on Benbecula and Barra. The main airport, just 4 miles (6km) east of Stornoway, is served by regular British Regional Airlines/Loganair flights from Glasgow, Edinburgh and Inverness (Monday to Saturday); return fares start at £103, £106 and £60 respectively. Note that single fares may be considerably dearer than returns!

From Monday to Saturday, the company also has flights to Benbecula and Barra from Glasgow – see their sections later for fare details. At Barra, the planes land on the beach, so the timetable depends on the tides. Buses meet the Barra flights. British Regional Airlines/Loganair also links Barra and Benbecula with Stornoway.

Bus
Regular bus services operating to Ullapool, Uig and Oban connect with the ferries. The principal operator is Scottish Citylink (☎ 0870 550 5050).

Train
Spectacular train services run as far as Oban, Mallaig and Kyle of Lochalsh from Glasgow and Edinburgh. In order to get to Ullapool for the Stornoway ferry, take the train to Inverness, then a bus to Ullapool. Phone ☎ 0845 748 4950 for rail details.

Boat
CalMac runs comfortable car and passenger ferries from Ullapool to Stornoway on Lewis (2¾ hours; two or three times Monday to Saturday); from Uig (Skye) to Tarbert on Harris and Lochmaddy on North Uist (around 1¾ hours; once or twice Monday to Saturday); and from Mallaig and Oban to Lochboisdale on South Uist and Castlebay on Barra (3¾ to seven hours; daily in summer).

Timetables are complicated and car space can fill up fast, especially during summer. Advance booking is essential, although foot and bicycle passengers should have no problems.

There are 12 different Island Hopscotch fares for set routes in the Outer Hebrides, offering a saving of around 10% (they're valid for one month). Island Rover Passes give unlimited travel on all CalMac routes for eight or 15 days; convenient certainly, but make sure you will use enough services to recoup the cost.

For reservations and service details, contact CalMac (☎ 0870 565 0000 car reservations, ☎ 01475-650100 enquiries), The Ferry Terminal, Gourock PA19 1QP.

A one-way ticket from Stornoway to Ullapool is £13 per person, plus £62 for a car. From Leverburgh to Berneray, it's £4.75/21.90; from Lochboisdale to Castlebay £5.30/30.50; and from Lochboisdale or Castlebay to Oban £18.75/67. For a passenger this totals £41.80, for a car £181.40 – as against £38 and £164 for the equivalent Hopscotch ticket. Allow at least a week to tackle this full north-south route. Bikes are carried free with a Hopscotch ticket (otherwise, £7 on this routing).

GETTING AROUND
Bus
Bus transport is extremely limited, although a bare-bones service allows crofters to get to the shops in the morning and return in the afternoon.

The TICs have up-to-date timetables and you can contact Stornoway bus station (☎ 01851-704327) for information about Lewis and Harris services. Visitors without their own transport should anticipate a fair amount of hitching and walking.

Car
Most roads are single track, but the main hazard is posed by sheep wandering about or sleeping on the road. Petrol stations are far apart, expensive and usually closed on Sunday.

Cars can be hired from around £18 per day from: Arnol Car Rentals (☎ 01851-710548), Arnol, Lewis; Mackinnon Self Drive (☎ 01851-702984), 18 Inaclete Rd, Stornoway; Farquhar McLeod (☎ 01859-520460), Leverburgh, Harris; Maclennan Brothers Ltd (☎ 01870-602191), Balivanich, Benbecula; Ask Car Hire (☎ 01870-602818), Liniclate, Benbecula; and Laing Motors (☎/fax 01878-700267), Lochboisdale, South Uist.

Hitching
Hitching is feasible, although traffic is light and virtually stops on Sunday, especially on Harris and Lewis.

The islanders are generally hospitable, and it's definitely safer than around big cities. See also Hitching in the Getting Around chapter.

Bicycle
Cycling from north to south is quite popular but allow at least a week for the trip. The main problems are difficult weather, strong winds (you hear stories of people cycling downhill and free-wheeling uphill) and sheep that believe they have the right of way.

Bikes can be hired from: Alex Dan's Cycle Centre (☎ 01851-704025), 67 Kenneth St, Stornoway, Lewis; Rothan Cycles (☎ 01870-620283), 9 Howmore, South Uist; and Barra Cycle Hire (☎ 01871-810284), 29 St Brendan's Rd, Castlebay, Barra. Booking is advisable.

LEWIS (LEODHAIS)
pop 19,634
The northern half of Lewis is low and flat, and dominated by the vast Black Moor, a peat moor dotted with numerous small lochs. The coastal fringes have some arable land and are surprisingly densely populated, if not particularly attractive.

The old black-houses may have gone, but most holdings are crofts that follow a traditional pattern dating back to medieval times. Most are narrow strips, designed to give everyone an equal share of good and bad land. Usually they run back from the foreshore (with its valuable seaweed), across the machair (the grassy sand dunes that were the best arable land), and back to the peaty grazing land.

Nowadays, few crofts are economically viable, so most islanders supplement what they make from the land with other jobs. Many go away to work on oil rigs or ships, and others work in the fishing industry (including fish farming), service industries, or the traditional tweed-weaving industry.

South of Stornoway and Barvas, the island is hilly and beautiful, reminiscent of parts of the mainland's north-west coast. Three of the Outer Hebrides' most important sights – the Arnol Blackhouse, Dun Carloway Broch and Callanish Standing Stones – are also here.

Stornoway (Steornabhagh)
☎ 01851 • pop 5975
The island's only sizeable town may lie on a beautiful natural harbour, but it's not one

of the most pleasant places in Scotland. There's a drink and drug problem, perhaps because there's so little else to do. For tourists there are reasonable facilities and several things to see.

Stornoway is the Outer Hebrides' administrative and commercial centre, and the base for the Western Isles Council (Comhairle nan Eilan), a hospital and the islands' Gaelic TV and radio stations. There's an airport and a ferry link with Ullapool.

Orientation & Information The ferry docks in the town centre, which is compact and easy to get around on foot. The bus station is on the foreshore next to the ferry terminal. For ferry information, phone CalMac (☎ 702361).

Some of the residential areas (and B&Bs) are a fair hike without a car, and many people commute in from communities around the island to work and shop, so there's more traffic than you might expect.

The main Western Isles Tourist Board (☎ 703088) is a short walk from the ferry pier. In theory you could use this office to book B&Bs around the islands (£1 fee), but you can take the free accommodation list and make the calls yourself.

There are banks with ATMs, as well as supermarkets, all near the TIC. The Western Isles Hospital (☎ 704704) is three-quarters of a mile (1.2km) north of the town centre.

Things to See The **Museum nan Eilean** (☎ 703773, Francis St; admission free; open 10am-5.30pm Mon-Sat, shorter winter hours) has a changing programme of exhibitions. The **Lewis Loom Centre** (☎ 704500, 3 Bayhead St; admission £2.50; open Mon-Sat), in the Old Grainstore, does good 40-minute tours, with demonstrations of Harris Tweed making. There's also the **An Lanntair** gallery (☎ 703307, South Beach; admission free; open 10am-5.30pm Mon-Sat), in the old Town Hall, which has temporary art exhibitions and a good-value cafe.

Lews Castle, the imposing mansion across the harbour, dating from 1563, is currently empty. It can be viewed from the surrounding park, which has some pleasant walking paths.

The roofless ruin of the 14th-century **St Columba's Church** (Aignish; admission free; open 24 hours year-round), 4 miles (6km) east of town on the Eye peninsula, has the interesting grave slabs of Roderick McLeod, 7th clan chief, (around 1498) and his daughter (1503). Hourly buses (not Sunday) to Point pass nearby.

Places to Stay There is a good range of places to stay in and around Stornoway.

Laxdale Holiday Park (☎ 703234, e gordon@laxdaleholidaypark.force9.co.uk, 6 Laxdale Lane) Tents from £6.50, bunkhouse beds £8-9. Camp site open Apr-Oct, bunkhouse open year-round. This camp site, 1½ miles (2.5km) north of town, off the A857, has a fine and quiet woodland setting.

Surf House Hostel (☎/fax 705862, 17 Keith St) Bunks £10, B&B from £12.50. Friendly Surf House Hostel offers bike hire (£5 per day), surfing equipment, transport, and historical bus tours. It also offers residents a three-course dinner for £7.50.

Stornoway Backpackers Hostel (☎ 703628, 47 Keith St) Dorm beds £9. This hostel is a five-minute walk from the ferry and bus station. The price includes a fairly basic breakfast but there's also a self-catering kitchen.

Hollsetr (☎ 702796, 29 Urquhart Gardens) B&B £17-20 per person. Hollsetr is a long walk from the centre, but it's an immaculate and welcoming B&B, with a single room, a double and a twin.

Fernlea (☎ 702125, 9 Matheson Rd) Rooms £18-25 per head. The recommended Fernlea, in a Victorian terrace, offers B&B with private bathrooms only five minutes' walk from the ferry.

Mrs MacDonald's (☎ 703254, e bookings@davinamacdonald.co.uk, 27 Springfield Rd) B&B £18-22. Mrs MacDonald offers three rooms with a private bathroom in a modern bungalow.

Kildun (☎ 703247, 14 Goathill Rd) Rooms £16-20. Kildun is a small but reasonable B&B in a quiet area; rooms have shared bathroom.

Park Guest House (☎ 702485, fax 703482, 30 James St) B&B £19-42 per person. Some rooms at this guesthouse have

An old bus stationed on Hoy, Orkney Islands

Evidence that Noss birds mess around

Turbulent seas batter Midhowe Broch on the Isle of Rousay, Orkney Islands.

Italian Church, Orkney Islands

A couple of curious cows on Shetland

Northern Europe's best-preserved prehistoric village, Skara Brae, Orkney Islands

If it's varied wildlife you're after, the Shetland Islands will fit the bill.

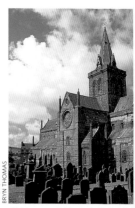

St Magnus Cathedral, Kirkwall

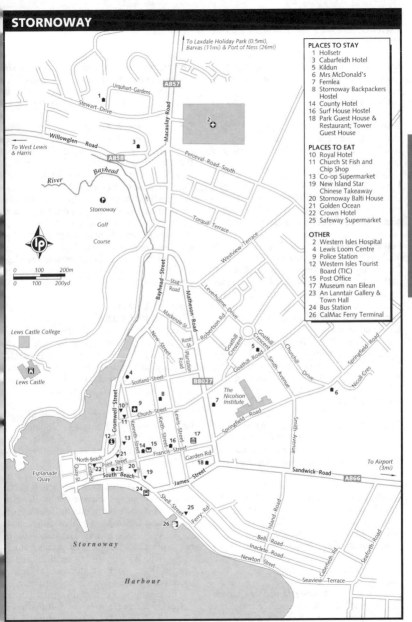

STORNOWAY

To Laxdale Holiday Park (0.5mi),
Barvas (11mi) & Port of Ness (26mi)

To West Lewis
& Harris

River

Bayhead

Stornoway

Golf

Course

Lews Castle College

Lews Castle

Esplanade
Quay

Stornoway

Harbour

To Airport
(3mi)

PLACES TO STAY
1 Hollsetr
3 Cabarfeidh Hotel
5 Kildun
6 Mrs McDonald's
7 Fernlea
8 Stornoway Backpackers
   Hostel
14 County Hotel
16 Surf House Hostel
18 Park Guest House &
   Restaurant; Tower
   Guest House

PLACES TO EAT
10 Royal Hotel
11 Church St Fish and
   Chip Shop
13 Co-op Supermarket
19 New Island Star
   Chinese Takeaway
20 Stornoway Balti House
21 Golden Ocean
22 Crown Hotel
25 Safeway Supermarket

OTHER
2 Western Isles Hospital
4 Lewis Loom Centre
9 Police Station
12 Western Isles Tourist
   Board (TIC)
15 Post Office
17 Museum nan Eilean
23 An Lanntair Gallery &
   Town Hall
24 Bus Station
26 CalMac Ferry Terminal

THE HEBRIDES

shared bathrooms but most are en suite. The restaurant here is highly recommended (see Places to Eat later).

Tower Guest House (☎/fax 703150, 32 James St) Singles/doubles £19/36. This friendly and comfortable guesthouse is in a Victorian villa.

County Hotel (☎ 703250, 12 Francis St) Singles/doubles from £45/65. The old-fashioned County Hotel is centrally located, just east of the pedestrian mall. It offers reasonable accommodation, but the meals are fairly average.

Cabarfeidh Hotel (☎ 702604, fax 705572, Manor Park) Singles/doubles £70/94. The Cabarfeidh Hotel offers high-standard modern hotel rooms and has a good restaurant with three-course set meals for £21.50.

Places to Eat After 6pm, you'll only get food at the hotels and a few takeaway places. On Sunday, most takeaways are closed.

Park Guest House (☎ 702485, 30 James St) 2-course dinner from £11.95. Park Guest House is one of the best places to eat in Stornoway; it specialises in local shellfish, game and lamb.

Royal Hotel (☎ 702109, Cromwell St) Bar meals £6-8, restaurant mains £8.50-15.50. At this place, the more expensive restaurant has a seafood slant; it's very pleasant, with half a boat attached to the ceiling.

Crown Hotel (☎ 703181, Castle St) Bar meals £5.95-13.95. The menu here includes fish, poultry, steaks and vegetarian dishes.

County Hotel (☎ 703250, 12 Francis St) Bar meals £5.25-9.80. Bar meals here are reasonable, but some items appear to have been cooked from frozen.

Golden Ocean (☎ 704422, 12-14 Cromwell St) During the day, Golden Ocean, near the TIC, does snacky meals in the day – baked potatoes start at £2 – but it's a Chinese restaurant in the evening.

Stornoway Balti House (☎ 706116, 24 South Beach St) Mains £5.50-6.95. Open daily. You can get a decent curry at this place, to eat in or take away.

There's also the *New Island Star* Chinese takeaway, at the southern end of Kenneth St, and a *fish and chip shop* on Church St.

For self-catering, there's a large *Safeway* supermarket on Shell St and a *Co-op* on Cromwell St (both closed Sunday).

Shopping The craft shop at the *Lewis Loom Centre* (☎ 704500, 3 Bayhead St) sells clothing made locally from Harris Tweed. It opens daily except Sunday.

Getting There & Away Buses from Stornoway to Tarbert and Leverburgh are run by Harris Coaches (☎ 01859-502441) three or four times Monday to Saturday. Galson Motors (☎ 840269) runs the service to Port of Ness six to ten times a day Monday to Saturday. Maclennan Coaches (☎ 702114) runs the circular route from Stornoway to Arnol, Carloway, Callanish and Stornoway (or reverse); three buses run Monday to Saturday in either direction.

For details on CalMac ferries, see Getting There & Away in the Outer Hebrides section earlier.

Butt of Lewis (Rubha Robhanais)

Lewis' northern tip is windswept and rugged, with a lighthouse, pounding surf, seals and large colonies of nesting fulmars. To get there, drive across the bleak expanse of Black Moor to **Barvas** (Barabhas), then follow the densely populated west coast to the north-east.

St Moluag's Church (Teampull Mholuidh), just north of Eoropie (Eoropaidh), is an austere, barn-like structure believed to date from the 12th century, but still used by the Episcopal Church.

Port of Ness (Port Nis) is an attractive harbour with a popular sandy beach. It's possible to walk along the east coast for 10 miles (16km) between the roads at Tolsta (Tolstaidh) and Cuisiadar (Cuidhaseadair), near Ness (four to six hours). The route passes ruins of a chapel and lots of summer shielings – until WWII, crofting families used to live on these moors in summer. There's a natural arch on the shore near Filiscleitir.

There are grocery shops in most villages.

Galson Farm Guesthouse & Bunkhouse (☎/fax 01851-850492, South Galson) B&B

singles/doubles from £35/58, dorm beds from £9. The recommended Galson Farm has B&B, pleasant hostel accommodation (with kitchen, shower and so on) and dinners for £16.

Arnol (Arnol) & Bragar

The most interesting and beautiful part of Lewis is south of Barvas and Stornoway. The coast has the best and most consistent surf in Europe.

Just west of Barvas, and off the A858, the **Arnol Blackhouse Museum** *(HS; ☎ 01851-710395, Arnol; adult/child £2.80/1; open 9.30am-6.30pm Mon-Sat Apr-Sept, 9.30am-4.30pm Mon-Sat Oct-Mar, last admission 30 minutes before closing)* is the only authentically maintained, traditional black-house – a combined byre, barn and home – left on the islands. Built in 1885, it was inhabited until 1964 and now offers a wonderful insight into the old crofting way of life. There's also a visitor centre with interpretative displays, a 1920s-style furnished croft and a black-house ruin.

At nearby **Bragar**, a pair of whalebones form an arch by the road, with the rusting harpoon that killed the whale dangling from the centre.

Dalbeg (Dail Beag)

West of Arnol, just before Carloway, lies this beautiful bay with a sandy beach backed by machair and flanked by cliffs and sea stacks.

Garenin (Na Gearrannan)
☎ 01851

The impressive **Gearrannan Blackhouse Village** *(W www.gearrannan.com)* consists of a street of nine restored thatch-roofed blackhouses at the end of the public road (well signposted from the main road). It's a fascinating place, with a cafe, hostel and upmarket self-catering options. The **museum** *(☎ 643416, Garenin; adult/child £2/1; open 11am-5.30pm Mon-Sat Apr-Oct)* is furnished as a traditional 1955 black-house and is well worth a visit. The live interpretation (with actors) includes spinning and peat cutting.

Garenin Crofters' Hostel (Garenin) Dorm beds £6.50/5. Open year-round. This wonderful thatch-roofed Gatliff Trust/SYHA hostel, in a restored black-house, is one of the most atmospheric hostels in Scotland (or anywhere else for that matter).

Taigh Thormoid 'an 'ic Iain (☎ 643416, fax 643488, Garenin) Self-catering doubles £25-43.75 per night. This place offers unique and highly recommended luxurious blackhouse accommodation, with attached kitchen and lounge.

The pleasant *Blackhouse Village Cafe (☎ 643416, Garenin)*, next to the museum, serves soup and snacks from £1.75.

Carloway (Carlabagh)

Carloway looks across a beautiful loch to the southern mountains and has a post office and small store.

Dun Carloway Broch (Dun Charlabhaigh) is a well-preserved, 2000-year-old dry-stone defensive tower, in a beautiful position with panoramic views. The subterranean grass-roofed **Doune Broch Centre** *(☎ 643338, Carloway; admission free; open 10am-5pm Mon-Sat late May–mid-Sept)* has interpretative displays and exhibitions about the history of the broch and the life of the people who lived there.

Callanish (Calanais)
☎ 01851

The construction of the **Callanish Standing Stones** *(☎ 621422, Callanish; admission free; open 24 hours year-round)* began around 5000 years ago, so they're similar in age to the earliest pyramids. Fifty-four large stones are arranged in the shape of a Celtic cross, with a circle and the remains of a chambered tomb where the arms cross, on a promontory overlooking Loch Roag. This is one of the most complete stone circles in Britain. Its great age, mystery, impressive scale and undeniable beauty have the dizzying effect of dislocating you from the present day.

The **Calanais Visitor Centre** *(☎ 621422, Callanish; admission free, exhibitions £1.75/75p; open 10am-6pm daily Apr-Sept, 10am-4pm Wed-Sat Oct-Mar)* is a *tour de force* of discreet design and provides a rare place to eat in the area. Snacks cost from

THE HEBRIDES

£1.15 (filled hoagies start at £2.60). There's an exhibition about the stones and a souvenir shop. Ask for permission to camp in the field.

Just north of Callanish, there's the **Stones, Sky and Sacred Landscape Exhibition** (*☎ 621277, New Park; admission free; open Mon-Sat, whenever someone is around*), with interesting displays, including astronomical items that relate to the Callanish stones. Tours of the stones cost £20 per group per hour.

There are a couple of pleasant B&Bs nearby including *Mrs Morrison's (☎ 621392, 27 Calanais)*, offering B&B from March to September for £20.

Eschol Guest House (☎/fax 621357, 21 Breascleit) B&B £29-31. The attractive Eschol Guest House, half a mile (800m) back towards Carloway, does good dinners (£18).

Tigh Mealros (☎ 621333, Garrynahine) Evening mains from £7.50. Tigh Mealros is noted for its wild local scallops.

Great Bernera
☎ 01851 • pop 262

This rocky island is connected to Lewis by another 'bridge over the Atlantic', which was built in 1953 (the islanders originally planned to destroy a small hill with explosives and use the material to build their own causeway). In the hamlet of **Breaclete**, there's a **folk history museum** (*☎ 612331, Breaclete; adult/child £1.50/50p; open noon-4pm Tues-Sat May-Sept*), with local temporary and permanent exhibits, and a tearoom serving home-baked goodies and snacks. You can walk a half mile (800m) from Breaclete to a restored mill. There's also a restored **Iron Age house** (*☎ 612331, Bosta; adult/child £1.50/50p; open noon-4pm Tues-Sat May-Sept*), where an entire village has been excavated and a guide will show you around. The beach at Bosta is excellent.

J MacDonald (*☎ 612224*) runs buses four or five times a day (Monday to Saturday) between Great Bernera and Stornoway.

Mealista (Mealasta)
The road to Mealista (the B8011 south-west of Callanish, signposted to Uig) takes you through the most remote parts of Lewis. Follow the road round towards Breanais for some truly spectacular white-sand beaches although the surf can make swimming treacherous. The famous 12th-century walrus-ivory Lewis chess pieces were discovered in the sand dunes here in 1831; of the 78 pieces, 67 ended up in the British Museum in London. You can buy replicas from various outlets around the island.

Bonaventure (☎ 01851-672474, Aird, Uig) 2-course/3-course lunch £6.50/8.50. Open Tues-Sat Jan, Mar-Oct & Dec. This Scottish-French restaurant and B&B (from £17 per person) is at Aird, just 3 miles (5km) north of the biggest beach, Uig Sands, at Timsgarry (Timsgearraidh). It serves snacks, lunches and a la carte evening meals – bookings are essential for dinner.

HARRIS (NA HEARADH)
pop 1866

Harris has the islands' most dramatic scenery, combining mountains, magnificent beaches, expanses of machair and weird rocky hills and coastline.

North Harris is actually the mountainous southern tip of Lewis, beyond the peat moors south of Stornoway – Clisham is the highest point. South Harris, across the land bridge at Tarbert, is also mountainous, but has a fascinating variety of landscapes and great beaches.

Harris is famous for Harris Tweed, high-quality woollen cloth still hand-woven in islanders' homes. The industry employs around 400 weavers; Tarbert TIC can tell you about the weavers and workshops you can visit.

Tarbert (An Tairbeart)
☎ 01859 • pop 480

Tarbert is a port village, midway between North and South Harris, with ferry connections to Uig on Skye.

Not in itself particularly inspiring, it has a spectacular location, overshadowed by mountains on the narrow land bridge between two lochs. Tarbert has basic facilities: a petrol station, a Bank of Scotland (no ATM) and two general stores. The Harris Tweed Shop stocks a wide range of books about the islands.

The year-round TIC (☎ 502011), Pier Rd, is signposted up the hill and to the right from the ferry. For ferry information, phone CalMac on ☎ 502444.

Rockview Bunkhouse (☎/fax 502626, Main St) Dorm beds £9. You'll find 32 beds, kitchen facilities and bike hire at this acceptable bunkhouse.

Tigh na Mara (☎ 502270, Tarbert) B&B £16 per person. This cosy B&B, with views of the eastern loch, is a five-minute walk from the ferry. The two-course dinner is good value at £10.

Hill Crest (☎ 502119, Tarbert) B&B with private bathroom £18. Hill Crest, 1½ miles (2.5km) west of the ferry, overlooks the west loch, and it's a good deal for the money. Dinner is available for an extra £11.

Waterstein House (☎ 502358, Main St) B&B £14 per person. Closer to the ferry terminal, Waterstein House is a bland building with four rooms.

Harris Hotel (☎ 502154, fax 502281, Tarbert) Singles £33.50-43.50, doubles £57-77. Between the eastern and western lochs, the Harris Hotel has a range of rooms, some en suite. It also has a good range of malt whiskies and serves good value pub meals (including vegetarian) for £6 to £9.

Harris Tweed

Warm, durable and relatively water-resistant, Harris Tweed is a luxury item hand-woven by some industrious Hebridean islanders in their own homes.

Weaving of Harris Tweed originated on the Amhuinnsuidhe Castle estate and it has now spread widely, with around 400 weavers throughout Lewis and Harris. Since clothes made from Harris Tweed have become expensive fashion statements, production in recent years has had to be cut back to avoid surpluses.

However, prices at outlets in the islands are much lower than in Edinburgh or London; typically, a jacket will cost around £110, a cap £16, or you can buy remnant cloth for £6.50 per metre.

Firstfruits (Pier Rd) Open Apr-Sept. This pleasant tearoom, opposite the TIC, is handy while you wait for a ferry. It does hot dishes, sandwiches and cakes.

Big D's (☎ 502098, Main St) Takeaways under £3.50. Big D's opens for lunch (not Sunday) and dinner (Friday and Saturday only). The fish and chips is OK but nothing to write home about.

North Harris

North Harris is the most mountainous part of the Outer Hebrides. Only a few roads run through the region, but there are many opportunities for climbing and walking. **Clisham** (799m) can be reached from the high point of the Stornoway to Tarbert road. The round trip takes about four hours and the views make it well worth the effort.

One road goes via **Amhuinnsuidhe Castle** to **Hushinish**, where there's a lovely silver-sand beach. Just north-west of Hushinish, the island of **Scarp**, now uninhabited, was the scene of bizarre attempts to send mail by rocket in 1934. The first rocket exploded, but the second actually reached its destination. A movie about the 'rocket post' was filmed in Harris in 2001.

The small village of **Rhenigidale** (Reinigeadal) has only recently become accessible by road.

Reinigeadal Crofters' Hostel (Rhenigidale) is a basic hostel, but it has toilets, shower, wood-burning stove and kitchen facilities. Beds costs £6.50/5. It can be reached on foot (three hours and 6 miles/9.5km from Tarbert). It's an excellent walk, but take all necessary supplies. From Tarbert, take the road to Kyles Scalpay for 2 miles (3km). Just beyond Laxdale Lochs, at a bend in the road, a signposted track, marked on OS maps, veers off to the left across the hills. The hostel is a white building standing above the road on the eastern side of the glen; the warden lives in the house closest to the shore.

The island of **Scalpay** (population 388), east of Tarbert, can now be reached by road. There are a couple of shops, B&Bs and interesting 'lazy-beds' on some of the crofts. Scalpay was the scene of great heroism during a storm in 1962 when local men set out in a small boat to rescue crew members of a ship that had run aground.

South Harris
☎ 01859

Beautiful South Harris is ringed by a tortuous 45-mile (72km) road. The beaches on the west coast, backed by rolling machair and mountains, with views across to North Harris and offshore islands, are stunning.

Seallam! (☎ *520258, Northton; adult/child £2.50/2; open 9am-6pm Mon-Sat*) has exhibits covering local and natural history; you can also trace your ancestors.

The town of **Leverburgh** (An t-Ob) is named after Lord Leverhulme (the founder of Unilever), who bought Lewis and Harris in 1918 and 1919. He had grand plans for the islands, and for Obbe, as Leverburgh was then known, which was to be a major fishing port, but it's now a sprawling, ordinary place. The An Clachan shop has a TIC (☎ 520370), tearoom and exhibition space.

Am Bothan (☎/*fax 520251, Leverburgh*), with dorm beds for £12, is a pleasant, quirky hostel.

Located near the ferry, *Caberfeidh House* (☎ *520276, Leverburgh*) has B&B for £17 to £20 and dinner for £10. Five minutes north from the ferry, *Garryknowe* (☎ *520246, Ferry Rd*) has B&B for £16 and offers dinner for £10; it opens February to October.

Also near the ferry is *Anchorage Restaurant* (☎ *520225, Leverburgh*), which serves pre-packed fast food (mains £4.95-6.20).

Three miles (5km) east, at attractive **Rodel** (Roghadal), stands **St Clement's Church** *(Rodel; admission free; open 24 hours year-round)*, which was mainly built between the 1520s and 1550s, only to be abandoned in 1560 after the Reformation. Inside, there's the fascinating tomb of Alexander MacLeod, the man responsible for the initial construction. Crude carvings show hunting scenes, a castle, a galleon and various saints, including St Clement clutching a skull.

The east, or Bays, coast is traversed by the Golden Road, derisively nicknamed by national newspapers that didn't think so much money should be spent on building it. This is a weird, rocky moonscape, still dotted with numerous crofts. It's difficult to imagine how anyone could have survived in such an inhospitable environment.

Hospitable *Drinishader Bunkhouse* (☎/*fax 511255, Drinishader*) is close to Tarbert. Dorm beds cost £7.

Getting There & Away
CalMac (☎ 502444) sails from Leverburgh to Berneray. In summer, it runs Monday to

---

For Peat's Sake

Visitors to the Outer Hebrides will not fail to notice peat stacks next to many houses. These interestingly constructed stacks are designed to allow wind to blow straight through, thus assisting the drying process before it can be used as fuel.

Peat is extremely wet in its raw state and it can take a few months to dry out. Initially it's cut from roadside sphagnum moss bogs, and cuttings are at least a metre deep. Rectangular blocks of peat are cut using a long-handled tool called a peat-iron (*tairsgeir* in Gaelic); this is extremely hard work and causes blisters, even on hands used to manual labour. Different types of tairsgeir are used on the islands. In Lewis, they cut relatively short brick-shaped blocks, while in Uist the blocks are somewhat longer. The peat blocks are transported to the cutter's house, then carefully built into a stack called a *cruach-mhonach*. The blocks are balanced on top of each other in a grid pattern so that there's a maximum air space. Once the peat is dry it can be stored in a shed.

Peat fires in Hebridean homes are becoming increasingly rare due to the popularity of oil-fuelled central heating. Peat burns much more slowly than wood or coal and it produces a pleasant smell and quite a lot of heat.

Saturday, three or four times a day; in winter, once or twice a day Monday to Saturday (£4.75, £21.90 for a car, one hour).

Getting Around

Buses from Tarbert to Scalpay, Stornoway and Leverburgh/Rodel (via the east or west coast) are run by Harris Coaches (☎ 01859-502441).

BERNERAY (BEARNARAIGH)
☎ 01876 • pop 140

The superb beaches of western Berneray are unparalleled in Scotland. The new causeway to North Uist opened in October 1998, but it hasn't altered the peace and beauty of this place.

Gatliff Hostel (Baile) Dorm beds £6.50/5. Open year-round. The excellent thatch-roofed Gatliff Hostel is just under 2 miles (3km) from the causeway.

Burnside Croft (☎/fax 540235, Borve) B&B from £20-26 per person. Open Feb-Nov. You'll get the finest island hospitality at this excellent B&B; it offers a four-course dinner for £20.

In summer, snacks are available at *The Lobster Pot*, the tearoom attached to Ardmarree Stores (near the causeway). There are two shops for groceries on Berneray.

There are Monday to Saturday postbus services (☎ 01246-546329), and Grenitote Travel (☎ 560244) buses, from Berneray (Gatliff Hostel) to Lochmaddy. For details of ferries to Leverburgh (Harris), see the preceding South Harris section.

NORTH UIST (UIBHIST A TUATH)
☎ 01876 • pop 1386

North Uist is half-drowned by lochs and has some magnificent beaches on the northern side. There are great views north to the mountains of Harris, especially from the top of hills such as **Crogarry Mór** (180m), which is 5 miles (8km) from Lochmaddy, towards Sollas. The landscape is a bit less wild than on Harris, but it has a sleepy, subtle appeal. For bird-watchers this is an earthly paradise, with huge populations of migrant waders – oystercatchers, lapwings, curlews and redshanks at every turn.

Lochmaddy (Loch nam Madadh)

Tiny Lochmaddy has the ferry terminal for sailings to Uig on Skye, and there are a couple of stores, a Bank of Scotland (with ATM), a petrol station, a post office and a pub.

The TIC (☎ 500321) opens 9am to 5pm Monday to Saturday April to mid-October, and for late ferry arrivals. For ferry information, phone CalMac on ☎ 500337.

The interesting **Taigh Chearsabhagh** *(☎ 500293, Lochmaddy; adult/child £1/50p; open 10am-5pm Mon-Sat Feb-Dec, 10am-8pm Fri in summer)* is a museum and arts centre that's worth a visit. The cafe next door offers free Internet access, and does soup and sandwiches.

Uist Outdoor Centre (☎ 500480, Ceann Dusgaidh, Lochmaddy) Beds £8-10. This independent hostel is often booked-out by large parties. Outdoor activities, including kayaking, can be arranged.

Old Courthouse (☎/fax 500358, Lochmaddy) En-suite B&B £21-25. The comfortable Old Courthouse offers good B&B in a historic building. You'll find it first on the right after the pier.

Stag Lodge (☎/fax 500364, Lochmaddy) En-suite B&B £23-25. The extremely comfortable and well-presented Stag Lodge is in a pleasing whitewashed building a mile (1.6km) from the ferry terminal; take the first right after the pier. There's also a small restaurant here serving meals for £6 to £12.75.

Lochmaddy Hotel (☎ 500331, fax 500210, Lochmaddy) En-suite B&B £35-65 per person. This traditional hotel has a range of rooms and offers bar meals for £4.25-£12.95. It's a good place to stay if you're into fishing (and North Uist is famous for fishing). You can buy permits here.

Balranald Nature Reserve

Eighteen miles (29km) west of Lochmaddy, off the A865, there's an RSPB nature reserve *(☎ 510372)*, where you can watch migrant waders and listen for rare corncrakes. A free visitor centre provides leaflets and information from April to September. Peter Rabbit (yes, really) can take you on a 2½-hour guided walk in the reserve on Tuesday at 6.30pm and Thursday at 11.30am, May to August (£2.50/1).

Bharpa Langass & Pobull Fhinn

The chambered Neolithic burial tomb of Bharpa Langass stands on a hillside 6 miles (10km) south-west of Lochmaddy, just off the A867. The 24m-diameter and 4.2m-high cairn is believed to date back 5000 years. Take care as the path can be boggy.

Pobull Fhinn (Finn's People) is a stone circle of similar age accessible from a path beside Langass Lodge Hotel. There are lovely views over the loch, where seals can sometimes be seen. A marked circular route from the hotel takes less than an hour and includes both sites.

Langass Lodge Hotel (☎ 580285, fax 580385, Locheport) Singles/doubles £45/75. This hotel is particularly noted for its food (three-course bar meals around £13). It's in a grand old lodge which feels remote from the rest of the world.

Clachan na Luib

This village has a shop and a few houses; *Mermaid Fish Supplies (☎ 580209)* does excellent smoked salmon. About a mile (1.6km) to the west, by the sandy tidal channel between North Uist and **Baleshare (Am Baile Sear) Island**, there's luxurious hostel accommodation in a tastefully modernised crofthouse, *Taigh mo Sheanair (☎ 580246, Claddach Baleshare)*. It has bunks from £9 and camping for £4.50 per person.

The nearest place to eat is in Langass, or you can try the modernised *Carinish Inn (☎ 580673, fax 580665, Carinish)*, where bar meals cost from £4.25 to £11.95. It also offers en-suite B&B for £35.

Bike hire can be organised with Iain Morrison (☎ 580211) for £7.50 per day.

Getting There & Away

Buses from Lochmaddy to Langass, Clachan na Luib, Berneray Hostel, Benbecula and Lochboisdale are run by Royal Mail (☎ 500330), Hebridean Coaches (☎ 01870-620345) and Macdonald Coaches (☎ 01870-620288). There are usually two runs a day Monday to Saturday.

BENBECULA (BEINN NA FAOGHLA)
☎ 01870 • pop 1883

Blink and you'll miss Benbecula, a low-lying island that's almost as much water as land, connected by bridge and causeway to both the Uists.

Although the number of British soldiers based here is declining, they still have a missile firing range. The troops and their families were quartered around functional **Balivanich** (Baile a'Mhanaich), but now most of their houses are empty. The Spar shop opens 8am to 8pm Monday to Saturday and 11am to 4pm Sunday. There's also a post office and a bank with an ATM. The new Uists hospital (☎ 603603) is in Balivanich.

The **Sgoil Lionacleit Leisure Centre** *(☎ 602211)*, about 4 miles (6km) south of Balivanich, has a pool, games hall and sauna. It opens to the public when not being used by the school.

Taigh na Cille Bunkhouse (☎ 602522, Balivanich) Dorm beds £10-11. The bunkhouse is near the airport – but don't worry, flights are infrequent!

Stepping Stone Restaurant (☎ 603377, Balivanich) Mains £4.25-13.75. Good food is available here, from pie, beans & chips to steamed halibut steak.

The *Café Bar* at the airport is reasonable, but the *Low Flyer (Balivanich)* pub is basic.

Monday to Saturday, there's one flight a day to Glasgow, from £104 return. For bus details, see the North Uist Getting There & Away section earlier.

SOUTH UIST (UIBHIST A DEAS)
pop 2064

Unassuming South Uist, the second largest island in the Outer Hebrides, has an expansiveness with its own magic. The low west coast, with machair backing an almost continuous sandy beach, offers excellent bird-watching prospects, and the multitude of lochs are great for trout fishing. The east coast, cut by four large sea lochs, is quite hilly, with spectacular **Beinn Mhor** reaching 620m. The main settlement and ferry port, Lochboisdale is the only place of any size on the east coast.

The island rewards those who go beyond the main north-south road. One of the best areas to explore is remote Usinish, on the east coast, where you'll find **Nicolson's Leap**.

As you drive from Benbecula, watch for the granite statue of **Our Lady of the Isles** standing on the slopes of the Rueval hill.

Lochboisdale (Loch Baghasdail)
☎ 01878

Lochboisdale has ferry links to Oban and Mallaig on the mainland and Castlebay on Barra.

The TIC (☎ 700286) opens 9am to 5pm Monday to Saturday April to mid-October and for late ferry arrivals. For ferry information phone CalMac on ☎ 700288. There's a Royal Bank of Scotland branch (no ATM) and petrol supplies. The nearest shop is at Daliburgh (Dalabrog), 3 miles (5km) west.

Friendly *Lochside Cottage* (☎ 700472, Lochboisdale) has B&B for £18. It is 1½ miles (2.5km) west of the ferry. Nearer the pier, *Bayview* (☎ 700329, Lochboisdale) offers B&B for £20 and opens March to October.

Mrs MacDonald (☎ 700517, Kilchoan Bay) B&B £18-20. Open Apr-Sept. This recommended B&B offers pick-up from the ferry.

Lochboisdale Hotel (☎ 700332, fax 700367, Lochboisdale) B&B £38-46.50. Lochboisdale Hotel, above the ferry terminal, has a variety of rooms and the pub lets good food for £2.25 to £14.95.

For bus details, see the North Uist Getting There & Away section.

Kildonan Museum

Kildonan, 7 miles (11km) north of Lochboisdale, has a fine folk and historical museum (☎ 01878-710343, Kildonan; adult/child £1.50/free; open 10am-5pm daily & 10am-2pm Sun Easter-Oct) detailing the life and work of the islanders. The adjacent *cafe* does basic snacks and meals from £1.50 to £4.20. There's an excellent craft shop on site.

Howmore (Tobha Mor)

The attractive west coast village of Howmore has the *Tobha Mor Crofters' Hostel* (Howmore), with dorm beds for £6.50/5. The Gatliff Trust/SYHA hostel is near the beach.

Bike hire is available from the shed (☎ 01870-620283) at the junction with the main road. There's a shop nearby.

Two miles (3km) north there's the **Loch Druidibeg Nature Reserve**. SNH has an information office by the roadside, and you can take a 5-mile (8km) hike (two hours). A more demanding walk follows the northeastern ridge of Beinn Mhor – beware of the precipitous cliffs on the northern side, and carry OS map No 22. Allow six hours for the round trip from the hostel.

The North

The best place to eat in the Uists is the *Orasay Inn* (☎ 01870-610298, fax 610390, Lochcarnan). It offers excellent bar and restaurant meals for £5.85 to £16.95, including salmon, scallops, langoustine, halibut, sole, beef, duck and vegetarian dishes. It also offers B&B for £30 to £85.

The South

The southern tip looks across to the islands of Eriskay and Barra. The scenery is particularly lovely at Polochar (Pol a'Charra).

The *Polochar Inn* (☎ 01878-700215, fax 700768, Polochar) is a comfortable hotel offering en-suite singles/doubles for £35/55 and bar and restaurant meals for £5 to £16.

Monday to Saturday, Hebridean Coaches (☎ 01870-620345) do at least three runs a day from Eriskay to Lochboisdale via Polochar.

The South Uist to Eriskay causeway, the longest in Scotland, is half a mile (800m) east of Ludag. It cost £10 million and opened in July 2001. The passenger ferry (☎ 01878-720238) from Ludag to Eoligarry/Ardveenish on Barra runs Monday to Saturday, two to four times a day (£5, one hour).

ERISKAY (EIRIOSGAIGH)
☎ 01878 • pop 173

This romantic and beautiful island is where Bonnie Prince Charlie first set foot in Scotland in 1745. More recently, the SS *Politician* sank just off the coast in 1941 and the islanders retrieved some of its cargo of around 250,000 bottles of whisky. After a binge of dramatic proportions, the police turned up and a number of the islanders landed in jail.

The story was immortalised in good humour by Sir Compton Mackenzie in his book *Whisky Galore*, later turned into a film.

The **Catholic church** in Haunn (the northernmost settlement) uses a boat's prow as its altar. There's a good view from **Ben Scrien** (186m); look out for Eriskay ponies on the way.

The island has a grocery store, post office and pub.

Mrs Cambell's Apartment (☎ 720274, 2 *Haunn*) £180 per week. This well-equipped apartment has an excellent beachside location. Its minimum letting period is one week.

Am Politician (☎ 720246, *Haunn*) Mains £5.50-6.75. Open 11am-8pm daily. Am Politician serves popular seafood meals.

BARRA (BARRAIGH)
☎ 01871 • pop 1212

Barra (W www.isleofbarra.com) is a small island, just 14 miles (22km) around and ideal for exploring on foot. With beautiful beaches, machair, hills, Neolithic remains and a strong sense of community, it encapsulates the Outer Hebridean experience. Barra is connected by causeway to **Vatersay** (Bhatarsaigh), where there's a 4-mile (6km) heritage trail (three hours).

The TIC (☎ 810336) in **Castlebay** (Bagh a'Chaisteil), the largest village, opens April to mid-October. Castlebay has ferry connections with Lochboisdale (South Uist), Mallaig and Oban. For information, phone CalMac on ☎ 810306. There's a post office, bank (no ATM), Co-op and Spar.

For a great view, walk up to the top of Heaval (383m) on Barra, a mile (1.6km) north-east of Castlebay. Allow about two hours from the road.

Things to See
On an islet in the bay at Castlebay, there's **Kisimul Castle** (HS; ☎ 810313, Castlebay; adult/child £3/1, including ferry; open 9.30am-6.30pm daily Apr-Sept), first built by the MacNeil clan in the 11th century. It was sold in the 19th century and restored in the 20th by American architect Robert Mac-Neil, who became the 45th clan chief. A standard flies above the castle when his son

and heir is in residence. A boat will collect you from Castlebay on request.

The **Barra Heritage Centre** (☎ 810413, Castlebay; adult/child £2/75p; open 11am-4pm Mon-Fri May-Sept, shorter hours Oct-Apr) has Gaelic-theme displays about the island, local art exhibitions and a tearoom. It also has a restored **19th-century cottage** (☎ 810413, Craigston, Borve; adult/child £2/75p; open 1pm-4pm Mon-Fri mid-May–Sept), 3 miles (5km) north of Castlebay.

Places to Stay & Eat
With only about 20 B&Bs scattered around the island, and some ferries arriving late in the evening, it's best to book ahead.

Isle of Barra Hostel (☎/fax 810443, Castlebay) Beds £10. This excellent and friendly hostel is 150m west of the pier; sea kayak tours cost £12/18 per half/full day.

Mrs Clelland (☎ 810438, 47 Glen) Singles/doubles £18/36. Open year-round. Just half a mile from the pier, this basic B&B dishes up a reasonable breakfast.

Faire Mhaoldonaich (☎ 810441, e fm@ isleofbarra.com, Nask) En-suite B&B £20-22. Open Apr-Oct. Located 1½ miles (2.5km) from Castlebay, by the Vatersay road, this is an excellent choice.

Craigard Hotel (☎ 810200, fax 810726, Castlebay) En-suite singles/doubles £34/62. This comfortable hotel does excellent meals for £5.75 to £10.95, including a catch of the day and vegetarian dishes.

Kismul Galley (☎ 810645, Castlebay) Meals £4-6.95. Open daily. Kismul Galley, in the village centre, does soup and a home-made roll for £2.10.

At the northern end of the island, the *airport tearoom* does snacks.

Getting There & Away
British Airways Express flies to Barra from Glasgow from Monday to Saturday (from £99/138 single/return).

See the Outer Hebrides Getting There & Away section earlier for CalMac ferry details. The small passenger ferry (☎ 01878-701702) to Ludag on South Uist (from Eoligarry/Ardveenish) runs Monday to Saturday, two to four times a day (£5, bikes £2.50).

Getting Around

There's a good postbus service (☎ 01246-546329) around the island, which connects with flights at the airport.

PABBAY (PABAIDH) & MINGULAY (MIUGHALAIGH)

Uninhabited Pabbay and Mingulay (along with two other islands) were acquired by the NTS in 2001.

Pabbay, roughly a mile (1.6km) across, was abandoned in 1912. The south-western cliffs and an immense natural arch attract rock climbers. Near the ruinous settlement at the eastern end of Pabbay, there are **symbol stones** (probably Pictish), one with a cross, a crescent and a lily.

Mingulay, measuring 2 miles (3km) by a mile (1.6km), is characterised by sea stacks, cliffs (over 200m high), huge caves and natural arches on its western side, and more gradual slopes in the east. The ruined village near the boat landing is a reminder of human occupation until 1912.

A trip to Mingulay, especially during the puffin season from June to early August, is highly recommended. *George McLeod (☎ 01871-810223)* in Castlebay, Barra, sails to Mingulay (usually at weekends) for around £10/20 per person without/with landing, depending on weather and numbers.

ST KILDA

St Kilda (**W** *www.kilda.org.uk*), owned by NTS and leased to SNH, is a UNESCO World Heritage Site and consists of four main islands and several smaller ones. You can easily exhaust all superlatives to describe this collection of volcanic rock stacks and islands about 40 miles (64km) west of North Uist. The largest island, **Hirta**, measures about 2 miles (3km) east-west by a mile (1.6km) north-south. It has huge cliffs along most of its coastline.

History

Hirta was inhabited by Gaelic-speaking people until the well-documented evacuation in 1930. Tourism and church influences in the 19th century assisted in the destruction of the community on St Kilda, but the islanders' habit of using fulmar oil on the umbilical cord of new-born babies killed about 80% of their infants. People survived here by keeping sheep, fishing, growing a few basic crops such as barley, and climbing the cliffs without boots to catch sea birds and collect their eggs. Over the centuries, this resulted in a genetic peculiarity – St Kildan men and their male descendants have unusually long big-toes.

Organised Tours

The NTS charges volunteers for doing archaeological and conservation work in and around the village ruins. Archaeology/restoration trips run mid-May to mid-August; you have to work 36/24 hours per week, and the cost is £450/500 (including transport from Oban in a converted lifeboat and full board in dorm accommodation). Volunteers must be fit. There are 11 in each party, and the selection process takes place in February for the following summer. Get your application form from the NTS (☎ 01631-570000) in November.

In your time off, you can wander up to the top of **Conachair** (430m) to admire the view of **Boreray** (384m) and the great rock towers of **Stac Lee** (172m) and **Stac an Armin** (196m). A visit will be arranged to the island of **Dun**.

Boat tours to St Kilda are expensive and landing is usually possible on Hirta. For a listing of tour operators, check out the Internet at **W** www.kilda.org.uk. *Western Edge (☎ 01224-210564, mobile ☎ 07761 400446,* **e** *Murrayiain@compuserve.com)* departs from Berneray on Saturday in summer and charges £450 for a six-day trip (possibly including the Monach Islands). Another possibility is *Island Cruising (☎ 01851-672381,* **e** *cuma@sol.co.uk)*, based in Uig, Lewis.

Getting There & Away

Apart from the aforementioned organised trips, the only access to St Kilda is by private boat. Landing on all of the islands, except Hirta, is virtually impossible due to the ocean swell; even Hirta can be difficult in a southerly to north-easterly wind.

THE HEBRIDES

Orkney & Shetland Islands

These two groups of islands lie north of the Scottish mainland. They're popular with walkers, bird-watchers, anglers and divers, and reward visitors who make the effort to get there with some spectacular scenery.

Orkney Islands

Just 6 miles (10km) off the north coast of the Scottish mainland, this magical group of islands is known for its dramatic coastal scenery, ranging from 300m-high cliffs to white, sandy beaches; for its abundant marine bird life; and for a plethora of prehistoric sites, including an entire 4500-year-old village at Skara Brae.

Sixteen of the 70 islands are inhabited. Kirkwall is the main town and Stromness is a major port – both are on the largest island, which is known as Mainland. The land is virtually treeless, but lush, level and cultivated rather than rugged. The climate, warmed by the Gulf Stream, is surprisingly mild, with April and May being the driest months.

Over 1000 prehistoric sites have been identified on Orkney, the greatest concentration in any place in Europe. Since there has always been a lack of timber, everything is made from stone. This explains the survival of ancient domestic architecture that includes a 5500-year-old house, Europe's oldest, on Papa Westray. The most impressive ancient monuments – the village of Skara Brae, the tomb of Maeshowe and the Ring of Brodgar – are all on Mainland.

Orkney's Pictish rulers were replaced by Norse earls in the 9th century. The Norse ruled until the mid-13th century and built the magnificent St Magnus Cathedral in Kirkwall. Even today, there are hints of those distant Scandinavian connections in the lilting accent with which Orcadians speak English.

Orkney is popular with bird-watchers and the Royal Society for the Protection of Birds (RSPB) runs several reserves. From

HIGHLIGHTS

- Exploring Orkney's evocative prehistoric sites
- Discovering the stunning coastal scenery of Eshaness (Shetland)
- Taking a day trip on a ferry to one of Orkney's Northern Isles
- Bird-watching at North Ronaldsay (Orkney), and sitting among the puffins at Hermaness on Unst (Shetland)
- Experiencing some of Europe's best scuba-diving among the sunken warships of Scapa Flow (Orkney)

May to mid-July, vast numbers of seabirds come to nest on the cliffs. The clear waters around the islands attract divers, and Scapa Flow, south of Mainland, offers the most interesting wreck dive site in Europe.

If you're anywhere in the area around mid-June, don't miss the St Magnus Arts

Festival. Sir Peter Maxwell Davies, one of the greatest living British composers, usually contributes to the festival – he lives on Hoy. The poet and writer George Mackay Brown lived in Stromness. His novel *Greenvoe* perfectly captures the special atmosphere of these islands.

INFORMATION

The Orkney Tourist Board (☎ 01856-872856, W www.visitorkney.com), 6 Broad St, Kirkwall KW15 1NX, publishes a useful brochure detailing visitor attractions, services and accommodation options on the islands. It also has a very helpful guide called *The Islands of Orkney*, which covers all the islands (except Mainland) in depth.

There are only two TICs, in Kirkwall and Stromness, but they're open year-round.

GETTING THERE & AWAY
Air

There are flights to Kirkwall airport on British Airways/Loganair (☎ 0845 773 3377) daily (except Sunday) from Aberdeen, Edinburgh, Glasgow, Inverness and Shetland, with connections to London Heathrow, Birmingham, Manchester and Belfast. The cheapest return tickets (which must usually be bought 14 days in advance and require at least a Saturday night stay in Orkney) cost around £230 from London, £140 from Glasgow and £100 from Inverness.

Bus

Scottish Citylink (☎ 0870 550 5050, W www.citylink.co.uk) has daily coaches from Inverness to Scrabster (£10, three hours), connecting with the ferries to Stromness. Early-morning departures from Glasgow or Edinburgh, and overnighters from London, connect with the Scrabster bus at Inverness.

John O'Groats Ferries (☎ 01955-611353) operates the summer-only Orkney Bus service from Inverness to Kirkwall. The ticket (single/return £28/40, five hours) includes bus travel from Inverness to John o'Groats, the passenger ferry to Burwick, and another bus from Burwick to Kirkwall. There's one bus daily in May and two daily from June to early September.

Boat

Car ferries to and from Orkney can be very busy in July and August – it's best to book ahead at these times.

Note that in October 2002, ferry services to Orkney and Shetland, currently run by P&O, will be taken over by NorthLink Ferries, a joint venture between Caledonian MacBrayne and the Royal Bank of Scotland. It will introduce three brand-new, purpose-built ferries, and plans to provide more frequent services with lower fares. Ferries from Aberdeen and Lerwick (Shetland) will dock at Kirkwall. For the latest details, check the Web site at W www.northlinkferries.co.uk.

From Scrabster P&O Scottish Ferries (☎ 01224-572615, fax 574411, W www.posf .co.uk) runs a regular car ferry from Scrabster, near Thurso, to Stromness (passenger/car £16.50/51, two hours). The return fare for passenger/car is £33/86. From April to October, there are at least two crossings daily Monday to Saturday (three Monday and Friday) and one Sunday. In winter, there are two daily Monday to Friday, one Saturday and none Sunday.

P&O also offers round-trip tickets on the following routes (in either direction):

Scrabster-Stromness-Aberdeen (£56/118)
Scrabster-Stromness-Lerwick (Shetland)-
  Stromness-Scrabster (£112/177)
Scrabster-Stromness-Lerwick (Shetland)-
  Aberdeen (£110/215).

From Shetland P&O sails from Lerwick to Stromness (passenger/car £40.50/95, eight to 10 hours) once a week (Friday) from March to December, and twice a week (Wednesday and Friday) from June to August. Ferries from Stromness to Lerwick leave on Tuesday and Sunday.

From Aberdeen P&O also sails to Stromness from Aberdeen (passenger/car £43.50/113, 10 hours) once a week (Saturday) from March to December, and twice a week (Tuesday and Saturday) from June to August. The minimum fare gets you a reclining seat; one-way passenger fares with a cabin berth cost from £48 to £76.50.

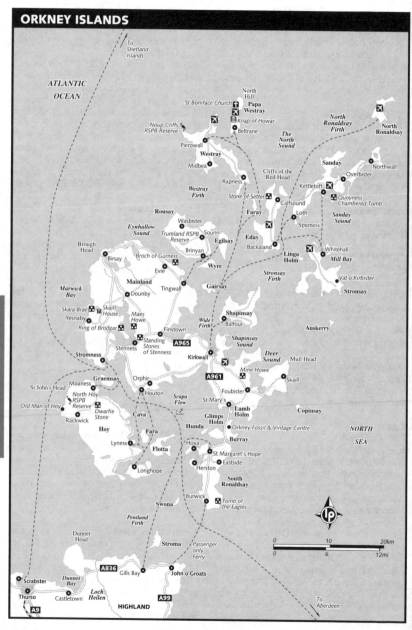

ORKNEY ISLANDS

ATLANTIC OCEAN

To Shetland Islands

North Hill

St Boniface Church **Papa Westray**

Noup Cliffs RSPB Reserve Knap of Howar

Beltrane

Pierowall

Westray

Midbea

Rapness

Westray Firth

The North Sound

North Ronaldsay Firth

North Ronaldsay

Sanday

Northwall

Overbister

Kettletoft

Cliffs of the Red Head

Stone of Setter

Calfsound

Quoyness Chambered Tomb

Sanday Sound

Faray

Loth

Spurness

Rousay

Wasbister

Eynhallow Sound

Trumland RSPB Reserve

Sourin

Brinyan

Egilsay

Eday

Backaland

Linga Holm

Whitehall

Mill Bay

Brough Head

Birsay

Broch of Gurness

Evie

Wyre

Stronsay Firth

Vat o'Kirbister

Stronsay

Marwick Bay

Mainland

Dounby

Tingwall

Gairsay

Skara Brae Skaill House

Yesnaby

Ring of Brodgar

Maes Howe

Stenness

Finstown

Standing Stones of Stenness

Shapinsay

Balfour

Wide Firth

Shapinsay Sound

Auskerry

A965

Kirkwall

Deer Sound

Mull Head

Stromness

A961

Mine Howe

Skaill

Moaness

Graemsay

Orphir

Houton

Scapa Flow

Foubister

St Mary's

Copinsay

NORTH SEA

St John's Head

North Hoy RSPB Reserve

Old Man of Hoy

Dwarfie Stone

Cava

Fara

Glimps Holm

Hunda

Lamb Holm

Orkney Fossil & Vintage Centre

Rackwick

Hoy

Lyness

Flotta

Hoxa

Burray

St Margaret's Hope

Eastside

Herston

Longhope

South Ronaldsay

Burwick

Tomb of the Eagles

Swona

Pentland Firth

Dunnet Head

Stroma

Passenger only Ferry

Scrabster

Dunnet Bay

Gills Bay

A836

John o'Groats

A99

Thurso

Castletown

Loch Heilen

HIGHLAND

A9

To Aberdeen

0   10   20km

0   6   12mi

You can also buy a round-trip ticket for the route Aberdeen-Stromness-Lerwick (Shetland)-Aberdeen (£135/250).

From Gills Bay Pentland Ferries (☎ 01856-831226, **W** www.pentlandferries.com) offers a shorter and less expensive car ferry crossing from Gills Bay, about 3 miles (5km) west of John o'Groats, to St Margaret's Hope in Orkney (passenger/car £10/25, one hour); return fares are double the single fare. There are at least three crossings daily in summer; call to check availability in winter.

From John o'Groats In summer, John o' Groats Ferries (☎ 01955-611353) operates a passenger-only ferry from John o'Groats to Burwick, on the southern tip of South Ronaldsay. For details, see the John o'Groats section of the Highlands chapter.

GETTING AROUND
Highland Council (☎ 01463-702695) publishes a public transport map *The Highlands, Orkney, Shetland and Western Isles* (10p), which lists air, bus and ferry services in Orkney. Also available is an annual public transport guide, *North Highland and Orkney* (£1), which includes detailed timetables.

The largest island, Mainland, is joined by road-bearing causeways to Burray and South Ronaldsay. The other islands can be reached by air and ferry services.

Air
British Airways/Loganair (☎ 0845 773 3377 or ☎ 01856-872494) operates inter-island air services between Kirkwall airport and North Ronaldsay, Westray, Papa Westray, Stronsay, Sanday and Eday. For details, see the relevant island entries in this chapter.

Bus
Orkney Coaches (☎ 01856-870555) runs a network of bus services on Mainland and South Ronaldsay. Most buses do not run on Sunday. A free timetable for all services is available from the TIC.

You can save money with Day Rover (£6) and 3-Day Rover (£15) tickets, which allow unlimited travel on Orkney Coaches bus routes.

Boat
Orkney Ferries Ltd (☎ 01856-872044, **W** www.orkneyferries.co.uk), Shore St, Kirkwall, operates car ferries from Mainland to Hoy, Flotta and the northern Orkney islands; for details see the relevant island sections later.

Car
There are several car-hire companies on Mainland, including Orkney Car Hire (☎ 01856-872866), Junction Rd, Kirkwall, and Norman Brass Car Hire (☎ 01856-850850), Blue Star Filling Station, North End Rd, Stromness. Rates for a small car begin at around £35 per day or £170 per week including VAT, CDW, insurance and unlimited mileage.

To hire a camper van, contact Orkney Motorhome Hire (☎ 01856-874391, **W** www.orkney-motorhome-hire.co.uk). The vans are comfy for two adults, but at a pinch will sleep two adults and three kids. Rates are £590 per week in July and August, £490 per week April to June, September and October, and £390 per week November to March.

Bicycle
You can hire bikes from various locations on the Mainland, including Bobby's Cycles

JANE SMITH

A sure sign that otters are present on Orkney

(☎ 01856-875777), Tankerness Lane, Kirkwall, which charges £8 per day or £50 per week; and Orkney Cycle Hire (☎ 01856-850255), 54 Dundas St, Stromness, which charges between £5 and £8.50 per day, depending on the type of bike.

ORGANISED TOURS

Orkney Island Wildlife (☎ 01856-711373, e *islandholidays@orkney.com, Shapinsay 20, Orkney)* offers holidays based on Shapinsay, with guided tours of archaeological sites, bird-watching and wildlife trips, and trips to other islands. One-week packages cost £599 to £650 and are all-inclusive.

Wildabout Orkney (☎/fax 01856-851011, mobile ☎ 0777 637 8966, e *wildabout@ orkney.com)* is a small tour company whose trips cover archaeology, history, folklore and wildlife. Day trips run from March to October and cost £14 to £18. The minibus tours pick up at Stromness ferry terminal, Palace Rd in Kirkwall and Kirkwall Youth Hostel.

Discover Orkney (☎/fax 01856-872865, 44 Clay Loan, Kirkwall) caters to individuals and small groups, and offers guided tours and walks throughout the islands in the company of a qualified guide.

Also, *Brass's Taxis (☎ 01856-850750)* at the ferry terminal in Stromness and *Peedie Cab (☎ 01856-741398)* in Deerness offer taxi tours of Mainland from around £15 per hour for up to four people.

KIRKWALL
☎ 01856 • pop 6100

Orkney's capital is a bustling market town set back from a wide bay. Founded in the early 11th century by Earl Rognvald Brusason, the original part is one of the best examples of an ancient Norse town.

St Magnus Cathedral, one of Scotland's finest medieval cathedrals, is certainly worth a visit, and there are a number of other things to see in the town; the whisky distillery tour is interesting.

Orientation

Kirkwall is a fairly compact town and it's easy enough to get around on foot. The cathedral and most of the shops are set back from the harbour on Broad St, which changes its name several times along its length. Ferries leave from the harbour for the northern Orkney islands.

Information

Kirkwall's TIC (☎ 872856), at 6 Broad St by the cathedral, opens 8.30am to 8pm daily April to September and 9.30am to 5pm Monday to Saturday the rest of the year. It's a helpful place with a good range of publications on Orkney.

There are banks with ATMs on Broad St and Albert St. The post office is on Junction Rd. You can check email at Orkney College (☎ 569000) on East Rd, a 10-minute walk from the TIC. It charges £4 per hour (no minimum) and opens 4pm to 9pm daily (except Friday) in term time and 9am to 4pm Monday to Friday during the holidays (July and August).

Launderama (☎ 872982), 47 Albert St, does a wash and dry for £3.50; it opens 8.30am to 5.30pm Monday to Friday and 9am to 5pm Saturday.

The Balfour Hospital (☎ 885400) is on New Scapa Rd.

St Magnus Cathedral

Founded in 1137, and constructed from local red sandstone and yellow Eday stone, St Magnus Cathedral *(☎ 874894; admission free; open 9am-6pm Mon-Sat & 2pm-6pm Sun Apr-Sept, 9am-1pm & 2pm-5pm Mon-Sat Oct-Mar)* was built by masons who had previously worked on Durham Cathedral. The interior is particularly impressive and, although much smaller than the great cathedral at Durham, the same powerful atmosphere of a very ancient faith pervades the place. There's a service at 11.15am on Sunday.

Earl Rognvald Brusason commissioned the cathedral in the name of his martyred uncle, Magnus Erlendsson, who was killed by Earl Hakon Paulsson on Egilsay in 1117. Work began in 1137, but the building is actually the result of 300 years of construction and alteration, and includes Romanesque, transitional and Gothic styles.

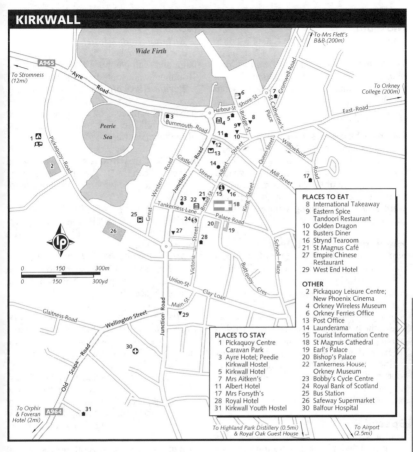

KIRKWALL

Wide Firth

To Stromness (12mi)

To Mrs Flett's B&B (200m)

To Orkney College (200m)

Peerie Sea

PLACES TO EAT
8 International Takeaway
9 Eastern Spice Tandoori Restaurant
10 Golden Dragon
12 Busters Diner
16 Strynd Tearoom
21 St Magnus Café
27 Empire Chinese Restaurant
29 West End Hotel

OTHER
2 Pickaquoy Leisure Centre; New Phoenix Cinema
4 Orkney Wireless Museum
6 Orkney Ferries Office
13 Post Office
14 Launderama
15 Tourist Information Centre
18 St Magnus Cathedral
19 Earl's Palace
20 Bishop's Palace
22 Tankerness House; Orkney Museum
23 Bobby's Cycle Centre
24 Royal Bank of Scotland
25 Bus Station
26 Safeway Supermarket
30 Balfour Hospital

PLACES TO STAY
1 Pickaquoy Centre Caravan Park
3 Ayre Hotel; Peedie Kirkwall Hostel
5 Kirkwall Hotel
7 Mrs Aitken's
11 Albert Hotel
17 Mrs Forsyth's
28 Royal Hotel
31 Kirkwall Youth Hostel

To Orphir & Foveran Hotel (2mi)

To Highland Park Distillery (0.5mi) & Royal Oak Guest House

To Airport (2.5mi)

The bones of Magnus are interred in one of the pillars in the cathedral. Other memorials include a statue of John Rae, the Arctic explorer, and the bell from HMS *Royal Oak*, torpedoed and sunk in Scapa Flow during WWII with the loss of 833 crew.

Earl's Palace & Bishop's Palace

Near the cathedral, and on opposite sides of the street, are these two ruined buildings (☎ 875461, Palace Rd; adult/child £2/75p; open 9.30am-6.30pm daily Apr-Oct), run by Historic Scotland (HS). A joint ticket for all staffed HS monuments in Orkney, including Maeshowe, Skara Brae, Skaill House, the Broch of Gurness and the Brough of Birsay, costs £11/3.50 in summer, £10/3 in winter.

The Bishop's Palace was built in the mid-12th century to provide comfortable lodgings for Bishop William the Old. There's a good view of the cathedral from the tower, and a plaque showing the different phases of the construction of the cathedral.

At one time, the Earl's Palace was known as the finest example of French Renaissance architecture in Scotland. It was begun in 1600 by Earl Patrick Stewart, but he ran out of money and the palace wasn't completed.

Tankerness House & Orkney Museum

This excellent restored merchant's house (☎ 873191, Broad St; admission free; open 10.30am-5pm Mon-Sat year-round, 2pm-5pm Sun May-Sept, closed 12.30pm-1.30pm Oct-Mar) contains an interesting museum of Orkney life over the last 5000 years. Guided tours are available.

Orkney Wireless Museum

This museum (☎ 874272, Junction Rd; adult/child £2/1; open 10am-4.30pm Mon-Sat & 2.30pm-4.30pm Sun Apr-Sept) is a fascinating jumble of communications equipment dating from around 1930 onwards, especially relating to the Scapa Flow naval base.

Highland Park Distillery

Not only is Highland Park a very fine single-malt, but the tour of the world's most northerly whisky distillery (☎ 874619, Holm Rd; guided tour £3; open 10am-5pm Mon-Fri Apr-Oct, noon-5pm Sat & Sun July & Aug, 1pm-5pm Mon-Fri Nov-Mar) is also one of the best. You'll see the whole whisky-making process – this is one of the few distilleries that still does its own barley malting, known as floor malting. There are tours of the distillery every half-hour during opening times from April to October, and one tour only at 2pm in winter.

Special Events

The St Magnus Festival (☎ 871445) takes place in June and is a celebration of music and the arts. An interesting event called The Ba' takes place on New Year's Day; two teams – the Uppies and the Doonies – chase a ball, and each other, around Broad St until one team reaches its goal.

Places to Stay

Camping There's a convenient camp site on the edge of town.

Pickaquoy Centre Caravan Park (☎ 879900, Pickaquoy Rd) Pitches £3.50-5.50. This camp site is on the western outskirts of Kirkwall, next to the town's leisure centre.

Hostels Kirkwall has two hostels for backpackers.

Kirkwall Youth Hostel (☎ 872243, Old Scapa Rd) Dorm beds £8.75/7.75. Kirkwall's large and well-equipped SYHA hostel is a 10-minute walk south from the bus station.

Peedie Kirkwall Hostel (☎ 875477, 1 Ayre Houses, Ayre Rd) Beds from £10 per person. This place is on the waterfront next to the Ayre Hotel, five minutes' walk west of the town centre.

B&Bs & Guesthouses There's a good range of cheap B&Bs, though most are very small and few have rooms with en-suite facilities.

Mrs Aitken's (☎ 874193, Whiteclett, St Catherine's Place) B&B from £16 per person. Mrs Aitken's is centrally located, with three doubles.

Mrs Forsyth's (☎ 874020, 21 Willowburn Rd) B&B £13-18 per person, dinner B&B £21-23 per person. This is a small, friendly place, 10 minutes' walk from the town centre.

Mrs Flett's (☎ 873160, Cumliebank, Cromwell Rd) B&B £15-17 per person. You'll get a warm welcome at this small B&B overlooking Kirkwall Bay, 10 minutes' walk east of the centre.

Royal Oak Guest House (☎/fax 877177, Holm Rd) B&B £22-26 per person. The Royal Oak, near the Highland Park distillery on the southern edge of town, is a large, modern guesthouse with eight en-suite rooms.

Hotels There are several hotels in and around Kirkwall.

Kirkwall Hotel (☎ 872232, fax 872812, ⒺE enquiries@kirkwallhotel.com, Harbour St) Singles £35-62, doubles £50-80. The grand, Victorian-era Kirkwall Hotel is slightly starchy and old-fashioned, but has a great location overlooking the harbour.

Ayre Hotel (☎ 873001, fax 876289, ⒺE ayre.hotel@orkney.com, Ayre Rd) Singles £54-64, doubles £80-108. The cheerful, family-run Ayre Hotel, at the western end of the harbour, is a very comfortable townhouse hotel, built 200 years ago. Try to get a room with a sea view.

Royal Hotel (☎ *873477, fax 872767,* e *royalhotel@supanet.com, 40 Victoria St)* Singles £35-50, doubles £50-80. The recently refurbished Royal is a friendly and homely little hotel, in the middle of Kirkwall's narrow main street.

Albert Hotel (☎ *876000, fax 875397,* e *enquiries@alberthotel.co.uk, Mounthoolie Lane)* Singles £35-75, doubles £50-100. The child-friendly Albert Hotel is centrally located and has a pleasantly traditional feel to it.

Foveran Hotel (☎ *872389, fax 876430,* e *foveranhotel@aol.com, St Ola)* Singles £35-45, doubles £60-70. Two miles (3.2km) south-west of Kirkwall on the Orphir road, the modern Foveran Hotel enjoys a peaceful location overlooking Scapa Flow.

Places to Eat

There's little in the way of gourmet dining in Kirkwall, but the restaurants at the *Ayre Hotel* and *Albert Hotel* are worth trying.

Foveran Hotel (☎ *872389, St Ola)* 3-course dinner £25. The Foveran Hotel (see Places to Stay earlier) has a fine restaurant serving fresh Orkney seafood and local beef and lamb. Specialities include prime fillet of beef with a whisky and cream sauce, and Orkney fudge cheesecake. There are good vegetarian dishes too.

West End Hotel (☎ *872368, Main St)* Lunch mains £5.90-6.70, dinner mains £8.60-13.25. Bar meals served noon-2pm Mon-Sat & 6pm-9pm daily. The West End Hotel serves great bar meals of the steak and seafood variety.

Busters Diner (☎ *876717, 1 Mounthoolie Lane)* Pizza £2.10-6. Open noon-2pm & 4.30pm-10pm Mon-Fri, noon-2am Sat, 4pm-10pm Sun. This is an American, Italian and Mexican place serving pizzas and burgers to eat in or takeaway.

St Magnus Café (☎ *873354, Broad St)* Open 7am-5pm Mon-Fri, 7am-noon & 1pm-3pm Sat. This place, in the Kirkwall and St Ola Community Centre across the road from the cathedral, has good, cheap food such as quiches and bacon rolls. It does an all-day breakfast, between 9am and 4.30pm, for £4.

Bridge St, near the harbour, has several fast-food and takeaway places, including

the *Eastern Spice Tandoori Restaurant* (☎ *876596, 7 Bridge St)*, open 4.30pm to 11pm daily. Directly across the street is the *International Takeaway* fish and chip shop.

There are also a couple of Chinese restaurants that do takeaways: the *Golden Dragon* (☎ *872933, 25a Bridge St)* and the *Empire Chinese Restaurant* (☎ *872300, 51 Junction Rd)*. Main courses cost around £3.60 to £5.50; the Empire does an all-you-can-eat buffet on Sunday (noon-2pm) for £5.90.

The *Strynd Tearoom*, up an alley beside the TIC, is a good place for a cup of tea and a scone.

The *Safeway* supermarket, Pickaquoy Rd, is the best place to stock up on provisions; it opens 8am to 9pm Monday to Friday, 8am to 8pm Saturday and 9am to 6pm Sunday.

Entertainment

The local weekly newspaper, *The Orcadian*, has useful listings of what's on.

The *Bothy Bar* in the Albert Hotel (see Places to Stay earlier) is probably the liveliest place for a drink, with occasional live music in the evenings. On Thursday, Friday and Saturday there's *Matchmakers* disco, also at the Albert.

Other good drinking places include the pleasant *West End Hotel* and the bar at the *Ayre Hotel*, which has live fiddle music on Wednesday nights. See earlier for details.

The *New Phoenix Cinema* (☎ *879900, Pickaquoy Rd)* is in the Pickaquoy Leisure Centre, known locally as 'the Picky'; tickets cost £4/2.70 per adult/child.

Getting There & Away

The airport (☎ 872494) is 2½ miles (4km) east of the town centre. For information on flying into Orkney, see Getting There & Away at the start of the Orkney section. For flights and ferries from Kirkwall to the northern islands, see the following island sections.

The bus station is south-west of the town centre; except for bus No 10, there are no bus services on Sunday. Bus No 1 runs from Kirkwall to Stromness direct (£2.35, 30 minutes, seven or eight daily); No 2 runs to Orphir and Houton (20 minutes, three or four daily), and No 7 from Kirkwall to Stromness

ORKNEY & SHETLAND ISLANDS

via Birsay (one hour). Bus No 6 runs four times daily from Kirkwall to Tingwall (30 minutes) and the ferry to Rousay, and on to Evie (35 minutes).

From May to September, bus No 10 runs between Kirkwall and the John o'Groats ferry at Burwick (£2.50, 50 minutes, four daily). From June to September, a special tourist service (No 8A) runs twice daily Monday to Friday between Kirkwall and Stromness via Stenness Standing Stones, the Ring of Brodgar and Skara Brae.

EAST MAINLAND TO SOUTH RONALDSAY
☎ 01856

The sinking of the battleship HMS *Royal Oak* in 1939 – torpedoed by a German U-boat which had sneaked through Kirk Sound into Scapa Flow – prompted Winston Churchill to commission better defences for this important naval harbour. Causeways made of concrete blocks were laid across the channels on the eastern side of Scapa Flow, linking Mainland to the islands of Lamb Holm, Glimps Holm, Burray and South Ronaldsay. The **Churchill Barriers**, flanked by the rusting wrecks of the old blockships that once guarded the channels, now carry the main road from Kirkwall to Burwick. There are good sandy beaches by Barrier Nos 3 and 4.

East Mainland
The land south-east of Kirkwall is mainly agricultural. On a farm at Tankerness is the mysterious Iron Age site of **Mine Howe** *(☎ 861234; adult/child £2.50/1.25; open 11am-3pm Wed & Sun May, 11am-5pm daily June-Aug, 11am-4pm daily early Sept, 11am-2pm Wed & Sun late Sept)*, discovered in 1946 but reopened by farmer Douglas Paterson in September 1999. The Howe is an underground chamber whose function is unknown – the Channel 4 TV series *Time Team* carried out an archaeological dig here in 2000 and concluded that it may have had some ritual significance, perhaps an oracle or shrine.

On the far eastern shore of Mainland, a mile (1.6km) north of Skaill, is **The Gloup**, a spectacular natural arch and sea cave. There are large colonies of nesting seabirds

at **Mull Head**, and the shores of **Deer Sound** attract wildfowl.

Lamb Holm
On the tiny island of Lamb Holm, the **Italian Chapel** *(☎ 781268; admission free; open daylight hours)* is all that remains of a POW camp that housed the Italian prisoners of war who worked on the Churchill Barriers. They built the chapel in their spare time, using two Nissen huts, scrap metal and their considerable artistic and decorative skills. One of the artists returned in 1960 to restore the paintwork. It's quite extraordinary inside and definitely worth seeing.

Burray
The **Orkney Fossil and Vintage Centre** *(☎ 731255, Viewforth; adult/child £2/1; open 10am-6pm daily Apr-Sept)* on Burray is a quirky collection of household and farming relics and 360-million-year-old fish fossils. The centre's coffee shop is excellent.

Burray village, on the southern side of the island, has a general store, a post office and a couple of places to stay.

Sands Hotel (☎/fax 731298, Burray) B&B £25-35 per person. The Sands, housed in a newly refurbished 19th-century herring station, has en-suite doubles and family rooms, plus six-person self-catering flats. There's also a good bar and restaurant.

Vestlaybanks (☎ 731305, fax 731401, e *vestlaybanks@btinternet.com, Burray)* B&B £22-25 per person. The modern bungalow overlooking Scapa Flow has two en-suite rooms, as well as a self-catering caravan (£150 per week for four people). Evening meals are available and vegetarians are catered for.

South Ronaldsay
The main village on South Ronaldsay is **St Margaret's Hope**, named after Margaret, the Maid of Norway, who died here in 1290 on the way from her homeland to marry Edward II of England. There are two grocery stores, a post office and several pubs.

Tomb of the Eagles A visit to this tomb *(☎ 831339, Liddle Farm, Isbister; adult/child*

£3/1.50; open 10am-8pm daily Apr-Oct, 10am-noon or by arrangement Nov-Mar), at the southern tip of South Ronaldsay, is highly recommended. The 5000-year-old chambered tomb was discovered by local farmers, the Simisons, who now run it privately as a visitor attraction. It's as interesting for their entertaining and informative guided tour as for the tomb itself. After handling some of the human skulls and sea-eagle talons found in the tomb, you walk across the fields, put on knee pads and crawl down the cramped entrance passage. It's possible that sky burials occurred here; there's evidence that the dead people had been stripped of their flesh before being put in the tomb, possibly by being placed on top of wooden platforms just outside the tomb entrance, providing the eagles with a feast. You'll also see a **burned mound**, an impressive Bronze Age kitchen. The tomb is a 20-minute walk east from Burwick.

Places to Stay & Eat South Ronaldsay has several options for food and accommodation. There is a very basic *camp site* at Wheems Hostel (see later), charging £3 per person.

Backpacker's Hostel (☎ 831205, St Margaret's Hope) Beds £10. This place is run by the neighbouring Murray Arms Hotel, and has good kitchen facilities and hot showers.

Bellevue Guest House (☎ 831294, St Margaret's Hope) B&B £20-25 per person. The two-room Bellevue is a lovely old stone-built house, with great views.

Creel Inn & Restaurant (☎ 831311, Front Rd, St Margaret's Hope) 3-course dinner £26. Open Apr-Sept. Arguably the best restaurant in Orkney, the Creel serves fresh local produce – fish, shellfish, beef, lamb, vegetables – simply but deliciously prepared. There are also five en-suite rooms (singles £40 to £45, doubles £60 to £70).

Wheems Hostel (☎ 831537, Eastside) Beds £6.50. Open Apr-Oct. Wheems, a mile (1.6km) south-east of St Margaret's Hope, is a very pleasant hostel offering basic accommodation and organic breakfast.

Getting There & Away
Orkney Coaches' (☎ 870555) bus No 4 from Kirkwall runs to Deerness in East Mainland

(25 minutes, three to five daily except Sunday), with one bus calling at Tankerness on Tuesday and Friday. May to September, bus No 10 runs from Kirkwall to Burwick (£2.50, 50 minutes, four daily).

Causeway Coaches (☎ 831444) operates a bus service between St Margaret's Hope and Kirkwall (£1.50, 30 minutes, three or four daily except Sunday).

SOUTH MAINLAND
☎ 01856

There are a few things to see at Orphir, a scattered community with no shop, about 9 miles (14.5km) west of Kirkwall. The **Orkneyinga Saga Centre** (admission free; open 9am-5pm daily) has displays relating to the Orkneyinga Saga (a story dating from 1136 about the Vikings in Orkney) and a wide-screen video show.

Just behind the centre is **The Earl's Bu** (admission free; open 24 hours year-round), the foundations of a 12th-century manor house belonging to the Norse earls of Orkney. There's also the remains of **St Nicholas' Church** (admission free; open 24 hours year-round), a unique circular building that was originally 9m in diameter. Built before 1136 and modelled on the rotunda of the Church of the Holy Sepulchre in Jerusalem, it was popular with pilgrims after the capture of the Holy Land by the first Crusade. The church remained in use until 1705, and was partly demolished in 1756. For bus details, see the Kirkwall Getting There & Away section earlier. From the main road, it's a 10-minute walk to the centre.

King Haakon of Norway beached his ship at **Houton** in 1263, after his defeat at the Battle of Largs, and he died in Orkney soon afterwards. There's not much in Houton apart from a ferry terminal and a hotel.

Roving Eye Enterprises (☎ 811360; adult/child £25/12.50; 1.20pm daily May-Aug) offers boat trips on Scapa Flow, with the opportunity to view some of the wrecks of the German High Seas Fleet (see the boxed text 'Scapa Flow Wrecks' later) using a video camera attached to a remotely operated vehicle (ROV) – a technology developed for use in the offshore oil industry.

The trips, which must be booked in advance, depart from Houton Pier, last around three hours and include a visit to Lyness (see the Hoy section later in this chapter).

Bus No 2 runs from Kirkwall to Houton (20 minutes, three or four daily except Sunday) via Orphir. For details of ferries from Houton to Hoy and Flotta, see Hoy later.

STROMNESS
☎ 01856 • pop 2400

Although Stromness was officially founded in 1620, it had been used as a port by the Vikings in the 12th century, as well as by earlier visitors. Its importance as a trading port grew in the 18th century, and in the 19th century it was a busy centre for the herring industry. Until the beginning of the

Scapa Flow Wrecks

The many wrecks that litter the floor of Scapa Flow make it one of the most popular diving locations in Europe. Enclosed by Mainland, Hoy and South Ronaldsay, this is one of the world's largest natural harbours and has been used by vessels as diverse as King Hakon's Viking ships in the 13th century and the NATO fleet of today.

It was from Scapa Flow that the British Home Fleet sailed to meet the German High Seas Fleet at the Battle of Jutland on 31 May 1916. After the war, 74 German ships were interned in Scapa. Conditions for the German sailors were poor and there were several mutinies as the negotiations for the fate of the ships dragged on. When the terms of the armistice were agreed on 6 May 1919, with the announcement of a severely reduced German navy, Admiral von Reuter, who was in charge of the German fleet in Scapa Flow, decided to take matters into his own hands. On 21 June, a secret signal to scuttle the ships was passed from vessel to vessel, and the British watched incredulously as every German ship began to sink.

Most of the ships were salvaged but seven remain on the sea floor, attracting divers from all over the world. There are three battleships – the *König*, the *Kronprinz Wilhelm* and the *Markgraf* – which are all over 25,000 tons. The first two were subjected to blasting for scrap metal, but the *Markgraf* is undamaged and considered one of the best dives in the area. Four light cruisers (4400 to 5600 tons) – the *Karlsruhe*, *Dresden*, *Brummer* and *Köln* – are particularly interesting as they lie on their sides and are very accessible to divers. The *Karlsruhe*, though severely damaged, is only 10m below the surface. Its twisted superstructure has now become a huge metal reef encrusted with diverse sea life.

As well as the German wrecks, numerous other ships rest on the sea bed in Scapa Flow. HMS *Royal Oak*, which was sunk by a German U-boat in October 1939, with the loss of 833 crew, is now an official war grave.

If you're interested in diving in Scapa Flow, contact the following: **European Technical Dive Centre** (ETDI; ☎ 01856-731269, fax 731345, e sue@techincaldivers.com, Garisle, Burray); the **Diving Cellar** (☎ 01856-850055, tel/fax 850395, e leigh@divescapaflow.co.uk, 4 Victoria St, Stromness); or **Scapa Scuba** (☎/fax 01856-851218, e diving@scapascuba.co.uk, 13 Ness Rd, Stromness).

ETDI and Scapa Scuba offer instruction as well as diving holidays. A one-day PADI Discover Scuba course costs around £80, including theory lecture, basic training, equipment hire and one scuba dive. A five-day Open Water Diver course costs £265.

JANE SMITH

20th century, ships from the Hudson's Bay Company would stop to take on fresh water from Login's Well.

It's an attractive little grey-stone town and is the main point of arrival for ferries from Scrabster. As a place to stay, many visitors prefer Stromness to Kirkwall – it's smaller, it has more of the feeling of a working fishing village and it's convenient for the island of Hoy. There are some excellent places to stay, including two hostels. The narrow, winding main street has an eclectic selection of shops, including no less than three bookshops and a place that does tarot readings.

Orientation & Information

The ferry terminal and TIC are at the northern end of the village. The main street – named variously John St, Victoria St and Dundas St – straggles south from here for almost a mile (1.6km) to the camp site at Ness Point – pretty much everything of interest lies along it.

The TIC (☎ 850716), at the ferry terminal, opens 8am-6pm Monday to Saturday and 9am to 4pm Sunday April to October, and 9am to 5pm Monday to Friday November to March. Ask for the *Stromness Heritage Guide* leaflet.

There's a Royal Bank of Scotland ATM on Victoria St near the pier. You can check email at Julia's Cafe (see Places to Eat later) near the ferry terminal for 10p per minute (minimum £1).

Things to See

The main occupation in Stromness is simply strolling back and forth along the narrow, atmospheric main street. The **Pier Arts Centre** (☎ 850209, 30 Victoria St; admission free; open 10.30am-12.30pm & 1.30pm-5pm Tues-Sat) is a gallery exhibiting 20th-century British and international art, including works by Barbara Hepworth and Ben Nicholson.

The interesting **Stromness Museum** (☎ 850925, 52 Alfred St; adult/child £2.50/50p; open 10am-5pm daily May-Sept) has maritime, natural history and temporary exhibitions covering (among other things) fishing, whaling, the Hudsons Bay Company and the sunken German fleet. Across the street

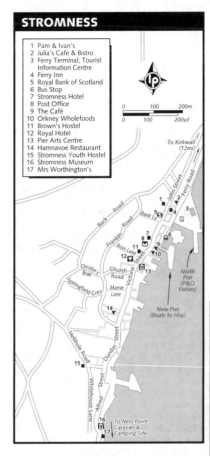

STROMNESS

1 Pam & Ivan's
2 Julia's Cafe & Bistro
3 Ferry Terminal; Tourist Information Centre
4 Ferry Inn
5 Royal Bank of Scotland
6 Bus Stop
7 Stromness Hotel
8 Post Office
9 The Café
10 Orkney Wholefoods
11 Brown's Hostel
12 Royal Hotel
13 Pier Arts Centre
14 Hamnavoe Restaurant
15 Stromness Youth Hostel
16 Stromness Museum
17 Mrs Worthington's

from the museum is the house where local poet and novelist **George Mackay Brown** lived from 1968 until his death in 1996.

Special Events

The annual Orkney Folk Festival (☎ 851331, W www.orkney.com/folkfestival) is a four-day event based in Stromness in the third week of May, with a programme of folk concerts and *ceilidhs* and informal pub sessions.

Places to Stay

Ness Point Caravan & Camping Site (☎ 873535) Pitches £4. Stromness' breezy camp site overlooks the bay at the southern end of town.

Brown's Hostel (☎ *850661, 45 Victoria St)* Beds £9. Brown's is a very popular 14-bed independent hostel, just five minute's walk from the ferry. It opens year-round and there's no curfew.

Stromness Youth Hostel (☎ *850589, Hellihole Rd)* Beds £8.25/7. Open May-Sept. The town's SYHA hostel is a 10-minute walk from the ferry terminal.

Pam & Ivan's (☎ *850642, 15 John St)* B&B £16 per person. This comfy B&B is directly opposite the ferry terminal. The basic rate includes a continental breakfast – a cooked brekkie is £2 extra.

Mrs Worthington's (☎ *850215, 2 South End)* B&B £18-25 per person. Open Apr-Oct. This is an attractive 19th-century house, set on its own pier next to the museum. Great breakfasts are served in the lovely old kitchen.

Stromness Hotel (☎ *850298, fax 850610, Pier Head)* Singles £35-42, doubles £70-84. The grandest place in town, the recently refurbished 19th-century Stromness Hotel lords it over the harbour. It has well-appointed rooms with harbour views and a good restaurant, and serves excellent bar meals.

Ferry Inn (☎ *850280, fax 851332* e *lyall@ ferryinn.com, John St)* Singles £18-30, doubles £34-50. The 11-room Ferry Inn, opposite the ferry terminal, has a good bar and restaurant.

Places to Eat
The Café (☎ *850368, 22 Victoria St)* Snacks £1.50-5. Open 7.30am-9pm Mon-Sat, 10am-7pm Sun. This place does toasties, pizzas, burgers and baked potatoes to eat in or take away.

Julia's Café & Bistro (☎ *850904, Ferry Rd)* Lunch mains £3.75-5.75, dinner mains £9.50-12.50. Cafe open 8am-5pm Mon-Sat & 9am-4pm Sun, bistro open 6.30pm-10pm Wed-Sat & 6pm-9.30pm Sun. This attractive eatery serves good cafe-style snacks and light meals during the day and more formal dinners in the evening.

Hamnavoe Restaurant (☎ *850606, 35 Graham Place)* Mains £9-15.50. Open 7pm-late Mon-Sat Apr-Sept. The Hamnavoe is

Stromness' gourmet choice with a menu of steak and seafood dishes, including fresh lobster and halibut, and one veggie option. Despite being fairly expensive, it doesn't accept credit cards.

The **Stromness Hotel**, **Ferry Inn** and **Royal Hotel** (☎ *850342, 55 Victoria St)* all serve good bar meals. There's also a **fish and chip shop** next to the Royal Hotel.

Orkney Wholefoods *(Victoria St)* sells delicious fresh and smoked seafood and other deli goods, and does excellent sandwiches, baguettes and wraps for £1.20 to £2.25.

Self-caterers can stock up at **Mill Stores** *(North End Rd)*, beyond the northern end of John St.

Getting There & Away
For information on ferries to Scrabster, Lerwick and Aberdeen, see Getting There & Away at the start of the Orkney section earlier. For boats to Hoy, see Hoy later.

For bus services, see Getting There & Away in the Kirkwall section earlier in this chapter.

WEST & NORTH MAINLAND
☎ 01856

This part of Orkney contains an amazing concentration of impressive prehistoric monuments, many of them in the care of Historic Scotland (HS). You can buy a joint ticket for admission to all staffed monuments in Orkney, including Maeshowe, Skara Brae, Skaill House, the Broch of Gurness and the Brough of Birsay; it costs £11/3.50 in summer and £10/3 in winter.

Stenness
The scattered village of Stenness, about 4 miles (7km) east of Stromness, consists of little more than some houses, a petrol station and a hotel. Around it, however, are some of the most interesting prehistoric monuments on Orkney, easily accessible using the regular bus service between Stromness and Kirkwall (see Getting There & Away in the Kirkwall section earlier in this chapter).

Just 500m north of the Stenness crossroads, on the B9055 road, are the **Standing Stones of Stenness**, a prehistoric stone circle dating from around 2500 BC. Only four of the original 12 mighty stones remain erect; one is over 5m high.

A short walk to the east are the excavated remains of **Barnhouse Neolithic Village**, thought to have been inhabited by the builders of Maeshowe.

Maeshowe

Constructed about 5000 years ago, Maeshowe *(☎ 761606; adult/child £2.80/1; open 9.30am-6.30pm daily Apr-Sept, 9.30am-4.30pm Mon-Sat & 2pm-4.30pm Sun Oct-Mar)* is the finest chambered tomb in western Europe. A long, low stone passage leads into a chamber in the centre of an earth-covered mound which is over 6.7m high and 35m across. The entrance passage is aligned with the direction of sunset at the winter solstice.

No remains were found when the tomb was excavated in the 19th century. It's not known how many people were originally buried here or whether they were buried with any of their worldly goods. In the 12th century, however, Vikings returning from the Crusades broke into the tomb, searching for treasure. They found none, but left a wonderfully earthy collection of graffiti, carved in runes on the walls of the tomb, including 'Thorni bedded Helgi' – some things never change. There's also some Viking artwork, including a crusader cross, a lion, a walrus and a knotted serpent.

Maeshowe is about 10 minutes' walk east of the Stenness crossroads. Buy your ticket at **Tormiston Mill**, across the road from the tomb, where there's a cafe serving snacks and light meals, a gift shop, a small exhibition and a 15-minute video about Orkney's prehistoric sites.

Ring of Brodgar

About a mile (1.6km) north of Stenness, along the road towards Skara Brae, is this wide circle of standing stones *(admission free; open 24 hours year-round)*, some over 5m tall. Thirty-six of the original 60 stones are still standing among the heather. It's an impressive sight and a powerful place. These old stones, raised skyward 4500 years ago, still attract the forces of nature –

on 5 June 1980, one was struck by lightning.

Skara Brae & Skaill House

Eight miles (13km) north of Stromness, overlooking a beautiful sandy bay, is Skara Brae *(HS; ☎ 841815, Bay of Skaill; adult/child £3.50/1.20, joint ticket with Skaill House £4.50/1.30; open 9.30am-6.30pm daily Apr-Sept, 9.30am-4.30pm Mon-Sat & 2pm-4.30pm Sun Oct-Mar)*, northern Europe's best preserved prehistoric village. Even the stone furniture – beds, boxes and dressers – has survived the 5000 years since people last lived here. It was hidden under the sand until 1850, when waves whipped up by a severe storm eroded the sand and grass above the beach, exposing the houses underneath. The official guidebook, available from the visitor centre, includes a good self-guided tour.

Skaill House *(☎ 841501; adult/child £3/1, joint ticket with Skara Brae £4.50/1.30; open 9.30am-6.30pm daily Apr-Sept, 10am-4pm Thur & Sat Oct)* is an early 17th-century mansion, the former home of the laird of Breckness, who discovered Skara Brae. The displays of period furniture and memorabilia include Captain Cook's dinner service.

Bus No 8A runs twice daily to Skara Brae from Kirkwall and Stromness (May to September only). It's possible to walk along the coast from Stromness to Skara Brae via Yesnaby and the Broch of Borwick (9 miles, 14.5km).

Yesnaby Sea Stacks

Six miles (10km) north of Stromness are some spectacular but easy coastal walks. Less than half a mile south of the car park at Yesnaby is the Yesnaby Castle sea stack. The ugly brick-built ruin at the car park was a WWII lookout post. Watch out during the nesting season in early summer, as seabirds will divebomb you to scare you away from their nests.

Birsay

The small village of Birsay, with a shop and a post office, is 6 miles (10km) north of Skara Brae. The ruins of the **Earl's Palace** *(admission free; open 24 hours year-round)*, built in the 16th century by the despotic Robert Stewart, earl of Orkney, dominate the village centre. Just beyond the palace is the *Heimdall Tearoom*, open 11am to 6pm daily.

At low tide (check times with a TIC) you can walk out to the **Brough of Birsay**, three-quarters of a mile (1.2km) north-west of the Earl's Palace. On the island, you'll find the extensive ruins of a Norse settlement and the 12th-century St Peter's Church. There's a replica of a Pictish symbol stone which was found here, with an eagle and human figures. St Magnus was buried here after his murder on Egilsay in 1117, and the island was a place of pilgrimage until a few centuries ago.

Barony Mills *(☎ 771276; adult/family £1/4; open 10am-1pm & 2pm-5pm daily Apr-Sept)*, 600m east of the Earl's Palace at the north-eastern end of the Loch of Boardhouse, is a working, water-powered meal mill.

Places to Stay Accommodation is scattered in and around the village centre.

Birsay Hostel (☎ 873535 ext 2404 office hours only, fax 876327, Birsay) Beds £7/6.25. Open year-round. Formerly the village school, this 30-bed, council-run hostel now provides group accommodation for a minimum of 12 people.

Primrose Cottage (☎/fax 721384, Ⓔⓘclouston@talk21.com, Birsay) B&B £14-19 per person, dinner B&B £22-27. Peaceful Primrose Cottage is a modern bungalow overlooking Marwick Bay, 2 miles (3.2km) south of the Earl's Palace.

Barony Hotel (☎ 721327, fax 721302, Birsay) B&B £25-30 per person. Open May-Sept. The Barony Hotel, overlooking the Loch of Boardhouse about half a mile south of Birsay, is an angler's favourite, with a good restaurant serving steaks and seafood.

Evie

On an exposed headland at Aikerness, a 1½-mile (2.5km) walk north-east from the straggling village of Evie, you'll find the **Broch of Gurness** *(☎ 751414; adult/child £2.80/1; open 9.30am-6.30pm daily Apr-Sept)*. Although not nearly as impressive as Mousa Broch in Shetland, this is the best preserved example of a fortified stone tower in Orkney.

Look out for the interesting stone dish – it was probably used as a grinder. Built around 100 BC, the broch is surrounded by a ditch and the remains of a large village.

Eviedale Campsite & Bothy (☎/fax 751270, Ⓔ colin.richardson@orkney.com, Dyke Farm, Evie) Pitches £3-4, bothy beds £5. Open Apr-Sept. Eviedale, at the northern end of the village, has a small, basic bothy with four beds (with toilet and stove, but no showers or bed linen), and a small camp site.

Woodwick House (☎ 751330, fax 751383, Ⓔ woodwickhouse@appleonline.net, Evie) B&B £27-38 per person. Woodwick is a country house set in beautiful wooded grounds overlooking the sea at the southern end of Evie. The food at the restaurant is superb; three-course dinners cost £22.

HOY
☎ 01856

Hoy (meaning 'high island') is the second-largest island in the Orkney archipelago, and the only one that is truly hilly. The highest point in Orkney is Ward Hill (479m), in the north of Hoy.

There are post offices at Moaness and Lyness.

Northern Hoy

There's spectacular sea-cliff scenery in the northern part of the island, including some of the highest vertical cliffs in Britain – St John's Head on the north-west coast rises 346m. Hoy is probably best known for the **Old Man of Hoy**, a 137m-high rock stack that can be seen from the Scrabster-Stromness ferry. It was first scaled in 1966 by a party led by the eminent mountaineer Chris Bonington, and still attracts rock climbers today. The northern part of Hoy has been maintained as a nature reserve by the RSPB since 1983.

The easiest approach to the Old Man is from Rackwick Bay, a two-hour walk by road from Moaness Pier through the beautiful **Rackwick Glen**. You'll pass the 5000-year-old **Dwarfie Stone**, the only example of a rock-cut tomb in Scotland, and, according to Sir Walter Scott, the favourite residence of Trolld, a dwarf from Norse legend. On your return, you can take the path via the **Glens of Kinnaird** and **Berriedale Wood**, Scotland's most northerly patch of native forest.

The most popular walk climbs steeply westwards from Rackwick Bay, then curves northwards, descending gradually to the edge of the cliffs opposite the Old Man of Hoy. Allow about seven hours for the return trip from Moaness, or three hours from Rackwick.

Lyness

Lyness, on the eastern side of Hoy, was an important naval base during both world wars, when the British Grand Fleet was based in Scapa Flow. With the dilapidated remains of buildings and an uninspiring outlook towards the Oil Terminal on Flotta Island, this isn't a pretty place, but the **Scapa Flow Visitor Centre** (☎ 791300; adult/child £2/1; open 9am-4pm Mon-Fri & 10am-4pm Sat & Sun mid-May–Sept) is well worth a visit. It's a fascinating naval museum and photographic display, located in an old pumphouse that once fed fuel to the ships.

On either side of Longhope Bay, 2 miles (3km) south of Lyness, you'll see defensive towers dating from the Napoleonic Wars, built to protect convoys heading for the Baltic. **Hackness Tower**, on the southern side of the bay, 3 miles (5km) from Longhope pier, is undergoing conservation work under the direction of Historic Scotland.

Organised Tours

Louise Budge (☎ 791234, Stoneyquoy Farm) offers guided tours (in a VW people carrier) for groups of up to six people, picking up from the ferry at Lyness; the price of £45 includes a light lunch at her farm.

Places to Stay & Eat

There are two SYHA hostels on Hoy, both owned and operated by Orkney Islands Council.

Hoy Youth Hostel (☎ 873535 ext 2415 office hours only, Moaness) Beds £7/6.25. Open May-Sept. This place is a 15-minute walk from Moaness Pier. Bring your own sleeping bag and supplies.

Rackwick Youth Hostel (☎ 873535 ext 2404 office hours only, Rackwick) Beds £7/6.25. Open Mar-Sept. The Rackwick hostel, 6 miles (9.5km) from the ferry at Moaness, has eight beds in two dorms; bring your own sleeping bag and food. The warden comes by to collect your money each evening.

There are several B&Bs on the island, with accommodation at around £18 per person, and dinner for around £10 extra, including *Mrs Rendall* (☎ 791262, The Glen) at Rackwick, *Stoneyquoy Farm* (☎ 791234, Lyness) at Lyness and *Mrs Taylor* (☎ 701358, Old Custom House, Longhope) at Longhope.

The *Hoy Inn* (☎ 791313, Moaness), near the ferry pier, is a bar with a restaurant serving good seafood from noon to 2pm and 6pm to 9pm daily.

There's a *cafe* serving snacks at the Scapa Flow Visitor Centre. Groceries can be bought at the shops in Lyness and in Longhope.

Getting There & Away

Orkney Ferries (☎ 850624) runs a passenger ferry between Stromness and Moaness pier on Hoy (£2.65, 30 minutes) at 7.45am, 10am and 4.30pm Monday to Friday, and 9.30am and 6pm at weekends, with a reduced schedule from mid-September to mid-May. In the other direction, the service departs five minutes after its arrival on Hoy.

There is also a car ferry to Lyness (Hoy) from Houton (Mainland). It sails up to six times daily Monday to Saturday (passenger/car £2.65/7.90, 45 minutes). A limited Sunday service runs May to September.

Getting Around

Transport on Hoy is very limited. North Hoy Transport (☎ 791315 or ☎ 791261) runs a minibus service between Rackwick and Moaness, meeting the 10am weekday ferry from Stromness. Otherwise, call the same number for a taxi service.

You can hire mountain bikes at Moaness pier (☎ 791225) for £7 per day. Hitching is possible, but there's not much traffic.

NORTHERN ISLANDS

The group of windswept islands that lies north of Mainland provides a refuge for migrating birds and a nesting ground for seabirds; there are several RSPB reserves. Some of the islands are also rich in archaeological sites.

However, the beautiful scenery, with wonderful white sandy beaches and turquoise seas, is the main attraction.

The TICs in Kirkwall and Stromness have a useful brochure, *The Islands of Orkney*, with maps and details of these islands. Note that the 'ay' at the end of each island name (from the Old Norse for 'island') is pronounced 'ee' (ie Shapinsay is pronounced **shap**-insee).

Orkney Ferries (☎ 872044) operates an efficient ferry service. From Kirkwall you can day-trip to many of the islands (except North Ronaldsay; see that section later) on most days of the week, but it's really worth staying for at least a few nights.

Shapinsay
☎ 01856

Just 20 minutes by ferry from Kirkwall, Shapinsay is a low-lying, intensively cultivated island. There are two general stores and a post office here.

Balfour Castle (☎ *872856; adult/child £16/8; tours at 2.15pm Wed May-Sept)*, completed in 1848 in the turreted Scottish baronial style, is the most impressive sight. Guided tours must be booked in advance at the TIC in Kirkwall; the price includes the ferry, admission to the castle and afternoon tea.

Shapinsay Heritage Centre (☎ *711258, The Smithy, Balfour Village; admission free; open noon-4.30pm daily Apr-Sept)* has a wide range of displays about the island's history, plus a cafe and a craft shop.

About 4 miles (7km) from the pier, at the far north-eastern corner of the island, is the Iron-Age **Burroughston Broch** (*admission free; open at all times)*, one of the best-preserved in Orkney. It has a central well.

Girnigoe (☎ *711256,* e *jean@girnigoe.f9 .co.uk, Girnigoe)* B&B £20 per person. The breakfasts at this friendly farmhouse, with Mrs Wallace's home-made bread and jam, are excellent. Dinner is also available for £12. Girnigoe is at the northern end of the island.

Balfour Castle (☎ *711282, fax 711283,* e *balfourcastle@btinternet.com, Balfour Village)* B&B £35-40 per person. Balfour Castle has a private chapel, seating about 20, which is becoming popular for weddings. A boat is available for residents for island trips, bird-watching and sea fishing.

There are about six ferries daily (plus three Sunday in summer) between Kirkwall and Shapinsay (passenger/car £2.65/7.90, 20 minutes).

Rousay
☎ 01856 • pop 200

This hilly island is famous for its numerous archaeological sites. Most of the island is classed as a site of special scientific interest (SSSI), but it also has the important RSPB **Trumland Reserve** and three trout-fishing lochs.

Marion's shop, and a post office that looks like a hen coop, are at Sourin, 2½ miles (4km) north of the pier. Bikes can be rented for £6 per day from ABC (☎ 821398), near the pier; the island's single road makes a pleasant circuit of about 13 miles (21km).

Things to See West of the pier are four **prehistoric burial cairns** and a **broch** (*admission free, open 24 hours year-round)*. Close to the road and near the hostel, the two-storey **Taversoe Tuick** contained the remains of at least five people and a large amount of pottery when it was excavated in Victorian times. It's an amazing and most unusual structure. **Blackhammer** is a stalled Neolithic chambered cairn dating from 2500 BC, less than a mile west of Taversoe Tuick. Like many of these structures, it originally had a corbelled roof. The **Knowe of Yarso** stalled cairn is a wet half-mile walk from the road; it contained the remains of 29 adults, and had been in use from 2900 BC to 1900 BC.

Midhowe Cairn is the most extraordinary of them all. It's housed inside a modern barn-like building, about 5½ miles (9km) west of the pier, and a half-mile walk down from the road. Containing the remains of 25 people and dating from the 3rd millennium BC, the 'Great Ship of Death', as it's called, is the longest chambered cairn in Orkney.

As well as the human remains, there were the bones of birds and animals too, perhaps meant as food for the deceased.

Nearby, **Midhowe Broch** is the best example of a broch in Orkney. It was built in the 1st century AD, probably by a powerful local family.

The TICs on Mainland have a useful leaflet, *Westness Walk*, describing the mile-long walk from Midhowe Cairn to Westness Farm via a Norse cemetery.

Organised Tours From June to August, *Rousay Traveller History Tours (☎/fax 821234)* will meet you off the 10.40am ferry from Tingwall. You'll be driven around the island in a minibus and you'll get to explore the main sites. Trips cost £15/6, excluding the ferry, and operate Tuesday to Thursday.

Places to Stay & Eat There are a couple of accommodation options on Rousay.

Rousay Farm Hostel (☎ 821252, Trumland Farm) Pitches £3.50, dorm beds from £6. This hostel is half a mile from the ferry. There's excellent dormitory accommodation (bring a sleeping bag) and a small camp site.

Blackhamar (☎ 821333, fax 821421, e jscott9616@aol.com, Rousay) B&B £25 per person, dinner B&B £45 per person. Blackhamar is a delightfully remote 19th-century crofting cottage, near Wasbister in the north of the island. It's a 10-minute uphill walk from the road (your bags are carried up by 4WD vehicle).

You can get bar meals, including vegetarian choices, at the *Pier Restaurant (☎ 821359)*, close to the ferry pier.

Getting There & Away A small car ferry (☎ 751360) connects Tingwall on Mainland with Rousay (passenger/car £2.65/7.90, 30 minutes) and the nearby islands of Egilsay and Wyre about six times daily. Booking is recommended if you want to take a car.

Egilsay & Wyre

These two small islands lie east of Rousay. On Egilsay, a cenotaph marks the spot where Earl Magnus was murdered in 1117. After his martyrdom, pilgrims flocked to the island, and **St Magnus Church**, now roofless, was built. It's a rare example of a round-towered Viking church. Much of Egilsay is an RSPB reserve; listen for the corncrakes at the southern end of the island.

Wyre is even smaller than Egilsay. It was the domain of the Viking baron Kolbein Hruga ('Cubbie Roo'); the ruins of his castle, built around 1145, and the nearby 12th-century St Mary's Chapel, can be visited free. You can spot seals at Taing, on the southern-western corner of Wyre.

These two islands are reached on the Rousay-Tingwall ferry (see the Rousay section earlier).

Stronsay
☎ 01857

In the 18th century, the major industry on this island was the collection and burning of seaweed to make kelp, which was exported for use in the production of glass, iodine and soap. In the 19th century, it was replaced by herring-curing, and Whitehall harbour became one of Scotland's major herring ports until the collapse of the fisheries in the 1930s. Currently, Whitehall has shops, a post office and a hotel. The old **Stronsay Fish Mart** *(☎ 616360, Whitehall; admission free; open 11am-5pm daily May-Sept)* now houses a herring industry interpretation centre, a hostel and a cafe.

Just across the harbour from Whitehall is the small island of **Papa Stronsay**, where Earl Rognvald Brusason was murdered in 1046. In 1999, the island was purchased by a monastic order, the Transalpine Redemptorists, who are building a new monastery; the monks will provide boat trips to the island by prior arrangement (☎ 616389).

A peaceful and attractive farming island, Stronsay now attracts seals, migratory birds and a few tourists. There are good coastal walks and some sandy beaches. In the east, the **Vat o'Kirbuster** is the best example of a gloup (natural arch) in Orkney. A new nature trail leads from the road to the Vat; it's a 10-mile (16km) round trip from Whitehall.

At the southern end of the island, you should visit the **seal-watch hide** on the beach

ORKNEY & SHETLAND ISLANDS

near the camping barn (see Places to Stay & Eat later in this section). There's also a chance to see otters at nearby **Loch Lea-shun.**

Places to Stay & Eat There are few good places to stay on the island.

Torness Camping Barn (☎ 616314) £3 per person. Down at the southern end of the island, the environmentally-friendly Holland Farm offers basic bunkhouse accommodation only a few metres from the beach. It's a pleasant place with kitchen and toilet, that sleeps about eight, but you'll need a sleeping bag. Phone from the pier for a lift.

Stronsay Fish Mart Hostel & Cafe (☎ 616360 or 616346, Whitehall) Beds £8. Part of the island's former herring station has been converted into a 10-bed hostel with shower and kitchen; you'll need your own sleeping bag. The neighbouring cafe opens all day for takeaways, snacks and meals.

Stronsay Hotel (☎ 616473, fax 616465, e *info@stronsayhotel.com, Whitehall)* B&B £35 per person. This tiny three-star hotel has three en-suite rooms – one four-bed family room, a twin and a single. You can get reasonable pub grub in the bar.

Stronsay Bird Reserve (☎ 616363, Castle, Mill Bay) B&B £16, tent pitches £5. John and Sue Holloway offer B&B and camping at the Stronsay Bird Reserve, a 40-minute walk south from the ferry.

Getting There & Away British Airways/Loganair (☎ 01856-872494) has two flights daily, Monday to Friday, from Kirkwall to Stronsay (single/return £31/62, 10 minutes).

A car ferry service links Kirkwall with Stronsay (passenger/car £5.25/11.75, 1½ hours, two daily) and Eday. There's a daily reduced service to Stronsay on Sunday.

Eday
☎ 01857

Eday supplied some of the stone for St Magnus Cathedral in Kirkwall, and peat for most of the other northern islands. It has a hilly centre and cultivated fields around the coast. Occupied for at least the last 5000 years, Eday has numerous chambered cairns, and also one of Orkney's most impressively located standing stones, the **Stone of Setter,** which is over 5m high. Close to the stone are the chambered cairns of **Braeside, Huntersquoy** and **Vinquoy.** Huntersquoy is a two-storeyed cairn, like Taversoe Tuick on Rousay. From nearby **Mill Loch bird hide** you can observe red-throated divers.

The early 17th-century **Carrick House** *(☎ 622260; small admission charge; open pm Sun June-Sept, other times by arrangement)* is worth a visit. The pirate John Gow was captured here in 1725, during a failed raid on the house (there's still a stain on the drawing room floor, said to be blood spilled during the raid). The pirates were later executed in London.

It's worth getting hold of the *Eday Heritage Walk* leaflet, which details an interesting four-hour ramble from the Community Enterprises shop up to the Cliffs of Red Head in the north of the island. There's also an easy one-hour walk to War Ness Point in the south of the island.

Organised Tours There's a couple of tours worth taking in Eday.

Eday Heritage Tour (☎ 622248 or 622260) offers a guided tour using your own vehicle. The guide meets you at 10.35am (Sundays between July and mid-September) at Eday pier and gives you a tour of the main sights until 5pm. Tours must be booked in advance; the price (£12 per person) includes refreshments and admission to Carrick House.

Eday Minibus Tour (☎ 622206) has guided tours that last for two hours; they begin and end at the ferry pier. Adult/child tickets cost £17.59/11.75 and tours run on Monday, Wednesday and Friday between May and August. The price doesn't include lunch, and the tour doesn't include Carrick House except by previous arrangement.

Places to Stay & Eat You can camp on the island provided you first ask permission from the local farmer.

Eday Hostel (☎ 622206 or 622311, Bay of London) Dorm beds £5. This recently renovated 24-bed hostel, run by the Eday Community Association, is 4 miles (7km) north of the ferry pier. You'll need your own sleeping bag.

Mrs Popplewell's (☎ 622248, Blett, Carrick Bay) Dinner B&B £23 per person. Mrs Popplewell's, opposite the Calf of Eday, has one single and one double. There's also a fully equipped self-catering croft-house nearby, for three people, at just £10 per person per night. Mrs Popplewell bakes fresh bread daily, and she serves snacks and meals at her craft shop.

Mrs Cockram's (☎ 622271, Skaill) Dinner B&B around £29 per person. This place is in a comfortable farmhouse at Skaill, near the church.

Getting There & Away There are two flights from Kirkwall (single/return £31/62, 30 minutes) to London airport – that's London, Eday – on Wednesday only. The ferry service from Kirkwall usually sails via Stronsay (passenger/car £5.25/11.75, 1¼ to two hours), but occasionally it's direct. There's a link between Sanday and Eday (20 minutes) on Monday, Wednesday and Friday.

Getting Around Alan Stewart (☎ 622206) runs the local minibus and taxi service. He charges around £3 for a trip along the length of Eday. Ask locally about bicycle hire.

Sanday
☎ 01857

This island is aptly named, for the best beaches in Orkney are here – dazzling white sand of the sort you'd expect in the Caribbean. The island is almost entirely flat, apart from the cliffs at Spurness; it's 12 miles (20km) long and growing due to sand build-up.

There are several archaeological sites, the most impressive being the **Quoyness chambered tomb** *(admission free; open 24 hours year-round)*, similar to Maeshowe and dating from the 3rd millennium BC. It has triple walls, a main chamber and six smaller cells. At the north-eastern tip of Sanday, there's **Tofts Ness**, with around 500 prehistoric burial mounds.

There are shops and post offices at Kettletoft, Lady and Cross. A bank service is

available at Kettletoft on Tuesday only. The island is known for its knitwear, which is sold in Lady village, at the Wool Hall.

Cars and taxis can be hired from Kettletoft Garage (☎ 600321). For bicycle hire, try Bernie Flett (☎ 600418) at Quivals.

Organised Tours From May to September, *Bernie Flett (☎ 600418, Quivals Garage)* offers minibus tours of the island. Tours operate on Wednesday and Friday, cost £30/22 (minimum four people), and leave Kirkwall (on Mainland) pier at 10.10am, returning at 7.40pm.

Places to Stay & Eat With permission, you can camp anywhere on the island, but there's no hostel. There are several B&Bs charging around £15 per person, including *Tina Flett (☎ 600467)* at Quivals and *Margaret Groat (☎ 600396)* at North Myre.

Kettletoft Hotel (☎/fax 600217, Kettletoft) B&B £18-20 per person, dinner B&B £25-27. The welcoming and family-friendly four-room Kettletoft is near the centre of the island, 8 miles (13km) north of the ferry terminal.

Belsair Orkney Healing Retreat (☎ 600206, e joy@sanday.quista.net, Kettletoft) B&B £18.50-25 per person. The Belsair, also at Kettletoft, offers comfortable accommodation combined with courses in 'spiritual healing, emotional clearance and personal insight through meditation'. A 1½-hour healing session costs £35.

The Kettletoft and Belsair are the only places to eat out on the island; main courses at Belsair cost between £5 and £15. The *Kettletoft Hotel* also does takeaway fish and chips on Wednesday and Saturday evenings.

Getting There & Away There are flights from Kirkwall to Sanday (single/return £31/62, 20 minutes) and Westray twice daily Monday to Friday, and once Saturday. There's at least one ferry daily between Kirkwall and Sanday (passenger/car £5.25/11.75, 1½ hours) year-round, most of which permit a day trip with about eight hours on the island.

ORKNEY & SHETLAND ISLANDS

Westray
☎ 01857

This is the largest of the northern islands, with a population of around 700. It's a varied island, with prehistoric sites, some sandy beaches and great cliff scenery.

The ferry docks at Rapness in the south of the island but Pierowall, 7 miles (11km) to the north, is the main village. It has grocery shops, a post office and a hotel. For information about island facilities, call the Westray & Papa Westray Tourist Association (☎ 677404).

Pierowall has one of the best natural harbours in Orkney – it was once an important Viking base. The **Westray Heritage Centre** *(☎ 677414, Pierowall; adult/child £2/50p; open 10am-noon & 2pm-5pm Tues-Sat & 11.30am-5pm Sun & Mon May-Sept)* has displays on local history and nature. Beside the ruins of the 17th-century **St Mary's Church** you'll find some interesting gravestones.

A half-mile west of Pierowall lie the impressive ruins of **Noltland Castle** *(admission free; open 24 hours year-round)*, a 16th-century fortified Z-plan tower house. The RSPB reserve at **Noup Head** sea cliffs, in the northwest of the island, attracts vast numbers of breeding seabirds from April to July. There are big puffin colonies here and at **Castle o'Burrian**, a mile (1.6km) north of Rapness.

Places to Stay & Eat With permission, you can camp almost anywhere. There are also a couple of backpacker hostels, B&Bs and hotels.

The Barn (☎ 677214, e thebarn@orkney.com, Chalmersquoy, Pierowall) Beds £11.75/8.80. Open year-round. This a modern 13-bed hostel in Pierowall village, with bunks in two-, three- and four-bed rooms. The price includes bed linen, shower and kitchen facilities, and there is one room with wheelchair access. You can camp here too.

Bis Geos Hostel (☎ 677420, Bis Geos) Beds £9 per person. Open May-Sept. Bis Geos is a 16-bed bothy, with bunks in one- and two-bed compartments, about 2 miles (3.2km) west of Pierowall and 30 minutes' hike from Noup Head. Facilities include showers, phone, Internet access, kitchen

and dining area, and an attractive conservatory overlooking the sea.

Pierowall Hotel (☎ 677472, fax 677707, e pierowall.hotel@norsecom.co.uk, Pierowall) Doubles £38-68. The comfortable eight-room Pierowall Hotel is famous throughout Orkney for its popular fish and chips (£3.80), available to take away.

Cleaton House Hotel (☎ 677508, fax 677442, e cleaton@orkney.com, Cleaton) Singles £36, doubles £64-80. The most comfortable place to stay on Westray is the Cleaton House Hotel, a refurbished Victorian manse about 2 miles (3.2km) south-east of Pierowall. The restaurant is very good.

Several places offer B&B for around £16 per person, including *Mrs Groat (☎ 677283, Arcadia)* in Pierowall and another *Mrs Groat (☎ 677374, Sand o'Gill)* about a mile north of Pierowall in Rackwick.

Getting There & Away For information on flights, see the Sanday section earlier. A ferry service links Kirkwall with Rapness (passenger/car £5.25/11.75, 1½ hours) with at least two crossings daily each way in summer. From mid-September to mid-May, boats operate once or twice daily.

There's also a passenger-only ferry from Pierowall to Papa Westray (£5.25, 25 minutes, two to six daily in summer); the crossing is free if you travel direct from the Rapness ferry. From late October to May, the boat sails by arrangement (☎ 677216).

Papa Westray
Known locally as Papay (pronounced **pa**-pee), this tiny island (4 miles long by a mile wide, 6.5km by 1.6km) attracts superlatives. It is home to Europe's oldest domestic building, the **Knap of Howar** (built about 5500 years ago), and to Europe's largest colony of arctic terns (about 6000 birds) at North Hill. Even the two-minute hop from Westray airfield is featured in *The Guinness Book of Records* as the world's shortest scheduled air service. The island was also the cradle of Christianity in Orkney – **St Boniface's Church** was founded in the 8th century, though most of the recently restored structure dates from the 12th century.

ORKNEY & SHETLAND ISLANDS

From May to September, Jim Davidson (☎ 644259) runs boat trips to the **Holm of Papay**, a small island about a half-mile east of Papa Westray, for £4 per person. The main reason for a visit is to see the huge **chambered cairn**, with 16 beehive cells and wall carvings. You enter through the roof – there's a torch so you can light your way as you crawl around in the gloomy interior.

Beltane House Hotel (☎ 644267) Dorm beds £7/6.25. B&B £23.50-26.50. Open year-round. Owned by the local community co-op, Beltane House comprises a 16-bed SYHA-approved hostel and a guesthouse with four comfortable en-suite rooms. There is also a small shop and a restaurant here; evening meals are available for £16.50 (book in advance). It's just over a mile north of the ferry.

Getting There & Away Flying to Papa Westray or North Ronaldsay from Kirkwall is a good deal compared with other flights in Orkney – about twice the distance for half the price. To either island it's £15/30 for a single/return, and there are flights twice daily Monday to Saturday.

For ferry details, see the Westray section earlier.

North Ronaldsay
☎ 01857 • pop 50

Pity the poor sheep on this remote, wind-swept island – they're kept off the rich farmland by a 13 mile-long (21km) wall all round the island, and forced to feed only on seaweed, which is said to give their meat a unique flavour.

North Ronaldsay is only 3 miles (5km) long and almost completely flat. The island has Scotland's tallest land-built **lighthouse** (33m), and seal and cormorant colonies nearby. North Ronaldsay is also an important stopover point for migratory birds.

There's a couple of accommodation options and, half a mile north of the ferry pier, there's a shop and a pub which serves meals.

Bird Observatory (☎ 633200, e *warden@ nrbo.prestel.co.uk*) Dorm beds £17 per person, guest rooms £25 per person. Powered by wind and solar energy, the observatory (next to the ferry pier) offers hostel and B&B

accommodation and ornithological activities. All prices include breakfast, dinner and bed linen; under-15s are half-price, under-fours are free. There's also a shop, cafe and licensed lounge bar.

Garso Guest House (☎/fax 633244) Dinner B&B £25 per person. Cottage £25 per night. Mrs Muir's B&B is at the northern end of the island, about 3 miles (5km) from the pier. She also has a self-catering cottage, sleeping up to five. Mr Muir offers a taxi and minibus service.

See the Papa Westray section earlier for details of flights. There's a weekly ferry from Kirkwall on Friday (passenger/car £5.75/11.75, 1½ hours). Phone ☎ 872044 for details.

Shetland Islands

Sixty miles (100km) north-east of Orkney, the Shetland Islands remained under Norse rule until 1469, when they were given to Scotland as part of a Danish princess' dowry. Even today, these remote, windswept, virtually treeless islands are almost as much a part of Scandinavia as of Britain – the nearest mainland town is Bergen, Norway.

Much bleaker than Orkney, Shetland is famous for its varied birdlife, teeming seabird colonies and a 4000-year-old archaeological heritage that includes the ancient settlement Jarlshof. Also, its rugged, indented coastline offers superb cliff-top walks and good fishing.

Almost everything of interest is on the coast rather than inland but it's impossible to get farther than 3 miles (5km) from the sea. There are some impressively located places to stay, and budget accommodation includes six camping *böds* (barns).

Shetland's 552-sq-mile (1408 sq km) area consists of over 100 islands, 15 of which are inhabited. Mainland is by far the largest and Lerwick is the capital. Shetland is the base for the North Sea oilfields, and pipelines feed Europe's largest oil refinery at Sullom Voe, in northern Mainland. Oil has brought some prosperity to these islands; there are well-equipped leisure centres in many villages.

ORKNEY & SHETLAND ISLANDS

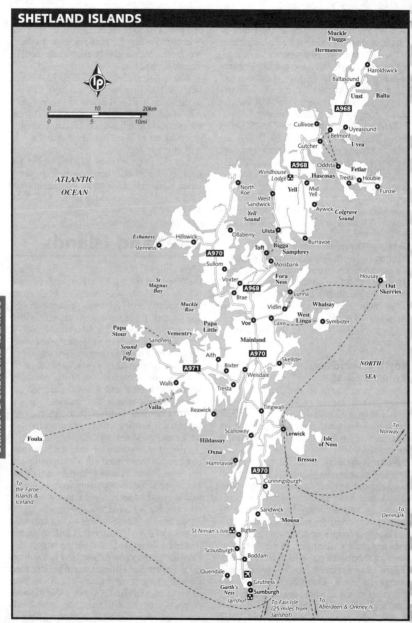

SHETLAND ISLANDS

ORKNEY & SHETLAND ISLANDS

ATLANTIC OCEAN

Muckle Flugga

Hermaness

Haroldswick

Baltasound

Unst

Balta

A968

Cullivoe

Uyeasound

Belmont

Gutcher

Uyea

Windhouse Lodge

A968

Oddsta

Fetlar

Hascosay

Tresta

Houbie

North Roe

Yell

Mid Yell

Funzie

West Sandwick

Eshaness

Hillswick

Yell Sound

Ollaberry

Aywick

Colgrave Sound

Stenness

A970

Ulsta

Burravoe

Toft

Bigga

Sullom

Samphrey

St Magnus Bay

Voxter

Mossbank

Fora Ness

Brae

A968

Muckle Roe

Lunna

Housay

Out Skerries

Vidlin

Whalsay

Papa Stour

Vementry

Papa Little

Voe

Laxo

West Linga

Symbister

Sandness

Mainland

A970

Sound of Papa

Aith

Bixter

Skellster

NORTH SEA

A971

Weisdale

Walls

Tresta

Vaila

Reawick

Tingwall

To Norway

Foula

Scalloway

Lerwick

Hildassay

Isle of Noss

Oxna

Hamnavoe

Bressay

To the Faroe Islands & Iceland

A970

Cunningsburgh

To Denmark

Sandwick

Mousa

St Ninian's Isle

Bigton

Scousburgh

Boddam

Quendale

Grutness

Garth's Ness

Sumburgh

Jarlshof

To Fair Isle (25 miles from Jarlshof)

To Aberdeen & Orkney Is

With the exceptions of Lerwick and Scalloway, most villages are collections of scattered settlements.

GETTING THERE & AWAY

Unlike Orkney, Shetland is relatively expensive to get to from mainland Scotland.

Air

The oil industry ensures that air connections are good. The main airport is at Sumburgh, 25 miles (40km) south of Lerwick. There are two to four flights daily between Sumburgh and Aberdeen (£119–176 return, one hour) with British Airways (BA; ☎ 0845 773 3377, W www.britishairways.com).

BA also flies daily (except Sunday) between Orkney and Shetland (£79–119 return, 35 minutes). You can also fly direct from Inverness, Glasgow and Edinburgh.

Boat

P&O Scottish Ferries (☎ 01224-572615, W www.posf.co.uk) runs car ferries between Lerwick and Stromness in Orkney – see the Orkney section earlier in this chapter for details.

P&O also operates overnight car ferries from Aberdeen to Lerwick (£60/148, 14 hours), with three to five services a week (Monday to Friday) departing Aberdeen at 6pm.

For details of the ferry link between Lerwick, Torshavn (Faroe Islands) and Bergen (Norway), see the Getting There & Away chapter.

GETTING AROUND

The *Shetland Transport Timetable*, an invaluable publication listing all local air, sea and bus services, costs 80p from the TIC.

Bus

There are several bus operators. For detailed information on all services call ☎ 01595-694100.

Car

The wide roads seem more like motorways after Orkney's tiny, winding lanes. It's cheaper to rent a car in Lerwick rather than

at the airport. Try Star Rent A Car (☎ 01595-692075), 22 Commercial Rd, opposite the bus station, or John Leask & Son (☎ 01595-693162), The Esplanade.

Bicycle

If it's fine, cycling on the islands' excellent roads can be an exhilarating way to experience the stark beauty of Shetland. It can, however, be very windy (wind speeds of up to 194mph have been recorded!) and there are few places to shelter. You hire bikes from Eric Brown at Grantfield Garage (☎ 01595-692709), North Rd, Lerwick, for £7.50/45 per day/week.

LERWICK

☎ 01595 • pop 7280

A pleasant town of grey-stone buildings built around a natural harbour, Lerwick is the only settlement of any size in Shetland.

Although the Shetland Islands have been occupied for around 5000 years, Lerwick was established only in the 17th century. Dutch herring fleets began to shelter in the harbour, in preference to Scalloway which was then the capital. A small community grew up to trade with them and by the late 19th century this was the largest herring town in northern Europe. Today, it's the main port of entry into Shetland and the centre has received a facelift paid for by money from the national lottery fund.

Orientation & Information

The old harbour, which forms the focus of the town, is a 20-minute walk south of the main ferry terminal; it's now used by visiting yachts and pleasure cruisers. Commercial St, one block back from the waterfront, is the main shopping street, dominated by the Victorian bulk of the Grand Hotel. The post office is on Commercial St and there's a bank with an ATM across the road. Internet facilities are available at the library (☎ 693868), Lower Hillhead.

The TIC (☎ 693434, W www.shetland-tourism.co.uk), Market Cross, opens 8am to 6pm Monday to Friday, 8am to 4pm Saturday and 10am to 1pm Sunday April to September; and 9am to 5pm Monday to Friday

ORKNEY & SHETLAND ISLANDS

the rest of the year. There's a bureau de change here. The TIC has a good range of books and maps, as well as brochures on everything from Shetland pony stud farms to lists of safe anchorages for yachts. *Walks on Shetland* (£6.50), by Mary Welsh, is a good walking guide.

Eight countries have consulates in Shetland. The consulates for Denmark, Iceland, Netherlands and Sweden can be contacted on ☎ 692533 (Hay & Co, 66 Commercial Rd); for Finland, France, Germany and Norway call ☎ 692556 (Shearer Shipping Services, off Commercial Rd).

Manson's Dry Cleaners (☎ 695335), Kantersted Rd, charges £5 for a wash and dry (including powder).

Things to See & Do

Above the town, there are good views from the battlements of **Fort Charlotte** *(Charlotte St; admission free; open 9am-10pm June-Sept, 9am-4pm Oct-May)*, built in 1665 to protect the harbour from the Dutch navy. There's not much to see in the fort itself, which housed the town prison from 1837 to 1875 and now provides the headquarters for the Territorial Army.

The **Town Hall** *(☎ 693535, Hillhead; admission free; open 9am-5pm Mon-Thur, 9am-4pm Fri)* has stained-glass windows with local historical scenes, and a great view from the clock tower.

It's worth visiting the **Shetland Museum** *(☎ 695057, Lower Hillhead; admission free; open 10am-7pm Mon, Wed & Fri, 10am-5pm Tues, Thur & Sat)* for an introduction to the islands' history and geology. There are replicas of the St Ninian's Isle treasure, and displays detailing the fishing, whaling and knitting industries.

The **Up Helly Aa Exhibition** *(St Sunniva St; adult/child £2.50/free; open 2pm-4pm Tues & Sat & 7pm-9pm Tues & Fri mid-May–mid-Sept)*, in the Galley Shed off St Sunniva St, explains the curious Viking fire festival (see Special Events later).

The fortified site of **Clickimin Broch** *(admission free; open 24 hours year-round)*, just under a mile west of the town centre, was occupied from the 7th century BC to the 6th

century AD. The entrance to the path leading to the site is opposite the BP service station.

The **Böd of Gremista** *(☎ 695057, Gremista; adult/child £2/1.50; open 10am-1pm & 2pm-5pm Wed-Sun June–mid-Sept)*, about a mile (1.6km) north of the ferry terminal, was the birthplace of Arthur Anderson, co-founder of P&O. It has been restored as an 18th-century fishing booth; there's also a small exhibition about Anderson.

There's a cliff-side walk south of Lerwick to the headland known as **The Knab**, where you can watch the ferries coming in.

Special Events

It's well worth being here for the Folk Festival in April/May, or the Fiddle and Accordion Festival in October. The Up Helly Aa festival takes place on the last Tuesday in January, when locals dress up as Vikings and set fire to a replica Viking ship in the harbour.

Places to Stay

Camping There's only one place for campers in Lerwick.

Clickimin Caravan & Camp Site (☎ 741000, fax 741001, Lochside) Small tents £6.30. This place is by the loch on the western edge of town. The price includes the use of the shower in the adjacent Clickimin Leisure Centre.

Hostels Lerwick has an excellent central SYHA hostel.

Lerwick Youth Hostel (☎ 692114, fax 696470, King Harald St) Beds from £9.25/8. Open Apr-Sept. This hostel, three-quarters of a mile (1.2km) from the ferry terminal, stays open for late ferry arrivals. It's clean and well maintained but the kitchen is small.

B&Bs & Hotels Most of Lerwick's B&Bs and guesthouses are small, cosy affairs with only two or three rooms.

Mrs Gifford's (☎ 693554, e cgifford@btinternet.com, 12 Burgh Rd) B&B £20-22 per person. Although Mrs Gifford's address is 12 Burgh Rd, the house is actually in a small lane off Burgh Rd. It's a four-star B&B with a nice garden, and vegetarians can be catered for.

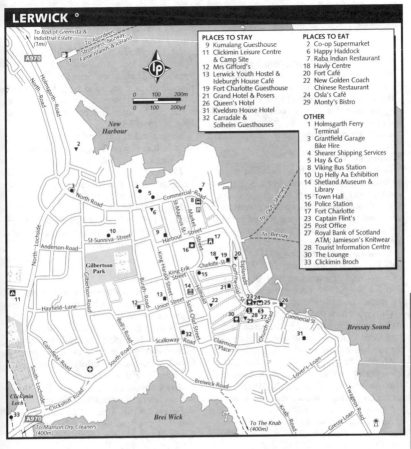

LERWICK

PLACES TO STAY
9 Kumalang Guesthouse
11 Clickimin Leisure Centre & Camp Site
12 Mrs Gifford's
13 Lerwick Youth Hostel & Isleburgh House Café
19 Fort Charlotte Guesthouse
21 Grand Hotel & Posers
26 Queen's Hotel
31 Kveldsro House Hotel
32 Carradale & Solheim Guesthouses

PLACES TO EAT
2 Co-op Supermarket
6 Happy Haddock
7 Raba Indian Restaurant
18 Havly Centre
20 Fort Café
22 New Golden Coach Chinese Restaurant
24 Osla's Café
29 Monty's Bistro

OTHER
1 Holmsgarth Ferry Terminal
3 Grantfield Garage Bike Hire
4 Shearer Shipping Services
5 Hay & Co
8 Viking Bus Station
10 Up Helly Aa Exhibition
14 Shetland Museum & Library
15 Town Hall
16 Police Station
17 Fort Charlotte
23 Captain Flint's
25 Post Office
27 Royal Bank of Scotland ATM; Jamieson's Knitwear
28 Tourist Information Centre
30 The Lounge
33 Clickimin Broch

ORKNEY & SHETLAND ISLANDS

Solheim Guest House (☎/fax 695275, 34 King Harald St) Singles £21-24, doubles £38-50. This excellent, friendly place offers a good breakfast and colour TVs in every room. The rooms, with shared bathrooms, are large and clean.

Carradale Guest House (☎ 692251, 36 King Harald St) Singles £20-35, doubles £40-60. Carradale Guest House is similar to its neighbour, Solheim. Dinner is available for an extra £10.

Kumalang Guest House (☎ 695731, 89 St Olaf St) B&B £20-25 per person. This is another friendly place, with dinner avail-

able on request. Bathrooms at Kumalang are shared.

Fort Charlotte Guesthouse (☎ 695956, e fortcharlotte.guesth@talk21.com, 1 Charlotte St) Singles/doubles £25-35 per person. Squeezed between Commercial St and the fort, this place has four en-suite rooms.

Queen's Hotel (☎ 692826, fax 694048, Commercial St) Singles/doubles £65/90. This hotel is right by the harbour and, if you can get a room with a view over the water, it's a pleasant place to stay. All rooms are en-suite.

Grand Hotel (☎ 692826, fax 694048, 24 Commercial St) En-suite singles/doubles

£65/90. Also in the centre, the modernised Grand Hotel includes Shetland's only nightclub.

Kveldsro House Hotel (☎ 692195, fax 696595, Greenfield Place) Singles/doubles £70/94. This top hotel overlooks the harbour, but the small, narrow streets can make it difficult to find. Pronounced kelro, it's a very comfortable, small hotel with 16 en-suite rooms. If it isn't busy at the weekend, you may be able to negotiate a special deal.

Places to Eat

Although there's good fresh fish, Shetland is no place for gastronomes. *Restit* is the best known local dish – lumps of mutton cured with salt and made into a soupy, salty stew traditionally eaten in the long winter months. It tastes quite as awful as it sounds and, consequently, rarely appears on menus.

Kveldsro House Hotel (☎ 692195, Greenfield Place) 3-course dinner £17.50. This is a fine place to go for a really special occasion, but there's also a cheaper and extensive bar menu.

Queen's Hotel (☎ 692826, Commercial St) 3-course dinner £15.25. The restaurant at the Queen's Hotel is good, but there are also bar meals available from £4.25 to £7.95.

Monty's Bistro (☎ 696555, 5 Mounthooly St) Evening mains £8-12. Open Mon-Sat. The recommended Monty's Bistro also serves good cheap snacks and meals during the day – pitta lamb toastie is £3.50.

New Golden Coach (☎ 693848, 17 Hillhead) Mains from £6.80. This large restaurant serves Chinese and Thai dishes.

Raba Indian Restaurant (☎ 695585, 26 Commercial Rd) Mains from £3.75. Located near the bus station, this is the best curry house in Shetland, with good vegetarian choices.

Osla's Cafe (☎ 696005, 88 Commercial St) Soup and snacks from £2.20. This small cafe serves a wide range of delicious coffees and teas; savoury and sweet pancakes start at £3.

Havly Centre (☎ 692100, 7 Charlotte St) Snacks from £2. Open Tues-Sat. The Havly Centre is a Norwegian Christian centre with an excellent cafe, and the staff don't quiz you on your religious beliefs. It serves mainly snacks and its gooey cakes are heavenly. Pizzas start at £3.50.

Islesburgh House Café (☎ 692114, King Harald St) Mains around £4. Open 11am-9pm Mon-Thur, 11am-5pm Fri & Sat. This place is in the same building as the Lerwick Youth Hostel. It serves good-value, wholesome food. Soup and bread costs £1.20, lasagne costs £3.95.

Several takeaways offer good fish and chips – just as you'd expect in the heart of a fishing community.

Fort Café (☎ 693125, 2 Commercial Rd) Fish and chips £3. This place has a cheap restaurant as well as a takeaway.

Happy Haddock (☎ 692414, 59 Commercial Rd) Fish and chips £2.65. Happy Haddock also offers vegetarian takeaways.

There's a *Co-op* supermarket on Holmsgarth Rd.

Entertainment

The Shetland Fiddlers play at a number of locations, and it's worth attending their sessions – enquire at the TIC.

The Lounge (☎ 692231, 4 Mounthooly St) This is the best place to drink in Lerwick. From mid-May to late September, there's live traditional music on Wednesday evenings.

Captain Flint's (☎ 692249, Market Cross) Captain Flint's also has live music and serves bar lunches and dinners.

Posers (☎ 692826, 24 Commercial St) Cover charge around £4. Posers, at the Grand Hotel, is Lerwick's only nightclub.

Shopping

Best buys are the woollen jerseys, cardigans and sweaters for which Shetland is world-famous. There are numerous shops selling woollens, but for bargains (from £20) you must go to the factories.

Jamieson's Knitwear (☎ 693114, 93 Commercial St) Here you'll find real Fair Isle sweaters with the distinctive OXOXO pattern, from £40.

Getting There & Away

See both the Getting There & Away chapter and Shetland's introductory Getting There &

Away information earlier. Ferries dock at Holmsgarth terminal, a 20-minute walk from the town centre (the terminal will be reconstructed by 2002 to allow larger ships to dock). From Sumburgh airport, Leask's (☎ 693162) runs regular buses to meet flights (£1.90 one way).

Getting Around

If you need a taxi, call Sinclair's Taxis (☎ 694617).

AROUND LERWICK
Bressay & Noss
☎ 01595 • pop 353

Two islands lie across Bressay Sound east of Lerwick. The 21-sq-mile (54-sq-km) island of Bressay (pronounced bressah) shelters Lerwick from the North Sea making the town's harbour one of the finest in Britain. There are some interesting walks, especially along the cliffs and up Ward Hill (226m), which offers good views of the island.

Colonies of birds can be seen at the Ord and Bard Head cliffs in the south. For serious **bird-watching** though, it's worth visiting Noss, a National Nature Reserve (NNR) east of Bressay, to see the huge number of seabirds nesting on the island's 183m cliffs. Noss can only be visited from mid-May to August when Scottish Natural Heritage (SNH) operates a small visitor centre at Gungstie.

From Lerwick, *Bressaboats* (☎ 693434) runs two-hour cruises daily (except Sunday), April to September, around Bressay and Noss for £20/10; book with the TIC.

Maryfield Hotel (☎ 820207), located by the ferry quay, offers bar meals with seafood specialities.

Getting There & Away From the dock below Fort Charlotte in Lerwick, there are hourly ferries (☎ 01426-980317) daily to Bressay (£1.25, five minutes). It's then 2½ miles (4km) across the island (some people bring rented bikes from Lerwick) to take the inflatable dinghy to Noss. The dinghy departs at 10.30am, returning at 2.30pm, Tuesday, Wednesday and Friday to Sunday, mid-May to August (£3/1.50 return), but

check with SNH (☎ 693345) before leaving Lerwick as it doesn't operate in bad weather.

CENTRAL & WEST MAINLAND
Scalloway
☎ 01595 • pop 1053

The former capital of Shetland, Scalloway (pronounced scallowah), on the west coast 6 miles (10km) from Lerwick, is now a busy fishing village. During WWII, the Norwegian resistance movement operated the 'Shetland Bus' from here, carrying arms and transporting refugees in fishing boats.

Things to See The ruins of **Scalloway Castle** *(HS; Castle St)* rise above the warehouses of the port. It was built in 1600 by the cruel Patrick Stewart, earl of Orkney and lord of Shetland, and consists of a four-storey rectangular main block, with a wing of the same height at one corner. If the gate is closed, get the key from the Shetland Woollen Company shop just up the hill. The small, volunteer-run **Scalloway Museum** *(☎ 880666, Main St; donation requested; open 11.30am-4.30pm Mon, 2pm-4.30pm Tues-Thur, 9.30am 12.30pm & 2pm-4.30pm Fri, 10am-12.30pm & 2pm-4.30pm Sat May-Sept)* is interesting for its displays on the 'Shetland Bus'.

Places to Stay & Eat There's a hotel in Scalloway but no hostel or camping.

Scalloway Hotel (☎ 880444, Main St) En-suite singles/doubles £50/70. Down in the village close to the waterfront, the Scalloway Hotel has 24 rooms. It's a fairly modern place and a trifle bland. Bar meals are available (£4.25 to £9.95).

Kiln Bar (☎ 880444, Main St) Bar meals around £4-10. Run by the Scalloway Hotel and located just across the street from it, the Kiln serves fairly average bar meals.

Da Haaf Restaurant (☎ 880747, Port Arthur) Fish dishes £5.25-8.50. Open 9am-8pm Mon-Fri. Located in the North Atlantic Fisheries College, this restaurant specialises in excellent local seafood.

Getting There & Away Buses run up to seven times daily (except Sunday) from Lerwick (95p, 20 minutes).

ORKNEY & SHETLAND ISLANDS

Tingwall Valley

North of Scalloway, the B9074 follows the western shores of the two lochs, Asta and Tingwall, through the fertile Tingwall Valley. In June and July, the wildflowers are particularly beautiful. Both lochs are good for trout fishing and home to several species of birds, including swans. The promontory at the northern end of the Loch of Tingwall is called the **Law Ting Holm**. In the days of Norse rule, this was where Shetland's annual parliament or *althing* was held.

Weisdale

North-west of Tingwall, on the A971, there are great views of Shetland from **Wormadale Hill**. Below, past the Loch of Strom, the head of **Weisdale Voe** is a good spot for viewing wading birds. Nearby, the restored **Weisdale Mill** (☎ *01595-830400, Weisdale*) is now a gallery and cafe.

In the 19th century, the mill was part of the estate of Kergord (then called Flemington), about half a mile (800m) north. No crofters' cottages are found here because in the 1850s tenants were 'cleared' by the laird to make way for sheep. Stones from the cottages were used to build the estate house which, in the 1940s, was the headquarters of the Shetland Bus operation. Today, tree plantations around Kergord attract woodland birds such as the rook and chaffinch.

On the western shore of Weisdale Voe, south of the mill, are the ruins of the house where John Clunies Ross (1786–1853) was born. In 1827, he settled in the Cocos Islands in the Indian Ocean where he proclaimed himself 'king'.

The Western Side

☎ 01595

The area west of Weisdale is notable for its varied scenery of bleak moors, sheer cliffs, rolling green hills and numerous cobalt-blue lochs and inlets. It is great for walking, cycling and fishing.

There are also a number of interesting archaeological sites including **Stanydale**, a Neolithic settlement, and the **Scord of Brewster**, a prehistoric farm at Brig of Waas, both signposted off the road between Bixter and Walls.

Bird-watching in Shetland

Lying on the north-south and east-west migration routes, this island group is internationally famous for its birdlife, and is one of Britain's top bird-watching locations. As well as being a stopover for migrating Arctic species, there are large seabird breeding colonies.

Out of the 24 seabird species that nest in the British Isles, 21 are found here; June is the height of the breeding season. The bird population vastly outnumbers the human population of 24,000 – there are said to be around 30,000 gannets, 140,000 guillemots, 250,000 puffins and 300,000 fulmars.

The Royal Society for the Protection of Birds (RSPB; W www.rspb.org.uk) maintains reserves on south Mainland at **Loch of Spiggie**, which attracts wildfowl in autumn and winter, **Sumburgh Head** and on the island of **Fetlar**, which supports the richest heathland bird community, but there are also cliffs with auks, gulls and shags.

There are national nature reserves at **Hermaness**, where you can't fail to be entertained by the clownish antics of the almost tame puffins – known here as the tammy norrie – and on the **Isle of Noss**, which can be reached from Lerwick. **Fair Isle**, owned by the National Trust for Scotland (NTS), supports large seabird populations and there's accommodation at the bird observatory.

Lerwick TIC has lots of ornithological leaflets. A useful Web site for bird-watchers is W www.wildlife.shetland.co.uk/birds/where.html. Take care when out bird-watching, as the cliff-edge sites can be dangerous. Also watch out for skuas (bonxies) that will dive-bomb you if you go near their nests. Since they aim for the highest part of your body, it's wise to walk with a stick, pointing it above your head if they approach. And don't get too close to nesting fulmars or you'll be the target for their smelly, oily spittle!

Out in the Atlantic Ocean, about 15 miles (24km) south-west of Walls, is the remote, windswept, 5-sq-mile (13 sq km) island of **Foula** (Bird Island). It competes with Fair Isle for the title of Scotland's most isolated inhabited island. It supports 42 people and 1500 sheep plus 500,000 seabirds, including the rare Leach's petrel and Scotland's largest colony of great skuas. All this amid dramatic cliff scenery, particularly the awesome, sheer Kame (372m). There's no shop on the island, but *Mrs Taylor's (☎/fax 753226, Leraback)* offers dinner B&B for £25 per person. It's centrally located with good food.

Foula is reached by twice-weekly ferries (£4.30 return, £21 for a car and driver, four hours) from Walls or Scalloway (☎ 753226) and flights (£42.60 return) from Tingwall (☎ 840246).

North-west from Walls, the road crosses desolate moorland then descends through green fields before arriving at the small crofting community of **Sandness**. The woollen spinning mill, Jamieson's Spinning *(☎ 870285, Sandness)* opens 8am to 5pm weekdays and sells knitted garments at factory prices (from £20). Visible about a mile (1.6km) offshore is the island of **Papa Stour**, home to huge colonies of auks, terns and skuas. It's mostly made up of volcanic rock that has eroded to form sea caves, underground passages, arches and columns. Access to the island is by ferry from West Burrafirth (east of Sandness), which runs four to seven times weekly (£4.40 return, £21 for a car and driver, one hour); book with W Clark (☎ 810460).

SOUTH MAINLAND

From Lerwick, the main road south winds 25 miles (40km) down the eastern side of this long, narrow, hilly tail of land that ends at Sumburgh Head. South of Sandwick, a minor road loops around to the west coast at Bigton before returning to the main road at Boddam.

Catpund

About 10 miles (16km) south of Lerwick, Catpund is an interesting archaeological site. From Neolithic to medieval times, this former large quarry was mined for soapstone

which was used to make various utensils and implements. It was excavated in the 1980s and evidence of the workings can be seen along the stream.

Sandwick & Around
☎ 01950 • pop 1352

Opposite the small scattered village of Sandwick, is the **Isle of Mousa**, a newly created RSPB reserve, on which stands the impressive double-walled fortified tower, **Mousa Broch** (13m). The well-preserved broch was built from local sandstone between 100 BC and AD 100 and features in two Viking sagas as a hideout for eloping couples! The island is also home to many seabirds and waders; around 6000 storm petrels nest on Mousa, but they're only on the island at night. Common and grey seals can be seen on the beach and among the rocks at West Voe.

From mid-April to mid-September, there are regular boat trips (£7/3.50 return, 15 minutes) from Leebitton harbour in Sandwick, allowing two hours on the island. Contact *Tom Jamieson (☎ 431367, W www.mousaboattrips.co.uk)* in advance for bookings.

Barclay Arms Hotel (☎ 431226, fax 431262, Hoswick) B&B singles £25-30, doubles £40-50. This place has full en-suite facilities and also offers evening meals.

Solbrekke (☎ 431410, Park Rd, Sandwick) B&B £15-17 per person. Solbrekke has one room available for guests.

There are two to nine buses daily between Lerwick and Sandwick (£1.30, 25 minutes).

Bigton & Around

Buses from Lerwick stop twice daily (except Sunday) in Bigton on the west coast, but it's another couple of miles (around 3km) to the **tombolo** (a narrow isthmus) that connects Mainland with St Ninian's Isle. The site is of geological importance and is an SSSI. It is the largest shell-and-sand tombolo in Britain; most other similar tombolos are made of gravel or shingle.

Across the tombolo is **St Ninian's Isle** where you'll find the ruins of a 12th-century church, beneath which are traces of an earlier Pictish church. In 1958 during excavations, Pictish treasure, probably dating from

AD 800 and consisting of 27 silver objects, including shallow bowls and dishes, was found beneath a broken sandstone slab. They're now kept in the Museum of Scotland in Edinburgh, but you can see replicas in the Shetland Museum, Lerwick.

Boddam

From this small village there's a side road that leads to the **Shetland Crofthouse Museum** (☎ *01595-695057, South Voe; adult/ child £2/1.50; open 10am-1pm & 2pm-5pm daily May-Sept)*. Built in 1870, it has been restored, thatched and furnished with 19th-century furniture and utensils. The Lerwick–Sumburgh bus stops right outside.

Quendale

South of Boddam, a minor road runs southwest to Quendale where you'll find the small but excellent, restored and fully working 19th-century **Quendale Watermill** (☎ *01950-460969; adult/child £1.50/50p; open 10am-5pm daily May-Sept)*, the last of Shetland's water mills. It's on a working farm and the admission cost includes an interesting 12-minute video. The bus stops in Quendale from where it's about a mile (1.6km) to the mill (signposted).

The village overlooks a long, sandy beach to the south in the Bay of Quendale. West of the bay there's dramatic cliff scenery and **diving** in the waters between Garth's Ness and Fitful Head and to the wreck of the oil tanker *Braer* off Garth's Ness. About 2 miles (3km) north of the village, the RSPB reserve of **Loch of Spiggie** is an autumn and winter refuge for wildfowl, especially whooper swans. Other migrating birds that stop over are kittiwakes, arctic terns and greylag geese. Nesting birds include ducks, oystercatchers and curlews. The reserve isn't open, but there are good views from the road.

From Lerwick there are two buses daily (except Sunday).

Sumburgh

At the southern tip of Mainland, this village is home to the international airport and **Jarlshof** *(HS;* ☎ *01950-460112; adult/child £2.80/1; open 9.30am-6.30pm daily Apr-*

Sept), Shetland's most impressive archaeological attraction. This large settlement, with buildings from prehistory through Norse times to the 16th century, was hidden under the sand until exposed by a gale at the end of the 19th century. The original Stone-Age settlement (dating from around 2500 BC) is topped by a broch, wheelhouses, a Norse farmhouse and the remains of a 16th-century mansion. The site gets its name from Sir Walter Scott; Jarlshof is what he called the mansion in his novel, *The Pirate*.

The 26-page guidebook (£2.50), available from the visitor centre, interprets the ruins from a number of vantage points. It's an interesting place, but the modern world impinges with the airport and hotel so close.

Near Jarlshof you can visit **Sumburgh Head**, an RSPB reserve. The lighthouse here isn't open to the public, but you can view the many birds that inhabit the cliffs below. At various times there are puffins (over 2000 pairs), kittiwakes (1000 pairs), fulmars, guillemots (over 13,000 breed here), razorbills and cormorants. The other important bird-watching area is the **Pool of Virkie**, the bay just east of the airport.

At Old Scatness, next to the airport, **Betty Mouat's Cottage**, a crofter's cottage, is now a camping böd. Betty became famous in 1886 when, on a routine sailing trip to Lerwick on board the fishing smack *Columbine*, the captain was swept overboard. His two crewmen went to rescue him, leaving Betty alone; they were unable to return to the smack, which drifted for nine days before ending up in Norway, but Betty survived the experience.

East of the airport, **Grutness** is the port for the ferry to Fair Isle.

Places to Stay There are a couple of options in Sumburgh.

Betty Mouat's Cottage (Old Scatness, Dunrossness) Beds £5. Open Apr-Oct. This camping böd by the airport sleeps up to eight people. Book in advance at Lerwick TIC.

Sumburgh Hotel (☎ *01950-460201, fax 460394, Sumburgh)* En-suite singles/doubles from £45/60. Next to Jarlshof and the airport, the large, upmarket Sumburgh Hotel serves bar and restaurant meals; set dinners are £15.50.

Getting There & Away To get to Sumburgh from Lerwick take the airport bus (£1.90, 50 minutes) and get off at the second-last stop.

FAIR ISLE
☎ 01595 • pop 68

Fair Isle is one of Scotland's most remote inhabited islands, 24 miles (39km) south-west of Sumburgh, about halfway to Orkney, and only three by 1½ miles (about 5km by 2.5km) in size. It's probably best known for its patterned knitwear, still produced in the island's co-operative, Fair Isle Crafts.

However, it's also a paradise for birdwatchers, who form the bulk of the island's visitors. Fair Isle is in the flight path of migrating birds, and thousands breed here. They're monitored by the **Bird Observatory** which collects and analyses information year-round; visitors are more than welcome to participate.

The island also has over 250 species of flowering plants, and grey and golden seals can be seen around its shores, especially in late summer.

Fair Isle was given to the NTS in 1954 by George Waterston, who bought it earlier and set up the first bird observatory. In the same year it was declared a National Scenic Area.

The small **George Waterston Memorial Centre** (☎ 760244, Taft; donations welcome; open 2pm-4pm Mon, 10.30am-noon Wed, 2pm-3.30pm Fri) has photos and exhibits on the island's natural history, crofting, fishing, archaeology and knitwear.

Places to Stay
Accommodation must be booked in advance and includes meals.

Fair Isle Lodge & Bird Observatory (☎/fax 760258) Full-board dorm beds/singles/doubles £30/42/74. The bird observatory offers home cooking and free guided walks; it's located about 400m from the ferry terminal.

Two places offering dinner B&B are *Mrs Riddiford* (☎/fax 760250, Schoolton) with two rooms for £28 to £30 per person, and *Mrs Coull* (☎ 760248, e kathleen.coull@lineone.net, Upper Leogh) for £30 to £34 per person, located near the southern harbour.

Getting There & Away
Air From Tingwall (☎ 840246) there are two return flights daily (£74.40 return, 25 minutes) on Monday, Wednesday and Friday. A day return allows about six hours on the island, eight on Monday. On Saturday, there's only one return flight from Tingwall, allowing just 2½ hours on Fair Isle, but from early May to mid-October there's also a return flight from Sumburgh.

Boat From May to September, the *Good Shepherd IV* ferry sails from Grutness (near Sumburgh) to Fair Isle (£2.20, 2½ hours) on Tuesday, Saturday and alternate Thursdays, and from Lerwick (£2.20, 4½ hours) on alternate Thursdays. In winter, there's one return trip on Tuesday. All sailings are return trips from Fair Isle, so day trips from mainland Shetland aren't possible. Book with JW Stout (☎ 760222). On the trip you may see dolphins and porpoises.

NORTH MAINLAND
Voe
Old Voe is a pretty collection of buildings beside a tranquil bay on the southern shore of Olna Firth. It's sheltered from the wind by the surrounding hills on which the newer part of the township has spread.

In old Voe, *Selkie Charters* (☎ 01806-588297) offers diving trips, training courses and equipment hire.

Sail Loft (Old Voe) Beds £5 per person. Open Apr-Oct. In previous incarnations, this red-painted building by the pier was a fishing shed and knitwear factory, but it's now a camping böd.

Pierhead Restaurant & Bar (☎ 01806-588332, Old Voe) 3-course meal £21.50. Excellent fish dishes are available opposite the Sail Loft; snacks start at £1.25 and the seafood selection is £8.50.

There are up to nine buses daily from Lerwick to Voe, Monday to Saturday (and two on Sunday during school terms).

ORKNEY & SHETLAND ISLANDS

Whalsay & Out Skerries
☎ 01806 • pop 1043

South of Voe, the B9071 branches east to Laxo, the ferry terminal for the island of Whalsay. This is one of the most prosperous of Shetland's islands owing to its large fishing industry whose fleet is based at the modern harbour of **Symbister**.

The Hanseatic League, a commercial association of German towns that existed between the 14th and early 18th centuries, set up trading booths at the harbour. One of these, **Pier House** *(☎ 566362, Symbister; adult/child £1/free; open 9am-1pm & 2pm-5pm Mon-Sat Apr-Sept)*, has been restored and inside is an exhibition on the trade and about the island.

Whalsay is popular for sea angling and for trout fishing in its lochs. There are also scenic walks in the south and east where colonies of seabirds breed and where you may catch sight of seals.

Grieve House (Sodom) Beds £5. At Sodom, not far from Symbister, the famous poet Hugh MacDiarmid's former home is now a camping böd. Book through Lerwick TIC.

There are regular ferries daily between Laxo and Symbister (£2.50 return, 30 minutes). To book, call ☎ 566259.

North-east of Whalsay, another thriving fishing community occupies the 2 sq miles (5 sq km) of Out Skerries (or just Skerries). It's made up of the three main islands of Housay, Bruray (these two connected by a road bridge) and Grunay, plus a number of islets. Their rugged cliffs teem with birdlife. There are ferries between Out Skerries and Lerwick on Tuesday and Thursday (2½ hours), and the rest of the week (except Wednesday) to Vidlin (1½ hours), about 3 miles (5km) north-east of Laxo. The return passenger fare is £4.30 (£6 for a car and driver). To book, call GW Henderson (☎ 515226).

Brae & Around

Apart from the swimming pool (80p), there's little in Brae itself, but there's accommodation and it would make a good base. There's fine **walking** on the peninsula west of Brae, and to the south on the red-granite island of **Muckle Roe**, which is connected to the peninsula by a bridge. Muckle Roe also offers good **diving** off its west and north coasts.

Places to Stay & Eat There are a few places to stay for visitors.

Mrs Wood (☎ 01806-522368, Westayre, Muckle Roe) B&B £20-22 per person. This working croft offers home cooking and evening meals are available for £12.

Valleyfield Guest House (☎ 01806-522563, fax 890257) En-suite rooms £25-35 per person. Friendly Valleyfield Guest House is 1½ miles (2.5km) south of Brae on the A970. It offers good three-course evening meals (£12.50) by reservation only, and there's space for tents (£3.50 per person) and caravans.

There are other places to stay, but they appeal mostly to oil workers.

Brae Stores, near the junction in the village centre, is a supermarket and post office.

Getting There & Away Buses from Lerwick to Eshaness and North Roe stop in Brae (£1.50, 35 minutes).

Eshaness & Hillswick

About 11 miles (18km) north-west of Brae, the road ends at the red, basalt lava cliffs of Eshaness which form some of the most impressive coastal scenery in Shetland. This is superb **walking** country and there are panoramic views from the lighthouse (closed to the public) on the headland.

A mile (1.6km) east, a side road leads south to the **Tangwick Haa Museum** *(☎ 503389, Tangwick Haa; admission free; open 1pm-5pm Mon-Fri & 11am-7pm Sat & Sun May-Sept)*, in a restored 17th-century house. The difficulties and dangers of fishing and whaling, and the hardship of domestic life, are shown through photographs and displays.

At **Hamnavoe**, which you reach from another side road heading north, about 3½ miles (6km) east of Eshaness, is **Johnny Notions Camping Böd** (£5, book through Lerwick TIC). This was the birthplace of Johnny 'Notions' Williamson, an 18th-century blacksmith who inoculated several thousand people against smallpox using a serum and method he devised himself.

Offshore from **Hillswick**, 7 miles (11km) east of Eshaness, there's excellent **diving** around The Drongs, a series of exposed sea stacks.

St Magnus Hotel *(☎ 01806-503372, fax 503373, Hillswick)* En-suite singles/doubles £33/60. Built of timber brought from Norway in 1900, this hotel also offers bar lunches and suppers from £4.95.

Booth Restaurant & Café *(☎ 01806-503348, Hillswick)* Open daily May-Aug, Sat & Sun Sept. Down on the quay, this restaurant is in one of Shetland's oldest buildings – a 300-year-old former Hanseatic trading post. It serves exclusively vegetarian food and has live music some nights. Proceeds go to the local wildlife sanctuary.

Buses from Lerwick run (evenings only) to Hillswick (£1.90, 1¼ hours) and Eshaness; contact Whites Coaches (☎ 01595-809443).

Sullom Voe

Sullom Voe is the name given to both the northern headland jutting into Yell Sound and the long sea inlet that provides a deep-water harbour for the huge Sullom Voe oil terminal. You can see the terminal to the left en route to **Toft**, the ferry terminal for Ulsta on Yell.

THE NORTH ISLES

The North Isles are made up of the three islands of Yell, Unst and Fetlar, all connected to each other by ferry.

Yell

☎ 01957 • pop 1083

Yell is a desolate island covered mostly by heather moors atop a deep layer of peat. There are, however, some good coastal and hill walks, especially around the **Herra Peninsula**, about halfway up the west coast.

Across Whale Firth from the peninsula is Lumbister, where red-throated divers (called 'rain geese' in Shetland), merlins, bonxies, arctic skuas and other bird species breed. The area is home to a large otter population too. The otters can be best viewed near the shores of Whale Firth, where you may also spot common and grey seals.

In the Daal of Lumbister, a short, narrow gorge between the Loch of Lumbister and the west coast, there are bright displays of wildflowers such as juniper, honeysuckle and thyme. The area immediately north of Lumbister provides some excellent walking along the coast and over remote moorland.

South of Lumbister, on the hillside above the main road, stand the reputedly haunted ruins of **Windhouse**, dating from 1707. About a mile (1.6km) east of here is **Mid Yell**, the island's largest village and a natural harbour. The road north to Gutcher passes **Basta Voe** where many otters inhabit the shores. In the north, around the village of **Cullovoe**, there's more good walking along the attractive coastline.

Look out for the bright and breezy **mural** by the Ulsta ferry terminal. From Ulsta, the road leads 5 miles (8km) east to Burravoe. The **Old Haa Visitor Centre** *(☎ 722339, Burravoe; admission free; open 10am-4pm Tues-Thur & Sat, 2pm-5pm Sun late April-Sept)* is in Yell's oldest building, built in 1672. There's an interesting exhibition on local flora, fauna and history and a small gallery.

Places to Stay & Eat Simple accommodation is available on Yell.

Windhouse Lodge *(By the A968 in Mid Yell)* Beds £5. Below the haunted ruins of Windhouse you'll find this camping böd. You can book beds at Lerwick TIC.

Gutcher Post Office *(☎ 744201, fax 744366, Gutcher)* B&B £17 per person. Friendly Gutcher Post Office, run by Margaret Tulloch, is close to the ferry terminal for Unst. Evening meals cost £8.

Mrs Leask's *(☎ 722274, Hillhead, Burravoe)* B&B £17 per person. There are good views and home-cooked dinners (£7) at this pleasant B&B.

Hilltop Restaurant & Bar *(☎ 702333, Mid Yell)* Mains £2.50-5. This place opens for lunch and dinner (to 10.45pm).

While you're waiting for the ferry in Gutcher, you can snack at the ***Seaview Café*** (burgers from only £1.20), while in Burravoe the Old Haa Visitor Centre has a small ***tearoom*** serving good home-made food. There are grocery stores in Mid Yell and Ulsta.

Getting There & Away Yell is connected with Mainland by ferry between Toft and Ulsta (£1.25, £3 for a car and driver, 20 minutes). Although you don't need to book in advance, from May to September traffic is constant so it's wise to do so. Call ☎ 722259.

Two or three buses daily (Sunday during school terms only) leave Lerwick for Toft ferry pier (£1.90, one hour). There are connecting buses at Ulsta for other parts of the island.

Unst
☎ 01957 • pop 1067
Unst has an area of 45 sq miles (117 sq km) and it's Scotland's northernmost inhabited island. A geological fault line runs from Belmont in the south to Burrafirth in the north; to the east of the line the rocks are serpentine and gabbro, to the west mainly gneiss and schist. As a result, there's a wide variety of vegetation – over 400 different plant species. Some of the most unusual examples can be seen at the 30-hectare **Keen of Hamar NNR** north-east of Baltasound.

In the north-west is the wonderfully wild and windy NNR reserve of **Hermaness**. Here you can sit on the high cliffs, commune with the thousands of seabirds and Shetland's largest colony of puffins (best seen in May and June), and gaze across the sea towards the Arctic Circle. The more energetic might enjoy the superb cliff-top walk along the west coast.

The **Hermaness Visitor Centre** (☎ 711278, Shore Station, Burrafirth; admission free; open 8.30am-6pm daily late Apr–mid-Sept), near the reserve's entrance, has a seabird exhibit and provides information on the island's wildlife.

Robert Louis Stevenson wrote *Treasure Island* while living on Unst and the map in the novel is reputedly based on Unst. Stevenson's uncle built the lighthouse on **Muckle Flugga**, one of the group of rocks off Hermaness; another of the rocks is **Out Stack**, Scotland's most northerly point.

On the way to Hermaness, you might want to pause to mail a card at Scotland's northernmost post box in **Haroldswick**.

Unst Boat Haven (☎ 711528, Haroldswick; admission free; open 2pm-5pm daily May-Sept) has an interesting collection of photographs, boats and maritime artefacts.

Unst Heritage Centre (☎ 711528, Haroldswick; admission free; open 2pm-5pm daily May-Sept) houses a museum on geology and local history, and has information on family trees.

There's an RAF radar at Saxavord and a base station near the heritage centre. North of Haroldswick there are some fine sandy beaches at Burrafirth, Norwick and Skaw. Scotland's oddest **bus shelter** (W www.unst busshelter.shetland.co.uk), complete with sofa and other accoutrements, is at Baltasound.

In the south, about 3 miles (5km) east of Uyeasound, are the remains of **Muness Castle** (HS), a late 16th-century tower house. There's some gentle walking around the bay a little to the north, past the beach at Sand Wick, with the chance to see some otters and seals.

Organised Tours In summer, *Shetland Wildlife* (☎ 01950-422483, W www.shet landwildlife.co.uk) runs very popular 7½-hour tours from Mid Yell to Muckle Flugga and Out Stack on Wednesday for £75, including minibus transport to Mid Yell.

Places to Stay & Eat Baltasound has the greatest range of accommodation, but there are other options.

Gardiesfauld Hostel (☎ 755259, fax 711211, Uyeasound) Dorm beds £8/6.50, tent & two persons £6. Open Apr-Sept. Gardiesfauld Hostel has modern facilities and can organise bicycle hire.

Mrs Ritch (☎ 711323, Gerratoun, Haroldswick) B&B £16-17 per person. Mrs Ritch offers B&B in a converted croft house. Dinner costs an extra £7.

Mrs Firmin (☎ 755234, Prestegaard, Uyeasound) Rooms £18 per person. Mrs Firmin offers two rooms in a large Victorian house. Evening meals are available for £8.

Buness Country House (☎ 711315, fax 711815, Baltasound) B&B £31.50-36.50 per person. The notorious Burke and Hare stayed at Buness House, and there are views of the otters down on the shore. Dinner costs £20 extra.

Baltasound Hotel (☎ *711334, fax 711358, Baltasound*) Singles/doubles with bathroom £39.50/59. This solid place has extensions in nearby chalets. Lunches and dinners are available (three courses around £10-15). Try the local real ale White Wife, named after a ghostly figure seen by the A968, just south of Baltasound.

Another recommended place is ***Clingera Guest House*** (☎/fax 711579, *Baltasound*) with en-suites for £18 to £20 per person.

Nornova Tearoom (☎ *755373, Muness*), near Muness Castle, serves sandwiches and snacks, while self-caterers can stock up at ***Skibhoul Store & Bakery*** (*Baltasound*).

Getting There & Away Flights from Sumburgh/Tingwall to Unst run Monday and Wednesday to Friday and cost £46.30/21 one way.

Unst is connected with Yell by a small car ferry between Gutcher and Belmont (£1.25 one way, £3 for a car and driver, 10 minutes). To book, call ☎ 722259.

Haroldswick is 55 miles (88km) from Lerwick and, if you don't have a car, you must spend the night on Unst as buses only run once daily. From Lerwick, you can make connections with ferries and other buses to reach Haroldswick by 10.55am if you catch the 8am bus. It's then only a couple of miles to either Hermaness or Keen of Hamar (5km or 3km respectively).

Fetlar
☎ 01957 • pop 87

Fetlar is the smallest (5 miles by 2 miles, 8 km by 3km) but most fertile of the North Isles. The name Fetlar is derived from old Norse meaning 'fat land' as there is good grazing and a rich variety of plant and bird life. Much of the island is designated as SSSI. There's great bird-watching, and the 705 hectares of grassy moorland around Vord Hill (159m) in the north form the **North Fetlar RSPB Reserve**. Large numbers

of auks, gulls and shags breed in the cliffs. Common and grey seals can also be seen on the shores. The reserve is closed during the breeding season, from May to August; contact the warden (☎ 733246) at Baelans.

Fetlar is home to one of Britain's rarest birds, the red-necked phalarope, which breeds in the loch near **Funzie** (pronounced finnie), in the island's east. From April to November, you can view them from an RSPB hide in the nearby marshes. The whimbrel, a cousin of the curlew, also breeds here.

Scenic **walking** is possible on much of the island, especially around the bay near Tresta, at Urie and Gruting in the north, and Funzie in the east.

There's no petrol on Fetlar, but there's a shop and a post office in **Houbie**, the main village. The excellent **Fetlar Interpretive Centre** (☎ *733206, Houbie; admission free; open noon-5pm Tues-Sun May-Sept*), near the post office, has photos, audio recordings and videos on the island and its history.

Places to Stay & Eat There's no hotel on Fetlar, but there are other accommodation possibilities.

Garth's Campsite (☎ *733227, Gord, Houbie*) Pitches from £4. Garth's Campsite, with flush toilets and showers, overlooks the beach at Tresta and is 2½ miles (4km) from the ferry.

Gord (☎ *733227, Gord, Houbie*) B&B £23 per person. All rooms have their own bathrooms at this friendly B&B. It also offers dinner for £7.

The Glebe (☎/fax *733242*) B&B £16-17 per person. The Glebe is a listed building overlooking Papil Water, about a mile (1.6km) west of Houbie.

The ***shop/cafe*** in Houbie serves homemade food, including lemon chicken pie and pasta dishes.

Getting There & Away Regular ferries (£1.25, £3 for car and driver, 25 minutes) from Oddsta in the island's north-west connect with Gutcher on Yell and Belmont on Unst.

ORKNEY & SHETLAND ISLANDS

Language

Scottish Gaelic (*Gàidhlig* – pronounced *gallic* in Scotland) is spoken by about 80,000 people in Scotland, mainly in the Highlands and islands, and by many native speakers and learners overseas. It is a member of the Celtic branch of the Indo-European family of languages, which has given us Gaelic, Irish, Manx, Welsh, Cornish and Breton.

Although Scottish Gaelic is the Celtic language most closely associated with Scotland it was quite a latecomer to those shores. Other Celtic languages in the form of Pictish and Brittonic had existed prior to the arrival and settlement by Gaelic-speaking Celts (Gaels) from Ireland from the 4th to the 6th centuries AD. These Irish settlers, known to the Romans as Scotti, were eventually to give their name to the entire country. Initially they settled in the area on the west coast of Scotland in which their name is perpetuated, Earra Ghaidheal (Argyll). As their territorial influence extended so did their language and from the 9th to the 11th centuries Gaelic was spoken throughout the country. For many centuries the language was the same as the language of Ireland; there is little evidence of much divergence before the 13th century. Even up to the 18th century the bards adhered to the strict literary standards of Old Irish.

The Viking invasions from AD 800 brought linguistic influences which are evident in many of the coastal place names of the Highlands.

Gaelic culture flourished in the Highlands until the 18th century and the Jacobite rebellions. After the Battle of Culloden in 1746 many Gaelic speakers were forced from their ancestral lands; this 'ethnic cleansing' by landlords and governments culminated in the Highland Clearances of the 19th century. Although still studied at academic level, the spoken language declined, being regarded as a mere 'peasant' language of no modern significance.

It was only in the 1970s that Gaelic began to make a comeback with a new generation of young enthusiasts who were determined that it should not be allowed to die. People from all over Scotland, and indeed worldwide, are beginning to appreciate their Gaelic heritage.

After two centuries of decline, the language is now being encouraged through financial help from government agencies and the EU. Gaelic education is flourishing from playgroups to tertiary levels. This renaissance flows out into the field of music, literature, cultural events and broadcasting.

The Gaelic language has a vital role to play in the life of modern Scotland.

Grammar

The usual word order in Gaelic is verb-subject-object; English, by comparison, has a subject-verb-object word order, eg, The girl (subject) reads (verb) the book (object).

There are two forms of the pronoun 'you' in Gaelic: the singular *thu*, and the plural form *sibh* which is also used as a formal (ie, polite) singular. We use the informal *thu* in the following phraselist.

English Borrowings from Gaelic

bard	bard – *baard* (poet)
ben	beinn – *beh-een* (hill)
bog	bog – *bohk* (soft, wet)
brogue	bròg – *bro-ck* (shoe)
caber	cabar – *cap-er* (pole)
claymore	claidheamh mòr – *cly-af mor* (big sword)
dune	dùn – *doo-n* (a heap)
galore	gu leòr – *gu lyor* (plenty)
loch	loch – *loch*
Sassenach	Sasannach – *Sasunach* (Englishman)
sporran	sporan – *sporan* (purse)
strath	strath – *strah* (mountain valley)

Pronunciation

Stress usually falls on the first syllable of a word. The Gaelic alphabet has only 18 letters.

Vowels

There are five vowels: **a, e, i, o** and **u** – **a, o** and **u** are known as broad vowels, **e** and **i** are known as slender vowels. A grave accent indicates that a vowel sound is lengthened, eg *bata* (a stick), *bàta* (a boat).

Consonants

There are 12 consonants: **b, c, d, f, g, l, m, n, p, r, s, t**, and the letter **h** (only used to change other sounds).

Consonants may be pronounced in different ways depending on the vowel beside them. The spelling rule in Gaelic is 'broad to broad and slender to slender'. This means that if, in a word, a consonant is preceded by a broad vowel it must be followed by a broad vowel, and if it is preceded by a slender vowel it must be followed by a slender vowel. Consequently, we speak about broad consonants and slender consonants, eg *balach* (a boy), *caileag* (a girl).

Broad consonants sound approximately as their English equivalents.

Slender consonants are often followed by a 'y' sound.

c	always a hard 'k' sound; never an 's' sound
d	when broad, thicker than English 'd'; when slender, as the 'j' in 'jet'
l, ll	when slender, as in 'value'
n, nn	when slender, as in 'new'
s	when slender, as 'sh'
t	when broad, thicker than English 't'; when slender, as the 'ch' in 'chin'

When consonants are followed by 'h', a change of sound occurs:

bh, mh	as 'v'
ch	when broad, as in *loch* (not 'lock'!); when slender, as the German *ich*
dh, gh	when broad, voiced at the back of the throat; when slender, as 'y' – there's no English equivalent
fh	silent
ph	as 'f'
sh	as 'h' if before a broad vowel
th	as 'h'

There are a number of Gaelic sounds, especially vowel combinations and consonantal changes brought about by the addition of the letter **h**, which cannot be reproduced satisfactorily in English. The help of a native speaker is invaluable in learning these.

Greetings & Civilities

Good morning.
  madding va
  Madainn mhath.
Good afternoon/Good evening.
  fesskurr ma
  Feasgar math.
Good night.
  uh eech uh va
  Oidhche mhath.
How are you?
  kimmer uh ha oo?
  Ciamar a tha thu?
Very well, thank you.
  gley va, tappuh let
  Glè mhath, tapadh leat.
I'm well, thank you.
  ha mee goo ma, tappuh let
  Tha mi gu math, tapadh leat.
That's good.
  sma shin
  'S math sin.
Please.
  mahs eh doh hawl eh
  Mas e do thoil e.
Thank you.
  tappuh let
  Tapadh leat.
Many thanks.
  moe ran ta eeng
  Mòran taing.
You're welcome.
  sheh doh veh huh
  'Se do bheatha.
I beg your pardon.
  baaluv
  B'àill leibh.
Excuse me.
  gav mo lishk yal
  Gabh mo leisgeul.
I'm sorry.
  ha mee dooleech
  Tha mi duilich.

Small Talk

Do you speak (have) Gaelic?
uh vil ga lick ackut?
A bheil Gàidhlig agad?

Yes, a little.
ha, beg an
Tha, beagan.

Not much.
chan yil moe ran
Chan eil mòran.

What's your name?
jae an tannam uh ha orsht?
De an t ainm a tha ort?

Who are you?
coe oosuh?
Co thusa?

I'm ...
is meeshuh ...
Is mise ...

Good health! (Cheers!)
slahntchuh va!
Slàinte mhath!

Goodbye. (lit: Blessings go with you)
B yan achd let
Beannachd leat.

Goodbye. (The same with you)
mar shin let
Mar sin leat.

Useful Phrases

It's warm today.
ha eh blah un joo
Tha e blàth an diugh.

It's cold today.
ha eh foo ur un joo
Tha e fuar an diugh.

The day is beautiful.
ha un la bree a uh
Tha an latha brèagha.

It's wet.
ha e flooch
Tha e fliuch.

It's raining.
ha un tooshku a woon
Tha an t uisge ann.

It's misty.
ha k yaw a woon
Tha ceò ann.

Has the rain stopped?
un daw skoor un tooshku?
An do sguir an t uisge?

Travel & Accommodation

Can you tell me ...?
un yee ish oo ghoe ...?
An innis thu dhomh ...?

I want to go to ...
ha mee ug ee urry uh gholl goo ...
Tha mi ag iarraidh a dhol gu ...

How do I get to ...?
kimmer uh yaev mee goo ...?
Ciamar a gheibh mi gu ...?

by bus		
ir uh vuss	air a' bhus	
by train		
ir un tren	air an trean	
by car		
a woon un car	ann an car	

a hotel		
tuh ee awstu	taigh òsda	
a bedroom		
roowm caddil	rùm cadail	
a toilet		
tuh ee beck	taigh beag	

rhinn (also 'rhin')   headland

Food

food and drink
bee ugh agus joch
biadh agus deoch

I'm hungry.
ha an tac russ orrom
Tha an t-acras orm.

I'm thirsty.
ha am pah ugh orrom
Tha am pathadh orm.

I want ...
ha mee ug ee uhree
Tha mi ag iarraidh ...

I'd like ...
boo tawl lehum
Bu toigh leam ...

I don't like ...
chah tawl lehum
Cha toigh leam ...

That was good.
va shood ma
Bha siud math.

Very good.
  gley va
  Glè mhath.

a biscuit
  briskatch   brioscaid
apple juice
  sooh ooh al   sùgh ubhal
bread
  aran   aran
broth, soup
  broht   brot
butter
  eem   ìm
cheese
  kashuh   càise
cream
  baahrr   bàrr
dessert
  meehlshuhn   mìlsean
fish
  eeusk   iasg
meat
  fehyawl   feòil
oatcakes
  aran korkuh   aran coirce
orange juice
  sooh awhrinsh   sùgh orains
peas
  pessir   peasair
porridge
  lee chuh   lite
potatoes
  boontahtuh   buntàta

salmon
  brahdan   bradan
vegetables
  glasreech   glasraich

Drinks

a cup of coffee
  coopa cawfee   cupa cofaidh
a cup of tea
  coopa tee   cupa tì
black coffee
  cawfee dooh   cofaidh dubh
black tea
  tee dhooh   tì dhubh
with milk
  leh bahnyuh   le bainne
with sugar
  leh shooh car   le siùcar
a drink of milk
  joch vahnyuh   deoch bhainne
a glass of water
  glahnyuh   glainne uisge
  ooshkuy
a glass of wine
  glahnyuh feeuhn   glainne fìon
beer
  lyawn   leann
red wine
  feeuhn jerrack   fìon dearg
white wine
  feeuhn gyahl   fìon geal
whisky
  ooshkuy beh huh   uisge beatha

Glossary

AA – Automobile Association
abhainn – river
ABTA – Association of British Travel Agents
BABA – book-a-bed-ahead scheme
bag – reach the top of (as in to 'bag a couple of peaks' or 'Munro-bagging')
bailey – the space enclosed by castle walls
bairn – child
ben – mountain
böd – originally a simple trading booth used by fishing communities, today it refers to basic accommodation for walkers etc
bothy – hut or mountain shelter
brae – hill
broch – defensive tower
BTA – British Tourist Authority
burgh – town
burn – stream
cairn – pile of stones to mark path or junction, also peak
ceilidh – pronounced **kay**-lay, informal entertainment and dance
clootie dumpling – a steamed fruit pudding, boiled in a 'cloot' (linen cloth)
close – entrance to an alley
craig – exposed rock
dene – valley
dirk – dagger
doocot – dovecote
dram – whisky measure
dun – fort
firth – estuary
glen – valley
haar – fog off the North Sea
Hogmanay – New Year's Eve
howff – pub or shelter
HS – Historic Scotland
kail – cabbage
ken – know
kipper – smoked herring
kirk – church
kyle – narrow strait of water
laird – estate owner
land – tenement
law – round hill
links – golf course
linn – waterfall
machair – grass and wildflower-covered dunes
MBA – Mountain Bothies Association
MCS – Mountaineering Council of Scotland
merse – saltmarsh
motte – early Norman fortification consisting

of a raised, flattened mound with a keep on top; when attached to a bailey it is known as a motte-and-bailey
muckle – big
Munro – mountain of 914m or higher
Munro-bagger – a hillwalker who tries to climb all the Munros in Scotland
neeps – turnips
ness – headland
NNR – National Nature Reserve, managed by the SNH
NTS – National Trust for Scotland
OS – Ordnance Survey
pend – arched gateway
Picts – early inhabitants of northern and eastern Scotland (from the Latin pictus, meaning painted, after their body paint decorations)
provost – mayor
RAC – Royal Automobile Association
reiver – raider
rhinn or **rhin** – headland
RNLI – Royal National Lifeboat Institute
rood – an old Scots word for cross
RSA – Royal Scottish Academy
RSPB – Royal Society for the Protection of Birds
Sassenach – from Gaelic Sasannach, meaning an English person
sett – tartan pattern, or cobblestone
SMC – Scottish Mountaineering Club
SNH – Scottish Natural Heritage, a government organisation responsible for safeguarding and improving Scotland's natural heritage
sporran – purse worn around waist with the kilt
SRWS – Scottish Rights of Way and Access Society
SSSI – Sight of Special Scientific Interest
STB – Scottish Tourist Board
strath – valley
SYHA – Scottish Youth Hostel Association
tatties – potatoes
TIC – Tourist Information Centre
tor – bare, rocky hill, or outcrop of granite
tron – public weighbridge
trows – mythical little people (Shetland)
twitcher – bird-watcher
uisge-beatha – whisky (literally, water of life)
vennel – narrow street
voe – inlet (Shetland)
way – walking trail
wean – child
wynd – lane

Lonely Planet Guides by Region

Lonely Planet is known worldwide for publishing practical, reliable and no-nonsense travel information in our guides and on our Web site. The Lonely Planet list covers just about every accessible part of the world. Currently there are 16 series: Travel guides, Shoestring guides, Condensed guides, Phrasebooks, Read This First, Healthy Travel, Walking guides, Cycling guides, Watching Wildlife guides, Pisces Diving & Snorkeling guides, City Maps, Road Atlases, Out to Eat, World Food, Journeys travel literature and Pictorials.

AFRICA Africa on a shoestring • Botswana • Cairo • Cairo City Map • Cape Town • Cape Town City Map • East Africa • Egypt • Egyptian Arabic phrasebook • Ethiopia, Eritrea & Djibouti • Ethiopian Amharic phrasebook • The Gambia & Senegal • Healthy Travel Africa • Kenya • Malawi • Morocco • Moroccan Arabic phrasebook • Mozambique • Namibia • Read This First: Africa • South Africa, Lesotho & Swaziland • Southern Africa • Southern Africa Road Atlas • Swahili phrasebook • Tanzania, Zanzibar & Pemba • Trekking in East Africa • Tunisia • Watching Wildlife East Africa • Watching Wildlife Southern Africa • West Africa • World Food Morocco • Zambia • Zimbabwe, Botswana & Namibia
Travel Literature: Mali Blues: Traveling to an African Beat • The Rainbird: A Central African Journey • Songs to an African Sunset: A Zimbabwean Story

AUSTRALIA & THE PACIFIC Aboriginal Australia & the Torres Strait Islands •Auckland • Australia • Australian phrasebook • Australia Road Atlas • Cycling Australia • Cycling New Zealand • Fiji • Fijian phrasebook • Healthy Travel Australia, NZ & the Pacific • Islands of Australia's Great Barrier Reef • Melbourne • Melbourne City Map • Micronesia • New Caledonia • New South Wales • New Zealand • Northern Territory • Outback Australia • Out to Eat – Melbourne • Out to Eat – Sydney • Papua New Guinea • Pidgin phrasebook • Queensland • Rarotonga & the Cook Islands • Samoa • Solomon Islands • South Australia • South Pacific • South Pacific phrasebook • Sydney • Sydney City Map • Sydney Condensed • Tahiti & French Polynesia • Tasmania • Tonga • Tramping in New Zealand • Vanuatu • Victoria • Walking in Australia • Watching Wildlife Australia • Western Australia
Travel Literature: Islands in the Clouds: Travels in the Highlands of New Guinea • Kiwi Tracks: A New Zealand Journey • Sean & David's Long Drive

CENTRAL AMERICA & THE CARIBBEAN Bahamas, Turks & Caicos • Baja California • Belize, Guatemala & Yucatán • Bermuda • Central America on a shoestring • Costa Rica • Costa Rica Spanish phrasebook • Cuba • Cycling Cuba • Dominican Republic & Haiti • Eastern Caribbean • Guatemala • Havana • Healthy Travel Central & South America • Jamaica • Mexico • Mexico City • Panama • Puerto Rico • Read This First: Central & South America • Virgin Islands • World Food Caribbean • World Food Mexico • Yucatán
Travel Literature: Green Dreams: Travels in Central America

EUROPE Amsterdam • Amsterdam City Map • Amsterdam Condensed • Andalucía • Athens • Austria • Baltic States phrasebook • Barcelona • Barcelona City Map • Belgium & Luxembourg • Berlin • Berlin City Map • Britain • British phrasebook • Brussels, Bruges & Antwerp • Brussels City Map • Budapest • Budapest City Map • Canary Islands • Catalunya & the Costa Brava • Central Europe • Central Europe phrasebook • Copenhagen • Corfu & the Ionians • Corsica • Crete • Crete Condensed • Croatia • Cycling Britain • Cycling France • Cyprus • Czech & Slovak Republics • Czech phrasebook • Denmark • Dublin • Dublin City Map • Dublin Condensed • Eastern Europe • Eastern Europe phrasebook • Edinburgh • Edinburgh City Map • England • Estonia, Latvia & Lithuania • Europe on a shoestring • Europe phrasebook • Finland • Florence • Florence City Map • France • Frankfurt City Map • Frankfurt Condensed • French phrasebook • Georgia, Armenia & Azerbaijan • Germany • German phrasebook • Greece • Greek Islands • Greek phrasebook • Hungary • Iceland, Greenland & the Faroe Islands • Ireland • Italian phrasebook • Italy • Kraków • Lisbon • The Loire • London • London City Map • London Condensed • Madrid • Madrid City Map • Malta • Mediterranean Europe • Milan, Turin & Genoa • Moscow • Munich • Netherlands • Normandy • Norway • Out to Eat – London • Out to Eat – Paris • Paris • Paris City Map • Paris Condensed • Poland • Polish phrasebook • Portugal • Portuguese phrasebook • Prague • Prague City Map • Provence & the Côte d'Azur • Read This First: Europe • Rhodes & the Dodecanese • Romania & Moldova • Rome • Rome City Map • Rome Condensed • Russia, Ukraine & Belarus • Russian phrasebook • Scandinavian & Baltic Europe • Scandinavian phrasebook • Scotland • Sicily • Slovenia • South-West France • Spain • Spanish phrasebook • Stockholm • St Petersburg • St Petersburg City Map • Sweden • Switzerland • Tuscany • Ukrainian phrasebook • Venice • Vienna • Wales • Walking in Britain • Walking in France • Walking in Ireland • Walking in Italy • Walking in Scotland • Walking in Spain • Walking in Switzerland • Western Europe • World Food France • World Food Greece • World Food Ireland • World Food Italy • World Food Spain **Travel Literature:** After Yugoslavia • Love and War in the Apennines • The Olive Grove: Travels in Greece • On the Shores of the Mediterranean • Round Ireland in Low Gear • A Small Place in Italy

Lonely Planet Mail Order

Lonely Planet products are distributed worldwide. They are also available by mail order from Lonely Planet, so if you have difficulty finding a title please write to us. North and South American residents should write to 150 Linden St, Oakland, CA 94607, USA; European and African residents should write to 10a Spring Place, London NW5 3BH, UK; and residents of other countries to Locked Bag 1, Footscray, Victoria 3011, Australia.

INDIAN SUBCONTINENT & THE INDIAN OCEAN Bangladesh • Bengali phrasebook • Bhutan • Delhi • Goa • Healthy Travel Asia & India • Hindi & Urdu phrasebook • India • India & Bangladesh City Map • Indian Himalaya • Karakoram Highway • Kathmandu City Map • Kerala • Madagascar • Maldives • Mauritius, Réunion & Seychelles • Mumbai (Bombay) • Nepal • Nepali phrasebook • North India • Pakistan • Rajasthan • Read This First: Asia & India • South India • Sri Lanka • Sri Lanka phrasebook • Tibet • Tibetan phrasebook • Trekking in the Indian Himalaya • Trekking in the Karakoram & Hindukush • Trekking in the Nepal Himalaya • World Food India **Travel Literature:** The Age of Kali: Indian Travels and Encounters • Hello Goodnight: A Life of Goa • In Rajasthan • Maverick in Madagascar • A Season in Heaven: True Tales from the Road to Kathmandu • Shopping for Buddhas • A Short Walk in the Hindu Kush • Slowly Down the Ganges

MIDDLE EAST & CENTRAL ASIA Bahrain, Kuwait & Qatar • Central Asia • Central Asia phrasebook • Dubai • Farsi (Persian) phrasebook • Hebrew phrasebook • Iran • Israel & the Palestinian Territories • Istanbul • Istanbul City Map • Istanbul to Cairo • Istanbul to Kathmandu • Jerusalem • Jerusalem City Map • Jordan • Lebanon • Middle East • Oman & the United Arab Emirates • Syria • Turkey • Turkish phrasebook • World Food Turkey • Yemen **Travel Literature:** Black on Black: Iran Revisited • Breaking Ranks: Turbulent Travels in the Promised Land • The Gates of Damascus • Kingdom of the Film Stars: Journey into Jordan

NORTH AMERICA Alaska • Boston • Boston City Map • Boston Condensed • British Columbia • California & Nevada • California Condensed • Canada • Chicago • Chicago City Map • Chicago Condensed • Florida • Georgia & the Carolinas • Great Lakes • Hawaii • Hiking in Alaska • Hiking in the USA • Honolulu & Oahu City Map • Las Vegas • Los Angeles • Los Angeles City Map • Louisiana & the Deep South • Miami • Miami City Map • Montreal • New England • New Orleans • New Orleans City Map • New York City • New York City City Map • New York City Condensed • New York, New Jersey & Pennsylvania • Oahu • Out to Eat – San Francisco • Pacific Northwest • Rocky Mountains • San Diego & Tijuana • San Francisco • San Francisco City Map • Seattle • Seattle City Map • Southwest • Texas • Toronto • USA • USA phrasebook • Vancouver • Vancouver City Map • Virginia & the Capital Region • Washington, DC • Washington, DC City Map • World Food New Orleans **Travel Literature:** Caught Inside: A Surfer's Year on the California Coast • Drive Thru America

NORTH-EAST ASIA Beijing • Beijing City Map • Cantonese phrasebook • China • Hiking in Japan • Hong Kong & Macau • Hong Kong City Map • Hong Kong Condensed • Japan • Japanese phrasebook • Korea • Korean phrasebook • Kyoto • Mandarin phrasebook • Mongolia • Mongolian phrasebook • Seoul • Shanghai • South-West China • Taiwan • Tokyo • Tokyo Condensed • World Food Hong Kong • World Food Japan **Travel Literature:** In Xanadu: A Quest • Lost Japan

SOUTH AMERICA Argentina, Uruguay & Paraguay • Bolivia • Brazil • Brazilian phrasebook • Buenos Aires • Buenos Aires City Map • Chile & Easter Island • Colombia • Ecuador & the Galapagos Islands • Healthy Travel Central & South America • Latin American Spanish phrasebook • Peru • Quechua phrasebook • Read This First: Central & South America • Rio de Janeiro • Rio de Janeiro City Map • Santiago de Chile • South America on a shoestring • Trekking in the Patagonian Andes • Venezuela **Travel Literature:** Full Circle: A South American Journey

SOUTH-EAST ASIA Bali & Lombok • Bangkok • Bangkok City Map • Burmese phrasebook • Cambodia • Cycling Vietnam, Laos & Cambodia • East Timor phrasebook • Hanoi • Healthy Travel Asia & India • Hill Tribes phrasebook • Ho Chi Minh City (Saigon) • Indonesia • Indonesian phrasebook • Indonesia's Eastern Islands • Java • Lao phrasebook • Laos • Malay phrasebook • Malaysia, Singapore & Brunei • Myanmar (Burma) • Philippines • Pilipino (Tagalog) phrasebook • Read This First: Asia & India • Singapore • Singapore City Map • South-East Asia on a shoestring • South-East Asia phrasebook • Thailand • Thailand's Islands & Beaches • Thailand, Vietnam, Laos & Cambodia Road Atlas • Thai phrasebook • Vietnam • Vietnamese phrasebook • World Food Indonesia • World Food Thailand • World Food Vietnam

ALSO AVAILABLE: Antarctica • The Arctic • The Blue Man: Tales of Travel, Love and Coffee • Brief Encounters: Stories of Love, Sex & Travel • Buddhist Stupas in Asia: The Shape of Perfection • Chasing Rickshaws • The Last Grain Race • Lonely Planet ... On the Edge: Adventurous Escapades from Around the World • Lonely Planet Unpacked • Lonely Planet Unpacked Again • Not the Only Planet: Science Fiction Travel Stories • Ports of Call: A Journey by Sea • Sacred India • Travel Photography: A Guide to Taking Better Pictures • Travel with Children • Tuvalu: Portrait of an Island Nation

Index

Text

Boxed Text

MAP LEGEND

BOUNDARIES

International
Provincial, State
Regional, Suburb

HYDROGRAPHY

Coastline
River, Creek
Lake
Canal

Building
Urban Area

ROUTES & TRANSPORT

Freeway
Highway
Major Road
Minor Road
Unsealed Road
City Freeway
City Highway
City Road
City Street, Lane

Pedestrian Mall
Tunnel
Train Route & Station
Metro & Station
Tramway & Tram Stop
Cable Car or Chairlift
Walking Track
Walking Tour
Ferry Route & Terminal

AREA FEATURES

Park, Gardens
Cemetery

Market
Beach, Desert

MAP SYMBOLS

⚙ EDINBURGH .... Large City
● Glasgow .... City
● Hawick .... Large Town
● Moniaive .... Town or Village

● .... Point of Interest

▪ .... Place to Stay
▲ .... Camp Site
⌂ .... Caravan Park
▼ .... Place to Eat
⬛ .... Pub or Bar

✈ .... Airport
Ancient or City Wall

Archaeological Site
Bank
Beach
Bus Stop, Station
Castle or Fort
Cave
Church or Cathedral
Cinema
Embassy
Fountain
Golf Course
Hospital
Internet Cafe
Lighthouse
Monument

▲ .... Mountain or Hill
🏛 .... Museum
🅿 .... Parking
✚ .... Police Station
✉ .... Post Office
⊗ .... Shopping Centre
🏠 .... Stately Home
🏊 .... Swimming Pool
☎ .... Telephone
🎭 .... Theatre
⊕ .... Toilet
⬛ .... Tomb
❶ .... Tourist Information
🚶 .... Trail Head
🐘 .... Zoo

Note: not all symbols displayed above appear in this book

LONELY PLANET OFFICES

Australia
Locked Bag 1, Footscray, Victoria 3011
☎ 03 8379 8000 fax 03 8379 8111
email: talk2us@lonelyplanet.com.au

USA
150 Linden St, Oakland, CA 94607
☎ 510 893 8555 TOLL FREE: 800 275 8555
fax 510 893 8572
email: info@lonelyplanet.com

UK
10a Spring Place, London NW5 3BH
☎ 020 7428 4800 fax 020 7428 4828
email: go@lonelyplanet.co.uk

France
1 rue du Dahomey, 75011 Paris
☎ 01 55 25 33 00 fax 01 55 25 33 01
email: bip@lonelyplanet.fr
www.lonelyplanet.fr

World Wide Web: www.lonelyplanet.com *or* AOL keyword: lp
Lonely Planet Images: lpi@lonelyplanet.com.au